classrooms around the world.

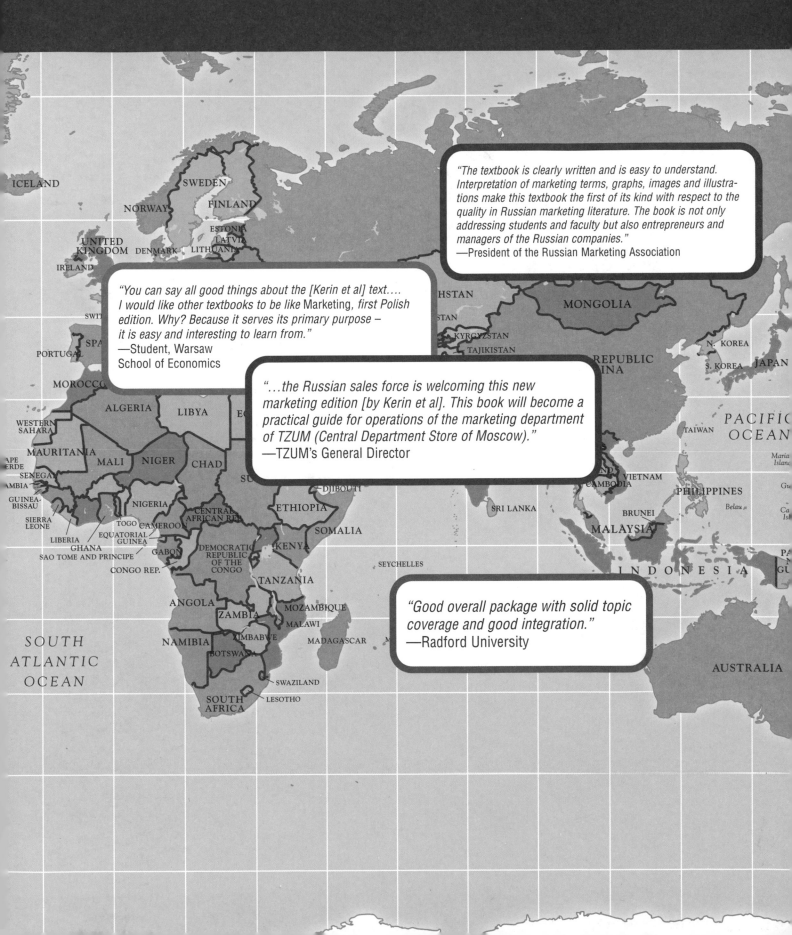

"The textbook is clearly written and is easy to understand. Interpretation of marketing terms, graphs, images and illustrations make this textbook the first of its kind with respect to the quality in Russian marketing literature. The book is not only addressing students and faculty but also entrepreneurs and managers of the Russian companies."
—President of the Russian Marketing Association

"You can say all good things about the [Kerin et al] text.... I would like other textbooks to be like Marketing, first Polish edition. Why? Because it serves its primary purpose – it is easy and interesting to learn from."
—Student, Warsaw School of Economics

"...the Russian sales force is welcoming this new marketing edition [by Kerin et al]. This book will become a practical guide for operations of the marketing department of TZUM (Central Department Store of Moscow)."
—TZUM's General Director

"Good overall package with solid topic coverage and good integration."
—Radford University

MARKETING

McGRAW-HILL/IRWIN SERIES IN MARKETING

Alreck & Settle
The Survey Research Handbook
Third Edition

Alsem & Wittink
Strategic Marketing: A Practical Approach
First Edition

Anderson, Beveridge, Lawton, & Scott
Merlin: A Marketing Simulation
First Edition

Arens
Contemporary Advertising
Tenth Edition

Arnould, Price, & Zinkhan
Consumers
Second Edition

Bearden, Ingram, & LaForge
Marketing: Principles & Perspectives
Fourth Edition

Belch & Belch
Advertising & Promotion: An Integrated
Marketing Communications Approach
Sixth Edition

Bingham & Gomes
Business Marketing
Third Edition

Cateora & Graham
International Marketing
Twelfth Edition

Cole & Mishler
Consumer and Business Credit Management
Eleventh Edition

Cooper & Schindler
Marketing Research
First Edition

Cravens & Piercy
Strategic Marketing
Eighth Edition

Cravens, Lamb, & Crittenden
Strategic Marketing Management Cases
Seventh Edition

Crawford & Di Benedetto
New Products Management
Eighth Edition

Duncan
Principles of Advertising and IMC
Second Edition

Dwyer & Tanner
Business Marketing
Third Edition

Eisenmann
Internet Business Models: Text and Cases
First Edition

Etzel, Walker, & Stanton
Marketing
Thirteenth Edition

Forrest
Internet Marketing Intelligence
First Edition

Futrell
ABC's of Relationship Selling
Eighth Edition

Futrell
Fundamentals of Selling
Ninth Edition

Gourville, Quelch, & Rangan
Cases in Health Care Marketing
First Edition

Hair, Bush, & Ortinau
Marketing Research
Third Edition

Hawkins, Best, & Coney
Consumer Behavior
Ninth Edition

Johansson
Global Marketing
Fourth Edition

Johnston & Marshall
Churchill/Ford/Walker's Sales
Force Management
Eighth Edition

Johnston & Marshall
Relationship Selling and Sales Management
First Edition

Kerin, Hartley, & Rudelius
Marketing: The Core
First Edition

Kerin, Hartley, Berkowitz, & Rudelius
Marketing
Eighth Edition

Lehmann & Winer
Analysis for Marketing Planning
Sixth Edition

Lehmann & Winer
Product Management
Fourth Edition

Levy & Weitz
Retailing Management
Fifth Edition

Mason & Perreault
The Marketing Game!
Third Edition

McDonald
Direct Marketing: An Integrated Approach
First Edition

**Mohammed, Fisher, Jaworski, &
Paddison**
Internet Marketing: Building Advantage in a
Networked Economy
Second Edition

Molinari
Marketing Research Project Manual
First Edition

Monroe
Pricing
Third Edition

Mullins, Walker, & Boyd
Marketing Management: A Strategic
Decision-Making Approach
Fifth Edition

Nentl & Miller
SimSeries Simulations:
SimSell
SimSales Management SimMarketing
SimMarketing Research
SimCRM
First Edition

Perreault & McCarthy
Basic Marketing: A Global Managerial
Approach
Fifteenth Edition

Perreault & McCarthy
Essentials of Marketing: A Global
Managerial Approach
Tenth Edition

Peter & Donnelly
A Preface to Marketing Management
Tenth Edition

Peter & Donnelly
Marketing Management: Knowledge and
Skills
Seventh Edition

Peter & Olson
Consumer Behavior
Seventh Edition

Purvis & Burton
Which Ad Pulled Best?
Ninth Edition

Quelch, Rangan, & Lal
Marketing Management Text and Cases
First Edition

Rayport & Jaworski
Introduction to e-Commerce
Second Edition

Rayport & Jaworski
e-Commerce
First Edition

Rayport & Jaworski
Cases in e-Commerce
First Edition

Richardson
Internet Marketing
First Edition

Roberts
Internet Marketing: Integrating Online and
Offline Strategies
First Edition

Spiro, Stanton, & Rich
Management of a Sales Force
Eleventh Edition

Stock & Lambert
Strategic Logistics Management
Fourth Edition

Ulrich & Eppinger
Product Design and Development
Third Edition

Walker, Boyd, Mullins, & Larreche
Marketing Strategy: A Decision-
Focused Approach
Fifth Edition

Weitz, Castleberry, & Tanner
Selling: Building Partnerships
Fifth Edition

Zeithaml & Bitner
Services Marketing
Fourth Edition

MARKETING

EDITION

Roger A. Kerin
Southern Methodist University

Steven W. Hartley
University of Denver

Eric N. Berkowitz
University of Massachusetts

William Rudelius
University of Minnesota

McGraw-Hill
Irwin

Boston   Burr Ridge, IL   Dubuque, IA   Madison, WI   New York   San Francisco   St. Louis
Bangkok   Bogotá   Caracas   Kuala Lumpur   Lisbon   London   Madrid   Mexico City
Milan   Montreal   New Delhi   Santiago   Seoul   Singapore   Sydney   Taipei   Toronto

**McGraw-Hill
Irwin**

MARKETING

Published by McGraw-Hill/Irwin, a business unit of The McGraw-Hill Companies, Inc., 1221 Avenue of the Americas, New York, NY, 10020. Copyright © 2006, 2003, 2000, 1997, 1994, 1992, 1989, 1986 by The McGraw-Hill Companies, Inc. All rights reserved. No part of this publication may be reproduced or distributed in any form or by any means, or stored in a database or retrieval system, without the prior written consent of The McGraw-Hill Companies, Inc., including, but not limited to, in any network or other electronic storage or transmission, or broadcast for distance learning.

Some ancillaries, including electronic and print components, may not be available to customers outside the United States.

This book is printed on acid-free paper.

2 3 4 5 6 7 8 9 0 CTP/CTP 0 9 8 7 6

ISBN-13: 978-0-07-282880-1 / ISBN-10: 0-07-282880-3 (Text)
ISBN-13: 978-0-07-308015-4 / ISBN-10: 0-07-308015-2 (Set)

Editorial director: *John E. Biernat*
Publisher: *Andy Winston*
Sponsoring editor: *Barrett Koger*
Developmental editors: *Sarah Crago/Gina M. Huck*
Executive marketing manager: *Dan Silverburg*
Producer, media technology: *Damian Moshak*
Senior project manager: *Christine A. Vaughan*
Manager, new book production: *Heather D. Burbridge*
Lead designer: *Matthew Baldwin*
Photo research coordinator: *Ira C. Roberts*
Photo researcher: *Michael Hruby*
Senior media project manager: *Susan Lombardi*
Developer, media technology: *Brian Nacik*
Cover illustration: *Ralph Kelliher*
Interior design: *Jenny El-Shamy*
Typeface: *10.5/12 Times Roman*
Compositor: *GTS – York, PA Campus*
Printer: *CTPS*

Library of Congress Cataloging-in-Publication Data

Marketing / Roger A. Kerin . . . [et al.]. — 8th ed.
     p. cm.—(McGraw-Hill/Irwin series in marketing)
   Includes bibliographical references and index.
   ISBN 0-07-282880-3 (alk. paper)
   1. Marketing. I. Kerin, Roger A.
  HF5415 .M29474 2006
  658.8—dc22

                                                                 2004065542

A MESSAGE FROM THE AUTHORS

Welcome to the eighth edition of **Marketing!** We are truly pleased to have an opportunity to share our enthusiasm for this exciting and dynamic field with students and instructors across the United States and throughout the world.

This edition of our book is designed to reflect the many recent and extraordinary events that have changed all aspects of our economy, particularly the field of marketing. The combination of the dot-com boom then bust, the instant success of interactive and wireless technologies, the immediate and dramatic response to international terrorism, the economic recession and recovery, the shock over the ethical lapses of many of our corporate leaders, and the rapid evolution from mass marketing to micromarketing have created a completely new business environment. We've worked hard to bring you the most up-to-date text that reflects today's world of marketing for consumers, managers, and students!

This edition of **Marketing,** like its previous editions, is the result of a detailed and rigorous development process that has been consistently successful at providing customer value. The process starts by building on the strengths of the active-learning approach that has evolved from our previous editions. Then we evaluate and integrate the most recent new ideas from education about how to engage today's students in learning activities. On that foundation we build a comprehensive presentation of traditional and contemporary marketing theories, concepts, approaches, and tools, based on our own expertise and the expert advice and input of many knowledgeable reviewers and users of previous editions. To bring the theories and concepts to life we use products, brands, and companies that students can relate to from their personal experiences but also less-known entrepreneurs and small businesses that may also stimulate career plans. Finally, we invest in the growing number of educational support technologies—from web-based testing, to real-time information updates, to interactive exercises and experiences.

Feedback from students and instructors from around the world has reinforced our commitment to this approach. The previous edition of **Marketing** became the best-selling marketing text in the United States and Canada; and it has been adapted with local cases and examples or translated into Russian, Polish, French, Spanish, Chinese, and Portuguese. This eighth edition of **Marketing** represents our efforts to continue our tradition of excellence and to guarantee an exceptional learning experience for marketing students. We hope you'll enjoy reading and using the text as much as we've enjoyed preparing it.

Roger A. Kerin
Steven W. Hartley
Eric N. Berkowitz
William Rudelius

PREFACE

DISTINCTIVE FEATURES OF OUR APPROACH

The innovative pedagogical approach used in *Marketing* and its supplements is the result of our combined experiences in a variety of classroom, college, and university settings. We introduced the approach in our first edition by integrating key elements from each of our teaching styles and preferences. Of course, like most instructors, we continuously monitor the changing learning styles of students, the growth and evolution of our discipline, and the efficacy of new instructional technologies to adapt and improve the approach. Its distinctive features include:

- **Assessment-Ready Elements.** Learning objectives and Chapter in Review summaries integrated to help instructors and programs address growing interest in assessment and assurance of learning.
- **High-Engagement Style.** An easy-to-read, high-involvement, interactive writing style that engages students through active learning techniques, timely and interesting examples, and challenging applications.
- **Personalized Marketing.** A vivid and accurate description of businesses, marketing professionals, and entrepreneurs—through cases, exercises, and testimonials—that allows students to personalize marketing and identify possible career interests and role models.
- **Marketing Decision Making.** The use of extended examples, cases, and videos involving people making marketing decisions, which students can easily relate to text concepts.
- **Traditional and Contemporary Coverage.** Comprehensive and integrated coverage of traditional and contemporary concepts illustrated through relevant popular business publications.
- **Rigorous Framework.** A rigorous pedagogical framework based on the use of learning objectives, concept checks, key terms, Chapter in Review summaries, and supportive student supplements such as the Student CD, Study Studio, and Study Guide.
- **Comprehensive Support Package.** A package of support materials to accommodate a wide variety of instructor teaching styles and student learning styles.

Feedback from many of the 3,000 instructors and 800,000 students who have used our text and package in the past has emphasized that the synergy of these features contributes to the success of each teaching and learning experience. We focused our efforts to build on these strengths as we developed the eighth edition of *Marketing*.

NEW AND REVISED CONTENT

- **Integrated Marketing Plan Activities.** Each chapter now includes an end-of-chapter section titled "Building Your Marketing Plan" that discusses an element of the strategic marketing process presented in Chapter 2 (see Figure 2–5) and the sample marketing plan presented in Appendix A. Each Building Your Marketing Plan assignment provides step-by-step activities corresponding to the topics discussed in that chapter. By completing the assignments students will have completed all of the key components of a marketing plan.
- **Assessment-Ready Objectives and Summaries.** Each chapter (1) begins with measurable learning objectives and (2) ends with the Chapter in Review, which is a summary of chapter content related to each objective. This direct link

between objectives and content facilitates now-common accreditation efforts necessary to meet assurance-of-learning requirements. The objectives are cross-referenced to specific test bank questions to allow construction of measurement instruments.

- **Increased Emphasis on Meeting Consumer Needs with New Products.** Chapter 1 presents an enhanced discussion of the difficulty of introducing successful new products and provides a variety of new-product examples as engaging topics of discussion for students. A complete update of Rollerblade's new product line and marketing program is also provided.

- **Expanded Coverage of Business Portfolio Analysis.** The Chapter 2 discussion of BCG's business portfolio analysis has been expanded and applied to Kodak's shift from film to digital technology. Students are asked to evaluate four opportunities—film, digital cameras, self-service kiosks, and printers—in terms of the BCG matrix alternatives.

- **Updated Overview of the Marketing Environment.** Chapter 3 now includes discussions of the digital revolution taking place in the music industry, global population trends, generational cohorts (including millennials) and the transition of Gen Y to economic adults, the two new types of "statistical areas" used by the Census Bureau, multicultural marketing, the growth of new technologies such as VOIP and Wi-Fi, and new regulations such as the Madrid Protocol, the Federal Dilution Act, and the CAN-SPAM Act.

- **Addition of Extended Examples to Ethics and Social Responsibility Discussion.** Detailed examples of situations, products, and companies familiar to students have been added to Chapter 4. A survey showing students' attitudes toward downloading music, Xerox's efforts at green marketing through its "Design for the Environment" program, and the growth of online fraud are examples used to help students relate to the concepts presented in the chapter. Chapter 4 also includes the new AMA Code of Ethics.

- **Updated Consumer Behavior Coverage.** Chapter 5 includes new examples related to MP3 players, an updated discussion of the new VALS typology (including innovators, thinkers, and survivors), a description of the word-of-mouth activity called *buzz marketing,* and an update on recent debates about subliminal advertising.

- **New Business-to-Business Content.** Chapter 6 now includes discussions of the forthcoming North American Product Classification system, Harley-Davidson's supplier collaboration efforts, and eBay's expansion into online business-to-business trading: eBayBusiness.com.

- **Updated Global Coverage.** Recent changes in tariffs and their cost to consumers, the latest membership of the European Union, the growing use of global brands by companies such as Coca-Cola, Gillette, L'Oréal, and McDonald's, and considerations when customizing versus standardizing marketing practices are part of the Chapter 7 discussion of global markets and global marketing.

- **New Marketing Research Framework.** The five-step marketing research approach presented in Chapter 8 now discusses three types of research—exploratory, descriptive, and causal—in the context of setting research objectives. Recent changes in Nielsen's method of obtaining TV viewing data from all TV viewers, and particularly from men and owners of DVRs such as TiVo, are also discussed.

- **New and Updated Extended Examples.** Reebok, Wendy's, and Apple are used as extended examples to illustrate segmentation and typical age, gender, price, and lifestyle segments in Chapter 9. 3M, Little Remedies, and Volvo are used to explain new-product development in Chapter 10.

- **New Brand Management Content.** The rapidly changing field of brand management includes new approaches to valuing brand equity, brand licensing, and the use of "fighting" brands now covered in Chapter 11.

- **Increased Emphasis on Services as Experiences.** Chapter 12 opens with a description of *Star Trek: The Experience,* a recently opened attraction at the Las Vegas Hilton, and one of many services designed to provide consumers with a strong experiential element (e.g., Hard Rock Cafe, Planet Hollywood, etc.). New e-services such as VOIP, retinal scan security services, and match-making are also included in the chapter.

- **Updated Channels, Wholesaling, Supply Chain, and Logistics Discussions.** The Chapter 15 opening example and the chapter Web Link use Apple Stores to illustrate the use of a high-touch environment to distribute high-tech products. Chapter 16 now includes a discussion of IBM's on-demand supply chain and an example of BMW's online site available to build your own automobile.

- **Updated Retailing and Category Management Coverage.** Chapter 17 provides a discussion of the growing demand for luxury products by the mass market. Other important new topics are also included, such as the replacement of bar codes with RFID technology, the trend toward self-service retailing, the growth of supercenters, the new regulations affecting telemarketing, and the use of category management to determine the assortment of merchandise in a store.

- **Revised Integrated Marketing Communications Content.** Chapter 18 opens with a description of Disney's $250 million integrated marketing campaign, which includes the popular "What's Next?" campaign, network and cable TV ads, print ads, newspaper inserts, direct marketing, a comprehensive website and campaign, a Disney Visa card, and many other partnerships and promotions. IMC is now introduced much earlier in the chapter, and other topics such as SIMM (simultaneous media usage), direct-to-consumer marketing, and assessment of program effectiveness are included.

- **New Forms of Advertising.** Important content describing the new world of advertising has been added to Chapter 19. As more consumers learn to multi-task, advertisers have turned to new attention-getting media. Internet promotions, online contests, virtual advertising, and *advergaming* (the integration of advertising messages in a video game) are all included with recent examples. In addition, the advertising content debate sparked by Janet Jackson's Super Bowl performance is presented for student debate.

- **Updated Chapter 21: "Implementing Interactive and Multichannel Marketing."** The reviews on this chapter, introduced in the seventh edition, were extraordinary. It is now updated to include recent examples and terms, such as new descriptions of Reflect.com, Nike's customized product configurator, new segments of online mothers, blogs, viral marketing, and multichannel marketing initiatives.

- **Increased Integration of Strategic Marketing Process.** The strategic marketing process introduced in Chapter 2 and used in Appendix A is integrated with the entire text in Chapter 22, "Pulling It All Together: The Strategic Marketing Process." A new section, "Finding and Using What Really Works," is based on the results of a five-year study of 160 companies.

ORGANIZATION

The eighth edition of *Marketing* is divided into five parts. Part 1, "Initiating the Marketing Process," looks first at what marketing is and how it creates customer value and customer relationships (Chapter 1). Then Chapter 2 provides an overview of the strategic marketing process that occurs in an organization—which provides a framework for the text. Appendix A provides a sample marketing plan as a reference for students. Chapter 3 analyzes the five major environmental factors in our changing marketing environment, and Chapter 4 provides a framework for including ethical and social responsibility considerations in marketing decisions.

Part 2, "Understanding Buyers and Markets," first describes, in Chapter 5, how individual consumers reach buying decisions. Next, Chapter 6 looks at organizational buyers and markets and how they make purchase decisions. And finally, in Chapter 7, the nature and scope of world trade and the influence of cultural differences on global marketing practices are explored.

In Part 3, "Targeting Marketing Opportunities," the marketing research function and how information about prospective consumers is linked to marketing strategy and decisions is discussed in Chapter 8. The process of segmenting and targeting markets and positioning products appears in Chapter 9.

Part 4, "Satisfying Marketing Opportunities," covers the four Ps, the marketing mix elements. The product element is divided into the natural chronological sequence of first developing new products and services (Chapter 10) and then managing existing products (Chapter 11) and services (Chapter 12). Pricing is covered in terms of underlying pricing analysis (Chapter 13), followed by actual price setting (Chapter 14) and Appendix B, "Financial Aspects of Marketing." Three chapters address the place (distribution) aspects of marketing: "Managing Marketing Channels and Wholesaling" (Chapter 15), "Integrating Supply Chain and Logistics Management" (Chapter 16), and "Retailing" (Chapter 17). Retailing is discussed in a separate chapter because of its importance and interest as a career for many of today's students. Promotion is also covered in three chapters. Chapter 18 discusses integrated marketing communications and direct marketing, topics that have grown in importance in the marketing discipline recently. The primary forms of mass market communication—advertising, sales promotion, and public relations—are covered in Chapter 19. Personal selling and sales management are covered in Chapter 20.

Part 5, "Managing the Marketing Process," discusses issues and techniques related to interactive marketing technologies and the strategic marketing process. Chapter 21 describes how interactive technologies influence customer value and the customer experience through context, content, community, customization, connectivity, and commerce. Chapter 22 expands on Chapter 2 to describe specific techniques and issues related to blending the four marketing mix elements to plan, implement, and control marketing programs.

The book closes with several useful supplemental sections. Appendix C, "Planning a Career in Marketing," discusses marketing jobs and how to get them, and Appendix D provides 22 alternate cases. In addition, a detailed glossary with page references and three indexes (name, company/product, and subject) complete the book.

ACKNOWLEDGMENTS

DEVELOPMENT OF THE TEXT AND PACKAGE

To ensure continuous improvement of our product we have utilized an extensive review and development process for each of our past editions. Building on that history, the eighth edition development process included several phases of evaluation and a variety of stakeholder audiences (e.g., students, instructors, etc.).

- The first phase of the review process asked adopters to suggest improvements to the text and supplements through a detailed review of each component. We also surveyed students to find out what they liked about the book and what changes they would suggest.
- The second phase included symposiums across the country, including users and nonusers. These sessions focused specifically on the supplements package and its effectiveness for instructors and students.

Reviewers who were vital in the changes that were made to this edition include:

Christie Amato
University of North Carolina, Charlotte

Carol Bienstock
Radford University

Larry Borgen
Normandale Community College

Nancy Boykin
Tarleton State University

Judy Bulin
Monroe Community College

Bruce Chadbourne
Embry Riddle Aeronautical University

Mark Collins
University of Tennessee

Howard Combs
San Jose State University

Sherry Cook
Southwest Missouri State University

Tino DeMarco
SUNY Albany

Jobie Devinney-Walsh
Northern Kentucky University

Bob Dwyer
University of Cincinnati

Ken Fairweather
Letourneau University

Larry Feick
University of Pittsburgh

Glen Gelderloos
Grand Rapids Community College

David Gerth
Nashville State Community College

James Gould
Pace University

Kimberly Grantham
University of Georgia

Nancy Grassilli
Tunxis Community College

Barnett Greenberg
Florida International University

Pamela Grimm
Kent State University

Ernan Haruvy
University of Texas, Dallas

Ken Herbst
St. Joseph's University

Jonathan Hibbard
Boston University

Rajesh Iyer
Valdosta State University

Katie Kemp
Middle Tennessee State University

Tim Landry
University of Oklahoma

Debbie Laverie
Texas Tech University

Yunchuan Liu
University of California, Riverside

Paul Londrigan
Mott Community College

Tom Marshall
Owens Community College

Tamara Masters
Brigham Young University

Charla Mathwick
Portland State University

Ed McLaughlin
Cornell University

Bob McMillen
James Madison University

Soon Hong Min
University of Oklahoma

Kim Montney
Kellogg Community College

Gordon Mosley
Troy State University

Jeanne Munger
University of Southern Maine

Linda Munilla
Georgia Southern University

Sunder Narayanan
New York University

Bob Newberry
Winona State University

Ben Oumlil
University of Dayton

Notis Pagiavlas
Embry Riddle Aeronautical University

Susan Peterson
Scottsdale Community College

Edna Ragins
North Carolina A&T

Daniel Rajaratnam
Baylor University

Joe Ricks
Xavier University

Teri Root
Southeastern Louisiana University

Heidi Rottier
Bradley University

Ken Shaw
State University of New York, Oswego

Dan Sherrel
University of Memphis

Norman Smothers
California State University, Hayward

Kathleen Stuenkel
Northeastern State University

Ruth Taylor
Texas State University

Tom Thompson
University of Maryland

Dan Toy
California State University, Chico

Erin Wilkinson
Johnson & Wales University
Janice Williams
University of Central Oklahoma

Joseph Wisenblit
Seton Hall University

Lauren Wright
California State University, Chico

The preceding section demonstrates the amount of feedback and developmental input that went into this project, and we are deeply grateful to the numerous people who have shared their ideas with us. Reviewing a book or supplement takes an incredible amount of energy and attention. We are glad so many of our colleagues took the time to do it. Their comments have inspired us to do our best.

Reviewers who contributed to the first seven editions of this book include:

Nadia J. Abgrab
Kerri Acheson
Roy Adler
Christie Amato
Linda Anglin
William D. Ash
Gerard Athaide
Andy Aylesworth
Patricia Baconride
Siva Balasubramanian
A. Diane Barlar
James H. Barnes
Karen Becker-Olsen
Frederick J. Beier
Thom J. Belich
Joseph Belonax
Thomas M. Bertsch
Parimal Bhagat
Kevin W. Bittle
Jeff Blodgett
Nancy Bloom
Charles Bodkin
Thomas Brashear
Martin Bressler
Bruce Brown
William Brown
William G. Browne
Alan Bush
Stephen Calcich
William J. Carner
Gerald O. Cavallo
S. Tamer Cavusgil
S. Choi Chan
Sang Choe
Kay Chomic
Clare Comm
Clark Compton
Cristanna Cook
John Coppett
John Cox
Scott Cragin
Ken Crocker
Joe Cronin
James Cross
Lowell E. Crow

John H. Cunningham
Bill Curtis
Dan Darrow
Hugh Daubek
Martin Decatur
Francis DeFea
Linda M. Delene
Tino DeMarco
Paul Dion
William B. Dodds
James H. Donnelly
Michael Drafke
Eddie V. Easley
Eric Ecklund
Roger W. Egerton
Steven Engel
Barbara Evans
Lori Feldman
Kevin Feldt
Theresa Flaherty
Charles Ford
Renee Foster
Donald Fuller
Stan Garfunkel
James Ginther
Susan Godar
Dan Goebel
Marc Goldberg
Leslie A. Goldgehn
Kenneth Goodenday
Darrell Goudge
James Gould
James L. Grimm
Pola B. Gupta
Richard Hansen
Donald V. Harper
Dotty Harpool
Lynn Harris
Robert C. Harris
James A. Henley, Jr.
Jonathan Hibbard
Richard M. Hill
Al Holden
Kristine Hovsepian
Jarrett Hudnal

Mike Hyman
Donald R. Jackson
Kenneth Jameson
Deb Jansky
James C. Johnson
Robert Jones
Mary Joyce
Jacqueline Karen
Sudhir Karunakaran
Herbert Katzenstein
George Kelley
Ram Kesaran
Roy Klages
Douglas Kornemann
Terry Kroeten
Nanda Kumar
Ann Kuzma
John Kuzma
Priscilla LaBarbera
Duncan G. LaBay
Jay Lambe
Irene Lange
Richard Lapidus
Ron Larson
Ed Laube
Debra Laverie
Gary Law
Robert Lawson
Wilton Lelund
Karen LeMasters
Richard C. Leventhal
Leonard Lindenmuth
Ann Little
James Lollar
Lynn Loudenback
Ann Lucht
Mike Luckett
Robert Luke
Michael R. Luthy
Richard J. Lutz
Marton L. Macchiete
Rhonda Mack
Patricia Manninen
Kenneth Maricle
Elena Martinez

James McAlexander	Michael Peters	Michael Swenson
Peter J. McClure	William S. Piper	Robert Swerdlow
Phyllis McGinnis	Stephen Pirog	Vincent P. Taiani
Jim McHugh	Gary Poorman	Clint Tankersley
Gary F. McKinnon	Vonda Powell	Ruth Taylor
Jo Ann McManamy	Joe Puzi	Andrew Thacker
Lee Meadow	James P. Rakowski	Fred Trawick
James Meszaros	Barbara Ribbens	Thomas L. Trittipo
George Miaoulis	Cathie Rich-Duval	Sue Umashankar
Ronald Michaels	Heikki Rinne	Ottilia Voegtli
Stephen W. Miller	William Rodgers	Jeff von Freymann
William G. Mitchell	Jean Romeo	Gerald Waddle
Melissa Moore	Vicki Rostedt	Randall E. Wade
Linda Morable	Larry Rottmeyer	Blaise Waguespack, Jr.
Fred Morgan	Robert W. Ruekert	Harlan Wallingford
William Motz	Maria Sanella	Mark Weber
Donald F. Mulvihill	Charles Schewe	Don Weinrauch
Bill Murphy	Starr F. Schlobohm	Robert S. Welsh
Janet Murray	Roberta Schultz	Ron Weston
Keith Murray	Stan Scott	Sheila Wexler
Joseph Myslivec	Eberhard Seheuling	Max White
Bob Newberry	Harold S. Sekiguchi	James Wilkins
Donald G. Norris	Doris M. Shaw	Janice Williams
Carl Obermiller	Eric Shaw	Kaylene Williams
Dave Olson	Bob E. Smiley	Robert Williams
James Olver	Allen Smith	Jerry W. Wilson
Allan Palmer	Ruth Ann Smith	Robert Witherspoon
Dennis Pappas	James V. Spiers	Van R. Wood
June E. Parr	Craig Stacey	Wendy Wood
Philip Parron	Miriam B. Stamps	William R. Wynd
Richard Penn	Joe Stasio	Mark Young
John Penrose	Tom Stevenson	Leon Zurawicki
William Pertula	Scott Swan	

Thanks are also due to many faculty members who contributed to the text chapters and cases. They include Linda Rochford of the University of Minnesota, Duluth; Robert Hansen of the University of Minnesota; Kenneth Goodpaster, Thomas Holloran, David Brennan, and Mark Spriggs of the University of St. Thomas; Thomas Belich of Capella University; and Kathy Chadwick of St. Olaf College. Krzysztof Przybylowski of the Warsaw School of Economics, and Olga Saguinova and Irina Skorobogatykn of the Plekhanov Academy of Economics provided a number of international materials. Michael Vessey provided cases, research assistance, many special images, and he led our efforts on the Instructor's Manual, In-Class Activities, and Instructor's Survival Kit. Rick Armstrong, Chris Cole, and Jennifer Cole produced the videos. William Carner of the University of Texas provided the study guide. Carol Johnson of the University of Denver was responsible for the revision of the text bank.

Many businesspeople also provided substantial assistance by making available information that appears in the text and supplements, much of it for the first time in college materials. Thanks are due to Jeremy Stonier and Nicholas Skally of Rollerblade; Carol Watzke of CNS; David Ford of Ford Consulting Group; Maureen Cahill of Mall of America; Jack McKeon and Frank Lynch of Golden Valley Microwave Foods; Wayne Johansen of HOM Furniture; Donald Dunham of BP plc; Dr. George Dierberger and David Windorski of 3M; and Keith Nowak of Nokia. We also acknowledge the special help of Fred Senn and Kim Eskro of Fallon Worldwide; Mathew Kornberg of Little Remedies; Kirk Hodgdon and Mary Brown of

Bolin; Robert Kierlan of Fastenal; Dr. Aelred (Al) J. Kurtenbach of Daktronics; and Dan Stephenson of the Philadelphia Phillies.

Staff support from the Southern Methodist University, the University of Denver, and the University of Minnesota was essential. We gratefully acknowledge the help of Wanda Hanson, Louise Holt, Jeanne Milazzo, and Gloria Valdez for their many contributions.

Finally, we acknowledge the professional efforts of the McGraw-Hill/Irwin staff. Completion of our book and its many supplements required the attention and commitment of many editorial, production, marketing, and research personnel. Our Burr Ridge—based team included John Biernat, Barrett Koger, Sarah Crago, Sue Lombardi, Christine Vaughan, Ira Roberts, Heather Burbridge, Dan Silverburg, Dave Kapoor, and many others. In addition, we relied on Michael Hruby for constant attention regarding photo elements of the text. Finally, our developmental editor, Gina Huck of Imaginative Solutions, Inc., provided outstanding assistance, advice, coordination, editing, and guidance with extraordinary professionalism and enthusiasm. Handling the countless details of our text, supplement, and support technologies has become an incredibly complex challenge. We thank all these people for their efforts.

Roger A. Kerin
Steven W. Hartley
Eric N. Berkowitz
William Rudelius

Your Guide to Marketing, 8/e

Marketing, 8/e is the centerpiece of a successful partnership between students, instructors, and the course materials. Users of these materials enjoy an array of features that engage students, bring the classroom to life, and ease the burden of the instructor's workload.

Check out these engaging features of Marketing, 8/e

Marketing Planning

"Building Your Marketing Plan" is a new end-of-chapter feature that reinforces the concepts presented in Appendix A, "Building an Effective Marketing Plan," while guiding students through the practical application of creating their own marketing plan. In addition the Instructors Manual contains helpful hints and materials for instructors having students write marketing plans.

BUILDING YOUR MARKETING PLAN

To do a consumer analysis for the product—the good, service, or idea—in your marketing plan:

1 Identify the consumers who are most likely to buy your product—the primary target market—in terms of (*a*) their demographic characteristics and (*b*) any other kind of characteristics you believe are important.

2 Describe (*a*) the main points of difference of your product for this group and (*b*) what problem they help

solve for the consumer, in terms of the first stage in the consumer purchase decision process in Figure 5–1.

3 Identify the one or two key influences for each of the four outside boxes in Figure 5–4: (*a*) marketing mix, (*b*) psychological, (*c*) sociocultural, and (*d*) situational influences.

This consumer analysis will provide the foundation for the marketing mix actions you develop later in your plan.

APPENDIX

A — BUILDING AN EFFECTIVE MARKETING PLAN

"New ideas are a dime a dozen," observes Arthur R. Kydd, "and so are new products and new technologies." Kydd should know. As chief executive officer of St. Croix Venture Partners, he and his firm have provided the seed money and venture capital to launch more than 60 startup firms in the last 25 years. Today, those firms have more than 5,000 employees. Kydd explains:

> I get 200 to 300 marketing and business plans a year to look at, and at St. Croix provides startup financing for only two or three. What sets a potentially successful idea, product, or technology apart from all the rest is markets and marketing. If you have a real product with a distinctive point of difference that satisfies the needs of customers, you may have a winner. And you get a real feel for this in a well-written marketing or business plan.[1]

This appendix (1) describes what marketing and business plans are, including the purposes and guidelines in writing effective plans, and (2) provides a sample marketing plan.

MARKETING PLANS AND BUSINESS PLANS

After explaining the meanings, purposes, and audiences of marketing plans and business plans, this section describes some writing guidelines for them and what external funders often look for in successful plans.

Meanings, Purposes, and Audiences

A marketing plan is a road map for the marketing activities of an organization for a specified future period of time, such as one year or five years.[2] It is important to note that no single "generic" marketing plan applies to all organizations and all situations. Rather, the specific format for a marketing plan for an organization depends on the following:

- *The target audience and purpose.* Elements included in a particular marketing plan depend heavily on (1) who the audience is and (2) what its purpose is. A marketing plan for an internal audience seeks to point the direction for future marketing activities and is sent to all individuals in the organization

who must implement the plan or who will be affected by it. If the plan is directed to an external audience, such as friends, banks, venture capitalists, or potential investors, for the purpose of raising capital, it has the additional function of being an important sales document. In this case, it contains elements such as the strategic plan/focus, organization, structure, and biographies of key personnel that would rarely appear in an internal marketing plan. Also, the financial information is far more detailed when the plan is used to obtain outside capital. The elements of a marketing plan for each of these two audiences are compared in Figure A–1 on the next page.

- *The kind and complexity of the organization.* A small neighborhood restaurant has a somewhat different marketing plan than Nestlé, which serves international markets. The restaurant's plan would be relatively simple and directed at serving customers in a local market. In Nestlé's case, because there is a hierarchy of marketing plans, various levels of detail would be used—such as the entire organization, the business unit, or the product/product line.

- *The industry.* Both the restaurant serving a local market and Medtronic, selling heart pacemakers globally, analyze competition. Not only are their geographic thrusts far different, but the complexities of their offerings and, hence, the time periods likely to be covered by their plans also differ. A one-year marketing plan may be adequate for the restaurant, but Medtronic may need a five-year planning horizon because product-development cycles for complex, new medical devices may be three or four years.

In contrast to a marketing plan, a **business plan** is a road map for the entire organization for a specified future period of time, such as one year or five years.[3] A key difference between a marketing plan and a business plan is that the business plan contains details on the research and development (R&D)/operations/manufacturing activities of the organization. Even for a manufacturing business,

53

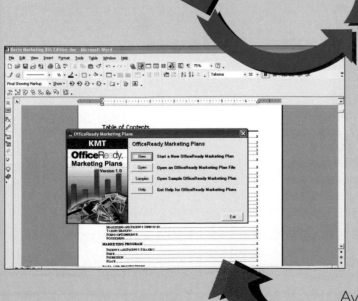

Available with the text, KMT Marketing Planning software follows the step-by-step building of a marketing plan, supporting the "Building Your Marketing Plan" feature and Appendix A, while reinforcing student learning.

Chapter-Opening Vignettes

Chapter-opening vignettes introduce students to the chapter concepts ahead, using an exciting company example. For instance, in Chapter 9, the authors use the S. Carter Collection (a shoe line named for hip-hop star Jay-Z, who was originally known as Shawn Carter) and the segmentation strategies of Reebok and Nike to grab student interest.

CHAPTER

9 IDENTIFYING MARKET SEGMENTS AND TARGETS

LEARNING OBJECTIVES

After reading this chapter you should be able to:

1   Explain what market segmentation is and when to use it.

2   Identify the five steps involved in segmenting and targeting markets.

3   Recognize the different factors used to segment consumer and organizational markets.

4   Know how to develop a market-product grid to identify a target market and recommend resulting actions.

5   Explain how marketing managers position products in the marketplace.

6   Describe three approaches to developing a sales forecast for a company.

SNEAKERS MARKETING WARS: HIP-HOP, YAO MING, AND 3 BILLION TRILLION CHOICES

In today's annual $16 billion U.S. sneakers war among Reebok, Nike, Adidas, and others, a new shoe introduction can have the effect of a toy pop gun—or a salvo across a battleship's bow. That's how serious the competition is. And Reebok recently launched a marketing strategy that challenges conventional wisdom.

New Segments and Strategies   Reebok is reaching a new market segment and getting publicity for its entire sneaker line by signing endorsements with popular rappers and hip-hop music stars. Example: S. Carter Collection by Rbk. Don't recognize the S. Carter name? The street-inspired S. Carter Collection is named for hip-hop star Jay-Z, who was originally known as Shawn Carter. With their flat soles and soft leather, the S. Carter low tops (opposite page) are a long way from the look of Reebok's traditional "performance" athletic shoes.[1]

231

The chapter-opening discussions are often integrated into narrative, exhibits, and boxed features throughout the chapter.

MARKETING NEWSNET

BzzAgent—The Business of Buzz

GLOBAL

Have you recently heard about a new product, movie, website, book, or restaurant from someone you know . . . or a complete stranger? If so, you may have been buzzed.

Marketers recognize the power of word of mouth. The challenge has been to harness that power. BzzAgent LLC does just that. Its nationwide volunteer army of 25,000 natural-born talkers channel their chatter toward products and services they deem authentically worth talking about. "Our goal is to capture honest word of mouth," says David Bolter, BzzAgent's founder, "and to build a network that turns passionate customers into brand evangelists."

BzzAgent's method is simple. Once a client signs on with BzzAgent, the company s___ ___hose for those

respond with encouragement and feedback on additional techniques.

Agents keep the products they promote. They also earn points redeemable for books, CDs, and other items by filing detailed reports. Who are the agents? About 65 percent are older than 25, 60 percent are women, and two are Fortune 500 CEOs. All are gregarious and genuinely like the product or service, otherwise they wouldn't participate in the buzz campaign.

Estée Lauder, Monster.com, Anheuser-Busch, Penguin Books, Lee jeans, and Rock Bottom Restaurants have used BzzAgent. But BzzAgent's buzz isn't cheap, and not everything is buzz worthy.

Deploy___ ___12-week c___

Marketing NewsNet

This boxed feature provides engaging, current examples of marketing applications in action, organized around the following themes: Technology and E-Commerce, Customer Value, Global, and Cross Functional.

Ethics and Social Responsibility Alert

These boxes increase awareness and assessment of current topics of ethical and social concern.

ETHICS AND SOCIAL RESPONSIBILITY ALERT

Student Credit Cards— What Is the Real Price?

ETHICS

Concept Check

Found at the end of each major chapter section, these checkpoints offer critical thinking and memory recall questions, helping students reflect on the text and test their comprehension of the material before reading on.

Concept Check

1. How does the development stage of the new-product process involve testing the product inside and outside the firm?

2. What is a test market?

3. What is commercialization of a new product?

These hands-on features bring the course to life

Instructor's Survival Kit (ISK): In-Class Activities and Product Props in a Box!

The ISK box contains an In-Class Activities Guide and product props for use in the classroom to illustrate marketing concepts and encourage student participation and collaboration. Today's students are more likely to learn and be motivated by active, participative experiences than by classic classroom lecture and discussion. The Instructor's Survival Kit contains these specific elements to enhance classroom interaction:

In-Class Activities: These in-class activities have received extremely positive feedback from our customers, both instructors and students. In-class activities may relate to a specific video case or example from the text.

Sample Products: *Marketing,* 8/e utilizes examples of offerings from both large and small firms that will interest today's students. A number of new products are included in the Survival Kit, such as a 3M Post-it Flag Highlighter. Also, when appropriate, sample ads are included among our transparencies and PowerPoint slides.

Real-world examples and today's technology bring the content to life

Video Case Studies

This end-of-chapter feature provides an up-close look at a company example, reinforcing the chapter content while bringing the material to life. Philadelphia Phillies, BMW, and Nokia are just a few of the exciting video cases available with the Eighth Edition.

Alternate Cases

An additional 22 alternate cases can be found in Appendix D, providing even more opportunity to bring the course content to life for students.

Website Addresses

The URLs of companies and organizations discussed in the text are easily located in the text margin, facilitating further exploration of these real-world examples.

California produce a hotter nacho cheese sauce than that produced in the other plants to serve their regions better.

- *Demographic customer characteristic: Household size.* More than half of all U.S. households are made up of only one or two persons, so Campbell's packages meals with only one or two servings—from Great Starts breakfasts to L'Orient dinners.
- *Psychographic customer characteristic: Lifestyle.* Claritas provides lifestyle segmentation services to marketers. Claritas's lifestyle segmentation is based on the belief that people of similar lifestyle characteristics tend to live near one another, have similar interests, and buy similar products and services. One of its services classifies every *household* in the United States into one of 48 unique market segments.

As shown at the bottom of Figure 9–4, *buying situations* are another way to segment consumer markets. These buying situations include benefits sought (product features, quality, service, warranty) and usage (heavy user, light user, nonuser). Two examples show how these buying situations can be used in developing consumer segments:

- *Benefits sought: Product features.* Understanding what benefits are important to different customers is often a useful way to segment markets because it can lead directly to specific marketing actions, such as a new product, ad campaign, or distribution system. For example, MicroFridge targets its combination microwave/refrigerator/freezer at college dorm residents, who are often woefully

What special benefit does a MicroFridge offer, and to which market segment might this appeal? The answer appears in the text.

Mac-Gray Corporation
www.microfridge.com

Web Link

Integrated throughout the text, Web Link boxes encourage students to explore digital strategies that innovative companies and organizations are employing online.

WEB LINK Customizing Your Own Designer Shoes

www.mhhe.com/Kerin

Going Online Exercises

These end-of-chapter exercises ask students to go online and think critically about a specific company's use of the Internet, helping students apply knowledge of key chapter concepts, terms, and topics, as well as evaluate the success or failure of the company's efforts.

GOING ONLINE Finding the Best Airline Ticket Price

It's Wednesday and you just completed your midterm exams. As a reward for your hard work, a friend has sent you a pair of free tickets to a popular Broadway show in New York City for 7:00 P.M. Saturday night. Check out the following online travel services to book a nonstop, round-trip ticket, leaving from Chicago's O'Hare (ORD) airport around 4:00 P.M. on Friday to City's LaGuardia (LGA) airport. On ... around 5:0...

- Expedia (www.expedia.com)—Lowest price: $280.00 from United Airlines.
- Orbitz (www.orbitz.com), the online travel service owned by the major airlines—Lowest price: $281.00 from United Airlines.
- Priceline (www.priceline.com)—Lowest price: $282.00 from United Airlines ... Lowest price:

Marketing, 8/e makes an instructor's life easier

Accreditation-Ready Book and Package

Proving your course satisfies learning outcomes is now easier. Revised and integrated learning objectives open each chapter and are tied to Chapter in Review summaries at the chapter's end.

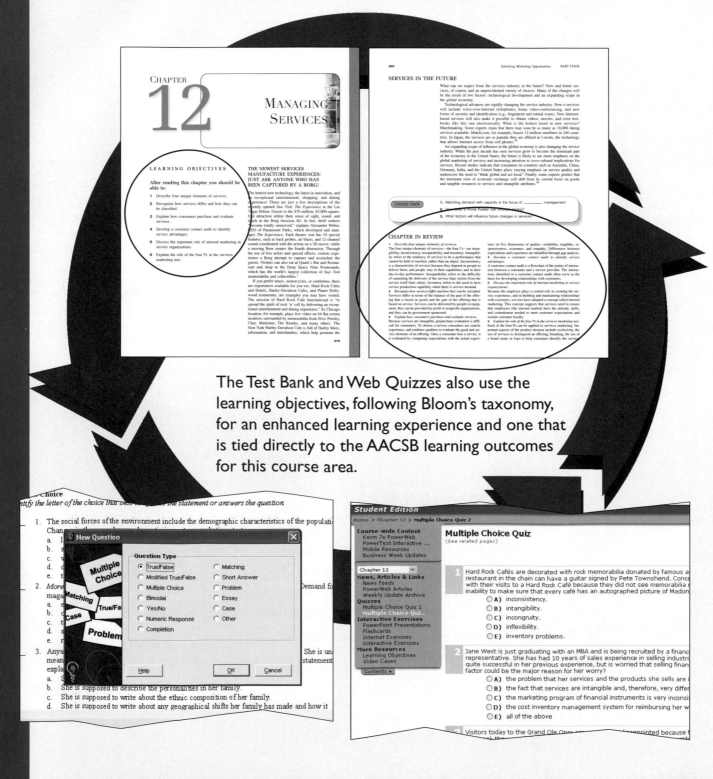

The Test Bank and Web Quizzes also use the learning objectives, following Bloom's taxonomy, for an enhanced learning experience and one that is tied directly to the AACSB learning outcomes for this course area.

Instructor Supplements

- **Instructor's Resource CD-ROM (IRCD):**
  The CD-ROM includes a digital version of the
  Instructor's Manual, PowerPoint slides, Test Bank
  and Computerized Test Bank.

- **Instructor's Manual:**
  The thoroughly revised Instructor's Manual includes
  lecture notes, discussions, and a description of all of the
  individual multimedia assets from which instructors can
  construct a custom presentation. The Instructor's
  Manual is also available in a hard-copy, looseleaf version.

- **PowerPoint Presentation:**
  The PowerPoint presentation, included on the IRCD, features
  slides that can be used by instructors to help present concepts
  to students in an efficient manner.

- **5,000+ Test Questions Correlated to
  Learning Outcomes:**
  We offer 5,000 test questions categorized by topic and level of
  learning (definitional, conceptual, or application) and correlated
  to the Learning Objectives and Chapter in Review within each
  chapter of the text.

- **Expanded Computerized Test Bank Program:**
  This Computerized Test Bank is revised to contain all of the
  multiple-choice questions from the Test Bank, Web Quizzes,
  Student CD-ROM, Study Guide, and PowerWeb readings so the
  instructor can include questions from these supplements in tests
  and quizzes.

- **Video Case and Appendix D Case Teaching Notes:**
  This manual includes helpful teaching suggestions for the video cases and alternate cases.

- **New and Revised Video Case Studies:**
  A unique series of 22 contemporary marketing cases is available on videotape (VHS) cassettes and DVD. Each video case corresponds with chapter-specific topics and the end-of-chapter case in the text. The video cases feature a variety of organizations and provide balanced coverage of services, consumer products, small businesses, Fortune 500 firms, and business-to-business examples. The 8/e package includes brand new videos including Philadelphia Phillies, 3M Greptile Grip™ golf glove, and more.

- **Weekly Updates:**
  Available when appropriate, this hot-off-the-press material provides instructors with current, fresh, and interesting examples not found in their students' textbooks.

- **Color Acetates:**
  A set of 100 four-color overhead transparency acetates is available free to adopters upon request.

- **PageOut Quizzes with Instructor Gradebook:**
  Assign quizzes in PageOut to give students incentive to read the text and prepare for class. Grades for each student will automatically post to the instructor's gradebook.

- **WebCT/BlackBoard/eCollege/TopClass Content:**
  Content from the Online Learning Center can be made available to adopting professors for delivery through several course management systems, including WebCT, BlackBoard, TopClass, or eCollege platforms.

Student Learning Tools

- **Print Study Guide.** The Study Guide enables students to learn and apply marketing principles instead of simply memorizing facts for an examination. The Study Guide includes chapter outlines for student note-taking, sample tests, critical thinking questions, and flash cards.

- **Student CD-ROM.** This CD-ROM contains the new KMT Marketing Planning Software. This high-quality commercial software contains detailed planning templates with extensive guidance provided for each section of the plan and includes a well-written marketing plan as an example. This product operates within the Microsoft Office Suite, so students work directly in Word and Excel to create professional looking documents.

- **Student Online Learning Center.** This rich book-specific website contains weekly updated *BusinessWeek* articles, an interactive Marketing Workshop, lots of self-study and quizzing resources, and the Kerin 8/e PowerWeb resources, including Daily News Feed, Weekly Case Updates, Readings in Marketing, PowerSearch research engine, Career Resources, Web Research guidance, and Study Tips. Visit **www.mhhe.com/kerin**.

BRIEF CONTENTS

Part 1   **Initiating the Marketing Process 2**

1   Creating Customer Relationships and Value through Marketing 4

2   Developing Successful Marketing and Corporate Strategies 28

APPENDIX A Building an Effective Marketing Plan 53

3   Scanning the Marketing Environment 70

4   Ethics and Social Responsibility in Marketing 96

Part 2   **Understanding Buyers and Markets 116**

5   Consumer Behavior 118

6   Organizational Markets and Buyer Behavior 146

7   Reaching Global Markets 168

Part 3   **Targeting Marketing Opportunities 200**

8   Marketing Research: From Information to Action 202

9   Identifying Market Segments and Targets 230

Part 4   **Satisfying Marketing Opportunities 258**

10   Developing New Products and Services 260

11   Managing Products and Brands 286

12   Managing Services 314

13   Building the Price Foundation 334

14   Arriving at the Final Price 360

APPENDIX B Financial Aspects of Marketing 386

15   Managing Marketing Channels and Wholesaling 394

16   Integrating Supply Chain and Logistics Management 420

17   Retailing 442

18   Integrated Marketing Communications and Direct Marketing 468

19   Advertising, Sales Promotion, and Public Relations 494

20   Personal Selling and Sales Management 526

Part 5   **Managing the Marketing Process 554**

21   Implementing Interactive and Multichannel Marketing 556

22   Pulling It All Together: The Strategic Marketing Process 580

APPENDIX C Planning a Career in Marketing 610

APPENDIX D Alternate Cases 628

Glossary *661*

Chapter Notes *673*

Credits *701*

Name Index *705*

Company/Product Index *711*

Subject Index *718*

DETAILED CONTENTS

Part 1　　Initiating the Marketing Process　2

1　CREATING CUSTOMER RELATIONSHIPS AND VALUE THROUGH MARKETING　4

Aero? Lightning? The Next Act after Launching an Industry?　5
What Is Marketing?　7
　Rollerblade Skates, Marketing, and You　8
　Marketing: Using Exchanges to Satisfy Needs　8
　The Diverse Factors Influencing Marketing Activities　8
　Requirements for Marketing to Occur　9
How Marketing Discovers and Satisfies Consumer Needs　10
　Discovering Consumer Needs　10

　Ethics and Social Responsibility Alert: Cell Phones and Distracted Driving—Just as Dangerous as Drunk Driving　13

　Satisfying Consumer Needs　14
The Marketing Program: How Customer Relationships Are Built　15
　Global Competition, Customer Value, and Customer Relationships　15
　Relationship Marketing　16
　The Marketing Program　16
　A Marketing Program for Rollerblade　16
How Marketing Became So Important　19
　Evolution of the Market Orientation　19
　Ethics and Social Responsibility: Balancing the Interests of
　　Different Groups　20
　The Breadth and Depth of Marketing　21

　Web Link: Marketing the Hermitage, a World-Class Russian Art Museum—with a Virtual Tour　23

Chapter in Review　24
Focusing on Key Terms　25
Discussion and Application Questions　25
Going Online: Your Personal Mechanized "Transporter"　25
Building Your Marketing Plan　26

Video Case 1 Rollerblade: Benefits Beyond Expectations　26

2　DEVELOPING SUCCESSFUL MARKETING AND CORPORATE STRATEGIES　28

Where Can an "A" in a Course in Ice Cream Making Lead?　29
Levels of Strategy in Organizations　30
　Today's Organizations: Kinds, Levels, and Teams　30
　Strategy Issues in Organizations　32

　Ethics and Social Responsibility Alert: The Global Dilemma: How to Achieve Sustainable Development　34

Setting Strategic Directions　35
　A Look Around: Where Are We Now?　35
　Growth Strategies: Where Do We Want to Go?　38

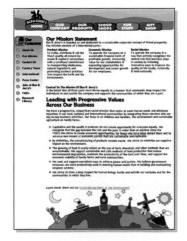

The Strategic Marketing Process 41
        Strategic Marketing Process: The Planning Phase   42

        *Web Link: Ben & Jerry's Flavors: From Chocolate Fudge Brownie Ice
        Cream and One Sweet Whirled Novelty Bars to . . . the Flavor Graveyard 43*

        Strategic Marketing Process: The Implementation Phase   46
        Strategic Marketing Process: The Control Phase   48
Chapter in Review   49
Focusing on Key Terms   50
Discussion and Application Questions   50
Going Online: How Mission Statements Compare   51
Building Your Marketing Plan   51

*Video Case 2 Specialized Bicycle Components, Inc.:
    Ride the Red "S"   51*

APPENDIX A: Building an Effective Management Plan   53

3   SCANNING THE MARKETING ENVIRONMENT   70
It's Show Time!   71
Environmental Scanning in the New Millennium   72
        Tracking Environmental Trends   72
        An Environmental Scan of Today's Marketplace   73
Social Forces   74
        Demographics   74

        *Marketing NewsNet: After Seeing 23 Million Ads,
        Generation Y Is Turning 21   76*

        Culture   78
Economic Forces   80
        Macroeconomic Forces   80
        Consumer Income   81

        Web Link: How Typical Is Your Home Town?   83

Technological Forces   83
        Technology of Tomorrow   83
        Technology's Impact on Customer Value   84
        Electronic Business Technologies   85
Competitive Forces   85
        Alternative Forms of Competition   85

        *Marketing NewsNet: Where Can You Go When You Are Wireless?
        Anywhere!   86*

        Components of Competition   86
        Small Businesses as Competitors   87
Regulatory Forces   87
        Protecting Competition   88
        Product-Related Legislation   88
        Pricing-Related Legislation   89
        Distribution-Related Legislation   90
        Advertising- and Promotion-Related Legislation   90

        *Ethics and Social Responsibility Alert: Is Telemarketing a First
        Amendment Right?   91*

        Control through Self-Regulation   91

Chapter in Review   92
Focusing on Key Terms   92
Discussion and Application Questions   92
Going Online: Using the Web to Scan the Environment   93
Building Your Marketing Plan   93

Video Case 3 Flyte Tyme Productions, Inc.: The Best Idea Wins   93

4   ETHICS AND SOCIAL RESPONSIBILITY IN MARKETING   96

There Is More Brewing at Anheuser-Busch than Beer   97
Nature and Significance of Marketing Ethics   98
  Ethical/Legal Framework in Marketing   98
  Current Perceptions of Ethical Behavior   99
Understanding Ethical Marketing Behavior   99
  Societal Culture and Norms   100
  Business Culture and Industry Practices   100

  Marketing NewsNet: Internet Piracy and Campus Pirates   101
  Web Link: The Corruption Perceptions Index   103

  Corporate Culture and Expectations   103
  Personal Moral Philosophy and Ethical Behavior   105
Understanding Social Responsibility in Marketing   106
  Concepts of Social Responsibility   107

  Marketing NewsNet: Will Consumers Switch Brands for a Cause?
  Yes, If . . .   109

  The Social Audit: Doing Well by Doing Good   109
  Turning the Table: Consumer Ethics and Social Responsibility   110
Chapter in Review   112
Focusing on Key Terms   112
Discussion and Application Questions   112
Going Online: Doing Well by Doing Good   113
Building Your Marketing Plan   113

Video Case 4 Starbucks Corporation: Serving More Than Coffee   113

Part 2   Understanding Buyers and Markets   116

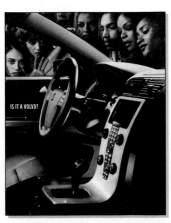

5   CONSUMER BEHAVIOR   118

Getting to Know the Automobile Custom(h)er and Influenc(h)er   119
Consumer Purchase Decision Process   120
  Problem Recognition: Perceiving a Need   120
  Information Search: Seeking Value   120
  Alternative Evaluation: Assessing Value   121
  Purchase Decision: Buying Value   122
  Postpurchase Behavior: Value in Consumption or Use   122

  Marketing NewsNet: The Value of a Satisfied Customer   123

  Involvement and Problem-Solving Variations   124
  Situation Influences   125
Psychological Influences on Consumer Behavior   126
  Motivation and Personality   126

  Ethics and Social Responsibility Alert: The Ethics of Subliminal
  Messages   128

Perception   128
Learning   130
Values, Beliefs, and Attitudes   131

Web Link: Identify Your VALS Profile   132

Lifestyle   132
Sociocultural Influences on Consumer Behavior   134
Personal Influence   134

Marketing NewsNet: BzzAgent—The Business of Buzz   135

Reference Groups   136
Family Influence   136
Social Class   138
Culture and Subculture   139
Chapter in Review   141
Focusing on Key Terms   142
Discussion and Application Questions   142
Going Online: Tracking Buying Power of Consumers   143
Building Your Marketing Plan   143

*Video Case 5 Ken Davis Products, Inc.: Sauces for
All Tastes   143*

6   ORGANIZATIONAL MARKETS AND BUYER BEHAVIOR   146

Buying Paper Is a Strategic Business Decision at JCPenney   147
The Nature and Size of Organizational Markets   148
Industrial Markets   149
Reseller Markets   149
Government Markets   149
Global Organizational Markets   149
Measuring Domestic and Global Industrial, Reseller, and
Government Markets   150
Characteristics of Organizational Buying   151
Demand Characteristics   151
Size of the Order or Purchase   151
Number of Potential Buyers   152
Organizational Buying Objectives   152

*Marketing NewsNet: The Airbus A380 Superjumbo Jet Is about to
Take Flight   153*

Organizational Buying Criteria   153

*Marketing NewsNet: Harley-Davidson's Supplier Collaboration Creates
Customer Value . . . and a Great Ride   154*

*Ethics and Social Responsibility Alert: Scratching Each Other's Back—The
Ethics of Reciprocity in Organizational Buying   155*

Buyer–Seller Relationships and Supply Partnerships   155
The Buying Center: A Cross-Functional Group   156
Charting the Organizational Buying Process   158
Stages in the Organizational Buying Process   158
Buying a Machine Vision System   159
Online Buying in Organizational Markets   161
Prominence of Online Buying in Organizational Markets   161

Web Link: eBay Means Business Too   162

E-Marketplaces: Virtual Organizational Markets   162
Online Auctions in Organizational Markets   163
Chapter in Review   164
Focusing on Key Terms   164
Discussion and Application Questions   164
Going Online: Navigating the NAICS   165
Building Your Marketing Plan   165

Video Case 6 Lands' End: Where Buyers Rule   166

7   REACHING GLOBAL MARKETS   168

Mattel's Global Marketing Is More than Child's Play   169
Dynamics of World Trade   170
World Trade Flows   170
Competitive Advantage of Nations   171
Marketing in a Borderless Economic World   174
Decline of Economic Protectionism   174

***Ethics and Social Responsibility Alert: Global Ethics and Global
Economics—The Case of Protectionism   175***

Rise of Economic Integration   176
A New Reality: Global Competition among Global Companies for
Global Consumers   177

***Marketing NewsNet: The Global Teenager—A Market of 500 Million
Consumers with $100 Billion to Spend   179***

Emergence of a Networked Global Marketspace   180
A Global Environmental Scan   181
Cultural Diversity   181
Economic Considerations   184

Web Link: Checking a Country's Political Risk   188

Political-Regulatory Climate   188
Global Market-Entry Strategies   189

***Marketing NewsNet: Creative Cosmetics and Creative Export Marketing
in Japan   190***

Exporting   190
Licensing   191
Joint Venture   191
Direct Investment   192
Crafting a Worldwide Marketing Program   193
Product and Promotion Strategies   193
Distribution Strategy   194
Pricing Strategy   195
Chapter in Review   196
Focusing on Key Terms   196
Discussion and Application Questions   197
Going Online: Getting to Know the WTO   197
Building Your Marketing Plan   197

Video Case 7 CNS Breath Right® Strips: Going Global   198

Part 3   Targeting Marketing Opportunities   200

8   **MARKETING RESEARCH: FROM INFORMATION TO ACTION   202**

Test Screenings: Listening to Consumers to Reduce Movie Risks   203
The Role of Marketing Research   205
    What Is Marketing Research?   205
    Why Good Marketing Research Is Difficult   206
    Five-Step Marketing Research Approach to Making
       Better Decisions   206
Step 1: Define the Problem   207
    Set the Research Objectives   207
    Identify Possible Marketing Actions   208
Step 2: Develop the Research Plan   209
    Specify Constraints   209
    Identify Data Needed for Marketing Actions   209
    Determine How to Collect Data   209
Step 3: Collect Relevant Information   210
    Secondary Data   210

    Web Link: Online Databases and Internet Resources Useful for Marketers   212

    Primary Data   213
    Using Information Technology to Trigger Marketing Actions   221
Step 4: Develop Findings   223
    Analyze the Data   223
    Present the Findings   223
Step 5: Take Marketing Actions   225
    Make Action Recommendations   225
    Implement the Action Recommendations   225
    Evaluate the Results   225
Chapter in Review   226
Focusing on Key Terms   226
Discussion and Application Questions   227
Going Online: What's New in Marketing Research?   227
Building Your Marketing Plan   228

*Video Case 8 Ford Consulting Group, Inc.: From Data to
    Actions   228*

9   **IDENTIFYING MARKET SEGMENTS AND TARGETS   230**

Sneakers Marketing Wars: Hip-Hop, Yao Ming, and 3 Billion
   Trillion Choices   231
Why Segment Markets?   233
    What Market Segmentation Means   233

    Marketing NewsNet: Sneaker Strategies—Who's Doing What   235

    When to Segment Markets   235

    Web Link: Customizing Your Own Designer Shoes   237

Steps in Segmenting and Targeting Markets   238
    Step 1: Group Potential Buyers into Segments   238
    Step 2: Group Products to Be Sold into Categories   244

Step 3: Develop a Market-Product Grid and Estimate Size
of Markets   244
Step 4: Select Target Markets   244
Step 5: Take Marketing Actions to Reach Target Markets   246
Market-Product Synergies: A Balancing Act   248

*Marketing NewsNet: Apple's Segmentation Strategy—Camp Runamok
No Longer   249*

Positioning the Product   249
Two Approaches to Product Positioning   250
Product Positioning Using Perceptual Maps   250
Sales Forecasting Techniques   252
Judgments of the Decision Maker   252
Surveys of Knowledgeable Groups   253
Statistical Methods   253
Chapter in Review   254
Focusing on Key Terms   254
Discussion and Application Questions   254
Going Online: Apple's Latest Market-Product Strategies   255
Building Your Marketing Plan   255

Video Case 9 Nokia: A Phone for Every Segment   255

Part 4   Satisfying Marketing Opportunities   258

10   DEVELOPING NEW PRODUCTS AND SERVICES   260

3M's New Grephite Grip Golf Glove: How to Get to the Top of the
Leader Board   261
The Variations of Products   262
Product Line and Product Mix   262
Classifying Products   263
Classifying Consumer and Business Groups   264
Classification of Consumer Groups   264
Classification of Business Groups   265
New Products and Why They Succeed or Fail   266
What Is a New Product?   266

*Marketing NewsNet: Blindsided in the Twenty-First Century—The
Convergence of Digital Devices   267*

Why Products Succeed or Fail   268

Marketing NewsNet: What Separates New-Product Winners and Losers   269

*Marketing NewsNet: When Less Is More—How Reducing the Number of
Features Can Open Up Huge Markets   271*

The New-Product Process   272
New-Product Strategy Development   272
Idea Generation   273

Web Link: IDEO—Where Design Is Not a Noun . . . It's a Verb   275

Screening and Evaluation   275
Business Analysis   277
Development   277

*Ethics and Social Responsibility Alert: SUVs and Pickups versus
Cars—Godzilla Meets a Chimp?   278*

Market Testing   279
Commercialization   280
Chapter in Review   282
Focusing on Key Terms   283
Discussion and Application Questions   283
Going Online: Jalapeño Soda, Anyone?   283
Building Your Marketing Plan   283

*Video Case 10 3M™ Greptile Grip™ Golf Glove:
Great Gripping!   284*

11   MANAGING PRODUCTS AND BRANDS   286

Gatorade: An Unquenchable Thirst for Competition   287
The Product Life Cycle   288
Introduction Stage   288
Growth Stage   290
Maturity Stage   292
Decline Stage   292

Marketing NewsNet: Will E-Mail Spell Doom for the Familiar Fax?   293

Some Dimensions of the Product Life Cycle   293
Managing the Product Life Cycle   296
Role of a Product Manager   296
Modifying the Product   297
Modifying the Market   297

***Ethics and Social Responsibility Alert: Consumer Economics of
Downsizing—Get Less, Pay More   298***

Repositioning the Product   298
Branding and Brand Management   299
Brand Personality and Brand Equity   300

Web Link: Have an Idea for a Brand or Trade Name? Check It Out   303

Picking a Good Brand Name   303
Branding Strategies   304

***Marketing NewsNet: Creating Customer Value through Packaging—Pez
Heads Dispense More Than Candy   306***

Packaging and Labeling   307
Creating Customer Value and Competitive Advantage through
Packaging and Labeling   307
Global Trends in Packaging   309
Product Warranty   309
Chapter in Review   310
Focusing on Key Terms   311
Discussion and Application Questions   311
Going Online: Brand News You Can Use   311
Building Your Marketing Plan   311

Video Case 11 BMW: "Newness" and the Product Life Cycle   312

12   MANAGING SERVICES   314

The Newest Services Manufacture Experiences: Just Ask Anyone Who
Has Been Captured by a Borg!   315

The Uniqueness of Services   316
   The Four I's of Services   317
   The Service Continuum   319

   Marketing NewsNet: Sports Get a Gold Medal—in Marketing!   321

   Classifying Services   321

   Web Link: Nonprofit Organizations Are Becoming Marketing Experts   323

How Consumers Purchase Services   323
   The Purchase Process   323
   Assessing Service Quality   324

   *Marketing NewsNet: What if Someone Complains? How Services Can
   Recover from Failure to Satisfy a Customer   325*

   Customer Contact and Relationship Marketing   325
Managing the Marketing of Services   327
   Product (Service)   327
   Pricing   328
   Place (Distribution)   329
   Promotion   329
Services in the Future   330
Chapter in Review   330
Focusing on Key Terms   331
Discussion and Application Questions   331
Going Online: Reviewing the Latest Services Marketing Strategies   331
Building Your Marketing Plan   331

Video Case 12 Philadelphia Phillies, Inc.: Sports Marketing 101   332

13   **BUILDING THE PRICE FOUNDATION   334**

Where Dot-Coms Still Thrive: Helping You Get a $100-a-Night Hotel
   Room Overlooking New York's Central Park   335
Nature and Importance of Price   336
   What Is a Price?   336

   *Ethics and Social Responsibility Alert: Student Credit Cards—What Is the
   Real Price?   338*

   Price as an Indicator of Value   338
   Price in the Marketing Mix   339
Step 1: Identify Pricing Objectives and Constraints   340
   Identifying Pricing Objectives   340
   Identifying Pricing Constraints   341

   *Web Link: Pricing 101: $4,205 for a 1969 Used Hotwheels Volkswagen
   Van, or $121,000 for a Mint-Condition 1952 Mickey Mantle Topps
   Baseball Card?   343*

Step 2: Estimate Demand and Revenue   344
   Fundamentals of Estimating Demand   344
   Fundamentals of Estimating Revenue   346

   *Marketing NewsNet: The Airbus versus Boeing Face-Off—How Many Can
   We Sell and at What Price . . . in 2006 and 2008?   348*

Step 3: Determine Cost, Volume, and Profit Relationships   350
   The Importance of Controlling Costs   350

Marketing NewsNet: Pricing Lessons from the Dot-Coms—Understand Revenues and Expenses 351

Marginal Analysis and Profit Maximization 351
Break-Even Analysis 351
Chapter in Review 355
Focusing on Key Terms 356
Discussion and Application Questions 356
Going Online: Finding the Best Airline Ticket Price 357
Building Your Marketing Plan 357

Video Case 13 Washburn International: Guitars and Break-Even 358

14   ARRIVING AT THE FINAL PRICE 360

Gillette Knows the Value of a Great Shave 361
Step 4: Select an Approximate Price Level 362
Demand-Oriented Approaches 362

Marketing NewsNet: Energizer's Lesson in Price Perception—Value Lies in the Eye of the Beholder 365

Cost-Oriented Approaches 365
Profit-Oriented Approaches 367
Competition-Oriented Approaches 370
Step 5: Set the List or Quoted Price 371
One-Price versus Flexible-Price Policy 371

Ethics and Social Responsibility Alert: Flexible Pricing—Is There Race and Gender Discrimination in Bargaining for a New Car? 372

Company, Customer, and Competitive Effects on Pricing 372
Balancing Incremental Costs and Revenues 374
Step 6: Make Special Adjustments to the List or Quoted Price 374
Discounts 375
Allowances 377

Marketing NewsNet: Everyday Low Prices at the Supermarket = Everyday Low Profits—Creating Customer Value at a Cost 378

Geographical Adjustments 378
Legal and Regulatory Aspects of Pricing 379

Web Link: And You Thought That "Free" Is Simply Defined 380

Chapter in Review 382
Focusing on Key Terms 382
Discussion and Application Questions 383
Going Online: The Cost of Price Discrimination 383
Building Your Marketing Plan 383

Video Case 14 Stuart Cellars: Price Is a Matter of Taste 384

APPENDIX B: Financial Aspects of Marketing 386

15   MANAGING MARKETING CHANNELS AND WHOLESALING 394

Apple Stores: Adding High-Touch to High-Tech Marketing Channels 395
Nature and Importance of Marketing Channels 396
What Is a Marketing Channel of Distribution? 396

Value Created by Intermediaries   397
Channel Structure and Organization   398
Marketing Channels for Consumer Goods and Services   398
Marketing Channels for Business Goods and Services   400
Electronic Marketing Channels   400
Direct Marketing Channels   401

Marketing NewsNet: Nestlé and General Mills—Cereal Partners Worldwide   402

Multiple Channels and Strategic Channel Alliances   402
A Closer Look at Channel Intermediaries   402
Vertical Marketing Systems and Channel Partnerships   405
Channel Choice and Management   407
Factors Affecting Channel Choice and Management   407

Marketing NewsNet: Wrigley Markets a Controlled Substance in Singapore—Chewing Gum   408

Channel Design Considerations   409

Web Link: Visit an Apple Store to See What All the Excitement Is About   411

Global Dimensions of Marketing Channels   411
Channel Relationships: Conflict, Cooperation, and Law   412

Ethics and Social Responsibility Alert: The Ethics of Slotting Allowances   413

Chapter in Review   415
Focusing on Key Terms   415
Discussion and Application Questions   416
Going Online: Finding a Franchise for You   416
Building Your Marketing Plan   416

Video Case 15 Golden Valley Microwave Foods: The Surprising Channel   417

16   **INTEGRATING SUPPLY CHAIN AND LOGISTICS MANAGEMENT   417**

Snap! Crack! Pop! Even World-Class Companies Like Nike Can Feel the Bullwhip's Sting   421
Significance of Supply Chain and Logistics Management   422
Relating Marketing Channels, Logistics, and Supply Chain Management   422
Supply Chains versus Marketing Channels   422
Sourcing, Assembling, and Delivering a New Car: The Automotive Supply Chain   423

Web Link: Build Your Own BMW with a Mouse   424

Supply Chain Management and Marketing Strategy   424

Marketing NewsNet: IBM—Creating an On-Demand Supply Chain   425

Objective of Information and Logistics Management in a Supply Chain   427
Information's Role in Supply Chain Responsiveness and Efficiency   427
Total Logistics Cost Concept   428
Customer Service Concept   429

Marketing NewsNet: For Fashion and Food Merchandising, Haste Is as Important as Taste **430**

Customer Service Standards   431
Key Logistics Functions in a Supply Chain   432
Transportation   432
Warehousing and Materials Handling   434
Order Processing   435
Inventory Management   436

Ethics and Social Responsibility Alert: Reverse Logistics and Green Marketing Go Together at Estée Lauder **438**

Closing the Loop: Reverse Logistics   438
Chapter in Review   439
Focusing on Key Terms   439
Discussion and Application Questions   439
Going Online: Tracking Supply Chain Trends   440
Building Your Marketing Plan   440

Video Case 16 Amazon: Delivering the Goods . . . Millions of Times a Day   440

17   RETAILING   442

Trading Up . . . at Target!   443
The Value of Retailing   444
Consumer Utilities Offered by Retailing   445
The Global Economic Impact of Retailing   445
Classifying Retail Outlets   446
Form of Ownership   446

Marketing NewsNet: Say Good-Bye to Bar Codes! **447**

Level of Service   448
Merchandise Line   449
Nonstore Retailing   450
Automatic Vending   451
Direct Mail and Catalogs   451
Television Home Shopping   452
Online Retailing   453

Web Link: Dress (Your Virtual Model) for Success! **454**

Telemarketing   454
Direct Selling   455
Retailing Strategy   455
Positioning a Retail Store   455
Retailing Mix   457

Ethics and Social Responsibility Alert: Who Takes the Five-Finger Discount? You'll Be Surprised! **458**

The Changing Nature of Retailing   461
The Wheel of Retailing   461
The Retail Life Cycle   462
Future Changes in Retailing   463
Multichannel Retailing   463
The Impact of Technology   463
Changing Shopping Behavior   464

Chapter in Review   464
Focusing on Key Terms   465
Discussion and Application Questions   465
Going Online: Consumers Can Now "Shop With Their Bot"!   465
Building Your Marketing Plan   465

*Video Case 17 Mall of America: Shopping and a Whole
Lot More   466*

**18   INTEGRATED MARKETING COMMUNICATIONS AND
DIRECT MARKETING   468**

Who Is Going to Disney World Next?   469
The Communication Process   470
   Encoding and Decoding   471
   Feedback   472
   Noise   472
The Promotional Elements   472
   Advertising   473
   Personal Selling   474
   Public Relations   474
   Sales Promotion   475
   Direct Marketing   475
Integrated Marketing Communications—Developing the
  Promotional Mix   476
   The Target Audience   476
   The Product Life Cycle   476

   *Marketing NewsNet: Gen Y Applies Multitasking to Media
   Consumption—29 Hours per Day!   477*

   Product Characteristics   478
   Stages of the Buying Decision   478
   Channel Strategies   480

   Web Link: Direct-to-Consumer Drug Marketing Moves to the Web   481

Developing an IMC Program   481
   Identifying the Target Audience   482
   Specifying Promotion Objectives   482
   Setting the Promotion Budget   483
   Selecting the Right Promotional Tools   484
   Designing the Promotion   485
   Scheduling the Promotion   485
Executing and Evaluating the Promotion Program   485
Direct Marketing   486
   The Growth of Direct Marketing   487
   The Value of Direct Marketing   487
   Technological, Global, and Ethical Issues in Direct
     Marketing   488

   *Ethics and Social Responsibility Alert: How Do You Like Your E-Mail?
   "Opt-out" or "Opt-in" Are Your Choices   489*

Chapter in Review   490
Focusing on Key Terms   490
Discussion and Application Questions   490

Going Online: Agencies Adopt IMC Approaches   491
Building Your Marketing Plan   491

Video Case 18 UPS: Repositioning a Business with IMC   492

**19   ADVERTISING, SALES PROMOTION, AND PUBLIC
RELATIONS   494**

Welcome to the New World of Advertising   495
Types of Advertisements   496
   Product Advertisements   497
   Institutional Advertisements   497
Developing the Advertising Program   498
   Identifying the Target Audience   498
   Specifying Advertising Objectives   499
   Setting the Advertising Budget   499

   Web Link: See Your Favorite Super Bowl Ad Again   500

   Designing the Advertisement   500

   **Ethics and Social Responsibility Alert: Who Decides What Is
"Appropriate" Advertising?   502**

   Selecting the Right Media   503
   Different Media Alternatives   505

   Marketing NewsNet: Does Internet Advertising Really Work?   510

   Scheduling the Advertising   511
Executing the Advertising Program   512
   Pretesting the Advertising   512
   Carrying Out the Advertising Program   512
Evaluating the Advertising Program   513
   Posttesting the Advertising   513
   Making Needed Changes   514
Sales Promotion   514
   Consumer-Oriented Sales Promotions   514
   Trade-Oriented Sales Promotions   519
Public Relations   520
   Publicity Tools   520
Increasing the Value of Promotion   521
   Building Long-Term Relationships with Promotion   521
   Self-Regulation   521
Chapter in Review   522
Focusing on Key Terms   522
Discussion and Application Questions   523
Going Online: Advertising on the Internet   523
Building Your Marketing Plan   523

Video Case 19 Fallon Worldwide: In the Creativity *Business   524*

20   PERSONAL SELLING AND SALES MANAGEMENT   526

Selling the Way Customers Want to Buy   527
Scope and Significance of Personal Selling and Sales
   Management   528
   Nature of Personal Selling and Sales Management   528
   Selling Happens Almost Everywhere   528

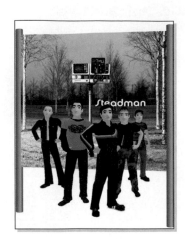

Personal Selling in Marketing   529
Creating Customer Value through Salespeople: Relationship and
    Partnership Selling   529
The Many Forms of Personal Selling   530
    Order Taking   531
    Order Getting   531
    Customer Sales Support Personnel   532

*Marketing NewsNet: Creating and Sustaining Customer Value through
Cross-Functional Team Selling   533*

The Personal Selling Process: Building Relationships   533
    Prospecting   534
    Preapproach   535
    Approach   536
    Presentation   536

Marketing NewsNet: The Subtlety of Saying Yes in East Asia   538

    Close   538
    Follow-Up   539
The Sales Management Process   539

*Ethics and Social Responsibility Alert: The Ethics of Asking Customers
about Competitors   540*

Sales Plan Formation: Setting Direction   540

Web Link: What Is Your Emotional Intelligence?   545

    Sales Plan Implementation: Putting the Plan into Action   545
    Salesforce Evaluation and Control: Measuring Results   547
    Salesforce Automation and Customer Relationship Management   548
Chapter in Review   550
Focusing on Key Terms   550
Discussion and Application Questions   550
Going Online: Selling News You Can Use   551
Building Your Marketing Plan   551

Video Case 20 Reebok: Relationship Selling and Customer Value   552

Part 5   Managing the Marketing Process   554

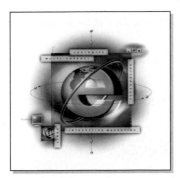

21   **IMPLEMENTING INTERACTIVE AND
     MULTICHANNEL MARKETING   556**

Reflect.com: Creating Customized Cosmetics   557
Creating Customer Value, Relationships, and Experiences
    in Marketspace   558
    Customer Value Creation in Marketspace   559
    Interactivity, Individuality, and Customer Relationships
        in Marketspace   560

*Web Link: Interactivity and Individuality—Your Nike iD Customized
Product   561*

    Creating an Online Customer Experience   561
Online Consumer Behavior and Marketing Practice in Marketspace   564
    The Online Consumer   564

What Online Consumers Buy   565

Marketing NewsNet: Meet Today's Internet Mom—All 31 Million!   *566*

Why Consumers Shop and Buy Online   567

Ethics and Social Responsibility Alert: Sweet and Sour Cookies in the New Marketspace   *571*

When and Where Online Consumers Shop and Buy   571
Multichannel Marketing to the Online Consumer   572
    Integrating and Leveraging Multiple Channels with Multichannel
        Marketing   572

Marketing NewsNet: The Multichannel Marketing Multiplier   *573*

    Implementing Multichannel Marketing   573
Chapter in Review   575
Focusing on Key Terms   576
Discussion and Application Questions   576
Going Online: Tracking Trends in Interactive Marketing   576
Building Your Marketing Plan   577

Video Case 21 McFarlane Toys: The Best of Interactive Marketing   577

**22   PULLING IT ALL TOGETHER: THE STRATEGIC
MARKETING PROCESS   580**

Marketing Strategy at General Mills: Tough Competition and
    Critical Decisions   581
Marketing Basics: Doing What Works and Allocating Resources   582
    Finding and Using What Really Works   582
    Allocating Marketing Resources Using Sales Response
        Functions   584
The Planning Phase of the Strategic Marketing Process   586
    The Variety of Marketing Plans   587

*Web Link: Want to Be a BCG Consultant? Solve the Trevor's Toys
Online Case*   *588*

    Marketing Planning Frameworks: The Search for Growth   588

*Marketing NewsNet: The Strategy Issue for the New
Millennium—Finding Synergies*   *592*

    Some Planning and Strategy Lessons   593

*Marketing NewsNet: Keeping Planning Simple at Big G: "One-Handed"
Convenience plus Cover All the Bases*   *595*

The Implementation Phase of the Strategic Marketing Process   596
    Is Planning or Implementation the Problem?   596

*Marketing NewsNet: GE's Implementation Strategies—How Neutron Jack
Became One of the Most Acclaimed CEOs of the Twentieth Century*   *597*

    Increasing Emphasis on Marketing Implementation   597
    Improving Implementation of Marketing Programs   598
    Organizing for Marketing   600
The Control Phase of the Strategic Marketing Process   602
    The Marketing Control Process   602
    Sales Analysis   603
    Profitability Analysis and ROI Marketing   604

Chapter in Review   604
Focusing on Key Terms   605
Discussion and Application Questions   605
Going Online: Strategic Actions of Three CEOs   606
Building Your Marketing Plan   606

Video Case 22 Yoplait® USA: Portrait of a Turnaround   607

APPENDIX C: Planning a Career in Marketing   610
APPENDIX D: Alternate Cases   628

Case D–1 Burton Snowboards: Building a Sport   628
Case D–2 Daktronics, Inc: Global Displays in 68 Billion Colors   629
Case D–3 Jamba Juice: Scanning the Marketing Environment   631
Case D–4 Ford and Firestone: Who's to Blame?   633
Case D–5 The Jamisons Buy an Espresso Machine   635
Case D–6 Motetronix Technology: Marketing Smart Dust   636
Case D–7 Callaway Golf: The Global Challenge   637
Case D–8 HOM Furniture: Where Keen Observation Pays   639
Case D–9 The Hummer: A Segmentation Challenge   641
Case D–10 Medtronic in China: Where "Simpler" Serves Patients
            Better   642
Case D–11 Pampered Pooches Travel in Style   644
Case D–12 DigitalThink: Marketing E-Learning Services   645
Case D–13 Health Cruises, Inc.: Estimating Cost, Volume, and Profit
            Relationships   646
Case D–14 Little Remedies® Brand: Vetco, Inc.: The Bad News
            E-mail   647
Case D–15 Fastenal Company: Bringing Retail Principles to the
            Wholesale Market   650
Case D–16 Dell Inc.: A Leader in Supply Chain Management   651
Case D–17 Nordstrom, Inc.: Retailing in a Competitive Environment   652
Case D–18 McDonald's Restaurants: An IMC Program to Reach
            Different Segments   653
Case D–19 Volkswagen: The Drivers Wanted Campaign   655
Case D–20 Manor Furniture: Making Promotion Trade-Offs   656
Case D–21 Crate and Barrel: Multichannel Marketing   658
Case D–22 BP Connect: Gasoline, Convenience, and . . .
            Just-Baked Bread   659

Glossary   661
Chapter Notes   673
Credits   701
Name Index   705
Company/Product Index   711
Subject Index   718

BOXED FEATURES

Stay up to date with these timely and interesting boxed features

MARKETING NEWSNET

Chapter 3	• After Seeing 23 Million Ads, Generation Y Is Turning 21 76
	• Where Can You Go When You Are Wireless? Anywhere! 86
Chapter 4	• Internet Piracy and Campus Pirates 101
	• Will Consumers Switch Brands for a Cause? Yes, If . . . 109
Chapter 5	• The Value of a Satisfied Customer 123
	• BzzAgent—The Business of Buzz 135
Chapter 6	• The Airbus A380 Superjumbo Jet Is about to Take Flight 153
	• Harley-Davidson's Supplier Collaboration Creates Customer Value . . . and a Great Ride 154
Chapter 7	• The Global Teenager—A Market of 500 Million Consumers with $100 Billion to Spend 179
	• Creative Cosmetics and Creative Export Marketing in Japan 190
Chapter 9	• Sneaker Strategies—Who's Doing What 235
	• Apple's Segmentation Strategy—Camp Runamok No Longer 249
Chapter 10	• Blindsided in the Twenty-First Century—The Convergence of Digital Devices 267
	• What Separates New-Product Winners and Losers 269
	• When Less Is More—How Reducing the Number of Features Can Open Up Huge Markets 271
Chapter 11	• Will E-Mail Spell Doom for the Familiar Fax? 293
	• Creating Customer Value through Packaging—Pez Heads Dispense More Than Candy 306
Chapter 12	• Sports Get a Gold Medal—in Marketing! 321
	• What if Someone Complains? How Services Can Recover from Failure to Satisfy a Customer 325
Chapter 13	• The Airbus versus Boeing Face-Off—How Many Can We Sell and at What Price . . . in 2006 and 2008? 348
	• Pricing Lessons from the Dot-Coms—Understand Revenues and Expenses 351
Chapter 14	• Energizer's Lesson in Price Perception—Value Lies in the Eye of the Beholder 365
	• Everyday Low Prices at the Supermarket = Everyday Low Profits—Creating Customer Value at a Cost 378
Chapter 15	• Nestlé and General Mills—Cereal Partners Worldwide 402
	• Wrigley Markets a Controlled Substance in Singapore—Chewing Gum 408

Chapter 16 • IBM—Creating an On-Demand Supply Chain 425

• For Fashion and Food Merchandising, Haste Is as Important as Taste 430

Chapter 17 • Say Good-Bye to Bar Codes! 447

Chapter 18 • Gen Y Applies Multitasking to Media Consumption—29 Hours per Day! 477

Chapter 19 • Does Internet Advertising Really Work? 510

Chapter 20 • Creating and Sustaining Customer Value through Cross-Functional Team Selling 533

• The Subtlety of Saying *Yes* in East Asia 539

Chapter 21 • Meet Today's Internet Mom—All 31 Million! 566

• The Multichannel Marketing Multiplier 573

Chapter 22 • The Strategy Issue for the New Millennium—Finding Synergies 592

• Keeping Planning Simple at Big G: "One-Handed" Convenience plus Cover All the Bases 595

• GE's Implementation Strategies—How Neutron Jack Became One of the Most Acclaimed CEOs of the Twentieth Century 597

WEB LINK

www.mhhe.com/Kerin

Chapter 1 • Marketing the Hermitage, a World-Class Russian Art Museum—with a Virtual Tour 23

Chapter 2 • Ben & Jerry's Flavors—From Chocolate Fudge Brownie Ice Cream and One Sweet Whirled Novelty Bars to . . . the Flavor Graveyard 43

Chapter 3 • How Typical Is Your Home Town? 83

Chapter 4 • The Corruption Perceptions Index 103

Chapter 5 • Identify Your VALS Profile 132

Chapter 6 • eBay Means Business Too 162

Chapter 7 • Checking a Country's Political Risk 188

Chapter 8 • Online Databases and Internet Resources Useful for Marketers 212

Chapter 9 • Customizing Your Own Designer Shoes 237

Chapter 10 • IDEO—Where Design Is Not a Noun . . . It's a Verb 275

Chapter 11 • Have an Idea for a Brand or Trade Name? Check It Out 303

Chapter 12 • Nonprofit Organizations Are Becoming Marketing Experts 323

Chapter 13 • Pricing 101—$4,205 for a 1969 Used Hotwheels Volkswagen Van, or $121,000 for a Mint-Condition 1952 Mickey Mantle Topps Baseball Card? 343

Chapter 14 • And You Thought That "Free" Is Simply Defined 380

Chapter 15 • Visit an Apple Store to See What All the Excitement Is About 411

Chapter 16 • Build Your Own BMW with a Mouse 424

Chapter 17 • Dress (Your Virtual Model) for Success! 454

Chapter 18 • Direct-to-Consumer Drug Marketing Moves to the Web 481

Chapter 19 • See Your Favorite Super Bowl Ad Again 500

Chapter 20 • What Is Your Emotional Intelligence? 545

Chapter 21 • Interactivity and Individuality—Your Nike iD Customized Product 561

Chapter 22 • Want to Be a BCG Consultant? Solve the Trevor's Toys Online Case 588

ETHICS AND SOCIAL RESPONSIBILITY ALERT

Chapter 1 • Cell Phones and Distracted Driving—Just as Dangerous as Drunk Driving 13

Chapter 2 • The Global Dilemma—How to Achieve Sustainable Development 34

Chapter 3 • Is Telemarketing a First Amendment Right? 91

Chapter 5 • The Ethics of Subliminal Messages 128

Chapter 6 • Scratching Each Other's Back—The Ethics of Reciprocity in Organizational Buying 155

Chapter 7 • Global Ethics and Global Economics—The Case of Protectionism 175

Chapter 10 • SUVs and Pickups versus Cars—Godzilla Meets a Chimp? 278

Chapter 11 • Consumer Economics of Downsizing—Get Less, Pay More 298

Chapter 13 • Student Credit Cards—What Is the Real Price? 338

Chapter 14 • Flexible Pricing—Is There Race and Gender Discrimination in Bargaining for a New Car? 372

Chapter 15 • The Ethics of Slotting Allowances 413

Chapter 16 • Reverse Logistics and Green Marketing Go Together at Estée Lauder 438

Chapter 17 • Who Takes the Five-Finger Discount? You'll Be Surprised! 458

Chapter 18 • How Do You Like Your E-Mail? "Opt-out" or "Opt-in" Are Your Choices 489

Chapter 19 • Who Decides What Is "Appropriate" Advertising? 502

Chapter 20 • The Ethics of Asking Customers about Competitors 540

Chapter 21 • Sweet and Sour Cookies in the New Marketspace 571

MARKETING

PART 1
Initiating the Marketing
Process

PART 2
Understanding Buyers
and Markets

PART 3
Targeting Marketing
Opportunities

PART 4
Satisfying Marketing
Opportunities

PART 5
Managing the
Marketing Process

1 INITIATING THE MARKETING PROCESS

HOW PART 1 FITS INTO THE BOOK

Laying the foundation for the entire book, chapters in Part 1 explain what marketing and the strategic marketing process are, and relate the importance of environmental, ethical, and social responsibility factors to a manager's marketing actions.

CHAPTER 1
Creating Customer Relationships and Value through Marketing

CHAPTER 2
Developing Successful Marketing and Corporate Strategies

APPENDIX A
Building an Effective Marketing Plan

CHAPTER 3
Scanning the Marketing Environment

CHAPTER 4
Ethics and Social Responsibility in Marketing

CREATING CUSTOMER RELATIONSHIPS AND VALUE THROUGH MARKETING

LEARNING OBJECTIVES

After reading this chapter you should be able to:

1 Define marketing and identify the requirements for marketing to occur.

2 Explain how marketing discovers and satisfies consumer needs.

3 Distinguish between marketing mix elements and environmental factors.

4 Explain how organizations build strong customer relationships and customer value through marketing.

5 Describe how today's customer era differs from prior eras oriented to production and selling.

6 Explain how marketing creates utilities for consumers.

AERO? LIGHTNING? THE NEXT ACT AFTER LAUNCHING AN INDUSTRY?

What do you do for the next act, for your encore, when you create an entire industry?

That's the challenge facing the company featured on the opposite page. It launched the in-line skate industry two decades ago. But such success attracts lots of competitors. So what does it do to provide exciting new products to build and maintain continuing, loyal customer relationships? A big part of the answer is its new Aero™, Lightning™, Zetrablade™, and Microblade™ lines of in-line skates. But that puts us ahead of the Rollerblade® story.

A New Idea That Wasn't So New   In the early 1700s, a Dutch inventor trying to simulate ice skating in the summer created the first roller skates by attaching spools in a single row to his shoes. His "in-line" arrangement was the standard design until 1863 when the first skates with rollers set as two pairs appeared. This two-pair design became the new standard, and in-line skates virtually disappeared from the market.

In 1980, two Minnesota hockey-playing brothers found an old pair of in-line skates while browsing through a sporting goods store. Working in their garage, they modified the design to add hard plastic wheels, a molded boot shell, and a toe brake. They sold their product, which they dubbed "Rollerblade skates," out of the back of their truck to off-season hockey players and skiers. In the mid-1980s, Rollerblade marketing executive Mary Horwath had to figure out how to market its in-line skates to a broader range of customers.

Understanding the Consumer   "When I came here," remembers Horwath, "I knew there had to be a change." By focusing only on hockey players and skiers who used in-line skates to train during the summer, Rollerblade had developed an image as a training product. Conversations with in-line skaters, however, convinced Horwath that using Rollerblade skates:

- Was incredible fun.
- Was a great aerobic workout and made the skater stronger and healthier.
- Was quite different from traditional roller skating, which was practiced alone, mostly inside, and mostly by young girls.
- Would appeal to more than just off-season ice hockey skaters and skiers.

Horwath set out to reposition Rollerblade, to change the image in people's minds from in-line skating as off-season training to in-line skating as a new kind of fun exercise that anyone could do.

It worked. As shown in Figure 1–1,[1] Horwath and the company succeeded in popularizing in-line skating and actually launched an entirely new industry that by 1997 had more than 27 million U.S. in-line skaters.

Success Invites Imitation, Which Stimulates Innovation   The marketing problems of Rollerblade today are far different than those faced by Mary Horwath in the late 1980s. Rollerblade's success in launching a new industry brought its own dangers: major competition in terms of not only more than 30 other skate manufacturers but also competing sports like skateboarding, biking, and snowboarding. Yet Rollerblade still has 35 percent of the industry sales, with no other competitor having more than 10 percent. Still, Figure 1–1 shows that the number of in-line skaters in the United States has declined from its 1997 peak, a concern for Rollerblade. If this declining trend continues, Rollerblade can only grow by increasing its share of the number of in-line skates sold annually, requiring innovation and creative marketing strategies to meet customer needs.

FIGURE 1–1

Number of in-line skaters in the United States. Where is the trend headed and what marketing actions might Rollerblade take? For some answers, see the text.

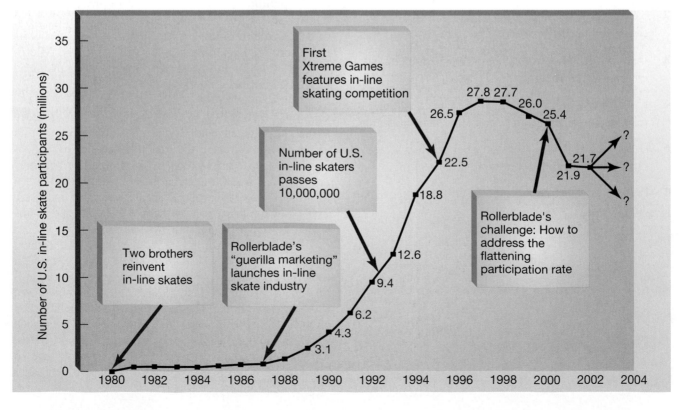

What special features might Rollerblade design into an in-line skate for the fitness/recreation segment? For children? Rollerblade's marketing programs for these two segments appear later in the chapter.

WHAT IS MARKETING?

Here's some good news: In many respects you are a marketing expert already because you do many marketing activities every day. For example, would you sell more 42-inch Panasonic Diagonal HDTV Plasma Displays for $6,499 or $499 each? You answered $499, right? So your experience in shopping for products already gives you great insights into the world of marketing. As a consumer, you've already been involved in thousands of marketing decisions—but mainly on the buying, not the selling, side. But just to test your expertise, try the "marketing expert" questions in Figure 1–2. You'll find the answers in the next few pages.

The bad news is, good marketing isn't always easy. In Rollerblade's case, it's easy to talk about making new and better skates for potential customers but not so simple to do. One of Rollerblade's strategies is to market skates designed for the special needs of different groups, or segments, of in-line skaters. What special features might Rollerblade build into an in-line skate for (1) the fitness/recreation segment that skates·mainly for fun and (2) the children segment? Give some thought to this. We'll analyze Rollerblade's strategies for these two segments later in the chapter.

FIGURE 1–2

The see-if-you're-really-a-marketing-expert test

Answer the questions below. The correct answers are given later in the chapter.

1. True or False. You can now buy a robotic floor vacuum that cleans as good or better than an upright vacuum—even when you're not there!
2. Eating, talking on a cell phone, changing a CD, and other distracted driving behaviors account for what percentage of auto accidents each year according to the National Highway Traffic Safety Administration?
   (a) 5%, (b) 10%, (c) 30%, (d) 50%.
3. True or False. The 60-year lifetime value of a loyal Kleenex customer is $994.
4. To be socially responsible, 3M puts what recycled material into its very successful ScotchBrite® Never Rust™ Soap Pads? (a) aluminum cans, (b) steel-belted tires, (c) plastic bottles, (d) computer screens.

Fast forward to today to hear Jeremy Stonier, Rollerblade's current director of product marketing, describe a key challenge he faces: "How do you continue to innovate and perfect something that's already a pretty darn good device?" Stonier's answer focuses on innovation and customer benefits: "We make Rollerblade skates better year by year by providing benefits that are beyond what people are expecting to have."[2]

Rollerblade's history presents a huge marketing lesson: Changing consumer tastes and changing competitive offerings require that an organization search continuously for ways to provide genuine value to customers, or sales will fall and the organization will die.

Rollerblade Skates, Marketing, and You

What marketing strategy is the Rollerblade marketing team using today? By the time you reach the end of this chapter, you will know some of the answers to this question.

One key to how well Rollerblade succeeds lies in the subject of this book: marketing. In this chapter and in the rest of the book, we'll introduce you to many of the people, organizations, ideas, and activities in marketing that have spawned the products and services that have been towering successes, shattering failures, or something in between.

Marketing affects all individuals, all organizations, all industries, and all countries. This book seeks to teach you marketing concepts, often by having you actually "do marketing"—by putting you in the shoes of a marketing manager facing actual marketing opportunities and problems. The book also shows marketing's many applications and how it affects our lives. This knowledge should make you a better consumer, help you in your career, and enable you to be a more informed citizen.

In this chapter and those that follow, you will feel the excitement of marketing. You will be introduced to the dynamic changes that will affect all of us in the future. You will also meet many men and women whose marketing creativity sometimes achieved brilliant, extraordinary results. And who knows? Somewhere in these pages you may find a career.

Marketing: Using Exchanges to Satisfy Needs

The American Marketing Association, representing marketing professionals, states that "**marketing** is an organizational function and a set of processes for creating, communicating, and delivering value to customers and for managing customer relationships in ways that benefit the organization and its stakeholders."[3] Many people incorrectly believe that marketing is the same thing as advertising or personal selling; this definition shows marketing to be a far broader activity. This definition stresses the importance of delivering genuine value in the goods, services, and ideas marketed to customers. Also, note that the organization doing the marketing and the stakeholders affected—such as customers, employees, suppliers, and shareholders—should both benefit.

To serve both buyers and sellers, marketing seeks (1) to discover the needs and wants of prospective customers and (2) to satisfy them. These prospective customers include both individuals buying for themselves and their households, and organizations that buy for their own use (such as manufacturers) or for resale (such as wholesalers and retailers). The key to achieving these two objectives is the idea of **exchange**, which is the trade of things of value between buyer and seller so that each is better off after the trade. This vital concept of exchange in marketing is covered below in more detail.

The Diverse Factors Influencing Marketing Activities

Although an organization's marketing activity focuses on assessing and satisfying consumer needs, countless other people, groups, and forces interact to shape the nature of its activities (Figure 1–3). Foremost is the organization itself, whose mission and objectives determine what business it is in and what goals it seeks. Within

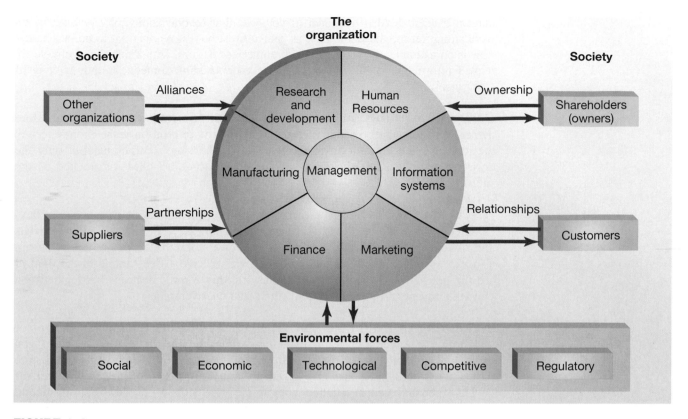

FIGURE 1–3

An organization's marketing department relates to many people, groups, and forces.

the organization, management is responsible for establishing these goals. The marketing department works closely with a network of other departments and employees to help provide the customer-satisfying products required for the organization to survive and prosper.

Figure 1–3 also shows the key people, groups, and forces outside the organization that influence marketing activities. The marketing department is responsible for facilitating relationships, partnerships, and alliances with the organization's customers, its shareholders (or often representatives of groups served by a nonprofit organization), its suppliers, and other organizations. Environmental forces such as social, technological, economic, competitive, and regulatory factors also shape an organization's marketing activities. Finally, an organization's marketing decisions are affected by and, in turn, often have an important impact on society as a whole.

The organization must strike a continual balance among the sometimes differing interests of these individuals and groups. For example, it is not possible to simultaneously provide the lowest-priced and highest-quality products to customers and pay the highest prices to suppliers, highest wages to employees, and maximum dividends to shareholders.

Requirements for Marketing to Occur

For marketing to occur, at least four factors are required: (1) two or more parties (individuals or organizations) with unsatisfied needs, (2) a desire and ability on their part to be satisfied, (3) a way for the parties to communicate, and (4) something to exchange.

Two or More Parties with Unsatisfied Needs   Suppose you've developed an unmet need—a desire for information about how computer and telecommunications are interacting to reshape the workplace—but you didn't yet know that *ComputerWorld* magazine existed. Also unknown to you was that several copies of *ComputerWorld* were sitting on the magazine rack at your nearest bookstore, waiting to be purchased. This is an example of two parties with unmet needs: you, with a need for technology-related information, and your bookstore owner, needing someone to buy a copy of *ComputerWorld.*

Desire and Ability to Satisfy These Needs   Both you and the bookstore owner want to satisfy these unmet needs. Furthermore, you have the money to buy the item and the time to get to the bookstore. The store's owner has not only the desire to sell *ComputerWorld* but also the ability to do so since it's stocked on the shelves.

A Way for the Parties to Communicate   The marketing transaction of buying a copy of *ComputerWorld* will never occur unless you know the product exists and its location. Similarly, the store owner won't stock the magazine unless there's a market of potential buyers nearby. When you receive a free sample in the mail or see the magazine on display in the bookstore, this communications barrier between you (the buyer) and your bookstore (the seller) is overcome.

Something to Exchange   Marketing occurs when the transaction takes place and both the buyer and seller exchange something of value. In this case, you exchange your money for the bookstore's magazine. Both you and the bookstore have gained something and also given up something, but you are both better off because you have each satisfied your unmet needs. You have the opportunity to read *ComputerWorld,* but you gave up some money; the store gave up the magazine but received money, which enables it to remain in business. This exchange process and, of course, the ethical and legal foundations of exchange are central to marketing.[4]

Concept Check

1. What is marketing?

2. Marketing focuses on _____ and _____ consumer needs.

3. What four factors are needed for marketing to occur?

HOW MARKETING DISCOVERS AND SATISFIES CONSUMER NEEDS

The importance of discovering and satisfying consumer needs is so critical to understanding marketing that we look at each of these two steps in detail next.

Discovering Consumer Needs

The first objective in marketing is discovering the needs of prospective consumers. Sound simple? Well, it's not.

Discovering consumer needs may look easy, but when you get down to the specifics of developing new products, problems crop up. For one thing, consumers may not always know or be able to describe what they need and want. When Apple built its first Apple II personal computer and started a new industry, consumers didn't really know what the benefits would be. So they had to be educated and to learn how to use personal computers. Also, knowing how to ask consumers the right questions to discover their real needs can be difficult. This is where effective marketing research, the topic of Chapter 8, can help.

For these four products, identify (1) what benefits the product provides buyers and (2) what "showstoppers" might kill the product in the marketplace. Answers are discussed in the text.

Vanilla-mint-flavored tooth-paste in an aerosol container

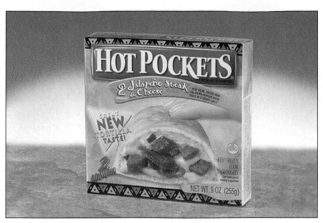

Meat and cheese microwaveable sandwiches

Robotic vacuum cleaner

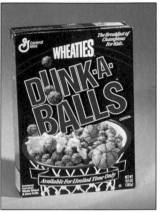

Basketball-shaped cereal that lets kids "shoot baskets" at breakfast

The Challenge of Meeting Consumer Needs with New Products

New-product experts generally estimate that up to 94 percent of the more than 33,000 new consumable products (food, beverage, health, beauty, and other household and pet products) introduced in the United States annually "don't succeed in the long run."[5] Robert M. McMath, who has studied more than 70,000 of these new-product launches, has two key suggestions: (1) focus on what the customer benefit is, and (2) learn from the past.[6]

The solution to preventing such product failures seems embarrassingly obvious. First, find out what consumers need and want. Second, produce what they need and want, and don't produce what they don't need and want. This is far more difficult than it sounds. The four products shown above illustrate just how hard it is with today's competition to achieve new-product success, a topic covered in more detail in Chapter 10.

Without reading further, think about the potential benefits to customers and possible "showstoppers" for each of the four products pictured. Some of the products may come out of your past, and others may be on your horizon. Here's a quick analysis of the four new products, with some comments adapted from McMath:

- *Dr. Care Toothpaste.* As a result of extensive research and development, Dr. Care family toothpaste in its aerosol container was introduced two decades ago. The vanilla-mint-flavored product's benefits were advertised as being easy to use and sanitary. But roll the clock back and pretend for a minute that you are five years old and left alone in the bathroom to brush your teeth using your new can of aerosol toothpaste. Hmm! Apparently, surprised parents were not enthusiastic about the paintings on their bathroom walls by their future Rembrandts—a parental showstopper that doomed this creative product.[7]

- *Hot Pockets.* Since 1983, these convenient, specially formulated meat and cheese microwavable sandwiches have been a favorite brand among students. More than 20 varieties have been introduced, from Hot Pockets Pizza Snacks to Hot Pockets Pot Pie Express. In 2002, Nestlé acquired Chef America, the firm that invented Hot Pockets, and has added its marketing muscle to promote the brand and gain valuable shelf space in the freezer sections of grocery and convenience stores. A none-too-serious potential showstopper: Excessive ice crystals can form on the product due to variations in freezer temperatures; if this happens and the sandwich is thawed before eaten, it may not taste as good.[8]

- *Roomba's Robotic FloorVac.* In head-to-head tests with upright vacuums from the major brands, the Roomba Robotic FloorVac cleaned kitty litter, crumbs, and other "dirt" better, was easier to use, and was quieter (question 1, Figure 1–2). Moreover, it goes where other vacuums can't: under the bed and other furniture. Retailing at $199.99 to $249.99, depending on the model, the Roomba sold 200,000 units in specialty retailers such as The Sharper Image and Brookstone in 2003. In 2004, Roomba appeared in retail chains. Possible showstoppers: Because the Roomba doesn't come with much "robotic intelligence," it can get stuck under furniture until the consumer releases it and dust in corners is a problem. Also, some consumers may be intimidated by its remote control—you need to program it like a VCR to use it.[9]

- *Wheaties Dunk-A-Balls Cereal.* Introduced by General Mills in the mid-1990s, it was a basketball-shaped, brown-sugar-sweetened corn and wheat puffs breakfast cereal. The box promoted the idea of having the kids "shoot baskets" with the cereal. People do love to shoot baskets, it's true. But think for three seconds about this product concept. Imagine kids taking jump shots with their cereal, picking the missed shots up off the floor, and stuffing these missed shots in their mouth—clearly a showstopper for this new product. Dunk-A-Balls quietly disappeared from the marketplace.[10]

Firms spend billions of dollars annually on marketing and technical research that significantly reduces, but doesn't eliminate, new-product failure. So meeting the constantly changing needs of consumers is a continuing challenge for firms around the world.

Consumer Needs and Consumer Wants   Should marketing try to satisfy consumer needs or consumer wants? The answer is both. Heated debates rage over this question, depending on the definitions of needs and wants and the amount of freedom given to prospective customers to make their own buying decisions.

A *need* occurs when a person feels deprived of basic necessities such as food, clothing, and shelter. A *want* is a need that is shaped by a person's knowledge, culture, and personality. So if you feel hungry, you have developed a basic need and desire to eat something. Let's say you then want to eat an apple or a candy bar because, based on your past experience and personality, you know these will satisfy your hunger need. Effective marketing, in the form of creating an awareness of good products at convenient locations, can clearly shape a person's wants.

At issue is whether marketing persuades prospective customers to buy the "wrong" things—say, a candy bar rather than an apple to satisfy hunger pangs. Of increasing concern, as described in the Ethics and Social Responsibility Alert, is the distracting effect of cell phones used by drivers, which significantly increases highway accidents.

Certainly, marketing tries to influence what we buy. A question then arises: At what point do we want government and society to step in to protect consumers? Most consumers would say they want government to protect us from harmful drugs and unsafe cars but not from candy bars and soft drinks. To protect vehicle drivers and

ETHICS AND SOCIAL RESPONSIBILITY ALERT

Cell Phones and Distracted Driving—Just as Dangerous as Drunk Driving

ETHICS

Using a cell phone, eating a burger, changing a CD, or reading a newspaper—normally, marketers want to encourage these behaviors. However, if done while driving a car, they can have disastrous consequences. Cell phones are an especially critical problem. In a recent study, researchers found that the distracting effect of using a cell phone exceeded that of a person with a 0.08 blood-alcohol level, the legal limit for drunk driving in most states.

Why do drivers engage in these dangerous behaviors? In 2002, they spent an average of 300 hours on the road and want that time to be productive. According to a recent study, more than 50 percent of drivers who have a cell phone admit to using it while driving. And a more sobering study from the National Highway Traffic Safety Administration estimated that distracted drivers accounted for almost 30 percent of all automobile crashes, or 1.2 million accidents a year—many of them fatal (question 2, Figure 1–2).

Many states, such as New York, and most European nations have enacted legislation to reduce or eliminate cell phone use and prohibit other distracting behaviors while driving. To reduce cell phone distractions, mobile phone manufacturers have introduced hands-free, voice-activated devices. Other organizations, such as the Cellular Telecommunications and Internet Association (CTIA), Cingular Wireless, and Shell, have developed public service announcements (PSAs) and driver-training videos to educate consumers on the dangers of distracted driving. Some states have created billboards to inform drivers of their moral if not legal obligation to drive attentively.[11]

Do you use your cell phone while driving? Should states be encouraged to restrict cell phone use by drivers? Are states restricting your individual rights? Or are these laws making you safer on the highway?

their passengers, should government restrict the use of cell phones by drivers? Such questions have no clear-cut answers, which is why legal and social issues are central to marketing. Because even psychologists and economists still debate the exact meanings of *need* and *want,* we shall avoid the semantic arguments and use the terms interchangeably throughout the rest of the book.

As shown in Figure 1–4 on the next page, discovering needs involves looking carefully at prospective customers, whether they are children buying M&M's candy, college students buying Rollerblade in-line skates, or firms buying Xerox photocopying machines. A principal activity of a firm's marketing department is to scrutinize carefully its consumers to understand what they need and want and the trends and factors that shape them.

What a Market Is   Potential consumers make up a **market**, which is people with both the desire and the ability to buy a specific product. All markets ultimately are people. Even when we say a firm bought a Xerox copier, we mean one or several people in the firm decided to buy it. People who are aware of their unmet needs may have the desire to buy the product, but that alone isn't sufficient. People must also have the ability to buy, such as the authority, time, and money. People may even "buy" an idea that results in an action, such as having their blood pressure checked annually or turning down their thermostat to save energy.

FIGURE 1–4
Marketing's first task:
discovering consumer needs

Satisfying Consumer Needs

Marketing doesn't stop with the discovery of consumer needs. Because the organization obviously can't satisfy all consumer needs, it must concentrate its efforts on certain needs of a specific group of potential consumers. This is the **target market**—one or more specific groups of potential consumers toward which an organization directs its marketing program.

The Four Ps: Controllable Marketing Mix Factors   Having selected the target market consumers, the firm must take steps to satisfy their needs. Someone in the organization's marketing department, often the marketing manager, must take action and develop a complete marketing program to reach consumers by using a combination of four tools, often called the four Ps—a useful shorthand reference to them first published by Professor E. Jerome McCarthy:[12]

- *Product.* A good, service, or idea to satisfy the consumer's needs.
- *Price.* What is exchanged for the product.
- *Promotion.* A means of communication between the seller and buyer.
- *Place.* A means of getting the product into the consumer's hands.

We'll define each of the four Ps more carefully later in the book, but for now it's important to remember that they are the elements of the marketing mix, or simply the **marketing mix**. These are the marketing manager's controllable factors—product, price, promotion, and place—that can be used to solve a marketing problem. The marketing mix elements are called controllable factors because they are under the control of the marketing department in an organization.

The Uncontrollable, Environmental Factors   There are a host of factors largely beyond the control of the marketing department and its organization. These factors can be placed into five groups (as shown in Figure 1–3): social, economic, technological, competitive, and regulatory forces. Examples are what consumers themselves want and need, changing technology, the state of the economy in terms of whether it is expanding or contracting, actions that competitors take, and government restrictions. These are the **environmental factors** in a marketing decision, the uncontrollable factors involving social, economic, technological, competitive, and regulatory forces. These five forces may serve as accelerators or brakes on marketing, sometimes expanding an organization's marketing opportunities and other times restricting them. These five environmental factors are covered in Chapter 3.

Traditionally, many marketing executives have treated these environmental factors as rigid, absolute constraints that are entirely outside their influence. However, recent

Costco and Starbucks provide customer value using two very different approaches. For their strategies, see the text.

Costco
www.costco.com

Starbucks
www.starbucks.com

studies and marketing successes have shown that a forward-looking, action-oriented firm can often affect some environmental factors, for example, by achieving technological or competitive breakthroughs.

THE MARKETING PROGRAM: HOW CUSTOMER RELATIONSHIPS ARE BUILT

A firm's marketing program connects the firm to its customers. To clarify this link, we shall first discuss the critically important concepts of customer value, customer relationships, and relationship marketing, and then illustrate these concepts with the marketing program at Rollerblade.

Global Competition, Customer Value, and Customer Relationships

Intense competition in today's fast-paced domestic and global markets has caused massive restructuring of many American industries and businesses. American managers are seeking ways to achieve success in this new, more intense level of global competition.[13]

This has prompted many successful U.S. firms to focus on "customer value." That firms gain loyal customers by providing unique value is the essence of successful marketing. What is new, however, is a more careful attempt at understanding how a firm's customers perceive value. For our purposes, **customer value** is the unique combination of benefits received by targeted buyers that includes quality, price, convenience, on-time delivery, and both before-sale and after-sale service. Firms now actually try to place a dollar value on a loyal, satisfied customer. As pointed out in Chapter 5, loyal Kleenex customers average 6.7 boxes a year, about $994 over 60 years in today's dollars (question 3, Figure 1–2).[14]

Research suggests that firms cannot succeed by being all things to all people.[15] Instead, firms must find ways to build long-term customer relationships to provide unique value that they alone can deliver to targeted markets. Many successful firms have chosen to deliver outstanding customer value with one of three value strategies: best price, best product, or best service.

Companies such as Wal-Mart, Southwest Airlines, Costco, and Dell Computer have all been successful offering consumers the best price. Other companies such as Starbucks, Nike, Microsoft, and Johnson & Johnson claim to provide the best products on the market. Finally, companies such as Lands' End and Home Depot deliver value by providing exceptional service.

But changing tastes can devastate once-successful marketing strategies. Lands' End, now part of Sears, must focus on strategies to defeat new groups of competitors: boutique specialty stores, catalog retailers, and Internet sellers (Chapter 2).

Relationship Marketing

Meaningful customer relationships are achieved by the firm's identifying creative ways to connect closely to its customers through specific marketing mix actions implemented in its marketing program.

Relationship Marketing: Easy to Understand
The hallmark of developing and maintaining effective customer relationships is today called **relationship marketing**, linking the organization to its individual customers, employees, suppliers, and other partners for their mutual long-term benefits. Note that these mutual long-term benefits between the organization and its customers require links to other vital stakeholders, including suppliers, employees, and "partners" such as wholesalers or retailers in a manufacturer's channel of distribution. In an ideal setting, relationship marketing involves a personal, ongoing relationship between the organization and an individual customer.

Relationship Marketing: Difficult to Implement
Huge manufacturers find this rigorous standard of relationship marketing difficult to achieve. Today's information technology, along with cutting-edge manufacturing and marketing processes, have led to tailoring goods or services to the tastes of individual customers in high volumes at a relatively low cost. Thus, you can place an Internet order for all the components of a Dell or Apple computer and have it delivered in four or five days—in a configuration tailored to your unique wants.

But there are other forces working against these kinds of personal relationships between company and customer. Researchers Fournier, Dobscha, and Mick observe that "the number of one-on-one relationships that companies ask consumers to maintain is untenable,"[16] as evidenced by the dozens of credit card and financing offers a typical consumer gets in a year. A decade ago you might have gone to a small store to buy a book or music record, being helped in your buying decision by a salesclerk or the store owner. With today's Internet purchases, you will probably have difficulty achieving the same personal, tender-loving-care connection that you once had with your own special book or music store.

The Marketing Program

Effective relationship marketing strategies help marketing managers discover what prospective customers need. They must translate this information into some concepts for products the firm might develop (Figure 1–5). These concepts must then be converted into a tangible **marketing program**—a plan that integrates the marketing mix to provide a good, service, or idea to prospective buyers. These prospects then react to the offering favorably (by buying) or unfavorably (by not buying), and the process is repeated. As shown in Figure 1–5, in an effective organization this process is continuous: Consumer needs trigger product concepts that are translated into actual products that stimulate further discovery of consumer needs.

A Marketing Program for Rollerblade

To see some specifics of an actual marketing program, let's return to the earlier example of Rollerblade and its in-line skates. Looking at the in-line skating horizon, Rollerblade's long-run strategy is to focus on three areas: (1) listening to consumers to

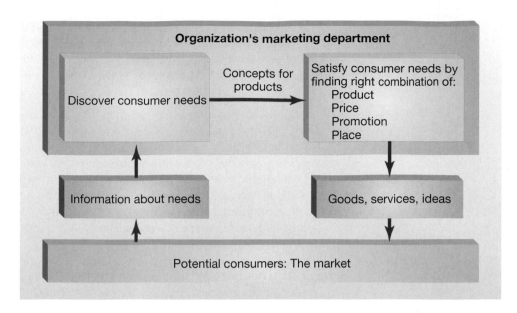

stay ahead of the trends, (2) focusing its marketing program on four key segments, and (3) using the company's strengths in technology. These three areas are covered below.

Listening to Consumers to Stay Ahead of the Trends   Consumer tastes change—and quickly. This is the reason for Rollerblade's concerns that it stay ahead of trends in the marketplace. Competition is coming from directions never anticipated even two or three years earlier. Rollerblade has always had to compete with skateboards and mountain bikes. But now it even competes with other active sports, as well as scooters and Heelys, a sneaker with an embedded, detachable wheel in the heel.[17]

Today, Rollerblade uses careful marketing research to listen to what various segments of Rollerblade customers want. For example, its website (www.rollerblade.com) enables its marketing executives to not only obtain detailed information about what skate features customers want but also link these wants to their individual characteristics like age, sex, and lifestyle (like hobbies and purchasing behaviors). Rollerblade's "Skate Selector" on its website not only helps consumers select the skate that's right for them but also provides timely data on consumer wants.

Focusing the Marketing Program on Four Key Segments   Three key benefits for customers remain the foundation for Rollerblade's marketing program: (1) fun, (2) fitness and health, and (3) excitement. Today, while the fundamental customer benefits remain the same, Rollerblade is now trying to reach narrower, more specialized segments of customers than in the past.[18] Jeremy Stonier, responsible for planning Rollerblade's product strategy, identifies four key market segments and typical Rollerblade skates designed for each segment:

- *Fitness/recreation segment.* Do you skate often and are you serious about a good aerobic workout? If so, you probably are a "fitness" in-line skater and should try the Lightning 05 (for women) or Aero 9 (for men)—skates for people whose feet demand a good fit and the shock dampening provided by Rollerblade's latest technology. The Aero 9 also has the Total Fit System™, the quick-closer mechanism that laces the skate instantly with a pull on the cord and that is shown on the chapter's opening page. Are you skating mainly for fun, like most in-line skaters? Then you are a "recreational" in-line skater and should use a Zetrablade skate designed for reliability, comfort, and ease of use.
- *Children segment.* Most parents can't afford to buy a new set of in-line skates each season as their children's feet grow. No problem now. Skates in the Microblade line extend up to four sizes with a simple push of a button.

- *Street/vert segment.* Are you the kind of stunt or grind skater seen on Xtreme Games on TV? Then try the new Team Rollerblade Series (TRS) line, reflecting design suggestions from Rollerblade's sponsored skating team members.
- *Speed segment.* Expert speed skaters wanting the best technical features and performance form this segment, skating on Rollerblade's ProBlade™ 100 model.

Rollerblade has more than 20 lines of skates targeted to different market segments. As illustrated in Figure 1–6 for the Zetrablade and Microblade lines, most Rollerblade brands require a slightly different marketing program to reach their targeted segments of potential customers. For example, expandable Microblade lines designed for growing children have a significantly lower price than the Zetrablade targeted at the fitness and recreation segment and use distinctly different promotional strategies: gym classes and ads in local newspapers versus gaining exposure in sports competitions and national magazines like *Shape* and *Mademoiselle.*

Exploiting Strengths in Technology   In 2003, Rollerblade was sold to Tecnica of Italy, which includes the Nordica brand. This provided huge technology synergies for the two firms by combining state-of-the-art R&D and manufacturing resources. An example of exploiting tomorrow's technology is ABT Lite®, a light, integral braking system that allows skaters to brake by sliding their heel downward, without compromising balance or performance.

Rollerblade's emphasis on the technology is reflected in the more than 200 patents it holds on key elements of its in-line skate line. The Rollerblade case at the end of the chapter lets us look in greater depth at the marketing strategies that Rollerblade is developing for the twenty-first century.

FIGURE 1–6
Marketing programs for two of Rollerblade's skates, targeted at two distinctly different customer segments: fitness/recreation skaters and children

MARKETING PROGRAM ACTIVITY TO REACH:

MARKETING MIX ELEMENT	FITNESS/ RECREATION SEGMENT	CHILDREN SEGMENT	RATIONALE FOR MARKETING PROGRAM ACTIVITY
Product	Offer Zetrablade in-line skates for beginning and intermediate skaters simply wanting fun and exercise	Offer the Microblade, a skate for children that extends so that its length changes as their feet grow	Use new-product research and the latest technology to offer high-quality skates to satisfy the needs of key customer segments
Price	Price up to $169.99 a pair	Price up to $109.99 a pair	Set prices that provide genuine value to the customer segment that is targeted
Promotion	Feature Rollerblade in sports competitions and magazines like *Shape* and *Mademoiselle* and local newspapers	Use gym classes to introduce children to in-line skating and place ads in local newspapers	Increase awareness to those new to the sport while offering ads and press releases for more advanced segments
Place	Distribute through specialty in-line skate, regular, and superstore sporting goods stores and the Internet	Distribute through regular and superstore sporting goods stores	Make it easy for buyers in the segment to buy at an outlet that is convenient and where they feel comfortable

Rollerblade in-line skate lines targeted at the fitness/recreation segment (left) and children segment (right).

Zetrablade Model   Microblade Model

Concept Check

1. An organization can't satisfy the needs of all consumers, so it must focus on one or more subgroups, which are its _____.

2. What are the four marketing mix elements that make up the organization's marketing program?

3. What are uncontrollable variables?

HOW MARKETING BECAME SO IMPORTANT

To understand why marketing is a driving force in the modern global economy, let us look at the (1) evolution of the market orientation, (2) ethics and social responsibility in marketing, and (3) breadth and depth of marketing activities.

Evolution of the Market Orientation

Many market-oriented manufacturing organizations have experienced four distinct stages in the life of their firms. We can use Pillsbury, now part of General Mills, and General Electric as examples.

Production Era   Goods were scarce in the early years of the United States, so buyers were willing to accept virtually any goods that were produced and make do with them as best they could. The central notion was that products would sell themselves, so the major concern of business firms was production, not marketing. Robert Keith, a Pillsbury president, described his company at this stage: "We are professional flour millers. . . . Our basic function is to mill quality flour."[19] As shown in Figure 1–7 on the next page, this production era generally continued in America through the 1920s.

Sales Era   About that time, many firms discovered that they could produce more goods than their regular buyers could consume. Competition grew. The usual solution was to hire more salespeople to find new buyers. Pillsbury's philosophy at this stage was summed up simply by Keith: "We must hire salespersons to sell it [the flour] just as we hire accountants to keep our books." The role of the Pillsbury salesforce was simply to find consumers for the goods that the firm could produce best. This sales era continued into the 1950s for Pillsbury and into the 1960s for many other American firms (see Figure 1–7).

FIGURE 1–7
Four different orientations in the history of American business

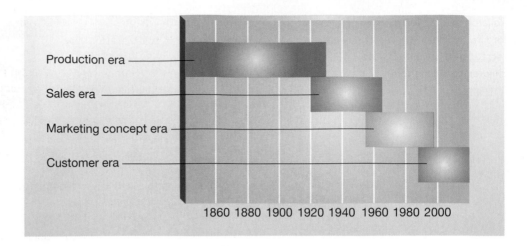

The Marketing Concept Era   In the 1960s, marketing became the motivating force among many American firms. Then the policy became, "we are in the business of satisfying needs and wants of consumers." This is really a brief statement of what has come to be known as the **marketing concept**, the idea that an organization should (1) strive to satisfy the needs of consumers (2) while also trying to achieve the organization's goals.

The statement of a firm's commitment to satisfying consumer wants and needs that probably launched the marketing concept appeared in a 1952 annual report of General Electric:[20] "The concept introduces . . . marketing . . . at the beginning rather than the end of the production cycle and integrates marketing into each phase of the business." This statement emphasizes that marketing ideas are fed into the production cycle *before* an item is designed, rather than *after* it is produced. Clearly, the marketing concept is a focus on the consumer. Unfortunately, many companies found that actually implementing the concept was very difficult.

The Customer Era   Firms such as General Electric, Marriott, and Toyota have achieved great success by putting huge effort into implementing the marketing concept, giving their firms what has been called a *market orientation*. An organization that has a **market orientation** focuses its efforts on (1) continuously collecting information about customers' needs, (2) sharing this information across departments, and (3) using it to create customer value.[21] The result is today's "customer era," in which firms seek continuously to satisfy the high expectations of customers.

An important outgrowth of this focus on the customer is the recent attention placed on **customer relationship management (CRM)**, the process of identifying prospective buyers, understanding them intimately, and developing favorable long-term perceptions of the organization and its offerings so that buyers will choose them in the marketplace.[22] This process requires the involvement and commitment of managers and employees throughout the organization and a growing application of information, communication, and Internet technology, as will be described throughout this book. Unfortunately, many expensive CRM computer systems have not provided the expected benefits because they failed to identify exactly which customer segments the company wanted to reach.[23]

Ethics and Social Responsibility: Balancing the Interests of Different Groups

As organizations have changed their orientation, society's expectations of marketers have also changed. Today, the standards of marketing practice have shifted from an emphasis on producers' interests to consumers' interests. In addition, organizations are increasingly encouraged to consider the social and environmental consequences of their actions for all parties. Guidelines for ethical and socially responsible behavior can help managers balance consumer, organizational, and societal interests.

Ethics   Many marketing issues are not specifically addressed by existing laws and regulations. Should information about a firm's customers be sold to other organizations? Should advertising by professional service providers, such as accountants and attorneys, be restricted? Should consumers be on their own to assess the safety of a product? These questions raise difficult ethical issues. Many companies, industries, and professional associations have developed codes of ethics to assist managers.

Social Responsibility   While many ethical issues involve only the buyer and seller, others involve society as a whole. For example, suppose you change the oil in your old Chevy yourself and dump the used oil in a corner of your backyard. Is this just a transaction between you and the oil manufacturer? Not quite! The used oil may contaminate the soil, so society will bear a portion of the cost of your behavior. This example illustrates the issue of social responsibility, the idea that organizations are accountable to a larger society. The well-being of society at large should also be recognized in an organization's marketing decisions. In fact, some marketing experts stress the **societal marketing concept**, the view that organizations should satisfy the needs of consumers in a way that provides for society's well-being.[24] For example, ScotchBrite® Never Rust™ Soap Pads from 3M—which are made from recycled plastic bottles—are more expensive than competitors (SOS and Brillo) but superior because they don't rust or scratch (question 4, Figure 1–2).

The societal marketing concept is directly related to **macromarketing**, which is the study of the aggregate flow of a nation's goods and services to benefit society.[25] Macromarketing addresses broad issues such as whether marketing costs too much, whether advertising is wasteful, and what resource scarcities and pollution side effects result from the marketing system. While macromarketing issues are addressed briefly in this book, the book's main focus is on how an individual organization directs its marketing activities and allocates its resources to benefit its customers, or **micromarketing**. Because of the importance of ethical and social responsibility issues in marketing today, Chapter 4 focuses on them, but they are touched on throughout the book.

The Breadth and Depth of Marketing

Marketing today affects every person and organization. To understand this, let's analyze (1) who markets, (2) what they market, (3) who buys and uses what is marketed, (4) who benefits from these marketing activities, and (5) how they benefit.

Who Markets?   Every organization markets. It's obvious that business firms involved in manufacturing (Tommy Hilfiger, Heinz), retailing (Abercrombie & Fitch, Target), and providing services (America Online, Chicago Cubs) market their offerings. Today, many other types of marketing are also popular. Nonprofit organizations (San Francisco Opera, your local hospital) also engage in marketing.[26] Your college or university, for example, probably has a marketing program to attract students, faculty members, and donations.

Places (cities, states, countries) often use marketing efforts to attract tourists, conventions, and new investment to provide local jobs. While *Arizona Highways* markets its state, entire countries—from the United States and New Zealand to Germany and Poland—market themselves. A special challenge: Economically prosperous Slovenia that joined the European Union in 2004 is often confused in foreign minds with Slovakia.[27] Special events or causes use marketing to inform and influence a target audience. These marketing activities range from government agencies discouraging smoking to private groups promoting social causes such as literacy.

Marketing is used by nonprofit organizations, causes, and places, as well as businesses. Direct messages like those illustrated here can reach their target audiences very effectively.

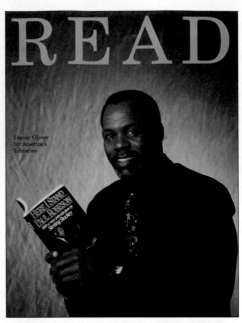

Finally, individuals such as political candidates often use marketing to gain attention and preference.

What Is Marketed?   Goods, services, and ideas are marketed. *Goods* are physical objects, such as toothpaste, cameras, or computers, that satisfy consumer needs. *Services* are intangible items such as airline trips, financial advice, or telephone calls. *Ideas* are intangibles involving thoughts about actions or causes.

Financial pressures have caused art museums to embark on creative marketing activities to attract visitors and generate revenues. New York's Guggenheim Museum challenged the concept of what an art museum is when it organized an exhibition on "The Art of the Motorcycle."[28] As described in the Web Link, Russia's Hermitage Museum has partnered with IBM to give you a computerized "virtual tour" of its exhibits in hopes that some day you may visit it personally.[29] The search for new revenues caused the Dallas Museum of Art to stay open for 100 consecutive hours to celebrate its centennial, and Chicago's Field Museum now offers a licensing program featuring Sue, its Tyrannosaurus rex skeleton.[30]

Who Buys and Uses What Is Marketed?   Both individuals and organizations buy and use goods and services that are marketed. **Ultimate consumers** are the people who use the goods and services purchased for a household. In contrast, **organizational buyers** are those manufacturers, wholesalers, retailers, and government agencies that buy goods and services for their own use or for resale. Although the terms *consumers, buyers,* and *customers* are sometimes used for both ultimate consumers and organizations, there is no consistency on this. In this book you will be able to tell from the example whether the buyers are ultimate consumers, organizations, or both.

Who Benefits?   In our free-enterprise society there are three specific groups that benefit from effective marketing: consumers who buy, organizations that sell, and society as a whole. True competition between products and services in the marketplace ensures that we consumers can find value from the best products, the lowest prices, or exceptional service. Providing choices leads to the consumer satisfaction and quality of life that we have come to expect from our economic system.

WEB LINK

Marketing the Hermitage, a World-Class Russian Art Museum—with a Virtual Tour

www.mhhe.com/Kerin

Founded in 1764 by Catherine the Great, the Hermitage is one of a handful of world-class museums—like the Louvre in Paris or the Metropolitan Museum in New York City—and is the main tourist attraction in St. Petersburg, Russia. Today, the Hermitage consists of five buildings of over 1,000 rooms that con-

tain more than 3 million items, only 5 percent ever exhibited at one time.

But since the Berlin Wall fell in 1989, the Hermitage has struggled financially. Gone is most of its government funding. As a result, the number of visitors to the Hermitage fell from 3.5 million in 1989 to under 2 million in 2000, far less than the Louvre's 6.2 million.

Dr. Mikhail Piotrovsky, the Hermitage's director since 1992, decided to face this funding crisis head on. By using innovative strategic alliances

and marketing initiatives, Piotrovsky has begun to bring in the resources needed to improve and expand the museum.

To take a "virtual tour" of the Hermitage, go to its Internet address, www.hermitagemuseum.org, and click on the "Virtual Visit" link.

This website allows people all over the world to view more Hermitage treasures and consider a personal visit. A $2 million IBM grant to the Hermitage made possible this state-of-the-art Internet website and a digital library of the Hermitage collection. The website allows users to "walk through" Hermitage rooms and see its artwork. Users can zoom in to examine the artwork more closely.

Organizations that provide need-satisfying products with effective marketing programs—for example, McDonald's, IBM, and Avon—have blossomed. But competition creates problems for ineffective competitors, such as eToys and hundreds of other dot-com businesses that failed in the last few years.[31] Effective marketing actions result in rewards for organizations that serve consumers and in millions of marketing jobs such as those described in Appendix C.

Finally, effective marketing benefits society. It enhances competition, which, in turn, improves both the quality of products and services and lowers their prices. This makes countries more competitive in world markets and provides jobs and a higher standard of living for their citizens.

How Do Consumers Benefit? Marketing creates **utility**, the benefits or customer value received by users of the product. This utility is the result of the marketing exchange process. There are four different utilities: form, place, time, and possession. The value to consumers that comes from the production or alteration of a good or service constitutes *form utility. Place utility* is the value to consumers of having a good or service available where needed, whereas *time utility* is the value to consumers of having a good or service available when needed. *Possession utility* is the value to consumers of making an item easy to purchase so consumers can use it.

Thus, marketing provides consumers with place, time, and possession utilities by making the good or service available at the right place and right time for the right consumer. Although form utility usually arises in manufacturing activity and could be seen as outside the scope of marketing, an organization's marketing activities influence the product features and packaging. Marketing creates its utilities by bridging space (place utility) and hours (time utility) to provide products (form utility) for consumers to own and use (possession utility).

> ### Concept Check
>
> **1.** Like Pillsbury and General Electric, many firms have gone through four distinct orientations for their business: starting with the _____ era and ending with today's _____ era.
>
> **2.** What are the two key characteristics of the marketing concept?

CHAPTER IN REVIEW

1 *Define marketing and identify the requirements for marketing to occur.*

Marketing is an organizational function and a set of processes for creating, communicating, and delivering value to customers and for managing customer relationships in ways that benefit the organization and its stakeholders. This definition relates to two primary goals of marketing: (*a*) assessing the needs of consumers and (*b*) satisfying them. For marketing to occur, it is necessary to have (*a*) two or more parties with unmet needs, (*b*) a desire and ability to satisfy them, (*c*) communication between the parties, and (*d*) something to exchange.

2 *Explain how marketing discovers and satisfies consumer needs.*

The first objective in marketing is discovering the needs of prospective consumers. This is not an easy task because consumers may not always know or be able to describe what they need and want. A need occurs when a person feels physiologically deprived of basic necessities such as food, clothing, and shelter. A want is a felt need that is shaped by a person's knowledge, culture, and personality. Effective marketing can clearly shape a person's wants and tries to influence what we buy. The second objective in marketing is satisfying the needs of targeted consumers. Because an organization obviously can't satisfy all consumer needs, it must concentrate its efforts on certain needs of a specific group of potential consumers or target market—one or more specific groups of potential consumers toward which an organization directs its marketing program. Having selected its target market consumers, the organization then takes action to satisfy their needs by developing a unique marketing program to reach them.

3 *Distinguish between marketing mix elements and environmental factors.*

Four elements in a marketing program designed to satisfy customer needs are product, price, promotion, and place. These elements are called the marketing mix, the four Ps, or the controllable variables because they are under the general control of the marketing department. Environmental factors, also called uncontrollable variables, are largely beyond the organization's control. These include social, economic, technological, competitive, and regulatory forces.

4 *Explain how organizations build strong customer relationships and customer value through marketing.*

The essence of successful marketing is to provide sufficient value to gain loyal, long-term customers. Customer value is the unique combination of benefits received by targeted buyers that usually includes quality, price, convenience, on-time delivery, and both before-sale and after-sale service. Marketers do this by using one of three value strategies: best price, best product, or best service.

5 *Describe how today's customer era differs from prior eras oriented to production and selling.*

U.S. business history is divided into four periods: the production era, the sales era, the marketing concept era, and the current customer era. The production era covers the period to the 1920s when buyers were willing to accept virtually any goods that were available. The central notion was that products would sell themselves. The sales era lasted from the 1920s to the 1960s. Manufacturers found they could produce more goods than buyers could consume, and competition grew, so the solution was to hire more salespeople to find new buyers. In the 1960s, the marketing concept era dawned, when organizations began to integrate marketing into each phase of the business. In today's customer era, organizations focus their efforts on (*a*) continuously collecting information about customers' needs, (*b*) sharing this information across departments, and (*c*) using it to create customer value.

6 *Explain how marketing creates utilities for consumers.*

Marketing creates utility, which consists of the benefits or customer value received by users of the product and is the result of the exchange process. Marketing provides four types of utilities that are designed to get the right product or service to consumers (form utility) where (place utility) and when (time utility) they need it so they can ultimately use or consume it (possession utility).

FOCUSING ON KEY TERMS

customer relationship management (CRM) p. 20
customer value p. 15
environmental factors p. 14
exchange p. 8
macromarketing p. 21
market p. 13
market orientation p. 20
marketing p. 8
marketing concept p. 20

marketing mix p. 14
marketing program p. 16
micromarketing p. 21
organizational buyers p. 22
relationship marketing p. 16
societal marketing concept p. 21
target market p. 14
ultimate consumers p. 22
utility p. 23

DISCUSSION AND APPLICATION QUESTIONS

1 What consumer wants (or benefits) are met by the following products or services? (*a*) Carnation Instant Breakfast, (*b*) Adidas running shoes, (*c*) Hertz Rent-A-Car, and (*d*) television home shopping programs.

2 Each of the four products, services, or programs in question 1 has substitutes. Respective examples are (*a*) a ham and egg breakfast, (*b*) regular tennis shoes, (*c*) taking a bus, and (*d*) a department store. What consumer benefits might these substitutes have in each case that some consumers might value more highly than those mentioned in question 1?

3 What are the characteristics (e.g., age, income, education) of the target market customers for the following products or services? (*a*) *National Geographic* magazine, (*b*) *Wired* magazine, (*c*) New York Giants football team, and (*d*) the U.S. Open tennis tournament.

4 A college in a metropolitan area wishes to increase its evening-school offerings of business-related courses such as marketing, accounting, finance, and management. Who are the target market customers (students) for these courses?

5 What actions involving the four marketing mix elements might be used to reach the target market in question 4?

6 What environmental factors (uncontrollable variables) must the college in question 4 consider in designing its marketing program?

7 Rollerblade is now trying to grow in-line skating globally. What are the advantages and disadvantages of trying to reach new global markets?

8 Does a firm have the right to "create" wants and try to persuade consumers to buy goods and services they didn't know about earlier? What are examples of "good" and "bad" want creation? Who should decide what is good and bad?

GOING ONLINE Your Personal Mechanized "Transporter"

"It!" "Ginger!" "Jetson's scooter!" These were early names given the revolutionary Segway™ Human Transporter (HT), a technology shrouded in secrecy until it was launched in 2001. The Segway HT relies on computers and gyroscopes to control its speed, balance, and direction. It can travel up to 15 miles on a six-hour battery charge.

Go to the Segway HT website (www.segway.com). View both the consumer and business models.

1 What do you see as the advantages and disadvantages of the Segway HT?
2 For businesses, what applications could the Segway HT be used for?
3 Why would consumers want to buy a Segway HT?

BUILDING YOUR MARKETING PLAN

If your instructor assigns a marketing plan for your class, don't make a face and complain about the work—for two special reasons. First, you will get insights into trying to actually "do marketing" that often go beyond what you can get by simply reading the textbook. Second, thousands of graduating students every year get their first job by showing prospective employers a "portfolio" of samples of their written work from college—often a marketing plan if they have one. This can work for you.

This "Building Your Marketing Plan" section at the end of each chapter gives you suggestions to improve and focus your marketing plan. You will use the sample marketing plan in Appendix A as a guide, and this section after each chapter will help you apply those Appendix A ideas to your own marketing plan. Depending on the topic of your marketing plan, some parts of Appendix A or some sections of Building Your Marketing Plan may not be relevant for your plan.

The first step in writing a good marketing plan is to have a business or product that enthuses you and for which you can get detailed information, so you can avoid glitter-ing generalities. Your instructor probably has guidelines on acceptable topics for marketing plans. Having worked with students on hundreds of marketing plans, we offer these additional bits of advice in selecting a topic:

1 *Do* pick a topic that has personal interest for you—a family business, a business or product you or a friend might want to launch, or a student organization needing marketing help.
2 *Do not* pick a topic that is so large it can't be covered adequately or so abstract it will lack specifics.

Now to get you started on your marketing plan, list four or five possible topics and compare these with the criteria your instructor suggests and those shown above. Think hard, because your decision will be with you all term long and may influence the quality of the resulting marketing plan you show to a prospective employer.

When you have selected your marketing plan topic, whether the plan is for an actual business, a possible business, or a student organization, write the "company description" in your plan, as shown in Appendix A.

VIDEO CASE 1   Rollerblade: Benefits Beyond Expectations

ABT, TRS, TFS . . . and SIS! Does this look like a spoon-ful of alphabet soup?

Perhaps. But it really refers to Rollerblade's technolo-gies, programs, and commitment to providing in-line skaters with the best quality of skates and skating experi-ences possible. Or "by providing benefits beyond what people are expecting to have," as Jeremy Stonier, Rollerblade's director of product marketing, describes it. In fact, Rollerblade's leading-edge technology is covered by more than 200 patents, with more on the way.

ROLLERBLADE'S LAUNCH

At Rollerblade's launch two decades ago only one in-line skate manufacturer existed—Rollerblade. The company had only a single skate line and there were few sales. No one had heard of in-line skating! So Rollerblade used a "guerrilla marketing" campaign to get the word out. It used a tiny budget to develop attention-getting promo-tions to make people aware of the skates and to try them. Promotions ranged from "Demo Vans" in supermarket parking lots, where prospects could try the skates for a half hour, to putting Rollerblade skates on Minnesota Viking cheerleaders at a football game or Arnold Schwarzeneg-ger. Marketing research was almost limited to what skaters told the Demo Van drivers.

A SKATE LINE FOR EACH SEGMENT

From the outset in-line skaters have been united by a common experience: the thrill and fun of the speed and freedom that comes from almost frictionless wheels on their feet. "As the market has matured, it has settled into four core groups of users," says Stonier. Each requires a number of unique skate features.

"The trickiest segment we sell to is probably the 'street/vert' skater—the 14- to 22-year-old in your neigh-borhood who is doing tricks you might see on ESPN's X Games," says Stonier. Members of Team Rollerblade, a skating group that gives demonstrations around the country, suggest and test new technologies that find their way first into skates for this segment. The TRS—for Team Rollerblade Series—line of skates contains every-thing from a PFS Specialized form-fit memory foot liner gel insert for extreme shock absorption to CoolMax© fabric to keep the skater's feet cool and dry.

Skate buyers overlap somewhat in the fitness/recreation segment. The "fitness" group probably skates two or three times a week and may even aspire to skate in an in-line marathon. "The fitness user is going at high speeds and skating frequently, so we've developed the Lightning series of skates for women and Aero series for men that are in-credibly light weight with an anatomical fit," says Stonier.

The Aero series have the Total Fit System (TFS) that incorporates a new shell, liner, and closure system. Don't want to waste time buckling the skates? Here you don't need to because you simply pull up on a cord at the back of the skate, giving you a customized fit in a matter of seconds. (That's Stonier in the photo demonstrating it to colleague Nicholas Skally.) A larger view of the Total Fit System appears in the Rollerblade ad on page 4.

Most adult skaters are "recreational" users, for which the Zetrablade skate line is designed. With this skate both beginner and intermediate skaters get the comfort and reliability they want.

Parents are always concerned about having to buy their children new shoes or skates as their feet grow. Not only does the Microblade extendable skate adjust four sizes with a push of a button, but it also has a quick-pull lacing system, padded liner, and shell ventilation designed specifically for children.

The "speed" segment is just what the name implies— expert speed skaters wanting the maximum in technical features and performance. The ProBlade 100 model meets the needs of this segment.

The segments don't stop there. Besides its flagship Rollerblade brand marketed through sporting goods and skate specialty stores, Rollerblade has a lower-priced Bladerunner line sold through mass merchant and sporting goods chain stores. Finally, the global market has enormous potential. With China and South Korea showing high growth today, who knows what new segments could be next?

A FOCUS ON EACH CONSUMER

"One of the big differences between marketing today and in the future is that we will be able to reach each person, such as designing your own personal workout program," says Nicholas Skally, Rollerblade's manager of marketing and public relations. Rollerblade's website (www.rollerblade.com) is a step in that direction. "An important benefit of the website is our ability to acquire marketing research data on individual consumers inexpensively," says Skally. This enables Rollerblade to get feedback and ideas from users very inexpensively. Website topics include everything from helping you choose which skate is right for you (Skate Selector) to helping you brush up on your braking technique.

In the past, Rollerblade often sent out millions of direct-mail pieces or buying commercials on national TV networks. Today, Skally points out that Rollerblade now focuses more narrowly by selecting magazines that link directly to the user segments or grassroots programs like Skate-in-School (SIS) that offer physical education class options to students in more than 750 schools.

ROLLERBLADE'S FIRSTS

"If you're going to buy a pair of in-line skates, it only make sense to buy from us," says Stonier, "because we're the ones who started it, perfected it, and continue to push the innovation." As evidence of Rollerblade's innovation, he points to a number of firsts, such as the use of polyurethane boots and wheels, metal frames, dual bearings, and heel brakes. Other firsts include breathable liners, push-button adjustable children's skates, skates designed specifically for women, and the award-winning Advanced Braking Technology (ABT) that allows braking without raising the toe of the skate.

Questions

1   What trends in the environmental forces (social, economic, technological, competitive, and regulatory) identified in Figure 1–3 in the chapter (*a*) work for and (*b*) work against Rollerblade's potential growth in the twenty-first century?

2   Compare the marketing goals for Rollerblade (*a*) in 1986 when Rollerblade was launched and (*b*) today.

3   What kind of focused communication and promotion actions might Rollerblade take to reach the (*a*) recreational and (*b*) children market segments? For some starting ideas, visit rollerblade.com.

4   In searching for global markets to enter, (*a*) what are some criteria that Rollerblade should use to select countries to enter, and (*b*) what three or four countries meet these criteria best and are the most likely candidates?

Our Company

- ⇨ About Us
- ⇨ Our Mission
- ⇨ Contact Us
- ⇨ Factory Tours
- ⇨ International
- ⇨ Press Center
- ⇨ Jobs at Ben & Jerry's
- ⇨ FAQ's
- ⇨ Research Library

Our Mission Statement

Ben & Jerry's is founded on and dedicated to a sustainable corporate concept of linked prosperity. Our mission consists of 3 interrelated parts::

Product Mission
To make, distribute & sell the finest quality all natural ice cream & euphoric concoctions with a continued commitment to incorporating wholesome, natural ingredients and promoting business practices that respect the Earth and the Environment.

Economic Mission
To operate the Company on a sustainable financial basis of profitable growth, increasing value for our stakeholders & expanding opportunities for development and career growth for our employees.

Social Mission
To operate the company in a way that actively recognizes the central role that business plays in society by initiating innovative ways to improve the quality of life locally, nationally & internationally.

Central To The Mission Of Ben & Jerry's
is the belief that all three parts must thrive equally in a manner that commands deep respect for individuals in and outside the company and supports the communities of which they are a part.

Leading with Progressive Values Across Our Business

We have a progressive, nonpartisan social mission that seeks to meet human needs and eliminate injustices in our local, national and international communities by integrating these concerns into our day-to-day business activities. Our focus is on children and families, the environment and sustainable agriculture on family farms.

- ○ Capitalism and the wealth it produces do not create opportunity for everyone equally. We recognize that the gap between the rich and the poor is wider than at anytime since the 1920's. We strive to create economic opportunities for those who have been denied them and to advance new models of economic justice that are sustainable and replicable.

- ○ By definition, the manufacturing of products creates waste. We strive to minimize our negative impact on the environment.

- ○ The growing of food is overly reliant on the use of toxic chemicals and other methods that are unsustainable. We support sustainable and safe methods of food production that reduce environmental degradation, maintain the productivity of the land over time, and support the economic viability of family farms and rural communities.

- ○ We seek and support nonviolent ways to achieve peace and justice. We believe government resources are more productively used in meeting human needs than in building and maintaining weapons systems.

- ○ We strive to show a deep respect for human beings inside and outside our company and for the communities in which they live.

Learn more! check out our <u>Social Mission News</u> or <u>Our Environment</u>

2

DEVELOPING SUCCESSFUL MARKETING AND CORPORATE STRATEGIES

LEARNING OBJECTIVES

After reading this chapter you should be able to:

1 Describe the three organizational levels of strategy.

2 Describe why business, mission, culture, and goals are important in organizations.

3 Explain how organizations set strategic directions by assessing where they are now and seek to be in the future.

4 Describe the strategic marketing process and its three key phases: planning, implementation, and control.

5 Explain how the marketing mix elements are blended into a cohesive marketing program.

WHERE CAN AN "A" IN A COURSE IN ICE CREAM MAKING LEAD?

These two entrepreneurs who aced their college course in ice cream making aren't just your typical Tom, Dick, or Harry! Consider the company they founded:

- It lets customers order "Ice Cream by Mail" from its website by creating "Custom Creation," "Scooper's Choice," or "Organic" six-pack flavor options.

- It contributes 7.5 percent of its pretax profits to philanthropic efforts.

- Its franchised PartnerShops are available to nonprofit organizations to provide training and job opportunities for people such as at-risk youth.

- It buys all of its milk and cream from one dairy cooperative whose members guarantee a supply that is bovine growth hormone-free.

Also, the company recently introduced two new lines: (1) organic (vanilla, chocolate, etc.), made from certified organic ingredients that have been cultivated in environmentally sustainable ways and (2) "low carb" ice cream flavors using a sugar substitute (Splenda) and containing ingredients obtained from family farmers or environmentally sensitive suppliers that pledge to uphold labor practices respecting children's and human rights.[1]

By now you know the company: Ben & Jerry's, or more formally, Ben & Jerry's Homemade, Inc. Its website (opposite page) reflects its creative, funky approach to business, linking its prosperity to a genuine concern for social causes.

Ben & Jerry's is proof that the American dream is still alive and well. Ben Cohen and Jerry Greenfield were grade school classmates on Long Island. In 1978 they headed north to Vermont and started an ice cream parlor in a renovated gas station.[2] Buoyed with enthusiasm, $12,000 they had borrowed and saved, and ideas from the $5 they spent on a Penn State correspondence course in ice cream making (with perfect scores on their openbook tests!) they were off and running.[3]

Today, Ben & Jerry's Homemade, Inc., now owned by Unilever N.V., has more than $200 million in annual sales worldwide, mainly from selling its incredibly rich ice cream. Ben & Jerry's has also been a leader with its social mission. For example, the company is committed to paying its employees a "livable wage" and providing top-quality benefits, as well as purchasing supplies from other socially responsible companies.[4] Customers love Cherry Garcia and One Sweet Whirled ice cream flavors, but many also want to support Ben & Jerry's social mission, too. The company has international sales in Europe, the Mideast, and Asia.

Chapter 2 describes how organizations set their mission and overall direction and link these activities to marketing strategies. As consumers become more concerned about a company's impact on society, marketing strategy may need to be linked to the social goals of the company's mission statement, as at Ben & Jerry's.

LEVELS OF STRATEGY IN ORGANIZATIONS

This chapter first distinguishes among different kinds of organizations and the different levels within them. We then compare strategies at three different levels in an organization, emphasizing the importance of activities at the functional level.

Today's Organizations: Kinds, Levels, and Teams

Large organizations today are extremely complex. All of us deal in some way with huge organizations every day, so it is useful to understand (1) the two basic kinds of organizations, (2) the levels that exist in them and their link to marketing, and (3) the functional areas and cross-functional teams.

Kinds of Organizations
Today's organizations can be divided into business firms and nonprofit organizations. A *business firm* is a privately owned organization that serves its customers in order to earn a profit. Business firms must earn profits to survive. **Profit** is the reward to a business firm for the risk it undertakes in offering a product for sale; the money left over after a firm's total expenses are subtracted from its total revenues. In contrast to business firms, a *nonprofit organization* is a nongovernmental organization that serves its customers but does not have profit as an organizational goal. For simplicity in the rest of the book, however, the terms *firm, company, corporation,* and *organization* are used to cover both business and nonprofit operations.

Levels in Organizations and How Marketing Links to Them
Whether explicit or implicit, organizations such as Ben & Jerry's have a strategic direction. Marketing not only helps set this direction but must also help the organization move there. Figure 2–1 summarizes the focus of this direction at each of the three levels in an organization.

The **corporate level** is where top management directs overall strategy for the entire organization. Multimarket, multiproduct firms such as General Electric or Johnson & Johnson really manage a portfolio of businesses, variously termed *strategic*

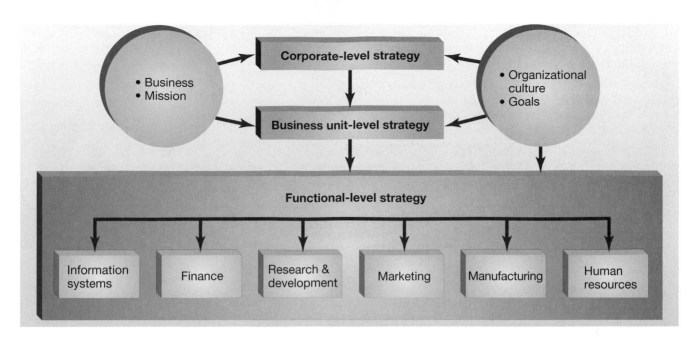

FIGURE 2–1

The three levels of strategy in organizations: corporate, business unit, and functional

business units (SBUs), strategic business segments, and *product-market units (PMUs).*[5] This level creates value for the shareholders of the firm, as measured by stock performance and profitability.

The term **business unit** refers to an organization that markets a set of related products to a clearly defined group of customers. The **business unit level** is the level at which business unit managers set the direction for their products and markets to exploit value-creating opportunities. The strategic direction is more specific at the business level of an organization. For less complex firms with a single business focus, such as Ben & Jerry's, the corporate and business unit levels may merge.

Each business unit has marketing and other specialized activities (e.g., finance, research and development, or human resource management) at the **functional level**, which is where groups of specialists *actually* create value for the organization. The term *department* generally refers to these specialized functions, such as the marketing department or information systems department. At the functional level, the strategic direction becomes more specific and focused. So just as there is a hierarchy of levels within organizations, there is also a hierarchy of strategic directions set by management at that level.

Because marketing's major role is to look outward—to keep the organization focused on contributing to customer value—its activities tie to each of the three levels in Figure 2–1. In a large corporation with multiple business units, marketing may be called on to assess consumer trends as an aid to corporate planning. At the business unit level, marketing may be asked to provide leadership in developing a new, integrated customer service program across all business units.

Where Things Happen: Functional Areas and Cross-Functional Teams   At the lowest level in Figure 2–1, marketing serves as part of a team of functional specialists. This is the level at which most of the organization's work gets done—customers are listened to, products are designed and produced, and customers' needs are satisfied. The marketing department does not work alone but works with *all* departments to deliver this customer value and satisfaction.

In practice, new-product development and other activities in many organizations involve **cross-functional teams**, a small number of people from different departments in an organization who are mutually accountable to a common set of performance goals. Boeing's cross-functional teams blend not only employees from different functional areas within the firm but also representatives from its suppliers and

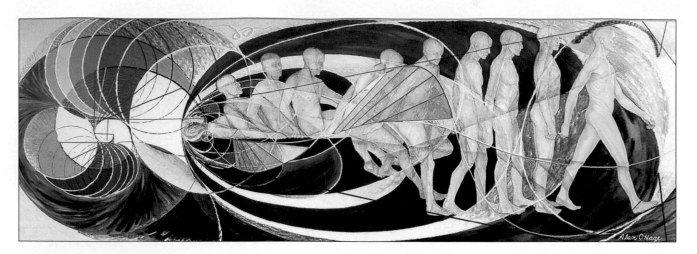

People see this "rising figure" mural in the headquarters of a world-class corporation. What does it signify? What does it say to employees? To others? For some insights and why it is important, see the text.

customers as well. Listening to airline passengers like you, one Boeing cross-functional team helped develop the Boeing 777, with customer-value innovations like more aisle headroom, TV screens in seatbacks, and seats 1.5 inches wider than most economy jetliner seats.

Cross-functional conflict can arise because in marketing's drive to implement the marketing concept and increase customer value, other departments may see this as making their jobs more difficult. For example, widening the Boeing 777 seats adds design and space problems for the engineering department and causes the finance department concerns about cost overruns. It is marketing's job to make these departments understand that without happy, satisfied customers who buy the organization's product, there is no company and there are no jobs.

Strategy Issues in Organizations

Organizations need a reason for their existence—and a direction. This is where their business, mission, organizational culture, and goals converge. We'll discuss each below. As shown in Figure 2–1, business and mission apply to the corporate and business unit levels, while organizational culture and goals relate to all three levels.

The Business   Organizations like Ben & Jerry's, the Red Cross, and your college exist for a purpose: to accomplish something for someone. At birth, most organizations have clear ideas about what "something" and "someone" mean. But as the organization grows over time, often its purpose gets fuzzy, unclear.

This is where the organization repeatedly asks some of the most difficult questions it ever faces: What is our business? Who are our customers? What offerings should we provide to give these customers value? One guideline in defining the company's business: Try to understand the people served by the organization and the value they receive, which emphasizes the critical customer-driven focus that successful organizations have.

In a now-famous article, Harvard professor Theodore Levitt cited American railroads as organizations that had a narrow, production-oriented statement of their business: "We are in the railroad business!" This narrow definition of their business lost sight of who their customers were and what their needs were. Railroads saw only other railroads as competitors and failed to design strategies to compete with airlines, barges, pipelines, trucks, bus lines, and cars. Railroads would probably have fared better over the past century by recognizing they are in "the transportation business."[6]

With this focus on the customer, Disney *is not* in the movie and theme park business, but rather it *is* in the business of creating fun and fantasy for customers.

Similarly, as we'll see shortly, Medtronic is *the* world leader in developing, producing, and marketing heart pacemakers and other implantable medical devices. Yet Medtronic *is not* in the medical device business. It *is* in the business of alleviating pain, restoring health, and extending life. In this respect Medtronic's business somewhat overlaps its mission, the next topic.

The Mission   By understanding its business, an organization can take steps to define its **mission**, a statement of the organization's scope, often identifying its customers, markets, products, technology, and values. Today, often used interchangeably with *vision,* the *mission statement* frequently has an inspirational theme—something that can ignite the loyalty of employees and others with whom the organization comes in contact. This is one of the better-known mission statements in America:

> To explore strange new worlds, to seek out new life and new civilizations, to boldly go where no one has gone before.

This continuing mission for the starship *Enterprise,* as Gene Rodenberry wrote it for the *Star Trek* adventure series, is inspirational and focuses the advanced technology, strong leadership, and skilled crew of the *Enterprise* on what is to be accomplished.

This inspiration and focus appears in the mission of many organizations, like the American Red Cross:

> To provide relief to victims of disasters and help people prevent, prepare for, and respond to emergencies.

Or like this first sentence from Medtronic's mission statement:

> To contribute to human welfare by application of biomedical engineering in the research, design, manufacture, and sale of instruments or appliances that alleviate pain, restore health, and extend life.

Organizational Culture   Organizations must connect not just with their customers but with all their **stakeholders**, who are the people who are affected by what the company does and how well it performs. This group includes employees, owners, and board members, as well as suppliers, distributors, unions, local communities, and, of course, customers. Communicating the mission statement is an important corporate-level marketing function. Some companies print their mission statement on cards or placards. Others take a more dramatic approach—like the "rising figure" wall painting at Medtronic's corporate headquarters, which powerfully communicates the inspiration and focus of its mission to employees, doctors, and patients alike.[7]

Whether at the corporate, business, or functional level, **organizational culture** exists in the unit, which is a set of values, ideas, and attitudes that is learned and shared among the members of an organization. At Medtronic, a corporate officer presents each new employee with a medallion with the "rising figure" on one side and the mission on the other. Each December five or six patients, accompanied by their physicians, describe to a large employee holiday celebration how Medtronic products have changed their lives. These activities send clear messages to employees and other stakeholders about Medtronic's cohesive organizational culture.

When corporations merge or are acquired, organizational cultures can collide, often resulting from conflicts in missions and goals (discussed in the following section). Ben & Jerry's is an example. When Unilever acquired Ben & Jerry's in April 2000, it had 180 times the annual sales of Ben & Jerry's and dozens of well-known brands (Wisk, Dove, Lipton). This really makes Ben & Jerry's only a small business unit in Unilever. How would Ben & Jerry's fare in its new corporate setting? The Going Online exercise at the end of the chapter asks you to compare the mission statements for both Ben & Jerry's and Unilever.

ETHICS AND SOCIAL RESPONSIBILITY ALERT

The Global Dilemma: How to Achieve Sustainable Development

ETHICS

Corporate executives and world leaders are increasingly asked to address the issue of "sustainable development." This term was formally defined in a 1987 United Nations report as meeting present needs "without compromising the ability of future generations to meet their own needs." What often happens is the achievement of profits for a firm and economic development for a country by adding jobs in highly polluting industries, thereby pushing cleanup actions into the future.

Eastern Europe and the nations of the former Soviet Union provide an example. Tragically, poisoned air and dead rivers are the legacies of seven decades of communist rule. With more than a third of the households of many of these nations below the poverty level, should the immediate goal be a cleaner environment or more food, clothing, housing, and consumer goods? What should the heads of these governments do? What should Western firms trying to enter these new, growing markets do? What will be the impact on future generations?

3M developed an innovative program called Pollution Prevent Pays (3P) to reduce harmful environmental impacts, making a profit doing so. 3M estimates that the 3P program in the last quarter century has cut its pollution by 1.6 billion pounds while saving almost $900 million in raw materials and avoiding fines. The company's current environmental goals: Improve energy efficiency per pound of product by 20 percent while reducing waste per pound by 25 percent.

Should the environment or economic growth come first? What are the societal trade-offs? Will profit-making firms adopt and implement a 3P kind of program?

Goals   **Goals** or **objectives** (terms used interchangeably in this textbook) convert the mission into targeted levels of performance to be achieved, often by a specific time. These goals measure how well the mission is being accomplished. As shown in Figure 2–1, goals exist at the corporate, business unit, and functional levels. All lower-level goals must contribute to achieving goals at the next, higher level.

Business firms can pursue several different types of goals:

- *Profit.* Classic economic theory assumes a firm seeks to get as high a financial return on its investment—profit—as possible.
- *Sales.* If profits are acceptable, a firm may elect to maintain or increase its sales level even though profitability may not be maximized.
- *Market share.* A firm may choose to maintain or increase its market share, sometimes at the expense of greater profits if industry status or prestige is at stake. **Market share** is the ratio of sales revenue of the firm to the total sales revenue of all firms in the industry, including the firm itself.
- *Quality.* A firm may target the highest quality, as Medtronic does with its implantable medical devices.
- *Customer satisfaction.* Customers are the reason the organization exists, so their perceptions and actions are of vital importance. Their satisfaction can be measured directly with surveys or tracked with proxy measures like number of customer complaints or percentage of orders shipped within 24 hours of receipt.
- *Employee welfare.* A firm may recognize the critical importance of its employees by having an explicit goal stating its commitment to good employment opportunities and working conditions for them.
- *Social responsibility.* A firm may seek to balance conflicting goals of consumers, employees, and stockholders to promote overall welfare of all these groups, even at the expense of profits. U.S. firms manufacturing products abroad increasingly seek to be "good global citizens" by paying reasonable wages and reducing pollution from their manufacturing plants. For example, as described in the Ethics and Social Responsibility Alert on sustainable development, today 3M has an environmental goal of reducing its waste per pound of product by 25 percent.[8]

Many private organizations that do not seek profits also exist. Examples are museums, symphony orchestras, and private hospitals. These organizations strive to serve consumers as efficiently as possible. Government agencies also perform marketing activities in trying to achieve their goal of serving the public good.

Concept Check

1. What are the three levels in today's large organizations?

2. What is the meaning of an organization's mission?

3. How do an organization's goals relate to its mission?

SETTING STRATEGIC DIRECTIONS

Setting strategic directions involves answering two other difficult questions: (1) Where are we now? and (2) Where do we want to go?

A Look Around: Where Are We Now?

Asking an organization where it is at the present time involves identifying its customers, competencies, and competitors. More detailed approaches of assessing "where are we now?" include SWOT analysis, discussed later in this chapter, and environmental scanning (Chapter 3). Both may be done at each of the three levels in the organization.

Customers   Ben & Jerry's customers are ice cream and frozen yogurt eaters. But they are not all the same, because they have different flavor preferences, fat preferences, convenience preferences, and so on. Medtronic's "customers" are cardiologists and heart surgeons who serve patients.

Lands' End's unconditional guarantee for its products highlights its focus on its customers.

Lands' End
www.landsend.com

Lands' End provides an example of a clear focus on customers. Its stores and website give a remarkable statement about its commitments to customer relationships and quality of its products with these unconditional words:

GUARANTEED. PERIOD.®

Its website points out the Lands' End guarantee has always been an unconditional one and it has read: "If you are not completely satisfied with any item you buy from us, at any time during your use of it, return it and we will refund your full purchase price." But to get the message across more clearly to its customers, it put it in the two-word guarantee above.

The crucial point: Strategic directions must be customer-focused and provide genuine value and benefits to present and prospective customers. This Lands' End customer focus was apparent to Sears, Roebuck & Co., which bought Lands' End in 2002. By early 2004, Sears had handed over much of its retail apparel operations to executives of Lands' End.[9]

Competencies   "What do we do best?" asks about our organization's capabilities, or competencies. **Competencies** are an organization's special capabilities, including skills, technologies, and resources that distinguish it from other organizations. Exploiting these competencies can lead to success.[10] In Medtronic's case, its competencies include world-class technology plus training, service, and marketing activities that respond to both standard and urgent, life-threatening medical needs and wants. Competencies should be distinctive enough to provide a **competitive advantage**, a unique strength relative to competitors, often based on quality, time, cost, or innovation.[11]

For example, if 3M has a goal of generating a specific portion of its sales from new products, it must have a supporting competency in research and development and new-product marketing. In the 1990s, Hewlett-Packard had a truly competitive advantage with its fast cycle time, which allowed it to bring innovative products to markets in large volume rapidly.[12]

Another strategy is to develop a competency in total quality management (TQM). **Quality** here means those features and characteristics of a product that influence its ability to satisfy customer needs. Firms often try to improve quality or reduce new product cycles through **benchmarking**—discovering how others do something better than your own firm so you can imitate or leapfrog competition. Benchmarking often involves studying operations in completely different businesses. When General Mills sought ideas on how to reduce the time to convert its production lines from one cereal to another, it sent a team to observe the pit crews at the Indianapolis 500 race. The result: General Mills cut its plant changeover time by more than half.

Competitors   In today's fierce global competition the lines among competitive sectors are increasingly blurred. Lands' End started as a catalog retailer. But defining its competitors simply as other catalog retailers (Figure 2–2) is a huge oversimplification. In what is called *intertype competition* in Chapter 17, Lands' End, now part of Sears, competes not only with other catalog retailers of clothing but with traditional department stores, mass merchandisers, specialty shops, and well-known brands of clothing sold in all these kinds of retailers.

While only parts of the clothing lines sold by these competitors overlap those of Lands' End, all have websites for Internet sales. In addition, thousands of other small clothing manufacturers, distributors, and liquidators sell through websites like eBay, adding more competition for Lands' End. In 2004, about 430,000 small businesses and individuals used eBay to earn their livings.[13]

Is everyone selling clothes? For a view of the intense competition Lands' End faces, ranging from catalogs to e-tailers, see Figure 2–2 and the text.

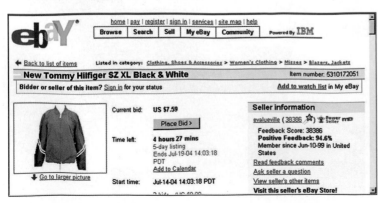

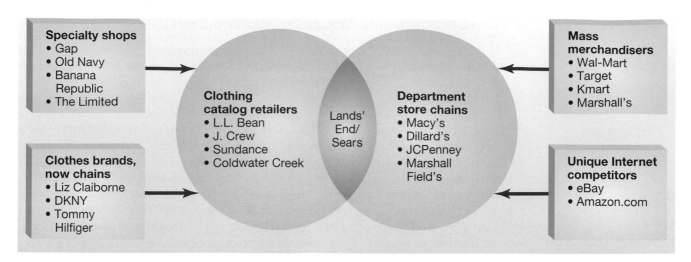

FIGURE 2-2

Who are Lands' End/Sears' competitors? Today, they go far beyond clothing catalog retailers and department store chains.

Like all Internet retailers, Lands' End has a goal of increasing its "conversion rate," the percentage of browsers who actually buy something on visits to the website. Compared to other big name e-tailers—or Internet retailers—Lands' End's conversion rate is among the best. This is because it has invested heavily in technology to make its site more consumer friendly (easier to move from the home page to the sales-confirmation window) with a "virtual model" of a customer to let him or her "try things on" online (see Chapter 17) and "synchronized screens" to let Lands' End's service rep see exactly the same screen the customer is viewing at home.[14] On the horizon for e-tailer customers: video and TV commercials made possible by improved computer and broadband technology.

Lands' End's experience is typical of the complex array of competitors today's business firms face. So successful firms continuously assess both who the competitors are and how they are changing in order to respond with their own strategies.

Kodak today must make a series of difficult marketing decisions. From what you know about cameras and photos, assess Kodak's sales opportunities for the four products shown here. For some possible answers and a way to show these opportunities graphically, see the text and Figure 2–3.

Eastman Kodak Company
www.kodak.com

Kodak digital cameras

Kodak printers (to print digital photos at home)

Kodak film sold in the U.S., Canada, and Western Europe

Kodak self-service kiosks in retail outlets

Growth Strategies: Where Do We Want to Go?

Knowing where the organization is at the present time enables managers to set a direction for the firm and start to allocate resources to move toward that direction. Two techniques to aid in these decisions are (1) business portfolio and (2) market-product analyses.

Business Portfolio Analysis The Boston Consulting Group's (BCG) *business portfolio analysis* uses quantified performance measures and growth targets to analyze a firm's business units (called strategic business units, or SBUs, in the BCG analysis) as though they were a collection of separate investments.[15] While used at the strategic business unit level here, this BCG analysis has also been applied at the product line or individual product or brand level. More than 75 percent of the largest U.S. firms have used it in some form. BCG, a nationally known management consulting firm, advises its clients to locate the position of each of its SBUs on a growth-share matrix (Figure 2–3).

The vertical axis is the *market growth rate,* which is the annual rate of growth of the specific market or industry in which a given SBU is competing. The horizontal axis is the *relative market share,* defined as the sales of the SBU divided by the sales of the largest firm in the industry. A relative market share of $10\times$ (at the left end of the scale) means that the SBU has 10 times the *share* of its largest competitor, whereas a share of $0.1\times$ (at the right end of the scale) means it has only 10 percent of the *sales* of its largest competitor.

BCG has given specific names and descriptions to the four resulting quadrants in its business portfolio analysis matrix based on the amount of cash they generate for or require from the firm:

- *Cash cows* are SBUs that typically generate large amounts of cash, far more than they can invest profitably in their own product line. They have a dominant share of a slow-growth market and provide cash to pay large amounts of company overhead and to invest in other SBUs.
- *Stars* are SBUs with a high share of high-growth markets that may need extra cash to finance their own rapid future growth. When their growth slows, they are likely to become cash cows.

FIGURE 2–3

Boston Consulting Group portfolio analysis for Kodak, as it might appear in 2004

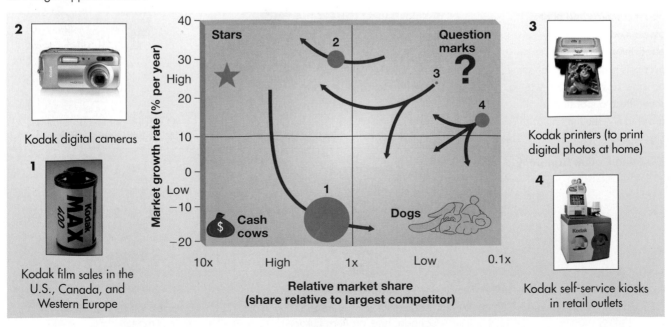

2 Kodak digital cameras

1 Kodak film sales in the U.S., Canada, and Western Europe

3 Kodak printers (to print digital photos at home)

4 Kodak self-service kiosks in retail outlets

- *Question marks* or *problem children* are SBUs with a low share of high-growth markets. They require large injections of cash just to maintain their market share, much less increase it. Their name implies management's dilemma for these SBUs: choosing the right ones to invest in and phasing out the rest.
- *Dogs* are SBUs with a low share of low-growth markets. Although they may generate enough cash to sustain themselves, they do not hold the promise of ever becoming real winners for the firm. Dropping SBUs that are dogs may be required, except when relationships with other SBUs, competitive considerations, or potential strategic alliances exist.[16]

A firm's SBUs often start as question marks and go counterclockwise around Figure 2–3 to become stars, then cash cows, and finally dogs. Because most firms have limited influence on the market growth rate, their main alternative in a business portfolio analysis framework is to try to change the relative market share. To accomplish this, management makes conscious decisions on what role each SBU should have in the future and either injects or removes cash from it.

Four Kodak SBUs are shown as they appeared in 2004 and can serve as an example of BCG analysis. The area of each circle in Figure 2–3 is roughly proportional to the corresponding SBU's 2004 sales revenue. In a more complete analysis, its other SBUs would be included. This Kodak example also shows the agonizing strategic decisions that must be made by executives in firms in an industry facing revolutionary change—the situation Kodak faces in the camera and film business with the arrival of digital technology.

More than a century ago, Kodak virtually invented the photography industry. Nicknamed "Big Yellow" for its film packages, until about 2000 Kodak relied not on its cameras for the bulk of its revenues and profits but on its film for the billions of photographs taken every year. Two factors changed that: (1) more competition from film manufacturers like Fuji and (2) the popularization of digital cameras that need no conventional film.

So in late 2003, Kodak's CEO Daniel Karp announced a shift in Kodak's strategic priorities from film to digital technology. Experts, both supporters and critics, have weighed in with their opinions of the new priorities. One thing, however, is eminently clear. The success of Kodak's strategy and its product lines shown in Figure 2–3 depends on how millions of consumers like you take pictures and convert your pictures into useful images over the next decade. Here is a snapshot of the sales opportunities of the four product lines reflected in the comments of analysts:

1. *Kodak film sales in the United States, Canada, and Western Europe.* An $8 billion per year "cash cow" in 2003, Kodak film sales are still its biggest single source of revenue. In its "death throes," Kodak film sales are expected to decline 10 to 12 percent per year through 2006.[17] Sales will not be helped by the 2004 announcement that Kodak will soon stop selling film cameras in these countries.[18]
2. *Kodak digital cameras.* A $1 billion business in 2003, Kodak's "filmless imaging market" is expected to grow from 30 percent of its 2003 revenues to 60 percent in 2006.[19] Sales of its popular line of EasyShare digital cameras grew 87 percent in 2003 over sales in 2002.[20] Kodak clearly expects its digital cameras to be a "star" soon. The challenge: It is #2 in market share behind Sony in the United States with new rivals emerging, like Nokia's cell phones with digital cameras.
3. *Kodak printers (to print digital photos at home).* With 82 percent of digital prints made this way in 2003, this might look like a clear BCG star with Kodak's expected new line of home printers. But industry analysts expect this in-home segment to decline substantially because of the hassle.[21] And with Kodak competing with established printer manufacturers like Hewlett-Packard and Canon, the future of this "question mark" could range from being a "dog" to a "star."

4. *Kodak self-service kiosks in retail outlets.* With only about 1 percent of the market in printed pictures in 2003, these self-service machines used to take up to four minutes to make an 8 × 10 photo. But in early 2004 Kodak announced a self-service kiosk that can convert a roll of 35 mm. film into prints in only seven minutes. As shown in Figure 2–3, an innovative technology (the kiosks) for a slowly dying product (the film) faces big unknowns, also because Japanese copiers are well entrenched in these outlets.[22]

Are these BCG projections valid? Your use of digital cameras and how you make their prints hold the answer. Kodak strategies on selling film in developing markets are discussed later in the chapter.

The primary strength of business portfolio analysis lies in forcing a firm to place each of its SBUs in the growth-share matrix, which in turn suggests which SBUs will be cash producers and cash users in the future. Weaknesses are that it is often difficult (1) to get the needed information and (2) to incorporate competitive information into business portfolio analysis.[23]

Market-Product Analysis   Firms can also view growth opportunities in terms of markets and products. Let's think of it this way: For any product there is both a current market (consisting of existing customers) and a new market (consisting of potential customers). And for any market, there is a current product (what they're now using) and a new product (something they might use if it were developed). These four market-product strategies are shown in Figure 2–4.[24]

As Unilever attempts to increase sales revenues of its Ben & Jerry's business, it must consider all four of the alternative market-product strategies shown in Figure 2–4. For example, it can try to use *market penetration*—a marketing strategy of increasing sales of present products in existing markets, in this case by increasing sales of Ben & Jerry's present ice cream products to U.S. consumers. There is no change in either the basic product line or the market served, but increased sales are possible—either by selling more ice cream (through better promotion or distribution) *or* by selling the same amount of ice cream at a higher price to its existing customers.

Market development, a marketing strategy of selling existing products to new markets, is a reasonable alternative for Ben & Jerry's. South America, for example, is a good possible new market. There is good news and bad news for this marketing strategy: As the income of South American households increases, consumers may be able to buy more ice cream, but the Ben & Jerry's brand is relatively unknown.

Product development is a marketing strategy of selling new products to existing markets. Figure 2–4 shows that the firm could try leveraging the Ben & Jerry's brand, as mentioned earlier, by selling its own Ben & Jerry's brand of children's clothing in the United States. This, of course, has dangers because Americans may not be

FIGURE 2–4
Four market-product strategies: alternative ways to expand sales revenues for Ben & Jerry's

Markets	PRODUCTS	
	Current	**New**
Current	**Market penetration** Selling more Ben & Jerry's super premium ice cream to Americans	**Product development** Selling a new product such as children's clothing under the Ben & Jerry's brand to Americans
New	**Market development** Selling more Ben & Jerry's super premium ice cream in South American markets for the first time	**Diversification** Selling a new product such as children's clothing in South American markets for the first time

able to see a clear connection between the company's expertise in ice cream and, say, children's clothing.

Diversification is a marketing strategy of developing new products and selling them in new markets. This is a potentially high-risk strategy for Ben & Jerry's, and for most firms, because the company has neither previous production experience nor marketing experience on which to draw. For example, in trying to sell a Ben & Jerry's brand of children's clothing in South America, the company has expertise neither in producing children's clothing nor in marketing to South American consumers.

Which strategies will Ben and Jerry's follow? Keep your eyes, ears, and taste buds working to discover the marketing answers.

Concept Check

1. What are competencies and why are they important?

2. What is business portfolio analysis?

3. What are the four market-product strategies?

THE STRATEGIC MARKETING PROCESS

After the organization assesses where it's at and where it wants to go, other questions emerge:

1. How do we allocate our resources to get where we want to go?
2. How do we convert our plans to actions?
3. How do our results compare with our plans, and do deviations require new plans?

How can Ben & Jerry's identify new ice cream flavors and social responsibility programs that contribute to its mission? The text describes how the strategic marketing process and its SWOT analysis can help.

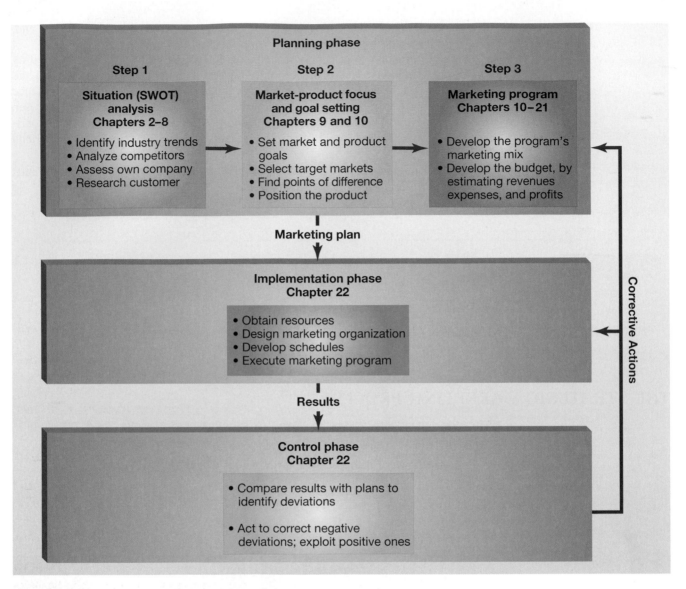

FIGURE 2–5

The strategic marketing process

This same approach is used in the **strategic marketing process**, whereby an organization allocates its marketing mix resources to reach its target markets. This process is divided into three phases: planning, implementation, and control (Figure 2–5).

The strategic marketing process is so central to the activities of most organizations that they formalize it as a **marketing plan**, which is a road map for the marketing activities of an organization for a specified future period of time, such as one year or five years. Appendix A at the end of this chapter provides guidelines for writing a marketing plan and also presents a sample marketing plan for Paradise Kitchens,® Inc., a firm that produces and distributes a line of spicy chilies under the Howlin' Coyote® brand name. The sequence of activities that follow parallels the elements of the marketing plan that appear in Appendix A.

Strategic Marketing Process: The Planning Phase

As shown in Figure 2–5, the planning phase of the strategic marketing process consists of the three steps shown at the top of the figure: (1) situation analysis, (2) market-product focus and goal setting, and (3) the marketing program. Let's use the recent marketing planning experiences of several companies to look at each of these steps.

WEB LINK

Ben & Jerry's Flavors: From Chocolate Fudge Brownie Ice Cream and One Sweet Whirled Novelty Bars to . . . the Flavor Graveyard

www.mhhe.com/Kerin

Ben & Jerry's markets its flavors of ice cream, frozen yogurt, sorbet, and novelty bars in response to both consumer . . . ahem! . . . tastes and important causes it supports, a practice continued even after being sold to Unilever in 2000. For more than a decade, the brownies for Ben & Jerry's popular Chocolate Fudge Brownie ice cream have been supplied by Greyston Bakery of Yonkers, NY, a nonprofit organization that trains, employs, and houses low-income people in the area. Recently, Ben & Jerry's teamed up with the award-winning Dave Matthews Band and SaveOurEnvironment.org to fight global warming by creating the One Sweet Whirled ice cream flavor in pints and novelty bars. But not all flavors last. The ones that don't survive wind up in Ben & Jerry's "Flavor Graveyard." To see Ben & Jerry's current flavors as well as those "dearly departed flavors" in the Flavor Graveyard, visit "Our Products" at www.benjerry.com. Have any of your favorite flavors been "laid to rest"?

Figure 2–5 also shows how the strategic marketing process integrates the chapters in this book. Chapters 2 through 8 provide the information for the situation (SWOT) analysis, step 1 of the planning phase. Step 2, developing a market-product focus and goals for the product, is covered in Chapters 9 and 10. The elements of the marketing program in step 3—the 4Ps—are discussed in Chapters 10 through 21. The book concludes with Chapter 22, which ties together the planning, implementation, and control phases of the strategic marketing process.

Step 1: Situation (SWOT) Analysis   The essence of **situation analysis** is taking stock of where the firm or product has been recently, where it is now, and where it is headed in terms of the organization's plans and the external factors and trends affecting it. The situation analysis box in Figure 2–5 is the first of the three steps in the planning phase.

An effective shorthand summary of the situation analysis is a **SWOT analysis**, an acronym describing an organization's appraisal of its internal **S**trengths and **W**eaknesses and its external **O**pportunities and **T**hreats. Both the situation and SWOT analyses can be done at the level of the entire organization, the business unit, the product line, or the specific product. As an analysis moves from the level of the entire organization to the specific product, it, of course, gets far more detailed. For small firms or those with basically a single product line, an analysis at the firm or product level is really the same thing.

The SWOT analysis is based on an exhaustive study of the four areas shown in step 1 of the planning phase of the strategic marketing process (Figure 2–5). Knowledge of these areas forms the foundation on which the firm builds its marketing program:

- Identifying trends in the firm's industry.
- Analyzing the firm's competitors.
- Assessing the firm itself.
- Researching the firm's present and prospective customers.

Let's assume you are the Unilever vice president responsible for integrating Ben & Jerry's into Unilever's business. You might do the SWOT analysis shown in Figure 2–6 on the next page. Note that your SWOT table has four cells formed by the combination of internal versus external factors (the rows) and favorable versus unfavorable factors (the columns) that summarize Ben & Jerry's strengths, weaknesses, opportunities, and threats. This SWOT analysis can identify Ben & Jerry's flavors that don't meet customer tastes and wind up in its "Flavor Graveyard," as described in the Web Link.

FIGURE 2–6

Ben & Jerry's: a SWOT analysis to get it growing again

Location of Factor	TYPE OF FACTOR	
	Favorable	**Unfavorable**
Internal	**Strengths** • Prestigious, well-known brand name among U.S. consumers • 40 percent share of the U.S. super premium ice cream market • Can complement Unilever's existing ice cream brands • Widely recognized for its social responsibility actions	**Weaknesses** • Danger that B&J's social responsibility actions may add costs, reduce focus on core business • Need for experienced managers to help growth • Flat sales and profits in recent years
External	**Opportunities** • Growing demand for quality ice cream in overseas markets • Increasing U.S. demand for frozen yogurt and other low-fat desserts • Success of many U.S. firms in extending successful brand in one product category to others	**Threats** • Consumer concern with fatty desserts; B&J customers are the type who read new government-ordered nutritional labels • Competes with giant Pillsbury and its Haagen-Dazs brand • International downturns increase the risks for B&J in European and Asian markets

A SWOT analysis helps a firm identify the strategy-related factors in these four cells that can have a major effect on the firm. The goal is not simply to develop the SWOT analysis but to translate the results of the analysis into specific actions to help the firm grow and succeed. The ultimate goal is to identify the *critical* factors affecting the firm and then build on vital strengths, correct glaring weaknesses, exploit significant opportunities, and avoid disaster-laden threats. That is a big order.

The Ben and Jerry's SWOT analysis in Figure 2–6 can be the basis for these kinds of specific actions. An action in each of the four cells might be:

- *Build on a strength.* Find specific efficiencies in distribution with Unilever's existing ice cream brands.
- *Correct a weakness.* Recruit experienced managers from other consumer product firms to help stimulate growth.
- *Exploit an opportunity.* Develop a new line of low-fat frozen yogurts to respond to consumer health concerns.
- *Avoid a disaster-laden threat.* Focus on less risky international markets, such as Canada and Mexico.

Examples of more in-depth study in these four areas appear in the SWOT analysis in Figure 1 in the marketing plan in Appendix A and the chapters in this textbook cited in that plan.

Step 2: Market-Product Focus and Goal Setting Determining which products will be directed toward which customers (step 2 of the planning phase in Figure 2–5) is essential for developing an effective marketing program (step 3). This decision is often based on **market segmentation**, which involves aggregating prospective buyers into groups, or segments, that (1) have common needs and (2) will respond similarly to a marketing action. Ideally, a firm can use market segmentation to identify the segments on which it will focus its efforts—its target market segments—and develop one or more marketing programs to reach them.

As always, understanding the customer is essential. In the case of Medtronic, executives researched a potential new market in Asia by talking extensively with

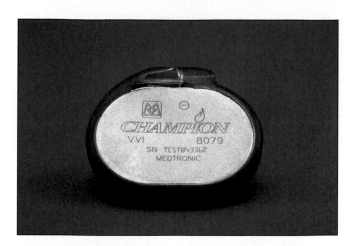

The Champion: Medtronic's high-quality, long-life, low-cost heart pacemaker for an Asian market segment.

doctors in India and China. They learned that these doctors saw some of the current state-of-the-art features of heart pacemakers as unnecessary and too expensive. Instead, they wanted an affordable pacemaker that was reliable and easy to implant. This information led Medtronic to develop and market a new product, the Champion heart pacemaker, directed at the needs of this Asian market segment.

Goal setting involves setting measurable marketing objectives to be achieved. Such objectives would be different depending on the level of marketing involved. For a specific market, the goal may be to introduce a new product, such as Medtronic's Champion pacemaker in Asia or Toyota's launch of its hybrid car, the Prius. For a specific brand or product, the goal may be to create a promotional campaign or pricing strategy that will get more consumers to purchase. For an entire marketing program, the objective is often a series of actions to be implemented over several years.

Using the strategic marketing process shown in Figure 2–5, let's examine Medtronic's five-year plan to reach the "affordable and reliable" segment of the pacemaker market:[25]

- *Set marketing and product goals.* The chances of new-product success are increased by specifying both market and product goals. Based on their market research showing the need for a reliable yet affordable pacemaker, Medtronic executives set the following as their goal: Design and market such a pacemaker in the next three years that could be manufactured in China for the Asian market.
- *Select target markets.* The Champion pacemaker will be targeted at cardiologists and medical clinics performing heart surgery in India, China, and other Asian countries.
- *Find points of difference.* **Points of difference** are those characteristics of a product that make it superior to competitive substitutes. Just as a competitive advantage is a unique strength of an entire organization compared to its competitors, points of difference are unique characteristics of one of its products that make it superior to competitive products it faces in the marketplace. For the Champion pacemaker, the key points of difference are *not* the state-of-the-art features that drive up production costs and are important to only a minority of patients. Instead, they are high quality, long life, reliability, ease of use, and low cost.
- *Position the product.* The pacemaker will be "positioned" in cardiologists' and patients' minds as a medical device that is high quality and reliable with a long, nine-year life. The name Champion is selected after testing acceptable names among doctors in India, China, Pakistan, Singapore, and Malaysia.

Details in these four elements of step 2 provide a solid foundation to use in developing the marketing program, the next step in the planning phase of the strategic marketing process.

Step 3: Marketing Program   Activities in step 2 tell the marketing manager which customers to target and which customer needs the firm's product offerings can satisfy—the *who* and *what* aspects of the strategic marketing process. The *how* aspect—step 3 in the planning phase—involves developing the program's marketing mix and its budget.

Figure 2–7 on the next page shows components of each marketing mix element that are combined to provide a cohesive marketing program. For the five-year marketing plan of Medtronic, these marketing mix activities include the following:

- *Product strategy.* Offer a Champion brand heart pacemaker with features needed by Asian patients at an affordable price.

FIGURE 2–7

Elements of the marketing mix
that comprise a cohesive
marketing program

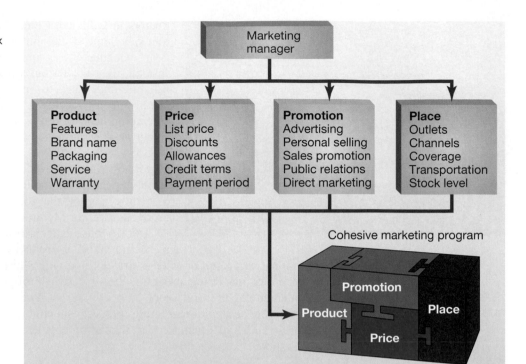

- *Price strategy.* Manufacture Champion to control costs so that it can be priced below $1,000 (in U.S. dollars)—a fraction of the price of the state-of-the-art pacemakers offered in Western markets.
- *Promotion strategy.* Feature demonstrations at cardiologist and medical conventions across Asia to introduce the Champion and highlight the device's features and application.
- *Place (distribution) strategy.* Search out, utilize, and train reputable medical distributors across Asia to call on cardiologists and medical clinics.

Putting this marketing program into effect requires that the firm commit time and money to it in the form of a sales forecast and budget that must be approved by top management.

Concept Check

1. What is the difference between a strength and an opportunity in a SWOT analysis?

2. What is market segmentation?

3. What are points of difference and why are they important?

Strategic Marketing Process: The Implementation Phase

As shown in Figure 2–5, the result of the tens or hundreds of hours spent in the planning phase of the strategic marketing process is the firm's marketing plan. Implementation, the second phase of the strategic marketing process, involves carrying out the marketing plan that emerges from the planning phase. If the firm cannot put the marketing plan into effect—in the implementation phase—the planning phase was a waste of time. Figure 2–5 also shows the four components of the implementation phase: (1) obtaining resources, (2) designing the marketing organization,

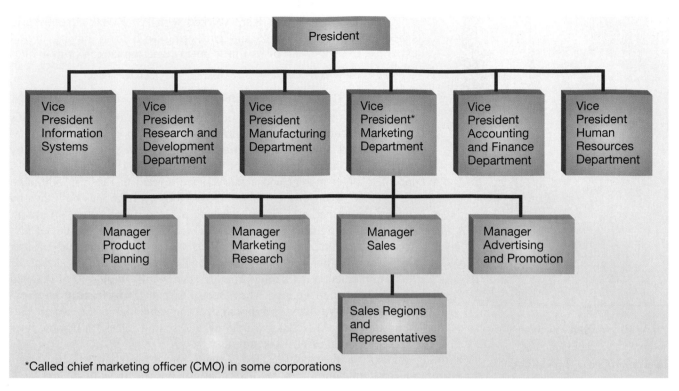

*Called chief marketing officer (CMO) in some corporations

FIGURE 2–8

Organization of a typical manufacturing firm, showing a breakdown of the marketing department

(3) developing schedules, and (4) actually executing the marketing program designed in the planning phase. Eastman Kodak provides a case example.

Obtaining Resources   In late 2003, Kodak CEO Daniel Karp announced his bold plan (discussed earlier) to reenergize the filmmaker for the new age of digital cameras and prints. Karp needed money to implement the plan, so he cut shareholder dividends by 72 percent to invest the $3 billion saved in Kodak's digital technologies.[26] And in early 2004, Karp announced a painful cut of up to 15,000 jobs over the next three years to provide additional money to invest in Kodak's digital future.[27]

Designing the Marketing Organization   A marketing program needs a marketing organization to implement it. Figure 2–8 shows the organization chart of a typical manufacturing firm, giving some details of the marketing department's structure. Four managers of marketing activities are shown to report to the vice president of marketing. Several regional sales managers and an international sales manager may report to the manager of sales. This marketing organization is responsible for converting marketing plans to reality as a part of the corporate team.

In the 1990s a number of large consumer products firms changed the title of the head of the marketing department from "vice president of marketing" to "chief marketing officer" (CMO), but the responsibilities have stayed largely the same.[28]

Developing Schedules   Effective implementation requires goals, deadlines, and schedules. To implement his plan to focus on Kodak's digital business opportunities, Karp set some key goals:[29]

- Boost sales from $13 billion in 2003 to $16 billion in 2006 and $20 billion in 2010.
- Increase the share of Kodak's revenues from its digital businesses from 30 percent in 2003 to 60 percent in 2006.

While Kodak is now pursuing immediate sales of film cameras in China, it also has a long-term strategy of selling digital cameras there, too.

To achieve these goals, Karp worked with key Kodak executives to schedule the acquisition of and partnering with firms having digital expertise, the phase-out of its film cameras, and the launch of new lines of digital cameras.

Executing the Marketing Program   Marketing plans are meaningless pieces of paper without effective execution of those plans. This effective execution requires attention to detail for both marketing strategies and marketing tactics. A **marketing strategy** is the means by which a marketing goal is to be achieved, usually characterized by a specified target market and a marketing program to reach it. Although the term *marketing strategy* is often used loosely, it implies both the end sought (target market) and the means to achieve it (marketing program). At this marketing strategy level, Kodak will seek to increase sales of film cameras and film in emerging markets like India, China, and Eastern Europe where low prices, simplicity, and convenience are important.[30]

To implement a marketing program successfully, hundreds of detailed decisions are often required. These decisions, called **marketing tactics**, are detailed day-to-day operational decisions essential to the overall success of marketing strategies. At Kodak, writing ads and setting prices for its new lines of digital cameras are examples of marketing tactics.

Marketing strategies and marketing tactics shade into each other. Effective marketing program implementation requires excruciating concern for both.

Strategic Marketing Process: The Control Phase

The control phase of the strategic marketing process seeks to keep the marketing program moving in the direction set for it (see Figure 2–5). Accomplishing this requires the marketing manager (1) to compare the results of the marketing program with the goals in the written plans to identify deviations and (2) to act on these deviations—correcting negative deviations and exploiting positive ones.

Comparing Results with Plans to Identify Deviations   In late 2003, as Daniel Karp looked at the company's sales revenues from 1998 through 2003, he didn't like what he saw: the very flat trend, or AB in Figure 2–9. Extending the 1998–2003 trend to 2010 along BC shows declining sales revenues, a totally unacceptable, no-growth strategy.

FIGURE 2–9
Evaluation and control of Kodak's marketing program

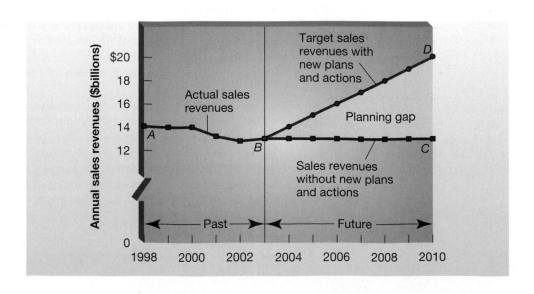

Karp set a growth target of 5 to 6 percent annually, the line BD in Figure 2–9 that will give sales revenues of $16 billion in 2006 and $20 billion in 2010. This reveals a wedge-shaped shaded gap in the figure. Planners call this the *planning gap,* the difference between the projection of the path to reach a new goal (line BD) and the projection of the path of the results of a plan already in place (line BC).

The ultimate purpose of the firm's marketing program is to "fill in" this planning gap—in Kodak's case, to move its future sales revenue line from the no-growth line BC up to the challenging target of line BD. But poor performance can result in actual sales revenues being far less than the targeted levels. This is the essence of evaluation: comparing actual results with planned objectives.

Acting on Deviations   When evaluation shows that actual performance fails to meet expectations, managers need to take corrective actions. And when actual results are far better than the plan called for, creative managers find ways to exploit the situation. Two possible Kodak midcourse corrections for both positive and negative deviations from targets illustrate these management actions:

- *Exploiting a positive deviation.* If Kodak's film strategy in India and China shows promise, it might partner with more local companies to produce cameras and film and to process film.
- *Correcting a negative deviation.* However, if Indian and Chinese consumers choose to skip film cameras and jump directly to digital ones, Kodak will likely need to partner with different business firms in these countries.

The strategic marketing process is discussed in greater detail again in Chapter 22.

Concept Check

1. What is the control phase of the strategic marketing process?

2. How do the objectives set for a marketing program in the planning phase relate to the control phase of the strategic marketing process?

CHAPTER IN REVIEW

1 *Describe the three organizational levels of strategy.*
Most large business firms and nonprofit organizations are divided into three levels of strategy: (*a*) the corporate level, where top management directs overall strategy for the entire organization; (*b*) the business unit level, where business unit managers set the direction for their products and markets to exploit value-creating opportunities; and (*c*) the functional level, where groups of specialists actually create value for the organization.

2 *Describe why business, mission, culture, and goals are important in organizations.*
Organizations exist to accomplish something for someone. To give organizations direction and focus, they continuously assess their business, mission, culture, and goals. First, an organization defines what its business is—the set of customer needs, such as transportation, it wants to satisfy. Next, an organization defines its mission, which is a statement that describes its customers, markets, and products and inspires loyalty from its stakeholders. An organization's culture serves to connect it with its stakeholders based on a set of shared values, ideas, and attitudes. Finally, the organization's goals measure how well it accomplishes its mission at

each organizational level by providing specific targeted levels of performance to be achieved, such as sales and profits, by a specific time period.

3 *Explain how organizations set strategic directions by assessing where they are now and seek to be in the future.*
Managers of an organization ask two key questions to set a strategic direction. The first question, Where are we now?, requires an organization to (*a*) assess its customers to determine whether its direction must be modified based on changes in consumer trends; (*b*) reevaluate its competencies to ensure that its special capabilities still provide a competitive advantage; and (*c*) analyze its current and potential competitors from a global perspective to determine whether any business definition modifications are needed. The second question, Where do we want to go?, requires an organization to actually set a direction and allocate resources to move it in that direction. Business portfolio and market-product analyses are two useful techniques to do this.

4 *Describe the strategic marketing process and its three key phases: planning, implementation, and control.*
An organization uses the strategic marketing process to allocate its marketing mix resources to reach its target markets.

This process consists of three phases, which are usually formalized in a marketing plan. The planning phase consists of (*a*) a situation (SWOT) analysis of the organization's strengths, weaknesses, opportunities, and threats; (*b*) a market-product focus through market segmentation, points of difference analysis, and goal setting; and (*c*) a marketing program that specifies the budget and activities (marketing strategies and tactics) for each marketing mix element. The implementation phase carries out the marketing plan that emerges from the planning phase. It has four key elements: obtaining resources, designing the marketing organization, developing schedules, and executing the marketing program. The control phase compares the results from the implemented marketing program with the marketing plan's goals to identify the "planning gaps" and take actions to exploit positive deviations or correct negative ones.

5 *Explain how the marketing mix elements are blended into a cohesive marketing program.*

A marketing manager uses information obtained during the SWOT analysis, market-product focus, and goal-setting steps in the planning process to develop marketing strategies and marketing tactics for each marketing mix element for a given product, which are then implemented, as specified in the marketing plan, as a marketing program.

FOCUSING ON KEY TERMS

benchmarking p. 36
business unit p. 31
business unit level p. 31
competencies p. 36
competitive advantage p. 36
corporate level p. 30
cross-functional teams p. 31
functional level p. 31
goals p. 34
market segmentation p. 44
market share p. 34
marketing plan p. 42

marketing strategy p. 48
marketing tactics p. 48
mission p. 33
objectives p. 34
organizational culture p. 33
points of difference p. 45
profit p. 30
quality p. 36
situation analysis p. 43
stakeholders p. 33
strategic marketing process p. 42
SWOT analysis p. 43

DISCUSSION AND APPLICATION QUESTIONS

1 (*a*) Explain what a mission statement is. (*b*) Using Medtronic as an example from the chapter, explain how it gives a strategic direction to its organization. (*c*) Create a mission statement for your own career.

2 What competencies best describe (*a*) your college or university, (*b*) your favorite restaurant, and (*c*) the company that manufactures the computer you own or use most often?

3 Look at Figure 2–2 that shows the four main groups of competitors Lands' End faces. For Wal-Mart, eBay, Old Navy, and Liz Claiborne, explain in which ways each is a competitor of Lands' End.

4 Why does a product often start as a question mark and then move counterclockwise around BCG's growth-share matrix shown in Figure 2–3?

5 Many American liberal arts colleges have traditionally offered an undergraduate degree in liberal arts

(the product) to full-time 18- to 22-year-old students (the market). How might such a college use the four market-product expansion strategies shown in Figure 2–4 to compete in the twenty-first century?

6 What is the main result of each of the three phases of the strategic marketing process? (*a*) planning, (*b*) implementation, and (*c*) control.

7 Select one strength, one weakness, one opportunity, and one threat from the SWOT analysis for Ben & Jerry's shown in Figure 2–6, and suggest a specific possible action that Unilever might take to exploit or address each one.

8 The goal-setting step in the planning phase of the strategic marketing process sets quantified objectives for use in the control phase. What actions are suggested for a marketing manager if measured results are below objectives? Above objectives?

GOING ONLINE   How Mission Statements Compare

In April 2000, Unilever N.V., a multinational consumer products firm, bought Ben & Jerry's, adding to its portfolio of other famous North American ice cream brands, such as Breyers All Natural, Good-Humor, Klondike, and Popsicle. As a condition of the buyout, Unilever must continue to donate 7.5 percent of all pretax profits to the Ben & Jerry's Foundation to fund organizations that engage in socially responsive activities, a critical aspect of Ben & Jerry's mission. In early 2004, Unilever revised its mission in response to its Path to Growth strategy that was launched in February 2000. Go to

Ben & Jerry's website (www.benjerry.com) and Unilever's website (www.unilever.com) to compare the mission statements of each firm.

1   How are the mission statements of these organizations similar? How are they different?
2   Which mission statement do you believe will lead to "sustainable, profitable growth for our businesses and long-term value creation for our shareholders and employees" (from the "Introducing Unilever" promotional brochure)?

BUILDING YOUR MARKETING PLAN

1   Read Appendix A, "Building an Effective Marketing Plan." Then write a 600-word executive summary for the Paradise Kitchens marketing plan using the numbered headings shown in the plan. When you have completed the draft of your own marketing plan, use what you learned in writing an executive summary for Paradise Kitchens to write a 600-word executive summary to go in the front of your own marketing plan.

2   Using Chapter 2 and Appendix A as guides, give focus to your marketing plan by (*a*) writing your mission statement in 25 words or less, (*b*) listing three nonfinancial goals and three financial goals, (*c*) writing your competitive advantage in 35 words or less, and (*d*) Doing a SWOT analysis table.

VIDEO CASE 2   Specialized Bicycle Components, Inc.: Ride the Red "S"

The speaker leans forward with both intensity and pride in his voice. "We're in the business of creating a bike that delivers the customer their best possible ride," he explains. "When the customer sees our red 'S,' they say this is the company that understands the cyclist. It's a company of riders. The products they make are the rider's products." The speaker is Chris Murphy, director of marketing for Specialized Bicycle Components, Inc.—or just "Specialized" to serious riders.

THE COMPANY

Specialized was founded in 1974 by Mike Sinyard, a cycling enthusiast who sold his VW van for the $1,500 start-up capital. Mike started out importing hard-to-find "specialized" bike components, but the company began to produce its own bike parts by 1976. Specialized introduced the first major production mountain bike in the world in 1980, revolutionizing the bike industry, and since then has maintained a reputation as the technological leader in the bike and bike accessory market. In fact, since the company's founding, its formal mission statement has remained unchanged: "To give everyone the best ride of their life!"

The company continues to innovate. In addition to hiring bicycling enthusiasts, Specialized created the first professional mountain bike racing team, a dedicated BMX program, and an elite road racing program. Racers often serve as design consultants and "test pilots" for new technologies. The company banks on the perception, and reality, that this race-proven technology trickles down to the entire line of Specialized bikes and products.

Today Specialized produces a full range of high-end and entry-level road bikes, mountain bikes, commuter/city bikes, children's bikes, and BMX bikes. The company also offers an extensive line of bike accessories, including helmets, water bottles, jerseys, tires, and shoes. As Chris says, "The customer is buying the ride from us, not just the bike."

THE ENVIRONMENT

The bike market is driven by innovation and technology, and with the market becoming more crowded and competitive. Specialized divides the bike market into two categories: (1) the retailer and (2) the end-user consumer. While its focus in designing the product is on the end-user consumer, it only sells directly to the retailer and realizes a strong relationship with the dealers is a key

factor for success. Steve Meineke, president of Specialized USA (the domestic unit of Specialized), refers to the on-floor salesperson as "our most important partner."

The end-user consumer is broken down into two target age groups: the 18- to 25-year-old college students and the 30- to 40-year-old professional "techies." To differentiate itself from the rest of the market, Specialized positioned itself as the innovator in bike design—its models are what the rest of the industry imitates.

Cycling is the seventh most popular recreational activity in the U.S. behind walking, swimming, camping, fishing, exercising with equipment, and bowling. About 11 million adults in the U.S. ride a bicycle regularly and spend approximately $5 billion each year on new bicycles, parts, and accessories. Bicycle sales have declined slightly in recent years, however, as the 1990s surge in mountain bike sales has slowed. One explanation is that mountain bikes—which account for one-third of all bicycle sales—are so durable that consumers haven't needed to replace them. Does Chris believe this trend will hurt Specialized? "We believe we will see growth in the next six or seven years as the entry level participants trade up—trade their lower end bikes for higher end bikes," he explains.

Other factors suggest that the industry will grow in the future. The popularity of Lance Armstrong has increased the interest in road bikes, which currently represent 5 percent of the market. In addition, new full-suspension technology and improved ergonomic frame designs have attracted many new customers to the "comfort" bike category. Finally, recent research shows that while 94 percent of people who ride bicycles do so for recreation or fitness, a growing number are using bicycles as a form of transportation.

The bicycle industry consists of four channels of distribution—independent bicycle retailers, mass merchants, sporting goods stores, and other outdoor retailers

and mail order merchants. Specialized now has an extensive global distribution network of 5,000 retailers in 35 countries in Asia, North America, South America, and Australia.

THE ISSUES

How can Specialized stay at the forefront of an industry that now includes more than 20 manufacturers? Strategic placement in the marketplace is one way. Specialized recently designed its own server, the World Ride Web, on the Internet (www.specialized.com). The website offers international mountain bike trail and road bike trail directories, e-mail access to Specialized engineers, a trail preservation network, and a dealer directory that connects users directly to dealer home pages. Specialized believes guest appearances on TV talk shows and displays in retail shops help to keep the Specialized name in front of the end-user consumer.

Targeting its other market segment, the dealers, Specialized launched a "Best Ride Tour." It loaded up trailers full of the new models and visited 30 cities nationwide, enabling retailers and shop employees to test ride the bikes they will be ordering for the coming year—"Ride Before You Buy."

Specialized is also eager to become involved in joint ventures to keep its technological edge, including one with Du Pont that led to a more aerodynamic wheel. Specialized also entered into a distribution relationship with GripShift, allowing the high-end gear manufacturer access to its extensive dealer network.

Specialized sponsors races, provides racer support teams, initiates mountain biking safety programs, and is involved in trail-access advocacy groups all over the world. Specialized supplies bicycles and equipment to many of the top racing teams in the world, such as Domina Vacanze that raced in the 2004 Tour de France.

But, as it was in Specialized's early years, Mike sees a commitment to top quality and design as the most important factor for future success: "Even though we've been around for 20 years, this company still feels like it has something to prove. I expect it will always be that way."

Questions

1 Do a SWOT analysis for Specialized. Use Figure 2–6 in Chapter 2 and Figure 1 in Appendix A as guides. In assessing internal factors (strengths and weaknesses), use the material provided in the case. In assessing external factors (opportunities and threats) augment the case material with what you see happening in the bicycle industry.

2 As part of step 2 of the planning phase, and using your SWOT analysis, select target markets on which you might focus for present and potential bikers.

3 As part of step 3 of the planning phase and using your answers in questions 1 and 2 above, outline Specialized's marketing programs for the target market segments you chose.

BUILDING AN EFFECTIVE MARKETING PLAN

"New ideas are a dime a dozen," observes Arthur R. Kydd, "and so are new products and new technologies." Kydd should know. As chief executive officer of St. Croix Venture Partners, he and his firm have provided the seed money and venture capital to launch more than 60 startup firms in the last 25 years. Today, those firms have more than 5,000 employees. Kydd explains:

> I get 200 to 300 marketing and business plans a year to look at, and St. Croix provides startup financing for only two or three. What sets a potentially successful idea, product, or technology apart from all the rest is markets and marketing. If you have a real product with a distinctive point of difference that satisfies the needs of customers, you may have a winner. And you get a real feel for this in a well-written marketing or business plan.[1]

This appendix (1) describes what marketing and business plans are, including the purposes and guidelines in writing effective plans, and (2) provides a sample marketing plan.

MARKETING PLANS AND BUSINESS PLANS

After explaining the meanings, purposes, and audiences of marketing plans and business plans, this section describes some writing guidelines for them and what external funders often look for in successful plans.

Meanings, Purposes, and Audiences

A marketing plan is a road map for the marketing activities of an organization for a specified future period of time, such as one year or five years.[2] It is important to note that no single "generic" marketing plan applies to all organizations and all situations. Rather, the specific format for a marketing plan for an organization depends on the following:

- *The target audience and purpose.* Elements included in a particular marketing plan depend heavily on (1) who the audience is and (2) what its purpose is. A marketing plan for an internal audience seeks to point the direction for future marketing activities and is sent to all individuals in the organization who must implement the plan or who will be affected by it. If the plan is directed to an external audience, such as friends, banks, venture capitalists, or potential investors, for the purpose of raising capital, it has the additional function of being an important sales document. In this case, it contains elements such as the strategic plan/focus, organization, structure, and biographies of key personnel that would rarely appear in an internal marketing plan. Also, the financial information is far more detailed when the plan is used to raise outside capital. The elements of a marketing plan for each of these two audiences are compared in Figure A–1 on the next page.
- *The kind and complexity of the organization.* A small neighborhood restaurant has a somewhat different marketing plan than Nestlé, which serves international markets. The restaurant's plan would be relatively simple and directed at serving customers in a local market. In Nestlé's case, because there is a hierarchy of marketing plans, various levels of detail would be used—such as the entire organization, the business unit, or the product/product line.
- *The industry.* Both the restaurant serving a local market and Medtronic, selling heart pacemakers globally, analyze competition. Not only are their geographic thrusts far different, but the complexities of their offerings and, hence, the time periods likely to be covered by their plans also differ. A one-year marketing plan may be adequate for the restaurant, but Medtronic may need a five-year planning horizon because product-development cycles for complex, new medical devices may be three or four years.

In contrast to a marketing plan, a **business plan** is a road map for the entire organization for a specified future period of time, such as one year or five years.[3] A key difference between a marketing plan and a business plan is that the business plan contains details on the research and development (R&D)/operations/manufacturing activities of the organization. Even for a manufacturing business,

Element of the plan	Marketing plan		Business plan	
	For internal audience (to direct the firm)	For external audience (to raise capital)	For internal audience (to direct the firm)	For external audience (to raise capital)
1. Executive summary	✓	✓	✓	✓
2. Description of company		✓		✓
3. Strategic plan/focus		✓		✓
4. Situation analysis	✓	✓	✓	✓
5. Market-product focus	✓	✓	✓	✓
6. Marketing program strategy and tactics	✓	✓	✓	✓
7. R&D and operations program			✓	✓
8. Financial projections	✓	✓	✓	✓
9. Organization structure		✓		✓
10. Implementation plan	✓	✓	✓	✓
11. Evaluation and control	✓		✓	
Appendix A: Biographies of key personnel		✓		✓
Appendix B, etc.: Details on other topics	✓	✓	✓	✓

the marketing plan is probably 60 or 70 percent of the entire business plan. For businesses like a small restaurant or an auto repair shop, their marketing and business plans are virtually identical. The elements of a business plan typically targeted at internal and external audiences appear in the two right-hand columns in Figure A–1.

The Most-Asked Questions by Outside Audiences

Lenders and prospective investors reading a business or marketing plan that is used to seek new capital are probably the toughest audiences to satisfy. Their most-asked questions include the following:

1. Is the business or marketing idea valid?
2. Is there something unique or distinctive about the product or service that separates it from substitutes and competitors?
3. Is there a clear market for the product or service?
4. Are the financial projections realistic and healthy?
5. Are the key management and technical personnel capable, and do they have a track record in the industry in which they must compete?
6. Does the plan clearly describe how those providing capital will get their money back and make a profit?

Rhonda M. Abrahms, author of *The Successful Business Plan*, observes that "within the first five minutes of reading your . . . plan, readers must perceive that the answers to these questions are favorable."[4] While her comments apply to plans seeking to raise capital, the first five questions just listed apply equally well to plans for internal audiences.

Writing and Style Suggestions

There are no magic one-size-fits-all guidelines for writing successful marketing and business plans. Still, the following writing and style guidelines generally apply:[5]

• Use a direct, professional writing style. Use appropriate business terms without jargon. Present and future tenses with active voice ("I will write an effective marketing plan.") are generally better than past tense and passive voice ("An effective marketing plan was written by me.").

- Be positive and specific to convey potential success. At the same time, avoid superlatives ("terrific," "wonderful"). Specifics are better than glittering generalities. Use numbers for impact, justifying projections with reasonable quantitative assumptions, where possible.
- Use bullet points for succinctness and emphasis. As with the list you are reading, bullets enable key points to be highlighted effectively.
- Use A-level (the first level) and B-level (the second level) headings under the numbered section headings to help readers make easy transitions from one topic to another. This also forces the writer to organize the plan more carefully. Use these headings liberally, at least one every 200 to 300 words.
- Use visuals where appropriate. Photos, illustrations, graphs, and charts enable massive amounts of information to be presented succinctly.
- Shoot for a plan 15 to 35 pages in length, not including financial projections and appendixes. An uncomplicated small business may require only 15 pages, while a high-technology start-up may require more than 35 pages.
- Use care in layout, design, and presentation. Laser printers give a more professional look than ink-jet printers do. Use 11- or 12-point type (you are now reading 10.5-point type) in the text. Use a serif type (with "feet," like that you are reading now) in the text because it is easier to read, and sans serif (without "feet") in graphs and charts like Figure A–1. A bound report with a nice cover and clear title page adds professionalism.

These guidelines are used, where possible, in the sample marketing plan that follows.

SAMPLE FIVE-YEAR MARKETING PLAN FOR PARADISE KITCHENS,® INC.

To help interpret the marketing plan for Paradise Kitchens, Inc., that follows, we will describe the company and suggest some guidelines in interpreting the plan.

Background on Paradise Kitchens, Inc.

With a degree in chemical engineering, Randall F. Peters spent 15 years working for General Foods and Pillsbury with a number of diverse responsibilities: plant operations, R&D, restaurant operations, and new business development. His wife Leah, with degrees in both molecular cellular biology and food science, held various Pillsbury executive positions in new category development and packaged goods, and restaurant R&D. In the company's start-up years, Paradise Kitchens survived on the savings of Randy and Leah, the cofounders. With their backgrounds, they decided Randy should serve as president and CEO of Paradise Kitchens, and Leah should focus on R&D and corporate strategy.

Interpreting the Marketing Plan

The marketing plan below, based on an actual Paradise Kitchens plan, is directed at an external audience (see Figure A–1). To protect proprietary information about the company, some details and dates have been altered, but the basic logic of the plan has been kept.

Notes in the margins next to the Paradise Kitchens plan fall into two categories:

1. *Substantive notes* are in blue boxes. These notes elaborate on the significance of an element in the marketing plan and are keyed to chapter references in this textbook.
2. *Writing style, format, and layout notes* are in red boxes and explain the editorial or visual rationale for the element.

A closing word of encouragement: Writing an effective marketing plan is hard, but challenging and satisfying, work. Dozens of the authors' students have used effective marketing plans they wrote for class in their interviewing portfolio to show prospective employers what they could do and to help them get their first job.

Color-coding Legend

Blue boxes explain significance of Marketing Plan elements

Red boxes give writing style, format, and layout guidelines

The Table of Contents provides quick access to the topics in the plan, usually organized by section and subsection headings.

Seen by many experts as the single most important element in the plan, the two-page Executive Summary "sells" the plan to readers through its clarity and brevity. For space reasons, it is not shown here, but the Building Your Marketing Plan exercise at the end of Chapter 2 asks the reader to write an Executive Summary for this plan.

The Company Description highlights the recent history and recent successes of the organization.

The Strategic Focus and Plan sets the strategic direction for the entire organization, a direction with which proposed actions of the marketing plan must be consistent. This section is not included in all marketing plans. See Chapter 2.

The qualitative Mission/Vision statement focuses the activities of Paradise Kitchens for the stakeholder groups to be served. See Chapter 2.

FIVE-YEAR MARKETING PLAN
Paradise Kitchens,® Inc.

Table of Contents

1. Executive Summary

2. Company Description

Paradise Kitchens®, Inc., was started by cofounders Randall F. Peters and Leah E. Peters to develop and market Howlin' Coyote® Chili, a unique line of single serve and microwaveable Southwestern/Mexican style frozen chili products. The Howlin' Coyote line of chili was first introduced into the Minneapolis–St. Paul market and expanded to Denver two years later and Phoenix two years after that.

To the Company's knowledge, Howlin' Coyote is the only premium-quality, authentic Southwestern/Mexican style, frozen chili sold in U.S. grocery stores. Its high quality has gained fast, widespread acceptance in these markets. In fact, same-store sales doubled in the last year for which data are available. The Company believes the Howlin' Coyote brand can be extended to other categories of Southwestern/Mexican food products, such as tacos, enchiladas, and burritos.

Paradise Kitchens believes its high-quality, high-price strategy has proven successful. This marketing plan outlines how the Company will extend its geographic coverage from 3 markets to 20 markets by the year 2010.

3. Strategic Focus and Plan

This section covers three aspects of corporate strategy that influence the marketing plan: (1) the mission/vision, (2) goals, and (3) core competence/sustainable competitive advantage of Paradise Kitchens.

Mission/Vision

The mission and vision of Paradise Kitchens is to market lines of high-quality Southwestern/Mexican food products at premium prices that satisfy consumers in this fast-growing food segment while providing challenging career opportunities for employees and above-average returns to stockholders.

Goals

For the coming five years Paradise Kitchens seeks to achieve the following goals:

- Nonfinancial goals
  1. To retain its present image as the highest-quality line of Southwestern/ Mexican products in the food categories in which it competes.
  2. To enter 17 new metropolitan markets.
  3. To achieve national distribution in two convenience store or supermarket chains by 2005 and five by 2006.
  4. To add a new product line every third year.
  5. To be among the top five chili lines—regardless of packaging (frozen or canned) in one-third of the metro markets in which it competes by 2006 and two-thirds by 2008.
- Financial goals
  1. To obtain a real (inflation-adjusted) growth in earnings per share of 8 percent per year over time.
  2. To obtain a return on equity of at least 20 percent.
  3. To have a public stock offering by the year 2006.

In keeping with the goal of achieving national distribution through chains, Paradise Kitchens recently obtained distribution through a convenience store chain where it uses this point-of-purchase ad that adheres statically to the glass door of the freezer case.

Core Competency and Sustainable Competitive Advantage

In terms of core competency, Paradise Kitchens seeks to achieve a unique ability to (1) provide distinctive, high-quality chilies and related products using Southwestern/Mexican recipes that appeal to and excite contemporary tastes for these products and (2) deliver these products to the customer's table using effective manufacturing and distribution systems that maintain the Company's quality standards.

To translate these core competencies into a sustainable competitive advantage, the Company will work closely with key suppliers and distributors to build the relationships and alliances necessary to satisfy the high taste standards of our customers.

To improve readability, each numbered section usually starts on a new page. (This is not done in this plan to save space.)

The Situation Analysis is a snapshot to answer the question, "Where are we now?" See Chapter 2.

The SWOT Analysis identifies strengths, weaknesses, opportunities, and threats to provide a solid foundation as a springboard to identify subsequent actions in the marketing plan. See Chapter 2.

Each long table, graph, or photo is given a figure number and title. It then appears as soon as possible after the first reference in the text, accommodating necessary page breaks. This also avoids breaking long tables like this one in the middle. Short tables or graphs that are less than 1 ½ inches are often inserted in the text without figure numbers because they don't cause serious problems with page breaks.

Effective tables seek to summarize a large amount of information in a short amount of space.

4. Situation Analysis

This situation analysis starts with a snapshot of the current environment in which Paradise Kitchens finds itself by providing a brief SWOT (strengths, weaknesses, opportunities, threats) analysis. After this overview, the analysis probes ever-finer levels of detail: industry, competitors, company, and consumers.

SWOT Analysis

Figure 1 shows the internal and external factors affecting the market opportunities for Paradise Kitchens. Stated briefly, this SWOT analysis highlights the great strides taken by the company since its products first appeared on grocers' shelves. In the

Figure 1. SWOT Analysis for Paradise Kitchens

Internal Factors	Strengths	Weaknesses
Management	Experienced and entrepreneurial management and board	Small size can restrict options
Offerings	Unique, high-quality, high-price products	Many lower-quality, lower-price competitors
Marketing	Distribution in three markets with excellent acceptance	No national awareness or distribution; restricted shelf space in the freezer section
Personnel	Good workforce, though small; little turnover	Big gap if key employee leaves
Finance	Excellent growth in sales revenues	Limited resources may restrict growth opportunities when compared to giant competitors
Manufacturing	Sole supplier ensures high quality	Lack economies of scale of huge competitors
R&D	Continuing efforts to ensure quality in delivered products	Lack of canning and microwavable food processing expertise

External Factors	Opportunities	Threats
Consumer/Social	Upscale market, likely to be stable; Southwestern/Mexican food category is fast-growing segment due to growth in Hispanic American population and desire for spicier foods	Premium price may limit access to mass markets; consumers value a strong brand name
Competitive	Distinctive name and packaging in its markets.	Not patentable; competitors can attempt to duplicate product; others better able to pay slotting fees
Technological	Technical breakthroughs enable smaller food producers to achieve many economies available to large competitors	Competitors have gained economies in canning and microwavable food processing
Economic	Consumer income is high; convenience important to U.S. households	More households "eating out," and bringing prepared take-out into home
Legal/Regulatory	High U.S. Food & Drug Admin. standards eliminate fly-by-night competitors	Mergers among large competitors being approved by government

The text discussion of Figure 1 (the SWOT Analysis table) elaborates on its more important elements. This "walks" the reader through the information from the vantage of the plan's writer. In terse plans this accompanying discussion is sometimes omitted, but is generally desirable to give the reader an understanding of what the company sees as the critical SWOT elements.

The Industry Analysis section provides the backdrop for the subsequent, more detailed analysis of competition, the company, and the company's customers. Without an in-depth understanding of the industry, the remaining analysis may be misdirected. See Chapter 2.

This summary of sales of key entrees in the prepared frozen food product category shows Mexican entrees are significant and provides a variety of future opportunities for Paradise Kitchens.

Company's favor internally are its strengths of an experienced management team and board of directors, excellent acceptance of its lines in the three metropolitan markets in which it competes, and a strong manufacturing and distribution system to serve these limited markets. Favorable external factors (opportunities) include the increasing appeal of Southwestern/Mexican foods, the strength of the upscale market for the Company's products, and food-processing technological breakthroughs that make is easier for smaller food producers to compete.

Among unfavorable factors, the main weakness is the limited size of Paradise Kitchens relative to its competitors in terms of the depth of the management team, available financial resources, and national awareness and distribution of product lines. Threats include the danger that the Company's premium prices may limit access to mass markets and competition from the "eating-out" and "take-out" markets.

Industry Analysis: Trends in Frozen and Mexican Foods

Frozen Foods. According to *Grocery Headquarters,* consumers are flocking to the frozen food section of grocery retailers. The reasons: hectic lifestyles demanding increased convenience and an abundance of new, tastier, and nutritious products.[6] By 2004, total sales of frozen food in supermarkets, drugstores, and mass merchandisers, such as Target and Costco (excluding Wal-Mart) reached $27.6 billion. Prepared frozen meals, which are defined as meals or entrees that are frozen and require minimal preparation, accounted for $7.3 billion, or 26 percent of the total frozen food market, which is shown in Figure 2 based on ACNielsen tracking data:

Figure 2. Some Frozen Entrees Included in the Prepared Frozen Food Product Category, 2004[7]

Item	Sales in Millions	Percent of Sales
Frozen dinners	$1,323	18%
Italian entrees	1,231	17
Meat entrees	721	10
Mexican entrees	**506**	**7**
Oriental entrees	479	7
Poultry entrees	1,617	22
Seafood entrees	190	3
Other entrees	1,281	16
Total	$7,348	100%

Handheld entrees, such as Hot Pockets ($1.1 billion), comprise a significant portion of the "Other entrees" category.[8] However, frozen pizza/snacks, which are not included in this category, accounted for an additional $3.3 billion in frozen food sales in 2004. Heavy consumers of frozen meals, those who eat five or more meals every two weeks, tend to be kids, teens, and young adults 35–44 years old.[9]

Even though relatively brief, this in-depth treatment of sales of Mexican foods in the United States demonstrates to the plan's readers the company's understanding of the industry in which it competes. It gives both external and internal readers confidence that the company thoroughly understands its own industry.

As with the Industry Analysis, the Competitors Analysis demonstrates that the company has a realistic understanding of who its major chili competitors are and what their marketing strategies are. Again, a realistic assessment gives confidence to both internal and external readers that subsequent marketing actions in the plan rest on a solid foundation. See Chapters 2, 3, 8, 9, and 21.

This page uses a "block" style and does *not* indent each paragraph, although an extra space separates each paragraph. Compare this page with page 61, which has indented paragraphs. Most readers find indented paragraphs in marketing plans and long reports are easier to follow.

Mexican Foods. Currently, Mexican foods such as burritos, enchiladas, and tacos are used in two-thirds of American households. These trends reflect a generally more favorable attitude on the part of all Americans toward spicy foods that include red chili peppers. Grocery marketers and retailers have tried to capitalize on this trend by developing meals targeted to those who desire this type of food. Considering the current desire for convenience, several major food processors, such as Hormel, Tyson Foods, and ConAgra, as well as Hispanic-owned firms, such as Goya (Mission Foods), Ruiz Foods, and Don Miguel's, have introduced many new frozen Mexican food entrees over the past few years. The growing Hispanic population in the U.S., about 36 million and almost $600 billion in purchasing power in 2004, partly explains the increasing demand for Mexican food.[10]

Competitors in the Chili Market

The chili market represents over $500 million in annual sales. On average, consumers buy five to six servings annually, according to the NPD Group.[11] The products fall primarily into two groups: canned chili (70 percent of sales) and dry chili (25 percent of sales). The remaining 5 percent of sales go to frozen chili products. Besides Howlin' Coyote, Stouffer's offers a frozen chili product (Slowfire Classic's Chunky Beef & Bean Chili) as part of its broad line of frozen dinners and entrees. Major canned chili brands include Hormel, Wolf, Dennison, Stagg, Austin's, and Castleberry's. Their retail prices range from $1.49 to $2.49. In the fall of 2004, Campbell's, the world's largest maker of soup, and Bush Brothers, a privately held marketer of baked beans, will enter the canned chili market. However, Bush will use a glass bottle to package its Homestyle Chili brand.[12]

Bluntly put, the major disadvantage of the segment's dominant product, canned chili, is that it does not taste very good. A taste test described in an issue of *Consumer Reports* magazine ranked 26 canned chili products "poor" to "fair" in overall sensory quality. The study concluded, "Chili doesn't have to be hot to be good. But really good chili, hot or mild, doesn't come out of a can."

Dry mix brands include such familiar spice brands as McCormick (which has 40 percent of this market), Lawry's, French's, and Durkee, along with smaller offerings such as Wick Fowler's and Carroll Shelby's. Their retail prices range from $0.99 to $1.49. The *Consumer Reports* study was more favorable about dry chili mixes, ranking them from "fair" to "very good."

The Company Analysis provides details of the company's strengths and marketing strategies that will enable it to achieve the mission, vision, and goals identified earlier. See Chapters 2, 8, and 22.

Company Analysis

The husband-and-wife team that cofounded Paradise Kitchens, Inc., has 44 years of experience between them in the food-processing business. Both have played key roles in the management of the Pillsbury Company. They are being advised by a highly seasoned group of business professionals, who have extensive understanding of the requirements for new product development.

Currently, Howlin' Coyote products compete in the chili and Mexican frozen entree segments of the Southwestern/Mexican food market. While the chili obviously competes as a stand-alone product, its exceptional quality means it can complement such dishes as burritos, nachos, and enchiladas and can be readily used as a smothering sauce for pasta, rice, or potatoes. This flexibility of use is relatively rare in the prepared food marketplace. With Howlin' Coyote, Paradise Kitchens is broadening the position of frozen chili in a way that can lead to impressive market share for the new product category.

The Company now uses a single outside producer with which it works closely to maintain the consistently high quality required in its products. The greater volume has increased production efficiencies, resulting in a steady decrease in the cost of goods sold.

The higher-level "A heading" of Customer Analysis has a more dominant typeface and position than the lower-level "B heading" of Customer Characteristics. These headings introduce the reader to the sequence and level of topics covered. The organization of this textbook uses this kind of structure and headings.

Customer Analysis

In terms of customer analysis, this section describes (1) the characteristics of customers expected to buy Howlin' Coyote products and (2) health and nutrition concerns of Americans today.

Customer Characteristics. Demographically, chili products in general are purchased by consumers representing a broad range of socioeconomic backgrounds. Howlin' Coyote chili is purchased chiefly by consumers who have achieved higher levels of education and whose income is $50,000 and higher. These consumers represent 50 percent of canned and dry mix chili users.

Satisfying customers and providing genuine value to them is why organizations exist in a market economy. This section addresses the question of "Who are the customers for Paradise Kitchens's products?" See Chapters 5, 6, 7, 8, and 9.

The five Howlin' Coyote entrees offer a quick, tasty meal with high-quality ingredients.

The household buying Howlin' Coyote has one to three people in it. Among married couples, Howlin' Coyote is predominantly bought by households in which both spouses work. While women are a majority of the buyers, single men represent a significant segment. Anecdotally, Howlin' Coyote has heard from fathers of teenaged boys who say they keep a freezer stocked with the chili because the boys devour it.

Because the chili offers a quick way to make a tasty meal, the product's biggest users tend to be those most pressed for time. Howlin' Coyote's premium pricing also means that its purchasers are skewed toward the higher end of the income range. Buyers range in age from 25 to 54. Because consumers in the western United States have adopted spicy foods more readily than the rest of the country, Howlin' Coyote's initial marketing expansion efforts will be concentrated in that region.

Health and Nutrition Concerns. Coverage of food issues in the U.S. media is often erratic and occasionally alarmist. Because Americans are concerned about their diets, studies from organizations of widely varying credibility frequently receive significant attention from the major news organizations. For instance, a study of fat levels of movie popcorn was reported in all the major media. Similarly, studies on the healthfulness of Mexican food have received prominent "play" in print and broadcast reports. The high caloric levels of much Mexican and Southwestern-style food have been widely reported and often exaggerated. Some Mexican frozen food competitors, such as Don Miguel, Mission Foods, Ruiz Foods, and Jose Ole, plan to offer or have recently offered more "carb-friendly" and "fat-friendly" products in response to this concern.

Howlin' Coyote is already lower in calories, fat, and sodium than its competitors, and those qualities are not currently being stressed in its promotions. Instead, in the space and time available for promotions, Howlin' Coyote's taste, convenience, and flexibility are stressed.

5. Market-Product Focus

This section describes the five-year marketing and product objectives for Paradise Kitchens and the target markets, points of difference, and positioning of its lines of Howlin' Coyote chilies.

Marketing and Product Objectives

Howlin' Coyote's marketing intent is to take full advantage of its brand potential

---

This section demonstrates the company's insights into a major trend that has a potentially large impact.

Size of headings should give a professional look to the report and not overwhelm the reader. These two headings are too large.

As noted in Chapter 10, the chances of success for a new product are significantly increased if objectives are set for the product itself and if target market segments are identified for it. This section makes these explicit for Paradise Kitchens. The objectives also serve as the planned targets against which marketing activities are measured in program implementation and control.

A heading should be spaced closer to the text that follows (and that it describes) than the preceding section to avoid confusion for the reader. This rule is not followed for the Target Markets heading, which now unfortunately appears to "float" between the preceding and following paragraphs.

This section identifies the specific niches or target markets toward which the company's products are directed. When appropriate and when space permits, this section often includes a market-product grid. See Chapter 9.

while building a base from which other revenues sources can be mined—both in and out of the retail grocery business. These are detailed in four areas below:

- Current markets. Current markets will be grown by expanding brand and flavor distribution at the retail level. In addition, same-store sales will be grown by increasing consumer awareness and repeat purchases. With this increase in same-store sales, the more desirable broker/warehouse distribution channel will become available, increasing efficiency and saving costs.

- New markets. By the end of Year 5, the chili, salsa, burrito, and enchilada business will be expanded to a total of 20 metropolitan areas. This will represent 70 percent of U.S. food store sales.

- Food service. Food service sales will include chili products and smothering sauces. Sales are expected to reach $693,000 by the end of Year 3 and $1.5 million by the end of Year 5.

- New products. Howlin' Coyote's brand presence will be expanded at the retail level through the addition of new products in the frozen-foods section. This will be accomplished through new product concept screening in Year 1 to identify new potential products. These products will be brought to market in Years 2 and 3. Additionally, the brand may be licensed in select categories.

Target Markets

The primary target market for Howlin' Coyote products is households with one to three people, where often both adults work, with individual income typically above $50,000 per year. These households contain more experienced, adventurous consumers of Southwestern/Mexican food and want premium quality products.

To help buyers see the many different uses for Howlin' Coyote chili, recipes are even printed on the *inside* of the packages.

An organization cannot grow by offering only "me-too products." The greatest single factor in a new product's failure is the lack of significant "points of difference" that sets it apart from competitors' substitutes. This section makes these points of difference explicit. See Chapter 10.

A positioning strategy helps communicate the company's unique points of difference of its products to prospective customers in a simple, clear way. This section describes this positioning. See Chapters 9 and 10.

Everything that has gone before in the marketing plan sets the stage for the marketing mix actions—the 4 Ps—covered in the marketing program. See Chapters 10 through 20.

The section describes in detail three key elements of the company's product strategy: the product line, its quality and how this is achieved, and its "cutting edge" packaging. See Chapters 10, 11, and 12.

Points of Difference

The "points of difference"—characteristics that make Howlin' Coyote chilies unique relative to competitors—fall into three important areas:

- Unique taste and convenience. No known competitor offers a high-quality, "authentic" frozen chili in a range of flavors. And no existing chili has the same combination of quick preparation and home-style taste.

- Taste trends. The American palate is increasingly intrigued by hot spices, and Howlin' Coyote brands offer more "kick" than most other prepared chilies.

- Premium packaging. Howlin' Coyote's high-value packaging graphics convey the unique, high-quality product contained inside and the product's nontraditional positioning.

Positioning

In the past chili products have been either convenient or tasty, but not both. Howlin' Coyote pairs these two desirable characteristics to obtain a positioning in consumers' minds as very high-quality "authentic Southwestern/Mexican tasting" chilies that can be prepared easily and quickly.

6. Marketing Program

The four marketing mix elements of the Howlin' Coyote chili marketing program are detailed below. Note that "chile" is the vegetable and "chili" is the dish.

Product Strategy

After first summarizing the product line, the approach to product quality and packaging are covered.

Product Line. Howlin' Coyote chili, retailing for $3.99 for an 11-ounce serving, is available in five flavors. The five are:

- Green Chile Chili: braised extra-lean pork with fire-roasted green chilies, onions, tomato chunks, bold spices, and jalapeno peppers, based on a Southwestern favorite.

- Red Chile Chili: extra-lean cubed pork, deep-red chilies, and sweet onions; known as the "Texas Bowl of Red."

- Beef and Black Bean Chili: lean braised beef with black beans, tomato chunks, and Howlin' Coyote's own blend of red chilies and authentic spicing.

> Using parallel structure, this bulleted list presents the product line efficiently and crisply.

- Chicken Chunk Chili: hearty chunks of tender chicken, fire-roasted green chilies, black beans, pinto beans, diced onions, and zesty spices.

- Mean Bean Chili: vegetarian, with nine distinctive bean varieties and fire-roasted green chilies, tomato chunks, onion, and a robust blend of spices and rich red chilies.

Unique Product Quality. The flavoring systems of the Howlin' Coyote chilies are proprietary. The products' tastiness is due to extra care lavished upon the ingredients during production. The ingredients used are of unusually high quality. Meats are low-fat cuts and are fresh, not frozen, to preserve cell structure and moistness. Chilies are fire-roasted for fresher taste, not the canned variety used by more mainstream products. Tomatoes and vegetables are select quality. No preservatives or artificial flavors are used.

Packaging. Reflecting the "cutting edge" marketing strategy of its producers, Howlin' Coyote bucks conventional wisdom in packaging. It avoids placing predictable photographs of the product on its containers. (Head to any grocer's freezer and you will be hardpressed to find a product that does not feature a heavily stylized photograph of the contents.) Instead, Howlin' Coyote's package shows a Southwestern motif that communicates the product's out-of-the-ordinary positioning. This approach signals the product's nontraditional qualities: "adventurous" eating with minimal fuss—a frozen meal for people who do not normally enjoy frozen meals.

> A brief caption on photos and sample ads ties them to the text and highlights the reason for being included.

The Southwestern motif makes Howlin' Coyote's packages stand out in a supermarket's freezer case.

Price Strategy

Howlin' Coyote Chili is, at $3.99 for an 11-ounce package, priced comparably to the other frozen offerings and higher than the canned and dried chili varieties. However, the significant taste advantages it has over canned chilies and the convenience advantages over dried chilies justify this pricing strategy.

> This Price Strategy section makes the company's price point very clear, along with its price position relative to potential substitutes. When appropriate and when space permits, this section might contain a break-even analysis. See Chapters 13 and 14.

This "introductory overview" sentence tells the reader the topics covered in the section—in this case in-store demonstrations, recipes, and cents-off coupons. While this sentence may be omitted in short memos or plans, it helps readers see where the text is leading. These sentences are used throughout this plan. This textbook also generally utilizes these introductory overview sentences to aid your comprehension.

Elements of the Promotion Strategy are highlighted in terms of the three key promotional activities the company is emphasizing: in-store demonstrations, recipes, and cents-off coupons. For space reasons the company's on-line strategies are not shown in the plan. See Chapters 18, 19, 20, and 21.

Photos or sample ads can illustrate key points effectively, even if they are not in color as they appear here.

Promotion Strategy

Key promotion programs feature in-store demonstrations, recipes, and cents-off coupons.

In-Store Demonstrations. In-store demonstrations will be conducted to give consumers a chance to try Howlin' Coyote products and learn about their unique qualities. Demos will be conducted regularly in all markets to increase awareness and trial purchases.

Recipes. Because the products' flexibility of use is a key selling point, recipes will be offered to consumers to stimulate use. The recipes will be given at all in-store demonstrations, on the back of packages, and through a mail-in recipe book offer. In addition, recipes will be included in coupons sent by direct-mail or free-standing inserts. For new markets, recipes will be included on in-pack coupon inserts.

Cents-Off Coupons. To generate trial and repeat-purchase of Howlin' Coyote products, coupons will be distributed in four ways:

- In Sunday newspaper inserts. These inserts are widely read and will help generate awareness. Coupled with in-store demonstrations, this has been a very successful technique so far.

Sunday newspaper inserts encourage consumer trial and provide recipes to show how Howlin' Coyote chili can be used in summer meals.

Another bulleted list adds many details for the reader, including methods of gaining customer awareness, trial, and repeat purchases as Howlin' Coyote enters new metropolitan areas.

- In-pack coupons. Inside each box of Howlin' Coyote chili will be coupons for $1 off two more packages of the chili. These coupons will be included for the first three months the product is shipped to a new market. Doing so encourages repeat purchases by new users.
- Direct-mail chili coupons. Those households that fit the Howlin' Coyote demographics described previously will be mailed coupons. This is likely to be an efficient promotion due to its greater audience selectivity.
- In-store demonstrations. Coupons will be passed out at in-store demonstrations to give an additional incentive to purchase.

The Place Strategy is described here in terms of both (1) the present method and (2) the new one to be used when the increased sales volume makes it feasible. See Chapters 15, 16, and 17.

Place (Distribution) Strategy

Howlin' Coyote is distributed in its present markets through a food distributor. The distributor buys the product, warehouses it, and then resells and delivers it to grocery retailers on a store-by-store basis. This is typical for products that have moderate sales—compared with, say, staples like milk or bread. As sales grow, we will shift to a more efficient system using a broker who sells the products to retail chains and grocery wholesalers.

All the marketing mix decisions covered in the just-described marketing program have both revenue and expense effects. These are summarized in this section of the marketing plan. See Appendix B.

7. Financial Data and Projections

Past Sales Revenues

Note that this section contains no introductory overview sentence. While the sentence is not essential, many readers prefer to see it to avoid the abrupt start with Past Sales Revenues.

Historically, Howlin' Coyote has had a steady increase in sales revenues since its introduction in 1997. In 2001, sales jumped spectacularly, due largely to new promotion strategies. Sales have continued to rise, but at a less dramatic rate. The trend in sales revenues appears in Figure 3.

Figure 3.   Sales Revenues for Paradise Kitchens, Inc.

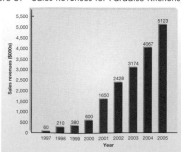

The graph shows more clearly the dramatic growth of sales revenue than data in a table would do.

<u>Five-Year Projections</u>

Five-year financial projections for Paradise Kitchens appear below:

			Projections				
		Actual	Year 1	Year 2	Year 3	Year 4	Year 5
<u>Financial Element</u>	<u>Units</u>	<u>2005</u>	<u>2006</u>	<u>2007</u>	<u>2008</u>	<u>2009</u>	<u>2010</u>
Cases sold	1,000	353	684	889	1,249	1,499	1,799
Net sales	$1,000	5,123	9,913	12,884	18,111	21,733	26,080
Gross profit	$1,000	2,545	4,820	6,527	8,831	10,597	12,717
Operating profit (loss)	$1,000	339	985	2,906	2,805	3,366	4,039

These projections reflect the continuing growth in number of cases sold (with 8 packages of Howlin' Coyote chili per case) and increasing production and distribution economies of scale as sales volume increases.

8. Organization

Paradise Kitchens's present organization appears in Figure 4. It shows the four people reporting to the President. Below this level are both the full-time and part-time employees of the Company.

At present Paradise Kitchens operates with full-time employees in only essential positions. It now augments its full-time staff with key advisors, consultants, and sub-contractors. As the firm grows, people with special expertise will be added to the staff.

Figure 4. The Paradise Kitchens Organization

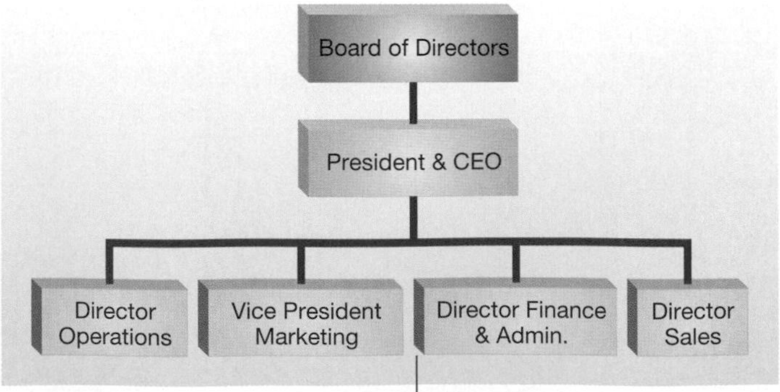

The following annotations appear in the left margin:

Because this table is very short, it is woven into the text, rather than given a figure number and title.

Because the plan proposes to enter 17 new metropolitan markets in the coming five years (for a total of 20), it is not possible to simply extrapolate the trend in Figure 3. Instead, management's judgment must be used. Methods of making sales forecasts—including the "lost horse" technique used here—are discussed in Chapter 9.

The Five-Year Financial Projections section starts with the judgment forecast of cases sold and the resulting net sales. Gross profit and then operating profit—critical for the company's survival—are projected. An actual plan often contains many pages of computer-generated spreadsheet projections, usually shown in an appendix to the plan.

The following annotation appears at the bottom:

The Organization of Paradise Kitchens appears here. It reflects the bare-bones organizational structure of successful small businesses. Often a more elaborate marketing plan will show the new positions expected to be added as the firm grows. See Chapter 22.

The Implementation Plan shows how the company will turn plans into results. Gantt charts are often used to set deadlines and assign responsibilities for the many tactical marketing decisions needed to enter a new market. See Chapter 22.

9. Implementation Plan

Introducing Howlin' Coyote chilies to 17 new metropolitan areas is a complex task and requires that creative promotional activities gain consumer awareness and initial trial among the target market households identified earlier. The anticipated rollout schedule to enter these metropolitan markets appears in Figure 5.

Figure 5.   Rollout Schedule to Enter New U.S. Markets

Year	New Markets Added	Cumulative Markets	Cumulative Percentage of U.S. Market
Today (2005)	2	5	16
Year 1 (2006)	3	8	21
Year 2 (2007)	4	12	29
Year 3 (2008)	2	14	37
Year 4 (2009)	3	17	45
Year 5 (2010)	3	20	53

The diverse regional tastes in chili will be monitored carefully to assess whether minor modifications may be required in the chili recipes. For example, what is seen as "hot" in Boston may not be seen as "hot" in Dallas. As the rollout to new metropolitan areas continues, Paradise Kitchens will assess manufacturing and distribution trade-offs. This is important in determining whether to start new production with selected high-quality regional contract packers.

The essence of Evaluation and Control is comparing actual sales with the targeted values set in the plan and taking appropriate actions. Note that the section briefly describes a contingency plan for alternative actions, depending on how successful the entry into a new market turns out to be. See Chapter 22.

10. Evaluation and Control

Monthly sales targets in cases have been set for Howlin' Coyote chili for each metropolitan area. Actual case sales will be compared with these targets and tactical marketing programs modified to reflect the unique sets of factors in each metropolitan area. The speed of the roll-out program will increase or decrease, depending on Paradise Kitchens's performance in the successive metropolitan markets it enters. Similarly, as described above in the section on the implementation plan, Paradise Kitchens may elect to respond to variations in regional tastes by using contract packers, which will reduce transportation and warehousing costs but will require special efforts to monitor production quality.

Various appendixes may appear at the end of the plan, depending on the purpose and audience for them. For example, resumes of key personnel or detailed financial spreadsheets often appear in appendixes. For space reasons these are not shown here.

Appendix A. Biographical Sketches of Key Personnel

Appendix B. Detailed Financial Projections

iPod

10,000 songs* in your pocket. Works with Mac or PC. The new iPod.

3

SCANNING THE MARKETING ENVIRONMENT

LEARNING OBJECTIVES

After reading this chapter you should be able to:

1 Explain how environmental scanning provides information about social, economic, technological, competitive, and regulatory forces.

2 Describe how social forces such as demographics and culture and economic forces such as macroeconomic conditions and consumer income affect marketing.

3 Describe how technological changes can affect marketing.

4 Discuss the forms of competition that exist in a market, key components of competition, and the impact of competition on corporate structures.

5 Explain the major legislation that ensures competition and regulates the elements of the marketing mix.

IT'S SHOW TIME!

Don't blink, because the world of entertainment is changing faster than anyone imagined possible. Online music, high-definition televisions, digital photography, computer-based media centers, and software for making movies are just some of the many products new to the entertainment industry. The revolution began with the combination of Apple's iPod music player, which can store 10,000 songs in a device smaller than a deck of cards, and its iTunes Music Store, which sells more than 10,000,000 songs each month for just $.99 each. Other new forms of digital entertainment products include digital video recorders (DVRs), which record TV shows on hard drives instead of tape, and home entertainment "hubs," which utilize wireless networks to link digital devices from around the home. Some experts even predict that there will probably be a version of iPod and iTunes for movies in the near future.

Suddenly the music, television, photography, movie, and computer industries are converging. Musicians, recording companies, television networks, camera companies, movie studios, computer companies, retail stores, and consumers like you are part of a completely different entertainment marketplace. How did this happen? The marketing environment changed!

First, consumers changed. They gradually made it clear that they prefer more convenient and customer-friendly approaches to purchasing music, television programming, movies, and photographs. Second, technology changed. High-speed Internet became available to millions of users, computers with improved storage capabilities and CD burners were introduced, high-resolution displays became smaller and less expensive, and file-transfer software was developed. Third, the regulatory environment changed. You may remember the first file-sharing service, Napster, was sued by the Recording Industry Association of

America (RIAA) and ordered to stop helping users exchange copyrighted material. The ruling led to new agreements between music labels and services like iTunes and sparked a worldwide debate about copyright protection. Finally, competitive forces have changed. Companies such as Disney, Pixar, Apple, Hewlett-Packard, Sony, Napster, A&M Records, and many others are now in an environment where they might be competitors or partners. Apple, for example, has created a partnership that allows Hewlett-Packard to resell its music player under the HP brand, but it is competing with Microsoft, Sony, and RealNetworks to become the industry standard in the music-downloading business. All of these changes, and the trends they suggest, led one expert to predict that "how we watch movies, look at photos, listen to music, even read a book promises to change profoundly in the next decade."[1]

Many businesses operate in environments where important forces change. Anticipating and responding to changes such as those experienced by the entertainment industry often means the difference between marketing success and failure. This chapter describes how the marketing environment has changed in the past and how it is likely to change in the future.

ENVIRONMENTAL SCANNING IN THE NEW MILLENNIUM

Changes in the marketing environment are a source of opportunities and threats to be managed. The process of continually acquiring information on events occurring outside the organization to identify and interpret potential trends is called **environmental scanning**.

Tracking Environmental Trends

Environmental trends typically arise from five sources: social, economic, technological, competitive, and regulatory forces. As shown in Figure 3–1 and described later in this chapter, these forces affect the marketing activities of a firm in numerous ways. To illustrate how environmental scanning is used, consider the following trend:[2]

> Coffee industry marketers have observed that the percentage of adults who drink coffee has declined from 75 percent in 1962 to 51 percent in 2003. Age-specific analysis, however, indicates that the percentage of 18- to 24-year-olds who drink coffee has risen from 19 percent in 1998 to 29 percent today.

FIGURE 3–1

Environmental forces affecting the organization, as well as its suppliers and customers

What types of businesses are likely to be influenced by this trend? What future would you predict for coffee?

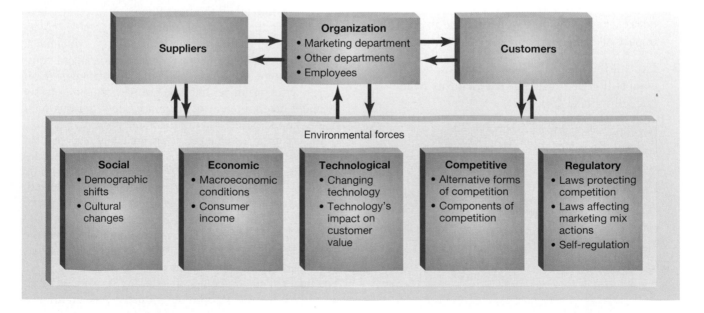

You may have concluded that this trend is likely to influence coffee manufacturers, coffee shops, and supermarkets. If so, you are absolutely correct—manufacturers have responded by offering new flavors and seasonal blends, coffee shops are automating to prepare drinks faster, and supermarkets have added coffee boutiques and gourmet brands to try to reverse the trend. Predicting the future of coffee requires assumptions about the number of years the trends will continue and the rate of increase or decline in various age groups. Did you consider these issues in your analysis? Because experts make different assumptions, their forecasts range from a 30 percent decline to a 7 percent increase by 2008, a range that probably includes your forecast.

Environmental scanning also involves explaining trends. Why has coffee consumption been declining? One explanation is that consumers are switching from coffee to other beverages such as soft drinks, juices, or water. This idea is supported by the fact that soft drink consumption has increased from 23 gallons per person in 1970 to 54 gallons in 2003. Another explanation is that preferences have shifted to more expensive types of coffee, and consumers have reduced their use to maintain the same level of expenditure. Identifying and interpreting trends, such as the decline in coffee consumption, and developing explanations, such as those offered in this paragraph, are essential to successful environmental scanning.[3]

An Environmental Scan of Today's Marketplace

What other trends might affect marketing in the future? A firm conducting an environmental scan of the marketplace might uncover key trends such as those listed in Figure 3–2 for each of the five environmental factors.[4] Although the list of trends is far from complete, it reveals the breadth of an environmental scan—from the growing diversity of the U.S. population, to the shift of white-collar work to offshore locations, to the increasing use of wireless technology. These trends affect consumers and the businesses and organizations that serve them. Trends such as these are covered as the five environmental forces are described in the following pages.

FIGURE 3–2
An environmental scan of today's marketplace

ENVIRONMENTAL FORCE	TREND IDENTIFIED BY AN ENVIRONMENTAL SCAN
Social	• Declining differences in gender roles and buying patterns • Growing diversity of the U.S. population • Decline in smoking and tobacco use throughout the world
Economic	• Increasing military and humanitarian expenditures related to the war on terrorism • The shift of white-collar work to offshore locations • Increase in savings and money management as many workers approach retirement
Technological	• Increasing use of wireless broadband technology • The dramatic growth of the open source (free) software movement, started by Linux • Advances in biotechnology, cosmetic surgery, and cancer drugs
Competitive	• The growing influence of China as the world leader in technology manufacturing • The development of corporate competitive intelligence departments and relationships with federal security agencies • Increased focus on empowering workers to improve performance
Regulatory	• New legislation related to digital copyright and intellectual property protection • Greater concern for privacy and personal information collection • New legislation on Internet taxation, e-mail spam, and domain names

SOCIAL FORCES

The **social forces** of the environment include the demographic characteristics of the population and its values. Changes in these forces can have a dramatic impact on marketing strategy.

Demographics

Describing a population according to selected characteristics such as age, gender, ethnicity, income, and occupation is referred to as **demographics**. Several organizations such as the Population Reference Bureau and the United Nations monitor the world population profile, while many other organizations such as the U.S. Census Bureau provide information about the American population.

The World Population at a Glance   The most recent estimates indicate that there are 6.3 billion people in the world today, and that the population is likely to grow to 9 billion by 2050. While this growth has led to the term *population explosion,* the increases have not occurred worldwide—they are primarily in the developing countries of Africa, Asia, and Latin America. In fact, India is predicted to have the world's largest population in 2050 with 1.6 billion people, and China will be a close second with 1.3 billion people. Figure 3–3 shows the declining proportion of the world's population in North America, Europe, Australia, and Japan.[5]

Another important global trend is the shifting age structure of the world population. It is expected that the number of people older than 65 will more than double in the coming decades, while the number of youth will grow at a much lower rate. Again, the magnitude of this trend varies by region, and developed countries such as the United States are expected to face the highest growth rates of the elderly age group. Global income levels and living standards have also been increasing, although the averages across countries are very different. Per capita income, for example, ranges from $43,000 in Luxembourg, to $24,000 in Canada, to $800 in Afghanistan.

For marketers, global trends such as these have many implications. Obviously, the relative size of countries such as India and China will mean they represent huge markets for many product categories. Elderly populations in developed countries are likely to save less and begin spending their funds on health care, travel, and other retirement-related products and services. Economic progress in developing countries will lead to growth in entrepreneurship, new markets for infrastructure related to manufacturing, communication, and distribution, and the growth of exports.[6]

FIGURE 3–3

The changing distribution of the world population

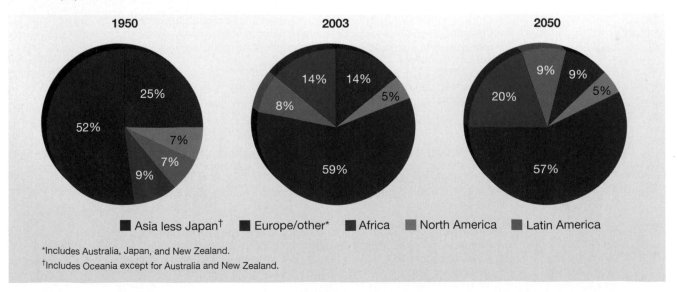

*Includes Australia, Japan, and New Zealand.
†Includes Oceania except for Australia and New Zealand.

The U.S. Population   Studies of the demographic characteristics of the U.S. population suggest several important trends. Generally, the population is becoming larger, older, and more diverse. In 2004, the U.S. population was estimated to be 294 million people. If current trends in life expectancy, birthrates, and immigration continue, by 2025 the U.S. population will exceed 350 million people. This growth suggests that niche markets based on age, life stage, family structure, geographic location, and ethnicity will become increasingly important. The global trend toward an older population is particularly true in the United States. Today, there are approximately 35 million people 65 and older. By 2025, this age group will include more than 70 million people, or 20 percent of the population. You may have noticed companies trying to attract older consumers without alienating younger ones. Pepsi, for example, ran an ad featuring a teenage boy at a rock concert who discovers his father is at the same concert. Finally, the term *minority* as it is currently used is likely to become obsolete as the size of most ethnic groups will double by 2025.[7]

Generational Cohorts   A major reason for the graying of America is that the **baby boomers**—the generation of children born between 1946 and 1964—are growing older. As the 78 million boomers have aged, their participation in the workforce and their earnings have increased, making them an important consumer market. It has been estimated that this group accounts for 56 to 58 percent of the purchases in most consumer product and service categories. In the future, boomers' interests will reflect concern for their children and grandchildren, their own health, and their retirement, and companies will need to position products to respond to these interests. Generally, baby boomers are receptive to anything that makes them feel younger. Olay's Total Effects product line, for example, includes anti-aging moisturizers, cleansing cloths, and restoration treatments designed for this age group.

The baby boom cohort is followed by **Generation X**, which includes the 15 percent of the population born between 1965 and 1976. This period is also known as the baby bust, because the number of children born each year was declining. This is a generation of consumers who are self-reliant, entrepreneurial, supportive of racial and ethnic diversity, and better educated than any previous generation. They are not prone to extravagance and are likely to pursue lifestyles that are a blend of caution, pragmatism, and traditionalism. For example, Generation X is saving, planning for retirement, and taking advantage of 401(k) plans much earlier than the boomer generation. As the baby boomers move into grandparenthood, Generation X is becoming the new parent market. In response, some brands that Generation X helped

Which generational cohorts are these advertisers trying to reach?

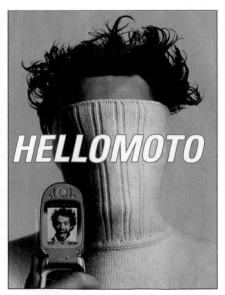

MARKETING NEWSNET

After Seeing 23 Million Ads, Generation Y Is Turning 21

CUSTOMER VALUE

There are 72 million members of the Generation Y cohort. About 20 percent of them have already reached the age of 21, and the rest are not far behind. Why is this important? Because much more than legal privileges begin when someone turns 21. This transition to adulthood signals a period when many people graduate from college, look for their first full-time job, start forming their own households, purchase their first new car and home, and select savings and retirement funds. They also begin developing brand loyalties that could last a lifetime. As a result, 21-year-olds are just beginning a path of extraordinary influence on the marketplace.

Generation Y is known as a savvy, demanding, and sometimes marketing-skeptical group, so marketers are eager to better understand them. Would you have guessed any of the following facts about 21-year-olds?

- Number of advertisements received in the past 21 years: 23 million
- Amount a 21-year-old will spend in his or her lifetime: $2,241,141
- Years until a 21-year-old will buy a vacation home: 22
- Percentage of 21-year-olds who have a credit card: 93%
- Hours each week a 21-year-old spends online: 10

Of course, there is a lot more to know about 21-year-olds, but if you watch closely you'll start seeing unique product and service offerings—and maybe a few more ads—designed with just that age in mind!

---

popularize are expanding their offerings. Tommy Hilfiger and DKNY, for example, have launched children's lines for the babies of Generation X parents.[8]

The generational cohort labeled **Generation Y** includes the 72 million Americans born between 1977 and 1994. This was a period of increasing births, which resulted from baby boomers having children, and it is often referred to as the echo-boom or baby boomlet. Generation Y exerts influence on music, sports, computers, videogames, and especially cell phones. Generation Y views wireless communication as a lifeline to friends and family and has been the first to use text messaging, cell phone games, and built-in cameras. This is also the group that includes recent and future 21-year-olds—the beginning of adult responsibilities and many new consumer activities. The accompanying Marketing NewsNet describes some of the important changes that many "Gen Ys" face.[9] The term *millennials* is also used, with inconsistent definitions, to refer to younger members of Generation Y and sometimes to Americans born since 1994.

Because the members of each generation are distinctive in their attitudes and consumer behavior, marketers have been studying the many groups or cohorts that make up the marketplace and have developed *generational marketing* programs for them. In addition, global marketers have discovered that many of the American generational differences also exist outside of the United States.[10]

The American Household As the population age profile has changed, so has the structure of the American household. In 1960, 75 percent of all households consisted of married couples. Today, that type of household is just 50 percent of the population. Just 25 percent of households are married couples with children, and only 10 percent are households with working fathers and stay-at-home moms. Some of the fastest-growing types of households are those with a single person, those with a single parent, and those with unmarried partners. Advertisers are trying to develop campaigns that reflect the changing structure of U.S. households. Schwab financial services, for example, used Sarah Ferguson, a single mother, to reach single women with an interest in personal finance.[11]

The increase in cohabitation (households with unmarried partners) may be one reason that the divorce rate has declined slightly in recent years. Even so, the likelihood that a couple will divorce exceeds 40 percent and the total number of divorced people is 21.6 million. The majority of divorced people eventually remarry, which has given rise to the **blended family**, one formed by the merging into a single household of two previously separated units. Today, one of every three Americans is a stepparent, stepchild, stepsibling, or some other member of a blended family. Hallmark Cards, Inc., now has specially designed cards and verses for blended families.[12]

Population Shifts   A major regional shift in the U.S. population toward western and southern states is underway. During the period from 1995 to 2025, California, New Mexico, Hawaii, Arizona, and Nevada are expected to grow at the fastest rates. Three states—California, Texas, and Florida—will account for 45 percent of the population change in the United States, gaining more than 6 million people in each state.[13]

Populations are also shifting within states. In the early 1900s, the population shifted from rural areas to cities. From the 1930s through the 1980s, the population shifted from the cities to suburbs. During the 1990s and 2000s, the population began to shift again, from suburbs to more remote suburbs called *exurbs* and to smaller towns called *penturbia*. Today, 30 percent of all Americans live in central cities, 50 percent live in suburbs, and 20 percent live in rural locations.[14]

To assist marketers in gathering data on the population, the Census Bureau has developed a classification system to describe the varying locations of the population. The system consists of two types of *statistical areas*:

- A *metropolitan statistical area* has at least one urbanized area of 50,000 or more people, and adjacent territory that has a high degree of social and economic integration.
- A *micropolitan statistical area* has at least one urban cluster of at least 10,000 but less than 50,000 people, and adjacent territory that has a high degree of social and economic integration.

If a metropolitan statistical area contains a population of 2.5 million or more, it may be subdivided into smaller areas called *metropolitan divisions*. In addition, adjacent metropolitan statistical areas and micropolitan statistical areas may be grouped into *combined statistical areas*.[15]

There are currently 362 metropolitan statistical areas, which include 83 percent of the population, and 573 micropolitan areas, which include 10 percent of the population.

Racial and Ethnic Diversity   A notable trend is the changing racial and ethnic composition of the U.S. population. Approximately one in four U.S. residents is African American, American Indian, Asian, Pacific Islander, or a representative of another racial or ethnic group. Diversity is further evident in the variety of peoples that make up these groups. For example, Asians consist of Asian Indians, Chinese, Filipinos, Japanese, Koreans, and Vietnamese. For the first time, the 2000 Census allowed respondents to choose more than one of the six race options, and more than 6 million reported more than one race. Hispanics, who may be from any race, currently make up 12 percent of the U.S. population and are represented by Mexicans, Puerto Ricans, Cubans, and others of Central and South American ancestry. While the United States is becoming more diverse, Figure 3–4 on the next page suggests that the racial and ethnic groups tend to be concentrated in geographic regions.[16]

The racial and ethnic composition of the United States is expected to change even more by 2025. Between 2000 and 2025, the Hispanic population will grow from 35 million to more than 68 million, or almost 20 percent of the total population. The number of Asian Americans in the United States will also double to 24 million, or 7 percent of the population, and the African American population will be approximately 45 million, or 13 percent of the population. The new Census category, *multiracials,* currently makes up 2.4 percent of the population, but because of the limited

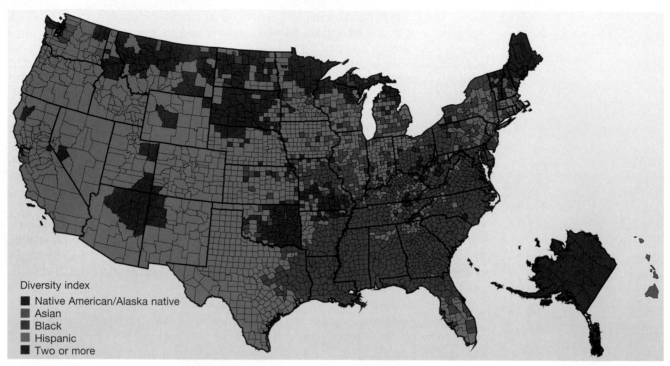

Diversity index
■ Native American/Alaska native
■ Asian
■ Black
■ Hispanic
■ Two or more

SOURCE: *American Demographics,* November 2002.

FIGURE 3–4

Racial and ethnic concentrations in the United States (excluding whites)

information about this group, growth forecasts are difficult to make. Overall, the trends in the composition of the population suggest that the U.S. market will no longer be dominated by one group and that non-Hispanic whites will be a declining majority over the next two decades.

While the growing size of these groups has been identified through new Census data, their economic impact on the marketplace is also very noticeable. By 2007, Hispanics, African Americans, and Asians will spend $900 billion, $850 billion, and $455 billion each year, respectively. To adapt to this new marketplace, many companies are developing **multicultural marketing** programs, which are combinations of the marketing mix that reflect the unique attitudes, ancestry, communication preferences, and lifestyles of different races. Because businesses must now market their products to a consumer base with many racial and ethnic identities, indepth marketing research that allows an accurate understanding of each culture is essential.[17]

Additional analysis of population demographic data, such as the information shown in Figure 3–4, suggests that racial and ethnic groups tend to be concentrated in geographic regions. This information allows companies to combine their multicultural marketing efforts with *regional marketing* activities. Consider, for example, that 48 percent of Asian Americans live in Los Angeles, New York City, and San Francisco, and that two-thirds of Hispanics live in Florida, Texas, and California. Saturn combined multicultural and regional marketing by running a Spanish-language advertising campaign, using a testimonial from San Antonio, Texas, firefighter Ernest Imperial, in Texas and California. The ads were not used in Florida, where more than 55 percent of the Hispanic population is Cuban, a group for which a different Spanish dialect was needed.[18] In Chapter 9 you will learn more about this approach to the market referred to as geographic segmentation.

Culture

A second social force, **culture**, incorporates the set of values, ideas, and attitudes that are learned and shared among the members of a group. Because many of the elements of culture influence consumer buying patterns, monitoring national and

Saturn combined ethnic and regional marketing by using Spanish-language promotions in some states.

Saturn

www.saturnbp.com

global cultural trends is important for marketing. Cross-cultural analysis needed for global marketing is discussed in Chapter 7.

The Changing Attitudes and Roles of Men and Women   One of the most notable cultural changes in the United States in the past 30 years has been in the attitudes and roles of men and women in the marketplace. In fact, some experts predict that as this trend continues, there will eventually be very few differences in the buying patterns of men and women.

Your mothers and grandmothers probably remember advertising targeted at them that focused on the characteristics of household products—like laundry detergent that got clothes "whiter than white." In the 1970s and 1980s, ads began to create a bridge between genders with messages such as Secret's "strong enough for a man, but made for a woman." In the 1990s, marketing to women focused on their challenge of balancing family and career interests. Since then, women and men have encouraged the slow movement toward equality in the marketplace. As a result, today's Generation Y represents the first generation of women who have no collective memory of the dramatic changes we have undergone. As one expert explains, "Feminism today is like fluoride, we scarcely notice that we have it."

Several factors have contributed to the shift in attitudes. First, many young women had career mothers who provided a reference point for lifestyle choices. Second, increased participation in organized sports eliminated one of the most visible inequalities in opportunities for women. And finally, the Internet has provided exposure to the marketplace through a mechanism that makes gender, race, and ethnicity invisible. Most of the 35 million Generation Y women view themselves as confident, strong, and feminine. They are not likely to respond to "we know you are busy" appeals; they know they are busy and thrive on it. In addition, research suggests that the majority of adults today believe men and women should equally share most responsibilities.[19]

Many U.S. companies that had a consumer base that was primarily men or primarily women in the past are preparing for growth from the other gender. Grocery stores, car dealers, investment services, and many others hope to appeal to both groups in the future. Burton Snowboard Company, for example, makes boards and clothing for men and women and redesigned its website to reflect feedback from female riders. Some industries are slower in making these changes. Explanations for lower use of video games than computer and Internet games by women suggest that video games often exaggerate and stereotype gender roles. Outside of the United States, gender roles may still be very prevalent. In India, for example, regulation has been introduced that specifies that women in advertising "must not be portrayed in a manner that emphasizes passive, submissive qualities and encourages them to play a subordinate role in the family and society."[20]

Changing Values　Culture also includes values, which vary with age but tend to be very similar for men and women. All age groups, for example, rank "protecting the family" and "honesty" as the most important values. Consumers under 20 rank "friendship" third, while the 20 to 29 and 30 to 39 age groups rank "self-esteem" and "health and fitness" as their third most important values, respectively. These values are reflected in the growth of products and services that consumers believe are consistent with their values. Concern for health and fitness is one reason 51 million people in the United States report that they are trying to control their weight. But they are less likely to "diet" than they are to create a healthy and balanced lifestyle. Stouffer's Lean Cuisine is trying to respond to the trend by suggesting that health-conscious consumers don't have to sacrifice taste for nutrition with its "Do something good for yourself" campaign. Similarly, Jenny Craig's primary market is 35- to 55-year-old people who are interested in a healthier lifestyle. Other products related to this trend include vitamins, exercise equipment, fitness drinks, and magazines such as *Fitness, Runner's World,* and *Walking.*[21]

A change in consumption orientation is also apparent. Today, and for the foreseeable future, **value consciousness**—or the concern for obtaining the best quality, features, and performance of a product or service for a given price—will drive consumption behavior. Innovative marketers have responded to this new orientation in numerous ways. Holiday Inn Worldwide has opened Holiday Express hotels, designed to offer comfortable accommodations with room rates lower than Holiday Inns. Revlon's Charles of the Ritz, known for its upscale and expensive cosmetics, has introduced the Express Bar, a collection of modified, medium-priced cosmetics. Even American Express is adding low-fee credit cards to its line of well-known, high-priced, and exclusive green, gold, and platinum charge cards.[22]

(Concept Check)

1. Describe three generational cohorts.

2. Why are many companies developing multicultural marketing programs?

3. How are important values such as "health and fitness" reflected in the marketplace today?

ECONOMIC FORCES

The second component of the environmental scan, the **economy**, pertains to the income, expenditures, and resources that affect the cost of running a business and household. We'll consider two aspects of these economic forces: a macroeconomic view of the marketplace and a microeconomic perspective of consumer income.

Macroeconomic Conditions

Of particular concern at the macroeconomic level is the inflationary or recessionary state of the economy, whether actual or perceived by consumers or businesses. In an inflationary economy, the cost to produce and buy products and services escalates

FIGURE 3–5

Percentage change in the annual growth rate of the Index of Consumer Sentiment (ICS) and GDP

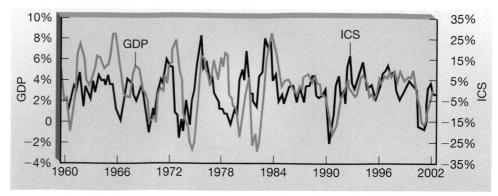

SOURCE: *American Demographics,* February 2003 and University of Michigan.

as prices increase. From a marketing standpoint, if prices rise faster than consumer incomes, the number of items consumers can buy decreases. This relationship is evident in the cost of a college education. Today, the average cost of one year of college is approximately 16 percent of the annual income of an average middle-class family, compared with 9 percent in 1976.[23]

Whereas inflation is a period of price increases, recession is a time of slow economic activity. Businesses decrease production, unemployment rises, and many consumers have less money to spend. The U.S. economy experienced recessions in the early 1970s, early 1980s, and early 1990s. From 1998 through early 2000 the U.S. economy grew rapidly as businesses invested in "new economy" technology and as consumers spent their stock market gains. Following this period of growth, however, the economy again entered a slow-growth recessionary period from 2001 through 2003.[24]

Consumer expectations of an inflationary and recessionary U.S. economy are an important element of environmental scanning. Consumer spending, which accounts for two-thirds of the U.S. economic activity, is affected by expectations of the future. There are many surveys of consumer expectations, but the two most popular are the Consumer Confidence Index, conducted by a nonprofit business research organization called the Conference Board, and the Index of Consumer Sentiment, conducted by the Survey Research Center at the University of Michigan. The surveys track the responses of consumers to specific questions about their expectations, and the results are reported once each month. For example, the Index of Consumer Sentiment asks, "Looking ahead, do you think that a year from now you will be better off financially, worse off or just about the same as now?" The answers to the questions are used to construct an index. The higher the index, the more favorable are consumer expectations. Figure 3–5 shows the fluctuation in the Index of Consumer Sentiment and its close relationship to GDP. The consumer expectations surveys are closely monitored by many companies, particularly manufacturers and retailers of cars, furniture, and major appliances. Chrysler, for example, uses the surveys to plan its automobile production and avoid producing too many or too few cars.[25]

Consumer Income

The microeconomic trends in terms of consumer income are also important issues for marketers. Having a product that meets the needs of consumers may be of little value if they are unable to purchase it. A consumer's ability to buy is related to income, which consists of gross, disposable, and discretionary components.

Gross Income   The total amount of money made in one year by a person, household, or family unit is referred to as **gross income** (or "money income" at the Census Bureau). While the typical U.S. household earned only about $8,700 of income in 1970, it earned about $43,318 in 2003. When gross income is adjusted for inflation, however, income of that typical U.S. household was relatively stable

FIGURE 3–6

Income distribution of U.S. households

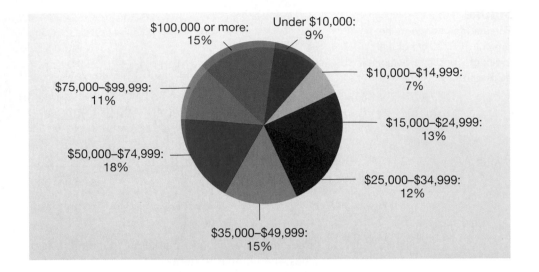

from 1970 to 2002 (e.g., adjusted for inflation the 1970 salary was $40,338). Figure 3–6 shows the distribution of annual income among U.S. households.[26] Are you from a typical household? Read the accompanying Web Link to learn how you can determine the median household income in your home town.

Disposable Income   The second income component, **disposable income**, is the money a consumer has left after paying taxes to use for food, shelter, clothing, and transportation. Thus, if taxes rise at a faster rate than does income, consumers must economize. In recent years, consumers' allocation of income has shifted. As the marketplace has become more efficient, producing products that are more durable and use less energy, consumers have increased their disposable income. Car maintenance costs, for example, have declined 28 percent since 1985, because automobile quality has improved. Much of the money is being spent on new categories of "necessities" such as vitamins and supplements; antibacterial bodywashes, lotions, and deodorants; antiwrinkle creams; and children's shampoos, toothpaste, and bath products.[27]

As consumers' discretionary income increases, so does the enjoyment of pleasure travel.

Cunard

www.cunard.com

WEB LINK   How Typical Is Your Home Town?

Marketers collect and use environmental information to better understand consumers. One way to begin an environmental scan is to compare economic data about a particular segment of the population to what is "typical" or "average" for the entire population. Do you think your town is typical? To find out, visit ESRI's website at www.esribis.com, look under the heading "Free Tapestry Report" and type in the zip code of your home town. ESRI provides a comparison of your zip code's population with the averages for the nation.

Discretionary Income   The third component of income is **discretionary income**, the money that remains after paying for taxes and necessities. Discretionary income is used for luxury items such as a cruise on the Queen Mary 2. An obvious problem in defining discretionary versus disposable income is determining what is a luxury and what is a necessity.

The Department of Labor monitors consumer expenditures through its annual Consumer Expenditure Survey. In 2002, consumers spent approximately 13 percent of their income on food, 33 percent on housing, and 4 percent on clothes. While an additional 36 percent is often spent on transportation, health care, and insurance, the remainder is generally viewed as discretionary. The percentage of income spent on food and housing typically declines as income increases, which can provide an increase in discretionary income. Discretionary expenditures can also be increased by reducing savings. The Bureau of Labor Statistics has observed that the percentage of income put into savings has been steadily declining and is expected to be only 2.7 percent in 2012, compared with 3.7 percent today.[28]

TECHNOLOGICAL FORCES

Our society is in a period of dramatic technological change. **Technology**, the third environmental force, refers to inventions or innovations from applied science or engineering research. Each new wave of technological innovation can replace existing products and companies. Do you recognize the items pictured on the next page and what they may replace?

Technology of Tomorrow

Technological change is the result of research, so it is difficult to predict. Some of the most dramatic technological changes occurring now, however, include the following:

1. Advances in nanotechnology, the science of unimaginably small electronics, will lead to smaller microprocessors, efficient fuel cells, and cancer-detection sensors.
2. High-definition televisions and programming will become the industry standard.
3. In the next five years as much as 50 percent of all telephone calls could be made over the Internet.
4. Companies will begin building software databases so that lines of code can be "reused."

Technological change leads to new products. What products might be replaced by these innovations?

These trends in technology are already seen in today's marketplace. Cablevision recently launched a high-definition-only service called Voom, which carries 25 HD channels. Voice over Internet protocol (VOIP) companies such as Vonage offer very low-cost, over-the-Internet telephone services, and Xerox has already saved $30 million in two years by "reusing" software. Other technologies such as flash memory, music downloading services, and plasma screen televisions are likely to replace or substitute for existing products and services such as floppy disks or CDRs, music stores and CDs, and televisions with CRT or projection screens.[29]

Technology's Impact on Customer Value

Advances in technology are having important effects on marketing. First, the cost of technology is plummeting, causing the customer value assessment of technology-based products to focus on other dimensions such as quality, service, and relationships. When Plaxo introduced its address book software, it gave the product away at no charge, reasoning that satisfied customers would later buy upgrades and related products. A similar approach is now used by many cellular telephone vendors, who charge little for the telephone if the purchase leads to a telephone service contract.[30]

Technology also provides value through the development of new products. Many automobile manufacturers now offer customers a navigation system that uses satellite signals to help the driver reach any destination. Under development are radar-like collision avoidance systems that disengage cruise control, reduce the engine speed, and even apply the brakes.[31] Other new products likely to be available soon include a "smart ski" with an embedded microprocessor that will adjust the flexibility of the ski to snow conditions; injectable health monitors that will send glucose, oxygen, and other clinical information to a wristwatch-like monitor; and electronic books that will allow you to download any volume and view it on pages coated with electronic "ink" and embedded electrodes.[32]

Technology can also change existing products and the ways they are produced. Many companies are using technological developments to allow *recycling* products through the manufacturing cycle several times. The National Association for Plastic Container Recovery, for example, estimates that 50 percent of all plastic bottles are now recycled, usually to make polyester fibers that are spun into everything from sweaters to upholstery. In Southern California, Tomra Systems has launched a chain of 200 rePlanet recycling kiosks that it hopes to spread across the United States. Consumers receive between 2.5 and 10 cents per recycled container. Another approach is *precycling*—efforts by manufacturers to reduce waste by decreasing the amount of packaging they use. The development of new packaging materials, for

Examples of recycling by rePlanet and precycling by Lever.

example, has allowed Du Pont to produce a collapsible pouch as an alternative to milk cartons in school lunch programs.[33]

Electronic Business Technologies

The transformative power of technology may be best illustrated by the rapid growth of the **marketspace**, an information- and communication-based electronic exchange environment mostly occupied by sophisticated computer and telecommunication technologies and digitized offerings. Any activity that uses some form of electronic communication in the inventory, exchange, advertisement, distribution, and payment of goods and services is often called **electronic commerce**. Network technologies are now used for everything from filing expense reports, to monitoring daily sales, to sharing information with employees, to communicating instantly with suppliers.

Many companies have adapted Internet-based technology internally to support their electronic business strategies. An **Intranet**, for example, is an Internet-based network used within the boundaries of an organization. It is a private Internet that may or may not be connected to the public Internet. **Extranets**, which use Internet-based technologies, permit communication between a company and its suppliers, distributors, and other partners (such as advertising agencies). The Marketing NewsNet on the next page describes how the latest Internet development—the Wi-Fi revolution—is transforming how companies do business.[34]

COMPETITIVE FORCES

The fourth component of the environmental scan, **competition**, refers to the alternative firms that could provide a product to satisfy a specific market's needs. There are various forms of competition, and each company must consider its present and potential competitors in designing its marketing strategy.

Alternative Forms of Competition

There are four basic forms of competition that form a continuum from pure competition to monopolistic competition to oligopoly to pure monopoly. Chapter 13 contains further discussions on pricing practices under these four forms of competition.

At one end of the continuum is *pure competition,* in which every company has a similar product. Companies that deal in commodities common to agribusiness

MARKETING NEWSNET

Where Can You Go When You Are Wireless? Anywhere!

TECHNOLOGY & E-COMMERCE

Electronic technologies are going through an incredible transformation. It started when network engineers were looking for a way to transmit an Internet connection without wires. The concept of "wireless fidelity" soon became "Wi-Fi," and businesses were eager to use it. Then two New York City residents started a free Wi-Fi node in midtown Manhattan's Bryant Park, and consumer demand skyrocketed. Soon there were nodes throughout the country: Levi Strauss Plaza in San Francisco, Tryst Coffeehouse in Washington, D.C., O'Hare Airport in Chicago, all Starbucks in Seattle, and the lobbies of Sheraton Four Points hotels around the nation. Currently, industry experts estimate that there are more than 12,000 nodes worldwide.

But this is just the beginning. Wi-Fi will soon grow beyond Internet connections and be found in most consumer electronics devices, including videogames, televisions, music players, cell phones, PDAs, digital cameras, and PCs. Then central servers will be able to record and store television programs, music, and video and play it back on any screen in the network.

Why is this revolution taking place so quickly? First, it is inexpensive: An access point is about $100 and a wireless card for a computer is about $60. Second, the technology is fast and powerful. Finally, it works. These three attributes combine to create an alluring option. At the current growth rate there will be 99 million people on Wi-Fi networks by 2006.

Several companies are working on devices that will hang on your key chain and glow when you are in signal range of an access point. So where can you go when you are wireless? Soon the answer will truly be anywhere!

(for example, wheat, rice, and grain) often are in a pure competition position in which distribution (in the sense of shipping products) is important but other elements of marketing have little impact.

In the second point on the continuum, *monopolistic competition,* the many sellers compete with their products on a substitutable basis. For example, if the price of coffee rises too much, consumers may switch to tea. Coupons or sales are frequently used marketing tactics.

Oligopoly, a common industry structure, occurs when a few companies control the majority of industry sales. For example, AT&T, MCI, Verizon, and Sprint control approximately 80 percent of the $16 billion international long-distance telephone service market. Similarly, the entertainment industry in the United States is dominated by Viacom, Disney, and AOL Time Warner, and the major firms in the U.S. defense contractor industry are Boeing, United Technologies, and Lockheed Martin. Critics of oligopolies suggest that because there are few sellers, price competition among firms is not desirable because it leads to reduced profits for all producers.[35]

The final point on the continuum, *pure monopoly,* occurs when only one firm sells the product. Monopolies are common for producers of goods considered essential to a community: water, electricity, and telephone service. Typically, marketing plays a small role in a monopolistic setting because it is regulated by the state or federal government. Government control usually seeks to ensure price protection for the buyer, although deregulation in recent years has encouraged price competition in the electricity market.[36] Concern that Microsoft's 86 percent share of the PC operating system market is a monopoly has led to lawsuits and consent decrees from the U.S. Justice Department and fines from the European Union.[37]

Components of Competition

In developing a marketing program, companies must consider the factors that drive competition: entry, bargaining power of buyers and suppliers, existing rivalries, and substitution possibilities.[38] Scanning the environment requires a look at all of them. These factors relate to a firm's marketing mix decisions and may be used to create a barrier to entry, increase brand awareness, or intensify a fight for market share.

Entry   In considering the competition, a firm must assess the likelihood of new entrants. Additional producers increase industry capacity and tend to lower prices. A company scanning its environment must consider the possible **barriers to entry** for other firms, which are business practices or conditions that make it difficult for new firms to enter the market. Barriers to entry can be in the form of capital requirements, advertising expenditures, product identity, distribution access, or switching costs. The higher the expense of the barrier, the more likely it will deter new entrants. For example, Lucent Technologies is one of the major suppliers of phone network equipment in the world, and its past customers find it less expensive to upgrade their equipment than switch to another supplier.[39]

Power of Buyers and Suppliers   A competitive analysis must consider the power of buyers and suppliers. Powerful buyers exist when they are few in number, there are low switching costs, or the product represents a significant share of the buyer's total costs. This last factor leads the buyer to exert significant pressure for price competition. A supplier gains power when the product is critical to the buyer and when it has built up the switching costs.

Existing Competitors and Substitutes   Competitive pressures among existing firms depend on the rate of industry growth. In slow-growth settings, competition is more heated for any possible gains in market share. High fixed costs also create competitive pressures for firms to fill production capacity. For example, airlines offer discounts for making early reservations and charge penalties for changes or cancellations in an effort to fill seats, which represent a high fixed cost.

Small Businesses as Competitors

While large companies provide familiar examples of the forms and components of competition, small businesses make up the majority of the competitive landscape for most businesses. Consider that there are approximately 23 million small businesses in the United States, which employ half of all private sector employees. In addition, small businesses generate 60 to 80 percent of all new jobs annually and 50 percent of the gross domestic product (GDP). Research has shown that there is a strong correlation between national economic growth and the level of new small business activity in the previous years.[40]

Concept Check

1. What is the difference between a consumer's disposable and discretionary income?

2. How does technology impact customer value?

3. In pure competition there are a _____ number of sellers.

REGULATORY FORCES

For any organization, the marketing and broader business decisions are constrained, directed, and influenced by regulatory forces. **Regulation** consists of restrictions state and federal laws place on business with regard to the conduct of its activities. Regulation exists to protect companies as well as consumers. Much of the regulation from the federal and state levels is the result of an active political process and has been passed to ensure competition and fair business practices. For consumers, the focus of legislation is to protect them from unfair trade practices and ensure their safety.

Protecting Competition

Major federal legislation has been passed to encourage competition, which is deemed desirable because it permits the consumer to determine which competitor will succeed and which will fail. The first such law was the *Sherman Antitrust Act* (1890). Lobbying by farmers in the Midwest against fixed railroad shipping prices led to the passage of this act, which forbids (1) contracts, combinations, or conspiracies in restraint of trade and (2) actual monopolies or attempts to monopolize any part of trade or commerce. Because of vague wording and government inactivity, however, there was only one successful case against a company in the nine years after the act became law, and the Sherman Act was supplemented with the *Clayton Act* (1914). This act forbids certain actions that are likely to lessen competition, although no actual harm has yet occurred.

In the 1930s, the federal government had to act again to ensure fair competition. During that time, large chain stores appeared, such as the Great Atlantic & Pacific Tea Company (A&P). Small businesses were threatened, and they lobbied for the *Robinson-Patman Act* (1936). This act makes it unlawful to discriminate in prices charged to different purchasers of the same product, where the effect may substantially lessen competition or help to create a monopoly.

Product-Related Legislation

Various federal laws in existence specifically address the product component of the marketing mix. Some are aimed at protecting the company, some at protecting the consumer, and at least one at protecting both.

Company Protection   A company can protect its competitive position in new and novel products under the patent law, which gives inventors the right to exclude others from making, using, or selling products that infringe the patented invention. The federal copyright law is another way for a company to protect its competitive position in a product. The copyright law gives the author of a literary, dramatic, musical, or artistic work the exclusive right to print, perform, or otherwise copy that work. Copyright is secured automatically when the work is created. However, the published work should bear an appropriate copyright notice, including the copyright symbol, the first year of publication, and the name of the copyright owner, and it must be registered under the federal copyright law. Digital technology has necessitated new copyright legislation, called the *Digital Millenium Copyright Act* (1998), to improve protection of copyrighted digital products. In addition, producers of DVD movies, music recordings, and software want protection from devices designed to circumvent antipiracy elements of their products.[41]

Consumer Protection   There are many consumer-oriented federal laws regarding products. The various laws include more than 30 amendments and separate laws relating to food, drugs, and cosmetics, such as the *Infant Formula Act* (1980), the *Nutritional Labeling and Education Act* (1990), new labeling requirements for dietary supplements (1997), and proposed labeling guidelines for trans fats (2006).[42] Various other consumer protection laws have a broader scope, such as the *Fair Packaging and Labeling Act* (1966), the *Child Protection Act* (1966), and the *Consumer Product Safety Act* (1972), which established the Consumer Product Safety Commission to monitor product safety and establish uniform product safety standards. Many of these laws came about because of **consumerism**, a grassroots movement started in the 1960s to increase the influence, power, and rights of consumers

These products are identified by protected trademarks. Are any of these trademarks in danger of becoming generic?

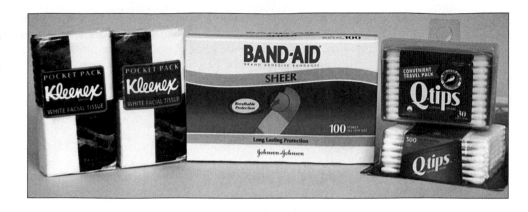

in dealing with institutions. This movement continues and is reflected in growing consumer demands for ecologically safe products, and ethical and socially responsible business practices. One hotly debated issue concerns liability for environmental abuse.

Both Company and Consumer Protection   Trademarks are intended to protect both the firm selling a trademarked product and the consumer buying it. A Senate report states:

> The purposes underlying any trademark statute [are] twofold. One is to protect the public so that it may be confident that, in purchasing a product bearing a particular trademark which it favorably knows, it will get the product which it asks for and wants to get. Secondly, where the owner of a trademark has spent energy, time, and money in presenting to the public the product, he is protected in this investment from misappropriation in pirates and cheats.

This statement was made in connection with another product-related law, the *Lanham Act* (1946), which provides for registration of a company's trademarks. Historically, the first user of a trademark in commerce had the exclusive right to use that particular word, name, or symbol in its business. Registration under the Lanham Act provides important advantages to a trademark owner that has used the trademark in interstate or foreign commerce, but it does not confer ownership. A company can lose its trademark if it becomes generic, which means that it has primarily come to be merely a common descriptive word for the product. Coca-Cola, Whopper, and Xerox are registered trademarks, and competitors cannot use these names. Aspirin and escalator are former trademarks that are now generic terms in the United States and can be used by anyone. In 1988, the *Trademark Law Revision Act* resulted in a major change to the Lanham Act, allowing a company to secure rights to a name before actual use by declaring an intent to use the name.[43] In 2003, the United States agreed to participate in the *Madrid Protocol,* which is a treaty that facilitates the protection of U.S. trademark rights throughout the world.[44]

One of the most recent changes in trademark law is the U.S. Supreme Court's ruling that companies may obtain trademarks for colors associated with their products. The reason is that, over time, consumers may begin to associate a particular color with a specific brand. Examples of products that may benefit from the new law include NutraSweet's sugar substitute in pastel blue packages and Owens-Corning Fiberglas Corporation's pink insulation.[45] Another recent addition to trademark law is the *Federal Dilution Act* (1995), which is used to prevent someone from using a trademark on a noncompeting product (e.g., "Cadillac" brushes).[46]

Pricing-Related Legislation

The pricing component of the marketing mix is the focus of regulation from two perspectives: price fixing and price discounting. Although the Sherman Act did not outlaw price fixing, the courts view this behavior as *per se illegal* (*per se* means "through or of itself"), which means the courts see price fixing itself as illegal.

Certain forms of price discounting are allowed. Quantity discounts are acceptable; that is, buyers can be charged different prices for a product provided there are differences in manufacturing or delivery costs. Promotional allowances or services may be given to buyers on an equal basis proportionate to volume purchased. Also, a firm can meet a competitor's price "in good faith." Legal and regulatory aspects of pricing are covered in more detail in Chapter 14.

Distribution-Related Legislation

The government has four concerns with regard to distribution—earlier referred to as "place" actions in the marketing mix—and the maintenance of competition. The first, *exclusive dealing,* is an arrangement a manufacturer makes with a reseller to handle only its products and not those of competitors. This practice is only illegal under the Clayton Act when it substantially lessens competition.

Requirement contracts require a buyer to purchase all or part of its needs for a product from one seller for a period of time. These contracts are not always illegal but depend on the court's interpretation of their impact on distribution.

Exclusive territorial distributorships are a third distribution issue often under regulatory scrutiny. In this situation, a manufacturer grants a distributor the sole rights to sell a product in a specific geographical area. The courts have found few violations with these arrangements.

The fourth distribution strategy is a *tying arrangement,* whereby a seller requires the purchaser of one product to also buy another item in the line. These contracts may be illegal when the seller has such economic power in the tying product that the seller can restrain trade in the tied product. Legal aspects of distribution are reviewed in greater detail in Chapter 15.

Advertising- and Promotion-Related Legislation

Promotion and advertising are aspects of marketing closely monitored by the Federal Trade Commission (FTC), which was established by the *FTC Act of 1914.* The FTC has been concerned with deceptive or misleading advertising and unfair business practices and has the power to (1) issue cease and desist orders and (2) order corrective advertising. In issuing a *cease and desist order,* the FTC orders a company to stop practices it considers unfair. With *corrective advertising,* the FTC can require a company to spend money on advertising to correct previous misleading ads. The enforcement powers of the FTC are so significant that often just an indication of concern from the commission can cause companies to revise their promotion.

A landmark legal battle regarding deceptive advertising involved the Federal Trade Commission and Campbell Soup Co. It had been Campbell's practice to insert clear glass marbles into the bottom of soup containers used in print advertisements to bring the soup ingredients (e.g., noodles or chicken) to the surface. The FTC ruled that the advertising was deceptive because it misrepresented the amount of solid ingredients in the soup, and it issued a cease and desist order. Campbell and its advertising agency agreed to discontinue the practice. Future ads used a ladle to show the ingredients.[47]

Other laws have been introduced to regulate promotion practices. The *Deceptive Mail Prevention and Enforcement Act* (1999), for example, provides specifications for direct-mail sweepstakes, such as the requirement that the statement "No purchase is necessary to enter" is displayed in the mailing, in the rules, and on the entry form. Similarly, the *Telephone Consumer Protection Act* (1991) provides requirements for telemarketing promotions, including fax promotions. Telemarketing is also subject to a law that created the *National Do Not Call Registry,* which

ETHICS AND SOCIAL RESPONSIBILITY ALERT

Is Telemarketing a First Amendment Right?

ETHICS

The Federal Trade Commission is responsible for managing the National Do Not Call Registry (www.donotcall.gov), the list of telephone numbers that telemarketers must not call. Proponents of the list argue that it will give consumers relief from unwanted telephone solicitations. Others have suggested that the registry violates free speech rights protected under the Constitution. A District Court ruled that the do-not-call list was not legal because it prevented calls from businesses but not charities. More recently, however, the Circuit Court of Appeals ruled that the registry does not violate the First Amendment. Meanwhile, more than 64 million people have placed their numbers on the registry, and 66 million people made purchases in response to telemarketing calls. Many experts believe the Supreme Court will eventually rule on the law. What is your opinion? Is your number on the "do-not-call" or the "call" list?

is a list of consumer phone numbers of people who do not want to receive unsolicited telemarketing calls. See the accompanying Ethics and Social Responsibility Alert for more information about the registry.[48] Finally, new laws such as the *Children's Online Privacy Protection Act* (1998) and the *Controlling the Assault of Non-Solicited Pornography and Marketing (CAN-SPAM) Act* (2004) are designed to restrict information collection and unsolicited e-mail promotions on the Internet.[49]

Control through Self-Regulation

www.bbbonline.com

The government has provided much legislation to create a competitive business climate and protect the consumer. An alternative to government control is **self-regulation**, where an industry attempts to police itself. The major television networks, for example, have used self-regulation to set their own guidelines for TV ads for children's toys. These guidelines have generally worked well. There are two problems with self-regulation, however: noncompliance by members and enforcement. In addition, if attempts at self-regulation are too strong, they may violate the Robinson-Patman Act. The best-known self-regulatory group is the Better Business Bureau (BBB). This agency is a voluntary alliance of companies whose goal is to help maintain fair practices. Although the BBB has no legal power, it does try to use "moral suasion" to get members to comply with its ruling. The BBB recently developed a reliability assurance program, called BBB Online, to provide objective consumer protection for Internet shoppers. Before they display the BBB Online logo on their website, participating companies must be members of their local Better Business Bureau, have been in business for at least one year, have agreed to abide by BBB standards of truth in advertising, and have committed to work with the BBB to resolve consumer disputes that arise over goods or services promoted or advertised on their site.[50]

Concept Check

1. The _____ Act was punitive toward monopolies, whereas the _____ Act was preventive.

2. Describe some of the recent changes in trademark law.

3. How does the Better Business Bureau encourage companies to follow its standards for commerce?

CHAPTER IN REVIEW

1 *Explain how environmental scanning provides information about social, economic, technological, competitive, and regulatory forces.*

Many businesses operate in environments where important forces change. Environmental scanning is the process of acquiring information about these changes to allow marketers to identify and interpret trends. There are five environmental forces businesses must monitor: social, economic, technological, competitive, and regulatory. By identifying trends related to each of these forces businesses can develop and maintain successful marketing programs. Several trends that most businesses are monitoring include the growing diversity of the U.S. population, the increasing use of wireless technology, and new legislation related to intellectual property and privacy.

2 *Describe how social forces such as demographics and culture and economic forces such as macroeconomic conditions and consumer income affect marketing.*

Demographic information describes the world population, the U.S. population, generational cohorts such as baby boomers, Generation X and Generation Y, the structure of the American household, geographic shifts of the population, and the racial and ethnic diversity of the population that has led to multicultural marketing programs. Cultural factors include the trend toward fewer differences in male and female consumer behavior and the impact of values such as "health and fitness" on consumer preferences. Economic forces include the strong relationship between consumers' expectations about the economy and their spending. Gross income has remained stable for more than 30 years although the rate of saving has been declining.

3 *Describe how technological changes can affect marketing.*

Technological innovations can replace existing products and services. Digital cameras, for example, have reduced the need

for film, and music downloading services are changing how consumers buy music. Changes in technology can also have an impact on customer value by reducing the cost of products, improving the quality of products, and providing new products that were not previously feasible. Electronic commerce, including the Wi-Fi revolution, is transforming how companies do business.

4 *Discuss the forms of competition that exist in a market, key components of competition, and the impact of small businesses as competitors.*

There are four forms of competition: pure competition, monopolistic competition, oligopoly, and monopoly. The key components of competition include the likelihood of new competitors, the power of buyers and suppliers, and the presence of competitors and possible substitutes. While large companies are often used as examples of marketplace competitors, there are 23 million small businesses in the United States, which have a significant impact on the economy.

5 *Explain the major legislation that ensures competition and regulates the elements of the marketing mix.*

Regulation exists to protect companies and consumers. Legislation that ensures a competitive marketplace includes the Sherman Antitrust Act. Product-related legislation includes copyright and trademark laws that protect companies and packaging and labeling laws that protect consumers. Pricing- and distribution-related laws are designed to create a competitive marketplace with fair prices and availability. Regulation related to promotion and advertising reduces deceptive practices and provides enforcement through the Federal Trade Commission. Self-regulation through organizations such as the Better Business Bureau provides an alternative to federal and state regulation.

FOCUSING ON KEY TERMS

baby boomers p. 75
barriers to entry p. 87
blended family p. 77
competition p. 85
consumerism p. 88
culture p. 78
demographics p. 74
discretionary income p. 83
disposable income p. 82
economy p. 80
electronic commerce p. 85
environmental scanning p. 72

Extranets p. 85
Generation X p. 75
Generation Y p. 76
gross income p. 81
Intranet p. 85
marketspace p. 85
multicultural marketing p. 78
regulation p. 87
self-regulation p. 91
social forces p. 74
technology p. 83
value consciousness p. 80

DISCUSSION AND APPLICATION QUESTIONS

1 For many years Gerber has manufactured baby food in small, single-sized containers. In conducting an environmental scan, identify three trends or factors that might significantly affect this company's future business, and then propose how Gerber might respond to these changes.

2 Describe the new features you would add to an automobile designed for consumers in the 55+ age group. In

what magazines would you advertise to appeal to this target market?

3 The population shift from suburbs to exurbs and penturbia was discussed in this chapter. What businesses and industries are likely to benefit from this trend? How will retailers need to change to accommodate these consumers?

4 New technologies are continuously improving and re-placing existing products. Although technological change is often difficult to predict, suggest how the following companies and products might be affected by the Internet and digital technologies: (*a*) Kodak cameras and film, (*b*) American Airlines, and (*c*) the Metropolitan Museum of Art.

5 In recent years in the brewing industry, a couple of large firms that have historically had most of the beer sales (Anheuser-Busch and Miller) have faced competition from many small "micro" brands. In terms of the continuum of competition, how would you explain this change?

6 The Johnson Company manufactures buttons and pins with slogans and designs. These pins are inexpensive to produce and are sold in retail outlets such as discount stores, hobby shops, and bookstores. Little equipment is needed for a new competitor to enter the market. What strategies should Johnson consider to create effective barriers to entry?

7 Why would Xerox be concerned about its name becoming generic?

8 Develop a "Code of Business Practices" for a new online vitamin store. Does your code address advertising? Privacy? Use by children? Why is self-regulation important?

GOING ONLINE   Using the Web to Scan the Environment

There are many sources of information that might be useful in an environmental scan. Two particularly useful websites include FEDSTATS (www.fedstats.gov) and the United Nations (www.un.org). The FEDSTATS page links 100 federal agencies, including the U.S. Census Bureau, the Department of Commerce, and the Bureau of Labor Statistics. The United Nations page provides links to its Economic and Social Development division, which supports programs related to population, development trends, statistics, and others.

Use the sites to help answer the following questions:

1 What is the current (to the minute) population of the United States? What is the projected population of the United States in 2050?

2 What population or social trends can be identified with UN information?

BUILDING YOUR MARKETING PLAN

Your marketing plan will include a situation analysis based on internal and external factors that are likely to affect your marketing program.

1 To summarize information about external factors, create a table similar to Figure 3–2 and identify three trends related to each of the five forces (social, eco-nomic, technological, competitive, and regulatory) that relate to your product or service.

2 When your table is completed, describe how each of the trends represents an opportunity or a threat for your business.

VIDEO CASE 3   Flyte Tyme Productions, Inc.: The Best Idea Wins

"Terry was looking for a keyboard player to be in the band he was just starting," remembers Jimmy Jam of Flyte Tyme Productions, Inc. "I had sort of rebelled because I had first thought of myself as a drummer," says Jam. But after he listened and heard how good the drummer was, he told Terry, "I'll be the keyboard player."

The conversation took place a few weeks after Terry Lewis and Jimmy Jam met at a summer math program for gifted junior high school students, sponsored by a local university. The two came to prominence in the early 1980s as members of the funk band "The Time" that appeared as the opener on many of Prince's early tours. The pair still credit Prince for much of their tenacious work ethic and eclectic musical tastes. After leaving the band, Terry and Jimmy started a music production company—Flyte Tyme—creating the new name by adapting the old one. Now in their early 40s, the two have worked together for 20 years, most of it in Flyte Tyme Productions (www.flytetyme.com), where their clients include Mary J. Blige, Boyz II Men, Mariah Carey, Aretha Franklin, Janet Jackson, Patti LaBelle, Usher, TLC, and many others.

THE MUSIC

Sunglasses, fedoras, and sharp suits are Jam and Lewis's signature image, but—curiously—they have no signature sound. Instead, their approach is to tailor tunes for each artist. Janet Jackson's steamy ballads don't sound

anything like Patti LaBelle's big Diane Warren ballads. They also work in a wide variety of music genres—from gospel (Yolanda Adams) and country (Rissi Palmer) to jazz (Herb Alpert) and pop (Mariah Carey).

Flyte Tyme's successes are impressive. They produced Usher's no. 1 pop hit "U Remind Me," which held the top spot on the charts for four weeks. They also produced an album for Japanese pop star, Hikaru Utada, which climbed to the top of Japan's pop charts, selling 4 million copies in two weeks. And then there are projects like creating music for the NBA All-Star game!

These and other hits put Flyte Tyme in extraordinary company. Having produced 16 no. 1 singles on *Billboard*'s pop chart, they are second only to the producer for the Beatles (with 23) and tied with the producer for Elvis Presley. Flyte Tyme has also produced more than 40 Top-10 hits and more than 100 albums that have reached gold, platinum, and multi-platinum status. They are three-time Grammy winners for Producer of the Year, Best R&B Song, and Best Dance Recording. Most recently they have been nominated for the fourth consecutive year for Producer of the Year. In an industry where consumers' preferences, technology, competition, and the regulatory environment change at an extraordinary pace, Flyte Tyme has managed to stay on top for more than 20 years!

THE TEAM AND ITS FORMULA FOR SUCCESS

How have Jam and Lewis stayed at the top of the music game so long? Janet Jackson's answer: "There are no egos involved." Terry Lewis echoes this and says about his relationship with Jam: "He's the best partner a person could have. We've never had a contract—we've never had one argument in twenty-something years, not saying we don't disagree about things but our attitudes are the *best* idea wins. Not the right, not the wrong, but the *best*!"

"What we try to do is get everybody relaxed—check the egos at the door, that kind of thing. We find that we do

it a lot more with new artists than with the older, more established artists," explains Jam. "Psychology is a big part of producing. Some artists like to work right away, others like to play pool, have lunch, talk on the phone, then they mosey in and record," he says. "If you think of Janet Jackson or Mariah Carey—the people who you would think of as superstars, you would think that they would bring a superstar ego with them. But it's almost the opposite," says Jam. "New artists often come to Flyte Tyme with a feeling they have to prove something. And what happens is, you don't really get a natural performance," says Jam.

Another of Flyte Tyme's special strengths: adapting the music and lyrics to an artist's unique talents, not the other way around. Their interest in many types of music and their experience with many artists allow them to add new ideas to the creative process. Still, Flyte Tyme may work on several different versions based on its perceptions of what radio stations or MTV will play.

Jam and Lewis work on both the music and lyrics for many of their songs, but Jam leans slightly more toward the melodies and Lewis toward the vocals and lyrics. In fact, Lewis keeps "The Book of Titles," and any time someone says something clever or in an interesting way it goes into the book. "Music is the soundtrack of life," says Lewis. "The inspiration for words I just take from watching people, and life has a lot of verses in it," he adds.

MARKETING, DISTRIBUTION, COMPETITION

Selecting the best music ideas requires an instinct to find the right blend of art and business. The elements of the art include a huge respect for and understanding of the artists, an interest in a broad palette of musical sounds, and a good ear for melodies and vocals. The business components of their formula include understanding many of the factors—such as consumers, technology, and competition—that influence their business.

Music artists walking in the door of Flyte Tyme receive an array of services: a studio facility with Jam, Lewis, and an experienced staff providing ideas, direction, and focus—"trying to get things out of them they didn't know they had in them," says Lewis. Flyte Tyme Records, the marketing arm, develops the artist's image, the marketing plan, advertising, and distribution—everything to get the record or CD on the rack to be sold. "If you have $100,000 to spend on promotion, you can

do a nice music video and then you can spend a lot of time trying to get it played on MTV or BET or VH1 or any of the appropriate video channels," says Jam. Or sometimes the music calls for a different strategy, Flyte Tyme's "groundhog approach." For example, in the early 1990s with one of its bands, Flyte Tyme piled the band in a Winnebago and hit college campuses.

Today, Flyte Tyme creates a lot of that same groundhog buzz with its website, where the music audience can learn about Flyte Tyme's artists and activities. Jam and Lewis note that the new fee-based online music services are a great tool for providing the public access to music. In addition, while the delivery system—buying a CD at a retail store, downloading music from the Internet, or burning a CD—doesn't affect the process of Flyte Tyme's making the music in the studio, adapting to the environmental changes is important. "Change doesn't frighten us," says Lewis, "and we change with time."

Questions

1   Based on the case information and what you know about today's music industry, conduct an environmental scan for Flyte Tyme to identify key trends. For each of the five environmental forces (social, economic, technological, competitive, and regulatory), identify trends likely to influence it in the near future.

2   About 80 percent of start-up businesses fail within five years. What reasons explain Flyte Tyme's continuing success?

3   What marketing factors and actions must Jimmy Jam and Terry Lewis consider in developing music (*a*) for a new, unknown artist and (*b*) an established artist like Janet Jackson?

4   What promotional and distribution strategies should Flyte Tyme use to get its music in front of prospective buyers?

MUSIC? UNLIKELY.

But you can influence your kids' decisions about drinking.

Kids do listen to parents about some things. In fact, on the subject of underage drinking, kids consider parents their number one influence*. Use that influence while you can. Talk to your kids about underage drinking now. For a free 'Family Talk' guide, visit familytalkonline.com or call 1-800-359-TALK.

RESPONSIBILITY MATTERS™
ANHEUSER-BUSCH, INC.

*73% of 8-17 year olds, 2003 Roper Youth Report.

CHAPTER

4 ETHICS AND SOCIAL RESPONSIBILITY IN MARKETING

LEARNING OBJECTIVES

After reading this chapter you should be able to:

1 Explain the differences between legal and ethical behavior in marketing.

2 Identify factors that influence ethical and unethical marketing decisions.

3 Describe the different concepts of social responsibility.

4 Recognize unethical and socially irresponsible consumer behavior.

THERE IS MORE BREWING AT ANHEUSER-BUSCH THAN BEER

Why would a company spend more than $430 million since 1982 trying to convince people not to abuse its products and millions more to decrease litter and solid waste? Ask Anheuser-Busch, the world's largest brewer.

Anheuser-Busch has been an advocate for responsible drinking for almost 25 years. The company began an aggressive campaign to fight alcohol abuse and underage drinking with its landmark "Know When to Say When" campaign in 1982. In 1989, a Consumer Awareness and Education Department was established within the company. This department was charged with developing and implementing programs, advertising and partnerships that promote responsible drinking, helping prevent alcohol abuse, and helping stop underage drinking before it starts. For example, more than 5.3 million copies of the company's *Family Talk about Drinking* guidebook have been distributed free to parents and educators in the past decade. In 1999, the brewer began a new chapter in its awareness and education efforts with the launch of its "We All Make a Difference" advertising campaign. This effort reinforced the good practices of drinkers who exercise personal responsibility, designate a driver or call a cab, and salutes parents who talk to their children about illegal underage drinking. Anheuser-Busch believes these efforts have contributed to a 37 percent decline in drunk-driving fatalities and a 61 percent drop in teenage drunk-driving deaths since 1982.

Responsibility at Anheuser-Busch is broader than its successful alcohol awareness and education initiatives. The company is an advocate and sponsor of numerous efforts to preserve the natural environment. A notable example is its massive recycling effort through

Anheuser-Busch Recycling Corporation (ABRC). ABRC is the world's largest recycler of aluminum cans. ABRC recycles over 685 million pounds of aluminum annually, the equivalent of about 130 percent of the beer cans Anheuser-Busch ships domestically. The rationale for founding ABRC was simple: Voluntary recycling reduces litter and solid waste while conserving natural resources.

Anheuser-Busch acts on what it views as an ethical obligation to its customers and the general public with its alcohol awareness and education programs. At the same time, the company's efforts to protect the environment reflect its broader social responsibility.[1]

NATURE AND SIGNIFICANCE OF MARKETING ETHICS

Ethics are the moral principles and values that govern the actions and decisions of an individual or group.[2] They serve as guidelines on how to act rightly and justly when faced with moral dilemmas.

Ethical/Legal Framework in Marketing

A good starting point for understanding the nature and significance of ethics is the distinction between legality and ethicality of marketing decisions. Figure 4–1 helps visualize the relationship between laws and ethics.[3] Whereas ethics deal with personal moral principles and values, **laws** are society's values and standards that are enforceable in the courts. This distinction can sometimes lead to the rationalization that if a behavior is within reasonable ethical and legal limits, then it is not really illegal or unethical. When a recent survey asked the question, "Is it OK to get around the law if you don't actually break it?" 61 percent of businesspeople who took part responded 'yes.'[4] How would you answer this question?

There are numerous situations in which judgment plays a large role in defining ethical and legal boundaries. Consider the following situations. After reading each, assign it to the cell in Figure 4–1 that you think best fits the situation along the ethical–legal continuum.[5]

1. More than 70 percent of the physicians in the Maricopa County (Arizona) Medical Society agreed to establish a maximum fee schedule for health services to curb rising medical costs. All physicians were required to adhere to this schedule as a condition for membership in the society. The U.S. Supreme Court ruled that this agreement to set prices violated the Sherman Act and represented price fixing, which is illegal.

2. A company in California sells a computer program to auto dealers showing that car buyers should finance their purchase rather than paying cash. The program omits the effect of income taxes and misstates the interest earned on savings over the loan period. The finance option always provides a net benefit over the cash option. Company employees agree that the program does mislead buyers, but say the company will "provide what [car dealers] want as long as it is not against the law."

3. China is the world's largest tobacco-producing country and has 300 million smokers. Approximately 700,000 Chinese die annually from smoking-related illnesses. This figure is expected to rise to more than 2 million by 2025. China restricts tobacco imports. U.S. trade negotiators advocate free trade, thus allowing U.S. tobacco companies to market their products in China. Critics say that the U.S. government should not assist in the promotion of smoking in China.

Did these situations fit neatly into Figure 4–1 as clearly ethical and legal or unethical and illegal? Probably not. As you read further in this chapter, you will be asked to consider other ethical dilemmas.

FIGURE 4–1
Classifying marketing
decisions according to ethical
and legal relationships

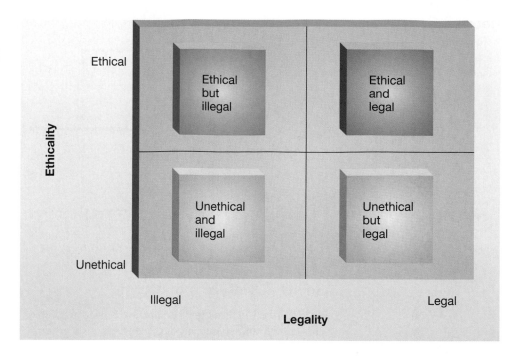

Current Perceptions of Ethical Behavior

There has been a public outcry about the ethical practices of businesspeople.[6] Public opinion surveys show that 58 percent of U.S. adults rate the ethical standards of business executives as only "fair" or "poor"; 90 percent think white-collar crime is "very common" or "somewhat common"; 76 percent say the lack of ethics in businesspeople contributes to tumbling societal moral standards; only the U.S. government is viewed as less trustworthy than corporations among institutions in the United States; and advertising practitioners, telemarketers, and car salespeople are thought to be among the least ethical occupations. Surveys of corporate employees generally confirm this public perception. When asked if they were aware of ethical problems in their companies, a third say, "yes."

There are at least four possible reasons the state of perceived ethical business conduct is at its present level. First, there is increased pressure on businesspeople to make decisions in a society characterized by diverse value systems. Second, there is a growing tendency for business decisions to be judged publicly by groups with different values and interests. Third, the public's expectations of ethical business behavior has increased. Finally, and most disturbing, ethical business conduct may have declined.

Concept Check

1. What are ethics?

2. What are four possible reasons for the present state of ethical conduct in the United States?

UNDERSTANDING ETHICAL MARKETING BEHAVIOR

Researchers have identified numerous factors that influence ethical marketing behavior.[7] Figure 4–2 on the next page presents a framework that shows these factors and their relationships.

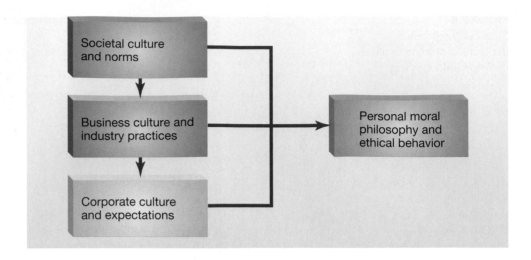

Societal Culture and Norms

As described in Chapter 3, *culture* refers to the set of values, ideas, and attitudes that are learned and shared among members of a group. Culture also serves as a socializing force that dictates what is morally right and just. This means that moral standards are relative to particular societies.[8] These standards often reflect the laws and regulations that affect social and economic behavior, which can create moral dilemmas. For example, Levi Strauss decided to end much of its business dealings in China because of what the company called "pervasive human rights abuses." According to its vice president for corporate marketing: "There are wonderful commercial opportunities in China. But when ethical issues collide with commercial appeal, we try to ensure ethics as the trump card. For us, ethical issues precede all others."[9]

Societal values and attitudes also affect ethical and legal relationships among individuals, groups, and business institutions and organizations. Consider the copying of another's copyright, trademark, or patent. These are viewed as intellectual property. Unauthorized use, reproduction, or distribution of intellectual property is illegal in the United States and most countries and can result in fines and prison terms of perpetrators. The owners of intellectual property also lose. For example, annual lost sales from the theft of intellectual property amount of $22 billion in the music industry, $3.5 billion in the movie industry, and $15 billion in the software industry.[10] Lost sales, in turn, result in lost jobs, royalties, wages, and tax revenue. But what about a person downloading copyrighted music and movies over the Internet or from peer-to-peer file-sharing programs, without paying the owner of this property? Is this an ethical or unethical act? It depends on who you ask. Surveys of the U.S. public indicate that the majority consider such acts unethical. The accompanying Marketing NewsNet describes college student views on the ethicality of downloading music and movies.[11]

Business Culture and Industry Practices

Societal culture provides a foundation for understanding moral behavior in business activities. *Business cultures* "comprise the effective rules of the game, the boundaries between competitive and unethical behavior, [and] the codes of conduct in business dealings."[12] Consumers have witnessed numerous instances where business cultures in the brokerage (inside trading), insurance (deceptive sales practices), and defense (bribery) industries went awry. Business culture affects ethical conduct both in the exchange relationship between sellers and buyers and in the competitive behavior among sellers.

Ethics of Exchange   The exchange process is central to the marketing concept. Ethical exchanges between sellers and buyers should result in both parties being better off after a transaction.

MARKETING NEWSNET

Internet Piracy and Campus Pirates

TECHNOLOGY & E-COMMERCE

Have you ever downloaded music or a movie from the Internet or from a peer-to-peer file-sharing program such as Kazaa or Morpheus without paying for it? This question was recently posed to a random sample of 1,000 U.S. college and university students. The findings described below may or may not surprise you.

Not surprisingly, most students (69 percent) download music. A smaller number (26 percent) download movies. For those students who download music, 92 percent admit to never or seldom paying for the copies they made. For students who download movies, 96 percent say they never or seldom pay for the copies made. In a related finding, 76 percent of students say it is okay to download music and movies from unauthorized sources to save money.

Downloading music and movies from unauthorized sources is illegal and unethical. The cost of a CD or the price of a movie ticket or rental seems small compared with the legal and ethical ramifications.

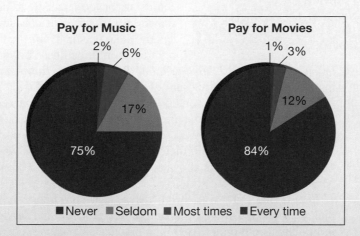

Q. How often do you pay for the music that you download? *Asked only of those who have downloaded music from the Internet.*

Q. How often do you pay for the movies that you download? *Asked only of those who have downloaded a movie from the Internet.*

Prior to the 1960s, the legal concept of **caveat emptor**—let the buyer beware—was pervasive in the American business culture. In 1962, President John F. Kennedy outlined a **Consumer Bill of Rights** that codified the ethics of exchange between buyers and sellers. These were the right (1) to safety, (2) to be informed, (3) to choose, and (4) to be heard. Consumers expect and often demand that these rights be protected, as have American businesses.

The right to safety manifests itself in industry and federal safety standards for most products sold in the United States. In fact, the U.S. Consumer Product Safety Commission routinely monitors the safety of 15,000 consumer products. However, even the most vigilant efforts to ensure safe products cannot foresee every possibility. Mattel's experience with its Cabbage Patch Snacktime Kids doll is a case in point.[13] The doll was designed to "eat" plastic french fries, celery, and other tidbits by drawing them into its motorized mouth. Despite exhaustive laboratory and in-home testing, Mattel executives did not consider that a child's hair might get caught in the doll's mouth and cause harm. It did! Mattel immediately informed buyers of the safety issue, pulled the dolls from store shelves, refunded buyers, and discontinued the product.

The Federal Trade Commission plays an active role in educating consumers and businesses about the importance of personal information privacy on the Internet. FTC initiatives are detailed on its website.

Federal Trade Commission
www.ftc.gov

The right to be informed means that marketers have an obligation to give consumers complete and accurate information about products and services, but this is not always the case. For example, three U.S. advertising agencies recently agreed to settle Federal Trade Commission (FTC) claims that they failed to disclose the actual costs of car leases and credit transactions in their advertising for three Japanese carmakers.[14] This right also applies to the solicitation of personal information over the Internet and its subsequent use by marketers.[15] A FTC survey of websites indicated that 92 percent collect personal information such as consumer e-mail addresses, telephone numbers, shopping habits, and financial data. Yet, only two-thirds of websites inform consumers of what is done with this information once obtained. The FTC wants more than posted privacy notices that merely inform consumers of a company's data-use policy, which critics say are often vague, confusing, or too legalistic to be understood. This view is shared by two-thirds of consumers who worry about protecting their personal information online. The consumer right to be informed has spawned numerous federal legislation, such as the *Children's Online Privacy Protection Act* (1998), and self-regulation initiatives restricting disclosure of personal information.

Relating to the right to choose, today many supermarket chains demand "slotting allowances" from manufacturers, in the form of cash or free goods, to stock new products.[16] This practice could limit the number of new products available to consumers and interfere with their right to choose. One critic of this practice remarked, "If we had had slotting allowances a few years ago, we might not have had granola, herbal tea, or yogurt."

Finally, the right to be heard means that consumers should have access to public-policy makers regarding complaints about products and services. This right is illustrated in limitations put on telemarketing practices. Consumer complaints about latenight and repeated calls resulted in the Telephone Consumer Protection Act of 1991. The FTC established the Do Not Call Registry in 2003 for consumers who do not want to receive unsolicited telemarketing calls. More than 64 million consumers have their telephone numbers listed in the registry, which is managed by the FTC. A telemarketer can be fined $11,000 for each call made to a telephone number posted on the registry.

Ethics of Competition   Business culture also affects ethical behavior in competition. Two kinds of unethical behavior are most common: (1) economic espionage and (2) bribery.

Economic espionage is the clandestine collection of trade secrets or proprietary information about a company's competitors. This practice is illegal and unethical and carries serious criminal penalties for the offending individual or business. Espionage activities include illegal trespassing, theft, fraud, misrepresentation, wiretapping, the search of a competitor's trash, and violations of written and implicit employment agreements with noncompete clauses. About 56 percent of the largest firms in the United States have uncovered espionage in some form, costing them $200 billion annually in lost sales.[17]

Economic espionage is most prevalent in high-technology industries, such as electronics, specialty chemicals, industrial equipment, aerospace, and pharmaceuticals, where technical know-how and trade secrets separate industry leaders from followers. But espionage can occur anywhere—even in the ready-to-eat cookie industry! Procter & Gamble charged that competitors photographed its plants and production lines, stole a sample of its cookie dough, and infiltrated a confidential sales presentation

WEB LINK   The Corruption Perceptions Index

Bribery as a means to win and retain business varies widely by country. Transparency International periodically polls employees of multinational firms and institutions and political analysts and ranks countries on the basis of their perceived level of bribery to win or retain business. To obtain the most recent ranking, visit the Transparency International website at www.transparency.org and click "Site Shortcuts for the Corruption Perceptions Index."

Scroll the Corruption Perceptions Index to see where the United States stands in the worldwide rankings as well as its neighbors, Canada and Mexico. Any surprises? Which country listed in the most recent ranking has the highest ranking and which has the lowest ranking?

to learn about its technology, recipe, and marketing plan. The competitors paid Procter & Gamble $120 million in damages after a lengthy dispute.[18]

The second form of unethical competitive behavior is giving and receiving bribes and kickbacks. Bribes and kickbacks are often disguised as gifts, consultant fees, and favors. This practice is more common in business-to-business and government marketing than in consumer marketing. For example, two American Honda Motor Company executives were fined and sentenced to prison for extracting $15 million in kickbacks from Honda dealers and advertising agencies, and a series of highly publicized trials uncovered widespread bribery in the U.S. Defense Department's awarding of $160 billion in military contracts.[19]

In general, bribery is most evident in industries experiencing intense competition and in countries in earlier stages of economic development. According to a recent United Nations' study, 15 percent of all companies in industrialized countries have to pay bribes to win or retain business. In Asia, this figure is 40 percent. In Eastern Europe, 60 percent of all companies must pay bribes to do business. A recent poll of senior executives engaged in global marketing revealed that Bangladesh and Nigeria were the most likely countries to evidence bribery to win or retain business. Iceland and Finland were the least likely.[20] Bribery on a worldwide scale is monitored by Transparency International. Visit its website described in the accompanying Web Link, and view the most recent country rankings on this practice.

The prevalence of economic espionage and bribery in international marketing has prompted laws to curb these practices. Two significant laws, the *Economic Espionage Act* (1996) and the *Foreign Corrupt Practices Act* (1977), address these practices in the United States. Both are detailed in Chapter 7.

Corporate Culture and Expectations

A third influence on ethical practices is corporate culture. *Corporate culture* is a set of values, ideas, and attitudes that is learned and shared among the members of an organization. The culture of a company demonstrates itself in the dress ("We don't wear tics"), sayings ("The IBM Way"), and manner of work (team efforts) of employees. Culture is also apparent in the expectations for ethical behavior present in formal codes of ethics and the ethical actions of top management and co-workers.

Codes of Ethics   A **code of ethics** is a formal statement of ethical principles and rules of conduct. It is estimated that 80 percent of U.S. companies have

American Marketing Association Code of Ethics

Preamble

The American Marketing Association commits itself to promoting the highest standard of professional ethical norms and values for its members. Norms are established standards of conduct that are expected and maintained by society and/or professional organizations. Values represent the collective conception of what people find desirable, important and morally proper. Values serve as the criteria for evaluating the actions of others. Marketing practitioners must recognize that they not only serve their enterprises but also act as stewards of society in creating, facilitating and executing the efficient and effective transactions that are part of the greater economy. In this role, marketers should embrace the highest ethical *norms* of practicing professionals and the ethical *values* implied by their responsibility toward stakeholders (e.g., customers, employees, investors, channel members, regulators and the host community).

General Norms

1. Marketers must do no harm. This means doing work for which they are appropriately trained or experienced so that they can actively add value to their organizations and customers. It also means adhering to all applicable laws and regulations and embodying high ethical standards in the choices they make.
2. Marketers must foster trust in the marketing system. This means that products are appropriate for their intended and promoted uses. It requires that marketing communications about goods and services are not intentionally deceptive or misleading. It suggests building relationships that provide for the equitable

adjustment and/or redress of customer grievances. It implies striving for good faith and fair dealing so as to contribute toward the efficacy of the exchange process.

3. Marketers must embrace, communicate and practice the fundamental ethical values that will improve consumer confidence in the integrity of the marketing exchange system. These basic *values* are intentionally aspirational and include honesty, responsibility, fairness, respect, openness and citizenship.

Ethical Values

Honesty—to be truthful and forthright in our dealings with customers and stakeholders.

- We will tell the truth in all situations and at all times.
- We will offer products of value that do what we claim in our communications.
- We will stand behind our products if they fail to deliver their claimed benfits.
- We will honor our explicit and implicit commitments and promises.

Responsibility—to accept the consequences of our marketing decisions and strategies.

- We will make strenuous efforts to serve the needs of our customers.
- We will avoid using coercion with all stakeholders.
- We will acknowledge the social obligations to stakeholders that come with increased marketing and economic power.
- We will recognize our special commitments to economically vulnerable segments of the market such as children, the elderly and others who may be substantially disadvantaged.

FIGURE 4–3

American Marketing Association Code of Ethics

American Marketing Association

www.marketingpower.com

some sort of ethics code and one of every five large companies has corporate ethics officers. At United Technologies, for example, 160 corporate ethics officers distribute the company's ethics code, translated into 24 languages, to employees who work for this defense and engineering giant around the world.[21] Ethics codes and committees typically address contributions to government officials and political parties, relations with customers and suppliers, conflicts of interest, and accurate recordkeeping. For example, General Mills provides guidelines for dealing with suppliers, competitors, and customers, and recruits new employees who share these views. However, an ethics code is rarely enough to ensure ethical behavior. Coca-Cola has an ethics code and emphasizes that its employees be ethical in their behavior. But that did not stop some Coca-Cola employees from rigging the results of a test market for a frozen soft drink to win Burger King's business. Coca-Cola subsequently agreed to pay Burger King and its operators more than $20 million to settle the matter.[22]

The lack of specificity is one of the major reasons for the violation of ethics codes. Employees must often judge whether a specific behavior is really unethical. The American Marketing Association has addressed this issue by providing a detailed code of ethics, which all members agree to follow. This code is shown in Figure 4–3.

Ethical Behavior of Top Management and Co-Workers   A second reason for violating ethics codes rests in the perceived behavior of top management and co-workers.[23] Observing peers and top management and gauging

FIGURE 4–3
(Continued)

Fairness—to try to balance justly the needs of the buyer with the interests of the seller.

- We will represent our products in a clear way in selling, advertising and other forms of communication; this includes the avoidance of false, misleading and deceptive promotion.
- We will reject manipulations and sales tactics that harm customer trust.
- We will not engage in price fixing, predatory pricing, price gouging or "bait-and-switch" tactics.
- We will not knowingly participate in material conflicts of interest.

Respect—to acknowledge the basic human dignity of all stakeholders.

- We will value individual differences even as we avoid stereotyping customers or depicting demographic groups (e.g., gender, race, sexual orientation) in a negative or dehumanizing way in our promotions.
- We will listen to the needs of our customers and make all reasonable efforts to monitor and improve their satisfaction on an ongoing basis.
- We will make a special effort to understand suppliers, intermediaries and distributors from other cultures.
- We will appropriately acknowledge the contributions of others, such as consultants, employees and coworkers, to our marketing endeavors.

Openness—to create transparency in our marketing operations.

- We will strive to communicate clearly with all our constituencies.
- We will accept constructive criticism from our customers and other stakeholders.
- We will explain significant product or service risks, component substitutions or other foreseeable eventualities that could affect customers or their perception of the purchase decision.
- We will fully disclose list prices and terms of financing as well as available price deals and adjustments.

Citizenship—to fulfill the economic, legal, philanthropic and societal responsibilities that serve stakeholders in a strategic manner.

- We will strive to protect the natural environment in the execution of marketing campaigns.
- We will give back to the community through volunteerism and charitable donations.
- We will work to contribute to the overall betterment of marketing and its reputation.
- We will encourage supply chain members to ensure that trade is fair for all participants, including producers in developing countries.

Implementation

Finally, we recognize that every industry sector and marketing subdiscipline (e.g., marketing research, e-commerce, direct selling, direct marketing, advertising) has its own specific ethical issues that require policies and commentary. An array of such codes can be accessed through links on the AMA web site. We encourage all such groups to develop and/or refine their industry and discipline-specific codes of ethics to supplement these general norms and values.

responses to unethical behavior play an important role in individual actions. A study of business executives reported that 40 percent had been implicitly or explicitly rewarded for engaging in ethically troubling behavior. Moreover, 31 percent of those who refused to engage in unethical behavior were penalized, either through outright punishment or a diminished status in the company.[24] Clearly, ethical dilemmas often bring personal and professional conflict. For this reason, numerous states have laws protecting **whistle-blowers**, employees who report unethical or illegal actions of their employers. Some firms, such as General Dynamics and Dun & Bradstreet, have appointed ethics officers responsible for safeguarding these individuals from recrimination.

Personal Moral Philosophy and Ethical Behavior

Ultimately, ethical choices are based on the personal moral philosophy of the decision maker. Moral philosophy is learned through the process of socialization with friends and family and by formal education. It is also influenced by the societal, business, and corporate culture in which a person finds him- or herself. Two prominent personal moral philosophies have direct bearing on marketing practice: (1) moral idealism and (2) utilitarianism.[25]

Moral Idealism   **Moral idealism** is a personal moral philosophy that considers certain individual rights or duties as universal, regardless of the outcome. This

philosophy exists in the Consumer Bill of Rights and is favored by moral philosophers and consumer interest groups. For example, the right to know applies to probable defects in an automobile that relate to safety.

This philosophy also applies to ethical duties. A fundamental ethical duty is to do no harm. Adherence to this duty prompted the recent decision by 3M executives to phase out production of a chemical 3M had manufactured for nearly 40 years. The substance, used in far-ranging products from pet food bags, candy wrappers, carpeting, and 3M's popular Scotchgard fabric protector, had no known harmful health or environmental effect. However, the company discovered that the chemical appeared in miniscule amounts in humans and animals around the world and accumulated in tissue. Believing that the substance could be possibly harmful in large doses, 3M voluntarily stopped its production acknowledging that the outcome of this action was a potential loss of $500 million in annual sales.[26]

Utilitarianism   An alternative perspective on moral philosophy is **utilitarianism**, which is a personal moral philosophy that focuses on "the greatest good for the greatest number," by assessing the costs and benefits of the consequences of ethical behavior. If the benefits exceed the costs, then the behavior is ethical. If not, then the behavior is unethical. This philosophy underlies the economic tenets of capitalism and, not surprisingly, is embraced by many business executives and students.[27]

Utilitarian reasoning was apparent in Nestlé Food Corporation's marketing of Good Start infant formula, sold by Nestlé's Carnation Company. The formula, promoted as hypoallergenic, was designed to prevent or reduce colic caused by an infant's allergic reaction to cow's milk, a condition suffered by 2 percent of babies. However, some severely milk-allergic infants experienced serious side effects after using Good Start, including convulsive vomiting. Physicians and parents charged that the hypoallergenic claim was misleading, and the Food and Drug Administration investigated the matter. A Nestlé vice president defended the claim and product, saying, "I don't understand why our product should work in 100 percent of cases. If we wanted to say it was foolproof, we would have called it allergy-free. We call it hypo-, or less, allergenic."[28] Nestlé officials seemingly believed that most allergic infants would benefit from Good Start—"the greatest good for the greatest number." However, other views prevailed, and the claim was dropped from the product label.

An appreciation for the nature of ethics, coupled with a basic understanding of why unethical behavior arises, alerts a person to when and how ethical issues exist in marketing decisions. Ultimately, ethical behavior rests with the individual, but the consequences affect many.

Concept Check

1. What rights are included in the Consumer Bill of Rights?

2. Economic espionage includes what kinds of activities?

3. What is meant by moral idealism?

UNDERSTANDING SOCIAL RESPONSIBILITY IN MARKETING

As we saw in Chapter 1, the societal marketing concept stresses marketing's social responsibility by not only satisfying the needs of consumers but also providing for society's welfare. **Social responsibility** means that organizations are part of a larger society and are accountable to that society for their actions. Like ethics, agreement on the nature and scope of social responsibility is often difficult to come by, given the diversity of values present in different societal, business, and corporate cultures.

Concepts of Social Responsibility

Figure 4–4 shows three concepts of social responsibility: (1) profit responsibility, (2) stakeholder responsibility, and (3) societal responsibility.

Profit Responsibility   *Profit responsibility* holds that companies have a simple duty: to maximize profits for their owners or stockholders. This view is expressed by Nobel Laureate Milton Friedman, who said, "There is one and only one social responsibility of business—to use its resources and engage in activities designed to increase its profits so long as it stays within the rules of the game, which is to say, engages in open and free competition without deception or fraud."[29] Genzyme, the maker of Cerezyme, a drug that treats a genetic illness called Gaucher's disease that affects 20,000 people worldwide, has been criticized for apparently adopting this view in its pricing practices. Genzyme charges up to $170,000 for a year's worth of Cerezyme. A Genzyme spokesperson responded saying the company spends about $150 million annually to manufacture Cerezyme and freely gives the drug to patients without insurance. Also, the company invested considerable dollars in research over several years to develop Cerezyme, and the drug's profits are reinvested in ongoing R&D programs.[30]

Stakeholder Responsibility   Criticism of the profit view has led to a broader concept of social responsibility. *Stakeholder responsibility* focuses on the obligations an organization has to those who can affect achievement of its objectives. These constituencies include consumers, employees, suppliers, and distributors. Source Perrier S.A., the supplier of Perrier bottled water, exercised this responsibility when it recalled 160 million bottles of water in 120 countries after traces of a toxic chemical were found in 13 bottles. The recall cost the company $35 million, and $40 million more in lost sales. Even though the chemical level was not harmful to humans, Source Perrier's president believed he acted in the best interests of the firm's consumers, distributors, and employees by removing "the least doubt, as minimal as it might be, to weigh on the image of the quality and purity of our product"—which it did.[31]

FIGURE 4–4

Three concepts of social responsibility

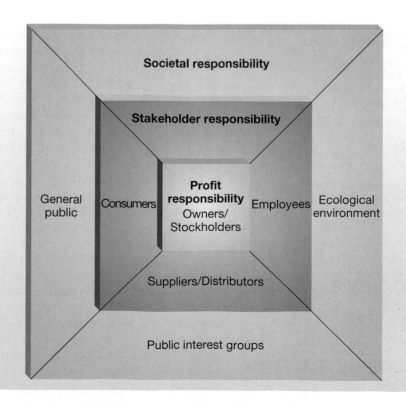

Failure to consider a company's broader constituencies can have negative consequences. For example, Bridgestone/Firestone, Inc., executives were widely criticized for how they responded to complaints about the safety of selected Firestone-brand tires. These tires had been linked to crashes that killed at least 174 people and injured more than 700 in the United States. In 2000, the company recalled 6.5 million tires under pressure from the National Highway Traffic Administration. After the recall, Firestone tire sales fell by nearly one-half, which affected Firestone employees, suppliers, and distributors as well. Ford Motor Company, a large buyer of Firestone tires, ended its exclusive contract with the tire producer.[32]

Societal Responsibility   An even broader concept of social responsibility has emerged in recent years. *Societal responsibility* refers to obligations that organizations have (1) to the preservation of the ecological environment and (2) to the general public. Concerns about the environment and public welfare are represented by interest and advocacy groups such as Greenpeace, an international environmental organization.

Chapter 3 detailed the importance of ecological issues in marketing. Companies have responded to this concern through what is termed **green marketing**—marketing efforts to produce, promote, and reclaim environmentally sensitive products.

Green marketing takes many forms.[33] At 3M, product development opportunities emanate both from consumer research and its "Pollution Prevention Pays" program. This program solicits employee suggestions on how to reduce pollution and recycle materials. Since 1975, this program has generated almost 5,000 ideas that eliminated more than 1.7 billion pounds of air, water, and solid-waste pollutants from the environment. Xerox's "Design for the Environment" program focuses on ways to make its equipment recyclable and remanufacturable. Today, 90 percent of Xerox-designed products are remanufacturable. This effort has kept more than 1.4 billion pounds of equipment from being discarded in U.S. landfills since 1991. Boise Cascade, a leading North American timber manufacturer and Lowe's and Home Depot, two home-and-garden center retail chains, have discontinued the sale of wood products from the world's endangered forests. FedEx and UPS are converting their delivery trucks with standard diesel engines to more fuel-efficient and cleaner technologies, such as hybrid electric vehicles. These vehicles can cut fuel costs by half and lower fuel emissions by 90 percent. These voluntary responses to environmental issues have been implemented with little or no additional cost to consumers and actually resulted in cost savings to companies.

A global undertaking to further green marketing efforts is the ISO 14000 initiative developed by the International Standards Organization (ISO) in Geneva, Switzerland. **ISO 14000** consists of worldwide standards for environmental quality and green marketing practices. These standards are embraced by 118 countries, including the United States, members of the European Union, and many Pacific Rim nations. More than 53,000 companies have met ISO 14000 standards for environmental quality and green marketing. About 23 percent of all ISO 14000 certified companies are Japanese firms, making Japan a world leader in environmental protection.[34]

Socially responsible efforts on behalf of the general public are becoming more common. A formal practice is **cause marketing**, which occurs when the charitable contributions of a firm are tied directly to the customer revenues produced through the promotion of one of its products.[35] This definition distinguishes cause marketing from a firm's standard charitable contributions, which are outright donations. For example, Procter & Gamble raises funds for the Special Olympics when consumers purchase selected company products, and MasterCard International links usage of its card with fund raising for institutions that combat cancer, heart disease, child abuse, drug abuse, and muscular dystrophy. Barnes & Noble promotes literacy, and Coca-Cola sponsors local Boys and Girls Clubs. Avon Products, Inc., focuses on different issues in different countries: breast cancer in the United States, Canada, Philippines, Mexico, Venezuela, Malaysia, and Spain; programs for women who care for senior citizens in

Avon Products, Inc. employs cause marketing programs in the fight against breast cancer.

Avon Products, Inc.
www.avon.com

MARKETING NEWSNET — Will Consumers Switch Brands for a Cause? Yes, If . . .

CUSTOMER VALUE

American Express Company pioneered cause marketing when it sponsored the renovation of the Statue of Liberty. This effort raised $1.7 million for the renovation, increased card usage among cardholders, and attracted new cardholders. In 2001, U.S. companies raised more than $5 billion for causes they champion. It is estimated that cause marketing will raise over $8 billion in 2006.

Cause marketing benefits companies as well as causes. Research indicates that 92 percent of U.S. consumers say they have a more favorable opinion of companies that support causes. Also, 84 percent of consumers say they will switch to a brand or retailer that supports a good cause if the price and quality of brands or retailers are equal. In short, cause marketing may be a valued point of difference for brands and companies, all other things being equal.

For more information, including news, links, and case studies, visit the Cause Marketing Forum website at www.causemarketingforum.com.

Japan; emotional and financial support for mothers in Germany; and AIDS in Thailand. Cause marketing programs incorporate all three concepts of social responsibility by addressing public concerns and satisfying customer needs. They can also enhance corporate sales and profits as described in the accompanying Marketing NewsNet.[36]

The Social Audit: Doing Well by Doing Good

Converting socially responsible ideas into actions involves careful planning and monitoring of programs. Many companies develop, implement, and evaluate their social responsibility efforts by means of a **social audit**, which is a systematic assessment of a firm's objectives, strategies, and performance in terms of social responsibility. Frequently, marketing and social responsibility programs are integrated, as is the case with McDonald's. The company's concern for the needs of families with children who are chronically or terminally ill was converted into 212 Ronald McDonald Houses around the world. These facilities, located near treatment centers, enable families to stay together during the child's care. In this case, McDonald's is contributing to the welfare of a portion of its target market.

A social audit consists of five steps:[37]

1. Recognition of a firm's social expectations and the rationale for engaging in social responsibility endeavors.
2. Identification of social responsibility causes or programs consistent with the company's mission.
3. Determination of organizational objectives and priorities for programs and activities it will undertake.

Marketing and social responsibility programs are often integrated, as is the case with McDonald's. Its concern for ill children is apparent in the opening of another Ronald McDonald House for children and their families.

McDonald's
www.mcdonalds.com

4. Specification of the type and amount of resources necessary to achieve social responsibility objectives.
5. Evaluation of social responsibility programs and activities undertaken and assessment of future involvement.

Corporate attention to social audits will increase as companies seek to achieve sustainable development and improve the quality of life in a global economy. **Sustainable development** involves conducting business in a way that protects the natural environment while making economic progress. Ecologically responsible initiatives such as green marketing represent one such initiative. Recent initiatives related to working conditions at offshore manufacturing sites that produce goods for U.S. companies focus on quality-of-life issues. Public opinion surveys show that 90 percent of U.S. citizens are concerned about working conditions under which products are made in Asia and Latin America. Companies such as Reebok, Nike, Liz Claiborne, Levi Strauss, and Mattel have responded by imposing codes of conduct to reduce harsh or abusive working conditions at offshore manufacturing facilities.[38] Reebok, for example, now monitors production of its sporting apparel and equipment to ensure that no child labor is used in making its products.

Companies that evidence societal responsibility have been rewarded for their efforts. Research has shown that these companies (1) benefit from favorable word-of-mouth among consumers and (2) typically outperform less responsible companies on financial performance.[39]

Turning the Table: Consumer Ethics and Social Responsibility

Consumers also have an obligation to act ethically and responsibly in the exchange process and in the use and disposition of products. Unfortunately, consumer behavior is spotty on both counts.

Unethical practices of consumers are a serious concern to marketers.[40] These practices include filing warranty claims after the claim period, misredeeming coupons, making fraudulent returns of merchandise, providing inaccurate information on credit applications, tampering with utility meters, tapping cable TV lines, pirating music, movies, and software from the Internet, and submitting phony insurance claims. Consumers also act unethically toward each other. According to the FBI, consumer complaints about online auction fraud, in which consumers misrepresent their goods to others, outnumbers all reports of online crime. The cost to marketers of such behavior in lost sales and prevention expenses is huge. For example, consumers who redeem coupons for

Reebok has been a leader in improving workplace conditions in factories that produce its sporting apparel and equipment.

Reebok
www.reebok.com

unpurchased products or use coupons for other products cost manufacturers $1 billion each year. Fraudulent automobile insurance claims cost insurance companies more than $10 billion annually. Unauthorized downloading of music, movies, and software from the Internet cost companies about $40 billion per year in lost sales. Electrical utilities lose between 1 and 3 percent of yearly revenues because of meter tampering. In addition, retailers lose about $30 billion yearly from shoplifting.

Research on unethical consumer behavior indicates that these acts are rarely motivated by economic need. This behavior appears to be influenced by (1) a belief that a consumer can get away with the act and it is worth doing and (2) the rationalization that the act is justified or driven by forces outside the individual—"everybody does it." These reasons were vividly expressed by a 24-year-old who pirated a movie, *The Hulk,* and was sentenced to six months of house arrest, three years of probation, and a $7,000 fine. He said, "I didn't like paying for movies," and added, "so many people do it, you never think you're going to get caught."[41]

Consumer purchase, use, and disposition of environmentally sensitive products relate to consumer social responsibility. Research indicates that consumers are sensitive to ecological issues.[42] However, research also shows that consumers (1) may be unwilling to sacrifice convenience and pay potentially higher prices to protect the environment and (2) lack the knowledge to make informed decisions dealing with the purchase, use, and disposition of products.[43]

Consumer confusion over which products are environmentally safe is also apparent, given marketers' rush to produce "green products." For example, few consumers realize that nonaerosol "pump" hairsprays are the second-largest cause of air pollution, after drying paint. In California alone, 27 tons of noxious hairspray fumes are expelled every day. And "biodegradable" claims on a variety of products, including trash bags, have not proven to be accurate, thus leading to buyer confusion. The FTC has drafted guidelines that describe the circumstances when environmental claims can be made and would not constitute misleading information. For example, an advertisement or product label touting a package as "50 percent more recycled content than before" could be misleading if the recycled content has increased from 2 percent to 3 percent.[44]

Ultimately, marketers and consumers are accountable for ethical and socially responsible behavior. The twenty-first century will prove to be a testing period for both.

Concept Check

1. What is meant by social responsibility?

2. Marketing efforts to produce, promote, and reclaim environmentally sensitive products are called _____.

3. What is a social audit?

CHAPTER IN REVIEW

1 *Explain the differences between legal and ethical behavior in marketing.*

A good starting point for understanding the nature and significance of ethics is the distinction between legality and ethicality of marketing decisions. Whereas ethics deal with personal moral principles and values, laws are society's values and standards that are enforceable in the courts. This distinction can lead to the rationalization that if a behavior is within reasonable ethical and legal limits, then it is not really illegal or unethical. Judgment plays a large role in defining ethical and legal boundaries in marketing. Ethical dilemmas arise when acts or situations are not clearly ethical and legal or unethical and illegal.

2 *Identify factors that influence ethical and unethical marketing decisions.*

Four factors influence ethical marketing behavior. First, societal culture and norms serve as socializing forces that dictate what is morally right and just. Second, business culture and industry practices affect ethical conduct both in the exchange relationships between buyers and sellers and the competitive behavior among sellers. Third, corporate culture and expectations are often defined by corporate ethics codes and the ethical behavior of top management and co-workers. Finally, an individual's personal moral philosophy, such as moral idealism or utilitarianism, will dictate ethical choices. Ultimately, ethical behavior rests with the individual, but the consequences affect many.

3 *Describe the different concepts of social responsibility.*

Social responsibility means that organizations are part of a larger society and are accountable to that society for their actions. There are three concepts of social responsibility. First, profit responsibility holds that companies have a simple duty: to maximize profits for their owners or stockholders. Second, stakeholder responsibility focuses on the obligations an organization has to those who can affect achievement of its objectives. Those constituencies include consumers, employees, suppliers, and distributors. Finally, societal responsibility focuses on obligations that organizations have to the preservation of the ecological environment and the general public. Companies are placing greater emphasis on societal responsibility today and are reaping the rewards of positive word-of-mouth from their consumers and favorable financial performance.

4 *Recognize unethical and socially irresponsible consumer behavior.*

Consumers, like marketers, have an obligation to act ethically and responsibly in the exchange process and in the use and disposition of products. Unfortunately, consumer behavior is spotty on both counts. Unethical consumer behavior include filing warranty claims after the claim period, misredeeming coupons, pirating music, movies, and software from the Internet, and submitting phony insurance claims, among other behaviors. Unethical behavior is rarely motivated by economic need. Rather, research indicates that this behavior is influenced by (*a*) a belief that a consumer can get away with the act and it is worth doing and (*b*) the rationalization that such acts are justified or driven by forces outside the individual—"everybody does it." Consumer purchase, use, and disposition of environmentally sensitive products relate to consumer social responsibility. Even though consumers are sensitive to ecological issues they (*a*) may be unwilling to sacrifice convictions and pay potentially higher prices to protect the environment and (*b*) lack the knowledge to make informed decisions dealing with the purchase, use, and disposition of products.

FOCUSING ON KEY TERMS

cause marketing p. 108
caveat emptor p. 101
code of ethics p. 103
Consumer Bill of Rights p. 101
economic espionage p. 102
ethics p. 98
green marketing p. 108
ISO 14000 p. 108

laws p. 98
moral idealism p. 105
social audit p. 109
social responsibility p. 106
sustainable development p. 110
utilitarianism p. 106
whistle-blowers p. 105

DISCUSSION AND APPLICATION QUESTIONS

1 What concepts of moral philosophy and social responsibility are applicable to the practices of Anheuser-Busch described in the introduction to this chapter? Why?

2 Four ethical situations were presented in this chapter: (*a*) a medical society's decision to set fee schedules, (*b*) the use of a computer program by auto dealers to arrange financing, (*c*) smoking in China, and (*d*) the pricing of Cerezyme for the treatment of a rare genetic illness. Where would each of these situations fit in Figure 4–1?

3 The American Marketing Association Code of Ethics shown in Figure 4–3 details the rights and duties of parties in the marketing exchange process. How do these rights and duties compare with the Consumer Bill of Rights?

4 Compare and contrast moral idealism and utilitarianism as alternative personal moral philosophies.

5 How would you evaluate Milton Friedman's view of the social responsibility of a firm?

6 The text lists several unethical practices of consumers. Can you name others? Why do you think consumers engage in unethical conduct?

7 Cause marketing programs have become popular. Describe two such programs with which you are familiar.

GOING ONLINE   Doing Well by Doing Good

Business for Social Responsibility (BSR) is a membership organization for companies seeking to sustain their commercial success in ways that demonstrate respect for ethical values, people, communities, and the environment. As part of its mission, BSR scans numerous publications and news services each month to identify what is new in corporate social responsibility.

Choose a topic from Chapter 4 pertaining to ethics or social responsibility that interests you, such as economic espionage, current perceptions of ethical behavior, sustainable development, or green marketing. Visit the BSR website at www.bsr.org and go to the "CSR Issue Areas and Information Links." Can you update at least one example in the text related to your chosen topic?

BUILDING YOUR MARKETING PLAN

Consider these potential stakeholders that may be affected in some way by the marketing plan on which you are working: shareholders (if any), suppliers, employees, customers, and society in general. For each group of stakeholders,

1 identify what, if any, ethical and social responsibility issues might arise and

2 describe, in one or two sentences, how your marketing plan addresses each potential issue.

VIDEO CASE 4   Starbucks Corporation: Serving More than Coffee

Wake up and smell the coffee—Starbucks is everywhere! As the world's number one specialty coffee retailer, Starbucks serves more than 25 million customers in its stores every week. The concept of Starbucks goes far beyond being a coffeehouse or coffee brand. It represents the dream of its founder, Howard Schultz, who wanted to take the experience of an Italian—specifically, Milan–espresso bar to every corner of every city block in the world. So what is the *Starbucks experience*? According to the company,

> You get more than the finest coffee when you visit Starbucks. You get great people, first-rate music, a comfortable and upbeat meeting place, and sound advice on brewing excellent coffee at home. At home you're part of a family. At work you're part of a company. And somewhere in between there's a place where you can sit back and be yourself. That's what a Starbucks store is to many of its customers—a kind of "third place" where they can escape, reflect, read, chat, or listen.

But there is more. Starbucks has embraced corporate social responsibility like few other companies. A recent Starbucks Corporate Social Responsibility Annual Report described the company's views on social responsibility:

> Starbucks defines corporate social responsibility as conducting our business in ways that produce social, environmental, and economic benefits to the communities in which we operate. In the end, it means being responsible to our stakeholders.

There is a growing recognition of the need for corporate accountability. Consumers are demanding more than "product" from their favorite brands. Employees are choosing to work for companies with strong values. Shareholders are more inclined to invest in business with outstanding corporate reputations. Quite simply, being socially responsible is not only the right thing to do; it can distinguish a company from its industry peers.

Starbucks not only recognizes the central role that social responsibility plays in its business. It also takes constructive action to be socially responsible.

THE COMPANY

Starbucks is the leading retailer, roaster, and brand of specialty coffee in the world, with more than 7,500 retail locations in North America, Latin America, Europe, the Middle East, and the Pacific Rim. Beginning in 1971 with a single retail location in Seattle, Washington, Starbucks became a Fortune 500 company in 2003 with annual sales exceeding $4 billion. In addition, Starbucks is ranked as one of the "Ten Most Admired Companies in America" and one of the "100 Best Companies to Work For" by *Fortune* magazine. It has been recognized as one of the "Most Trusted Brands" by *Ad Week* magazine. *Business Ethics* magazine placed Starbucks twenty-first in its list of the "100 Best Citizens" in 2003. Starbucks' performance can be attributed to a passionate pursuit of its mission and adherence to six guiding principles. Both appear in Figure 1.

FIGURE 1
Starbucks Mission Statement
and Guiding Principles

> **Establish Starbucks as the premier purveyor of the finest coffee in the world while maintaining our uncompromising principles as we grow.**
>
> **The following six principles will help us measure the appropriateness of our decisions:**
>
> 1. Provide a great work environment and treat each other with respect and dignity.
> 2. Embrace diversity as an essential component in the way we do business.
> 3. Apply the highest standards of excellence to the purchasing, roasting, and fresh delivery of our coffee.
> 4. Develop enthusiastically satisfied customers all the time.
> 5. Contribute positively to our communities and our environment.
> 6. Recognize that profitability is essential to our future success.

COMMITMENT TO CORPORATE SOCIAL RESPONSIBILITY

Starbucks continually emphasizes its commitment to corporate social responsibility. Speaking at the annual shareholders meeting in March 2004, Howard Schultz said,

> From the beginning, Starbucks has built a company that balances profitability with a social conscience. Starbucks business practices are even more relevant today as consumers take a cultural audit of the goods and services they use. Starbucks is known not only for serving the highest quality coffee, but for enriching the daily lives of its people, customers, and coffee farmers. This is the key to Starbucks ongoing success and we are pleased to report our positive results to shareholders and partners (employees).

Each year, Starbucks makes public a comprehensive report on its corporate social responsibility initiatives. A central feature of this annual report is the alignment of the company's social responsibility decisions and actions with Starbucks Mission Statement and Guiding Principles. The Starbucks 2003 Corporate Social Responsibility Report, titled "Living Our Values," focused on six topical areas: (*a*) partners, (*b*) diversity, (*c*) coffee, (*d*) customers, (*e*) community and environment, and (*g*) profitability.

Partners

Starbucks employs some 74,000 people around the world. The company considers its employees as partners following the creation of Starbucks stock option plan in 1991, called "Bean Stock." The company believes that giving eligible full- and part-time employees an ownership in the company and sharing the rewards of Starbucks' financial success has made the sense of partnership real. In addition, the company has one of the most competitive employee benefits and compensation packages in the retail industry. Ongoing training, career advancement opportunities, partner recognition programs, and diligent efforts to ensure a healthy and safe work environment have all contributed to the fact that Starbucks has one of the lowest employee turnover rates within the restaurant and fast food industry.

Diversity

Starbucks strives to mirror the customers and communities it serves. On a quarterly basis, the company monitors the demographics of its workforce to determine whether they reflect the communities in which Starbucks operates. In 2003, Starbucks' U.S. workforce was comprised of 63 percent women and 24 percent people of color. The company also is engaged in a joint venture called Urban Coffee Opportunities (UCO) created to bring Starbucks stores to diverse neighborhoods. There were 52 UCO locations employing almost 1,000 Starbucks partners at the end of 2003.

Supplier diversity is also emphasized. To do business with Starbucks as a diverse supplier, that company must be 51 percent owned, operated, and managed by women, minorities, or socially disadvantaged individuals and meet Starbucks requirements of quality, service, value, stability, and sound business practice. The company spent $80 million with diverse suppliers in 2003 and expects to spend $95 million with diverse suppliers in 2004.

Coffee

Starbucks attention to quality coffee extends to its coffee growers located in more than 20 countries. Sustainable development is emphasized. This means that Starbucks pays coffee farmers a fair price for the beans; that the coffee is grown in an ecologically sound manner; and that Starbucks invests in the farming communities where its coffees are produced.

One long-standing initiative is Starbucks' partnership with Conservation International, a nonprofit organization dedicated to protecting soil, water, energy, and biological diversity worldwide. Starbucks is particularly focused on environmental protection and helping local farmers earn more for their crops. In 2003, Starbucks invested more than $1 million in social programs, notably health and education projects, that benefited farming communities in nine countries, from Columbia to Indonesia.

Customers

Starbucks served customers in 32 countries in 2003. The company and its partners are committed to providing each customer the optimal Starbucks experience every time they visit a store. For very loyal Starbucks customers, that translates into 18 visits per month on average.

Making a connection with customers at each store and building the relationship a customer has with Starbucks *baristas,* or coffee brewers, is important in creating the Starbucks experience. Each barista receives 24 hours of training in customer service and basic retail skills, as well as "Coffee Knowledge" and "Brewing the Perfect Cup" classes. Baristas are taught to anticipate the customers' needs and to make eye contact while carefully explaining the various coffee flavors and blends. Starbucks also enhances the customer relationship by soliciting feedback and responding to patrons' experiences and concerns. Starbucks Customer Relations reviews and responds to every inquiry or comment, often within 24 hours for telephone calls and e-mails.

Community and Environment

Efforts to contribute positively to the communities it serves and the environments in which it operates are emphasized in Starbucks' guiding principles. "We aren't in the coffee business, serving people. We are in the people business, serving coffee," says Howard Schultz. Starbucks and its partners have been recognized for volunteer support and financial contributions to a wide variety of local, national, and international social, economic, and environmental initiatives. For example, the "Make Your Mark" program rewards partners' gifts of time for volunteer work with charitable donations from Starbucks. In addition, Starbucks is a supporter of CARE International, a nonprofit organization dedicated to fighting global poverty.

Starbucks is also committed to environmental responsibility. Starbucks has been a long-time involvement with Earth Day activities. It has instituted companywide energy and water conservation programs and waste reduction, recycling, and reuse initiatives proposed by partner *Green Teams.*

Profitability

At Starbucks, profitability is viewed as essential to its future success. When Starbucks' guiding principles were conceived, profitability was included but intentionally placed last on the list. This was done not because profitability was the least important. Instead, it was believed that adherence to the five other principles would ultimately lead to good financial performance. In fact, it has.

Questions

1 How does Starbucks' approach to social responsibility relate to the three concepts of social responsibility described in the text?

2 What role does sustainable development play in Starbucks' approach to social responsibility?

PART

PART 1
Initiating the Marketing
Process

PART 2
Understanding
Buyers and Markets

PART 3
Targeting Marketing
Opportunities

PART 4
Satisfying Marketing
Opportunities

PART 5
Managing the
Marketing Process

2 UNDERSTANDING BUYERS AND MARKETS

HOW PART 2 FITS INTO THE BOOK

Chapters in Part 2 stress how marketing seeks to serve the needs and wants of potential buyers, whether they are individuals and household consumers, organizations, or global customers.

CHAPTER 5
Consumer Behavior

CHAPTER 6
Organizational Markets and Buyer Behavior

CHAPTER 7
Reaching Global Markets

CHAPTER

5

CONSUMER BEHAVIOR

After reading this chapter you should be able to:

1 Describe the stages in the consumer purchase decision process.

2 Distinguish among three variations of the consumer purchase decision process: routine, limited, and extended problem solving.

3 Identify major psychological influences on consumer behavior.

4 Identify the major sociocultural influences on consumer behavior.

GETTING TO KNOW THE AUTOMOBILE CUSTOM(H)ER AND INFLUENC(H)ER

Who buys about 67 percent of new cars and light trucks? Who spends about $100 billion on new and used cars and trucks and automotive accessories? Who influences 85 percent of all vehicle buying decisions? Women. Yes, women.

Women are a driving force in the U.S. automotive industry. Enlightened automakers such as Volvo have hired women designers, engineers, and marketing executives to better understand and serve this valuable automobile consum(h)er and influenc(h)er of purchase decisions. What have they learned? First, women cast the deciding vote in the family-car purchase and, of course, make the final decision in all of their own purchase decisions. Second, sleek exteriors and interior designs that fit a driver's proportions as well as easy vehicular entry and exit, minimal maintenance, good visibility, storage space, and effortless parking are important to women . . . and men. "We have found that by meeting women's expectations, we exceeded those of most men," says Hans-Olov Olsson, president and CEO of Volvo Cars, a unit of Ford Motor Company. Not surprisingly, 54 percent of Volvo buyers in North America are women.

Third, women approach car buying in a deliberate manner. They frequently visit auto-buying websites and scan car advertisements to gather information, but recommendations of friends and relatives matter most. Women shop an average of three dealerships before making a purchase decision—one more than men. While only a third of women say that price is the most influential factor when they shop for a car, 73 percent say price determines their final decision. Finally, automakers have learned that the great majority of women dislike the car-buying process.

Recognition of women as purchasers and influencers in car and truck buying has also altered the behavior of dealers. Many dealers now use a one-price policy and have stopped negotiating a vehicle's price. Industry research indicates that 68 percent of new-car buyers dread the price negotiation process involved in buying a car, and women often refuse to do it at all.[1]

This chapter examines **consumer behavior**, the actions a person takes in purchasing and using products and services, including the mental and social processes that come before and after these actions. This chapter shows how the behavioral sciences help answer questions such as why people choose one product or brand over another, how they make these choices, and how companies use this knowledge to provide value to consumers.

CONSUMER PURCHASE DECISION PROCESS

Behind the visible act of making a purchase lies an important decision process that must be investigated. The stages a buyer passes through in making choices about which products and services to buy is the **purchase decision process**. This process has the five stages shown in Figure 5–1: (1) problem recognition, (2) information search, (3) alternative evaluation, (4) purchase decision, and (5) postpurchase behavior.

Problem Recognition: Perceiving a Need

Problem recognition, the initial step in the purchase decision, is perceiving a difference between a person's ideal and actual situations big enough to trigger a decision.[2] This can be as simple as finding an empty milk carton in the refrigerator; noting, as a first-year college student, that your high school clothes are not in the style that other students are wearing; or realizing that your laptop computer may not be working properly.

In marketing, advertisements or salespeople can activate a consumer's decision process by showing the shortcomings of competing (or currently owned) products. For instance, an advertisement for a portable MP3-capable CD player could stimulate problem recognition because it emphasizes "maximum music from one device."

Information Search: Seeking Value

After recognizing a problem, a consumer begins to search for information, the next stage in the purchase decision process. First, you may scan your memory for previous experiences with products or brands.[3] This action is called *internal search.* For frequently purchased products such as shampoo and conditioner, this may be enough. Or a consumer may undertake an *external search* for information.[4] This is especially needed when past experience or knowledge is insufficient, the risk of making a wrong purchase decision is high, and the cost of gathering information is low. The primary sources of external information are: (1) *personal sources,* such as relatives and friends whom the consumer trusts; (2) *public sources,* including various product-rating organizations such as *Consumer Reports,* government agencies, and TV

FIGURE 5–1
Purchase decision process

| Problem recognition: Perceiving a need | Information search: Seeking value | Alternative evaluation: Assessing value | Purchase decision: Buying value | Postpurchase behavior: Value in consumption or use |

BRAND	MODEL	PRICE	SOUND QUALITY	BUMP IMMUNITY	BATTERY LIFE (HOURS) CD	MP3	EASE OF USE
Sony	D-CJ01	$130	◉	○	30	23	◑
Philips	EXP503/17	180	◉	◒	17	15	◉
Panasonic	SL-MP50	100	◉	○	29	11	◑
Philips	EXP203	100	◉	◑	7	11	◉
RCA	RP-2415	120	○	◒	6	8	○
Samsung	MCD-SM60	80	◐	○	17	15	◉
SonicBlue	Rio Volt SP90	100	◐	◒	6	15	◑
SonicBlue	Rio Volt SP250	180	○	○	5	13	◑

Rating:	◉	◑	○	◔	●
	Excellent	Very Good	Good	Fair	Poor

FIGURE 5–2

Consumer Reports' evaluation of portable MP3-capable CD players (abridged)

Consumer Reports

www.consumerreports.org

"consumer programs"; and (3) *marketer-dominated sources,* such as information from sellers that include advertising, company websites, salespeople, and point-of-purchase displays in stores.

Suppose you consider buying a portable MP3-capable CD player. You will probably tap several of these information sources: friends and relatives, portable MP3-capable advertisements, brand and company websites, and stores carrying these CD players (for demonstrations). You might study the comparative evaluation of portable MP3-capable CD players that appeared in *Consumer Reports,* a portion of which appears in Figure 5–2.[5]

Alternative Evaluation: Assessing Value

The information search stage clarifies the problem for the consumer by (1) suggesting criteria to use for the purchase, (2) yielding brand names that might meet the criteria, and (3) developing consumer value perceptions. Given only the information shown in Figure 5–2, what selection criteria would you use in buying a portable MP3-capable CD player? Would you use price, sound quality, ease of use, or some other combination of these and other criteria?

For some of you, the information provided may be inadequate because it does not contain all the factors you might consider when evaluating portable MP3-capable CD players. These factors are a consumer's **evaluative criteria**, which represent both the objective attributes of a brand (such as the locate speed) and the subjective ones (such as prestige) you use to compare different products and brands.[6] Firms try to identify and capitalize on both types of criteria to create the best value for the money sought by you and other consumers. These criteria are often displayed in advertisements.

Consumers often have several criteria for evaluating brands. (Didn't you in the preceding exercise?) Knowing this, companies seek to identify the most important evaluative criteria that consumers use when judging brands. For example, among the evaluative criteria shown in the columns of Figure 5–2, suppose you use three in considering brands of portable MP3-capable CD players: (1) a list price under $150, (2) sound quality, and (3) battery life of more than 10 hours. These criteria establish the brands in your **consideration set**—the group of brands that a consumer would consider acceptable from among all the brands in the product class of which he or she is aware.[7] Your evaluative criteria result in five models and five brands (Panasonic, Philips, Samsung, SonicBlue, and Sony) in your consideration set. If these alternatives don't satisfy you, you can change your evaluative criteria to create a different consideration set of models and brands. For example, bump immunity might join the list of evaluative criteria if you are a jogger.

Purchase Decision: Buying Value

Having examined the alternatives in the consideration set, you are almost ready to make a purchase decision. Two choices remain: (1) from whom to buy and (2) when to buy. For a product like a portable MP3-capable CD player, the information search process probably involved visiting retail stores, seeing different brands in catalogs, and viewing a portable MP3-capable CD-player on a seller's website. The choice of which seller to buy from will depend on such considerations as the terms of sale, your past experience buying from the seller, and the return policy. Often a purchase decision involves a simultaneous evaluation of both product attributes and seller characteristics. For example, you might choose the second-most preferred portable MP3-capable CD player brand at a store with a liberal refund and return policy versus the most preferred brand at a store with more conservative policies.

Deciding when to buy is frequently determined by a number of factors. For instance, you might buy sooner if one of your preferred brands is on sale or its manufacturer offers a rebate. Other factors such as the store atmosphere, pleasantness of the shopping experience, salesperson persuasiveness, time pressure, and financial circumstances could also affect whether a purchase decision is made or postponed.[8]

Use of the Internet to gather information, evaluate alternatives, and make buying decisions adds a technological dimension to the consumer purchase decision process. Consumer benefits and costs associated with this technology and its marketing implications are detailed in Chapter 21.

Postpurchase Behavior: Value in Consumption or Use

After buying a product, the consumer compares it with his or her expectations and is either satisfied or dissatisfied. If the consumer is dissatisfied, marketers must decide whether the product was deficient or consumer expectations too high. Product deficiency may require a design change; if expectations are too high, perhaps the company's advertising or the salesperson oversold the product's features.

Sensitivity to a customer's consumption or use experience is extremely important in a consumer's value perception. For example, research on long-distance telephone services provided by Sprint and AT&T indicates that satisfaction or dissatisfaction affects consumer value perceptions.[9] Studies show that satisfaction or dissatisfaction affects consumer communications and repeat-purchase behavior. Satisfied buyers tell three other people about their experience. Dissatisfied buyers complain to nine people.[10] Satisfied buyers also tend to buy from the same seller each time a purchase occasion arises. The financial impact of repeat-purchase behavior is significant, as described in the accompanying Marketing NewsNet.[11] Accordingly, firms such as General Electric (GE), Johnson & Johnson, Coca-Cola, and British Airways focus attention on postpurchase behavior to maximize customer satisfaction and retention. These firms, among many others, now provide toll-free telephone numbers, offer liberalized return and refund policies, and engage in staff training to handle complaints,

A satisfactory or unsatisfactory consumption or use experience is an important factor in postpurchase behavior. Marketer attention to this stage can pay huge dividends as described in the text.

MARKETING NEWSNET   The Value of a Satisfied Customer

Customer satisfaction is an important focus of the marketing concept. But how much is a satisfied customer worth? This question has prompted firms to calculate the financial value of a satisfied customer over time. Frito-Lay, for example, estimates that the average loyal consumer in the southwestern United States eats 21 pounds of salty snack chips a year. At a price of $2.50 a pound, this customer spends $52.50 annually on the company's salty snacks such as Lays and Ruffles potato chips and Doritos and Tostitos tortilla chips. Exxon estimates that a loyal customer will spend $500 annually for its branded gasoline, not including candy, snacks, oil, or repair services purchased at its gasoline stations. Kimberly-Clark reports that a loyal customer will buy 6.7 boxes of its Kleenex tissues each year and will spend $994 on facial tissues over 60 years, in today's dollars.

These calculations have focused marketer attention on customer satisfaction and retention. Ford Motor Company has set a target of increasing customer retention—the percentage of Ford owners whose next car is also a Ford—from 60 percent to 80 percent. Why? Ford executives say that each additional percentage point is worth a staggering $100 million in profits. This calculation is not unique to Ford. Research shows that a 5 percent improvement in customer retention can increase a company's profits by 70 to 80 percent.

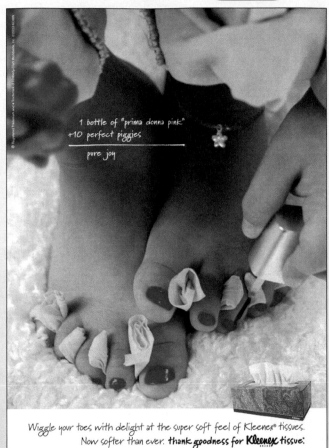

1 bottle of "prima donna pink"
+10 perfect piggies
_____
pure joy

Wiggle your toes with delight at the super soft feel of Kleenex® tissues. Now softer than ever. **thank goodness for Kleenex tissue.**

answer questions, and record suggestions. For example, GE operates a database that stores 750,000 answers about 8,500 of its models in 120 product lines to handle 3 million calls annually. Such efforts produce positive postpurchase communications among consumers and contribute to relationship building between sellers and buyers.

Often a consumer is faced with two or more highly attractive alternatives, such as a Panasonic or Sony portable MP3-capable CD player. If you choose the Panasonic, you may think, "Should I have purchased the Sony?" This feeling of postpurchase psychological tension or anxiety is called **cognitive dissonance**. To alleviate it, consumers often attempt to applaud themselves for making the right choice. So after your purchase, you may seek information to confirm your choice by asking friends questions like, "Don't you like my new CD player?" or by reading ads of the brand you chose. You might even look for negative features about the brand you didn't buy and decide that the Philips headphones didn't feel right. Firms often use ads or follow-up calls from salespeople in this postpurchase stage to comfort buyers that they made the right decision. For many years, Buick ran an advertising campaign with the message, "Aren't you really glad you bought a Buick?"

Involvement and Problem-Solving Variations

Sometimes consumers don't engage in the five-stage purchase decision process. Instead, they skip or minimize one or more stages depending on the level of **involvement**, the personal, social, and economic significance of the purchase to the consumer.[12] High-involvement purchase occasions typically have at least one of three characteristics: The item to be purchased (1) is expensive, (2) can have serious personal consequences, or (3) could reflect on one's social image. For these occasions, consumers engage in extensive information search, consider many product attributes and brands, form attitudes, and participate in word-of-mouth communication. Low-involvement purchases, such as toothpaste and soap, barely involve most of us, but audio and video systems and automobiles are very involving. There are three general variations in the consumer purchase decision process based on consumer involvement and product knowledge. Figure 5–3 shows some of the important differences between the three problem-solving variations.[13]

Extended Problem Solving   In extended problem solving, each of the five stages of the consumer purchase decision process is used in the purchase, including considerable time and effort on external information search and in identifying and evaluating alternatives. Several brands are in the consideration set, and these are evaluated on many attributes. Extended problem solving exists in high-involvement purchase situations for items such as automobiles and elaborate audio systems.

Limited Problem Solving   In limited problem solving, consumers typically seek some information or rely on a friend to help them evaluate alternatives. In general, several brands might be evaluated using a moderate number of different attributes. You might use limited problem solving in choosing a toaster, a restaurant for lunch, and other purchase situations in which you have little time or effort to spend.

Routine Problem Solving   For products such as table salt and milk, consumers recognize a problem, make a decision, and spend little effort seeking external information and evaluating alternatives. The purchase process for such items is virtually a habit and typifies low-involvement decision making. Routine problem solving is typically the case for low-priced, frequently purchased products.

FIGURE 5–3

Comparison of problem-solving variations

HIGH ◄ CONSUMER INVOLVEMENT ► LOW			
CHARACTERISTICS OF THE CONSUMER PURCHASE DECISION PROCESS	**EXTENDED PROBLEM SOLVING**	**LIMITED PROBLEM SOLVING**	**ROUTINE PROBLEM SOLVING**
Number of brands examined	Many	Several	One
Number of sellers considered	Many	Several	Few
Number of product attributes evaluated	Many	Moderate	One
Number of external information sources used	Many	Few	None
Time spent searching	Considerable	Little	Minimal

Involvement and Marketing Strategy   Low and high consumer involvement has important implications for marketing strategy. If a company markets a low-involvement product and its brand is a market leader, attention is placed on (1) maintaining product quality, (2) avoiding stockout situations so that buyers don't substitute a competing brand, and (3) advertising messages that reinforce a consumer's knowledge or assures buyers they made the right choice. Market challengers have a different task. They must break buying habits and use free samples, coupons, and rebates to encourage trial of their brand. Advertising messages will focus on getting their brand into a consumer's consideration set. For example, Campbell's V8 vegetable juice advertising message—"I could have had a V8!"—was targeted at consumers who routinely purchased fruit juices and soft drinks. Challengers can also link their brand attributes with high involvement issues. Tropicana does this by linking the natural attributes of orange juice with adult health concerns.

Help keep your heart running strong:
New Tropicana® Healthy Heart.™

Marketers of high-involvement products recognize that their consumers constantly seek and process information about objective and subjective brand attributes, form evaluative criteria, rate product attributes in various brands, and combine these ratings for an overall brand evaluation—like that described in the portable MP3-capable CD player purchase decision. Market leaders freely ply consumers with product information through advertising and personal selling and create chat rooms on their company or brand websites. Market challengers capitalize on this behavior through comparative advertising that focuses on existing product attributes and often introduce novel evaluative criteria for judging competing brands. Increasingly, challengers benefit from Internet search engines such as MSN Search and Google that assist buyers of high-involvement products.

Situational Influences

Often the purchase situation will affect the purchase decision process. Five **situational influences** have an impact on your purchase decision process: (1) the purchase task, (2) social surroundings, (3) physical surroundings, (4) temporal effects, and (5) antecedent states.[14] The purchase task is the reason for engaging in the decision in the first place. Information searching and evaluating alternatives may differ depending on whether the purchase is a gift, which often involves social visibility, or for the buyer's own use. Social surroundings, including the other people present when a purchase decision is made, may also affect what is purchased. Physical surroundings such as decor, music, and crowding in retail stores may alter how purchase decisions are made. Temporal effects such as time of day or the amount of time available will influence where consumers have breakfast and lunch and what is ordered. Finally, antecedent states, which include the consumer's mood or the amount of cash on hand, can influence purchase behavior and choice.

Figure 5–4 on the next page shows the many influences that affect the consumer purchase decision process. The decision to buy a product also involves important psychological and sociocultural influences, the two important topics discussed during the remainder of this chapter. Marketing mix influences are described in Chapters 10 through 20.

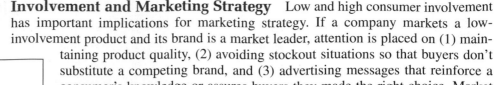

Concept Check

1. What is the first stage in the consumer purchase decision process?

2. The brands a consumer considers buying out of the set of brands in a product class of which the consumer is aware is called the _____.

3. What is the term for postpurchase anxiety?

FIGURE 5–4

Influences on the consumer purchase decision process

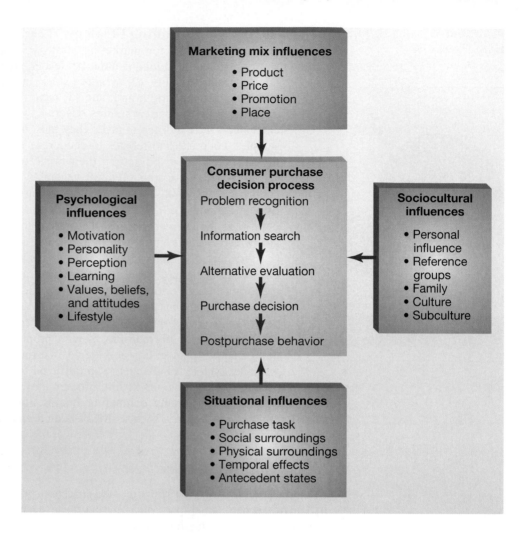

PSYCHOLOGICAL INFLUENCES ON CONSUMER BEHAVIOR

Psychology helps marketers understand why and how consumers behave as they do. In particular, psychological concepts such as motivation and personality; perception; learning; values, beliefs, and attitudes; and lifestyle are useful for interpreting buying processes and directing marketing efforts.

Motivation and Personality

Motivation and personality are two familiar psychological concepts that have specific meanings and marketing implications. These concepts are closely related and are used to explain why people do some things and not others.

Motivation   **Motivation** is the energizing force that stimulates behavior to satisfy a need. Because consumer needs are the focus of the marketing concept, marketers try to arouse these needs.

An individual's needs are boundless. People possess physiological needs for basics such as water, sex, and food. They also have learned needs, including self-esteem, achievement, and affection. Psychologists point out that these needs may be hierarchical; that is, once physiological needs are met, people seek to satisfy their learned needs. Figure 5–5 shows one need hierarchy and classification scheme that contains five need classes.[15] *Physiological needs* are basic to survival and must be satisfied first. A Red Lobster advertisement featuring a seafood salad attempts to

FIGURE 5-5
Hierarchy of needs

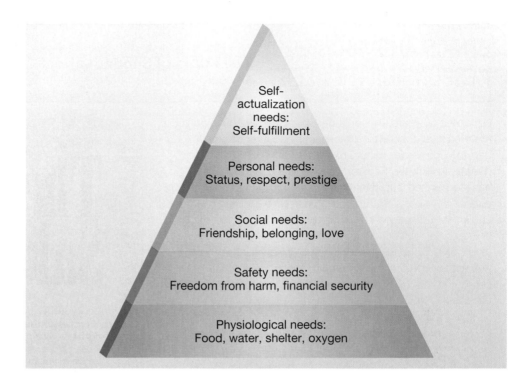

activate the need for food. *Safety needs* involve self-preservation and physical well-being. Smoke detector and burglar alarm manufacturers focus on these needs. *Social needs* are concerned with love and friendship. Dating services and fragrance companies try to arouse these needs. *Personal needs* include the need for achievement, status, prestige, and self-respect. The American Express Gold Card and Brooks Brothers Clothiers appeal to these needs. Sometimes firms try to arouse multiple needs to stimulate problem recognition. Michelin combined safety with parental love to promote tire replacement for automobiles. *Self-actualization needs* involve personal fulfillment. For example, a long-running U.S. Army recruiting program invited enlistees to "Be all you can be."

Personality   While motivation is the energizing force that makes consumer behavior purposeful, a consumer's personality guides and directs behavior. **Personality** refers to a person's consistent behaviors or responses to recurring situations. Although many personality theories exist, most identify key traits—enduring characteristics within a person or in his or her relationship with others. Such traits include assertiveness, extroversion, compliance, dominance, and aggression, among others. These traits are inherited or formed at an early age and change little over the years. Research suggests that compliant people prefer known brand names and use more mouthwash and toilet soaps. In contrast, aggressive types use razors, not electric shavers, apply more cologne and after-shave lotions, and purchase signature goods such as Gucci, Yves St. Laurent, and Donna Karan as an indicator of status.[16] Cross-cultural analysis also suggests that residents of different countries have a *national character,* or a distinct set of personality characteristics common among people of a country or society.[17] For example, North Americans and Germans are relatively more assertive than Russians and the English.

These personality characteristics are often revealed in a person's **self-concept**, which is the way people see themselves and the way they believe others see them. Marketers recognize that people have an actual self-concept and an ideal self-concept. The actual self refers to how people actually see themselves. The ideal self describes how people would like to see themselves. These two self-images are reflected in the products and brands a person buys, including automobiles, home

ETHICS AND SOCIAL RESPONSIBILITY ALERT

The Ethics of Subliminal Messages

ETHICS

For about 50 years, the topic of subliminal perception and the presence of subliminal messages and images embedded in commercial communications has sparked heated debate. In fact, the Federal Communications Commission has denounced subliminal messages as deceptive. Still, consumers spend $50 million a year for audiotapes with subliminal messages designed to help them raise their self-esteem, quit smoking, or lose weight. Almost two-thirds of U.S. consumers think subliminal messages are present in commercial communications; about half are convinced that this practice can cause them to buy things they don't want.

Subliminal messages are not illegal in the United States, however, and marketers are often criticized for pursuing opportunities to create these messages in both electronic and print media. A recent book by August Bullock, *The Secret Sales Pitch: An Overview of Subliminal Advertising,* is devoted to this topic. Bullock identifies images and advertisements that he claims contain subliminal messages and describes techniques that can be used for conveying these messages.

Do you believe that attempts to implant subliminal messages in electronic and print media are a deceptive practice and unethical, regardless of their intent?

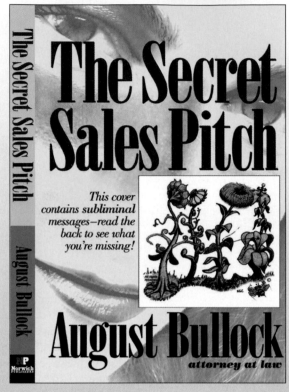

appliances and furnishings, magazines, clothing, grooming and leisure products, and frequently, the stores a person shops. The importance of self-concept is summed up by a senior executive at Barnes & Noble: "People buy books for what the purchase says about them—their taste, their cultivation, their trendiness."[18]

Perception

One person sees a Cadillac as a mark of achievement; another sees it as ostentatious. This is the result of **perception**—the process by which an individual selects, organizes, and interprets information to create a meaningful picture of the world.

Selective Perception   Because the average consumer operates in a complex environment, the human brain attempts to organize and interpret information with a process called *selective perception,* a filtering of exposure, comprehension, and retention. *Selective exposure* occurs when people pay attention to messages that are consistent with their attitudes and beliefs and ignore messages that are inconsistent. Selective exposure often occurs in the postpurchase stage of the consumer decision process, when consumers read advertisements for the brand they just bought. It also occurs when a need exists—you are more likely to "see" a McDonald's advertisement when you are hungry rather than after you have eaten a pizza.

Why does the Good Housekeeping seal for Clorox's new Fresh Step Crystals cat litter appear in the ad, and why does Mary Kay, Inc., offer a free sample of its new Velocity brand fragrance through its mkvelocity.com website? The answer appears in the text.

The Clorox Company
www.freshstep.org

Mary Kay, Inc.
www.mkvelocity.com

Selective comprehension involves interpreting information so that it is consistent with your attitudes and beliefs. A marketer's failure to understand this can have disastrous results. For example, Toro introduced a small, lightweight snowblower called the Snow Pup. Even though the product worked, sales failed to meet expectations. Why? Toro later found out that consumers perceived the name to mean that Snow Pup was a toy or too light to do any serious snow removal. When the product was renamed Snow Master, sales increased sharply.[19]

Selective retention means that consumers do not remember all the information they see, read, or hear, even minutes after exposure to it. This affects the internal and external information search stage of the purchase decision process. This is why furniture and automobile retailers often give consumers product brochures to take home when they leave the showroom.

Because perception plays such an important role in consumer behavior, it is not surprising that the topic of subliminal perception is a popular item for discussion. **Subliminal perception** means that you see or hear messages without being aware of them. The presence and effect of subliminal perception on behavior is a hotly debated issue, with more popular appeal than scientific support. Indeed, evidence suggests that such messages have limited effects on behavior.[20] If these messages did influence behavior, would their use be an ethical practice? (See the accompanying Ethics and Social Responsibility Alert.[21])

Perceived Risk   Perception plays a major role in the perceived risk in purchasing a product or service. **Perceived risk** represents the anxieties felt because the consumer cannot anticipate the outcomes of a purchase but believes that there may be negative consequences. Examples of possible negative consequences are the size of the financial outlay required to buy the product (Can I afford $500 for those skis?), the risk of physical harm (Is bungee jumping safe?), and the performance of the product (Will the hair coloring work?). A more abstract form is psychosocial (What will my friends say if I wear that sweater?). Perceived risk affects information search, because the greater the perceived risk, the more extensive the external search stage is likely to be.

Recognizing the importance of perceived risk, companies develop strategies to reduce the consumer's risk and encourage purchases. These strategies and examples of firms using them include the following:

- *Obtaining seals of approval:* the Good Housekeeping seal for Fresh Step Crystals cat litter.
- *Securing endorsements from influential people:* the National Fluid Milk Processor Promotion Board "Got Milk" advertising campaign.
- *Providing free trials of the product:* samples of Mary Kay's Velocity fragrance.
- *Giving extensive usage instructions:* Clairol hair coloring.
- *Providing warranties and guarantees:* Cadillac's four-year, 50,000-mile, Gold Key Bumper-to-Bumper warranty.

Learning

Much consumer behavior is learned. Consumers learn which information sources to consult for information about products and services, which evaluative criteria to use when assessing alternatives, and, more generally, how to make purchase decisions. **Learning** refers to those behaviors that result from (1) repeated experience and (2) reasoning.

Behavioral Learning   *Behavioral learning* is the process of developing automatic responses to a situation built up through repeated exposure to it. Four variables are central to how consumers learn from repeated experience: drive, cue, response, and reinforcement. A *drive* is a need that moves an individual to action. Drives, such as hunger, might be represented by motives. A *cue* is a stimulus or symbol perceived by consumers. A *response* is the action taken by a consumer to satisfy the drive, whereas a *reinforcement* is the reward. Being hungry (drive), a consumer sees a cue (a billboard), takes action (buys a sandwich), and receives a reward (it tastes great!).

Marketers use two concepts from behavioral learning theory. *Stimulus generalization* occurs when a response elicited by one stimulus (cue) is generalized to another stimulus. Using the same brand name for different products is an application of this concept, such as Tylenol Cold & Flu and Tylenol P.M. *Stimulus discrimination* refers to a person's ability to perceive differences in stimuli. Consumers' tendency to perceive all light beers as being alike led to Budweiser Light commercials that distinguished between many types of "lights" and Bud Light.

Cognitive Learning   Consumers also learn through thinking, reasoning, and mental problem solving without direct experience. This type of learning, called *cognitive learning,* involves making connections between two or more ideas or simply observing the outcomes of others' behaviors and adjusting your own accordingly. Firms also influence this type of learning. Through repetition in advertising, messages such as "Advil is a headache remedy" attempt to link a brand (Advil) and an idea (headache remedy) by showing someone using the brand and finding relief.

Brand Loyalty   Learning is also important because it relates to habit formation—the basis of routine problem solving. Furthermore, there is a close link between habits and **brand loyalty**, which is a favorable attitude toward and consistent purchase of a single brand over time. Brand loyalty results from the positive reinforcement of previous actions. So a consumer reduces risk and saves time by consistently purchasing the same brand of shampoo and has favorable results—healthy, shining hair. There is evidence of brand loyalty in many commonly purchased products in the United States and the global marketplace. However, the incidence of brand loyalty appears to be declining in North America, Mexico, Western European nations, and Japan.[22]

Attitudes toward Colgate Total toothpaste and Extra Strength Bayer aspirin were successfully changed by these ads. How? Read the text to find out how marketers can change consumer attitudes toward products and brands.

Colgate-Palmolive
www.colgate.com

Bayer Corporation
www.bayerus.com

Values, Beliefs, and Attitudes

Values, beliefs, and attitudes play a central role in consumer decision making and related marketing actions.

Attitude Formation   An **attitude** is a "learned predisposition to respond to an object or class of objects in a consistently favorable or unfavorable way."[23] Attitudes are shaped by our values and beliefs, which are learned. Values vary by level of specificity. We speak of American core values, including material well-being and humanitarianism. We also have personal values, such as thriftiness and ambition. Marketers are concerned with both but focus mostly on personal values. Personal values affect attitudes by influencing the importance assigned to specific product attributes. Suppose thriftiness is one of your personal values. When you evaluate cars, fuel economy (a product attribute) becomes important. If you believe a specific car has this attribute, you are likely to have a favorable attitude toward it.

Beliefs also play a part in attitude formation. **Beliefs** are a consumer's subjective perception of how a product or brand performs on different attributes. Beliefs are based on personal experience, advertising, and discussions with other people. Beliefs about product attributes are important because, along with personal values, they create the favorable or unfavorable attitude the consumer has toward certain products, services, and brands.

Attitude Change   Marketers use three approaches to try to change consumer attitudes toward products and brands, as shown in the following examples.[24]

1. *Changing beliefs about the extent to which a brand has certain attributes.* To allay consumer concern that aspirin use causes an upset stomach, Bayer Corporation successfully promoted the gentleness of its Extra Strength Bayer Plus aspirin.

2. *Changing the perceived importance of attributes.* Pepsi-Cola made freshness an important product attribute when it stamped freshness dates on its cans. Prior to doing so, few consumers considered cola freshness an issue. After Pepsi spent about $25 million on advertising and promotion, a consumer survey found that 61 percent of cola drinkers believed freshness dating was an important attribute.

3. *Adding new attributes to the product.* Colgate-Palmolive included a new antibacterial ingredient, tricloson, in its Colgate Total toothpaste and spent $100 million marketing the brand. The result? Colgate replaced Crest as the market leader for the first time in 25 years.

Lifestyle

Lifestyle is a mode of living that is identified by how people spend their time and resources, what they consider important in their environment, and what they think of themselves and the world around them. The analysis of consumer lifestyles, called *psychographics,* provides insights into consumer needs and wants. Lifestyle analysis has proven useful in segmenting and targeting consumers for new and existing products and services (see Chapter 9).

Psychographics, the practice of combining psychology, lifestyle, and demographics, is often used to uncover consumer motivations for buying and using products and services. A prominent psychographic system is VALS from SRI Consulting Business Intelligence (SRIC-BI).[25] The VALS system identifies eight consumer segments based on (1) their primary motivation for buying and having certain products and services and (2) their resources. According to SRIC-BI researchers, consumers are motivated to buy products and services and seek experiences that give shape, substance, and satisfaction to their lives. But not all consumers are alike. Consumers are inspired by one of three primary motivations—ideals, achievement, and self-expression—that give meaning to their self or the world and governs their activities. The different levels of resources enhance or constrain a person's expression of his or her primary motivation. A person's resources include psychological, physical, demographic, and material capacities such as income, self confidence, and risk-taking. Before reading further, visit the VALS website shown in the accompanying Web Link. Complete the short survey to learn which segment best describes you.

The VALS system seeks to explain why and how consumers make purchase decisions. Consumers motivated by ideals are guided by knowledge and principle. These consumers divide into two segments. *Thinkers* are mature, reflective, and well-educated

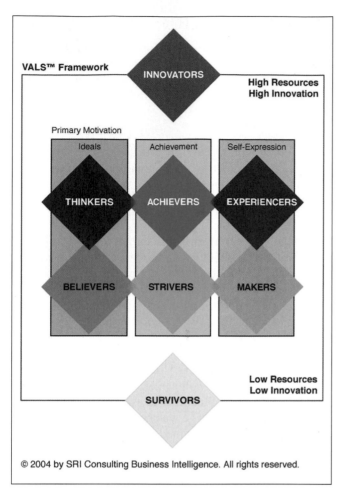

VALS™ Framework

INNOVATORS   High Resources
High Innovation

Primary Motivation

| Ideals | Achievement | Self-Expression |

THINKERS   ACHIEVERS   EXPERIENCERS

BELIEVERS   STRIVERS   MAKERS

Low Resources
Low Innovation

SURVIVORS

VALS consumer
segments

people who value order, knowledge, and responsibility. They are practical consumers, deliberate information-seekers, who value durability and functionality in products over styling and newness. *Believers,* with fewer resources, are conservative, conventional people with concrete beliefs based on traditional, established codes: family, religion, community, and the nation. They choose familiar products and brands, favor American-made products, and are generally brand loyal.

Consumers motivated by achievement look for products and services that demonstrate success to their peers or to a peer group they aspire to. These consumers include *Achievers,* who have a busy, goal-directed lifestyle and a deep commitment to career and family. Image is important to them. They favor established, prestige products and services and are interested in time-saving devices given their hectic schedules. *Strivers* are trendy, fun-loving, and less self confident than achievers. They also have lower levels of education and household income. Money defines success for them. They favor stylish products and are as impulsive as their financial circumstances permit.

Consumers motivated by self-expression desire social or physical activity, variety, and risk. *Experiencers* are young, enthusiastic, and impulsive consumers who become excited about new possibilities but are equally quick to cool. They savor the new, the offbeat, and the risky. Their energy finds an outlet in exercise, sports, outdoor recreation, and social activities. Much of their income is spent on fashion items, entertainment, and socializing and particularly on looking good and having the latest things. *Makers,* with fewer resources, express themselves and experience the world by working on it—building a house, raising children, or fixing a car. They are practical people who have constructive skills, value self-sufficiency, and are unimpressed by material possessions except those with a practical or functional purpose.

Two segments stand apart. *Innovators* are successful, sophisticated, take-charge people with high self-esteem and abundant resources of all kinds. Image is important to them, not as evidence of power or status, but as an expression of cultivated tastes, independence, and character. They are receptive to new ideas and technologies and their lives are characterized by variety. *Survivors,* with the least resources of any segment, focus on meeting basic needs (safety and security) rather than fulfilling desires. They represent a very modest market for most products and services and are loyal to favorite brands, especially if they can be purchased at a discount.

Each of these segments exhibits unique media preferences. Experiencers and Strivers are the most likely to visit Internet chat rooms. Innovators, Thinkers, and Achievers tend to read business and news magazines such as *Fortune* and *Time.* Experiencers read sports magazines, whereas Makers read automotive magazines. Believers are the heaviest readers of *Reader's Digest.*

Concept Check

1. The problem with the Toro Snow Pup was an example of selective _____.

2. What three attitude-change approaches are most common?

3. What does *lifestyle* mean?

SOCIOCULTURAL INFLUENCES ON CONSUMER BEHAVIOR

Sociocultural influences, which evolve from a consumer's formal and informal relationships with other people, also exert a significant impact on consumer behavior. These involve personal influence, reference groups, the family, social class, culture, and subculture.

Personal Influence

A consumer's purchases are often influenced by the views, opinions, or behaviors of others. Two aspects of personal influence are important to marketing: opinion leadership and word-of-mouth activity.

Opinion Leadership   Individuals who exert direct or indirect social influence over others are called **opinion leaders**. Opinion leaders are considered to be knowledgeable about or users of particular products and services, so their opinions influences others' choices. Opinion leadership is widespread in the purchase of cars and trucks, clothing and accessories, club membership, consumer electronics, vacation locations, and financial investments. A study by *Popular Mechanics* magazine identified 18 million opinion leaders who influence the purchases of some 85 million consumers for do-it-yourself products.

About 10 percent of U.S. adults are opinion leaders.[26] Identifying, reaching, and influencing opinion leaders is a major challenge for companies. Some firms use sports figures or celebrities as spokespersons to represent their products, such as actor Pierce Brosnan and tennis player Anna Kournikova for Omega watches, in the hope that they are opinion leaders. Others promote their products in media believed to reach opinion leaders. Still others use more direct approaches. For example, DaimlerChrysler Corporation invited influential community leaders and business executives to test-drive its new models. Some 6,000 accepted the offer, and 98 percent said they would recommend their tested car. The company estimated that the number of favorable recommendations totaled 32,000.

Firms use actors or athletes as spokespersons to represent their products, such as Pierce Brosnan and Anna Kournikova for Omega watches, in the hope that they are opinion leaders.

Omega
www.omegawatches.com

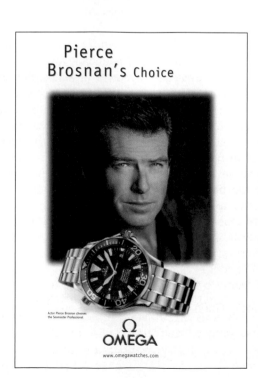

MARKETING NEWSNET

BzzAgent—The Business of Buzz

GLOBAL

Have you recently heard about a new product, movie, website, book, or restaurant from someone you know . . . or a complete stranger? If so, you may have been buzzed.

Marketers recognize the power of word of mouth. The challenge has been to harness that power. BzzAgent LLC does just that. Its nationwide volunteer army of 25,000 natural-born talkers channel their chatter toward products and services they deem authentically worth talking about. "Our goal is to capture honest word of mouth," says David Bolter, BzzAgent's founder, "and to build a network that turns passionate customers into brand evangelists."

BzzAgent's method is simple. Once a client signs on with BzzAgent, the company searches its "agent" database for those who match the demographic and psychographic profile of the target market for a client's offering. Agents then can sign up for a buzz campaign and receive a sample product and a training manual for buzz-creating strategies. Each time an agent completes an activity, he or she is expected to file an online report describing the nature of the buzz and its effectiveness. BzzAgent coaches

respond with encouragement and feedback on additional techniques.

Agents keep the products they promote. They also earn points redeemable for books, CDs, and other items by filing detailed reports. Who are the agents? About 65 percent are older than 25, 60 percent are women, and two are Fortune 500 CEOs. All are gregarious and genuinely like the product or service, otherwise they wouldn't participate in the buzz campaign.

Estée Lauder, Monster.com, Anheuser-Busch, Penguin Books, Lee jeans, and Rock Bottom Restaurants have used BzzAgent. But BzzAgent's buzz isn't cheap, and not everything is buzz worthy. Deploying 1,000 agents on a 12-week campaign can cost a company $85,000, exclusive of product samples. BzzAgent researches a product or service before committing to a campaign and rejects about 80 percent of the companies that seek its service. It also refuses campaigns for politicians, religious groups, and certain products, like firearms. Interested in BzzAgent? Visit its website at www.bzzagent.com.

Word of Mouth   The influencing of people during conversations is called **word of mouth**. Word of mouth is the most powerful and authentic information source for consumers because it typically involves friends viewed as trustworthy. According to a recent study, 67 percent of U.S. consumer product sales are directly based on word-of-mouth activity among friends, family, and colleagues.[27]

The power of personal influence has prompted firms to promote positive and retard negative word of mouth. For instance, "teaser" advertising campaigns are run in advance of new-product introductions to stimulate conversations. Other techniques such as advertising slogans, music, and humor also heighten positive word of mouth. Many commercials shown during the Super Bowl, for instance, are created expressly to initiate conversations about the advertisements and featured product or service the next day. Increasingly, companies recruit and deploy people to produce *buzz*— popularity created by consumer word of mouth. Read the accompanying Marketing NewsNet to learn how this is done by BzzAgent.[28]

On the other hand, rumors about Kmart (snake eggs in clothing), McDonald's (worms in hamburgers), Corona Extra beer (contaminated beer), and Snickers candy bars in Russia (a cause of diabetes) have resulted in negative word of mouth, none of which was based on fact. Overcoming or neutralizing negative word of mouth is difficult and costly. Marketers have found that supplying factual information, providing toll-free numbers for consumers to call the company, and giving appropriate product demonstrations have proven helpful.

The power of word of mouth has been magnified by the Internet through online forums, chat rooms, bulletin boards, and websites. In fact, Ford uses special software to monitor online messages and find out what consumers are saying about its vehicles. Chapter 21 describes how marketers track, initiate, and manage word of mouth in an online environment.

Reference Groups

Reference groups are people to whom an individual looks as a basis for self-appraisal or as a source of personal standards. Reference groups affect consumer purchases because they influence the information, attitudes, and aspiration levels that help set a consumer's standards. For example, one of the first questions one asks others when planning to attend a social occasion is, "What are you going to wear?" Reference groups have an important influence on the purchase of luxury products but not of necessities—reference groups exert a strong influence on the brand chosen when its use or consumption is highly visible to others.

Consumers have many reference groups, but three groups have clear marketing implications. A *membership group* is one to which a person actually belongs, including fraternities and sororities, social clubs, and the family. Such groups are easily identifiable and are targeted by firms selling insurance, insignia products, and charter vacations. An *aspiration group* is one that a person wishes to be a member of or wishes to be identified with, such as a professional society. Firms frequently rely on spokespeople or settings associated with their target market's aspiration group in their advertising. A *dissociative group* is one that a person wishes to maintain a distance from because of differences in values or behaviors.

Family Influence

Family influences on consumer behavior result from three sources: consumer socialization, passage through the family life cycle, and decision making within the family or household.

Consumer Socialization   The process by which people acquire the skills, knowledge, and attitudes necessary to function as consumers is **consumer socialization**.[29] Children learn how to purchase (1) by interacting with adults in purchase situations and (2) through their own purchasing and product usage experiences. Research shows that children evidence brand preferences at age two, and these preferences often last a lifetime.[30] This knowledge prompted Sony to introduce "My First Sony," a line of portable audio equipment for children; Time, Inc., to launch *Sports Illustrated for Kids;* Polaroid to develop the Cool Cam camcorder for children between ages 9 and 14; and Yahoo! and America Online to offer special areas where young audiences can view their children's menu—Yahooligans! and Kids Only, respectively.

Family Life Cycle   Consumers act and purchase differently as they go through life. The **family life cycle** concept describes the distinct phases that a family progresses through from formation to retirement, each phase bringing with it identifiable purchasing behaviors.[31] Figure 5–6 illustrates the traditional progression as well as contemporary variations of the family life cycle. Today, the traditional family—married couples with children younger than 18 years—constitute just 24 percent of all U.S. households. The remaining 76 percent of U.S. households include single parents, unmarried couples, divorced, never-married, or widowed individuals, and older married couples whose children no longer live at home.

Young singles' buying preferences are for nondurable items, including prepared foods, clothing, personal care products, and entertainment. They represent a target market for recreational travel, automobile, and consumer electronics firms. Young

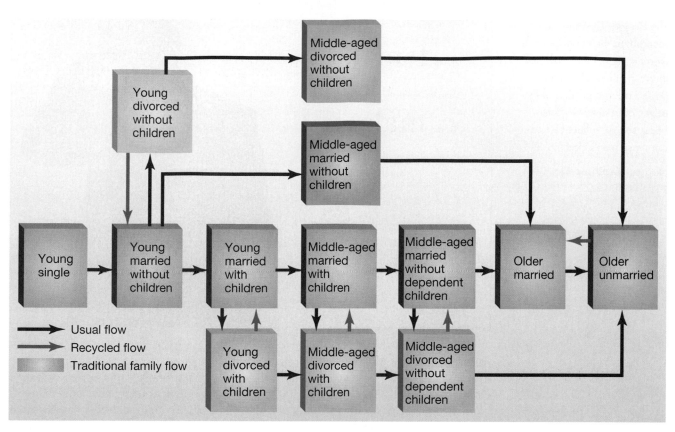

FIGURE 5-6

Modern family life cycle

married couples without children are typically more affluent than young singles because usually both spouses are employed. These couples exhibit preferences for furniture, housewares, and gift items for each other. Young marrieds with children are driven by the needs of their children. They make up a sizable market for life insurance, various children's products, and home furnishings. Single parents with children are the least financially secure of households with children. Their buying preferences are affected by a limited economic status and tend toward convenience foods, child care services, and personal care items.

Middle-aged married couples with children are typically better off financially than their younger counterparts. They are a significant market for leisure products and home improvement items. Middle-aged couples without children typically have a large amount of discretionary income. These couples buy better home furnishings, status automobiles, and financial services. Persons in the last two phases—older married and older unmarried—make up a sizable market for prescription drugs, medical services, vacation trips, and gifts for younger relatives.

Family Decision Making   A third influence in the decision-making process occurs within the family. Two decision-making styles exist: spouse-dominant and joint decision making. With a joint decision-making style, most decisions are made by both husband and wife. Spouse-dominant decisions are those for which either the husband or the wife is responsible. Research indicates that wives tend to have the most say when purchasing groceries, children's toys, clothing, and medicines. Husbands tend to be more influential in home and car maintenance purchases. Joint decision making is common for cars, vacations, houses, home appliances and electronics, and medical care. As a rule, joint decision making increases with the education of the spouses.[32]

Roles of individual family members in the purchase process are another element of family decision making. Five roles exist: (1) information gatherer, (2) influencer, (3) decision maker, (4) purchaser, and (5) user. Family members assume different

The Haggar Clothing Co. recognizes the important role women play in the choice of men's clothing. The company directs a large portion of its advertising toward women because they influence and purchase men's clothing.

Haggar Clothing Co.
www.haggar.com

In the **female** the ability to match colors comes at an early age. In the **male** it comes when he marries a female.

The City Casuals three-button, crepe jacket, 100% cotton, French-yarn shirt, Bedford cord pants, and a touch of color.

roles for different products and services. This knowledge is important to firms.[33] For example, 89 percent of wives either influence or make outright purchases of men's clothing. Knowing this, Haggar Clothing, a menswear marketer, now advertises in women's magazines such as *Vanity Fair* and *Redbook*. Even though women are often the grocery decision maker, they are not necessarily the purchaser. More than 40 percent of all food-shopping dollars are spent by male customers. Increasingly, preteens and teenagers are the information gatherers, influencers, decision makers, and purchasers of products and services for the family, given the prevalence of working parents and single-parent households.[34] Children under 12 directly influence more than $300 billion in annual family purchases. Teenagers influence another $500 billion and spend another $175 million of their own money annually. These figures help explain why, for example, Nabisco, Johnson & Johnson, Apple Computer, Kellogg, P&G, Sony, and Oscar Mayer, among countless other companies, spend more than $32 billion annually in media that reach preteens and teens.

Social Class

A more subtle influence on consumer behavior than direct contact with others is the social class to which people belong. **Social class** may be defined as the relatively permanent, homogeneous divisions in a society into which people sharing similar values, interests, and behavior can be grouped. A person's occupation, source of income (not level of income), and education determine his or her social class. Generally speaking, three major social class categories exist—upper, middle, and lower—with subcategories within each. This structure has been observed in the United States, Great Britain, Western Europe, and Latin America.[35]

To some degree, persons within social classes exhibit common values, attitudes, beliefs, lifestyles, and buying behaviors. Compared with the middle classes, people in the lower classes have a more short-term time orientation, are more emotional than rational in their reasoning, think in concrete rather than abstract terms, and see fewer personal opportunities. Members of the upper classes focus on achievements and the future and think in abstract or symbolic terms.

Companies use social class as a basis for identifying and reaching particularly good prospects for their products and services. For instance, JCPenney has historically appealed to the middle classes. *New Yorker* magazine reaches the upper classes. In general, people in the upper classes are targeted by companies for items such as financial investments, expensive cars, and formal evening wear. The middle classes represent a target market for home improvement centers, automobile parts stores, and personal hygiene products. Firms also recognize differences in media preferences among classes: lower and working classes prefer tabloid magazines; middle classes read fashion, romance, and celebrity (*People*) magazines; and upper classes tend to subscribe to literary, travel, and news magazines.

Culture and Subculture

As described in Chapter 3, *culture* refers to the set of values, ideas, and attitudes that are learned and shared among the members of a group. Thus, we often refer to the American culture, the Latin American culture, or the Japanese culture. Cultural underpinnings of American buying patterns were described in Chapter 3; Chapter 7 will explore the role of culture in global marketing.

Subgroups within the larger, or national, culture with unique values, ideas, and attitudes are referred to as **subcultures**. Various subcultures exist within the American culture. The three largest racial/ethnic subcultures in the United States are African Americans, Hispanics, and Asian Americans. Collectively, they annually spend about $2.4 trillion for goods and services. Each group exhibits sophisticated social and cultural behaviors that affect buying patterns, which provides the basis for multicultural marketing programs described in Chapter 3.

African American Buying Patterns   African Americans have the second-largest spending power of the three racial/ethnic subcultures in the United States. Consumer research on African American buying patterns have focused on similarities and differences with whites. When socioeconomic status differences between African Americans and whites are removed, there are more similarities than points of difference. Differences in buying patterns are greater within the African American subculture, due to levels of socioeconomic status, than between African Americans and whites of similar status.

Even though similarities outweigh differences, there are consumption patterns that do differ between African Americans and whites.[36] For example, African Americans spend far more than whites on boy's clothing, rental goods, and audio equipment. Adult African Americans are twice as likely to own a pager and spend twice as much for online services, on a per capita basis, than whites. African American women spend three times more on health and beauty products than white women. Furthermore, the typical African American family is five years younger than the typical white family. This factor alone accounts for some of the observed differences in preferences for clothing, music, shelter, cars, and many other products, services, and activities. Finally, it must be emphasized that, historically, African Americans have been deprived of employment and educational opportunities in the United States. Both factors have resulted in income disparities between African Americans and whites, which influence purchase behavior.

Recent research indicates that while African Americans are price conscious, they are strongly motivated by quality and choice. They respond more to products such as apparel and cosmetics and advertising that appeal to their African American pride and heritage as well as address their ethnic features and needs regardless of socioeconomic status.

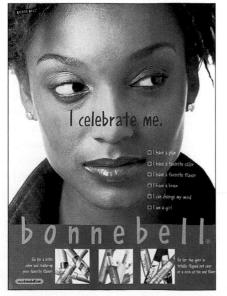

African American women represent a large market for health and beauty products. Cosmetic companies such as Bonne Bell Cosmetics, Inc. actively seek to serve this market.

Bonne Bell Cosmetics, Inc.
www.bonnebell.com

Appreciation for the context in which African American consumers make purchase decisions is a necessary first step in understanding their buying patterns. Current research on African American purchase behavior reveals that stereotypes are often misleading, as they also are for the Hispanic and Asian American subcultures.

Hispanic Buying Patterns   Hispanics represent the largest racial/ethnic subculture in the United States in terms of population and spending power. About 50 percent of Hispanics in the United States are immigrants, and the majority are under the age of 25.

Research on Hispanic buying practices has uncovered several consistent patterns:[37]

1. Hispanics are quality and brand conscious. They are willing to pay a premium price for premium quality and are often brand loyal.
2. Hispanics prefer buying American-made products, especially those offered by firms that cater to Hispanic needs.
3. Hispanic buying preferences are strongly influenced by family and peers.
4. Hispanics consider advertising a credible product information source, and U.S. firms spend more than $3 billion annually on advertising to Hispanics.
5. Convenience is not an important product attribute to Hispanic homemakers with respect to food preparation or consumption, nor is low caffeine in coffee and soft drinks, low fat in dairy products, and low cholesterol in packaged foods.

Despite some consistent buying patterns, marketing to Hispanics has proven to be a challenge for two reasons. First, the Hispanic subculture is diverse and composed of Mexicans, Puerto Ricans, Cubans, and others of Central and South American ancestry. Cultural differences among these nationalities often affect product preferences. For example, Campbell Soup Company sells its Casera line of soups, beans, and sauces using different recipes to appeal to Puerto Ricans on the East Coast and Mexicans in the Southwest. Second, a language barrier exists, and commercial messages are frequently misinterpreted when translated into Spanish. Volkswagen learned this lesson when the Spanish translation of its "Driver's Wanted" slogan suggested "chauffeurs wanted." The Spanish slogan is now *Agarra calle,* a slang expression that can be loosely translated as "let's hit the road."[38]

Sensitivity to the unique needs of Hispanics by firms has paid huge dividends. For example, Metropolitan Life Insurance is the largest insurer of Hispanics. Goya Foods dominates the market for ethnic food products sold to Hispanics. Best Foods' Mazola Corn Oil captures two-thirds of the Hispanic market for this product category. Time, Inc., has more than 400,000 subscribers to its *People en Espanol.*

Asian American Buying Patterns   About 70 percent of Asian Americans are immigrants, and most are under the age of 30. Asian Americans are the fastest-growing racial/ethnic subculture in the United States.

The Asian subculture is composed of Chinese, Japanese, Filipinos, Koreans, Asian Indians, people from Southeast Asia, and Pacific Islanders. The diversity of the Asian subculture is so great that generalizations about buying patterns of this group are difficult to make.[39] Consumer research on Asian Americans suggests that individuals and families divide into two groups. *Assimilated* Asian Americans are conversant in English, highly educated, hold professional and managerial positions, and exhibit buying patterns very much like the typical American consumer. *Nonassimilated* Asian Americans are recent immigrants who still cling to their native languages and customs. The diversity of Asian Americans evident in language, customs, and tastes requires marketers to be sensitive to different Asian nationalities. For example, Anheuser-Busch's agricultural products division sells eight different varieties of California-grown rice, each with a different Asian label to cover a range of nationalities and tastes. The company's advertising also addresses the preferences of Chinese, Japanese, and Koreans for different kinds of rice bowls.

Target often uses Spanish language advertising to communicate to the Hispanic community in the United States.

Target
www.target.com

Studies show that the Asian American subculture as a whole is characterized by hard work, strong family ties, appreciation for education, and median family incomes exceeding those of any other ethnic group. This subculture is also the most entrepreneurial in the United States, as evidenced by the number of Asian-owned businesses. These qualities led Metropolitan Life Insurance to identify Asian Americans as a target for insurance following the company's success in marketing to Hispanics.

Concept Check

1. What are the two primary forms of personal influence?

2. Marketers are concerned with which types of reference groups?

3. What two challenges must marketers overcome when marketing to Hispanics?

CHAPTER IN REVIEW

1 *Describe the stages in the consumer purchase decision process.*
The consumer purchase decision process consists of five stages. They are problem recognition, information search, alternative evaluation, purchase decision, and postpurchase behavior. Problem recognition is perceiving a difference between a person's ideal and actual situation big enough to trigger a decision. Information search involves remembering previous purchase experiences (internal search) and external search behavior such as seeking information from other sources.

Alternative evaluation clarifies the problem for the consumer by (*a*) suggesting the evaluative criteria to use for the purchase, (*b*) yielding brand names that might meet the criteria, and (*c*) developing consumer value perceptions. The purchase decision involves the choice of an alternative, including from whom to buy and when to buy. Postpurchase behavior involves the comparison of the chosen alternative with a consumer's expectations, which leads to satisfaction or dissatisfaction and subsequent purchase behavior.

2 *Distinguish among three variations of the consumer purchase decision process: routine, limited, and extended problem solving.*

Consumers don't always engage in the five-stage purchase decision process. Instead, they skip or minimize one or more stages depending on the level of involvement—the personal, social, and economic significance of the purchase. For low-involvement purchase occasions, consumers engage in routine problem solving. They recognize a problem, make a decision, and spend little effort seeking external information and evaluating alternatives. For high-involvement purchase occasions, each of the five stages of the consumer purchase decision process is used, including considerable time and effort on external information search and in identifying and evaluating alternatives. With limited problem solving, consumers typically seek some information or rely on a friend to help them evaluate alternatives.

3 *Identify major psychological influences on consumer behavior.*

Psychology helps marketers understand why and how consumers behave as they do. In particular, psychological concepts such as motivation and personality; perception; learning; values, beliefs, and attitudes; and lifestyle are useful for interpreting buying processes. Motivation is the energizing force that stimulates behavior to satisfy a need. Personality refers to a person's consistent behaviors or responses to recurring situations. Perception is the process by which an individual selects, organizes, and interprets information to create a meaningful picture of the world. Consumers filter information through selective exposure, comprehension, and retention.

Much consumer behavior is learned. Learning refers to those behaviors that result from (*a*) repeated experience and (*b*) reasoning. Brand loyalty results from learning. Values, beliefs, and attitudes are also learned and influence how consumers evaluate products, services, and brands. A more general concept is lifestyle. Lifestyle, also called psychographics, combines psychology and demographics and focuses on how people spend their time and resources, what they consider important in their environment, and what they think of themselves and the world around them.

4 *Identify major sociocultural influences on consumer behavior.*

Sociocultural influences, which evolve from a consumer's formal and informal relationships with other people, also affect consumer behavior. These involve personal influence, reference groups, the family, social class, culture, and subculture. Opinion leadership and word-of-mouth behavior are two major sources of personal influence on consumer behavior. Reference groups are people to whom an individual looks as a basis for self-approval or as source of personal standards. Family influences on consumer behavior result from three sources: consumer socialization; passage through the family life cycle; and decision making within the family or household. A more subtle influence on consumer behavior than direct contact with others is the social class to which people belong. Persons within social classes tend to exhibit common values, attitudes, beliefs, lifestyles, and buying behaviors. Finally, a person's culture and subculture have been shown to influence product preferences and buying patterns.

FOCUSING ON KEY TERMS

attitude p. 131
beliefs p. 131
brand loyalty p. 130
cognitive dissonance p. 123
consideration set p. 122
consumer behavior p. 120
consumer socialization p. 136
evaluative criteria p. 121
family life cycle p. 136
involvement p. 124
learning p. 130
lifestyle p. 132
motivation p. 126

opinion leaders p. 134
perceived risk p. 129
perception p. 128
personality p. 127
purchase decision process p. 120
reference groups p. 136
self-concept p. 127
situational influences p. 125
social class p. 138
subcultures p. 139
subliminal perception p. 129
word of mouth p. 135

DISCUSSION AND APPLICATION QUESTIONS

1 Review Figure 5–2 in the text, which shows the MP3-capable CD player attributes identified by *Consumer Reports*. Which attributes are important to you? What other attributes might you consider? Which brand would you prefer?

2 Suppose research at Panasonic reveals that prospective buyers are anxious about buying high-definition television sets. What strategies might you recommend to the company to reduce consumer anxiety?

3 A Porsche salesperson was taking orders on new cars because he was unable to satisfy the demand with the limited number of cars in the showroom and lot. Several persons had backed out of the contract within two weeks of signing the order. What explanation can you give for this behavior, and what remedies would you recommend?

4 Which social class would you associate with each of the following items or actions: (*a*) tennis club membership, (*b*) an arrangement of plastic flowers in the kitchen,

(c) *True Romance* magazine, (d) *Smithsonian* magazine, (e) formally dressing for dinner frequently, and (f) being a member of a bowling team.

5 Assign one or more levels of the hierarchy of needs and the motives described in Figure 5–5 to the following products: (a) life insurance, (b) cosmetics, (c) *The Wall Street Journal*, and (d) hamburgers.

6 With which stage in the family life cycle would the purchase of the following products and services be most closely identified: (a) bedroom furniture, (b) life insurance, (c) a Caribbean cruise, (d) a house mortgage, and (e) children's toys?

7 "The greater the perceived risk in a purchase situation, the more likely that cognitive dissonance will result." Does this statement have any basis given the discussion in the text? Why?

GOING ONLINE Tracking Buying Power of Consumers

www.mhhe.com/Kerin

The size and economic significance of racial/ethnic subcultures in the United States has been documented by the 2000 Census. Population statistics supplied by the U.S. Census are readily accessible at www.census.gov. These statistics coupled with data useful for marketing purposes offer valuable insights into the growing diversity of the U.S. population.

The Selig Center for Economic Growth at the University of Georgia provides useful information on the buying power of African Americans, Hispanics, and Asian Americans, the three largest racial/ethnic subcultures in the United States. Visit the Center's website at www.selig. uga.edu for answers to the following questions.

1 What is the most recent estimate of the buying power of African Americans, Hispanics, and Asian Americans in the United States?

2 In which states is African American buying power the highest? Which states have the highest Hispanic and Asian American buying power?

BUILDING YOUR MARKETING PLAN

To do a consumer analysis for the product—the good, service, or idea—in your marketing plan:

1 Identify the consumers who are most likely to buy your product—the primary target market—in terms of (a) their demographic characteristics and (b) any other kind of characteristics you believe are important.

2 Describe (a) the main points of difference of your product for this group and (b) what problem they help solve for the consumer, in terms of the first stage in the consumer purchase decision process in Figure 5–1.

3 Identify the one or two key influences for each of the four outside boxes in Figure 5–4: (a) marketing mix, (b) psychological, (c) sociocultural, and (d) situational influences.

This consumer analysis will provide the foundation for the marketing mix actions you develop later in your plan.

VIDEO CASE 5   Ken Davis Products, Inc.: Sauces for All Tastes

"Cooking is a lot like music," explains Barbara Jo Davis. "There are musicians who are excellent musicians and they can play any of the classical music to perfection, but they don't know how to improvise. And then there are the jazz musicians who can do both of these things."

"The same thing is true of cooks," continues Barbara. "There are the cooks who can follow a recipe . . . and will be the best cooks in the world as long as they have a recipe. But if they have to improvise, then they're lost. So what we want to do is help those who aren't the improvisers."

THE COMPANY

Barbara Jo Davis is president of Ken Davis Products, Inc., a small regional business that develops and markets barbe-

cue sauces. The company was founded by Barbara Davis's late spouse Ken Davis. Ken owned a restaurant where he served his grandmother's recipe for barbecue sauce, and he received such positive feedback from his customers he decided to write the recipe down to ensure it would taste the same every time he made it. He called in Barbara, then a home economist for a large consumer foods corporation, to help him do it. Shortly afterward, Ken closed the restaurant, married Barbara, and began marketing his barbecue sauce full-time. Barbara Davis stayed with the consumer foods corporation, becoming a manager for the test kitchens and for the cookbooks, until 1988 when she left to work for Ken Davis Products full-time.

While Ken Davis Products is a market leader in its region, it has not expanded nationwide. Barbara Davis

explains, "What I hear consumers say again and again is the reason they buy Ken Davis barbecue sauces is because it's a local company. I think the reason we're the market leaders is because it's a personal product. People know who the person is. They can see me driving around in my car."

PRODUCTS, CUSTOMERS, AND ENVIRONMENT

In addition to the Original Ken Davis Barbecue Sauce, the company also sells Smooth and Spicy Barbecue Sauce, with jalapeño peppers added to it, and a line of marinade sauces called Jazz It Up. Through consumer testing and focus groups, Barbara Davis discovered the real problem consumers are facing when they cook is how to add flavor to the meats they are eating. Hence, the Jazz It Up line of marinade sauces was born. Ken Davis Products now offers four varieties of cooking sauces: Orange Citrus, Lemon Lime, Southwestern, and Mesquite. "They're really a hybrid between marinades and cooking sauces because you can use them as an ingredient, a marinade, or even as a dipping sauce," explains Barbara Davis. This was a natural product line extension for Ken Davis Products based on its reputation in the barbecue sauce market.

The company does not target specific consumer segments because it seems the consumers are just about everybody. Barbara Davis has discovered through consumer focus groups that the barbecue sauce buying decision is still made by the female head of the household, but everybody in the family seems to participate in the decision. "Kids especially like our sauce a lot," explains Barbara Davis, "and elderly people like the Original Recipe because it's got a lot of flavor but it's not hot or spicy."

The Food and Drug Administration (FDA) recently passed legislation requiring all consumer food products to nutrition label their products in a standardized way. For small companies such as Ken Davis Products, this meant the added expense of finding an independent laboratory to analyze the products and redesigning the labels. Barbara Davis thinks this new legislation works to the advantage of Ken Davis Products, though. "New people can compare and see Ken Davis is indeed lower in sodium than most of the other barbecue sauces on the market."

THE ISSUES

Ken Davis Products prides itself on staying abreast of changing consumer tastes and trends. In addition to conducting focus groups, Barbara Davis solicits informal feedback from current and potential Ken Davis customers. She will talk to testers at an in-store sampling or even walk up to shoppers in the barbecue sauce aisle and ask them about their purchases. Barbara Davis believes, "You have to listen to your consumer because you're not in this business to please yourself. You're in business to please your consumer." In addition to discovering the latest tastes, she has learned from her customers that the primary promotional vehicle used to spread the word about Ken Davis Products is word of mouth.

To make the most of this strategy, Ken Davis Products participates in event marketing and in-store sampling. Ken Davis used to always say, "The best way to sell a food product is to get people to taste it, because it's ultimately the taste that will keep them as customers." Barbara Davis has found that another successful strategy to get people talking about Ken Davis Products is to become involved in the community. She regularly talks to groups of young entrepreneurs or

completely unrehearsed. "That way I don't have to pay talent," she chuckles.

THE MULTIPLE ROLES OF A SMALL BUSINESSPERSON

After working for a large corporation and then becoming a small business entrepreneur, Barbara Davis is in a unique position to comment on the satisfactions and hardships of owning your own business. She stresses that you have to know everything about your business—you can't specialize as in a large corporation. You also get to make all the decisions and have the satisfaction of being a part of the process every step of the way. "But," Barbara adds, "you have to work harder than you have ever worked in your life. You have to always be working. When I was working for a corporation, I resented working all those hours because it wasn't for me. But now when I'm working all these hours I love it because I am doing it for myself. That's the reward—it's all for you."

invites school children to her test kitchen to learn how to cook. "You do all of these little things just to get people thinking Ken Davis. And they don't even know they're thinking Ken Davis half the time. But it's so ingrained that when they go to the grocery store, why would they look at those other brands?" Barbara Davis also sends out a newsletter twice a year to Ken Davis Products users with new recipe ideas and stories about the company. Today's busy family is always on the look out for quick and easy recipes.

Ken Davis Products also uses some more traditional promotional vehicles, such as freestanding inserts (FSIs) in Sunday newspaper and radio advertising. The FSIs include a coupon to induce new customers to try the product. The radio ads reflect the local, homegrown differentiation strategy used by Ken Davis Products. Barbara Davis does the commercials herself, which are

Questions

1   In what ways have American eating habits changed over the past decade that affect a barbecue sauce manufacturer?

2   What are the two or three main (*a*) objective evaluative criteria and (*b*) subjective evaluative criteria consumers of Ken Davis barbecue sauces might use?

3   How can Ken Davis Products do marketing research on consumers to find out what they eat, to learn how they use barbecue sauces, and to get ideas for new products?

4   (*a*) Do you think a small, local company such as Ken Davis Products should have entered the market as a premium-priced product or a low-priced product? (*b*) What should its pricing strategy be today?

5   What do you see are the (*a*) satisfactions and (*b*) concerns of being in business for yourself?

it's all inside:

JCPenney

catalog | .com

fall&winter '04

6 ORGANIZATIONAL MARKETS AND BUYER BEHAVIOR

LEARNING OBJECTIVES

After reading this chapter you should be able to:

1 Distinguish among industrial, reseller, and government organizational markets.

2 Describe the key characteristics of organizational buying that make it different from consumer buying.

3 Explain how buying centers and buying situations influence organizational purchasing.

4 Recognize the importance and nature of online buying in industrial, reseller, and government organizational markets.

BUYING PAPER IS A STRATEGIC BUSINESS DECISION AT JCPENNEY

Kim Nagele views paper differently than most people do. As the senior procurement agent at JCPMedia, he and a team of purchasing professionals buy more than 260,000 tons of paper annually at a cost of hundreds of millions of dollars.

JCPMedia is the print and paper purchasing arm for JCPenney, the fifth-largest retailer in the United States and the largest catalog merchant of general merchandise in the Western Hemisphere. Paper is serious business at JCPMedia, which buys paper for JCPenney catalogs (see opposite page), newspaper inserts, and direct-mail pieces. Some 10 companies from around the world, including International Paper in the United States, Stora Enso in Sweden, and UPM-Kymmene, Inc., a Finnish paper company, supply paper to JCPMedia.

The choice of paper and suppliers is a strategic business decision given its revenue and expense consequences. Therefore, JCPMedia paper buyers work closely with JCPenney marketing personnel and within budget constraints to assure that the right quality and quantity of paper is purchased at the right price point for merchandise featured in the millions of catalogs, newspaper inserts, and direct-mail pieces distributed every year. In addition to paper quality and price, buyers formally evaluate supplier capabilities. These include a supplier's capacity to deliver selected grades of paper from specialty items to magazine papers, the availability of specific types of paper to meet printing deadlines, and ongoing environmental programs. For example, a supplier's forestry management and antipollution practices are considered in the JCPMedia buying process.[1]

The next time you thumb through a JCPenney catalog, newspaper insert, or direct-mail piece, take a moment to notice the paper. Considerable effort and attention was given to its selection and purchase.

Purchasing paper for JCPMedia is one example of organizational buying. This chapter examines the types of organizational buyers; key characteristics of organizational buying, including online buying; and some typical buying decisions in organizational markets.

THE NATURE AND SIZE OF ORGANIZATIONAL MARKETS

Understanding organizational markets and buying behavior is a necessary prerequisite for effective business marketing. **Business marketing** is the marketing of goods and services to companies, governments, or not-for-profit organizations for use in the creation of goods and services that they can produce and market to others. Because over half of all U.S. business school graduates take jobs in firms that engage in business marketing, it is important to understand the characteristics of organizational buyers and their buying behavior.

Organizational buyers are those manufacturers, wholesalers, retailers, and government agencies that buy goods and services for their own use or for resale. For example, these organizations buy computers and telephone services for their own use. However, manufacturers buy raw materials and parts that they reprocess into the finished goods they sell. Wholesalers and retailers resell the goods they buy without reprocessing them. Organizational buyers include all buyers in a nation except ultimate consumers. These organizational buyers purchase and lease large volumes of capital equipment, raw materials, manufactured parts, supplies, and business services. In fact, because they often buy raw materials and parts, process them, and sell the upgraded product several times before it is purchased by the final organizational buyer or ultimate consumer, the total annual purchases of organizational buyers are far greater than those of ultimate consumers.

Organizational buyers are divided into three different markets: (1) industrial, (2) reseller, and (3) government markets (Figure 6–1).[2]

FIGURE 6–1

Type and number of organizational customers in the United States

KIND OF MARKET	TYPE OF ORGANIZATION	NUMBER
Industrial (business) markets— 11,967,000	Manufacturers	355,000
	Mining	25,000
	Construction	710,000
	Farms, timber, and fisheries	2,054,000
	Service	7,707,000
	Finance, insurance, and real estate	724,000
	Transportation, communications, and public utilities	336,000
	Not-for-profit associations	56,000
Reseller markets—3,810,000	Wholesalers	860,000
	Retailers	2,950,000
Government markets—88,000	Government units	88,000

Industrial Markets

There are about 12 million firms in the industrial, or business, market. These **industrial firms** in some way reprocess a product or service they buy before selling it again to the next buyer. This is certainly true of Corning, Inc., which transforms an exotic blend of materials to create optical fiber capable of carrying much of the telephone traffic in the United States at once on a single strand. It is also true (if you stretch your imagination) of a firm selling services, such as a bank that takes money from its depositors, reprocesses it, and "sells" it as loans to borrowers.

The importance of services in the United States today is emphasized by the composition of the industrial markets shown in Figure 6–1. The first four types of industrial firms (manufacturers; mining; construction; and farms, timber, and fisheries) sell physical products and represent 26 percent of all the industrial firms, or about 3.1 million. The services market sells diverse services such as legal advice, auto repair, and dry cleaning. Along with finance, insurance, and real estate businesses, and transportation, communication, and public utility firms, these service firms represent about 73 percent of all industrial firms, or about 8.8 million. Because of the size and importance of service firms and some 56,000 not-for-profit organizations (such as the American Red Cross), services marketing is discussed in detail in Chapter 12.

Reseller Markets

Wholesalers and retailers that buy physical products and resell them again without any reprocessing are **resellers**. In the United States there are almost 3 million retailers and 860,000 wholesalers. In Chapters 15 through 17 we shall see how manufacturers use wholesalers and retailers in their distribution ("place") strategies as channels through which their products reach ultimate consumers. In this chapter we look at these resellers mainly as organizational buyers in terms of (1) how they make their own buying decisions and (2) which products they choose to carry.

Government Markets

Government units are the federal, state, and local agencies that buy goods and services for the constituents they serve. There are about 88,000 of these government units in the United States. Their annual purchases vary in size from the $898 million the Federal Aviation Administration intends to spend for 3,000 computerized workstations for 22 major air traffic control centers in the United States to lesser amounts spent by local school or sanitation districts.[3]

Global Organizational Markets

Industrial, reseller, and government markets also exist on a global scale. International trade statistics indicate that the largest exporting industries in the United States focus on organizational customers, not ultimate consumers.

The majority of world trade involves manufacturers, resellers, and government agencies buying goods and services for their own use or for resale to others. The exchange relationships often involve numerous transactions spanning the globe.[4] For example, Volvo Aero of Sweden, Ishikawajima-Harima Heavy Industries of Japan, and Chemical Automatics Design Bureau of Russia provide key components used in the high-performance liquid hydrogen-fueled rocket engine made for space exploration by U.S.-based Pratt & Whitney. This engine is deployed in the Atlas, Titan, and Delta launch vehicles made by Lockheed-Martin and Boeing, which are sold to space agencies of many countries for use in deploying communication satellites. Even the familiar Yellow Pages, sold in Moscow, is the product of a global purchasing and marketing effort. The Moscow Yellow Pages lists more than 10,000 telephone numbers and addresses for shops, restaurants, hotels, businesses, and cultural, trade, and government institutions classified under 500 categories of goods and services. A collaborative effort between U.S.- and Russian-based companies solicits advertising for the directory, which is printed in Russia for resale to individuals and businesses through stores, hotels, and international trade centers such as the Armand Hammer Center in Red Square.

MEASURING DOMESTIC AND GLOBAL INDUSTRIAL, RESELLER, AND GOVERNMENT MARKETS

The measurement of industrial, reseller, and government markets is an important first step for a firm interested in gauging the size of one, two, or all three of these markets in the United States and around the world. This task has been made easier with the **North American Industry Classification System (NAICS)**.[5] The NAICS provides common industry definitions for Canada, Mexico, and the United States, which makes easier the measurement of economic activity in the three member countries of the North American Free Trade Agreement (NAFTA). The NAICS replaced the Standard Industrial Classification (SIC) system, a version of which has been in place for more than 50 years in the three NAFTA member countries. The SIC neither permitted comparability across countries nor accurately measured new or emerging industries. Furthermore, the NAICS is consistent with the International Standard Industrial Classification of All Economic Activities, published by the United Nations, to facilitate measurement of global economic activity.

The NAICS groups economic activity to permit studies of market share, demand for goods and services, import competition in domestic markets, and similar studies. It designates industries with a numerical code in a defined structure. A six-digit coding system is used. The first two digits designate a sector of the economy, the third digit designates a subsector, and the fourth digit represents an industry group. The fifth digit designates a specific industry and is the most detailed level at which comparable data is available for Canada, Mexico, and the United States. The sixth digit designates individual country-level national industries. Figure 6–2 presents an abbreviated breakdown within the information industries sector (code 51) to illustrate the classification scheme.

FIGURE 6–2
NAICS breakdown for information industries sector: NAICS code 51 (abbreviated)

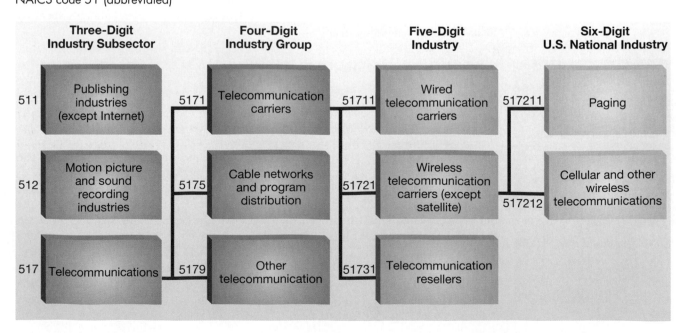

The NAICS permits a firm to find the NAICS codes of its present customers and then obtain NAICS-coded lists for similar firms. Also, it is possible to monitor NAICS categories to determine the growth in various sectors and industries to identify promising marketing opportunities. However, NAICS codes, like the earlier SIC codes, have important limitations. The NAICS assigns one code to each organization based on its major economic activity, so large firms that engage in many different activities are still given only one NAICS code. A second limitation is that five-digit national industry codes are not available for all three countries because the respective governments will not reveal data when too few organizations exist in a category.

A further refinement in the measurement of organizational markets is expected in 2007 with the publication of the *North American Product Classification System* (NAPCS). The NAPCS will provide a classification system for products and services that is consistent across Canada, Mexico, and the United States and international classification systems, such as the Central Product Classification System of the United Nations. The NAICS and NAPCS represent the continued effort toward economic integration in North America and the world.

Concept Check

1. What are the three main types of organizational buyers?

2. What is the North American Industry Classification System (NAICS)?

CHARACTERISTICS OF ORGANIZATIONAL BUYING

Organizations are different from individuals, so buying for an organization is different from buying for yourself or your family. True, in both cases the objective in making the purchase is to solve the buyer's problem—to satisfy a need or want. But unique objectives and policies of an organization put special constraints on how it makes buying decisions. Understanding the characteristics of organizational buying is essential in designing effective marketing programs to reach these buyers. Key characteristics of organizational buying are listed in Figure 6–3 on the next page and discussed next.[6]

Demand Characteristics

Consumer demand for products and services is affected by their price and availability and by consumers' personal tastes and discretionary income. By comparison, industrial demand is derived. **Derived demand** means that the demand for industrial products and services is driven by, or derived from, demand for consumer products and services. For example, the demand for Weyerhaeuser's pulp and paper products is based on consumer demand for newspapers, Domino's "keep warm" pizza-to-go boxes, Federal Express packages, and disposable diapers. Derived demand is often based on expectations of future consumer demand. For instance, Whirlpool purchases parts for its washers and dryers in anticipation of consumer demand, which is affected by the replacement cycle for these products and by consumer income.

Size of the Order or Purchase

The size of the purchase involved in organizational buying is typically much larger than that in consumer buying. The dollar value of a single purchase made by an organization often runs into the thousands or millions of dollars. For example, Motorola was paid $63 million to install a cellular phone system in Brazil.[7] With so

CHARACTERISTICS	DIMENSIONS
Market characteristics	• Demand for industrial products and services is derived. • Few customers typically exist, and their purchase orders are large.
Product or service characteristics	• Products or services are technical in nature and purchased on the basis of specifications. • There is a predominance of raw and semifinished goods purchased. • Heavy emphasis is placed on delivery time, technical assistance, postsale service, and financing assistance.
Buying process characteristics	• Technically qualified and professional buyers exist and follow established purchasing policies and procedures. • Buying objectives and criteria are typically spelled out, as are procedures for evaluating sellers and products (services). • Multiple buying influences exist, and multiple parties participate in purchase decisions. • Reciprocal arrangements exist, and negotiation between buyers and sellers is commonplace. • Online buying over the Internet is widespread.
Marketing mix characteristics	• Direct selling to organizational buyers is the rule, and physical distribution is very important. • Advertising and other forms of promotion are technical in nature. • Price is often negotiated, evaluated as part of broader seller and product (service) qualities, typically inelastic owing to derived demand, and frequently affected by trade and quantity discounts.

FIGURE 6–3

Key characteristics of organizational buying behavior

much money at stake, most organizations place constraints on their buyers in the form of purchasing policies or procedures. Buyers must often get competitive bids from at least three prospective suppliers when the order is above a specific amount, such as $5,000. When the order is above an even higher amount, such as $50,000, it may require the review and approval of a vice president or even the president of the company. Knowing how the size of the order affects buying practices is important in determining who participates in the purchase decision and makes the final decision, and also the length of time required to arrive at a purchase agreement.

Number of Potential Buyers

Firms selling consumer products or services often try to reach thousands or millions of individuals or households. For example, your local supermarket or bank probably serves thousands of people, and Kellogg tries to reach 80 million American households with its breakfast cereals and probably succeeds in selling to a third or half of these in any given year. In contrast, firms selling to organizations are often restricted to far fewer buyers. Gulfstream Aerospace Corporation can sell its business jets to a few thousand organizations throughout the world, and B. F. Goodrich sells its original equipment tires to fewer than 10 car manufacturers.

Derived demand, the size of the purchase order, and the number of potential buyers will play a part in the commercial success of the new A380 superjumbo jet being developed by Europe's Airbus. Read the accompanying Marketing NewsNet to learn more about the largest airplane ever built.[8]

Organizational Buying Objectives

Organizations buy products and services for one main reason: to help them achieve their objectives. For business firms the buying objective is usually to increase profits

MARKETING NEWSNET

The Airbus A380 Superjumbo Jet Is about to Take Flight

GLOBAL

Rapidly expanding demand for intercontinental passenger air traffic and the growth of the global air freight industry bodes well for aircraft manufacturers. Europe's Airbus expects to transport future air travelers and cargo in the largest airplane ever built—its A380 superjumbo jet. Scheduled to begin service in 2006, the A380 features passenger models seating more than 555 people, spread over two full decks, and a freightliner model capable of delivering 331,000 pounds of cargo. The A380 has a list price of about $250 million.

The demand for the A380 will depend on prospective buyers' expectation of future air transport traffic. If initial orders are an indication, the future is bright for superjumbo jet aircraft. Airbus has already taken orders for the A380 from buyers on five continents, including Singapore Airlines, Qantas Airways, Lufthansa, Virgin Atlantic Airways, Air

France, Emirates Airlines, and FedEx, which has 10 freight-liners on order with an option to buy even more.

through reducing costs or increasing revenues. 7-Eleven buys automated inventory systems to increase the number of products that can be sold through its convenience stores and to keep them fresh. Nissan Motor Company switched its advertising agency because it expects the new agency to devise a more effective ad campaign to help it sell more cars and increase revenues. To improve executive decision making, many firms buy advanced computer systems to process data. The objectives of nonprofit firms and government agencies are usually to meet the needs of the groups they serve. Thus, a hospital buys a high-technology diagnostic device to serve its patients better. Recognizing the high costs of energy, Sylvania promotes to prospective buyers cost savings and increased profits made possible by its fluorescent and halogen lights.

Many companies today have broadened their buying objectives to include an emphasis on buying from minority- and women-owned suppliers and vendors. Companies such as Pitney Bowes, PepsiCo, Coors, and JCPenney report that sales, profits, and customer satisfaction have increased because of their minority- and women-owned supplier and vendor initiatives. Other companies include environmental initiatives. For example, Lowe's and Home Depot, two home-and-garden center chains, no longer purchase lumber from companies that harvest timber from the world's endangered forests.[9] Successful business marketers recognize that understanding buying objectives is a necessary first step in marketing to organizations.

Organizational Buying Criteria

In making a purchase, the buying organization must weigh key buying criteria that apply to the potential supplier and what it wants to sell. **Organizational buying criteria** are the objective attributes of the supplier's products and services and the capabilities of the supplier itself. These criteria serve the same purpose as the evaluative criteria used by consumers and described in Chapter 5. Seven of the most commonly used criteria are: (1) price, (2) ability to meet the quality specifications required for the item, (3) ability to meet required delivery schedules, (4) technical capability, (5) warranties and claim policies in the event of poor performance,

It's nice to be admired. Harley-Davidson's well-deserved reputation for innovation, product quality, and talented management and employees has made it a perennial member of *Fortune* magazine's list of "America's Most Admired Companies."

Harley-Davidson is also respected by suppliers for the way it collaborates with them in product design. According to Jeff Bluestein, the company's chairman and CEO: "We involve our suppliers as much as possible in future products, new-product development, and get them working with us." Emphasis is placed on quality benchmarks, cost control, delivery schedules, and technological innovation as well as building mutually beneficial, long-term relationships. Face-to-face communication is encouraged, and many suppliers have personnel officed at Harley-Davidson's Product Development Center.

The relationship between Harley-Davidson and Milsco Manufacturing is a case in point. Milsco has been the sole source of original equipment motorcycle seats and a major supplier of aftermarket parts and accessories, such as saddlebags, for Harley-Davidson since 1934. Milsco engineers and designers work closely with their Harley counterparts in the design of each year's new products. The notion of a mutually beneficial relationship is expressed by Ron Priem, Milsco's manager of industrial design: "Harley-Davidson refers to us as stakeholders, someone who can win or lose from a successful or failed program. We all share responsibility toward one another." Priem also notes that Harley-Davidson is not Milsco's only customer. It is simply the customer that he most respects.

(6) past performance on previous contracts, and (7) production facilities and capacity.[10] Suppliers that meet or exceed these criteria create customer value.

Organizational buyers who purchase products and services in the global marketplace often supplement their buying criteria with supplier ISO 9000 standards certification. **ISO 9000** standards, developed by the International Standards Organization (ISO) in Geneva, Switzerland, refer to standards for registration and certification of a manufacturer's quality management and assurance system based on an on-site audit of practices and procedures. 3M, which buys and markets its products globally, has over 80 percent of its manufacturing and service facilities ISO 9000 certified. According to the company's director of quality control, certification also gives 3M confidence in the consistent quality of its suppliers' manufacturing systems and products.[11]

Many organizational buyers today are transforming their buying criteria into specific requirements that are communicated to prospective suppliers. This practice, called **reverse marketing**, involves the deliberate effort by organizational buyers to build relationships that shape suppliers' products, services, and capabilities to fit a buyer's needs and those of its customers.[12] For example, consider Deere & Company, the maker of John Deere farm, construction, and lawn-care equipment. Deere employs 94 supplier-development engineers who work full-time with the company's suppliers to improve their efficiency and quality and reduce their costs. According to a Deere senior executive, "Their quality, delivery, and costs are, after all, our quality, delivery, and costs."[13] Read the accompanying Marketing NewsNet to learn how Harley-Davidson emphasizes supplier collaboration in its product design.[14]

ETHICS AND SOCIAL RESPONSIBILITY ALERT

Scratching Each Other's Back— The Ethics of Reciprocity in Organizational Buying

ETHICS

Reciprocity, the buying practice in which two organizations agree to purchase each other's products and services, is frowned upon by the U.S. Justice Department because it restricts the normal operation of the free market. Reciprocal buying practices do exist, however, in a variety of forms, including certain types of trade arrangements in international marketing. Furthermore, the extent to which reciprocity is viewed as an ethical issue varies across cultures. In many Asian countries, for instance, reciprocity is often a positive and widespread practice.

Reciprocity is occasionally addressed in the ethics codes of companies or their purchasing policies. For instance, IBM describes its reciprocity policy in the company's Global Procurement Principles and Practices Statement:

> IBM's goal is to buy goods and services which have the best prices, quality, delivery, and technology. IBM has a policy against reciprocal buying arrangements because those arrangements can interfere with this goal.

Do you think reciprocal buying is unethical?

With many U.S. manufacturers using a *just-in-time* (JIT) inventory system that reduces the inventory of production parts to those to be used within hours or days, on-time delivery is becoming an even more important buying criterion and, in some instances, a requirement. Caterpillar trains its key suppliers at its Quality Institute in JIT inventory systems and conducts supplier seminars on how to diagnose, correct, and implement continuous quality improvement programs. The just-in-time inventory system is discussed further in Chapter 16.

Buyer–Seller Relationships and Supply Partnerships

Another distinction between organizational and consumer buying behavior lies in the nature of the relationship between organizational buyers and suppliers. Specifically, organizational buying is more likely to involve complex negotiations concerning delivery schedules, price, technical specifications, warranties, and claim policies. These negotiations also can last for an extended period of time. This was the case when the Lawrence Livermore National Laboratory recently acquired two IBM supercomputers—each with capacity to perform 360 trillion mathematical operations per second—at a cost of $290 million.[15]

Reciprocal arrangements also exist in organizational buying. **Reciprocity** is an industrial buying practice in which two organizations agree to purchase each other's products and services. The U.S. Justice Department frowns on reciprocal buying because it restricts the normal operation of the free market. However, the practice exists and can limit the flexibility of organizational buyers in choosing alternative suppliers. Regardless of the legality of reciprocal buying, do you believe this practice is ethical? See the Ethics and Social Responsibility Alert.[16]

Long-term contracts are also prevalent.[17] As an example, the U.S. Department of Defense recently announced it intends to spend $6.9 billion over five years for computer and computer technology provided by Electronic Data Systems. Hewlett-Packard is engaged in a 10-year, $3 billion contract to manage Procter & Gamble's information technology in 160 countries.

In some cases, buyer–seller relationships evolve into supply partnerships.[18] A **supply partnership** exists when a buyer and its supplier adopt mutually beneficial objectives, policies, and procedures for the purpose of lowering the cost or increasing the value of products and services delivered to the ultimate consumer. Intel, the world's largest manufacturer of microprocessors and the "computer inside" most personal computers, is a case in point. Intel supports its suppliers by offering them quality management programs and by investing in supplier equipment that produces fewer product defects and boosts supplier productivity. Suppliers, in turn, provide Intel with consistent high-quality products at a lower cost for its customers, the makers of personal computers, and finally you, the ultimate customer. Retailers, too, have forged partnerships with their suppliers. Wal-Mart and Kmart have such a relationship with Procter & Gamble for ordering and replenishing P&G's products in their stores. By using computerized cash register scanning equipment and direct electronic linkages to P&G, these retailers can tell P&G what merchandise is needed, along with how much, when, and to which store to deliver it on a daily basis. Because supply partnerships also involve the physical distribution of goods, they are again discussed in Chapter 16 in the context of supply chains.

The Buying Center: A Cross-Functional Group

For routine purchases with a small dollar value, a single buyer or purchasing manager often makes the purchase decision alone. In many instances, however, several people in the organization participate in the buying process. The individuals in this group, called a **buying center**, share common goals, risks, and knowledge important to a purchase decision. For most large multistore chain resellers, such as Sears, 7-Eleven convenience stores, Target, or Safeway, the buying center is highly formalized and is called a *buying committee*. However, most industrial firms or government units use informal groups of people or call meetings to arrive at buying decisions.

The importance of the buying center requires that a firm marketing to many industrial firms and government units understand the structure, technical and business functions represented, and behavior of these groups. One researcher has suggested four questions to provide guidance in understanding the buying center in these organizations:[19] Which individuals are in the buying center for the product or service? What is the relative influence of each member of the group? What are the buying criteria of each member? How does each member of the group perceive our firm, our products and services, and our salespeople?

Answers to these questions are difficult to come by, particularly when dealing with industrial firms, resellers, and governments outside the United States.[20] For example, U.S. firms are often frustrated by the fact that Japanese buyers "ask a thousand questions" but give few answers, sometimes rely on third-party individuals to convey views on proposals, are prone to not "talk business," and often say yes to be courteous when they mean no. U.S. firms in the global chemical industry recognize that production engineering personnel have a great deal of influence in Hungarian buying groups, whereas purchasing agents in the Canadian chemical industry have relatively more influence in buying decisions.

People in the Buying Center The composition of the buying center in a given organization depends on the specific item being bought. Although a buyer or

purchasing manager is almost always a member of the buying center, individuals from other functional areas are included, depending on what is to be purchased. In buying a million-dollar machine tool, the president (because of the size of the purchase) and the production vice president or manager would probably be members. For key components to be incorporated in a final manufactured product, a cross-functional group of individuals from research and development (R&D), engineering, and quality control are likely to be added. For new word-processing equipment, experienced secretaries who will use the equipment would be members. Still, a major question in penetrating the buying center is finding and reaching the people who will initiate, influence, and actually make the buying decision.

Roles in the Buying Center

Roles in the Buying Center   Researchers have identified five specific roles that an individual in a buying center can play.[21] In some purchases the same person may perform two or more of these roles.

- *Users* are the people in the organization who actually use the product or service, such as a secretary who will use a new word processor.
- *Influencers* affect the buying decision, usually by helping define the specifications for what is bought. The information systems manager would be a key influencer in the purchase of a new mainframe computer.
- *Buyers* have formal authority and responsibility to select the supplier and negotiate the terms of the contract. The purchasing manager probably would perform this role in the purchase of a mainframe computer.
- *Deciders* have the formal or informal power to select or approve the supplier that receives the contract. Whereas in routine orders the decider is usually the buyer or purchasing manager, in important technical purchases it is more likely to be someone from R&D, engineering, or quality control. The decider for a key component being incorporated in a final manufactured product might be any of these three people.
- *Gatekeepers* control the flow of information in the buying center. Purchasing personnel, technical experts, and secretaries can all keep salespeople or information from reaching people performing the other four roles.

Buying Situations and the Buying Center   The number of people in the buying center largely depends on the specific buying situation. Researchers who have studied organizational buying identify three types of buying situations, called **buy classes**. These buy classes vary from the routine reorder, or *straight rebuy,* to the completely new purchase, termed *new buy.* In between these extremes is the *modified rebuy.* Some examples will clarify the differences.[22]

- *Straight rebuy.* Here the buyer or purchasing manager reorders an existing product or service from the list of acceptable suppliers, probably without even checking with users or influencers from the engineering, production, or quality control departments. Office supplies and maintenance services are usually obtained as straight rebuys.
- *Modified rebuy.* In this buying situation the users, influencers, or deciders in the buying center want to change the product specifications, price, delivery schedule, or supplier. Although the item purchased is largely the same as with the straight rebuy, the changes usually necessitate enlarging the buying center to include people outside the purchasing department.
- *New buy.* Here the organization is a first-time buyer of the product or service. This involves greater potential risks in the purchase, so the buying center is enlarged to include all those who have a stake in the new buy. Procter & Gamble's recent purchase of a multimillion-dollar fiber-optic network from Corning, Inc., linking its corporate offices in Cincinnati, represented a new buy.[23]

Figure 6–4 on the next page summarizes how buy classes affect buying center tendencies in different ways.[24]

The marketing strategies of sellers facing each of these three buying situations can vary greatly because the importance of personnel from functional areas such as purchasing, engineering, production, and R&D often varies with (1) the type of buying situation and (2) the stage of the purchasing process.[25] If it is a new buy for the manufacturer, you should be prepared to act as a consultant to the buyer, work with technical personnel, and expect a long time for a buying decision to be reached. However, if the manufacturer has bought the item from you before (a straight or modified rebuy), you might emphasize a competitive price and a reliable supply in meetings with the purchasing agent.

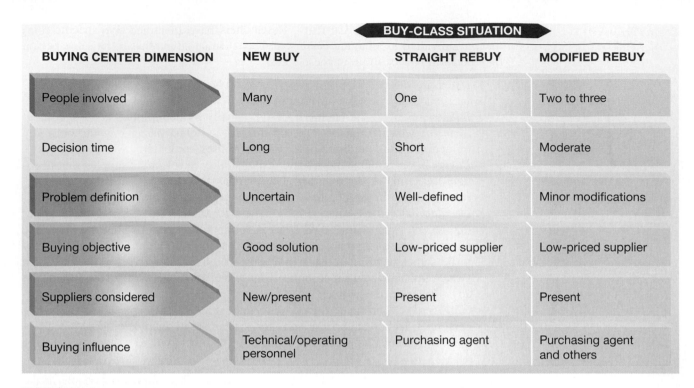

FIGURE 6–4
How the buying situation
affects buying center behavior

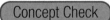 **Concept Check**

1. What one department is almost always represented by a person in the buying center?

2. What are the three types of buying situations or buy classes?

CHARTING THE ORGANIZATIONAL BUYING PROCESS

Organizational buyers, like consumers, engage in a decision process when selecting products and services. **Organizational buying behavior** is the decision-making process that organizations use to establish the need for products and services and identify, evaluate, and choose among alternative brands and suppliers. There are important similarities and differences between the two decision-making processes. To better understand the nature of organizational buying behavior, we first compare it with consumer buying behavior and then describe an actual organizational purchase in detail.

Stages in the Organizational Buying Process

As shown in Figure 6–5 (and covered in Chapter 5), the five stages a student might use in buying a portable MP3-capable CD player also apply to organizational purchases. However, comparing the two right-hand columns in Figure 6–5 reveals some key differences. For example, when a portable MP3-capable CD player manufacturer buys earphones for its units from a supplier, more individuals are involved, supplier capability becomes more important, and the postpurchase evaluation behavior is more formalized.

The earphone-buying decision process is typical of the steps made by organizational buyers. Let's now examine in detail the decision-making process for a more complex product—machine vision systems.

STAGE IN THE BUYING DECISION PROCESS	CONSUMER PURCHASE: PORTABLE MP3-CAPABLE CD PLAYER FOR A STUDENT	ORGANIZATIONAL PURCHASE: EARPHONES FOR A PORTABLE MP3-CAPABLE CD PLAYER
Problem recognition	Student doesn't like the features of the portable CD player now owned and desires a new one.	Marketing research and sales departments observe that competitors are improving the earphones on their portable CD models. The firm decides to improve the earphones on their own new models, which will be purchased from an outside supplier.
Information search	Student uses past experience, that of friends, ads, the Internet, and *Consumer Reports* to collect information and uncover alternatives.	Design and production engineers draft specifications for earphones. The purchasing department identifies suppliers of portable CD player earphones.
Alternative evaluation	Alternative portable CD players are evaluated on the basis of important attributes desired in one, and several stores are visited.	Purchasing and engineering personnel visit with suppliers and assess (1) facilities, (2) capacity, (3) quality control, and (4) financial status. They drop any suppliers not satisfactory on these factors.
Purchase decision	A specific brand of portable CD player is selected, the price is paid, and the student leaves the store.	They use (1) quality, (2) price, (3) delivery, and (4) technical capability as key buying criteria to select a supplier. Then they negotiate terms and award a contract.
Postpurchase behavior	Student reevaluates the purchase decision, may return the player to the store if it is unsatisfactory, and looks for supportive information to justify the purchase.	They evaluate suppliers using a formal vendor rating system and notify a supplier if earphones do not meet their quality standard. If the problem is not corrected, they drop the firm as a future supplier.

FIGURE 6–5

Comparing the stages in consumer and organizational purchases

Buying a Machine Vision System

Machine vision is widely regarded as one of the keys to the factory of the future. The chief elements of a machine vision system are its optics, light source, camera, video processor, and computer software. Vision systems are mainly used for product inspection. They are also becoming important as one of the chief elements in the information feedback loop of systems that control manufacturing processes. Vision systems, selling in the price range of $25,000, are mostly sold to original equipment manufacturers (OEMs) who incorporate them in still larger industrial automation systems, which sell for $200,000 to $300,000. Companies worldwide are expected to spend more than $9.1 billion for machine vision systems in 2007.[26]

Finding productive applications for machine vision involves the constant search for technology and designs that satisfy user needs. The buying process for machine vision components and assemblies is frequently a new buy because many machine vision systems contain elements that require some custom design. Let's track five purchasing stages that a company such as the Industrial Automation Division of Siemens, a large German industrial firm, would follow when purchasing components and assemblies for the machine vision systems it produces and installs.

Problem Recognition   Sales engineers constantly canvass industrial automation equipment users such as American National Can, Ford Motor Company, Grumman Aircraft, and many Asian and European firms for leads on upcoming industrial automation projects. They also keep these firms current on Siemens' technology, products, and services. When a firm needing a machine vision capability identifies a

The purchase of machine vision systems involves a lengthy organizational buying process.

project that would benefit from Siemens' expertise, company engineers typically work with the firm to determine the kind of system required to meet the customer's need.

After a contract is won, project personnel must often make a **make-buy decision**—an evaluation of whether components and assemblies will be purchased from outside suppliers or built by the company itself. (Siemens produces many components and assemblies.) When these items are to be purchased from outside suppliers, the company engages in a thorough supplier search and evaluation process.

Information Search   Companies such as Siemens employ a sophisticated process for identifying outside suppliers of components and assemblies. For standard items such as connectors, printed circuit boards, and components such as resistors and capacitors, the purchasing agent consults the company's purchasing databank, which contains information on hundreds of suppliers and thousands of products. All products in the databank have been prenegotiated as to price, quality, and delivery time, and many have been assessed using **value analysis**—a systematic appraisal of the design, quality, and performance of a product to reduce purchasing costs.

For one-of-a-kind components or assemblies such as new optics, cameras, and light sources, the company relies on its engineers to keep current on new developments in product technology. This information is often found in technical journals and industry magazines or at international trade shows where suppliers display their most recent innovations. In some instances, supplier representatives might be asked to make presentations to the buying center at Siemens. Such a group often consists of a project engineer; several design, system, and manufacturing engineers; and a purchasing agent.

Alternative Evaluation   Three main buying criteria are used to select suppliers: price, performance, and delivery. Other important criteria include assurance that a supplier will not go out of business during the contractual period, assurance that the supplier will meet product quality and performance specifications, and service during the contractual period. Typically, two or three suppliers for each standard component and assembly are identified from a **bidder's list**—a list of firms believed to be qualified to supply a given item. This list is generated from the company's purchasing databank as well as from engineering inputs. Specific items that are unique or one-of-a-kind may be obtained from a single supplier after careful evaluation by the buying center.

Firms selected from the bidder's list are sent a quotation request from the purchasing agent, describing the desired quantity, delivery date(s), and specifications of the components or assemblies. Suppliers are expected to respond within 30 days.

Purchase Decision   Unlike the short purchase stage in a consumer purchase, the period from supplier selection to order placement to product delivery can take several weeks or even months. Even after bids for components and assemblies are submitted, further negotiation concerning price, performance, and delivery terms is likely. Sometimes conditions related to warranties, indemnities, and payment schedules have to be agreed on. The purchase decision is further complicated by the fact that two or more suppliers of the same item might be awarded contracts. This practice can occur when large orders are requested. Furthermore, suppliers who are not chosen are informed why their bids were not selected.

Postpurchase Behavior   As in the consumer purchase decision process, postpurchase evaluation occurs in the industrial purchase decision process, but it is formalized and often more sophisticated. All items purchased are examined in a formal product acceptance process. The performance of the supplier is also monitored and recorded. Performance on past contracts determines a supplier's chances of being asked to bid on future purchases, and poor performance may result in a supplier's name being dropped from the bidder's list.

   This example of an organizational purchase suggests four lessons for marketers who want to increase their chances of selling products and services to organizations. Firms selling to organizations must: (1) understand the organization's needs, (2) get on the right bidder's list, (3) find the right people in the buying center, and (4) provide value to organizational buyers.

Concept Check

1. What is a make-buy decision?

2. What is a bidder's list?

ONLINE BUYING IN ORGANIZATIONAL MARKETS

Organizational buying behavior and business marketing continues to evolve with the application of Internet technology. Organizations dwarf consumers both in terms of online transactions made and purchase volume.[27] In fact, organizational buyers account for about 80 percent of the total worldwide dollar value of all online transactions. Online organizational buyers around the world will purchase between $6 and $7.5 trillion worth of products and services by 2007. Organizational buyers in the United States will account for about 60 percent of these purchases.

Prominence of Online Buying in Organizational Markets

Online buying in organizational markets is prominent for three major reasons.[28] First, organizational buyers depend heavily on timely supplier information that describes product availability, technical specifications, application uses, price, and delivery schedules. This information can be conveyed quickly via Internet technology. Second, this technology has been shown to substantially reduce buyer order processing costs. At General Electric, online buying has cut the cost of a transaction from $50 to $100 per purchase to about $5. Third, business marketers have found that Internet technology can reduce marketing costs, particularly sales and advertising expense, and broaden their potential customer base for many types of products and services. For these reasons, online buying is popular in all three kinds of organizational markets. For example, airlines electronically order over $400 million in spare parts from the Boeing Company each year. Customers of W. W. Grainger, a large U.S. wholesaler of maintenance, repair, and operating supplies, buy more than $425 million worth of these products annually online. Supply and service purchases totaling $650 million each year are made online by the Los Angeles County government.

WEB LINK   eBay Means Business Too

San Jose, California–based eBay, Inc., is a true Internet phenomenon. By any measure, it is the predominant person-to-person trading community in the world.

eBay recently introduced a trading platform for the nearly 23 million small businesses in the United States and even greater numbers around the world. When you go to the eBayBusiness website (www.ebaybusiness.com), you will find a homepage structured for the small business marketplace. The site is easy for small business buyers and sellers to

"I save so much on eBay, I recommend it to my clients"

navigate and features more than 20 industry marketplaces and a dozen cross-industry products, such as office equipment, metalworking, and professional photography. Transactions on eBayBusiness exceed sales of $2 billion annually.

eBay is always updating its industry marketplaces. Go to the industry listing on the homepage. What type of industries are most prominent? Are products for all three kinds of organizational markets—industrial, reseller, and government—available?

Online buying can assume many forms. Organizational buyers can purchase directly from suppliers. For instance, a buyer might acquire a dozen desktop photocopiers from Xerox.com. This same buyer might purchase office furniture and supplies through a reseller such as Office Depot at officedepot.com. Increasingly, organizational buyers and business marketers are using e-marketplaces and online auctions to purchase and sell products and services.

E-Marketplaces: Virtual Organizational Markets

A significant development in organizational buying has been the creation of online trading communities, called **e-marketplaces**, that bring together buyers and supplier organizations. These online communities go by a variety of names, including B2B exchanges and e-hubs, and make possible the real-time exchange of information, money, products, and services.

E-marketplaces can be independent trading communities or private exchanges.[29] Independent e-marketplaces act as a neutral third-party and provide an Internet technology trading platform and a centralized market that enable exchanges between buyers and sellers. They charge a fee for their service and exist in settings that have one or more of the following features: (1) thousands of geographically dispersed buyers and sellers, (2) volatile prices caused by demand and supply fluctuations, (3) time sensitivity due to perishable offerings and changing technologies, and (4) easily comparable offerings between a variety of suppliers. Well-known independent e-marketplaces include PlasticsNet (plastics), FreeMarkets (industrial parts, raw material, and commodities), and XSAg.com (agricultural products). Small business buyers and sellers, in particular, benefit from independent e-marketplaces. These e-marketplaces offer them an economical way to expand their customer base and reduce the cost of products and services. eBay recently launched eBayBusiness to serve the small businesses market in the United States. You can learn about how B2B exchanges work and eBayBusiness in the accompanying Web Link.[30]

Large companies tend to favor private exchanges that link them with their network of qualified suppliers and customers. Private exchanges focus on streamlining a company's purchase transactions with its suppliers and customers. Like independent e-marketplaces, they provide a technology trading platform and central market for buyer–seller interactions. They are not a neutral third party, however, but represent the interests of their owners. For example, Worldwide Retail Exchange performs the buying function for its 62 retail members, including Best Buy, The Gap, Radio Shack, Safeway, Target, and

Walgreen. The Global Healthcare Exchange engages in the buying and selling of health care products for 1,400 hospitals and more than 100 health care suppliers, such as Abbott Laboratories, Johnson & Johnson, and U.S. Surgical. Each of these private exchanges has saved their members $1 billion due to efficiencies in purchase transactions.

Online Auctions in Organizational Markets

Online auctions have grown in popularity among organizational buyers and business marketers. Many e-marketplaces offer this service. Two general types of auctions are common: (1) a traditional auction and (2) a reverse auction.[31] Figure 6–6 shows how buyer and seller participants and price behavior differ by type of auction. Let's look at each auction type more closely to understand the implications of each for buyers and sellers.

In a **traditional auction** a seller puts an item up for sale and would-be buyers are invited to bid in competition with each other. As more would-be buyers become involved, there is an upward pressure on bid prices. Why? Bidding is sequential. Prospective buyers observe the bids of others and decide whether or not to increase the bid price. The auction ends when a single bidder remains and "wins" the item with its highest price. For example, eBayBusiness uses a traditional auction. Traditional auctions are also used to dispose of excess merchandise. For example, Dell, Inc., sells surplus, refurbished, or closeout computer merchandise at its dellauction.com website.

A reverse auction works in the opposite direction from a traditional auction. In a **reverse auction**, a buyer communicates a need for a product or service and would-be suppliers are invited to bid in competition with each other. As more would-be suppliers become involved, there is a downward pressure on bid prices for the buyer's business. Why? Like traditional auctions, bidding is sequential and prospective suppliers observe the bids of others and decide whether or not to decrease the bid price. The auction ends when a single bidder remains and "wins" the business with its lowest price. Reverse auctions benefit organizational buyers by reducing the cost of their purchases. As an example, Global eXchange Services, which runs online reverse auctions, claims it saved General Electric $780 million on the purchase of $6 billion worth of products and services.

FIGURE 6–6

How buyer and seller participants and price behavior differ by type of online auction

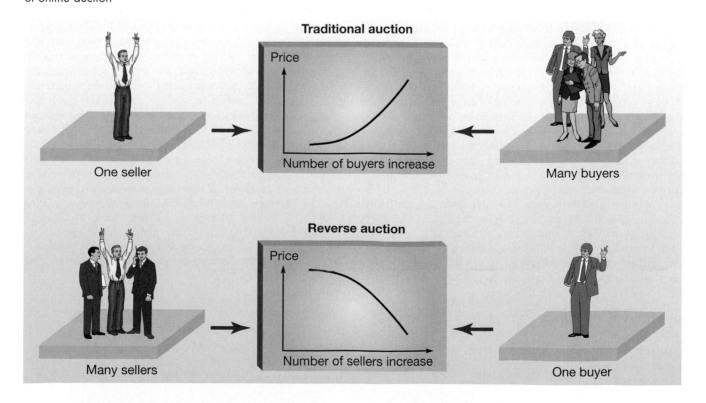

Clearly, buyers welcome the lower prices generated by reverse auctions. Some suppliers also favor reverse auctions because they give them a chance to capture business that they might not have otherwise had because of a long-standing purchase relationship between the buyer and another supplier. On the other hand, suppliers say that reverse auctions put too much emphasis on prices, discourage consideration of other important buying criteria, and threaten supply partnership opportunities.[32]

Concept Check

1. What are e-marketplaces?

2. In general, which type of online auction creates upward pressure on bid prices and which type creates downward pressure on bid prices?

CHAPTER IN REVIEW

1 *Distinguish among industrial, reseller, and government organizational markets.*

There are three different organizational markets: industrial, reseller, and government. Industrial firms in some way reprocess a product or service they buy before selling it to the next buyer. Resellers—wholesalers and retailers—buy physical products and resell them again without any reprocessing. Government agencies, at the federal, state, and local levels, buy goods and services for the constituents they serve. The North American Industry Classification System (NAICS) provides common industry definitions for Canada, Mexico, and the United States, which facilitates the measurement of economic activity for these three organizational markets.

2 *Describe the key characteristics of organizational buying that make it different from consumer buying.*

Seven major characteristics of organizational buying make it different from consumer buying. These include demand characteristics, size of the order or purchase, number of potential buyers, buying objectives, buying criteria, buyer–seller relationships and supply partnerships, and multiple buying influences within organizations. The organizational buying process itself is more formalized, more individuals are involved, supplier capability is more important, and the postpurchase evaluation behavior often includes performance of the supplier and the item purchased. Figure 6–5 details how the purchase of an MP3-capable CD player differs between a consumer and organizational purchase. The case study describing the purchase of machine vision systems by an industrial firm illustrates this process in greater depth.

3 *Explain how buying centers and buying situations influence organizational purchasing.*

Buying centers and buying situations have an important influence on organizational purchasing. A buying center consists of a group of individuals who share common goals, risks, and knowledge important to a purchase decision. A buyer or purchasing manager is almost always a member of a buying center. However, other individuals may affect organizational purchasing

due to their unique roles in a purchase decision. Five specific roles that a person may play in a buying center include users, influencers, buyers, deciders, and gatekeepers. The specific buying situation will influence the number of people in and the different roles played in a buying center. For a routine reorder of an item—a straight rebuy situation—a purchasing manager or buyer will typically act alone in making a purchasing decision. When an organization is a first-time purchaser of a product or service—a new buy situation—a buying center is enlarged and all five roles in a buying center often emerge. A modified rebuy buying situation lies between these two extremes. Figure 6–4 offers additional insights into how buying centers and buying situations influence organization purchasing.

4 *Recognize the importance and nature of online buying in industrial, reseller, and government organizational markets.*

Organizations dwarf consumers in terms of online transactions made and purchase volume. Online buying in organizational markets is popular for three reasons. First, organizational buyers depend on timely supplier information that describes product availability, technical specifications, application uses, price, and delivery schedules. This information can be conveyed quickly via Internet technology. Second, this technology substantially reduces buyer order processing costs. Third, business marketers have found that Internet technology can reduce marketing costs, particularly sales and advertising expense, and broaden their customer base. Two developments in online buying have been the creation of e-marketplaces and online auctions. E-marketplaces provide a technology trading platform and a centralized market for buyer–seller transactions and make possible the real-time exchange of information, money, products, and services. These e-marketplaces can be independent trading communities, such as FreeMarkets, or private exchanges such as the Worldwide Retail Exchange. Online traditional and reverse auctions represent a second major development. With traditional auctions, the highest-priced bidder "wins." Conversely, the lowest-priced bidder "wins" with reverse auctions.

FOCUSING ON KEY TERMS

bidder's list p. 160
business marketing p. 148
buy classes p. 157

buying center p. 156
derived demand p. 151
e-marketplaces p. 162

government units p. 149
industrial firms p. 149
ISO 9000 p. 154
make-buy decision p. 160
North American Industry Classification System (NAICS) p. 150
organizational buyers p. 148
organizational buying behavior p. 158

organizational buying criteria p. 153
reciprocity p. 155
resellers p. 149
reverse auction p. 163
reverse marketing p. 154
supply partnership p. 155
traditional auction p. 163
value analysis p. 160

DISCUSSION AND APPLICATION QUESTIONS

1   Describe the major differences among industrial firms, resellers, and government units in the United States.

2   Explain how the North American Industry Classification System (NAICS) might be helpful in understanding industrial, reseller, and government markets, and discuss the limitations inherent in this system.

3   List and discuss the key characteristics of organizational buying that make it different from consumer buying.

4   What is a buying center? Describe the roles assumed by people in a buying center and what useful questions should be raised to guide any analysis of the structure and behavior of a buying center.

5   Effective marketing is of increasing importance in today's competitive environment. How can firms more effectively market to organizations?

6   A firm that is marketing multimillion-dollar wastewater treatment systems to cities has been unable to sell a new type of system. This setback has occurred even though the firm's systems are cheaper than competitive systems and meet U.S. Environmental Protection Agency (EPA) specifications. To date, the firm's marketing efforts have been directed to city purchasing departments and the various state EPAs to get on approved bidder's lists. Talks with city-employed personnel have indicated that the new system is very different from current systems and therefore city sanitary and sewer department engineers, directors of these two departments, and city council members are unfamiliar with the workings of the system. Consulting engineers, hired by cities to work on the engineering and design features of these systems and paid on a percentage of system cost, are also reluctant to favor the new system. (*a*) What roles do the various individuals play in the purchase process for a wastewater treatment system? (*b*) How could the firm improve the marketing effort behind the new system?

GOING ONLINE   Navigating the NAICS

The North American Industrial Classification System (NAICS) structures industrial sectors into their component industries. The NAICS can be accessed at www.census.gov by clicking "NAICS." Industry information can be obtained by navigating through the codes.

You have been hired as a market analyst by a snack food company that is looking for opportunities outside its normal business. The vice president of marketing has asked you to look into the dog and cat food manufacturing industry to determine its size. She suggests that a good place to start is the NAICS, beginning with the two-digit manufacturing sectors (codes 31–33).

1   What is the three-digit industry subsector code for food manufacturing?

2   What is the six-digit U.S. code for dog and cat food manufacturing?

3   How many establishments and what is the value of shipments sold by the U.S. dog and cat food manufacturing industry based on the latest government statistics? (*Hint:* You will need to click "Economic Census" to get this information.)

BUILDING YOUR MARKETING PLAN

Your marketing plan may need an estimate of the size of the market potential or industry potential (see Chapter 9) for a particular product-market in which you compete. Use these steps:

1   Define the product-market precisely, such as ice cream.

2   Visit the NAICS website at www.census.gov.

3   Click "NAICS" and enter a keyword that describes your product-market (e.g., ice cream).

4   Follow the instructions to the specific NAICS code and economic census data that details the dollar sales and provides the estimate of market or industry potential.

VIDEO CASE 6   Lands' End: Where Buyers Rule

Organizational buying is a part of the marketing effort that influences every aspect of business at Lands' End. As senior vice president of operations Phil Schaecher explains, "When we talk about purchasing at Lands' End, most people think of the purchase of merchandise for resale, but we buy many other things aside from merchandise, everything from the simplest office supply to the most sophisticated piece of material-handling equipment." As a result, Lands' End has developed a sophisticated approach to organizational buying, which is one of the keys to its incredible success.

THE COMPANY

The company started by selling sailboat equipment, duffle bags, rainsuits, and sweaters from a basement location in Chicago's old tannery district. In its first catalog, the company name was printed with a typing error—the apostrophe in the wrong place—but the fledgling company couldn't afford to correct and reprint it. So ever since, the company name has been Lands' End—with the misplaced apostrophe.

When the company outgrew its Chicago location, founder Gary Comer relocated it to Dodgeville, Wisconsin, where he had fallen in love with the rolling hills and changing seasons. The original business ideas were simple: "Sell only things we believe in, ship every order the day it arrives, and unconditionally guarantee everything." Over time, the company developed eight principles of doing business:

1. Never reduce the quality of a product to make it cheaper.
2. Price products fairly and honestly.
3. Accept any return for any reason.
4. Ship items in stock the day after the order is received.
5. What is best for the customer is best for Lands' End.
6. Place contracts with manufacturers who are cost-conscious and efficient.
7. Operate efficiently.
8. Keep overhead low.

These principles became the guidelines for the company's dedicated local employees and helped create extraordinary expectations from Lands' End customers.

Today, Lands' End is one of the world's largest direct merchants, with annual sales of traditionally styled clothing, luggage, and home products exceeding $1.4 billion. The products are offered through catalogs, the Internet, and retail stores. Last year, Lands' End distributed more than 260 million catalogs designed for specific segments,

including *The Lands' End Catalog, Lands' End Men, Lands' End Women, Lands' End Kids, Lands' End for School, Lands' End Home,* and *Lands' End Corporate*. In a typical day, catalog shoppers place more than 40,000 telephone calls to the company. The Lands' End website (www.landsend.com) also offers every Lands' End product and a wide variety of Internet shopping innovations such as a 3-D model customized to each customer (called My Virtual Model™); a "personal shopper," to suggest products that match the consumer's preferences; and a feature that allows customers to "chat" online directly with a customer service representative. Lands' End also operates stores in the United States, the United Kingdom, and Japan. Selected Lands' End merchandise is also sold at Sears following the purchase of Lands' End by Sears in 2002.

The company's goal is to please customers with the highest levels of quality and service in the industry. Lands' End maintains the high quality of its products through several important activities. For example, the company works directly with mills and manufacturers to retain control of quality and design. "The biggest difference between Lands' End and some other retailers or catalog businesses is that we actually design all the product here and we do all the specifications. Therefore, the manufacturer is building that product directly to our specs, we are not buying off of somebody else's line," explains Joan Mudget, vice president of quality assurance. In addition, Lands' End tests its products for comfort and fit by paying real people (local residents and children) to "wear-test" and "fit-test" all types of garments.

Service has also become an important part of the Lands' End reputation. Customers expect prompt, professional service at every step—initiating the order, making selections, shipping, and follow-up (if necessary). Some of the ways Lands' End meets these expectations include offering the simplest guarantee in the industry—"Guaranteed. Period."—toll-free telephone lines open 24 hours-a-day, 364 days a year, continuous product training for telephone representatives, and two-day shipping. Lands' End operators even send personal responses to all e-mail messages, approximately 230,000 per year.

ORGANIZATIONAL BUYING AT LANDS' END

The sixth Lands' End business principle (described above) is accomplished through the company's organizational buying process. First, its buyers specify fabric quality, construction, and sizing standards, which typically

exceed industry standards, for current and potential Lands' End products. Then the buyers literally search around the world for the best possible source of fabrics and products. Once a potential supplier is identified, one of the company's 150 quality assurance personnel makes an information-gathering visit. The purpose of the visit is to understand the supplier's values, to assess four criteria (economic, quality, service, and vendor), and to determine if the Lands' End standards can be achieved.

Lands' End evaluations of potential suppliers lead to the selection of what the company hopes will become long-term partners. As Mudget explains, "When we're looking for new manufacturers we are looking for the long term. I think one of the most interesting things is we're not out there looking for new vendors every year to fill the same products." In fact, Lands' End believes that the term *supplier* does not adequately describe the importance the company places on the relationships. Lands' End suppliers are viewed as allies, supporters, associates, colleagues, and stakeholders in the future of the company. Once an alliance is formed the product specifications and the performance on those specifications are regularly evaluated.

Lands' End buyers face a variety of buying situations. Straight rebuys involve reordering an existing product—such as shipping boxes—without evaluating or changing specifications. Modified rebuys involve changing some aspect of a previously ordered product—such as the collar of a knit shirt—based on input from consumers, retailers, or other people involved in the purchase decision. Finally, new buys involve first-time purchases—such as Lands' End addition of men's suits to its product line. The complexity of the process can vary with the type of purchase. Schaecher explains, "As you get more complicated in the purchase there are more things you look at to decide on a vendor."

FUTURE CHALLENGES FOR LANDS' END

Lands' End faces several challenges as it pursues improvements in its organizational buying process. First, new technologies offer opportunities for fast, efficient, and accurate communication with suppliers. Ed Smidebush, general inventory manager, describes a new system at Lands' End: "Our quick response system is a computerized system where we transmit electronically to our vendors each Sunday night, forecast information as well as stock positions and purchase order information so that on Monday morning this information will be incorporated directly into their manufacturing reports so that they can prioritize their production." Occasionally Lands' End must work with its suppliers to improve their technology and information system capabilities.

Another challenge for Lands' End is to anticipate changes in consumer interests. While it has many years of experience with retail consumers, preferences for colors, fabrics, and styles change frequently, requiring buyers to constantly monitor the marketplace. In addition, Lands' End's more recent offerings to corporate customers require constant attention "because business customers' wants and incentives, and the environment in which they're shopping, are very different from consumers at home," explains marketing manager Hilary Kleese.

Finally, Lands' End must anticipate the quantities of each of its products consumers are likely to order. To do this, historical information is used to develop forecasts. One of the best tests of their forecast accuracy is the holiday season, when Lands' End receives more than 100,000 calls each day. Having the right products available is important because, as every employee knows from Principle 4, every order must be shipped the day after it is received.

Questions

1 Who is likely to comprise the buying center in the decision to select a new supplier for Lands' End? Which of the buying center members are likely to play the roles of users, influencers, buyers, deciders, and gatekeepers?

2 Which stages of the organizational buying decision process does Lands' End follow when it selects a new supplier? What selection criteria does the company utilize in the process?

3 Describe purchases Lands' End buyers typically face in each of the three buying situations: straight rebuy, modified rebuy, new buy.

CHAPTER

7 REACHING GLOBAL MARKETS

LEARNING OBJECTIVES

After reading this chapter you should be able to:

1 Describe the nature and scope of world trade from a global perspective and its implications for the United States.

2 Identify the major trends that have influenced the landscape of global marketing in the past decade.

3 Identify the environmental factors that shape global marketing efforts.

4 Name and describe the alternative approaches companies use to enter global markets.

5 Explain the distinction between standardization and customization when companies craft worldwide marketing programs.

MATTEL'S GLOBAL MARKETING IS MORE THAN CHILD'S PLAY

Mattel is rewriting the rules for toy marketing on a global scale. As the worldwide leader in the design, manufacture, and marketing of toys and family products, Mattel successfully markets its best-selling Barbie®, Hot Wheels®, Fisher-Price®, and American Girl® brands in more than 150 countries.

Mattel's global marketing success can be linked to its new-product development effort. Toy developers are encouraged to think globally from the moment a new toy is conceived, with an eye to developing products that are likely to have universal appeal. Why? Mattel's research with children in dozens of countries has yielded a novel insight: Children are more alike than they are different in their product preferences. Today, Mattel markets as much as 80 percent of its product offerings to a global audience, with just 20 percent geared to individual country markets. Mattel's product introductions as well are global in scope. For example, Mattel recently launched Rapunzel Barbie on the same day in 59 countries supported by a televised advertising campaign broadcast in 35 languages. The widening international reach of retailing giants such as Wal-Mart, Target, and French-based Carrefour SA (the world's second-largest retailer) also permits Mattel to coordinate its store merchandising campaigns on a global scale.

Mattel's global marketing orientation has paid huge dividends. About 40 percent of the company's sales come from outside the United States. One Barbie is sold every three seconds somewhere in the world.[1]

This chapter describes the global marketing environment at the dawn of the twenty-first century. It also highlights the many ways successful companies like Mattel engage in global marketing.

DYNAMICS OF WORLD TRADE

The dollar value of world trade has more than doubled in the past decade and will exceed $11.5 trillion in 2008. Manufactured goods and commodities account for 75 percent of world trade. Service industries, including telecommunications, transportation, insurance, education, banking, and tourism, represent the other 25 percent of world trade.

World Trade Flows

All nations and regions of the world do not participate equally in world trade. World trade flows reflect interdependencies among industries, countries, and regions and manifest themselves in country, company, industry, and regional exports and imports.

Global Perspective   Figure 7–1 shows the estimated dollar value of exports and imports among North American countries, Europe, Asian/Pacific Rim countries, and the rest of the world, including intraregional trade flows.[2] The United States, Europe, Canada, China, and Japan together account for more than two-thirds of world trade.

Not all trade involves the exchange of money for goods or services. In a world where 70 percent of all countries do not have convertible currencies or where government-owned enterprises lack sufficient cash or credit for imports, other means of payment are used. An estimated 15 to 20 percent of world trade involves **countertrade**, the practice of using barter rather than money for making global sales.[3]

FIGURE 7–1
Illustrative world trade flows for manufactured goods and commodities (billions of dollars)

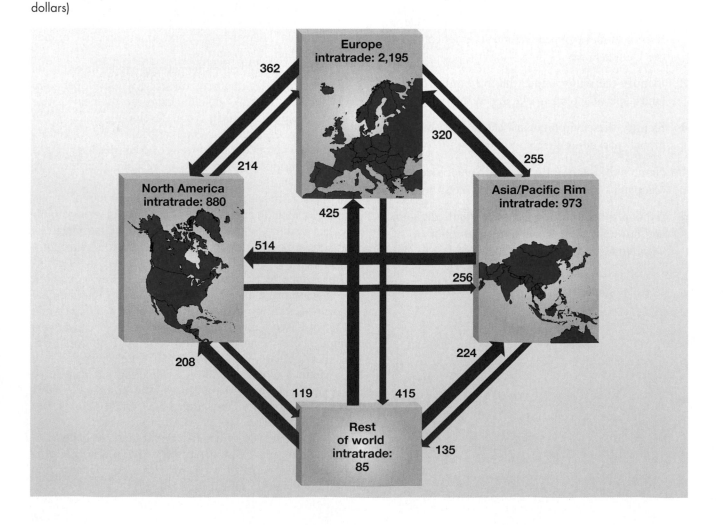

Countertrade is popular with many Eastern European nations, Russia, and Asian countries. For example, the Malaysian government recently exchanged 20,000 tons of rice for an equivalent amount of Philippine corn. Volvo of North America delivered automobiles to the Siberian police force when Siberia had no cash to pay for them. It accepted payment in oil, which it then sold for cash to pay for media advertising in the United States.[4]

A global perspective on world trade views exports and imports as complementary economic flows: A country's imports affect its exports and exports affect its imports. Every nation's imports arise from the exports of other nations. As the exports of one country increase, its national output and income rise, which in turn leads to an increase in the demand for imports. This nation's greater demand for imports stimulates the exports of other countries. Increased demand for exports of other nations energizes their economic activity, resulting in higher national income, which stimulates their demand for imports. In short, imports affect exports and vice versa. This phenomenon is called the *trade feedback effect* and is one argument for free trade among nations.

United States Perspective   The United States is the world's perennial leader in terms of **gross domestic product** (GDP), which is the monetary value of all goods and services produced in a country during one year. The United States is also among the world's leaders in exports due in large part to its global prominence in the aerospace, chemical, office equipment, information technology, pharmaceutical, telecommunications, and professional service industries. However, the U.S. percentage share of world exports has shifted downward over the past 30 years, whereas its percentage share of world imports has increased. Therefore, the relative position of the United States as a supplier to the world has diminished despite an absolute growth in exports. At the same time, its relative role as a marketplace for the world has increased, particularly for automobile, oil, textile, apparel, and consumer electronics products.

The difference between the monetary value of a nation's exports and imports is called the **balance of trade**. When a country's exports exceed its imports, it incurs a surplus in its balance of trade. When imports exceed exports, a deficit results. World trade trends in U.S. exports and imports are reflected in the U.S. balance of trade. Since 1975, two important things have happened in U.S. exports and imports. First, imports have significantly exceeded exports each year, indicating that the United States has a continuing balance of trade deficit. Second, the volume of both exports and imports is about 10 to 15 times what it was in the mid-1970s, showing why almost every American is significantly affected. The effect varies from the products they buy (Samsung DVD players from South Korea, Waterford crystal from Ireland, Louis Vuitton luggage from France) to those they sell (Cisco Systems' Internet technology to Europe, Du Pont's chemicals to the Far East) and the additional jobs and improved standard of living that result.

World trade flows to and from the United States reflect demand and supply interdependencies for goods and services among nations and industries. The three largest importers of U.S. goods and services are Canada, Mexico, and Japan. These countries purchase approximately 44 percent of U.S. exports. The four largest exporters to the United States are Canada, China, Mexico, and Japan, in that order.

The United States is Asia's largest export market, buying about one-third of the exports of Japan, Taiwan, South Korea, and China, a quarter of Hong Kong's exports, and 40 percent of the Philippines's exports. The trade imbalance between the United States and Asia is illustrated by the fact that Japan, South Korea, and China combine for about 80 percent of the total U.S. balance of trade deficit.

Competitive Advantage of Nations

As companies in many industries find themselves competing against foreign competitors at home and abroad, government policy makers around the world are increasingly asking why some companies and industries in a country succeed globally while

FIGURE 7–2

Porter's diamond of national competitive advantage

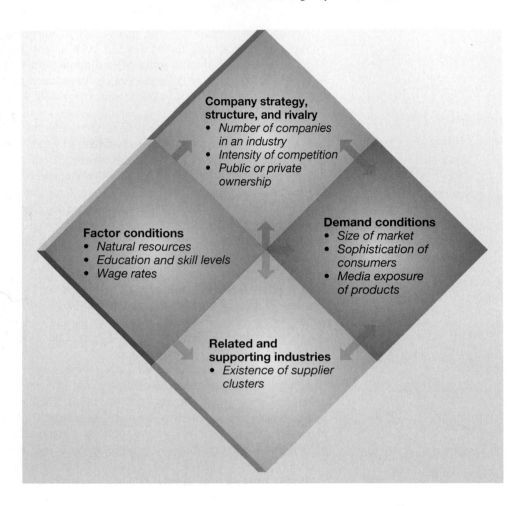

others lose ground or fail. Harvard Business School professor Michael Porter suggests a "diamond" to explain a nation's competitive advantage and why some industries and firms become world leaders.[5] He identified four key elements, which appear in Figure 7–2:

1. *Factor conditions.* These reflect a nation's ability to turn its natural resources, education, and infrastructure into a competitive advantage. Consider Holland, which exports 59 percent of the world's cut flowers. The Dutch lead the world in the cut-flower industry because of their research in flower cultivation, packaging, and shipping—not because of their weather.

2. *Demand conditions.* These include both the number and sophistication of domestic customers for an industry's product. Japan's sophisticated consumers demand quality in their TVs and radios, thereby making Japan's producers such as Sony, Sanyo, Matsushita, and Hitachi among the world leaders in the electronics industry.

3. *Related and supporting industries.* Firms and industries seeking leadership in global markets need clusters of world-class suppliers that accelerate innovation. The German leadership in scientific and industrial instrumentation relates directly to the cluster of supporting German precision engineering suppliers.

4. *Company strategy, structure, and rivalry.* These factors include the conditions governing the way a nation's businesses are organized and managed, along with the intensity of domestic competition. The Italian shoe industry has become a world leader because of intense domestic competition among firms such as MAB, Bruno Magli, and Rossimoda, which has made shoes for Christian Dior and Anne Klein Couture.

Sharp and Bruno Magli have succeeded in the global marketplace as well as in their domestic markets.

Sharp
www.sharpusa.com

Bruno Magli
www.brunomagli.it

In Porter's study, case histories of firms in more than 100 industries were analyzed. While the strategies employed by the most successful global competitors were different in many respects, a common theme emerged: A firm that succeeds in global markets has first succeeded in intense domestic competition. Hence, competitive advantage for global firms grows out of relentless, continuing improvement, innovation, and change.

However, pursuit of a country's competitive advantage in global markets has a dark side—economic espionage.[6] Economic espionage is the clandestine collection of trade secrets or proprietary information about competitors. This practice is common in high-technology industries such as electronics, specialty chemicals, industrial equipment, aerospace, and pharmaceuticals, where technical know-how and trade secrets separate global industry leaders from followers. It has been estimated that the intelligence services of some 23 nations routinely target U.S. firms for information about research and development strategies, manufacturing and marketing plans, and customer lists. To counteract this threat, the **Economic Espionage Act (1996)** makes the theft of trade secrets by foreign entities a federal crime in the United States. This act prescribes prison sentences of up to 15 years and fines up to $500,000 for individuals. Agents of foreign governments found guilty of economic espionage face a 25-year prison sentence and a $10 million fine.

Concept Check

1. What is the trade feedback effect?

2. What variables influence why some companies and industries in a country succeed globally while others lose ground or fail?

MARKETING IN A BORDERLESS ECONOMIC WORLD

Global marketing has and continues to be affected by a growing borderless economic world. Four trends in the past decade have significantly influenced the landscape of global marketing:

Trend 1: Gradual decline of economic protectionism by individual countries.
Trend 2: Formal economic integration and free trade among nations.
Trend 3: Global competition among global companies for global customers.
Trend 4: Development of networked global marketspace.

Decline of Economic Protectionism

Protectionism is the practice of shielding one or more industries within a country's economy from foreign competition through the use of tariffs or quotas. The economic argument for protectionism is that it limits the outsourcing of jobs, protects a nation's political security, discourages economic dependency on other countries, and encourages the development of domestic industries. Read the accompanying Ethics and Social Responsibility Alert and ask yourself if protectionism has an ethical and social responsibility dimension.[7]

Tariffs and quotas discourage world trade as depicted in Figure 7–3. **Tariffs**, which are a government tax on goods or services entering a country, primarily serve to raise prices on imports. The average tariff on manufactured goods in industrialized countries is 4 percent. However, wide differences exist across nations. For example, European Union countries have a 10 percent tariff on cars imported from Japan, which is about four times higher than the tariff imposed by the United States on Japanese cars.

The effect of tariffs on world trade and consumer prices is substantial. Consider U.S. rice exports to Japan. The U.S. Rice Millers' Association claims that if the Japanese rice market were opened to imports by lowering tariffs, lower prices would save Japanese consumers $6 billion annually, and the United States would gain a large share of the Japanese rice market. Similarly, tariffs imposed on bananas by European Union countries cost consumers $2 billion a year. Ecuador (the world's largest banana exporter), Mexico, Guatemala, and Honduras have negotiated a reduction in this levy before 2007.

FIGURE 7–3
How protectionism affects world trade

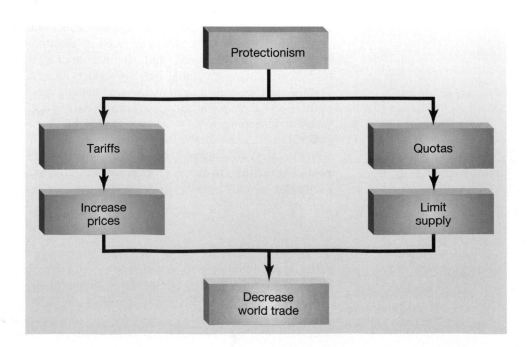

ETHICS AND SOCIAL RESPONSIBILITY ALERT

Global Ethics and Global Economics—The Case of Protectionism

ETHICS

World trade benefits from free and fair trade among nations. Nevertheless, governments of many countries continue to use tariffs and quotas to protect their various domestic industries. Why? Protectionism earns profits for domestic producers and tariff revenue for the government. There is a cost, however. Protectionist policies cost Japanese consumers between $75 billion and $110 billion annually. U.S. consumers pay about $70 billion each year in higher prices because of tariffs and other protective restrictions.

Sugar and textile import quotas in the United States, automobile and banana import tariffs in many European countries, beer import tariffs in Canada, and rice import tariffs in Japan protect domestic industries but also interfere with world trade for these products. Regional trade agreements, such as those found in the provisions of the European Union and the North American Free Trade Agreement, may also pose a situation whereby member nations can obtain preferential treatment in quotas and tariffs but nonmember nations cannot.

Protectionism, in its many forms, raises an interesting global ethical question. Is protectionism, no matter how applied, an ethical practice?

A **quota** is a restriction placed on the amount of a product allowed to enter or leave a country. Quotas can be mandated or voluntary and may be legislated or negotiated by governments. Import quotas seek to guarantee domestic industries access to a certain percentage of their domestic market. For example, there is a limit on imported television sets to Great Britain and Italian quotas on Japanese motorcycles. The United States also imposes quotas. For instance, U.S. sugar import quotas have existed for more than 50 years and preserve about half of the U.S. sugar market for domestic producers. American consumers pay almost $3 billion annually in extra food costs because of this quota. Import quotas on textiles and apparel from Asian countries cost U.S. consumers almost $20 billion per year in higher prices.

Every country engages in some form of protectionism. However, protectionism has declined over the past 50 years due in large part to the *General Agreement on Tariffs and Trade (GATT)*. This international treaty was intended to limit trade barriers and promote world trade through the reduction of tariffs, which it did. However, GATT did not explicitly address nontariff trade barriers, such as quotas and world trade in services, which often sparked heated trade disputes between nations.

World Trade Organization
www.wto.org

As a consequence, the major industrialized nations of the world formed the **World Trade Organization** (WTO) in 1995 to address a broad array of world trade issues.[8] There are 147 WTO member countries, including the United States, which account for more than 90 percent of world trade. The WTO is a permanent institution that sets rules governing trade between its members through panels of trade experts who decide on trade disputes between members and issue binding decisions. The WTO reviews more than 200 disputes annually. For instance, the WTO denied Kodak's multimillion-dollar damage claim that the Japanese government protected Fuji Photo from import competition. In another decision, the WTO allowed Britain, Ireland, and the European Union to reclassify U.S.-produced local area network (LAN) computer equipment as telecommunications gear. The new classification effectively doubled the import tariff on these U.S. goods.

FIGURE 7–4
The countries of the European Union in 2005

European Union
www.europa.eu.int

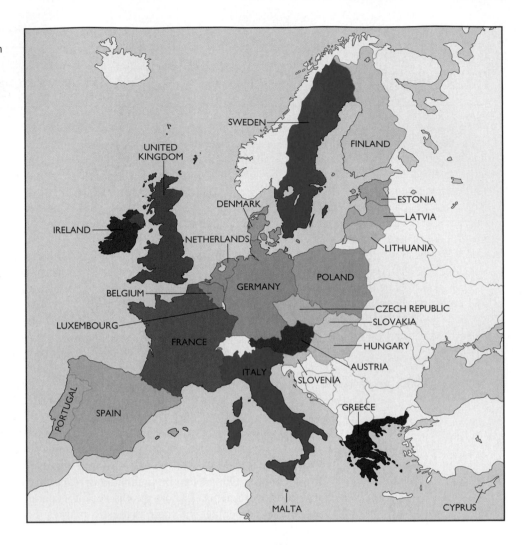

Rise of Economic Integration

In recent years, a number of countries with similar economic goals have formed transnational trade groups or signed trade agreements for the purpose of promoting free trade among member nations and enhancing their individual economies. Three of the best-known examples are the European Union (or simply EU), the North American Free Trade Agreement (NAFTA), and Asian Free Trade Areas.

European Union   The European Union consists of 25-member countries that have eliminated most barriers to the free flow of goods, services, capital, and labor across their borders (see Figure 7–4).[9] This single market houses more than 380 million consumers with a combined gross domestic product larger than that of the United States. In addition, 12 countries have adopted a common currency called the *euro*. Adoption of the euro has been a boon to electronic commerce in the EU by eliminating the need to continually monitor currency exchange rates.

The EU creates abundant marketing opportunities because firms no longer find it necessary to market their products and services on a nation-by-nation basis. Rather, pan-European marketing strategies are possible due to greater uniformity in product and packaging standards; fewer regulatory restriction on transportation, advertising, and promotion imposed by countries; and removal of most tariffs that affect pricing practices. For example, Colgate-Palmolive Company now markets its Colgate toothpaste with one formula and package across EU countries at one price. Similarly,

Black & Decker—the maker of electrical hand tools, appliances, and other consumer products—now produces 8, not 20, motor sizes for the European market, resulting in production and marketing cost savings. These practices were previously impossible because of different government and trade regulations. Europeanwide distribution from fewer locations is also feasible given open borders. French tire maker Michelin has closed 180 of its European distribution centers and now uses just 20 to serve all EU countries.

North American Free Trade Agreement   The North American Free Trade Agreement lifted many trade barriers between Canada, Mexico, and the United States and created a marketplace with more than 400 million consumers.[10] Negotiations are under way to expand NAFTA to create a 34-country Free Trade Area of the Americas. This agreement would include the United States, Canada, Mexico, and Latin America and Caribbean countries.

NAFTA has stimulated trade flows among member nations as well as cross-border retailing, manufacturing, and investment. For example, NAFTA paved the way for Wal-Mart to move to Mexico and Mexican supermarket giant, Gigante, to move into the United States. Whirlpool Corporation's Canadian subsidiary stopped making washing machines in Canada and moved that operation to Ohio. Whirlpool then shifted the production of kitchen ranges and compact dryers to Canada. Ford invested $60 million in its Mexico City manufacturing plant to produce smaller cars and light trucks for global sales.

Asian Free Trade Agreements   Efforts to liberalize trade in East Asia—from Japan and the four "Little Dragons" (Hong Kong, Singapore, South Korea, and Taiwan) through Thailand, Malaysia, and Indonesia—are also growing. Although the trade agreements are less formal than those underlying the EU and NAFTA, they have reduced tariffs among countries and promoted trade.

A New Reality: Global Competition among Global Companies for Global Consumers

The emergence of a largely borderless economic world has created a new reality for marketers of all shapes and sizes. Today, world trade is driven by global competition among global companies for global consumers.

Global Competition   **Global competition** exists when firms originate, produce, and market their products and services worldwide. The automobile, pharmaceutical, apparel, electronics, aerospace, and telecommunication fields represent well-known industries with sellers and buyers on every continent. Other industries that are increasingly global in scope include soft drinks, cosmetics, ready-to-eat cereals, snack chips, and retailing.

Global competition broadens the competitive landscape for marketers. The familiar "cola war" waged by Pepsi-Cola and Coca-Cola in the United States has been repeated around the world, including India, China, and Argentina. Procter & Gamble's Pampers and Kimberly-Clark's Huggies have taken their disposable diaper rivalry from the United States to Western Europe. Boeing and Europe's Airbus vie for lucrative commercial aircraft contracts on virtually every continent.

Collaborative relationships also are becoming a common way to meet the demands of global competition. Global **strategic alliances** are agreements among two or more independent firms to cooperate for the purpose of achieving common goals such as a competitive advantage or customer value creation. For instance, several of the world's largest telecommunication equipment makers, including Ericsson (Sweden), Nortel (Canada), Siemens (Germany), and 3Com and Worldcom (two U.S. firms), formed Juniper Networks, Inc., an alliance created to build devices to speed global Internet communications. General Mills and Nestlé of Switzerland created

Pepsi-Cola, now available in more than 190 countries and territories, accounts for a quarter of all soft drinks sold internationally. This Brazilian ad—"How to make jeans last 10 years"—features the popular Diet Pepsi brand targeted at weight-conscious consumers.

PepsiCo, Inc.

www.pepsico.com

Cereal Partners Worldwide for the purpose of fine-tuning Nestlé's European cereal marketing and distributing of General Mills cereals worldwide. This global alliance produces more than $1 billion in sales in 130 countries.[11]

Global Companies   Three types of companies populate and compete in the global marketplace: (1) international firms, (2) multinational firms, and (3) transnational firms.[12] All three employ people in different countries, and many have administrative, marketing, and manufacturing operations (often called *divisions* or *subsidiaries*) around the world. However, a firm's orientation toward and strategy for global markets and marketing defines the type of company it is or attempts to be.

An *international firm* engages in trade and marketing in different countries as an extension of the marketing strategy in its home country. Generally speaking, these firms market their existing products and services in other countries the same way they do in their home country. Avon, for example, successfully distributes its product line through direct selling in Asia, Europe, and South America, employing virtually the same marketing strategy used in the United States.

A *multinational firm* views the world as consisting of unique parts and markets to each part differently. Multinationals use a **multidomestic marketing strategy**, which means that they have as many different product variations, brand names, and advertising programs as countries in which they do business. For example, Lever Europe, a division of Unilever, markets its fabric softener known as Snuggle in the United States in 10 different European countries under seven brand names, including Kuschelweich in Germany, Coccolino in Italy, and Mimosin in France. These products have different packages, different advertising programs, and occasionally different formulas. Procter & Gamble markets Mr. Clean, its multipurpose cleaner, in North America and Asia. But you won't find Mr. Clean in other parts of the world. In Latin America, Mr. Clean is Mastro Limpio. Mr. Clean is Mr. Proper in Europe, Africa, and the Middle East.

A *transnational firm* views the world as one market and emphasizes cultural similarities across countries or universal consumer needs and wants more than differences. Transnational marketers employ a **global marketing strategy**—the practice of standardizing marketing activities when there are cultural similarities and adapting them when cultures differ. This approach benefits marketers by allowing them to realize economies of scale from their production and marketing activities.

MARKETING NEWSNET

The Global Teenager—A Market of 500 Million Consumers with $100 Billion to Spend

GLOBAL

The "global teenager" market consists of 500 million 13- to 19-year-olds in Europe, North and South America, and industrialized nations of Asia and the Pacific Rim who have experienced intense exposure to television (MTV broadcasts in 166 countries), movies, travel, the Internet, and global advertising by companies such as Benetton, Sony, Nike, and Coca-Cola. The similarities among teens across these countries are greater than their differences. For example, a global study of middle-class teenagers' rooms in 25 industrialized countries indicated it was difficult, if not impossible, to tell whether the rooms were in Los Angeles, Mexico City, Tokyo, Rio de Janeiro, Sidney, or Paris. Why? Teens spend $100 billion annually for a common gallery of products: Sony video games, Tommy Hilfiger apparel, Levi's

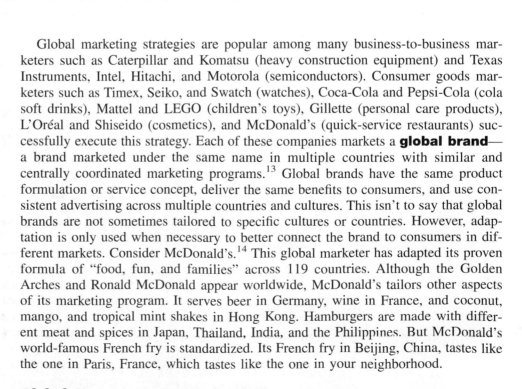

blue jeans, Nike athletic shoes, Swatch watches, and Procter & Gamble Clearasil facial medicine.

Teenagers around the world appreciate fashion and music, and desire novelty and trendier designs and images. They also acknowledge an Americanization of fashion and culture based on another study of 6,500 teens in 26 countries. When asked what country had the most influence on their attitudes and purchase behavior, 54 percent of teens from the United States, 87 percent of those from Latin America, 80 percent of the Europeans, and 80 percent of those from Asia named the United States. This phenomenon has not gone unnoticed by parents. As one parent in India said, "Now the youngsters dress, talk, and eat like Americans."

Global marketing strategies are popular among many business-to-business marketers such as Caterpillar and Komatsu (heavy construction equipment) and Texas Instruments, Intel, Hitachi, and Motorola (semiconductors). Consumer goods marketers such as Timex, Seiko, and Swatch (watches), Coca-Cola and Pepsi-Cola (cola soft drinks), Mattel and LEGO (children's toys), Gillette (personal care products), L'Oréal and Shiseido (cosmetics), and McDonald's (quick-service restaurants) successfully execute this strategy. Each of these companies markets a **global brand**—a brand marketed under the same name in multiple countries with similar and centrally coordinated marketing programs.[13] Global brands have the same product formulation or service concept, deliver the same benefits to consumers, and use consistent advertising across multiple countries and cultures. This isn't to say that global brands are not sometimes tailored to specific cultures or countries. However, adaptation is only used when necessary to better connect the brand to consumers in different markets. Consider McDonald's.[14] This global marketer has adapted its proven formula of "food, fun, and families" across 119 countries. Although the Golden Arches and Ronald McDonald appear worldwide, McDonald's tailors other aspects of its marketing program. It serves beer in Germany, wine in France, and coconut, mango, and tropical mint shakes in Hong Kong. Hamburgers are made with different meat and spices in Japan, Thailand, India, and the Philippines. But McDonald's world-famous French fry is standardized. Its French fry in Beijing, China, tastes like the one in Paris, France, which tastes like the one in your neighborhood.

Global Consumers Global competition among global companies often focuses on the identification and pursuit of global consumers as described in the accompanying Marketing NewsNet.[15] **Global consumers** consist of consumer groups living in many countries or regions of the world who have similar needs or seek similar features and benefits from products or services.[16] Evidence suggests the emergence of a global middle-income class, a youth market, and an elite segment, each consuming or using a common assortment of products and services, regardless of geographic location. A variety of companies have capitalized on the global consumer. Whirlpool, Sony, and IKEA have benefited from the growing global middle-income class desire for kitchen appliances, consumer electronics, and home furnishings, respectively. Levi's, Nike, Coca-Cola, and Benetton have tapped the global youth market. DeBeers, Chanel, Gucci, Rolls Royce, and Sotheby's and Christie's, the world's largest fine art and antique auction houses, cater to the elite segment for luxury goods worldwide.

Emergence of a Networked Global Marketspace

The use of Internet technology as a tool for exchanging goods, services, and information on a global scale is the fourth trend affecting world trade.[17] Some 1 billion businesses, educational institutions, government agencies, and households worldwide are expected to have Internet access by 2007. The broad reach of this technology suggests that its potential for promoting world trade is huge. In fact, sales arising from electronic commerce are projected to represent 10 percent of world trade in 2007, up from about 1 percent in 2001.

The promise of a networked global marketspace is that it enables the exchange of goods, services, and information from companies *anywhere* to customers *anywhere* at *any time* and at a lower cost. This promise has become a reality for buyers and sellers in industrialized countries that possess the telecommunications infrastructure necessary to support Internet technology. In particular, companies engaged in business-to-business marketing have spurred the growth of global electronic commerce. Ninety percent of global electronic commerce revenue arises from business-to-business transactions among a dozen countries in North America, Western Europe, and the Asia/Pacific Rim region. Industries that have benefited from this technology include industrial chemicals and controls, maintenance, repair, and operating supplies, computer and electronic equipment and components, aerospace parts, and agricultural and energy products. The United States, Canada,

Nestlé features multiple country and language websites that customize content and communicate with consumers in their native tongue. The website for Peru shown here is an example. Read the text to learn how many websites and languages Nestlé uses.

Nestlé S. A.
www.nestle.com

United Kingdom, Germany, Sweden, Japan, China, and Taiwan are among the most active participants in worldwide business-to-business electronic commerce.

Marketers recognize that the networked global marketspace offers unprecedented access to prospective buyers on every continent. Companies that have successfully capitalized on this access manage multiple country and language websites that customize content and communicate with consumers in their native tongue. Nestlé, the world's largest packaged food manufacturer, coffee roaster, and chocolate maker is a case in point. The company operates 53 individual country websites in 20 languages that span five continents.

Concept Check

1. What is protectionism?

2. The North American Free Trade Agreement was designed to promote free trade among which countries?

3. What is the difference between a multidomestic marketing strategy and a global marketing strategy?

A GLOBAL ENVIRONMENTAL SCAN

Global companies conduct continuing environmental scans of the five sets of environmental factors described earlier in Figure 3–1 (social, economic, technological, competitive, and regulatory forces). This section focuses on three kinds of uncontrollable environmental variables—cultural, economic, and political-regulatory—that affect global marketing practices in strikingly different ways than those in domestic markets.

Cultural Diversity

Marketers must be sensitive to the cultural underpinnings of different societies if they are to initiate and consummate mutually beneficial exchange relationships with global consumers. A necessary step in this process is **cross-cultural analysis**, which involves the study of similarities and differences among consumers in two or more nations or societies.[18] A thorough cross-cultural analysis involves an understanding of and an appreciation for the values, customs, symbols, and language of other societies.

Values   A society's **values** represent personally or socially preferable modes of conduct or states of existence that tend to persist over time. Understanding and working with these aspects of a society are important factors in global marketing. For example,

- McDonald's does not sell beef hamburgers in its restaurants in India because the cow is considered sacred by almost 85 percent of the population. Instead, McDonald's sells the McMaharajah: two all-mutton patties, special sauce, lettuce, cheese, pickles, onions on a sesame-seed bun.
- Germans have not been overly receptive to the use of credit cards such as Visa or MasterCard and installment debt to purchase goods and services. Indeed, the German word for debt, *Schuld,* is the same as the German word for guilt.

These examples illustrate how cultural values can influence behavior in different societies. Cultural values become apparent in the personal values of individuals that affect their attitudes and beliefs and the importance assigned to specific behaviors and attributes of goods and services. These personal values affect consumption-specific values, such as the use of installment debt by Germans, and product-specific values, such as the importance assigned to credit card interest rates.

What cultural lesson did Coca-Cola executives learn when they used the Eiffel Tower and the Parthenon in a recent global advertising campaign?

Customs **Customs** are what is considered normal and expected about the way people do things in a specific country. Clearly customs can vary significantly from country to country. For example, 3M Company executives were perplexed when the company's Scotch-Brite floor-cleaning product initially produced lukewarm sales in the Philippines. When a Filipino employee explained that consumers there customarily clean floors by pushing coconut shells around with their feet, 3M changed the shape of the pad to a foot and sales soared. Some other customs may seem unusual to Americans. Consider, for example, that in France, men wear more than twice the number of cosmetics than women do and that Japanese women give Japanese men chocolates on Valentine's Day.

The custom of giving token business gifts is popular in many countries where they are expected and accepted.[19] However, bribes, kickbacks, and payoffs offered to entice someone to commit an illegal or improper act on behalf of the giver for economic gain is considered corrupt in any culture. The prevalence of bribery in global marketing has led to an agreement among the world's major exporting nations to make bribery of foreign government officials a criminal offense. This agreement is patterned after the **Foreign Corrupt Practices Act (1977)**, as amended by the *International Anti-Dumping and Fair Competition Act* (1998). These acts make it a crime for U.S. corporations to bribe an official of a foreign government or political party to obtain or retain business in a foreign country. Bribery paid to foreign companies is another matter. In France and Greece, bribes paid to foreign companies are a tax-deductible expense!

Customs also relate to nonverbal behavior of individuals in different cultural settings. The story is told of U.S. executives negotiating a purchase agreement with their Japanese counterparts. The chief American negotiator made a proposal that was met with silence by the Japanese head negotiator. The American assumed the offer was not acceptable and raised the offer, which again was met with silence. A third offer was made, and an agreement was struck. Unknown to the American, the silence of the Japanese head negotiator meant that the offer was being considered, not rejected. The Japanese negotiator obtained several concessions from the American because of a misreading of silence. Unlike U.S. businesspeople, who tend to express opinions early in meetings and negotiations, Japanese executives prefer to wait and listen. The higher their position, such as chief negotiator, the more they listen.[20]

Cultural Symbols **Cultural symbols** are things that represent ideas and concepts. Symbols and symbolism play an important role in cross-cultural analysis because different cultures attach different meanings to things. So important is the role of symbols that a field of study, called **semiotics**, has emerged that examines

In Canada, all packages and labels must be printed in both English and French, and most major companies also run their ads in both languages. Here are both the English and French versions of a service ad for Hewlett-Packard. The company's website is multilingual too.

Hewlett-Packard
www.hp.com

the correspondence between symbols and their role in the assignment of meaning for people. By adroitly using cultural symbols, global marketers can tie positive symbolism to their products, services, and brands to enhance their attractiveness to consumers. However, improper use of symbols can spell disaster. A culturally sensitive global marketer will know that[21]

- North Americans are superstitious about the number 13, and Japanese feel the same way about the number 4. *Shi,* the Japanese word for four, is also the word for death. Knowing this, Tiffany & Company sells its fine glassware and china in sets of five, not four, in Japan.
- "Thumbs-up" is a positive sign in the United States. However, in Russia and Poland, this gesture has an offensive meaning when the palm of the hand is shown, as AT&T learned. The company reversed the gesture depicted in ads, showing the back of the hand, not the palm.

Cultural symbols evoke deep feelings. Consider how executives at Coca-Cola Company's Italian office learned this lesson. In a series of advertisements directed at Italian vacationers, the Eiffel Tower, Empire State Building, and the Tower of Pisa were turned into the familiar Coca-Cola bottle. However, when the white marble columns in the Parthenon that crowns Athens's Acropolis were turned into Coca-Cola bottles, the Greeks were outraged. Greeks refer to the Acropolis as the "holy rock," and a government official said the Parthenon is an "international symbol of excellence" and that "whoever insults the Parthenon insults international culture." Coca-Cola apologized for the ad.[22]

Global marketers are also sensitive to the fact that the country of origin or manufacture of products and services can symbolize superior or poor quality in some countries. For example, Russian consumers believe products made in Japan and Germany are superior in quality to products from the United States and the United Kingdom. Japanese consumers believe Japanese products are superior to those made in Europe and the United States. About half of Americans say the quality of products from Asia is not as good as products made in the United States.[23]

Language Global marketers should not only know the native tongues of countries in which they market their products and services but also the nuances and idioms of a language. Even though about 100 official languages exist in the world, anthropologists estimate that at least 3,000 different languages are spoken. There are 20 official languages spoken in the European Union, and Canada has two official languages (English and French). Seventeen major languages are spoken in India alone.

English, French, and Spanish are the principal languages used in global diplomacy and commerce. However, the best language to communicate with consumers is their own, as any seasoned global marketer will attest to. Unintended meanings of brand names and messages have ranged from the absurd to the obscene:

- When the advertising agency responsible for launching Procter & Gamble's successful Pert shampoo in Canada realized that the name means "lost" in French, it substituted the brand name Pret, which means "ready."
- In Italy, Cadbury Schweppes, the world's third-largest soft-drink manufacturer, realized that its Schweppes Tonic Water brand had to be renamed Schweppes Tonica because "il water" turned out to be the idiom for a bathroom.
- The Vicks brand name common in the United States is German slang for sexual intimacy; therefore, Vicks is called Wicks in Germany.

Experienced global marketers use **back translation**, where a translated word or phrase is retranslated into the original language by a different interpreter to catch errors. For example, IBM's first Japanese translation of its "Solution for a small planet" advertising message yielded "Answers that make people smaller." The error was caught and corrected. Nevertheless, unintended meanings still occur in the most unlikely situations. Just ask the logo designers for a line of Nike athletic shoes. The designers intended to portray "air" with stylized flames on the shoe heel. Unfortunately, the logo inadvertently resembled the Arabic script for the word "Allah," the Arabic word for God. After receiving complaints from Muslim leaders, Nike apologized and withdrew the offending shoes from the market.

The importance of language in global marketing is assuming greater importance in an increasingly networked and borderless economic world. For example, Oracle Corporation, a leading worldwide supplier of software, now markets its products by language groups instead of through 145 country-specific efforts. The French group markets to France, Belgium, Switzerland, and Canada. A Spanish-language group oversees Spain and Latin America. Eight other language groups—English, Japanese, Korean, Chinese, Portuguese, Italian, Dutch, and German—cover Oracle's top revenue-producing countries.[24]

Cultural Ethnocentricity   The tendency for people to view their own values, customs, symbols, and language favorably is well-known. However, the belief that aspects of one's culture are superior to another's is called *cultural ethnocentricity* and is a sure impediment to successful global marketing.

An outgrowth of cultural ethnocentricity exists in the purchase and use of goods and services produced outside of a country. Global marketers are acutely aware that certain groups within countries disfavor imported products, not on the basis of price, features, or performance, but purely because of their foreign origin. **Consumer ethnocentrism** is the tendency to believe that it is inappropriate, indeed immoral, to purchase foreign-made products.[25] Ethnocentric consumers believe that buying imported products is wrong because such purchases are unpatriotic, harm domestic industries, and cause domestic unemployment. Consumer ethnocentrism has been observed among a segment of the population in the United States, France, Japan, Korea, and Germany as well as other parts of Europe and Asia. The prevalence of consumer ethnocentrism makes the task of global marketers more difficult.[26]

Economic Considerations

Global marketing is also affected by economic considerations. Therefore, a scan of the global marketplace should include (1) a comparative analysis of the economic development in different countries, (2) an assessment of the economic infrastructure in these countries, (3) measurement of consumer income in different countries, and (4) recognition of a country's currency exchange rates.

Stage of Economic Development   There are about 260 countries in the world today, each of which is at a slightly different point in terms of its stage of economic development. However, they can be classified into two major groupings that will help the global marketer better understand their needs:

- *Developed* countries have somewhat mixed economies. Private enterprise dominates, although they have substantial public sectors as well. The United States, Canada, Japan, and most of Western Europe can be considered developed.
- *Developing* countries are in the process of moving from an agricultural to an industrial economy. There are two subgroups within the developing category: (1) those that have already made the move and (2) those that remain locked in a preindustrial economy. Countries such as Brazil, Poland, Hungary, China, Slovenia, Australia, Israel, Venezuela, and South Africa fall into the first group. In the second group are Afghanistan, Sri Lanka, Tanzania, and Chad, where living standards are low and improvement will be slow.

A country's stage of economic development affects and is affected by other economic factors, as described next.

Economic Infrastructure   The *economic infrastructure*—a country's communications, transportation, financial, and distribution systems—is a critical consideration in determining whether to try to market to a country's consumers and organizations. Parts of the infrastructure that North Americans or Western Europeans take for granted can be huge problems elsewhere—not only in developing nations but even in countries of the former Soviet Union, Eastern Europe, the Indian subcontinent, and China where such an infrastructure is assumed to be in place. Two-lane roads outside major urban centers that limit average speeds to 35 to 40 miles per hour are commonplace and a nightmare for firms requiring prompt truck delivery in these countries. In China, the bicycle is the preferred mode of transportation. This is understandable because China has few navigable roads outside its major cities where 80 percent of the population lives. In India, Coca-Cola uses large tricycles to distribute cases of Coke along narrow streets in many cities. Wholesale and retail institutions tend to be small, and

Procter & Gamble has successfully adapted to the economic infrastructure in China since beginning operations in that country in 1988.

Procter & Gamble
www.pg.com

The Coca-Cola Company has made a huge financial investment in bottling and distribution facilities in Russia.

The Coca-Cola Company
www.thecoca-colacompany.
com

a majority are operated by new owner–managers in many of these countries who are still learning the ways of a free market system.

The communication infrastructure in these countries also differ. This infrastructure includes telecommunication systems and networks in use, such as telephones, cable television, broadcast radio and television, computer, satellite, and wireless telephone. In general, the communication infrastructure in many developing countries is limited or antiquated compared with that of developed countries. But notable exceptions exist. China will have the most Internet users in the world in 2007, thus surpassing the United States.[27]

Even the financial and legal system can cause problems. Formal operating procedures among financial institutions and private properties did not exist under communism and are still limited. As a consequence, it is estimated that two-thirds of the commercial transactions in Russia involve nonmonetary forms of payment. The legal red tape involved in obtaining titles to buildings and land for manufacturing, wholesaling, and retailing operations also has been a huge problem. Nevertheless, the Coca-Cola Company has invested $750 million from 1991 through 1998 to build bottling and distribution facilities in Russia, Allied Lyons has spent $30 million to build a plant to make Baskin-Robbins ice cream, and Mars recently opened a $200 million candy factory outside Moscow.[28]

Consumer Income and Purchasing Power A global marketer selling consumer goods must also consider what the average per capita or household income is among a country's consumers and how the income is distributed to determine a nation's purchasing power. Per capita income varies greatly between nations. Average yearly per capita income in EU countries is more than $20,000 and is less than $300 in some developing countries such as Vietnam. A country's income distribution is important because it gives a more reliable picture of a country's purchasing power. Generally speaking, as the proportion of middle-income households in a country increases, the greater a nation's purchasing power tends to be. Figure 7–5 shows the worldwide disparity in the percentage distribution of households by level of purchasing power. In established market economies such as those in North America and Western Europe, 65 percent of households have an annual purchasing capability of $20,000 or more. In comparison, 75 percent of households in the developing countries of South Asia have an annual purchasing power of less than $5,000.[29]

Seasoned global marketers recognize that people in developing countries often have government subsidies for food, housing, and health care that supplement their

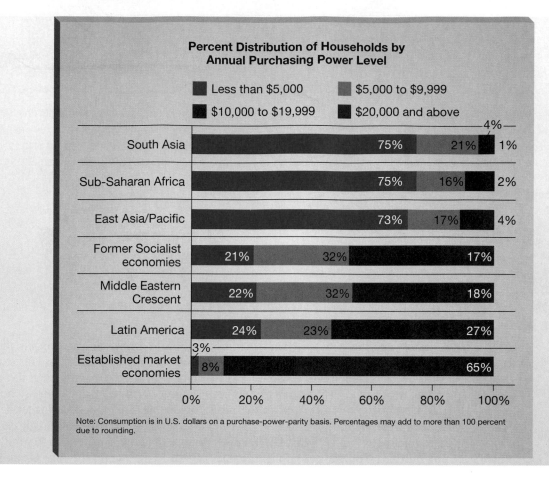

**Percent Distribution of Households by
Annual Purchasing Power Level**

■ Less than $5,000   ■ $5,000 to $9,999
■ $10,000 to $19,999   ■ $20,000 and above

South Asia	75% 21% 4% 1%
Sub-Saharan Africa	75% 16% 2%
East Asia/Pacific	73% 17% 4%
Former Socialist economies	21% 32% 17%
Middle Eastern Crescent	22% 32% 18%
Latin America	24% 23% 27%
Established market economies	3% 8% 65%

0%   20%   40%   60%   80%   100%

Note: Consumption is in U.S. dollars on a purchase-power-parity basis. Percentages may add to more than 100 percent due to rounding.

FIGURE 7–5

How purchasing power differs around the world

income. So people with seemingly low incomes are actually promising customers for a variety of products. For example, a consumer in South Asia earning the equivalent of $250 per year can afford Gillette razors. When that consumer's income rises to $1,000, a Sony television becomes affordable, and a new Volkswagen or Nissan can be bought with an annual income of $10,000. In developing countries of Eastern Europe, a $1,000 annual income makes a refrigerator affordable, and $2,000 brings an automatic washer within reach—good news for Whirlpool, the world's leading manufacturer and marketer of major home appliances.

Income growth in developing countries of Asia, Latin America, and Eastern Europe is expected to stimulate world trade well into the twenty-first century. The number of consumers in these countries earning the equivalent of $10,000 per year is expected to surpass the number of consumers in the United States, Japan, and Western Europe combined by 2007.

Currency Exchange Rates   Fluctuations in exchange rates among the world's currencies are of critical importance in global marketing. Such fluctuations affect everyone, from international tourists to global companies.

A **currency exchange rate** is the price of one country's currency expressed in terms of another country's currency, such as the U.S. dollar expressed in Brazilian reals, Japanese yen, or Swiss francs. Failure to consider exchange rates when pricing products for global markets can have dire consequences. Mattel learned this lesson the hard way. The company was recently unable to sell its popular Holiday Barbie doll and accessories in some international markets because they were too expensive. Why? Barbie prices, expressed in U.S. dollars, were set without regard for how they would translate into foreign currencies and were too high for many buyers.[30]

WEB LINK   Checking a Country's Political Risk Rating

The political climate in every country is regularly changing. Governments can make new laws or enforce existing policies differently. Numerous consulting firms prepare political risk analyses that incorporate a variety of variables such as the risk of internal turmoil, external conflict, government restrictions on company operations, and tariff and nontariff trade barriers.

The PRS Group maintains multiple databases of country-specific information and projections, including country political risk ratings. These ratings can be accessed at www.prsgroup.com. Click "Intl. Country Risk Guide" followed by "Sample Tables." Then click "Table 1: Country Risk, Ranked by Composite Risk Rating" (you will need to give your name and e-mail address to obtain the table). Which three countries have the highest rating (lowest risk), and which three have the lowest rating (highest risk)? Which countries have risk ratings closest to the United States?

Exchange rate fluctuations have a direct impact on the sales and profits made by global companies. When foreign currencies can buy more U.S. dollars, for example, U.S. products are less expensive for the foreign customer. This has been the case in recent years, and U.S. exports grew accordingly. Short-term fluctuations, however, can have a significant effect on the profits of global companies.[31] Hewlett-Packard recently gained nearly a half million dollars of additional profit through exchange rate fluctuation in one year. On the other hand, Honda recently lost $408 million on its European operations alone because of currency swings in the Japanese yen compared with the euro and British pound. Severe and protracted fluctuations in a country's currency can affect trade as well. For example, Procter & Gamble briefly suspended product shipments to Turkey, one of its largest export markets, because of instability of the Turkish currency.

Political-Regulatory Climate

The political and regulatory climate for marketing in a country or region of the world lies not only in identifying the current climate but in determining how long a favorable or unfavorable climate will last. An assessment of a country or regional political-regulatory climate includes an analysis of its political stability and trade regulations.

Political Stability   Trade among nations or regions depends on political stability. Billions of dollars have been lost in the Middle East and Africa as a result of internal political strife, terrorism, and war. Losses such as these encourage careful selection of politically stable countries and regions of the world for trade.

Political stability in a country is affected by numerous factors, including a government's orientation toward foreign companies and trade with other countries. These factors combine to create a political climate that is favorable or unfavorable for marketing and financial investment in a country or region of the world. Marketing managers monitor political stability using a variety of measures and often track country risk ratings supplied by agencies such as the PRS Group. Visit the PRS Group website shown in the accompanying Web Link to see political risk ratings for 140 countries.

Trade Regulations   Countries have a variety of rules that govern business practices within their borders. These rules often serve as trade barriers.[32] For example, Japan has some 11,000 trade regulations. Japanese car safety rules effectively require all automobile replacement parts to be Japanese and not American or European;

public health rules make it illegal to sell aspirin or cold medicine without a pharmacist present. The Malaysian government has advertising regulations stating that "advertisements must not project or promote an excessively aspirational lifestyle," Greece bans toy advertising, and Sweden outlaws all advertisements to children.

Trade regulations also appear in free trade agreements among countries. EU nations abide by some 10,000 rules that specify how goods are to be made and marketed. For instance, the rules for a washing machine's electrical system are detailed on more than 100 typed pages. Regulations related to contacting consumers via telephone, fax, and e-mail without their prior consent also exist. The European Union's ISO 9000 quality standards, though not a trade regulation, have the same effect on business practice. These standards, described in Chapter 6, involve registration and certification of a manufacturer's quality management and quality assurance system. Many European companies require suppliers to be ISO 9000 certified as a condition of doing business with them. Certified companies have undergone an on-site audit that includes an inspection of its facilities to ensure that documented quality control procedures are in place and that all employees understand and follow them.

Concept Check

1. Semiotics involves the study of _____.

2. When foreign currencies can buy more U.S. dollars, are U.S. products more or less expensive for a foreign consumer?

GLOBAL MARKET-ENTRY STRATEGIES

Once a company has decided to enter the global marketplace, it must select a means of market entry. Four general options exist: (1) exporting, (2) licensing, (3) joint venture, and (4) direct investment.[33] As Figure 7–6 demonstrates, the amount of financial commitment, risk, marketing control, and profit potential increases as the firm moves from exporting to direct investment.

FIGURE 7–6
Alternative global market-entry strategies

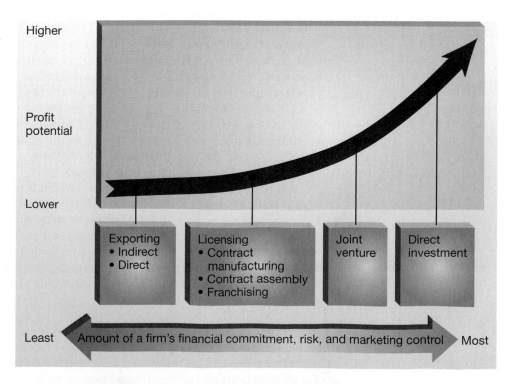

MARKETING NEWSNET

Creative Cosmetics and Creative Export Marketing in Japan

GLOBAL

How does a medium-sized U.S. cosmetics firm sell 1.5 million tubes of lipstick in Japan annually? Fran Wilson Creative Cosmetics can attribute its success to a top-quality product, effective advertising, and a novel export marketing program. The firm's Moodmatcher lip coloring comes in green, orange, silver, black, and six other hues that change to a shade of pink, coral, or red, depending on a woman's chemistry when it's applied.

The company does not sell to department stores. According to a company spokesperson, "Shiseido and Kanebo (two large Japanese cosmetics firms) keep all the other Japanese or import brands out of the major department stores." Rather, the company sells its Moodmatcher lipstick through Japanese distributors that reach Japan's 40,000 beauty salons. The result? The company, with its savvy Japanese distributors, accounts for 20 percent of the $4.3 million of lipsticks exported annually to Japan by U.S. companies.

Exporting

Exporting is producing goods in one country and selling them in another country. This entry option allows a company to make the least number of changes in terms of its product, its organization, and even its corporate goals. Host countries usually do not like this practice because it provides less local employment than under alternative means of entry.

Indirect exporting is when a firm sells its domestically produced goods in a foreign country through an intermediary. It has the least amount of commitment and risk but will probably return the least profit. Indirect exporting is ideal for a company that has no overseas contacts but wants to market abroad. The intermediary is often a distributor that has the marketing know-how and resources necessary for the effort to succeed. Fran Wilson Creative Cosmetics of New York uses an indirect exporting approach to sell its products in Japan. Read the accompanying Marketing NewsNet to find out how this innovative marketer and its Japanese distributors sell 20 percent of the lipsticks exported to Japan by U.S. companies.[34]

Direct exporting is when a firm sells its domestically produced goods in a foreign country without intermediaries. Most companies become involved in direct exporting when they believe their volume of sales will be sufficiently large and easy to obtain so that they do not require intermediaries. For example, the exporter may be approached by foreign buyers that are willing to contract for a large volume of purchases. Direct exporting involves more risk than indirect exporting for the company but also opens the door to increased profits. The Boeing Company applies a direct exporting approach. Boeing is not only one of the world's largest aerospace companies but also the largest U.S. exporter.

Even though exporting is commonly employed by large firms, it is the prominent global market-entry strategy among small- and medium-sized companies. For example, 60 percent of U.S. firms exporting products have fewer than 100 employees. These firms account for about 30 percent of total U.S. merchandise exports.[35]

McDonald's uses franchising as a market-entry strategy and over 70 percent of the company's sales come from non-U.S. operations.

McDonald's
www.mcdonalds.com

Licensing

Under licensing, a company offers the right to a trademark, patent, trade secret, or other similarly valued items of intellectual property in return for a royalty or a fee. The advantages to the company granting the license are low risk and a capital-free entry into a foreign country. The licensee gains information that allows it to start with a competitive advantage, and the foreign country gains employment by having the product manufactured locally. For instance, Yoplait yogurt is licensed from Sodima, a French cooperative, by General Mills for sales in the United States.

There are some serious drawbacks to this mode of entry, however. The licensor forgoes control of its product and reduces the potential profits gained from it. In addition, while the relationship lasts, the licensor may be creating its own competition. Some licensees are able to modify the product somehow and enter the market with product and marketing knowledge gained at the expense of the company that got them started. To offset this disadvantage, many companies strive to stay innovative so that the licensee remains dependent on them for improvements and successful operation. Finally, should the licensee prove to be a poor choice, the name or reputation of the company may be harmed.

Two variations of licensing, *contract manufacturing* and *contract assembly,* represent alternative ways to produce a product within the foreign country. With contract manufacturing, a U.S. company may contract with a foreign firm to manufacture products according to stated specifications. The product is then sold in the foreign country or exported back to the United States. With contract assembly, the U.S. company may contract with a foreign firm to assemble (not manufacture) parts and components that have been shipped to that country. In both cases, the advantage to the foreign country is the employment of its people, and the U.S. firm benefits from the lower wage rates in the foreign country. Contract manufacturing and assembly in developing countries has sparked controversy in the toy, textile, and apparel industries where poor working conditions, low pay, and child labor practices have been documented. However, this practice has been an economic boon to Taiwan where 55 percent of the world's notebook computers are made. In a typical year, U.S. companies such as Dell and IBM will have Taiwanese firms supply more than half of their notebook computer needs.[36]

A third variation of licensing is *franchising.* Franchising is one of the fastest-growing market-entry strategies. More than 35,000 franchises of U.S. firms are located in countries throughout the world. Franchises include soft-drink, motel, retailing, fast-food, and car rental operation and a variety of business services. McDonald's is a premier global franchiser. More than 70 percent of the company's stores are franchised, and over 70 percent of the company's sales come from non-U.S. operations.[37]

Joint Venture

When a foreign company and a local firm invest together to create a local business, it is called a **joint venture**. These two companies share ownership, control, and profits

of the new company. For example, Elite Foods is a joint venture between Elite Industries and PepsiCo created to market Frito-Lay's Cheetos, Ruffles, and Doritos and other snacks in Israel.[38]

The advantages of this option are twofold. First, one company may not have the necessary financial, physical, or managerial resources to enter a foreign market alone. The joint venture between Ericsson, a Swedish telecommunications firm, and CGCT, a French switch maker, enabled them together to beat out AT&T for a $100 million French contract. Ericsson's money and technology combined with CGCT's knowledge of the French market helped them to win the contract that neither of them could have won alone. Similarly, Ford and Volkswagen formed a joint venture to make four-wheel-drive vehicles in Portugal. Second, a government may require or strongly encourage a joint venture before it allows a foreign company to enter its market. This is the case in China. Today, more than 75,000 Chinese-foreign joint ventures operate in China.[39]

The disadvantages arise when the two companies disagree about policies or courses of action for their joint venture or when governmental bureaucracy bogs down the effort. For example, U.S. firms often prefer to reinvest earnings gained, whereas some foreign companies may want to spend those earnings. Or a U.S. firm may want to return profits earned to the United States, while the local firm or its government may oppose this—the problem faced by many potential joint ventures in Eastern Europe, Russia, Latin America, and South Asia.

Direct Investment

The biggest commitment a company can make when entering the global market is **direct investment**, which entails a domestic firm actually investing in and owning a foreign subsidiary or division. Examples of direct investment are Nissan's Smyrna, Tennessee, plant that produces pickup trucks and the Mercedes-Benz factory in Vance, Alabama, that makes the DaimlerChrysler M-class sports utility vehicle. Many U.S.-based global companies also use this mode of entry. Reebok entered Russia by creating a subsidiary known as Reebok Russia, Motorola established a wholly owned Chinese subsidiary that manufactures mobile phones and other telecommunication equipment, and Ford built a $1.9 billion automobile plant in Brazil.

For many firms, direct investment often follows one of the other three market-entry strategies. For example, Ernst & Young, an international accounting and management consulting firm, entered Hungary first by establishing a joint venture with a local company. Ernst & Young later acquired the company, making it a subsidiary with headquarters in Budapest. Following on the success of its European and Asian exporting strategy, Harley-Davidson now operates wholly owned marketing and sales subsidiaries in Germany, Italy, the United Kingdom, and Japan, among other countries.

The advantages to direct investment include cost savings, better understanding of local market conditions, and fewer local restrictions. Firms entering foreign markets using direct investment believe that these advantages outweigh the financial commitments and risks involved.

Concept Check

1. What mode of entry could a company follow if it has no previous experience in global marketing?

2. How does licensing differ from a joint venture?

CRAFTING A WORLDWIDE MARKETING PROGRAM

The choice of a market-entry strategy is a necessary first step for a marketer when joining the community of global companies. The next step involves the challenging task of designing, implementing, and controlling marketing programs worldwide.

Successful global marketers standardize global marketing programs whenever possible and customize them wherever necessary. The extent of standardization and customization is often rooted in a careful global environment scan supplemented with judgment based on experience and marketing research.

Product and Promotion Strategies

Global companies have five strategies for matching products and their promotion efforts to global markets. As Figure 7–7 shows, the strategies focus on whether a company extends or adapts its product and promotion message for consumers in different countries and cultures.

A product may be sold globally in one of three ways: (1) in the same form as in its home market, (2) with some adaptations, or (3) as a totally new product:[40]

1. *Product extension.* Selling virtually the same product in other countries is a product extension strategy. It works well for products such as Coca-Cola, Gillette razors, Wrigley's gum, Levi's jeans, Sony consumer electronics, Harley-Davidson motorcycles, and Nokia cell phones. As a general rule, product extension seems to work best when the consumer market target for the product is alike across countries and cultures—that is, consumers share the same desires, needs and uses for the product.

2. *Product adaptation.* Changing a product in some way to make it more appropriate for a country's climate or consumer preferences is a product adaptation strategy. Exxon sells different gasoline blends based on each country's climate. Gerber baby food comes in different varieties in different countries. Vegetable and Rabbit Meat is a favorite food in Poland. Freeze-Dried Sardines and Rice is popular in Japan. Maybelline's makeup is formulaically adapted in labs to local skin types and weather across the globe, including an Asia-specific mascara that doesn't run during the rainy season.

3. *Product invention.* Alternatively, companies can invent totally new products designed to satisfy common needs across countries. Black & Decker did this with its Snake Light Flexible Flashlight. Created to address a global need for portable lighting, the product became a best seller in North America, Europe,

FIGURE 7-7

Five product and promotion strategies for global marketing

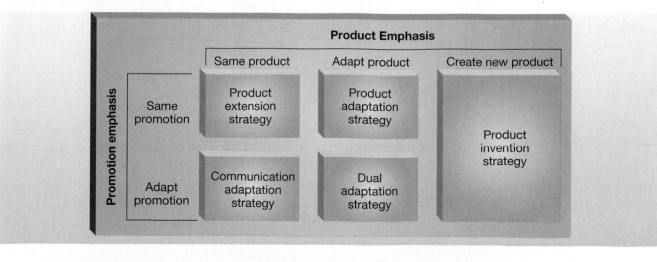

Latin America, and Australia and is the most successful new product developed by Black & Decker. Similarly, Whirlpool developed a compact, automatic clothes washer specifically for households in developing countries with annual household incomes of $2,000. Called Ideale, the washer features bright colors because washers are often placed in home living areas, not hid in laundry rooms (which don't exist in many homes in developing countries). Demand for this product exceeded forecasts when it was introduced in Brazil, China, and India.

An identical promotion message is used for the product extension and product adaptation strategies around the world. Gillette uses the same global message for its men's toiletries: "Gillette, the Best a Man Can Get." Even though Exxon adapts its gasoline blends for different countries based on climate, the promotion message is unchanged: "Put a Tiger in Your Tank."

Global companies may also adapt their promotion message. For instance, the same product may be sold in many countries but advertised differently. As an example, L'Oréal, a French health and beauty products marketer, introduced its Golden Beauty brand of sun care products through its Helena Rubenstein subsidiary in Western Europe with a communication adaptation strategy. Recognizing that cultural and buying motive differences related to skin care and tanning exist, Golden Beauty advertising features dark tanning for northern Europeans, skin protection to avoid wrinkles among Latin Europeans, and beautiful skin for Europeans living along the Mediterranean Sea, even though the products are the same.

Other companies use a dual adaptation strategy by modifying both their products and promotion messages. Nestlé does this with Nescafé coffee. Nescafé is marketed using different coffee blends and promotional campaigns to match consumer preferences in different countries. For example, Nescafé, the world's largest brand of coffee, generally emphasizes the taste, aroma, and warmth of shared moments in its advertising around the world. However, Nescafé is advertised in Thailand as a way to relax from the pressures of daily life.

These examples illustrate the simple rule applied by global companies: Standardize product and promotion strategies whenever possible and customize them wherever necessary. This is the art of global marketing.[41]

Distribution Strategy

Distribution is of critical importance in global marketing. The availability and quality of retailers and wholesalers as well as transportation, communication, and warehousing

Gillette delivers the same global message whenever possible, as shown in the Gillette for Women Venus ads from Greece, Germany, and the United States.

The Gillette Company
www.gillette.com

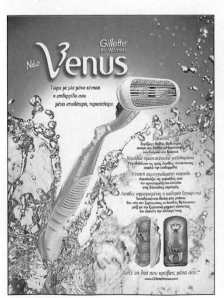
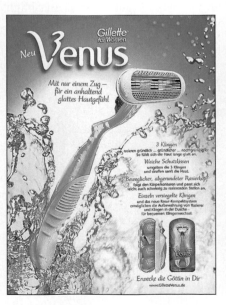
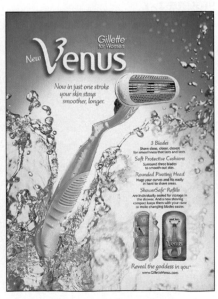

FIGURE 7–8
Channels of distribution in global marketing

facilities are often determined by a country's stage of economic development. Figure 7–8 outlines the channel through which a product manufactured in one country must travel to reach its destination in another country. The first step involves the seller; its headquarters is the starting point and is responsible for the successful distribution to the ultimate consumer.

The next step is the channel between two nations, moving the product from one country to another. Intermediaries that can handle this responsibility include resident buyers in a foreign country, independent merchant wholesalers who buy and sell the product, or agents who bring buyers and sellers together.

Once the product is in the foreign nation, that country's distribution channels take over.[42] These channels can be very long or surprisingly short, depending on the product line. In Japan, fresh fish go through three intermediaries before getting to a retail outlet. Conversely, shoes only go through one intermediary. In other cases, the channel does not even involve the host country. Procter & Gamble sells its soap door to door in the Philippines because there are no other alternatives in many parts of that country. The sophistication of a country's distribution channels increase as its economic infrastructure develops. Supermarkets facilitate selling products in many nations, but they are not popular or available in many others where culture and lack of refrigeration dictate shopping on a daily rather than a weekly basis. For example, when Coke and Pepsi entered China, both had to create direct-distribution channels, investing in refrigerator units for small retailers.

Pricing Strategy

Global companies also face many challenges in determining a pricing strategy as part of their worldwide marketing effort. Individual countries, even those with free trade agreements, may impose considerable competitive, political, and legal constraints on the pricing latitude of global companies. For example, Wal-Mart was told by German antitrust authorities that the prices in its stores were too low, relative to competitors, and faced a fine for violating the country's trade if the prices weren't raised.[43] Of course, economic factors such as the costs of production, selling, and tariffs, plus transportation and storage costs, also affect global pricing decisions.

Pricing too low or too high can have dire consequences. When prices appear too low in one country, companies can be charged with dumping, a practice subject to severe penalties and fines. **Dumping** is when a firm sells a product in a foreign country below its domestic price or below its actual cost. This is often done to build a company's share of the market by pricing at a competitive level. Another reason is that the products being sold may be surplus or cannot be sold domestically and, therefore, are already a burden to the company. The firm may be glad to sell them at almost any price. A recent trade dispute involving U.S. apple growers and Mexico is a case in point. Mexican trade officials claimed that U.S. growers were selling their red and golden delicious apples in Mexico below the actual cost of production. They imposed a 101 percent tariff on U.S. apples, and a severe drop in U.S. apple exports to Mexico resulted. Subsequent negotiations set a price floor on the price of U.S. apples sold to Mexico.[44]

When companies price their products very high in some countries but competitively in others, they face a gray market problem. A **gray market**, also called *parallel importing,* is a situation where products are sold through unauthorized channels of distribution. A gray market comes about when individuals buy products in a lower-priced country from a manufacturer's authorized retailer, ship them to higher-priced countries, and then sell them below the manufacturer's suggested retail price through unauthorized retailers. Many well-known products have been sold through gray markets, including Olympus cameras, Seiko watches, IBM personal computers, and Mercedes-Benz cars. Parallel importing is legal in the United States. It is illegal in the European Union.

Concept Check

1. Products may be sold globally in three ways. What are they?

2. What is dumping?

CHAPTER IN REVIEW

1 *Describe the nature and scope of world trade from a global perspective and its implications for the United States.*

A global perspective on world trade views exports and imports as complementary economic flows: A country's imports affect its exports and exports affects its imports. World trade flows to and from the United States reflect demand and supply interdependencies for goods among nations and industries. The three largest importers of U.S. goods and services are Canada, Mexico, and Japan. The four largest exporters to the United States are Canada, China, Mexico, and Japan. The United States imports more goods than it exports.

2 *Identify the major trends that have influenced the landscape of global marketing in the past decade.*

Four major trends have influenced the landscape of global marketing in the past decade. First, there has been a gradual decline of economic protectionism by individual countries, leading to a reduction in tariffs and quotas. Second, there is growing economic integration and free trade among nations, reflected in the creation of the European Union and the North American Free Trade Agreement. Third, there is increased global competition among global companies for global consumers, resulting in firms adopting global marketing strategies and promoting global brands. And finally, a networked global marketspace has emerged using Internet technology as a tool for exchanging goods, services, and information on a global scale.

3 *Identify the environmental factors that shape global marketing efforts.*

Three major environmental factors shape global marketing efforts. First, there are cultural factors, including values, customs, cultural symbols, and language. Economic factors also

shape global marketing efforts. These include a country's stage of economic development and economic infrastructure, consumer income and purchasing power, and currency exchange rates. Finally, political-regulatory factors in a country or region of the world create a favorable or unfavorable climate for global marketing efforts.

4 *Name and describe the alternative approaches companies use to enter global markets.*

Companies have four alternative approaches for entering global markets. These are exporting, licensing, joint venture, and direct investment. Exporting involves producing goods in one country and selling them in another country. Under licensing, a company offers the right to a trademark, patent, trade secret, or similarly valued items of intellectual property in return for a royalty or fee. In a joint venture, a foreign company and a local firm invest together to create a local business. Direct investment entails a domestic firm actually investing in and owning a foreign subsidiary or division.

5 *Explain the distinction between standardization and customization when companies craft worldwide marketing programs.*

Companies distinguish between standardization and customization when crafting worldwide marketing programs. Standardization means that all elements of the marketing program are the same across countries and cultures. Customization means that one or more elements of the marketing program are adapted to meet the needs or preferences of consumers in a particular country or culture. Global marketers apply a simple rule when crafting worldwide marketing programs: Standardize marketing programs whenever possible and customize them wherever necessary.

FOCUSING ON KEY TERMS

back translation p. 184
balance of trade p. 171
consumer ethnocentrism p. 184

countertrade p. 170
cross-cultural analysis p. 181
cultural symbols p. 182

currency exchange rate p. 187
customs p. 182
direct investment p. 192
dumping p. 195
Economic Espionage Act (1996) p. 173
exporting p. 190
Foreign Corrupt Practices Act (1977) p. 182
global brand p. 179
global competition p. 177
global consumers p. 179
global marketing strategy p. 178

gray market p. 196
gross domestic product p. 171
joint venture p. 191
multidomestic marketing strategy p. 178
protectionism p. 174
quota p. 175
semiotics p. 182
strategic alliances p. 177
tariffs p. 174
values p. 181
World Trade Organization p. 175

DISCUSSION AND APPLICATION QUESTIONS

1 What is meant by this statement: "Quotas are a hidden tax on consumers, whereas tariffs are a more obvious one"?

2 Is the trade feedback effect described in the text a long-run or short-run view on world trade flows? Explain your answer.

3 The United States is considered to be a global leader in the development and marketing of pharmaceutical products, and Merck & Co. of New Jersey is a world leader in prescription drug sales. What explanation can you give for this situation based on the text discussion concerning the competitive advantage of nations?

4 How successful would a television commercial in Japan be if it featured a husband surprising his wife in her dressing area on Valentine's Day with a small box of chocolates containing four candies? Why?

5 As a novice in global marketing, which alternative for global market-entry strategy would you be likely to start with? Why? What other alternatives do you have for a global market entry?

6 Coca-Cola is sold worldwide. In some countries, Coca-Cola owns the bottling facilities; in others, it has signed contracts with licensees or relies on joint ventures. When selecting a licensee in each country, what factors should Coca-Cola consider?

GOING ONLINE   Getting to Know the WTO

The World Trade Organization is the only international organization dealing with the global rules of trade between nations. Its intended function is to ensure that trade flows as smoothly, predictably, and freely as possible. Understanding how the WTO operates is a necessary prerequisite for global marketing.

Visit the WTO website at www.wto.org to learn more about how this organization functions and the issues it faces. A useful starting point for familiarizing yourself with the WTO is to find answers to the following questions:

1 Countries are constantly seeking WTO membership. How many countries are now members of this organization? Which country is the newest member?

2 What are the 10 most common misunderstandings about the WTO identified by this organization?

BUILDING YOUR MARKETING PLAN

Does your marketing plan involve reaching global customers outside the United States? If the answer is no, read no further and do not include a global element in your plan.

If the answer is yes, try to identify:

1 what features of your product are especially important to potential customers,

2 in which countries these potential customers live, and

3 special marketing issues that are involved in trying to reach them. Answers to these questions will help in developing more detailed marketing mix strategies described in later chapters.

VIDEO CASE 7 CNS Breathe Right® Strips: Going Global

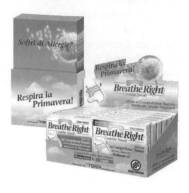

"It's naive to treat 'international' as one big market—particularly within OTC," explains Marti Morfitt, president and CEO of CNS, the company that manufactures Breathe Right® nasal strips. "There are many discrete, unique markets, and local expertise is needed to understand the dynamics within each and address them effectively."

"OTC" refers to over-the-counter medical products like aspirin or cough syrup that customers can buy without a doctor's prescription. Breathe Right nasal strips qualify as an OTC product. But, that doesn't mean there isn't a lot of technology and medical science behind it.

Breathe Right® nasal strips are innovative adhesive strips with patented dual flex bars inside. When attached to the nose, they gently lift and hold open nasal passages, making it easier to breathe. Breathe Right strips are used for a variety of reasons, all to help breathe better through the nose: athletes hoping to play their best (particularly when wearing mouth guards); snorers (and their spouses) hoping for a quiet night's sleep; and allergy, sinusitis, and cold sufferers looking for drug-free relief from nasal congestion.

HOW IT ALL BEGAN

Breathe Right strips were invented by Bruce Johnson, a chronic nasal congestion sufferer. At times Johnson put straws or paper clips in his nose at night to keep his nasal passages open. He eventually came up with a prototype for Breathe Right strips. He brought his invention to CNS, Inc., which recognized its market potential. CNS took the strips to the Food and Drug Administration for approval of claims for relief of snoring and nasal congestion.

CNS, a small company, had a limited marketing budget. However, it got a big public relations break when Jerry Rice, the wide receiver for the San Francisco 49ers, wore a Breathe Right strip on national TV and scored two touchdowns during the 49ers' 1995 Super Bowl victory. Demand for the strips soared.

"What really helped sales of Breathe Right strips was that CNS had done a very effective job of getting press kits in the hands of news and sports media," says Morfitt. "When people on television asked, 'What is that funny looking thing on his nose?' the reporters could talk about how the strip was an effective consumer product for everyone. And a $1.4 million business turned into a $45 million business in just one year," she explains.

THE DECISION TO GO GLOBAL

As awareness and trial in the U.S. was building, CNS began to get inquiries from people in other countries asking where they could buy strips. In 1995 CNS decided to take advantage of global interest and introduce Breathe Right strips internationally.

What countries did CNS choose to enter with its Breathe Right strips? "Countries we focus on are those with a large OTC market, high per-capita spending in the OTC market, and future prospects for growth," says Kevin McKenna, vice president for international at CNS. All these factors relate to market size. "But the real key to success in a market is a local partner that is entrepreneurial and has an ability to execute in terms of achieving distribution and sales."

IMPORTANCE OF LOCAL PARTNERS

Dynamic world market changes in the last 30 years have influenced opportunities for global sales of Breathe Right strips. Key trends include increased availability of OTC products formerly available only by prescription; and a global push toward self-care, spurred by the increasing cost of health and medical care. Additionally, OTC products have extended beyond the traditional boundary of the pharmacy and into grocery and other channels; and the role of the pharmacist has expanded from that of medical professional to one that includes selling and marketing OTC products to consumers.

At the same time, changes were taking place within CNS. When Morfitt joined CNS in 1998, she began pulling together a new management group with extensive experience in marketing consumer packaged goods, both in the U.S. and abroad. CNS began seeking "hungry" international partners who would bring greater localized market expertise and direct-selling capabilities than past partners. Morfitt also wanted partners with demonstrated entrepreneurial spirit to match that of the new management team.

The company's partner in Italy, BluFarm Group, uses its local knowledge and direct selling skills to partner with pharmacists to teach them how to increase sales of Breathe Right strips in their stores. In Italy, as throughout much of Europe, OTC products such as antacids, aspirin, and nasal strips are typically placed behind pharmacy counters and therefore not visible to customers. The only way to sell a product is for a customer to ask for it by name. BluFarm Group recognized the importance of in-store advertising and sales execution to build awareness and created point-of-sale materials such as window and counter displays (see photo) to let customers know that Breathe Right strips were available in the store. "BluFarm's ability to capture consumers' awareness of Breathe Right strips as they walk in the retailer's door has beneficial results for CNS, BluFarm, pharmacists, and consumers," says McKenna.

"Working with an experienced local partner helps overcome surprises in global markets," says Nick Naumann, senior marketing communications manager at CNS. One surprise: Universal Product Codes (UPC) on packaging aren't "universal"—they are used only in the U.S. and Canada. "Different forms of those codes in other countries can take a few weeks to six months or more of government review to obtain," he says.

Even the same packaging colors don't work around the globe. Research with U.S. consumers revealed they wanted darker packaging to suggest the strips' use at night by snorers and those with stuffed noses. "'Too grim and negative' Asian and European consumers told us," says Naumann. Breathe Right strips in those countries have a lighter, airier look than in the U.S. to convey the open feeling one gets from the nasal strips.

MANAGING GLOBAL GROWTH

Today, Breathe Right strips are sold in over 25 countries, and global sales make up a growing percentage of CNS business each year. To ensure the Breathe Right brand continues to meet growth expectations, CNS now uses a three-stage approach to penetrate and develop new markets:

- Stage 1: Explore/test the concept
  — Use screening criteria to identify high-potential markets
  — Identify potential partners
  — Validate concept with research
  — Develop strategy and launch test market

- Stage 2: Establish the product
  — Penetrate the marketplace

  — Refine messages for local market
  — Evaluate partnership and marketing strategies

- Stage 3: Manage the product
  — Achieve sustainability/profitability
  — Exploit new product and new use opportunities

Overall, this approach starts with what works in the U.S. and extends it into new markets, paying close attention to local needs and customs. Throughout the three stages CNS conducts market research and makes financial projections.

As shown in the figure, at each stage of the market development process, performance must be met for the product to enter the next stage. Once success with Breathe Right nasal strips is established in a country, the groundwork is laid and international partners have the ability to introduce other Breathe Right products, such as Snore Relief™ Throat Spray, and Vapor Shot™ personal vaporizer.

LOOKING FORWARD

"We believe the Breathe Right brand has great potential, both domestically and around the world," says Morfitt. "Growth will come both from further expansion of Breathe Right nasal strips and from other drug-free, better-breathing line extensions," says Morfitt.

Questions

1 What are the advantages and disadvantages for CNS taking Breathe Right strips into international markets?

2 What are the advantages to CNS of (a) using its three-stage process to enter new global markets and (b) having specific criteria to move through the stages?

3 Using the CNS criteria, with what you know, which countries should have highest priority for CNS?

4 Which single segment of potential Breathe Right strip users would you target to enter new markets?

5 Which marketing mix variables should CNS emphasize the most to succeed in a global arena? Why?

Stage 1: Explore/Test

Stage 1 to Stage 2 Criteria Screen
- Relevant market: Cough/cold category size, GDP and GDP growth
- Quality of partners
- Product acceptance
- Cost to launch/support
- Political stability

Stage 2: Establish the Product

Stage 2 to Stage 3 Criteria Screen
- Proven partner and distribution strength
- Effective consumer ad and education programs
- Met initial trial and repeat targets
- Clear path to profits

Stage 3: Manage the Product

PART

PART 1
Initiating the Marketing Process

PART 2
Understanding Buyers and Markets

PART 3
Targeting Marketing Opportunities

PART 4
Satisfying Marketing Opportunities

PART 5
Managing the Marketing Process

3

TARGETING MARKETING OPPORTUNITIES

HOW PART 3 FITS INTO THE BOOK

The two chapters in Part 3 discuss key marketing methods—techniques to help discover the potential buyers for a product and determine their needs and wants; then focusing marketing efforts on those key segments most likely to buy the product.

CHAPTER 8
Marketing Research: From Information to Action

CHAPTER 9
Identifying Market Segments and Targets

CHAPTER

8

MARKETING RESEARCH: FROM INFORMATION TO ACTION

LEARNING OBJECTIVES

After reading this chapter you should be able to:

1 Identify the reason for doing marketing research, and describe the five-step marketing research approach leading to marketing actions.

2 Describe how secondary and primary data are used in marketing, including the uses of questionnaires, observations, experiments, and panels.

3 Explain how information technology and data mining link massive amounts of marketing information to meaningful marketing actions.

TEST SCREENINGS: LISTENING TO CONSUMERS TO REDUCE MOVIE RISKS

Blockbuster movies are essential for today's fiercely competitive world of filmmaking, examples being *Spider-Man 2, Tough Love, Shoeless Joe,* and *3000.*

What's in a Movie Name?   Can't remember those last three movies, even after scratching your head? Well, test screenings by the studios—a form of marketing research—found that moviegoers had problems with those titles, too. Here's what happened:

- *Tough Love* became *Gigli* when audiences didn't like the name for the 2004 mob comedy starring Jennifer Lopez and Ben Affleck. (More on this below.)

- *Shoeless Joe* became *Field of Dreams* because audiences thought Kevin Costner might be playing a homeless person.

- *3000* became *Pretty Woman* when audiences didn't have a clue what the number meant. *Hint:* It was the number of dollars to spend an evening with Julia Roberts.[1]

Filmmakers want movie titles that are concise, attention-getting, capture the essence of the film, and have no legal restrictions—basically, the same factors that make a good brand name.

The Risks in Today's Blockbuster Movies
Bad weather, poor scripts, temperamental stars who stomp off the set, and too-costly special effects are just some of the nightmares faced by movie producers. Today's films average more than $103 million to produce

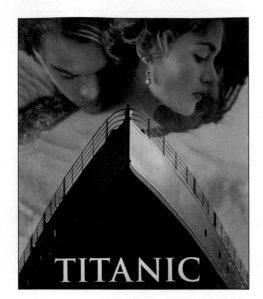

and market.[2] So some studios try to reduce their new-movie gamble by planning a multiepisode film series—*Harry Potter, Matrix, Lord of the Rings,* and *Spider-Man 2* being examples. But there are hidden dangers. As Harry Potter and Hermione Granger age, will their characters be credible and will young moviegoers, the target audience, still buy tickets? Shooting all the movies in a sequence at one time, like was done for the *Lord of the Rings* trilogy, also poses huge marketing and marketing research issues. Most of the $320 million invested in the three movies would have been lost had the first in the sequence, *The Fellowship of the Ring,* been a disaster. The third film in the *Matrix* trilogy, *The Matrix Revolutions,* highlights the multifilm problem: U.S. ticket sales didn't reach the $175 million production costs, to say nothing of the tens of millions of dollars of marketing costs.[3]

Spider-Man 2 was a pleasant shock among multiepisode film series by outselling the original movie. Its $500 million gross sales the first three weeks in theaters around the world easily covered its $200 million production budget and $50 million marketing costs. But some movies like *Titanic,* the biggest blockbuster ever, don't lend themselves to a follow-up movie: So if you can write a credible screenplay for *Titanic 2,* take off for Hollywood where your future is secure! Hmmm![4]

Using Marketing Research to Reduce Movie Risk

Is research on movie titles and content expensive? Very! But the greater expense is selecting a bad title that can kill a movie and cost the studio millions of dollars, not to mention the careers of producers and directors. So movie studios use market research to reduce their risk of losses by hiring firms like the National Research Group to conduct test screenings and tracking studies.

For test screenings, 300 to 400 prospective moviegoers are recruited to attend a "sneak preview" of a film before its release. After viewing the movie, the audience fills out an exhaustive survey to critique the title, plot, characters, music, and ending as well as the marketing program (posters, trailers, etc.) to identify improvements to make in the final edit of the movie.[5]

Without reading ahead, think about the answers to these questions:

- Whom would you recruit for movie test screenings?
- What questions would you ask to help you edit or modify the title or other aspects of a film?

Virtually every major U.S. movie produced today uses test screenings to obtain the key reactions of consumers likely to be in the target audience. Figure 8–1 summarizes some of the key questions that are used in these test screenings, both to select the people for the screenings and to obtain key reactions of those sitting in the screenings. Note how specific the studio's action is for each question asked, like change the title or ending. This is an example of effective, action-oriented marketing research.

Here are some changes to movies that have resulted from this kind of marketing research:

- *Making the plot move faster.* Disney cut a duet by Pocahontas and John Smith in *Pocahontas* because it got in the way of the action and confused test audiences.[6]
- *Changing an ending. Fatal Attraction* had probably the most commercially successful "ending-switch" of all time. In its sneak previews, audiences liked everything but the ending, which had Alex (Glenn Close) committing suicide and managing to frame Dan (Michael Douglas) as her murderer by leaving his fingerprints on the knife she used. The studio shot $1.3 million of new scenes for the ending that audiences eventually saw.[7]

POINT WHEN ASKED	KEY QUESTIONS	USE OF QUESTION(S)
Before the test screening	• How old are you? • How frequently do you pay to see movies?	• Find people who fit profile of target audience for movie. • Find people who frequently attend movies.
After the test screening	• What do you think of the title? What title would you suggest? • Were there any characters too distasteful? Who? How? • Did you like the ending? If not, how would you change it? • Would you recommend the movie to a friend?	• Change movie title. • Change aspects of some characters. • Change or clarify ending. • Overall indicator of liking and/or satisfaction with movie.

FIGURE 8–1

Marketing research questions asked in test screenings of movies, and how they are used

The switch in endings for *Fatal Attraction* that resulted from audience reactions to test screenings reduced the studio's risk and undoubtedly contributed to the movie's box-office success. But even good marketing research can't guarantee success. Test screenings caused the studio to shoot a new ending for JLo and Ben Affleck in *Gigli*. Audiences hated that Ben Affleck's character died in the original ending, which they felt was too dark and inconsistent with the rest of the movie. The reshoot wasn't enough. Besides being a disaster at the box office, *Gigli* was nominated for "worst picture" and eight other "Razzies," the highest-profile bad-movie anti-Oscars given by voters of the Golden Raspberry Awards.[8]

Movie studios also use tracking studies, in which prospective moviegoers in the target audience are asked three key questions about an upcoming film release:[9]

- Are you aware of a particular film?
- Are you interested in seeing it?
- Would it be your first choice on a certain weekend?

Studios then use the data collected to forecast the movie's opening weekend box office sales; if necessary, they run last minute ads to increase its awareness and interest—the "buzz" or word of mouth for the film. In some cases, a studio may postpone or advance a movie's release date, depending on the results for other movies scheduled for release at that time.

These examples show how marketing research is the link between marketing strategy and decisive actions, the main topic of this chapter. Also, marketing research is often used to help a firm develop sales forecasts, the final topic in Chapter 9.

THE ROLE OF MARKETING RESEARCH

To place marketing research in perspective, we can describe (1) what it is, (2) some of the difficulties in conducting it, and (3) the five steps marketing executives can use in conducting marketing research.

What Is Marketing Research?

Marketing research is the process of defining a marketing problem and opportunity, systematically collecting and analyzing information, and recommending actions.[10] The broad goal of marketing research is to identify and define both

How can Fisher-Price do marketing research on young children who can't even fill out a questionnaire? For the answer, see the text.

Fisher-Price
www.fisherprice.com

marketing problems and opportunities and to generate and improve marketing actions. Although marketing research isn't perfect, it seeks to reduce risk and uncertainty to improve decisions made by marketing managers.

Why Good Marketing Research Is Difficult

Ask a moviegoer if she liked the title for a film she just saw and you'll probably get a straightforward answer. But often marketing researchers face difficulties in asking consumers questions about new, unknown products. For example,

- Suppose your company is developing a brand new product, never before seen by consumers. Would consumers really know whether they are likely to buy a particular product that they probably have never thought about before?
- Imagine if you, as a consumer, were asked about your personal hygiene habits. Even though you knew the answer, would you reveal it? When personal or status questions are involved, will people give honest answers?
- Will consumers' actual purchase behavior be the same as their stated interest or intentions? Will they buy the same brand they say they will?

A task of marketing research is to overcome these difficulties and to obtain the information needed to make reasonable estimates about what consumers will or won't buy.

Five-Step Marketing Research Approach to Making Better Decisions

A **decision** is a conscious choice from among two or more alternatives. All of us make many such decisions daily. At work we choose from alternative ways to accomplish an assigned task. At college we choose from alternative courses. As consumers we choose from alternative brands. No magic formula guarantees correct decisions.

Managers and researchers have tried to improve the outcomes of decisions by using more formal, structured approaches to *decision making,* the act of consciously choosing from alternatives. The systematic marketing research approach used to collect information to improve marketing decisions and actions described in this chapter uses five steps and is shown in Figure 8–2. Although the five-step approach described here focuses on marketing decisions, it provides a systematic checklist for making both business and personal decisions.

Concept Check

1. What is marketing research?

2. What are the five steps marketing research uses to help lead to marketing actions?

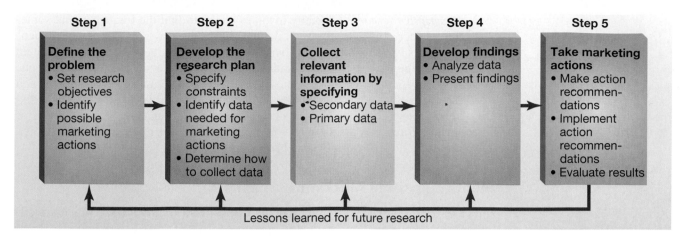

Step 1	Step 2	Step 3	Step 4	Step 5
Define the problem • Set research objectives • Identify possible marketing actions	**Develop the research plan** • Specify constraints • Identify data needed for marketing actions • Determine how to collect data	**Collect relevant information by specifying** • Secondary data • Primary data	**Develop findings** • Analyze data • Present findings	**Take marketing actions** • Make action recommendations • Implement action recommendations • Evaluate results

Lessons learned for future research

FIGURE 8–2

Five-step marketing research approach leading to marketing actions

STEP 1: DEFINE THE PROBLEM

Designers at Fisher-Price, the nation's top marketer of infant and preschool toys, seek to develop toys they think kids will like, but the problem is: How can they be certain kids will like the toys? As part of their marketing research, Fisher-Price gets children to play at its state-licensed nursery school in East Aurora, New York. From behind one-way mirrors, Fisher-Price designers and marketing researchers watch the children use, and abuse, the toys to develop better products.

The original model of a classic Fisher-Price toy, the Chatter Telephone™, was simply a wooden phone with a dial that rang a bell. Observers noted, however, that the children kept grabbing the receiver like a handle to pull the phone along behind them, so a designer added wheels, a noisemaker, and eyes that bobbed up and down.

Fisher-Price's toy testing shows how to define the problem and its two key elements: setting the research objectives and identifying possible marketing actions suggested by the research.

Set the Research Objectives

Objectives are specific, measurable goals the decision maker—in this case, an executive at Fisher-Price—seeks to achieve in solving a problem. Typical marketing objectives are increasing sales and profits, discovering what consumers are aware of and want, and finding out why a product isn't selling well. For Fisher-Price, the immediate research objective was to decide whether to market the old or new telephone design.

In setting these research objectives, marketers have to be clear on the kind of research they are about to do. The three kinds of research, with examples explained in more detail later in the chapter, are:[11]

1. *Exploratory research* provides ideas about a relatively vague problem. General Mills discovered that the initial version of its Hamburger Helper wasn't satisfactory for many consumers, so it interviewed them to get ideas to improve the product.

2. *Descriptive research* generally involves trying to find the frequency that something occurs or the extent of a relationship between two factors. So when General Mills wants to study how loyal consumers are to its Wheaties, it can obtain data on the number of households buying Wheaties and competitive products.

3. *Causal research,* the most sophisticated, tries to determine the extent to which the change in one factor changes another one. In the Fisher-Price example discussed next, changing the toy designs is related to changes in the amount of time children play with the toy. Experiments and test markets, discussed later, are examples of causal research.

Identify Possible Marketing Actions

Effective decision makers develop specific **measures of success**, which are criteria or standards used in evaluating proposed solutions to a problem. Different research outcomes—based on the measure of success—lead to different marketing actions. For the Fisher-Price problem, if a measure of success were the total time children spent playing with each of the two telephone designs, the results of observing them would lead to clear-cut actions as follows:

Measure of Success: Playtime	**Possible Marketing Action**
• Children spent more time playing with old design.	• Continue with old design; don't introduce new design.
• Children spent more time playing with new design.	• Introduce new design; drop old design.

One test of whether marketing research should be done is if different outcomes will lead to different marketing actions. If all the research outcomes lead to the same action—such as top management sticking with the older design regardless of what the observed children liked—the research is useless and a waste of money. In this causal research study, results showed that kids liked the new design, so Fisher-Price introduced its noisemaking pull-toy Chatter Telephone, which became a toy classic and sold millions.

Digital Research, Inc., a marketing research firm, evaluates almost 500 new toys from more than 160 toy manufacturers to select *Family Fun* magazine's Toy of the Year award. More than 700 children "toy testers" are involved. And they've been right on the money in selecting Barney the TV dinosaur, Tickle Me Elmo, and Fisher-Price's Love to Dance Bear™ as hot toys—ones that jumped off retailers' shelves. But sometimes they are wrong.[12] Forecasting which toys are hot is critical for retailers, which must place orders to manufacturers 8 to 10 months before Christmas shoppers walk into their stores. Bad forecasts can lead to lost sales for understocks and severe losses for overstocks.

Marketing research turned up these "hot toys" for the Christmas 2004 shopping season: Rainbow Brite™, Aquapets™, Star Wars® Original Trilogy Collection™, and Dora the Explorer™. For the importance of good forecasts, see the text.

Marketing researchers know that defining a problem is an incredibly difficult task. For example, if the objectives are too broad, the problem may not be researchable. If they are too narrow, the value of the research results may be seriously lessened. This is why marketing researchers spend so much time in defining a marketing problem precisely and writing a formal proposal that describes the research to be done.[13]

STEP 2: DEVELOP THE RESEARCH PLAN

The second step in the marketing research process involves (1) specifying the constraints on the marketing research activity, (2) identifying the data needed for marketing decisions, and (3) determining how to collect the data.

Specify Constraints

The **constraints** in a decision are the restrictions placed on potential solutions to a problem. Common constraints in marketing problems are limitations on the time and money available to solve the problem. Thus, Fisher-Price might set two constraints on its decision to select either the old or new version of the Chatter Telephone: The decision must be made in 10 weeks and no research budget is available beyond that needed for collecting data in its nursery school.

Identify Data Needed for Marketing Actions

Often marketing research studies wind up collecting a lot of data that are interesting but irrelevant for marketing decisions that result in marketing actions. In the Fisher-Price Chatter Telephone case, it might be nice to know the children's favorite colors, whether they like wood or plastic toys better, and so on. In fact, knowing answers to these questions might result in later modifications of the toy, but right now the problem is to select one of two toy designs. So this study must focus on collecting data that help managers make a clear choice between the two telephone designs.

Determine How to Collect Data

Determining how to collect useful marketing research data is often as important as actually collecting the data—step 3 in the process, which is discussed later. Two key elements in deciding how to collect the data are (1) concepts and (2) methods.

Concepts   In the world of marketing, *concepts* are ideas about products or services. To find out about consumer reaction to a potential new product, marketing researchers frequently develop a *new-product concept*, that is, a picture or verbal description of a product or service the firm might offer for sale. For example, with the Chatter Telephone, Fisher-Price managers developed a new-product concept that involved adding a noisemaker, wheels, and eyes to the basic design, which would make the toy more fun for children and increase sales.

Methods   *Methods* are the approaches that can be used to collect data to solve all or part of a problem. For example, if you are the marketing researcher at Fisher-Price responsible for the Chatter Telephone, you face a number of methods issues in developing your research plan, including the following:

- Can we actually ask three- or four-year-olds meaningful questions they can answer about their liking or disliking of the two designs?
- Are we better off not asking them questions but simply observing their behavior?
- If we simply observe the children's behavior, how can we do this in a way to get the best information without biasing the results?

Millions of other people have asked similar questions about millions of other products and services. How can you find and use the methodologies that other marketing researchers have found successful? Information on useful methods is available in tradebooks, textbooks, and handbooks that relate to marketing and marketing research. Some periodicals and technical journals, such as the *Journal of Marketing* and the *Journal of Marketing Research* published by the American Marketing Association, summarize methods and techniques valuable in addressing marketing problems. Special methods vital to marketing are (1) sampling and (2) statistical inference.

Marketing researchers often select a group of distributors, customers, or prospects, ask them questions, and treat their answers as typical of all those in whom they are interested. There are two ways of **sampling**, or selecting representative elements from a population: probability and nonprobability sampling. **Probability sampling** involves using precise rules to select the sample such that each element of the population has a specific known chance of being selected. For example, if a college wants to know how last year's 1,000 graduates are doing, it can put their names in a bowl and randomly select 50 names to contact. The chance of being selected—50/1,000, or 0.05—is known in advance, and all graduates have an equal chance of being contacted. This procedure helps select a sample (the 50 graduates) that is representative of the entire population (the 1,000 graduates) and allows conclusions to be drawn about the entire population.

When time and budget are limited, researchers may opt for **nonprobability sampling** and use arbitrary judgments to select the sample so that the chance of selecting a particular element may be unknown or 0. If the college decides to select the 50 graduates from last year's class who live closest to the college, many members of the class have been arbitrarily excluded. This has introduced a bias that makes it dangerous to draw conclusions about the population from this geographically restricted sample.

The method of **statistical inference** involves drawing conclusions about a *population* (the "universe" of all people, stores, or salespeople about which researchers wish to generalize) from a *sample* (some elements of the universe) taken from that population. To draw accurate inferences about the population, the sample elements should be representative of that universe. If the sample is not typical, bias can be introduced, resulting in bad marketing decisions.

Concept Check

1. What are the three kinds of marketing research?

2. What does *constraints* mean?

3. What is the difference between concepts and methods?

STEP 3: COLLECT RELEVANT INFORMATION

Collecting enough relevant information to make a rational, informed marketing decision sometimes simply means using your knowledge to decide immediately. At other times it entails collecting an enormous amount of information at great expense.

Figure 8–3 shows how the different kinds of marketing information fit together. **Data**, the facts and figures related to the problem, are divided into two main parts: secondary data and primary data. **Secondary data** are facts and figures that have already been recorded before the project at hand, whereas **primary data** are facts and figures that are newly collected for the project.

Secondary Data

Secondary data divide into two parts—internal and external secondary data—depending on whether the data come from inside or outside the organization needing the research.

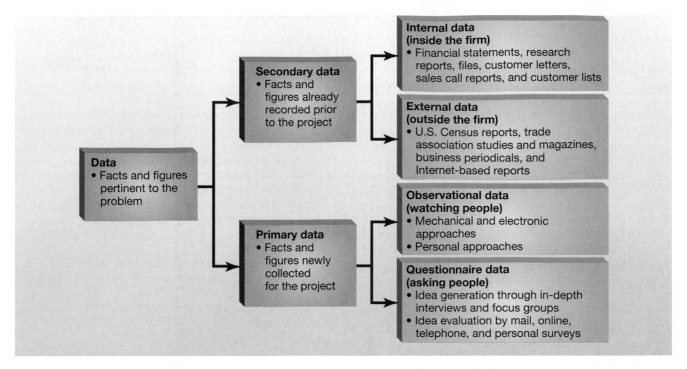

FIGURE 8–3
Types of marketing
information

Internal Secondary Data   Data that have already been collected and exist inside the business firm or other organization are internal secondary data. These include product sales data and sales reports on customer calls.

External Secondary Data   Published data from outside the organization are external secondary data. The U.S. Census Bureau publishes a variety of useful reports. Best known is the Census 2000, which is a decennial count of the U.S. population containing detailed information on American households, such as the number of people per household and their age, sex, race/ethnic background, income, occupation, and education. Marketers use these data to identify characteristics and trends of ultimate consumers.

The Census Bureau also publishes other reports that are vital to business firms selling products and services to organizations. The Economic Census, which now encompasses the former U.S. Census of Manufacturers, U.S. Census of Retail Trade, and others, is conducted every five years. The 2002 Economic Census contains data on the number and size of establishments in the United States that produce a good or service on the basis of its North American Industry Classification (NAICS) and the new North American Product Classification System (NAPCS). The Current Industrial Reports are periodic studies that provide data on the production quantity and shipment value of selected products. Finally, trade associations, universities, and business periodicals provide detailed data of value to market researchers and planners. These data are now available online via the Internet, which can be identified and located using a search engine like Google. The Web Link on the next page provides examples.

A variety of marketing research organizations serves the needs of marketers. Specialized syndicated services provide a standard set of data on a regular basis, such as the Nielsen Media Research's TV ratings or J. D. Powers with its automotive quality and customer satisfaction research. Other market research suppliers contract with clients to conduct complete marketing research projects.

Several data services provide comprehensive information on household demographics and lifestyle, product purchases, TV viewing behavior, and responses to coupon and free-sample promotions. Their principal advantage is the ability of one service to collect, analyze, interrelate, and present all this information. For consumer product firms like Procter & Gamble, sales data from various channels are critical to allocate scarce

WEB LINK   Online Databases and Internet Resources Useful for Marketers

www.mhhe.com/Kerin

Information contained in online databases available via the Internet consists of indexes to articles in periodicals and statistical or financial data on markets, products, and organizations that are accessed either directly or via Internet search engines or portals through key word searches.

Online databases of indexes, abstracts, and full-text information from periodicals include:

- LexisNexis™ Academic (www.lexisnexis.com), which provides full-text documents from over 5,600 news, business, legal, and reference publications.
- ProQuest databases (www.proquest.com), which provide summaries of management, marketing, and other business articles from over 8,500 publishers.

Statistical and financial data on markets, products, and organizations include:

- Bloomberg (www.bloomberg.com), *Investor's Business Daily* (www.investors.com), and *The Wall Street Journal* (www.wsj.com), all providing up-to-the-minute business news and security prices plus research reports on companies, industries, and countries.

- FISonline (www.fisonline.com), which has created a database that contains information on over 28,000 companies worldwide (15,000 U.S. public companies and 20,000 non-U.S. public companies).
- STAT-USA (www.stat-usa.gov) from the Department of Commerce, which provides information on U.S. business, economic, and trade activity collected by the federal government.

Portals and search engines include:

- Firstgov.gov (www.firstgov.gov), a portal to all U.S. government websites. Users click on links to browse by topic or enter keywords for specific searches.
- Google (www.google.com), a portal to the entire Internet. Users click on links to browse by topic or enter key words for specific searches.

Some of these websites are accessible only if your educational institution has paid a subscription fee. To see if you can access these sites for free, check with your institution's website.

---

marketing resources. As a result, they use firms such as Information Resources' Info-Scan and AC Nielsen's ScanTrack to collect product sales and coupon/free-sample redemptions that have been scanned at the checkout counters of supermarket, drug, convenience, and mass merchandise retailers in the United States and other international markets. Campbell Soup, maker of Swanson frozen dinners, used the information from one of these single-source data providers to shift a TV ad campaign from a serious to a light theme, which increased sales of Swanson dinners by 14 percent.[14]

Advantage and Disadvantages of Secondary Data   A general rule among marketing people is to obtain secondary data first and then collect primary data. Two important advantages of secondary data are (1) the tremendous time savings if the data have already been collected and published and (2) the low cost, such as free or inexpensive Census reports. Furthermore, a greater level of detail is often available through secondary data, especially U.S. Census Bureau data.

However, these advantages must be weighed against some significant disadvantages. First, the secondary data may be out of date, especially if they are U.S. Census data collected only every 5 or 10 years. Second, the definitions or categories might not be quite right for your project. For example, the age groupings might be wrong for your project. Finally, because the data are collected for another purpose, they may not be specific enough for your project. In such cases it may be necessary to collect primary data.

Concept Check

1. What is the difference between secondary and primary data?

2. What are some advantages and disadvantages of secondary data?

Primary Data

The two principal ways to collect new or primary data for a marketing study are by (1) observing people and (2) asking them questions.

Observational Data   Facts and figures obtained by watching, either mechanically or in person, how people actually behave is the way marketing researchers collect **observational data**. National TV ratings, such as those of Nielsen Media Research

shown in Figure 8–4, are an example of mechanical observational data collected by a "people meter." The people meter is a box that (1) is attached to TV sets, VCRs, cable boxes, and satellite dishes in over 6,000 homes across the country; (2) has a remote that operates the meter when a viewer begins and finishes watching a TV program; and (3) stores and then transmits the viewing information each night to Nielsen Media Research. Also, Nielsen Media Research employs a much larger sample of households in 210 TV markets in the United States to record their viewing behavior in TV diaries or booklets (not a mechanical but a manual measurement system) during the months of February, May, July, and November, which are known as "the sweeps."[15]

On the basis of all this observational data, Nielsen Media Research then calculates the "rating" and "share" of each TV program. With 109.6 million TV households in the United States based on the 2000 U.S. Census, a single ratings point equals 1 percent, or 1,096,000 TV households.[16] In TV viewing a share point is the percentage of TV sets in use tuned to a particular program. Because TV networks and cable sell more than $32 billion annually in advertising and set advertising rates to advertisers on the basis of those data, precision in the Nielsen data is critical. Thus, a change of one percentage point in a rating can mean gaining or losing up to $50 million in advertising revenue because advertisers pay rates on the basis of the size of the audience for a TV program. So from Figure 8–4, we might expect to pay more for a 30-second TV ad on *CSI: Miami* than one on *Survivor: Vanuatu*. Broadcast and cable networks may change the time slot or even cancel a TV program if its ratings are

FIGURE 8–4
Nielsen ratings of the top 10 national television programs from September 27, 2004, through October 3, 2004.

RANK	PROGRAM	NETWORK	RATING	SHARE
1	*Desperate Housewives*	ABC	13.6	20.0
2	*CSI: Miami*	CBS	13.0	21.0
2	*NFL Monday Night Football*	ABC	13.0	22.0
4	*CSI: NY*	CBS	12.5	20.0
5	*Everybody Loves Raymond*	CBS	12.1	18.0
6	*Survivor: Vanuatu*	CBS	11.5	18.0
7	*Two and a Half Men*	CBS	10.9	16.0
8	*CSI Special(s)*	CBS	10.8	17.0
9	*Lost*	ABC	10.5	17.0
10	*60 Minutes*	CBS	10.2	17.0

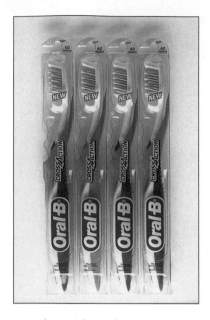

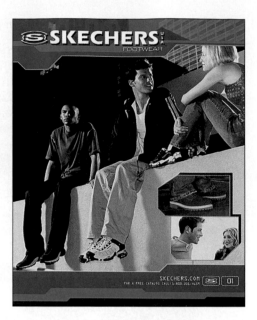

How do you do marketing research on things as diverse as toothbrushes, soap pads, and fashion products for teenagers? For some creative answers, see the text.

Oral-B Laboratories
www.oralb.com

3M Company
www.scotchbrite.com

Skechers USA, Inc.
www.skechers.com

consistently poor and advertisers are unwilling to pay a rate based on a higher guaranteed rating.

The people meter's limitations—as with all observational data collected mechanically (or manually)—relate to how the measurements are taken. In 2003, Nielsen reported a 7 to 12 percent annual decline from 2002 in the prime-time TV watched by men from 18 to 34. This has caused chaos among networks and advertisers alike because of the size of this market segment. This is the very group most likely to watch TV at sports bars, on the treadmill at their athletic club, or on DVDs, or skip regular TV entirely to play videogames or surf the Web. Because of pressure to get more accurate viewing data, Nielsen is putting more technology into its people meter and increasing the sample of homes from 6,000 to 10,000 by 2006. In 2004, Nielsen also started collecting data from users of TiVo's increasingly popular digital video recorders that allow viewers to pause live TV programming and to fast forward through commercials. This enables Nielsen to tell not only which TV commercials viewers skip but also whether they skip only 10 or 20 seconds into the commercial.[17]

Nielsen//NetRatings also uses an electronic meter to record Internet user behavior. These data are collected by tracking the actual mouse clicks made by users from more than 100,000 individuals in 13 countries as they surf the Internet via a meter installed on their home or work computers. Nielsen//NetRatings identifies the top websites that have the largest unique audiences, the top advertising banners viewed, the top Internet advertisers, and global Internet usage for selected European and Asian countries. Figure 8–5, showing the top 10 Internet websites, gives interesting comparisons about Internet usage. For example, while eBay reaches about one-fourth fewer users than Google in a month, the typical eBay user spends more than three times the minutes per month than a Google user.

Observational data can take some strange twists. Jennifer Voitle, a laid-off investment bank employee with four advanced degrees, responded to an Internet ad and found a new career: *mystery shopper*. Companies pay her to check on the quality of their products and services and write a detailed report on what she finds. She gets paid to travel to Mexican and Hawaiian hotels, eat at restaurants, play golf, test-drive new cars at auto dealerships, shop for groceries and clothes, and play arcade games. But her role posing as a customer gives her client unique marketing research information that can be obtained in no other way. Says Jennifer, "Can you believe they call this work?"[18]

Watching consumers in person and videotaping them are other observational approaches. For example, Aurora Foods observes how consumers bake cakes in its

FIGURE 8–5

Nielsen//NetRatings of the top 10 Internet websites for September, 2004

RANK	PROPERTY	UNIQUE AUDIENCE (000s)	REACH %	HOURS AND MINUTES PER PERSON PER WEEK
1	Yahoo	88,732	60.73	2:47
2	MSN	88,630	60.66	1:39
3	Microsoft	84,581	57.88	0:40
4	AOL	70,487	48.24	6:48
5	Google	61,897	42.36	0:29
6	eBay	45,386	31.06	1:45
7	MapQuest	31,142	21.31	0:12
8	Amazon	29,868	20.44	0:19
9	Weather Channel	29,730	20.35	0:21
10	Real	29,428	20.14	0:38

test kitchens to see if baking instructions on the cake box are understood and followed correctly. Gillette marketing researchers actually videotaped consumers brushing their teeth in their own bathrooms to see how they really brush—not just how they *say* they brush. The new-product result: Gillette's new Oral-B CrossAction toothbrush that's supposed to do a better job, at $4.99 each.[19]

A specialized observational approach is *ethnographic research,* in which anthropologists and other trained observers seek to discover subtle emotional reactions as consumers encounter products in their "natural use environment," such as in their home, car, or hotel. For example, Best Western International, Inc., a national hotel chain, paid couples to videotape themselves as they spent three to seven days on a cross-country car trip. From this, Best Western found that women usually decide when to pull off the road and where to stay—the reverse of focus group research. The result: target more promotional messages to women.[20]

Personal observation is both useful and flexible, but it can be costly and unreliable when different observers report different conclusions in watching the same event. Also, although observation can reveal what people do, it cannot easily determine why they do it, such as why they are buying or not buying a product. This is the principal reason for using questionnaires.

Questionnaire Data   Questionnaire data are facts and figures obtained by asking people about their attitudes, awareness, intentions, and behaviors. Because so many questions might be asked in questionnaires, it is essential that the researcher concentrate on those directly related to the marketing problem being studied and potential marketing actions that might result.

General Mills did exploratory research to search for ideas about why Hamburger Helper didn't fare too well with consumers when introduced. Initial instructions called for cooking a half pound of hamburger separately from the noodles or potatoes, which were later mixed with the hamburger. *Individual interviews* (a single researcher asking questions of one respondent) showed that consumers (1) didn't think it contained enough meat and (2) didn't want the hassle of cooking in two different pots. So the Hamburger Helper product manager changed the recipe to call for a full pound of meat and to allow users to prepare it in one dish; this converted a potential failure into a success.[21]

Focus groups are informal sessions of 6 to 10 past, present, or prospective customers in which a discussion leader, or moderator, asks their opinions about the firm's and its competitors' products, how they use these products, and special needs they have that these products don't address. Often video-recorded and conducted in special interviewing rooms with a one-way mirror, these groups enable marketing researchers and managers to hear and watch consumer reactions. The informality and peer support in an effective focus group uncover ideas that are often difficult to obtain with individual interviews.

In the mid-1990s, 3M sought ways to push further into the home-care business and decided to target the wool soap pads niche, which was dominated by giants SOS and Brillo. 3M ran eight focus groups around the United States and heard consumers complain that standard wool pads scratched their expensive cookware. These interviews led to 3M's internationally successful Scotch-Brite® Never Scratch wool soap pad.[22]

Finding "the next big thing" for consumers has become the obsession not only for consumer product firms but also for firms in many other industries. The result is that marketing researchers have come to rely on techniques that are far more basic—many would say bizarre—than more traditional individual or focus group interviews. These "fuzzy front end" methods attempt to identify elusive consumer tastes or trends far before typical consumers have recognized them themselves. Three examples of unusual ways to collect consumer data and their results include the following:

- Having consumers take a photo of themselves every time they snack. This resulted in General Mills' Homestyle Pop Secret popcorn, which delivers the real butter and bursts of salt in microwave popcorn that consumers thought they could only get from the stovetop variety.[23]
- Having teenagers complete a drawing. This is used by researchers at Teenage Research Unlimited (TRU) to help discover what teenagers like, wear, listen to, read, and watch. TRU surveys 2,000 teens twice a year to identify their lifestyles, attitudes, trends, and behaviors. With its Coolest Brand Meter™, TRU asks teens to specify the coolest brands within specific product categories, such as sneakers and clothing.[24]
- Hiring "cool hunters," people with tastes far ahead of the curve. This is used to identify the next big things likely to sweep popular teen culture. Many marketers consult Look-Look, a marketing research firm that can call on up to 20,000 "field correspondents" who specialize in hunting for "trendsetters" for ideas, products, and fashions that are deemed to be "cool" in large cities around the world. Look-Look provides these teenage field correspondents with digital cameras to send back uploaded images from parties, concerts, and sporting events.[25] For example, Wet Seal uses this method to anticipate teenage girls' fashions while Skechers uses it to spot footwear trends.

More conventional questionnaire studies use personal, mail, telephone, e-mail, fax, or Internet surveys of a large sample of past, present, or prospective consumers. In choosing between these alternatives, the marketing researcher must balance cost against the expected quality of information obtained. Personal interview surveys have a major advantage of enabling the interviewer to be flexible in asking probing questions or getting reactions to visual materials, but are very costly to conduct. Mail surveys are usually biased because those most likely to respond have had especially positive or negative experiences with the product or brand. While telephone interviews allow flexibility, they are increasingly difficult to complete because respondents may hang up on the interviewer. E-mail, fax, and Internet surveys are restricted to respondents having the technologies but are expanding rapidly.[26]

The high cost of reaching respondents in their homes using personal interviews has led to a dramatic increase in the use of *mall intercept interviews,* which are personal interviews of consumers while on visits to shopping centers. These face-to-face interviews reduce the cost of personal visits to consumers in their homes while providing the flexibility to show respondents visual cues such as ads or actual product samples. However, a critical disadvantage of mall intercept interviews is that the people selected for the interviews may not be representative of the consumers targeted for the interviews, giving a biased result.

Figure 8–6 shows typical problems to guard against in wording questions to obtain meaningful answers from respondents. For example, in a question of whether you eat at fast-food restaurants regularly, the word *regularly* is ambiguous. Two people might answer "yes" to the question, but one might mean "once a day" while the other means "once or twice a month." Both answers appear as "yes" to the researcher who tabulates them, but they suggest that dramatically different marketing actions be directed to each of these two prospective consumers. Therefore, it is essential that marketing research questions be worded precisely so that all respondents interpret the same question similarly.

FIGURE 8–6

Typical problems in wording questions

PROBLEM	SAMPLE QUESTION	EXPLANATION OF PROBLEM
Leading question	Why do you like Wendy's fresh meat hamburgers better than those of competitors?	Consumer is led to make statement favoring Wendy's hamburgers.
Ambiguous question	Do you eat at fast-food restaurants regularly? ☐ Yes ☐ No	What is meant by word *regularly*—once a day, once a month, or what?
Unanswerable question	What was the occasion for eating your first hamburger?	Who can remember the answer? Does it matter?
Two questions in one	Do you eat Wendy's hamburgers and chili? ☐ Yes ☐ No	How do you answer if you eat Wendy's hamburgers but not chili?
Nonexhaustive question	Where do you live? ☐ At home ☐ In dormitory	What do you check if you live in an apartment?
Nonmutually exclusive answers	What is your age? ☐ Under 20 ☐ 20–40 ☐ 40 and over	What answer does a 40-year-old check?

1. What things are most important to you when you decide to eat out and go to a fast-food restaurant?

_____

_____

_____

2. Have you eaten at a fast-food restaurant in the past month?

☐ Yes   ☐ No

3. If you answered yes to question 2, how often do you eat fast food?

☐ Once a week   ☐ 2 to 3 times a month   ☐ Once a month or less

4. How important is it to you that a fast-food restaurant satisfies you on the following characteristics? [Check the box that describes your feelings for each item listed]

CHARACTERISTIC	VERY IMPORTANT	SOMEWHAT IMPORTANT	IMPORTANT	UNIMPORTANT	SOMEWHAT UNIMPORTANT	VERY UNIMPORTANT
• Taste of food	☐	☐	☐	☐	☐	☐
• Cleanliness	☐	☐	☐	☐	☐	☐
• Price	☐	☐	☐	☐	☐	☐
• Variety of menu	☐	☐	☐	☐	☐	☐

5. For each of the characteristics listed below, check the space on the scale that describes how you feel about Wendy's. Mark an X on only **one** of the five spaces listed for each item listed.

CHARACTERISTIC   CHECK THE SPACE THAT DESCRIBES THE DEGREE TO WHICH WENDY'S IS . . .

• Taste of food	Tasty	____	____	____	____	____	Not tasty
• Cleanliness	Clean	____	____	____	____	____	Dirty
• Price	Inexpensive	____	____	____	____	____	Expensive
• Variety of menu	Broad	____	____	____	____	____	Narrow

FIGURE 8–7

Sample questions from Wendy's survey

Figure 8–7 shows a number of different formats for questions taken from a Wendy's survey that assessed fast-food restaurant preferences among present and prospective consumers. Question 1 is an example of an *open-ended question,* which allows respondents to express opinions, ideas, or behaviors in their own words without being forced to choose among alternatives that have been predetermined by a marketing researcher. This information is invaluable to marketers because it captures the "voice" of respondents, which is useful in understanding consumer behavior, identifying product benefits, or developing advertising messages. In contrast, *closed-end* or *fixed alternative questions* require respondents to select one or more response options from a set of predetermined choices. Question 2 is an example of a *dichotomous question,* the simplest form of a fixed alternative question that allows only a "yes" or "no" response.

A fixed alternative question with three or more choices uses a *scale.* Question 5 is an example of a question that uses a *semantic differential scale,* a five-point scale in which the opposite ends have one- or two-word adjectives that have opposite meanings. For example, depending on how clean the respondent feels that

6. Check one box that describes your agreement or disagreement with each statement listed below:

STATEMENT	STRONGLY AGREE	AGREE	DON'T KNOW	DISAGREE	STRONGLY DISAGREE
• Adults like to take their families to fast-food restaurants	☐	☐	☐	☐	☐
• Our children have a say in where the family chooses to eat	☐	☐	☐	☐	☐

7. How important are each of the following sources of information to you when selecting a fast-food restaurant to eat at? [Check one box for each source listed]

SOURCE OF INFORMATION	VERY IMPORTANT	SOMEWHAT IMPORTANT	NOT AT ALL IMPORTANT
• Television	☐	☐	☐
• Newspapers	☐	☐	☐
• Radio	☐	☐	☐
• Billboards	☐	☐	☐
• Flyers	☐	☐	☐

8. How often do you eat out at each of the following fast-food restaurants? [Check one box for each restaurant listed]

RESTAURANT	ONCE A WEEK OR MORE	2 TO 3 TIMES A MONTH	ONCE A MONTH OR LESS
• Burger King	☐	☐	☐
• McDonald's	☐	☐	☐
• Wendy's	☐	☐	☐

9. Please answer the following questions about you and your household. [Check only one for each item]

a. What is your gender? ☐ Male ☐ Female

b. What is your marital status? ☐ Single ☐ Married ☐ Other (widowed, divorced, etc.)

c. How many children under age 18 live in your home? ☐ 0 ☐ 1 ☐ 2 ☐ 3 or more

d. What is your age? ☐ Under 25 ☐ 25–44 ☐ 45 or older

e. What is your total annual individual or household income?
☐ <$15,000   ☐ $15,000–49,000   ☐ $50,000 or more

FIGURE 8–7
(Continued)

Wendy's is, he or she would check the left-hand space on the scale, the right-hand space, or one of the five intervening points. Question 6 uses a *Likert scale,* in which the respondent indicates the extent to which he or she agrees or disagrees with a statement.

The questionnaire in Figure 8–7 is an excerpt of a precisely worded survey that provides valuable information to the marketing researcher at Wendy's.[27] Questions 1 to 8 inform him or her about the likes and dislikes in eating out, frequency of eating out at fast-food restaurants generally and at Wendy's specifically, and sources of information used in making decisions about fast-food restaurants. Question 9 gives details about the personal or household characteristics, which can be used in trying to segment the fast-food market, a topic discussed in Chapter 9.

Electronic technology has revolutionized traditional concepts of interviews or surveys. Today, respondents can walk up to a kiosk in a shopping center, read questions off a screen, and key their answers into a computer on a touch screen. Even fully automated telephone interviews exist: An automated voice questions respondents over the telephone, who then key their replies on a touch-tone telephone.

Wendy's changes continuously in response to changing customer wants, while keeping its "Fresh, hot'n juicy®" image.

Wendy's Restaurant
www.wendys.com

Panels and Experiments Two special ways that observations and questionnaires are sometimes used are panels and experiments.

Marketing researchers often want to know if consumers change their behavior over time, and so they take successive measurements of the same people. A *panel* is a sample of consumers or stores from which researchers take a series of measurements. For example, the NPD Group collects data about consumer purchases such as apparel, food, and electronics from its Online Panel, which consists of more than 2.5 million individuals worldwide. So a firm like General Mills can use descriptive research—counting the frequency of consumer purchases—to measure switching behavior from one brand of its breakfast cereal (Wheaties) to another (Cheerios) or to a competitor's (Kellogg's Special K). A disadvantage of panels is that the marketing research firm needs to recruit new members continually to replace those who drop out. These new recruits must match the characteristics of those they replace to keep the panel representative of the marketplace.

An *experiment* involves obtaining data by manipulating factors under tightly controlled conditions to test cause and effect, an example of causal research. The interest is in whether changing one of the independent variables (a cause) will change the behavior of the dependent variable that is studied (the result). In marketing experiments, the independent variables of interest—sometimes called the marketing *drivers*—are often one or more of the marketing mix elements, such as a product's features, price, or promotion (like advertising messages or coupons). The ideal dependent variable usually is a change in purchases (incremental unit or dollar sales) of individuals, households, or organizations. For example, food companies often use *test markets,* which is offering a product for sale on a limited basis in a defined area to help decide the likely effectiveness of potential marketing actions. So a test market is really a kind of marketing experiment to reduce risks. In 1988, Wal-Mart opened three experimental stand-alone supercenters to gauge consumer acceptance before deciding to open others. Today, Wal-Mart operates over 1,000 supercenters nationwide.[28]

A potential difficulty with experiments is that outside factors (such as actions of competitors) can distort the results of an experiment and affect the dependent variable (such as sales). A researcher's task is to identify the effect of the marketing variable of interest on the dependent variable when the effects of outside factors in an experiment might hide it.

Advantages and Disadvantages of Primary Data   Compared with secondary data, primary data have the advantage of being more specific to the problem being studied. The main disadvantages are that primary data are usually far more costly and time consuming to collect than secondary data.

Concept Check

1. What is the difference between observational and questionnaire data?

2. Which survey provides the greatest flexibility for asking probing questions: mail, telephone, or personal interview?

3. What is the difference between a panel and an experiment?

Using Information Technology to Trigger Marketing Actions

Today's marketing managers can be drowned in such an ocean of data that they need to adopt strategies for dealing with complex, changing views of the competition, the market, and the consumer. The Internet and the PC power of today provide a gateway to exhaustive data sources that vary from well organized and correct to disorganized and incorrect.

The Marketing Manager's View of Sales Drivers   Figure 8–8 shows a marketing manager's view of the product or brand "drivers," the factors that influence buying decisions of a household or organization and, hence, sales. These drivers

FIGURE 8–8
Product and brand drivers: factors that influence sales

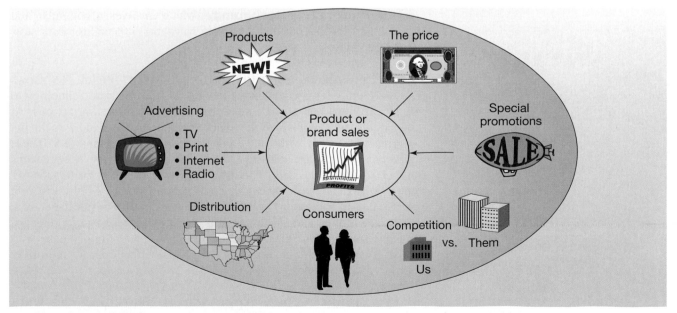

SOURCE: Ford Consulting Group, Inc.

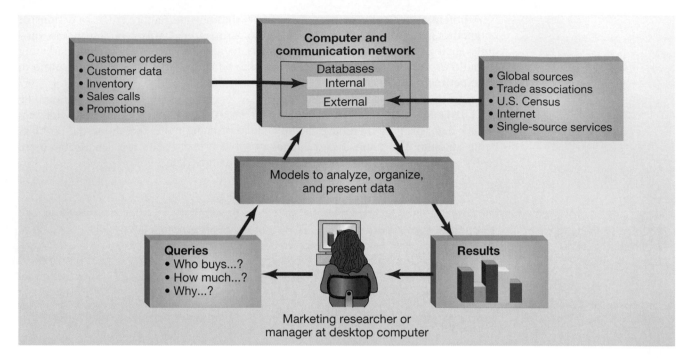

FIGURE 8–9

How marketing researchers and managers use information technology to turn information into action

include both the controllable marketing mix factors like product and distribution as well as uncontrollable factors like competition and the changing tastes of households or organizational buyers.

Understanding these drivers involves managing this ocean of data. Sometimes hundreds of thousands of bits of data are created each week. Sources feeding this database ocean range from internal data about sales and customers to external data from syndication services and TV ratings. The marketer's task is to convert this data ocean into useful information on which to base informed decisions. In practice, some market researchers distinguish *data*—the facts and figures—from *information*—the distilled facts and figures whose interpretation leads to marketing actions.

Current information about products, competitors, and customers is almost always accessed and analyzed by computer. So today, these activities fall under the broader term of **information technology**, which involves a computer and communication system to satisfy an organization's needs for data storage, processing, and access.

Key Elements of an Information System   Figure 8–9 shows how marketing researchers and managers use information technology to frame questions that provide answers leading to marketing actions. At the bottom of Figure 8–9 the marketer queries the databases in the information system with marketing questions needing answers. These questions go through statistical models that analyze the relationships that exist among the data. The databases form the core, or *data warehouse,* where the ocean of data is collected and stored. After the search of this data warehouse, the models select and link the pertinent data, often presenting them in tables and graphics for easy interpretation. Marketers can also use *sensitivity analysis* to query the database with "what if" questions to determine how a hypothetical change in a driver like advertising can affect sales.

Data Mining: A New Approach to Searching the Data Ocean   Traditional marketing research typically involves identifying

possible drivers and then collecting data: Increasing couponing (the driver) during spring will increase trial by first-time buyers (the result). Marketing researchers then try to collect information to attempt to verify the truth of the relationship.

In contrast, **data mining** is the extraction of hidden predictive information from large databases. Catalog companies such as Lands' End, Fingerhut, and Spiegel use data mining to find statistical links that suggest marketing actions. For example, Fingerhut studies about 3,500 variables over the lifetime of a consumer's relationship. It has found that customers who change residences are three times as likely as regular customers to buy tables, fax machines, and decorative products but no more likely to buy jewelry or footwear. So Fingerhut has created a catalog especially targeted at consumers who have recently moved.[29]

Some of these purchase patterns are common sense: Peanut butter and grape jelly purchases are linked and might suggest a joint promotion between Skippy peanut butter and Welch's grape jelly. Other patterns link seemingly unrelated purchases: Supermarkets mined checkout data from scanners and discovered men buying diapers in the evening sometimes buy a six-pack of beer as well. So they placed diapers and beer near each other. Placing potato chips between them increased sales of all three.

Still, the success in data mining ultimately depends on humans—the judgments of the marketing managers and researchers in how to select, analyze, and interpret the information.

STEP 4: DEVELOP FINDINGS

Mark Twain once observed, "Collecting data is like collecting garbage. You've got to know what you're going to do with the stuff before you collect it." Thus, marketing data and information have little more value than garbage unless they are analyzed carefully and translated into logical findings, step 4 in the marketing research approach.[30]

Analyze the Data

How are sales doing? To see how marketers at Tony's Pizza assessed this question and the reasons they came up with this ad, read the text.

Let's consider the case of Tony's Pizza and Teré Carral, the marketing manager responsible for the Tony's brand. We will use hypothetical data to protect Tony's proprietary information.

Teré is concerned about the limited growth in the Tony's brand over the past four years. She hires a consultant to collect and analyze data to explain what's going on with her brand and to recommend ways to improve its growth. Teré asks the consultant to put together a proposal that includes the answers to two key questions:

1. How are Tony's sales doing on a household basis? For example, are fewer households buying Tony's pizzas, *or* is each household buying fewer Tony's? Or both?
2. What factors might be contributing to Tony's very flat sales over the past four years?

Facts uncovered by the consultant are vital. For example, is the average household consuming more or less Tony's pizza than in previous years? Is Tony's flat sales performance related to a specific factor? With answers to these questions Teré can identify actions in her marketing plan and implement them over the coming year.

Present the Findings

Findings should be clear and understandable from the way the data are presented. Managers are responsible for *actions*. Often it means delivering the results in clear pictures and, if possible, in a single page.

The consultant gives Teré the answers to her questions using Figure 8–10 on the next page, a creative way to present findings graphically.

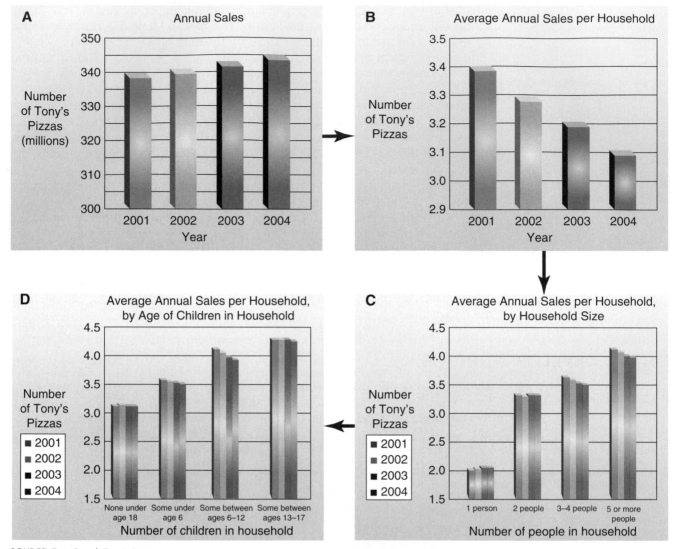

SOURCE: Teré Carral, Tony's Pizza.

FIGURE 8–10

Presenting findings to Tony's marketing manager that lead to recommendations and actions

Let's look over the shoulders of Teré and the consultant while they interpret these findings:

- Figure 8–10A, the chart showing Annual Sales. This shows the annual growth of the Tony's Pizza brand is stable but virtually flat from 2001 through 2004.
- Figure 8–10B, the chart showing Average Annual Sales per Household. Look closely at this graph. At first glance, it may seem like sales in 2004 are *half* what they were in 2001, right? But be careful to read the numbers on the vertical axis. They show that household purchases of Tony's have been steadily declining over the past four years, from an average of 3.4 pizzas per household in 2001 to 3.1 pizzas per household in 2004. (Significant, but hardly a 50 percent drop.) Now the question is, if Tony's annual sales are stable, yet the average individual household is buying fewer Tony's pizzas, what's going on? The answer is, more households are buying pizzas—it's just that each household is buying fewer Tony's pizzas. That households aren't choosing Tony's is a genuine source of concern. But again, here's a classic example of a marketing problem representing a marketing opportunity. The number of households buying pizza is *growing,* and that's good news for Tony's.

- Figure 8–10C, the chart showing Average Annual Sales per Household, by Household Size. Oh, Oh! This chart starts to show a source of the problem: Even though average sales of pizza to households with only one or two people is stable, households with three or four people and those with five or more are declining in average annual pizza consumption. Which households tend to have more than two people? Answer: Households *with children.* Therefore, we should look more closely at the pizza-buying behavior of households with children.
- Figure 8–10D, the chart showing Average Annual Sales per Household, by Age of Children in the Household. Oh, oh, oh! The picture is becoming very clear now: The real problem is in the serious decline in average consumption in the households with younger children, especially in households with children in the 6- to 12-year-old age group.

Identifying a sales problem in households with children 6- to 12-years-old is an important discovery, as Tony's sales are declining in a market segment that is known to be one of the heaviest in buying pizzas.

STEP 5: TAKE MARKETING ACTIONS

Effective marketing research doesn't stop with findings and recommendations—someone has to identify the marketing actions, put them into effect, and monitor how the decisions turn out, which is the essence of step 5.

Make Action Recommendations

Teré Carral, the marketing manager for Tony's Pizza, met with her team to convert the market research findings into specific marketing recommendations with a clear objective: Target families with children ages 6 to 12 to reverse the trend among this segment and gain strength in one of the most important segments in the frozen pizza category. Her recommendation is to develop:

- An advertising campaign that will target children 6 to 12.
- A monthly promotion calendar with this 6 to 12 age group target in mind.
- A special event program reaching children 6 to 12.

Implement the Action Recommendations

As her first marketing action, Teré undertakes advertising research to develop ads that appeal to children in the 6 to 12 age group and their families. The research shows that children like colorful ads with funny, friendly characters. She gives these research results to her advertising agency, which develops several sample ads for her review. Teré selects three that are tested on children to try to identify the most appealing one. The one that gets the best results appeared earlier on page 223. Teré uses this ad in her next advertising campaign for Tony's Pizza.

Evaluate the Results

Evaluating results is a continuing way of life for effective marketing managers. There are really two aspects of this evaluation process:

- *Evaluating the decision itself.* This involves monitoring the marketplace to determine if action is necessary in the future. For Teré, is her new ad successful in appealing to 6- to 12-year-olds and their families? Are sales increasing to this target segment? The success of this strategy suggests Teré add more follow-up ads with colorful, funny, friendly characters.

• *Evaluating the decision process used.* Was the marketing research and analysis used to develop the recommendations effective? Was it flawed? Could it be improved for similar situations in the future? Teré and her marketing team must be vigilant for ways to improve the analysis and results—to learn lessons that might apply to future marketing research efforts at Tony's.

Again, systematic analysis does not guarantee success. But, as in the case of Tony's Pizza, it can improve a firm's success rate for its marketing decisions.

Concept Check

1. What does a marketing manager mean when she talks about a sales driver?

2. How does data mining differ from traditional marketing research?

3. In the marketing research for Tony's Pizza, what is an example of (*a*) a finding and (*b*) a marketing action?

CHAPTER IN REVIEW

1 *Identify the reason for doing marketing research, and describe the five-step marketing research approach leading to marketing actions.*

To be successful, products and marketing programs must meet the wants and needs of potential customers. So marketing research provides the vital information to help marketing managers understand those wants and needs and translate them into actions in their marketing activities. This information reduces the risk and uncertainty marketing managers face and helps them make better decisions.

The first step of the five-step marketing research approach involves defining the problem, which requires setting the research objectives and identifying possible marketing actions. The second step, developing the research plan, requires specifying the constraints in solving the problem, identifying data needed, and determining how to collect the data. The third step involves collecting the relevant information, which includes considering pertinent secondary and primary data. Analyzing the data and presenting findings based on the data is the fourth step. The fifth step in the marketing research sequence involves identifying and implementing marketing action recommendations and evaluating the results—how the decisions turned out.

2 *Describe how secondary and primary data are used in marketing, including the uses of questionnaires, observations, experiments, and panels.*

Secondary data have been recorded prior to the project. Internal secondary data come from within the organization, such as

sales reports and customer comments. The most widely used external secondary data are reports from the U.S. Bureau of the Census on characteristics of the country's population, manufacturers, and retailers. Primary data are collected specifically for the project and are obtained by either observing or questioning people. Observing people in marketing is done in various ways, including electronically with Nielsen people meters to measure TV viewing habits or personally, say, with mystery shoppers. Questionnaires involve asking people questions—in person, by telephone or fax, in a printed survey, or by Internet. Panels involve a sample of consumers or stores that are measured repeatedly through time to see if behavior changes. Experiments, such as test markets, involve measuring the effect of marketing variables like price or advertising on sales.

3 *Explain how information technology and data mining link massive amounts of marketing information to meaningful marketing actions.*

Today's marketing managers are often overloaded with data—from internal data to those provided by services on, say, TV-viewing habits or grocery purchases from the scanner data at checkout counters. This can involve millions of bits of new information in a week or month. So information technology enables massive amounts of marketing data to be stored, processed, and accessed. Using this information technology, databases can be queried using data mining to find statistical relationships useful for marketing decisions and actions.

FOCUSING ON KEY TERMS

constraints p. 209
data p. 210
data mining p. 223
decision p. 206
information technology p. 222
marketing research p. 205
measures of success p. 208
nonprobability sampling p. 210

observational data p. 213
primary data p. 210
probability sampling p. 210
questionnaire data p. 215
sampling p. 210
secondary data p. 210
statistical inference p. 210

DISCUSSION AND APPLICATION QUESTIONS

1 Look at Figure 8–1. (*a*) What kind of questions are these? (*b*) What difficulties might you have in tabulating answers to the questions about the movie title? (*c*) How might you address these problems?

2 (*a*) Why might a marketing researcher prefer to use secondary data rather than primary data in a study? (*b*) Why might the reverse be true?

3 Suppose your dean of admissions is considering surveying high school seniors about their perceptions of your school to design better informational brochures for them. What are the advantages and disadvantages of doing (*a*) telephone interviews and (*b*) an Internet survey of seniors who have requested information on the school?

4 Nielsen Media Research obtains ratings of local TV stations by having households fill out diary questionnaires. These give information on (*a*) who is watching TV and (*b*) what program. What are the limitations of this questionnaire method?

5 The format in which information is presented to a harried marketing manager is often vital. (*a*) If you were a marketing manager and queried your information system, would you rather see the results in tables or charts and graphs? (*b*) What are one or two strengths and weaknesses of each format?

6 Right out of school you get your dream job that relates to your favor sport: You're the marketing manager for a small company that gives flying lessons in ultralight planes to college students. A summer intern shows you the questionnaire below. In terms of Figure 8–6, (*i*) identify the problem with each question and (*ii*) correct it. *Note:* Some questions may have more than one problem.

a. Have you ever flown in commercial airliners and in ultralight planes?　　□ Yes　　□ No

b. Why do you think ultralights are so much safer than hang gliders?_____

c. At what age did you first know you liked to fly?
　□ Under 10　□ 10 to 20　□ 21 to 30　□ Over 30

d. How much did you spend on recreational activities last year?
　□ $100 or less　　□ $801 to $1,201
　□ $101 to $400　　□ $1,201 to $1,600
　□ $401 to $800　　□ $1,600 or more

e. How much would you pay for ultralight flying lessons?
_____

f. Would you sign up for a class that met regularly?
　□ Yes　　□ No

7 Wisk detergent decides to run a test market to see the effect of coupons and in-store advertising on sales. The index of sales is as follows:

ELEMENT IN TEST MARKET	WEEKS BEFORE COUPON	WEEK OF COUPON	WEEK AFTER COUPON
Without in-store ads	100	144	108
With in-store ads	100	268	203

What are your conclusions and recommendations?

8 Suppose Fisher-Price wants to run a simple experiment to evaluate a proposed chatter telephone design. It has two different groups of children on which to run its experiment for one week each. The first group has the old toy telephone, whereas the second group is exposed to the newly designed pull toy with wheels, a noisemaker, and bobbing eyes. The dependent variable is the average number of minutes during the two-hour play period that one of the children is playing with the toy, and the results are as follows:

ELEMENT IN EXPERIMENT	FIRST GROUP	SECOND GROUP
Independent variable	Old design	New design
Dependent variable	13 minutes	62 minutes

Should Fisher-Price introduce the new design? Why?

GOING ONLINE   What's New in Marketing Research?

WorldOpinion calls its website "The World's Market Research Web Site." To check out the latest marketing research news, job opportunities, and directories of more than 8,500 research locations in 99 countries, go to www.worldopinion.com and do the following:

1 Click on the "News" link on WorldOpinion's home page to read about the current news and issues facing the market research industry.

2 Click on the "The Frame" link, a set of online articles published by Survey Sampling, International.

BUILDING YOUR MARKETING PLAN

To help you collect the most useful data for your marketing plan, develop a three-column table:

1 In column 1, list the information you would ideally like to have to fill holes in your marketing plan.

2 In column 2, identify the source for each bit of information in column 1, such as a Web search, talking to prospective customers, looking at internal data, and so forth.

3 In column 3, set a priority on information you will have time to spend collecting by ranking them: 1 = most important; 2 = next most important, and so forth.

VIDEO CASE 8 Ford Consulting Group, Inc.: From Data to Actions

"The fast pace of working as a marketing professional isn't getting any easier," agrees David Ford, as he talks with Mark Rehborg, Tony's Pizza brand manager. "The speed of communication, the availability of real-time market information, and the responsibility for a brand's profit make marketing one of the most challenging professional jobs today."

Mark responds, "Ten years ago, we could reach 80 percent of our target market with 3 television spots—but today, to reach the same 80 percent, we would have to buy 97 spots. We haven't the luxury to be complacent—our core consumer, the 6- to 12-year-old 'big kid,' is part of a savvy, wired culture that is changing rapidly."

THE COMPANY AND ITS CLIENTS

David Ford, president of Ford Consulting Group (FCG), assists clients such as Tony's in translating the market and sales information into marketing actions. Mark executes ideas that will draw consumers to Tony's and manages sales and profit performance. He distributes budgeted funds to promote the product. Feedback from the sales force requesting promotion funds is a common occurrence.

The information that FCG consultants and Tony's use most often for this analysis comes from places like AC Nielsen's ScanTrack and Information Resources' InfoScan (IRI) that summarize sales data from grocery stores and other outlets that scan purchases at the checkout.

FCG's typical consulting project involves helping clients make sense of their existing information, *not* in helping clients collect more information. Most often the client has a critical time deadline for FCG's data analysis and action recommendations: The client "wants" the answer a week ago, about four days *before* it hires FCG!

The project that follows is typical of the work Ford Consulting Group (www.fordconsultinggroup.com) undertakes for a client. The data are hypothetical, but the situation is a very typical one in the grocery products industry. Here's a snapshot of some of the terms in the case:

- "You" have just come on the job, as the new marketing person.
- "NE" is the Northeastern sales region of Tony's.
- "SE, NW, SW" are the other sales regions.

PART 1: A TYPICAL QUESTION, ON A TYPICAL DAY

Let's dive into the background of a typical question you might face, on a typical day. On the opposite page are some memos you are given (one from Mark to you) as background.

You dig into Lauretta's data files and develop Table 1 that shows how Tony's is doing in the company's four sales regions and the entire United States on key marketing dimensions. Without reading further, take a deep breath and try to answer question 1 below.

PART 2: UNCOVERING THE TRUTH

Let's assume your analysis (question 1) shows NE is a problem, so we need to understand what's going on in the NE. You dig into the data and develop Table 2. It shows the situation for the four largest supermarket chains in the Northeast sales region that carry Tony's. Now answer question 2.

Questions

1 Study Table 1. (*a*) How does the situation in the Northeast compare with the other regions in the United States? (*b*) What appears to be the reason(s) that sales are soft? (*c*) Write a 150-word e-mail with attachments to Mark Rehborg, your boss, giving your answers to *b*.

2 Study Table 2. (*a*) What do you conclude from this information? (*b*) Summarize your conclusions in a 150-word e-mail with attachments to Mark, who needs them for a meeting tomorrow with Margaret, the Northeast sales region manager. (*c*) What marketing actions might your memo suggest?

TO: Mark Rehborg, Tony's Brand Manager
FROM: Steve Quam, Tony's Field Sales
CC: Margaret Loiaza, NE Sales Region Manager

RE: Feedback on Sales Call at Food-Fast

Hi Mark—

Our sales call at Food-Fast wasn't so great. They don't see how our Tony's is going to sell well enough to justify the additional shelf-space. I also talked to Margaret and she said that second quarter may be weaker than planned across all the NE, and I should give you a heads-up. (She's on vacation this week, Aruba!) She's planning to schedule some time with you to talk about additional promotion money to do catch-up in the third quarter. She'll be there next week.

Steve

TO: You, the New Marketing Person
FROM: Mark Rehborg, Tony's Brand Manager (Your Boss)

RE: Small Project due Friday

Hi You,

Can you help out here? I've got a meeting with Margaret on Friday afternoon, and she's concerned that Food-Fast and the whole NE is going to need some additional promotion dollars.

Lauretta started the analysis and was hurt in a kick-boxing accident yesterday and won't be back to work for a week. Her files are attached. Can you look through her files and summarize what's going on in the NE and the rest of the U.S.? Does Margaret need more promotion money?

Let's discuss Friday AM.

Mark

TABLE 1. COMPARISON OF TONY'S PERFORMANCE, BY REGION

| REGION | QUARTERLY CHANGE IN VOLUME (%) | DISTRIBUTION[a] (%) | PRICE ($) | PRICE GAP[b] ($) | PROMOTION | |
					SUPPORT[c] (%)	VOLUME[d] (%)
NE	3%	93%	$1.29	+8	7%	14%
SE	5	95	1.11	−1	9	16
NW	8	98	1.19	+1	8	15
SW	6	96	1.25	0	8	15
U.S.	6	97	1.19	0	8	15

[a] % of outlets carrying Tony's.
[b] Price gap = (Our price) − (Competitor's price).
[c] Promotion support = % of the time brand was promoted.
[d] Promotion volume = % of the volume sold on promotion.

TABLE 2. COMPARISON OF MAJOR SUPERMARKET CHAINS IN THE NORTHEAST

| SUPER-MARKET CHAIN | QUARTERLY CHANGE IN VOLUME (%) | DISTRIBUTION[a] (%) | PRICE ($) | PRICE GAP[b] ($) | PROMOTION | |
					SUPPORT[c] (%)	VOLUME[d] (%)
Save-a-lot	5%	95%	$1.39	+10	10%	19%
Food-Fast	0	90	1.28	−1	3	4
Get-Fresh	0	90	1.30	+1	3	4
Dollars-Off	7	97	1.34	+5	7	14

CHAPTER 9

IDENTIFYING MARKET SEGMENTS AND TARGETS

LEARNING OBJECTIVES

After reading this chapter you should be able to:

1 Explain what market segmentation is and when to use it.

2 Identify the five steps involved in segmenting and targeting markets.

3 Recognize the different factors used to segment consumer and organizational markets.

4 Know how to develop a market-product grid to identify a target market and recommend resulting actions.

5 Explain how marketing managers position products in the marketplace.

6 Describe three approaches to developing a sales forecast for a company.

SNEAKERS MARKETING WARS: HIP-HOP, YAO MING, AND 3 BILLION TRILLION CHOICES

In today's annual $16 billion U.S. sneakers war among Reebok, Nike, Adidas, and others, a new shoe introduction can have the effect of a toy pop gun—or a salvo across a battleship's bow. That's how serious the competition is. And Reebok recently launched a marketing strategy that challenges conventional wisdom.

New Segments and Strategies Reebok is reaching a new market segment and getting publicity for its entire sneaker line by signing endorsements with popular rappers and hip-hop music stars. Example: S. Carter Collection by Rbk. Don't recognize the S. Carter name? The street-inspired S. Carter Collection is named for hip-hop star Jay-Z, who was originally known as Shawn Carter. With their flat soles and soft leather, the S. Carter low tops (opposite page) are a long way from the look of Reebok's traditional "performance" athletic shoes.[1]

The look is not all that's unusual about Jay-Z's endorsement agreement with Reebok. Basketball star Yao Ming and tennis star Venus Williams have endorsement agreements with Reebok not only for their own footwear lines but also to promote its entire line and not to wear products from competitors. Yao Ming's $70 million contract with Reebok also will help it market its sports lines in his native China. But Jay-Z agrees to promote only his line of Reebok shoes, which means he is allowed to wear competing brands in public. Can you imagine Tiger Woods wearing a Reebok hat in the U.S. Open golf tournament—and his Nike sponsor being happy about it? Reebok says the "standard, more restrictive deal would have risked tagging its rapper allies as walking billboards for the corporation, hurting their countercultural appeal."[2]

What do you need in the sneaker business to stand out from the pack when consumers are faced with hundreds of athletic shoe choices, often on sneaker "walls" in sporting goods stores? The answer: All sneaker manufacturers are searching for new market segments of consumers and ways to differentiate their products from their global competitors. This challenge applies to the giants like Reebok and Nike, which is aggressively marketing new lines of superfast sneakers for track athletes, sleek soccer shoes, and sporty street apparel.[3] Competitive sneaker upstarts frequently target narrow market niches. For example, Heelys sneakers come with an imbedded, detachable wheel in the shoe's heel. In 2001, its first year of operation, Heelys sneakers were so hot that retailers sold 1 million pairs.

And what about the "3 billion trillion choices" mentioned in the heading of this section? This was the number of different athletic shoe designs that Customatix claimed was possible if you ordered from its design-your-own-customized-shoes website. Customatix's strategy targeted a niche segment of athletic shoe buyers who wanted a shoe designed to their unique wants and needs. And where are Customatix and its 3 billion trillion choices today? Gone—a silent victim in early 2004 to the sneaker marketing wars that proved too competitive.

Competitive Trends

Reebok also has recently signed deals with the NBA ($175 million) and the NFL ($250 million) to be their exclusive team uniform providers while offering branded apparel to consumers. And beginning in 2005, Reebok will be the provider of footwear to Major League Baseball players not under contract with other manufacturers. As a result of intense competition in the sneaker market, Nike acquired Converse, maker of basketball shoes worn by legends Magic Johnson and Larry Bird. The Sporting Goods Manufacturers Association (SGMA) and the NPD Group identified the following U.S. trends to consider in planning for the sneaker wars for 2005 and beyond:[4]

- *Age segments.* Teenagers/college-aged consumers comprise more than 32 percent of total sales, are the largest segment, and spend more for sneakers than older consumers.
- *Gender segments.* Both men and women are important segments—women because their sales growth is higher than men, and men because they still buy more in total (double) at higher average prices.
- *Price segments.* More than 62 percent of sneakers purchased today cost less than $50 per pair.
- *Sport segments.* In the United States, running shoes are number one ($4.5 billion today and 29 percent market share); basketball shoes are number two ($3.2 billion and 21 percent); and cross-training shoes number three ($2.0 billion and 13 percent). Basketball sales are up, but cross-training is down slightly.

- *Lifestyle segments.* Most recent sales growth in sneakers is due to casual styles that have a strong fashion component, where the retro look is prominent. Almost three-fourths of all sneakers are purchased for casual rather than for sports or fitness purposes. However, sales of higher-priced performance shoes has risen dramatically in 2003 and 2004.

The strategies sneaker manufacturers use to satisfy needs of different customers illustrate successful market segmentation, the main topic of this chapter. After discussing why markets need to be segmented, this chapter covers the steps a firm uses in segmenting and targeting a market, positioning its offering to the marketplace, and forecasting sales.

WHY SEGMENT MARKETS?

A business firm segments its markets so it can respond more effectively to the wants of groups of potential buyers and thus increase its sales and profits. Not-for-profit organizations also segment the clients they serve to satisfy client needs more effectively while achieving the organization's goals. Let's use the dilemma of sneaker buyers finding their ideal Reebok shoes to describe (1) what market segmentation is and (2) when it is necessary to segment markets.

What Market Segmentation Means

People have different needs and wants, even though it would be easier for marketers if they didn't. Market segmentation involves aggregating prospective buyers into groups that (1) have common needs and (2) will respond similarly to a marketing action. **Market segments** are the relatively homogeneous groups of prospective buyers that result from the market segmentation process. Each market segment consists of people who are relatively similar to each other in terms of their consumption behavior.

The existence of different market segments has caused firms to use a marketing strategy of **product differentiation**. This strategy involves a firm's using different marketing mix activities, such as product features and advertising, to help consumers perceive the product as being different and better than competing products. The perceived differences may involve physical features or nonphysical ones, such as image or price. The Reebok example discussed below shows how the company is using market segmentation, product differentiation, and market-product grids to develop effective marketing strategies.

Segmentation: Linking Needs to Actions   The process of segmenting a market and selecting specific segments as targets is the link between the various buyers' needs and the organization's marketing program (Figure 9–1). Market segmentation is only a means to an end: to lead to tangible marketing actions that can increase sales and profitability.

Market segmentation first stresses the importance of grouping people or organizations in a market according to the similarity of their needs and the benefits they are looking for in making a purchase. Second, such needs and benefits must be

FIGURE 9–1

Market segmentation—linking market needs to an organization's marketing program

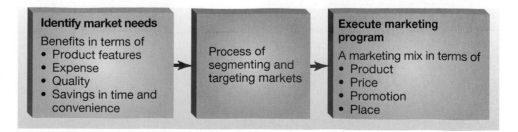

related to specific marketing actions the organization can take. These actions may involve separate products or other aspects of the marketing mix such as price, advertising, or distribution strategies.

How Reebok's Segmentation Strategy Developed

In 1979, Paul Fireman, who had dropped out of college to run his family's business, wandered through an international trade fair and saw Reebok's custom track shoes. He bought the U.S. license from the British manufacturer and started selling running shoes in 1981.

In a brilliant marketing decision, Fireman introduced soft-leather aerobic dance shoes in flamboyant colors—the Reebok Freestyle—in 1982. Figure 9–2 shows that Reebok has introduced a variety of shoes since 1982—from tennis and basketball shoes in 1984 to cross-training shoes in 1988 and golf shoes in 1997. For simplicity, Figure 9–2 covers only shoes and does not show nonshoe lines, like fitness water (2001) and NBA/NFL apparel (2002).

Reebok's $3 billion-a-year sneaker business has a huge need to generate sales from new opportunities. As a result, Reebok has expanded both the markets it targets and the products it develops to satisfy this need, as detailed in Figure 9–2.

Using Market-Product Grids

A **market-product grid** is a framework to relate the market segments of potential buyers to products offered or potential marketing actions by the firm. The market-product grid in Figure 9–2 shows different market segments of sneaker users as rows in the grid, whereas the columns show the different shoe product lines chosen by Reebok. In a complete market-product grid analysis, each cell in the grid can show the estimated market size of a given product sold to a specific market segment.

The cells with red boxes in Figure 9–2, labeled P, represent Reebok's primary target market segment when it introduced each type of shoe. The blue boxes, labeled S, represent the secondary target market segments that also bought these products. In some cases, Reebok discovered that large numbers of people in a segment not

FIGURE 9–2
Market-product grid showing how different Reebok shoes reach segments of customers with different needs

MARKET SEGMENT		PRODUCT								
GENERAL	GROUP WITH NEED	RUNNING SHOES (1981)	AEROBIC SHOES (1982)	TENNIS SHOES (1984)	BASKETBALL SHOES (1984)	KIDS SHOES (1984)	WALKING SHOES (1986)	CROSS-TRAINING SHOES (1988)	GOLF SHOES (1997)	S. CARTER SHOES (2003)
Performance-oriented 30%	Runners	P						P		
	Aerobic/fitness exercisers		P					P		
	Tennis players			P				P		
	Basketball players				P			P		
	Golfers								P	
	Adventure seekers							P		
Nonathletic-oriented 70%	Walkers	S	S	S	S		P	P		
	Children					P				
	Comfort/style-conscious	S	S	S	S		S	S		
	Street fashion									P

Key: P = Primary market   S = Secondary market

MARKETING NEWSNET

Sneaker Strategies—Who's Doing What

CUSTOMER VALUE

Cross beams, shock absorbers, and cushions. Off-the-shelf versus design-your-own-shoe with numerous design combinations. These are some of the innovative technologies and strategies used by sneaker manufacturers to attract new consumers and differentiate their products from those offered by competitors.

Reebok

Reebok's Premier Series of shoes targets the specific needs of runners and features the new DMX Shear and Foam cushioning and Play Dry™ moisture management technologies. Because one style does not fit all, Reebok designed the Premier Control ($100) for runners whose feet tend to turn outward and the Premier Road ($85) with extra cushioning for pavement runners, two of several in the Premier line. From its new NFL® Collection, the Reebok NFL Game Day DMX cross-training shoe ($80) displays the official NFL logo and features an "X-Beam," similar to a cross beam used in buildings, to hold the foot in place and a "tongue pull ring" to tighten the laces of the shoe.

Nike

The "Michael-inspired" Air Jordan basketball shoe was originally launched in 1985. Today's Air Jordan XIX ($165) basketball shoe incorporates the latest Zoom Air cushioning technology. The Air Jordan XIX also features the radically new "Tech-Flex" lace cover for instep support, a carbon fiber midfoot shank plate for lateral support, and an adjustable strap for a more snug fit. Nike also lets you design your own running or basketball shoes at www.nikeid.com. Nike's MJ replacement? Basketball phenom LeBron James, with a reported $90 million basketball shoe and jersey contract.

Vans

Vans has targeted the rising wave of skateboard, snowboard, biking, and outdoor enthusiasts. To reach its skateboard shoe market, Vans relies on its endorsing athletes to design and market its signature lines and promote its skateboard events. Vans had a breakthrough when Foot Locker carried its shoes in more than 2,700 retail outlets.

originally targeted for a particular shoe style bought it anyway. Today, Reebok products are purchased by two types of segments: performance-oriented consumers (30 percent), who buy sneakers and apparel for athletic purposes; and nonathletic-oriented consumers (70 percent), who buy sneakers and apparel for comfort, style, price, or other nonathletic reasons. But as Figure 9–2 depicts, two segments of consumers in the nonathletic-oriented category, comfort/style conscious and walker, bought running, aerobic, and cross-trainer shoes not initially targeted at their respective segments. When this trend became apparent to Reebok in 1986, it introduced its walking shoe line directly at the walker segment.

Reebok tries to upgrade its products continuously, so that the years shown in Figure 9–2 are the first year that Reebok entered that segment. For example, in 2003, it upgraded many of its kids and adult shoes using microprocessor technologies. Figure 9–2 shows its 2003 introduction of the S. Carter Collection by Rbk, designed for a street fashion target market.

What segmentation strategy will Reebok use to take it further into the twenty-first century? Only Reebok knows, but it will certainly involve trying to differentiate its products more clearly from its global competitors and perhaps target new or retarget existing global consumers. The Marketing NewsNet[5] describes how Reebok, Nike, and Vans have succeeded in using market segmentation and product differentiation strategies to reach special groups of customers.

When to Segment Markets

A business firm goes to the trouble and expense of segmenting its markets when it expects that this will increase its sales, profit, and return on investment. When expenses are greater than the potentially increased sales from segmentation, a firm should not attempt to segment its market. However, three specific situations that illustrate effective use of market segmentation are the cases of: (1) one product and multiple market segments, (2) multiple products and multiple market segments, and (3) "segments of one," or mass customization.

One Product and Multiple Market Segments

When a firm produces only a single product or service and attempts to sell it to two or more market segments, it

avoids the extra costs of developing and producing additional versions of the product, which often entail extremely high research, engineering, and manufacturing expenses. In this case, the incremental costs of taking the product into new market segments are typically those of a separate promotional campaign or a new channel of distribution. Although these expenses can be high, they are rarely as large as those for developing an entirely new product.

Movies, magazines, and books are single products frequently directed to two or more distinct market segments. Movie companies often run different TV commercials or magazine ads featuring different aspects of a newly released film (love, or drama, or spectacular scenery) that are targeted to different market segments. *Time* magazine now publishes more than 200 different U.S. editions and more than 100 international editions, each targeted at

Does Harry Potter appeal only to the kids' segment? See the text for the answer to this amazing publishing success.

unique geographic and demographic segments using a special mix of advertisements. As shown below, Street & Smith's spring *Baseball* issue uses different covers in different regions of the United States, featuring a baseball star from that region.

Harry Potter's phenomenal five-book success is based both on author J. K. Rowling's fiction-writing wizardry and her publisher's creativity in marketing to preteen, teen, and adult segments of readers. By the end of 2003, more than 250 million Harry Potter books had been sold globally, and in the United States the books were often at the top of *The New York Times* fiction best-seller list—for *adults. Harry Potter and the Order of the Phoenix,* the fifth book in the series, had a record-shattering initial press run of 8.5 million copies in the United States.[6] Although multiple TV commercials for movies and separate covers or advertisements for magazines or books are expensive, they are minor compared with the costs of producing an entirely new movie, magazine, or book for another market segment.

Multiple Products and Multiple Market Segments

Reebok's different styles of shoes, each targeted at a different type of user, are an example of multiple products aimed at multiple markets. Manufacturing these different styles of shoes is clearly more expensive than producing only a single style but seems worthwhile if it serves customers' needs better, doesn't reduce quality or increase price, and adds to the sales revenues and profits.

Marketing experts increasingly emphasize the two-tier marketing strategies—what some call "Tiffany/Wal-Mart strategies." Many firms are now offering different variations of the same basic product or service to high-end and low-end segments. Gap's

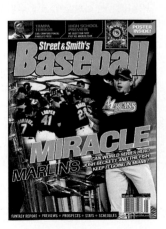
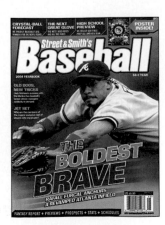

WEB LINK   Customizing Your Own Designer Shoes

www.mhhe.com/Kerin

Don't like the looks of those things on your feet right now?

If you think your style instincts could design you a better running or basketball shoe, go to www.nikeid.com. There you can design your own shoe, customizing up to 11 elements for one of four shoe models. All possible combinations of these 11 design elements should create enough design variations for shoes to fit your unique style and feet.

Banana Republic chain sells blue jeans for $58, whereas its Old Navy stores sell a slightly different version for $22. The Walt Disney Company carefully markets two distinct Winnie-the-Poohs—such as the original line-drawn figures on fine china sold at Nordstrom and a cartoonlike Pooh on polyester bedsheets sold at Wal-Mart. The lines between customer segments often blur, however, as shown by the Cadillacs and Mercedes in Wal-Mart parking lots.[7]

Segments of One: Mass Customization   American marketers are redis-covering today what their ancestors running the corner general store knew a cen-tury ago: Every customer is unique, has unique wants and needs, and desires special tender loving care from the seller—the essence of customer relationship management (CRM). Economies of scale in manufacturing and marketing during the past century made mass-produced goods so affordable that most customers were willing to compromise their individual tastes and settle for standardized products. Today's Internet ordering and flexible manufacturing and marketing processes have made *mass customization* possible, tailoring goods or services to the tastes of individual customers on a high-volume scale. The Web Link shows how mass customization lets you design your own personalized running shoe.

Mass customization is the next step beyond *build-to-order* (BTO), manufactur-ing a product only when there is an order from a customer. Dell Computer uses BTO systems that trim work-in-progress inventories and shorten delivery times to customers. Dell's three-day deliveries are made possible by restricting its computer line to only a few basic modules and stocking a variety of each. This gives customers a good choice with quick delivery—Dell PCs can be assembled in four minutes. Most Dell customization comes from spending 90 minutes loading the unique software each customer selects. But even this system falls a bit short of total mass customization with virtually unlimited specification of features by customers.[8]

The key to successful product differentiation and market segmentation strategies is finding the ideal balance between satisfying a customer's individual wants and achieving organizational **synergy**, the increased customer value achieved through performing organizational functions more efficiently. The "increased customer value" can take many forms: more products, improved quality on existing products, lower prices, easier access to product through improved distribution, and so on. So the ultimate criterion for an organization's marketing success is that customers should be better off as a result of the increased synergies.

Concept Check

1. Market segmentation involves aggregating prospective buyers into groups that have two key characteristics. What are they?

2. When should a firm segment its markets?

STEPS IN SEGMENTING AND TARGETING MARKETS

The process of segmenting a market and then selecting and reaching the target segments is divided into the five steps discussed in this section, as shown in Figure 9–3. Segmenting a market is not an exact science—it requires large doses of common sense and managerial judgment.

Let's have you put on your entrepreneur's hat to use the market segmentation process to choose target markets and take useful marketing actions. Suppose you own a Wendy's fast-food restaurant next to a large urban university that offers both day and evening classes. Your restaurant specializes in the Wendy's basics: hamburgers, french fries, Frosty desserts, and chili. Even though you are part of a chain and have some restrictions on menu and decor, you are free to set your hours of business and to undertake local advertising. How can market segmentation help?

Step 1: Group Potential Buyers into Segments

It's not always a good idea to segment a market. Grouping potential buyers into meaningful segments involves meeting some specific criteria that answer the question, Would segmentation be worth doing and is it possible? If so, the next step is to find specific variables that can be used to create the various segments.

Criteria to Use in Forming the Segments
A marketing manager should develop segments for a market that meet five main criteria:

- *Potential for increased profit.* The best segmentation approach is the one that maximizes the opportunity for future profit and ROI. If this potential is maximized without segmentation, don't segment. For not-for-profit organizations, the criterion is the potential for serving client users more effectively.
- *Similarity of needs of potential buyers within a segment.* Potential buyers within a segment should be similar in terms of a marketing action, such as product features sought or advertising media used.
- *Difference of needs of buyers among segments.* If the needs of the various segments aren't very different, combine them into fewer segments. A different segment usually requires a different marketing action that, in turn, means greater costs. If increased sales don't offset extra costs, combine segments and reduce the number of marketing actions.
- *Potential of a marketing action to reach a segment.* Reaching a segment requires a simple but effective marketing action. If no such action exists, don't segment.
- *Simplicity and cost of assigning potential buyers to segments.* A marketing manager must be able to put a market segmentation plan into effect. This means being able to recognize the characteristics of potential buyers and then assigning them to a segment without encountering excessive costs.

FIGURE 9–3
The five key steps in segmenting and targeting markets link market needs of customers to the organization's marketing program

Steps in segmenting and targeting markets

Identify market needs →

1 Group potential buyers into segments
2 Group products to be sold into categories
3 Develop a market-product grid and estimate size of markets
4 Select target markets
5 Take marketing actions to reach target markets

→ Execute marketing program

The global market for chicken is an example of how the five criteria can be used effectively to segment a market. While Americans (one segment) tend to prefer the white chicken meat, Russians (another segment) prefer the dark. Because it's easy to separate the white and dark meat portions of the chicken, it made sense—and increased profits—to market the dark meat to Russia. Today, about one-fourth of all U.S. chicken legs are eaten by Russians.[9]

Ways to Segment Consumer Markets   Figure 9–4 on the next page shows a number of variables that can be used to segment U.S. consumer markets, many based on those from the 2000 U.S. Census. They are divided into two general categories: customer characteristics and buying situations. Here are some examples of how certain *customer characteristics* can be used to segment specific markets:

- *Geographic customer characteristic: Region.* Campbell's found that its canned nacho cheese sauce, which could be heated and poured directly onto nacho chips, was too hot for Americans in the East and not hot enough for those in the West and Southwest. The result: Today, Campbell's plants in Texas and California produce a hotter nacho cheese sauce than that produced in the other plants to serve their regions better.
- *Demographic customer characteristic: Household size.* More than half of all U.S. households are made up of only one or two persons, so Campbell's packages meals with only one or two servings—from Great Starts breakfasts to L'Orient dinners.
- *Psychographic customer characteristic: Lifestyle.* Claritas provides lifestyle segmentation services to marketers. Claritas's lifestyle segmentation is based on the belief that people of similar lifestyle characteristics tend to live near one another, have similar interests, and buy similar products and services. One of its services classifies every *household* in the United States into one of 48 unique market segments.

What special benefit does a MicroFridge offer, and to which market segment might this appeal? The answer appears in the text.

Mac-Gray Corporation
www.microfridge.com

As shown at the bottom of Figure 9–4, *buying situations* are another way to segment consumer markets. These buying situations include benefits sought (product features, quality, service, warranty) and usage (heavy user, light user, nonuser). Two examples show how these buying situations can be used in developing consumer segments:

- *Benefits sought: Product features.* Understanding what benefits are important to different customers is often a useful way to segment markets because it can lead directly to specific marketing actions, such as a new product, ad campaign, or distribution system. For example, MicroFridge targets its combination microwave/refrigerator/freezer at college dorm residents, who are often woefully short of space. Busy, convenience-oriented consumers are beginning to use online grocery shopping and delivery from services like Peapod, which is currently located in Chicago, Boston, Washington, D.C., among other markets.[10]
- *Usage/patronage: Usage rate.* **Usage rate** is the quantity consumed or patronage—store visits—during a specific period. It varies significantly among different customer groups. Airlines have developed frequent-flier programs to encourage passengers to use the same airline repeatedly, a technique sometimes called *frequency marketing,* which focuses on usage rate.

One key conclusion emerges about usage: In market segmentation studies, some measure of usage by, or sales obtained from, various segments is central to the analysis.

MAIN DIMENSION	SEGMENTATION VARIABLES	TYPICAL BREAKDOWNS
CUSTOMER CHARACTERISTICS		
Geographic	Region	Northeast; Midwest; South; West; etc.
	City size	Under 10,000; 10,000–24,999; 25,000–49,999; 50,000–99,999; etc.
	Statistical area	Metropolitan statistical areas; micropolitan statistical areas; etc.
	Density	Urban; suburban; small town; rural
Demographic	Gender	Male; Female
	Age	Under 6 yrs; 6–11 yrs; 12–17 yrs; 18–24 yrs; 25–34 yrs; etc.
	Race	African American; Asian; Hispanic; white/Caucasian; etc.
	Life stage	Infant; preschool; child; youth; collegiate; adult; senior
	Birth era	Baby boomer (1946–1964); Generation X (1965–1976); baby boomlet/Generation Y (1977–1994)
	Household size	1; 2; 3–4; 5 or more
	Marital status	Never married; married; separated; divorced; widowed
	Income	<$15,000; $15,000–$24,999; $25,000–34,999; etc.
	Education	Some high school or less; high school graduate (or GED); etc.
	Occupation	Managerial and professional specialty; technical; sales; etc.
Psychographic	Personality	Gregarious; compulsive; introverted; aggressive; ambitious; etc.
	Values (VALS)	Innovators; thinkers; achievers; experiencers; believers; strivers; etc.
	Lifestyle (Claritas)	Settled in; white picket fence; and 46 other household segments
BUYING SITUATIONS		
Outlet type	In-store	Department; specialty; outlet; convenience; mass merchandiser, etc.
	Direct	Mail order/catalog; door-to-door; direct response; Internet
Benefits sought	Product features	Situation specific; general
	Needs	Quality; service; price/value; financing; convenience; etc.
Usage/patronage	Usage rate	Light user; medium user; heavy user
	User status	Nonuser; ex-user; prospect; first-time user; regular user
Awareness/intentions	Product knowledge	Unaware; aware; interested; intending to buy; purchaser; rejection
Behavior	Involvement	Minimum effort; comparison; special effort

FIGURE 9–4

Segmentation variables and breakdowns for U.S. consumer markets

To obtain usage rate data, the Simmons Market Research Bureau semi-annually surveys about 33,000 adults 18 years of age and older to discover how the products and services they buy and the media they watch relate to their lifestyle and demographic characteristics. Figure 9–5 shows the results of a question Simmons asks about the respondent's frequency of use (or patronage) of fast-food restaurants.[11]

As shown in the right column of Figure 9–5, the importance of the segment increases as we move up the table. Among nonusers of these restaurants, prospects (who *might become* users) are more important than nonprospects (who are *never likely* to become users). Moving up the rows to the users, it seems logical that light users of these restaurants (5 times per month or less) are important but less so than medium users (6 to 13 times per month), who, in turn, are a less important segment than the critical group, the heavy users (14 or more times per month).

The Actual Consumption column in Figure 9–5 shows how much of the total monthly usage of these restaurants are accounted for by the heavy, medium, and light users.

Usage rate is sometimes referred to in terms of the **80/20 rule**, a concept that suggests 80 percent of a firm's sales are obtained from 20 percent of its customers. The percentages in the 80/20 rule are not really fixed at exactly 80 percent and 20 percent but suggest that a small fraction of customers provide a large fraction of a firm's sales. For example, Figure 9–5 shows that the 17.7 percent of the U.S. population who are heavy users of fast-food restaurants provide 37.9 percent of the consumption volume.

The Usage Index per Person column in Figure 9–5 emphasizes the importance of the heavy-user group even more. Giving the light users (5 or less restaurant visits per month) an index of 100, the heavy users have an index of 400. In other words, for every $1.00 spent by a light user in one of these restaurants in a month, each heavy user spends $4.00. This is the reason for the emphasis in almost all marketing strategies on effective ways to reach these heavy users. Thus, as a Wendy's restaurant owner you want to keep the heavy-user segment constantly in mind.

As part of the Simmons fast-food survey, restaurant patrons were asked if each restaurant was (1) the sole restaurant they went to, (2) the primary one, or (3) one of several secondary ones. This national information, shown in Figure 9–6 on the next page, might give you, as a Wendy's owner, some ideas in developing your local strategy. The Wendy's bar in Figure 9–6 shows that your sole (0.8 percent), primary (21.9 percent), and secondary (12.4 percent) user segments are somewhat behind Burger King and far behind McDonald's, so a natural strategy is to look at these two competitors and devise a marketing program to win customers from them.

The nonusers part of the Wendy's bar in Figure 9–6 also provides ideas. It shows that 10.9 percent of adult Americans don't go to fast-food restaurants in a typical month (also shown in Figure 9–5) and are really nonprospects—unlikely to ever patronize your restaurant. But the 54.0 percent of the Wendy's bar shown as prospects may be worth detailed thought. These adults use the product category (fast-food restaurants) but *do not* go to Wendy's. New menu items or new promotional strategies might succeed in converting these prospects into users.

Variables to Use in Forming Segments for Wendy's In determining one or two variables to segment the market for your Wendy's restaurant, very broadly

FIGURE 9–5
Patronage of fast-food restaurants by adults 18 years and older: Simmons Market Research Bureau NCS/NHCS Spring 2004 Adult Full-Year Choices System Cross-tabulation Report based on visits within the past 30 days

USER OR NONUSER	SPECIFIC SEGMENT	NUMBER (1,000s)	PERCENTAGE	ACTUAL CONSUMPTION (%)	USAGE INDEX PER PERSON	IMPORTANCE OF SEGMENT
Users	Heavy users (14+ per month)	37,251	17.7%	37.9%	400	High
	Medium users (6–13 per month)	57,064	27.1	39.3	271	
	Light users (5 or less per month)	89,759	42.6	22.8	100	
Total users		184,074	87.4	100.0	214	
Nonusers	Prospects	3,677	1.7	0	0	
	Nonprospects	23,018	10.9	0	0	
Total nonusers		26,695	12.6	0	0	Low
Total	Users and nonusers	210,769	100.0	100.0	—	

FIGURE 9–6

Comparison of various kinds of users and nonusers for Wendy's, Burger King, and McDonald's fast-food restaurants

Simmons Market Research Bureau

www.smrb.com

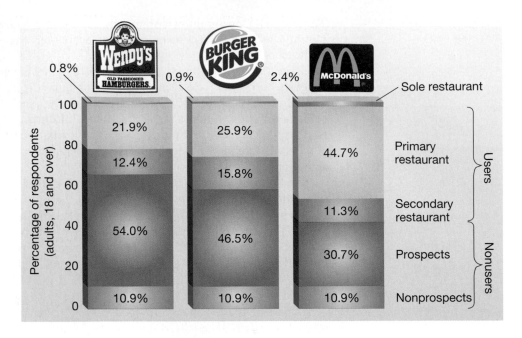

we find two main market segments: students and nonstudents. To segment the students, we could try a variety of demographic variables, such as age, sex, year in school, or college major, or psychographic variables, such as personality characteristics, attitudes, or interests. But none of these variables really meets the five criteria listed previously—particularly, the fourth criterion about leading to a doable marketing action to reach the various segments. Four student segments that *do* meet these criteria include the following:

- Students living in dormitories (college residence halls, sororities, fraternities).
- Students living near the college in apartments.
- Day commuter students living outside the area.
- Night commuter students living outside the area.

These segmentation variables are really a combination of where the student lives and the time he or she is on campus (and near your restaurant). For nonstudents who might be customers, similar variables might be used:

- Faculty and staff members at the university.
- People who live in the area but aren't connected with the university.
- People who work in the area but aren't connected with the university.

People in each of these segments aren't quite as similar as those in the student segments, which makes them harder to reach with a marketing program or action. Think about (1) whether the needs of all these segments are different and (2) how various advertising media can be used to reach these groups effectively.

Ways to Segment Organizational Markets   Variables to segment organizational markets are shown in Figure 9–7. For example, a product manager at Xerox responsible for its new solid-ink color printer might use several of these segmentation variables, as follows:

- *Geographic customer characteristic: Statistical area.* Firms located in a metropolitan statistical area might receive a personal sales call, whereas those in a micropolitan statistical area might be contacted by telephone.
- *Demographic customer characteristic: NAICS code.* Firms categorized by the North American Industry Classification System code as manufacturers that deal with customers throughout the world might have different document printing needs than do retailers or lawyers serving local customers.

What variables might Xerox use to segment the organizational markets for its answer to color copying problems? For the possible answer and related marketing actions, see the text.

Xerox Corporation
www.xerox.com

FIGURE 9–7
Segmentation variables and breakdowns for U.S. organizational markets

- *Demographic customer characteristic: Number of employees.* The size of the firm is related to the volume of digital documents produced for a given industry or NAICS, so firms with varying numbers of employees might be specific target markets for different Xerox systems.
- *Benefits sought: Product features.* Similar to this segmentation variable for consumer markets, features are often of major importance in organizational

MAIN DIMENSION	SEGMENTATION VARIABLES	TYPICAL BREAKDOWNS
CUSTOMER CHARACTERISTICS		
Geographic	U.S. region	Northeast; Midwest; South; West; etc.
	Statistical area	Metropolitan statistical areas; micropolitan statistical areas; etc.
	Density	Urban; suburban; small town; rural
Demographic	NAICS code	2-digit: Sector (Information—51); 3-digit: Subsector; 4-digit: Industry group
	NAICS sector	Agriculture, Forestry, etc. (11); Mining (21); Utilities (22), etc.
	Number of employees	1–99; 100–499; 500–999; 1,000–4,999; 5,000+
	Annual sales	<$1 million; $1 million–9.9 million; $10 million–49.9 million; etc.
	Number of locations	1–9; 10–49; 50–99; 100–499; 500–999; 1,000 and over
BUYING SITUATIONS*		
Nature of good	Kind	Product; service
	Where used	Installation; component; supplies
	Application	Office use; limited production use; heavy production use
Buying condition	Purchase location	Centralized; decentralized
	Who buys	Individual buyer; groups of buyers
	Type of buy	New buy; modified rebuy; straight rebuy

*Outlet type, benefits sought, usage/patronage, and awareness/intentions are similar to consumer market variables in Figure 9–4.

markets. So Xerox can target organizations needing different benefits from its new solid-ink color printer, such as speed and low cost, the benefits and features emphasized in the ad for its Xerox Phaser® 8400.

Concept Check

1. The process of segmenting and targeting markets is a bridge between what two marketing activities?

2. What are two main ways to segment consumer and organizational markets?

Step 2: Group Products to Be Sold into Categories

Finding a means of grouping the products a firm sells into meaningful categories is as important as grouping customers into segments. If the firm has only one product or service, this isn't a problem, but when it has dozens or hundreds, these must be grouped in some way so buyers can relate to them. This is why department stores and supermarkets are organized into product groups, with the departments or aisles containing related merchandise. Likewise, manufacturers have product lines that are the groupings they use in the catalogs sent to customers.

What are the product groupings for your Wendy's restaurant? It could be the item purchased, such as a Frosty, chili, hamburgers, and french fries. This is where judgment—the qualitative aspect of marketing—comes in. Students really buy an eating experience, or a meal that satisfies a need at a particular time of day, so the product grouping can be defined by meal or time of day as breakfast, lunch, between-meal snack, dinner, and after-dinner snack. These groupings are more closely related to the way purchases are actually made and permit you to market the entire meal, not just your french fries or Frosties.

Step 3: Develop a Market-Product Grid and Estimate Size of Markets

Developing a market-product grid means labeling the markets (or horizontal rows) and products (or vertical columns), as shown in Figure 9–8. In addition, the size of the market in each cell (the market-product combination) must be estimated. For your restaurant, this involves estimating the sales of each kind of meal that can reasonably be expected to be sold to each market segment. This is a form of the usage rate analysis discussed earlier in the chapter.

The market sizes in Figure 9–8 may be simple "guesstimates" if you don't have time for formal marketing research (as discussed in Chapter 8). But even such crude estimates of the size of specific markets using a market-product grid are helpful in determining which target market segments to select and which product groupings to offer.

Step 4: Select Target Markets

A firm must take care to choose its target market segments carefully. If it picks too narrow a set of segments, it may fail to reach the volume of sales and profits it needs. If it selects too broad a set of segments, it may spread its marketing efforts so thin that the extra expenses are more than the increased sales and profits.

Criteria to Use in Picking the Target Segments   There are two different kinds of criteria in the market segmentation process: (1) those to use in dividing the market into segments (discussed earlier) and (2) those to use in actually picking the target segments. Even experienced marketing executives often confuse

FIGURE 9–8
Selecting a target market for your Wendy's fast-food restaurant next to an urban university (target market is shaded)

MARKETS	PRODUCTS: MEALS				
	BREAK-FAST	LUNCH	BETWEEN-MEAL SNACK	DINNER	AFTER-DINNER SNACK
Student					
Dormitory	0	1	3	0	3
Apartment	1	3	3	1	1
Day commuter	0	3	2	1	0
Night commuter	0	0	1	3	2
Nonstudent					
Faculty or staff	0	3	1	1	0
Live in area	0	1	2	2	1
Work in area	1	3	0	1	0

Key: 3 = Large market; 2 = Medium market; 1 = Small market; 0 = No market.

these two different sets of criteria. The five criteria to use in actually selecting the target segments apply to your Wendy's restaurant this way:

- *Market size.* The estimated size of the market in the segment is an important factor in deciding whether it's worth going after. There is really no market for breakfasts among dormitory students (Figure 9–8), so why devote any marketing effort toward reaching a small or nonexistent segment?
- *Expected growth.* Although the size of the market in the segment may be small now, perhaps it is growing significantly or is expected to grow in the future. Between now and 2007, sales of fast-food meals eaten outside the restaurants are projected to grow three times as fast as those eaten inside. And Wendy's is the fast-food leader in average time to serve a drive-thru order—for example, 16.7 seconds faster than McDonald's. This speed and convenience is potentially very important to night commuters in adult education programs.[12]
- *Competitive position.* Is there a lot of competition in the segment now or is there likely to be in the future? The less the competition, the more attractive the segment is. For example, if the college dormitories announce a new policy of "no meals on weekends," this segment is suddenly more promising for your restaurant. With McDonald's recent introduction of pay-by-credit-card processing at its restaurants, will Wendy's have to offer the same option to its customers?
- *Cost of reaching the segment.* A segment that is inaccessible to a firm's marketing actions should not be pursued. For example, the few nonstudents who live in the area may not be reachable with ads in newspapers or other media. As a result, do not waste money trying to advertise to them.
- *Compatibility with the organization's objectives and resources.* If your restaurant doesn't have the cooking equipment to make breakfasts and has a policy against spending more money on restaurant equipment, then don't try to reach the breakfast segment.

As is often the case in marketing decisions, a particular segment may appear attractive according to some criteria and very unattractive according to others.

Choose the Segments   Ultimately, a marketing executive has to use these criteria to choose the segments for special marketing efforts. As shown in Figure 9–8, let's assume you've written off the breakfast product grouping for two reasons: too

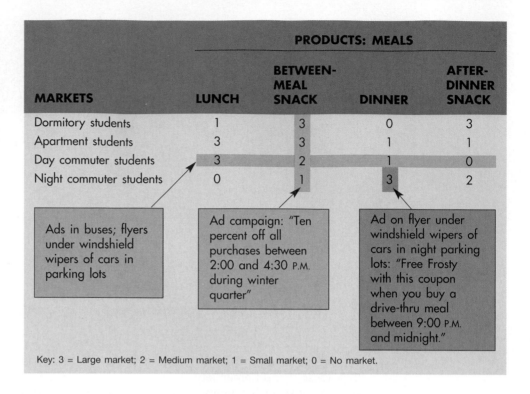

MARKETS	LUNCH	BETWEEN-MEAL SNACK	DINNER	AFTER-DINNER SNACK
Dormitory students	1	3	0	3
Apartment students	3	3	1	1
Day commuter students	3	2	1	0
Night commuter students	0	1	3	2

Ads in buses; flyers under windshield wipers of cars in parking lots

Ad campaign: "Ten percent off all purchases between 2:00 and 4:30 P.M. during winter quarter"

Ad on flyer under windshield wipers of cars in night parking lots: "Free Frosty with this coupon when you buy a drive-thru meal between 9:00 P.M. and midnight."

Key: 3 = Large market; 2 = Medium market; 1 = Small market; 0 = No market.

small of a market size and incompatibility with your objectives and resources. In terms of competitive position and cost of reaching the segment, you choose to focus on the four student segments and not the three nonstudent segments (although you're certainly not going to turn away business from the nonstudent segments). This combination of market-product segments—your target market—is shaded in Figure 9–8.

How can Wendy's target different market segments like drive-thru customers or commuting college students with different advertising programs? For the answer, see the text and Figure 9–9.

A late night oasis on the highway of hunger.

Step 5: Take Marketing Actions to Reach Target Markets

The purpose of developing a market-product grid is to trigger marketing actions to increase sales and profits. This means that someone must develop and execute an action plan.

Your Wendy's Segmentation Strategy With your Wendy's restaurant you've already reached one significant decision: There is a limited market for breakfast, so you won't open for business until 10:30 A.M. In fact, Wendy's first attempt at a breakfast menu was a disaster and was discontinued in 1986. Wendy's evaluates possible new menu items continuously, not only to compete with McDonald's and Burger King but with a complex array of supermarkets, convenience stores, and gas stations that sell reheatable packaged foods as well as new "easy-lunch" products.

Another essential decision is where and what meals to advertise to reach specific market segments. An ad in the student newspaper could reach all the student segments, but you might consider this approach too expensive and want a more focused effort to reach smaller segments. If you choose three segments for special actions (Figure 9–9), advertising actions to reach them might include:

- *Day commuters* (an entire market segment). Run ads inside commuter buses and put flyers under the windshield wipers of cars in parking lots used by day commuters. These ads and flyers promote all the meals at your restaurant to a single segment of students, a horizontal cut through the market-product grid.

- *Between-meals snacks* (directed to all four student markets). To promote eating during this downtime for your restaurant, offer "Ten percent off all purchases between 2:00 and 4:30 P.M. during winter quarter." This ad promotes a single meal to all four student segments, a vertical cut through the market-product grid.
- *Dinners to night commuters.* The most focused of all three campaigns, this ad promotes a single meal to the single segment of night commuter students. The campaign might consist of a windshield flyer offering a free Frosty with the coupon when the person buys a drive-thru meal between 9:00 P.M. and midnight.

Depending on how your advertising actions work, you can repeat, modify, or drop them and design new campaigns for other segments you feel are worth the effort.

This example of advertising your Wendy's restaurant is just a small piece of a complete marketing program using all the elements of the marketing mix. For example, in 2004 Wendy's reported its most profitable year in history. It introduced new menu items to appeal to segments in the various nutritional concerns, from Homestyle Chicken Strips to Garden Sensations Salads. And a special success is Wendy's new focus on the after-dinner snack column in Figure 9–9: As shown in Wendy's ad on the opposite page, its late-night pickup window is open until midnight or later, even though most of its restaurants close their doors to customers at 10:00 P.M.

Apple's Ever-Changing Segmentation Strategy   Steve Jobs and Steve Wozniak didn't realize they were developing today's multibillion-dollar PC industry when they invented the Apple I in a garage on April Fool's Day, 1976. Hobbyists, the initial target market, were not interested in the product. However, when the

What market segments for Apple's computers are represented by these products? The Marketing NewsNet and text discussion provide insights into Apple's market segmentation strategy.

Apple Computer
www.apple.com

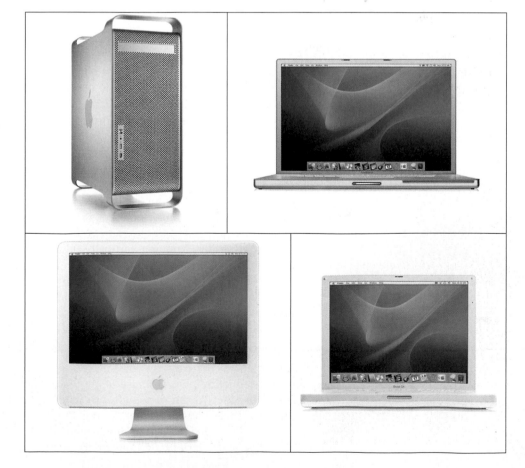

Apple II was displayed at a computer trade show in 1977, consumers loved it and Apple Computer was born. Typical of young companies, Apple focused on its products and had little concern for its markets. When IBM—"Big Blue"—entered the PC market in 1981, Apple was forced to become a "real company," much to the disappointment of its creative young engineers who were likened to "Boy Scouts without adult supervision."[13]

Fast-forward to the twenty-first century. Jobs believes that the personal computer entered the Age of the Digital Lifestyle in 2001. In a keynote address, Jobs said that "the proliferation of digital devices—CD players, MP3 players, cell phones, hand-held organizers, digital cameras, digital camcorders, and more—will never have enough processing power and memory to stand alone." Jobs enthusiastically proclaimed, "the Mac can become the digital hub of this new digital lifestyle." By repositioning Apple as the "digital hub" with "killer apps," such as iTunes, iMovie, iDVD, iPhoto, and GarageBand—now bundled as iLife—Jobs believes consumers can take full advantage of the new digital lifestyle era.[14]

In most segmentation situations, a single product does not fit into an exclusive market niche. Rather, there is overlap among products in the product line and also among the markets to which they are directed. But a market segmentation strategy enables Apple to offer different products to meet the needs of different market segments, as shown in the accompanying Marketing NewsNet. Stay tuned to see if Steve Jobs and these market-product strategies for his vision of the digital lifestyle era are on target. He's betting the company on it![15]

Market-Product Synergies: A Balancing Act

Recognizing opportunities for key synergies—that is, efficiencies—is vital to success in selecting target market segments and making marketing decisions. Market-product grids illustrate where such synergies can be found. How? Let's consider Apple's market-product grid in the accompanying Marketing NewsNet and examine the difference between marketing synergies and product synergies shown there.

- *Marketing synergies.* Running horizontally across the grid, each row represents an opportunity for efficiency in terms of a market segment. Were Apple to focus on just one group of consumers, such as the Medium/Large Business segment, its marketing efforts could be streamlined. Time would not have to be spent learning about the buying habits of students or college faculty. So it could probably do a single ad piece to reach the Medium/Large Business target segment (the yellow row), highlighting the only products they'd need to worry about developing: Power Mac G5, the PowerBook G4, and the iMac G5. Although clearly this is not Apple's strategy today, focusing on a single customer segment is a common marketing strategy for new companies.
- *Product synergies.* Running vertically down the market-product grid, each column represents an opportunity for efficiency in research and development (R&D) and production. If Apple wanted to simplify its product line, reduce R&D and production expenses, and manufacture only one computer, which might it choose? Based on the market-product grid, Apple might do well to focus on the iMac G5 (the brown column), since the iMac G5 is purchased by the most consumer segments—in this case, every segment.

A choice to take advantage of marketing synergies can often come at the expense of production ones because a single customer segment will likely require a variety of products, each of which will have to be designed and manufactured. The company saves money on marketing but spends more in production. Conversely, if product synergies are emphasized, marketing will have to address the concerns of a wide variety of consumers, which costs more time and money.

MARKETING NEWSNET

Apple's Segmentation Strategy— Camp Runamok No Longer

CUSTOMER VALUE

Camp Runamok was the nickname given to Apple Computer in the early 1980s because the innovative company had no coherent series of product lines directed at identifiable market segments.

Today, Apple has targeted its various lines of Macintosh computers at specific market segments, as shown in the market-product grid below. Because the market-product grid shifts as a firm's strategy changes, the one below is based on Apple's product lines in late 2004. This market-product grid is a simplification because each product grouping consists of a line of Apple hardware products. Nevertheless, the grid suggests the market segmentation strategy Steve Jobs is using to compete in what he sees as the Age of the Digital Lifestyle, as described in the text.

MARKETS		HARDWARE PRODUCTS					
SECTOR	**SEGMENT**	Power Macintosh G5	PowerBook G4	iMac G5	iBook	eMac	iPod
CONSUMER	Individuals	✓	✓	✓	✓	✓	✓
	Small/home office	✓	✓	✓	✓	✓	
	Students			✓	✓	✓	✓
	Teachers	✓	✓	✓		✓	
PROFESSIONAL	Medium/large business	✓	✓	✓			
	Creative	✓	✓	✓			✓
	College faculty	✓	✓	✓			✓
	College staff			✓	✓	✓	

Marketing managers responsible for developing a company's product line must balance both product and marketing synergies as they try to increase the company's profits.

Concept Check

1. What are some criteria used to decide which segments to choose for targets?

2. In a market-product grid, what factor is estimated or measured for each of the cells?

3. What is the difference between marketing synergies and product synergies in a market-product grid?

POSITIONING THE PRODUCT

When a company introduces a new product, a decision critical to its long-term success is how prospective buyers view it in relation to those products offered by its competitors. **Product positioning** refers to the place an offering occupies in consumers' minds on important attributes relative to competitive products. In contrast, **product repositioning** involves *changing* the place an offering occupies in a consumer's mind relative to competitive products.

How can dairies put more zip into chocolate milk sales? To discover their successful positioning strategy, see the text.

FIGURE 9–10
Using positioning and perceptual maps to increase milk sales to children and adults

Two Approaches to Product Positioning

There are two main approaches to positioning a new product in the market. *Head-to-head positioning* involves competing directly with competitors on similar product attributes in the same target market. Using this strategy, Dollar competes directly with Avis and Hertz.

Differentiation positioning involves seeking a less competitive, smaller market niche in which to locate a brand. McDonald's initially tried to appeal to the health-conscious segment and introduced its low-fat McLean Deluxe hamburger to avoid direct competition with Wendy's and Burger King. Companies also follow a differentiation positioning strategy among brands within their own product line to try to minimize cannibalization of a brand's sales or shares.

Product Positioning Using Perceptual Maps

A key to positioning a product effectively is the perceptions of consumers. In determining a brand's position and the preferences of consumers, companies obtain three types of data from consumers:

1. Identification of the important attributes for a product class.
2. Judgments of existing brands with respect to these important attributes.
3. Ratings of an "ideal" brand's attributes.

From these data, it is possible to develop a **perceptual map**, a means of displaying or graphing in two dimensions the location of products or brands in the minds of consumers to enable a manager to see how consumers perceive competing products or brands relative to its own and then take marketing actions.

Figure 9–10 shows how a perceptual map can be used to develop positioning strategies for (1) milk drinks for children and (2) chocolate milk for adults. The perceptual map in Figure 9–10 shows the positions that consumer beverages might occupy in the minds of Americans. Note that even these positions vary from one

Good nutrition is an increasing concern of Americans. It gets highlighted in comparing recent U.S. annual capita consumption of soft drinks versus milk: 52 gallons of soft drinks versus 25 gallons of milk, even with all milk's benefits of calcium and vitamins.[16] Here are two product positioning actions featuring milk products to address these nutrition concerns.

MILK DRINKS FOR KIDS: POSITIONING A NEW PRODUCT Nutrition is a special concern for American school children, where childhood obesity is growing. Soft-drink companies, criticized heavily for pushing soda sales in schools, are seeking both to "buff their image and build sales."[17] Study the perceptual map at the right and identify (a) in which lettered location a beverage company might position new milk drinks and (b) what the product and some flavors might be to appeal to schoolchildren.

CHOCOLATE MILK FOR ADULTS: REPOSITIONING AN EXISTING PRODUCT Several years ago dairies got the idea to target chocolate milk sales at a new market—adults. Note on the perceptual map where adults positioned chocolate milk then and suggest (a) in which lettered location dairies might reposition chocolate milk targeted at adults and (b) what kind of packaging might appeal to them.

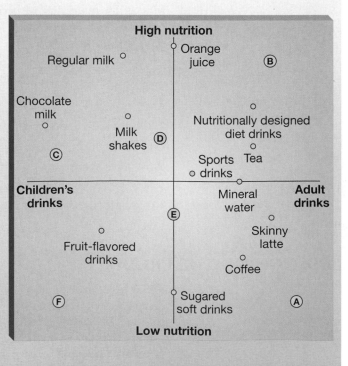

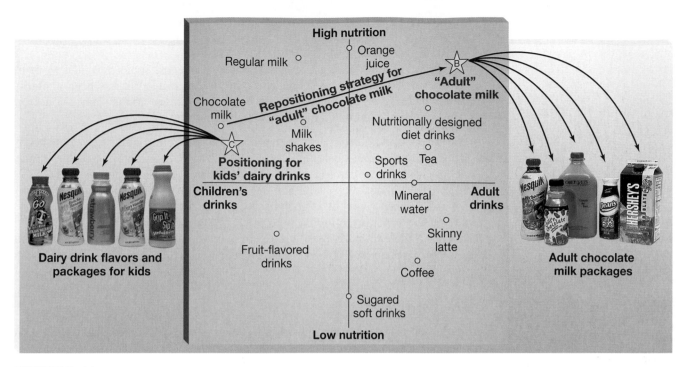

FIGURE 9–11

Strategies for positioning dairy drinks for kids and repositioning chocolate milk to reach adults

consumer to another. But for simplicity, let's assume these are the positions on the beverage perceptual map of typical Americans.

Positioning Milk Drinks for Children
Assume you work for a dairy or soft-drink company trying to develop milk drinks for school children that have more nutrition than soft drinks but more appeal than regular or chocolate milk. You can start by looking for holes or gaps in the perceptual map in Figure 9–10 that suggest a possible position for a milk drink that would have more nutritional value than soft drinks. Here's what companies did:

- *Finding a position for milk drinks.* Marketing managers looked at this kind of perceptual map and picked a position about at point C in Figure 9–10. This is in a relatively big gap between regular milk and fruit-flavored drinks and shows the increased nutritional value of the milk drinks.
- *Developing the product and flavors.* In mid-2003, Coca-Cola and Cadbury Schweppes PLC both developed "dairy drinks" positioned at point C, with just over half being regular milk and the rest being water, sugar, and flavorings. Although calories and sugar are concerns, these drinks have nutritional value missing in soft drinks. Sample flavors? Cadbury's Raging Cow started with five flavors, including Chocolate Insanity, Piña Colada Chaos, and Jamocha Frenzy.[18]

Not to be left behind, some dairies have responded with new 100 percent milk drinks with extra sugar and flavors like Pleasin' Punch and Root Beer Float. The position of these milk drinks, sample flavors, and their packaging appear in Figure 9–11.

Repositioning Chocolate Milk for Adults
In mid-2000, U.S. dairies, struggling to increase milk sales, hit on a wild idea: Try to reposition chocolate milk to make it appeal to adults. The term *adults* in this sense probably means 18 years old and older. The dairies' arguments are nutritionally powerful. For example, chocolate milk provides calcium and vitamins, critically important in adult diets. And dieters get a more filling, nutritious beverage than with a soft drink for about the same calories.[19] Here's what some dairies have done:

- *Finding a new position for chocolate milk in the minds of adults.* In Figure 9–10, dairies sought to do two things: (1) move chocolate milk to the right to make it a more respectable "adult drink" and (2) move it up on the nutrition scale. The result is a repositioning at about point B in Figure 9–10, a dramatic move as shown in Figure 9–11.

- *Packaging "adult" chocolate milk.* Sample packages, some designed to fit in car beverage holders, are shown in Figure 9–11. The result has been a significant increase in chocolate milk consumption among adults. Have you seen chocolate milk in containers like these in your college cafeteria?

With the success of these drinks, dairies are now offering other new, nonchocolate grown-up milks like a caramel Dulce de Leche milk and a coffee-flavored milk with decaffeinated Brazilian roast coffee that tastes like coffee ice cream. And Krispy Kreme in its doughnut shops sells hot and cold milk in such flavors as vanilla, cinnamon, and raspberry, plus its signature "original Kreme."[20]

And for the superadventurous there are *carbonated* flavored milk beverages.[21] Question 6 in the end-of-chapter Discussion and Application Questions asks you to identify the target market and positioning strategies for these beverages.

SALES FORECASTING TECHNIQUES

Forecasting or estimating potential sales is often a key goal in a marketing research study. Good sales forecasts are important for a firm as it schedules production.[22]

The term **market potential**, or **industry potential**, refers to the maximum total sales of a product by all firms to a segment during a specified time period under specified environmental conditions and marketing efforts of the firms. For example, the market potential for cake mix sales to U.S. consumers in 2008 might be 12 million cases—what Pillsbury, Betty Crocker, Aurora Foods, and other cake mix producers would sell to American consumers under the assumptions that (1) past patterns of dessert consumption continue and (2) the same level of promotional effort continues relative to other desserts. The term **sales forecast**, or **company forecast**, refers to the total sales of a product that a firm expects to sell during a specified time period under specified environmental conditions and its own marketing efforts. For example, Betty Crocker might develop a sales forecast of 4 million cases of cake mix for U.S. consumers in 2008, assuming consumers' dessert preferences remain constant and competitors don't change prices.

Three main sales forecasting techniques are often used: (1) judgments of the decision maker, (2) surveys of knowledgeable groups, and (3) statistical methods.

Judgments of the Decision Maker

Probably 99 percent of all sales forecasts are simply the judgment of the person who must act on the results of the forecast—the individual decision maker. A **direct forecast** involves estimating the value to be forecast without any intervening steps. Examples appear daily: How many quarts of milk should I buy? How much money should I get out of the ATM?

You probably get the same cash withdrawal most times you use the ATM. But if you need to withdraw more than the usual amount, you would probably make some intervening steps (such as counting the cash in your pocket or estimating what you'll need for special events this week) to obtain your direct forecast.

A **lost-horse forecast** involves making a forecast using the last known value and modifying it according to positive or negative factors expected in the future. The technique gets its name from how you'd find a lost horse: Go to where it was last seen, put yourself in its shoes, consider those factors that could affect where you might go (to the pond if you're thirsty, the hayfield if you're hungry, and so on), and go there. For example, a product manager for Wilson's tennis rackets in 2004 who needed to make a sales forecast through 2007 would start with the known value of 2004 sales and list the positive factors (more tennis courts, more TV publicity) and

How might a marketing manager for Wilson tennis rackets forecast sales through 2007? Use a lost-horse forecast, as described in the text.

the negative ones (competition from other sports, high prices of graphite and ceramic rackets) to arrive at the final series of annual sales forecasts.

Surveys of Knowledgeable Groups

If you wonder what your firm's sales will be next year, ask people who are likely to know something about future sales. Two common groups that are surveyed to develop sales forecasts are prospective buyers and the firm's salesforce.

A **survey of buyers' intentions forecast** involves asking prospective customers if they are likely to buy the product during some future time period. For industrial products with few prospective buyers, this can be effective. There are only a few hundred customers in the entire world for Boeing's largest airplanes, so Boeing surveys them to develop its sales forecasts and production schedules.

A **salesforce survey forecast** involves asking the firm's salespeople to estimate sales during a coming period. Because these people are in contact with customers and are likely to know what customers like and dislike, there is logic to this approach. However, salespeople can be unreliable forecasters—painting too rosy a picture if they are enthusiastic about a new product and too grim a forecast if their sales quota and future compensation are based on it.

Statistical Methods

The best-known statistical method of forecasting is **trend extrapolation**, which involves extending a pattern observed in past data into the future. When the pattern is described with a straight line, it is **linear trend extrapolation**. Suppose that in early 2000 you were a sales forecaster for the Xerox Corporation and had actual sales running from 1988 to 1999 (Figure 9–12). Using linear trend extrapolation, you draw a line to fit the past data and project it into the future to give the forecast values shown for 2000 to 2006.[23]

If in 2004 you want to compare your forecasts with actual results, you are in for a surprise—illustrating the strength and weakness of trend extrapolation. Trend extrapolation assumes that the underlying relationships in the past will continue into the future, which is the basis of the method's key strength: simplicity. If this assumption proves correct, you have an accurate forecast. However, if this proves wrong, the forecast is likely to be wrong. In this case, your forecasts from 2001 through 2003 were too high, as shown in Figure 9–12, largely because of fierce competition in the photocopying industry.

FIGURE 9–12

Linear trend extrapolation of sales revenues of Xerox, made at the start of 2000

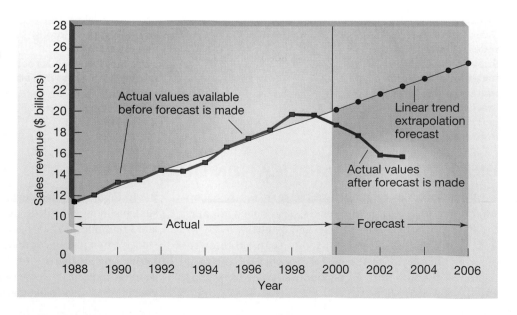

Concept Check

1. Why do marketers use perceptual maps in product positioning decisions?

2. What are the three kinds of sales forecasting techniques?

3. How do you make a lost-horse forecast?

CHAPTER IN REVIEW

1 *Explain what market segmentation is and when to use it.*
Market segmentation involves aggregating prospective buyers into groups that (*a*) have common needs and (*b*) will respond similarly to a marketing action. Organizations go to the trouble and expense of segmenting their markets when it increases their sales, profits, and ability to serve customers better.

2 *Identify the five steps involved in segmenting and targeting markets.*
Step 1 is to group potential buyers into segments. Buyers within a segment should have similar characteristics to each other and respond similarly to marketing actions like a new product or a lower price. Step 2 involves putting related products to be sold into groups. In step 3, organizations develop a market-product grid with estimated size of markets in each of the market-product cells of the resulting table. Step 4 involves selecting the target market segments on which the organization should focus. Step 5 involves taking marketing mix actions—often in the form of a marketing program—to reach the target market segments.

3 *Recognize the different factors used to segment consumer and organizational markets.*
Factors used to segment consumer markets include customer characteristics (geographic, demographic, and psychographic variables) and buying situations. Organizational markets use related variables except for psychographic ones.

4 *Know how to develop a market-product grid to identify a target market and recommend resulting actions.*
Organizations use five key criteria to segment markets, whose groupings appear in the rows of the market-product grid. Groups of related products appear in the columns. After estimating the size of market in each cell in the grid, they select the target market segments on which to focus. They then identify marketing mix actions—often in a marketing program—to reach the target market most efficiently.

5 *Explain how marketing managers position products in the marketplace.*
Marketing managers often locate competing products on two-dimensional perceptual maps to visualize the products in the minds of consumers. They then try to position new products or reposition existing products in this space to attain the maximum sales and profits.

6 *Describe three approaches to developing a sales forecast for a company.*
One approach uses subjective judgments of the decision maker, such as direct or lost-horse forecasts. Surveys of knowledgeable groups is a second method. It involves obtaining information such as the intentions of potential buyers or estimates of the salesforce. Statistical methods involving extending a pattern observed in past data into the future is a third example. The best-known example is linear trend extrapolation.

FOCUSING ON KEY TERMS

company forecast p. 252
80/20 rule p. 241
direct forecast p. 252
industry potential p. 252
linear trend extrapolation p. 253
lost-horse forecast p. 252
market potential p. 252
market-product grid p. 234
market segments p. 233
perceptual map p. 250

product differentiation p. 233
product positioning p. 249
product repositioning p. 249
sales forecast p. 252
salesforce survey forecast p. 253
survey of buyers' intentions forecast p. 253
synergy p. 237
trend extrapolation p. 253
usage rate p. 239

DISCUSSION AND APPLICATION QUESTIONS

1 What variables might be used to segment these consumer markets? (*a*) lawnmowers, (*b*) frozen dinners, (*c*) dry breakfast cereals, and (*d*) soft drinks.

2 What variables might be used to segment these industrial markets? (*a*) industrial sweepers, (*b*) photocopiers, (*c*) computerized production control systems, and (*d*) car rental agencies.

3 In Figure 9–8, the dormitory market segment includes students living in college-owned residence halls, sororities, and fraternities. What market needs are common to these students that justify combining them into a single segment in studying the market for your Wendy's restaurant?

4 You may disagree with the estimates of market size given for the rows in the market-product grid in Figure 9–8.

Estimate the market size, and give a brief justification for these market segments: (*a*) dormitory students, (*b*) day commuters, and (*c*) people who work in the area.

5 Suppose you want to increase revenues for your fast-food restaurant even further. Referring to Figure 9–9, what advertising actions might you take to increase revenues from (*a*) dormitory students, (*b*) dinners, and (*c*) after-dinner snacks from night commuters?

6 In 1999, entrepreneurs Mary Ann and George Clark founded MacFarms, Inc., to introduce milk beverages with enough appeal to wean children from soft drinks and athlete-oriented drinks. Their patented invention: carbonated milk beverages in various flavors. Look again at Figure 9–10 and (*a*) select one of the lettered positions on the perceptual map and (*b*) suggest packaging for these drinks.

7 Which of the following variables would linear trend extrapolation be more accurate for? (*a*) Annual population of the United States or (*b*) annual sales of cars produced in the United States by General Motors. Why?

GOING ONLINE   Apple's Latest Market-Product Strategies

In its 25-year history, Apple Computer has initiated a series of creative market segmentation strategies, with new product lines targeted at specific market segments. For the latest updates of Apple's market-product strategies, go to www.apple-history.com and click on the "Intro" and "History" menu options. As you read the narrative, identify the new and remaining markets Apple has targeted with new and existing products compared to those described in the text and the Marketing NewsNet. Do you think Apple will succeed in its quest to lead us into the digital lifestyle age? Can Apple survive as a niche PC marketer like BMW has with autos? Why or why not?

BUILDING YOUR MARKETING PLAN

Your marketing plan needs (*a*) a market-product grid to focus your marketing efforts and also (*b*) leads to a forecast of sales for the company. Use these steps:

1 Define the market segments (the rows in your grid) using the factors in Figures 9–4 or 9–7.

2 Define the groupings of related products (the columns in your grid).

3 Form your grid and estimate the size of market in each market-product cell.

4 Select the target market segments on which to focus your efforts with your marketing program.

5 Use the information and the lost-horse forecasting technique to make a sales forecast (company forecast).

VIDEO CASE 9   Nokia: A Phone for Every Segment

"While practically everybody today is a potential mobile phone customer, everybody is simultaneously different in terms of usage, needs, lifestyles, and individual preferences," explains Keith Nowak, Nokia's Media Relations Manager. Understanding those differences requires that Nokia conduct ongoing research among different consumer groups throughout the world. The approach is reflected in the company's business strategy:

> "We intend to exploit our leadership role by continuing to target and enter segments of the communications market that we believe will experience rapid growth or grow faster than the industry as a whole and that cater to the diverse needs, lifestyles, and preferences of our customers."

In fact, Nowak believes that "to be successful in the mobile phone business of today and tomorrow, Nokia has to fully understand the fundamental nature and rationale of segmentation."

THE COMPANY

Nokia started in 1865, when a mining engineer built a wood-pulp mill in southern Finland to manufacture paper. Over the next century, the company diversified into industries ranging from paper to chemicals and rubber. In the 1960s, Nokia ventured into telecommunications by developing a digital telephone exchange switch. In the 1980s, Nokia developed its first "transportable" car mobile phone and the first "handportable" one. During the early 1990s, Nokia divested all of its nontelecommunications operations to focus on its telecommunications and mobile handset businesses.

Today, Nokia is the world leader in mobile communications. Globally, the company generates sales of about $40 billion in over 130 countries and employs more than 51,000 people. Its Mobile Phones, Enterprise Solutions, and Multimedia business groups account for over 75 percent of sales. Nokia's mission is simple: "Connecting People," which is accomplished by understanding consumer needs and providing offerings that meet or exceed those needs. Nokia believes that designing state-of-the-art mobile phones for its global customers is critical to its continued success in the rapidly changing mobile phone market.

THE MOBILE PHONE MARKET

In the 1980s, first generation (1G) mobile phones consisted of voice-only analog devices with limited roaming and features that were sold mainly in North America. In the 1990s, second generation (2G and 2.5G) devices consisted of voice/data digital mobile phones with higher data transfer rates, expanded range, and more features. Sales of these devices grew initially in Europe and Asia. In the twenty-first century, Nokia and other companies are combining digital audio, video, and data technologies into third generation (3G) communication devices that reach consumers globally. The convergence of the mobile phone (audio), digital camera (video), personal digital assistant (PDA), Internet and e-mail services (data), and other multimedia technologies will usher in the fourth generation (4G) of global communication devices.

The annual global demand for mobile phones has increased significantly over the years—from over 400 million units in 2000 to about 650 million units shipped in 2004. In 2008, mobile phone shipments could exceed 950 million units. Marketers of 1G and 2G mobile phones used a geographic segmentation strategy as wireless communication networks were developed. Most started with the U.S. and then proceeded to Europe and Asia. However, each market grew at different rates. In 2004, Asia was the largest mobile phone market with 240 million or 37% of all handsets sold that year. Europe was second with 240 million shipments (19%), followed by North America at 110 million shipments (17%).

Nokia led all marketers with a 29 percent market share in mid-2004, followed by Motorola (16%), Samsung (14%), Siemens (7%), and Sony Ericsson (6%). The total number of worldwide wireless subscribers reached 1.5 billion in 2004 and is expected to increase to 2.0 billion by 2008. The increase is due to the growing demand by teens for high-speed handsets that will provide digital audio, video, and data applications. According to Cellular Telecommunications & Internet Association (CTIA), U.S. wireless subscribers reached 170 million by 2004 and spent an average of $50 per month on calls.

HOW NOKIA SEGMENTS ITS MARKETS

According to Keith Nowak, "Different people have different usage needs. Some people want and need all of the latest and most advanced data-related features and functions, while others are happy with basic voice connectivity. Even people with similar usage needs often have differing lifestyles representing various value sets. For example, some people have an active lifestyle in which sports and fitness play an important role, while for others arts, fashion, and trends may be very important."

Based on its information about consumer usage, lifestyles, price sensitivity, and individual preferences, Nokia currently defines and markets mobile phone handsets to the following six segments: "Basic" consumers, first-time buyers who are very price driven and only need voice connectivity; "Expression" consumers, younger buyers who want to customize and personalize features; "Active" consumers, who are looking for a rugged product to stand up to an active lifestyle; "Classic" consumers, who prefer a more traditional mobile phone with some features at a modest price; "Fashion" consumers, who want a very small phone as a fashion item; and "Premium" consumers, who are interested in all the high-end technological and service features. Nokia also markets a number of very focused products including the "Communicator" line, for business users who want more sophisticated convergent devices that contain telephone, pager, PDA, Internet, streaming multimedia, and other functions, and the "N-Gage" line of mobile game decks, designed to provide a mobile, connected video game platform.

NOKIA'S PRODUCT LINES

Nokia has recently introduced several innovative products to meet the needs of these segments. To target the Basic segment, Nokia provides very easy-to-use, low-priced phones, such as the 1000 and 2000 series. "The idea behind a product like this is to bring voice communication to emerging markets and help people take life mobile," explains Nowak.

Products designed for the Expression segment are still in the lower price range but allow young adults to have fun while communicating with friends. These products often feature changeable covers, color displays, embedded lights or game controls, and a wide selection of high-fidelity ring tones and downloadable games. Examples include the 3000 series of mobile phones, which offers all of these features, plus the unique option for owners to design their own custom cover inserts.

For the sports enthusiast segment, Nokia designs products in the Active segment. The 5000 series of mobile phones offer a youthful and vibrant style with improved durability. Features include a removable shell, built-in timers and stopwatch, a digital compass, a digital camera, a "Fitness Monitor" that monitors activity level and calorie consumption, and "Fitness Coach" personal trainer software.

Nokia's 6000 series of mobile phones allow Classic consumers to roam between various global networks. Some models have Bluetooth technology, voice dialing, voice recording, and Internet access while others have a camera, a document viewer to read e-mails, a browser, and a wireless keyboard for entering data into a personal information manager (phone book and calendar).

Nokia also designs phones for the Fashion segment—people who want a phone to "show off." The Nokia 7000 series of mobile phones are in this category. They allow these consumers to have a device with unique styling and materials that allow the owner to communicate their individual sense of style. In addition, Nokia offers phones for the Premium segment—people who also want a distinctive and elegant design, but as a functional phone to use rather than to show off. The Nokia 8000 series features titanium or stainless steel construction and a color screen.

THE FUTURE FOR NOKIA AND THE MOBILE PHONE INDUSTRY

By the end of 2010, the total number of mobile phone users worldwide could approach 3 billion due to the growth in emerging markets like China, India, and Latin America. This will spur the development of mobile phones that will work in all geographic markets. Nokia, Motorola, and Samsung have recently introduced phones, initially targeted at business users, which will work regardless of the location of the user.

3G mobile phone products and services continue to be rolled out in the United States. Wireless services providers, such as AT&T Wireless and Verizon Wireless, have introduced 3G services in selected U.S. cities in 2004. The convergence of digital devices may accelerate as key features from mobile phones, higher resolution digital cameras, TV-quality video streaming, PDAs, the Internet, music players, games, etc. become standard in the offerings of mobile phone marketers. What's on the horizon? The development of 4G! A forum of the top 15 mobile phone marketers recently gathered to plan for the offering of high-speed wireless technology that will allow for mobile shopping and video streaming at reasonable prices.

Finally, a fast-growing segment for mobile phones is the automobile. Many automobile manufacturers, in partnership with mobile phone marketers like Nokia, have recently introduced products that integrate "hands-free, voice-activated" technology to reduce mobile phone-related automobile accidents. The CTIA has recently developed public service announcements (PSAs) to promote more responsible behavior and forestall federal and state legislation designed to eliminate mobile phone use in the car.

Questions

1 Why has segmentation been a successful marketing strategy for Nokia?

2 What customer characteristics were used by mobile phone marketers during the industry's early stages of growth? Which customer characteristics and segmentation variables does Nokia use today?

3 Create a market-product grid for Nokia today. What potential new markets could you add to the grid?

PART

PART 1
Initiating the Marketing
Process

PART 2
Understanding Buyers
and Markets

PART 3
Targeting Marketing
Opportunities

PART 4
Satisfying Marketing
Opportunities

PART 5
Managing the
Marketing Process

4 SATISFYING MARKETING OPPORTUNITIES

HOW PART 4 FITS INTO THE BOOK

The chapters in Part 4 cover the marketing mix—the four Ps that are the key product, price, place, and promotion actions marketing managers use to implement their marketing program.

CHAPTER 10
Developing New Products and Services

CHAPTER 11
Managing Products and Brands

CHAPTER 12
Managing Services

CHAPTER 13
Building the Price Foundation

CHAPTER 14
Arriving at the Final Price

APPENDIX B
Financial Aspects of Marketing

CHAPTER 15
Managing Marketing Channels and Wholesaling

CHAPTER 16
Integrating Supply Chain and Logistics Management

CHAPTER 17
Retailing

CHAPTER 18
Integrated Marketing Communications and Direct Marketing

CHAPTER 19
Advertising, Sales Promotion, and Public Relations

CHAPTER 20
Personal Selling and Sales Management

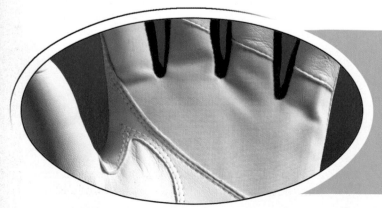
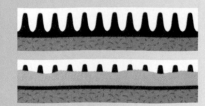

10

DEVELOPING NEW PRODUCTS AND SERVICES

LEARNING OBJECTIVES

After reading this chapter you should be able to:

1 Recognize the various terms that pertain to products and services.

2 Identify the ways in which consumer and business goods and services can be classified.

3 Explain the implications of alternative ways of viewing "newness" in new products and services.

4 Describe the factors contributing to a product's or service's failure.

5 Explain the purposes of each step of the new-product process.

3M'S NEW GREPTILE GRIP GOLF GLOVE: HOW TO GET TO THE TOP OF THE LEADER BOARD

"We look around the company for underutilized technologies that can result in exciting new products for niche markets," says Dr. George Dierberger, marketing and international manager for Sports and Leisure Products at 3M™. Turning 3M's micro-replication technology into a golf glove is a prime example.

To ensure that retailers will carry the innovative 3M Greptile™ Grip golf glove and that prospective golfers will buy and use it, Dierberger helps them discover its benefits and learn about the technology behind it. The benefits: To help golfers wearing the glove to hit longer drives and more accurate shots, thus getting lower scores through improved control of the golf club swing under both wet and dry conditions. Here's a quick take on the marketing issues Dierberger faced when introducing this new product in 2004:[1]

- *The product*? A golf glove that integrates 3M's revolutionary Greptile urethane gripping material, a technology that consists of thousands of "microscopic fingers," into a golf glove. The material is sewn in the "gripping channel" of the lower fingers and upper palm on the underside of the glove to reduce the slip of a golfer's grip when swinging the club.
- *The target market*? Golfers who want to improve their scores—only, say, 100 percent of the market. But then the market segments get more specific: golfers playing in hot or humid conditions, or those needing a stronger grip due to their skill level, age, or arthritis.
- *The special marketing task*? Leverage 3M's strong brand reputation for using its world-class technologies to introduce innovative, high-quality products

in the adhesives, office supply, health care, and other markets as a means of entering the intensely competitive golf equipment market.

Dierberger and his marketing and engineering staff created the ad for distributors and retailers shown on page 260. 3M has developed a two-stage marketing program for the golf glove: Initially, a moderately priced 3M Greptile Grip golf glove will be sold in mass merchandise retailers, such as Wal-Mart. Then, 3M will introduce a premium version of the golf glove in golf course pro shops, golf superstores like Golfsmith, sporting goods superstores like Sportmart, and sporting goods retailers like Modell's. The team's continuing challenge is to communicate the product's benefits in its packaging and promotions to its targeted retailers and customers to overcome the lack of 3M brand recognition in a market dominated by FootJoy, Titleist, Nike, and other golf glove marketers.

A brief look at some 3M products shows how its new-product research has enabled the company to become a global leader in adhesive technology. This has led to dozens of 3M adhesive products. Some examples, varying by the degree of adhesive stickiness, include:

- *Permanent adhesive bonding.* VHB™ (for "very high bond") tape made with high-strength acrylic, pressure-sensitive adhesives that can make a continuous bond stronger than spot welds or rivets for applications such as for cargo trailers and highway signs.
- *One-time adhesion.* Nexcare™ Tattoo™ Waterproof Bandages for kids that combine superior, waterproof wound protection with fun designs.
- *Multiple-time adhesion.* Post-it® Notes that enable you to stick and unstick that note to your friend over and over again.
- *No adhesion, but better gripping.* The Greptile Grip golf glove with its urethane gripping material that was discussed above.

The essence of marketing is in developing products such as a new, technologically advanced adhesive to meet buyer needs. A **product** is a good, service, or idea consisting of a bundle of tangible and intangible attributes that satisfies consumers and is received in exchange for money or some other unit of value. Tangible attributes include physical characteristics such as color or sweetness, and intangible attributes include becoming healthier or wealthier. Hence, a product includes the breakfast cereal you eat, the accountant who fills out your tax return, or your local art museum.

The life of a company often depends on how it conceives, produces, and markets new products. This is the exact reason that 3M spends $1.1 billion on research annually and has over 5,000 engineers and scientists around the globe looking for what *BusinessWeek* calls the Next Big Thing for 3M.[2] Later we describe how 3M strives to "delight its customers" using cross-functional teams and "Six Sigma" initiatives.

This chapter covers decisions involved in developing and marketing new products and services. Chapters 11 and 12 discuss the process of managing existing products and services, respectively.

THE VARIATIONS OF PRODUCTS

A product varies in terms of whether it is a consumer or business good. For most organizations the product decision is not made in isolation because companies often offer a range of products. To better appreciate the product decision, let's first define some terms pertaining to products.

Product Line and Product Mix

A **product line** is a group of products that are closely related because they satisfy a class of needs, are used together, are sold to the same customer group, are

An extensive product line can benefit both consumers and retailers. To discover how Little Remedies' product line helps achieve this, see the text.

distributed through the same type of outlets, or fall within a given price range. Within a firm, each product line usually has its own marketing strategy. Nike's product lines are shoes and clothing, whereas the Mayo Clinic's product lines consist of inpatient hospital care, outpatient physician services, and medical research.

The product line for the Little Remedies® Products from Vetco, Inc., shown above, is nonprescription medicines for infants and children 6 years old and younger. An important benefit of having a broad product line like that for Little Remedies is it enables both consumers and retailers to simplify their buying decisions. For example, if a family has a good experience with its four-year-old's sore throat with Little Colds® Saf-T-Pops® from Little Remedies, the family might consider its Little Noses® Decongestant Nose Drops if the child's cold causes a stuffed nose. Also, Vetco can obtain distribution in retail chains like Babies "Я" Us and Wal-Mart because its extensive product line enables these chains to contract with a single supplier and avoid having to deal with several different suppliers, often an expensive and time-consuming process.

Within each product line is the *product item,* a specific product as noted by a unique brand, size, or price. For example, Downy softener for clothes comes in 20-ounce and 40-ounce sizes; each size is considered a separate item or *stock keeping unit* (SKU), which is a unique identification number that defines an item for ordering or inventory purposes.

The third way to look at products is by the **product mix**, or the number of product lines offered by a company. Cray, Inc., has a single product line consisting of supercomputers, which are sold mostly to governments and large businesses. Fortune Brands, however, has many product lines such as sporting equipment (Titleist golf balls) and office products (Swingline staplers).

Classifying Products

Both the federal government and companies classify products, but for different purposes. The government's classification method helps it collect information on industrial activity. Companies classify products to help develop similar marketing strategies for the wide range of products offered. Two major ways to classify products are by type of user and degree of product tangibility.

Type of User   The first major type of product classification is according to the user. **Consumer goods** are products purchased by the ultimate consumer, whereas **business goods** (also called *B2B goods, industrial goods, or organizational goods*) are products that assist directly or indirectly in providing products for resale.

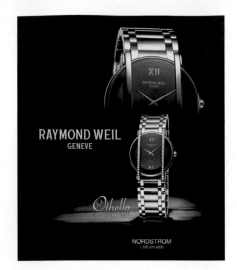

Specialty goods like Raymond Weil watches require distinct marketing programs to reach narrow target markets.

Raymond Weil
www.raymondweil.com

There are difficulties, however, with this classification because some products can be considered both consumer and business items. An Apple computer can be sold to consumers as a final product or to business firms for office use. Each classification results in different marketing actions. Viewed as a consumer product, the Apple computer would be sold through computer stores or directly from the company website. As a business product, the Apple computer might be sold by a salesperson offering discounts for multiple purchases.

Degree of Tangibility   Classification by degree of tangibility divides products into one of three categories. First is a *nondurable* good, an item consumed in one or a few uses, such as food products and fuel. A *durable* good is one that usually lasts over an extended number of uses, such as appliances, automobiles, and stereo equipment. *Services* are defined as activities, benefits, or satisfactions offered for sale, such as marketing research, health care, and education. According to this classification government data indicate that the United States is becoming a service economy, which is the reason for a separate chapter (Chapter 12) on the topic.

This classification method also provides direction for marketing actions. For nondurable products like Wrigley's gum, inexpensive and purchased frequently, consumer advertising and wide distribution in retail outlets is essential. Durable products like cars, however, generally cost more than nondurable goods and last longer, so personal selling is an important marketing activity in answering consumer questions and concerns. Because services are intangible, special marketing effort is usually needed to communicate their benefits to potential buyers.

Services and New-Product Development   "New-product" development in services like buying a stock or airline ticket or watching TV occurs but, being intangible, is often difficult to observe step by step. Nevertheless, service innovations can have a huge impact on our lives. For example, online brokerage firms have revolutionized the financial services industry, as have travel reservation firms like Expedia.

CLASSIFYING CONSUMER AND BUSINESS GOODS

Because the buyer is the key to marketing, consumer and business product classifications are discussed in greater detail.

Classification of Consumer Goods

Convenience, shopping, specialty, and unsought products are the four types of consumer goods. They differ in terms of (1) effort the consumer spends on the decision, (2) attributes used in purchase, and (3) frequency of purchase.

Convenience goods are items that the consumer purchases frequently, conveniently, and with a minimum of shopping effort. **Shopping goods** are items for which the consumer compares several alternatives on criteria, such as price, quality, or style. **Specialty goods** are items, such as Raymond Weil watches, that a consumer makes a special effort to search out and buy. **Unsought goods** are items that the consumer either does not know about or knows about but does not initially want. Figure 10–1 shows how the classification of a consumer product into one of these four types results in different aspects of the marketing mix being stressed. Different degrees of brand loyalty and amounts of shopping effort by the consumer are displayed for sample products in each of the four types of consumer goods.

The manner in which a consumer good is classified depends on the individual. One person may view a camera as a shopping good and visit several stores before deciding on a brand, whereas a friend may view cameras as a specialty good and will only buy a Nikon.

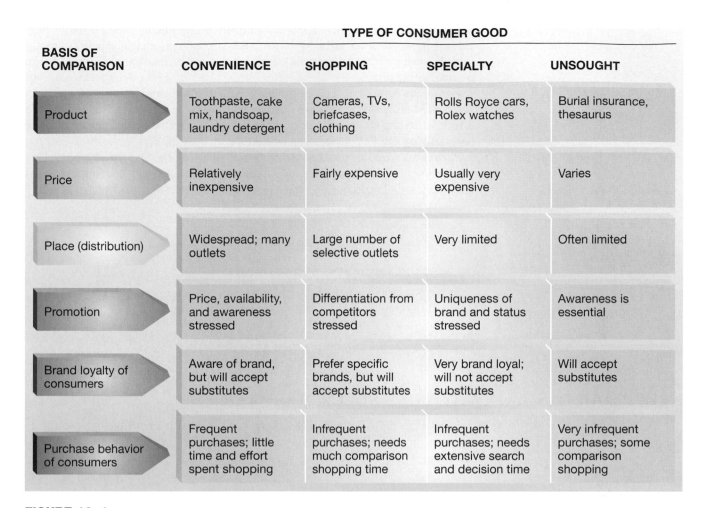

FIGURE 10–1
Classification of consumer goods

Classification of Business Goods

A major characteristic of business goods is that their sales are often the result of derived demand; that is, sales of business and industrial goods frequently result (or are derived) from the sale of consumer goods. For example, if consumer demand for Ford cars (a consumer product) increases, the company may increase its demand for paint spraying equipment (a business product). Business goods may be classified as production or support goods.

Production Goods   Items used in the manufacturing process that become part of the final product are **production goods**. These include raw materials such as grain or lumber, as well as component parts. For example, a company that manufactures door hinges used by Ford in its car doors is producing a component part. As noted in Chapter 6, the marketing of production goods is based on factors such as price, quality, delivery, and service. Marketers of these products tend to sell directly to industrial users.

Support Goods   The second class of business goods is **support goods**, which are items used to assist in producing other goods and services. Support goods include installations, accessory equipment, supplies, and services.

- *Installations* consist of buildings and fixed equipment. Because a significant amount of capital is required to purchase installations, the industrial buyer deals directly with construction companies and manufacturers through sales representatives. The pricing of installations is often by competitive bidding.

- *Accessory equipment* includes tools and office equipment and is usually purchased in small-order sizes by buyers. As a result, instead of dealing directly with buyers, sellers of industrial accessories use distributors to contact a large number of buyers.
- *Supplies* are similar to consumer convenience goods and consist of products such as stationery, paper clips, and brooms. These are purchased with little effort, using the straight rebuy decision sequence discussed in Chapter 6. Price and delivery are key factors considered by the buyers of supplies.
- *Industrial services* are intangible activities to assist the industrial buyer. This category can include maintenance and repair services and advisory services such as tax or legal counsel, where the seller's reputation is critical.

Concept Check

1. Explain the difference between product mix and product line.

2. What are the four main types of consumer goods?

3. To which type of good (business or consumer) does the term *derived demand* generally apply?

NEW PRODUCTS AND WHY THEY SUCCEED OR FAIL

New products are the lifeblood of a company and keep it growing, but the financial risks are large. Before discussing how new products reach the stage of commercialization when they are in the market, we'll begin by looking at *what* a new product is.

What Is a New Product?

The term *new* is difficult to define. Is Sony's PlayStation 2 *new* when there was a PlayStation 1? Is Microsoft's Xbox *new* when Microsoft hasn't been a big player in video games before? What does *new* mean for new-product marketing? Newness from several points of view and some marketing implications of this newness are discussed below.

As you read the discussion about what "new" means in new-product development, think about how it affects the marketing strategies of Sony and Microsoft in their *new* video-game launches.

Sony Corporation
www.sony.com

Microsoft Corporation
www.microsoft.com

MARKETING NEWSNET

Blindsided in the Twenty-First Century— The Convergence of Digital Devices

TECHNOLOGY & E-COMMERCE

Mobile phones that provide wireless voice communications virtually anywhere. Personal digital assistants, or PDAs, that give handheld computerized organization of appointments, addresses, telephone numbers, and so on. Digital cameras that can electronically capture and distribute digitized images. Portable music players that will store and play back hundreds of tunes. In the late 1990s, companies selling these digital products had it relatively easy: Just deliver the *single* core benefit that defined their respective product classes.

But that was the twentieth century—when electronic devices "stayed at home" in their own industry. But in today's twenty-first century, whole industries—industries that used to be completely separate—are colliding and their products often overlap.

What has happened is that improvements in key technologies have transformed the landscape of the digital consumer electronics marketplace. Consumers, who in the past had purchased these devices separately, now want features

Announcing an incredibly compact, folding PDA phone. The amazing, new Samsung i500.

The Samsung family of PDA phones. That's DigitAll ingenuity.

from each to be incorporated into a unified product. This collision of these industries has birthed what some call the "convergent digital device."

Blindsided by the revolutionary changes in technology and consumer tastes, digital device marketers now face competition from unexpected places. Motorola, Nokia, and Samsung now market mobile phones that integrate a digital camera, voice recorder, phonebook organizer, and Internet and e-mail access. PalmOne now offers a PDA with a mobile phone and Internet and e-mail access. Apple's iPod may soon have the capability to store and play video images in addition to voice and music, and Nokia recently introduced a mobile phone that plays CD-quality music.

Some experts believe that television, handheld gaming, integrated hands-free mobile phone, and satellite radio will be the next set of convergent digital devices to appear on the horizon and integrate voice, data, and video communication technologies to meet the future needs of consumers.

Newness Compared with Existing Products   If a product is functionally different from existing products, it can be defined as new. Sometimes this newness is revolutionary and creates a whole new industry, as in the case of the Apple II computer. At other times additional features are added to an existing product to try to make it appeal to more customers. An example appearing in the accompanying Marketing NewsNet describes the convergence of cell phones, PDAs, digital cameras, and portable music players in a single device.[3] So digital device manufacturers are suddenly facing competitors from completely different industries than they faced a decade ago. But another result is that today's consumers face difficult decisions about which of almost countless features they want in buying their new digital devices.

Newness in Legal Terms   The U.S. Federal Trade Commission (FTC) advises that the term *new* be limited to use with a product up to six months after it enters regular distribution. The difficulty with this suggestion is in the interpretation of the term *regular distribution.*

Newness from the Company's Perspective   Successful companies are starting to view newness and innovation in their products at three levels. At the lowest level, which usually involves the least risk, is a product line extension. This is an incremental improvement of an existing product for the company, such as Frosted Cheerios or Diet Cherry Coke or Gillette Venus for Women—extensions of the basic Cheerios or Diet Coke or men's Gillette MACH 3 product lines, respectively.

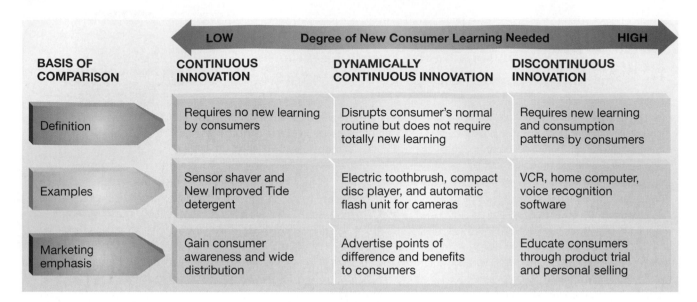

FIGURE 10–2

Consumption effects define newness

At the next level is a significant jump in the innovation or technology, such as Sony's leap from the micro tape recorder to the Walkman. The third level is true innovation, a truly revolutionary new product, like the first Apple computer in 1976. Effective new-product programs in large firms deal at all three levels.

Newness from the Consumer's Perspective   A fourth way to define new products is in terms of their effects on consumption. This approach classifies new products according to the degree of learning required by the consumer, as shown in Figure 10–2.

With *continuous innovation,* no new behaviors must be learned. Gateway's introduction of the first plasma flat-panel TV started a revolution among TV buyers.[4] Gateway's new TV does not require buyers to learn new TV-watching behaviors and therefore is a continuous innovation. Under these conditions, the beauty of this innovation is that effective marketing simply depends on generating awareness and having strong distribution in appropriate outlets, not completely reeducating customers.

With *dynamically continuous innovation,* only minor changes in behavior are required for use. An example is built-in, fold-down child seats such as those available in Chrysler minivans. Built-in car seats for children require only minor bits of education and changes in behavior, so the marketing strategy is to educate prospective buyers on their benefits, advantages, and proper use.

A *discontinuous innovation* involves making the consumer learn entirely new consumption patterns in order to use the product. After decades of research, IBM introduced its ViaVoice speech recognition software. If you are using ViaVoice today, you speak to your computer and watch your own words appear on your computer screen. You also can open Microsoft Office programs with your voice. The risk that IBM faced in introducing this discontinuous innovation was that you had to learn new behaviors in producing your word-processed memos and reports. Hence, marketing efforts for discontinuous innovations involve not only gaining initial consumer awareness but also educating consumers on both the benefits and proper use of the innovative product, activities that can cost millions of dollars.

Why Products Succeed or Fail

We all know the giant product successes—such as Microsoft Windows, Swatch watches, CNN. Yet the thousands of failures every year that slide quietly into oblivion cost American businesses billions of dollars. Recent research suggests that it takes about 3,000 raw unwritten ideas to produce a single commercially successful new

MARKETING NEWSNET

What Separates New-Product Winners and Losers

CUSTOMER VALUE

What makes some products winners and others losers? Knowing this answer is a key to a new-product strategy. R. G. Cooper and E. J. Kleinschmidt studied 203 new industrial products to find the answers shown below.

The researchers defined the "product success rate" of new products as the percentage of products that reached the company's own profitability criteria. Product "winners" are the best 20 percent of performers and "losers" are the worst 20 percent. For example, for the first factor in the table below, 98 percent of the winners had a major point of difference compared with only 18 percent of the losers, giving a difference of 80 percent.

Note that the table below includes both marketing and nonmarketing factors. Most of the marketing factors tie directly to the reasons cited in the text for new-product failures that are taken from a number of research studies.

FACTOR AFFECTING PRODUCT SUCCESS RATE	PRODUCT "WINNERS" (BEST 20%)	−	PRODUCT "LOSERS" (WORST 20%)	=	% DIFFERENCE (WINNERS− LOSERS)
• Point of difference, or uniquely superior product	98%	−	18%	=	80%
• Well-defined product before actual development starts	85	−	26	=	59
• Synergy, or fit, with firm's R&D and manufacturing capabilities	80	−	29	=	51
• Quality of execution of technological activities	76	−	30	=	46
• Quality of execution of activities before actual development starts	75	−	31	=	44
• Synergy, or fit, with marketing mix activities	71	−	31	=	40
• Quality of execution of marketing mix activities	71	−	32	=	39
• Market attractiveness, ones with large markets, high growth	74	−	43	=	31

product.[5] To learn marketing lessons and convert potential failures to successes, we can analyze why new products fail and then study several failures in detail. As we go through the new-product process later in the chapter, we can identify ways such failures might have been avoided—admitting that hindsight is clearer than foresight.

Marketing Reasons for New-Product Failures   Both marketing and nonmarketing factors contribute to new-product failures, as shown in the accompanying Marketing NewsNet. Using the research results from several studies[6] on new-product success and failure and also those described in the Marketing NewsNet, we can identify critical marketing factors—sometimes overlapping—that often separate new-product winners and losers:

  1. *Insignificant point of difference.* Shown as the most important factor in the Marketing NewsNet, a distinctive point of difference is essential for a new

New-product success or
failure? For the special
problems these products
face, see the text.

product to defeat competitive ones—through having superior characteristics that deliver unique benefits to the user. In the mid-1990s, General Mills introduced Fingos, a sweetened cereal flake about the size of a corn chip. Consumers were supposed to snack on them dry, but they didn't.[7] The point of difference was not important enough to get consumers to give up eating competing snacks such as popcorn, potato chips, or Cheerios from the box late at night.

2. *Incomplete market and product definition before product development starts.* Ideally, a new product needs a precise **protocol**, a statement that, before product development begins, identifies: (1) a well-defined target market; (2) specific customers' needs, wants, and preferences; and (3) what the product will be and do. Without this precision, loads of money disappear as research and development (R&D) tries to design a vague product for a phantom market. Apple Computer's hand-sized Newton personal digital assistant (PDA) that was supposed to help keep the user organized fizzled badly because no clear protocol existed.

3. *Too little market attractiveness.* Market attractiveness refers to the ideal situation every new-product manager looks for: a large target market with high growth and real buyer need. But often, when looking for ideal market niches, the target market is too small and competitive to warrant the R&D, production, and marketing expenses necessary to reach it. In the early 1990s, Kodak discontinued its Ultralife lithium battery with its 10-year shelf life, although the battery was touted as lasting twice as long as an alkaline battery. Yet the product was only available in the 9-volt size, which accounted for less than 10 percent of the U.S. battery market.

4. *Poor execution of the marketing mix: name, package, price, promotion, distribution.* Coca-Cola thought its Minute Maid Squeeze-Fresh frozen orange juice concentrate in a squeeze bottle was a hit. The idea was that consumers could make one glass of juice at a time, and the concentrate stayed fresh in the refrigerator for over a month. After two test markets, the product was finished. Consumers loved the idea, but the product was messy to use, and the advertising and packaging didn't educate them effectively on how much concentrate to mix.

5. *Poor product quality or sensitivity to customer needs on critical factors.* Overlapping somewhat with point 1, this factor stresses that problems on one or two critical factors can kill the product, even though the general quality is high. For example, the Japanese, like the British, drive on the left side of the road. Until 1996, U.S. carmakers sent Japan few right-drive cars—unlike German carmakers who exported right-drive models in a number of their brands.[8] As described

MARKETING NEWSNET

When Less Is More—How Reducing the Number of Features Can Open Up Huge Markets

TECHNOLOGY & E-COMMERCE

New products! To invent them the natural thing is to add more features, new technologies, more glitz. Many new-product successes described in the chapter do just that.

But huge new markets can open up if firms move the opposite direction by taking features away and simplifying the product. Here are some less-is-more new-product breakthroughs that revolutionized national or global markets:

1. *Canon's tabletop copiers.* Canon found it couldn't sell its little copiers to big companies, which were happy with their large Xerox machines. So Canon sold its little machines to little companies with limited copying needs by the zillions.

2. *Palm Computing's PalmPilot PDA.* Apple Computer's Newton personal digital assistant (PDA) was a great idea but was too complicated for users. Enter: PalmPilot inventors Donna Dubinsky and Jeff Hawkins, who deleted features to achieve the market breakthrough.

3. *Intuit's QuickBooks accounting software.* Competitors offered complex accounting software containing every feature professional accountants might possibly want. Intuit then introduced QuickBooks, a smaller, cheaper program with less functionality that won 70 percent of the huge market for small-business accounting software within two years.

4. *Swatch watches.* In 1983, a slim plastic watch with only 51 components appeared on the global market. That simplicity—plus top quality, affordable price, and creative designs—is the reason that more than 250 million Swatch watches have been sold.

Sometimes much less is much, much more!

One surprise: Innovation research shows that firms using disruptive innovation and creating newness by simplifying the product are often *not* the industry leaders selling the more sophisticated high-end products with more features.

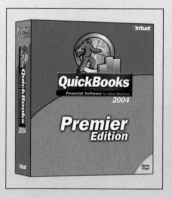

in the Marketing NewsNet "When Less Is More," sometimes large markets can be served by taking features *out* of a product and actually making it simpler.[9]

6. *Bad timing.* The product is introduced too soon, too late, or at a time when consumer tastes are shifting dramatically. Bad timing gives new-product managers nightmares. IBM, for example, killed several laptop computer prototypes because competitors introduced better, more advanced machines to the marketplace before IBM could get there.

7. *No economical access to buyers.* Grocery products provide an example. Today's mega-supermarkets carry more than 30,000 different SKUs. With more than 33,000 new packaged goods products (food, beverage, health and beauty aids, household, and pet items) introduced in 2003, the fight for exposure is tremendous in terms of costs for advertising, distribution, and shelf space.[10] Because shelf space is judged in terms of sales per square foot, Thirsty Dog! (a zesty beef-flavored, vitamin-enriched, mineral-loaded, lightly carbonated bottled water for your dog) must displace an existing product on the supermarket shelves, a difficult task with the precise measures of revenues per square foot these stores use.

FIGURE 10–3
Why did these new products
fail?

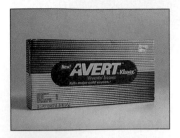

As explained in detail in the text, new products often fail because of one or a combination of seven reasons. Look at the two products described below, and try to identify
which reason explains why they failed in the marketplace.

- Kimberly Clark's Avert Virucidal tissues that contained vitamin C derivatives scien-
  tifically designed to kill cold and flu germs when users sneezed, coughed, or blew
  their nose into them.
- OUT! International's Hey! There's A Monster In My Room spray that was designed
  to rid scary creatures from kids' rooms and had a bubble-gum fragrance.

Compare your insights with those in the text.

A Look at Some Failures   Before reading the next two paragraphs, study the
product failures described in Figure 10–3. Then think for several minutes to try to
identify which of the seven reasons listed in the text is the most likely explanation
for their failure. The two examples are discussed in greater detail below.

Kimberly Clark's Avert Virucidal tissues lasted 10 months in a test market in
upstate New York before being pulled from the shelves. People didn't believe the
claims and were frightened by the "-cidal" in the name, which they connected to
events like "suicidal." So the tissue probably failed because of not having a clear point
of difference and a bad name, and, hence, bad marketing mix execution—probably
reasons 1 and 4 in the list in the text.

OUT! International's Hey! There's A Monster In My Room spray was creative
and cute when introduced in 1993. But the name probably kept the kids awake at
night more than their fear of the monsters because it suggested the monster was still
hiding in the room. Question: Wouldn't calling it the Monster-Buster Spray—the
secondary name shown at the bottom of the package—have licked the name problem? It looks like the spray was never really defined well in a protocol (reason 2)
and definitely had poor name execution (reason 4).[11]

Simple marketing research on consumers should have revealed the problems. Developing successful new products may sometimes involve luck, but more often it involves
having a product that really meets a need and has significant points of difference over
competitive products. The likelihood of success is improved by paying attention to the
early steps of the new-product process described in the next section of the text.

Concept Check

1. From a consumer's viewpoint, what kind of innovation would an improved
electric toothbrush be?

2. What does "insignificant point of difference" mean as a reason for new-product
failure?

THE NEW-PRODUCT PROCESS

Companies such as General Electric, Sony, and 3M take a specific sequence of steps
before their products are ready for market. Figure 10–4 shows the seven stages of
the **new-product process**, the stages a firm goes through to identify business
opportunities and convert them to a salable good or service. This sequence begins
with new-product strategy development and ends with commercialization.

New-Product Strategy Development

For companies, **new-product strategy development** is the stage of the new-
product process that defines the role for a new product in terms of the firm's overall

FIGURE 10–4
Stages in the new-product process

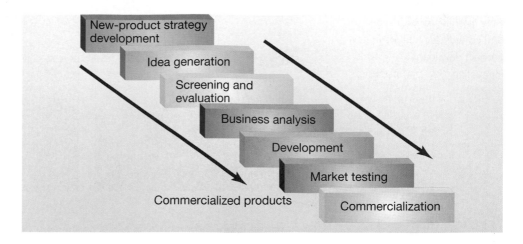

New-product strategy development

Idea generation

Screening and evaluation

Business analysis

Development

Market testing

Commercialization

Commercialized products

corporate objectives. This step in the new-product process has been added by many companies recently to provide a needed focus for ideas and concepts developed in later stages.

Objectives of the Stage: Identify Markets and Strategic Roles   During this new-product strategy development stage the company uses the environmental scanning process described in Chapter 3 to identify trends that pose either opportunities or threats. Relevant company strengths and weaknesses are also identified. The outcome of new-product strategy development is not only new-product ideas but also identifying markets for which new products will be developed and strategic roles new products might serve—the vital protocol activity explained earlier in the discussion of the Marketing NewsNet on new-product winners and losers.

3M: Cross-Functional Teams and Six Sigma   When James McNerney left General Electric to become chairman and CEO of 3M in 2001, he soon made a major discovery: 3M's legendary success using its vaunted labs and scientists to turn out commercial hits had bogged down. His immediate actions were to refocus 3M's research and development efforts on technologies that would result in commercially successful products and getting 3M scientists to communicate earlier in the new-product sequence with its marketing and manufacturing people to focus 3M's lab work better.

One key to success in new-product development is 3M's use of *cross-functional teams,* a small number of people from different departments in an organization who are mutually accountable to a common set of performance goals. Today in 3M, these teams are especially important so that individuals from R&D, marketing, sales, and manufacturing can simultaneously work together to focus on new product and market opportunities. In the past, 3M and other firms often utilized these department people in sequence— possibly resulting in R&D designing new products that the manufacturing department couldn't produce economically and that the marketing department couldn't sell.

Important today in 3M's cross-functional teams is **Six Sigma**, a means to "delight the customer" by achieving quality through a highly disciplined process to focus on developing and delivering near-perfect products and services. "Near perfect" here means being 99.9997 percent perfect or allowing 3.4 defects per million products produced or transactions processed—getting as close as possible to zero defects. Six Sigma's success lies in determining what variables impact the results, measuring them, and making decisions based on data, not gut feelings.[12] In 2004, 3M had a cross-functional Six Sigma team charged with finding ways to streamline and standardize ways for conducting its marketing research. Worldwide that year 3M had 130 Six Sigma projects underway with major customers.

Idea Generation

The stage of the new-product process that involves developing a pool of concepts as candidates for new products, or **idea generation**, must build on the previous

How listening to employees and co-workers matters in new product development: Volvo's innovative YCC and its design team.

stage's results. New-product ideas are generated by customers, suppliers, employees, basic R&D, and competitors.

Customer and Supplier Suggestions   Companies often analyze customer complaints or supplier ideas to discover new-product opportunities. Whirlpool, trying to reduce costs by cutting the number of different product platforms in half, got ideas from customers on ways to standardize components.[13] Business researchers now emphasize that firms must actively involve customers and suppliers in the product development process.[14] This often means focusing on what the new product will actually *do* for them rather than simply *what they want*.[15]

Employee and Co-Worker Suggestions   Employees may be encouraged to suggest new-product ideas through suggestion boxes or contests. The idea for Nature Valley Granola Bars from General Mills came when one of its marketing managers observed co-workers bringing granola to work in plastic bags.

As described at the start of Chapter 5, auto industry studies show that women buy about two-thirds of all vehicles and also influence about 85 percent of all sales. However, many auto manufacturers get ideas on new-car features by doing marketing research on gear-head guys who love cars. That's *exactly opposite* to what Volvo did recently in trying to bridge the gender gap. Volvo first obtained ideas on new-car features from all-female focus groups drawn from its Swedish workforce. It then named a five-woman team of Volvo managers to design a "concept car"— what the auto industry uses to test new designs, technical innovations, and consumer reactions. Shown in the photos above with its all-women design team, here are some features of Volvo's YCC (Your Concept Car) that appeared in auto shows in 2004:

- *Automatically opening doors.* Press a button on the car key and the gull-wing doors pop open, the chassis rises a few inches, and the steering pulls in to make a wide path in for the driver.
- *Ergovision system for automatic fit to the driver.* At a dealership the driver's body is laser-scanned so that the car automatically sets the optimal positions for the seat belt, pedals, headrest, steering wheel, and seat—information saved in memory in the car key.
- *Parallel parking aid.* When the car stops in front of an empty spot, sensors confirm the space is big enough and the system automatically self-steers the car into the space while the driver controls the brake and gas.
- *Care and cleanliness.* The no-stick paint on body panels repels dirt and customized seat covers can be removed and washed.

You may never see the YCC in your local Volvo showroom because its likely $65,000 price tag may be too high for the market. But you *will* see many of these women-designed features on future Volvos, testimony to the importance of listening to consumers in developing new products.[16]

WEB LINK   IDEO—Where Design Is Not a Noun... It's a Verb

The Apple mouse. The Palm V PDA. The Crest Neat Squeeze toothpaste dispenser. The Steelecase Leap adjustable office chair. These are just some of the thousands of new products designed by a firm you've probably never heard of but benefit from everyday. For David Kelley, cofounder of IDEO, product design includes both artistic and functional elements. And to foster this creativity, IDEO allows its designers and engineers much freedom—its offices look like schoolrooms; employees can hang their bicycles from the ceiling; there are rubber-band fights; and on Monday mornings, there are show-and-tell sessions.

Visit IDEO's website (www.ideo.com) to view its recent inventions and innovations for clients such as McDonald's self-ordering kiosk, the Zyliss' Mandolin fruit and vegetable slicer, LifePort's kidney transporter, Pepsi's High Visibility vending machine, and Nike's all-terrain sunglasses.

Research and Development Breakthroughs   Another source of new products is a firm's basic research, but the costs can be huge. Sony is a world leader in new-product development in electronics. Sony's research and development breakthroughs have made it a legend in the electronics industry, popularizing VCRs, the Walkman, and—coming into your future?—flat-panel Organic Electroluminescence (OEL) monitors about the thickness of a credit card providing brighter images on large, 30-inch screens.

Not all R&D labs have Sony's genius for moving electronic breakthroughs into the marketplace. Take Xerox Corporation's Palo Alto Research Center (PARC). In maybe the greatest electronic fumble of all time, by 1979 PARC had what's in your computer system now: graphical user interfaces, mice, windows and pull-down menus, laser printers, and distributed computing. Concerned with aggressive competition from Japan in its core photocopier business, Xerox didn't even bother to patent these breakthroughs. Apple Computer's Steven Jobs visited PARC in 1979, adapted many of the ideas for the Macintosh, and the rest is history.

Professional R&D laboratories also provide new-product ideas. Labs at Arthur D. Little helped put the crunch in Cap'n Crunch cereal and the flavor in Carnation Instant Breakfast. As described in the Web Link, IDEO is a world-class new-product development firm, having designed more than 4,000 of them.

Brainstorming sessions run at IDEO can generate 100 new ideas in an hour. Its "shop-a-long" visits with managers of client firms let the managers experience firsthand what one of its customers does. A sample recommendation from a shop-a-long with managers from a large U.S. health maintenance organization who actually could play the part of a patient: Make examining rooms larger to enable the nervous patient to have a friend or relative in the room while waiting for the doctor.[17]

Competitive Products   New-product ideas can also be found by analyzing the competition. A six-person intelligence team from the Marriott Corporation spent six months traveling around the country staying at economy hotels. The team assessed the competition's strengths and weaknesses on everything from the soundproof qualities of the rooms to the softness of the towels. Marriott then budgeted $500 million for a new economy hotel chain, Fairfield Inns.

Screening and Evaluation

Screening and evaluation is the stage of the new-product process that involves internal and external evaluations of the new-product ideas to eliminate those that warrant no further effort.

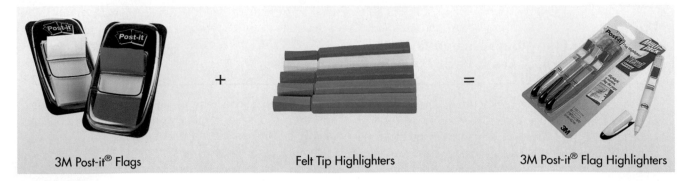

3M Post-it® Flags   Felt Tip Highlighters   3M Post-it® Flag Highlighters

For the creative way a student project helped lead to 3M's new Post-it® Flag Highlighter, see the text.

Internal Approach Internally, the firm evaluates the technical feasibility of the proposal and whether the idea meets the objectives defined in the new-product strategy development step. In a recent project, 3M researcher David Windorski worked with a team of local university students to find new applications for Post-it® Flags in their studying activities. Student suggestions reinforced some ideas Windorski had been working on in his lab. Students said that combining Post-it® Flags with colored felt-tip highlighters could be used as bookmarks on key pages in their textbooks that they highlighted. Windorski and the team worked on a few different prototypes: Post-it® Flags on top, on the side, and so on. He knew the basic idea was sound, but the designs were not.

Windorski then hit on his breakthrough idea: Put small Post-it® Flags *inside* pens and highlighters that students use! After much engineering, consumer testing, and evaluation, the result was the launch of 3M's Post-it® Flag Highlighter and Post-it® Flag Pen in June 2003—a credit to global cross-functional collaboration among research, manufacturing and marketing. In these two 3M products, the pen and highlighter components were sourced worldwide. The new product development team then coordinated the commercialization for a global introduction.

The final, marketable Post-it® Flag Highlighter version is shown in the photo above. But earlier prototypes were first mocked up in cardboard, then modeling clay, then components screwed together—a far cry from the final product you probably see in your student bookstore. By the end of 2004, 3M had sold over a million units of the two new products.[18]

External Approach Concept tests are external evaluations that consist of preliminary testing of the new-product idea (rather than the actual product) with consumers. Generally, these tests are more useful with minor modifications of existing products than with really new, innovative products not familiar to consumers.[19] Concept tests usually rely on written descriptions of the product but may be augmented with sketches, mockups, or promotional literature. Several key questions are asked during concept testing: How does the customer perceive the product? Who would use it? How would it be used?

Snacks with no trans fats? To see how Frito-Lay uses consumer ideas, read the text.

Frito-Lay spent a year interviewing 10,000 consumers about the concept of a multigrain snack chip before introducing its highly successful Sun Chips.

But the consumers are now changing, concerned about healthy snacks, low-carb foods, Atkin's diets, trans fats, and so on—topics few Americans even thought about a couple of years ago. Frito-Lay is now focusing efforts on a critical research issue: healthy snacks that taste good. Frito-Lay's big challenge is that healthy snacks taste distinctly. . . uh. . . healthy because they lack the salt, fats, and sugars that give the taste that is the reason most Americans eat them.

So Frito-Lay in 2003 launched a line of natural snacks, including such consumer favorites as Ruffles, Tostitos, and Cheetos. In fall 2003, Frito-Lay announced that it cooks these snacks in oils without trans fat, a big benefit for health because research shows trans fats raise the level of LDL, what doctors call the "bad cholesterol." The company was one of the first to put nutrition labels on the front of its snacks that included fat content. Purchase decisions by consumers like you will determine the success of this new line of Frito-Lay healthier snacks.[20]

Concept Check

1. What step in the new-product process has been added in recent years?

2. What are the main sources of new-product ideas?

3. What is the difference between internal and external screening and evaluation approaches used by a firm in the new-product process?

Business Analysis

Business analysis is the stage of the new-product process that involves specifying the product features and marketing strategy and making necessary financial projections needed to commercialize a product. This is the last checkpoint before significant capital is invested in creating a *prototype,* a full-scale operating model of the product under development. Economic analysis, marketing strategy review, and legal examination of the proposed product are conducted at this stage. The product is also analyzed relative to the firm's marketing and technological synergies, two criteria noted in the Marketing NewsNet shown earlier on page 269.

The marketing strategy review studies the new-product idea in relation to the marketing program to support it. The proposed product is assessed to determine whether it will help or hurt sales of existing products. Likewise, the product is examined to assess whether it can be sold through existing channels or if new outlets will be needed. Profit projections involve estimating the number of units expected to be sold but also the costs of R&D, production, and marketing.

As an important aspect of the business analysis, the proposed new product is studied to determine whether it can be protected with a patent or copyright. An attractive new-product proposal is one in which the technology, product, or brand cannot easily be copied. All of these critical business issues emerge in huge research and development gambles on new drug compounds by pharmaceutical companies like Eli Lilly & Company, discussed in the next section.

Development

Product ideas that survive the business analysis proceed to actual **development**, the stage of the new-product process that involves turning the idea on paper into a prototype. This results in a demonstrable, producible product in hand. Outsiders seldom understand the technical complexities of the development stage, which involves not only manufacturing the product but also performing laboratory and consumer tests to ensure that it meets the standards set. Design of the product becomes an important element.

Some new products can be so important and costly that the company is literally betting its very existence on success. And creative, out-of-the-box thinking can be critical. In the pharmaceutical industry, no more than one out of every 5,000 to 10,000 new compounds developed in the labs emerges as an approved drug.[21]

With the success rate on new drug compounds so low, pharmaceutical giant Eli Lilly has initiated "failure parties" to recognize excellent scientific work that unfortunately resulted in products that failed anyway. But the failed drug compound doesn't end with the party. Instead, Lilly usually names a team of doctors and scientists to look back objectively at every compound that failed at any point in human clinical trials to learn the specific reasons for the failure.

ETHICS AND SOCIAL RESPONSIBILITY ALERT

SUVs and Pickups versus Cars—Godzilla Meets a Chimp?

ETHICS

Make car collisions safe. Sound silly? But. . . the problem is death! The high-bumper pickups and sport utility vehicles (SUVs)—termed "light trucks" in the industry—are now involved in about 20 percent of all U.S. highway deaths.

When one of these light trucks, which is often a ton heavier than a car, collides with a car, the car comes off second best. A special problem is that the bumper of the pickup truck or SUV is as much as nine inches higher than the car's bumper, a problem referred to as "compatibility" in the auto industry.

How serious is the problem? Highway data from 2003 show that in a head-on collision between a car and a light truck, the car occupants were 3.3 times more likely to die than those in the light truck. Occupants in a car struck in the side by a light truck are 21 times as likely to be killed than the truck occupants.

The problem is also money. These light trucks now account for more than half of Detroit's sales and most of its profits. Improving the cars—with side air bags and steel supports—is expensive, as is lowering the frame or adding a crumple zone for the bumper of the bigger vehicle. Nothing is easy.

What to do? In late 2003, 15 automakers from four countries voluntarily agreed to redesign their light trucks to make their bumper height more compatible with cars. They are also likely to protect car passengers from side impacts from light trucks by making side air bags standard equipment in cars sold in the United States. The new designs will start appearing in 2007, with all vehicles meeting the standards for the 2010 model year. The design changes are expected to save thousands of lives annually.

Are the voluntary agreements from automakers good enough? Or should federal laws be passed? Or insurance companies lobby Congress?

To see how your vehicle measures up on various crash tests, go to the website of the Insurance Institute of Highway Safety (www.hwysafety.org) and click on "Vehicle Ratings."

This "failure analysis" has resulted in Lilly's sometimes finding ways to make the compound succeed in addressing the original disease for which it was designed. For example, in 1999 Lilly halted trials of Alimta, an experimental chemotherapy drug, when three patients died. Extensive failure analysis revealed that patients with the most severe side effects had reduced folic acid in their blood. The solution: Simply give all patients suffering from a rare type of cancer caused by exposure to asbestos *both* Alimta *and* folic acid pills.

More surprisingly, a number of successful Lilly drugs trace their origins back to trials that demonstrated the drug was a flop for the initial medical problem it was intended to address. Examples are a failed antidepressant drug now used in treating attention deficit/hyperactivity disorders and a drug that flopped in addressing asthma but works for cardiovascular diseases. Some of these breakthroughs come from researchers using a Lilly "blue sky" fund that enables them to spend 10 to 20 percent of their time on projects with no clear immediate commercial value.[22]

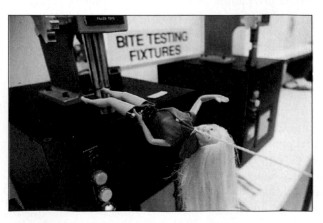

Lilly's drug prototypes go through exhaustive lab and clinical tests to see if they meet design criteria set for them if used the way intended. But safety tests are also critical for when the product isn't used as planned. To make sure seven-year-olds can't bite Barbie's head off and choke, Mattel clamps her foot in steel jaws in a test stand and then pulls on her head with a wire. Similarly, car manufacturers have done extensive safety tests by crashing their cars into concrete walls. As mentioned in the Ethics and Social Responsibility Alert, consumer groups are increasingly concerned about what happens when a pickup truck or sport utility vehicle hits a small car when their bumpers don't line up.[23] Auto industry tests are identifying some feasible, but costly, solutions.

Market Testing

Market testing is the stage of the new-product process that involves exposing actual products to prospective consumers under realistic purchase conditions to see if they will buy. Often a product is developed, tested, refined, and then tested again to get consumer reactions through either test marketing or simulated test markets.

Test Marketing   *Test marketing* involves offering a product for sale on a limited basis in a defined area. This test is done to determine whether consumers will actually buy the product and to try different ways of marketing it. Only about a third of the products test marketed do well enough to go on to the next phase. These market tests are usually conducted in cities that are viewed as being representative of U.S. consumers like the six shown in Figure 10–5. Of these cities, Wichita Falls, Texas, most closely matches the U.S. average found in the 2000 Census. Other criteria used in selecting test market cities are brand purchase patterns resembling the U.S. average, small towns far enough from big markets to allow low-cost advertising purchases, cable systems to deliver different ads to different homes, and tracking systems like those of AC Nielsen to measure sales resulting from different advertising campaigns.[24]

This gives the company an indication of potential sales volume and market share in the test area. Market tests are also used to check other elements of the marketing mix besides the product itself such as price, level of advertising support, and distribution. These market tests also are time consuming and expensive because production lines as well as promotion and sales programs must be set up. Costs can run several million dollars. Market tests also reveal plans to competitors, sometimes enabling them to get a product into national distribution first. Competitors can also try to sabotage test markets. With such problems, some firms skip test markets completely or use simulated test markets.

Simulated Test Markets   Because of the time, cost, and confidentiality problems of test markets, consumer packaged goods companies often turn to *simulated* (or *laboratory*) *test markets* (*STM*), a technique that simulates a full-scale test market but in a limited fashion. STMs are often run in shopping malls, where consumers are questioned to identify who uses the product class being tested. Willing participants are questioned on usage, reasons for purchase, and important product attributes. Qualified persons are then shown TV commercials or print ads for the test product along with competitors' advertising and are given money to make a decision to buy or not

FIGURE 10–5

Six important U.S. test markets and the "demographics winner": Wichita Falls, Texas, metropolitan statistical area

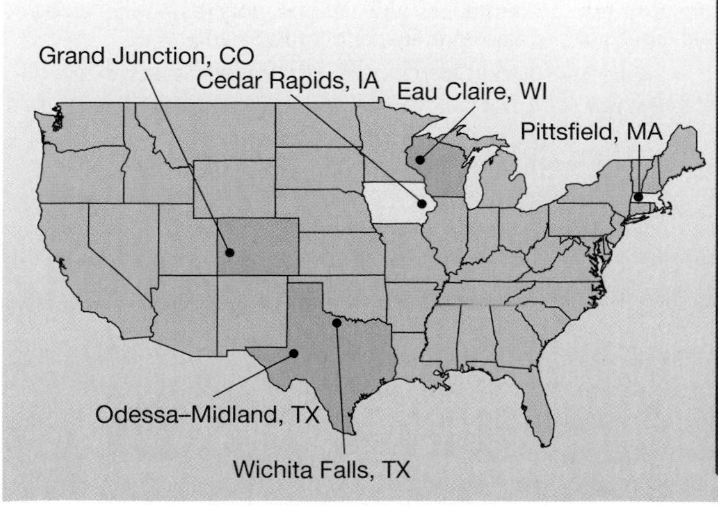

Demographic Characteristic	USA	Wichita Falls, TX
2000 population	281.4 mil.	140,518
Median age (years)	35.3	33.6
% of family households with children under 18	32.8%	33.8%
% Hispanic or Latino of any race	12.5%	11.8%
% African American	12.3%	9.6%
% Asian American	3.6%	1.7%
% Native American	1.5%	1.7%

buy the firm's product—or the competitors' product—from a real or simulated store environment. STMs are used early in the development process to screen new-product ideas and later in the process to make sales projections.

When Test Markets Don't Work   Test marketing is a valuable step in the new-product process, but not all products can use it. Testing a service beyond the concept level is very difficult because the service is intangible and consumers can't see what they are buying. For example, how could Google easily have test marketed the mid-2004 launch of its Gmail, an e-mail service users get free in exchange for accepting ads with its Gmail?[25]

Similarly, test markets for expensive consumer products such as cars or VCRs or costly industrial products such as jet engines or computers are impractical. For these products consumer reactions to mockup designs or one-of-a-kind prototypes are all that is feasible. Carmakers test new style designs on early adopters (discussed in Chapter 11) who are more willing than the average customer to buy new designs or products.[26]

Commercialization

Finally, the product is brought to the point of **commercialization**—the stage of the new-product process that involves positioning and launching a new product in full-scale production and sales. Companies proceed very carefully at the commer-

FIGURE 10–6
Marketing information and methods used in the new-product process

STAGE OF PROCESS	PURPOSE OF STAGE	MARKETING INFORMATION AND METHODS USED
New-product strategy development	Identify new-product niches to reach in light of company objectives	Company objectives; assessment of firm's current strengths and weaknesses in terms of market and product
Idea generation	Develop concepts for possible products	Ideas from employees and co-workers, consumers, R&D, and competitors; methods of brainstorming and focus groups
Screening and evaluation	Separate good product ideas from bad ones inexpensively	Screening criteria, concept tests, and weighted point systems
Business analysis	Identify the product's features and its marketing strategy, and make financial projections	Product's key features, anticipated marketing mix strategy; economic, marketing, production, legal, and profitability analyses
Development	Create the prototype product, and test it in the laboratory and on consumers	Laboratory and consumer tests on product prototypes
Market testing	Test product and marketing strategy in the marketplace on a limited scale	Test markets, simulated test markets (STMs)
Commercialization	Position and offer product in the marketplace	Perceptual maps, product positioning, regional rollouts

Commercializing a new french fry: To learn how Burger King's improved french fries confronted McDonald's fries, see the text.

Effective cross-functional teams at Hewlett-Packard have reduced new-product development times significantly.

cialization stage because this is the most expensive stage for most new products, especially consumer products. If competitors introduce a product that leapfrogs the firm's own new product or if cannibalization of its own existing products look significant, the firm may halt the new-product launch permanently.[27] Large companies use *regional rollouts,* introducing the product sequentially into geographical areas of the United States to allow production levels and marketing activities to build up gradually to minimize the risk of new-product failure. Grocery product manufacturers and some telephone service providers are two examples of firms that use this strategy.

Figure 10–6 identifies the purpose of each stage of the new-product process and the kinds of marketing information and methods used. The third column of the figure also suggests information that might help avoid some new-product failures. Although using the new-product process does not guarantee successful products, it does increase a firm's success rate.

Burger King's French Fries: The Complexities of Commercialization

Burger King's "improved french fries" are an example of what can go wrong at the commercialization stage. In the fast-food industry, McDonald's french fries are the gold standard against which all other fries are measured. In 1996, Burger King decided to take on McDonald's fries and spent millions of R&D dollars developing a starch-coated fry designed to retain heat longer and add crunch.

A 100-person team set to work and developed the starch-coated fry that beat McDonald's fries in taste tests, 57 percent to 35 percent, with 8 percent no opinion. After "certifrying" 300,000 managers and employees on the new frying procedures, the fries were launched in early 1998 with a $70 million marketing budget. The launch turned to disaster. The reason: The new fry proved too complicated to get right day after day in Burger King restaurants, except under ideal conditions.[28]

By summer 2000, Burger King realized something had to be done. Solution: Launch a "new," coated fry in early 2001 that is easier for its kitchens to prepare. A commercialization stage success? You be the judge.

The Risks and Uncertainties of the Commercialization Stage   As the Burger King french fries show, the job is far from over when the new product gets to the commercialization stage. In spite of brilliant technologies, the hundreds of dot-com failures in 2000 and 2001 show the difficulty of launching successful new products.

Grocery products pose special commercialization problems. Because shelf space is so limited, many supermarkets require a **slotting fee** for new products, a payment a manufacturer makes to place a new item on a retailer's shelf. This can run to several million dollars for a single product. But there's even another potential expense. If a new grocery product does not achieve a predetermined sales target, some retailers require a **failure fee**, a penalty payment a manufacturer makes to compensate a retailer for sales its valuable shelf space failed to make. These costly slotting fees and failure fees are further examples of why large grocery product manufacturers use regional rollouts.

Speed as a Factor in New-Product Success   In recent years, companies have discovered that speed or *time to market* (TtM) is often vital in introducing a new product. Recent studies have shown that high-tech products coming to market on time are far more profitable than those arriving late. So some companies—such as Sony, Honda, 3M, and Hewlett-Packard—have overlapped the sequence of stages described in this chapter.

With this approach, termed *parallel development,* cross-functional team members who conduct the simultaneous development of both the product and the production process stay with the product from conception to production. This has enabled Hewlett-Packard (HP) to reduce the development time for computer printers from 54 months to 22. In software development, *fast prototyping* uses a "do it, try it, fix it" approach—encouraging continuing improvements even after the initial design. One result: HP introduced 100 new printer products in late 2003.[29]

Hewlett-Packard's new-product success can be traced to its founders' innovative management style that shunned the traditional rigid hierarchical structure. Instead, HP uses a decentralized system where the brainpower of its employees is freed to let them talk to whoever is needed to get the job done. This HP system is often referred to as the "birthplace of Silicon Valley."[30]

Concept Check

1. How does the development stage of the new-product process involve testing the product inside and outside the firm?

2. What is a test market?

3. What is commercialization of a new product?

CHAPTER IN REVIEW

1 *Recognize the various terms that pertain to products and services.*

A product is a good, service, or idea consisting of a bundle of tangible and intangible attributes that satisfies consumers and is received in exchange for money or some other unit of value. Firms can offer a range of products, which involve decisions regarding the product item, product line, and product mix.

2 *Identify the ways in which consumer and business goods and services can be classified.*

Products can be classified by type of user and tangibility. By user, the major distinctions are consumer goods, which are products purchased by the ultimate consumer, and business goods, which are products that assist in providing other products for resale. By degree of tangibility, products may be classified as (*a*) nondurable goods, which are consumed in one or a few uses, (*b*) durable goods, which are items that usually last over an extended number of uses, or (*c*) services, which are activities, benefits, or satisfactions offered for sale.

Consumer goods can further be broken down based on the effort involved in the purchase decision process, marketing mix attributes used in the purchase, and the frequency of purchase: (*a*) convenience goods are items that consumers purchase frequently and with a minimum of shopping effort, (*b*) shopping goods are items for which consumers compare several alternatives on selected criteria, (*c*) specialty goods are items that consumers make special efforts to seek out and buy, and (*d*) unsought goods are items that consumers do not either know about or initially want.

Business goods can further be broken down into (*a*) production goods, which are items used in the manufacturing process that become part of the final product, such as raw materials or component parts, and (*b*) support goods, which are items used to assist in producing other goods and services and include installations, accessory equipment, supplies, and services.

3 *Explain the implications of alternative ways of viewing "newness" in new products and services.*

A product may be defined as "new" if it (*a*) is functionally different from the firm's existing products, (*b*) falls within the FTC's definition, (*c*) is a product line extension, a significant innovation, or a revolutionary new product, or (*d*) affects the degree of learning that consumers must engage in to use the product. With a continuous innovation, no new behaviors must be learned. With a dynamically continuous innovation, only minor behavioral changes are needed. With a discontinuous innovation, consumers must learn entirely new consumption patterns.

4 *Describe the factors contributing to a product's or service's failure.*

A new product often fails for these marketing reasons: (*a*) insignificant points of difference, (*b*) incomplete market and product definition before product development begins, (*c*) too little market attractiveness, (*d*) poor execution of the marketing mix, (*e*) poor product quality on critical factors, (*f*) bad timing, and (*g*) no economical access to buyers.

5 *Explain the purposes of each step of the new-product process.*

The new-product process consists of seven stages a firm uses to develop a salable good or service: (1) New-product strategy development involves defining the role for the new product within the firm's overall objectives. (2) Idea generation involves developing a pool of concepts from consumers, employees, basic R&D, and competitors to serve as candidates for new products. (3) Screening and evaluation involves evaluating new product ideas to eliminate those that are not feasible from a technical or consumer perspective. (4) Business analysis involves defining the features of the new product, developing the marketing strategy and marketing program to introduce it, and making a financial forecast. (5) Development involves not only producing a prototype product but also testing it in the lab and on consumers to see that it meets the standards set for it. (6) Market testing involves exposing actual products to prospective consumers under realistic purchasing conditions to see if they will buy the product. (7) Commercialization involves positioning and launching a product in full-scale production and sales with a specific marketing program.

FOCUSING ON KEY TERMS

business analysis p. 277
business goods p. 263
commercialization p. 280
consumer goods p. 263
convenience goods p. 264
development p. 277
failure fee p. 281
idea generation p. 273
market testing p. 279
new-product process p. 272
new-product strategy development p. 272
product p. 262

product line p. 262
product mix p. 263
production goods p. 265
protocol p. 270
screening and evaluation p. 275
shopping goods p. 264
Six Sigma p. 273
slotting fee p. 281
specialty goods p. 264
support goods p. 265
unsought goods p. 264

DISCUSSION AND APPLICATION QUESTIONS

1 Products can be classified as either consumer or business goods. How would you classify the following products? (*a*) Johnson's baby shampoo, (*b*) a Black & Decker two-speed drill, and (*c*) an arc welder.

2 Are products such as Nature Valley Granola bars and Eddie Bauer hiking boots convenience, shopping, specialty, or unsought goods?

3 Based on your answer to question 2, how would the marketing actions differ for each product and the classification to which you assigned it?

4 In terms of the behavioral effect on consumers, how would a PC, such as an Apple PowerBook be classified? In light of this classification, what actions would you suggest to the manufacturers of these products to increase their sales in the market?

5 Several alternative definitions were presented for a new product. How would a company's marketing strategy be affected if it used (*a*) the legal definition or (*b*) a behavioral definition?

6 What methods would you suggest to assess the potential commercial success for the following new products? (*a*) a new, improved ketchup, (*b*) a three-dimensional television system that took the company 10 years to develop, and (*c*) a new children's toy on which the company holds a patent.

7 Concept testing is an important step in the new-product process. Outline the concept tests for (*a*) an electrically powered car and (*b*) a new loan payment system for automobiles that is based on a variable interest rate. What are the differences in developing concept tests for products as opposed to services?

GOING ONLINE   Jalapeño Soda, Anyone?

Jalapeño soda? Aerosol mustard? Fingos? These are just three of the more than 70,000 products (both successes and failures) on the shelves of the NewProductWorks Showcase in Ann Arbor, Michigan. Visit its new website (www.newproductworks.com). Study the "Hits & Misses" categories such as "We Expect Them to Be Successes," which are those that probably will be commercial successes; "Jury Is Out," products whose future is in doubt; "Failures," which are recent products that have failed miserably; and "Favorite Failures," which are those that cause people to ask "What *were* they thinking?" Pick

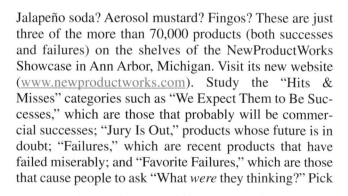

two of the failed products and try to identify the reasons discussed earlier in the chapter that may have led to their failure. Contrast these failed products with those that are deemed successes to learn why they became "sure-fire winners."

BUILDING YOUR MARKETING PLAN

In fine-tuning the product strategy for your marketing plan, do these two things:

1 Develop a simple two-column table in which (*a*) market segments of potential customers are in the first column and (*b*) the one or two key points of differences of the product to satisfy the segment's needs are in the second column.

2 Look back at Figure 2–4, which describes four alternative market-product strategies to expand sales revenues. Write specific ideas for market and product opportunities for your business in each of the four cells in the figure.

VIDEO CASE 10   3M™ Greptile Grip™ Golf Glove: Great Gripping!

"Marketing is not brain surgery," says Dr. George Dierberger, Marketing and International Manager of 3M's Sports and Leisure Products Project. "We tend to make it a lot more difficult than it is. 3M wins with its technology. We're not in the 'me-too' business and in marketing we've got to remember that."

3M'S MICROREPLICATION TECHNOLOGY AND ITS GREPTILE GOLF GLOVE

3M is a $20 billion global, diversified technology company. Among its well-known brands are Post-it Notes, Scotch tape, Scotch Brite scouring pads, and Nexcare bandages. The key to 3M's marketing successes is its commitment to innovation. For more than a century, 3M's management has given its employees the freedom to try new ideas. This "culture of creativity" has led to the commercialization of more than 50,000 products.

The Sports and Leisure Products Project is a business unit managed by Dierberger and his marketing staff. Recently, Dierberger and his staff changed the conventional thinking about golfing. Using 3M's proprietary "microreplication" technology, and applying it to a golf glove, the new Greptile gripping material 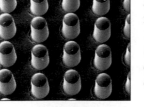 consists of thousands of tiny "gripping fingers" sewn into the upper palm and lower fingers of a golf glove. According to Dierberger, "It is the only glove on the market that actively improves a golfer's hold on the club by allowing a more relaxed grip, leading to greater driving distance with less grip pressure, even under wet conditions." Laboratory tests found that the Greptile material offers 610 percent greater gripping power than leather and 340 percent greater than tackified (sticky) grips. The result: On drives, the golf ball travels an average 10.5 feet farther!

Introduced in 2004, the new 3M Greptile Grip golf glove is made primarily of high-quality Cabretta sheep leather to give it a soft feel. Initially, 3M sold the Greptile Grip golf glove through Wal-Mart and other mass merchandisers for a suggested retail price of $11.95 to $15.95. And now it's also being stocked by golf retailers across the country like Nevada Bob's, Golfsmith, and Austad's. The golf glove is available in both men's and women's left hand versions and in small, medium, medium/large, large, and extra-large hand sizes. A right hand version for both genders appeared in 2005. 3M projected first year sales of $1 million in the U.S.

THE GOLF MARKET

Several socioeconomic and demographic trends impact the golf glove market favorably. First, the huge baby boomer population (those born between 1946 and 1964) has matured, reaching its prime earning potential. This allows for greater discretionary spending on leisure activities, such as golf. According to the National Golf Foundation (NGF), most spending on golf equipment (clubs, bags, balls, shoes, gloves, etc.) is by consumers 50 and older—today's baby boomers. Second, according to the U.S. Census, the U.S. population has shifted regionally from the East and North to the South and West, where golfing is popular year around due to the temperate weather. Third, the number of U.S. golf courses has been growing, totaling about 15,000 at the end of 2004.

Finally, golf is becoming an increasingly popular leisure activity for all age groups and ethnic backgrounds. According to the NGF, golf participants in the U.S. totaled 37.9 million in 2003, an all-time high. Female golfers now account for about 25 percent of all golfers while minority participation has increased to over 10 percent. According to the National Sporting Goods Association, sales of golf equipment was $3.1 billion in 2004, an increase of 2 percent from 2003.

THE GOLF GLOVE MARKET

The global market for golf gloves is estimated at $300 million, with the U.S. at $180 million or 60 percent of worldwide sales. Historically, about 80 percent of golf gloves are sold through public and private on- and off-course golf pro specialty shops, golf superstores, and sporting good superstores. However, mass merchandisers have recently increased their shares due to the typically lower prices offered by these retailers. FootJoy and Titleist, both owned by Acushnet, are the top two golf glove market share leaders. Nike, which recently entered the golf equipment market with Tiger Woods as its spokesperson, has a measurable share of the golf glove market. These golf glove marketers focus on technology and comfort to create points of difference from its competitors, such as the recently introduced FootJoy SciFlex™ glove ($18), the Titleist Perma-Tech™ glove ($19), and the Nike DriFit glove ($18).

3M'S NEW PRODUCT PROCESS

Since about half of 3M's products are less than five years old, the process used by 3M to develop new product innovations is critical to its success and continued growth.

Every innovation must meet 3M's new product criteria: (1) be a patentable or trademarked technology; (2) offer a superior value proposition to consumers; and (3) change the basis of competition by achieving a significant point of difference.

When developing a new product innovation such as the 3M Greptile Grip golf glove, 3M uses a rigorous seven-step process: (1) ideas, (2) concept, (3) feasibility, (4) development, (5) scale-up, (6) launch, and (7) post-launch. "But innovation is not a linear path—not just A, then B, then C," says Dierberger. "It's the adjustments you make after you've developed the product that determines your success. And it's learning lessons from testing on real customers to make the final 'tweaks'— changing the price points, improving the benefits statement on the packaging, and sharpening the advertising appeals."

In the case of the 3M Greptile Grip golf glove, countless other examples of these adjustments appeared. Mike Kuhl, marketing coordinator at 3M, points out, "Consumer testing labs said the information on the back of our package was incomplete so we had dozens of golfers hit drives using our glove and competitive gloves to compare driving distance." And says 3M packaging engineer Travis Strom, "Our first glove package 'pillowed'—bulked up—on the shelf, had hard-to-read text, and wasn't appealing to golfers, so we had to redesign it. After all, you only have a few seconds to capture the customer's attention with the package and make a sale."

THE FUTURE OF 3M GOLF AND GREPTILE

In 2005, 3M Golf launched a premium golf glove consisting of the highest quality Cabretta leather and selling for a suggested retail price of $16.95 to $19.95. On the

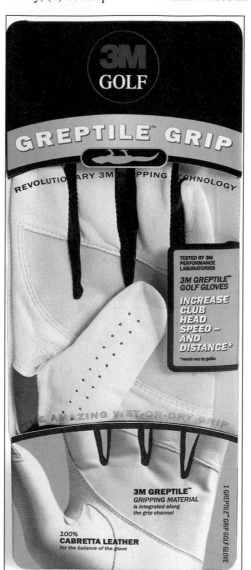

drawing board: 3M Greptile Grip golf tape that can be applied to golf club grips and possibly a line of Greptile Grip golf grips to double the gripping power when used in conjunction with the Greptile Grip golf glove. In 2006, 3M intends to launch versions of its Greptile Grip golf gloves in Japan and Europe, the second and third largest golf markets behind the U.S. Finally, 3M may develop and market baseball and softball batting gloves using the Greptile material in 2006 if the manufacturing and channels for golf gloves can been augmented.

Questions

1   What are the characteristics of the target market for the 3M Greptile Grip golf glove?

2   What are the key points of difference of the 3M Greptile Grip golf glove when compared to competitors' products, such as FootJoy and Nike? Substitute products, such as golf grips?

3   How does the Greptile Grip golf glove meet 3M's three criteria for new products?

4   Since 3M has no prior products for the golf market, what special promotion and distribution problems might 3M have?

5   How would you rate the 3M Greptile Grip golf glove on the following reasons for success and failure: (*a*) significant points of difference; (*b*) size and growth of the golf market; (*c*) product quality; (*d*) market timing; (*e*) execution of the marketing mix; (*f*) synergy or fit with 3M's R&D, manufacturing, and/or marketing capabilities; and (*g*) access to consumers?

PROPER HYDRATION
ISN'T ROCKET SCIENCE.
IT'S CHEMISTRY.

Athletes perform at their best when they replace the essential elements they sweat out.
Water doesn't have them. Gatorade does. Nothing rehydrates, replenishes, and refuels athletes better.

is it in you?

11

MANAGING PRODUCTS AND BRANDS

LEARNING OBJECTIVES

After reading this chapter you should be able to:

1 Explain the product life-cycle concept.

2 Identify ways that marketing executives manage a product's life cycle.

3 Recognize the importance of branding and alternative branding strategies.

4 Describe the role of packaging, labeling, and warranties in the marketing of a product.

GATORADE: AN UNQUENCHABLE THIRST FOR COMPETITION

The thirst for Gatorade is unquenchable. This brand powerhouse has posted yearly sales gains over four decades and commands 85 percent of the sports beverage market in the United States.

Like Kleenex in the tissue market and Jello among gelatin desserts, Gatorade has become synonymous with sports beverages. Concocted in 1965 at the University of Florida as a rehydration beverage for the school's football team, the drink was coined "Gatorade" by an opposing team's coach after watching his team lose to the Florida Gators in the Orange Bowl. The name stuck, and a new beverage product class was born.

Stokely–Van Camp Inc. made a deal for the Gatorade formula in 1967 and commercialized the product. The original Gatorade was a liquid with a lemon-lime flavor. An orange flavor was introduced in 1971 and a fruit punch flavor in 1983. Instant Gatorade was launched in 1979. The Quaker Oats Company purchased Stokely–Van Camp in 1983, and Quaker Oats executives quickly grew sales through a variety of means. More flavors were added and multiple package sizes were offered using different containers—glass and plastic bottles and aluminum cans. Regional distribution expanded first including new distribution in convenience stores and supermarkets, followed by vending machines and fountain service. Consistent advertising and promotion effectively conveyed the product's unique benefits and links to athletic competition using popular athletes such as Michael Jordan and Mia Hamm as spokespersons. International opportunities were vigorously pursued. Today, Gatorade is sold in 78 countries in North America, Europe, Latin America, the Middle East, Africa, and Australasia and has become a global brand.

Gatorade's success is a direct result of masterful product and brand management.

Gatorade
www.gatorade.com

Brand development has been a key factor in Gatorade's success. Quaker Oats introduced Gatorade Frost in 1997, with a "lighter, crisper," taste aimed at expanding the brand's reach beyond participants in organized sports to other usage occasions. Gatorade Fierce with a "bolder" taste was launched in 1999. In the same year, Gatorade entered the bottled-water category with Propel Fitness Water, a lightly flavored water fortified with vitamins. In 2001, the Gatorade Performance Series was introduced, featuring the Gatorade Energy Bar, Gatorade Energy Drink, and Gatorade Nutritional Shake. Brand development continued after PepsiCo, Inc., purchased Quaker Oats and the Gatorade brand in 2001. Gatorade All Stars, specifically designed for teens, and Gatorade Xtremo, developed for Latino consumers with an exotic blend of flavors and a bilingual label, were introduced in 2002. Gatorade X-Factor, with three unique flavors of its own, followed in 2003, bringing the total number of Gatorade flavors to 30. Today, some 40 years after its creation, Gatorade remains a multimillion dollar growth brand with seemingly unlimited potential.[1]

The marketing of Gatorade illustrates effective product and brand management in a dynamic marketplace. This chapter shows how the actions taken by Gatorade executives are typical of those made by successful marketers.

THE PRODUCT LIFE CYCLE

Products, like people, have been viewed as having a life cycle. The concept of the **product life cycle** describes the stages a new product goes through in the marketplace: introduction, growth, maturity, and decline (Figure 11–1).[2] There are two curves shown in this figure, total industry sales revenue and total industry profit, which represent the sum of sales revenue and profit of all firms producing the product. The reasons for the changes in each curve and the marketing decisions involved are discussed in the following pages.

Introduction Stage

The introduction stage of the product life cycle occurs when a product is first introduced to its intended target market. During this period, sales grow slowly, and profit is minimal. The lack of profit is often the result of large investment costs in product development, such as the $1 billion spent by Gillette to develop and launch the MACH3 razor shaving system. The marketing objective for the company at this stage is to create consumer awareness and stimulate *trial*—the initial purchase of a product by a consumer.

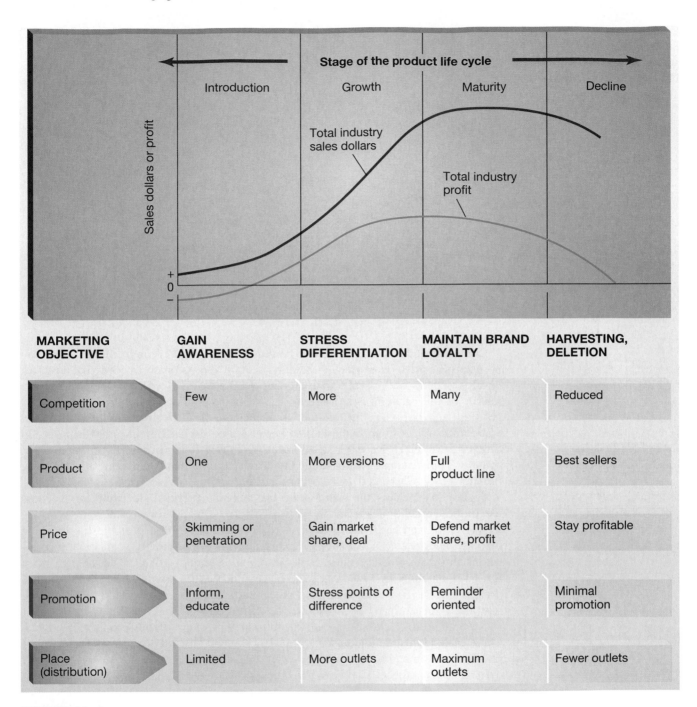

MARKETING OBJECTIVE	GAIN AWARENESS	STRESS DIFFERENTIATION	MAINTAIN BRAND LOYALTY	HARVESTING, DELETION
Competition	Few	More	Many	Reduced
Product	One	More versions	Full product line	Best sellers
Price	Skimming or penetration	Gain market share, deal	Defend market share, profit	Stay profitable
Promotion	Inform, educate	Stress points of difference	Reminder oriented	Minimal promotion
Place (distribution)	Limited	More outlets	Maximum outlets	Fewer outlets

FIGURE 11–1

How stages of the product life cycle relate to a firm's marketing objectives and marketing mix actions

Companies often spend heavily on advertising and other promotion tools to build awareness among consumers in the introduction stage. For example, Gillette budgeted $300 million in advertising alone to introduce the MACH3 razor to consumers.[3] These expenditures are often made to stimulate *primary demand,* the desire for the product class rather than for a specific brand, since there are few competitors with the same product. As more competitors introduce their own products and the product progresses along its life cycle, company attention is focused on creating *selective demand,* the preference for a specific brand.

Other marketing mix variables also are important at this stage. Gaining distribution can be a challenge because channel intermediaries may be hesitant to carry a new product. Moreover, in this stage a company often restricts the number of variations of the product to ensure control of product quality. For example, Gatorade came in only one flavor. Gillette offered only a single version of the MACH3 razor.

FIGURE 11-2

Product life cycle for the stand-alone fax machine for business use: 1970–2006

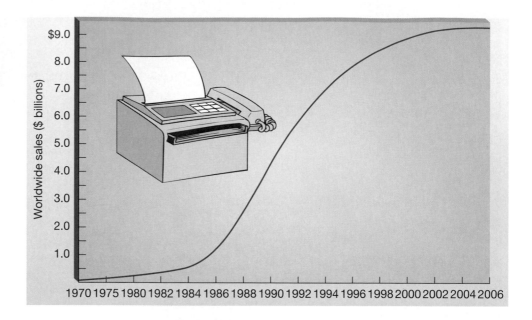

During introduction, pricing can be either high or low. A high initial price may be used as part of a *skimming* strategy to help the company recover the costs of development as well as capitalize on the price insensitivity of early buyers. 3M is a master of this strategy. According to a 3M manager, "We hit fast, price high, and get the heck out when the me-too products pour in."[4] High prices tend to attract competitors eager to enter the market because they see the opportunity for profit. To discourage competitive entry, a company can price low, referred to as *penetration pricing*. This pricing strategy helps build unit volume, but a company must closely monitor costs. These and other pricing techniques are covered in Chapter 14.

Figure 11–2 charts the stand-alone fax machine product life cycle for business use in the United States from the early 1970s to 2006.[5] As shown, sales grew slowly in the 1970s and early 1980s after Xerox pioneered the first portable fax machine that sent and received documents. Fax machines were originally sold direct to businesses through company salespeople and were premium priced. The average price for a fax machine in 1980 was $12,700. By today's standards, those fax machines were primitive. They contained mechanical parts, not electronic circuitry, and offered few features seen in today's models.

Several product classes are in the introductory stage of the product life cycle. These include high-definition television (HDTV) and "hybrid" (gasoline- and electric-powered) automobiles.

Growth Stage

The second stage of the product life cycle, growth, is characterized by rapid increases in sales. It is in this stage that competitors appear. For example, Figure 11–2 shows the dramatic increase in sales of fax machines from 1986 to 1995. The number of companies selling fax machines was also increasing, from one in the early 1970s to four in the late 1970s to seven manufacturers in 1983, which sold nine brands. By 1995 there were some 25 manufacturers and 60 brands from which to choose.

The result of more competitors and more aggressive pricing is that profit usually peaks during the growth stage. For instance, the average price for a fax machine declined from $3,300 in 1985 to $500 in 1995. At this stage, the emphasis of advertising shifts to stimulating selective demand, in which product benefits are compared with those of competitors' offerings for the purpose of gaining market share.

Product sales in the growth stage grow at an increasing rate because of new people trying or using the product and a growing proportion of *repeat purchasers*—people who tried the product, were satisfied, and bought again. As a product moves through the life cycle, the ratio of repeat to trial purchasers grows. Failure to achieve substantial repeat purchasers usually means an early death for a product. This happened to Alberto-Culver's Mr. Culver's Sparklers, which were solid air fresheners that looked like stained glass. The product moved quickly from the introduction to the growth stage, but then sales plummeted. Why? There were almost no repeat purchasers because buyers treated the product like cheap window decorations, left them there, and didn't buy new ones. Durable fax machines meant that replacement purchases were rare; however, it was common for more than one machine to populate a business as their use became more widespread. In 1995, there was one fax machine for every eight people in a business in the United States.

Changes start to appear in the product during the growth stage. To help differentiate a company's brand from its competitors, an improved version or new features are added to the original design, and product proliferation occurs. Changes in fax machines included: (1) models with built-in telephones; (2) models that used plain, rather than thermal, paper for copies; (3) models that integrated telex for electronic mail purposes; and (4) models that allowed for secure (confidential) transmissions. For Gatorade, new flavors and package sizes were added during the growth stage.

In the growth stage it is important to gain as much distribution for the product as possible. In the retail store, for example, this often means that competing companies fight for display and shelf space. Expanded distribution in the fax industry is an example. In 1986, early in the growth stage, only 11 percent of office machine dealers carried this equipment. By the mid-1990s, more than 70 percent of these dealers sold fax equipment, distribution was expanded to other stores selling electronic equipment, and the fight continues for market share.

Hybrid automobiles made by Ford are in the introductory stage of the product life cycle. Digital cameras produced by Canon are in the growth stage. Each product and company faces unique challenges based on its product life-cycle stage.

Ford
www.ford.com

Canon
www.canon.com

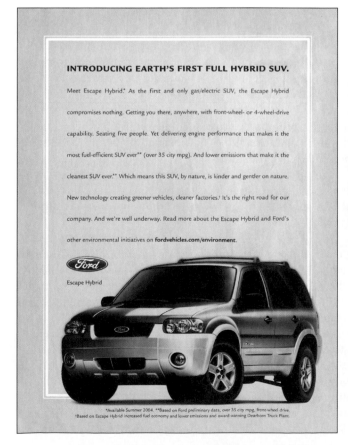

Numerous product classes or industries are in the growth stage of the product life cycle. Examples include DVD players and digital cameras.

Maturity Stage

The third stage, maturity, is characterized by a slowing of total industry sales or product class revenue. Also, marginal competitors begin to leave the market. Most consumers who would buy the product are either repeat purchasers of the item or have tried and abandoned it. Sales increase at a decreasing rate in the maturity stage as fewer new buyers enter the market. Profit declines because there is fierce price competition among many sellers and the cost of gaining new buyers at this stage increases. By 2005, the average price for a fax machine had dropped below $100.

Marketing attention in the maturity stage is often directed toward holding market share through further product differentiation and finding new buyers. Gillette, for example, differentiated its MACH3 razor through new product features specifically designed for women and then launched the Gillette for Women Venus razor just as the MACH3 razor entered its maturity stage. Fax machine manufacturers developed Internet-enabled multifunctional models that include product features suitable for small and home businesses, which today represent a substantial portion of industry sales. Still, a major consideration in a company's strategy in this stage is to reduce overall marketing cost by improving promotional and distribution efficiency.

Fax machines for business use entered the maturity stage in the late 1990s. By 2006, 90 percent of industry sales were captured by five producers (Hewlett-Packard, Matsushita, Lexmark, Brother, and Sharp), reflecting the departure of marginal competitors. By early 2006, 100 million stand-alone fax machines for business use were installed throughout the world.

Numerous product classes and industries are in the maturity stage of their product life cycle. These include soft drinks, automobiles, and conventional TVs.

Decline Stage

The decline stage occurs when sales and profits begin to drop. Frequently, a product enters this stage not because of any wrong strategy on the part of the company but because of environmental changes. Technological innovation often precedes the decline stage as newer technologies replace older technologies. The word-processing capability of personal computers pushed typewriters into decline. Compact discs did the same to cassette tapes in the prerecorded music industry. Will Internet technology and e-mail spell doom for fax machines? The accompanying Marketing NewsNet offers one perspective on this question.[6]

Products in the decline stage tend to consume a disproportionate share of management time and financial resources relative to their potential future worth. A company will follow one of two strategies to handle a declining product: deletion or harvesting.

Deletion   Product *deletion,* or dropping the product from the company's product line, is the most drastic strategy. Because a residual core of consumers still consume or use a product even in the decline stage, product elimination decisions are not taken lightly. For example, Gillette continues to sell its Liquid Paper correction fluid for use with typewriters in the era of word-processing equipment.

Harvesting   A second strategy, *harvesting,* is when a company retains the product but reduces marketing costs. The product continues to be offered, but salespeople do not allocate time in selling nor are advertising dollars spent. The purpose of harvesting is to maintain the ability to meet customer requests. Coca-Cola, for instance, still sells Tab, its first diet cola, to a small group of die-hard fans. According to Coke's CEO, "It shows you care. We want to make sure those who want Tab, get Tab."[7]

MARKETING NEWSNET

Will E-Mail Spell Doom for the Familiar Fax?

TECHNOLOGY & E-COMMERCE

Technological substitution often causes the decline stage in the product life cycle. Will the Internet and e-mail replace fax machines?

This question has caused heated debates. Even though sales of computers with Internet access are in the growth stage of the product life cycle, fax machine sales continue to grow as well. Industry analysts estimate that there are 1.5 billion e-mail mailboxes worldwide. However, the growth of e-mail has not affected faxing because the two technologies do not directly compete for the same messaging applications.

E-mail is used for text messages and faxing is predominately used for communicating formatted documents by business users. Fax usage is expected to increase through 2007, even though unit sales of fax machines has plateaued on a worldwide basis. Internet technology may eventually replace facsimile technology, but not in the immediate future.

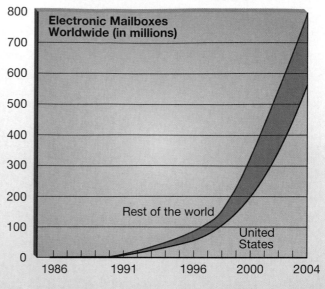

Some Dimensions of the Product Life Cycle

Some important aspects of product life cycles are (1) their length, (2) the shape of their sales curves, (3) how they vary with different levels of products, and (4) the rate at which consumers adopt products.

Length of the Product Life Cycle   There is no exact time that a product takes to move through its life cycle. As a rule, consumer products have shorter life cycles than business products. For example, many new consumer food products such as Frito-Lay's WOW brand potato chips move from the introduction stage to maturity in 18 months. The availability of mass communication vehicles informs consumers faster and shortens life cycles. Also, technological change tends to shorten product life cycles as new product innovation replaces existing products.

Shape of the Product Life Cycle   The product life-cycle sales curve shown in Figure 11–1 is the *generalized life cycle,* but not all products have the same shape to their curve. In fact, there are several different life-cycle curves, each type suggesting different marketing strategies. Figure 11–3 on the next page shows the shape of life-cycle sales curves for four different types of products: high-learning, low-learning, fashion, and fad products.

A *high-learning product* is one for which significant education of the customer is required and there is an extended introductory period (Figure 11–3A). It may surprise you, but personal computers had this type of life-cycle curve because consumers in the 1980s had to understand the benefits of purchasing the product or be educated in a new way of performing familiar tasks. Convection ovens, for example, required consumers to learn a new way of cooking and alter familiar recipes used with conventional ovens. As a result, these ovens spent years in the introductory period.

In contrast, for a *low-learning product* sales begin immediately because little learning is required by the consumer, and the benefits of purchase are readily understood

FIGURE 11–3

Alternative product life cycles

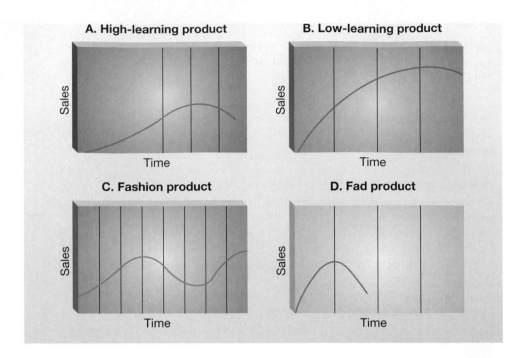

A. High-learning product

B. Low-learning product

C. Fashion product

D. Fad product

(Figure 11–3B). This product often can be easily imitated by competitors, so the marketing strategy is to broaden distribution quickly. In this way, as competitors rapidly enter, most retail outlets already have the innovator's product. It is also important to have the manufacturing capacity to meet demand. An example of a successful low-learning product is Gillette's MACH3 razor. MACH3 recorded $9 billion in worldwide sales in the brief span of five years.[8]

A *fashion product* (Figure 11–3C), such as hemline lengths on skirts or lapel widths on jackets, is introduced, declines, and then seems to return. Life cycles for fashion products most often appear in women's and men's clothing styles. The length of the cycles may be years or decades.

A *fad* experiences rapid sales on introduction and then an equally rapid decline (Figure 11–3D). These products are typically novelties and have a short life cycle. They include car tattoos sold in southern California and described as the first removable and reusable graphics for automobiles, and vinyl dresses, fleece bikinis, and an AstroTurf miniskirt made by Thump, Inc., a Minnesota clothing company.[9]

The Product Level: Class and Form   The product life cycle shown in Figure 11–1 is a total industry or product class sales curve. Yet, in managing a product it is important to often distinguish among the multiple life cycles (class and form) that may exist. **Product class** refers to the entire product category or industry, such as video game consoles and software shown in Figure 11–4.[10] **Product form** pertains to variations within the class. For video games, product form exists in the computing capability of game consoles such as 8-, 16-, 32/64-, and 128-bit machines such as Sony's PlayStation 2, Nintendo's GameCube, and Microsoft's Xbox. Game consoles and software have a life cycle of their own. They typically move from the introduction stage to maturity in five years. PlayStation 3 and rival game consoles and software arrived in 2005 on schedule.

The Life Cycle and Consumers   The life cycle of a product depends on sales to consumers. Not all consumers rush to buy a product in the introductory stage, and the shapes of the life-cycle curves indicate that most sales occur after the product has been on the market for some time. In essence, a product diffuses, or spreads, through the population, a concept called the *diffusion of innovation.*[11]

FIGURE 11–4
Video game console and
software life cycles by product
class and product form

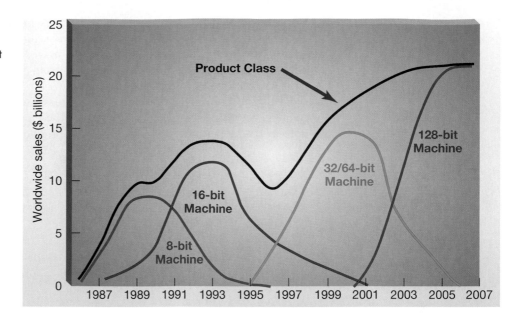

Some people are attracted to a product early, while others buy it only after they see their friends with the item. Figure 11–5 shows the consumer population divided into five categories of product adopters based on when they adopt a new product. Brief profiles accompany each category. For any product to be successful, it must be purchased by innovators and early adopters. This is why manufacturers of new pharmaceuticals try to gain adoption by leading hospitals, clinics, and physicians that are widely respected in the medical field. Once accepted by innovators and early adopters, the adoption of new products moves on to the early majority, late majority, and laggard categories.

Several factors affect whether a consumer will adopt a new product or not. Common reasons for resisting a product in the introduction stage are usage barriers (the product is not compatible with existing habits), value barriers (the product provides no incentive to change), risk barriers (physical, economic, or social), and psychological barriers (cultural differences or image).[12]

FIGURE 11–5
Five categories and profiles of
product adopters

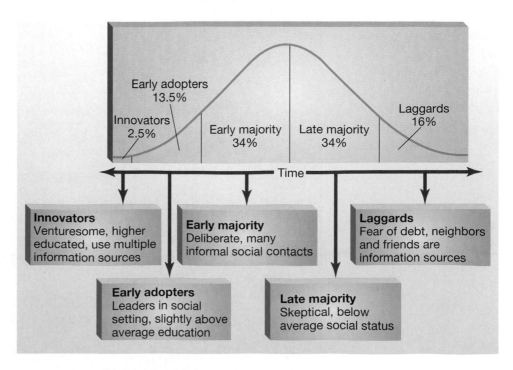

Companies attempt to overcome these barriers in numerous ways. They provide warranties, money-back guarantees, extensive usage instructions, demonstrations, and free samples to stimulate initial trial of new products. For example, software developers offer demonstrations downloaded from the Internet. Maybelline allows consumers to browse through the Cover Girl Color Match system on its website to find out how certain makeup products will look. Free samples are one of the most popular means to gain consumer trial. In fact, 71 percent of consumers consider a sample to be the best way to evaluate a new product.[13]

Concept Check

1. Advertising plays a major role in the _____ stage of the product life cycle, and _____ plays a major role in maturity.

2. How do high-learning and low-learning products differ?

3. What does the life cycle of a fashion product look like?

MANAGING THE PRODUCT LIFE CYCLE

An important task for a firm is to manage its products through the successive stages of their life cycles. This section describes the role of the product manager who is usually responsible for this, and analyzes three ways to manage a product through its life cycle: modifying the product, modifying the market, and repositioning the product.

Role of a Product Manager

The product manager, sometimes called *brand manager*, manages the marketing efforts for a close-knit family of products or brands.[14] Introduced by Procter & Gamble in 1928, the product manager style of marketing organization is used by consumer goods

Harley-Davidson's redesigned Sportster motorcycle features smaller hand grips, a lower seat, and an easier-to-pull clutch lever to create an even more comfortable ride for first-time motorcycle buyers.

Harley-Davidson, Inc.
www.harley-davidson.com

firms, including General Mills and PepsiCo, and by industrial firms such as Intel and Hewlett-Packard. The U.S. Postal Service employs product managers as well. All product managers are responsible for managing existing products through the stages of the life cycle. Some are also responsible for developing new products. Product managers' marketing responsibilities include developing and executing a marketing program for the product line described in an annual marketing plan and approving ad copy, media selection, and package design. The role of product managers in planning, implementing, and controlling marketing strategy is covered in Chapter 22.

Modifying the Product

Product modification involves altering a product's characteristic, such as its quality, performance, or appearance, to try to increase the product's sales. Wrinkle-free and stain-resistant clothing made possible by nanotechnology has revolutionized the men's and women's apparel business and stimulated industry sales of casual pants, shirts, and blouses. Harley-Davidson modified its entry-level Sportster line of motorcycles by including smaller hand grips, a lower seat, and an easier-to-pull clutch lever to create a more comfortable ride for first-time motorcycle buyers.[15]

New features, packages, or scents can be used to change a product's characteristics and give the sense of a revised product. Procter & Gamble revamped Pantene shampoo and conditioner with a new vitamin formula and relaunched the brand with a multimillion-dollar advertising and promotion campaign. The result? Pantene, a brand first introduced in the 1940s, became the top-selling shampoo and conditioner in the United States in an industry with more than 1,000 competitors.

Modifying the Market

With **market modification** strategies, a company tries to find new customers, increase a product's use among existing customers, or create new use situations.

Finding New Users   Produce companies have begun marketing and packaging prunes as dried plums for the purpose of attracting younger buyers. Sony expanded its user base by developing PlayStation 2 video games for children under 13 years old.[16]

Increasing Use   Promoting more frequent usage has been a strategy of Campbell Soup Company. Because soup consumption rises in the winter and declines during the summer, the company now advertises more heavily in warm months to encourage consumers to think of soup as more than a cold-weather food. Similarly, the Florida

The Milk Processor Education Program (MilkPEP) promotes the use of milk rather than water or other ingredients in preparing food. According to a MilkPEP executive, "If every household one day a week added milk rather than water to instant coffee and made a caffe latte, it would add [up to] $100 million to the bottom line of the milk industry."

The Milk Processor Education Program
www.whymilk.com

ETHICS AND SOCIAL RESPONSIBILITY ALERT

Consumer Economics of Downsizing—Get Less, Pay More

ETHICS

For more than 30 years, Starkist put 6.5 ounces of tuna into its regular-sized can. Today, Starkist puts 6.125 ounces of tuna into its can, but charges the same price. Frito-Lay (Doritos and Lay's snack chips), Procter & Gamble (Pampers and Luvs disposable diapers), Nestlé (Poland Spring and Calistoga bottled waters) have whittled away at package contents 5 to 10 percent while maintaining their products' package size, dimensions, and prices. Kimberly-Clark cut its retail price on its jumbo pack of Huggies diapers from $13.50 to $12.50, but reduced the number of diapers per pack from 48 to 42. Georgia-Pacific reduced the content of its Brawny paper towel six-roll pack by 20 percent without lowering the price.

Consumer advocates charge that downsizing the content of packages while maintaining prices is a subtle and unannounced way of taking advantage of consumer buying habits. They also say downsizing is a price increase in

disguise and deceptive, but legal. Manufacturers argue that this practice is a way of keeping prices from rising beyond psychological barriers for their products.

Is downsizing an unethical practice if manufacturers do not inform consumers that the package contents are less than they were previously?

Orange Growers Association advocates drinking orange juice throughout the day rather than for breakfast only.

Creating New Use Situations   Finding new uses for an existing product has been the strategy behind Woolite, a laundry soap. Originally intended for the hand washing of woolen material, Woolite now promotes itself for use with all fine clothing items. The Milk Processor Education Program suggests a new use situation by substituting milk for water or other ingredients in preparing food.

Repositioning the Product

Often a company decides to reposition its product or product line in an attempt to bolster sales. *Product repositioning* is changing the place a product occupies in a consumer's mind relative to competitive products. A firm can reposition a product by changing one or more of the four marketing mix elements. Four factors that trigger a repositioning action are discussed next.

Reacting to a Competitor's Position   One reason to reposition a product is because a competitor's entrenched position is adversely affecting sales and market share. New Balance, Inc., successfully repositioned its athletic shoes to focus on fit and comfort rather than competing head-on against Nike and Reebok on fashion and sport. The company offers an expansive range of shoe widths with the message, "N is for fit," and it networks with podiatrists, not sport celebrities.[17]

Reaching a New Market   When Unilever introduced iced tea in Britain in the mid-1990s, sales were disappointing. British consumers viewed it as leftover hot tea, not suitable for drinking. The company made its tea carbonated and repositioned it as a cold soft drink to compete as a carbonated beverage and sales improved. Johnson & Johnson effectively repositioned St. Joseph Aspirin from one for infants to an adult low-strength aspirin to reduce the risk of heart problems or strokes.[18]

Catching a Rising Trend Changing consumer trends can also lead to repositioning. Growing consumer interest in foods that offer health and dietary benefits is an example and many products have been repositioned to capitalize on this trend. Quaker Oats makes the FDA-approved claim that oatmeal, as part of a low-saturated-fat, low-cholesterol diet, may reduce the risk of heart disease. Calcium-enriched products, such as Kraft American cheese and Uncle Ben's Calcium Plus rice, emphasize healthy bone structure for children and adults. Weight-conscious consumers have embraced low-carbohydrate diets in growing numbers. Today, every major consumer food and beverage company offers and advertises reduced-carbohydrate versions of their products, producing sales of $1 billion in 2005.[19]

Changing the Value Offered In repositioning a product, a company can decide to change the value it offers buyers and trade up or down. **Trading up** involves adding value to the product (or line) through additional features or higher-quality materials. Michelin and Goodyear have done this with a "run-flat" tire that can travel up to 50 miles at 55 miles-per-hour after suffering total air loss. Dog food manufacturers, such as Ralston Purina, also have traded up by offering superpremium foods based on "life-stage nutrition." Mass merchandisers, such as Sears and JCPenney, can trade up by adding a designer clothes section to their stores.

Trading down involves reducing the number of features, quality, or price. For example, airlines have added more seats, thus reducing leg room, and eliminated extras, such as snack service and food portions. Trading down often exists when companies engage in **downsizing**—reducing the content of packages without changing package size and maintaining or increasing the package price. Firms have been criticized for this practice, as described in the accompanying Ethics and Social Responsibility Alert.[20]

Concept Check

1. How does a product manager help manage a product's life cycle?

2. What does "creating new use situations" mean in managing a product's life cycle?

3. Explain the difference between trading up and trading down in repositioning.

BRANDING AND BRAND MANAGEMENT

A basic decision in marketing products is **branding**, in which an organization uses a name, phrase, design, symbols, or combination of these to identify its products and distinguish them from those of competitors. A **brand name** is any word, device (design, sound, shape, or color), or combination of these used to distinguish a seller's goods or services. Some brand names can be spoken, such as a Gatorade or Rollerblade. Other brand names cannot be spoken, such as the rainbow-colored apple (the *logotype* or *logo*) that Apple Computer originally put on its machines and in its ads. A **trade name** is a commercial, legal name under which a company does business. The Campbell Soup Company is the trade name of that firm.

A **trademark** identifies that a firm has legally registered its brand name or trade name so the firm has its exclusive use, thereby preventing others from using it. In the United States, more than a million trademarks are registered with the U.S. Patent and Trademark Office, and these trademarks are protected under the Lanham Act. A well-known trademark can help a company advertise its offerings to customers and develop their brand loyalty.

Because a good trademark can help sell a product, *product counterfeiting,* which involves low-cost copies of popular brands not manufactured by the original producer, has been a growing problem. Counterfeit products can steal sales from the

Can you describe the brand personality traits for these two brands? Not sure? Try visiting their websites for more information.

got2b
www.got2b.com

Mambo
www.lizclaiborne.com/mambo

original manufacturer or harm the company's reputation. U.S. companies lose between $200 billion and $250 billion each year to counterfeit products.[21] To protect against counterfeiting, the U.S. government passed the *Trademark Counterfeiting Act* (1984), which makes counterfeiting a federal offense with offenders subject to prison sentences, damage payments, and seizure of counterfeit merchandise.

Consumers may benefit most from branding. Recognizing competing products by distinct trademarks allows them to be more efficient shoppers. Consumers can recognize and avoid products with which they are dissatisfied, while becoming loyal to other, more satisfying brands. As discussed in Chapter 5, brand loyalty often eases consumers' decision making by eliminating the need for an external search.

Brand Personality and Brand Equity

Product managers recognize that brands offer more than product identification and a means to distinguish their products from competitors.[22] Successful and established brands take on a **brand personality**, a set of human characteristics associated with a brand name. Research shows that consumers often assign personality traits to products—traditional, romantic, rugged, sophisticated, rebellious—and choose brands that are consistent with their own or desired self-image. Marketers can and do imbue a brand with a personality through advertising that depicts a certain user or usage situation and conveys certain emotions or feelings to be associated with the brand. For example, the personality traits associated with Coca-Cola are all-American, real, and cool; with Pepsi, young, exciting, and hip; and with Dr Pepper, nonconforming, unique, and fun.

Brand name importance to a company has led to a concept called **brand equity**, the added value a given brand name gives to a product beyond the functional benefits provided. This value has two distinct advantages. First, brand equity provides a competitive advantage. The Sunkist brand implies quality fruit, and the Disney name defines children's entertainment. A second advantage is that consumers are often willing to pay a higher price for a product with brand equity. Brand equity, in this instance, is represented by the premium a consumer will pay for one brand over another when the functional benefits provided are identical. Intel microchips, Bose audio systems, Duracell batteries, Microsoft computer software, and Louis Vuitton luggage all enjoy a price premium arising from brand equity.

Creating Brand Equity Brand equity doesn't just happen. It is carefully crafted and nurtured by marketing programs that forge strong, favorable, and unique consumer associations and experiences with a brand. Brand equity resides in the minds of consumers and results from what they have learned, felt, seen, and heard about a brand over time. Marketers recognize that brand equity is not easily or quickly achieved. Rather, it arises from a sequential building process consisting of four steps (Figure 11–6).[23]

- The first step is to develop positive brand awareness and an association of the brand in consumers' minds with a product class or need to give the brand an identity. Gatorade and Kleenex have done this in the sports drink and facial tissue product classes, respectively.
- Next, a marketer must establish a brand's meaning in the minds of consumers. Meaning arises from what a brand stands for and has two dimensions—a functional, performance-related dimension and an abstract, imagery-related dimension. Nike has done this through continuous product development and improvement and its links to peak athletic performance in its integrated marketing communications program.
- The third step is to elicit the proper consumer responses to a brand's identity and meaning. Here attention is placed on how consumers think and feel about a brand. Thinking focuses on a brand's perceived quality, credibility, and superiority relative to other brands. Feeling relates to the consumer's emotional reaction to a brand. Michelin elicits both responses for its tires. Not only is Michelin thought of as a credible and superior-quality brand, but consumers also acknowledge a warm and secure feeling of safety, comfort, and self-assurance without worry or concern about the brand.

FIGURE 11–6
Customer-based brand equity pyramid

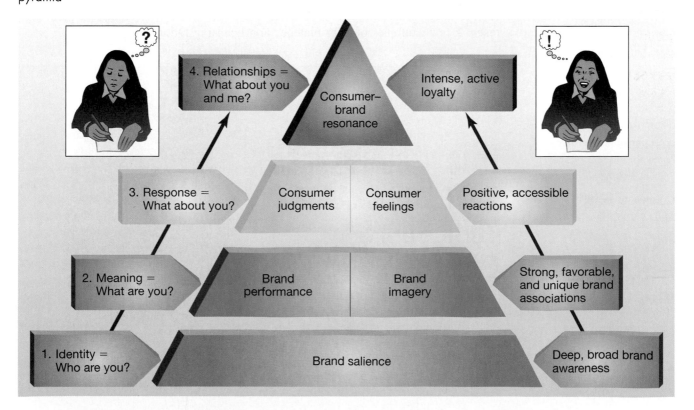

- The final, and most difficult, step is to create a consumer-brand resonance evident in an intense, active loyalty relationship between consumers and the brand. A deep psychological bond characterizes consumer-brand resonance and the personal identification consumers have with the brand. Examples of brands that have achieved this status include Harley-Davidson, Apple, and eBay.

Valuing Brand Equity Brand equity also provides a financial advantage for the brand owner.[24] Successful, established brand names, such as Gillette, Nike, Gatorade, and Nokia, have an economic value in the sense that they are intangible assets. The recognition that brands are assets is apparent in the decision to buy and sell brands. For example, Triarc Companies bought the Snapple brand from Quaker Oats in 1997 for $300 million and sold it to Cadbury Schweppes in 2000 for $900 million. This example illustrates that brands, unlike physical assets that depreciate with time and use, can appreciate in value when effectively marketed. However, brands can lose value when they are not managed properly. Consider the purchase and sale of Lender's Bagels. Kellogg bought the brand for $466 million only to sell it to Aurora Foods for $275 million three years later following deteriorating sales and profits.

Financially lucrative brand licensing opportunities arise from brand equity. **Brand licensing** is a contractual agreement whereby one company (licensor) allows its brand name(s) or trademark(s) to be used with products or services offered by another company (licensee) for a royalty or fee. For example, Playboy earns more than $260 million licensing its name for merchandise ranging from wallpaper in Europe to cooking classes in Brazil. Disney makes billions of dollars each year licensing its characters for children's toys, apparel, and games. Licensing fees for Winnie the Pooh alone exceed $3 billion annually. General Motors sells more than $2 billion in licensed products each year.[25]

Successful brand licensing requires careful marketing analysis to assure a proper match between the licensor's brand and the licensee's products. World-renowned designer Ralph Lauren has built a $5 billion business licensing his Ralph Lauren, Polo, and Chaps brands for dozens of products, including paint by Sherwin-Williams, furniture by Hendredon, footwear by Rockport, and fragrances by Cosmair. Mistakes, such as Kleenex diapers, Bic perfume, and Domino's fruit-favored bubble gum, represent a few examples of poor matches and licensing failures.

General Motors is the worldwide leader in licensed product sales among automakers. A recent licensing arrangement is for Hummer® Footwear made by Roper Footwear & Apparel.

General Motors
www.hummer.com

WEB LINK   Have an Idea for a Brand or Trade Name?
Check It Out

www.mhhe.com/Kerin

More than a million brand names or trade names are registered with the U.S. Patent and Trademark Office. Thousands more are registered each year.

An important step in choosing a brand or trade name is to determine whether the name has been already registered. The U.S. Patent and Trademark Office (www.uspto.gov) offers a valuable service by allowing individuals and companies to quickly check to see if a name has been registered.

Do you have an idea for a brand or trade name for a new snack, software package, retail outlet, or service? Check to see if the name has been registered by clicking "Trademarks," then "Search." Enter your brand name to find out if someone has registered your chosen name(s).

Picking a Good Brand Name

We take brand names such as Dial, Sanyo, Porsche, and Adidas for granted, but it is often a difficult and expensive process to pick a good name. Companies will spend between $25,000 and $100,000 to identify and test a new brand name. For instance, Intel spent $45,000 for the Pentium name given its family of microchips.[26] There are five criteria mentioned most often when selecting a good brand name.[27]

- *The name should suggest the product benefits.* For example, Accutron (watches), Easy Off (oven cleaner), Glass Plus (glass cleaner), Cling-Free (anti-static cloth for drying clothes), PowerBook (laptop computer), and Tidy Bowl (toilet bowl cleaner) all clearly describe the benefits of purchasing the product.
- *The name should be memorable, distinctive, and positive.* In the auto industry, when a competitor has a memorable name, others quickly imitate. When Ford named a car the Mustang, Pintos, Colts, and Broncos soon followed. The Thunderbird name led to the Phoenix, Eagle, Sunbird, and Firebird.
- *The name should fit the company or product image.* Sharp is a name that can apply to audio and video equipment. Excedrin, Anacin, and Nuprin are scientific-sounding names, good for an analgesic. However, naming a personal computer PCjr, as IBM did with its first computer for home use, neither fit the company nor the product. PCjr, sounded like a toy and stalled IBM's initial entry into the home-use market.
- *The name should have no legal or regulatory restrictions.* Legal restrictions produce trademark infringement suits, and regulatory restrictions arise through improper use of words. For example, the U.S. Food and Drug Administration discourages the use of the word *heart* in food brand names. This restriction led to changing the name of Kellogg's Heartwise cereal to Fiberwise, and Clorox's Hidden Valley Ranch Take Heart Salad Dressing had to be modified to Hidden Valley Ranch Low-Fat Salad Dressing. Increasingly, brand names need a corresponding address on the Internet. This further complicates name selection because millions of domain names are already registered.
- *Finally, the name should be simple* (such as Bold laundry detergent, Sure deodorant, and Bic pens) *and should be emotional* (such as Joy and Obsession perfumes). In the development of names for international use, having a non-meaningful brand name has been considered a benefit. A name such as Exxon does not have any prior impressions or undesirable images among a diverse world population of different languages and cultures. The 7Up name is another matter. In Shanghai, China, the phrase means "death through drinking" in the local dialect, and sales have suffered as a result.

Do you have an idea for a brand name? If you do, check to see if the name has been already registered with the U.S. Patent and Trademark Office by visiting its website described in the accompanying Web Link.

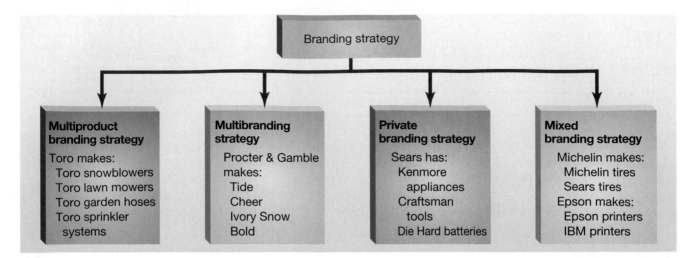

FIGURE 11–7

Alternative branding strategies

Branding Strategies

Companies can employ several different branding strategies, including multiproduct branding, multibranding, private branding, or mixed branding (Figure 11–7).

Multiproduct Branding   With **multiproduct branding**, a company uses one name for all its products in a product class. This approach is sometimes called *family branding,* or *corporate branding* when the company's trade name is used. For example, General Electric, Gerber, and Sony engage in corporate branding—the company's trade name and brand name are identical. Church & Dwight employs the Arm & Hammer family brand name for all its products featuring baking soda as the primary ingredient.

There are several advantages to multiproduct branding. Capitalizing again on brand equity, consumers who have a good experience with the product will transfer this favorable attitude to other items in the product class with the same name. Therefore, this brand strategy makes possible *line extensions,* the practice of using a current brand name to enter a new market segment in its product class. Campbell Soup Company effectively employs a multiproduct branding strategy with soup line extensions. It offers regular Campbell soup, home-cooking style, and chunky varieties and more than 100 soup flavors. This strategy can also result in lower advertising and promotion costs because the same name is used on all products, thus raising the level of brand awareness. A risk with line extension is that sales of an extension may come at the expense of other items in the company's product line. Therefore, line extensions work best when they provide incremental company revenue by taking sales away from competing brands or attracting new buyers.

Some companies employ *subbranding,* which combines a corporate or family brand with a new brand. Gatorade has successfully used subbranding with the introduction of Gatorade Frost, Gatorade Fierce, and Gatorade X-Factor, with unique flavors developed for each.

A strong brand equity also allows for *brand extension,* the practice of using a current brand name to enter a completely different product class. For instance, the equity in the Tylenol name as a trusted pain reliever allowed Johnson & Johnson to successfully extend this name to Tylenol Cold & Flu and Tylenol PM, a sleep aid. Honda's established name for motor vehicles has extended easily to snowblowers, lawn mowers, marine engines, and snowmobiles.

However, there is a risk with brand extensions. Too many uses for one brand name can dilute the meaning of a brand for consumers. Marketing experts claim this has happened to the Arm & Hammer brand given its use for toothpaste, laundry detergent, gum, cat litter, air freshener, carpet deodorizer, and antiperspirant.[28]

Black & Decker uses a multibranding strategy to reach different market segments. Black & Decker markets its line of tools for the do-it-yourselfer market with the Black & Decker name but uses the DeWalt name for its professional tool line.

Black & Decker
www.blackanddecker.com

A variation on brand extensions is the practice of **co-branding**, the pairing of two brand names of two manufacturers on a single product.[29] For example, Hershey Foods has teamed with General Mills to offer a co-branded breakfast cereal called Reese's Peanut Butter Puffs and with Nabisco to provide Chips Ahoy cookies using Hershey's chocolate morsels. Citibank co-brands MasterCard and Visa with American Airlines and Ford. Co-branding benefits firms by allowing them to enter new product classes and capitalize on an already established brand name in that product class.

Multibranding   Alternately, a company can engage in **multibranding**, which involves giving each product a distinct name. Multibranding is a useful strategy when each brand is intended for a different market segment. P&G makes Camay soap for those concerned with soft skin and Safeguard for those who want deodorant protection. Black & Decker markets its line of tools for the household do-it-yourselfer segment with the Black & Decker name but uses the DeWalt name for its professional tool line. Disney uses the Miramax and Touchstone Pictures names for films directed at adults and its Disney name for children's films.

Multibranding is applied in a variety of ways. Some companies array their brands on the basis of price-quality segments.[30] Marriott International offers 14 hotel and resort brands, each suited for a particular traveler experience and budget. To illustrate, Marriott Marquis hotels and Vacation Clubs offer luxury amenities at a premium price. Marriott and Renaissance hotels offer medium- to high-priced accommodations. Courtyard hotels and Town Place Suites appeal to economy-minded travelers, whereas the Fairfield Inn is for those on a very low travel budget. Other multibrand companies introduce new product brands as defensive moves to counteract competition. Called *fighting brands,* their chief purpose is to confront competitor brands. For instance, Frito-Lay introduced Santitas brand tortilla chip to go head-to-head against regional tortilla chip brands that were biting into sales of its

MARKETING NEWSNET

Creating Customer Value through Packaging—Pez Heads Dispense More Than Candy

CUSTOMER VALUE

Customer value can assume numerous forms. For Pez Candy, Inc. (www.pez.com), customer value manifests itself in some 250 Pez character candy dispensers. Each 99 cent refillable dispenser ejects tasty candy tablets in a variety of flavors that delight preteens and teens alike.

Pez was formulated in 1927 by Austrian food mogul Edward Haas III and successfully sold in Europe as an adult breath mint. Pez, which comes from the German word for peppermint, *pfefferminz,* was originally packaged in a hygienic, headless plastic dispenser. Pez first appeared in the United States in 1953 with a headless dispenser, marketed to adults. After conducting extensive marketing research, Pez was repositioned with fruit flavors, repackaged with licensed character heads on top of the dispenser, and remarketed as a children's product in the mid-1950s. Since then, most top-level licensed characters and hundreds of other characters have become Pez heads. Consumers eat more than 3 billion Pez tablets annually, and company sales growth exceeds that of the candy industry as a whole.

The unique Pez package dispenses a "use experience" for its customers beyond the candy itself, namely, fun. And

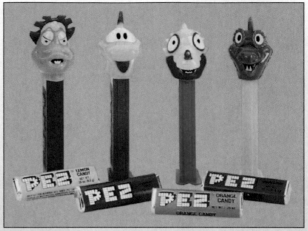

fun translates into a 98 percent awareness level for Pez among teenagers and 89 percent among mothers with children. Pez has not advertised its product for years. With that kind of awareness, who needs advertising?

flagship Doritos and Tostitos brand tortilla chips. Mattel launched its Flava brand of hip-hop fashion dolls in response to the popularity of Bratz brand dolls sold by MGA Entertainment, which were attracting the 8-to-12-year-old girl segment of Barbie brand sales.

Compared with the multiproduct approach, promotional costs tend to be higher with multibranding. The company must generate awareness among consumers and retailers for each new brand name without the benefit of any previous impressions. The advantages of this approach are that each brand is unique to each market segment and there is no risk that a product failure will affect other products in the line. Nevertheless, some large multibrand firms have found that the complexity and expense of implementing this strategy can outweigh the benefits. For example, Unilever recently pruned its brands from some 1,600 to 400 through product deletion and sales to other companies.[31]

Private Branding   A company uses **private branding**, often called *private labeling* or *reseller branding,* when it manufactures products but sells them under the brand name of a wholesaler or retailer. Rayovac, Paragon Trade Brands, and Ralcorp Holding are major suppliers of private label alkaline batteries, diapers, and grocery products, respectively. Radio Shack, Sears, Wal-Mart, and Kroger are large retailers that have their own brand names. Private branding is popular because it typically produces high profits for manufacturers and resellers. Consumers also buy them. It is estimated that one of every five items purchased at U.S. supermarkets, drugstores, and mass merchandisers bears a private brand.[32]

Mixed Branding   A fourth branding strategy is **mixed branding**, where a firm markets products under its own name(s) and that of a reseller because the segment attracted to the reseller is different from its own market. Beauty and fragrance marketer

Elizabeth Arden is a case in point. The company sells its Elizabeth Arden brand through department stores and a line of skin care products at Wal-Mart with the "skinsimple" brand name. Kodak uses a mixed branding approach in Japan to increase its sales of 35-mm film. In addition to selling its Kodak brand, the company now makes "COOP" private label film for the Japanese Consumer Cooperative Union, which is a group of 2,500 stores. Priced significantly below its Kodak brand, the private label seeks to attract the price-sensitive Japanese consumer.[33]

PACKAGING AND LABELING

The **packaging** component of a product refers to any container in which it is offered for sale and on which label information is conveyed. A **label** is an integral part of the package and typically identifies the product or brand, who made it, where and when it was made, how it is to be used, and package contents and ingredients. To a great extent, the customer's first exposure to a product is the package and label and both are an expensive and important part of marketing strategy. For Pez Candy, Inc., the character head-on-a-stick plastic container that dispenses a miniature tablet candy is the central element of its marketing strategy as described in the accompanying Marketing NewsNet.[34]

Creating Customer Value and Competitive Advantage through Packaging and Labeling

Packaging and labeling costs companies more than $100 billion annually and account for about 15 cents of every dollar spent by consumers for products.[35] Despite the cost, packaging and labeling are essential because both provide important benefits for the manufacturer, retailer, and ultimate consumer. Packaging and labeling also can provide a competitive advantage.

Communication Benefits   A major benefit of packaging is the label information on it conveyed to the consumer, such as directions on how and when to use the product and the composition of the product, which is needed to satisfy legal requirements of product disclosure. For example, the labeling system for packaged and processed

Can you name this soft-drink brand? If you can, then the package has fulfilled its purpose.

Which chip stacks up better? Frito-Lay's recent introduction of Lay's Stax potato crisps to compete against Procter & Gamble's Pringles illustrates the role of packaging in product and brand management.

Lay's Stax
www.laysstax.com

Pringles
www.pringles.com

The distinctive design of Celestial Seasonings' tea boxes reinforces the brand's positioning as a New Age, natural herbal tea.

Celestial Seasonings
www.celestialseasonings.com

foods in the United States provides a uniform format for nutritional and dietary information. Other information consists of seals and symbols, either government required or commercial seals of approval (such as the Good Housekeeping seal).

Packaging also can have brand equity benefits for a company. According to the director of marketing for L'eggs hosiery, "Packaging is important to the equity of the L'eggs brand." Why? Packaging has been shown to enhance brand recognition and facilitate the formation of strong, favorable, and unique brand associations.[36]

Functional Benefits Packaging often plays an important functional role, such as storage, convenience, protection, or product quality. Storing food containers is one example, and beverage companies have developed lighter and easier ways to stack products on shelves and in refrigerators. Examples include Coca-Cola beverage packs designed to fit neatly onto refrigerator shelves and Ocean Spray Cranberries' rectangular juice bottles that allow 10 units per package versus 8 of its former round bottles.[37]

The convenience dimension of packaging is becoming increasingly important. Kraft Miracle Whip salad dressing, Heinz ketchup, and Skippy Squeez'It peanut butter are sold in squeeze bottles; microwave popcorn has been a major market success; and Chicken of the Sea tuna and Folgers coffee are packaged in single-serving portions.

Consumer protection has become an important function of packaging, including the development of tamper-resistant containers. Today, companies commonly use safety seals or pop-tops that reveal previous opening. Nevertheless, no package is truly tamper resistant. U.S. law now provides for maximum penalties of life imprisonment and $250,000 fines for package tampering. Consumer protection through labeling exists in "open dating," which states the expected shelf life of the product.

Functional features of packaging also can affect product quality. Procter & Gamble's Pringles, with its cylindrical packaging, offers uniform chips, minimal breakage, and for some consumers, better value for the money than flex-bag packages for chips. Not to be outdone, Frito-Lay, the world's leading producer of snack chips recently decided to "stand up" to Pringles with its new line of Lay's Stax potato crisps.[38] Consumers will be the final judge of which chip stacks up better.

Perceptual Benefits A third component of packaging and labeling is the perception created in the consumer's mind. Just Born Inc., a candy manufacturer of such brands as Jolly Joes and Mike and Ike Treats, discovered the importance of this component of packaging. For many years the brands were sold in old-fashioned black and white packages, but when the packaging was changed to four color, with animated grape and cherry characters, sales increased 25 percent. Coca-Cola brought back its famous and universally recognized contoured bottle shape, this time in a 20-ounce plastic container, to further differentiate itself from competitors. Celestial Seasonings' packaging and labeling uses delicate illustrations, soft and warm colors, and quotations about life to reinforce the brand's positioning as a New Age, natural herbal tea.

Because labels list a product's source, brands competing in the global marketplace can benefit from "country of origin or manufacture" perceptions as described in Chapter 7. Consumers tend to have stereotypes about country-product pairings that they judge "best"—English tea, French perfume, Italian leather, and Japanese electronics—which can affect a brand's image. Increasingly today, Chinese firms are adopting the English language and Roman letters for their brand labels. This is being done because of the perception in many Asian countries that "things Western are good," even if consumers cannot understand the meaning of the English words.[39]

Global Trends in Packaging

Two global trends in packaging originating in the mid-1990s continue into the twenty-first century. One trend involves the environmental effects of packaging; the other focuses on packaging health and safety concerns.

Environmental Sensitivity

Environmental Sensitivity   Because of widespread worldwide concern about the growth of solid waste and the shortage of viable landfill sites, the amount, composition, and disposal of packaging material continues to receive much attention.[40] Recycling packaging material is a major thrust. Procter & Gamble now uses recycled cardboard in 70 percent of its paper packaging and is packaging Tide, Cheer, Era, and Dash detergents in jugs that contain 25 percent recycled plastic. Spic and Span liquid cleaner is packaged in 100 percent recycled material. Other firms, such as the large U.K. retailer Sainsbury, emphasize the use of less packaging material. Sainsbury examines every product it sells to ensure that each uses only the minimum material necessary for shipping and display.

European countries have been trendsetters concerning packaging guidelines and environmental sensitivity. Many of these guidelines now exist in provisions governing trade to and within the European Union. In Germany, 80 percent of packaging material must be collected, and 80 percent of this amount must be recycled or reused to reduce solid waste in landfills. U.S. firms marketing in Europe have responded to these guidelines, and ultimately benefited U.S. consumers.

Increasingly, firms are using life-cycle analysis (LCA) to examine the environmental effect of their packaging at every stage from raw material sources and production through distribution and disposal. A classic use of LCA was the decision by McDonald's to abandon the polystyrene clam shell it used to package its hamburger. LCA indicated that the environment would be better served if the amount of solid waste packaging was reduced than if the polystyrene shells were recycled. McDonald's elected to package its hamburgers in a light wrap made of paper and polyethylene and eliminate the polystyrene package altogether.

Health and Safety Concerns

Health and Safety Concerns   A second trend involves the growing health and safety concerns of packaging materials. Today, a majority of U.S. and European consumers believe companies should make sure products and their packages are safe, regardless of the cost, and companies are responding to this view in numerous ways. Most butane lighters sold today, such as those made by Scripto, contain a child-resistant safety latch to prevent misuse and accidental fire. Child-proof caps on pharmaceutical products and household cleaners and sealed lids on food packages are now common. New packaging technology and materials that extend a product's *shelf life* (the time a product can be stored) and prevent spoilage continue to be developed with special applications for less-developed countries.

PRODUCT WARRANTY

A final component for product consideration is the **warranty**, which is a statement indicating the liability of the manufacturer for product deficiencies. There are various types of product warranties with different implications for manufacturers and customers.

Some companies offer *express warranties,* which are written statements of liabilities. In recent years, the FTC has required greater disclosure on express warranties to indicate whether the warranty is a limited-coverage or full-coverage alternative. A *limited-coverage warranty* specifically states the bounds of coverage and, more important, areas of noncoverage. A *full warranty* has no limits of noncoverage. Cadillac is a company that boldly touts its warranty coverage. The *Magnuson-Moss Warranty/FTC Improvement Act* (1975) regulates the content of consumer warranties and so has strengthened consumer rights with regard to warranties.

With greater frequency, manufacturers are being held to *implied warranties,* which assign responsibility for product deficiencies to the manufacturer. Studies show that warranties are important and affect a consumer's product evaluation. Brands that have limited warranties tend to receive less positive evaluations compared with full-warranty items.

Warranties are also important in light of increasing product liability claims. In the early part of this century, the courts protected companies, but the trend now is toward "strict liability" rulings, where a manufacturer is liable for any product defect, whether it followed reasonable research standards or not. This issue is hotly contested between companies and consumer advocates.

Warranties represent much more to the buyer than just protection from negative consequences—they can hold a significant marketing advantage for the producer. Sears has built a strong reputation for its Craftsman tool line with a simple warranty: If you break a tool, it's replaced with no questions asked. Zippo has an equally simple guarantee: "If it ever fails, we'll fix it free."

Concept Check

1. What are the five criteria mentioned most often when selecting a good brand name?
2. Explain the role of packaging in terms of perception.
3. What is the difference between an expressed and an implied warranty?

CHAPTER IN REVIEW

1 *Explain the product life-cycle concept.*
The product life cycle describes the stages a new product goes through in the marketplace: introduction, growth, maturity, and decline. Product sales growth and profitability differ at each stage, and marketing managers have marketing objectives and marketing mix strategies unique to each stage based on consumer behavior and competitive factors. In the introductory stage, the need is to establish primary demand, whereas the growth stage requires selective demand strategies. In the maturity stage, the need is to maintain market share; the decline stage necessitates a deletion or harvesting strategy. Some important aspects of product life cycles are (*a*) their length, (*b*) the shape of the sales curve, (*c*) how they vary by product classes and forms, and (*d*) the rate at which consumers adopt products.

2 *Identify ways that marketing executives manage a product's life cycle.*
Marketing executives manage a product's life cycle three ways. First, they can modify the product itself by altering its characteristics, such as product quality, performance, or appearance. Second, they can modify the market by finding new customers for the product, increasing a product's use among existing customers, or creating new use situations for the product. Finally, they can reposition the product using any one or a combination of marketing mix elements. Four factors trigger a repositioning action. They include reacting to a competitor's position, reaching a new market, catching a rising trend, and changing the value offered to consumers.

3 *Recognize the importance of branding and alternative branding strategies.*
A basic decision in marketing products is branding, in which an organization uses a name, phrase, design, symbols, or a combination of these to identify its products and distinguish them from those of its competitors. Product managers recognize that brands offer more than product identification and a means to distinguish their products from competitors. Successful and established brands take on a brand personality and acquire brand equity—the added value a given brand name gives to a product beyond the functional benefits provided—that is crafted and nurtured by marketing programs that forge strong, favorable, and unique consumer associations with a brand. A good brand name should suggest the product benefits, be memorable, fit the company or product image, be free of legal restrictions, and be simple and emotional. Companies can and do employ several different branding strategies. With multiproduct branding, a company uses one name for all its products in a product class. A multibranding strategy involves giving each product a distinct name. A company uses private branding when it manufactures products but sells them under the brand name of a wholesaler or retailer. Finally, a company can employ mixed branding, where it markets products under its own name(s) and that of a reseller.

4 *Describe the role of packaging, labeling, and warranties in the marketing of a product.*
Packaging, labeling, and warranties play numerous roles in the marketing of a product. The packaging component of a product

refers to any container in which it is offered for sale and on which label information is conveyed. Manufacturers, retailers, and consumers acknowledge that packaging and labeling provide

communication, functional, and perceptual benefits. Warranties indicate the liability of the manufacturer for product deficiencies and are an important element of product and brand management.

FOCUSING ON KEY TERMS

brand equity p. 300
brand licensing p. 302
brand name p. 299
brand personality p. 300
branding p. 299
co-branding p. 305
downsizing p. 299
label p. 307
market modification p. 297
mixed branding p. 306
multibranding p. 305
multiproduct branding p. 304

packaging p. 307
private branding p. 306
product class p. 294
product form p. 294
product life cycle p. 288
product modification p. 297
trade name p. 299
trademark p. 299
trading down p. 299
trading up p. 299
warranty p. 309

DISCUSSION AND APPLICATION QUESTIONS

1 Listed here are three different products in various stages of the product life cycle. What marketing strategies would you suggest to these companies? (*a*) Canon digital cameras—growth stage, (*b*) Panasonic high-definition television—introductory stage, and (*c*) hand-held manual can openers—decline stage.

2 It has often been suggested that products are intentionally made to break down or wear out. Is this strategy a planned product modification approach?

3 The product manager of GE is reviewing the penetration of trash compactors in American homes. After more than two decades in existence, this product is in relatively few homes. What problems can account for this

poor acceptance? What is the shape of the trash compactor life cycle?

4 For years, Ferrari has been known as the manufacturer of expensive luxury automobiles. The company plans to attract the major segment of the car-buying market who purchase medium-priced automobiles. As Ferrari considers this trading-down strategy, what branding strategy would you recommend? What are the trade-offs to consider with your strategy?

5 The nature of product warranties has changed as the federal court system reassesses the meaning of warranties. How does the regulatory trend toward warranties affect product development?

GOING ONLINE   Brand News You Can Use

Branding and brand management is a challenging task. Brandchannel.com seeks to inform its readers on the important issues facing brands now and in the future from a global perspective. Of particular interest are (1) "features," which discuss the success and failure of particular brands, and (2) "debate," which presents a point/counterpoint discussion related to a brand's strategy.

Visit brandchannel.com (www.brandchannel.com) to complete the following assignment:

1 Pick a brand appearing in Chapter 11 and find a feature or debate pertaining to it either in the archives or from the current page. Summarize the views expressed in brandchannel.com.

2 Click the "papers" icon and read a paper on a topic covered in Chapter 11. Compare and contrast the views in this paper with the coverage found in the chapter.

BUILDING YOUR MARKETING PLAN

For the product offering in your marketing plan,

1 Identify (*a*) its stage in the product life cycle and (*b*) key marketing mix actions that might be appropriate, as shown in Figure 11–1.

2 Develop (*a*) branding and (*b*) packaging strategies, if appropriate for your offering.

VIDEO CASE 11   BMW: "Newness" and the Product Life Cycle

"We're fortunate right now at BMW in that all of our products are new and competitive," says Jim McDowell, vice president of marketing at BMW, as he explains BMW's product life cycle. "Now, how do you do that? You have to introduce new models over time. You have to logically plan out the introductions over time, so you're not changing a whole model range at the same time you're changing another model range."

BMW's strategy is to keep its products in the introduction and growth stages by periodically introducing new models in each of its product lines. In fact, in contrast to many auto manufacturers that launch a new model and then leave it unchanged, BMW works continually to improve its existing products. Explains McDowell, "Anyone can sell a lot of cars the first year, when a car is new. It is our challenge to constantly improve the car and to continuously find new innovative ways to market it."

BMW—THE COMPANY AND ITS PRODUCTS

BMW started in 1916 as a manufacturer of airplane engines. "When you look at our roundel, the BMW symbol, it is a blue and white circle," says McDowell, "that is meant to represent the spinning propeller on a plane, to remind us of our heritage." Since then the company has added motorcycle and automobile production. Today, BMW is one of the preeminent luxury car manufacturers in Europe, North America, and the world.

BMW produces several lines of cars including the 3, 5, 6, and 7 series, the Z line of roadsters, the X line of "sport activity vehicles," and the M line of "motor sport" sedans. Currently, the U.S., Germany, and the United Kingdom are BMW's largest markets. In Europe, BMW recently introduced its 1 series—a compact car designed to compete with the Volkswagen Golf—to attract a new younger audience. In addition, BMW owns the MINI and Rolls-Royce brands. Combined sales of BMW, MINI, and Rolls-Royce exceed $50 billion and have been growing at a rate of 3.5%. Reasons for the growing popularity of BMW include high-performance products, unique advertising, an award winning website, and innovations such as its partnership with Apple that provides a cable to plug an iPod into the auto's stereo system.

PRODUCT LIFE CYCLE

BMW cars typically have a product life cycle of seven years. To keep products in the introductory and growth stages, BMW regularly introduces new models for each of its series to keep the entire series "new." For instance, with the 3 series, it will introduce the new sedan model

one year, the new coupe the next year, then the convertible, then the station wagon, and then the sport hatchback. That's a new product introduction for five of the seven years of the product life cycle. McDowell explains, "So, even though we have seven-year life cycles, we constantly try and make the cars meaningfully different and new about every three years. And that involves adding features and other capabilities to the cars as well." How well does this strategy work? BMW often sees its best sales numbers in either the sixth or seventh year after the product introduction.

As global sales have increased, BMW has become aware of some international product life-cycle differences. For example, it has discovered that some competitive products have life cycles that are shorter or longer than seven years. In Sweden and Britain, automotive product life cycles are eight years, while in Japan they are typically only four years long.

BMW uses a system of "product advocates" to manage the marketing efforts of its product lines. McDowell explains that a series advocate would actually use and drive that series and would constantly be thinking "How can I better serve my customer?" In addition to modifying each model throughout the product life cycle, BMW modifies the markets it serves. For example, during the past ten years BMW has expanded its market by appealing to a much larger percentage of women, African Americans, Asians, and Hispanics. BMW's positioning strategy is the same worldwide and that is to offer high-performance, luxury vehicles to individuals. "You won't find it as a taxi or a fleet car," says McDowell. Generally, once a model is positioned and introduced, BMW avoids trying to reposition it.

BRANDING

"BMW is fortunate—we don't have too much of a dilemma as to what we're going to call our cars." McDowell is referring to BMW's trademark naming system that consists of the product line number and the motor type. For example, the designation "328" tells you the car is in the 3 series and the engine is 2.8 liters in size. BMW has found this naming system to be clear and logical and can be easily understood around the world.

The Z, X, and M series don't quite fit in with this system. BMW had a tradition of building experimental, open-air cars and calling them Z's, and hence when the prototype for the Z3 was built, BMW decided to continue with the Z name. For the sport activity vehicle, BMW also used a letter name—the X series—since the four-wheel drive vehicle didn't fit with the sedan-oriented 3, 5, 6, and 7 series. The M series has a 20-year history with BMW as the line with luxury and racing-level performance. The lettered series now includes the Z4, X3, X5, M3 and M5. Compared to the evocative names many car manufacturers choose to garner excitement for their new models, the BMW numbers and letters are viewed as a simple and effective branding strategy.

In the past BMW has built a brand personality for its vehicles with high-visibility product placements. The Z3, for example, was driven by Pierce Brosnan as James Bond in the movie *Goldeneye*. More recently, however, BMW has used a series of Internet-based mini movies—called "The Hire"—which feature "the ultimate driving machine." The movies (see www.bmwfilms.com) allow web surfers to avoid annoying pop-up ads and be entertained by engaging movies made by master directors using edgy actors. The movies have been so successful and attracted so much attention from consumers and industry experts that the movies have been inducted into the Museum of Modern Art.

MANAGING THE PRODUCT THROUGH THE WEB—THE WAVE OF THE FUTURE

One of the ways BMW is improving its product offerings even further is through its innovative website (www.bmwusa.com). At the site, customers can learn about the particular models, e-mail questions, and request literature or test-drives from their local BMW dealership. What really sets BMW's website apart from other car manufacturers, though, is the ability for customers to configure a car to their own specifications (interior choices, exterior choices, engine, packages, and options) and then transfer that information to their local dealer. As Carol Burrows, product communications manager for BMW, explains, "The BMW website is an integrated part of the overall marketing strategy for BMW. The full range of products can be seen and interacted with online. We offer pricing options online. Customers can go to their local dealership via the website to further discuss costs for purchase of a car. And it is a distribution channel for information that allows people access to the information 24 hours a day at their convenience." The ultimate extravagance in buying a car is having everything customized to the owner's preferences. Today, 80% of European buyers and 30% of U.S. buyers use the BMW website to choose from 350 model variations, 500 options, 90 exterior colors, and 170 interior trims to create their perfect vehicle!

Questions

1 Compare the product life cycle described by BMW for its cars to the product life cycle shown in Figure 11–1. How are they (*a*) similar and (*b*) dissimilar?

2 Based on BMW's typical product life cycle, what marketing strategies are appropriate for the 3 series? The X5?

3 Which of the three ways to manage the product life cycle does BMW utilize with its products—modifying the product, modifying the market, or repositioning the product?

4 How would you describe BMW's branding strategy (manufacturer branding, private branding, or mixed branding)? Why?

5 Go to the BMW website (www.bmwusa.com) and design a car to your own specifications. How does this enable you as a customer to evaluate the product differently than would be otherwise possible?

STAR TREK
THE EXPERIENCE
LAS VEGAS HILTON

CHAPTER 12

MANAGING SERVICES

LEARNING OBJECTIVES

After reading this chapter you should be able to:

1. Describe four unique elements of services.

2. Recognize how services differ and how they can be classified.

3. Explain how consumers purchase and evaluate services.

4. Develop a customer contact audit to identify service advantages.

5. Discuss the important role of internal marketing in service organizations.

6. Explain the role of the four Ps in the services marketing mix.

THE NEWEST SERVICES MANUFACTURE EXPERIENCES: JUST ASK ANYONE WHO HAS BEEN CAPTURED BY A BORG!

The hottest new technology, the latest in innovation, and an exceptional entertainment, shopping, and dining experience! These are just a few descriptions of the recently opened *Star Trek: The Experience* at the Las Vegas Hilton. Guests to the $70 million, 65,000-square-foot attraction utilize their sense of sight, sound, and touch at the Borg Invasion 4D. In fact, thrill seekers "become totally immersed," explains Alexander Weber, CEO of Paramount Parks, which developed and manages *The Experience*. Each theater seat has 10 special features, such as back probes, air blasts, and 12-channel sound coordinated with the action on a 3D movie, while a moving floor creates the fourth dimension. Through the use of live actors and special effects, visitors experience a Borg attempt to capture and assimilate the guests. Visitors can also eat at Quark's Bar and Restaurant and shop at the Deep Space Nine Promenade, which has the world's largest collection of *Star Trek* memorabilia and collectibles.[1]

If you prefer music, motorcycles, or celebrities, there are experiences available for you too. Hard Rock Cafes and Hotels, Harley-Davidson Cafes, and Planet Hollywood restaurants, are examples you may have visited. The mission of Hard Rock Cafe International is "to spread the spirit of rock 'n' roll by delivering an exceptional entertainment and dining experience." Its Chicago location, for example, plays live video on 64 flat-screen monitors surrounded by memorabilia from Elvis Presley, Cher, Madonna, The Beatles, and many others. The New York Harley-Davidson Cafe is full of Harley bikes, information, and merchandise, which help promote the

Harley lifestyle and experience. Planet Hollywood recently built a 2,500-room resort with a $30 million movie-memorabilia collection, where guests can make reservations to sleep on Austin Powers's shagadelic revolving bed.[2]

These are just a few of many service organizations competing for customers by offering enjoyable, memorable experiences rather than traditional service transactions. Walt Disney was one of the first to recognize the importance of sights, sounds, tastes, aromas, and textures to provide a unique experience when he created Disneyland. Chuck E. Cheese's uses a similar approach to sell birthday party experiences that include entertainment, food, music, and a fun environment. Companies that sell goods with a service element are also offering experiences. Nike, for example, offers fun activities and promotional events in its own store, Niketown, and Steinway provides a free concert including a pianist, invitations, and hors d'oeuvres in its customers' homes. These businesses are increasing the value of their offering to customers by engaging them in experiential elements of their service.

Some experts believe we are on the verge of a new economic era driven by an *experience economy*.[3] Coffee can be purchased as a commodity in a grocery store and brewed at home at a cost of about 10 cents per cup. Coffee can also be purchased from 7-Eleven, where consumers pay for the convenience of the service, for a cost of about 75 cents per cup. But most of us have often paid about $3 per cup at a Starbucks where the look of the shop, the jazz music, and the barrista's knowledge of the beans creates a "coffee experience" that is still a good value. ESPN Zone, Home Depot, Apple (stores), and many other companies are also responding to consumers' preferences for compelling experiences.

As the actions of *Star Trek: The Experience* and the other examples above illustrate, the marketing of services is dynamic and challenging. In this chapter, we discuss how services differ from traditional products (goods), how consumers make purchase decisions, and the ways in which the marketing mix is used.

THE UNIQUENESS OF SERVICES

Services are intangible activities or benefits that an organization provides to consumers (such as airline trips, financial advice, or automobile repair) in exchange for money or something else of value.

Services have become a significant component of the global economy and one of the most important components of the U.S. economy. The World Trade Organization estimates that in 2003 all countries exported merchandise valued at $7.3 trillion and commercial services valued at $1.8 trillion. In the United States, more than 40 percent of the gross domestic product (GDP) now comes from services. As shown in Figure 12–1, services accounted for $4.6 trillion in 2003, which was an increase of more than 80 percent since 1990. While goods-producing firms employ approximately 23.8 million people, service firms employ more than 84 million. Services also represent a large export business—the $323 billion of services exports in 2003 is one of the few areas in which the United States has a trade surplus.[4]

The growth in this sector is the result of increased demand for services that have been available in the past and the increasing interest in new services. Concierge services, for example, have been popular in hotels such as the Breakers in Palm Beach, Florida, which has a staff of 11 concierges who serve the hotel's guests. Some hotels, such as the Ritz-Carlton, even have a technology concierge to help with questions about wireless cards, firewalls, and software. Concierge services have also expanded beyond hotels and are now popular in department stores such as Nordstrom, at country clubs such as the Gainey Ranch in Scottsdale, Arizona, and on the Internet. Vipdesk.com, for example, can assist customers with reservations, gift purchases, travel destination research, or even finding a plumber. Other new services include MusicID, which tells you the name of a song within seconds if you hold your phone so that the song can be heard; "Search Inside the Book," Amazon's new

FIGURE 12-1
Importance of services in the U.S. gross domestic product (GDP)

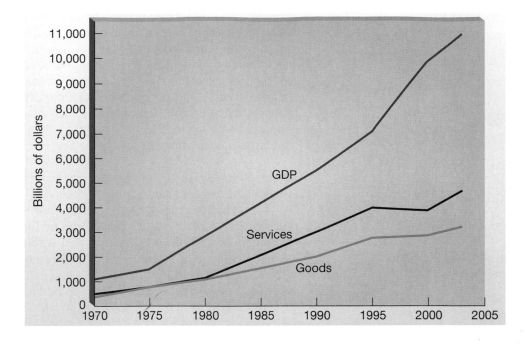

search service that allows customers to search every page of 120,000 books; and the DNA Copyright Institute service of copyrighting the unique DNA contained in your genes. These firms and many others like them are examples of the imaginative services that will play a role in our economy in the future.[5]

The Four I's of Services

There are four unique elements to services: *intangibility, inconsistency, inseparability,* and *inventory.* These four elements are referred to as the **four I's of services.**

Intangibility   Services are intangible; that is, they can't be held, touched, or seen before the purchase decision. In contrast, before purchasing a traditional product, a consumer can touch a box of laundry detergent, kick the tire of an automobile, or

4 Is
. intangibility
. inconsistency
. inseparability
. inventory

Why do many services emphasize their tangible benefits? The answer appears in the text.

Lufthansa
www.lufthansa-usa.com

ANA
www.fly-ana.com

American Express Co.
www.americanexpress.com

sample a new breakfast cereal. Because services tend to be a performance rather than an object, they are much more difficult for consumers to evaluate. To help consumers assess and compare services, marketers try to make them tangible or show the benefits of using the service.

The Lufthansa and ANA ads on the previous page show travelers sleeping in the airlines' new seats and also emphasize broadband Internet connections, in-seat entertainment, built-in tables, and other tangible benefits. American Express also provides tangible benefits by offering cardholders points and cash through its bonus rewards program.

Inconsistency   Developing, pricing, promoting, and delivering services is challenging because the quality of a service is often inconsistent. Because services depend on the people who provide them, their quality varies with each person's capabilities and day-to-day job performance. Inconsistency is much more of a problem in services than it is with tangible goods. Tangible products can be good or bad in terms of quality, but with modern production lines the quality will at least be consistent. On the other hand, one day the Philadelphia Phillies baseball team may have great hitting and pitching and look like a pennant winner and the next day lose by 10 runs. Or a soprano at New York's Metropolitan Opera may have a bad cold and give a less-than-perfect performance. Whether the service involves tax assistance at H&R Block or guest relations at the Ritz-Carlton, organizations attempt to reduce inconsistency through standardization and training.[6]

Inseparability   A third difference between services and goods, and related to problems of consistency, is inseparability. In most cases, the consumer cannot (and does not) separate the deliverer of the service from the service itself. For example, to receive an education, a person may attend a university. The quality of the education may be high, but if the student has difficulty interacting with instructors, finds counseling services poor, or does not receive adequate library or computer assistance, he or she may not be satisfied with the educational experience. Students' evaluations of their education will be influenced primarily by their perceptions of instructors, counselors, librarians, and other people at the university. Allstate's reminder that "You're in good hands" emphasizes the importance of its agents.

People play an important role in the delivery of many services.

Allstate
www.allstate.com

The amount of interaction between the consumer and the service provider depends on the extent to which the consumer must be physically present to receive the service. Some services such as haircuts, golf lessons, medical diagnoses, and food service require the customer to participate in the delivery of the services. Other services such as car repair, dry cleaning, and waste disposal process tangible objects with less involvement from the customer. Finally, services such as banking, consulting, and insurance can now be delivered electronically, often requiring no face-to-face customer interaction.[7]

Inventory Inventory of services is different from that of goods. Inventory problems exist with goods because many items are perishable and because there are costs associated with handling inventory. With services, inventory carrying costs are more subjective and are related to **idle production capacity**, which is when the service provider is available but there is no demand. The inventory cost of a service is the cost of paying the person used to provide the service along with any needed equipment. If a physician is paid to see patients but no one schedules an appointment, the fixed cost of the idle physician's salary is a high inventory carrying cost. In some service businesses, however, the provider of the service is on commission (a Merrill Lynch stockbroker) or is a part-time employee (a clerk at Sears). In these businesses, inventory carrying costs can be significantly lower or nonexistent because the idle production capacity can be cut back by reducing hours or having no salary to pay because of the commission compensation system. Figure 12–2 shows a scale of inventory carrying costs represented on the low end by real estate agencies and hair salons, and on the high end by airlines and hospitals. The inventory carrying costs of airlines is high because of high-salaried pilots and very expensive equipment. In contrast, real estate agencies and hair salons have employees who work on commission and need little expensive equipment to conduct business. One reason service providers must maintain production capacity is because of the importance of time to today's customers. People don't want to wait long at the emergency room!

The Service Continuum

The four I's differentiate services from goods in most cases, but many companies are not clearly service-based or good-based organizations. Is Hewlett-Packard a computer company or service business? Although Hewlett-Packard manufactures computers and other goods, many of the company's employees work in its services division providing systems integration, networking, consulting, education, and product support.[8] As companies look at what they bring to the market, there is a range from the tangible to the intangible or good-dominant to service-dominant offerings referred to as the **service continuum** (Figure 12–3 on the next page).

Teaching, nursing, and the theater are intangible, service-dominant activities, and intangibility, inconsistency, inseparability, and inventory are major concerns in their marketing. Salt, neckties, and dog food are tangible goods, and the problems represented

FIGURE 12–2

Inventory carrying costs of services

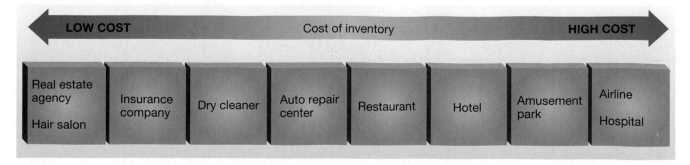

FIGURE 12–3
Service continuum

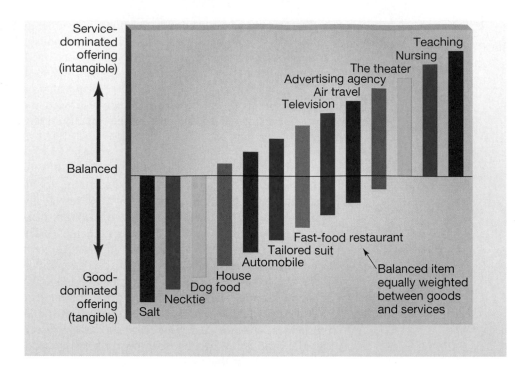

by the four I's are not relevant in their marketing. However, some businesses are a mix of intangible service and tangible good factors. A clothing tailor provides a service but also a good, the finished suit. How pleasant, courteous, and attentive the tailor is to the customer is an important component of the service, and how well the clothes fit is an important part of the product. As shown in Figure 12–3, a fast-food restaurant is about half tangible goods (the food) and half intangible services (courtesy, cleanliness, speed, and convenience).

For many businesses today it is useful to distinguish between their core product—either a good or a service—and supplementary services. A core service offering such as a bank account, for example, also has supplementary services such as deposit assistance, parking or drive-through availability, ATMs, and monthly statements. Supplementary services often allow service providers to differentiate their offering from competitors, and they may add value for consumers. While there are many

FIGURE 12–4
Service classifications

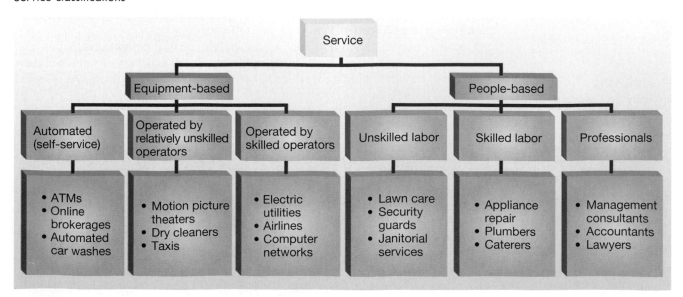

MARKETING NEWSNET
Sports Get a Gold Medal—in Marketing!

CUSTOMER VALUE

Like most services, sports teams know that inconsistency can reduce consumer interest. How well a team will play from game to game or year to year is difficult to control and predict. So in addition to providing a core service such as football or baseball games, many teams have invested in marketing programs that build an image and increase the entertainment value for fans. Promotional events, merchandise licensing, and new facilities have all become important marketing activities for sports teams. The home of the San Francisco Giants, SBC Park, for example, has added 121 high-speed Wi-Fi access points so fans can log-in from anyplace in the stadium.

While individual teams compete with each other, they also compete with other sports. According to NFL vice president of marketing John Collins, "we compete with all entertainment options that are out there." The big five—football, auto racing, baseball, basketball, and hockey—have all made efforts to improve their popularity. Football has become the most popular sport in the United States through strong promotion of Monday Night Football and Sunday afternoon programs. Auto racing claims 75 million fans and has moved north into markets such as Chicago

Greece 2004. On your marks, get set, visit.

It's our historic record-breaking Olympic year. Visit Greece in 2004 and experience your personal best time whether sightseeing, sunbathing or at an epic Olympic event. On your marks, get set, visit Greece.

Your best time yet.

Olympic Games ATHENS 2004. There 's no place like home.

GREEK NATIONAL TOURISM ORGANIZATION: OLYMPIC TOWER 645 FIFTH AVENUE, SUITE 903 · NEW YORK, NY 10022. TEL.: (00121O) 4210777, FAX: (00121O) 8298940, E-MAIL: info@greektourism.com, WEBSITES: www.greektourism.com, www.gnto.gr

by building new race tracks. Hockey has moved south by adding expansion teams in southern states. And the fastest-growing sport, basketball, has expanded globally by drafting players from Germany, China, and Spain and then playing preseason games overseas.

The competition isn't limited to major sports though. Marketing efforts by many familiar sports such as tennis, golf, soccer, and figure skating have been increasing. In addition, many "new" or less familiar sports such as arena football, lacrosse, bull riding, and bass fishing are developing growing fan interest.

Which sports marketing program is the most sophisticated? Probably the Olympics. Companies such as Coca-Cola, McDonald's, and Visa pay $55 million for the privilege of being official Olympic sponsors, and TV rights sell for $1.3 billion. Chinese computer manufacturer Lenovo joined the marketing program to become the official computer equipment provider for the 2006 Winter Games in Torino and the 2008 Summer Games in Beijing. Overall, the $600 million Olympic marketing program has made the five rings the most recognizable sports logo on earth!

potential supplementary services, key categories of supplementary services include information delivery, consultation, order taking, billing procedures, and payment options.[9] See the accompanying Marketing NewsNet to learn why sports teams try to augment their core offering.[10]

Classifying Services

Throughout this book, marketing organizations, techniques, and concepts are classified to show the differences and similarities in an organized framework. Services can also be classified in several ways, according to whether they are (1) delivered by people or equipment, (2) profit or nonprofit organizations, or (3) government sponsored.

- Delivery
- profit
- gov. sponsored

Delivery by People or Equipment   As seen in Figure 12–4, many companies offer services. Professional services include management consulting firms such as Booz, Allen & Hamilton or Accenture. Skilled labor is required to offer services such as Sears appliance repair or Sheraton catering service. Unskilled labor such as that used by Brinks store-security forces is also a service provided by people.

Equipment-based services do not have the marketing concerns of inconsistency because people are removed from the provision of the service. Electric utilities, for example, can provide service without frequent personal contact with customers. Motion picture theaters have projector operators that consumers never see. And a growing number of customers use self-service technologies such as Schwab's online stock trading service without interacting with any service employees.[11]

Profit or Nonprofit Organizations   Many organizations involved in services also distinguish themselves by their tax status as profit or nonprofit organizations. In contrast to *profit organizations, nonprofit organizations'* excesses in revenue over expenses are not taxed or distributed to shareholders. When excess revenue exists, the money goes back into the organization's treasury to allow continuation of the service. Based on the corporate structure of the nonprofit organization, it may pay tax on revenue-generating holdings not directly related to its core mission. The 1.1 million nonprofit organizations in the United States now generate 7 percent of the gross domestic product.[12]

The United Way, Greenpeace, Outward Bound, the Salvation Army, and the Nature Conservancy are examples of nonprofit organizations. Historically, misconceptions have limited the use of marketing practices by such organizations.[13] In recent years, however, nonprofit organizations have turned to marketing to help achieve their goals. The American Red Cross is a good example. To encourage blood donations in December and January, a time when donations typically decline, the American Red Cross launched a marketing campaign called "One Good Reason," which encouraged potential donors to think of giving blood as a gift of life.[14] Where can you get ideas for nonprofit marketing programs? See the Web Link to learn about several excellent resources.

Government Sponsored   A third way to classify services is based on whether they are government sponsored. Although there is no direct ownership and they are nonprofit organizations, governments at the federal, state, and local levels provide a broad range of services. The United States Postal Service, for example, has adopted many marketing activities. Its "Easy Come. Easy Go" campaign is designed to allow it to compete with UPS, FedEx, foreign postal services, and electronic communication technologies. Because faxes and e-mail have reduced first-class postage revenue, the Postal Service now tries to attract customers to its global package delivery service. Another marketing program has converted 700 postal offices to retail outlets that sell

Nonprofit and government-sponsored services often advertise.

The Nature Conservancy
www.nature.org

United States Postal Service
www.usps.com

collector stamps, Pony Express sweatshirts, and even neckties. Government sponsorship does not limit competition, however. Britain's Royal Mail recently opened an office in Manhattan to compete for international direct-mail business.[15]

Concept Check

1. What are the four I's of services?

2. Would inventory carrying costs for an accounting firm with certified public accountants be (*a*) high, (*b*) low, or (*c*) nonexistent?

3. To eliminate service inconsistencies, companies rely on _____ and _____.

HOW CONSUMERS PURCHASE SERVICES

Colleges, hospitals, hotels, and even charities are facing an increasingly competitive environment. Successful service organizations, like successful product-oriented firms, must understand how the consumer makes a service purchase decision and quality evaluation and in what ways a company can present a differential advantage relative to competing offerings.

The Purchase Process

Many aspects of services affect the consumer's evaluation of the purchase. Because services cannot be displayed, demonstrated, or illustrated, consumers cannot make a prepurchase evaluation of all the characteristics of services.[16] Similarly, because service providers may vary in their delivery of a service, an evaluation of a service may change with each purchase. Figure 12–5 on the next page portrays how different types of goods and services are evaluated by consumers. Tangible goods such as clothing, jewelry, and furniture have *search* properties, such as color, size, and style, which can be determined before purchase. Services such as restaurants and child care have *experience* properties, which can only be discerned after purchase or during consumption. Finally, services provided by specialized professionals such as medical diagnoses and legal services have *credence* properties, or characteristics that the consumer may find impossible to evaluate even after purchase and consumption.[17] To reduce the uncertainty created by these properties, service consumers turn to personal sources of information such as early adopters, opinion leaders, and reference group members during the purchase decision process.[18] The Mayo Clinic uses an organized, explicit approach called "evidence management" to present customers with concrete and convincing evidence of its strengths.[19]

- Search
- experience
- credence

FIGURE 12–5

How consumers evaluate goods and services

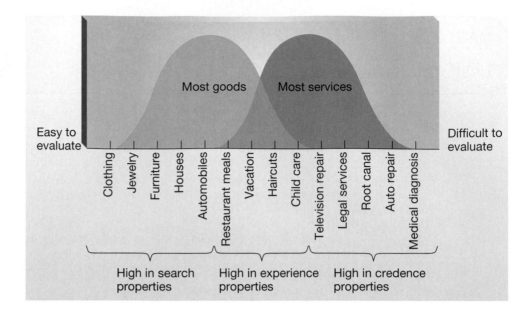

Assessing Service Quality

Once a consumer tries a service, how is it evaluated? Primarily by comparing expectations about a service offering to the actual experience a consumer has with the service.[20] Differences between the consumer's expectations and experience are identified through **gap analysis**. This type of analysis asks consumers to assess their expectations and experiences on dimensions of service quality such as those described in Figure 12–6.[21] Expectations are influenced by word-of-mouth communications, personal needs, past experiences, and promotional activities, while actual experiences are determined by the way an organization delivers its service.[22] The relative importance of the various dimensions of service quality varies by the type of service.[23] What if someone is dissatisfied and complains? See the accompanying Marketing NewsNet for four steps that can help.[24] Recent studies suggest that customers who

FIGURE 12–6

Dimensions of service quality

DIMENSION	DEFINITION	EXAMPLES OF QUESTIONS AIRLINE CUSTOMERS MIGHT ASK
Reliability	Ability to perform the promised service dependably and accurately	Is my flight on time?
Tangibles	Appearance of physical facilities, equipment, personnel, and communication materials	Are the gate, the plane, and the baggage area clean?
Responsiveness	Willingness to help customers and provide prompt service	Are the flight attendants willing to answer my questions?
Assurance	Knowledge and courtesy of employees and their ability to convey trust and confidence	Are the ticket counter attendants, flight attendants, and pilots knowledgeable about their jobs?
Empathy	Caring, individualized attention provided to customers	Do the employees determine if I have special seating, meal, baggage, transfer or rebooking needs?

MARKETING NEWSNET

What if Someone Complains? How Services Can Recover from Failure to Satisfy a Customer

CUSTOMER VALUE

Many service companies have developed strategies to encourage customer satisfaction and loyalty. Despite these efforts, however, every company has some service failures that lead to customer complaints. How can services recover from these situations? Professors Stephen Tax and Stephen Brown suggest four steps:

Step 1: Identify service failures. Only 5 to 10 percent of dissatisfied customers choose to complain—the rest simply switch companies or make negative comments to other people. One way companies encourage customers to express concerns is through 800 numbers.

Step 2: Resolve customer problems. Once customers complain, they want fair procedures, interactions, and outcomes. Because most complaints are first expressed to front-line employees, a key to resolving complaints is training employees to handle likely situations and giving them the authority to resolve problems. Federal Express, for example, gives new customer service representatives five weeks of training before assigning them to a location.

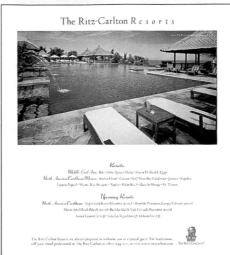

Step 3: Communicate and classify service failures. This step reflects the concept of organizational learning, or the capacity to improve performance based on experience. AT&T, for example, adds all complaints to its database in real time.

Step 4: Integrate data and improve overall service. Information from customer satisfaction surveys, focus groups, advisory panels, and other sources must be integrated with the complaint information to identify areas for service quality improvement.

Many firms are improving their methods of dealing with feedback and complaints. Scandanavian Airlines set up kiosks outside arrival gates to collect feedback from passengers. Xerox uses a Customer Action Request Form to facilitate its response to complaints. And at the Ritz-Carlton Hotels all 19,000 employees carry a plastic laminated card with the company's "Gold Standards." Number 13 of 20 guidelines: "Never lose a guest. Instant guest pacification is the responsibility of each employee. Whoever receives a complaint will own it, resolve it to the guest's satisfaction, and record it."

experience a "service failure" will increase their satisfaction if the service makes a satisfactory service recovery effort, but not if there is a second failure.[25]

Customer Contact and Relationship Marketing

Consumers judge services on the entire sequence of steps that make up the service process. To focus on these steps, or "service encounters," a firm can develop a **customer contact audit**—a flowchart of the points of interaction between consumer and service provider.[26] This is particularly important in high-contact services such as hotels, educational institutions, and automobile rental agencies. Figure 12–7 on the next page is a consumer contact audit for renting a car from Hertz. The interactions identified in a customer contact audit often serve as the basis for developing relationships with customers.

A Customer's Car Rental Activities   A customer decides to rent a car and (1) contacts the rental company (see Figure 12–7). A customer service representative receives the information (2) and checks the availability of the car at the desired location. When the customer arrives at the rental site (3), the reservation system is again accessed, and the customer provides information regarding payment, address, and driver's license (4). A car is assigned to the customer (5), who proceeds by bus to the car pickup (6). On return to the rental location (7), the customer checks in (8), a customer service representative collects information on mileage, gas consumption, and damages (9), and a bill is printed (10).

Each of the steps numbered 1 to 10 is a customer contact point where the tangible aspects of Hertz service are seen by the customer. Figure 12–7, however, also shows

FIGURE 12-7
Customer contact audit for a car rental (green shaded boxes indicate customer activity)

The Hertz Corporation
www.hertz.com

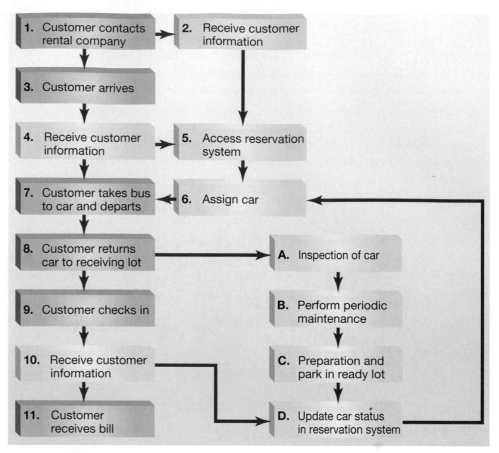

a series of steps lettered A to D that involve an inspection, maintenance, preparation for the next customer, and an update of the reservation system. These steps are essential in providing a clean, well-maintained car, but they are not points of customer interaction. To create a service advantage, Hertz must create a competitive advantage in the sequence of interactions with the customer. For example, Hertz has attempted to eliminate step 4 for some customers with its Hertz #1 Club—these customers simply show their drivers license and pick up the car's keys.

Relationship Marketing   The contact between a service provider and a customer represents a service encounter that is likely to influence the customer's assessment of the purchase. The number of encounters in a service experience may vary. Disney, for example, estimates that a park visitor will have 74 encounters with Disney employees in a single visit. These encounters represent opportunities to develop social bonds, or relationships, with customers. The relationship may also be developed through loyalty incentives such as airline frequent flyer programs. Relationship marketing provides several benefits for service customers including the continuity of a single provider, customized service delivery, reduced stress due to a repetitive purchase process, and an absence of switching costs. Recent surveys of consumers have indicated that while customers of many services are interested in being "relationship customers," they require that the relationship be balanced in terms of loyalty, benefits, and respect for privacy,[27] and that there is a higher expectation of future use of the service.[28]

Concept Check

1. What are the differences between search, experience, and credence properties?

2. Hertz created its differential advantage at the points of _____ in their customer contact audit.

MANAGING THE MARKETING OF SERVICES

Just as the unique aspects of services necessitate changes in the consumer's purchase process, the marketing management process requires special adaptation.[29] As emphasized earlier in the chapter, in services marketing the employee plays a central role in creating the service experience, and in building and maintaining relationships with customers.[30] This aspect of services marketing has led to a concept called internal marketing.[31]

[handwritten: employee satisfact.]

Internal marketing is based on the notion that a service organization must focus on its employees, or internal market, before successful programs can be directed at customers.[32] Services need to ensure that employees have the attitude, skills, and commitment needed to meet customer expectations and sustain customer loyalty. This idea suggests that employee development through recruitment, training, communication, coaching, management, and leadership are critical to the success of service organizations.[33]

Let's use the four Ps framework for discussing the marketing mix for services.

Product (Service)

The concepts of the product component of the marketing mix discussed in Chapters 10 and 11 apply equally well to Cheerios (a good) and to American Express (a service). Yet there are three aspects of the product/service element of the marketing mix that warrant special attention: exclusivity, brand name, and capacity management.

[handwritten: Services cannot be patented.]

Exclusivity   Chapter 10 pointed out that one favorable dimension in a new product is its ability to be patented. Remember that a patent gives the manufacturer of a product exclusive rights to its production for 17 years. A major difference between products and services is that services cannot be patented. Hence, the creator of a successful fast-food hamburger chain could quickly discover the concept being copied by others. Domino's Pizza, for example, has seen many competitors copy the quick delivery advantage that propelled the company to success. Many businesses today try to distinguish their core product with new or improved supplementary services through outsourcing: Hotels outsource concierge services, airlines outsource maintenance, and banks outsource the mailing of monthly statements.[34]

Logos create service identities.

[handwritten: important due to intangibility]

Branding   An important aspect in marketing goods is the branding strategy used. However, because services are intangible and, therefore, more difficult to describe, the brand name or identifying logo of the service organization is particularly important in consumer decisions.[35] The financial services industry, for example, has failed to use branding to distinguish what consumers perceive to be similar offerings by banks, mutual fund companies, brokerage firms, and insurance companies. UPS, however, recently changed its logo after 42 years, to communicate the addition of supply chain management services to its package delivery service.[36] Take a look at the logos to determine how successful some companies have been in branding their service with a name and symbol.

Capacity Management   Most services have a limited capacity due to the inseparability of the service from the service provider and the perishable nature of the service. For example, to "buy" an appendectomy, a patient must be in the hospital at the same time as the surgeon and only one patient can be helped at that time. Similarly, no additional surgery can be conducted tomorrow because of an unused operating room or an available surgeon today—the service capacity is lost if it is not used. So the service component of the marketing mix must be integrated with efforts to influence consumer demand.[37] This is referred to as **capacity management**.

Service organizations must manage the availability of the offering so that (1) demand matches capacity over the duration of the demand cycle (for example, one day, week, month, or year), and (2) the organization's assets are used in ways that will maximize

FIGURE 12–8

Managing capacity in a hotel

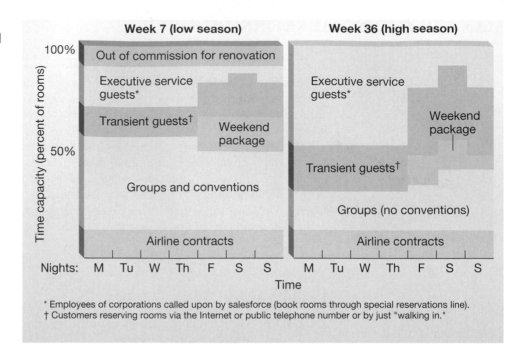

* Employees of corporations called upon by salesforce (book rooms through special reservations line).
† Customers reserving rooms via the Internet or public telephone number or by just "walking in."

the return on investment (ROI).[38] Figure 12–8 shows how a hotel tries to manage its capacity during the high and low seasons. Differing price structures are assigned to each segment of consumers to help moderate or adjust demand for the service. Airline contracts fill a fixed number of rooms throughout the year. In the low season, when more rooms are available, tour packages at appealing prices are used to attract groups or conventions, such as an offer for seven nights in Orlando at a reduced price. Weekend packages are also offered to vacationers. In the high-demand season, groups are less desirable because guests who will pay high prices travel to Florida on their own.

Price

- quality perception and capacity management

Price influences perceptions of services.

In the service industries, *price* is referred to in various ways. Hospitals refer to charges; consultants, lawyers, physicians, and accountants to fees; airlines to fares; and hotels to rates. Regardless of the term used, price plays two essential roles: (1) to affect consumer perceptions and (2) to be used in capacity management. Because of the intangible nature of services, price can indicate the quality of the service. Would you wonder about the quality of a $100 surgery? Studies have shown that when there are few well-known cues by which to judge a product, consumers use price.[39] Look at the accompanying ad for eye surgery. Would you have concerns about the offer or think it's a good value for the money?

The capacity management role of price is also important to movie theaters, airlines, restaurants, and hotels. Many service businesses use **off-peak pricing**, which consists of charging different prices during different times of the day or days of the week to reflect variations in demand for the service. Airlines offer discounts for weekend travel, and movie theaters offer matinee prices. Cellular telephone pricing plans typically offer peak (sometimes called "anytime") minutes for calls made during the day and off-peak minutes for calls made at night or on weekends. The different prices reflect the cell phone company's effort to shift demand to low-volume time periods.[40]

Place (Distribution) *access of service*

Place or distribution is a major factor in developing a service marketing strategy because of the inseparability of services from the producer. Historically in services marketing, little attention has been paid to distribution. But as competition grows, the value of convenient distribution, or access, is being recognized. Hairstyling chains such as Cost Cutters Family Hair Care, tax preparation offices such as H&R Block, and accounting firms such as Deloitte Touche Tohmatsu all use multiple locations for the distribution of services. In the banking industry, customers of participating banks using the Cirrus system can access any one of thousands of automatic teller systems throughout the United States. The availability of electronic distribution through the Internet now provides global coverage for travel services, banking, entertainment, insurance services, stock trading, and many other information-based services.[41]

Promotion *— especially advertising, publicity*

The value of promotion, specifically advertising, for many services is to show the benefits of purchasing the service. It is valuable to stress availability, location, consistent quality, and efficient, courteous service.[42] The *Princeton Review* ad below, for example, describes the benefits available to its customers—higher test scores. In addition, services must be concerned with their image. Promotional efforts, such as Accenture's "High performance. Delivered." campaign or Merrill Lynch's use of the bull in its ads, contribute to image and positioning strategies.[43] In most cases promotional concerns of services are similar to those of products.

Another form of promotion, *publicity,* has played a major role in the promotional strategy of nonprofit services and some professional organizations. Nonprofit organizations such as public school districts, the Chicago Symphony Orchestra, religious organizations, and hospitals have used publicity to disseminate their messages. Because of the heavy reliance on publicity, many services use *public service announcements* (PSAs), and because PSAs are free, nonprofit groups have tended to rely on them as the foundation of their media plan.[44] However, as discussed in Chapter 19, the timing and location of a PSA are under the control of the medium, not the organization. So the nonprofit service group cannot control who sees the message or when the message is given.

Services use promotional programs to communicate benefits and create an image.

The Princeton Review
www.princetonreview.com

Accenture
www.accenture.com

SERVICES IN THE FUTURE

What can we expect from the services industry in the future? New and better services, of course, and an unprecedented variety of choices. Many of the changes will be the result of two factors: technological development and an expanding scope in the global economy.

Technological advances are rapidly changing the service industry. New e-services will include voice-over-Internet (telephone), home video-conferencing, and new forms of security and identification (e.g., fingerprint and retinal scans). New Internet-based services will also make it possible to obtain videos, movies, and even textbooks like this one electronically. What is the hottest trend in new services? Matchmaking. Some experts claim that there may soon be as many as 10,000 dating services available. Match.com, for example, boasts 12 million members in 246 countries. In Japan, the services are so popular they are offered in I-mode, the technology that allows Internet access from cell phones.[45]

An expanding scope of influence in the global economy is also changing the service industry. While the past decade has seen services grow to become the dominant part of the economy in the United States, the future is likely to see more emphasis on the global marketing of services and increasing attention to cross-cultural implications for services. Recent studies indicate that consumers in countries such as Australia, China, Germany, India, and the United States place varying emphasis on service quality and underscore the need to "think global and act local." Finally, some experts predict that the dominant view of economic exchange will shift from its current focus on goods and tangible resources to services and intangible attributes.[46]

Concept Check

1. Matching demand with capacity is the focus of _____ management.

2. How does a movie theater use off-peak pricing?

3. What factors will influence future changes in services?

CHAPTER IN REVIEW

1 *Describe four unique elements of services.*
The four unique elements of services—the four I's—are intangibility, inconsistency, inseparability, and inventory. Intangibility refers to the tendency of services to be a performance that cannot be held or touched, rather than an object. Inconsistency is a characteristic of services because they depend on people to deliver them, and people vary in their capabilities and in their day-to-day performance. Inseparability refers to the difficulty of separating the deliverer of the service (hair stylist) from the service itself (hair salon). Inventory refers to the need to have service production capability when there is service demand.

2 *Recognize how services differ and how they can be classified.*
Services differ in terms of the balance of the part of the offering that is based on goods and the part of the offering that is based on service. Services can be delivered by people or equipment, they can be provided by profit or nonprofit organizations, and they can be government sponsored.

3 *Explain how consumers purchase and evaluate services.*
Because services are intangible, prepurchase evaluation is difficult for consumers. To choose a service consumers use search, experience, and credence qualities to evaluate the good and service elements of an offering. Once a consumer tries a service, it is evaluated by comparing expectations with the actual experience on five dimensions of quality—reliability, tangibles, responsiveness, assurance, and empathy. Differences between expectations and experience are identified through gap analysis.

4 *Develop a customer contact audit to identify service advantages.*
A customer contact audit is a flowchart of the points of interaction between a consumer and a service provider. The interactions identified in a customer contact audit often serve as the basis for developing relationships with customers.

5 *Discuss the important role of internal marketing in service organizations.*
Because the employee plays a central role in creating the service experience, and in building and maintaining relationships with customers, services have adopted a concept called internal marketing. This concept suggests that services need to ensure that employees (the internal market) have the attitude, skills, and commitment needed to meet customer expectations and sustain customer loyalty.

6 *Explain the role of the four Ps in the services marketing mix.*
Each of the four Ps can be applied to services marketing. Important aspects of the product element include exclusivity, the use of services to distinguish an offering; branding, the use of a brand name or logo to help consumer identify the service;

and capacity management, the efforts designed to influence the timing of consumer demand. Pricing is reflected in charges, fees, fares, and rates and can be used to influence perceptions of the quality of a service and to manage capacity. Place (or distribution) is used to provide access and convenience. Promotional tools such as advertising and publicity are a means of communicating the benefits of a service.

FOCUSING ON KEY TERMS

capacity management p. 327
customer contact audit p. 325
four I's of services p. 317
gap analysis p. 324
idle production capacity p. 319

internal marketing p. 327
off-peak pricing p. 328
service continuum p. 319
services p. 316

DISCUSSION AND APPLICATION QUESTIONS

1 Explain how the four I's of services would apply to a Marriott Hotel.

2 Idle production capacity may be related to inventory or capacity management. How would the pricing component of the marketing mix reduce idle production capacity for (*a*) a car wash, (*b*) a stage theater group, and (*c*) a university?

3 Look back at the service continuum in Figure 12–3. Explain how the following points in the continuum differ in terms of consistency: (*a*) salt, (*b*) automobile, (*c*) advertising agency, and (*d*) teaching.

4 What are the search, experience, and credence properties of an airline for the business traveler and pleasure traveler? What properties are most important to each group?

5 Outline the customer contact audit for the typical deposit you make at your neighborhood bank.

6 The text suggests that internal marketing is necessary before a successful marketing program can be directed at consumers. Why is this particularly true for service organizations?

7 Outline the capacity management strategies that an airline must consider.

8 How does off-peak pricing influence demand for services?

9 Draw the channel of distribution for the following services: (*a*) a restaurant, (*b*) a hospital, and (*c*) a hotel.

10 In recent years, many service businesses have begun to provide their employees with uniforms. Explain the rationale behind this strategy in terms of the concepts discussed in this chapter.

GOING ONLINE   Reviewing the Latest Services Marketing Strategies

The American Marketing Association provides a variety of useful services for anyone interested in the latest services marketing concepts and strategies. Go to AMA's home page (www.marketingpower.com), type "services marketing" in the search engine to review the information and services available. If you click on "AMA info" and "publications," articles from a variety of publications, including *Marketing Health Services,* can be reviewed. Another good site is www.emeraldinsight.com, where you can read abstracts of articles from *The Journal of Services Marketing.* Investigate a services marketing topic of interest to you.

1 What publications are available regarding the topic you selected?

2 Describe two insights you obtained from the summaries of the publications.

BUILDING YOUR MARKETING PLAN

In this section of your marketing plan you should distinguish between your core product—a good or a service— and supplementary services.

1 Develop an internal marketing program that will ensure that employees are prepared to deliver the core and supplementary services.

2 Conduct a customer contact audit and create a flowchart similar to Figure 12–7 to identify specific points of interaction with customers.

3 Describe marketing activities that will (*a*) address each of the four I's as they relate to your service and (*b*) encourage the development of relationships with your customers.

Add this as an appendix to your marketing plan and use the results in developing your marketing mix strategy.

VIDEO CASE 12 Philadelphia Phillies, Inc.: Sports Marketing 101

"Bring everyone in closer. Have fans feel 'I'm not alone here; lots of others are in the seats. This is a *happening*!'" chuckles David Montgomery, President and Chief Executive Officer of the Philadelphia Phillies, Inc.

He continues, "Old Veterans Stadium had too big an inventory of seats for baseball. The new facility and the fact that it's a game played in summer out in the open air really takes you to a much broader audience. Our challenge is to appeal to all the segments in that audience." What Montgomery is referring to is the Phillies' new world-class Citizens Bank Park baseball stadium that opened in 2004. It is a baseball-only ballpark, seating 43,500 fans, where every seat is angled toward home plate to give fans the best view of the action. This contrasts the 62,000-seat Veterans Stadium that both the Phillies and the Philadelphia Eagles football team shared from 1971 to 2003 where sightlines were always a compromise for the two sports.

The new fan-friendly Phillies stadium is just one element in today's complex strategy to market the Philadelphia Phillies effectively to many different segments of fans—a far different challenge than in the past. A century ago major-league baseball was pretty simple. You built a stadium. You hired the ballplayers. You printed tickets—hoping and praying a winning team would bring in fans and sell those tickets. And your advertising consisted of printing the team's home schedule in the local paper.

THE PHILLIES TODAY: APPEALS, SEGMENTS, AND ACTIVITIES

Marketing a major-league baseball team is far different today.

"How do you market a product that is all over the board?" asks David Buck, the Phillies' vice president of marketing. He first gives a general answer to his question: "The ballpark experience is the key. As long as you project an image of a fun ballpark experience in everything you do, you're going to be in good shape. Our best advertising is word-of-mouth from happy fans."

Next come the specifics. Marketing the appeal of a fun ballpark experience to all segments of fans is critical because the Phillies can't promise a winning baseball team. Every team, even the New York Yankees, has its ups and downs. The Phillies are no different.

Reaching the different segments of fans is a special challenge because each segment is often looking for different things. Segments often break down by why the fan is there, many tied to special promotions:

- The die-hards. Intense baseball fans that are there to watch the strategy and see the Phillies win.
- Kids 14 years and under. At the game with the family, also to get bat or bobble-head doll premiums and have a "run-the-bases" day.
- Women and men 15 years and older. Special "days out," such as for Mother's Day or Father's Day.
- Seniors, 60 years and over. A "stroll-the-bases" day.
- 20-somethings and 30-somethings. Meet some friends at the ballpark for a fun night out.
- Corporate and community groups. At the game to have fun but also to get to know members of their organization better.

It's clear that not all fans are there for exactly the same "fun ballpark experience."

The segments don't stop there. Marisol Lezeano, the Phillies' community outreach coordinator, says, "In the Philadelphia area we've got a lot of different ethnic groups and we want to make all of them Phillies fans." So she plans special nights for these groups—Latino Family Celebration night with a Latino Legends poster of Phillies Hispanic players; Asia Pacific night with a giant cloth dragon dancing its way across the outfield; and The Sound of Philadelphia night honoring Black Music Month featuring various African-American music groups. "We want all communities to come to the ballpark. We're all fans. It's great. Please be with us," she emphasizes.

The "fun ballpark experience" today also goes beyond simply watching the Phillies play a baseball game. Fans at Citizens Bank Park can also:

- Buy souvenirs at the Phillies store—the "Phanatic Attic."
- Romp in the largest soft-play area for kids in Major League Baseball and scale a giant, inflatable baseball rock-climbing wall.
- Test their skills in a pitching game.
- Play a giant pinball game.
- Stroll through Ashburn Alley (named for a famous Phillie), an outdoor food and entertainment area to see the All-Star Walk and the Wall of Fame.
- Eat at McFadden's Restaurant and Saloon or Harry the K's Bar & Grill.

PROMOTIONAL ACTIVITIES

The range of the Phillies' promotional activities today is mind numbing. They start with "special promotion days," which typically increase fan attendance by 30 to 35 percent for a game, according to David Buck. These days often generate first-time visits by people who have never seen a major league baseball game. They generally fall into two categories: (1) event days and (2) premium gift days.

Event days can involve camera days where fans can take players' photos—three FUJIFILM Fridays each season for the Phillies. Or they can involve fireworks, an old-timers' game, or running or strolling the bases. Some events are especially memorable. Phillies fans still talk about the ostrich race in which a terrified Phillies' broadcaster wound up in the first row of stands when the ostrich pulling him and his cart panicked due to crowd noise.

"Our premiums or giveaways are directed at specific groups," says Scott Brandreth, the Phillies' merchandising manager. "During the year, we probably have 2 or 3 for all fans, 6 or 7 for children 14 years or younger, and maybe 1 for women over 15, and 1 for men over 15—often for Mother's Day and Father's Day." These giveaways range from bobble-head dolls and nesting dolls to baseball caps, rally towels, and Louisville Slugger bats. "A special premium we had that was very successful was a DVD celebrating the tenth anniversary of the Phillies 1993 National League pennant," he says. To control expenses, the Phillies try to keep the cost of the premiums in the range of $1 to $3.

Other promotional activities fall in both the traditional and nontraditional categories. Personal appearances at public and charity events by Phillies' players and their wives, radio and TV ads, and special events paid for by sponsors have been used by baseball teams for decades. But newer, more nontraditional promotions include naming rights (Citizens Bank Park) for the stadium, Phillies Phantasy Camp, luxury suite and special "infield club seats," and Phillies youth baseball clubs and leagues. And getting Phillies updates and ordering tickets on its website (phillies.com) are only a few years old.

Probably the best-known mascot in professional sports, the Phillie Phanatic is almost a Philadelphia legend. This oversized, green furry mascot has been around for over 25 years. Not only does he appear in the ballpark at all Phillies' home games, but also he makes appearances at charity and public events year round. Or rather the *three* Phanatics do so, because the demand is too great for a single Phanatic. "The Phanatic is a great character because he doesn't carry wins or losses," says David Montgomery. "Fans young and old can relate to him. . . He makes you smile, makes you laugh, and adds to the enjoyment of the game."

BOTTOM LINE: REVENUES AND EXPENSES

"We're a private business that serves the public," David Montgomery points out. "And we've got to make sure

our revenues more than cover our expenses." He identifies these key sources of revenues and gives the approximate annual percentages of each:

SOURCES OF REVENUE	APPROX. %
1. Ticket sales (home and away games)	52%
2. National media (network TV and radio)	13%
3. Local media (over-the-air TV, pay TV, radio)	13%
4. Advertising (publications, co-sponsorship promotions)	12%
5. Concessions (food, souvenirs, restaurants)	10%
Total	100%

Balanced against these revenues are some major expenses that include players' salaries (exceeding $93 million in 2004) and salaries of more than 150 full-time employees. Other expenses are those for scouting and drafting 40 to 60 new players per year, operating six minor-league farm clubs, and operating (with a labor force of 400 persons per game) Citizens Bank Park for the Phillies' 81 home games.

David Montgomery never gets bored. "When I finished business school, I had to choose between a marketing research job at a large paper products company or marketing the Philadelphia Phillies," explains Montgomery, who started with the Phillies by selling season and group tickets. "And it was no real decision because there never has been one day on this job that wasn't different and exciting," he says.

Questions

1 (*a*) What is the "product" that the Phillies market? (*b*) What "products" are the Phillies careful not to market?

2 How does the "quality" dimension in marketing the Philadelphia Phillies differ from that in marketing a consumer product such as a breakfast cereal or cake mix?

3 When David Montgomery talks about reducing the "inventory of seats" in the new versus old stadium, what does he recognize as (*a*) advantages and (*b*) disadvantages?

4 Considering all five elements of the promotional mix (advertising, personal selling, public relations, sales promotion, and direct marketing), what specific promotional activities should the Phillies use? Which should be used off-season? On-season?

5 What kind of special promotion gift days (with premiums) and event days (no premiums) can the Phillies use to increase attendance by targeting these segments: (*a*) 14 and under, (*b*) 15 and over, (*c*) other special fan segments, and (*d*) all fans?

priceline.com

<u>Sign-In</u>   <u>My Profile</u>   <u>My Trips</u>   <u>Help</u>   <u>Check Your Request</u>

 Airfare   Hotels   Rental Cars On Sale!   Vacation Packages   Cruises

New to priceline? <u>Find out more</u>.

Huge Rental Car Sale!
- <u>Save big on ALL car types</u>
- <u>Book by Nov. 7</u>
- <u>Best Prices Guaranteed</u>

Weekend Getaway Deals
Big Savings on Weekend
<u>Airfares</u>, <u>Hotels</u>, <u>Packages</u>,
<u>Rental Cars</u> and <u>Cruises</u>.

Last Minute Deals
- <u>Save up to 60% on airfare</u>
- <u>Hotels up to 6pm same day</u>
- <u>Air+Hotel packages</u>

Home Financing
Great Deals on <u>mortgages</u>,
and online <u>bank accounts</u>.
Save on Rates Now!

Nationwide Rental Car Sale!*

<u>Compact Car</u>
from **$17** /day

<u>Mid-Size Car</u>
from **$19** /day

<u>Full-Size Car</u>
from **$20** /day

Find Your Next Travel Deal

● Airfare   ○ <u>Hotels</u>   ○ <u>Rental Cars</u>   ○ <u>Packages</u>   ○ <u>Cruises</u>

Book Together and Save More!   ○ Air+Hotel   ○ Air+Hotel+Car

Departure City: [   ]

Arrival City: [   ]

Departure Date: [1/5/2005]

Return Date: [1/15/2005]

Number of Tickets: [1 ticket ▾]

NEW!
More Ways To Save!
▶ <u>One-Way</u>
▶ <u>Multi-Destination</u>
▶ <u>Advanced Search</u>

NEXT ▸

Great Savings - Our Best Deals and Sales
- <u>Flight Deals to Las Vegas</u>
- <u>Midwest's Big Air Sale</u>
- <u>All Inclusive Packages</u>
- <u>Ted on Sale from $165 round-trip</u>
- <u>Flights under $150 round-trip</u>
- <u>Great Weekend Getaways</u>

Great Weekend Escapes ▸▸   WESTERN UNION
westernunion.com   TEXAS

Get Exclusive Email Deals!
Your e-mail address:
[   ] **Go ▸**

Priceline City Guides
- <u>Best Places to Eat</u>
- <u>Shopping Hot Spots</u>
- <u>Parks, Tours, Golf...</u>
- <u>More Ideas for Your Trip</u>

13

BUILDING THE PRICE FOUNDATION

LEARNING OBJECTIVES

After reading this chapter you should be able to:

1 Identify the elements that make up a price.

2 Recognize the objectives a firm has in setting prices and the constraints that restrict the range of prices a firm can charge.

3 Explain what a demand curve is and the role of revenues in pricing decisions.

4 Describe what price elasticity of demand means to a manager facing a pricing decision.

5 Explain the role of costs in pricing decisions.

6 Describe how various combinations of price, fixed cost, and unit variable cost affect a firm's break-even point.

WHERE DOT-COMS STILL THRIVE: HELPING YOU GET A $100-A-NIGHT HOTEL ROOM OVERLOOKING NEW YORK'S CENTRAL PARK

"When I travel, I always go through Internet sites," Utah State student Catherine C. Woolley tells *BusinessWeek* magazine.[1] She used this strategy recently with Priceline.com to reserve a $100-a-night hotel room overlooking Central Park, a glitzy area in New York City. Despite the effects of the September 11, 2001, attacks had on the travel industry, online bookings are expected to rise to $75 billion in 2005, according to Internet travel research firm PhoCusWright. These online websites book airline tickets, hotel rooms, rental cars, and special travel and cruise packages for leisure and business travelers. In terms of market share, the top four online travel websites are Orbitz, Travelocity, Expedia, and Priceline, Catherine Woolley's hotel reservation supplier.

Why Travel Dot-Coms Haven't Tanked "There are a bunch of businesses that don't make sense at all on the Internet," says Mitchell J. Rubin, a money manager who has a lot of his fund invested in Internet travel companies. "Travel is the quintessential one that does," he continues.[2] Travel companies have beaten the dot-com odds by providing two key benefits to customers:

1. *Saving time.* User friendliness makes getting Internet travel reservations easy, often saving much time and misunderstanding.
2. *Saving money.* Customers can achieve substantial price savings using the travel dot-coms instead of using conventional booking services, such as travel agents.

Answer the questions below. The correct answers are given later in the chapter.

1. If you are marketing vice president of Airbus planning to introduce your 555-seat A380 Super Jumbo passenger jet in 2006, which price would you set? (*a*) $125 million, (*b*) $275 million, (*c*) $400 million, (*d*) $500 million.
2. In terms of long-run sensitivity to price, rank these commodities from the most sensitive to least sensitive: (*a*) jewelry and watches, (*b*) gasoline, (*c*) wine, (*d*) clothing.
3. As an airline, what are the circumstances under which you'd be happy to have Priceline sell a ticket at half the regular full-fare price?
4. In automating a manufacturing plant, which of these would definitely increase in the short run? (*a*) price, (*b*) fixed cost, (*c*) total revenue, (*d*) variable cost.

FIGURE 13–1

Quick-take quiz on price: Answers that are part numbers, part good judgment

Travel Dot-Com Prices: A Win-Win for Both Buyers and Sellers

The benefits to customers buying airline tickets and hotel reservations from dot-com travel companies are clear. But what are the benefits for airlines and hotels? The easy answer: The extra money United Airlines or Marriott Hotels receives when Orbitz or Priceline books their services more than offsets the expenses United or Marriott incurs if their tickets or rooms are sold through travel agencies or its own channels (agents or website).

But it's a bit more complex than that and involves carefully assessing prices, revenues, fixed costs, and variable costs. And if the answers were that easy, hundreds of failed dot-com firms with brilliant ideas, technologies, and marketing plans would still be going strong today. So question 3 in Figure 13–1 asks you when an airline would be happy to have, say, Priceline sell low-priced tickets. Spend a couple of minutes on the "quiz" and then compare your answers to those given throughout the chapter.

Among all marketing and operations factors in a business firm, price is unique. It is the place where all other business decisions come together. The price must be "right"—in the sense that customers must be willing to pay it and it must generate enough sales dollars to pay for the cost of developing, producing, and marketing the product *and* earn a profit for the company. Small changes in price can have big effects on both the number of units sold and company profit. In fact, among 1,000 large U.S. companies, research shows that a 1 percent price increase translates to a 12 percent increase in profitability, other factors remaining the same.[3]

Welcome to the fascinating—and intense—world of pricing, where many forces come together in the price potential buyers are asked to pay. This chapter covers important factors used in setting prices.

NATURE AND IMPORTANCE OF PRICE

The price paid for goods and services goes by many names. You pay *tuition* for your education, *rent* for an apartment, *interest* on a bank credit card, and a *premium* for car insurance. Your dentist or physician charges you a *fee,* a professional or social organization charges *dues,* and airlines charge a *fare.* In business, an executive is given a *salary,* a salesperson receives a *commission,* and a worker is paid a *wage.* And what you pay for clothes or a haircut is termed a *price.*

What Is a Price?

These examples highlight the many varied ways that price plays a part in our daily lives. From a marketing viewpoint, **price** is the money or other considerations

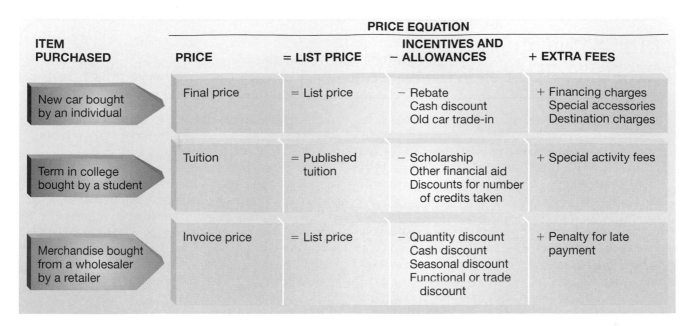

ITEM PURCHASED	PRICE EQUATION			
	PRICE	= LIST PRICE	INCENTIVES AND − ALLOWANCES	+ EXTRA FEES
New car bought by an individual	Final price	= List price	− Rebate Cash discount Old car trade-in	+ Financing charges Special accessories Destination charges
Term in college bought by a student	Tuition	= Published tuition	− Scholarship Other financial aid Discounts for number of credits taken	+ Special activity fees
Merchandise bought from a wholesaler by a retailer	Invoice price	= List price	− Quantity discount Cash discount Seasonal discount Functional or trade discount	+ Penalty for late payment

FIGURE 13–2

The price of three different purchases

(including other goods and services) exchanged for the ownership or use of a good or service. Recently, Wilkinson Sword exchanged some of its knives for advertising used to promote its razor blades. This practice of exchanging goods and services for other goods and services rather than for money is called **barter**. These transactions account for billions of dollars annually in domestic and international trade.

For most products, money is exchanged. However, the amount paid is not always the same as the list, or quoted, price because of discounts, allowances, and extra fees. While discounts, allowances, and rebates make the effective price lower, other marketing tactics raise the real price. One new twenty-first century pricing tactic is to use "special fees" and "surcharges." This practice is driven by consumers' zeal for low prices combined with the ease of making price comparisons on the Internet. Buyers are more willing to pay extra fees than a higher list price, so sellers use add-on charges as a way of having the consumer pay more without raising the list price.[4] Examples of such special fees include a Green Bay Packer "user fee" that can add $1,400 to the price of a season ticket or a 5 percent "environmental surcharge" by dry cleaners around the country.

All these different factors that increase or decrease the price are put together in a "price equation," which is shown for several different products in Figure 13–2. Suppose you decide you want to buy the newly introduced 2004 Bugatti Veyron, the

world's fastest production car, because its 8.0 litre, 1,001-horsepower V-16 engine moves you from 0 to 62 mph in 2.9 seconds at a top speed of 252 mph. The Veyron has a list price of $1.2 million, and only 300 are expected to be crafted. However, if you put $500,000 down now and finance the balance over the next year, you will receive a rebate of $100,000 off the list price and pay a finance charge of $26,317. To ship the car from France, you will pay a $5,000 destination charge. For your 2000 Honda Civic DX four-door sedan that has 60,000 miles and is in fair condition, you are given a trade-in allowance of $5,395, which is the *Kelley Blue Book* (www.kbb.com) trade-in value of your car.

ETHICS AND SOCIAL RESPONSIBILITY ALERT

Student Credit Cards— What Is the Real Price?

ETHICS

Thousands of college students and other adults across the nation are drowning in credit card debt. In 2003, the median credit card balance among college students was $1,770, up 43 percent from 2000. And the average college freshman receives 50 applications from credit card companies during the year.

College students are part of the under-25 age group that represents the fastest-growing bankruptcy filers in the country. When adding in student loans—exempt from bankruptcy—rent, car payments, utilities, telephone, taxes, and interest, few starting salaries of college graduates will be high enough to cover much beyond minimum payments on the $5,000 of average credit card debt they have at graduation.

The real price of student credit cards goes far beyond the 19.8 percent annual interest rate many companies charge. This interest is far higher than students with good credit ratings would pay for loans from their local bank. But the nonfinancial price for students may be even higher: College health services that offer psychological counseling report that many students suffer from serious depression be-

cause of their credit card debt. Other students are forced to drop out of college to go to work to repay their credit card debt.

What can students do who are over their heads in credit card debt? Some universities offer on-campus financial counseling. Or students can find savings in their utilities, wireless, long-distance and Internet services, insurance, and credit cards by logging onto www.lowermybills.com. Nellie Mae, the nation's lending education funder, provides students with debt-management tools and help at www.nelliemae.com. Financial counselors have two other bits of advice for students: (1) reduce the number of credit cards you have and (2) pay cash. Paying cash forces some hard thinking that is avoided by simply bringing out a plastic credit card.

What should be done to help students address their credit card debt problems? Require them to take personal finance training? Restrict the number of cards they own? Lower the maximum credit line? Have Congress pass laws to rein in credit card companies? What do you think?

Applying the price equation (as shown in Figure 13–2) to your purchase, your final price is:

$$\text{Final price} = \text{List price} - (\text{Incentives} + \text{Allowances}) + \text{Extra fees}$$
$$= \$1,200,000 - (\$100,000 + \$5,395) + (\$26,317 + \$5,000)$$
$$= \$1,135,922$$

Your monthly payment for the one-year loan of $600,000 is $52,193.06.[5] Are you still interested?

That monthly payment a bit too high for your credit card? Of course, and it's a silly question. But study the Ethics and Social Responsibility Alert to see some very difficult issues concerning student credit card debt that are not silly and that students should be aware of when using their credit cards.[6]

Price as an Indicator of Value

From a consumer's standpoint, price is often used to indicate value when it is compared with the perceived benefits of a product or service. Specifically, **value** is the ratio of perceived benefits to price, or[7]

$$\text{Value} = \frac{\text{Perceived benefits}}{\text{Price}}$$

This relationship shows that for a given price, as perceived benefits increase, value increases. For example, if you're used to paying $9.99 for a medium pizza, wouldn't a large pizza at the same price be more valuable? Conversely, for a given price, value decreases when perceived benefits decrease.

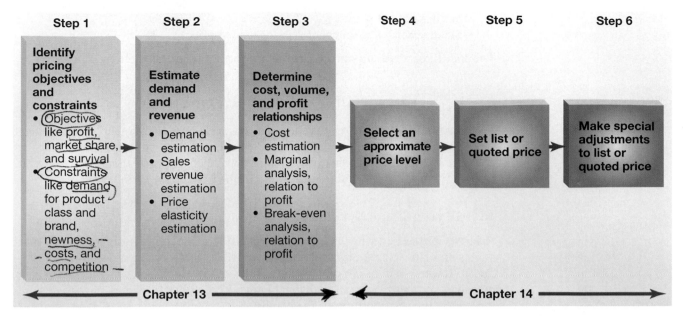

FIGURE 13–3

Steps in setting price

Creative marketers engage in **value-pricing**, the practice of simultaneously increasing product and service benefits while maintaining or decreasing price. For some products, price influences consumers' perception of overall quality and ultimately its value to consumers.[8] In a survey of home furnishing buyers, 84 percent agreed with the statement: "The higher the price, the higher the quality."[9] For example, Kohler introduced a walk-in bathtub that is safer for children and the elderly. Although priced higher than conventional step-in bathtubs, it has proven very successful because buyers are willing to pay more for what they perceive as the value of the extra safety. Here value involves the judgment by a consumer of the worth and desirability of a product or service relative to substitutes that satisfy the same need. In this instance a "reference value" emerges, which involves comparing the costs and benefits of substitute items. In another example, the value of "supersizing" at fast-food restaurants comes from getting more bang for your buck—generally, a larger quantity for about the same price.

Price in the Marketing Mix

Pricing is a critical decision made by a marketing executive because price has a direct effect on a firm's profits. This is apparent from a firm's **profit equation**:

$$\text{Profit} = \text{Total revenue} - \text{Total cost}$$
$$= (\text{Unit price} \times \text{Quantity sold}) - \text{Total cost}$$

What makes this relationship even more complicated is that price affects the quantity sold, as illustrated with demand curves later in this chapter. Furthermore, since the quantity sold sometimes affects a firm's costs because of efficiency of production, price also indirectly affects costs. Thus, pricing decisions influence both total revenue (sales) and total cost, which makes pricing one of the most important decisions marketing executives face.

The importance of price in the marketing mix necessitates an understanding of six major steps involved in the process organizations go through in setting prices (Figure 13–3):

- Identify pricing objectives and constraints.
- Estimate demand and revenue.
- Determine cost, volume, and profit relationships.
- Select an approximate price level.

- Set list or quoted price.
- Make special adjustments to list or quoted price.

The first three steps are covered in this chapter and the last three in Chapter 14.

STEP 1: IDENTIFY PRICING OBJECTIVES AND CONSTRAINTS

With such a variety of alternative pricing strategies available, a marketing manager must consider the pricing objectives and constraints that will narrow the range of choices. While pricing objectives frequently reflect corporate goals, pricing constraints often relate to conditions existing in the marketplace.

Identifying Pricing Objectives

Pricing objectives involve specifying the role of price in an organization's marketing and strategic plans. To the extent possible, these pricing objectives are carried to lower levels in the organization, such as in setting objectives for marketing managers responsible for an individual brand. These objectives may change depending on the financial position of the company as a whole, the success of its products, or the segments in which it is doing business. H. J. Heinz, for example, has specific pricing objectives for its Heinz ketchup brand that vary by country. Chapter 2 discussed six broad objectives that an organization may pursue, which tie in directly to the organization's pricing policies.

Profit   Three different objectives relate to a firm's profit, which is often measured in terms of return on investment (ROI) or return on assets (ROA). These objectives have different implications for pricing strategy. One objective is *managing for long-run profits,* in which a company—such as many Japanese car or TV set manufacturers—gives up immediate profit in exchange for achieving a higher market share by developing quality products to penetrate competitive markets. Products are priced relatively low compared to their cost to develop, but the firm expects to make greater profits later because of its high market share.

A *maximizing current profit* objective, such as for a quarter or year, is common in many firms because the targets can be set and performance measured quickly. American firms are sometimes criticized for this short-run orientation. As noted earlier, a *target return* objective occurs when a firm sets a profit goal (such as 20 percent for pretax ROI), usually determined by its board of directors. These three profit objectives have different implications for a firm's pricing objectives.

Another profit consideration for firms such as movie studios and manufacturers is to ensure that those firms in their channels of distribution make adequate profits. Without profits for these channel members, the movie studio or manufacturer is cut off from its customers. For example, Figure 13–4 shows where each dollar of your movie ticket goes. The 51 cents the movie studio gets must cover its profit plus the cost of making and marketing the movie, which averaged an all-time high of $103 million in 2003.[10] Although the studio would like more than 51 cents of your dollar, it settles for this amount to make sure theaters and distributors are satisfied and willing to handle its movies.

FIGURE 13–4
Where each dollar of your movie ticket goes

Theater 19¢

Distributor 30¢

Movie studio 51¢

10¢ = Theater expenses
9¢ = Left for theater
6¢ = Misc. expenses
24¢ = Left for distributor
20¢ = Advertising and publicity expenses
8¢ = Actors' share of gross
23¢ = Left for movie studio

Sales   Given that a firm's profit is high enough for it to remain in business, an objective may be to increase sales revenue, which will in turn lead to increases in market share and profit. Objectives related to sales revenue or

Are these real "collectibles" or "trashables"? The text describes factors that affect a product's price. And you can check the Web Link to see if those old Beanie Babies or Nikes in your attic or a recent Ichiro Suzuki bobble head doll have value.

unit sales have the advantage of being translated more easily into meaningful targets for marketing managers responsible for a product line or brand than profit objectives. However, cutting price on one product in a firm's line may increase its sales revenue but reduce those of related products.

Market Share   Market share is the ratio of the firm's sales revenues or unit sales to those of the industry (competitors plus the firm itself). Companies often pursue a market share objective when industry sales are relatively flat or declining. In the late 1990s, Boeing cut prices drastically to try to maintain its 60 percent market share and encountered huge losses. Although increased market share is a primary goal of some firms, others see it as a means to other ends: increasing sales and profits.

Unit Volume   Many firms use *unit volume,* the quantity produced or sold, as a pricing objective. These firms often sell multiple products at very different prices and need to match the unit volume demanded by customers with price and production capacity. Using unit volume as an objective can be counterproductive if a volume objective is achieved, say, by drastic price cutting that drives down profit.

Survival   In some instances, profits, sales, and market share are less important objectives of the firm than mere survival. Specialty-toy retailers increasingly are facing survival problems because they can't match price cuts by big discount retailers like Wal-Mart and Target, the reason FAO Schwartz filed for bankruptcy in late 2003.[11]

Social Responsibility   A firm may forgo higher profit on sales and follow a pricing objective that recognizes its obligations to customers and society in general. Medtronics followed this pricing policy when it introduced the world's first heart pacemaker. A critical social responsibility issue today is drug pricing—setting a price low enough to make the drug affordable by consumers needing it but high enough for drug companies to cover research costs and make a profit.[12]

Identifying Pricing Constraints

Factors that limit the range of prices a firm may set are **pricing constraints**. Consumer demand for the product clearly affects the price that can be charged. Other constraints on price vary from factors within the organization to competitive factors outside the organization. Legal and regulatory constraints on pricing are discussed in Chapter 14.

Demand for the Product Class, Product, and Brand   The number of potential buyers for the product class (cars), product (sports cars), and brand (Bugatti

Veyron) clearly affects the price a seller can charge. So does whether the item is a luxury—like a Veyron—or a necessity—like bread and a roof over your head. Generally, the greater the demand for a product, the higher the price that can be set. The nature of demand is discussed later in the chapter.

Newness of the Product: Stage in the Product Life Cycle The newer a product and the earlier it is in its life cycle, the higher is the price that can usually be charged. Willing to spend up to $2,000 for a new tablet PC? The high initial price is possible because of patents and limited competition early in its product life cycle. By the time you read this, the price will probably be much lower.

Sometimes—when nostalgia or fad factors come into play—prices may rise later in the product's life cycle. As described in the Web Link, collectibles such as a 1952 Mickey Mantle baseball card or old sneakers can experience skyrocketing prices.[13] But they can take a nosedive too. Publishing competitive prices on the Internet for the same or similar brands of products has revolutionized access to price comparisons for both collectors and buyers of more traditional products.[14]

Single Product versus a Product Line When Sony introduced its Walkman CD player, it was not only unique and in the introductory stage of its product life cycle but also the *only* CD player Sony sold, so the firm had great latitude in setting a price. Now, with a wide range of Sony CD products and technologies, the price of individual models has to be consistent with the others based on features provided, and meaningful price differentials must communicate value to consumers.

Cost of Producing and Marketing the Product In the long run, a firm's price must cover all the costs of producing and marketing a product. If the price doesn't cover these costs, the firm will fail; so in the long run, a firm's costs set a floor under its price. No-frills airlines like Southwest, JetBlue, and AirTran that set low airfares are forcing large competing U.S. airlines to cut costs and lower ticket prices.[15]

THE TERRITORY AHEAD
Exceptional Clothing for Life's Adventures
www.territoryahead.com

Setting hundreds of prices that will be valid for the life of a catalog involves many risky decisions.

Cost of Changing Prices and Time Period They Apply If Scandinavian Airlines asks General Electric (GE) to provide spare jet engines to power the new Boeing 737 it just bought, GE can easily set a new price for the engines to reflect its latest information since only one buyer has to be informed. But if The Territory Ahead decides that sweater prices are too low in its catalogs after thousands of catalogs have been mailed to customers, it has a big problem, so it must consider the cost of changing prices and the time period for which they apply in developing the price list for its catalog items. A recent study of four supermarket chains found the average annual cost of these price changes was $105,887, which represents 0.70 percent of revenues and an astounding 35.2 percent of net margins.[16] In actual practice, research indicates that most firms change the prices of their major products once a year.[17] But on a website, prices can change from minute to minute.[18]

Type of Competitive Markets The seller's price is constrained by the type of market in which it competes. Economists generally delineate four types of competitive markets: pure monopoly, oligopoly, monopolistic competition, and pure competition. Figure 13–5 shows that the type of competition dramatically influences the range of price competition and, in turn, the nature of product differentiation and extent of advertising. A firm must recognize the general type of competitive market it is in to understand the range of both its price and nonprice strategies. For example, prices can be significantly affected by four competitive situations:

- *Pure monopoly.* In 1994, Johnson & Johnson (J&J) revolutionized the treatment of coronary heart diseases by introducing the stent—a tiny mesh tube "spring"

WEB LINK

Pricing 101: $4,205 for a 1969 Used Hotwheels Volkswagen Van, or $121,000 for a Mint-Condition 1952 Mickey Mantle Topps Baseball Card?

www.mhhe.com/Kerin

Prices of collectibles, such as toys or old sneakers, are set by demand and supply forces discussed in this chapter. And for fads, the prices can fluctuate wildly. Here are some other recent collectibles prices, besides those mentioned above:

- Zip the Cat Beanie Baby: $260 (if it has black paws).
- 1985 Nike Dunks, high-top, blue-and-black basketball shoes: $2,300.
- 2001 Ichiro Suzuki bobble head doll: $305.

To get a feel for prices of some of these collectibles, visit www.ebay.com.

Marathon runner Malcolm East now wishes he had done a little more research on sneaker prices. At his wife's insistence he threw out six pairs of old shoes—that he now thinks would have fetched $15,000.

Want in on the collectibles business? Think twice. Zip the Cat Beanie Baby sold for $2,250 in 1998, about $2,000 more than in 2004.

that props open clogged arteries. Initially a monopolist, J&J stuck with its early $1,595 price and achieved $1 billion in sales and 91 percent market share by the end of 1996. But its reluctance to give price reductions for large-volume purchases to hospitals antagonized them. When competitors introduced an improved stent at lower prices, J&J's market share plummeted to 8 percent two years later.[19] Microsoft is another example. Its competitors and customers have argued in court that it engaged in illegal acts that reduced competition and increased prices.[20]

- *Oligopoly.* The few sellers of aluminum (Reynolds, Alcoa) or large jetliners (Boeing, Airbus) try to avoid price competition because it can lead to disastrous price wars in which all lose money. Yet firms in such industries stay aware of a competitor's price cuts or increases and may follow suit. The products can be undifferentiated (aluminum) or differentiated (large jetliners), and informative advertising that avoids head-to-head price competition is used.[21]

FIGURE 13–5

Pricing, product, and advertising strategies available to firms in four types of competitive markets

TYPE OF COMPETITIVE MARKET

STRATEGIES AVAILABLE	PURE MONOPOLY (One seller who sets the price for a unique product)	OLIGOPOLY (Few sellers who are sensitive to each other's prices)	MONOPOLISTIC COMPETITION (Many sellers who compete on nonprice factors)	PURE COMPETITION (Many sellers who follow the market price for identical, commodity products)
Extent of price competition	None: sole seller sets price	Some: price leader or follower of competitors	Some: compete over range of prices	Almost none: market sets price
Extent of product differentiation	None: no other producers	Various: depends on industry	Some: differentiate products from competitors	None: products are identical
Extent of advertising	Little: purpose is to increase demand for product class	Some: purpose is to inform but avoid price competition	Much: purpose is to differentiate firm's products from competitors	Little: purpose is to inform prospects that seller's products are available

- *Monopolistic competition.* Dozens of regional, private brands of peanut butter compete with national brands like Skippy and Jif. Both price competition (regional, private brands being lower than national brands) and nonprice competition (product features and advertising) exist.
- *Pure competition.* Hundreds of local grain elevators sell corn whose price per bushel is set by the marketplace. Within strains, the corn is identical, so advertising only informs buyers that the seller's corn is available.

Competitors' Prices   A firm must know or anticipate what specific price its present and potential competitors are charging now or will charge. In 2004, U.S. auto manufacturers wanted to raise prices but seldom did because of competitors' prices and the price "deals" that had become almost standard in the industry the last several years.[22]

Concept Check

1. What factors impact the list price to determine the final price?
2. What is the difference between pricing objectives and pricing constraints?
3. How does the type of competitive market a firm is in affect its range in setting price?

STEP 2: ESTIMATE DEMAND AND REVENUE

Basic to setting a product's price is the extent of customer demand for it. Marketing executives must also translate this estimate of customer demand into estimates of revenues the firm expects to receive.

Newsweek

Fundamentals of Estimating Demand

How much money would you pay for your favorite magazine? If the price kept going up, at some point you would probably quit buying it. Conversely, if the price kept going down, you might eventually decide not only to keep buying your magazine but also to get your friend a subscription too. The lower the price, the higher the demand. The publisher wants to sell more magazines, but will it sell enough additional copies to make up for the lower price per copy? That is an important question for marketing managers. Here's how one firm decided to find out.

Newsweek conducted a pricing experiment at newsstands in 11 cities throughout the United States. At that time, Houston newsstand buyers paid $2.25, while in Fort Worth, New York, Los Angeles, and Atlanta they paid the regular $2.00 price. In San Diego, the price was $1.50, while in Minneapolis–St. Paul, New Orleans, and Detroit it was only $1.00. By comparison, the regular newsstand price for *Time* and *U.S. News & World Report, Newsweek*'s competitors, was $1.95. Why did *Newsweek* conduct the experiment? According to a *Newsweek* executive, "We want to figure out what the demand curve for our magazine at the newsstand is."[23]

The Demand Curve   A **demand curve** is a graph relating the quantity sold and price, which shows the maximum number of units that will be sold at a given price. Demand curve D_1 in Figure 13–6A shows the newsstand demand for *Newsweek* under the existing conditions. Note that as price falls, more people decide

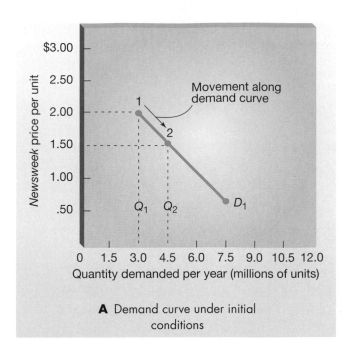

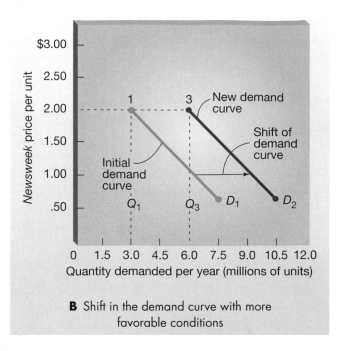

FIGURE 13–6

Illustrative demand curves for *Newsweek*

to buy and unit sales increase. But price is not the complete story in estimating demand. Economists emphasize three other key factors:

1. *Consumer tastes.* As we saw in Chapter 3, these depend on many factors such as demographics, culture, and technology. Because consumer tastes can change quickly, up-to-date marketing research is essential.
2. *Price and availability of similar products.* The laws of demand work for one's competitors, too. If the price of *Time* magazine falls, more people will buy it. That then means fewer people will buy *Newsweek. Time* is considered by economists to be a substitute for *Newsweek.* Online magazines are also a substitute, one whose availability has increased tremendously in recent years. The point to remember is, as the price of substitutes falls or their availability increases, the demand for a product (*Newsweek,* in this case) will fall.
3. *Consumer income.* In general, as real consumer income (allowing for inflation) increases, demand for a product also increases.

The first two factors influence what consumers *want* to buy, and the third affects what they *can* buy. Along with price, these are often called **demand factors**, or factors that determine consumers' willingness and ability to pay for goods and services. As discussed earlier in Chapters 8 and 10, it is often very difficult to estimate demand for new products, especially because consumer likes and dislikes are often so difficult to read clearly. For example, Campbell Soup spent seven years and $55 million on a supersecret project to produce a line of Intelligent Quisine (IQ) food products. The company expected that its line of 41 breakfasts, lunches, dinners, and snacks would be the first foods "scientifically proven to lower high levels of cholesterol, blood sugar, and blood pressure."[24] After 15 months in an Ohio test market, Campbell Soup yanked the entire IQ line when it fell far short of expectations because customers found the line too pricey and lacking in variety.

Movement Along versus Shift of a Demand Curve   Demand curve D_1 in Figure 13–6A shows that as the price is lowered from $2.00 to $1.50, the quantity demanded increases from 3.0 million (Q_1) to 4.5 million (Q_2) units per year. This is an example of a *movement along a demand curve* and assumes that other factors (consumer tastes, price and availability of substitutes, and consumer income) remain unchanged.

FIGURE 13–7

Fundamental revenue concepts

Total revenue (TR) is the total money received from the sale of product. If

    TR = Total revenue
    P = Unit price of the product
    Q = Quantity of the product sold

Then

    $TR = P \times Q$

Average revenue (AR) is the average amount of money received for selling one unit of a product, or simply the price of that unit. Average revenue is the total revenue divided by the quantity sold:

$$AR = \frac{TR}{Q} = P$$

Marginal revenue (MR) is the change in total revenue that results from producing and marketing one additional unit:

$$MR = \frac{\text{Change in TR}}{\text{1 unit increase in Q}} = \frac{\Delta TR}{\Delta Q} = \text{slope of TR curve}$$

What if some of these factors do change? For example, if advertising causes more people to want *Newsweek,* newsstand distribution is increased; or if consumer incomes rise, then the demand for all magazines, including *Newsweek,* increases. Now the original curve, D_1 (the blue line in Figure 13–6B), no longer represents the demand; instead, a new curve, D_2, must be drawn. D_2 (the red line in Figure 13–6B) represents the new demand for *Newsweek.* Economists call this a *shift in the demand curve*—in this case, a shift to the right, from D_1 to D_2. This increased demand means that more *Newsweek* magazines are wanted for a given price: At a price of $2.00, the demand is 6 million units per year (Q_3) on D_2 rather than 3 million units per year (Q_1) on D_1.

Fundamentals of Estimating Revenue

While economists may talk about "demand curves," marketing executives are more likely to speak in terms of "revenues generated," which are the monies received by the firm for selling its products. Demand curves lead directly to three related revenue concepts critical to pricing decisions: **total revenue**, **average revenue**, and **marginal revenue** (Figure 13–7).

Demand Curves and Revenue Figure 13–8A again shows the demand curve for *Newsweek,* but it is now extended to intersect both the price and quantity axes. The demand curve shows that as price is changed, the quantity of *Newsweek* magazines sold throughout the United States changes. This relationship holds whether the price is increased from $2.50 to $3.00 on the demand curve or is reduced from $1 to $0 on the curve. In the former case the market demands no *Newsweek* magazines, whereas in the latter case 9 million could be given away at $0 per unit.

It is likely that if *Newsweek* was given away, more than 9 million would be demanded. This fact illustrates two important points. First, it can be dangerous to extend a demand curve beyond the range of prices for which it really applies. Second, most demand curves are rounded (or convex) to the origin, thereby avoiding an unrealistic picture of what demand looks like when a straight-line curve intersects either the price axis or the quantity axis.

Figure 13–8B shows the total revenue curve for *Newsweek* calculated from the demand curve shown in Figure 13–8A. The total revenue curve is developed by

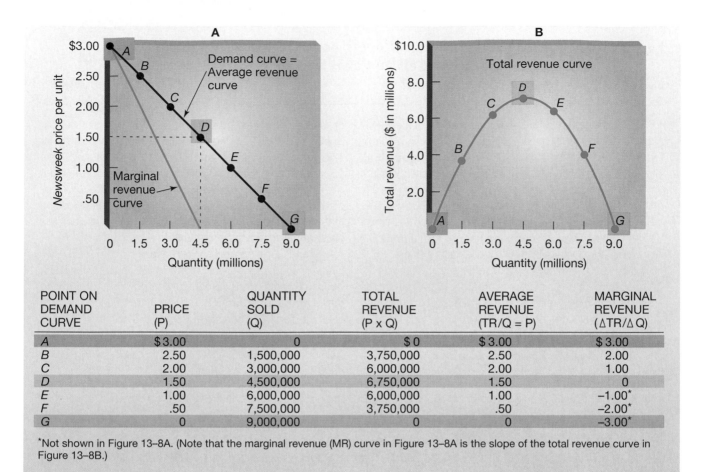

POINT ON DEMAND CURVE	PRICE (P)	QUANTITY SOLD (Q)	TOTAL REVENUE (P x Q)	AVERAGE REVENUE (TR/Q = P)	MARGINAL REVENUE (ΔTR/ΔQ)
A	$3.00	0	$0	$3.00	$3.00
B	2.50	1,500,000	3,750,000	2.50	2.00
C	2.00	3,000,000	6,000,000	2.00	1.00
D	1.50	4,500,000	6,750,000	1.50	0
E	1.00	6,000,000	6,000,000	1.00	−1.00*
F	.50	7,500,000	3,750,000	.50	−2.00*
G	0	9,000,000	0	0	−3.00*

*Not shown in Figure 13–8A. (Note that the marginal revenue (MR) curve in Figure 13–8A is the slope of the total revenue curve in Figure 13–8B.)

FIGURE 13–8

How a downward-sloping demand curve affects total, average, and marginal revenue

simply multiplying the unit price times the quantity for each of the points on the demand curve. Total revenue starts at $0 (point *A*), reaches a maximum of $6,750,000 at point *D*, and returns to $0 at point *G*. This shows that as price is reduced in the *A*-to-*D* segment of the curve, total revenue is increased. However, cutting price in the *D*-to-*G* segment results in a decline in total revenue.

Marginal revenue, which is the slope of the total revenue curve, is positive but decreasing when the price lies in the range from $3 to above $1.50 per unit. Below $1.50 per unit, though, marginal revenue is actually negative, so the extra quantity of magazines sold is more than offset by the decrease in the price per unit.

For any downward-sloping, straight-line demand curve, the marginal revenue curve always falls at a rate twice as fast as the demand curve. As shown in Figure 13–8A, the marginal revenue becomes $0 per unit at a quantity sold of 4.5 million units—the very point at which total revenue is maximum (see Figure 13–8B). A rational marketing manager would never operate in the region of the demand curve in which marginal revenue is negative. This means that in Figure 13–8A this manager would set prices only in the *A*-to-*D* segment of the demand curve. Also, when market share falls, the easy answer is to cut price, often with devastating results: A 1 percent price cut in the food and drug industry results in a 24 percent decline in profits, other factors being equal.[25]

What price did *Newsweek* select after conducting its experiment? It kept the price at $2.00. However, through expanded newsstand distribution and more aggressive advertising, *Newsweek* was later able to shift its demand curve to the right and charge a price of $2.50 without affecting its newsstand volume.

The Airbus versus Boeing Face-Off—How Many Can We Sell and at What Price . . . in 2006 and 2008?

GLOBAL

Are you interested in flying the eighth wonder of the world? Airbus is counting on it, when it introduces the new $275 million A380 super jumbo jet in 2006 (question 1, Figure 13–1). The A380 (below left) will carry at least 555 passengers in a double-decker bus design that may include sleeping berths, restaurants, and a casino. Airbus must sell 250 A380s to break even because development costs may reach $12 billion.

The A380 targets the growing market for large (500+ seats) passenger jets, which Airbus forecasts will total 1,535 planes by 2020. To stimulate initial demand, Airbus gave early A380 customers deep discounts of up to 40 percent off the list price. Airbus believes that the A380's economics provides a strong incentive for many airlines to buy the huge airplane: Only 323 passengers are needed to break even—the rest of the seats provide the potential of additional profits. As a result, Airbus had firm orders for 139 of its A380s by late 2004.

Boeing, too, carefully assessed the passenger jet market and came to a significantly different conclusion. As a result

of in-depth marketing research over a two-year period, Boeing decided (1) to defer work on a "stretch" version of its 747 (known as the 747X) in 2001 to compete with the A380, believing that consumers did not really care about sleeping berths or restaurants, and (2) to halt the development of its Sonic Cruiser in 2003 based on the conclusions that airlines were more interested in a super-efficient airplane rather than a faster airplane.

Instead, Boeing announced plans for its new 787 Dreamliner passenger jet (below right), one that will reduce fuel costs by 20 percent while significantly improving the environment through more efficient and powerful engines. The 787 Dreamliner targets the mid-size (200- to 300-passenger-seat) jet market, which Boeing forecasts will total 3,500 airplanes by 2023. In mid-2004 Boeing had orders for 62 Dreamliners, which will enter service in 2008. Time will tell whether Airbus or Boeing read their customers better.

Does forecasting future demand and revenue sound easy? Study the Marketing NewsNet above to understand the special difficulties that Airbus and Boeing face trying to forecast the demand and revenue for their revolutionary airliners five or six years before they roll off the production line.[26]

Price Elasticity of Demand With a downward-sloping demand curve, marketing managers are especially interested in how sensitive consumer demand and the firm's revenues are to changes in the product's price. This can be conveniently measured by **price elasticity of demand**, or the percentage change in quantity demanded relative to a percentage change in price. Price elasticity of demand (E) is expressed as follows:

$$E = \frac{\text{Percentage change in quantity demanded}}{\text{Percentage change in price}}$$

Is clothing or gasoline more sensitive to price changes? For the answer see the text and its discussion of price elasticity of demand.

Because quantity demanded usually decreases as price increases, price elasticity of demand is usually a negative number. However, for the sake of simplicity and by convention, elasticity figures are shown as positive numbers. Finally, price elasticity of demand assumes three forms: elastic demand, inelastic demand, and unitary demand.

Elastic demand exists when a 1 percent decrease in price produces more than a 1 percent increase in quantity demanded, thereby actually increasing sales revenue. This results in a price elasticity that is greater than 1 with elastic demand. In other words, a product with elastic demand is one in which a slight decrease in price results in a relatively large increase in demand or units sold. The reverse is also true; with elastic demand, a slight increase in price results in a relatively large decrease in demand. So marketers may cut price to increase consumer demand, the units sold, and total revenue for one of these products, depending on what competitors' prices are.

Inelastic demand exists when a 1 percent decrease in price produces less than a 1 percent increase in quantity demanded, thereby actually decreasing sales revenue. This results in a price elasticity that is less than 1 with inelastic demand. So a product with inelastic demand means that slight increases or decreases in price will not significantly affect the demand, or units sold, for the product. The concern for marketers is that while lowering price will increase the quantity sold, revenues will actually fall. *Unitary demand* exists when the percentage change in price is identical to the percentage change in quantity demanded so that sales revenue remains the same. In this instance, price elasticity is equal to 1.

The price elasticity of CDs is the reason that Vivendi Universal ran a series of test markets across the United States to find what it calls the maximum pricing "sweet spot" among shoppers. The ideal retail price for CDs was found to be $12.98—what you are probably paying now at a music store. To implement this pricing structure in late 2003, Vivendi cut the top wholesale price it charges retailers from $12.02 to $9.09, which should lead to retail price reductions up to 32 percent. Two other factors probably influenced Vivendi's pricing decision: (1) the widespread online music piracy and (2) the price cuts in DVDs several years earlier, which caused people to start buying DVDs rather than renting them and to discover they are sometimes cheaper than buying CDs.[27]

Price elasticity of demand is determined by a number of factors. First, the more substitutes a product or service has, the more likely it is to be price elastic. For example, a new sweater, shirt, or blouse has many possible substitutes and is price elastic, but gasoline has almost no substitutes and is price inelastic. Second, products and services considered to be necessities are price inelastic, so open-heart surgery is price inelastic, whereas airline tickets for a vacation are price elastic. Third, items that require a large cash outlay compared with a person's disposable income are price elastic. Accordingly, cars and yachts are price elastic; books tend to be price inelastic.

Price elasticity is important to marketing managers because of its relationship to total revenue, so it is important that marketing managers recognize that price elasticity of demand is not the same over all possible prices of a product. Figure 13–8B illustrates this point using the *Newsweek* demand curve shown in Figure 13–8A. As the price decreases from $2.50 to $2.00, total revenue increases, indicating an elastic demand. However, when the price decreases from $1.00 to 50 cents, total revenue declines, indicating an inelastic demand. Unitary demand elasticity exists at a price of $1.50.

Because 12- to 17-year-olds often have limited "spending money," this group is very price elastic in its demand for cigarettes. As a result, many legislators recommend far higher excise taxes on cigarettes to increase their prices significantly with the goal of reducing teenage smoking. Thus, price elasticity is not only a relevant concept for marketing managers, but it also important for public policy affecting pricing practices.[28]

STEP 3: DETERMINE COST, VOLUME, AND PROFIT RELATIONSHIPS

Why is Pets.com only a memory while its sock puppet has found new life? For the answers, see the text and the Marketing NewsNet.

While revenues are the monies received by the firm from selling its products or services to customers, costs or expenses are the monies the firm pays out to its employees and suppliers. Marketing managers often use marginal analysis and break-even analysis to relate revenues and costs, topics covered in this section.

The Importance of Controlling Costs

Understanding the role and behavior of costs is critical for all marketing decisions, particularly pricing decisions. Five cost concepts are important in pricing decisions: **total cost**, **fixed cost**, **variable cost**, **unit variable cost**, and **marginal cost** (Figure 13–9).

Many firms go bankrupt because their costs get out of control, causing their total costs to exceed their total revenues over an extended period of time. This is why sophisticated marketing managers make pricing decisions that balance both their revenues and costs. As described in the Marketing NewsNet, travel dot-com firms have been more successful than their brick-and-mortar counterparts at least partly because of far lower fixed costs.[29] But the high fixed costs tied up in an airline's planes is the reason an airline is delighted to sell last-day tickets for half of the full fare because the revenue obtained by filling the seat far exceeds the low unit variable cost of the passenger's meal and baggage handling (question 3, Figure 13–1).

FIGURE 13–9
Fundamental cost concepts

Total cost (TC) is the total expense incurred by a firm in producing and marketing a product. Total cost is the sum of fixed cost and variable cost.

Fixed cost (FC) is the sum of the expenses of the firm that are stable and do not change with the quantity of a product that is produced and sold. Examples of fixed costs are rent on the building, executive salaries, and insurance.

Variable cost (VC) is the sum of the expenses of the firm that vary directly with the quantity of a product that is produced and sold. For example, as the quantity sold doubles, the variable cost doubles. Examples are the direct labor and direct materials used in producing the product and the sales commissions that are tied directly to the quantity sold. As mentioned above:

$$TC = FC + VC$$

Variable cost expressed on a per unit basis is called **unit variable cost (UVC)**, or:

$$UVC = \frac{VC}{Q}$$

Marginal cost (MC) is the change in total cost that results from producing and marketing one additional unit of a product:

$$MC = \frac{\text{Change in TC}}{\text{1 unit increase in Q}} = \frac{\Delta TC}{\Delta Q} = \text{slope of TC curve}$$

MARKETING NEWSNET   Pricing Lessons from the Dot-Coms— Understand Revenues and Expenses   **TECHNOLOGY & E-COMMERCE**

Price, revenue, fixed cost, variable cost. Boring topics from finance or economics? But they are also critical to marketing success, as shown by lessons learned by the successful travel dot-coms so far.

Brick-and-Mortar Dot-Com Failures
During the past decade, hundreds of dot-coms have failed, many of them brick-and-mortar businesses like Pets.com (pet products) and Webvan (online groceries). Here are some reasons for these failures:

- Setting prices too low to cover the huge brick-and-mortar fixed costs of inventory, warehouses, and order fulfillment, especially on low-margin goods like groceries (Webvan).
- Spending too much on promotion, such as Pets.com's $2.2 million on Super Bowl XXXV ads.
- Believing people would forgo shopping at traditional stores, a problem, for example, with Pets.com competing with Petsmart.

As a result, Pets.com was liquidated. However, the Pets.com sock puppet, because of its visibility, was bought

by and serves as the "spokespuppet" for BarNone, a firm that helps consumers with poor credit obtain automobiles.

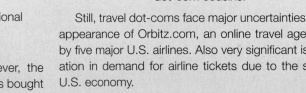

Everyone Deserves a Second Chance, BarNone

Travel Dot-Com Successes (So Far)
Besides time and money savings for customers, the travel dot-coms have special strategies for success:

- Reaching key customer segments that will actually pay *higher* prices for hotel rooms or airline tickets.
- Reaching customer segments (students, senior citizens) whose last-minute or last-week flexibility enables them to reserve hotel rooms or airline seats that would otherwise go unsold.
- Being able to conduct almost all operations electronically, without the warehousing and order fulfillment problems of their brick-and-mortar dot-com cousins.

Still, travel dot-coms face major uncertainties. One is the appearance of Orbitz.com, an online travel agency owned by five major U.S. airlines. Also very significant is the fluctuation in demand for airline tickets due to the state of the U.S. economy.

Marginal Analysis and Profit Maximization

A basic idea in business, economics, and indeed everyday life is **marginal analysis**, which is a continuing, concise trade-off of incremental costs against incremental revenues. In personal terms, marginal analysis means that people will continue to do something as long as the incremental return exceeds the incremental cost. This same idea holds true in marketing and pricing decisions. In this setting, marginal analysis means that as long as revenue received from the sale of an additional product (marginal revenue) is greater than the additional cost of producing and selling it (marginal cost), a firm will expand its output of that product.

Break-Even Analysis

Marketing managers often employ an approach that considers cost, volume, and profit relationships based on the profit equation. **Break-even analysis** is a technique that analyzes the relationship between total revenue and total cost to determine profitability at various levels of output. The **break-even point (BEP)** is the quantity at which total revenue and total cost are equal. Profit then comes from all units sold beyond the BEP. In terms of the definitions in Figure 13–9,

$$\text{BEP}_{\text{Quantity}} = \frac{\text{Fixed cost}}{\text{Unit price} - \text{Unit variable cost}} = \frac{\text{FC}}{\text{P} - \text{UVC}}$$

FIGURE 13–10

Profit maximization pricing

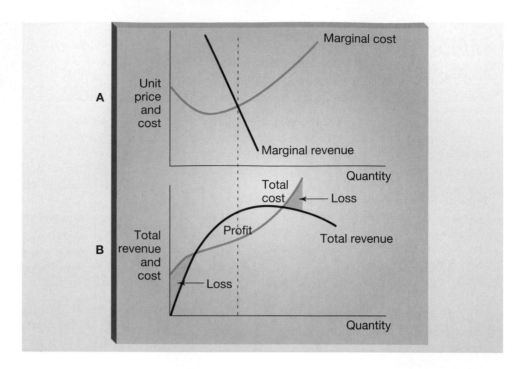

Calculating a Break-Even Point Consider a picture frame store. Suppose you wish to identify how many pictures you must sell to cover your fixed cost at a given price. Let's assume demand for your framed pictures has increased so the average price customers are willing to pay for each picture is $100. Also, suppose your fixed cost (FC) has grown to $28,000 (for real estate taxes, interest on a bank loan, and other fixed expenses) and unit variable cost (UVC) for a picture is now $30 (for labor, glass, frame, and matting). Your break-even quantity (BEP$_{Quantity}$) is 400 pictures, as follows:

$$BEP_{Quantity} = \frac{Fixed\ cost}{Unit\ price - Unit\ variable\ cost} = \frac{FC}{P - UVC}$$

$$= \frac{\$28,000}{\$100 - \$30}$$

$$= 400\ pictures$$

Marginal analysis is central to the concept of maximizing profits. In Figure 13–10A, marginal revenue and marginal cost are graphed. Marginal cost starts out high at lower quantity levels, decreases to a minimum through production and marketing efficiencies, and then rises again due to the inefficiencies of overworked labor and equipment. Marginal revenue follows a downward slope. In Figure 13–10B, total cost and total revenue curves corresponding to the marginal cost and marginal revenue curves are graphed. Total cost initially rises as quantity increases but increases at the slowest rate at the quantity where marginal cost is lowest. The total revenue curve increases to a maximum and then starts to decline, as shown in Figure 13–8B.

The message of marginal analysis, then, is to operate up to the quantity and price level where marginal revenue equals marginal cost (MR = MC). Up to the output quantity at which MR = MC, each increase in total revenue resulting from selling one additional unit exceeds the increase in the total cost of producing and marketing that unit. Beyond the point at which MR = MC, however, the increase in total revenue from selling one more unit is less than the cost of producing and marketing that unit. At the quantity at which MR = MC, the total revenue curve lies farthest above the total cost curve, they are parallel, and profit is a maximum.

QUANTITY OF PICTURES SOLD (Q)	PRICE PER PICTURE (P)	TOTAL REVENUE (TR) = (P × Q)	UNIT VARIABLE COST (UVC)	TOTAL VARIABLE COST (VC) = (UVC × Q)	FIXED COST (FC)	TOTAL COST (TC) = (FC + VC)	PROFIT = (TR − TC)
0	$100	$0	$30	$0	$28,000	$28,000	−$28,000
200	100	20,000	30	6,000	28,000	34,000	−14,000
400	100	40,000	30	12,000	28,000	40,000	0
600	100	60,000	30	18,000	28,000	46,000	14,000
800	100	80,000	30	24,000	28,000	52,000	28,000
1,000	100	100,000	30	30,000	28,000	58,000	42,000
1,200	100	120,000	30	36,000	28,000	64,000	56,000

FIGURE 13–11

Calculating a break-even point for a picture frame store

The row shaded in brown in Figure 13–11 shows that your break-even quantity at a price of $100 per picture is 400 pictures. At less than 400 pictures, your picture frame store incurs a loss, and at more than 400 pictures it makes a profit. Figure 13–11 also shows that if you could double your annual picture sales to 800, your store would make a profit of $28,000—the row shaded in green in the figure.

Figure 13–12 shows a graphic presentation of the break-even analysis, called a **break-even chart**. It shows that total revenue and total cost intersect and are equal at a quantity of 400 pictures sold, which is the break-even point at which profit is exactly $0. You want to do better? If your frame store could double the quantity sold annually to 800 pictures, the graph in Figure 13–12 shows you can earn an annual profit of $28,000, just as shown by the row shaded in green in Figure 13–11. Other financial aspects of a picture frame store appear in Appendix B.

FIGURE 13–12

Break-even analysis chart for a picture frame store

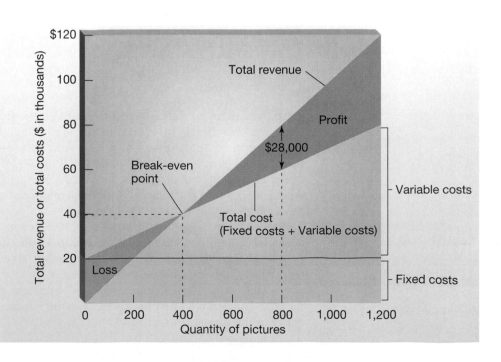

FIGURE 13–13

The cost trade-off: fixed versus variable costs

Executives in virtually every mass-production industry—from locomotives and cars to electronic calculators and breakfast cereals—are searching for ways to increase quality and reduce production costs to remain competitive in world markets. Increasingly they are substituting robots, automation, and computer-controlled manufacturing systems for blue- and white-collar workers.

To understand the implications of this on the break-even point and profit, consider this example of an electronic calculator manufacturer:

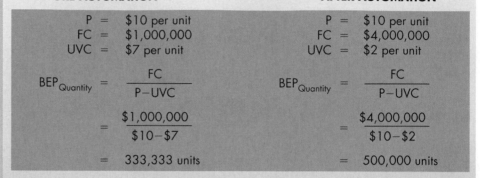

BEFORE AUTOMATION	**AFTER AUTOMATION**
$P = \$10$ per unit	$P = \$10$ per unit
$FC = \$1,000,000$	$FC = \$4,000,000$
$UVC = \$7$ per unit	$UVC = \$2$ per unit
$BEP_{Quantity} = \dfrac{FC}{P-UVC}$	$BEP_{Quantity} = \dfrac{FC}{P-UVC}$
$= \dfrac{\$1,000,000}{\$10-\$7}$	$= \dfrac{\$4,000,000}{\$10-\$2}$
$= 333,333$ units	$= 500,000$ units

The automation increases the fixed cost and increases the break-even quantity from 333,333 to 500,000 units per year. So if annual sales fall within this range, the calculator manufacturer will incur a loss with the automated plant, whereas it would have made a profit if it had not automated.

But what about its potential profit if it sells 1 million units a year? Look carefully at the two break-even charts below, and see the text to check your conclusions.

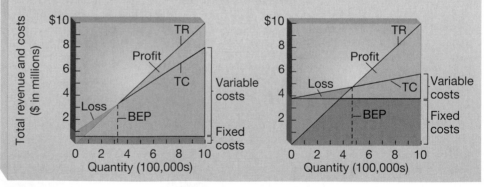

Applications of Break-Even Analysis

Because of its simplicity, break-even analysis is used extensively in marketing, most frequently to study the impact on profit of changes in price, fixed cost, and variable cost. The mechanics of break-even analysis are the basis of the widely used electronic spreadsheets offered by computer programs such as Microsoft Excel that permit managers to answer hypothetical "what if" questions about the effect of changes in prices and costs on their profit.

An example will show the power of break-even analysis. As described in Figure 13–13, if an electronic calculator manufacturer automates its production, thereby increasing fixed cost and reducing variable cost by substituting machines for workers, this increases the break-even point from 333,333 to 500,000 units per year. Note in this example that in the short run only the fixed costs definitely increase (question 4, Figure 13–1), hopefully offset in the longer run by reduced unit variable costs.

But what about the impact of the higher level of fixed costs on profit? Remember, profit at any output quantity is given by:

Profit = Total revenue − Total cost

$$= (P \times Q) - [FC + (UVC \times Q)]$$

So profit at 1 million units of sales before automation is:

Profit $= (P \times Q) - [FC + (UVC \times Q)]$

$$= (\$10 \times 1{,}000{,}000) - [\$1{,}000{,}000 + (\$7 \times 1{,}000{,}000)]$$

$$= \$10{,}000{,}000 - \$8{,}000{,}000$$

$$= \$2{,}000{,}000$$

After automation, profit is:

Profit $= (P \times Q) - [FC + (UVC \times Q)]$

$$= (\$10 \times 1{,}000{,}000) - [\$4{,}000{,}000 + (\$2 \times 1{,}000{,}000)]$$

$$= \$10{,}000{,}000 - \$6{,}000{,}000$$

$$= \$4{,}000{,}000$$

Automation, by adding to fixed costs, increases profit by $2 million at 1 million units of sales. Thus, as the quantity sold increases for the automated plant, the potential increase or leverage on profit is tremendous. This is why with large production and sales volumes, automated plants for Ford cars or Texas Instruments calculators produce large profits. Also, firms in other industries, such as airline, railroad, and hotel and motel industries, that require high fixed costs can reap large profits when they go even slightly beyond the break-even point.

Concept Check

1. What is the difference between fixed costs and variable costs?

2. What is a break-even point?

CHAPTER IN REVIEW

1 *Identify the elements that make up a price.*
Price is the money or other considerations (such as barter) exchanged for the ownership or use of a good or service. Although price typically involves money, the amount exchanged is often different from the list or quoted price because of incentives (rebates, discounts, etc.), allowances (trade), and extra fees (finance charges, surcharges, etc.).

2 *Recognize the objectives a firm has in setting prices and the constraints that restrict the range of prices a firm can charge.*
Pricing objectives specify the role of price in a firm's marketing strategy and may include profit, sales revenue, market share, unit volume, survival, or some socially responsible price level. Pricing constraints that restrict a firm's pricing flexibility include demand, product newness, other products sold by the firm, production and marketing costs, cost of price changes, type of competitive market, and the prices of competitive substitutes.

3 *Explain what a demand curve is and the role of revenues in pricing decisions.*
A demand curve is a graph relating the quantity sold and price, which shows the maximum number of units that will be sold at a given price. Three demand factors affect price: (*a*) consumer tastes, (*b*) price and availability of substitute products, and (*c*) consumer income. These demand factors determine consumers' willingness and ability to pay for goods and services. Assuming these demand factors remain unchanged, if the price of a product is lowered or raised, then the quantity demanded for it will increase or decrease, respectively.

Three important forms of revenues impact a firm's pricing decisions: (*a*) total revenue, which is the total money received from the sale of a product; (*b*) average revenue, which is the average amount of money received for selling one unit of a product (which is simply the price of the unit); and (*c*) marginal revenue, which is the change in total revenue that results from producing and marketing one additional unit.

4 *Describe what price elasticity of demand means to a manager facing a pricing decision.*

Price elasticity of demand measures the responsiveness of units of a product sold to a change in price, which is expressed as the percentage change in the quantity of a product demanded divided by the percentage change in price. Price elasticity is important to marketing managers because a change in price usually has an important effect on the number of units of the product sold and on total revenue.

5 *Explain the role of costs in pricing decisions.*

Five important costs impact a firm's pricing decisions: (*a*) total cost, or total expenses, the sum of fixed cost and variable cost incurred by a firm in producing and marketing a product; (*b*) fixed cost, the sum of expenses of the firm that are stable and do not change with the quantity of a product that is produced and sold; (*c*) variable cost, the sum of expenses of the firm that vary directly with the quantity of a product that is produced and sold; (*d*) unit variable cost, variable cost expressed on a per unit basis; and (*e*) marginal cost, the change in total cost that results from producing and marketing one additional unit of the product.

6 *Describe how various combinations of price, fixed cost, and unit variable cost affect a firm's break-even point.*

Break-even analysis is a technique that analyzes the relationship between total revenue and total cost to determine profitability at various levels of output. The break-even point is the quantity at which total revenue and total cost are equal. Assuming no change in price, if the costs of a firm's product increase due to higher fixed costs (manufacturing or advertising) or variable costs (direct labor or materials), then its break-even point will be higher. And if total cost is unchanged, an increase in price will reduce the break-even point.

FOCUSING ON KEY TERMS

average revenue (AR) p. 346
barter p. 337
break-even analysis p. 351
break-even chart p. 353
break-even point (BEP) p. 351
demand curve p. 344
demand factors p. 345
fixed cost (FC) p. 350
marginal analysis p. 351
marginal cost (MC) p. 350
marginal revenue (MR) p. 346

price (P) p. 336
price elasticity of demand p. 348
pricing constraints p. 341
pricing objectives p. 340
profit equation p. 339
total cost (TC) p. 350
total revenue (TR) p. 346
unit variable cost (UVC) p. 350
value p. 338
value-pricing p. 339
variable cost (VC) p. 350

DISCUSSION AND APPLICATION QUESTIONS

1 How would the price equation apply to the purchase price of (*a*) gasoline, (*b*) an airline ticket, and (*c*) a checking account?

2 What would be your response to the statement, "Profit maximization is the only legitimate pricing objective for the firm"?

3 How is a downward-sloping demand curve related to total revenue and marginal revenue?

4 A marketing executive once said, "If the price elasticity of demand for your product is inelastic, then your price is probably too low." What is this executive saying in terms of the economic principles discussed in this chapter?

5 A marketing manager reduced the price on a brand of cereal by 10 percent and observed a 25 percent increase in quantity sold. The manager then thought that if the price were reduced by another 20 percent, a 50 percent increase in quantity sold would occur. What would be your response to the marketing manager's reasoning?

6 A student theater group at a university has developed a demand schedule that shows the relationship between ticket prices and demand based on a student survey, as follows:

TICKET PRICE	NUMBER OF STUDENTS WHO WOULD BUY
$1	300
2	250
3	200
4	150
5	100

(*a*) Graph the demand curve and the total revenue curve based on these data. What ticket price might be set based on this analysis? (*b*) What other factors should be considered before the final price is set?

7 Touché Toiletries, Inc., has developed an addition to its Lizardman Cologne line tentatively branded Ode d'Toade Cologne. Unit variable costs are 45 cents for a three-ounce bottle, and heavy advertising expenditures in the first year would result in total fixed costs of $900,000. Ode d'Toade Cologne is priced at $7.50 for a three-ounce bottle. How many bottles of Ode d'Toade must be sold to break even?

8 Suppose that marketing executives for Touché Toiletries reduced the price to $6.50 for a three-ounce bottle of Ode d'Toade and the fixed costs were $1,100,000. Suppose further that the unit variable cost remained at 45 cents for a three-ounce bottle. (*a*) How many bottles must be sold to break even? (*b*) What dollar profit level would Ode d'Toade achieve if 200,000 bottles were sold?

9 Executives of Random Recordings, Inc., produced an album entitled *Sunshine/Moonshine* by the Starshine Sisters Band.

(*a*) Using the price and cost information in the table, prepare a chart like that in Figure 13–11 showing total cost, fixed cost, and total revenue for album quantity sold levels starting at 10,000 albums through 100,000

albums at 10,000 album intervals, that is, 10,000; 20,000; 30,000; and so on. (*b*) What is the break-even point for the album?

Selling price	$7.00 per album
Album cover	$1.00 per album
Songwriter's royalties	$0.30 per album
Recording artists' royalties	$0.70 per album
Direct material and labor costs to produce the album	$1.00 per album
Fixed cost of producing an album (advertising, studio fee, etc.)	$100,000

GOING ONLINE   Finding the Best Airline Ticket Price

It's Wednesday and you just completed your midterm exams. As a reward for your hard work, a friend has sent you a pair of free tickets to a popular Broadway show in New York City for 7:00 P.M. Saturday night. Check out the following online travel services to book a nonstop, round-trip ticket, leaving from Chicago's O'Hare (ORD) airport around 4:00 P.M. on Friday to New York City's LaGuardia (LGA) airport. On Sunday, you'll leave La Guardia around 5:00 P.M. and return to O'Hare.

Which of the following online travel services provides the cheapest fare and is easiest to use? Check out our search and see if you can beat the prices we obtained in late 2004. You may also want to book a hotel room for your stay. And don't forget to eat at the Carnegie Deli while you're in New York!

- Expedia (www.expedia.com)—Lowest price: $280.00 from United Airlines.
- Orbitz (www.orbitz.com), the online travel service owned by the major airlines—Lowest price: $281.00 from United Airlines.
- Priceline (www.priceline.com)—Lowest price: $282.00 from United Airlines.
- Travelocity (www.travelocity.com)—Lowest price: $280.00 from United Airlines.

(*Note:* You were not asked to search Priceline.com's Name Your Own Price® because you are required to make a purchase before receiving information on your bid for a ticket.)

BUILDING YOUR MARKETING PLAN

In starting to set a final price:
1 List two pricing objectives and three pricing constraints.
2 Think about your customers and competitors and set three possible prices.

3 Assume a fixed cost and unit variable cost and (*a*) calculate the break-even points and (*b*) plot a break-even chart for the three prices specified in step 2.

VIDEO CASE 13 Washburn International: Guitars and Break-Even

"The relationship between musicians and their guitars is something really extraordinary—and is a fairly strange one," says Brady Breen in a carefully understated tone of voice. Breen has the experience to know. He's production manager of Washburn International, one of the most prestigious guitar manufacturers in the world. Washburn's instruments range from one-of-a-kind, custom-made acoustic and electric guitars and basses to less-expensive, mass-produced ones.

THE COMPANY

The modern Washburn International started in 1977 when a small Chicago firm bought the century-old Washburn brand name and a small inventory of guitars, parts, and promotional supplies. At that time, annual revenues of the company were $300,000 for the sale of about 2,500 guitars. Washburn's first catalog, appearing in 1978, told a frightening truth:

> Our designs are translated by Japan's most experienced craftsmen, assuring the consistent quality and craftmanship for which they are known.

At that time, the American guitar-making craft was at an all-time low. Guitars made by Japanese firms such as Ibane and Yamaha were in use by an increasing number of professionals.

Times have changed for Washburn. Today, the company sells about 250,000 guitars a year. Annual sales exceed $50 million. All this resulted from Washburn's aggressive marketing strategies to develop product lines with different price points targeted at musicians in distinctly different market segments.

THE PRODUCTS AND MARKET SEGMENTS

Arguably the most trendsetting guitar developed by the modern Washburn company appeared in 1980. This was the Festival Series of cutaway, thin-bodied flattops, with built-in bridge pickups and controls, which went on to become the virtual standard for live performances. John Lodge of the Moody Blues endorsed the 12-string version—his gleaming white guitar appearing in both concerts and ads for years. In the time since the Festival Series appeared, countless rock and country stars have used these instruments including Bob Dylan, Dolly Parton, Greg Allman, and the late George Harrison of the Beatles.

Until 1991, all Washburn guitars were manufactured in Asia. That year Washburn started building its high-end guitars in the United States. Today, Washburn marketing executives divide its product line into four levels. From high end to low end these are:

- One-of-a-kind, custom units.
- Batch-custom units.
- Mass-customized units.
- Mass-produced units.

The one-of-a-kind custom units are for the many stars that use Washburn instruments. The mass-produced units targeted at first-time buyers are still manufactured in Asian factories.

PRICING ISSUES

Setting prices for its various lines presents a continuing challenge for Washburn. Not only do the prices have to reflect the changing tastes of its various segments of musicians, but the prices must also be competitive with the prices set for guitars manufactured and marketed globally. In fact, Washburn and other well-known guitar manufacturers have a prestige-niche strategy. For Washburn this involves endorsements by internationally known musicians who play its instruments and lend their names to lines of Washburn signature guitars. This has the effect of reducing the price elasticity or price sensitivity for these guitars. Stars playing Washburn guitars like Nuno Bettencourt, formerly of Pink Floyd now with Population 1; Dimebag Darrell of Damageplan; Joe Perry of Aerosmith; and Darryl Jones of the Rolling Stones have their own lines of signature guitars—the "batch-custom" units mentioned earlier.

Joe Baksha, Washburn's executive vice president, is responsible for reviewing and approving prices for the company's lines of guitars. Setting a sales target of 2,000 units for a new line of guitars, he is considering a suggested retail price of $329 per unit for customers at one of the hundreds of retail outlets carrying the Washburn line. For planning purposes, Baksha estimates half of the final retail price will be the price Washburn nets when it sells its guitar to the wholesalers and dealers in its channel of distribution.

Looking at Washburn's financial data for its present Chicago plant, Baksha estimates that this line of guitars must bear these fixed costs:

Rent and taxes	= $12,000
Depreciation of equipment	= $ 4,000
Management and quality control program	= $20,000

In addition, he estimates the variable costs for each unit to be:

Direct materials = $25/unit
Direct labor   = 8 hours/unit @ $14/hour

Carefully kept production records at Washburn's Chicago plant make Baksha believe that these are reasonable estimates. He explains, "Before we begin a production run, we have a good feel for what our costs will be. The U.S.-built N-4, for example, simply costs more than one of our foreign-produced Mercury or Wing series electrics."

Caught in the global competition for guitar sales, Washburn searches for ways to reduce and control costs. After much agonizing, the company decided to move to Nashville, Tennessee. In this home of country music, Washburn expects to lower its manufacturing costs because there are many skilled workers in the region, and its fixed costs will be reduced by avoiding some of the expenses of having a big city location. Specifically, Washburn projects that it will reduce its rent and taxes expense by 40 percent and the wage rate it pays by 15 percent in relocating from Chicago to Nashville.

Questions

1 What factors are most likely to affect the demand for the lines of Washburn guitars (*a*) bought by a first-time guitar buyer and (*b*) bought by a sophisticated musician who wants a signature model?

2 For Washburn, what are examples of (*a*) shifting the demand curve to the right to get a higher price for a guitar line (movement *of* the demand curve) and (*b*) pricing decisions involving moving *along* a demand curve?

3 In Washburn's Chicago plant, what is the break-even point for the new line of guitars if the retail price is (*a*) $329, (*b*) $359, and (*c*) $299? Also, (*d*) if Washburn achieves the sales target of 2,000 units at the $329 retail price, what will its profit be?

4 Assume that Washburn moves its production to Nashville and that the costs are reduced as projected in the case. Then, what will be the (*a*) new break-even point at a $329 retail price for this line of guitars and (*b*) the new profit if it sells 2,000 units?

5 If for competitive reasons, Washburn eventually has to move all its production back to Asia, (*a*) which specific fixed and variable costs might be lowered and (*b*) what additional fixed and variable costs might it expect to incur?

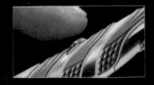

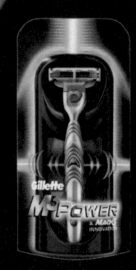

CHAPTER

14

ARRIVING AT THE FINAL PRICE

LEARNING OBJECTIVES

After reading this chapter you should be able to:

1 Describe how to establish the initial "approximate price level" using demand-oriented, cost-oriented, profit-oriented, and competition-oriented approaches.

2 Recognize the major factors considered in deriving a final list or quoted price from the approximate price level.

3 Identify the adjustments made to the approximate price level on the basis of discounts, allowances, and geography.

4 Name the principal laws and regulations affecting specific pricing practices.

GILLETTE KNOWS THE VALUE OF A GREAT SHAVE

How much is a close and comfortable shave worth? Ask the Gillette Company, the world leader in shaving technology and marketing. Gillette commands 74 percent of the $7 billion global wet-shaving market and is a respected global brand.

Product innovation that benefits consumers is a critical ingredient in Gillette's success. Gillette's latest breakthrough is M3Power, a revolutionary wet-shaving system upgrade to its MACH3 line of razors and blades. M3Power has a tiny motor powered by an AAA battery mounted in the razor's handle that emits gentle pulses to the shaving cartridge. The result? A totally new shaving experience that delivers the world's best shave. Extensive company research confirmed that men preferred M3Power nearly two-to-one over Gillette's best-selling MACH3 Turbo shaving system and by a still larger margin over rival products. In addition, M3Power outperformed other shaving systems on every one of 68 shaving attributes tested, including closeness, comfort, efficiency, safety, and less irritation. M3Power is also shower safe, so men can shave wherever they prefer.

Such innovation naturally translates into the price consumers are willing to pay. The M3Power handle sells for $14.99 with two blade cartridges and an AAA battery, or 67 percent higher than MACH3 Turbo razor. A four-pack of replacement cartridges are priced 20 percent higher than MACH3 Turbo replacement cartridges. According to Mary Ann Resce, Gillette's vice president of new shaving products, "Men have demonstrated over and over a willingness to pay if we perform, and we do."[1]

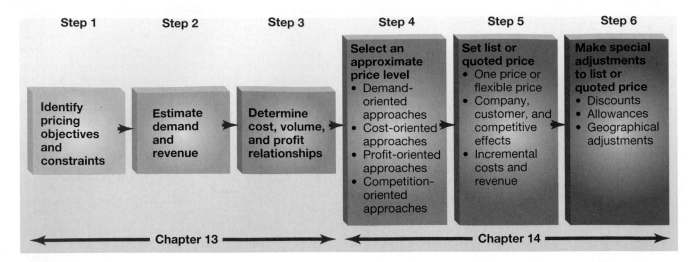

FIGURE 14–1
Steps in setting price

This chapter describes how companies like Gillette set an approximate price level for their offerings, highlights important considerations in setting a list or quoted price, and identifies various price adjustments that can be made to prices set by a company—the last three steps involved in setting prices (Figure 14–1). In addition, important legal and regulatory aspects of pricing are described.

STEP 4: SELECT AN APPROXIMATE PRICE LEVEL

A key to a marketing manager's setting a final price for a product is to find an approximate price level to use as a reasonable starting point. Four common approaches to helping find this approximate price level are (1) demand-oriented, (2) cost-oriented, (3) profit-oriented, and (4) competition-oriented approaches (Figure 14–2). Although these approaches are discussed separately below, some of them overlap, and an effective marketing manager will consider several in searching for an approximate price level.

Demand-Oriented Approaches

Demand-oriented approaches weigh factors underlying expected customer tastes and preferences more heavily than such factors as cost, profit, and competition when selecting a price level.

Skimming Pricing   A firm introducing a new or innovative product can use **skimming pricing**, setting the highest initial price that customers really desiring the product are willing to pay. These customers are not very price sensitive because they weigh the new product's price, quality, and ability to satisfy their needs against the same characteristics of substitutes. As the demand of these customers is satisfied, the firm lowers the price to attract another, more price-sensitive segment. Thus, skimming pricing gets its name from skimming successive layers of "cream," or customer segments, as prices are lowered in a series of steps.

Skimming pricing is an effective strategy when: (1) enough prospective customers are willing to buy the product immediately at the high initial price to make these sales profitable, (2) the high initial price will not attract competitors, (3) lowering price has only a minor effect on increasing the sales volume and reducing the unit costs, and (4) customers interpret the high price as signifying high quality. These four conditions are most likely to exist when the new product is protected by patents or copyrights or its uniqueness is understood and valued by consumers. Gillette

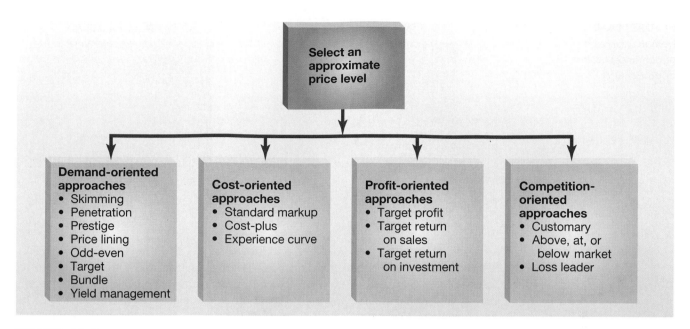

FIGURE 14–2

Four approaches for selecting an approximate price level

adopted a skimming strategy for the M3Power shaving system since many of these conditions applied. The M3Power shaving system has 62 patents that protect its product technology.

Penetration Pricing   Setting a low initial price on a new product to appeal immediately to the mass market is **penetration pricing**, the exact opposite of skimming pricing. Nintendo consciously chose a penetration strategy when it introduced Nintendo DS, its newest generation handheld video game player, to compete with Sony's PSP handheld player, which used a skimming pricing strategy.[2]

The conditions favoring penetration pricing are the reverse of those supporting skimming pricing: (1) many segments of the market are price sensitive, (2) a low initial price discourages competitors from entering the market, and (3) unit production and marketing costs fall dramatically as production volumes increase. A firm using penetration pricing may (1) maintain the initial price for a time to gain profit lost from its low introductory level or (2) lower the price further, counting on the new volume to generate the necessary profit.

In some situations, penetration pricing may follow skimming pricing. A company might initially price a product high to attract price-insensitive consumers and recoup initial research and development costs and introductory promotional expenditures. Once this is done, penetration pricing is used to appeal to a broader segment of the population and increase market share.[3]

Prestige Pricing   As noted in Chapter 13, consumers may use price as a measure of the quality or prestige of an item so that as price is lowered beyond some point, demand for the item actually falls. **Prestige pricing** involves setting a high price so that quality- or status-conscious consumers will be attracted to the product and buy it (Figure 14–3A on the next page). The demand curve slopes downward and to the right between points A and B but turns back to the left between points B and C because demand is actually reduced between points B and C. From A to B buyers see the lowering of price as a bargain and buy more; from B to C they become dubious about the quality and prestige and buy less. A marketing manager's pricing strategy here is to stay above price P_0 (the initial price).

Rolls-Royce cars, Chanel perfume, Cartier jewelry, Lalique crystal, and Swiss watches have an element of prestige pricing in them and may sell worse at lower prices than at higher ones.[4] The recent success of Swiss watchmaker TAG Heuer is an example.

FIGURE 14–3
Demand curves for two types
of demand-oriented
approaches

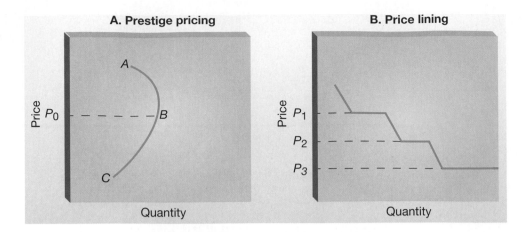

The company raised the average price of its watches from $250 to $1,000, and its sales volume increased sevenfold.[5] Recently, Energizer learned that buyers of high-performance alkaline batteries tend to associate a lower price with lower quality. The accompanying Marketing NewsNet describes the pricing lesson learned by Energizer.[6]

Price Lining   Often a firm that is selling not just a single product but a line of products may price them at a number of different specific pricing points, which is called **price lining**. For example, a department store manager may price a line of women's casual slacks at $59, $79, and $99. As shown in Figure 14–3B, this assumes that demand is elastic at each of these price points but inelastic between these price points. In some instances, all the items might be purchased for the same cost and then marked up at different percentages to achieve these price points based on color, style, and expected demand. In other instances, manufacturers design products for different price points, and retailers apply approximately the same markup percentages to achieve the three or four different price points offered to consumers. Sellers often feel that a limited number (such as three or four) of price points is preferable to 8 or 10 different ones, which may only confuse prospective buyers.[7]

Odd-Even Pricing   Sears offers a Craftsman radial saw for $499.99, the suggested retail price for a M3Power shaving system is $14.99, and Kmart sells Windex glass cleaner on sale for 99 cents. Why not simply price these items at $500, $15, and $1, respectively? These firms are using **odd-even pricing**, which involves setting prices a few dollars or cents under an even number. The presumption is that consumers see the Sears radial saw as priced at "something over $400" rather than "about $500." In theory, demand increases if the price drops from $500 to $499.99. There is some evidence to suggest this does happen. However, research suggests that overuse of odd-ending prices tends to mute its effect on demand.[8]

Target Pricing   Manufacturers will sometimes estimate the price that the ultimate consumer would be willing to pay for a product. They then work backward through markups taken by retailers and wholesalers to determine what price they can charge wholesalers for the product. This practice, called **target pricing**, results in the manufacturer deliberately adjusting the composition and features of a product to achieve the target price to consumers. Canon uses this practice for pricing its cameras, as does Heinz for its complete line of pet foods.[9]

Bundle Pricing   A frequently used demand-oriented pricing practice is **bundle pricing**—the marketing of two or more products in a single package price. For example, Delta Air Lines offers vacation packages that include airfare, car rental, and lodging. Bundle pricing is based on the idea that consumers value the package more than the individual items. This is due to benefits received from not having to

MARKETING NEWSNET

Energizer's Lesson in Price Perception— Value Lies in the Eye of the Beholder

CUSTOMER VALUE

Battery manufacturers are as tireless as a certain drum-thumping bunny in their efforts to create products that perform better, last longer, and not incidentally, outsell the competition. The commercialization of new alkaline battery technology at a price that creates value for consumers is not always obvious or easy. Just ask the marketing executives at Energizer about their experience with pricing Energizer Advanced Formula and Energizer e^2 AA alkaline batteries.

When Duracell launched its high-performance Ultra brand AA alkaline battery with a 25 percent price premium over standard Duracell batteries, Energizer quickly countered with its own high-performance battery—Energizer Advanced Formula. Believing that consumers would not pay the premium price,

Energizer priced its Advanced Formula brand at the same price as its standard AA alkaline battery, expecting to gain market share from Duracell. It did not happen. Why? According to industry analysts, consumers associated Energizer's low price with inferior quality in the high-performance segment. Instead of gaining market share, Energizer lost market share to Duracell and Rayovac, the number three battery manufacturer.

Having learned its lesson, Energizer subsequently released its e^2 high-performance battery, this time priced 4 percent higher than Duracell Ultra and about 50 percent higher than Advanced Formula. The result? Energizer recovered lost sales and market share. The lesson learned? Value lies in the eye of the beholder.

make separate purchases and enhanced satisfaction from one item given the presence of another. Moreover, bundle pricing often provides a lower total cost to buyers and lower marketing costs to sellers.[10]

Yield Management Pricing   Have you noticed seats on airline flights are priced differently within coach class? What you observed is **yield management pricing**— the charging of different prices to maximize revenue for a set amount of capacity at any given time.[11] As described in Chapter 12, service businesses engage in capacity management, and an effective way to do this is by varying prices by time, day, week, or season. Yield management pricing is a complex approach that continually matches demand and supply to customize the price for a service. Airlines, hotels, cruise ships, and car rental companies frequently use it. American Airlines estimates that yield management pricing produces an annual revenue that exceeds $500 million.[12]

Concept Check

1. What are the circumstances in pricing a new product that might support skimming or penetration pricing?

2. What is odd-even pricing?

Cost-Oriented Approaches

With cost-oriented approaches a price setter stresses the cost side of the pricing problem, not the demand side. Price is set by looking at the production and marketing costs and then adding enough to cover direct expenses, overhead, and profit.

Standard Markup Pricing Managers of supermarkets and other retail stores have such a large number of products that estimating the demand for each product as a means of setting price is impossible. Therefore, they use **standard markup pricing**, which entails adding a fixed percentage to the cost of all items in a specific product class. This percentage markup varies depending on the type of retail store (such as furniture, clothing, or grocery) and on the product involved. High-volume products usually have smaller markups than do low-volume products. Supermarkets such as Kroger, Safeway, and Jewel have different markups for staple items and discretionary items. The markup on staple items like sugar, flour, and dairy products varies from 10 percent to 23 percent, whereas markups on discretionary items like snack foods and candy ranges from 27 percent to 47 percent. These markups must cover all expenses of the store, pay for overhead costs, and contribute something to profits. For supermarkets these markups, which may appear very large, result in only a 1 percent profit on sales revenue if the store is operating efficiently. By comparison, consider the markups on snacks and beverages purchased at your local movie theater. The markup is 87 percent on soft drinks, 65 percent on candy bars, and a whopping 90 percent on popcorn. An explanation of how to compute a markup, along with operating statement data and other ratios, is given in Appendix B to this chapter.

Cost-Plus Pricing Many manufacturing, professional services, and construction firms use a variation of standard markup pricing. **Cost-plus pricing** involves summing the total unit cost of providing a product or service and adding a specific

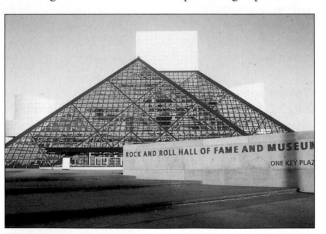

amount to the cost to arrive at a price. Cost-plus pricing generally assumes two forms. With *cost-plus percentage-of-cost pricing,* a fixed percentage is added to the total unit cost. This is often used to price one- or few-of-a-kind items, as when an architectural firm charges a percentage of the construction costs of, say, the $92 million Rock and Roll Hall of Fame and Museum in Cleveland, Ohio. In buying highly technical, few-of-a-kind products such as hydroelectric power plants or space satellites, country governments have found that general contractors are reluctant to specify a formal, fixed price for the procurement. Therefore, they use *cost-plus fixed-fee pricing,* which means that a supplier is reimbursed for all costs, regardless of what they turn out to be, but is allowed only a fixed fee as profit that is independent of the final cost of the project. For example, suppose that the National Aeronautics and Space Administration agreed to pay Boeing $1.2 billion as the cost of a space shuttle and agreed to a $100 million fee for providing that space shuttle. Even if Boeing's cost increased to $2 billion for the space shuttle, its fee would remain $100 million.

Cost-plus pricing is the most commonly used method to set prices for business products.[13] Increasingly, however, this method is finding favor among business-to-business marketers in the service sector. For example, the rising cost of legal fees has prompted some law firms to adopt a cost-plus pricing approach. Rather than billing business clients on an hourly basis, lawyers and their clients agree on a fixed fee based on expected costs plus a profit for the law firm. Many advertising agencies now use this approach. Here, the client agrees to pay the agency a fee based on the cost of its work plus some agreed-on profit, which is often a percentage of total cost.[14]

Experience Curve Pricing   The method of **experience curve pricing** is based on the learning effect, which holds that the unit cost of many products and services declines by 10 percent to 30 percent each time a firm's experience at producing and selling them doubles.[15] This reduction is regular or predictable enough that the average cost per unit can be mathematically estimated. For example, if the firm estimates that costs will fall by 15 percent each time volume doubles, then the cost of the 100th unit produced and sold will be about 85 percent of the cost of the 50th unit, and the 200th unit will be 85 percent of the cost of the 100th unit. Therefore, if the cost of the 50th unit is $100, the 100th unit would cost $85, the 200th unit would be $72.25, and so on. Because prices often follow costs with experience curve pricing, a rapid decline in price is possible. Japanese, Korean, and U.S. firms in the electronics industry often adopt this pricing approach. This cost-based pricing approach complements the demand-based pricing strategy of skimming followed by penetration pricing. For example, DVD player prices have decreased from $900 to less than $100, fax machine prices have declined from $1,000 to under $100, and cellular telephones that once sold for $4,000 are now priced below $99. Panasonic, Sony, Samsung, Zenith, and other television manufacturers will use experience curve pricing for HDTV sets. Consumers will benefit because prices will decline as cumulative sales volume grows.

Profit-Oriented Approaches

A price setter may choose to balance both revenues and costs to set price using profit-oriented approaches. These might either involve a target of a specific dollar volume of profit or express this target profit as a percentage of sales or investment.

Target Profit Pricing   A firm may set an annual target of a specific dollar volume of profit, which is called **target profit pricing**. Suppose a picture framing

Panasonic expects to be a leader in the successful commercialization of HDTV.

Panasonic
www.panasonic.com

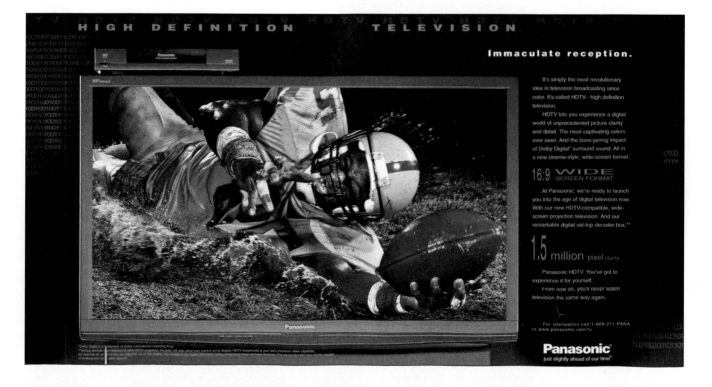

store owner wishes to use target profit pricing to establish a price for a typical framed picture and assumes the following:

- Variable cost is a constant $22 per unit.
- Fixed cost is a constant $26,000.
- Demand is insensitive to price up to $60 per unit.
- A target profit of $7,000 is sought at an annual volume of 1,000 units (framed pictures).

The price can be calculated as follows:

$$\text{Profit} = \text{Total revenue} - \text{Total cost}$$

$$\text{Profit} = (P \times Q) - [FC + (UVC \times Q)]$$

$$\$7,000 = (P \times 1,000) - [\$26,000 + (\$22 \times 1,000)]$$

$$\$7,000 = 1,000P - (\$26,000 + \$22,000)$$

$$1,000P = \$7,000 + \$48,000$$

$$P = \$55$$

Note that a critical assumption is that this higher average price of a framed picture will not cause the demand to fall.

Target Return-on-Sales Pricing A difficulty with target profit pricing is that although it is simple and the target involves only a specific dollar volume, there is no benchmark of sales or investment used to show how much of the firm's effort is needed to achieve the target. Firms such as supermarket chains often use **target return-on-sales pricing** to set typical prices that will give them a profit that is a specified percentage, say, 1 percent, of the sales volume. Suppose the owner decides to use target return-on-sales pricing for the frame shop and makes the same first three assumptions shown previously. The owner now sets a target of 20 percent return on sales at an annual volume of 1,250 units. This gives

$$\text{Target return on sales} = \frac{\text{Target profit}}{\text{Total revenue}}$$

$$20\% = \frac{TR - TC}{TR}$$

$$0.20 = \frac{P \times Q - [FC + (UVC \times Q)]}{TR}$$

$$0.20 = \frac{P \times 1,250 - [\$26,000 + (\$22 \times 1,250)]}{P \times 1,250}$$

$$P = \$53.50$$

So at a price of $53.50 per unit and an annual quantity of 1,250 frames,

$$TR = P \times Q = \$53.50 \times 1,250 = \$66,875$$

$$TC = FC + (UVC \times Q) = \$26,000 + (\$22 \times 1,250) = \$53,500$$

$$\text{Profit} = TR - TC = \$66,875 - \$53,500 = \$13,375$$

As a check,

$$\text{Target return on sales} = \frac{\text{Target profit}}{\text{Total revenue}} = \frac{\$13,375}{\$66,875} = 20\%$$

Target Return-on-Investment Pricing Firms such as General Motors and many public utilities set annual return-on-investment (ROI) targets such as ROI of 20 percent. **Target return-on-investment pricing** is a method of setting prices to achieve this target.

ASSUMPTIONS OR RESULTS	FINANCIAL ELEMENT	LAST YEAR	SIMULATION A	B	C	D
ASSUMPTIONS	Price per unit (P)	$50	$54	$54	$58	$58
	Units sold (Q)	1,000	1,200	1,100	1,100	1,000
	Change in unit variable cost (UVC)	0%	+10%	+10%	+20%	+20%
	Unit variable cost	$22.00	$24.20	$24.20	$26.20	$26.40
	Total expenses	$8,000	Same	Same	Same	Same
	Owner's salary	$18,000	Same	Same	Same	Same
	Investment	$20,000	Same	Same	Same	Same
	State and federal taxes	50%	Same	Same	Same	Same
SPREADSHEET SIMULATION	Net sales (P × Q)	$50,000	$64,800	$59,400	$63,800	$58,000
	Less: COGS (Q × UVC)	22,000	29,040	26,620	29,040	26,400
	Gross margin	$28,000	$35,760	$32,780	$34,760	$31,600
	Less: total expenses	8,000	8,000	8,000	8,000	8,000
	Less: owner's salary	18,000	18,000	18,000	18,000	18,000
	Net profit before taxes	$2,000	$9,760	$6,780	$8,760	$5,600
	Less: taxes	1,000	4,880	3,390	4,380	2,800
	Net profit after taxes	$1,000	$4,880	$3,390	$4,380	$2,800
	Investment	$20,000	$20,000	$20,000	$20,000	$20,000
	Return on investment	5.0%	24.4%	17.0%	21.9%	14.0%

FIGURE 14–4

Results of computer spreadsheet simulation to select price to achieve a target return on investment

Suppose the store owner sets a target ROI of 10 percent, which is twice that achieved the previous year. She considers raising the average price of a framed picture to $54 or $58—up from last year's average of $50. To do this, she might improve product quality by offering better frames and higher-quality matting, which will increase the cost but will probably offset the decreased revenue from the lower number of units that can be sold next year.

To handle this wide variety of assumptions, today's managers use computerized spreadsheets to project operating statements based on a diverse set of assumptions. Figure 14–4 shows the results of computerized spreadsheet simulation, with assumptions shown at the top and the projected results at the bottom. A previous year's operating statement results are shown in the column headed "Last Year," and the assumptions and spreadsheet results for four different sets of assumptions are shown in columns A, B, C, and D.

In choosing a price or another action using spreadsheet results, the decision maker must (1) study the results of the computer simulation projections and (2) assess the realism of the assumptions underlying each set of projections. For example, the store owner sees from the bottom row of Figure 14–4 that all four spreadsheet simulations exceed the after-tax target ROI of 10 percent. But after more thought, she judges it to be more realistic to set an average price of $58 per unit, allow the unit variable cost to increase by 20 percent to account for more expensive framing and matting, and settle for the same unit sales as the 1,000 units sold last year. She selects simulation D in this computerized spreadsheet approach to target ROI pricing and has a goal of 14 percent after-tax ROI. Of course, these same calculations can be done by hand, but this is far more time consuming.

Competition-Oriented Approaches

Rather than emphasize demand, cost, or profit factors, a price setter can stress what competitors or "the market" is doing.

Customary Pricing   For some products where tradition, a standardized channel of distribution, or other competitive factors dictate the price, **customary pricing** is used. Tradition prevails in the pricing of Swatch watches. The $40 customary price for the basic model changed little in 10 years. Candy bars offered through standard vending machines have a customary price of 75 cents, and a significant departure from this price may result in a loss of sales for the manufacturer. Hershey typically has changed the amount of chocolate in its candy bars depending on the price of raw chocolate rather than vary its customary retail price so that it can continue selling through vending machines.

Above-, At-, or Below-Market Pricing   For most products, it is difficult to identify a specific market price for a product or product class. Still, marketing managers often have a subjective feel for the competitors' price or market price. Using this benchmark, they then may deliberately choose a strategy of **above-, at-, or below-market pricing**.

Among watch manufacturers, Rolex takes pride in emphasizing that it makes one of the most expensive watches you can buy, a clear example of above-market pricing. Manufacturers of national brands of clothing such as Hart Schaffner & Marx and Christian Dior and retailers such as Neiman-Marcus deliberately set premium prices for their products.

Large department store chains such as JCPenney generally use at-market pricing. These chains often establish the going market price in the minds of their competitors. Similarly, Revlon and Cluett Peabody & Company (the maker of Arrow shirts) generally price their products "at market." They also provide a reference price for competitors that use above- and below-market pricing.

In contrast, a number of firms use below-market pricing. Manufacturers and retailers that offer private brands of products ranging from peanut butter to shampoo deliberately set prices for these products about 8 percent to 10 percent below the prices of nationally branded competitive products such as Skippy peanut butter, Vidal Sassoon shampoo, or Crest toothpaste. Below-market pricing also exists in business-to-business marketing. Hewlett-Packard, for instance, initially priced its line of office personal computers below IBM to promote a value image among corporate buyers.[16]

Loss-Leader Pricing   For a special promotion retail stores deliberately sell a product below its customary price to attract attention to it. The purpose of this **loss-leader pricing** is not to increase sales but to attract customers in hopes they will buy other products as well, particularly the discretionary items with large markups. Mass merchandisers such as Best Buy, Target, and Wal-Mart sell CDs at about half of their suggested retail price to attract customers to their stores.[17]

Concept Check

1. What is standard markup pricing?

2. What profit-based pricing approach should a manager use if he or she wants to reflect the percentage of the firm's resources used in obtaining the profit?

3. What is the purpose of loss-leader pricing when used by a retail firm?

STEP 5: SET THE LIST OR QUOTED PRICE

The first four steps in setting price covered in Chapter 13 and this chapter result in an approximate price level for the product that appears reasonable. But it still remains for the manager to set a specific list or quoted price in light of all relevant factors.

One-Price versus Flexible-Price Policy

A seller must decide whether to follow a one-price or flexible-price policy. A **one-price policy**, also called *fixed pricing,* is setting one price for all buyers of

a product or service. For example, when you buy a Wilson Sting tennis racket from a discount store, you are offered the product at a single price. You can buy it or not, but there is no variation in the price under the seller's one-price policy. Saturn Corporation uses this approach in its stores and features a "no haggle, one price" price for its cars. Some retailers such as Dollar Tree Stores and 99¢ Only Stores have married this policy with a below-market approach and sell everything in their stores for $1 or less!

In contrast, a **flexible-price policy**, also called *dynamic pricing,* involves setting different prices for products and services depending on individual buyers and purchase situations. A flexible-price policy gives sellers considerable discretion in setting the final price in light of demand, cost, and competitive factors. Yield management pricing is a form of flexible pricing because prices vary by an individual buyer's purchase situation, company cost considerations, and competitive conditions. Dell Inc. uses flexible pricing. It continually adjusts prices in response to changes in its own costs, competitive pressures, and demand from customers, from one segment of the personal computer market to another. "Our flexibility allows us to be [priced] different even within a day," says a Dell spokesperson.[18]

Most companies use a one-price policy. However, flexible pricing has grown in popularity because of increasingly sophisticated information technology. Today, many marketers have the ability to customize a price for an individual on the basis of his or her purchasing patterns, product preferences, and price-sensitivity, all of which are stored in company data warehouses. Price customization is particularly prevalent for products and services bought online.[19] Online marketers routinely adjust prices in response to purchase situations and past purchase behaviors of online buyers. Some online marketers monitor an online shopper's *"clickstream"*—the way that person navigates through the website. If the visitor behaves like a price-sensitive shopper—perhaps by comparing many different products and prices—that person may be offered a lower price.

Flexible pricing means that some customers pay more and others less for the same product or service. And flexible pricing is not without its critics because of this discriminatory potential. For example, car dealers have traditionally used flexible pricing on the basis of buyer–seller negotiations to agree on a final sales price. However,

ETHICS AND SOCIAL RESPONSIBILITY ALERT

Flexible Pricing—Is There Race and Gender Discrimination in Bargaining for a New Car?

What do 60 percent of prospective buyers dread when looking for a new car? That's right! They dread negotiating the price. Price bargaining has a more serious side and demonstrates shortcomings of flexible pricing when purchasing a new car: the potential for minority price discrimination. A National Bureau of Economic Research study of 750,000 car purchases indicated that blacks, Hispanics, and women, on average, paid roughly $423, $483, and $105 more, respectively, for a new car in the $21,000 range than the typical purchaser. Smaller price premiums remained after adjusting for income, education, and other factors that may affect price negotiations.

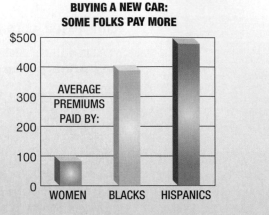

BUYING A NEW CAR: SOME FOLKS PAY MORE

AVERAGE PREMIUMS PAID BY: WOMEN, BLACKS, HISPANICS

flexible pricing may result in discriminatory practices in car buying as detailed in the Ethics and Social Responsibility Alert.[20] There are also legal issues associated with flexible pricing. As noted at the end of this chapter, there are constraints under the Robinson-Patman Act to prevent carrying a flexible-price policy to the extreme of price discrimination.

Company, Customer, and Competitive Effects on Pricing

As the final list or quoted price is set, the effects on the company, customers, and competitors must be assessed.

Company Effects   For a firm with more than one product, a decision on the price of a single product must consider the price of other items in its product line or related product lines in its product mix. Within a product line or mix there are usually some products that are substitutes for one another and some that complement each other.[21] Frito-Lay recognizes that its tortilla chip product line consisting of Baked Tostitos, Tostitos, and Doritos brands are partial substitutes for one another and its bean and cheese chip dip line and salsa sauces complement the tortilla chip line.

A manager's challenge when marketing multiple products is **product-line pricing**, the setting of prices for all items in a product line. When setting prices, the manager seeks to cover the total cost and produce a profit for the complete line, not necessarily for each item. For example, the penetration price for Nintendo's DS handheld video game player was likely at or below its cost, but the price of its video games (complementary products) was set high enough to cover the loss and deliver a profit for the Nintendo product line.

Product-line pricing involves determining (1) the lowest-priced product and price, (2) the highest-priced product and price, and (3) price differentials for all other products in the line.[22] The lowest- and highest-priced items in the product line play important roles. The highest-priced item is typically positioned as the premium item in quality and features. The lowest-priced item is the traffic builder designed to capture the attention of the hesitant or first-time buyer. Price differentials between items in the line should make sense to customers and reflect differences in their perceived value of the products offered. Behavioral research also suggests that the price differentials should get larger as one moves up the product line.

Frito-Lay recognizes that its tortilla chip products are partial substitutes for one another and its bean and cheese dips and salsa sauces complement tortilla chips. This knowledge is used for Frito-Lay product-line pricing.

Frito-Lay, Inc.
www.frito-lay.com

Customer Effects   In setting price, retailers weigh factors heavily that satisfy the perceptions or expectations of ultimate consumers, such as the customary prices for a variety of consumer products. Retailers have found that they should not price their store brands 20 to 25 percent below manufacturers' brands.[23] When they do, consumers often view the lower price as signaling lower quality and don't buy. Manufacturers and wholesalers must choose prices that result in profit for resellers in the channel to gain their cooperation and support. Toro failed to do this on its lines of lawn mowers and snow throwers. It decided to augment its traditional hardware outlet distribution by also selling through mass merchandisers such as Kmart and Target. To do so, it set prices for the mass merchandisers substantially below those for its traditional hardware outlets. Many unhappy hardware stores abandoned Toro products in favor of mowers and snow throwers from other manufacturers.

Competitive Effects   A manager's pricing decision is immediately apparent to most competitors, who may retaliate with price changes of their own. Therefore, a manager who sets a final list or quoted price must anticipate potential price responses from competitors. Regardless of whether a firm is a price leader or follower, it wants to avoid cutthroat price wars in which no firm in the industry makes a satisfactory profit. A **price war** involves successive price cutting by competitors to increase or maintain their unit sales or market share. Price wars erupt in a variety of industries, from consumer electronics to disposable diapers, from soft drinks to airlines, and from grocery retailing to telephone services. Managers expecting that a lower price will result in a larger market share, higher unit sales, and greater profit for their company often initiate them. This may occur. However, if competitors match the lower price, other things being equal, the expected market share, sales, and intended profit gain are lost. According to a recent analysis of large U.S. companies, a 1 percent price cut—assuming no change in unit volume or costs—lowers a company's net profit by an average of 8 percent.[24] Marketers are advised to consider price cutting only when one or more conditions exist: (1) the company has a cost or technological advantage over its competitors, (2) primary demand for a product class will grow if prices are lowered, and (3) the price cut is confined to specific products or customers (as with airline tickets), and not across-the-board.[25]

FIGURE 14–5

The power of marginal analysis in real-world decisions

Suppose the owner of a picture framing store is considering buying a series of magazine ads to reach her upscale target market. The cost of the ads is $1,000, the average price of a framed picture is $50, and the unit variable cost (materials plus labor) is $30.

This is a direct application of marginal analysis that an astute manager uses to estimate the incremental revenue or incremental number of units that must be obtained to at least cover the incremental cost. In this example, the number of extra picture frames that must be sold is obtained as follows:

$$\text{Incremental number of frames} = \frac{\text{Extra fixed cost}}{\text{Price} - \text{Unit variable cost}}$$

$$= \frac{\$1,000 \text{ of advertising}}{\$50 - \$30}$$

$$= 50 \text{ frames}$$

So unless there are other benefits of the ads, such as long-term goodwill, she should only buy the ads if she expects they will increase frame sales by at least 50 units.

Balancing Incremental Costs and Revenues

When a price is changed or new advertising or selling programs are planned, their effect on the quantity sold must be considered. This assessment, called *marginal analysis* (Chapter 13), involves a continuing, concise trade-off of incremental costs against incremental revenues.

Do marketing and business managers really use marginal analysis? Yes, they do, but they often don't use phrases such as *marginal revenue, marginal cost,* and *elasticity of demand.*

Think about these managerial questions:

• How many extra units do we have to sell to pay for that $1,000 advertisement?
• How much savings on unit variable cost do we have to get to keep the break-even point the same if we invest in a $10,000 labor-saving machine?
• Should we hire three more salespeople or not?

All these questions are a form of marginal or incremental analysis, even though these exact words are not used.

Figure 14–5 shows the power, and some limitations, of marginal analysis applied to a marketing decision. Note that the frame store owner must either conclude that a simple advertising campaign will more than pay for itself in additional sales or not undertake the campaign. The decision could also have been made to increase the average price of a framed picture to cover the cost of the campaign, but the principle still applies: Expected incremental revenues from pricing and other marketing actions must more than offset incremental costs.

The example in Figure 14–5 shows both the main advantage and difficulty of marginal analysis. The advantage is its commonsense usefulness, and the difficulty is obtaining the necessary data to make decisions. The owner can measure the cost quite easily, but the incremental revenue generated by the ads is difficult to measure. She could partly solve this problem by offering $2 off the purchase price with use of a coupon printed in the ad to see which sales resulted from the ad.

STEP 6: MAKE SPECIAL ADJUSTMENTS TO THE LIST OR QUOTED PRICE

When you pay 75 cents for a bag of M&Ms in a vending machine or receive a quoted price of $10,000 from a contractor to renovate a kitchen, the pricing sequence ends with the last step just described: setting the list or quoted price. But when you are a manufacturer of M&M candies or gas grills and sell your product to dozens or

FIGURE 14–6
Three special adjustments to list or quoted price

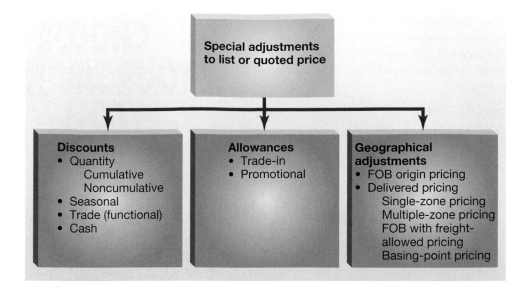

hundreds of wholesalers and retailers in your channel of distribution, you may need to make a variety of special adjustments to the list or quoted price. Wholesalers also must adjust list or quoted prices they set for retailers. Three special adjustments to the list or quoted price are (1) discounts, (2) allowances, and (3) geographical adjustments (Figure 14–6).

Discounts

Discounts are reductions from the list price that a seller gives a buyer as a reward for some activity of the buyer that is favorable to the seller. Four kinds of discounts are especially important in marketing strategy: (1) quantity, (2) seasonal, (3) trade (functional), and (4) cash discounts.[26]

Quantity Discounts   To encourage customers to buy larger quantities of a product, firms at all levels in the channel of distribution offer **quantity discounts**, which are reductions in unit costs for a larger order. For example, an instant photocopying service might set a price of 10 cents a copy for 1 to 25 copies, 9 cents a copy for 26 to 100, and 8 cents a copy for 101 or more. Because the photocopying service gets more of the buyer's business and has longer production runs that reduce its order-handling costs, it is willing to pass on some of the cost savings in the form of quantity discounts to the buyer.

Quantity discounts are of two general kinds: noncumulative and cumulative. *Noncumulative quantity discounts* are based on the size of an individual purchase order. They encourage large individual purchase orders, not a series of orders. This discount is used by FedEx to encourage companies to ship a large number of packages at one time. *Cumulative quantity discounts* apply to the accumulation of purchases of a product over a given time period, typically a year. Cumulative quantity discounts encourage repeat buying by a single customer to a far greater degree than do noncumulative quantity discounts.

Seasonal Discounts   To encourage buyers to stock inventory earlier than their normal demand would require, manufacturers often use seasonal discounts. A firm such as Toro that manufactures lawn mowers and snow throwers offers seasonal discounts to encourage wholesalers and retailers to stock up on lawn mowers in January and February and on snow throwers in July and August—five or six months before the seasonal demand by ultimate consumers. This enables Toro to smooth out seasonal manufacturing peaks and troughs, thereby contributing to more efficient

Toro uses seasonal discounts to stimulate consumer demand and smooth out seasonal manufacturing peaks and troughs.

The Toro Company
www.toro.com

production. It also rewards wholesalers and retailers for the risk they accept in assuming increased inventory carrying costs and having supplies in stock at the time they are wanted by customers.

Trade (Functional) Discounts   To reward wholesalers and retailers for marketing functions they will perform in the future, a manufacturer often gives *trade,* or *functional, discounts*. These reductions off the list or base price are offered to resellers in the channel of distribution on the basis of (1) where they are in the channel and (2) the marketing activities they are expected to perform in the future.

Suppose a manufacturer quotes price in the following form: list price—$100 less 30/10/5. The first number in the percentage sequence always refers to the retail end of the channel, and the last number always refers to the wholesaler or jobber closest to the manufacturer in the channel. The trade discounts are simply subtracted one at a time. This price quote shows $100 is the manufacturer's suggested retail price; 30 percent of the suggested retail price is available to the retailer to cover costs and provide a profit of $30 ($100 × 0.3 = $30); wholesalers closest to the retailer in the channel get 10 percent of their selling price ($70 × 0.1 = $7); and the final group of wholesalers in the channel (probably jobbers) that are closest to the manufacturer get 5 percent of their selling price ($63 × 0.05 = $3.15). Thus, starting with the manufacturer's retail price and subtracting the three trade discounts shows that the manufacturer's selling price to the wholesaler or jobber closest to it is $59.85 (Figure 14–7).

Traditional trade discounts have been established in various product lines such as hardware, food, and pharmaceutical items. Although the manufacturer may suggest the trade discounts shown in the example just cited, the sellers are free to alter the discount schedule depending on their competitive situation.

Cash Discounts   To encourage retailers to pay their bills quickly, manufacturers offer them *cash discounts*. Suppose a retailer receives a bill quoted at $1,000, 2/10 net 30. This means that the bill for the product is $1,000, but the retailer can

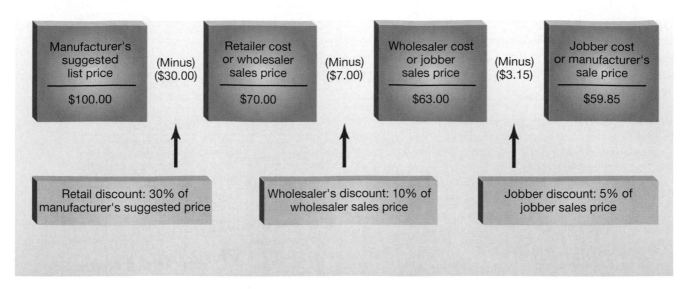

FIGURE 14–7

The structure of trade discounts

take a 2 percent discount ($1,000 × 0.02 = $20) if payment is made within 10 days and send a check for $980. If the payment cannot be made within 10 days, the total amount of $1,000 is due within 30 days. It is usually understood by the buyer that an interest charge will be added after the first 30 days of free credit.

Naive buyers may think that the 2 percent discount offered is not substantial. What this means is that the buyer pays 2 percent on the total amount to be able to use that amount an extra 20 days—from day 11 to day 30. In a 360-day business year, this is an effective annual interest rate of 36 percent (2% × 360/20 = 36%). Because the effective interest rate is so high, firms that cannot take advantage of a 2/10 net 30 cash discount often try to borrow money from their local banks at rates far lower than the 36 percent they must pay by not taking advantage of the cash discount.

Retailers provide cash discounts to consumers as well to eliminate the cost of credit granted to consumers. These discounts take the form of discount-for-cash policies.

Allowances

Allowances, like discounts, are reductions from list or quoted prices to buyers for performing some activity. They include trade-in and promotional allowances.

Trade-in Allowances   A new-car dealer can offer a substantial reduction in the list price of that new Toyota Camry by offering you a trade-in allowance of $1,000 for your Chevrolet Cavalier. A *trade-in allowance* is a price reduction given when a used product is part of the payment on a new product. Trade-ins are an effective way to lower the price a buyer has to pay without formally reducing the list price.

Promotional Allowances   Sellers in the channel of distribution can qualify for **promotional allowances** for undertaking certain advertising or selling activities to promote a product. Various types of allowances include an actual cash payment or an extra amount of "free goods" (as with a free case of pizzas to a retailer for every dozen cases purchased). Frequently, a portion of these savings is passed on to the consumer by retailers.

Some companies, such as Procter & Gamble, have chosen to reduce promotional allowances for retailers by using everyday low pricing. **Everyday low pricing** (EDLP) is the practice of replacing promotional allowances with lower manufacturer list prices. EDLP promises to reduce the average price to consumers while minimizing promotional allowances that cost manufacturers billions of dollars every year. However, EDLP does not necessarily benefit supermarkets as described in the Marketing NewsNet[27] on the next page.

MARKETING NEWSNET

Everyday Low Prices at the Supermarket = Everyday Low Profits— Creating Customer Value at a Cost

CUSTOMER VALUE

Who wouldn't welcome low retail prices every day? The answer is supermarket chains—76 percent of U.S. grocery stores have not adopted this practice. Supermarkets prefer Hi-Lo pricing based on frequent specials where prices are temporarily lowered then raised again. Hi-Lo pricing reflects allowances that manufacturers give supermarkets to push their product. Consider a New York City supermarket whose advertisement is shown here. It regularly pays $1.15 for a can of Bumble Bee white tuna ($55.43 ÷ 48 = $1.15), but the allowances reduce the cost to 96 cents. A price special of 99 cents still provides a 3 cent retail markup ($0.99 retail price in ad – $0.96 cost). When the price on tuna returns to its regular level, the store's gross margin on tuna increases substantially on those cans that were bought with the allowance but not sold during the price special promotion.

Everyday low pricing (EDLP) eliminates manufacturer allowances and can reduce average retail prices by up to 10 percent. While EDLP provides lower average prices than Hi-Lo pricing, EDLP does not allow for deeply discounted price specials. EDLP can create everyday customer value and modestly increase supermarket sales—but at a cost. Already slim supermarket chain profits can slip by 18 percent

with EDLP without the benefit of allowances as described earlier. Also, some argue that EDLP without price specials is boring for many grocery shoppers who welcome price specials. EDLP has been hailed as "value pricing" by manufacturers, but supermarkets view it differently. For them, EDLP means "Everyday Low Profits!"

Geographical Adjustments

Geographical adjustments are made by manufacturers or even wholesalers to list or quoted prices to reflect the cost of transportation of the products from seller to buyer. The two general methods for quoting prices related to transportation costs are (1) FOB origin pricing and (2) uniform delivered pricing.

FOB Origin Pricing FOB means "free on board" some vehicle at some location, which means the seller pays the cost of loading the product onto the vehicle that is used (such as a barge, railroad car, or truck). **FOB origin pricing** usually involves the seller's naming the location of this loading as the seller's factory or warehouse (such as "FOB Detroit" or "FOB factory"). The title to the goods passes to the buyer at the point of loading, so the buyer becomes responsible for picking the specific mode of transportation, for all the transportation costs, and for subsequent handling of the product. Buyers farthest from the seller face the big disadvantage of paying the higher transportation costs.

Uniform Delivered Pricing When a **uniform delivered pricing** method is used, the price the seller quotes includes all transportation costs. It is quoted in a contract as "FOB buyer's location," and the seller selects the mode of transportation, pays the freight charges, and is responsible for any damage that may occur because the seller retains title to the goods until delivered to the buyer. Although they go by various names, there are four kinds of delivered pricing methods: (1) single-zone pricing, (2) multiple-zone pricing, (3) FOB with freight-allowed pricing, and (4) basing-point pricing.

In *single-zone pricing* all buyers pay the same delivered price for the products, regardless of their distance from the seller. This method is also called *postage stamp pricing* because it is the way that the U.S. Postal Service sets rates for first-class mail. So, although a store offering free delivery in a metropolitan area has lower transportation costs for goods shipped to customers nearer the store than for those shipped to distant ones, customers pay the same delivered price.

In *multiple-zone pricing* a firm divides its selling territory into geographic areas or zones. The delivered price to all buyers within any one zone is the same, but prices across zones vary depending on the transportation cost to the zone and the level of competition and demand within the zone. The U.S. Postal Service uses multiple-zone pricing for mailing certain packages. This system is sometimes used in setting prices on long-distance phone calls.

With *FOB with freight-allowed pricing,* also called *freight absorption pricing,* the price is quoted by the seller as "FOB plant—freight allowed." The buyer is allowed to deduct freight expenses from the list price of the goods, so the seller agrees to pay, or "absorb," the transportation costs.

Basing-point pricing involves selecting one or more geographical locations (basing point) from which the list price for products plus freight expenses are charged to the buyer. For example, a company might designate St. Louis as the basing point and charge all buyers a list price of $100 plus freight from St. Louis to their location. Basing-point pricing methods have been used in the steel, cement, and lumber industries where freight expenses are a significant part of the total cost to the buyer and products are largely undifferentiated.

Legal and Regulatory Aspects of Pricing

Arriving at a final price is clearly a complex process. The task is further complicated by legal and regulatory restrictions. Five pricing practices have received the most scrutiny: (1) price fixing, (2) price discrimination, (3) deceptive pricing, (4) geographical pricing, and (5) predatory pricing[28] (Figure 14–8).

Price Fixing   A conspiracy among firms to set prices for a product is termed **price fixing**. Price fixing is illegal per se under the Sherman Act (*per se* means in and of itself). When two or more competitors explicitly or implicitly set prices, this practice is called *horizontal price fixing*. For example, six foreign vitamin companies

FIGURE 14–8
Pricing practices affected by legal restrictions

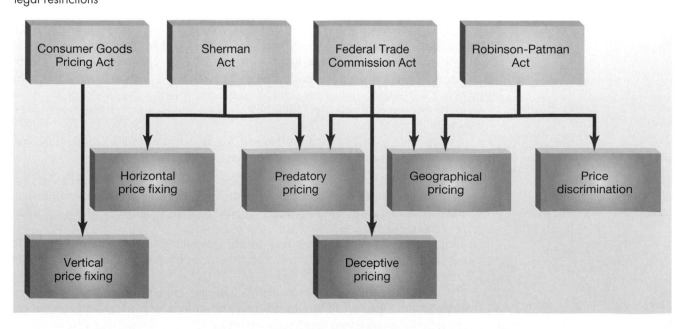

recently pled guilty to price fixing in the human and animal vitamin industry and paid the largest fine in U.S. history, $335 million.[29]

Vertical price fixing involves controlling agreements between independent buyers and sellers (a manufacturer and a retailer) whereby sellers are required to not sell products below a minimum retail price. This practice, called *resale price maintenance,* was declared illegal per se in 1975 under provisions of the *Consumer Goods Pricing Act.* Nevertheless, shoe supplier Nine West recently agreed to settle government charges that the company restricted competition by coercing retailers to adhere to its resale prices. Nine West agreed to pay $34 million in the settlement.[30] However, manufacturers and wholesalers can fix the maximum retail price for their products provided the price agreement does not create an "unreasonable restraint of trade" or is anticompetitive.

It is important to recognize that a "manufacturer's suggested retail price," or MSRP, is not illegal per se. The issue of legality only arises when manufacturers enforce such a practice by coercion. Furthermore, there appears to be a movement toward a *"rule of reason"* in pricing cases. This rule holds that circumstances surrounding a practice must be considered before making a judgment about its legality. The rule of reason perspective is the direct opposite of the per se rule.

Price Discrimination   The Clayton Act as amended by the Robinson-Patman Act prohibits **price discrimination**—the practice of charging different prices to different buyers for goods of like grade and quality. However, not all price differences are illegal; only those that substantially lessen competition or create a monopoly are deemed unlawful. Moreover, "goods" is narrowly defined and does not include discrimination in services.

A unique feature of the Robinson-Patman Act is that it allows for price differentials to different customers under the following conditions:

1. When price differences charged to different customers do not exceed the differences in the cost of manufacture, sale, or delivery resulting from differing methods or quantities in which such goods are sold or delivered to buyers. This condition is called the *cost justification defense.*
2. When price differences result from meeting changing market conditions, avoiding obsolescence of seasonal merchandise, including perishables, or closing out sales.
3. When price differences are quoted to selected buyers in good faith to meet competitors' prices and are not intended to injure competition. This condition is called the *meet-the-competition defense.*

DECEPTIVE PRACTICE   **DESCRIPTION**

Bait and switch	A deceptive practice exists when a firm offers a very low price on a product (the bait) to attract customers to a store. Once in the store, the customer is persuaded to purchase a higher-priced item (the switch) using a variety of tricks, including (1) downgrading the promoted item, (2) not having the item in stock, or (3) refusing to take orders for the item.
Bargains conditional on other purchases	This practice may exist when a buyer is offered "1-Cent Sales," "Buy 1, Get 1 Free," and "Get 2 for the Price of 1." Such pricing is legal only if the first items are sold at the regular price, not a price inflated for the offer. Substituting lower-quality items on either the first or second purchase is also considered deceptive.
Comparable value comparisons	Advertising such as "Retail Value $100.00, Our Price $85.00" is deceptive if a verified and substantial number of stores in the market area did not price the item at $100.
Comparisons with suggested prices	A claim that a price is below a manufacturer's suggested or list price may be deceptive if few or no sales occur at that price in a retailer's market area.
Former price comparisons	When a seller represents a price as reduced, the item must have been offered in good faith at a higher price for a substantial previous period. Setting a high price for the purpose of establishing a reference for a price reduction is deceptive.

FIGURE 14–9

Five most common deceptive pricing practices

The Robinson-Patman Act also covers promotional allowances. To legally offer promotional allowances to buyers, the seller must do so on a proportionally equal basis to all buyers distributing the seller's products. In general, the rule of reason applies frequently in price discrimination cases and is often applied to cases involving flexible pricing practices of firms.

Deceptive Pricing   Price deals that mislead consumers fall into the category of *deceptive pricing*. Deceptive pricing is outlawed by the Federal Trade Commission Act. The FTC monitors such practices and has published a regulation titled "Guides against Deceptive Pricing" designed to help businesspeople avoid a charge of deception. The five most common deceptive pricing practices are described in Figure 14–9. As you read about these practices it should be clear that laws cannot be passed and enforced to protect consumers and competitors against all of these practices, so it is essential to rely on the ethical standards of those making and publicizing pricing decisions. A frequently used pricing practice is to offer products and services for free—a great price! It would seem that the meaning of "free" is obvious. Think again. Visit the FTC website described in the accompanying Web Link to learn what *free* means.

Geographical Pricing   FOB origin pricing is legal, as are FOB freight-allowed pricing practices, providing no conspiracy to set prices exists. Basing-point pricing can be viewed as illegal under the Robinson-Patman Act and the Federal Trade Commission Act if there is clear-cut evidence of a conspiracy to set prices. In general, geographical pricing practices have been immune from legal and regulatory restrictions, except in those instances in which a conspiracy to lessen competition exists under the Sherman Act or price discrimination exists under the Robinson-Patman Act.

Predatory Pricing   **Predatory pricing** is the practice of charging a very low price for a product with the intent of driving competitors out of business. Once competitors have been driven out, the firm raises its prices. This practice is illegal under the Sherman Act and the Federal Trade Commission Act. Proving the presence of this practice has been difficult and expensive because it must be shown that the predator explicitly attempted to destroy a competitor and the predatory price was below the defendant's average cost.[31]

Concept Check

1. Why would a seller choose a flexible-price policy over a one-price policy?

2. If a firm wished to encourage repeat purchases by a buyer throughout a year, would a cumulative or noncumulative quantity discount be a better strategy?

3. Which pricing practices are covered by the Sherman Act?

CHAPTER IN REVIEW

1 *Describe how to establish the initial "approximate price level" using demand-oriented, cost-oriented, profit-oriented, and competition-oriented approaches.*

Demand, cost, profit, and competition influence the initial consideration of the approximate price level for a product or service. Demand-oriented pricing approaches stress consumer demand and revenue implications of pricing and include eight types: skimming, penetration, prestige, price lining, odd-even, target, bundle, and yield management. Cost-oriented pricing approaches emphasize the cost aspects of pricing and include three types: standard markup, cost-plus, and experience curve pricing. Profit-oriented pricing approaches focus on a balance between revenues and costs to set a price and include three types: target profit, target return-on-sales, and target return-on-investment pricing. And finally, competition-oriented pricing approaches stress what competitors or the marketplace are doing and include three types: customary; above-, at-, or below-market; and loss-leader pricing. Although these approaches are described separately, some of them overlap, and an effective marketing manager will consider several in searching for an approximate price level.

2 *Recognize the major factors considered in deriving a final list or quoted price from the approximate price level.*

Given an approximate price level for a product or service, a manager sets a list or quoted price by considering three additional factors. First, a manager must decide whether to follow a one-price versus a flexible-price policy. Second, the manager should consider the effects of the proposed price on the company, customer, and competitors. Finally, consideration should

be given to balancing incremental costs and revenues, particularly when price and cost changes are planned.

3 *Identify the adjustments made to the approximate price level on the basis of discounts, allowances, and geography.*

Numerous adjustments can be made to the approximate price level. Discounts are reductions from the list or quoted price that a seller gives a buyer as a reward for some activity of the buyer that is favorable to the seller. These include quantity, seasonal, trade (functional), and cash discounts. Allowances offered to buyers also reduce list or quoted prices. Trade-in allowances and promotional allowances are most common. Finally, geographical adjustments are made to list or quoted prices to reflect transportation costs from sellers to buyers. The two general methods for quoting prices related to transportation costs are FOB origin pricing and uniform delivered pricing.

4 *Name the principal laws and regulations affecting specific pricing practices.*

There are four principal laws that affect six major pricing practices. The Sherman Act specifically prohibits horizontal price fixing and predatory pricing. The Consumer Goods Pricing Act makes it illegal for companies to engage in vertical price fixing or resale price maintenance agreements. The Federal Trade Commission Act outlaws deceptive pricing. Provisions in this act also address aspects of predatory pricing and geographical pricing. Finally, the Robinson-Patman Act prohibits price discrimination for goods of like grade and quality, covers the use of promotional allowances, and addresses certain aspects of geographical pricing.

FOCUSING ON KEY TERMS

above-, at-, or below-market pricing p. 370
basing-point pricing p. 379
bundle pricing p. 364
cost-plus pricing p. 366
customary pricing p. 370
everyday low pricing p. 377
experience curve pricing p. 367
flexible-price policy p. 371
FOB origin pricing p. 378
loss-leader pricing p. 370
odd-even pricing p. 364

one-price policy p. 371
penetration pricing p. 363
predatory pricing p. 381
prestige pricing p. 363
price discrimination p. 380
price fixing p. 379
price lining p. 364
price war p. 373
product-line pricing p. 372
promotional allowances p. 377
quantity discounts p. 375

skimming pricing p. 362
standard markup pricing p. 366
target pricing p. 364
target profit pricing p. 367

target return-on-investment pricing p. 368
target return-on-sales pricing p. 368
uniform delivered pricing p. 378
yield management pricing p. 365

DISCUSSION AND APPLICATION QUESTIONS

1   Under what conditions would a digital camera manufacturer adopt a skimming price approach for a new product? A penetration approach?

2   What are some similarities and differences between skimming pricing, prestige pricing, and above-market pricing?

3   A producer of microwave ovens has adopted an experience curve pricing approach for its new model. The firm believes it can reduce the cost of producing the model by 20 percent each time volume doubles. The cost to produce the first unit was $1,000. What would be the approximate cost of the 4,096th unit?

4   The Hesper Corporation is a leading manufacturer of high-quality upholstered sofas. Current plans call for an increase of $600,000 in the advertising budget. If the firm sells its sofas for an average price of $850 and the unit variable costs are $550, then what dollar sales increase will be necessary to cover the additional advertising?

5   Suppose executives estimate that the unit variable cost for their VCR is $100, the fixed cost related to the product is $10 million annually, and the target volume for next year is 100,000 recorders. What sales price will be necessary to achieve a target profit of $1 million?

6   A manufacturer of motor oil has a trade discount policy whereby the manufacturer's suggested retail price is $30 per case with the terms of 40/20/10. The manufacturer sells its products through jobbers, who sell to wholesalers, who sell to gasoline stations. What will the manufacturer's sale price be?

7   What are the effective annual interest rates for the following cash discount terms? (*a*) 1/10 net 30, (*b*) 2/10 net 30, and (*c*) 2/10 net 60.

8   Suppose a manufacturer of exercise equipment sets a suggested price to the consumer of $395 for a particular piece of equipment to be competitive with similar equipment. The manufacturer sells its equipment to a sporting goods wholesaler who receives 25 percent of the selling price and a retailer who receives 50 percent of the selling price. What demand-oriented pricing approach is being used, and at what price will the manufacturer sell the equipment to the wholesaler?

9   Is there any truth in the statement, "Geographical pricing schemes will always be unfair to some buyers"? Why or why not?

GOING ONLINE   The Cost of Price Discrimination

Price discrimination, as defined by the Robinson-Patman Act, has been the subject of an enormous amount of litigation between buyers and sellers since its enactment in 1936. A unique website (www.lawmall.com/rpa) provides an up-to-date summary of price discrimination issues that is targeted toward businesspeople.

Visit the LawMall website to find answers to three frequently asked questions concerning Robinson-Patman Act lawsuits:

1   What are the litigation stages and estimated length of a Robinson-Patman Act lawsuit?

2   What are the estimated expenses of a Robinson-Patman Act price discrimination lawsuit?

3   What remedies are afforded plaintiffs in a Robinson-Patman Act price discrimination lawsuit?

BUILDING YOUR MARKETING PLAN

To arrive at the final price(s) for your offering(s):

1   Modify the three prices from your Chapter 13 analysis in light of (*a*) pricing considerations for demand-, cost-, profit-, and competition-oriented Chapter 14 approaches and (*b*) possibilities for discounts, allowances, and geographic adjustments.

2   Do a break-even analysis for each of these three new prices.

3   Choose the final price(s).

VIDEO CASE 14 Stuart Cellars: Price Is a Matter of Taste

Stuart Cellars is a family-owned winery located in Temecula, California. The winery marked its first harvest in 1999. Forty acres are available for cultivation, giving Stuart Cellars a capacity of some 150 tons of grapes and yielding about 16,000 cases of wine per year. Stuart Cellars offers its Chardonnay, Merlot, Cabernet Sauvignon, Cabernet Franc, Zinfandel, Viognier, and other wines for sale through its tasting room, its website (www.stuartcellars.com), and retailers in California.

Retail prices for Stuart Cellars products range from $13 per bottle for a Chardonnay, Viognier, Sauvignon Blanc, and White Merlot blend, to $46 per bottle for a 2002 Zinfandel Vintage Port. The average retail price for a Stuart Cellar wine is about $28 per bottle. Stuart Cellar Wine Club members enjoy a 20 percent discount and receive additional benefits such as complimentary tasting at the winery, special "member only" wines, additional discounts for reorders of the monthly wine selection, and quantity discounts.

PRICING WINE: CONSIDERING COSTS AND PROFITS

How does Stuart Cellars arrive at its pricing? What factors enter into the pricing decision?

The price floor is usually set by costs. Costs vary widely depending on winery location and number of years in business. There are tremendous economies of scale for larger producers versus smaller boutique wineries such as Stuart Cellars. Grapes, including labor to grow and harvest, can represent up to 60 percent of production expenses. One rule of thumb is that a bottle of wine should be priced at 1/1000 the cost of a ton of grapes. Paying $40,000 for a ton of Cabernet grapes would yield a bottle price of $40. Napa Valley growers' costs range from $2,800 per ton to $10,000 per ton.

Buying land adds to winery costs but provides more operational control. Even wineries that do grow grapes may need to buy grapes on the market to meet their production needs. The impact of land ownership depends on the size of the mortgage and the interest rate to finance the property. Planting costs can be as much as $30,000 per acre, depending on such factors as density of plantings, trellising, and irrigation methods. Winery facilities and equipment—grape press, tanks, barrel racks—can be significant. Winemaking barrels are the second-highest production cost for many wineries. American oak barrels ($300 per barrel) or French oak ($700 per barrel) may have a useful life of two to three years. On the other hand, a stainless tank may last 20 years. And of course, repair and maintenance costs for equipment and facilities can add up.

Because it can be a three-year wait to harvest grapes from new plantings, followed by barrel and bottle aging, wineries can easily have five and a half years of capital and cash flow for red wines–less for white wines that require less aging. Packaging is also important and a reflection of the wine's image. Will the winery use flat-bottomed, Burgundy-style bottles at $.50 each, or thick-glass, thick-neck, deep-punt bottles at $3? Corks can range in price from pennies to dollars a piece.

Advertising, public relations, point-of-sale materials, promotions, salesforce, wine tastings, samples for the wine press, warehousing, shipping, distribution, and excise taxes all mount up and can be about 15 percent of the retail price. Warehousing and shipping are significant because wine is a heavy product.

Many states have regulated distribution systems such as California's three-tier system of wineries, wholesalers, and retailers. Wholesaler markups range from 20–35 percent of what the distributor pays for the wine, with high-volume wines having lower margins as this means less inventory. Retailer markups can vary from 10–50 percent, depending on the type of outlet. Some states have mandated minimum markup to prevent predatory pricing.

The wine business is not known as a highly profitable business. Success comes over the long term as initial investments and expenses are spread out over a number of years and over increasing unit volume.

CONSUMER DEMAND AND COMPETITION

Costs and profit objectives are only part of the pricing formula. Wineries also have to consider buyer characteristics—retailers and consumers. According to Steven Bombola, consulting general manager, Stuart Cellars is targeting the "upper end of wine connoisseurs, people who can afford a premium product at a premium price" and represents perhaps "the top 10–15 percent of the wine purchasing public." These are savvy consumers; they read and follow wine reviews. Wineries also need to consider and compare pricing from competitive wineries. Wine buyers certainly will make these comparisons. And while price is often a cue for quality, there are many great-tasting wines at reasonable prices.

If a wine is priced too low, it will affect consumers' perceptions of quality. However, charging a price significantly higher than competitor prices can drive consumers away to lower-priced competitor products.

"People's perceptions are driven by wine pricing," states Robert Mondavi's senior vice president, Gayle Dargan. "If all consumer decisions were driven by blind-tasting, it would be a very different world. That's not reality. Price is a signal to people of our commitment and the efforts we are taking through out vineyards and our winemaking to put out the best wines."

The average bottle price for wine has been dropping, in large part due to the popularity of Australian and New Zealand wines. Most popular wine brands retail for less than $10 per bottle.

Image is very important in wine marketing. Fancy bottles, elegant and artistic labels, advertising, celebrity endorsements, and wine reviews can all impact consumers' perceptions of the value of a wine. There is often greater prestige from small-production, boutique wineries than larger-volume operations. Scarcity, the real or perceived rarity of a wine, can drive up prices. Demand can be influenced by global supply, those all-important ratings from publications such as the *Wine Spectator*, and the quality of the vintage. All the marketing efforts in the world can't make a poor wine taste good.

Questions

1 What factors related to (*a*) demand, (*b*) cost, (*c*) profit, and (*d*) competition are used by Stuart Cellars to arrive at an approximate price level?

2 If the average Stuart Cellars wine retails for $28 per bottle, what does Stuart Cellars sell the wine for if retailers take a 15 percent margin and wholesalers take a 20 percent margin?

3 Assume that Stuart Cellars annual fixed costs are $1,000,000. With an average retail price of $28 per bottle and assuming estimated unit variable costs of $11.50, calculate break-even volume. If there are 12 bottles per case, how does the break-even unit volume compare to Stuart Cellars' capacity?

4 You are a Stuart Cellars Wine Club member. You want to order Cabernet Sauvignon that normally retails for $45 per bottle. The following discount structure applies: 20 percent discount for purchases of 11 bottles or less; 30 percent discount for purchase of 12 bottles or more. Add 7.75 percent sales tax for California residents.

What price, before shipping and handling, would you pay if (*a*) you order 10 bottles? (*b*) you order 12 bottles? (*c*) What are the implications of this discounting structure?

5 What pricing strategy(ies) does Stuart Cellars appear to be following? What will be the key factors in making these strategies a success?

FINANCIAL ASPECTS OF MARKETING

Basic concepts from accounting and finance provide valuable tools for marketing executives. This appendix describes an actual company's use of accounting and financial concepts and illustrates how they assist the owner in making marketing decisions.

THE CAPLOW COMPANY

An accomplished artist and calligrapher, Jane Westerlund, decided to apply some of her experience to the picture framing business in Minneapolis. She bought an existing retail frame store, The Caplow Company, from a friend who owned the business and wanted to retire. She avoided the do-it-yourself end of the framing business and chose three kinds of business activities: (1) cutting the frame, mats, and glass for customers who brought in their own pictures or prints to be framed; (2) selling prints and posters that she had purchased from wholesalers; and (3) restoring high-quality frames and paintings.

To understand how accounting, finance, and marketing relate to each other, let's analyze (1) the operating statement for her frame shop, (2) some general ratios of interest that are derived from the operating statement, and (3) some ratios that pertain specifically to her pricing decisions.

The Operating Statement

The *operating statement* (also called an *income statement* or *profit-and-loss statement*) summarizes the profitability of a business firm for a specific time period, usually a month, quarter, or year. The title of the operating statement for The Caplow Company shows it is for a one-year period (Figure B–1). The purpose of an operating statement is to show the profit of the firm and the revenues and expenses that led to that profit. This information tells the owner or manager what has happened in the past and suggests actions to improve future profitability.

The left side of Figure B–1 shows that there are three key elements to all operating statements: (1) sales of the firm's goods and services, (2) costs incurred in making

and selling the goods and services, and (3) profit or loss, which is the difference between sales and costs.

Sales Elements The sales element of Figure B–1 has four terms that need explanation:

- *Gross sales* are the total amount billed to customers. Dissatisfied customers or errors may reduce the gross sales through returns or allowances.
- *Returns* occur when a customer gives the item purchased back to the seller, who either refunds the purchase price or allows the customer a credit on subsequent purchases. In any event, the seller now owns the item again.
- *Allowances* are given when a customer is dissatisfied with the item purchased and the seller reduces the original purchase price. Unlike returns, in the case of allowances the buyer owns the item.
- *Net sales* are simply gross sales minus returns and allowances.

The operating statement for The Caplow Company shows that

Gross sales	$80,500
Less: Returns and allowances	500
Net sales	$80,000

The low level of returns and allowances shows the shop generally has done a good job in satisfying customers, which is essential in building the repeat business necessary for success.

Cost Elements The *cost of goods sold* (COGS) is the total cost of the products sold during the period. This item varies according to the kind of business. A retail store purchases finished goods and resells them to customers without reworking them in any way. In contrast, a manufacturing firm combines raw and semifinished materials and parts, uses labor and overhead to rework these into finished goods, and then sells them to customers. All these activities are reflected in the cost of goods sold item on a manufacturer's operating statement.

FIGURE B–1

Examples of an operating statement

	THE CAPLOW COMPANY			
	Operating Statement			
	For the Year Ending December 31, 2005			
Sales	Gross sales			$80,500
	Less: Returns and allowances			500
	Net sales			$80,000
Costs	Cost of goods sold:			
	Beginning inventory at cost		$ 6,000	
	Purchases at billed cost	$21,000		
	Less: Purchase discounts	300		
	Purchases at net cost	20,700		
	Plus: freight-in	100		
	Net cost of delivered purchases		20,800	
	Direct labor (framing)		14,200	
	Cost of goods available for sale		41,000	
	Less: Ending inventory at cost		5,000	
	Cost of goods sold			36,000
	Gross margin (gross profit)			$44,000
	Expenses:			
	Selling expenses:			
	Sales salaries	2,000		
	Advertising expense	3,000		
	Total selling expense		5,000	
	Administrative expenses:			
	Owner's salary	18,000		
	Bookkeeper's salary	1,200		
	Office supplies	300		
	Total administrative expense		19,500	
	General expenses:			
	Depreciation expense	1,000		
	Interest expense	500		
	Rent expense	2,100		
	Utility expenses (heat, electricity)	3,000		
	Repairs and maintenance	2,300		
	Insurance	2,000		
	Social security taxes	2,200		
	Total general expense		13,100	
	Total expenses			37,600
Profit or loss	Profit before taxes			$ 6,400

Note that the frame shop has some features of a pure retailer (prints and posters it buys that are resold without alteration) and a pure manufacturer (assembling the raw materials of molding, matting, and glass to form a completed frame).

Some terms that relate to cost of goods sold need clarification:

- *Inventory* is the physical material that is purchased from suppliers, may or may not be reworked, and is available for sale to customers. In the frame shop, inventory includes molding, matting, glass, prints, and posters.
- *Purchase discounts* are reductions in the original billed price for reasons such as prompt payment of the bill or the quantity bought.
- *Direct labor* is the cost of the labor used in producing the finished product. For the frame shop, this is the cost of producing the completed frames from the molding, matting, and glass.
- *Gross margin (gross profit)* is the money remaining to manage the business, sell the products or services, and give some profit. Gross margin is net sales minus cost of goods sold.

The two right-hand columns in Figure B–1 between "Net sales" and "Gross margin" calculate the cost of goods sold:

Net sales		$80,000
Cost of goods sold		
Beginning inventory at cost	$ 6,000	
Net cost of delivered purchases	20,800	
Direct labor (framing)	14,200	
Cost of goods available for sale	41,000	
Less: ending inventory at cost	5,000	
Cost of goods sold		36,000
Gross margin (gross profit)		$44,000

This section considers the beginning and ending inventories, the net cost of purchases delivered during the year, and the cost of the direct labor going into making the frames. Subtracting the $36,000 cost of goods sold from the $80,000 net sales gives the $44,000 gross margin.

Three major categories of expenses are shown in Figure B–1 below the gross margin:

- *Selling expenses* are the costs of selling the product or service produced by the firm. For The Caplow Company there are two such selling expenses: sales salaries of part-time employees waiting on customers and the advertising expense of simple newspaper ads and direct-mail ads sent to customers.
- *Administrative expenses* are the costs of managing the business, and for The Caplow Company include three expenses: the owner's salary, a part-time bookkeeper's salary, and office supplies expense.
- *General expenses* are miscellaneous costs not covered elsewhere; for the frame shop these include seven items: depreciation expense (on her equipment),

Jane Westerlund (left) and an assistant assess the restoration of a gold frame for regilding.

interest expense, rent expense, utility expenses, repairs and maintenance expense, insurance expense, and social security taxes.

As shown in Figure B–1, selling, administrative, and general expenses total $37,600 for The Caplow Company.

Profit Element   What the company has earned, the *profit before taxes,* is found by subtracting cost of goods sold and expenses from net sales. For The Caplow Company, Figure B–1 shows that profit before taxes is $6,400.

General Operating Ratios to Analyze Operations

Looking only at the elements of Caplow's operating statement that extend to the right-hand column highlights the firm's performance on some important dimensions. Using operating ratios such as *expense-to-sales ratios* for expressing basic expense or profit elements as a percentage of net sales gives further insights:

ELEMENT IN OPERATING STATEMENT	DOLLAR VALUE	PERCENTAGE OF NET SALES
Gross sales	$80,500	
Less: Returns and allowances	500	
Net sales	80,000	100%
Less: Cost of goods sold	36,000	45
Gross margin	44,000	55
Less: Total expenses	37,600	47
Profit (or loss) before taxes	$ 6,400	8%

Westerlund can use this information to compare her firm's performance from one time period to the next. To do so, it is especially important that she keep the same definitions for each element of her operating statement, also a significant factor in using the electronic spreadsheets discussed in Chapter 14. Performance comparisons between periods are more difficult if she changes definitions for the accounting elements in the operating statement.

She can use either the dollar values or the operating ratios (the value of the element of the operating statement divided by net sales) to analyze the firm's performance. However, the operating ratios are more valuable than the dollar values for two reasons: (1) the simplicity of working with percentages rather than dollars and (2) the availability of operating ratios of typical firms in the same industry, which are published by Dun & Bradstreet and trade associations. Thus, Westerlund can compare her firm's performance not only with that of *other* frame shops but also with that of *small* frame shops that have annual net sales, for example, under $100,000. In this way, she can identify where her operations are better or worse than other similar firms. For example, if trade association data showed a typical frame shop of her size had a ratio of cost of goods sold to net sales of 37 percent, compared with her 45 percent, she might consider steps to reduce this cost through purchase discounts, reducing inbound freight charges, finding lower-cost suppliers, and so on.

Ratios to Use in Setting and Evaluating Price

Using The Caplow Company as an example, we can study four ratios that relate closely to setting a price: (1) markup, (2) markdown, (3) stockturns, and (4) return on investment. These terms are defined in Figure B–2 on the next page and explained below.

Markup   Both *markup* and gross margin refer to the amount added to the cost of goods sold to arrive at the selling price, and they may be expressed either in dollar

NAME OF FINANCIAL ELEMENT OR RATIO	WHAT IT MEASURES	EQUATION
Selling price ($)	Price customer sees	Cost of goods sold (COGS) + Markup
Markup ($)	Dollars added to COGS to arrive at selling price	Selling price − COGS
Markup on selling price (%)	Relates markup to selling price	$\dfrac{\text{Markup}}{\text{Selling price}} \times 100 = \dfrac{\text{Selling price} - \text{COGS}}{\text{Selling price}} \times 100$
Markup on cost (%)	Relates markup to cost	$\dfrac{\text{Markup}}{\text{COGS}} \times 100 = \dfrac{\text{Selling price} - \text{COGS}}{\text{COGS}} \times 100$
Markdown (%)	Ability of firm to sell its products at initial selling price	$\dfrac{\text{Markdowns}}{\text{Net sales}} \times 100$
Stockturn rate	Ability of firm to move its inventory quickly	$\dfrac{\text{COGS}}{\text{Average inventory at cost}}$ or $\dfrac{\text{Net sales}}{\text{Average inventory at selling price}}$
Return on investment (%)	Profit performance of firm compared with money invested in it	$\dfrac{\text{Net profit after taxes}}{\text{Investment}} \times 100$

FIGURE B–2

How to calculate selling price, markups, markdown, stockturn rate, and return on investment

or percentage terms. However, the term *markup* is more commonly used in setting retail prices. Suppose the average price Westerlund charges for a framed picture is $80. Then in terms of the first two definitions in Figure B–2 and the earlier information from the operating statement,

ELEMENT OF PRICE	DOLLAR VALUE
Cost of goods sold	$36
Markup (or gross margin)	44
Selling price	$80

The third definition in Figure B–2 gives the percentage markup on selling price:

$$\text{Markup on selling price (\%)} = \frac{\text{Markup}}{\text{Selling price}} \times 100$$

$$= \frac{44}{80} \times 100 = 55\%$$

And the percentage markup on cost is obtained as follows:

$$\text{Markup on cost (\%)} = \frac{\text{Markup}}{\text{Cost of goods sold}} \times 100$$

$$= \frac{44}{36} \times 100 = 122.2\%$$

Inexperienced retail clerks sometimes fail to distinguish between the two definitions of markup, which (as the preceding calculations show) can represent a tremendous difference, so it is essential to know whether the base is cost or selling price. Marketers generally use selling price as the base for talking about markups unless they specifically state that they are using cost as a base.

Retailers and wholesalers that rely heavily on markup pricing (discussed in Chapter 14) often use standardized tables that convert markup on selling price to markup on cost, and vice versa. The two equations below show how to convert one to the other:

$$\text{Markup on selling price (\%)} = \frac{\text{Markup on cost (\%)}}{100\% + \text{Markup on cost (\%)}} \times 100$$

$$\text{Markup on cost (\%)} = \frac{\text{Markup on selling price (\%)}}{100\% - \text{Markup on selling price (\%)}}$$

Using the data from The Caplow Company gives:

$$\text{Markup on selling price (\%)} = \frac{\text{Markup on cost (\%)}}{100\% + \text{Markup on cost (\%)}} \times 100$$

$$= \frac{122.2}{100 + 122.2} \times 100 = 55\%$$

$$\text{Markup on cost (\%)} = \frac{\text{Markup on selling price (\%)}}{100\% - \text{Markup on selling price (\%)}} \times 100$$

$$= \frac{55}{100 - 55} \times 100 = 122.2\%$$

The use of an incorrect markup base is shown in Westerlund's business. A markup of 122.2 percent on her cost of goods sold for a typical frame she sells gives 122.2% × $36 = $44 of markup. Added to the $36 cost of goods sold, this gives her selling price of $80 for the framed picture. However, a new clerk working for her who erroneously priced the framed picture at 55 percent of cost of goods sold set the final price at $55.80 ($36 of cost of goods sold plus 55% × $36 = $19.80). The error, if repeated, can be disastrous: frames would be accidentally sold at $55.80, or $24.20 below the intended selling price of $80.

Markdown   A *markdown* is a reduction in a retail price that is necessary if the item will not sell at the full selling price to which it has been marked up. The item might not sell for a variety of reasons: the selling price was set too high or the item is out of style or has become soiled or damaged. The seller "takes a markdown" by lowering the price to sell it, thereby converting it to cash to buy future inventory that will sell faster.

The markdown percentage cannot be calculated directly from the operating statement. As shown in the fifth item of Figure B–2, the numerator of the markdown percentage is the total dollar markdowns. Markdowns are reductions in the prices of goods that are purchased by customers. The denominator is net sales.

Suppose The Caplow Company had a total of $700 in markdowns on the prints and posters that are stocked and available for sale. Since the frames are custom made for individual customers, there is little reason for a markdown there. Caplow's markdown percent is then:

$$\text{Markdown (\%)} = \frac{\text{Markdowns}}{\text{Net sales}} \times 100$$

$$= \frac{\$700}{\$80,000} \times 100$$

$$= 0.875\%$$

Other kinds of retailers often have markdown ratios several times this amount. For example, women's dress stores have markdowns of about 25 percent, and menswear stores have markdowns of about 2 percent.

A customer discusses choices of framing and matting for her print with Jane Westerlund.

Stockturn Rate   A business firm is anxious to have its inventory move quickly, or "turn over." *Stockturn rate,* or simply stockturns, measures this inventory movement. For a retailer a slow stockturn rate may show it is buying merchandise customers don't want, so this is a critical measure of performance. When a firm sells only a single product, one convenient way to measure stockturn rate is simply to divide its cost of goods sold by average inventory at cost. The sixth item in Figure B–2 shows how to calculate stockturn rate using information in the operating statement:

$$\text{Stockturn rate} = \frac{\text{Cost of goods sold}}{\text{Average inventory at cost}}$$

The dollar amount of average inventory at cost is calculated by adding the beginning and ending inventories for the year and dividing by 2 to get the average. From Caplow's operating statement, we have:

$$\text{Stockturn rate} = \frac{\text{Cost of goods sold}}{\text{Average inventory at cost}}$$

$$= \frac{\text{Cost of goods sold}}{\dfrac{\text{Beginning inventory} + \text{Ending inventory}}{2}}$$

$$= \frac{\$36,000}{\dfrac{\$6,000 + \$5,000}{2}}$$

$$= \frac{\$36,000}{\$5,500}$$

$$= 6.5 \text{ stockturns per year}$$

What is considered a "good stockturn" varies by the kind of industry. For example, supermarkets have limited shelf space for thousands of new products from manufacturers each year, so they watch stockturn carefully by product line. The stockturn rate in supermarkets for breakfast foods is about 17 times per year, for pet food about 22 times per year, and for paper products about 25 times per year.

Return on Investment   A better measure of the performance of a firm than the amount of profit it makes in a year is its *return on investment* (ROI), which is the ratio of net income to the investment used to earn that net income. To calculate ROI, it is necessary to subtract income taxes from profit before taxes to obtain net income, then divide this figure by the investment that can be found on a firm's balance sheet (which is another accounting statement that shows the firm's assets, liabilities, and net worth). While financial and accounting experts have many definitions for *investment,* an often-used definition is "total assets."

For our purposes, let's assume that Westerlund has total assets (investment) of $20,000 in The Caplow Company, which covers inventory, store fixtures, and framing equipment. If she pays $1,000 in income taxes, her store's net income is $5,400, so her ROI is given by the seventh item in Figure B–2:

$$\text{Return on investment} = \text{Net income/Investment} \times 100$$

$$= \$5,400/\$20,000 \times 100$$

$$= 27\%$$

If Westerlund wants to improve her ROI next year, the strategies she might take are found in this alternative equation for ROI:

$$\text{ROI} = \text{Net sales/Investment} \times \text{Net income/Net sales}$$

$$= \text{Investment turnover} \times \text{Profit margin}$$

This equation suggests that The Caplow Company's ROI can be improved by raising investment turnover or increasing profit margin. Increasing stockturns will accomplish the former, whereas lowering cost of goods sold to net sales will cause the latter.

CHAPTER 15

MANAGING MARKETING CHANNELS AND WHOLESALING

LEARNING OBJECTIVES

After reading this chapter you should be able to:

1 Explain what is meant by a marketing channel of distribution and why intermediaries are needed.

2 Distinguish among traditional marketing channels, electronic marketing channels, and different types of vertical marketing systems.

3 Describe the factors and considerations that affect a company's choice and management of a marketing channel.

4 Recognize how conflict, cooperation, and legal considerations affect marketing channel relationships.

APPLE STORES: ADDING HIGH-TOUCH TO HIGH-TECH MARKETING CHANNELS

Apple Computer thrives on innovation. Apple ignited the personal computer revolution in the 1970s with the Apple II, reinvented the personal computer in the 1980s with the Macintosh, and captured the imagination of personal computer buyers worldwide in the 1990s with the introduction of the iMac, a design and technological breakthrough. Today, Apple's hot-selling iPod digital music players and popular online music store, iTunes, plus ongoing development projects promise to revolutionize digital entertainment.

But there's more. Apple Computer is changing the way consumer electronics are marketed with its company-owned Apple Stores. The thinking behind Apple Stores was to create an atmosphere where consumers can experience the thrill of owning and using Apple's complete line of Macintosh computers and an amazing array of digital cameras, camcorders, the entire iPod family, and more with the assistance of knowledgeable Apple personnel. Beginning with two stores in May 2001, Apple has been opening about 25 stores per year, mostly in upscale shopping malls in the United States. By 2004, about half of the U.S. population resided within 15 miles of an Apple Store. Success with an Apple Store in Tokyo in 2003 suggests future growth opportunities outside the United States as well.

Was Apple's decision to open its own stores a wise move? So far, yes. Apple Stores achieved $1 billion in sales faster than any retail business in history, taking just three years to reach that mark. About 40 percent of the people purchasing items at Apple Stores are new customers. Equally important, Apple Stores are profitable.[1]

This chapter focuses on marketing channels of distribution and why they are an important component in the marketing mix. It then shows how such channels benefit consumers and the sequence of firms that make up a marketing channel. Finally, it describes factors that influence the choice and management of marketing channels, including channel conflict and legal restrictions.

NATURE AND IMPORTANCE OF MARKETING CHANNELS

Reaching prospective buyers, either directly or indirectly, is a prerequisite for successful marketing. At the same time, buyers benefit from distribution systems used by companies.

What Is a Marketing Channel of Distribution?

You see the results of distribution every day. You may have purchased Lay's Potato Chips at a 7-Eleven store, a book through Amazon.com, and Levi's jeans at Sears. Each of these items was brought to you by a marketing channel of distribution, or simply a **marketing channel**, which consists of individuals and firms involved in the process of making a product or service available for use or consumption by consumers or industrial users.

Marketing channels can be compared with a pipeline through which water flows from a source to terminus. Marketing channels make possible the flow of goods from a producer, through intermediaries, to a buyer. Intermediaries go by various names (Figure 15–1) and perform various functions. Some intermediaries actually purchase items from the seller, store them, and resell them to buyers. For example, Sunshine Biscuits produces cookies and sells them to food wholesalers. The wholesalers then sell the cookies to supermarkets and grocery stores, which, in turn, sell them to consumers. Other intermediaries such as brokers and agents represent sellers but do not actually take title to products—their role is to bring a seller and buyer together. Century 21 real estate agents are examples of this type of intermediary. The

FIGURE 15–1

Terms used for marketing intermediaries

TERM	DESCRIPTION
Middleman	Any intermediary between manufacturer and end-user markets
Agent or broker	Any intermediary with legal authority to act on behalf of the manufacturer
Wholesaler	An intermediary who sells to other intermediaries, usually to retailers; usually applies to consumer markets
Retailer	An intermediary who sells to consumers
Distributor	An imprecise term, usually used to describe intermediaries who perform a variety of distribution functions, including selling, maintaining inventories, extending credit, and so on; a more common term in business markets but may also be used to refer to wholesalers
Dealer	An even more imprecise term that can mean the same as distributor, retailer, wholesaler, and so forth

importance of intermediaries is made even clearer when we consider the functions they perform and the value they create for buyers.

Value Created by Intermediaries

Few consumers appreciate the value created by intermediaries; however, producers recognize that intermediaries make selling goods and services more efficient because they minimize the number of sales contacts necessary to reach a target market. Figure 15–2 shows a simple example of how this comes about in the digital camera industry. Without a retail intermediary (such as Sears), Kodak, Sony, Panasonic, and Hewlett-Packard would each have to make four contacts to reach the four buyers shown who are in the target market. However, each producer has to make only one contact when Sears acts as an intermediary. Equally important from a macro marketing perspective, the total number of industry transactions is reduced from 16 to 8, which reduces producer cost and hence benefits the customer.

Functions Performed by Intermediaries
Intermediaries make possible the flow of products from producers to buyers by performing three basic functions (Figure 15–3 on the next page). Intermediaries perform a *transactional function* that involves buying, selling, and risk taking because they stock merchandise in anticipation of sales. Intermediaries perform a *logistical function* evident in the gathering, storing, and dispersing of products (see Chapter 16 on supply chain and logistics management). Finally, intermediaries perform *facilitating functions,* which assist producers in making goods and services more attractive to buyers.

All three groups of functions must be performed in a marketing channel, even though each channel member may not participate in all three. Channel members often negotiate about which specific functions they will perform. Borders, a leading U.S. book retailer, is a case in point. It has negotiated agreements with major book publishers whereby they assume responsibility for choosing books for Borders to buy, displaying the assortment of books on its shelves, and providing information on new titles and consumer reading preferences in specific book categories. For example, HarperCollins has responsibility for cookbooks, Random House for children's books, and Pearson for computer books.[2]

Consumer Benefits from Intermediaries
Consumers also benefit from intermediaries. Having the goods and services you want, when you want them, where you want them, and in the form you want them is the ideal result of

FIGURE 15–2

How intermediaries minimize transactions

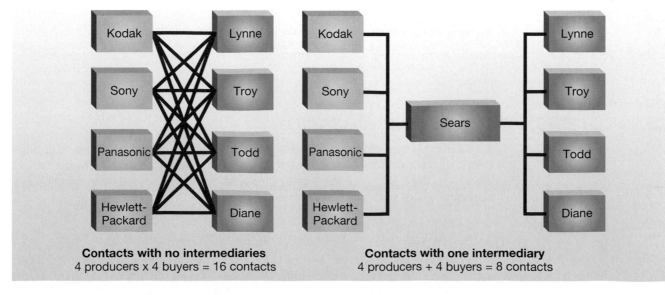

Contacts with no intermediaries
4 producers × 4 buyers = 16 contacts

Contacts with one intermediary
4 producers + 4 buyers = 8 contacts

TYPE OF FUNCTION   ACTIVITIES RELATED TO FUNCTION

Transactional function

- *Buying*: Purchasing products for resale or as an agent for supply of a product
- *Selling*: Contacting potential customers, promoting products, and soliciting orders
- *Risk taking*: Assuming business risks in the ownership of inventory that can become obsolete or deteriorate

Logistical function

- *Assorting*: Creating product assortments from several sources to serve customers
- *Storing*: Assembling and protecting products at a convenient location to offer better customer service
- *Sorting*: Purchasing in large quantities and breaking into smaller amounts desired by customers
- *Transporting*: Physically moving a product to customers

Facilitating function

- *Financing*: Extending credit to customers
- *Grading*: Inspecting, testing, or judging products, and assigning them quality grades
- *Marketing information and research*: Providing information to customers and suppliers, including competitive conditions and trends

FIGURE 15–3
Marketing channel functions
performed by intermediaries

marketing channels. In more specific terms, marketing channels help create value for consumers through the four utilities described in Chapter 1: time, place, form, and possession. Time utility refers to having a product or service when you want it. For example, FedEx provides next-morning delivery. Place utility means having a product or service available where consumers want it, such as having a Texaco gas station located on a long stretch of lonely highway. Form utility involves enhancing a product or service to make it more appealing to buyers. Consider the importance of bottlers in the soft-drink industry. Coca-Cola and Pepsi-Cola manufacture the flavor concentrate (cola, lemon-lime) and sell it to bottlers—intermediaries—which then add sweetener and the concentrate to carbonated water and package the beverage in bottles and cans, which are then sold to retailers. Possession utility entails efforts by intermediaries to help buyers take possession of a product or service, such as having airline tickets delivered by a travel agency.

Concept Check

1. What is meant by a marketing channel?

2. What are the three basic functions performed by intermediaries?

CHANNEL STRUCTURE AND ORGANIZATION

A product can take many routes on its journey from a producer to buyers, and marketers search for the most efficient route from the many alternatives available. As you'll see, there are some important differences between the marketing channels for consumer goods and those for business goods.

Marketing Channels for Consumer Goods and Services

Figure 15–4 shows the four most common marketing channels for consumer goods and services. It also shows the number of levels in each marketing channel, as

FIGURE 15–4

Common marketing channels for consumer goods and services

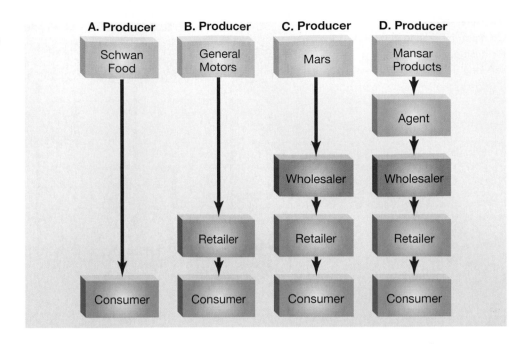

evidenced by the number of intermediaries between a producer and ultimate buyers. As the number of intermediaries between a producer and buyer increases, the channel is viewed as increasing in length. Thus, the producer → wholesaler → retailer → consumer channel is longer than the producer → consumer channel.

Channel A represents a **direct channel** because a producer and ultimate consumers deal directly with each other. Many products and services are distributed this way. A number of insurance companies sell their financial services using a direct channel and branch sales offices. The Schwan Food Company of Marshall, Minnesota, markets a full line of frozen foods in 48 states using door-to-door salespeople who sell from refrigerated trucks. Because there are no intermediaries with a direct channel, the producer must perform all channel functions.

The remaining three channel forms are **indirect channels** because intermediaries are inserted between the producer and consumers and perform numerous channel functions. Channel B, with a retailer added, is most common when a retailer is large and can buy in large quantities from a producer or when the cost of inventory makes it too expensive to use a wholesaler. Manufacturers such as General Motors, Ford, and DaimlerChrysler use this channel, and a local car dealer acts as a retailer. Why is there no wholesaler? So many variations exist in the product that it would be impossible for a wholesaler to stock all the models required to satisfy buyers; in addition, the cost of maintaining an inventory would be too high. However, large retailers such as Sears, 7-Eleven, Safeway, and Home Depot buy in sufficient quantities to make it cost effective for a producer to deal with only a retail intermediary.

Adding a wholesaler in Channel C is most common for low-cost, low-unit value items that are frequently purchased by consumers, such as candy, confectionary items, and magazines. For example, Mars sells its line of candies to wholesalers in case quantities, who then break down (sort) the cases so that individual retailers can order in boxes or much smaller quantities.

Channel D, the most indirect channel, is employed when there are many small manufacturers and many small retailers, and an agent is used to help coordinate a large supply of the product. Mansar Products, Ltd., is a Belgian producer of specialty jewelry that uses agents to sell to wholesalers in the United States, which then sell to many small retailers.

FIGURE 15–5

Common marketing channels for business goods and services

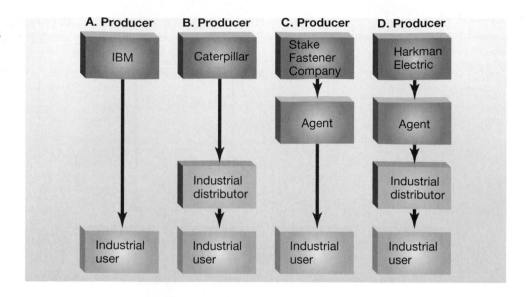

Marketing Channels for Business Goods and Services

The four most common channels for business goods and services are shown in Figure 15–5. In contrast with channels for consumer products, business channels typically are shorter and rely on one intermediary or none at all because business users are fewer in number, tend to be more concentrated geographically, and buy in larger quantities (see Chapter 6).

Channel A, represented by IBM's large, mainframe computer business, is a direct channel. Firms using this channel maintain their own salesforce and perform all channel functions. This channel is employed when buyers are large and well defined, the sales effort requires extensive negotiations, and the products are of high unit value and require hands-on expertise in terms of installation or use. Lockheed Martin and Airbus, in the aerospace industry, would be other examples.

Channels B, C, and D are indirect channels with one or more intermediaries to reach industrial users. In Channel B an **industrial distributor** performs a variety of marketing channel functions, including selling, stocking, delivering a full product assortment, and financing. In many ways, industrial distributors are like wholesalers in consumer channels. Caterpillar relies on industrial distributors to sell its construction and mining equipment in 200 countries. In addition to selling, Caterpillar distributors stock 40,000 to 50,000 parts and service equipment using highly trained technicians.

Channel C introduces a second intermediary, an *agent,* who serves primarily as the independent selling arm of producers and represents a producer to industrial users. For example, Stake Fastener Company, a California-based producer of industrial fasteners, has an agent call on industrial users rather than employing its own salesforce.

Channel D is the longest channel and includes both agents and distributors. For instance, Harkman Electric, a small Texas-based producer of electric products, uses agents to call on distributors who sell to industrial users.

Electronic Marketing Channels

These common marketing channels for consumer and business goods and services are not the only routes to the marketplace. Advances in electronic commerce have opened new avenues for reaching buyers and creating customer value.

Interactive electronic technology has made possible **electronic marketing channels**, which employ the Internet to make goods and services available for consumption or use by consumers or business buyers. A unique feature of these

FIGURE 15–6

Representative consumer electronic marketing channels

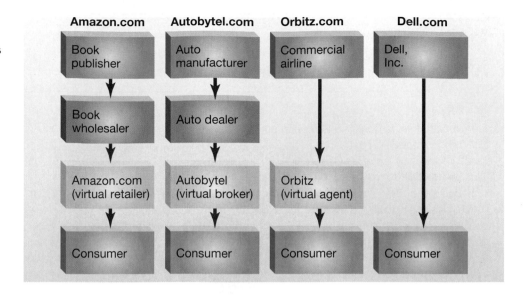

channels is that they combine electronic and traditional intermediaries to create time, place, form, and possession utility for buyers.[3]

Figure 15–6 shows the electronic marketing channels for books (Amazon.com), automobiles (Autobytel.com), reservation services (Orbitz.com), and personal computers (Dell.com). Are you surprised that they look a lot like common marketing channels? An important reason for the similarity resides in channel functions detailed in Figure 15–3. Electronic intermediaries can and do perform transactional and facilitating functions effectively and at a relatively lower cost than traditional intermediaries because of efficiencies made possible by information technology. However, electronic intermediaries are incapable of performing elements of the logistical function, particularly for products such as books and automobiles. This function remains with traditional intermediaries or with the producer, as evident with Dell, Inc., and its direct channel.

Many services can be distributed through electronic marketing channels, such as car rentals marketed by Alamo.com, financial securities by Schwab.com, and insurance by MetLife.com. Software too can be marketed this way. However, many other services such as health care and auto repair still involve traditional intermediaries.

Direct Marketing Channels

Many firms also use direct marketing channels to reach buyers. **Direct marketing channels** allow consumers to buy products by interacting with various advertising media without a face-to-face meeting with a salesperson. Direct marketing channels include mail-order selling, direct-mail sales, catalog sales, telemarketing, interactive media, and televised home shopping (for example, the Home Shopping Network). U.S. sales revenue attributed to direct marketing channels exceeds $1.75 trillion.[4]

Some firms sell products almost entirely through direct marketing channels. These firms include L.L. Bean (apparel), Sharper Image (expensive gifts and novelties), and Egghead.com (consumer electronics). Manufacturers such as Nestlé and Sunkist, in addition to using traditional channels composed of wholesalers and retailers, employ direct marketing through catalogs and telemarketing to reach more buyers. At the same time, retailers such as JCPenney use direct marketing techniques to augment conventional store merchandising activities. Some experts believe that direct marketing accounts for 20 percent of all retail transactions in the United States and 10 percent of retail transactions in Europe. Direct marketing is covered in greater depth in Chapter 18.

MARKETING NEWSNET

Nestlé and General Mills— Cereal Partners Worldwide

GLOBAL

Can you say Nestlé Cheerios *miel amandes*? Millions of French start their day with this European equivalent of General Mills' Honey Nut Cheerios, made possible by Cereal Partners Worldwide (CPW). CPW is the food industry's first strategic alliance designed to be a global business. It joined the cereal manufacturing and marketing capability of U.S.-based General Mills with the worldwide distribution clout of Swiss-based Nestlé.

From its headquarters near Lake Geneva, Switzerland, CPW

first launched General Mills cereals under the Nestlé label in France, the United Kingdom, Spain, and Portugal in 1991. Today, CPW competes in 75 international markets.

The General Mills–Nestlé strategic channel alliance is also likely to increase the ready-to-eat cereal worldwide market share of these companies, which are already rated as the two best-managed firms in the world. CPW is on track to reach its goal of a 20 percent worldwide share.

Multiple Channels and Strategic Channel Alliances

In some situations producers use **dual distribution**, an arrangement whereby a firm reaches different buyers by employing two or more different types of channels for the same basic product. For example, GE sells its large appliances directly to home and apartment builders but uses retail stores, including Lowe's home centers, to sell to consumers. In some instances, firms pair multiple channels with a multibrand strategy (see Chapter 11). This is done to minimize cannibalization of the firm's family brand and differentiate the channels. For example, Hallmark sells its Hallmark greeting cards through Hallmark stores and select department stores, and its Ambassador brand of cards through discount and drugstore chains. Levi Strauss sells its Signature brand of jeans only through Wal-Mart. In other instances, a firm will distribute modified products through different channels. Zoecon Corporation sells its insect control chemicals to professional pest-control operators such as Orkin and Terminex. A modified compound is sold to Boyle-Midway for use in its Black-Flag Roach Ender brand.

A recent innovation in marketing channels is the use of **strategic channel alliances**, whereby one firm's marketing channel is used to sell another firm's products. An alliance between Kraft Foods and Starbucks is a case in point. Kraft distributes Starbucks coffee in U.S. supermarkets and internationally. Strategic alliances are popular in global marketing, where the creation of marketing channel relationships is expensive and time consuming. For example, General Motors distributes the Swedish Saab through its Saturn dealers in Canada. General Mills and Nestlé have an extensive alliance that spans 75 international markets from Brazil to Poland to Thailand. Read the accompanying Marketing NewsNet so you won't be surprised when you are served Nestlé (not General Mills) Cheerios in Europe, South America, and parts of Asia.[5]

A Closer Look at Channel Intermediaries

Channel structures for consumer and business products assume various forms based on the number and type of intermediaries. Knowledge of the roles played by these intermediaries is important for understanding how channels operate in practice.

The terms *wholesaler, agent,* and *retailer* have been used in a general fashion consistent with the meanings given in Figure 15–1. However, on closer inspection, a

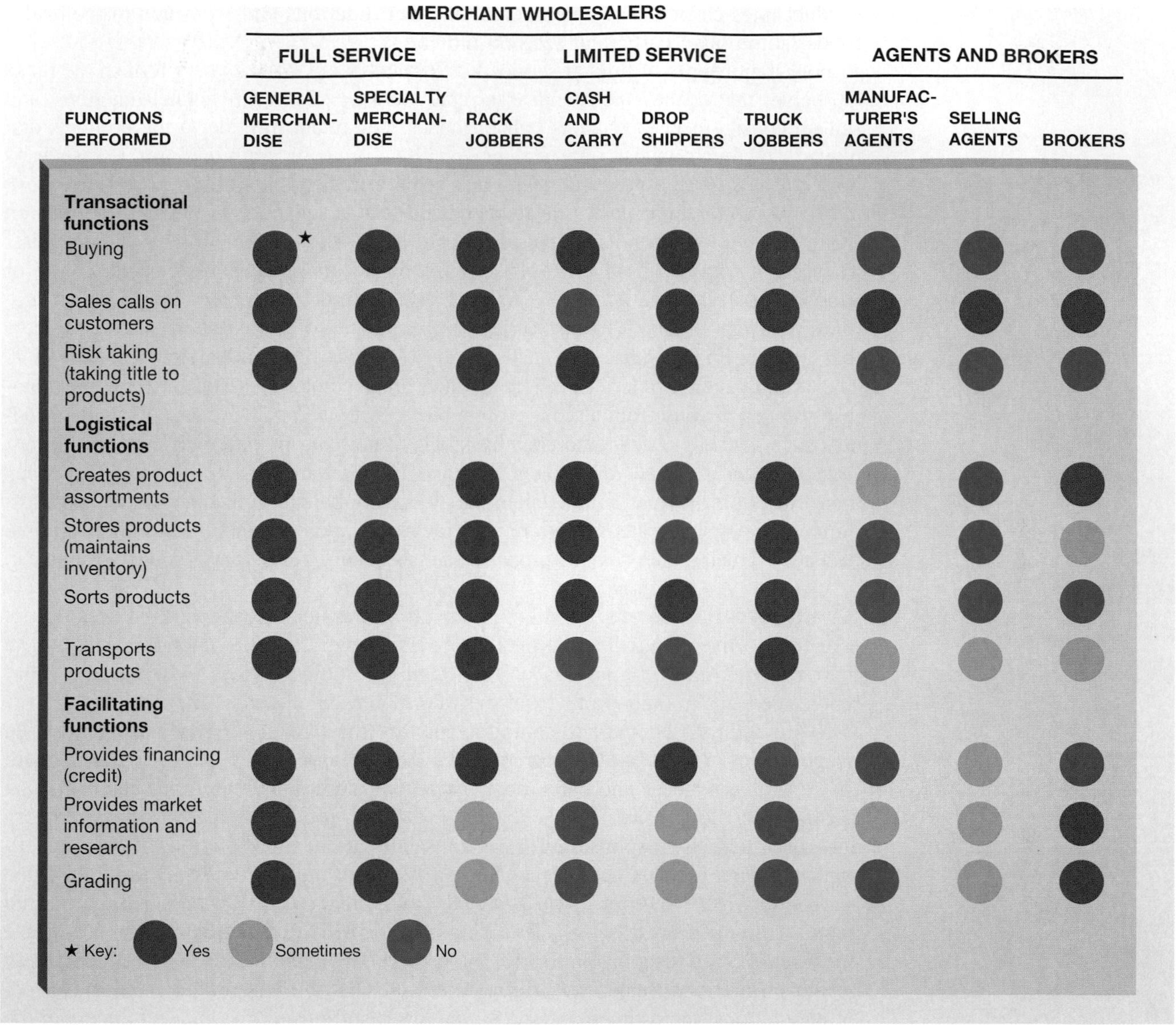

MERCHANT WHOLESALERS

FUNCTIONS PERFORMED	FULL SERVICE		LIMITED SERVICE				AGENTS AND BROKERS		
	GENERAL MERCHAN-DISE	SPECIALTY MERCHAN-DISE	RACK JOBBERS	CASH AND CARRY	DROP SHIPPERS	TRUCK JOBBERS	MANUFAC-TURER'S AGENTS	SELLING AGENTS	BROKERS

Transactional functions
- Buying
- Sales calls on customers
- Risk taking (taking title to products)

Logistical functions
- Creates product assortments
- Stores products (maintains inventory)
- Sorts products
- Transports products

Facilitating functions
- Provides financing (credit)
- Provides market information and research
- Grading

★ Key: ● Yes   ● Sometimes   ● No

FIGURE 15–7

Functions performed by independent wholesaler types

variety of specific types of intermediaries emerges. These intermediaries engage in wholesaling activities—those activities involved in selling products and services to those who are buying for the purposes of resale or business use. Intermediaries engaged in retailing activities are discussed in detail in Chapter 17. Figure 15–7 describes the functions performed by major types of independent wholesalers.[6]

Merchant Wholesalers   **Merchant wholesalers** are independently owned firms that take title to the merchandise they handle. They go by various names, including industrial distributor (described earlier). About 83 percent of the firms engaged in wholesaling activities are merchant wholesalers.

Merchant wholesalers are classified as either full-service or limited-service wholesalers, depending on the number of functions performed. Two major types of full-service wholesalers exist. *General merchandise* (or *full-line*) *wholesalers* carry a broad assortment of merchandise and perform all channel functions. This type of wholesaler is most prevalent in the hardware, drug, and clothing industries. However, these wholesalers do not maintain much depth of assortment within specific product lines. *Specialty merchandise* (or *limited-line*) *wholesalers* offer a relatively narrow range of products but have an extensive assortment within the product lines carried. They perform all channel functions and are found in the health foods, automotive parts, and seafood industries.

Four major types of limited-service wholesalers exist. *Rack jobbers* furnish the racks or shelves that display merchandise in retail stores, perform all channel functions, and sell on consignment to retailers, which means they retain the title to the products displayed and bill retailers only for the merchandise sold. Familiar products such as hosiery, toys, housewares, and health and beauty items are sold by rack jobbers. *Cash and carry wholesalers* take title to merchandise but sell only to buyers who call on them, pay cash for merchandise, and furnish their own transportation for merchandise. They carry a limited product assortment and do not make deliveries, extend credit, or supply market information. This wholesaler is common in electric supplies, office supplies, hardware products, and groceries. *Drop shippers,* or *desk jobbers,* are wholesalers that own the merchandise they sell but do not physically handle, stock, or deliver it. They simply solicit orders from retailers and other wholesalers and have the merchandise shipped directly from a producer to a buyer. Drop shippers are used for bulky products such as coal, lumber, and chemicals, which are sold in extremely large quantities. *Truck jobbers* are small wholesalers that have a small warehouse from which they stock their trucks for distribution to retailers. They usually handle limited assortments of fast-moving or perishable items that are sold for cash directly from trucks in their original packages. Truck jobbers handle products such as bakery items, dairy products, and meat.

Agents and Brokers   Unlike merchant wholesalers, agents and brokers do not take title to merchandise and typically provide fewer channel functions. They make their profit from commissions or fees paid for their services, whereas merchant wholesalers make their profit from the sale of the merchandise they own.

Manufacturer's agents and selling agents are the two major types of agents used by producers. **Manufacturer's agents**, or *manufacturer's representatives,* work for several producers and carry noncompetitive, complementary merchandise in an exclusive territory. Manufacturer's agents act as a producer's sales arm in a territory and are principally responsible for the transactional channel functions, primarily selling. They are used extensively in the automotive supply, footwear, and fabricated steel industries. However, Swank Jewelry and Japanese computer firms have used manufacturer's agents as well. By comparison, **selling agents** represent a single producer and are responsible for the entire marketing function of that producer. They design promotional plans, set prices, determine distribution policies, and make recommendations on product strategy. Selling agents are used by small producers in the textile, apparel, food, and home furnishing industries.

Brokers are independent firms or individuals whose principal function is to bring buyers and sellers together to make sales. Brokers, unlike agents, usually have no continuous relationship with the buyer or seller but negotiate a contract between two parties and then move on to another task. Brokers are used extensively by producers of seasonal products (such as fruits and vegetables) and in the real estate industry.

A unique broker that acts in many ways like a manufacturer's agent is a food broker, representing buyers and sellers in the grocery industry. Food brokers differ from conventional brokers because they act on behalf of producers on a permanent basis and receive a commission for their services. For example, Nabisco uses food brokers to sell its candies, margarine, and Planters peanuts, but it sells its line of cookies and crackers directly to retail stores.

Manufacturer's Branches and Offices   Unlike merchant wholesalers, agents, and brokers, manufacturer's branches and sales offices are wholly owned extensions of the producer that perform wholesaling activities. Producers assume wholesaling functions when there are no intermediaries to perform these activities, customers are few in number and geographically concentrated, or orders are large or require significant attention. A *manufacturer's branch office* carries a producer's inventory and performs the functions of a full-service wholesaler. A *manufacturer's* *sales office* does not carry inventory, typically performs only a sales function, and serves as an alternative to agents and brokers.

Vertical Marketing Systems and Channel Partnerships

The traditional marketing channels described so far represent a loosely knit network of independent producers and intermediaries brought together to distribute goods and services. However, new channel arrangements have emerged for the purpose of improving efficiency in performing channel functions and achieving greater marketing effectiveness. These new arrangements are called vertical marketing systems and channel partnerships. **Vertical marketing systems** are professionally managed and centrally coordinated marketing channels designed to achieve channel economies and maximum marketing impact.[7] Figure 15–8 depicts the major types of vertical marketing systems: corporate, contractual, and administered.

Corporate Systems   The combination of successive stages of production and distribution under a single ownership is a *corporate vertical marketing system.* For example, a producer might own the intermediary at the next level down in the channel. This practice, called *forward integration,* is exemplified by Polo/Ralph Lauren, which manufactures clothing and also owns apparel shops. Other examples of forward integration include Goodyear, Apple Computer, and Sherwin Williams. Alternatively, a retailer might own a manufacturing operation, a practice called *backward integration.* For example, Kroger supermarkets operate manufacturing facilities that produce everything from aspirin to cottage cheese, for sale under the Kroger label. Tiffany & Co., the exclusive jewelry retailer, manufactures about half of the fine jewelry items for sale through its 100 stores worldwide.

Companies seeking to reduce distribution costs and gain greater control over supply sources or resale of their products pursue forward and backward integration. However, both types of integration increase a company's capital investment and fixed

FIGURE 15–8

Types of vertical marketing systems

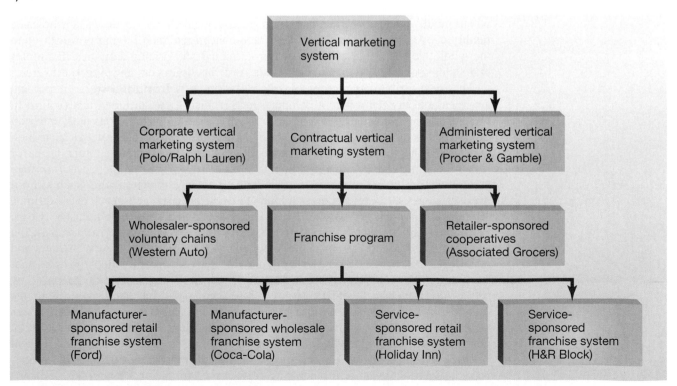

Sherwin-Williams and H&R
Block represent two different
types of vertical marketing
systems. Read the text to find
out how they differ.

Sherwin-Williams
www.sherwin-williams.com

H&R Block
www.hrblock.com

costs. For this reason, many companies favor contractual vertical marketing systems to achieve channel efficiencies and marketing effectiveness.

Contractual Systems   Under a *contractual vertical marketing system,* independent production and distribution firms integrate their efforts on a contractual basis to obtain greater functional economies and marketing impact than they could achieve alone. Contractual systems are the most popular among the three types of vertical marketing systems. They account for about 40 percent of all retail sales.

Three variations of contractual systems exist. *Wholesaler-sponsored voluntary chains* involve a wholesaler that develops a contractual relationship with small, independent retailers to standardize and coordinate buying practices, merchandising programs, and inventory management efforts. With the organization of a large number of independent retailers, economies of scale and volume discounts can be achieved to compete with chain stores. IGA and Ben Franklin variety and craft stores represent wholesaler-sponsored voluntary chains. *Retailer-sponsored cooperatives* exist when small, independent retailers form an organization that operates a wholesale facility cooperatively. Member retailers then concentrate their buying power through the wholesaler and plan collaborative promotional and pricing activities. Examples of retailer-sponsored cooperatives include Associated Grocers and Ace Hardware.

The most visible variation of contractual systems is **franchising**, a contractual arrangement between a parent company (a franchisor) and an individual or firm (a franchisee) that allows the franchisee to operate a certain type of business under an established name and according to specific rules. Franchises generate $1.53 trillion in sales through 760,000 outlets annually in the United States.[8] Four types of franchise arrangements are most popular. *Manufacturer-sponsored retail franchise systems* are prominent in the automobile industry, where a manufacturer such as Ford licenses dealers to sell its cars subject to various sales and service conditions. *Manufacturer-sponsored wholesale systems* exist in the soft-drink industry, where Pepsi-Cola licenses wholesalers (bottlers) that purchase concentrate from Pepsi-Cola and then carbonate, bottle, promote, and distribute its products to supermarkets and restaurants. *Service-sponsored retail franchise systems* are provided by firms that have designed a unique approach for performing a service and wish to profit by selling the franchise to others. Holiday Inn, Avis, and McDonald's represent this franchising approach. *Service-sponsored franchise systems* exist when franchisors license individuals or firms to dispense a service under a trade name and specific guidelines. Examples include Snelling and Snelling, Inc., employment services and H&R Block tax services. Service-sponsored franchise arrangements are the fastest-growing type of franchise. Franchising is discussed further in Chapter 17.

Administered Systems   In comparison, *administered vertical marketing systems* achieve coordination at successive stages of production and distribution by the size and influence of one channel member rather than through ownership. Procter & Gamble, given its broad product assortment ranging from disposable diapers to detergents, is able to obtain cooperation from supermarkets in displaying, promoting, and pricing its products. Wal-Mart can obtain cooperation from manufacturers in terms of product specifications, price levels, and promotional support, given its position as the world's largest retailer.

Channel Partnerships   Increasingly, channel members are forging channel partnerships akin to supply partnerships described in Chapter 6. A **channel partnership** consists of agreements and procedures among channel members for ordering and physically distributing a producer's products through the channel to the ultimate consumer.[9] A central feature of channel partnerships is the collaborative use of information and communication technology to better serve customers and reduce the time and cost of performing channel functions.

The partnership Levi Strauss has with Modell's Sporting Goods in New York is a case in point.[10] By using point-of-sale scanning equipment and direct electronic linkage to Levi Strauss in San Francisco, Modell's can instantaneously inform Levi Strauss what styles and sizes of jeans are needed, create purchase orders, and convey shipping instructions without any human involvement. The result? The costs of performing transaction, logistic, and facilitating functions are substantially reduced, and the customer is virtually assured of having his or her preferred 501 Levi jeans in stock. The role of information and communication technology in supply chain and logistics management is discussed further in Chapter 16.

Concept Check

1. What is the difference between a direct and an indirect channel?

2. Why are channels for business products typically shorter than channels for consumer products?

3. What is the principal distinction between a corporate vertical marketing system and an administered vertical marketing system?

CHANNEL CHOICE AND MANAGEMENT

Marketing channels not only link a producer to its buyers but also provide the means through which a firm implements various elements of its marketing strategy. Therefore, choosing a marketing channel is a critical decision.

Factors Affecting Channel Choice and Management

The final choice of a marketing channel by a producer depends on a number of factors that often interact with each other.

Environmental Factors   Environmental factors described in Chapter 3 have an important effect on the choice and management of a marketing channel. For example, Tupperware Corporation, a name synonymous with kitchen utensils and plastic storage containers sold in the home at Tupperware parties, now uses shopping mall kiosks to sell its wares. Changing family lifestyles with high employment among women prompted this action.[11] Advances in the technology of growing, transporting, and storing perishable cut flowers has allowed Kroger to eliminate flower wholesalers and buy direct from flower growers around the world. Kroger's annual cut flower sales exceed $100 million, making it the largest flower retailer in the world. The Internet

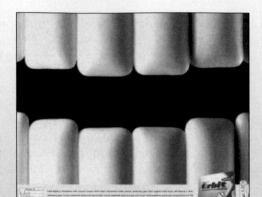
has created new marketing channel opportunities for a variety of products, including consumer electronics, books, music, video, and clothing and accessory items. Regulatory factors also influence marketing channels, notably in global markets. China, for example, lifted its ban on direct selling in 2005, thus creating a new marketing channel. However, the distribution of chewing gum in Singapore remains a sticky issue as described in the accompanying Marketing NewsNet.[12]

Consumer Factors   Consumer characteristics have a direct bearing on the choice and management of a marketing channel. Determining which channel is most appropriate is based on answers to fundamental questions such as: Who are potential customers? Where do they buy? When do they buy? How do they buy? What do they buy? These answers also indicate the type of intermediary best suited to reaching target buyers. For example, Ricoh Company, Ltd., studied the serious (as opposed to recreational) camera user and concluded that a change in marketing channels was necessary. The company terminated its contract with a wholesaler that sold to mass merchandise stores and began using manufacturer's agents who sold to photo specialty stores. These stores agreed to stock and display Ricoh's full line and promote it prominently. Sales volume tripled within 18 months. Recognizing that car buyers now comparison shop on the Internet, automakers now have their own websites to provide price and model information.

Product Factors   In general, highly sophisticated products such as large, scientific computers, unstandardized products such as custom-built machinery, and products of high unit value are distributed directly to buyers. Unsophisticated, standardized products with low unit value, such as table salt, are typically distributed through indirect channels. A product's stage in the life cycle also affects marketing channels. This was shown in the description of the fax machine product life cycle in Chapter 11.

Company Factors   A firm's financial, human, or technological capabilities affect channel choice. For example, firms that are unable to employ a salesforce might use manufacturer's agents or selling agents to reach wholesalers or buyers. If a

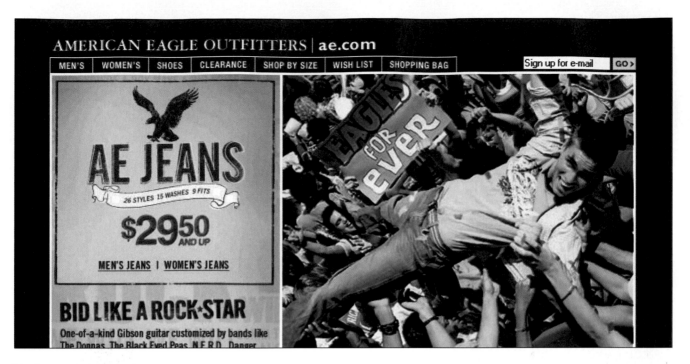

The Internet has created new marketing channel opportunities for the distribution of apparel.

American Eagle Outfitters
www.ae.com

firm has multiple products for a particular target market, it might use a direct channel. Firms with a limited product line might use intermediaries to reach buyers.

Company factors also apply to intermediaries. For example, personal computer hardware and software producers wishing to reach business users might look to value-added resellers such as Micro Age, which has its own salesforce and service staff that calls on businesses.

Channel Design Considerations

Recognizing that numerous routes to buyers exist and also recognizing the factors just described, marketing executives typically consider three questions when choosing a marketing channel and intermediaries:

1. Which channel and intermediaries will provide the best coverage of the target market?
2. Which channel and intermediaries will best satisfy the buying requirements of the target market?
3. Which channel and intermediaries will be the most profitable?

Target Market Coverage   Achieving the best coverage of the target market requires attention to the density—that is, the number of stores in a geographical area—and type of intermediaries to be used at the retail level of distribution.[13] Three degrees of distribution density exist: intensive, exclusive, and selective.

Intensive distribution means that a firm tries to place its products and services in as many outlets as possible. Intensive distribution is usually chosen for convenience products or services such as candy, fast food, newspapers, and soft drinks. For example, Coca-Cola's retail distribution objective is to place its products "within an arm's reach of desire." Cash, yes cash, is also distributed intensively by Visa. It operates over 810,000 automatic teller machines in more than 150 countries.

Exclusive distribution is the extreme opposite of intensive distribution because only one retail outlet in a specified geographical area carries the firm's products. Exclusive distribution is typically chosen for specialty products or services such as automobiles, some women's fragrances, men's and women's apparel and accessories, and yachts. Gucci, one of the world's leading luxury goods companies, uses

Read the text to learn which buying requirements are satisfied by Jiffy Lube and PETCO.

Jiffy Lube International
www.jiffylube.com

PETCO Animal Supplies
www.petco.com

exclusive distribution in the marketing of its Yves Saint Laurent, Sergio Rossi, Boucheron, Opium, and Gucci brands.[14] Sometimes retailers sign exclusive distribution agreements with manufacturers and suppliers.[15] For instance, Radio Shack sells only Compaq and Hewlett-Packard personal computers and Thomson SA's RCA brand of audio and video products in its 7,000 stores.

Selective distribution lies between these two extremes and means that a firm selects a few retail outlets in a specific geographical area to carry its products. Selective distribution weds some of the market coverage benefits of intensive distribution to the control over resale evident with exclusive distribution. For this reason, selective distribution is the most common form of distribution intensity. It is usually associated with shopping goods or services such as Rolex watches, Ben Hogan golf clubs, and Hendredon furniture.

Satisfying Buyer Requirements   A second consideration in channel design is gaining access to channels and intermediaries that satisfy at least some of the interests buyers might want fulfilled when they purchase a firm's products or services. These interests fall into four categories: (1) information, (2) convenience, (3) variety, and (4) attendant services.

Information is an important requirement when buyers have limited knowledge or desire specific data about a product or service. Properly chosen intermediaries communicate with buyers through in-store displays, demonstrations, and personal selling. Consumer electronics manufacturers such as Sony, palmOne, and Apple Computer have opened their own retail outlets staffed with highly trained personnel, to inform buyers how their products can better meet each customer's needs.[16]

Convenience has multiple meanings for buyers, such as proximity or driving time to a retail outlet. For example, 7-Eleven stores, with more than 24,000 outlets worldwide, satisfy this interest for buyers, and candy and snack food firms benefit by gaining display space in these stores. For other consumers, convenience means a minimum of time and hassle. Jiffy Lube, which promises to change engine oil and filters quickly, appeals to this aspect of convenience. For those who shop on the Internet, convenience means that websites must be easy to locate and navigate, and image downloads must be fast. A commonly held view among website developers is the "eight second rule": Consumers will abandon their efforts to enter or navigate a website if download time exceeds eight seconds.[17]

Variety reflects buyers' interest in having numerous competing and complementary items from which to choose. Variety is evident in both the breadth and depth of products and brands carried by intermediaries, which enhances their attraction to

WEB LINK   Visit an Apple Store to See What All the Excitement Is About

Interested in visiting an Apple Store to see what all the excitement is about? Is a store situated near you? If you answered yes to the first question and no to the second, then log on to www.ifoapplestore.com and click "Videos & Links." Here you will find exterior and interior photographs and video tours of various Apple Stores, including a walking tour led by Steven Jobs himself. If you are interested in learning whether or not an Apple Store is planned for your area, visit this website to find announcements of grand openings.

buyers. Thus, manufacturers of pet food and supplies seek distribution through pet superstores such as PETCO and PetsMart, which offer a wide array of pet products.

Attendant services provided by intermediaries are an important buying requirement for products such as large household appliances that require delivery, installation, and credit. Therefore, Whirlpool seeks dealers that provide such services.

Steven Jobs, Apple Computer's CEO, is one person who believes that computer retailers have failed to satisfy the buying requirements of today's consumer. Believing that "Buying a car is no longer the worst purchasing experience. Buying a computer is no. 1," he launched Apple Stores in 2001 with the intent of operating as many as 110 in the United States and still more worldwide.[18] Visit the website described in the Web Link to learn what all the excitement is about at Apple Stores.

Profitability   The third consideration in designing a channel is profitability, which is determined by the margins earned (revenue minus cost) for each channel member and for the channel as a whole. Channel cost is the critical dimension of profitability. These costs include distribution, advertising, and selling expenses associated with different types of marketing channels. The extent to which channel members share these costs determines the margins received by each member and by the channel as a whole.

Global Dimensions of Marketing Channels

Marketing channels around the world reflect traditions, customs, geography, and the economic history of individual countries and societies. Even so, the basic marketing channel functions must be performed. But differences do exist and are illustrated by marketing channels in Japan, one of the world's largest economies and the third-largest U.S.–world trade partner.

Intermediaries outside Western Europe and North America tend to be small, numerous, and often owner operated as described in Chapter 7. Japan, for example, has less than one-half of the population and a land mass less than 5 percent of the United States. However, Japan and the United States have about the same number of wholesalers and retailers. Why? Japanese marketing channels tend to include many intermediaries based on tradition and lack of storage space. As many as five intermediaries are involved in the distribution of soap in Japan compared with one or two in the United States.

Understanding marketing channels in global markets is often a prerequisite to successful marketing. For example, Gillette attempted to sell its razors and blades through company salespeople in Japan as it does in the United States, thus eliminating wholesalers traditionally involved in marketing toiletries. However, Schick

For the answer to how Schick became a razor and blade market share leader in Japan read the text.

Schick
www.schick.com

sold its razors and blades through the traditional Japanese channel involving wholesalers. The result? Schick achieved a commanding lead over Gillette in the Japanese razor and blade market.[19]

Channel relationships also must be considered. In Japan, the distribution *keiretsu* (translated as "alignments") bonds producers and intermediaries together. The bond, through vertical integration and social and economic ties, ensures that each channel member benefits from the distribution alignment. The dominant member of the distribution *keiretsu,* which is typically a producer, has considerable influence over channel member behavior, including which competing products are sold by other channel members. Well-known Japanese companies such as Matsushita (electronics), Nissan and Toyota (automotive products), Nippon Gakki (musical instruments), and Kirin (and other brewers and distillers) employ the distribution *keiretsu* extensively. Shiseido and Kanebo, for instance, influence the distribution of cosmetics through Japanese department stores.

Channel Relationships: Conflict, Cooperation, and Law

Unfortunately, because channels consist of independent individuals and firms, there is always potential for disagreements concerning who performs which channel functions, how profits are allocated, which products and services will be provided by whom, and who makes critical channel-related decisions. These channel conflicts necessitate measures for dealing with them. Sometimes they result in legal action.

Conflict in Marketing Channels

Channel conflict arises when one channel member believes another channel member is engaged in behavior that prevents it from achieving its goals. Two types of conflict occur in marketing channels: vertical conflict and horizontal conflict.

Vertical conflict occurs between different levels in a marketing channel—for example, between a manufacturer and a wholesaler or retailer or between a wholesaler and a retailer. Three sources of vertical conflict are most common.[20] First, conflict arises when a channel member bypasses another member and sells or buys products direct, a practice called **disintermediation**. This conflict emerged when Jenn-Air, a producer of kitchen appliances, decided to terminate its distributors and sell directly to retailers. Second, disagreements over how profit margins are distributed among channel members produce conflict. This happened when the world's biggest music company, Universal Music Group, adopted a pricing policy for CDs that squeezed the profit margins for music retailers, such as Tower Records. A third conflict situation arises when manufacturers believe wholesalers or retailers are not giving their products adequate attention. For example, Nike stopped shipping popular sneakers such as Nike Shox NZ to Foot Locker in retaliation for the retailer's decision to give more shelf space to shoes costing under $120.

Horizontal conflict occurs between intermediaries at the same level in a marketing channel, such as between two or more retailers (Target and Kmart) or two or more wholesalers that handle the same manufacturer's brands. Two sources of horizontal conflict are common. First, horizontal conflict arises when a manufacturer increases its distribution coverage in a geographical area. For example, a franchised Cadillac dealer in Chicago might complain to General Motors that another franchised Cadillac dealer has located too close to its dealership. Second, dual distribution causes conflict when different types of retailers carry the same brands. For instance, the launch of Elizabeth Taylor's Black Pearls fragrance by Elizabeth Arden was put on hold when department store chains such as May and Dillard's refused to stock the item once they learned that mass merchants Sears and JCPenney would also carry the brand. Elizabeth Arden subsequently introduced the brand only through department stores.[21]

Cooperation in Marketing Channels

Conflict can have destructive effects on the workings of a marketing channel, so it is necessary to secure cooperation among

ETHICS AND SOCIAL RESPONSIBILITY ALERT

The Ethics of Slotting Allowances

ETHICS

Have you ever wondered why your favorite cookies are no longer to be found at your local supermarket? Or that delicious tortilla chip you like to serve at parties is missing from the shelf and replaced by another brand?

Blame it on slotting allowances. Some large supermarket chains demand slotting allowances from food manufacturers, paid in the form of money or free goods to stock and display products. These allowances, which can run up to $25,000 per item for a supermarket chain, cost U.S. food makers about $1 billion annually. Not surprisingly, slotting allowances have been labeled "ransom," "extortional allowances," and "commercial bribery" by manufacturers because they already pay supermarkets $25 billion a year in "trade dollars" to promote and discount their products. Small food manufacturers, in particular, view slotting allowances as an economic barrier to distribution for their products. Supermarket operators see these allowances as a reasonable cost of handling business for manufacturers.

Is the practice of charging slotting allowances unethical behavior?

channel members. One means is through a **channel captain**, a channel member that coordinates, directs, and supports other channel members. Channel captains can be producers, wholesalers, or retailers. P&G assumes this role because it has a strong consumer following in brands such as Crest, Tide, and Pampers. Therefore, it can set policies or terms that supermarkets will follow. McKesson, a pharmaceutical drug wholesaler, is a channel captain because it coordinates and supports the product flow from numerous small drug manufacturers to more than 25,000 drugstores and some 6,000 hospitals nationwide. Wal-Mart and Office Depot are retail channel captains because of their strong consumer image, number of outlets, and purchasing volume.

A firm becomes a channel captain because it is typically the channel member with the ability to influence the behavior of other members.[22] Influence can take four forms. First, economic influence arises from the ability of a firm to reward other members given its strong financial position or customer franchise. Microsoft Corporation and Wal-Mart have such influence. Expertise is a second source of influence over other channel members. For example, American Hospital Supply helps its customers (hospitals) manage inventory and streamline order processing for hundreds of medical supplies. Third, identification with a particular channel member may also create influence for that channel member. For instance, retailers may compete to carry the Ralph Lauren line, or clothing manufacturers may compete to be carried by Neiman-Marcus, Nordstrom, or Bloomingdale's. In both instances, the desire to be associated with a channel member gives that firm influence over others. Finally, influence can arise from the legitimate right of one channel member to direct the behavior of other members. This situation would occur under contractual vertical marketing systems where a franchisor could legitimately direct how a franchisee behaves. Other means for securing cooperation in marketing channels rest in the different variations of vertical marketing systems.

Channel influence can be used to gain concessions from other channel members. For instance, some large supermarket chains expect manufacturers to pay allowances, in the form of cash or free goods, to stock and display their products. Some manufacturers call these allowances "extortion" as described in the Ethics and Social Responsibility Alert.[23]

Legal Considerations   Conflict in marketing channels is typically resolved through negotiation or the exercise of influence by channel members. Sometimes conflict produces legal action. Therefore, knowledge of legal restrictions affecting channel strategies and practices is important. Some restrictions were described in Chapter 14, namely vertical price fixing and price discrimination. However, other legal considerations unique to marketing channels warrant attention.[24]

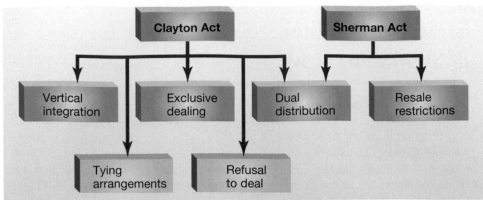

In general, suppliers can select whomever they want as channel intermediaries and may refuse to deal with whomever they choose. However, the Federal Trade Commission and the Justice Department monitor channel practices that restrain competition, create monopolies, or otherwise represent unfair methods of competition under the Sherman Act (1890) and the Clayton Act (1914). Six practices have received the most attention (Figure 15–9).

Dual distribution, although not illegal, can be viewed as anticompetitive in some situations. The most common situation arises when a manufacturer distributes through its own vertically integrated channel in competition with independent wholesalers and retailers that also sell its products. If the manufacturer's behavior is viewed as an attempt to lessen competition by eliminating wholesalers or retailers, then such action would violate both the Sherman and Clayton Acts.

Vertical integration is viewed in a similar light. Although not illegal, this practice is sometimes subject to legal action under the Clayton Act if it has the potential to lessen competition or foster monopoly.

The Clayton Act specifically prohibits exclusive dealing and tying arrangements when they lessen competition or create monopolies. *Exclusive dealing* exists when a supplier requires channel members to sell only its products or restricts distributors from selling directly competitive products. *Tying arrangements* occur when a supplier requires a distributor purchasing some products to buy others from the supplier. These arrangements often arise in franchising. They are illegal if the tied products could be purchased at fair market values from other suppliers at desired quality standards of the franchiser. Full-line forcing is a special kind of tying arrangement. This practice involves a supplier requiring that a channel member carry its full line of products in order to sell a specific item in the supplier's line.

Even though a supplier has a legal right to choose intermediaries to carry and represent its products, a *refusal to deal* with existing channel members may be illegal under the Clayton Act. *Resale restrictions* refer to a supplier's attempt to stipulate to whom distributors may resell the supplier's products and in what specific geographical areas or territories they may be sold. These practices have been prosecuted under the Sherman Act. Today, however, the courts apply the "rule of reason" in such cases and consider whether such restrictions have a "demonstrable economic effect."

Concept Check

1. What are the three degrees of distribution density?

2. What are the three questions marketing executives consider when choosing a marketing channel and intermediaries?

3. What is meant by *exclusive dealing*?

CHAPTER IN REVIEW

1 *Explain what is meant by a marketing channel of distribution and why intermediaries are needed.*

A marketing channel of distribution, or simply a marketing channel, consists of individuals and firms involved in the process of making a product or service available for use or consumption by consumers or industrial users. Intermediaries make possible the flow of products from producers to buyers by performing three basic functions. The transactional function involves buying, selling, and risk taking because intermediaries stock merchandise in anticipation of sales. The logistical function involves the gathering, storing, and dispensing of products. The facilitating function assists producers in making goods and services more attractive to buyers. The performance of these functions by intermediaries creates time, place, form, and possession utility for consumers.

2 *Distinguish among traditional marketing channels, electronic marketing channels, and different types of vertical marketing systems.*

Traditional marketing channels describe the route taken by products and services from producers to buyers. This route can range from a direct channel with no intermediaries, because a producer and ultimate consumers deal directly with each other, to indirect channels where intermediaries (agents, wholesalers, distributors, or retailers) are inserted between a producer and consumer and perform numerous channel functions. Electronic marketing channels employ the Internet to make goods and services available for consumption or use by consumer or business buyers. Vertical marketing systems are professionally managed and centrally coordinated marketing channels designed to achieve channel economics and maximum marketing impact. There are three major types of vertical marketing systems (VMS). A corporate VMS combines successive stages of production and distribution under a single ownership. A contractual VMS exists when independent production and distribution firms integrate their efforts on a contractual basis to obtain greater functional economies and marketing impact than they could achieve alone. An administered VMS achieves coordination at successive stages of production and distribution by the size and influence of one channel member rather than through ownership.

3 *Describe the factors and considerations that affect a company's choice and management of a marketing channel.*

Four factors affect a company's choice and management of a marketing channel. These are environmental factors, consumer factors, product factors, and company factors, all of which interact with each other. Recognizing that numerous routes to buyers exist and also recognizing the factors just described, marketers consider three questions when choosing and managing a marketing channel and intermediaries. First, which channel and intermediaries will provide the best coverage of the target market? Marketers typically choose one of three levels of market coverage: intensive, selective, or exclusive distribution. Second, which channel and intermediaries will best satisfy the buying requirements of the target market? These buying requirements fall into four categories: information, convenience, variety, and attendant services. Finally, which channel and intermediaries will be the most profitable? Here marketers look at the margins earned (revenues minus cost) for each channel member and for the channel as a whole.

4 *Recognize how conflict, cooperation, and legal considerations affect marketing channel relationships.*

Because marketing channels consist of independent individuals and firms, there is always potential for conflict which sometimes results in legal action. So channel members try to find ways to cooperate for their mutual benefit. Two types of conflict occur in marketing channels. Vertical conflict occurs between different levels in a marketing channel, for example, between a manufacturer and a wholesaler or retailer, or between a wholesaler and a retailer. Horizontal conflict occurs between intermediaries at the same level in a marketing channel, such as between two retailers or two or more wholesalers that handle the same manufacturer's brands. Because conflict can have destructive effects on the workings of a marketing channel, channel members seek ways to cooperate. One way is through a channel captain—a channel member that coordinates, directs, and supports other channel members. A firm becomes a channel captain because of its ability to influence the behavior of other channel members. Nevertheless, channel conflict can result in legal action. The most common legal actions arise from channel practices that restrain competition, create monopolies, or represent unfair methods of competition.

FOCUSING ON KEY TERMS

brokers p. 404
channel captain p. 413
channel conflict p. 412
channel partnership p. 407
direct channel p. 399
direct marketing channels p. 401
disintermediation p. 412
dual distribution p. 402
electronic marketing channels p. 400
exclusive distribution p. 409
franchising p. 406

indirect channels p. 399
industrial distributor p. 400
intensive distribution p. 409
manufacturer's agents p. 404
marketing channel p. 396
merchant wholesalers p. 403
selective distribution p. 410
selling agents p. 404
strategic channel alliances p. 402
vertical marketing systems p. 405

DISCUSSION AND APPLICATION QUESTIONS

1 A distributor for Celanese Chemical Company stores large quantities of chemicals, blends these chemicals to satisfy requests of customers, and delivers the blends to a customer's warehouse within 24 hours of receiving an order. What utilities does this distributor provide?

2 Suppose the president of a carpet manufacturing firm has asked you to look into the possibility of bypassing the firm's wholesalers (who sell to carpet, department, and furniture stores) and selling direct to these stores. What caution would you voice on this matter, and what type of information would you gather before making this decision?

3 What type of channel conflict is likely to be caused by dual distribution, and what type of conflict can be reduced by direct distribution? Why?

4 How does the channel captain idea differ among corporate, administered, and contractual vertical marketing systems with particular reference to the use of the different forms of influence available to firms?

5 Comment on this statement: "The only distinction among merchant wholesalers and agents and brokers is that merchant wholesalers take title to the products they sell."

6 How do specialty, shopping, and convenience goods generally relate to intensive, selective, and exclusive distribution? Give a brand name that is an example of each goods-distribution matchup.

GOING ONLINE   **Finding a Franchise for You**

www.mhhe.com/Kerin

Franchising is a large and growing industry both inside and outside the United States. For many individuals, franchising offers an opportunity to operate one's own business.

The Internet provides a number of websites that feature franchising opportunities. The International Franchise Association (www.franchise.org) features an extensive array of information, including answers to questions about franchising. Franchise.com (www.franchise.com) shows franchise opportunities for the aspiring franchisee.

1 Visit the Franchise.com website, and click on the "Franchise Buyer" link. Which franchise opportunities fit you?

2 Visit the International Franchise Association website, and click on the "Resource Center" link. Then, click on the "News" link. What are the current trends in franchising?

BUILDING YOUR MARKETING PLAN

Does your marketing plan involve selecting channels and intermediaries? If the answer is no, read no further and do not include this element in your plan. If the answer is yes:

1 Identify which channel and intermediaries will provide the best coverage of the target market for your product or service.

2 Specify which channel and intermediaries will best satisfy the important buying requirements of the target market.

3 Determine which channel and intermediaries will be the most profitable.

4 Select your channel(s) and intermediary(ies).

VIDEO CASE 15   Golden Valley Microwave Foods: The Surprising Channel

"We developed the technology that launched the microwave popcorn business and helped make ACT II the number one brand in the world," says Jack McKeon, president of Golden Valley Microwave Foods, a division of ConAgra Foods, Inc. "But we were also lucky along the way, as we backed into what has become one of the biggest distribution channels in the industry today, one that no one ever saw coming."

Founded in 1978, today Golden Valley is the global leader in producing and marketing microwave popcorn. Its ACT II brand is No. 1 in the industry. But it hasn't always been easy.

THE LAUNCH: THE IDEA AND THE TECHNOLOGY

In 1978 only about 15 percent of U.S. households had microwave ovens, so launching a microwave foods business was risky. Golden Valley's initial marketing research turned up two key points of difference or benefits that people wanted in their microwave popcorn: (1) fewer unpopped kernels and (2) good popping results in all types of microwave ovens, even low-powered ovens—the kind that many households with microwaves had at the time. Golden Valley's research and development (R&D) staff successfully addressed these wants by developing a microwave popcorn bag utilizing a thin strip of material laminated between layers of paper, which focused the microwave energy to produce high-quality popped corn,

regardless of an oven's power. This breakthrough significantly increased the size of the microwave popcorn market (and is still used in all microwave popcorn bags today). Using its revolutionary package, Golden Valley introduced ACT II in 1984.

THE LUCKY DAY: BOTH CAPITAL AND MASS MERCHANDISERS

From its founding in 1978 until a public offering of its stock in September 1986, Golden Valley was privately owned and, like most startups, was severely undercapitalized. Due to the cost of developing and introducing ACT II, Golden Valley needed a partner to help develop the business. Its solution was to enter into a licensing agreement to share its technology for packaging microwave popcorn with one of the largest food manufacturers in the industry. The licensing partner would sell the popcorn under its own brand name in grocery stores and supermarkets. In turn, Golden Valley agreed it would not distribute its ACT II brand in U.S. grocery stores or supermarkets for ten years. This meant that Golden Valley had to find other channels of distribution in which to sell its microwave popcorn.

For the next ten years the company developed many new channels. ACT II products were sold through vending machines, video stores (e.g., Blockbuster), institutions (e.g., movie theaters, colleges, military bases), drug stores (e.g., Walgreen's, Rite-Aid, Eckerd Drugs), club stores (e.g., Sam's, Costco, and BJ's), and convenience

stores. "But the huge opportunity we discovered and developed was the mass-merchandiser channel through chains like Wal-Mart and Target," says McKeon. "ACT II microwave popcorn was the first item of any kind to sell a million units in a week for Target, and that happened in 1987. Wal-Mart, too, was on the front end of this market and today is the top seller of microwave popcorn in any channel, selling far more popcorn than the leading grocery chains. Mass merchandisers now account for over a third of all the microwave popcorn sold in the U.S. They created the ACT II business as we know it today, and it was accomplished without a dime of conventional consumer promotions. That's one of the really unique parts of the ACT II story."

THE SITUATION TODAY

In the U.S. today, over 90 percent of households own microwave ovens, and more than 60 percent of households are microwave popcorn consumers who spend more than $688 million on the product each year. "Our marketing research shows ACT II is especially strong in young families with kids," says Frank Lynch, vice president of marketing at Golden Valley. This conjures up an image of mom and dad watching a movie on TV with the kids and eating ACT II popcorn, a picture close to reality. "ACT II has good market penetration in almost all age, income, urban versus rural, and ethnic segments," he continues.

"From the beginning, Golden Valley has been the leader in the microwave popcorn industry," says McKeon, "and we plan to continue that record." As evidence, he cites a number of Golden Valley's "firsts":

- First mass-marketed microwave popcorn
- First flavored microwave popcorn
- First microwave popcorn tub
- First fat-free microwave popcorn
- First extra-butter microwave popcorn
- First one-step sweetened microwave popcorn

This list highlights a curious market segmentation phenomenon that has emerged in the last five years—the no-butter versus plenty-of-butter consumers. Originally popcorn was seen as junk food. Later studies by nutritionists pointed out its health benefits: low calories and high fiber. This caused Golden Valley to introduce its low-fat popcorn in the late 1990s to appeal to the health-conscious segment of consumers. When it comes to eating popcorn while watching a movie at home on TV, however, the more butter on their popcorn, the better. Recently, much of the growth in popcorn sales has been in the spoil-yourself-with-a lot-of-butter-on-your-popcorn segment.

Because of these diverse consumer tastes in popcorn, Golden Valley has developed a variety of popcorn products around its ACT II brand. Besides the low-fat and extra butter versions, these include the original flavors (natural and butter), sweet glazed products, popcorn in tubs, and Kettle Corn. In 2004, ACT II Big Boy was introduced to appeal to the economy segment. It also has a line of ACT II non-popcorn snacks such as soft pretzels and snack mixes.

Golden Valley positions ACT II as unpretentious, fun, and youthful—a great product at a reasonable price. By stressing the value aspect of ACT II, Golden Valley has positioned the brand to appeal to today's growing value consciousness of consumers seeking quality products at reasonable prices. In terms of market share, these strategies have enabled ACT II to become the leader in the microwave popcorn market.

OPPORTUNITIES FOR FUTURE GROWTH

For many years the growth of the microwave popcorn industry closely followed the growth of household ownership of microwave ovens—from under 20 percent to over 90 percent. But now, with a microwave oven in virtually every U.S. home, Golden Valley is trying to identify new market segments, new products, and innovative ways to appeal to all the major marketing channels.

In the U.S., Golden Valley's strategy must include finding creative ways to continue to work with existing channels where it has special strength, such as the mass merchandiser channel. It also needs to further develop opportunities in the grocery store and supermarket channel. Now that the 10-year restriction on sales in grocery stores and supermarkets has expired, distribution through wholesalers which reach grocery stores and supermarkets is possible.

Global markets, too, present opportunities. Golden Valley has followed the penetration of microwave ovens in countries around the world, and used brokers to help gain distribution in those markets. Currently, Golden Valley has sales in more than 32 countries and the leading share in most of those markets. However, foreign markets represent foreign tastes, something that does not always lend itself to standardized products. United Kingdom consumers, for example, think of popcorn as a candy or child's food rather than the salty snack it is in the United States. Even in the Disney Park in Paris, American-style popcorn is absent, as French consumers sprinkle sugar on their popcorn. Swedes like theirs very buttery while many Mexicans like jalapeno-flavored popcorn.

Questions

1   Visit ACT II's website at www.ACTII.com and examine the assortment of products offered today. Are (*a*) the assortment or (*b*) the packaging related to Golden Valley's distribution channels or the segments they serve?

2   Use Figure 15–4 to create a description of the channels of distribution being used by Golden Valley today.

3   Compared to selling through the non-grocery channels, what kind of product, price, and promotion strategies might Golden Valley use to reach the grocery channel more effectively?

4   What special marketing issues does Golden Valley face as it pursues growth in global markets?

Supply Chain:
Managing Logistics
For the 21st Century

CHAPTER 16

INTEGRATING SUPPLY CHAIN AND LOGISTICS MANAGEMENT

LEARNING OBJECTIVES

After reading this chapter you should be able to:

1 Recognize the relationship between marketing channels, logistics, and supply chain management.

2 Describe how a company's supply chain aligns with its marketing strategy.

3 Identify the major logistics cost and customer service factors that managers consider when making supply chain decisions.

4 Describe the key logistics functions in a supply chain.

SNAP! CRACK! POP! EVEN WORLD-CLASS COMPANIES LIKE NIKE CAN FEEL THE BULLWHIP'S STING

Bad things can happen to great companies. Just ask Nike about the bullwhip's sting.

What is the bullwhip, and why does its sting hurt so bad? Companies define the *bullwhip* as too much or too little inventory to satisfy customer needs, missed production schedules, and ineffective transportation or delivery caused by miscommunication among material suppliers, manufacturers, and resellers of consumer and industrial goods. Its sting is poor customer service and lost revenue and profit opportunities.

So what does this have to do with Nike, well known for delivering the right athletic shoes, at the right time, place, and quantity to satisfy the fashion and functional needs of its buyers? Nike mistakenly sent double orders to its overseas factories, resulting in an oversupply of shoes. Meanwhile, production of its hot-selling shoes did not keep pace with customer demand. To offset shipping delays for its popular shoes, Nike transported them by plane at $4 to $8 a pair from Asia, compared with about 75 cents a pair by boat. Customers were displeased and company sales and profitability suffered.[1]

Welcome to the critical world of supply chain and logistics management. The essence of the problem is simple: It makes no sense to have brilliant marketing programs to sell world-class products if the products aren't available at the right time, at the right place, and in the right form and condition that customers want them. It's finding the continuing solutions through time that's always the problem. This chapter describes the role of supply chains and logistics management in marketing and how a firm balances distribution costs against the need for effective customer service.

SIGNIFICANCE OF SUPPLY CHAIN AND LOGISTICS MANAGEMENT

We often hear or use the term *distribution* but seldom appreciate its significance in marketing. U.S. companies spend $560 billion transporting raw materials and finished goods each year, another $332 billion on material handling, warehousing, storage, and holding inventory, and $40 billion managing the distribution process, including the cost of information technology. Worldwide, these activities and investments cost companies about $2 trillion each year.[2] In this section, we highlight contemporary perspectives on distribution, including supply chains and logistics, and describe the linkage between supply chain management and marketing strategy.

Relating Marketing Channels, Logistics, and Supply Chain Management

A marketing channel relies on logistics to make products available to consumers and industrial users, a point emphasized in Chapter 15. **Logistics** involves those activities that focus on getting the right amount of the right products to the right place at the right time at the lowest possible cost. The performance of these activities is **logistics management**, the practice of organizing the *cost-effective flow* of raw materials, in-process inventory, finished goods, and related information from point of origin to point of consumption to satisfy *customer requirements.*

Three elements of this definition deserve emphasis. First, logistics deals with decisions needed to move a product from the source of raw materials to consumption, or the *flow* of the product. Second, those decisions have to be made in a *cost-effective* manner. While it is important to drive down logistics costs, there is a limit—the third point of emphasis. A firm needs to drive down logistics costs as long as it can deliver expected *customer service,* which means satisfying customer requirements. The role of management is to see that customer needs are satisfied in the most cost-effective manner. When properly done, the results can be spectacular. Procter & Gamble is a case in point. The company set out to meet the needs of consumers more effectively by collaborating and partnering with its suppliers and retailers to ensure that the right products reached store shelves at the right time and at a lower cost. The effort was judged a success when, during a recent 18-month period, P&G's retail customers recorded a $65 million savings in logistics costs while customer service increased.[3]

The Procter & Gamble experience is not an isolated incident. Today, logistics management is embedded in a broader view of distribution, consistent with the emphasis on supply and channel partnering described in Chapters 6 and 15. Companies now recognize that getting the right items needed for consumption or production to the right place at the right time in the right condition at the right cost is often beyond their individual capabilities and control. Instead, collaboration, coordination, and information sharing among manufacturers, suppliers, and distributors are necessary to create a seamless flow of goods and services to customers. This perspective is represented in the concept of a supply chain and the practice of supply chain management.

Supply Chains versus Marketing Channels

A **supply chain** is a sequence of firms that perform activities required to create and deliver a good or service to consumers or industrial users. It differs from a marketing channel in terms of membership. A supply chain includes suppliers that provide raw material inputs to a manufacturer as well as the wholesalers and retailers that deliver finished goods to you. The management process is also different. **Supply chain management** is the integration and organization of information and logistics activities *across firms* in a supply chain for the purpose of creating and delivering goods and services that provide value to consumers. The relation among marketing channels, logistics management, and supply chain management is shown

FIGURE 16–1

Relating logistics management and supply chain management to supplier networks and marketing channels

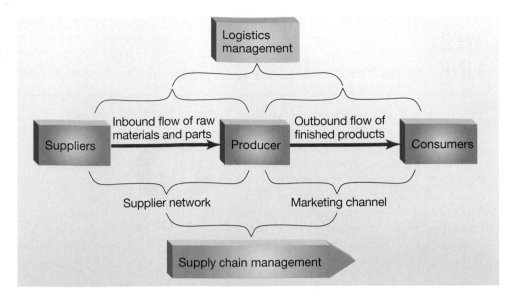

in Figure 16–1. An important feature of supply chain management is its application of sophisticated information technology that allow companies to share and operate systems for order processing, transportation scheduling, and inventory and facility management.

Sourcing, Assembling, and Delivering a New Car: The Automotive Supply Chain

All companies are members of one or more supply chains. A supply chain is essentially a sequence of linked suppliers and customers in which every customer is, in turn, a supplier to another customer until a finished product reaches the final consumer. Even a simplified supply chain diagram for carmakers shown in Figure 16–2 illustrates how complex a supply chain can be.[4] A carmaker's supplier network includes thousands of firms that provide the 5,000 or so parts in a typical automobile. They provide items ranging from raw materials such as steel and rubber to components, including transmissions, tires, brakes, and seats, to complex subassemblies and assemblies evident in chassis and suspension systems that make for a smooth, stable ride. Coordinating and scheduling material and component flows for their assembly into actual automobiles by carmakers is dependent on logistical activities, including transportation, order processing, inventory control, materials handling, and information technology. A central link is the car maker supply chain manager, who is responsible for translating customer requirements into actual orders and arranging

FIGURE 16–2

The automotive supply chain

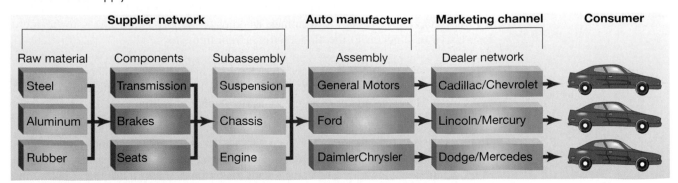

WEB LINK   Build Your Own BMW with a Mouse

The Ultimate Driving Machine®

Supply chain managers are responsible for having the right products at the right place at the right time at the right price for customers. In the automotive industry, this task is complex given the variety of car options available. To appreciate the challenge, visit the BMW website at www.bmwusa.com. Click the "Build Your BMW" link and choose a model. Then, select your exterior, interior, packages, options, and accessories. You will immediately obtain the manufacturer's suggested retail price (MSRP).

This easy task for you represents a sizable undertaking for a BMW supply manager. You may not realize it, but a BMW comes in thousands of versions, including dealer-installed options you might want. A supply of these items has to be at the BMW dealer for installation when you pick your new car.

for delivery dates and financial arrangements for car dealers. This is not an easy task given different consumer preferences and how much consumers are willing to pay. To appreciate the challenge facing supply chain managers, visit the BMW website described in the accompanying Web Link, and assemble your own "Ultimate Driving Machine™" based on your preferences and price.

Logistical aspects of the automobile marketing channel are also an integral part of the supply chain. Major responsibilities include transportation (which involves the selection and oversight of external carriers—trucking, airline, railroad, and shipping companies—for cars and parts to dealers), the operation of distribution centers, the management of finished goods inventories, and order processing for sales. Supply chain managers also play an important role in the marketing channel. They work with car dealers to ensure that the right mix of automobiles are delivered to different locations. In addition, they make sure that spare and service parts are available so that dealers can meet the car maintenance and repair needs of consumers. All of this is done with the help of information technology that links the entire automotive supply chain. What does all of this cost? Logistics costs represent 25 percent to 30 percent of the retail price of a typical new car.

Supply Chain Management and Marketing Strategy

The automotive supply chain illustration shows how information and logistics activities are integrated and organized across firms to create and deliver a car for you. What's missing from this illustration is the linkage between a specific company's supply chain and its marketing strategy. Just as companies have different marketing strategies, they also manage supply chains differently. The goals to be achieved by a firm's marketing strategy determines whether its supply chain needs to be more responsive or efficient in meeting customer requirements.

Aligning a Supply Chain with Marketing Strategy   There are a variety of supply chain configurations, each of which is designated to perform different tasks well. Marketers today recognize that the choice of a supply chain follows from a clearly defined marketing strategy and involves three steps:[5]

1. *Understand the customer.* To understand the customer, a company must identify the needs of the customer segment being served. These needs, such as a desire for a low price or convenience of purchase, help a company define the

MARKETING NEWSNET

IBM—Creating an On-Demand Supply Chain

CUSTOMER VALUE

Have you seen IBM's "On-Demand Business" advertising campaign? This campaign features IBM's commitment to being responsive and flexible to changes in customer requirements and the marketplace. The campaign reflects IBM's companywide marketing initiative to be the world's premier on-demand business.

What you probably haven't seen is IBM's transformed supply chain that makes on-demand business possible. Beginning in 2001, IBM set about to build a single integrated supply chain that would handle raw material procurement, manufacturing, logistics, customer support, order entry, and customer fulfillment across all of IBM—something that had never been done before. Why would IBM undertake this task? According to IBM's CEO, Samuel J. Palmisano, "You cannot hope to thrive in the IT industry if you are a high-cost, slow-moving company. Supply chain is one of the new competitive battlegrounds. We are committed to being the most efficient and productive player in our industry."

The task wasn't easy. With factories in 10 countries, IBM buys 2 billion parts a year from 33,000 suppliers, offers 78,000 products available in 3 million possible variations, processes 1.7 million customer orders annually, and operates

in 150 countries. Yet with surprising efficiency, IBM overhauled its supply chain end-to-end from raw material sourcing to postsales support by 2004. Along the way, IBM posted cost savings of $5.6 billion in 2002 and $7 billion in 2003.

Today, IBM is uniquely poised to configure and deliver a tailored mix of hardware, software, and service to customers on demand. This would have been impossible without the changes made in IBM's supply chain.

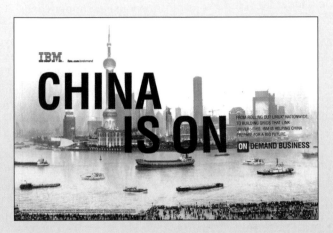

relative importance of efficiency and responsiveness in meeting customer requirements.

2. *Understand the supply chain.* Second, a company must understand what a supply chain is designed to do well. Supply chains range from those that emphasize being responsive to customer requirements and demand to those that emphasize efficiency with a goal of supplying products at the lowest possible delivered cost.

3. *Harmonize the supply chain with the marketing strategy.* Finally, a company needs to ensure that what the supply chain is capable of doing well is consistent with the targeted customer's needs and its marketing strategy. If a mismatch exists between what the supply chain does particularly well and a company's marketing strategy, the company will either need to redesign the supply chain to support the marketing strategy or change the marketing strategy. Read the accompanying Marketing NewsNet to learn how IBM overhauled its complete supply chain to support its new "On-Demand Business" marketing strategy.[6]

How are these steps applied and how are efficiency and responsive considerations built into a supply chain? Let's look at how two market leaders—Dell and Wal-Mart—have harmonized their supply chain and marketing strategy.[7]

Dell: A Responsive Supply Chain   The Dell marketing strategy targets customers who desire having the most up-to-date computer systems customized to their needs. These customers are also willing to: (1) wait to have their customized

World-class marketers Dell
and Wal-Mart emphasize
responsiveness and efficiency in
their supply chains, respectively.

Dell, Inc.
www.dell.com

Wal-Mart, Inc.
www.walmartstores.com

computer system delivered in a few days, rather than picking out a model at a retail store; and (2) pay a reasonable, though not the lowest price in the marketplace. Given Dell's customer segment, the company has the option of adopting an efficient or responsive supply chain. An efficient supply chain may use inexpensive, but slower, modes of transportation, emphasize economies of scale in its production process by reducing the variety of system configurations offered, and limit its assembly and inventory storage facilities to a single location, say Austin, Texas, where the company is headquartered. If Dell opted only for efficiency in its supply chain, it would be difficult if not impossible to satisfy its target customer's desire for rapid delivery and a wide variety of customizable products. Dell instead has opted for a responsive supply chain. It relies on more expensive express transportation for receipt of components from suppliers and delivery of finished products to customers. The company achieves product variety and manufacturing efficiency by designing common platforms across several products and using common components. Dell operates manufacturing facilities in Texas, Tennessee, Brazil, Ireland, Malaysia, and China to assure rapid delivery. Moreover, Dell has invested heavily in information technology to link itself with suppliers and customers.

Wal-Mart: An Efficient Supply Chain Now let's consider Wal-Mart. Wal-Mart's marketing strategy is to be a reliable, lower-price retailer for a wide variety of mass consumption consumer goods. This strategy favors an efficient supply chain designed to deliver products to consumers at the lowest possible cost. Efficiency is achieved in a variety of ways. For instance, Wal-Mart keeps relatively low inventory levels, and most is stocked in stores available for sale, not in warehouses gathering dust. The low inventory arises from Wal-Mart's innovative use of *cross-docking*—a practice that involves unloading products from suppliers, sorting products for individual stores, and quickly reloading products onto its trucks for a particular store. No warehousing or storing of products occurs, except for a few hours or, at most, a day. Cross-docking allows Wal-Mart to operate only a small number of distribution centers to service its vast network of Wal-Mart Stores, Supercenters, Neighborhood Markets, and Sam's Clubs which contributes to efficiency. On the other hand, the company runs its own fleet of trucks to service its stores. This does increase cost and investment, but the benefits in terms of responsiveness justify the cost in Wal-Mart's case. Wal-Mart has invested significantly more than its competitors in information technology to operate its supply chain. The company feeds information about customer requirements and demand from its stores back to its suppliers, which manufacture only what is being demanded. This large investment has improved the efficiency of Wal-Mart's supply chain and made it responsive to customer needs.

Three lessons can be learned from these two examples. First, there is no one best supply chain for every company. Second, the best supply chain is the one that is consistent with the needs of the customer segment being served and complements a company's marketing strategy. And finally, supply chain managers are often called upon to make trade-offs between efficiency and responsiveness on various elements of a company's supply chain.

Concept Check

1. What is the principal difference between a marketing channel and a supply chain?

2. The choice of a supply chain involves what three steps?

OBJECTIVE OF INFORMATION AND LOGISTICS MANAGEMENT IN A SUPPLY CHAIN

The objective of information and logistics management in a supply chain is to minimize logistics costs while delivering maximum customer service. The Dell and Wal-Mart examples highlighted how two market leaders have realized this objective by different means. An important similarity between these two companies is that both use information to leverage logistics activities, reduce logistics costs, and improve customer service.

Information's Role in Supply Chain Responsiveness and Efficiency

Hewlett-Packard is a leader in the application of information technology to supply chain management.

Hewlett-Packard
www.hp.com

Information consists of data and analysis regarding inventory, transportation, distribution facilities, and customers throughout the supply chain.[8] Continuing advances in information technology make it possible to track logistics activities and customer service variables and manage them for efficiency and responsiveness. For example, information on customer demand patterns allows pharmaceutical companies such as

How to light up a supply chain.

Advance Transformer, a leading component manufacturer for lighting systems, had legacy IT systems that no longer kept up with production demands. They turned to HP to help them better manage their supply chain. Now, with a unified management of the whole infrastructure, their systems automatically solve problems as they occur. All this has reduced production time from 28 to 5 days, cut inventory levels by 50% and revealed the bright side of change. www.hp.com/adapt

Solutions for the adaptive enterprise.

change + hp

hp invent

Eli Lilly and GlaxoSmithKline to produce and stock drugs in anticipation of customer needs. This improves supply chain responsiveness because customers will find the drugs when and where they want them. Demand information improves supply chain efficiency because pharmaceutical firms are better able to forecast customer needs and produce, transport, and store the required amount of inventory.

A variety of technologies are used to transmit and manage information in a supply chain. **Electronic data interchanges** (EDIs) combine proprietary computer and telecommunication technologies to exchange electronic invoices, payments, and information among suppliers, manufacturers, and retailers. When linked with store scanning equipment and systems, EDI provides a seamless electronic link from a retail checkout counter to suppliers and manufacturers. EDI is commonly used in retail, apparel, transportation, pharmaceutical, grocery, health care, and insurance industries, as well as by local, state, and federal government agencies. About 95 percent of the companies listed in the Fortune 1000 use EDI. At Hewlett-Packard, for example, 1 million EDI transactions are made every month.

Another technology is the *Extranet,* which is an Internet-based network that permits secure business-to-business communication between a manufacturer and its suppliers, distributors, and sometimes other partners (such as advertising agencies). Extranets are less expensive and more flexible to operate than EDI because of their connection to the public Internet. This technology is prominent in private electronic exchanges described in Chapter 6. For example, WhirlpoolWebWorld.com allows Whirlpool to fulfill retailer orders quickly and inexpensively and better match appliance demand and supply.

Whereas EDI and Extranets transmit information, other technologies help manage information in a supply chain. Enterprise resource planning (ERP) technology and supply chain management software track logistics cost and customer service variables, both of which are described next.

Total Logistics Cost Concept

For our purposes, **total logistics cost** includes expenses associated with transportation, materials handling and warehousing, inventory, stockouts (being out of inventory), order processing, and return goods handling. Note that many of these costs are interrelated so that changes in one will impact the others. For example, as the firm attempts to minimize its transportation costs by shipping in larger quantities, it will also experience an increase in inventory levels. Larger inventory levels will not only increase inventory costs but should also reduce stockouts. It is important, therefore, to study the impact on all of the logistics decision areas when considering a change.

Figure 16–3 provides a graphic example. An oft-used supply chain strategy is for a firm to have a number of warehouses, which receive shipments in large quantities and then redistribute smaller shipments to local customers. As the

FIGURE 16–3

How total logistics cost varies with number of warehouses used

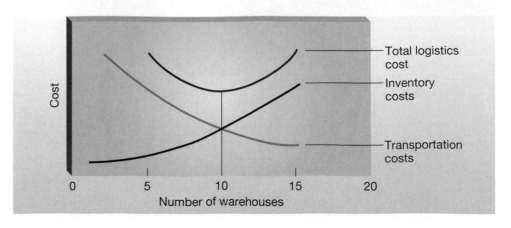

number of warehouses increases, inventory costs rise and transportation costs fall. That is, more inventory is warehoused, but it is transported in volume closer to customers. The net effect is to minimize the total costs of logistics shown in Figure 16–3 by having 10 warehouses. This means the total cost curve is minimized at a point where neither of the two individual cost elements is at a minimum but the overall system is.

Studying its total logistics cost has had revolutionary consequences for National Semiconductor, which produces computer chips. In two years it cut its standard delivery time 47 percent, reduced distribution costs 2.5 percent, and increased sales 34 percent by shutting down six warehouses around the world and air-freighting its microchips from its huge distribution center in Singapore. It does this even though it has six factories in Israel, Britain, and the United States. National also discovered that a lot of its chips were actually profit-losers, and it cut the number of products it sells by 45 percent, thereby simplifying logistics and increasing profits.[9]

Customer Service Concept

If a supply chain is a *flow,* the end of it—or *output*—is the service delivered to customers. However, service can be expensive. One company found that to increase on-time delivery from a 95 percent rate to a 100 percent rate tripled total logistics costs. Higher levels of service require tactics such as more inventory to reduce stockouts, more expensive transportation to improve speed and lessen damage, and double or triple checking of orders to ensure correctness. A firm's goal should be to provide superior customer service while controlling logistics costs. Customer service is now seen not merely as an expense but as a means to increase customer satisfaction and sales. For example, a 3M survey about customer service among 18,000 European customers in 16 countries revealed surprising agreement in all countries about the importance of customer service. Respondents stressed factors such as condition of product delivered, on-time delivery, quick delivery after order placement, and effective handling of problems.[10]

Within the context of a supply chain, **customer service** is the ability of logistics management to satisfy users in terms of time, dependability, communication, and convenience. As suggested by Figure 16–4, a supply chain manager's key task is to balance these four customer service factors against total logistics cost factors.

FIGURE 16–4

Supply chain managers balance total logistics cost factors against customer service factors

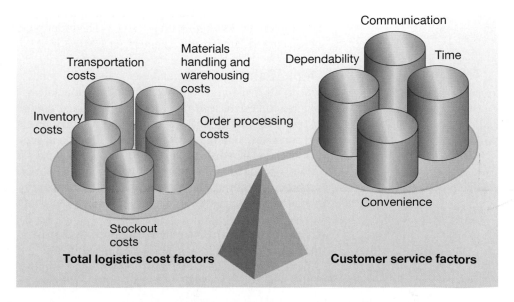

Total logistics cost factors

Transportation costs
Materials handling and warehousing costs
Inventory costs
Order processing costs
Stockout costs

Customer service factors

Communication
Dependability
Time
Convenience

MARKETING NEWSNET

For Fashion and Food Merchandising, Haste Is as Important as Taste

TECHNOLOGY & E-COMMERCE

Fashion and food have a lot in common. Both depend a lot on taste and both require timely merchandising. By its nature, fashion dictates that suppliers and retailers be able to adjust to new styles, colors, and different seasons. Fashion retailers need to identify what's hot so it can be ordered quickly and what's not to avoid markdowns. Saks Fifth Avenue has employed a *quick response* delivery system for fashion merchandise since the mid-1990s. Saks' point-of-sale scanner system records each day's sales. When stock falls below a minimum level, the system automatically generates a replenishment order. Vendors of fashion merchandise, such as Donna Karan (DKNY), receive an electronic order, which is processed within 48 hours.

Food marketers and retailers use the term *efficient consumer response* to describe their replenishment systems. All major food companies, including General Mills, Del Monte,

Heinz, Nestlé, and Beatrice Foods, and many supermarket chains such as Kroger, Safeway, and A&P rely on electronic replenishment systems to minimize stockouts of popular items and overstocks of slow-moving items. Lowered retailer inventories and efficient logistics practices have been projected to save U.S. grocery shoppers $30 billion a year.

Time   In a supply chain setting, time refers to **lead time** for an item, which means the lag from ordering an item until it is received and ready for use or sale. This is also referred to as *order cycle time* or *replenishment time* and may be more important to retailers or wholesalers than consumers. The various elements that make up the typical order cycle include recognition of the need to order, order transmittal, order processing, documentation, and transportation. A current emphasis in supply chain management is to reduce lead time so that the inventory levels of customers may be minimized. Another emphasis is to make the process of reordering and receiving products as simple as possible, often through electronic data and inventory systems called **quick response** and **efficient consumer response** delivery systems. These inventory management systems are designed to reduce the retailer's lead time for receiving merchandise, thereby lowering a retailer's inventory investment, improving customer service levels, and reducing logistics expense (see the accompanying Marketing NewsNet).[11] The order processing portion of lead time will be discussed later in this chapter.

Dependability   Dependability is the consistency of replenishment. This is important to all firms in a supply chain and to consumers. It can be broken into three elements: consistent lead time, safe delivery, and complete delivery. Consistent service allows planning (such as appropriate inventory levels), whereas inconsistencies create surprises. Intermediaries may be willing to accept longer lead times if they know about them in advance and can thus make plans. While surprise delays may shut down a production line, early deliveries will be almost as troublesome because of the problems of storing the extra inventory. Dependability is essential for the just-in-time inventory strategies discussed at the end of the chapter.

Communication   Communication is a two-way link between buyer and seller that helps in monitoring service and anticipating future needs. Status reports on orders are a typical example of improved communication between buyer and seller. The increased communication capability of transportation carriers has enhanced the accuracy of such tracing information and improved the ability of buyers to schedule shipments. Note, however, that such information is still reactive and is not a substitute for consistent on-time deliveries. Therefore, some firms have partnered with firms specializing in logistics in an effort to institutionalize a more proactive flow of useful information that, in turn, improves on-time deliveries. Hewlett-Packard (HP) turned its inbound raw materials for its printers over to a logistics firm, Roadway Logistics. HP lets Roadway manage the warehousing and coordinate printer parts delivery. In the process, HP estimates it has cut its warehouse operating costs by about 10 percent.[12]

Convenience   The concept of convenience for a supply chain manager means that there should be a minimum of effort on the part of the buyer in doing business with the seller. Is it easy for the customer to order? Are the products available from many outlets? Does the buyer have to buy huge quantities of the product? Will the seller arrange all necessary details, such as transportation? The seller must concentrate on removing unnecessary barriers to customer convenience. This customer service factor has promoted the use of vendor-managed inventory practices discussed later in the chapter.

Customer Service Standards

Firms that operate effective supply chains usually develop a set of written customer service standards. These serve as objectives and provide a benchmark against which results can be measured for control purposes. In developing these standards, information is collected on customers' needs. It is also necessary to know what competitors offer as well as the willingness of customers to pay a bit more for better service. After these and similar questions are answered, realistic standards are set and an ongoing monitoring program is established. The examples below suggest that customer service standards will differ by type of firm.

TYPE OF FIRM	CUSTOMER SERVICE STANDARD
Wholesaler	At least 98 percent of orders filled accurately
Manufacturer	Order cycle time of no more than five days
Retailer	Returns accepted within 30 days
Airline	At least 90 percent of arrivals on time
Trucker	A maximum of 5 percent loss and damage per year
Restaurant	Lunch served within five minutes of order

Effective customer service can yield substantial returns. The head of IBM's integrated supply chain group estimates that a 1 percent increase in customer service satisfaction translates into $2 billion to $3 billion of additional revenue to his company.[13]

Concept Check

1. The objective of information and logistics management in a supply chain is to _____.

2. How does consumer demand information increase supply chain responsiveness and efficiency?

3. What is the relationship between the number of warehouses a company operates, its inventory costs, and its transportation costs?

KEY LOGISTICS FUNCTIONS IN A SUPPLY CHAIN

The four key logistic functions in a supply chain include (1) transportation, (2) warehousing and materials handling, (3) order processing, and (4) inventory management. These functions have become so complex and interrelated that many companies have outsourced them to third-party logistics providers. **Third-party logistics providers** are firms that perform most or all of the logistics functions that manufacturers, suppliers, and distributors would normally perform themselves.[14] Today, 82 percent of manufacturers listed in the Fortune 500 outsource one or more logistics functions, at least on a limited basis. Ryder, UPS Logistics, FedEx, Roadway Logistics, Emery Worldwide, Global Logistics, and Penske are just a few of the companies that specialize in handling logistics functions for their clients. For example, Ryder manages the four key logistics functions for the Snapple Beverage Corporation, a unit of Cadbury Schweppes.

The four major logistics functions and the involvement of third-party logistics providers are described in detail next.

Transportation

Transportation provides the movement of goods necessary in a supply chain. There are five basic modes of transportation: railroads, motor carriers, air carriers, pipelines, and water carriers, and modal combinations involving two or more modes, such as truck trailers on a rail flatcar.

All transportation modes can be evaluated on six basic service criteria:

- *Cost.* Charges for transportation.
- *Time.* Speed of transit.
- *Capability.* What can be realistically carried with this mode.
- *Dependability.* Reliability of service regarding time, loss, and damage.
- *Accessibility.* Convenience of the mode's routes (such as pipeline availability).
- *Frequency.* Scheduling.

FedEx and Emery Worldwide are two third-party logistics providers that perform most or all of the logistics functions that manufacturers, suppliers, and distributors would normally perform.

FedEx
www.fedex.com

Emery Worldwide
www.emeryworld.com

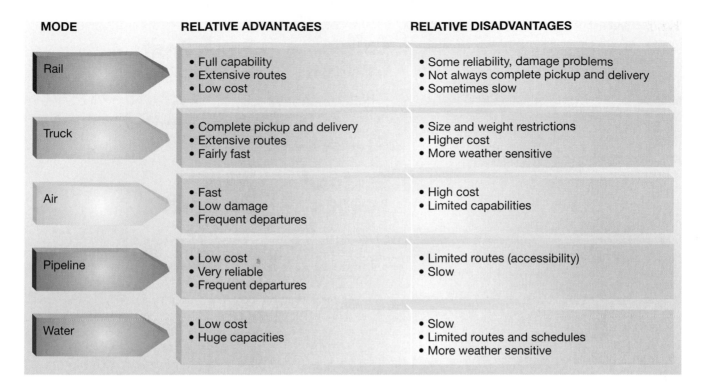

MODE	RELATIVE ADVANTAGES	RELATIVE DISADVANTAGES
Rail	• Full capability • Extensive routes • Low cost	• Some reliability, damage problems • Not always complete pickup and delivery • Sometimes slow
Truck	• Complete pickup and delivery • Extensive routes • Fairly fast	• Size and weight restrictions • Higher cost • More weather sensitive
Air	• Fast • Low damage • Frequent departures	• High cost • Limited capabilities
Pipeline	• Low cost • Very reliable • Frequent departures	• Limited routes (accessibility) • Slow
Water	• Low cost • Huge capacities	• Slow • Limited routes and schedules • More weather sensitive

FIGURE 16–5

Advantages and disadvantages of five modes of transportation

Figure 16–5 summarizes the relative service advantages and disadvantages of five modes of transportation available.[15]

Railroads Railroads carry heavy, bulky items over long distances. Of the commodities tracked by the rail industry, coal, farm products, chemicals, and nonmetallic minerals represent about 70 percent of the total tonnage. Railroads can carry larger shipments than trucks (in terms of total weight per vehicle), but their routes are less extensive. Service innovations include unit trains and intermodal service. A *unit train* is dedicated to one commodity (often coal), using permanently coupled cars that run a continuous loop from a single origin to a single destination and back. Even though the train returns empty, the process captures enough operating efficiencies to make it one of the lowest-cost transportation alternatives available. Unit trains keep to a specific schedule so that the customers can plan on reliable delivery and usually carry products that can be loaded and unloaded quickly and automatically.

Railroads also apply the unit train concept to *intermodal transportation,* which involves combining different transportation modes to get the best features of each. The result is a service that attracts high-valued freight, which would normally go by truck. The most popular combination is truck-rail, called *piggyback* or *trailer on flat-car (TOFC).* The other popular use of an intermodal combination is associated with export/import traffic and uses containers in place of trailers. These containers can be loaded on ships, trains, and truck trailers, so in terms of the on-land segment of international shipments, a container is handled the same way as a trailer. Containers are used in international trade because they use less space on oceangoing vessels.

Motor Carriers In contrast to the railroad industry, the for-hire motor carrier industry is composed of many small firms, including as many as 500,000 independent truckers and firms that own their own trucks for transporting their own products.

The greatest advantage of motor carriers is the complete door-to-door service. Trucks can go almost anywhere there is a road, and with the design of specialized equipment, they can carry most commodities. Their physical limitations are size and weight restrictions enforced by the states. Trucks have the reputation for maintaining a better record than rail for loss and damage and providing faster, more reliable

service, especially for shorter distances. As a result, trucks carry higher-valued goods that are time-sensitive and expensive to carry in inventory. The trade-off is that truck rates are substantially higher than rail rates.

Air Carriers and Express Companies Air freight is costly, but its speed may create savings in lower inventory. The items that can be carried are limited by space constraints and are usually valuable, time-sensitive, and lightweight, such as perishable flowers, clothing, and electronic parts. Specialized firms provide ground support in terms of collecting shipments and delivering them to the air terminal. When air freight is handled by major airlines—such as American, United, Delta, or Northwest—it is often carried as cargo using the excess luggage space of scheduled passenger flights.

Freight Forwarders *Freight forwarders* are firms that accumulate small shipments into larger lots and then hire a carrier to move them, usually at reduced rates. Recall that transportation companies provide rate incentives for larger quantities. Forwarders collect many small shipments consigned to a common destination and pay the carrier the lower rate based on larger volume, so they often convert shipments that are less-than-truckload (LTL) into full truckloads, thereby receiving better shipping rates. The rates charged by the forwarder to the individual shippers, in turn, are somewhat less than the small quantity rate, and the difference is the forwarder's margin. In general, the shipment receives improved service at lower cost.

Air freight forwarders are an example of specialization in one transportation mode. In some cases, airlines will subcontract excess space to *air freight forwarders or express companies,* which are firms that market air express services to the general public. Where markets are large enough, major airlines have responded with pure air freight service between specific airports, often involving international destinations.

Warehousing and Materials Handling

Warehouses may be classified in one of two ways: (1) storage warehouses and (2) distribution centers. In *storage warehouses* the goods are intended to come to rest

United Airlines Cargo provides fast, global delivery, often utilizing containers.

United Airlines
www.unitedcargo.com

for some period of time, as in the aging of products or in storing household goods. *Distribution centers,* on the other hand, are designed to facilitate the timely movement of goods and represent a very important part of a supply chain. They represent the second most significant cost in a supply chain after transportation.

Distribution centers not only allow firms to hold their stock in decentralized locations but are also used to facilitate sorting and consolidating products from different plants or different suppliers. Some physical transformation can also take place in distribution centers such as mixing or blending different ingredients, labeling, and repackaging. Paint companies such as Sherwin-Williams and Benjamin Moore use distribution centers for this purpose. In addition, distribution centers may serve as manufacturers' sales offices, described in Chapter 15, and order processing centers.

Materials handling, which involves moving goods over short distances into, within, and out of warehouses and manufacturing plants, is a key part of warehouse operations. The two major problems with this activity are high labor costs and high rates of loss and damage. Every time an item is handled, there is a chance for loss or damage. Common materials handling equipment includes forklifts, cranes, and conveyors. Today, materials handling in warehouses is automated by using computers and robots to reduce the cost of holding, moving, and recording inventories.

Order Processing

There are several stages in the processing of an order, and a failure at any one of them can cause a problem with the customer. The process starts with transmitting the order by a variety of means such as the Internet, an extranet, or electronic data interchange. This is followed by entering the order in the appropriate databases and sending the information to those needing it. For example, a regional warehouse is notified to prepare an order. After checking inventory, a new quantity may need to be reordered from the production line, or purchasing may be requested to reorder from a vendor. If the item is currently out of stock, a *backorder* is created, and the whole process of keeping track of a small part of the original order must be managed. In addition, credit may have to be checked for some customers, all documentation for the order must be prepared, transportation must be arranged, and an order confirmation must be sent. Order processing systems are evaluated in terms of speed and accuracy.

Electronic order processing has replaced manual processing for most large companies.[16] For example, 96 percent of IBM's purchase transactions with suppliers are conducted on the Internet. Kiwi Brands, the Douglassville, Pennsylvania, marketer

Materials handling through automation is now common in distribution centers.

of Kiwi shoe polish, Endust, and Behold, receives 75 percent of its retailers' purchase orders via EDI. The company has also implemented financial EDI, sending invoices to retailers and receiving payment order/remittance advice documents and electronic funds transfer (EFT) payments. Shippers as well are linked to the system, allowing Kiwi to receive shipment status messages electronically.

Inventory Management

Inventory management is one of the primary responsibilities of the supply chain manager. The major problem is maintaining the delicate balance between too little and too much. Too little inventory may result in poor service, stockouts, brand switching, and loss of market share; too much leads to higher costs because of the money tied up in inventory and the chance that it may become obsolete. Remember the sting of the bullwhip described at the beginning of the chapter?

Reasons for Inventory   Traditionally, carrying inventory has been justified on several grounds: (1) to offer a buffer against variations in supply and demand, often caused by uncertainty in forecasting demand; (2) to provide better service for those customers who wish to be served on demand; (3) to promote production efficiencies; (4) to provide a hedge against price increases by suppliers; (5) to promote purchasing and transportation discounts; and (6) to protect the firm from contingencies such as strikes and shortages. However, companies today view inventory as something to be moved, not stored, and more of a liability than an asset. The traditional justification for inventory has resulted in excessive inventories that have proven costly to maintain. Consider the U.S. automobile industry. Despite efforts to streamline its supply chain, industry analysts estimate that $230 billion worth of excess inventory piles up annually in the form of unused raw materials, parts waiting to be delivered, and vehicles sitting on dealers' lots.[17]

Inventory Costs   Specific inventory costs are often hard to detect because they are difficult to measure and occur in many different parts of the firm. A classification of inventory costs includes the following:

- *Capital costs.* The opportunity costs resulting from tying up funds in inventory instead of using them in other, more profitable investments; these are related to interest rates.

The key to Saturn's JIT system: a Ryder truck driver downloads a key-shaped floppy disk from an onboard computer to get delivery instructions.

Ryder System, Inc.
www.ryder.com

- *Inventory service costs.* Items such as insurance and taxes that are present in many states.
- *Storage costs.* Warehousing space and materials handling.
- *Risk costs.* Possible loss, damage, pilferage, perishability, and obsolescence.

Storage costs, risk costs, and some inventory service costs vary according to the characteristics of the item inventoried. For example, perishable products or highly seasonal items have higher risk costs than a commodity type product such as lumber. Capital costs are always present and are proportional to the *values* of the item and prevailing interest rates. The costs of carrying inventory vary with the particular circumstances but quite easily could range from 10 to 35 percent for different firms.

Supply Chain Inventory Strategies   Conventional wisdom a decade ago was that a firm should protect itself against uncertainty by maintaining a reserve inventory at each of its production and stocking points. This has been described as a "just-in-case" philosophy of inventory management and led to unnecessary high levels of inventory. In contrast is the **just-in-time (JIT) concept**, which is an inventory supply system that operates with very low inventories and requires fast, on-time delivery. When parts are needed for production, they arrive from suppliers "just in time," which means neither before nor after they are needed. Note that JIT is used in situations where demand forecasting is reliable, such as when supplying an automobile production line, and is not suitable for inventories that are to be stored over significant periods of time.

Saturn's manufacturing operation in Spring Hill, Tennessee, uses a sophisticated JIT system.[18] A central computerized system directs trucks to deliver preinspected parts at specific times 21 hours a day, six days a week to one of the plant's 56 receiving docks. Incredibly, the JIT system must coordinate Saturn's 300 suppliers located in the United States, Canada, and Mexico. Does the JIT system work for Saturn? The answer is a resounding yes. The Saturn production line has been shut down only once—for 18 minutes!—because the right part was not delivered at the right place and time.

Ryder Integrated Logistics is charged with making Saturn's JIT system work smoothly. Ryder long-haul trucks and their drivers are the most expensive part of the system. The key—very literally—to this JIT system is a computer disk in the form of a plastic key that drivers plug into an on-truck computer. The computer screen then tells the driver where to go, the route to use, and how much time to spend getting there.

Electronic data interchange and electronic messaging technology coupled with the constant pressure for faster response time in replenishing inventory have also changed the way suppliers and customers do business in a supply chain. The approach, called **vendor-managed inventory** (VMI), is an inventory-management system whereby the *supplier* determines the product amount and assortment a customer (such as a retailer) needs and automatically delivers the appropriate items.

ETHICS AND SOCIAL RESPONSIBILITY ALERT

Reverse Logistics and Green Marketing Go Together at Estée Lauder

ETHICS

Retailing industry research firms and trade groups report that U.S. consumers return an estimated $62 billion in merchandise to retailers each year. Until recently, returned merchandise was often disposed of in solid-waste landfills.

Estée Lauder, Inc., used to dump about $60 million worth of its products into landfills each year, destroying more than one-third of its name-brand cosmetics returned by retailers. That changed recently when Estée Lauder developed a sophisticated reverse logistics system that cut the volume of destroyed products in half. During the system's first year of operation, the company was able to evaluate 24 percent more returned products, redistribute 150 percent more of its returns, and save $475,000 in labor costs. Estée Lauder still destroyed 27 percent of returned products because their shelf life had expired, but that was down from 37 percent the previ-

ous year. The company expects to reduce its disposal rate to 15 percent as the reverse logistics system becomes even more efficient. The net effect of Estée Lauder's initiative has been a reduction in costs and a cleaner environment.

Campbell Soup's system illustrates how VMI works.[19] Campbell first establishes EDI links with retailers. Every morning, retailers electronically inform the company of their demand for all Campbell products and the inventory levels in their distribution centers. Campbell uses that information to forecast future demand and determine which products need replenishment based on upper and lower inventory limits established with each retailer. Trucks leave the Campbell shipping plant that afternoon and arrive at the retailer's distribution centers with the required replenishments the same day.

CLOSING THE LOOP: REVERSE LOGISTICS

The flow of goods in a supply chain does not end with the consumer or industrial user. Companies today recognize that a supply chain can work in reverse. **Reverse logistics** is a process of reclaiming recyclable and reusable materials, returns, and reworks from the point of consumption or use for repair, remanufacturing, redistribution, or disposal. The effect of reverse logistics can be seen in the reduced waste in landfills and lowered operating costs for companies. The accompanying Ethics and Social Responsibility Alert describes the successful reverse logistics initiative at Estée Lauder, Inc.[20]

Companies such as Eastman Kodak (reusable cameras), Hewlett-Packard (printer toner cartridges returned for filling), and Xerox and IBM (remanufacturing and recycling equipment parts) have implemented acclaimed reverse logistics programs.[21] Other firms have enlisted third-party logistics providers to handle this process along with other supply chain functions. GNB Technologies, Inc., a manufacturer of lead-acid batteries for automobiles and boats, has outsourced much of its supply chain activity to UPS Logistics.[22] The company contracts with UPS to manage its shipments between plants, distribution centers, recycling centers, and retailers. This includes movement of both new batteries and used products destined for recycling and covers both truck and railroad shipments. This partnership along with the initiatives of other battery makers has paid economic and ecological dividends. By recycling 90 percent of the lead from used batteries, manufacturers have kept the demand for new lead in check, thereby holding down costs to consumers. Also, solid waste management costs and the environmental impact of lead in landfills is reduced.

Concept Check	**1.** What are the basic trade-offs between the five modes of transportation?
	2. What types of inventory should use storage warehouses and which type should use distribution centers?
	3. What are the strengths and weaknesses of a just-in-time system?

CHAPTER IN REVIEW

1 *Recognize the relationship between marketing channels, logistics, and supply chain management.*

A marketing channel relies on logistics to make products available to consumers and industrial users. Logistics involves those activities that focus on getting the right amount of the right products to the right place at the right time at the lowest possible cost. The performance of these activities is logistics management—the practice of organizing the cost-effective flow of raw materials, in-process inventory, finished goods, and related information from point of origin to point of consumption to satisfy customer requirements.

A supply chain is a sequence of firms that perform activities required to create and deliver a good or service to consumers or industrial users. It differs from a marketing channel in terms of membership. A supply chain includes suppliers that provide raw material inputs to a manufacturer as well as the wholesalers and retailers that deliver goods. The management process is also different. Supply chain management is the integration and organization of information and logistics activities across firms in a supply chain for the purpose of creating and delivering goods and services that provide value to consumers.

2 *Describe how a company's supply chain aligns with its marketing strategy.*

A company's supply chain follows from a clearly defined marketing strategy. The alignment of a company's supply chain with its marketing strategy involves three steps. First, a supply chain must reflect the needs of the customer segment being served. Second, a company must understand what a supply chain is designed to do well. Supply chains range from those that emphasize being responsive to customer requirements and

demands to those that emphasize efficiency with the goal of supplying products at the lowest possible delivered cost. Finally, a supply chain must be consistent with the targeted customer's needs and the company's marketing strategy. The Dell and Wal-Mart examples in the chapter illustrate how this alignment is achieved by two market leaders.

3 *Identify the major logistics cost and customer service factors that managers consider when making supply chain decisions.*

Companies strive to provide superior customer service while controlling logistics cost. The major customer service factors include the length of time between orders and deliveries, dependability in replenishing inventory, communication between buyers and sellers, and convenience in buying from the seller. Logistics cost factors include transportation, materials handling and warehousing, order processing, inventory, and stockouts.

4 *Describe the key logistics functions in a supply chain.*

The four key logistics functions in a supply chain include transportation, warehousing and materials handling, order processing, and inventory management. Transportation provides the movement of goods necessary in a supply chain. The five major transportation modes are railroads, motor carriers, air carriers, pipelines, and water carriers. Warehousing and materials handling include the storing, sorting, and handling of products at storage warehouses or distribution centers. Order processing includes order receipt, delivery, invoicing, and collection from customers. Inventory management involves minimizing inventory-carrying costs while maintaining sufficient stocks of products to satisfy anticipated customer needs. Two popular inventory management practices are just-in-time (JIT) and vendor-managed inventory (VMI) systems.

FOCUSING ON KEY TERMS

customer service p. 429
efficient consumer response p. 430
electronic data interchange (EDI) p. 428
just-in-time (JIT) concept p. 437
lead time p. 430
logistics p. 422
logistics management p. 422

quick response p. 430
reverse logistics p. 438
supply chain p. 422
supply chain management p. 422
third-party logistics providers p. 432
total logistics cost p. 428
vendor-managed inventory (VMI) p. 437

DISCUSSION AND APPLICATION QUESTIONS

1 List several companies to which logistical activities might be unimportant. Also list several whose focus is only on the inbound or outbound side.

2 What are some types of businesses in which order processing may be among the paramount success factors?

3 What behavioral problems might arise to negate the logistics concept within the firm?

4 List the customer service factors that would be vital to buyers in the following types of companies: (*a*) manufacturing, (*b*) retailing, (*c*) hospitals, and (*d*) construction.

5 Name some cases when extremely high service levels (e.g., 99 percent) would be warranted.

6 Name the mode of transportation that would be the best for the following products: (*a*) farm machinery, (*b*) cut flowers, (*c*) frozen meat, and (*d*) coal.

7 The auto industry is a heavy user of the just-in-time concept. Why? What other industries would be good

candidates for its application? What do they have in common?

8 Look again at Figure 16–3. Explain why as the number of warehouses increases, (*a*) inventory costs rise and (*b*) transportation costs fall.

GOING ONLINE   Tracking Supply Chain Trends

What are the latest developments in supply chain and logistics management? Look no further than SupplyChainBrain.com, a repository of short articles related to supply chain news, developments, and innovative thinking. When you visit this website at www.supplychainbrain.com, you will find links to case studies and trends in "The Library," "Newsletters," and "Online Magazines" sections.

Your assignment is to:

1 Choose a topic (such as vendor-managed inventory) or a company (like IBM or Wal-Mart) featured in the chapter and update the text.

2 Go to the "Case Studies" link and summarize a specific company's application of one or more concepts described in the chapter.

BUILDING YOUR MARKETING PLAN

Does your marketing plan involve a product? If the answer is no, read no further and do not include this element in your plan. If the answer is yes:

1 (*a*) If inventory is involved, identify the three or four major kinds of inventory needed for your organization (retail stock, finished goods, raw materials, supplies, and so on), and (*b*) suggest ways to reduce their costs.

2 (*a*) Rank the four customer service factors (time, dependability, communication, and convenience) from most important to least important from your customers' point of view, and (*b*) identify actions for the one or two most important to serve customers better.

VIDEO CASE 16   Amazon: Delivering the Goods . . . Millions of Times a Day

"The new economy means that the balance of power has shifted toward the consumer," explains Jeff Bezos, CEO of Amazon.com, Inc. The global online retailer is a pioneer of fast, convenient, low-cost virtual shopping that has attracted millions of consumers. Of course, while Amazon has changed the way many people shop, the company still faces the traditional and daunting task of creating a seamless flow of deliveries to its customers—often millions of times each day.

THE COMPANY

Bezos started Amazon.com with a simple idea: to use the Internet to transform book buying into the fastest, easiest, and most enjoyable shopping experience possible. The company was incorporated in 1994 and opened its virtual doors in July 1995. At the forefront of a huge growth of dot-com businesses, Amazon pursued a get-big-fast business strategy. Sales grew rapidly and Amazon began

adding products and services other than books. In fact, Amazon soon set its goal on being the world's most customer-centric company, where customers can find and discover anything they might want to buy online!

Today Amazon claims to have the "Earth's Biggest Selection™" of products and services, including books, CDs, videos, toys and games, electronics, kitchenware, computers, free electronic greeting cards, and auctions. Other services allow customers to:

- Search for books, music, and videos with any word from the title or any part of the artist's name.
- Browse hundreds of product categories.
- Receive personalized recommendations, based on past purchases, through e-mail or when they log on.

These products and services have attracted millions of people in more than 220 countries and made Amazon.com, along with its international sites in the United Kingdom, Germany, Japan, and France, the leading online retailer.

Despite its incredible success with consumers and continuing growth in sales to more than $5 billion annually, Amazon.com found it difficult to be profitable. Many industry observers questioned the viability of online retailing and Amazon's business model. Then, Amazon shocked many people by becoming profitable. There are a variety of explanations for the turnaround. Generally, Bezos suggests that "efficiencies allow for lower prices, spurring sales growth across the board, which can be handled by existing facilities without much additional cost." More specifically, the facilities Bezos is referring to are the elements of its supply chain, which are one of the most complex and expensive aspects of the company's business.

SUPPLY CHAIN AND LOGISTICS MANAGEMENT AT AMAZON.COM

What happens after an order is submitted on Amazon's website but before it arrives at the customer's door? A lot. Amazon.com maintains huge distribution, or "fulfillment," centers where it keeps inventory of more than 2.7 million products. This is one of the key differences between Amazon.com and some of its competitors—it actually stocks products. So Amazon must manage the flow of products from its suppliers to its distribution centers and the flow of customer orders from the distribution centers to individuals' homes or offices.

The process begins with the suppliers. "Amazon's goal is to collaborate with our suppliers to increase efficiencies and improve inventory turnover," explains Jim Miller, vice president of supply chain at Amazon.com. "We want to bring to suppliers the kind of interactive relationship that has inspired customers to shop with us," he adds. For example, Amazon is using software to more accurately forecast purchasing patterns by region, which allows it to give its suppliers better information about delivery dates and volumes. Prior to the development of this software, 12 percent of incoming inventory was sent to the wrong location, leading to lost time and delayed orders. Now only 4 percent of the incoming inventory is mishandled.

At the same time, Amazon has been improving the part of the process that sorts the products into the individual orders. Jeffrey Wilke, Amazon's senior vice president of operations, says, "We spent the whole year really focused on increasing productivity." Again, technology has been essential. "The speed at which telecommunications networks allow us to pass information back and forth has enabled us to do the real-time work that we keep talking about. In the past, it would have taken too long to get this many items through a system," explains Wilke. Once the order is in the system, computers ensure that all items are included in the box before it is taped and labeled. A network of trucks and regional postal hubs then conclude the process with delivery of the order.

The success of Amazon's logistics and supply chain management activities may be most evident during the year-end holiday shopping season. Amazon received orders for 37.9 million items between November 9 and December 21, including orders for 450,000 Harry Potter books and products, and orders for 36,000 items placed just before the holiday delivery deadline. Well over 99 percent of the orders were shipped and delivered on time.

AMAZON'S CHALLENGES

Despite all of Amazon's recent improvements, logistics experts estimate that the company's distribution centers are operating at approximately 40 percent of their capacity. This situation suggests that Amazon must reduce its capacity or increase its sales.

Several sales growth options are possible. First, Amazon can continue to pursue growth through sales of books, CDs, and videos. Expanded lists of books, music, and movies from throughout the world and convenient selection services may appeal to current and potential customers. Second, Amazon can continue its expansion into new product and service categories. This approach would prevent Amazon from becoming a niche merchant of books, music, and movies, and position it as an online department store. Finally, Amazon can pursue a strategy of providing access to its existing operations to other retailers. For example, Amazon took over the Toys "Я" Us website, adding it as a store on Amazon's site. Borders, Expedia, and Circuit City have begun similar partnerships.

Amazon.com has come a long way toward proving that online retailing can work. As the company strives to maintain profitability and continue its growth, its future success is likely to depend on the success of its logistics and supply chain management activities.

Questions

1 How do Amazon.com's logistics and supply chain management activities help the company create value for its customers?

2 What systems did Amazon develop to improve the flow of products from suppliers to Amazon distribution centers? What systems improved the flow of orders from the distribution centers to customers?

3 Why will logistics and supply chain management play an important role in the future success of Amazon.com?

The lamp shade you need. 14.99

CHAPTER 17

RETAILING

LEARNING OBJECTIVES

After reading this chapter you should be able to:

1 Identify retailers in terms of the utilities they provide.

2 Explain the alternative ways to classify retail outlets.

3 Describe the many methods of nonstore retailing.

4 Classify retailers in terms of the retail positioning matrix.

5 Develop retailing mix strategies over the life cycle of a retail store.

TRADING UP . . . AT TARGET!

Are you one of the millions of consumers who selectively trade up to better products in some categories? Have you noticed the growing preference for brands that provide higher quality and emotional value? Consultants Michael Silverstein and Neil Fiske noticed, and they wrote about it in their book *Trading Up: The New American Luxury,* in which they describe the success of businesses that offer "new luxury" items, which can include clothing, appliances, and even personal care products. Target Stores noticed too and has repositioned the store as an "upscale discounter."

The first step in the strategy was to establish the red Target logo as a recognizable symbol of quality and value. The first campaign, called "Bulls-Eye World," featured the Target logo on everything in print and television ads—clothing, wallpaper, dogs—everything! Other promotions emphasized the high-quality brands available in Target stores. Then, Target added exclusive lines by well-known designers such as Michael Graves housewares, Swell bed and bath products, Amy Coe infant bedding, Sean Conway outdoor furniture and garden products, Mossimo clothing, and Sonia Kashuk makeup. You may remember the familiar "Everything You Want, You've Got It" campaign that showed the broad range of products available in the stores.

In 2004, Target began opening stores with a new design that includes a Starbucks café at the front of the store; a larger food area, which includes the Target food brand, Archer Farms; destination areas for categories such as baby merchandise; and more convenient locations of related categories such as movies, books, and music. Other marketing activities include Target's bridal registry, Club Wedd, and the Target Baby registry for new parents. Its website, Target.com, provides access to its brands for consumers in locales where no stores exist. Target has also developed partnerships with FTD, AOL, and Napster.

Target's most recent campaign builds on the trading-up theme by encouraging customers to "Expect More. Pay Less." One industry expert observed that Target has "been able to carve out the ultimate retail positioning with both a perception of having the highest-quality products and, at the same time, a perception of being a "low-price leader." Of course, Target is facing direct competition from Wal-Mart, but to attract and keep upscale consumers who like high-quality bargains, it also faces competition from traditional department stores. In what may be the most dramatic statement of its repositioning strategy, watch for Target to try new locations in suburban malls.[1]

Target is just one example of many dynamic and exciting retailers you may encounter today. This chapter examines the critical role of retailing in the marketplace and the challenging decisions retailers face as they strive to create value for customers.

What types of products will consumers buy through catalogs, television, the Web, or by telephone? In what type of store will consumers look for products they don't buy directly? How important is the location of the store? Will customers expect services such as alterations, delivery, installation, or repair? What price should be charged for each product? These are difficult and important questions that are an integral part of retailing. In the channel of distribution, retailing is where the customer meets the product. It is through retailing that exchange (a central aspect of marketing) occurs. **Retailing** includes all activities involved in selling, renting, and providing goods and services to ultimate consumers for personal, family, or household use.

THE VALUE OF RETAILING

FIGURE 17–1
Which company best represents which utilities?

Retailing is an important marketing activity. Not only do producers and consumers meet through retailing actions, but retailing also creates customer value and has a significant impact on the economy. To consumers, the value of retailing is in the form of utilities provided (Figure 17–1). Retailing's economic value is represented

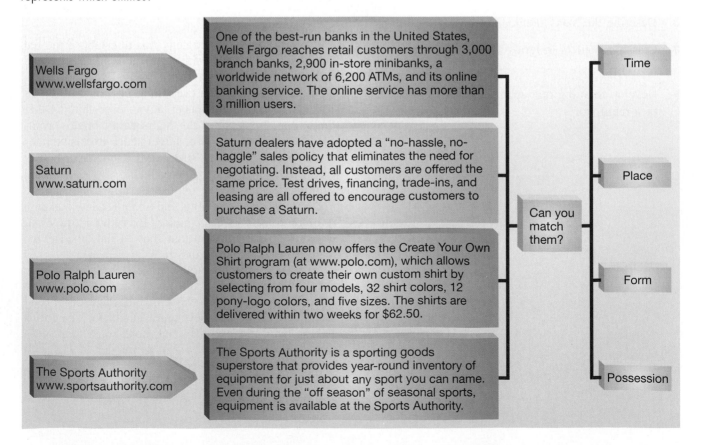

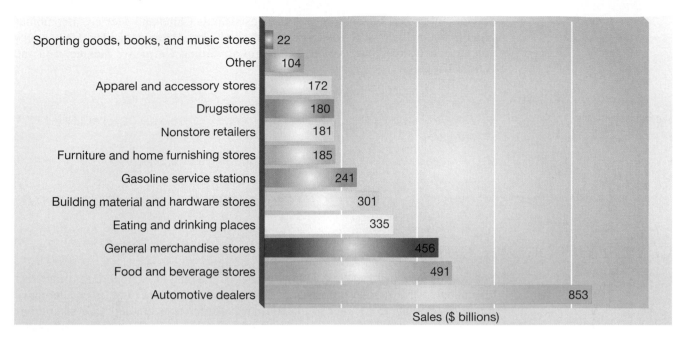

FIGURE 17–2
Retail sales ($ billions), by type of business

by the people employed in retailing as well as by the total amount of money exchanged in retail sales (Figure 17–2).

Consumer Utilities Offered by Retailing

The utilities provided by retailers create value for consumers. Time, place, form, and possession utilities are offered by most retailers in varying degrees, but one utility is often emphasized more than others. Look at Figure 17–1 to see how well you can match the retailer with the utility being emphasized in the description.

Providing minibanks in supermarkets, as Wells Fargo does, puts the bank's products and services close to the consumer, providing place utility. By providing financing or leasing and taking used cars as trade-ins, Saturn makes the purchase easier and provides possession utility. Form utility—production or alteration of a product—is offered by Polo Ralph Lauren through its online Create Your Own Shirt program, which offers shirts that meet each customer's specifications. Finding the right sporting equipment during the off-season is the time utility provided by the Sports Authority. Many retailers offer a combination of the four basic utilities. Some supermarkets, for example, offer convenient locations (place utility) and are open 24 hours (time utility). In addition, consumers may seek additional utilities such as entertainment, recreation, or information.[2]

The Global Economic Impact of Retailing

Retailing is also important to the U.S. and global economies. Three of the 25 largest businesses in the United States are retailers (Wal-Mart, Home Depot, and Target).[3] Wal-Mart's $258 billion of sales in 2003 surpassed the gross domestic product of Sweden for that same year. Wal-Mart, Home Depot, and Target together have more than 2.1 million employees—more than the number of people who live in Austin, Texas, Spokane, Washington, and Norwich, Connecticut, combined. Figure 17–2 shows that many other retailers, including food stores, automobile dealers, and general merchandise outlets, are also significant contributors to the U.S. economy.[4]

Outside the United States, large retailers include Daiei in Japan, Pinault-Printemps in France, Karstadtquelle in Germany, and Marks &

Spencer in Britain.[5] In emerging economies such as China and Mexico, a combination of local and global retailers is evolving. Wal-Mart, for example, has 1,300 stores outside the United States, including stores in China, Germany, Mexico, and the United Kingdom.

Concept Check

1. When Polo makes shirts cut to a customer's exact preferences, what utility is provided?

2. Two measures of the impact of retailing in the global economy are _____ and _____.

CLASSIFYING RETAIL OUTLETS

For manufacturers, consumers, and the economy, retailing is an important component of marketing that has several variations. Because of the large number of alternative forms of retailing, it is easier to understand the differences among retail institutions by recognizing that outlets can be classified in several ways. First, **form of ownership** distinguishes retail outlets based on whether individuals, corporate chains, or contractual systems own the outlet. Second, **level of service** is used to describe the degree of service provided to the customer. Three levels of service are provided by self-, limited-, and full-service retailers. Finally, the type of **merchandise line** describes how many different types of products a store carries and in what assortment. The alternative types of outlets are discussed in greater detail in the following pages.

Form of Ownership

There are three general forms of retail ownership—individual, corporate chain, and contractual system.

Independent Retailer
One of the most common forms of retail ownership is the independent business, owned by an individual. Small retailers account for most of the 1.5 million retail establishments in the United States and include hardware stores, bakeries, clothing stores, and restaurants. In addition, there are 29,000 jewelry stores, 26,000 florists, and 43,000 sporting good and hobby stores. The advantage of this form of ownership for the owner is that he or she can be his or her own boss. For customers, the independent store can offer convenience, quality personal service, and lifestyle compatibility.[6]

Corporate Chain
A second form of ownership, the corporate chain, involves multiple outlets under common ownership. If you've ever shopped at Bloomingdale's, Macy's, or Burdine's, you've shopped at a chain outlet owned by Federated Department Stores, Inc.

In a chain operation, centralization in decision making and purchasing is common. Chain stores have advantages in dealing with manufacturers, particularly as the size of the chain grows. A large chain can bargain with a manufacturer to obtain good service or volume discounts on orders. Target's large volume makes it a strong negotiator with manufacturers of most products. The buying power of chains is seen when consumers compare chain store prices with other types of stores. Consumers also benefit in dealing with chains because there are multiple outlets with similar merchandise and consistent management policies.

Retailing has become a high-tech business for many large chains. Wal-Mart, for example, has developed a sophisticated inventory management and cost control system

MARKETING NEWSNET   Say Good-Bye to Bar Codes!

New technologies are continually changing the marketing and retailing environment. The next big thing, however, may be tiny microchips known as radio frequency identification (RFID) tags, which are so small and inexpensive that they can be attached to pallets, cases, cartons, or even individual items. The new technology allows manufacturers, distributors, and retailers to collect detailed information about a product's origin, distribution path, and price, eliminating the need for the current bar codes used to track goods. Wal-Mart and Target have already

mandated that their top vendors begin using RFID tags, and manufacturers such as Gillette, Procter & Gamble, Nestlé, and Unilever are actively involved in implementing the technology. Companies such as Hewlett-Packard and Sun Microsystems are also getting involved, offering consulting services to companies that are developing RFID technology strategies. Some experts even predict that RFID could soon be used in driver's licenses, passports, and even money.

that allows rapid price changes for each product in every store. In addition, stores such as Wal-Mart and Target are implementing pioneering new technologies such as radio frequency identification (RFID) tags to improve the quality of information available about products. The accompanying Marketing NewsNet describes the trend.[7]

Contractual Systems   Contractual systems involve independently owned stores that band together to act like a chain. The three kinds described in Chapter 15 are retailer-sponsored cooperatives, wholesaler-sponsored voluntary chains, and franchises. One retailer-sponsored cooperative is the Associated Grocers, which consists of neighborhood grocers that all agree with several other independent grocers to buy their meat from the same wholesaler. In this way, members can take advantage of volume discounts commonly available to chains and also give the impression of being a large chain, which may be viewed more favorably by some consumers. Wholesaler-sponsored voluntary chains such as Ace Hardware and Independent Grocers' Alliance (IGA) try to achieve similar benefits.

As noted in Chapter 15, in a franchise system an individual or firm (the franchisee) contracts with a parent company (the franchisor) to set up a business or retail

outlet. The franchisor usually assists in selecting the location, setting up the store or facility, advertising, and training personnel. The franchisee usually pays a onetime franchise fee and an annual royalty, usually tied to franchise's sales. There are two general types of franchises: *business-format franchises,* such as McDonald's, Radio Shack, and Blockbuster, and *product-distribution franchises,* such as a Ford dealership or a Coca-Cola distributor. In business-format franchising, the franchisor provides step-by-step procedures for most aspects of the business and guidelines for the most likely decisions a franchisee will face.

Franchising is attractive because it offers an opportunity for people to enter a well-known, established business for which managerial advice is provided. Also, the franchise fee may be less than the cost of setting up an independent business. The International Franchise Association

FRANCHISE	TYPE OF BUSINESS	TOTAL START-UP COST	NUMBER OF FRANCHISES
Subway	Sandwich restaurant	$86,000–213,000	21,000
Curves	Women-only fitness center	$36,000–43,000	7,500
Quizno's	Sandwich restaurant	$208,000–244,000	3,500
7-Eleven	Convenience store	$65,000–227,000	25,800
Jackson Hewitt Tax Service	Income tax preparation	$47,000–75,000	4,900

FIGURE 17–3

The top five franchises in the United States

recently reported that there are 760,000 franchised businesses in the United States, which generate $1.53 trillion in annual sales and employ more than 9.7 million people. Franchising is popular in international markets also—more than half of all U.S. franchisors have operations in other countries. What is the fastest-growing franchise? For the past year it has been Subway, which now has 21,000 locations, including 4,000 stores outside of the United States.[8]

Franchise fees paid to the franchisor can range from $10,000 for a Subway franchise to $45,000 for a McDonald's restaurant franchise. When the fees are combined with other costs such as real estate and equipment, however, the total investment can be much higher. Figure 17–3 shows the top five franchises, as rated by *Entrepreneur* magazine, based on factors such as size, financial strength, stability, years in business, and costs. By selling franchises, an organization reduces the cost of expansion but loses some control. A good franchisor, however, will maintain strong control of the outlets in terms of delivery and presentation of merchandise and try to enhance recognition of the franchise name.[9]

Level of Service

Even though most customers perceive little variation in retail outlets by form of ownership, differences among retailers are more obvious in terms of level of service. In some department stores, such as Loehman's, very few services are provided. Some grocery stores, such as the Cub chain, allow customers to bag the food themselves. Other outlets, such as Neiman Marcus, provide a wide range of customer services from gift wrapping to wardrobe consultation.

Self-Service Self-service requires that the customer performs many functions and little is provided by the outlet. Warehouse stores, for example, are usually self-service, with all nonessential customer services eliminated. Similarly, most gas stations today are self-service. New forms of self-service are being developed in grocery stores, airlines, camera/photo stores, and hotels. Delta Airlines has installed more than 600 self-service kiosks in all 81 of its U.S. terminals to allow passengers to find a seat and print out a boarding pass without the help of an attendant. Hilton is currently testing self-service kiosks in its Chicago and New York hotels. Customers swipe a credit card, select from room availability options, and then receive an encoded key card.[10]

Limited Service Limited-service outlets provide some services, such as credit and merchandise return, but not others, such as clothing alterations. General merchandise stores such as Wal-Mart, Kmart, and Target are usually considered limited service outlets. Customers are responsible for most shopping activities, although salespeople are available in departments such as consumer electronics, jewelry, and lawn and garden.

Full-Service   Full-service retailers, which include most specialty stores and department stores, provide many services to their customers. Neiman Marcus, Nordstrom, and Saks Fifth Avenue, for example, all rely on better service to sell more distinctive, higher-margin goods. Nordstrom offers a wide variety of services, including free exchanges, easy returns, credit cards, Nordstrom bank, a live help line, an online gift finder, catalogs, and a beauty hotline. Some Nordstrom stores also offer a "Personal Touch" department, which provides shopping assistants for consumers who need help with style, color, and size selection, and a concierge service for assistance with anything else. Nordstrom stores typically have 50 percent more salespeople on the floor than similarly sized stores, and the salespeople are renowned for their professional and personalized attention to customers.[11]

Type of Merchandise Line

Retail outlets also vary by their merchandise lines, the key distinction being the breadth and depth of the items offered to customers (Figure 17–4). **Depth of product line** means that the store carries a large assortment of each item, such as a shoe store that offers running shoes, dress shoes, and children's shoes. **Breadth of product line** refers to the variety of different items a store carries, such as appliances and CDs.

Depth of Line   Stores that carry a considerable assortment (depth) of a related line of items are limited-line stores. Oshman's sporting goods stores carry considerable depth in sports equipment ranging from weight-lifting accessories to running shoes. Stores that carry tremendous depth in one primary line of merchandise are single-line stores. Victoria's Secret, a nationwide chain, carries great depth in women's lingerie. Both limited- and single-line stores are often referred to as *specialty outlets.*

Specialty discount outlets focus on one type of product, such as electronics (Circuit City), office supplies (Staples), or books (Barnes and Noble) at very competitive prices. These outlets are referred to in the trade as *category killers* because they often dominate the market. Staples, for example, controls 37 percent of the office supply market.[12]

Breadth of Line   Stores that carry a broad product line, with limited depth, are referred to as *general merchandise stores.* For example, large department stores such as Dillard's, Macy's, Marshall Field's, and Neiman Marcus carry a wide range of different types of products but not unusual sizes. The breadth and depth of merchandise lines are important decisions for a retailer. Traditionally, outlets carried related lines of goods. Today, however, **scrambled merchandising**, offering several unrelated product lines in a single store, is common. The modern drugstore

FIGURE 17–4
Breadth versus depth of merchandise lines

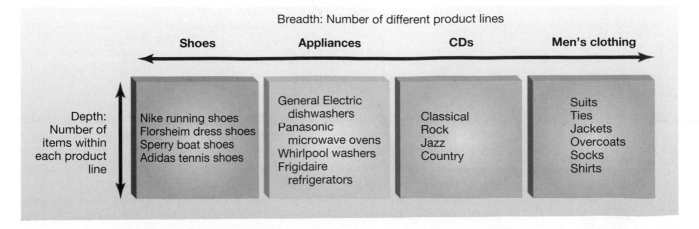

	HYPERMARKET		**SUPERCENTER**	
Region of popularity	Europe		United States	
Average size	200–300,000 sq. ft.		100–220,000 sq. ft.	
Number of products	50,000		40,000	
Annual revenue	$100,000,000 per store		$60,000,000 per store	

FIGURE 17–5
Differences between hypermarkets and supercenters

carries food, camera equipment, magazines, paper products, toys, small hardware items, and pharmaceuticals. Supermarkets rent videos, print photos, and sell flowers.

A form of scrambled merchandising, the **hypermarket**, has been successful in Europe. These hypermarkets are large stores (more than 200,000 square feet) based on a simple concept: Offer consumers everything in a single outlet, eliminating the need to stop at more than one location. The stores provide variety, quality, and low price for food and groceries and general merchandise. In France, the concept is so successful that hypermarkets maintain a 51 percent share of the grocery market. Carrefour, one of the largest hypermarket retailers, is introducing private-label items to help keep prices low, while it also adds upscale touches such as in-store butchers and extensive cheese selections.[13]

In the United States, retailers discovered that shoppers were uncomfortable with the huge size of hypermarkets. They developed a variation of the hypermarket called the *supercenter,* which combines a typical merchandise store (approximately 70,000 square feet) with a full-size grocery. Wal-Mart, Kmart, and Target are now using the concept very successfully. Wal-Mart currently operates 1,600 supercenters and is the nation's largest grocer and third-largest pharmacy, with 19 and 16 percent market shares, respectively. The concept is so successful that Wal-Mart plans to open an additional 1,000 supercenters in the United States during the next five years.[14] Figure 17–5 shows the differences between the supercenter and hypermarket concepts.

Scrambled merchandising is convenient for consumers because it eliminates the number of stops required in a shopping trip. However, for the retailer this merchandising policy means there is competition between very dissimilar types of retail outlets, or **intertype competition**. A local bakery may compete with a department store, discount outlet, or even a local gas station. Scrambled merchandising and intertype competition make it more difficult to be a retailer.

Concept Check

1. Centralized decision making and purchasing are an advantage of _____ ownership.

2. What are some examples of new forms of self-service retailers?

3. Would a shop for big men's clothes carrying pants in sizes 40 to 60 have a broad or deep product line?

NONSTORE RETAILING

Most of the retailing examples discussed earlier in the chapter, such as corporate chains, department stores, and limited- and single-line specialty stores, involve store retailing. Many retailing activities today, however, are not limited to sales in a store. Nonstore retailing occurs outside a retail outlet through activities that involve varying levels of customer and retailer involvement. Figure 17–6 shows six forms of nonstore retailing: automatic vending, direct mail and catalogs, television home shopping, online retailing, telemarketing, and direct selling.

FIGURE 17–6
Forms of nonstore retailing

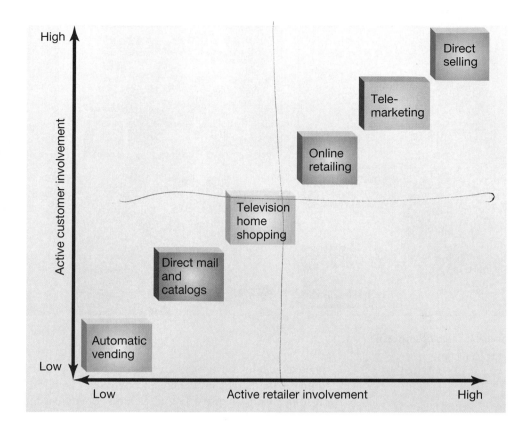

Automatic Vending

Nonstore retailing includes vending machines, which make it possible to serve customers when and where stores cannot. Machine maintenance, operating costs, and location leases can add to the cost of the products, so prices in vending machines tend to be higher than those in stores. About 29 percent of the products sold from vending machines are cold beverages, another 26 percent are candy and snacks, and another 29 percent is food. Other products are likely to be available in vending machines soon, however. Staples recently installed vending machines with office supplies in Boston's Logan International Airport and on several college campuses. Similarly, Flickstation Media is placing DVD vending machines in high-rise office complexes. The 5.6 million vending machines currently in use in the United States generated more than $21 billion in sales last year.[15]

Improved technology is making vending machines easier to use by reducing the need for cash. Many machines already accept credit cards, and cashless purchases using cell phones are likely in the near future. Japan's largest mobile phone company, DoCoMo, is working with Sony to introduce cell phones equipped with an electronic cash system called Edy (*e*uro, *d*ollar, *y*en), which will allow consumers to charge vending machine purchases to their cell phone accounts. Another improvement in vending machines is the use of wireless technology to notify vendors when their machines are empty. Nestlé, for example, is installing hundreds of ice cream vending machines in France and England that send wireless messages to supply truck drivers. Finally, one of the biggest developments in vending is being tested by Vision Inc.—it is experimenting with huge vending machines for parking lots that will be fully automated convenience stores.[16]

Direct Mail and Catalogs

Direct-mail and catalog retailing is attractive because it eliminates the cost of a store and clerks. For example, it costs a traditional retail store $34 to acquire a new customer,

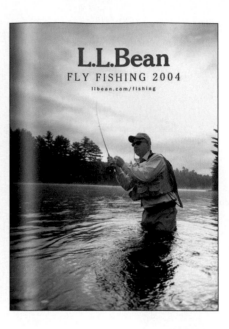

Specialty catalogs appeal to market niches.

whereas catalog customers are acquired for approximately $14. In addition, catalogs improve marketing efficiency through segmentation and targeting, and they create customer value by providing a fast and convenient means of making a purchase. The Direct Marketing Association predicts that catalog sales will reach $175 billion by 2008. Catalogs are popular outside of the United States also. Furniture retailer IKEA delivered 130 million copies of its catalog to 36 countries in 28 languages. Five million copies went to Canada, 11 million to the United States, 14 million to Britain, and every household in Sweden received a copy.[17]

One reason for the growth in catalog sales is that traditional retailers such as Crate and Barrel, OfficeMax, and Sears are adding catalog operations. As consumer's direct-mail purchases have increased, the number of catalogs and the number of products sold through catalogs have increased. A typical household now receives more than 50 of the 16 billion catalogs mailed each year. The competition, combined with increases in postal rates, however, have caused catalog retailers to focus on proven customers rather than prospective customers. Another successful approach used by many catalog retailers is to send specialty catalogs to market niches identified in their databases. L. L. Bean, a long-standing catalog retailer, has developed an individual catalog for fly-fishing enthusiasts. Similarly, Lillian Vernon Corporation sends a specialty catalog called "Lilly's Kids" to customers with children or grandchildren, and Sears sends a catalog called "Big and Tall" to customers who have purchased large-size clothing.[18]

Creative forms of catalog retailing are also being developed. Victoria's Secret mails as many as 45 catalogs a year to its customers to generate mail-order and 800-number business and to increase traffic in its 900 stores. Many catalog retailers such as Sharper Image now allow telephone orders, mail orders, and online orders. Each year, *Catalog Age* magazine evaluates more than 300 entries to select the winners of the Annual Catalog Awards. Some of this year's winners might be catalogs you have used—they included the Patagonia catalog, the Wilderness Travel catalog, and the Harry and David catalog.[19]

Television Home Shopping

Television home shopping is possible when consumers watch a shopping channel on which products are displayed; orders are then placed over the telephone or the Internet. Currently, the three largest programs are QVC, HSN, and ShopNBC. QVC

("quality, value, convenience") broadcasts live 24 hours each day, 364 days a year and reaches 145 million households in the United States, United Kingdom, Germany, and Japan. The company generates sales of more than $4.8 billion from its 29 million customers by offering 250 new products each week and shipping more than 120 million packages each year. You might be surprised to know that one of the most popular and fastest-growing product categories is footwear—more than 50 different brands of shoes are currently sold on the three channels.[20]

Because television home shopping programs typically attract women over age 35, other programs such as MTV's *House of Style* with host Molly Sims, and the complementary website, MTV Shop, are designed to attract a younger audience. The television shopping programs are using other forms of retailing also. QVC now has three types of retail stores: a studio store at its headquarters, QVC @ the Mall in the Mall of America, and six outlet stores. Similarly, the Home Shopping Network has added catalogs to its online and television offerings. Finally, several television shopping programs are testing interactive television technology that allows viewers to place orders with their remote control rather than the telephone.[21]

Online Retailing

Online retailing allows consumers to search for, evaluate, and order products through the Internet. For many consumers the advantages of this form of retailing are the 24-hour access, the ability to comparison shop, in-home privacy, and variety. Studies of online shoppers indicated that men were initially more likely than women to buy something online. As the number of online households increased, however, the profile of online shoppers changed to include all shoppers. In addition, the number of online retailers grew rapidly for several years and then declined as many standalone, Internet-only businesses failed or consolidated. Today, there has been a melding of traditional and online retailers—"bricks and clicks"—that are using experiences from both approaches to create better value and experiences for customers. At Walmart.com, for example, CEO Jeanne Jackson has advocated a streamlined and intuitive website layout and new services such as real-time inventories in individual stores that allow customers to decide whether to go to the store or to buy online. Experts predict that online sales will reach $255 billion by 2007.[22]

Online retail purchases can be the result of several very different approaches. First, consumers can pay dues to become a member of an online discount service such as

www.netMarket.com. The service offers more than 800,000 items at very low prices to its 25 million subscribers. Another approach to online retailing is to use a shopping "bot" such as www.mysimon.com. This site searches the Web for a product specified by the consumer and provides a report on the locations of the best prices available. Consumers can also use the Internet to go directly to online malls (www.fashionmall.com), apparel retailers (www.gap.com), book stores (www.amazon.com), computer manufacturers (www.dell.com), grocery stores (www.peapod.com), music and video stores (www.cdnow.com), and travel agencies (www.travelocity.com). A final approach to online retailing is the online auction, such as www.ebay.com, where consumers bid on more than 1,000 categories of products.[23]

One of the biggest problems online retailers face is that nearly two-thirds of online shoppers make it to "checkout" and then leave the website to compare shipping costs and prices on other sites. Of the shoppers who leave, 70 percent do not return. One way online retailers are addressing this issue is to offer consumers a comparison of competitors' offerings. At booksamillion.com,

for example, consumers can use a "comparison engine" to compare prices with Amazon.com, Barnesandnoble.com, and Borders.com.[24] Experts suggest that online retailers should think of their websites as dynamic billboards if they are to attract and retain customers.[25]

Online retailers are also trying to improve the online retailing experience by adding experiential or interactive activities to their websites. The Web Link describes how apparel stores use virtual models to involve consumers in the purchase process and help with product selection.[26] Similarly, car manufacturers like BMW, Mercedes, and Jaguar encourage website visitors to "build" a vehicle by selecting interior and exterior colors, packages, and options and then view the customized virtual car. In addition, the merger of television home shopping and online retailing will be possible through TV-based Internet platforms such as Microsoft's MSN TV, which uses an Internet appliance attached to a television to connect to the Internet. Owning a television or a computer isn't a necessity for online retailing, however, as 15,000 Internet cafés in 171 countries now provide guests with access to computer stations linked to the Internet.[27]

Telemarketing

Another form of nonstore retailing, called **telemarketing**, involves using the telephone to interact with and sell directly to consumers. Compared with direct mail, telemarketing is often viewed as a more efficient means of targeting consumers. Insurance companies, brokerage firms, and newspapers have often used this form of retailing as a way to cut costs but still maintain access to their customers. According to the Direct Marketing Association, annual telemarketing sales exceed $500 billion.[28]

Internet cafés provide access to the Web.

The telemarketing industry has recently gone through dramatic changes as a result of new legislation related to telephone solicitations. Issues such as consumer privacy, industry standards, and ethical guidelines have encouraged discussion among consumers, Congress, the Federal Trade Commission, and businesses. The result was legislation that created the National Do-Not-Call registry (www.donotcall.gov) for consumers who do not want to receive telephone calls related to company sales efforts. The American Teleservices Association asked the Supreme Court to review the implications of the legislation in terms of its restrictions on free speech. Although the Supreme Court decided not to review the case, companies that use telemarketing have already adapted by adding compliance software to ensure that numbers on the list are not called. In addition, some firms are considering shifting their telemarketing budgets to direct-mail and door-to-door techniques.[29]

Direct Selling

Direct selling, sometimes called door-to-door retailing, involves direct sales of goods and services to consumers through personal interactions and demonstrations in their home or office. A variety of companies, including familiar names such as Fuller Brush, Avon, World Book, and Mary Kay Cosmetics, have created an industry with more than $16 billion in sales by providing consumers with personalized service and convenience. In the United States, however, sales have been declining as retail chains such as Wal-Mart begin to carry similar products at discount prices and as the increasing number of dual-career households reduces the number of potential buyers at home.

In response to the changes in the United States, many direct selling retailers are expanding into other markets. Avon, for example, already has 4 million sales representatives in 137 countries including Mexico, Poland, Argentina, and China.[30] Similarly, other retailers such as Amway, Herbalife, and Electrolux are rapidly expanding. More than 70 percent of Amway's $7 billion in sales now comes from outside the United States, and sales in Japan alone exceed sales in North America.[31] Direct selling is likely to continue to grow in markets where the lack of effective distribution channels increases the importance of door-to-door convenience and where the lack of consumer knowledge about products and brands will increase the need for a person-to-person approach.[32]

Concept Check

1. Successful catalog retailers often send _____ catalogs to _____ markets identified in their databases.

2. How are retailers increasing consumer interest and involvement in online retailing?

3. Where are direct selling retail sales growing? Why?

RETAILING STRATEGY

This section describes how a retailer develops and implements a retailing strategy by positioning the store and taking specific retailing mix actions. Figure 17–7 on the next page identifies the relationship between positioning and the retailing mix.

Positioning a Retail Store

The classification alternatives presented in the previous sections help determine one store's position relative to its competitors.

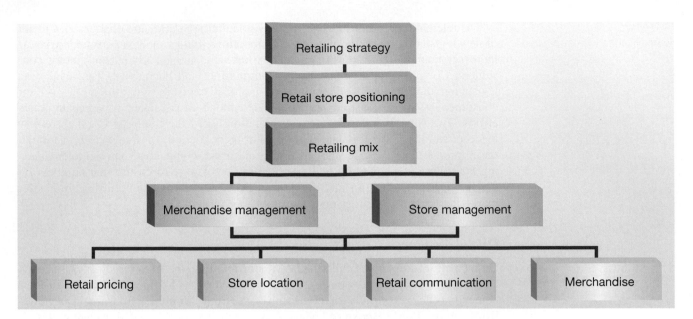

FIGURE 17–7
Elements of a retailing strategy

Retail Positioning Matrix The **retail positioning matrix** is a matrix developed by the MAC Group, Inc., a management consulting firm.[33] This matrix positions retail outlets on two dimensions: breadth of product line and value added. As defined previously, *breadth of product line* is the range of products sold through each outlet. The second dimension, *value added,* includes elements such as location (as with 7-Eleven stores), product reliability (as with Holiday Inn or McDonald's), or prestige (as with Saks Fifth Avenue or Brooks Brothers).

The retail positioning matrix in Figure 17–8 shows four possible positions. An organization can be successful in any position, but unique strategies are required within each quadrant. Consider the four stores shown in the matrix:

1. Bloomingdale's has high value added and a broad product line. Retailers in this quadrant pay great attention to store design and product lines. Merchandise often has a high margin of profit and is of high quality. The stores in this position typically provide high levels of service.
2. Wal-Mart has low value added and a broad line. Wal-Mart and similar firms typically trade a lower price for increased volume in sales. Retailers in this position focus on price with low service levels and an image of being a place for good buys.
3. Tiffany & Co. has high value added and a narrow line. Retailers of this type typically sell a very restricted range of products that are of high-status quality. Customers are also provided with high levels of service.
4. Payless ShoeSource has low value added and a narrow line. Such retailers are specialty mass merchandisers. Payless ShoeSource, for example, carries athletic shoes at a discount.[34] These outlets appeal to value-conscious consumers. Economies of scale are achieved through centralized advertising, merchandising, buying, and distribution. Stores are usually the same in design, layout, and merchandise; hence they are often referred to as "cookie-cutter" stores.

Keys to Positioning To successfully position a store, it must have an identity that has some advantages over the competitors yet is recognized by consumers. A company can have outlets in several positions on the matrix, but this approach is usually done with different store names. Federated Inc., for example, owns Bloomingdale's department stores (with high value added and a broad line) and Macy's Home Stores (high value added and a narrow line). Shifting from one box

FIGURE 17–8
Retail positioning matrix

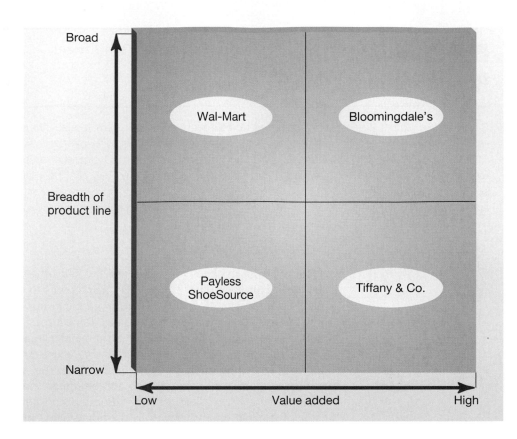

in the retail positioning matrix to another is also possible, but all elements of retailing strategy must be reexamined. For example, JCPenney has modified the visual presentation of its stores and changed the assortment of its merchandise to reposition itself from a mass merchandiser competing with Sears to a contemporary department store competing with stores such as Bloomingdale's.[35]

Retailing Mix

In developing retailing strategy, managers work with the **retailing mix**, which includes activities related to managing the store and the merchandise in the store. The retailing mix is similar to the marketing mix and includes retail pricing, store location, retail communication, and merchandise.

Retail Pricing   In setting prices for merchandise, retailers must decide on the markup, markdown, and timing for markdowns. As mentioned in the appendix to Chapter 14 (Appendix B), the *markup* refers to how much should be added to the cost the retailer paid for a product to reach the final selling price. Retailers decide on the *original markup*, but by the time the product is sold, they end up with a *maintained markup*. The original markup is the difference between retailer cost and initial selling price. When products do not sell as quickly as anticipated, their price is reduced. The difference between the final selling price and retailer cost is the maintained markup, which is also called the *gross margin.*

Discounting a product, or taking a *markdown,* occurs when the product does not sell at the original price and an adjustment is necessary. Often new models or styles force the price of existing models to be marked down. Discounts may also be used to increase demand for complementary products.[36] For example, retailers might take a markdown on CD players to increase sales of CDs or reduce the price of cake mix to generate frosting purchases. The *timing* of a markdown can be important. Many

ETHICS AND SOCIAL RESPONSIBILITY ALERT

Who Takes the Five-Finger Discount? You'll Be Surprised!

ETHICS

Retailers lose almost 2 percent of their sales to theft each year. To combat the problem many stores attempt to discourage consumers from shoplifting with magnetic detectors, locked cases, and other deterrents. What you may find surprising, though, is that more than 50 percent of the thefts are not made by consumers but by employees. The most popular items to steal are candy from convenience stores, shirts from department stores, batteries from discount stores, and cigarettes from drugstores. When does this happen? The most popular time is between 3 and 6 P.M. Why do you think shoplifting is such a large problem? What recommendations would you make to retailers?

retailers take a markdown as soon as sales fall off to free up valuable selling space and cash. However, other stores delay markdowns to discourage bargain hunters and maintain an image of quality. There is no clear answer, but retailers must consider how the timing might affect future sales. Recent research indicates that frequent promotions increase consumers' ability to remember regular prices.[37]

Although most retailers plan markdowns, many retailers use price discounts as a part of their regular merchandising policy. Wal-Mart and Home Depot, for example, emphasize consistently low prices and eliminate most markdowns with a strategy often called *everyday low pricing.*[38] Because consumers often use price as an indicator of product quality, however, the brand name of the product and the image of the store become important decision factors in these situations.[39] Another strategy, *everyday fair pricing,* is advocated by retailers which may not offer the lowest price but try to create value for customers through its service and the total buying experience.[40] Consumers often use the prices of *benchmark* or *signpost* items, such as a can of Coke, to form an overall impression of the store's prices.[41] In addition, price is the most likely to influence consumers' assessment of merchandise value.[42]

A special issue for retailers trying to keep prices low is **shrinkage**, or breakage and theft of merchandise by customers and employees. Who do you think steals more? For the answer see the accompanying Ethics and Social Responsibility Alert.[43]

Off-price retailing is a retail pricing practice that is used by retailers such as T.J. Maxx, Burlington Coat Factory, and Ross Stores. **Off-price retailing** involves selling brand-name merchandise at lower than regular prices. The difference between the off-price retailer and a discount store is that off-price merchandise is bought by the retailer from manufacturers with excess inventory at prices below wholesale prices, while the discounter buys at full wholesale price (but takes less of a markup than do traditional department stores). Because of this difference in the way merchandise is purchased by the retailer, selection at an off-price retailer is unpredictable, and searching for bargains has become a popular activity for many consumers. "It's more like a sport than it is like ordinary shopping," says Christopher Boring of Columbus, Ohio's Retail Planning Associates.[44] Savings to the consumer at off-price retailers are reported as high as 70 percent off the prices of a traditional department store.

There are several variations of off-price retailing. One is the *warehouse club.* These large stores (more than 100,000 square feet) began as rather stark outlets with no elaborate displays, customer service, or home delivery. They require an annual membership fee (ranging from $30 to $100) for the privilege of shopping there. While a typical Wal-Mart stocks 30,000 items, warehouse clubs carry about 3,500 items and usually stock just one brand of appliance or food product. Service is minimal, and customers usually must pay by cash or check. Customers are attracted by the ultralow prices and surprise deals on selected merchandise, although several of the clubs have recently started to add ancillary services such as optical shops and pharmacies to differentiate themselves from competitors. The major warehouse clubs in the United States include Wal-Mart's Sam's Club, BJ's Wholesale Club, and

Costco's Warehouse Club. Sales of these off-price retailers have grown faster than the rest of the retail industry and exceeded $77 billion in 2003.[45]

A second variation is the *outlet store*. Factory outlets, such as Van Heusen Factory Store, Bass Shoe Outlet, and Oneida Factory Store, offer products for 25 to 30 percent off the suggested retail price. Manufacturers use the stores to clear excess merchandise and to reach consumers who focus on value shopping. Retail outlets such as Nordstrom Rack and Brooks Brothers Outlet Store allow retailers to sell excess merchandise and still maintain an image of offering merchandise at full price in their primary store. The number of factory outlet centers has increased from 183 in 1990 to 312, with sales of $11.2 billion. Some experts expect the next trend to combine the various types of off-price retailers in "value-retail centers."[46]

A third variation of off-price retailing is offered by single-price, or extreme value, retailers such as Family Dollar, Dollar General, and Dollar Tree. These stores average about 6,000 square feet in size and attract customers who want value and a "corner store" environment rather than a large supercenter experience. Some experts predict extraordinary growth of these types of retailers. Dollar General, for example, already has 6,200 stores and plans for 625 new stores in the next year.[47]

Store Location   A second aspect of the retailing mix involves deciding where to locate the store and how many stores to have. Department stores, which started downtown in most cities, have followed customers to the suburbs, and in recent years more stores have been opened in large regional malls. Most stores today are near several others in one of five settings: the central business district, the regional center, the community shopping center, the strip, or the power center.

The **central business district** is the oldest retail setting, the community's downtown area. Until the regional outflow to suburbs, it was the major shopping area, but the suburban population has grown at the expense of the downtown shopping area. Consumers often view central business district shopping as less convenient because of lack of parking, higher crime rates, and exposure to the weather. Many cities such as Cincinnati, Denver, and San Antonio have implemented plans to revitalize shopping in central business districts by attracting new offices, entertainment, and residents to downtown locations.

Regional shopping centers consist of 50 to 150 stores that typically attract customers who live or work within a 5- to 10-mile range. These large shopping areas often contain two or three *anchor stores,* which are well-known national or regional stores such as Sears, Saks Fifth Avenue, and Bloomingdale's. The largest variation of a regional center is the West Edmonton Mall in Alberta, Canada. The shopping center is a conglomerate of 800 stores, seven amusement centers, 110 restaurants, and a 355-room Fantasyland hotel.[48]

A more limited approach to retail location is the **community shopping center**, which typically has one primary store (usually a department store branch) and often about 20 to 40 smaller outlets. Generally, these centers serve a population of consumers who are within a 10- to 20-minute drive.

Not every suburban store is located in a shopping mall. Many neighborhoods have clusters of stores, referred to as a **strip location**, to serve people who are within a 5- to 10-minute drive. Gas station, hardware, laundry, grocery, and pharmacy outlets are commonly found in a strip location. Unlike the larger shopping centers, the composition of these stores is usually unplanned. A variation of the strip shopping location is called the **power center**, which is a huge shopping strip with multiple anchor (or national) stores. Power centers are seen as having the convenient location found in many strip centers and the additional power of national stores. These large strips often have two to five anchor stores and often contain a supermarket, which brings the shopper to the power center on a weekly basis.[49]

Several new types of retail locations include carts, kiosks, and wall units. These forms of retailing have been popular in airports and mall common areas because they provide consumers with easy access and rental income for the property owner. Retailers benefit from the relatively low cost compared with a regular store.

Retail Communication As the chapter's opening example about Target illustrates, a retailer's communication activities can play an important role in positioning a store and creating its image. While the traditional elements of communication and promotion are discussed in Chapter 19 on advertising and Chapter 20 on personal selling, the message communicated by the many other elements of the retailing mix are also important.

Deciding on the image of a retail outlet is an important retailing mix factor that has been widely recognized and studied since the late 1950s. Pierre Martineau described image as "the way in which the store is defined in the shopper's mind," partly by its functional qualities and partly by an aura of psychological attributes.[50] In this definition, *functional* refers to mix elements such as price ranges, store layouts, and breadth and depth of merchandise lines. The psychological attributes are the intangibles such as a sense of belonging, excitement, style, or warmth. Image has been found to include impressions of the corporation that operates the store, the category or type of store, the product categories in the store, the brands in each category, merchandise and service quality, and the marketing activities of the store.[51]

Closely related to the concept of image is the store's atmosphere or ambiance. Many retailers believe that sales are affected by layout, color, lighting, and music in the store as well as by how crowded it is. In addition, the physical surroundings that influence customers may affect the store's employees.[52] In creating the right image and atmosphere, a retail store tries to attract its target audience with what those consumers seek from the buying experience, so the store will fortify the beliefs and the emotional reactions buyers are seeking.[53] Sears, for example, is attempting to shift from its appliance and tool image with advertising that speaks to all members of a family. The new "Good Life. Great Price." campaign emphasizes a broad range of brand-name merchandise and one-stop shopping.[54]

Merchandise A final element of the retailing mix is the merchandise offering. Managing the breadth and depth of the product line requires retail buyers who are familiar with the needs of the target market and the alternative products available from the many manufacturers that might be interested in having a product available in the store. A popular approach to managing the assortment of merchandise today is called **category management**. This approach assigns a manager with the responsibility for selecting all products that consumers in a market segment might view as substitutes for each other, with the objective of maximizing sales and profits in the category. For example, a category manager might be responsible for shoes in a department store or paper products in a grocery store.

Many retailers are developing an advanced form of category management called *consumer marketing at retail* (CMAR). Recent surveys show that, as part of their CMAR programs, retailers are conducting research, analyzing the data to identify shopper problems, translating the data into retailing mix actions, executing shopper-friendly in-store programs, and monitoring the performance of the merchandise. Wal-Mart, for example, has used the approach to test baby-product and dollar-product categories. Grocery stores such as Safeway and Kroger use the approach to determine the appropriate mix of brand name and private label products. Specialty retailer Barnes & Noble recently won a best practice award for its application of the approach to the selection, presentation, and promotion of magazines.[55]

Concept Check

1. What are the two dimensions of the retail positioning matrix?

2. How does original markup differ from maintained markup?

3. A huge shopping strip with multiple anchor stores is a _____ center.

THE CHANGING NATURE OF RETAILING

Retailing is the most dynamic aspect of a channel of distribution. Stores such as factory outlets show that new retailers are always entering the market, searching for a new position that will attract customers. The reason for this continual change is explained by two concepts: the wheel of retailing and the retail life cycle.

The Wheel of Retailing

The **wheel of retailing** describes how new forms of retail outlets enter the market.[56] Usually they enter as low-status, low-margin stores such as a drive-in hamburger stand with no indoor seating and a limited menu (Figure 17–9, box 1). Gradually these outlets add fixtures and more embellishments to their stores (in-store seating, plants, and chicken sandwiches as well as hamburgers) to increase the attractiveness for customers. With these additions, prices and status rise (box 2). As time passes, these outlets add still more services and their prices and status increase even further (box 3). These retail outlets now face some new form of retail outlet that again appears as a low-status, low-margin operator (box 4), and the wheel of retailing turns as the cycle starts to repeat itself.

In the 1950s, McDonald's and Burger King had very limited menus of hamburgers and french fries. Most stores had no inside seating for customers. Over time, the wheel of retailing for fast-food restaurants has turned. These chains have changed by altering their stores and expanding their menus. Today, McDonald's is testing new products such as its all white-meat Chicken McNuggets, chicken breast strips called Big Dippers, and the Go Active Happy Meal for adults; new formats such as its coffee, pastry, and sandwich outlets called McCafe; and new service options such as wireless Internet connections.[57] The changes are leaving room for new forms of outlets such as Checkers Drive-In Restaurants. The chain opened fast-food stores that offered only basics—burgers, fries, and cola, a drive-through window, and no inside seating—and now has more than 775 stores.[58] The wheel is turning for other outlets too—Boston Market has

FIGURE 17–9

The wheel of retailing

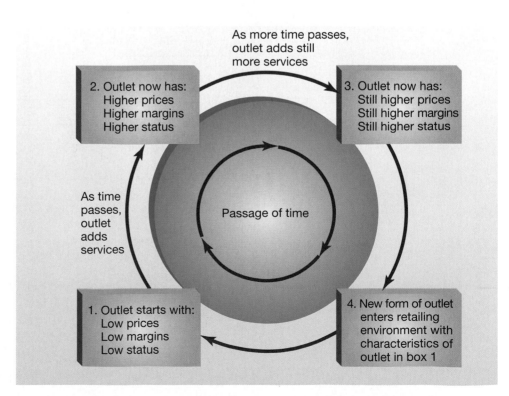

added sophisticated soups, salads, and desserts to its original menu, is testing home delivery in Washington, D.C., and recently introduced a full-service format called Rotisserie Grill in Tallahassee, Florida. For still others, the wheel has come full circle. Taco Bell is now opening small, limited-offering outlets in gas stations, discount stores, or "wherever a burrito and a mouth might possibly intersect."[59]

Discount stores were a major new retailing form in the 1960s and priced their products below those of department stores. As prices in discount stores rose, in the 1980s they found themselves overpriced compared with a new form of retail outlet—the warehouse club. Today, off-price retailers and factory outlets are offering prices even lower than warehouses.

The Retail Life Cycle

The process of growth and decline that retail outlets, like products, experience is described by the **retail life cycle**.[60] Figure 17–10 shows the retail life cycle and the position of various current forms of retail outlets on it. Early growth is the stage of emergence of a retail outlet, with a sharp departure from existing competition. Market share rises gradually, although profits may be low because of start-up costs. In the next stage, accelerated development, both market share and profit achieve their greatest growth rates. Usually multiple outlets are established as companies focus on the distribution element of the retailing mix. In this stage, some later competitors may enter. Wendy's, for example, appeared on the hamburger chain scene almost 20 years after McDonald's had begun operation. The key goal for the retailer in this stage is to establish a dominant position in the fight for market share.

The battle for market share is usually fought before the maturity stage, and some competitors drop out of the market. In the wars among hamburger chains, Jack in the Box, Gino Marchetti's, and Burger Chef used to be more dominant outlets. New retail forms enter in the maturity stage, stores try to maintain their market share,

FIGURE 17–10
The retail life cycle

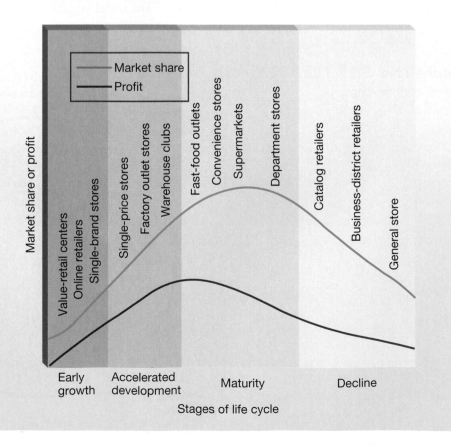

and price discounting occurs. For example, when McDonald's introduced its Extra Value Meal, a discounted package of burger, fries, and drink, Wendy's followed with a kid's Value Menu.

The challenge facing retailers is to delay entering the decline stage in which market share and profit fall rapidly. Specialty apparel retailers, such as the Gap, Limited, Benetton, and Ann Taylor, have noticed a decline in market share after a decade of growth. To prevent further decline, these retailers will need to find ways of discouraging their customers from moving to low-margin, mass-volume outlets or high-price, high-service boutiques.[61]

FUTURE CHANGES IN RETAILING

Three exciting trends in retailing—the growth of multichannel retailing, the increasing impact of technology, the dramatic changes in the way we shop—are likely to lead to many changes for retailers and consumers in the future.

Multichannel Retailing

The retailing formats described previously in this chapter represent an exciting menu of choices for creating customer value in the marketplace. Each format allows retailers to offer unique benefits and meet particular needs of various customer groups. While each format has many successful applications, retailers in the future are likely to combine many of the formats to offer a broader spectrum of benefits and experiences.[62] These **multichannel retailers** will utilize and integrate a combination of traditional store formats and nonstore formats such as catalogs, television, and online retailing.[63] Barnes & Noble, for example, created Barnesandnoble.com to compete with Amazon.com. Similarly, Office Depot has integrated its store, catalog, and Internet operations.

Integrated channels can make shopping simpler and more convenient. A consumer can research choices online or in a catalog and then make a purchase online, over the telephone, or at the closest store. In addition, the use of multiple channels allows retailers to reach a broader profile of customers. While online retailing may cannibalize catalog business to some degree, an online transaction costs about half as much to process as a catalog order. Multichannel retailers also benefit from the synergy of sharing information among the different channel operations. Online retailers, for example, have recognized that the Internet is more of a transactional medium than a relationship-building medium and are working to find ways to complement traditional customer interactions.[64]

The Impact of Technology

One of the most significant changes retailers may face in the future is the way consumers pay for purchases. Today, one of the most convenient and popular methods of payment is a credit card. Credit cards, however, are likely to be replaced by smart cards, which store information on computer chips instead of magnetic strips. They will hold information about bank accounts and amounts of available funds, and they will contain customer purchase information such as airline seat preferences and clothing sizes. The idea is already popular in Europe and Asia, where more than 33 million smart cards are in use. Benefits for consumers include faster service—a smart card transaction is much faster than having a check or credit card approved—and they are a convenient method of paying for small-dollar-amount transactions. Merchants will also benefit because they will save the 5 to 7 percent usually paid to credit card companies or lost in handling. Versions of smart cards are being developed for use in the memory slot in cell phones, PDAs, and computers. The St. Louis Rams are testing FastBreak cards, which use the same technology as E-ZPass tollway equipment, to help fans get through food lines quickly.[65]

Changing Shopping Behavior

In recent years, consumers have become precision shoppers. The number of stores consumers visit and the number of times they visit those stores each month is declining. Shoppers are demanding convenient hours and locations, outstanding service, and reasonable prices from retailers. As a result, familiar forms of retailers such as supermarkets, travel agencies, and car dealerships are likely to change or be replaced by new types of retailers. Byerly's, a supermarket chain with 12 stores in Minneapolis, offers rushed shoppers a wide variety of premium ready-to-eat entrees, in a carpeted store. *Vertical malls* such as the Shops at Columbus Circle in New York City and the Emporium in San Francisco are being developed to appeal to urban workers and residents.[66] Even car dealers are changing. CarMax offers no-haggle pricing, an inventory of 500 to 1,000 cars, written offers on trade-in vehicles, guarantees and extended warranties, financing, and one-hour transactions if a car is purchased.

Another response to the changes in consumers' preferences is a form of co-branding in which two retailers share a location. For example, McDonald's has developed partnerships with Wal-Mart, Home Depot, and Chevron that will lead to thousands of satellite outlets in retail stores and gas stations. Starbucks Coffee Co. has opened cafés in more than 100 Barnes & Noble bookstores. And KFC, which attracts a strong dinner crowd, now also includes Taco Bell, which is stronger in the lunch market, at 800 of its stores. Retailers hope that consumers will appreciate the convenience of the new locations.[67]

Concept Check

1. According to the wheel of retailing, when a new retail form appears, how would you characterize its image?

2. Market share is usually fought out before the _____ stage of the retail life cycle.

3. What is a smart card?

CHAPTER IN REVIEW

1 *Identify retailers in terms of the utilities they provide.*
Retailers provide time, place, form, and possession utilities. Time utility is provided by stores with convenient time-of-day (e.g., open 24 hours) or time-of-year (e.g., seasonal sports equipment available all year) availability. Place utility is provided by the number and location of the stores. Possession utility is provided by making a purchase possible (e.g., financing) or easier (e.g., delivery). Form utility is provided by producing or altering a product to meet the customer's specifications (e.g., custom-made shirts).

2 *Explain the alternative ways to classify retail outlets.*
Retail outlets can be classified by their form of ownership, level of service, and type of merchandise line. The forms of ownership include independent retailers, corporate chains, and contractual systems that include retailer-sponsored cooperatives, wholesaler-sponsored voluntary chains, and franchises. The levels of service include self-service, limited-service, and full-service outlets. Stores classified by their merchandise line include stores with depth, such as sporting good specialty stores, and stores with breadth, such as large department stores.

3 *Describe the many methods of nonstore retailing.*
Nonstore retailing includes automatic vending, direct mail and catalogs, television home shopping, online retailing, telemarketing, and direct selling. The methods of nonstore retailing

vary by the level of involvement of the retailer and the level of involvement of the customer. Vending, for example, has low involvement, whereas both the consumer and the retailer have high involvement in direct selling.

4 *Classify retailers in terms of the retail positioning matrix.*
The retail positioning matrix positions retail outlets on two dimensions: breadth of product line and value added. There are four possible positions in the matrix. Stores such as Bloomingdale's have a broad product line and high value added. Stores such as Wal-Mart also have a broad product line but have low value added because they offer fewer services. Tiffany & Co. represents a narrow product line and high value added. Finally, stores such as Payless ShoeSource offer a narrow product line and low value added.

5 *Develop retailing mix strategies over the life cycle of a retail store.*
The retail life cycle describes the process of growth and decline for retail outlets through four stages: early growth, accelerated development, maturity, and decline. The retail mix—pricing, store location, communication, and merchandise—can be managed to match the retail strategy with the stage of the life cycle. The challenge facing retailers is to delay entering the decline stage, where market share and profit fall rapidly.

FOCUSING ON KEY TERMS

breadth of product line p. 449
category management p. 460
central business district p. 459
community shopping center p. 459
depth of product line p. 449
form of ownership p. 446
hypermarket p. 450
intertype competition p. 450
level of service p. 446
merchandise line p. 446
multichannel retailers p. 463
off-price retailing p. 458

power center p. 459
regional shopping centers p. 459
retail life cycle p. 462
retail positioning matrix p. 456
retailing p. 444
retailing mix p. 457
scrambled merchandising p. 449
shrinkage p. 458
strip location p. 459
telemarketing p. 454
wheel of retailing p. 461

DISCUSSION AND APPLICATION QUESTIONS

1 Discuss the impact of the growing number of dual-income households on (*a*) nonstore retailing and (*b*) the retail mix.

2 How does value added affect a store's competitive position?

3 In retail pricing, retailers often have a maintained markup. Explain how this maintained markup differs from original markup and why it is so important.

4 What are the similarities and differences between the product and retail life cycles?

5 How would you classify Wal-Mart in terms of its position on the wheel of retailing versus that of an off-price retailer?

6 Develop a chart to highlight the role of each of the four main elements of the retailing mix across the four stages of the retail life cycle.

7 In Figure 17–8 Payless ShoeSource was placed on the retail positioning matrix. What strategies should Payless ShoeSource follow to move itself into the same position as Tiffany?

8 Breadth and depth are two important components in distinguishing among types of retailers. Discuss the breadth and depth implications of the following retailers discussed in this chapter: (*a*) Levi Strauss, (*b*) Wal-Mart, (*c*) L. L. Bean, and (*d*) Circuit City.

9 According to the wheel of retailing and the retail life cycle, what will happen to factory outlet stores?

10 The text discusses the development of online retailing in the United States. How does the development of this retailing form agree with the implications of the retail life cycle?

GOING ONLINE Consumers Can Now "Shop With Their Bot"!

For many consumers, comparison shopping is not appealing because of the inconvenience of traveling to multiple locations. Even on the Internet, finding and searching multiple websites can be tedious. One solution is a form of software called an *intelligent agent* or *bot* (derived from robot), which automatically searches for the best price. Try each of the following shopping bots—www.mysimon.com and www.shopping.com—to find the best price for one of the following products:

1 Wilson tennis racket
2 Sony TV
3 Guess jeans

How did the two bots differ? What range of prices did you obtain? What shipping and handling charges would apply to each purchase? Why are different recommendations made by the agents?

BUILDING YOUR MARKETING PLAN

Does your marketing plan involve using retailers? If the answer is no, read no further and do not include a retailing element in your plan. If the answer is yes:

1 Use Figure 17–7 to develop your retailing strategy by (*a*) selecting a position in the retail positioning matrix and (*b*) specifying the details of the retailing mix.

2 Develop a positioning statement describing the breadth of the product line (broad versus narrow) and value added (low versus high).

3 Describe an appropriate combination of retail pricing, store location, retail communication, and merchandise assortment.

VIDEO CASE 17   Mall of America: Shopping and a Whole Lot More

"Build it and they will come" not only worked in the movie *Field of Dreams* but applies—big time—to Mall of America.

Located in a suburb of Minneapolis, Mall of America (www.mallofamerica.com) is the largest completely enclosed retail and family-entertainment complex in the United States. "We're more than a mall, we're a destination," explains Maureen Cahill, an executive at Mall of America. More than 100,000 people each day—40 million visitors each year—visit the one-stop complex offering retail shopping, guest services, convenience, a huge variety of entertainment, and fun for all. "Guest services" include everything from high school and college classrooms to a doctor's office and wedding chapel.

THE CONCEPT AND CHALLENGE

The idea for the Mall of America came from the West Edmonton Mall in Alberta, Canada. The Ghermezian Brothers, who developed that mall, sought to create a unique mall that would attract not only local families but tourists from the Upper Midwest, nation, and even abroad.

The two challenges for Mall of America: How can it (1) attract and keep the large number of retail establishments needed to (2) continue to attract even more millions of visitors than today? A big part of the answer is in Mall of America's positioning—"There is a place for fun in your life!"

THE STAGGERING SIZE AND OFFERINGS

Opened August 1992 amid tremendous worldwide publicity, Mall of America faced skeptics who had their doubts because of its size, its unique retail-entertainment mix, and the nationwide recession. Despite these concerns, it

opened with more than 80 percent of its space leased and attracted more than one million visitors its first week.

Mall of America is 4.2 million square feet, the equivalent of 88 football fields. This makes it three to four times the size of most other regional malls. It includes four anchor department stores: Nordstrom, Macy's, Bloomingdale's, and Sears. It also includes more than 520 specialty stores, from Brooks Brothers and Sharper Image to Marshall's and DSW Shoe Warehouse. Approximately 36 percent of Mall of America's space is devoted to anchors and 64 percent to specialty stores. This makes the space allocation the reverse of most regional malls.

The retail-entertainment mix of Mall of America is incredibly diverse. For example, there are more than 100 apparel and accessory stores, 17 jewelry stores, and 24 shoe stores. Two food courts with 27 restaurants plus more than 30 other restaurants scattered throughout the building meet most food preferences of visitors. Another surprise: Mall of America is home to many "concept stores," where retailers introduce a new type of store or design. Because of its incredible size, the mall has 194 stores not found at competing regional malls. In addition, it has an entrepreneurial program for people with an innovative retail idea and limited resources. They can open up a kiosk, wall unit, or small store for a specified time period or as a temporary seasonal tenant.

Unique features of Mall of America include:

- Camp Snoopy, a seven-acre theme park with more than 50 attractions and rides, including a roller coaster, Ferris wheel, and games in a glass-enclosed, skylighted area with more than 400 trees.
- Underwater Adventures, where visitors are surrounded by tropical sharks, stingrays, and sea turtles; can adventure among fish native to the north woods; and can discover what lurks at the bottom of the Mississippi River.

- The Upper East Side, on the fourth floor, with its bars, nightclubs, game rooms, 14-screen theater, comedy club, and state-of-the-art bowling alley.
- The LEGO Land Imagination Center, a 6,000 square foot showplace with more than 30 full-sized models that include dinosaurs and astronauts.

As a host to corporate events and private parties, Mall of America has a rotunda that opens to all four floors that facilitates presentations, demonstrations, and exhibits. Organizations like Pepsi, Visa-USA, and the U.S. Postal Service have used the facilities to gain shopper awareness. Mall of America is a rectangle with the anchor department stores at the corners and Camp Snoopy in the skylighted central area, making it easy for shoppers to understand and navigate. It has 12,750 free parking ramp spaces on site and another 7,000 spaces nearby during peak times.

THE MARKET

The Minneapolis–St. Paul metropolitan area is a market with 3 million people. A total of 28 million people live within 400 miles or a day's drive of Mall of America. A survey of its shoppers showed that 43 percent of the shoppers come from outside Minnesota and account for 56 percent of the sales revenues. Located three miles from the thirteenth busiest international airport in the world, Mall of America provides a shuttle bus from the airport every half hour. Light-rail service from the airport and downtown Minneapolis begins in late 2004.

About 6 percent of visitors come from outside the United States. Some come just to see and experience Mall of America, while others take advantage of the cost savings available on goods (Japan) or taxes (Canada and states with sales taxes on clothing).

THE FUTURE: FACING THE CHALLENGES

Where does Mall of America head in the future?

"We just did a brand study and found that Mall of America is one of the most recognized brands in the world," says Maureen Cahill. "They might not know where we are sometimes, but they've heard of Mall of America and they know they want to come."

"What we've learned since 1992 is to keep the Mall of America fresh and exciting," she explains. "We're constantly looking at what attracts people and adding to that. We're adding new stores, new attractions, and new events. We hold more than 350 events a year and with everyone from Garth Brooks to Sara Ferguson to N Sync."

Mall of America recently announced a plan for a 5.7 million square foot expansion, the area of another 117 football fields, connected by pedestrian skyway to the present building. "The second phase will not be a duplicate of what we have," says Cahill. "We have plans for at least three hotels, a performing arts center, a business office complex, an art or history museum, and possibly even a television broadcast facility."

IKEA just opened a 336,000 square foot furniture store in the expansion phase, and Caesar's is exploring adding a casino, hotel, and entertainment complex. Both reinforce that Mall of America is a destination for shopping and a whole lot more. In addition, the mall has taken out a $100 million terrorist insurance policy and moved the transit hub outside the mall in the wake of 9/11.

Questions

1 Why has Mall of America been such a marketing success so far?

2 What (*a*) retail and (*b*) consumer trends have occurred since Mall of America was opened in 1992 that it should consider when making future plans?

3 (*a*) What criteria should Mall of America use in adding new facilities to its complex? (*b*) Evaluate (*i*) retail stores, (*ii*) entertainment offerings, and (*iii*) hotels on these criteria.

4 What specific marketing actions would you propose that Mall of America managers take to ensure its continuing success in attracting visitors (*a*) from the local metropolitan area and (*b*) from outside of it?

INTEGRATED MARKETING COMMUNICATIONS AND DIRECT MARKETING

LEARNING OBJECTIVES

After reading this chapter you should be able to:

1 Discuss integrated marketing communication and the communication process.

2 Describe the promotional mix and the uniqueness of each component.

3 Select the promotional approach appropriate to a product's life-cycle stage and characteristics.

4 Discuss the characteristics of push and pull strategies.

5 Describe the elements of the promotion decision process.

6 Explain the value of direct marketing for consumers and sellers.

WHO IS GOING TO DISNEY WORLD NEXT?

Since 1987 there have been more than 34 episodes of Disney's "What's Next?" campaign—you know, the commercials where a successful athlete is asked "What are you going to do next?" and they shout, "I'm going to Disney World!" The first to go was New York Giants' quarterback Phil Simms, and since then athletes such as Michael Jordan, Barry Bonds, Joe Montana, John Elway, Mark McGwire, and Tom Brady have been featured in the campaign. Ken Potrock, senior vice president of Walt Disney World Alliance Marketing, explains that "we select players based on success on the field and a Cinderella-type story." While players have been selected from the last 18 Super Bowls, standouts from Major League Baseball, the NBA, the NHL, the Olympics, and World Cup events have also been in the commercials.

The What's Next? campaign is just one of many forms of communication Disney uses to get its message to Disney fans. Other forms of communication include partnerships with other companies, direct marketing, Internet promotions, online games, and additional advertising. Disney uses its marketing expertise to integrate the plan and provide a consistent message and image to its many consumers.

The most recent plan calls for a $250 million, 15-month campaign targeted at people who travel in large groups or as an extended family. The advertising includes five different spots for network and cable TV, print ads, and newspaper inserts. The partnerships include agreements with Visa, Bank One, Kellogg's, Nestlé, Smuckers, and others who will be part of the

"Magical Gatherings" campaign. Direct-marketing activities include special offers mailed to many of the 31 million households in Disney's database. The website disneyworld.com provides information and services to help groups plan vacations and offers special events such as private breakfasts with costumed characters, evening cruises to watch fireworks, and after-hours safari treks.

Disney applies a similar, integrated approach to the marketing of all its products, services, and events. Other promotional activities include advertising on Radio Disney, sponsorship of documentaries on the ABC television network, Internet-linked kiosks to allow potential customers to check for location and availability of products at its stores, and contests and giveaways. Another component of Disney's promotion plan is a Visa card that allows users to accumulate "Disney Dream Reward Dollars" they can redeem for merchandise, tickets, and hotel rooms at Disney's theme parks and stores. In addition, Disney stores use in-store promotion that complements the online offerings (at disneystore.com) and the Disney catalogs.

Disney also uses "team" promotion deals, partnerships, and joint ventures. A team of companies, for example, was used to promote the movie *Finding Nemo*. Frito-Lay put 50 million stickers announcing a Nemo sweepstakes on packages of Lay's and Doritos; Wal-Mart distributed 3-D glasses to children to use to find hidden images of Nemo; and McDonald's offered plastic versions of the Nemo characters as Happy Meal premiums. Disney's partnerships have led to Disney On Ice, Disney's Broadway shows, and, most recently, Disney Live, which takes live stage shows to Asia and Africa and other locations where there is difficulty transporting the ice show and Broadway show. And Disney used a joint venture with Oriental Land to create and promote the new marine-themed DisneySea in Tokyo.[1]

The many types of promotion used by Disney demonstrate the opportunity for creativity in communicating with potential customers and the importance of integrating the various elements of a communication program. Promotion represents the fourth element in the marketing mix. The promotional element consists of communication tools, including advertising, personal selling, sales promotion, public relations, and direct marketing. The combination of one or more of these communication tools is called the **promotional mix**. All of these tools can be used to: (1) inform prospective buyers about the benefits of the product, (2) persuade them to try it, and (3) remind them later about the benefits they enjoyed by using the product. In the past, marketers often viewed the communication tools as separate and independent. The advertising department, for example, often designed and managed its activities without consulting departments or agencies that had responsibility for sales promotion or public relations. The result was often an overall communication effort that was uncoordinated and, in some cases, inconsistent. Today, the concept of designing marketing communications programs that coordinate all promotional activities—advertising, personal selling, sales promotion, public relations, and direct marketing—to provide a consistent message across all audiences is referred to as **integrated marketing communications (IMC)**.

This chapter provides an overview of the communication process, a description of the promotional mix elements, several tools for integrating the promotional mix, and a process for developing a comprehensive promotion program. One of the promotional mix elements, direct marketing, is also discussed in this chapter. Chapter 19 covers advertising, sales promotion, and public relations, and Chapter 20 discusses personal selling.

THE COMMUNICATION PROCESS

Communication is the process of conveying a message to others and requires six elements: a source, a message, a channel of communication, a receiver, and the processes of encoding and decoding[2] (Figure 18–1). The **source** may be a company or person who has information to convey. The information sent by a source, such as a description of a new cellular telephone, forms the **message**. The message is

FIGURE 18–1

The communication process

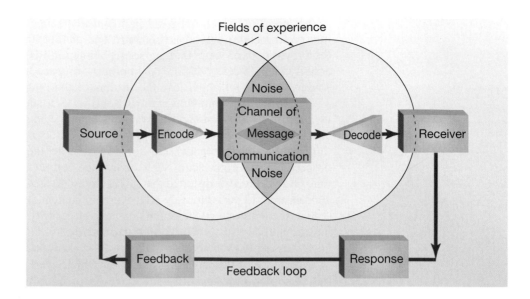

conveyed by means of a **channel of communication** such as a salesperson, advertising media, or public relations tools. Consumers who read, hear, or see the message are the **receivers**.

Encoding and Decoding

Encoding and decoding are essential to communication. **Encoding** is the process of having the sender transform an idea into a set of symbols. **Decoding** is the reverse, or the process of having the receiver take a set of symbols, the message, and transform them back to an idea. Look at the accompanying automobile advertisement: Who is the source, and what is the message?

Decoding is performed by the receivers according to their own frame of reference: their attitudes, values, and beliefs.[3] BMW is the source and the advertisement

A source and a message.

BMW

www.bmwusa.com

is the message, which appeared in *Wired* magazine (the channel). How would you interpret (decode) this advertisement? The picture and text in the advertisement on the previous page show that the source's intention is to generate interest in a sports activity vehicle designed for "Any corner. Any pace. Any passion."—a statement the source believes will appeal to the readers of the magazine.

The process of communication is not always a successful one. Errors in communication can happen in several ways. The source may not adequately transform the abstract idea into an effective set of symbols, a properly encoded message may be sent through the wrong channel and never make it to the receiver, the receiver may not properly transform the set of symbols into the correct abstract idea, or finally, feedback may be so delayed or distorted that it is of no use to the sender. Although communication appears easy to perform, truly effective communication can be very difficult.

For the message to be communicated effectively, the sender and receiver must have a mutually shared **field of experience**—a similar understanding and knowledge they apply to the message. Figure 18–1 shows two circles representing the fields of experience of the sender and receiver, which overlap in the message. Some of the better-known message problems have occurred when U.S. companies have taken their messages to cultures with different fields of experience. Many misinterpretations are merely the result of bad translations. For example, KFC made a mistake when its "finger-lickin' good" slogan was translated into Mandarin Chinese as "eat your fingers off!"[4]

Feedback

Figure 18–1 shows a line labeled *feedback loop,* which consists of a response and feedback. A **response** is the impact the message had on the receiver's knowledge, attitudes, or behaviors. **Feedback** is the sender's interpretation of the response and indicates whether the message was decoded and understood as intended. Chapter 19 reviews approaches called *pretesting* that ensure that messages are decoded properly.

Noise

Noise includes extraneous factors that can work against effective communication by distorting a message or the feedback received (Figure 18–1). Noise can be a simple error, such as a printing mistake that affects the meaning of a newspaper advertisement, or using words or pictures that fail to communicate the message clearly. Noise can also occur when a salesperson's message is misunderstood by a prospective buyer, such as when a salesperson's accent, use of slang terms, or communication style make hearing and understanding the message difficult.

(Concept Check)

1. What are the six elements required for communication to occur?

2. A difficulty for U.S. companies advertising in international markets is that the audience does not share the same _____.

3. A misprint in a newspaper ad is an example of _____.

THE PROMOTIONAL ELEMENTS

To communicate with consumers, a company can use one or more of five promotional alternatives: advertising, personal selling, public relations, sales promotion, and direct marketing. Figure 18–2 summarizes the distinctions among these five elements. Three of these elements—advertising, sales promotion, and public relations—are often said to use *mass selling* because they are used with groups of prospective

PROMOTIONAL ELEMENT	MASS VERSUS CUSTOMIZED	PAYMENT	STRENGTHS	WEAKNESSES
Advertising	Mass	Fees paid for space or time	• Efficient means for reaching large numbers of people	• High absolute costs • Difficult to receive good feedback
Personal selling	Customized	Fees paid to salespeople as either salaries or commissions	• Immediate feedback • Very persuasive • Can select audience • Can give complex information	• Extremely expensive per exposure • Messages may differ between salespeople
Public relations	Mass	No direct payment to media	• Often most credible source in the consumer's mind	• Difficult to get media cooperation
Sales promotion	Mass	Wide range of fees paid, depending on promotion selected	• Effective at changing behavior in short run • Very flexible	• Easily abused • Can lead to promotion wars • Easily duplicated
Direct marketing	Customized	Cost of communication through mail, telephone, or computer	• Messages can be prepared quickly • Facilitates relationship with customer	• Declining customer response • Database management is expensive

FIGURE 18–2

The promotional mix

buyers. In contrast, personal selling uses *customized interaction* between a seller and a prospective buyer. Personal selling activities include face-to-face, telephone, and interactive electronic communication. Direct marketing also uses messages customized for specific customers.

Advertising

Advertising is any paid form of nonpersonal communication about an organization, good, service, or idea by an identified sponsor. The *paid* aspect of this definition is important because the space for the advertising message normally must be bought. An occasional exception is the public service announcement, where the advertising time or space is donated. A full-page, four-color ad in *Time* magazine, for example, costs $223,000. The *nonpersonal* component of advertising is also important. Advertising involves mass media (such as TV, radio, and magazines), which are nonpersonal and do not have an immediate feedback loop as does personal selling. So before the message is sent, marketing research plays a valuable role; for example, it determines that the target market will actually see the medium chosen, and that the message will be understood.

There are several advantages to a firm using advertising in its promotional mix. It can be attention-getting—as with this Best Buy ad—and also can communicate specific product benefits to prospective buyers. By paying for the advertising space, a company can control *what* it wants to say and, to some extent, to *whom* the message is sent. If an electronics company wants college students to receive its message about CD players, advertising space is purchased in a college campus newspaper. Advertising also allows the company to decide *when* to send its message (which includes how often). The nonpersonal aspect of advertising also has its advantages. Once the message is created, the same message is sent to all receivers in a market segment. If the pictorial, text, and brand elements of an advertisement are properly pretested, an advertiser can ensure the ad's ability to capture consumers' attention[5] and trust that the same message will be decoded by all receivers in the market segment.

Advertising has some disadvantages. As shown in Figure 18–2 and discussed in depth in Chapter 19, the costs to produce and place a message are significant, and the lack of direct feedback makes it difficult to know how well the message was received.

Personal Selling

The second major promotional alternative is **personal selling**, defined as the two-way flow of communication between a buyer and seller, designed to influence a person's or group's purchase decision. Unlike advertising, personal selling is usually face-to-face communication between the sender and receiver. Why do companies use personal selling?

There are important advantages to personal selling, as summarized in Figure 18–2. A salesperson can control to *whom* the presentation is made. Although some control is available in advertising by choosing the medium, some people may read the college newspaper, for example, who are not in the target audience for CD players. For the CD-player manufacturer, those readers outside the target audience are *wasted coverage*. Wasted coverage can be reduced with personal selling. The personal component of selling has another advantage over advertising in that the seller can see or hear the potential buyer's reaction to the message. If the feedback is unfavorable, the salesperson can modify the message.

The flexibility of personal selling can also be a disadvantage. Different salespeople can change the message so that no consistent communication is given to all customers. The high cost of personal selling is probably its major disadvantage. On a cost-per-contact basis, it is generally the most expensive of the five promotional elements.

Public Relations

Public relations is a form of communication management that seeks to influence the feelings, opinions, or beliefs held by customers, prospective customers, stockholders, suppliers, employees, and other publics about a company and its products or services.[6] Many tools such as special events, lobbying efforts, annual reports, press conferences,[7] and image management may be used by a public relations department, although publicity often plays the most important role. **Publicity** is a nonpersonal, indirectly paid presentation of an organization, good, or service. It can take the form of a news story, editorial, or product announcement. A difference between publicity and both advertising and personal selling is the "indirectly paid" dimension. With publicity a company does not pay for space in a mass medium (such as television or radio) but attempts to get the medium to run a favorable story on the company. In this sense, there is an indirect payment for publicity in that a company must support a public relations staff.

An advantage of publicity is credibility. When you read a favorable story about a company's product (such as a glowing restaurant review), there is a tendency to believe it. Travelers throughout the world have relied on Arthur Frommer's guides such as *Ireland from $80 a Day*. These books outline out-of-the-way, inexpensive restaurants, hotels, inns, and bed-and-breakfast rooms, giving invaluable publicity to these establishments. Such businesses do not (nor can they) buy a mention in the guide, which in recent years has sold millions of copies.

The disadvantage of publicity relates to the lack of the user's control over it. A company can invite a news team to preview its innovative exercise equipment and hope for a favorable mention on the 6 P.M. newscasts. But without buying advertising time, there is no guarantee of any mention of the new equipment or that it will be aired when the target audience is watching. The company representative who calls the station and asks for a replay of the story may be told, "Sorry, it's only news once." With publicity there is little control over what is said, to whom, or when. As a result, publicity is rarely the main component of a promotional campaign.

Sales Promotion

A fourth promotional element is **sales promotion**, a short-term inducement of value offered to arouse interest in buying a good or service. Used in conjunction with advertising or personal selling, sales promotions are offered to intermediaries as well as to ultimate consumers. Coupons, rebates, samples, and sweepstakes are just a few examples of sales promotions discussed later in this chapter.

The advantage of sales promotion is that the short-term nature of these programs (such as a coupon or sweepstakes with an expiration date) often stimulates sales for their duration. Offering value to the consumer in terms of a cents-off coupon or rebate may increase store traffic from consumers who are not store-loyal.[8]

Sales promotions cannot be the sole basis for a campaign because gains are often temporary and sales drop off when the deal ends.[9] Advertising support is needed to convert the customer who tried the product because of a sales promotion into a long-term buyer.[10] If sales promotions are conducted continuously, they lose their effectiveness. Customers begin to delay purchase until a coupon is offered, or they question the product's value. Some aspects of sales promotions also are regulated by the federal government. These issues are reviewed in detail later in Chapter 19.

Direct Marketing

Another promotional alternative, **direct marketing**, uses direct communication with consumers to generate a response in the form of an order, a request for further information, or a visit to a retail outlet.[11] The communication can take many forms including face-to-face selling, direct mail, catalogs, telephone solicitations, direct response advertising (on television and radio and in print), and online marketing. Like personal selling, direct marketing often consists of interactive communication. It also has the advantage of being customized to match the needs of specific target markets. Messages can be developed and adapted quickly to facilitate one-to-one relationships with customers.

While direct marketing has been one of the fastest-growing forms of promotion, it has several disadvantages. First, most forms of direct marketing require a comprehensive and up-to-date database with information about the target market. Developing and maintaining the database can be expensive and time consuming. In addition, growing concern about privacy has led to a decline in response rates among some customer groups. Companies with successful direct marketing programs are sensitive to these issues and often use a combination of direct marketing alternatives together, or direct marketing combined with other promotional tools, to increase value for customers.

Concept Check

1. Explain the difference between advertising and publicity when both appear on television.

2. Which promotional element should be offered only on a short-term basis?

3. Cost per contact is high with the _____ element of the promotional mix.

INTEGRATED MARKETING COMMUNICATIONS— DEVELOPING THE PROMOTIONAL MIX

A firm's promotional mix is the combination of one or more of the promotional tools it chooses to use. In putting together the promotional mix, a marketer must consider two issues. First, the balance of the elements must be determined. Should advertising be emphasized more than personal selling? Should a promotional rebate be offered? Would public relations activities be effective? Several factors affect such decisions: the target audience for the promotion,[12] the stage of the product's life cycle, characteristics of the product, decision stage of the buyer, and even the channel of distribution. Second, because the various promotional elements are often the responsibility of different departments, coordinating a consistent promotional effort is necessary. A promotional planning process designed to ensure integrated marketing communications can facilitate this goal.

The Target Audience

Promotional programs are directed to the ultimate consumer, to an intermediary (retailer, wholesaler, or industrial distributor), or to both. Promotional programs directed to buyers of consumer products often use mass media because the number of potential buyers is large. Personal selling is used at the place of purchase, generally the retail store. Direct marketing may be used to encourage first-time or repeat purchases. Combinations of many media alternatives are a necessity for some target audiences today. The Marketing NewsNet describes how Generation Y consumers give media only partial attention but can be reached through integrated programs.[13]

Advertising directed to business buyers is used selectively in trade publications, such as *Fence* magazine for buyers of fencing material. Because business buyers often have specialized needs or technical questions, personal selling is particularly important. The salesperson can provide information and the necessary support after sales.

Intermediaries are often the focus of promotional efforts. As with business buyers, personal selling is the major promotional ingredient. The salespeople assist intermediaries in making a profit by coordinating promotional campaigns sponsored by the manufacturer and by providing marketing advice and expertise. Intermediaries' questions often pertain to the allowed markup, merchandising support, and return policies.

The Product Life Cycle

All products have a product life cycle (see Chapter 11), and the composition of the promotional mix changes over the four life-cycle stages, as shown for Purina Dog Chow in Figure 18–3 on page 478.

Introduction Stage Informing consumers in an effort to increase their level of awareness is the primary promotional objective in the introduction stage of the product life cycle. In general, all the promotional mix elements are used at this time, although the use of specific mix elements during any stage depends on the product and situation. News releases about Purina's new nutritional product are sent to veterinary magazines, trial samples are sent to registered dog owners, advertisements are placed in *Dog World* magazine, and the salesforce begins to approach supermarkets to get orders. Advertising is particularly important as a means of reaching as many people as possible to build up awareness and interest. Publicity may even begin slightly before the product is commercially available.

Growth Stage The primary promotional objective of the growth stage is to persuade the consumer to buy the product—Purina Dog Chow—rather than substitutes,

MARKETING NEWSNET

Gen Y Applies Multitasking to Media Consumption—29 Hours per Day!

CROSS FUNCTIONAL

Consumers are increasingly multitasking, or doing many things at the same time. The concept of multitasking applied to communication—watching TV while surfing the Internet, or reading a magazine while listening to the radio—has led to the term *simultaneous media usage* (SIMM). Generation Y seems to be particularly adept at SIMM as recent research found that 75 percent of the age group does something else while watching TV. In fact, SIMM has created 29.8 hour "media days" for this group. One reason is that media are pervasive—the average student may be exposed to 5,000 messages each day—but other reasons are the desires to be informed and to keep in touch. As a result, consumers in this group probably don't give full attention to any single message. Instead, they use continuous partial attention to scan the media.

Marketers can still communicate with Gen Y by utilizing a variety of promotional tools—from advertising to packaging to word-of-mouth communication—with an integrated message. Which media work particularly well with Gen Y? The most popular television channel is MTV. The most popular magazines are *Sports Illustrated* and *Seventeen*. Favorite websites include anything with content related to

their interests: celebrities, music, sports, and games. Another approach growing in popularity is viral, or "buzz," marketing. When BMW dealers started selling the new MINI convertible, for example, they held contests to see how long drivers could go before putting the top up. The drivers and potential buyers started talking about the contests and the new car, for at least part of the 29.8 hour day.

so the marketing manager seeks to gain brand preference and solidify distribution. Sales promotion assumes less importance in this stage, and publicity is not a factor because it depends on novelty of the product. The primary promotional element is advertising, which stresses brand differences. Personal selling is used to solidify the channel of distribution. For consumer products such as dog food, the salesforce calls on the wholesalers and retailers in hopes of increasing inventory levels and gaining shelf space. For business products, the salesforce often tries to get contractual arrangements to be the sole source of supply for the buyer.

Purina Dog Chow: in the maturity stage of its product life cycle.

Maturity Stage   In the maturity stage, the need is to maintain existing buyers, and advertising's role is to remind buyers of the product's existence. Sales promotion, in the form of discounts and coupons offered to both ultimate consumers and intermediaries, is important in maintaining loyal buyers. In a test of one mature consumer product, it was found that 80 percent of the product's sales at this stage resulted from sales promotions.[14] For the past eight years, Purina has sponsored the Incredible Dog Challenge, which is now covered by ESPN and USA Network.[15] Direct marketing actions such as direct mail are used to maintain involvement with existing customers and to encourage repeat purchases. Price cuts and discounts can also significantly increase a mature brand's sales. The salesforce at this stage seeks to satisfy intermediaries. An unsatisfied customer who switches brands is hard to replace.

Decline Stage   The decline stage of the product life cycle is usually a period of phaseout for the product, and little money is spent in the promotional mix. The rate

FIGURE 18–3

Promotional tools used over
the product life cycle of Purina
Dog Chow

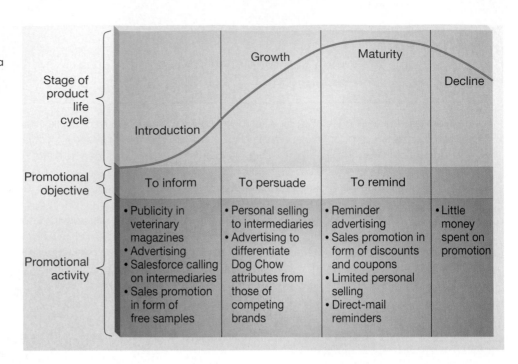

of decline can be rapid when a product is replaced by an improved or lower cost product, for example, or slow if there is a loyal group of customers.

Product Characteristics

The proper blend of elements in the promotional mix also depends on the type of product. Three specific characteristics should be considered: complexity, risk, and ancillary services. *Complexity* refers to the technical sophistication of the product and hence the amount of understanding required to use it. It's hard to provide much information in a one-page magazine ad or a 30-second television ad, so the more complex the product, the greater the emphasis on personal selling. Gulfstream asks potential customers to call their senior vice president in its ads. No information is provided for simple products such as Heinz ketchup.

A second element is the degree of risk represented by the product's purchase. *Risk* for the buyer can be assessed in terms of financial risk, social risk, and physical risk. A private jet, for example, might represent all three risks—it is expensive, employees and customers may see and evaluate the purchase, and safety and reliability are important. Although advertising helps, the greater the risk, the greater the need for personal selling. Consumers are unlikely to associate any of these risks with ketchup.

The level of ancillary services required by a product also affects the promotional strategy. *Ancillary services* pertain to the degree of service or support required after the sale. This characteristic is common to many industrial products and consumer purchases. Who will provide maintenance for the plane? Advertising's role is to establish the seller's reputation. Direct marketing can be used to describe how a product or service can be customized to individual needs. However, personal selling is essential to build buyer confidence and provide evidence of customer service.

Stages of the Buying Decision

Knowing the customer's stage of decision making can also affect the promotional mix. Figure 18–4 shows how the importance of the promotional elements varies with the three stages in a consumer's purchase decision.

How do Gulfstream aircraft and Heinz ketchup differ on complexity, risk, and ancillary services?

Gulfstream
www.gulfstreamvsp.com

Heinz
www.heinz.com

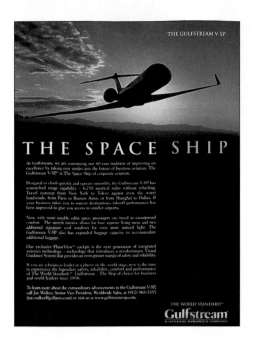

Prepurchase Stage   In the prepurchase stage, advertising is more helpful than personal selling because advertising informs the potential customer of the existence of the product and the seller. Sales promotion in the form of free samples also can play an important role to gain low-risk trial. When the salesperson calls on the customer after heavy advertising, there is some recognition of what the salesperson represents. This is particularly important in industrial settings in which sampling of the product is usually not possible.

Purchase Stage   At the purchase stage, the importance of personal selling is highest, whereas the impact of advertising is lowest. Sales promotion in the form of coupons, deals, point-of-purchase displays, and rebates can be very helpful in encouraging demand. In this stage, although advertising is not an active influence on the purchase, it is the means of delivering the coupons, deals, and rebates that are often important.

FIGURE 18–4
How the importance of promotional elements varies during the stages of a consumer's purchase decision

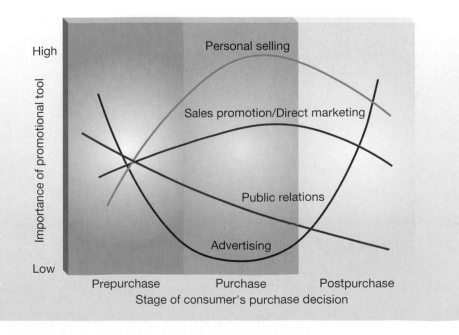

Postpurchase Stage   In the postpurchase stage, the salesperson is still important. In fact, the more personal contact after the sale, the more the buyer is satisfied. Advertising is also important to assure the buyer that the right purchase was made. Advertising and personal selling help reduce the buyer's postpurchase anxiety.[16] Sales promotion in the form of coupons and direct marketing reminders can help encourage repeat purchases from satisfied first-time triers. Public relations plays a small role in the postpurchase stage.

Channel Strategies

Chapter 15 discussed the channel flow from a producer to intermediaries to consumers. Achieving control of the channel is often difficult for the manufacturer, and promotional strategies can assist in moving a product through the channel of distribution. This is where a manufacturer has to make an important decision about whether to use a push strategy, pull strategy, or both in its channel of distribution.[17]

Push Strategy   Figure 18–5A shows how a manufacturer uses a **push strategy**, directing the promotional mix to channel members to gain their cooperation in ordering and stocking the product. In this approach, personal selling and sales promotions play major roles. Salespeople call on wholesalers to encourage orders and provide sales assistance. Sales promotions, such as case discount allowances (20 percent off the regular case price), are offered to stimulate demand. By pushing the product through the channel, the goal is to get channel members to push it to their customers.

Anheuser-Busch, for example, spends a significant amount of its marketing resources on maintaining its relationship with its distributors, and through them, with retailers. At a meeting of its wholesalers and salespeople, Anheuser-Busch announced that it would provide $250 million of marketing support for its Budweiser brand—an action designed to maintain channel dominance. The company also arranges group discounts on purchase of trucks, insurance, and the computers that wholesalers use to order beer. Even specialized computer software is provided to help retailers maximize the shelf space of Anheuser-Busch products.[18]

FIGURE 18–5

A comparison of push and pull promotional strategies

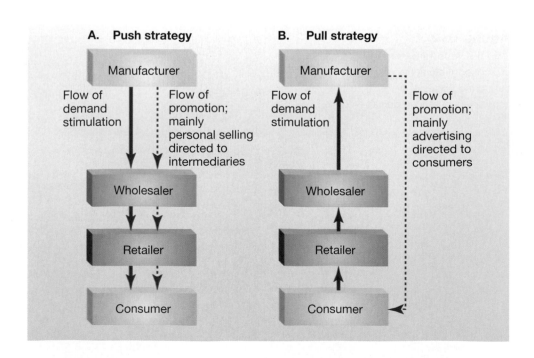

WEB LINK   Direct-to-Consumer Drug Marketing Moves to the Internet

www.mhhe.com/Kerin

Direct-to-consumer prescription drug advertising has made many drugs well-known brand names, such as Lipitor, Zocor, Prevacid, and Celebrex. The success of the approach has prompted pharmaceutical companies to expand to the Internet. Many drugs now have their own websites (e.g., www.lipitor.com, www.zocor.com), and there are many websites that provide information or fill prescriptions.

Drugstore.com, for example, was recently selected as one of the top 50 retailing websites, and the state of New Hampshire has a link on its website to www.canadadrugs.com. Choose a drug you or a family member has used and visit two websites to collect and compare information about side effects, prices, delivery, and so forth.

Transderm Scop
www.transdermscop.com

Pull Strategy   In some instances, manufacturers face resistance from channel members who do not want to order a new product or increase inventory levels of an existing brand. As shown in Figure 18–5B, a manufacturer may then elect to implement a **pull strategy** by directing its promotional mix at ultimate consumers to encourage them to ask the retailer for a product. Seeing demand from ultimate consumers, retailers order the product from wholesalers and thus the item is pulled through the intermediaries. Pharmaceutical companies, for example, now spend more than $1.2 billion annually on *direct-to-consumer* prescription drug advertising, to complement traditional personal selling and free samples directed only at doctors.[19] The strategy is designed to encourage consumers to ask their doctor for a specific drug by name—pulling it through the channel. Successful campaigns such as the adjacent print ad, which says "Ask your doctor about Transderm Scop, The Travel Patch," can have dramatic effects on the sales of a product. The accompanying Web Link describes how direct-to-consumer campaigns also utilize the Internet.[20]

Concept Check

1. Describe the promotional objective for each stage of the product life cycle.

2. At what stage of the consumer purchase decision is the importance of personal selling highest? Why?

3. Explain the differences between a push strategy and a pull strategy.

DEVELOPING AN IMC PROGRAM

Because media costs are high, promotion decisions must be made carefully, using a systematic approach. Paralleling the planning, implementation, and control steps described in the strategic marketing process (Chapter 2), the promotion decision process is divided into (1) developing, (2) executing, and (3) evaluating the promotion program (Figure 18–6 on the next page). Development of the promotion program focuses on the four *W*s:

- *Who* is the target audience?
- *What* are (1) the promotion objectives, (2) the amounts of money that can be budgeted for the promotion program, and (3) the kinds of promotion to use?
- *Where* should the promotion be run?
- *When* should the promotion be run?

FIGURE 18-6

The promotion decision process

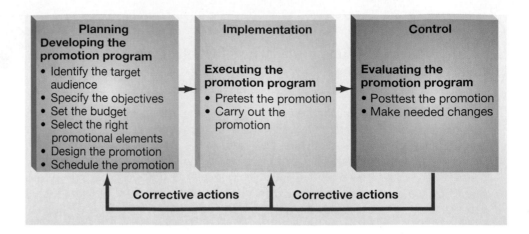

Identifying the Target Audience

The first decision in developing the promotion program is identifying the *target audience,* the group of prospective buyers toward which a promotion program is directed. To the extent that time and money permit, the target audience for the promotion program is the target market for the firm's product, which is identified from marketing research and market segmentation studies. The more a firm knows about its target audiences—including their lifestyle, attitudes, and values—the easier it is to develop a promotion program. If a firm wanted to reach you with television and magazine ads, for example, it would need to know what TV shows you watch and what magazines you read.

Specifying Promotion Objectives

After the target audience is identified, a decision must be reached on what the promotion should accomplish. Consumers can be said to respond in terms of a **hierarchy of effects**, which is the sequence of stages a prospective buyer goes through from initial awareness of a product to eventual action (either trial or adoption of the product).[21] The five stages are:

- *Awareness.* The consumer's ability to recognize and remember the product or brand name.
- *Interest.* An increase in the consumer's desire to learn about some of the features of the product or brand.
- *Evaluation.* The consumer's appraisal of the product or brand on important attributes.
- *Trial.* The consumer's actual first purchase and use of the product or brand.
- *Adoption.* Through a favorable experience on the first trial, the consumer's repeated purchase and use of the product or brand.

For a totally new product, the sequence applies to the entire product category, but for a new brand competing in an established product category it applies to the brand itself. These steps can serve as guidelines for developing promotion objectives.

Although sometimes an objective for a promotion program involves several steps in the hierarchy of effects, it often focuses on a single stage. Regardless of what the specific objective might be, from building awareness to increasing repeat purchases,[22] promotion objectives should possess three important qualities. They should (1) be designed for a well-defined target audience, (2) be measurable, and (3) cover a specified time period.

Setting the Promotion Budget

From Figure 18–7 it is clear that the promotion expenditures needed to reach U.S. households are enormous. Note that seven companies—General Motors, Procter & Gamble, Time Warner, Pfizer, DaimlerChrysler, Ford, and Disney—each spend a total of more than $2 billion annually on promotion.[23]

After setting the promotion objectives, a company must decide on how much to spend. Determining the ideal amount for the budget is difficult because there is no precise way to measure the exact results of spending promotion dollars. However, there are several methods used to set the promotion budget.[24]

Percentage of Sales   In the **percentage of sales budgeting** approach, funds are allocated to promotion as a percentage of past or anticipated sales, in terms of either dollars or units sold. A common budgeting method,[25] this approach is often stated in terms such as "Our promotion budget for this year is 3 percent of last year's gross sales." The advantage of this approach is obvious: It is simple and provides a financial safeguard by tying the promotion budget to sales. However, there is a major fallacy in this approach, which implies that sales cause promotion. Using this method, a company may reduce its promotion budget because of a downturn in past sales or an anticipated downturn in future sales—situations in which it may need promotion the most.

Competitive Parity   A second common approach, **competitive parity budgeting**, is matching the competitor's absolute level of spending or the proportion per point of market share. This approach has also been referred to as *matching competitors* or *share of market*. It is important to consider the competition in budgeting.[26] Consumer responses to promotion are affected by competing promotional activities, so if a competitor runs 30 radio ads each week, it may be difficult for a firm to get its message across with only five messages.[27] The competitor's budget level, however, should not be the only determinant in setting a company's budget. The competition might have very different promotional objectives, which require a different level of promotion expenditures.

FIGURE 18–7

U.S. promotion expenditures by companies in 2003

RANK	COMPANY	ADVERTISING (MILLIONS)	+	ALL OTHER PROMOTION (MILLIONS)	=	TOTAL (MILLIONS)
1	General Motors	$2,367		$1,063		$3,430
2	Procter & Gamble	2,684		639		3,323
3	Time Warner	1,847		1,250		3,097
4	Pfizer	1,012		1,827		2,839
5	DaimlerChrysler	1,608		710		2,318
6	Ford	1,445		789		2,234
7	Disney	1,392		737		2,129
8	Johnson & Johnson	1,252		744		1,996
9	Sony	1,004		811		1,815
10	Toyota	1,014		669		1,683
11	Verizon	1,198		476		1,674
12	Sears	786		848		1,634
13	General Electric	788		788		1,576
14	GlaxoSmithKline	776		778		1,554
15	SBC Communications	1,038		473		1,511

All You Can Afford   Common to many small businesses is **all-you-can-afford budgeting**, in which money is allocated to promotion only after all other budget items are covered. As one company executive said in reference to this budgeting process, "Why, it's simple. First, I go upstairs to the controller and ask how much they can afford to give us this year. She says a million and a half. Later, the boss comes to me and asks how much we should spend, and I say 'Oh, about a million and a half.' Then we have our promotion appropriation."[28]

Fiscally conservative, this approach has little else to offer. Using this budgeting philosophy, a company acts as though it doesn't know anything about a promotion-sales relationship or what its promotion objectives are.

Objective and Task   The best approach to budgeting is **objective and task budgeting**, whereby the company (1) determines its promotion objectives, (2) outlines the tasks to accomplish these objectives, and (3) determines the promotion cost of performing these tasks.[29]

This method takes into account what the company wants to accomplish and requires that the objectives be specified.[30] Strengths of the other budgeting methods are integrated into this approach because each previous method's strength is tied to the objectives. For example, if the costs are beyond what the company can afford, objectives are reworked and the tasks revised. The difficulty with this method is the judgment required to determine the tasks needed to accomplish objectives. Would two or four insertions in *Time* magazine be needed to achieve a specific awareness level? Figure 18–8 shows a sample media plan with objectives, tasks, and budget outlined. The total amount to be budgeted is $430,000. If the company can only afford $300,000, the objectives must be reworked, tasks redefined, and the total budget recalculated.

Selecting the Right Promotional Tools

Once a budget has been determined, the combination of the five basic IMC tools—advertising, personal selling, sales promotion, public relations, and direct marketing—can be specified. While many factors provide direction for selection of the appropriate mix, the large number of possible combinations of the promotional tools means that many combinations can achieve the same objective. Therefore, an analytical approach and experience are particularly important in this step of the promotion decision process. The specific mix can vary from a simple program using a single tool to a comprehensive program using all forms of promotion. The Olympics have become a very visible example of a comprehensive integrated communication program. Because the Games are repeated every two years, the promotion is almost continuous. Included in the program are advertising campaigns, personal selling efforts by the Olympic committee and organizers, sales promotion activities such as product tie-ins and sponsorships, public relations programs managed by the host cities, and direct marketing efforts targeted at a variety of audiences including governments, organizations, firms, athletes, and individuals.[31] At this stage, it is also important to assess the relative importance of the various tools. While it may be desirable to utilize and

FIGURE 18–8

The objective and task approach

OBJECTIVE	
To increase awareness among college students for a new video game. Awareness at the end of one semester should be 20 percent of all students from the existing 0 percent today.	
TASKS	**COSTS**
Advertisements once a week for a semester in 500 college papers	$280,000
Direct-mail samples to student leaders on 500 college campuses	50,000
Sponsor a national contest for video-game players	100,000
Total budget	$430,000

integrate several forms of promotion, one may deserve emphasis. The Olympics, for example, place exceptional importance on public relations and publicity.

Designing the Promotion

The central element of a promotion program is the promotion itself. Advertising consists of advertising copy and the artwork that the target audience is intended to see or hear. Personal selling efforts depend on the characteristics and skills of the salesperson. Sales promotion activities consist of the specific details of inducements such as coupons, samples, and sweepstakes. Public relations efforts are readily seen in tangible elements such as news releases, and direct marketing actions depend on written, verbal, and electronic forms of delivery. The design of the promotion will play a primary role in determining the message that is communicated to the audience. This design activity is frequently viewed as the step requiring the most creativity. In addition, successful designs are often the result of insight regarding consumer's interests and purchasing behavior. All of the promotion tools have many design alternatives. Advertising, for example, can utilize fear, humor, attractiveness, or other themes in its appeal.[32] Similarly, direct marketing can be designed for varying levels of personal or customized appeals. One of the challenges of IMC is to design each promotional activity to communicate the same message.

Scheduling the Promotion

Once the design of each of the promotional program elements is complete, it is important to determine the most effective timing of their use. The promotion schedule describes the order in which each promotional tool is introduced and the frequency of its use during the campaign. New Line Cinema, for example, developed one of the longest promotion schedules on record for its *Lord of the Rings* movie trilogy. To generate interest in each movie before its release, a movie "trailer" was shown on television and in theaters. Then movie-related products were released, followed by special promotions by Burger King, General Mills, and the NBA. Now that all three movies have been released, New Line is running a 30-second ad with high-definition footage to promote DVD sales.[33]

Overall, the scheduling of the various promotions was designed to generate interest, bring consumers into theaters, and then encourage additional purchases after seeing the movie. Several factors such as seasonality and competitive promotion activity can also influence the promotion schedule. Businesses such as ski resorts, airlines, and professional sports teams are likely to reduce their promotional activity during the "off" season. Similarly, restaurants, retail stores, and health clubs are likely to increase their promotional activity when new competitors enter the market.

EXECUTING AND EVALUATING THE PROMOTION PROGRAM

Carrying out the promotion program can be expensive and time consuming. One researcher estimates that "an organization with sales less than $10 million can successfully implement an IMC program in one year, one with sales between $200 million and $500 million will need about three years, and one with sales between $2 billion and $5 billion will need five years." To facilitate the transition, there are approximately 200 integrated marketing communications agencies in operation. In addition, some of the largest agencies are adopting approaches that embrace "total communications solutions." Starcom MediaVest, which recently won *Advertising Age* magazine's Media Agency of the Year award, for example, has created an integrated network of 3,800 employees who specialize in media management, Internet and digital communications, direct response media, entertainment marketing, sports sponsorships, event marketing, and multicultural marketing. One of their integrated campaigns for Coca-Cola Venezuela created a partnership with the *Who Wants to Be a Millionare* television program that led to increased awareness and preference for Coca-Cola in the teen market.[34] While many agencies still have departments dedicated to promotion, direct marketing, and other specialties, the trend today is clearly toward a long-term perspective in which all forms of promotion are integrated.[35]

An important factor in developing successful IMC programs is to create a process that facilitates their design and use. A tool used to evaluate a company's current process is the IMC audit. The audit analyzes the internal communication network of the company; identifies key audiences; evaluates customer databases; assesses messages in recent ads, public relations releases, packaging, video news releases, signage, sales promotion pieces, and direct mail; and determines the IMC expertise of company and agency personnel.[36] Although many organizations are interested in improving their IMC process, surveys suggest that fewer than one-third have been successful at implementing IMC. The reasons include lack of expertise, lack of budget, and lack of management approval.[37]

As shown earlier in Figure 18–6, the ideal execution of a promotion program involves pretesting each design before it is actually used to allow for changes and modifications which improve its effectiveness. Similarly, posttests are recommended to evaluate the impact of each promotion and the contribution of the promotion toward achieving the program objectives. The most sophisticated pretest and posttest procedures have been developed for advertising and are discussed in Chapter 19. Testing procedures for sales promotion and direct marketing efforts currently focus on comparisons of different designs or responses of different segments. To fully benefit from IMC programs, companies must create and maintain a test-result database that allows comparisons of the relative impact of the promotional tools and their execution options in varying situations. Information from the database will allow informed design and execution decisions and provide support for IMC activities during internal reviews by financial or administrative personnel. The San Diego Padres baseball team, for example, developed a database of information relating attendance to its integrated campaign using a new logo, special events, merchandise sales, and a loyalty program.

Currently, about one-fourth of all businesses assess program effectiveness by measuring "most of their communication tactics."[38] For most organizations, the assessment focuses on trying to determine which element of promotion works better. In an integrated program, however, media advertising might be used to build awareness, sales promotion to generate an inquiry, direct mail to provide additional information to individual prospects, and a personal sales call to complete the transaction. The tools are used for different reasons, and their combined use creates a synergy that should be the focus of the assessment.[39] Another level of assessment is necessary when firms have international promotion programs.

Concept Check

1. What are the characteristics of good promotion objectives?
2. What is the weakness of the percentage of sales budgeting approach?
3. How have advertising agencies changed to facilitate the use of IMC programs?

DIRECT MARKETING

Direct marketing has many forms and utilizes a variety of media. Several forms of direct marketing—direct mail and catalogs, television, telemarketing, and direct selling—were discussed as methods of nonstore retailing in Chapter 17. In addition, although advertising is discussed in Chapter 19, a form of advertising—direct response advertising—is an important form of direct marketing. Finally, interactive or online marketing is discussed in detail in Chapter 21. In this section, the growth of direct marketing, its value for consumers and sellers, and key global, technological, and ethical issues are discussed.

The Growth of Direct Marketing

The increasing interest in customer relationship management is reflected in the dramatic growth of direct marketing. The ability to customize communication efforts and create one-to-one interactions is appealing to most marketers, particularly those with IMC programs. While direct marketing methods are not new, the ability to design and use them has increased with the availability of databases. In recent years, direct marketing growth—in terms of spending, revenue generated, and employment—has outpaced total economic growth. Direct marketing expenditures of $217 billion in 2004 are expected to grow 18 percent by 2007. Similarly, 2004 revenues of $2.3 trillion are expected to grow to $3 trillion by 2007. Employment has also grown and now numbers more than 17 million employees. Figure 18–9 shows how the various forms of direct marketing contribute to the overall industry.[40]

Columbia House is one example of the kinds of companies fueling the growth in direct marketing. You may have received the company's letters in the mail offering 12 free music CDs if you agree to buy 5 additional CDs over the next two years. Columbia House also has similar offers for DVDs and videos. With more than 16 million club members, Columbia House is the largest direct marketer of entertainment products. Because one of its largest customer bases is the college student, its business typically surges about 30 percent in August when students return to college.[41]

Another component of the growth in direct marketing is the increasing popularity of the newest direct marketing channel—the Internet. As discussed in Chapter 21, total online sales have risen from close to nothing in 1996 to projections approaching $144 billion today. Continued growth in the number of consumers with Internet access and the number of businesses with websites and electronic commerce offerings is likely to contribute to the future growth of direct marketing.

The Value of Direct Marketing

FIGURE 18–9
Direct marketing expenditures, sales, and employment by medium

One of the most visible indicators of the value of direct marketing for consumers is the level of use of various forms of direct marketing. For example, 68 percent of the U.S. population has ordered merchandise or services by phone or mail; more

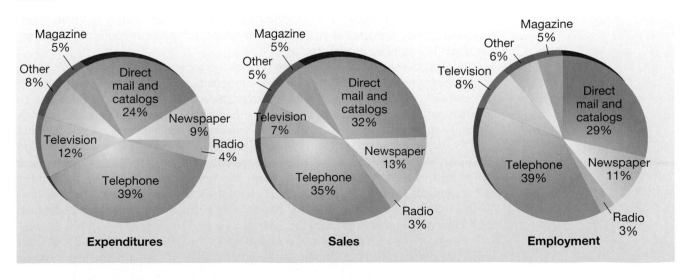

than 12 million adults have purchased items from a television offer; the average adult spends more than 30 hours per year accessing online services; and more than 21 percent of all adults make three to five purchases from a catalog each year. Consumers report many benefits, including the following: They don't have to go to a store, they can usually shop 24 hours a day, buying direct saves time, they avoid hassles with salespeople, they can save money, it's fun and entertaining, and direct marketing offers more privacy than in-store shopping. Many consumers also believe that direct marketing provides excellent customer service.[42] Toll-free telephone numbers, customer service representatives with access to information regarding purchasing preferences, overnight delivery services, and unconditional guarantees all help create value for direct marketing customers. At Landsend.com, when customers need assistance they can click a "help" icon and a sales rep will take control of their browser until the correct product is found. "It's like we were walking down the aisle in a store," says one Lands' End customer![43]

The value of direct marketing for sellers can be described in terms of the responses it generates.[44] **Direct orders** are the result of offers that contain all the information necessary for a prospective buyer to make a decision to purchase and complete the transaction. Club Med, for example, uses direct e-mail offers to sell "last-minute specials" to people in its database. The messages, which are sent midweek, describe rooms and air transportation available at a 30 to 40 percent discount if the customer can make the decision to travel on such short notice.[45] **Lead generation** is the result of an offer designed to generate interest in a product or service and a request for additional information. America Online announced a contest with direct advertising and used a direct-mail trial offer to generate interest in its latest release.[46] Finally, **traffic generation** is the outcome of an offer designed to motivate people to visit a business. Mitsubishi recently mailed a sweepstakes offer to 1 million prospective buyers to encourage them to visit a Mitsubishi dealer and test drive the new Galant. The names of prospects who took test drives were entered in the sweepstakes, which included a Galant, a trip to Hawaii, and large-screen TVs as prizes.[47]

Technological, Global, and Ethical Issues in Direct Marketing

The information technology and databases described in Chapter 8 are key elements in any direct marketing program. Databases are the result of organizations' efforts to collect demographic, media, and consumption profiles of customers so that direct marketing tools, such as catalogs, can be directed at specific customers. For example, Lillian Vernon started her very successful mail-order company four decades ago at her kitchen table by putting all her merchandise in a single catalog: Laundry baskets and men's slippers on one page might be followed by toys on the next. But in the last few years Lillian Vernon has shifted to a database approach with the 150 million catalogs she mails annually. There are now home-oriented, children's, and Christmas-ornament catalogs targeted at customers who have purchased these kinds of merchandise from her main catalog in the past.[48]

While most companies try to keep records of their customers' past purchases, many other types of data are needed to use direct marketing to develop one-to-one relationships with customers. Data, however, have little value by themselves. To translate data into information the data must be unbiased, timely, pertinent, accessible, and organized in a way that helps the marketing manager make decisions that lead to direct marketing actions. Some data, such as lifestyles, media use, and consumption behavior, must be collected in consumers' homes. Other types of data can be collected from the businesses where purchases are made. Today, technology such as optical scanners helps collect data with as little intrusion on the customer as possible. Safeway supermarkets, for example, use scanners to read bar codes and track customers' purchases in its database.

Technology may also prove to be important in the global growth of direct marketing. Compared with the United States, other countries' direct marketing systems

ETHICS AND SOCIAL RESPONSIBILITY ALERT

How Do You Like Your E-Mail? "Opt-out" or "Opt-in" Are Your Choices

ETHICS

More than 1 billion e-mail messages are sent each day in the United States. You've probably noticed that many of them are direct marketing messages—personalized offers from companies such as Pepsi, Victoria's Secret, Toyota, and the Phoenix Suns. In fact, e-mail advertisers spend more than $2 billion on their campaigns each year. One reason is that e-mail offers one-to-one conversations with each prospective consumer. Another reason is that the average cost per e-mail message is less than $.01 compared to $0.75 to $2.00 for direct mail and $1 to $3 for telemarketing.

Some consumers have complained that they are inundated with unsolicited messages, sometimes called "spam," and ignore them, while marketers believe that better management of e-mail campaigns will improve the value of e-mail advertising for customers. Two general approaches to

managing e-mail are being discussed. The "opt-out" system allows recipients to decline future messages after the first contact. The "opt-in" system requires advertisers to obtain e-mail addresses from registration questions on websites, business-reply cards, and even entry forms for contests or sweepstakes. Surveys indicate that about 77 percent of the unsolicited e-mails are deleted without being read, while only 2 percent of the e-mails received with the consumer's permission are deleted.

In January 2004, the Controlling the Assault of Non-Solicited Pornography and Marketing Act (CAN-SPAM) went into effect. The law does not prohibit spam but requires it to be truthful and to provide an opt-out return e-mail address. Some companies, however, have adopted opt-in policies. What is your opinion? Why?

are undeveloped. The mail and telephone systems in many countries are likely to improve, however, creating many new direct marketing opportunities. Developments in international marketing research and database management will also facilitate global growth. In Argentina, for example, mail service is very slow, telephone service is poor, and response to some forms of direct marketing such as coupons is negligible. The country is the first, however, to fully deregulate its postal service and expects rapid improvement from the private company, Correo Argentino. In Mexico, direct marketing activities are more advanced. Pond's recently mailed 20,000 direct-mail offers within Mexico and was surprised by a 33 percent response.[49] Another issue for global direct marketers is payment. Because fewer consumers have credit cards, alternatives such as C.O.D. and bank deposits are needed.

Global and domestic direct marketers both face challenging ethical issues today. Of course there has been considerable attention given to some annoying direct marketing activities such as telephone solicitations during dinner and evening hours. Concerns about privacy, however, have led to various attempts to provide guidelines that balance consumer and business interests. The European Union recently passed a consumer privacy law, called the Data Protection Directive, after several years of discussion with the Federation of European Direct Marketing and the U.K.'s Direct Marketing Association. In the United States, the Federal Trade Commission and many state legislatures have also been concerned about privacy.[50] Another issue, the proliferation of e-mail advertising, has received increasing attention from consumers and marketers recently. The accompanying Ethics and Social Responsibility Alert offers some of the details of the debate.[51]

Concept Check

1. The ability to design and use direct marketing programs has increased with the availability of _____ and _____.

2. What are the three types of responses generated by direct marketing activities?

CHAPTER IN REVIEW

1 *Discuss integrated marketing communication and the communication process.*

Integrated marketing communication is the concept of designing marketing communications programs that coordinate all promotional activities—advertising, personal selling, sales promotion, public relations, and direct marketing—to provide a consistent message across all audiences. The communication process conveys messages with six elements: a source, a message, a channel of communication, a receiver, and encoding and decoding. The communication process also includes a feedback loop and can be distorted by noise.

2 *Describe the promotional mix and the uniqueness of each component.*

There are five promotional alternatives. Advertising, sales promotion, and public relations are mass selling approaches, whereas personal selling and direct marketing use customized messages. Advertising can have high absolute costs but reaches large numbers of people. Personal selling has a high cost per contact but provides immediate feedback. Public relations is often difficult to obtain but is very credible. Sales promotion influences short-term consumer behavior. Direct marketing can help develop customer relationships although maintaining a database can be very expensive.

3 *Select the promotional approach appropriate to a product's life-cycle stage and characteristics.*

The promotional mix changes over the four product life-cycle stages. During the introduction stage, all the promotional mix elements are used. In the growth stage, the primary promotional element is advertising. The maturity stage utilizes sales promotion and direct marketing. During the decline stage, little money is spent on the promotional mix.

4 *Discuss the characteristics of push and pull strategies.*

A push strategy directs the promotional mix to channel members to gain their cooperation in ordering and stocking the product. Personal selling and sales promotion are commonly used in push strategies. A pull strategy directs the promotional mix at ultimate customers to encourage them to ask the retailer for the product. Direct-to-consumer advertising is typically used in pull strategies.

5 *Describe the elements of the promotion decision process.*

The promotional decision process consists of three steps: planning, implementation, and control. The planning step consists of six elements: identify the target audience, specify the objectives, set the budget, select the right promotional elements, design the promotion, and schedule the promotion. The implementation step includes pretesting. The control step includes posttesting.

6 *Explain the value of direct marketing for consumers and sellers.*

The value of direct marketing for consumers is indicated by its level of use. For example, 68 percent of them made a purchase by phone or mail, and 12 million people have purchased items from a television offer. The value of direct marketing for sellers can be measured in terms of three types of responses: direct orders, lead generation, and traffic generation.

FOCUSING ON KEY TERMS

advertising p. 473
all-you-can-afford budgeting p. 484
channel of communication p. 471
communication p. 470
competitive parity budgeting p. 483
decoding p. 471
direct marketing p. 475
direct orders p. 488
encoding p. 471
feedback p. 472
field of experience p. 472
hierarchy of effects p. 482
integrated marketing communications (IMC) p. 470
lead generation p. 488
message p. 470

noise p. 472
objective and task budgeting p. 484
percentage of sales budgeting p. 483
personal selling p. 474
promotional mix p. 470
public relations p. 474
publicity p. 474
pull strategy p. 481
push strategy p. 480
receivers p. 471
response p. 472
sales promotion p. 475
source p. 470
traffic generation p. 488

DISCUSSION AND APPLICATION QUESTIONS

1 After listening to a recent sales presentation, Mary Smith signed up for membership at the local health club. On arriving at the facility, she learned there was an additional fee for racquetball court rentals. "I don't remember that in the sales talk; I thought they said all facilities were included with the membership fee," complained Mary. Describe the problem in terms of the communication process.

2 Develop a matrix to compare the five elements of the promotional mix on three criteria—to *whom* you deliver the message, *what* you say, and *when* you say it.

3 Explain how the promotional tools used by an airline would differ if the target audience were (*a*) consumers who travel for pleasure and (*b*) corporate travel departments that select the airlines to be used by company employees.

4 Suppose you introduced a new consumer food product and invested heavily both in national advertising (pull strategy) and in training and motivating your field salesforce to sell the product to food stores (push strategy). What kinds of feedback would you receive from both the advertising and your salesforce? How could you increase both the quality and quantity of each?

5 Fisher-Price Company, long known as a manufacturer of children's toys, has introduced a line of clothing for children. Outline a promotional plan to get this product introduced in the marketplace.

6 Many insurance companies sell health insurance plans to companies. In these companies the employees pick the plan, but the set of offered plans is determined by the company. Recently Blue Cross–Blue Shield, a health insurance company, ran a television ad stating, "If your employer doesn't offer you Blue Cross–Blue Shield coverage, ask why." Explain the promotional strategy behind the advertisement.

7 Identify the sales promotion tools that might be useful for (*a*) Tastee Yogurt, a new brand introduction, (*b*) 3M self-sticking Post-it notes, and (*c*) Wrigley's Spearmint Gum.

8 Design an integrated marketing communications program—using each of the five promotional elements—for Music Boulevard, the online music store.

9 BMW recently introduced its first sport utility vehicle, the X5, to compete with other popular 4 × 4 vehicles such as the Mercedes-Benz M-class and Jeep Grand Cherokee. Design a direct marketing program to generate (*a*) leads, (*b*) traffic in dealerships, and (*c*) direct orders.

10 Develop a privacy policy for database managers that provides a balance of consumer and seller perspectives. How would you encourage voluntary compliance with your policy? What methods of enforcement would you recommend?

GOING ONLINE   Agencies Adopt IMC Approaches

Several large advertising agencies have described shifts in their philosophies to include IMC approaches to communication. In many cases, the outcome has been campaigns that utilize a combination of the five promotional elements. Go to Digitas' website at www.digitas.com and review the case studies (click on "Our Results," then "Our Case Studies").

1 Describe the promotional elements of one of the campaigns. Why were these elements selected? How are they integrated?

2 How would you evaluate the effectiveness of each of the promotional elements used? How would you evaluate the effectiveness of the entire campaign?

BUILDING YOUR MARKETING PLAN

To develop the promotion strategy for your marketing plan, follow the steps suggested in the planning phase of the promotion decision process described in Figure 18–6.

1 You should (*a*) identify the target audience, (*b*) specify the promotion objectives, (*c*) set the promotion budget, (*d*) select the right promotion tools, (*e*) design the promotion, and (*f*) schedule the promotion.

2 Also specify the pretesting and posttesting procedures needed in the implementation and control phases.

3 Finally, describe how each of your promotion tools are integrated to provide a consistent message.

VIDEO CASE 18   UPS: Repositioning a Business with IMC

"As a business we have, for decades, been primarily in the business of small package transportation and delivery," observes Paul Meyer, group manager of UPS Brand Communications, "which is how the vast majority of our customers and the population at large know us today." Now UPS is undertaking the challenge of expanding into new businesses and it must change the perceptions of the services it provides. As Meyers explains, the question he faces is "How do we position UPS as an enterprise . . . into a new space that we can define?"

THE COMPANY

UPS was founded in Seattle by 19-year-old James Casey in 1907 as a messenger service called the American Messenger Company. As the use of telephones and automobiles increased, the demand for message delivery declined, and Casey began to focus his business on package delivery for retail stores. In 1919 the company expanded into California and adopted its present name, United Parcel Service. The expansion continued to the East coast and Canada, necessitating the development of air and ground delivery routes. As retail stores moved to large suburban shopping centers with large parking lots, however, the demand for retail package delivery began to decline and UPS decided to expand its delivery service to include all possible customers, both private and commercial.

The decision to become a "common carrier" put UPS in direct competition with the U.S. Postal Service and in conflict with regulations of the Interstate Commerce Commission. Federal authority was needed to cross state borders and each state had to authorize the movement of packages within its borders. Over 30 years UPS made hundreds of applications to regulatory commissions and the courts for shipping rights. Finally, in 1975, UPS became the first package delivery company with federal and state authorization to serve every address in the 48 contiguous United States.

Today, UPS has grown into a $33 billion corporation and the world's largest package delivery service. The company consists of 357,000 employees, 88,000 package cars, vans, and motorcycles, and 269 airplanes which operate in 200 countries and territories worldwide. UPS now ships more than 13.6 million packages and documents each day to more than 7.9 million customers!

REPOSITIONING UPS

During the late 1990s UPS began to evaluate its core business—the distribution and delivery of goods—and the possibility of expanding into new services. Managers at UPS realized that commerce consisted of more than the flow of goods; it also included the flow of information and capital, so they began to build a network of services to help UPS customers with all three components. UPS began a series of acquisitions which created UPS Supply Chain Solutions, UPS Capital, UPS Mail Innovations, and UPS Consulting. In addition, it acquired the Mail Boxes Etc. franchise. UPS hoped that these new offerings would reposition UPS into a marketspace the company called "synchronized commerce."

Through its acquisitions UPS had the potential to be a comprehensive enabler of global commerce. It hoped to offer customized supply chain, information, and financial product solutions for each individual customer. Despite its new services, however, the company was challenged by the perception that it only provided package delivery. "We found that we needed to help our customers, and the different decision makers that we engage," explains Meyers. "We had to find a way to build a bridge for them from what they knew us to be as a small package transportation company into something larger than that. We do more than just deliver packages was the basic proposition," he says.

THE UPS IMC CAMPAIGN

UPS needed to convey its new capabilities, and its transformation to the "synchronized" commerce positioning, to current and potential customers. An integrated marketing communications campaign was needed. UPS started by conducting two years of strategic research and planning to guide the new communication activities. The result was a comprehensive campaign that included advertising, public relations, personal selling and promotional efforts.

The first announcement was the new logo. UPS had utilized four logos in its history. The first logo was adopted in 1916 and featured an eagle carrying a package on a shield with the words "Safe, Swift, Sure." The second logo retained the shield, added the letters "UPS" and the phrase "The Delivery System for Stores of Quality." The third logo, simplified UPS's identity by adding a bow-tied package above the shield and the letters UPS, and eliminating all words and phrases. This logo was used without change for 42 years! Finally, the new logo removed the bow-tied package to underscore the company's expanded services, and simply retained the shield and the letters "UPS." The new logo now appears on all UPS vehicles and aircraft, and its 45,000 drop-off boxes and 1 million uniform pieces.

Another element of the communication campaign was to rename 3,300 U.S. locations of Mail Boxes Etc. as *The UPS Store*—with the new logo prominent in the new store signage. The retail presence gave UPS the world's largest and fastest-growing shipping and business services

outlet, and access to a variety of small businesses, sales personnel, and retail consumers. In response, competitor FedEx purchased Kinko's 1,200 retail outlets for $2.4 billion dollars in the hope that it would add new locations to pick up packages.

Advertising also supports the changes at UPS. The company's largest national campaign "What Can Brown Do for You?" emphasizes the color that was selected by one of the company's founders because it reflected class, elegance, and professionalism. The color is viewed as a creative platform that ties all pieces of the campaign together. It is part of the presentation of all vehicles, planes, uniforms, and packaging. In addition, although brown will remain the primary color representing UPS, other new complementary colors will become part of new designs of company assets. The advertising also emphasizes the theme of "synchronizing the world of commerce."

UPS has identified five segments it tries to reach with its advertising. They are shipping decision makers, front office decision makers, small business owners, senior level managers, and retail consumers. Each campaign has a specific context and emphasizes benefits important to that segment. All campaigns, however, utilize the color brown theme as a means of integration.

The color brown is such an important part of the UPS image that UPS registered two trademarks on the color brown which prevent other delivery companies from using the color for vehicles or clothing if it creates confusion in the marketplace. It takes more than 142,000 gallons of brown paint to keep UPS's fleet of vehicles brown, and 1,673,000 yards of brown cloth to make the 188,000 hats, 459,000 shirts, 303,000 pants, and 192,000 pairs of shorts needed to keep all UPS drivers in uniform.

Another element of the integrated program is the web page (www.ups.com) which now receives 115 million hits per day, including 9.1 million online tracking requests. UPS's new CampusShip service allows consumers to operate a virtual post office online. From any location, customers can build an online address list, print labels, track a package, and e-mail shipping notifications. UPS even uses its online capabilities to manage online orders for companies such as Jockey International. Apparel bought on the Jockey Web site is boxed by UPS employees managing the Jockey warehouse, and delivered by UPS drivers.

Other elements of the campaign include promotions, personal selling activities, and public relations efforts which influence executives' public appearances and copy in popular business press such as *The Wall Street Journal* and *Fortune*.

Future Strategy

How can UPS managers assess the success of their campaign? There are several measures that give an indication of the impact of the various message activities. First, there have been a variety of awards. For example, the "What Can Brown Do for You?" advertising was selected for an American Marketing Association EFFIE award, and *BtoB Magazine* cited the campaign as one of the best integrated advertising campaigns. Meyer explains, "people across all of our target audiences have such a powerful association of the color brown with the company UPS, and the brand UPS, that we can use the color to personify the brand without even mentioning the brand and still get nearly 100% recall on all of our messaging."

Another measure of success is the new revenue being generated by logistics customers—a market growing at a rate of about 20 percent. In addition, some experts estimate that the new logistics business generates an additional $2 billion in shipping volume. Finally, a growing number of businesses such as Ford and Birkenstock Footprint Sandals have given UPS complete responsibility for their distribution networks. At Ford, UPS cut the time it takes a car to move from product to the dealer by 40 percent, 14 to 10 days, and at Birkenstock, UPS cut the time it takes shoes to get to stores by 50 percent.

For UPS it's all about helping customers effectively operate their supply chains by simultaneously managing the flow of goods, information, and money. In the future UPS will need to continue to evolve by developing new capabilities and by continuing to ask "What Can Brown Do for You?"

Questions

1 What information about consumer perceptions of UPS led the company to pursue an integrated marketing communications campaign? What was UPS's promotional objective as it repositioned itself in the "synchronized commerce" marketspace?

2 Which of the promotional elements described in Figure 18–2 were used by UPS in its integrated campaign? Describe how UPS might use different media or promotional elements to reach each of the five segments.

3 Why does the color brown provide a useful "creative platform" for UPS's IMC campaign? What is your first reaction to the advertising theme "What Can Brown Do for You?"

4 As UPS has expanded throughout the world it has chosen to use a global marketing strategy, as defined in Chapter 7. What are the advantages and disadvantages of this strategy for UPS?

19 ADVERTISING, SALES PROMOTION, AND PUBLIC RELATIONS

LEARNING OBJECTIVES

After reading this chapter you should be able to:

1 Explain the differences between product advertising and institutional advertising and the variations within each type.

2 Describe the steps used to develop, execute, and evaluate an advertising program.

3 Explain the advantages and disadvantages of alternative advertising media.

4 Discuss the strengths and weaknesses of consumer-oriented and trade-oriented sales promotions.

5 Recognize public relations as an important form of communication.

WELCOME TO THE NEW WORLD OF ADVERTISING

Consumers like you are changing the way they use media, and those changes are creating an entirely new world of advertising. Recent studies show that many consumers often use more than one potential source of advertising at the same time. While watching television, 67 percent of young consumers also use the Internet, 66 percent sometimes read a magazine, 56 percent are instant-messaging, and 34 percent are listening to the radio. While this means consumers may be exposed to many more ads, it also suggests that consumers may not be paying close attention to them. As a result, advertisers are adding attention-getting media such as Internet promotions, direct mail, and events to their campaigns, using technology to personalize their messages, and integrating their ads with the media.

To get New York City consumers' attention, for example, Target created a store in a boat that it moored at the West Side waterfront and then sent "crew members" out on Vespa scooters to distribute "boarding passes." When BMW introduced the MINI Cooper in the United States, it didn't use television advertising. Instead, it put giant pay phones in airports next to billboards with the message "Makes Everything Else Seem a Little Too Big." To introduce Sprite ReMix, Sprite distributed new editions of out-of-print music to disc jockeys on green vinyl with the Sprite logo. And Audi sponsored an online contest where visitors are asked to "mash up" two of rock legend David Bowie's songs into one to win an Audi TT coupe.

Technology is also allowing advertisers to match messages with consumers' personal interests. By 2007, 50 percent of the nation's households are expected to have personal video recorders like TiVo, which enable viewers to specify the type of programs that should be recorded. Personalization software will enable an advertiser to insert ads that are specific to the viewer of that television. So if parents typically watch a different television than their children, the ads on the two TVs are likely to be different even if the same program is tuned in.

One of the newest forms of advertising, however, is the integration of the message directly into the programming or a product. Using the same technology that places the yellow first-down line on the television screen when you watch football games, ESPN's coverage of baseball games lets television viewers see virtual ads that appear to be on the backstop behind home plate, invisible to players and fans at the game. Similarly, BMW puts its logo and virtual vehicles on soccer fields during half time and breaks of matches broadcast on television.

The popularity of video games and the growing interest in massive multiplayer games (MMPs) has led to *advergaming,* or the integration of advertising messages in the virtual world of the games. Currently, advertisers spend more than $100 million to be included in game settings. Nike and Levi's, for example, are included in a popular game called *There,* which allows players to use Therebucks to purchase in-game products. Manufacturers such as Atari are now designing video games with predetermined spots in the games, such as billboards along the track in a driving game, so advertisers can send messages into the game over the Internet in real time. According to one expert, advergaming will become much more sophisticated than signs. Chad Stoller, director of communications solutions at Arnell Group in New York, suggests that games such as Tony Hawk Underground might be designed so that "a skateboarder has to do a trick off the Jeep Liberty to accomplish a goal" in the game.[1]

Advergaming, virtual advertising, and the use of new media are just a few of the many exciting changes taking place in the field of advertising today. They also illustrate the importance of advertising as one of the five promotional mix elements in marketing communications programs. This chapter describes three of the promotional mix elements—advertising, sales promotion, and public relations. Direct marketing was covered in Chapter 18, and personal selling is covered in Chapter 20.

TYPES OF ADVERTISEMENTS

Advertisements serve varying purposes. Which ad would be considered a (1) pioneering, (2) competitive, and (3) reminder ad?

Chapter 18 described **advertising** as any paid form of nonpersonal communication about an organization, a good, a service, or an idea by an identified sponsor. As you look through any magazine, watch television, listen to the radio, or browse the Internet, the variety of advertisements you see or hear may give you the impression that

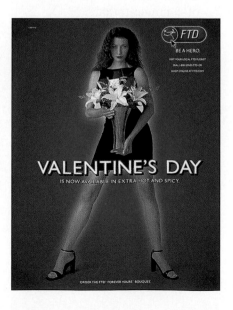

Dial soap uses reinforcement ads to encourage consumers to keep using the product.

they have few similarities. Advertisements are prepared for different purposes, but they basically consist of two types: product advertisements and institutional advertisements.

Product Advertisements

Focused on selling a good or service, **product advertisements** take three forms: (1) pioneering (or informational), (2) competitive (or persuasive), and (3) reminder. Look at the ads by Verizon, Allegra, and FTD, to determine the type and objective of each ad.

Used in the introductory stage of the product life cycle, *pioneering* advertisements tell people what a product is, what it can do, and where it can be found. The key objective of a pioneering advertisement (such as the ad for Verizon's new Mobile IM service) is to inform the target market. Informative ads have been found to be interesting, convincing, and effective.[2]

Advertising that promotes a specific brand's features and benefits is *competitive.* The objective of these messages is to persuade the target market to select the firm's brand rather than that of a competitor. An increasingly common form of competitive advertising is *comparative* advertising, which shows one brand's strengths relative to those of competitors.[3] The Allegra ad, for example, highlights the competitive advantage of Allegra over its primary competitors Benadryl, Tylenol, and Chlor-Trimeton. Studies indicate that comparative ads attract more attention and increase the perceived quality of the advertiser's brand.[4] Firms that use comparative advertising need market research to provide legal support for their claims.[5]

Reminder advertising is used to reinforce previous knowledge of a product. The FTD ad shown reminds consumers about the association between its product and a special event, in this case, Valentine's Day. Reminder advertising is good for products that have achieved a well-recognized position and are in the mature phase of their product life cycle. Another type of reminder ad, *reinforcement,* is used to assure current users they made the right choice. One example: "Aren't you glad you use Dial. Don't you wish everybody did?"

Institutional Advertisements

The objective of **institutional advertisements** is to build goodwill or an image for an organization rather than promote a specific good or service. Institutional advertising has been used by companies such as Texaco, Pfizer, and IBM to build confidence in the company name.[6] Often this form of advertising is used to support the public relations plan or counter adverse publicity. Four alternative forms of institutional advertisements are often used:

1. *Advocacy* advertisements state the position of a company on an issue. Lorillard Tobacco Company places ads discouraging teenagers from smoking. Another

A pioneering ad by Altria informs readers of the company's new name, and a competitive institutional ad by dairy farmers tries to increase demand for milk.

form of advocacy advertisement is used when organizations make a request related to a particular action or behavior, such as a request by American Red Cross for blood donations.

2. *Pioneering institutional* advertisements, like the pioneering ads for products discussed earlier, are used for announcements about what a company is, what it can do, or where it is located. Recent Bayer ads stating "We cure more headaches than you think" are intended to inform consumers that the company produces many products in addition to aspirin. When Philip Morris changed its name to Altria, it ran pioneering institutional ads to inform consumers.

3. *Competitive institutional* advertisements promote the advantages of one product class over another and are used in markets where different product classes compete for the same buyers. America's milk processors and dairy farmers use their "Got Milk?" campaign to increase demand for milk as it competes against other beverages.

4. *Reminder institutional* advertisements, like the product form, simply bring the company's name to the attention of the target market again. The four branches of the U.S. military sponsor the "Today's Military" campaign to remind potential recruits of the opportunities in the active military, the National Guard, and the reserves.

Concept Check

1. What is the difference between pioneering and competitive ads?

2. What is the purpose of an institutional advertisement?

DEVELOPING THE ADVERTISING PROGRAM

The promotion decision process described in Chapter 18 can be applied to each of the promotional elements. Advertising, for example, can be managed by following the three steps (developing, executing, and evaluating) of the process.

Identifying the Target Audience

To develop an effective advertising program advertisers must identify the target audience. All aspects of an advertising program are likely to be influenced by the characteristics of the prospective consumer. Understanding the lifestyles, attitudes, and demographics of the target market is essential. Mary Quinlan, vice chair of the MacManus Group advertising agency, suggests that when women are the target it is important that the ad content reflects that women "like to see other women who are diverse, confident, and naturally beautiful" and that "women respond to emotional truth and real-life experience."[7] Similarly, the placement of ads depends on the audience. When Hummer, the biggest and most expensive sport utility vehicle in the market, began its $3 million campaign targeted at "rugged individualists" with incomes above $200,000, it selected *Wired, Spin, Red Herring, BusinessWeek, Skiing,* and *Cigar Aficionado* to carry the ads.[8] Even scheduling can depend on the audience. Claritin, a popular allergy medication, schedules its use of brochures, in-store displays, coupons, and advertising to correspond to the allergy season, which varies by geographic region.[9] To eliminate possible bias that might result from subjective judgments about some population segments, the Federal Communications Commission suggests that advertising program decisions be based on market research about the target audience.[10]

Specifying Advertising Objectives

The guidelines for setting promotion objectives described in Chapter 18 also apply to setting advertising objectives. This step helps advertisers with other choices in the promotion decision process such as selecting media and evaluating a campaign. Advertising with an objective of creating awareness, for example, would be better matched with a magazine than a directory such as the Yellow Pages.[11] The Magazine Publishers of America believe objectives are so important that they offer a $100,000 prize each year to the campaign that best meets its objectives. The last winner, Apple, won with its "Silhouettes" campaign, which helped achieve the objective of making the iPod the number one MP3 player.[12] Similarly, the Advertising Research Foundation is collecting information about the effectiveness of advertising, particularly new forms such as online advertising.[13] Experts believe that factors such as product category, brand, and consumer involvement in the purchase decision may change the importance—and, possibly, the sequence—of the stages of the hierarchy of effects. Snickers, for example, knew that its consumers were unlikely to engage in elaborate information processing when it designed a recent campaign. The result was ads with simple humorous messages rather than extensive factual information.[14]

Setting the Advertising Budget

You might not remember who advertised during the 1990 Super Bowl, but it cost the companies $700,000 to place a 30-second ad. By 2004, the cost of placing a 30-second ad during Super Bowl XXXVIII was $2.25 million (Figure 19–1 on the next page). The reason for the escalating cost is the growing number of viewers: 41.4 million homes and 89.8 million people tune in. In addition, the audience is attractive to advertisers because research indicates that it is equally split between men and women and that prior to the game 54 percent of survey respondents were "looking forward" to watching the 59 spots. The ads are effective too: Movies promoted on the Super Bowl achieve 40 percent more revenue than movies not promoted on the Super Bowl. As a result, the Super Bowl attracts relatively new advertisers such as Levitra and Staples and regular advertisers such as Anheuser-Busch and Visa. Which ads were rated the highest? Budweiser, Chevrolet, Pepsi, and AOL.[15] To see your favorite Super Bowl ad again, read the Web Link on the next page.

Do you remember this Sierra Mist ad from the Super Bowl?

While not all advertising options are as expensive as the Super Bowl, most alternatives still represent substantial financial commitments and require a formal budgeting process. In the luxury car market, for example, the BMW 7 series and the Jaguar S-type have market shares of 5.0 and 3.6 percent and advertising budgets of $38.9 and $27.0 million, respectively. Using a competitive parity budgeting approach, each company spends between $7 and $8 million for each percent of market share. Using an objective and task approach, Coca-Cola allocated $50 million to introduce C2, its new 70-calorie, low-carb soft drink.[16]

Designing the Advertisement

An advertising message usually focuses on the key benefits of the product that are important to a prospective buyer in making trial and adoption decisions. The message depends on the general form or appeal used in the ad and the actual words included in the ad.

Message Content   Most advertising messages are made up of both informational and persuasional elements. These two elements, in fact, are so intertwined that it is sometimes difficult to tell them apart. For example, basic information contained in many ads such as the product name, benefits, features, and price are presented in a way that tries to attract attention and encourage purchase. On the other hand, even

FIGURE 19–1

Super Bowl, super dollars, super audience

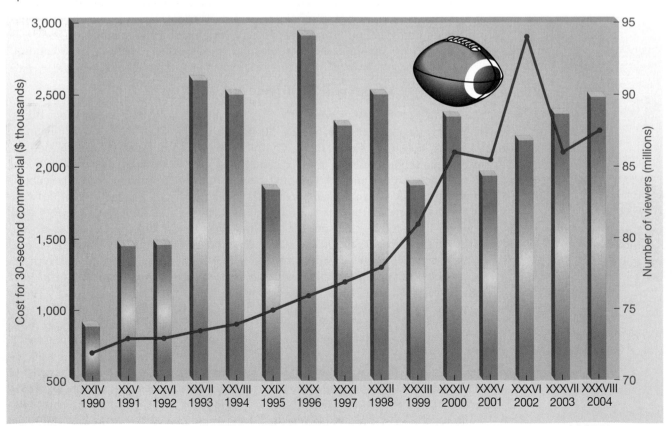

the most persuasive advertisements have to contain at least some basic information to be successful.

Information and persuasive content can be combined in the form of an appeal to provide a basic reason for the consumer to act. Although the marketer can use many different types of appeals, common advertising appeals include fear appeals,[17] sex appeals, and humorous appeals.

Fear appeals suggest to the consumer that he or she can avoid some negative experience through the purchase and use of a product or service, a change in behavior, or a reduction in the use of a product. Examples with which you may be familiar include: fire or smoke detector ads that depict a home burning; political candidate endorsements that warn against the rise of other, unpopular ideologies; or social cause ads warning of the serious consequences of drug and alcohol use or AIDS. Insurance companies often try to show the negative effects of premature death on the relatives of those who don't carry enough life or mortgage insurance. Food producers encourage the purchase of low-carb, low-fat, and high-fiber products as a means of reducing weight, cholesterol levels, and the possibility of a heart attack.[18] The Partnership for a Drug-Free America recently ran an ad with a fear appeal: The headline reads "Sniffing can harm your nervous system." When using fear appeals, the advertiser must be sure that the appeal is strong enough get the audience's attention and concern but not so strong that it will lead them to tune out the message. In fact, recent research on antismoking ads indicates that stressing the severity of long-term health risks may actually enhance smoking's allure among youth.[19]

In contrast, *sex appeals* suggest to the audience that the product will increase the attractiveness of the user. Sex appeals can be found in almost any product category, from automobiles to toothpaste. The contemporary women's clothing store bebe, for example, designs its advertising to "attract customers who are intrigued by the playfully sensual and evocative imagery of the bebe lifestyle." Unfortunately, many commercials that use sex appeals are only successful at gaining the attention of the audience; they have little impact on how consumers think, feel, or act. Some advertising experts even argue that such appeals get in the way of successful communication by distracting the audience from the purpose of the ad. Public response to a performance by Janet Jackson during a Super Bowl halftime show has led many advertisers to modify the content of their promotions.[20] See the Ethics and Social Responsibility Alert on the next page for a discussion of the complexity of the issues involved.[21]

These ads are examples of a fear appeal and a humor appeal, respectively.

ETHICS AND SOCIAL RESPONSIBILITY ALERT   Who Decides What Is "Appropriate" Advertising?

ETHICS

The controversy created by Janet Jackson's halftime performance in Super Bowl XXXVIII has sparked a complicated debate about what is appropriate content for media and advertising and who should decide what is appropriate. The Federal Communications Commission is legally responsible for policing the airwaves. Congress can also influence the industry with laws such as the recently proposed Clean Airwaves Act. Large media and retailing companies are also weighing in: Wal-Mart banned some magazines such as *Maxim* and *Stuff* from its stores, and six Clear Channel radio stations dropped Howard Stern from their programming. Finally, companies have made changes in their marketing activities: Anheuser-Busch has decided to stop using several popular ads, Victoria's Secret has canceled its TV fashion show, and Abercrombie & Fitch is dropping its suggestive quarterly catalog.

For each group, the difficulty is in trying to match content with consumer preferences, because preferences vary from segment to segment. The FCC, Congress, and large and small companies have all received complaints about advertising content from conservative segments of the population. At the same time, a recent survey reported that 74 percent of consumers ages 12–20 think that many people have overreacted to the issue. Some experts are anticipating that the result will be a continuum of media and content options from children's programming, to network television, to cable TV and satellite radio, to pay-per-view and Internet options. What is your opinion?

Humorous appeals imply either directly or subtly that the product is more fun or exciting than competitors' offerings. As with fear and sex appeals, the use of humor is widespread in advertising and can be found in many product categories. The Cannes Advertising Festival, held in June each year, recognized Burger King for its use of humor in websites designed to support messages also promoted in TV ads. For example, the "Have it your way" message is the theme of a site (www.subserviantchicken.com) where millions of visitors have commanded a chicken to do stunts. You may have a favorite humorous ad character, such as the Energizer battery bunny, the AFLAC duck, or the Geico gecko. Unfortunately for the advertiser, humor tends to wear out quickly, eventually boring the consumer. Another problem with humorous appeals is that their effectiveness may vary across cultures if used in a global campaign.[22]

Creating the Actual Message   Advertising agency Berlin Cameron was recently designated as *Advertising Age* magazine's U.S. Agency of the Year for its "rare combination of new-business savvy, strategic insight, creative prowess, and big personality." One example of the agency's approach is the "Real" campaign for Coca-Cola, which includes the Courteney Cox and David Arquette "pinball/true love" ad. Other successful campaigns include the Dasani bottled water "living with excitement" ads, the Mello Yellow "How would you stay smooth?" ads, and Tidy Cat ads.[23]

Berlin Cameron's use of well-known personalities such as Cox and Arquette in the Coca-Cola ad is an example of a popular form of advertising today: the use of a celebrity spokesperson. Many companies use athletes, movie and television stars, musicians, and other celebrities to talk to consumers through their ads. Advertisers who use a celebrity spokesperson believe that the ads are more likely to influence sales. The popular "Got Milk?" campaign reversed a steady decline in milk consumption with celebrities such as actress Angelina Jolie, author Dr. Phil McGraw, MTV star Carson Daly, supermodel Gisele Bundchen, Ronald McDonald, and many others. The two top celebrity spokespersons in recent years have been Tiger Woods, who appears in American Express, Nike, Titleist, and Buick ads, and Michael Jordan, who appears in Nike, Hanes, Rayovac, Gatorade, and Ballpark hotdog ads. Hershey Foods recently signed Jessica Simpson to endorse its new product Ice Breakers Liquid Ice. Thomas Hernquist, Hershey's chief marketing officer, says Jessica was selected because she "is energetic, fun, and sociable, so she's a perfect match for our new product."

Creative advertisements by Berlin Cameron for (clockwise from top left) Coca-Cola, Dasani, Mello Yello, and Tidy Cat.

One potential shortcoming of this form of advertising is that the spokesperson's image may change to be inconsistent with the image of the company or brand. NBA star Kobe Bryant's court appearances caused many companies to probe the backgrounds of potential endorsers and to consider retired athletes and legacy (deceased) athletes who are low risk and still have lasting appeal in the marketplace.[24]

Another issue involved in creating the message is the complex process of translating the copywriter's ideas into an actual advertisement. Designing quality artwork, layout, and production for the advertisements is costly and time consuming. High-quality TV commercials typically cost about $372,000 to produce a 30-second ad, a task done by about 2,000 small commercial production companies across the United States. One reason for the high costs is that as companies have developed global campaigns, the need to shoot commercials in exotic locations has increased. Audi recently filmed commercials in Germany, Australia, and Morocco. Actors are expensive also. The Screen Actors Guild reports that an actor in a typical network TV car ad would earn between $12,000 and $15,000.[25]

Concept Check

1. What are characteristics of good advertising objectives?

2. What is a potential shortcoming of using a celebrity spokesperson?

Selecting the Right Media

Every advertiser must decide where to place its advertisements. The alternatives are the *advertising media,* the means by which the message is communicated to the target audience. Newspapers, magazines, radio, and TV are examples of advertising media. This decision on media selection is related to the target audience, type of product, nature of the message, campaign objectives, available budget, and the costs of the alternative media. Figure 19–2 on the next page shows the distribution of the $245 billion spent on advertising among the many media alternatives.[26]

Choosing a Medium and a Vehicle within That Medium In deciding where to place advertisements, a company has several media to choose from and

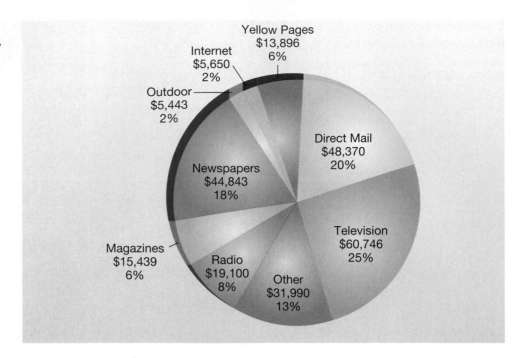

a number of alternatives, or vehicles, within each medium. Often advertisers use a mix of media forms and vehicles to maximize the exposure of the message to the target audience while at the same time minimizing costs. These two conflicting goals of (1) maximizing exposure and (2) minimizing costs are of central importance to media planning.

Basic Terms   Media buyers speak a language of their own, so every advertiser involved in selecting the right media for their campaigns must be familiar with some common terms used in the advertising industry. Figure 19–3 shows the most common terms used in media decisions.

Because advertisers try to maximize the number of individuals in the target market exposed to the message, they must be concerned with reach. **Reach** is the number of different people or households exposed to an advertisement. The exact definition of reach sometimes varies among alternative media. Newspapers often use reach to describe their total circulation or the number of different households that buy the paper. Television and radio stations, in contrast, describe their reach using the term **rating**—the percentage of households in a market that are tuned to a particular TV show or radio station. In general, advertisers try to maximize reach in their target market at the lowest cost.

Although reach is important, advertisers are also interested in exposing their target audience to a message more than once. This is because consumers often do not pay close attention to advertising messages, some of which contain large amounts of relatively complex information. When advertisers want to reach the same audience more than once, they are concerned with **frequency**, the average number of times a person in the target audience is exposed to a message or advertisement. Like reach, greater frequency is generally viewed as desirable.[27] Studies indicate that with repeated exposure to advertisements consumers respond more favorably to brand extensions.[28]

When reach (expressed as a percentage of the total market) is multiplied by frequency, an advertiser will obtain a commonly used reference number called **gross rating points** (GRPs). To obtain the appropriate number of GRPs to achieve an advertising campaign's objectives, the media planner must balance reach and frequency. The balance will also be influenced by cost. **Cost per thousand** (CPM) refers to the cost of reaching 1,000 individuals or households with the advertising message in a given medium (*M* is the Roman numeral for 1,000).

FIGURE 19–3
The language of the media buyer

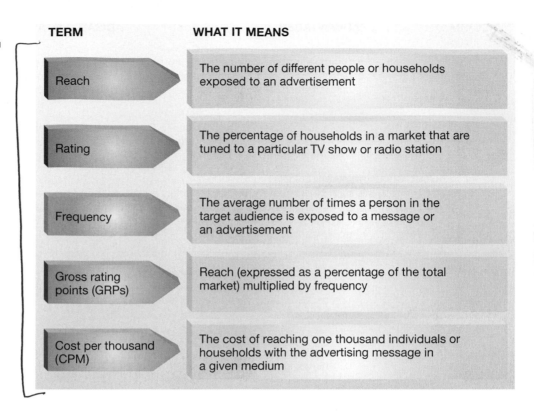

TERM	WHAT IT MEANS
Reach	The number of different people or households exposed to an advertisement
Rating	The percentage of households in a market that are tuned to a particular TV show or radio station
Frequency	The average number of times a person in the target audience is exposed to a message or an advertisement
Gross rating points (GRPs)	Reach (expressed as a percentage of the total market) multiplied by frequency
Cost per thousand (CPM)	The cost of reaching one thousand individuals or households with the advertising message in a given medium

Different Media Alternatives

Figure 19–4 on the next page summarizes the advantages and disadvantages of the major advertising media, which are described in more detail below. Direct mail was discussed in Chapter 18.

Television   Television is a valuable medium because it communicates with sight, sound, and motion. Print advertisements alone could never give you the sense of a sports car accelerating from a stop or cornering at high speed. In addition, network television is the only medium that can reach 95 percent of the homes in the United States.[29] Recent studies have shown that *out-of-home TV* reaches another 20 million viewers in bars, hotels, offices, and college campuses each week.[30]

Television's major disadvantage is cost: The price of a prime-time, 30-second ad run on *American Idol* is $658,333 and the average price for all prime-time programs is $147,986.[31] Because of these high charges, many advertisers choose less expensive "spot" ads, which run between programs in 10-, 15-, 30-, or 60-second lengths. Shorter ads reduce costs but severely restrict the amount of information and emotion that can be conveyed. Research indicates, however, that two different versions of a 15-second commercial, run back-to-back, will increase recall over long intervals.[32]

Another problem with television advertising is the likelihood of *wasted coverage*— having people outside the market for the product see the advertisement. The cost and wasted coverage problems of TV advertising can be reduced through the specialized cable and direct broadcast (satellite) channels. Advertising time is often less expensive on cable and direct broadcast channels than on the major networks. There are currently about 150 options—such as ESPN, MTV, Lifetime, We, the Speed Channel, the History Channel, Home and Garden Television, and the Outdoor Life Network— that reach very narrowly defined audiences. Other forms of television are changing television advertising also. Pay-per-view movie services and digital video recorders (DVRs), for example, offer the potential of commercial-free viewing. Many cable and satellite TV services now offer boxes with built-in DVRs and remotes with "30-second skip" buttons for ad-zapping.

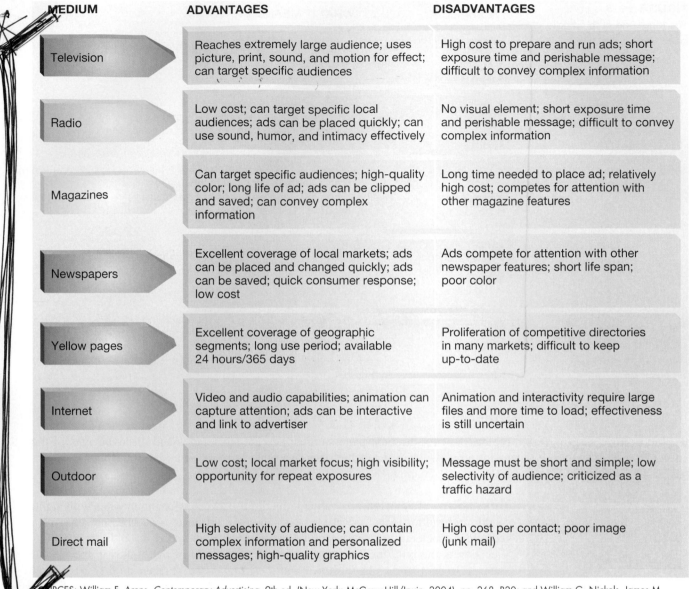

MEDIUM	ADVANTAGES	DISADVANTAGES
Television	Reaches extremely large audience; uses picture, print, sound, and motion for effect; can target specific audiences	High cost to prepare and run ads; short exposure time and perishable message; difficult to convey complex information
Radio	Low cost; can target specific local audiences; ads can be placed quickly; can use sound, humor, and intimacy effectively	No visual element; short exposure time and perishable message; difficult to convey complex information
Magazines	Can target specific audiences; high-quality color; long life of ad; ads can be clipped and saved; can convey complex information	Long time needed to place ad; relatively high cost; competes for attention with other magazine features
Newspapers	Excellent coverage of local markets; ads can be placed and changed quickly; ads can be saved; quick consumer response; low cost	Ads compete for attention with other newspaper features; short life span; poor color
Yellow pages	Excellent coverage of geographic segments; long use period; available 24 hours/365 days	Proliferation of competitive directories in many markets; difficult to keep up-to-date
Internet	Video and audio capabilities; animation can capture attention; ads can be interactive and link to advertiser	Animation and interactivity require large files and more time to load; effectiveness is still uncertain
Outdoor	Low cost; local market focus; high visibility; opportunity for repeat exposures	Message must be short and simple; low selectivity of audience; criticized as a traffic hazard
Direct mail	High selectivity of audience; can contain complex information and personalized messages; high-quality graphics	High cost per contact; poor image (junk mail)

SOURCES: William F. Arens, *Contemporary Advertising*, 9th ed. (New York: McGraw-Hill/Irwin, 2004), pp. 268, R20; and William G. Nickels, James M. McHugh, and Susan M. McHugh, *Understanding Business*, 7th ed. (Burr Ridge, IL: McGraw-Hill/Irwin, 2005), p. 493.

FIGURE 19–4

Advantages and disadvantages of major advertising media

Another popular form of television advertising is the infomercial. **Infomercials** are program-length (30-minute) advertisements that take an educational approach to communication with potential customers. Today, more than 90 percent of all TV stations air infomercials, and more than 25 percent of all consumers have purchased a product as a result of seeing an infomercial. Volvo, Club Med, General Motors, Bank of America, Mattel, Revlon, Texaco, and many other companies have used infomercials as a means of providing information that is relevant, useful, and entertaining to prospective customers. TiVo, the DVR manufacturer, for example, is using infomercials to show "how the DVR works, with vignettes on how it adds value to the TV-viewing experience."[33]

Radio   There are seven times as many radio stations as television stations in the United States. The major advantage of radio is that it is a segmented medium. There are the Farm Radio Network, the Physicians' Network, all-talk shows, and hard rock stations, all listened to by different market segments. The average college student is a surprisingly heavy radio listener and spends more time during the day listening to radio than watching network television—2.2 hours versus 1.6 hours. Thus, advertisers with college students as their target market must consider radio.

The disadvantage of radio is that it has limited use for products that must be seen. Another problem is the ease with which consumers can tune out a commercial by switching stations. A new form of radio available through satellite services offers up to 100 digital-quality coast-to-coast radio channels to consumers for a monthly subscription fee. Sirius Satellite Radio and XM Satellite Radio offer commercial-free channels and channels with only about 6 minutes of advertising per hour compared with 15 to 20 minutes heard on "free" channels.[34] Radio is also a medium that competes for people's attention as they do other activities such as driving, working, or relaxing. Peak radio listening time is during the drive times (6 to 10 A.M. and 4 to 7 P.M.).

Magazines Magazines have become a very specialized medium, primarily because there are currently more than 6,200 magazines. New magazines are introduced each year, such as *Budget Living,* a personal finance magazine for women; *All You,* a general topics magazine sold only through Wal-Mart; and *American Thunder,* a magazine about NASCAR racing for men.

The marketing advantage of this medium is the great number of special-interest publications that appeal to narrowly defined segments. Runners read *Runner's World,* sailors buy *Yachting,* gardeners subscribe to *Garden Design,* and teenagers peruse *Teen People.* More than 675 publications focus on computers and technology, 669 are dedicated to travel, and 500 magazine titles are related to music.[35] Each magazine's readers often represent a unique profile. Take the *Rolling Stone* reader, who tends to listen to music more than most people—so Sony knows an ad for its CLIE Handheld (which includes an MP3 audio player) in *Rolling Stone* is reaching the desired target audience. In addition to the distinct audience profiles of magazines, good color production is an advantage that allows magazines to create strong images.[36]

The cost of advertising in national magazines is a disadvantage, but many national publications publish regional and even metro editions, which reduce the absolute cost and wasted coverage. *Time* publishes well over 400 different editions, including Latin American, Canadian, Asian, South Pacific, European, and U.S. editions. The U.S. editions include national, demographic, regional, state, and city options. In addition to cost, another limitation to magazines is their infrequency. At best, magazines are printed on a weekly basis, with many specialized publications appearing only monthly or less often. Although specialization can be an advantage of this medium, consumer interests can be difficult to translate into a magazine theme—a fact made clear by the hundreds of magazine failures during the past decade. *Virtual City, Mouth 2 Mouth, Top Model,* and *Esquire Sportsman,* for example, all failed to attract and keep a substantial number of readers or advertisers.[37] Which magazine has the highest circulation? It's *AARP The Magazine* with 20 million readers.

Newspapers Newspapers are an important local medium with excellent reach potential. Because of the daily publication of most papers, they allow advertisements to focus on specific current events, such as a 24-hour sale. Local retailers often use newspapers as their sole advertising medium. Newspapers are rarely saved by the purchaser, however, so companies are generally limited to ads that call for an immediate customer response (although customers can clip and save ads they select). Companies also cannot depend on newspapers for color reproduction as good as that in most magazines.

National advertising campaigns rarely include this medium except in conjunction with local distributors of their products. In these instances, both parties often share the advertising costs using a cooperative advertising program, which is described later in this chapter. Another exception is the use of newspapers such as *The Wall Street Journal* and *USA Today*, each of which have national distribution of more than 2 million readers.

Print ads help attract readers to *The Wall Street Journal*.

Three trends are influencing newspapers today. The first is the dramatic increase in their cost of production and distribution. As printing and paper cost have increased, newspapers in cities such as Seattle and Denver have attempted to cut costs by merging their printing operations with another newspaper under a legal arrangement called a joint operating agreement (JOA). In cities such as Phoenix and Houston, population growth and suburban sprawl have increased the cost of distribution, requiring the newspapers to print outlying editions earlier, run multiple printing facilities, and use digital displays on the delivery vehicles to help control costs. The second trend is the growth in online newspapers. More than 60 newspapers, including the *Chicago Tribune, New York Times, Dallas Morning News, San Jose Mercury News,* and *Washington Post,* are already online, and many others are expected soon. Finally, in many large cities free tabloid newspapers such as Boston's *Metro* and New York's *am NewYork* are targeting commuters and creating new competition for traditional paid-for newspapers.[38]

Yellow Pages   Yellow pages represent an advertising media alternative comparable to radio and magazines in terms of expenditures—about $14 billion in the United States and $25 billion globally. According to the Yellow Pages Integrated Media Association, consumers turn to print yellow pages more than 15 billion times annually and online yellow pages an additional 1.6 billion times per year. One reason for this high level of use is that the 6,500 yellow pages directories reach almost all households with telephones. Yellow pages are a *directional* medium because they help consumers know where purchases can be made after other media have created awareness and demand.

The yellow pages have several other advantages. First, they are available 24 hours each day and 365 days each year. In addition, yellow pages have a long life span—directories are typically published once each year and provide advertisers with many advertisement size options. A disadvantage of yellow pages advertising is the proliferation of directories. In fact, many major cities are now covered by six or more directories, including directories for specific neighborhoods and ethnic groups. Another disadvantage is the lack of timeliness, because yellow pages can only be updated with new information once each year. Yellow pages are typically used for local advertising—85 percent of all yellow pages expenditures are local—because of the difficulty of coordinating a nationwide campaign in yellow pages directories.[39]

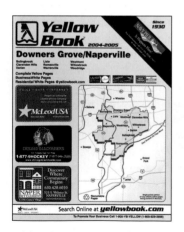

Internet   The Internet represents a relatively new medium for advertisers although it has already attracted a wide variety of industries. Online advertising is similar to print advertising in that it offers a visual message. It has additional advantages, however, because it can also use the audio and video capabilities of the Internet. Sound and movement may simply attract more attention from viewers, or they may provide an element of entertainment to the message. Online advertising also has the unique feature of being interactive. Called *rich media,* these interactive ads have drop-down menus, built-in

Internet advertising must
engage and entertain viewers.

games, or search engines to engage viewers.[40] Although online advertising is relatively small compared to other traditional media, it offers an opportunity to reach younger consumers who have developed a preference for online communication.[41]

There are a variety of online advertising options. The most common—banner ads—represent approximately 50 percent of online ad expenditures, although their effectiveness has declined to a current click-through rate of 0.3 percent. IBM used a banner ad with the question "What's on your mind?" to engage viewers by encouraging them to view a larger ad and then click through to IBM's website. Other forms of online advertising include skyscrapers, pop-ups, interstitials, and minisites that use streaming video and audio and are becoming similar to television advertising. Many advertisers are also adding entertainment elements.

Levi Strauss used banner ads to support a website announcing the debut of its recut 501 Re-Born jeans. The site featured an online music mixer that let visitors listen to "Ain't Nothing but the Real Thing" and other songs, record their own version, and send it to friends. Advertising executive Lucy McCabe explains that the online promotion "enables consumers to interact with the site and they spend a lot longer with your brand. The average length of time on the Re-Born site is five minutes." Nokia uses the same concept by providing a website where visitors can design their own phone covers and enter design competitions (www.nokia.com). The most popular locations for online advertising are the home pages of Yahoo!, MSN, and America Online, which, combined, reach 40 percent of all adults online.[42]

One disadvantage of online advertising is that because the medium is relatively new, technical and administrative standards for the various formats are still evolving. This situation makes it difficult for advertisers to run national online campaigns across multiple sites. The Interactive Advertising Bureau provides some guidance for online advertising standards and makes recommendations for new formats. Another disadvantage to online advertising is the difficulty of measuring impact. Online advertising lags behind radio, TV, and print in offering advertisers proof of effectiveness. To address this issue several companies are testing methods of tracking where viewers go on their computer in the days and weeks after seeing an ad. Nielsen's rating service, for example, measures actual click-by-click behavior through meters installed on the computers of 225,000 individuals in 26 countries both at home and at work (see www.nielsen-netratings.com for recent ratings). The Marketing NewsNet on the next page suggests that marketers should consider other measures of effectiveness also.[43] Another suggestion being tested by Volvo and Unilever is *permission-based* advertising, where viewers agree to watch a commercial online in exchange for points, samples, or access to premium content and advertisers only pay for completed views. Internet advertising is discussed further in Chapter 21 in the context of interactive marketing.[44]

MARKETING NEWSNET

Does Internet Advertising Really Work?

TECHNOLOGY & E-COMMERCE

The Internet has had a tremendous impact on many industries, including book retailing, music distribution, and travel services. While the $5.6 billion currently spent on Internet advertising represents only 2 percent of all advertising expenditures, the growing link between Internet advertising and other promotional activities has many marketers increasing their Internet budgets and wondering if they are making a good investment.

Currently, the most widely used measure of Internet advertising effectiveness is the percentage of people who are exposed to an ad who actually click on the ad—the *click-through* rate. Recent research using eye-tracking technology and a large-scale survey of Internet users provides some insight for marketing managers. First, the eye-tracking study indicates that many Internet users avoid looking at the ads, but the likelihood of looking at an ad can be increased by managing the size and location of the ad. Second, although click-through rates are typically low, traditional measures of advertising effectiveness such as unaided recall, brand recognition, and brand awareness suggest that the ads are effective for those who see the ads. In addition, repetition appears to have a positive influence on the traditional measures.

Despite these insights, Internet advertisers face another problem: Programs and filters that block ads on websites, like recently released AdSubtract PRO 3, are spreading fast. So do Internet ads work? For the moment the answer is yes . . . if anyone sees them.

Outdoor A very effective medium for reminding consumers about your product is outdoor advertising, such as the scoreboard at San Diego's Qualcomm Stadium.

The most common form of outdoor advertising, called *billboards,* often results in good reach and frequency and has been shown to increase purchase rates.[45] The visibility of this medium is good supplemental reinforcement for well-known products, and it is a relatively low-cost, flexible alternative. A company can buy space just in the desired geographical market. A disadvantage to billboards, however, is that no opportunity exists for lengthy advertising copy. Also, a good billboard site depends on traffic patterns and sight lines. In many areas, environmental laws have limited the use of this medium.

If you have ever lived in a metropolitan area, chances are you might have seen another form of outdoor advertising, *transit advertising.* This medium includes messages on the interior and exterior of buses, subway cars, and taxis. As use of mass transit grows, transit advertising may become increasingly important. Selectivity is available to advertisers, who can buy space by neighborhood or bus route. One disadvantage to this medium is that the heavy travel times, when the audiences are the largest, are not conducive to reading advertising copy. People are standing shoulder to shoulder on the subway, hoping not to miss their stop, and little attention is paid to the advertising.

The outdoor advertising industry has experienced a surge of growth recently. Lower costs, faster technology, and a lot of creativity have attracted large, national advertisers such as Sony, Microsoft, and America Online.[46] Orlando's Transportation Authority utilizes a wireless system to receive advertising for flat-screen monitors mounted in its 240 buses. Streetbeam is developing a service that will allow commuters with personal digital assistants (e.g., a Palm handheld) to receive enhanced messages from the displays.[47] Although outdoor advertising expenditures grew to more than $5 billion in 2004, the industry must address environmental concerns through self-regulation or be restricted by legislation. For example, four states have banned billboards, and New York City's Metropolitan Transportation Authority has banned tobacco advertising on buses and subways.[48]

Captivate TV Network offers "TV in Elevators."

Other Media   As traditional media have become more expensive and cluttered, advertisers have been attracted to a variety of nontraditional advertising options, called *place-based media.* Messages are placed in locations that attract a specific target audience such as airports, doctors' offices, health clubs, theaters (where ads are played on the screen before the movies are shown), even bathrooms of bars, restaurants, and nightclubs.[49] Soon there will be advertising on video screens on gas pumps, ATMs, and in elevators. New York's La Guardia airport has started putting ads on baggage conveyors, and Beach 'n Billboard will even imprint ads in the sand on a beach.[50]

Selection Criteria   Choosing between these alternative media is difficult and depends on several factors. First, knowing the media habits of the target audience is essential to deciding among the alternatives. Second, occasionally product attributes necessitate that certain media be used. For example, if color is a major aspect of product appeal, radio is excluded. Newspapers allow advertising for quick actions to confront competitors, and magazines are more appropriate for complicated messages because the reader can spend more time reading the message. The final factor in selecting a medium is cost. When possible, alternative media are compared using a common denominator that reflects both reach and cost—a measure such as CPM.

Scheduling the Advertising

There is no correct schedule to advertise a product, but three factors must be considered. First is the issue of *buyer turnover,* which is how often new buyers enter the market to buy the product. The higher the buyer turnover, the greater is the amount of advertising required. A second issue in scheduling is the *purchase frequency;* the more frequently the product is purchased, the less repetition is required. Finally, companies must consider the *forgetting rate,* the speed with which buyers forget the brand if advertising is not seen.

Setting schedules requires an understanding of how the market behaves. Most companies tend to follow one of three basic approaches:

1. *Continuous (steady) schedule.* When seasonal factors are unimportant, advertising is run at a continuous or steady schedule throughout the year.
2. *Flighting (intermittent) schedule.* Periods of advertising are scheduled between periods of no advertising to reflect seasonal demand.
3. *Pulse (burst) schedule.* A flighting schedule is combined with a continuous schedule because of increases in demand, heavy periods of promotion, or introduction of a new product.

For example, products such as dry breakfast cereals have a stable demand throughout the year and would typically use a continuous schedule of advertising. In contrast, products such as snow skis and suntan lotions have seasonal demands and receive flighting-schedule advertising during the seasonal demand period. Some products such as toys or automobiles require pulse-schedule advertising to facilitate sales throughout the year and during special periods of increased demand (such as holidays or new car introductions). Some evidence suggests that pulsing schedules are superior to other advertising strategies.[51] In addition, recent research findings indicate that the effectiveness of a particular ad wears out quickly and, therefore, many alternative forms of a commercial may be more effective.[52]

Concept Check

1. You see the same ad in *Time* and *Fortune* magazines and on billboards and TV. Is this an example of reach or frequency?

2. Why has the Internet become a popular advertising medium?

3. What factors must be considered when choosing among alternative media?

EXECUTING THE ADVERTISING PROGRAM

Executing the advertising program involves pretesting the advertising copy and actually carrying out the advertising program. John Wanamaker, the founder of Wanamaker's Department Store in Philadelphia, remarked, "I know half my advertising is wasted, but I don't know what half." By evaluating advertising efforts, marketers can try to ensure that their advertising expenditures are not wasted.[53] Evaluation is done usually at two separate times: before and after the advertisements are run in the actual campaign. Several methods used in the evaluation process at the stages of idea formulation and copy development are discussed below.

Pretesting the Advertising

To determine whether the advertisement communicates the intended message or to select among alternative versions of the advertisement, **pretests** are conducted before the advertisements are placed in any medium.

Portfolio Tests   Portfolio tests are used to test copy alternatives. The test ad is placed in a portfolio with several other ads and stories, and consumers are asked to read through the portfolio. Afterward, subjects are asked for their impressions of the ads on several evaluative scales, such as from "very informative" to "not very informative."

Jury Tests   Jury tests involve showing the ad copy to a panel of consumers and having them rate how they liked it, how much it drew their attention, and how attractive they thought it was. This approach is similar to the portfolio test in that consumer reactions are obtained. However, unlike the portfolio test, a test advertisement is not hidden within other ads.

Theater Tests   Theater testing is the most sophisticated form of pretesting. Consumers are invited to view new television shows or movies in which test commercials are also shown. Viewers register their feelings about the advertisements either on handheld electronic recording devices used during the viewing or on questionnaires afterward.

Carrying Out the Advertising Program

The responsibility for actually carrying out the advertising program can be handled in one of three ways, as shown in Figure 19–5. The **full-service agency** provides the most complete range of services, including market research, media selection, copy development, artwork, and production. Agencies that assist a client by both developing and placing advertisements have traditionally charged a commission of

FIGURE 19–5

Alternative structures of advertising agencies used to carry out the advertising program

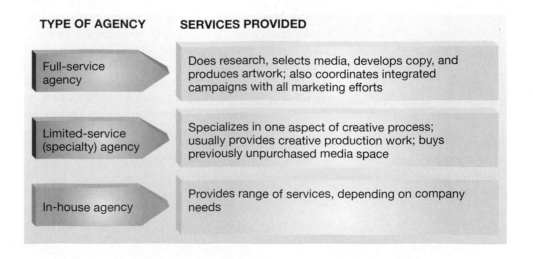

TYPE OF AGENCY	SERVICES PROVIDED
Full-service agency	Does research, selects media, develops copy, and produces artwork; also coordinates integrated campaigns with all marketing efforts
Limited-service (specialty) agency	Specializes in one aspect of creative process; usually provides creative production work; buys previously unpurchased media space
In-house agency	Provides range of services, depending on company needs

15 percent of media costs. As corporations have introduced integrated marketing approaches, however, most (70 percent) advertisers have switched from paying commissions to incentives or fees based on performance. Brad Brinegar, former CEO of advertising agency Leo Burnett USA, suggests that "a lot of value we offer is in strategic thinking, and how to pay for that is very different from traditional media spending." The most common performance criteria used are sales, brand and ad awareness, market share, and copy test results. Procter and Gamble's switch to sales-based incentives actually turned out better for its agency than media commissions would have. Global marketing director Bob Wehling explains: "P&G's goal in changing compensation wasn't to cut costs, the goal was to increase sales and support agencies in developing more comprehensive marketing plans that focus less exclusively on TV advertising and more on a broad array of reaching consumers."[54]

Limited-service agencies specialize in one aspect of the advertising process such as providing creative services to develop the advertising copy or buying previously unpurchased media space. Limited-service agencies that deal in creative work are compensated by a contractual agreement for the services performed. Finally, **in-house agencies** made up of the company's own advertising staff may provide full services or a limited range of services.

EVALUATING THE ADVERTISING PROGRAM

The advertising decision process does not stop with executing the advertising program. The advertisements must be posttested to determine whether they are achieving their intended objectives, and results may indicate that changes must be made in the advertising program.

Posttesting the Advertising

An advertisement may go through **posttests** after it has been shown to the target audience to determine whether it accomplished its intended purpose. Five approaches common in posttesting are discussed here.[55]

Starch scores an advertisement.

Aided Recall (Recognition-Readership)   After being shown an ad, respondents are asked whether their previous exposure to it was through reading, viewing, or listening. The Starch test shown in the accompanying photo uses aided recall to determine the percentage of those (1) who remember seeing a specific magazine ad (*noted*), (2) who saw or read any part of the ad identifying the product or brand (*seen-associated*), and (3) who read at least half of the ad (*read most*). Elements of the ad are then tagged with the results, as shown in the picture.

Unaided Recall   A question such as "What ads do you remember seeing yesterday?" is asked of respondents without any prompting to determine whether they saw or heard advertising messages.

Attitude Tests   Respondents are asked questions to measure changes in their attitudes after an advertising campaign, such as whether they have a more favorable attitude toward the product advertised.[56]

Inquiry Tests   Additional product information, product samples, or premiums are offered to an ad's readers or viewers. Ads generating the most inquiries are presumed to be the most effective.

Sales Tests   Sales tests involve studies such as controlled experiments (e.g., using radio ads in one market and newspaper ads in another and comparing the results) and consumer purchase tests (measuring retail sales that result from a given advertising campaign). The most sophisticated experimental methods today allow a manufacturer, a distributor, or an advertising agency to manipulate an advertising variable (such as schedule or copy) through cable systems and observe subsequent sales effects by monitoring data collected from checkout scanners in supermarkets.[57]

Making Needed Changes

Results of posttesting the advertising copy are used to reach decisions about changes in the advertising program. If the posttest results show that an advertisement is doing poorly in terms of awareness or cost efficiency, it may be dropped and other ads run in its place in the future. On the other hand, sometimes an advertisement may be so successful it is run repeatedly or used as the basis of a larger advertising program.

Concept Check

1. Explain the difference between pretesting and posttesting advertising copy.

2. What is the difference between aided and unaided recall posttests?

SALES PROMOTION

Sales promotion has become a key element of the promotional mix, which now accounts for more than $288 billion in annual expenditures. In a recent survey by the Promotion Marketing Association, marketing professionals reported that approximately 23 percent of their budgets were allocated to advertising, 15 percent to consumer promotion, 19 percent to trade promotion, and 7 percent to public relations and customer service.[58] The allocation of marketing expenditures reflects the trend toward integrated promotion programs which include a variety of promotion elements. Selection and integration of the many promotion techniques require a good understanding of the advantages and disadvantages of each kind of promotion.[59]

Consumer-Oriented Sales Promotions

Directed to ultimate consumers, **consumer-oriented sales promotions**, or simply *consumer promotions,* are sales tools used to support a company's advertising and personal selling. The alternative consumer-oriented sales promotion tools include coupons, deals, premiums, contests, sweepstakes, samples, loyalty programs, point-of-purchase displays, rebates, and product placement (see Figure 19–6).

Coupons   Coupons are sales promotions that usually offer a discounted price to the consumer, which encourages trial. Approximately 258 billion coupons are distributed in the United States each year. The redemption rate is typically about 2 percent, although in 2003 consumers redeemed only 3.6 billion coupons, or about 1.4 percent. One explanation for the decline is that the average expiration period has been declining—to about three months—giving consumers less time to redeem coupons. The average face value of redeemed coupons is about $.80. Companies that have increased their use of coupons include Procter & Gamble, H.J. Heinz, Nestlé,

ConAgra, and Kraft. In addition, the number of coupons generated at Internet sites (e.g., www.valpak.com and www.couponsonline.com) has been increasing. Coupons are often viewed as a key element of an integrated marketing program. When Duracell signed Jon Bon Jovi as a spokesperson, for example, coupons on Duracell battery packs offered $3 to $5 off Bon Jovi CDs and coupons on the CDs offered discounts on batteries.[60]

Do coupons help increase sales? Studies suggest that market share does increase during the period immediately after coupons are distributed.[61]

KIND OF SALES PROMOTION	OBJECTIVES	ADVANTAGES	DISADVANTAGES
Coupons	Stimulate demand	Encourage retailer support	Consumers delay purchases
Deals	Increase trial; retaliate against competitor's actions	Reduce consumer risk	Consumers delay purchases; reduce perceived product value
Premiums	Build goodwill	Consumers like free or reduced-price merchandise	Consumers buy for premium, not product
Contests	Increase consumer purchases; build business inventory	Encourage consumer involvement with product	Require creative or analytical thinking
Sweepstakes	Encourage present customers to buy more; minimize brand switching	Get customer to use product and store more often	Sales drop after sweepstakes
Samples	Encourage new product trial	Low risk for consumer	High cost for company
Loyalty programs	Encourage repeat purchases	Help create loyalty	High cost for company
Point-of-purchase displays	Increase product trial; provide in-store support for other promotions	Provide good product visibility	Hard to get retailer to allocate high-traffic space
Rebates	Encourage customers to purchase; stop sales decline	Effective at stimulating demand	Easily copied; steal sales from future; reduce perceived product value
Product placement	Introduce new products; demonstrate product use	Positive message in a noncommercial setting	Little control over presentation of product

FIGURE 19–6
Sales promotion alternatives

There are also indications, however, that couponing can reduce gross revenues by lowering the price paid by already-loyal consumers.[62] Therefore, the 9,000 manufacturers who currently use coupons are particularly interested in coupon programs directed at potential first-time buyers. One means of focusing on these potential buyers is through electronic in-store coupon machines that match coupons to your most recent purchases. A recent survey suggests that 81 percent of Americans use coupons when grocery shopping.[63]

Coupons are often far more expensive than the face value of the coupon; a 25 cent coupon can cost three times that after paying for the advertisement to deliver it, dealer handling, clearinghouse costs, and redemption. In addition, misredemption, or paying the face value of the coupon even though the product was not purchased, should be added to the cost of the coupon. The Coupon Information Corporation estimates that companies pay out refunds of more than $500 million each year as a result of coupon fraud.[64]

Deals   Deals are short-term price reductions, commonly used to increase trial among potential customers or to retaliate against a competitor's actions. For example, if a rival manufacturer introduces a new cake mix, the company responds with a "two packages for the price of one" deal. This short-term price reduction builds up the stock on the kitchen shelves of cake mix buyers and makes the competitor's introduction more difficult.

Premiums   A promotional tool often used with consumers is the premium, which consists of merchandise offered free or at a significant savings over its retail price. This latter type of premium is called *self-liquidating* because the cost charged to the consumer covers the cost of the item. McDonald's, for example, used a free premium in a promotional partnership with Disney during the release of the movie *The Incredibles*. Collectable toys that portrayed movie characters were given away free with the purchase of a Happy Meal. Milk-Bone dog biscuits used a self-liquidating premium when it offered a ball toy for $8.99 and two proofs of purchase.[65] By offering a premium, companies encourage customers to return frequently or to use more of the product.

Contests   A fourth sales promotion in Figure 19–6, the contest, is where consumers apply their skill or analytical or creative thinking to try to win a prize. For example, Brawny paper towel brand sponsored the "Do You Know a Brawny Man?" contest, which asked participants to send photos and a 150-word description explaining why the nominee was as rugged as the product. The winning nominee got a Dodge Durango and his photo on the Brawny packages. The contest increased the number of households using the product by 10 percent and increased sales by 12 percent.[66] If you like contests, you can even enter online now at websites such as www.playhere.com.

Sweepstakes   *Readers Digest* and Publisher's Clearing House are two well-known sweepstakes. These sales promotions require participants to submit some kind of entry but are purely games of chance requiring no analytical or creative effort by the consumer. The approach is very effective—*Time* magazine obtained 1.4 million new subscribers in one year through sweepstakes promotions.[67]

Two variations of sweepstakes are popular now. First is the instant-win game such as Pepsi's "Music Giveaway" promotion. The game offers millions of free downloads from Apple iTunes to Pepsi drinkers with winning bottle caps. Coca-Cola has a

Consumer-oriented promotions use sweepstakes to attract prospective customers and loyalty programs to reward repeat customers.

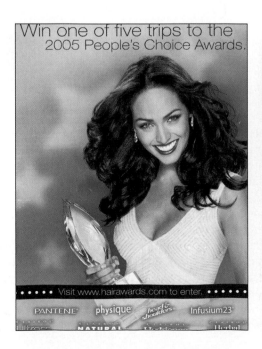

similar instant-win sweepstakes; some cans and bottles will have imbedded GPS receivers that winners can activate to alert a prize delivery team that could deliver $1 million in gold. The second is the sweepstakes that offers an "experience" as the prize. For example, AT&T's "Live Like an Idol" sweepstakes asked viewers of *American Idol* to use text messaging to vote for contestants, and each text message doubled as a sweepstakes entry. The grand prize for the sweepstakes was a trip for 10 friends to New York City or Los Angeles with first-class accommodations.[68] Federal laws, the Federal Trade Commission, and state legislatures have issued rules covering sweepstakes, contests, and games to regulate fairness, ensure that the chance for winning is represented honestly, and guarantee that the prizes are actually awarded.[69]

Samples   Another common consumer sales promotion is sampling, which is offering the product free or at a greatly reduced price. Often used for new products, sampling puts the product in the consumer's hands. A trial size is generally offered that is smaller than the regular package size. If consumers like the sample, it is hoped they will remember and buy the product. When Mars changed its Milky Way Dark to Milky Way Midnight, it gave away more than 1 million samples to college students at night clubs, several hundred campuses, and popular spring break locations. Awareness of the candy bar rose to 60 percent, trial rose 166 percent, and sales rose 25 percent. Recent research indicates that 63 percent of college students who receive a sample will also purchase the product. Overall, companies invest more than $1.5 billion in sampling programs each year.[70]

Loyalty Programs   Loyalty programs are a sales promotion tool used to encourage and reward repeat purchases by acknowledging each purchase made by a consumer and offering a premium as purchases accumulate. The most popular loyalty programs today are the frequent-flier and frequent-traveler programs used by airlines, hotels, and car rental services to reward loyal customers. American Airlines customers, for example, earn points for each mile they fly and can then redeem the accumulated points for free tickets or upgrades on the airline. American Airlines also offers a credit card that provides points for all charges made on it.

Loyalty programs are also becoming popular in other product categories. The Food Marketing Institute reports that 76 percent of all large grocery retailers offer a frequent-shopper program. Online auction retailer eBay offers its member a loyalty benefit through its Anything Points program. Even Kellogg Co. created a points program where cereal consumers visit a website to enter a code found on the package to earn downloadable awards. How many people participate in loyalty programs? There are now more than 4 billion memberships, for an average of four for each adult in the United States.[71]

Point-of-Purchase Displays   In a store aisle, you often encounter a sales promotion called a *point-of-purchase display*. These product displays take the form

of advertising signs, which sometimes actually hold or display the product, and are often located in high-traffic areas near the cash register or the end of an aisle. The accompanying picture shows a point-of-purchase display for Nabisco's annual back-to-school program. The display is designed to maximize the consumer's attention to lunch box and after-school snacks, and to provide storage for the products. A recent survey of retailers found that 87 percent plan to use more point-of-purchase materials in the future, particularly for products that can be purchased on impulse.[72]

Some studies estimate that two-thirds of a consumer's buying decisions are made in the store. This means that grocery product manufacturers want to get their message to you at the instant you are next to their brand in your supermarket aisle, perhaps through a point-of-purchase display. At a growing number of supermarkets this may be done with "floorgraphics"—floor displays with animation and sound—and "shelfscents"—displays that release a product's scent to potential consumers.[73] The advantage of these methods of promotion is that they do not rely on the consumers' ability to remember the message for long periods of time. Other in-store promotions such as interactive kiosks are also becoming popular.

Rebates   Another consumer sales promotion in Figure 19–6, the cash rebate, offers the return of money based on proof of purchase. This tool has been used heavily by car manufacturers facing increased competition. For example, Ford offers recent college graduates a $400 rebate on many of its vehicles, as part of its College Graduate Purchase Program.[74]

When a rebate is offered on lower-priced items, the time and trouble of mailing in a proof of purchase to get the rebate check often means that many buyers never take advantage of it. However, this "slippage" is less likely to occur with frequent users of rebate promotions.[75] In addition, online consumers are more likely to take advantage of rebates.

Product Placement   A final consumer promotion, **product placement**, involves the use of a brand-name product in a movie, television show, video, or commercial for another product. It was Steven Spielberg's placement of Hershey's Reese's Pieces in *E.T.* that first brought a lot of interest to the candy. Similarly, when Tom Cruise wore Bausch and Lomb's Ray-Ban sunglasses in *Risky Business* and its Aviator glasses in *Top Gun,* sales skyrocketed from 100,000 pairs to 7,000,000 pairs in five years. More recently, you might remember seeing participants in the television show *Survivor* eating Doritos and drinking Mountain Dew, actors in the *Matrix* movies using Samsung cellular telephones, and women in the cast of *All My Children* using Revlon products. The James Bond movie *Die Another Day* features Jaguars, Aston Martins, and Thunderbirds, all Ford products. Similarly, Cameron Diaz and Shirley MacLaine drive Jaguars in *In Her Shoes.* Another form of product placement uses new digital technology that can make virtual placements in an existing program. Reruns of *Seinfeld,* for example, could insert a Pepsi on a desktop, a Lexus parked on the street, or a box of Tide on the countertop.[76]

Companies are usually eager to gain exposure for their products, and studios believe that product placements add authenticity to the film or program. The studios receive fees—Sears paid $1 million for product placements in six episodes of ABC's *Extreme Makeover: Home Edition*—in exchange for the in-program exposure. How are product placements arranged? Many companies simply send brochures and catalogs to the studio resource departments; others are approached by agents who review scripts to find promising scenes where a product might be used.[77]

Can you identify these product placements?

Trade-Oriented Sales Promotions

Trade-oriented sales promotions, or simply *trade promotions,* are sales tools used to support a company's advertising and personal selling directed to wholesalers, retailers, or distributors. Some of the sales promotions just reviewed are used for this purpose, but there are three other common approaches targeted uniquely to these intermediaries: (1) allowances and discounts, (2) cooperative advertising, and (3) training of distributors' salesforces.

Allowances and Discounts
Trade promotions often focus on maintaining or increasing inventory levels in the channel of distribution. An effective method for encouraging such increased purchases by intermediaries is the use of allowances and discounts. However, overuse of these price reductions can lead to retailers changing their ordering patterns in the expectation of such offerings. Although there are many variations that manufacturers can use with discounts and allowances, three common approaches are the merchandise allowance, the case allowance, and the finance allowance.[78]

Reimbursing a retailer for extra in-store support or special featuring of the brand is a *merchandise allowance.* Performance contracts between the manufacturer and trade member usually specify the activity to be performed, such as a picture of the product in a newspaper with a coupon good at only one store. The merchandise allowance then consists of a percentage deduction from the list case price ordered during the promotional period. Allowances are not paid by the manufacturer until it sees proof of performance (such as a copy of the ad placed by the retailer in the local newspaper).

A second common trade promotion, a *case allowance,* is a discount on each case ordered during a specific time period. These allowances are usually deducted from the invoice. A variation of the case allowance is the "free goods" approach, whereby retailers receive some amount of the product free based on the amount ordered, such as 1 case free for every 10 cases ordered.[79]

A final trade promotion, the *finance allowance,* involves paying retailers for financing costs or financial losses associated with consumer sales promotions. This trade promotion is regularly used and has several variations. One type is the floor stock protection program—manufacturers give retailers a case allowance price for products in their warehouse, which prevents shelf stock from running down during the promotional period. Also common are freight allowances, which compensate retailers that transport orders from the manufacturer's warehouse.

Cooperative Advertising
Resellers often perform the important function of promoting the manufacturer's products at the local level. One common sales promotional activity is to encourage both better quality and greater quantity in the local advertising efforts of resellers through **cooperative advertising**. These are programs by which a manufacturer pays a percentage of the retailer's local advertising expense for advertising the manufacturer's products.

Usually the manufacturer pays a percentage, often 50 percent, of the cost of advertising up to a certain dollar limit, which is based on the amount of the purchases the retailer makes of the manufacturer's products. In addition to paying for the advertising, the manufacturer often furnishes the retailer with a selection of different ad executions, sometimes suited for several different media. A manufacturer may provide, for example, several different print layouts as well as a few broadcast ads for the retailer to adapt and use.[80]

Training of Distributors' Salesforces
One of the many functions the intermediaries perform is customer contact and selling for the producers they represent. Both retailers and wholesalers employ and manage their own sales personnel. A manufacturer's success often rests on the ability of the reseller's salesforce to represent its products.

Thus, it is in the best interest of the manufacturer to help train the reseller's salesforce. Because the reseller's salesforce is often less sophisticated and knowledgeable about the products than the manufacturer might like, training can increase their sales performance. Training activities include producing manuals and brochures to educate the reseller's salesforce. The salesforce then uses these aids in selling situations. Other activities include national sales meetings sponsored by the manufacturer and field visits to the reseller's location to inform and motivate the salesperson to sell the products. Manufacturers also develop incentive and recognition programs to motivate reseller's salespeople to sell their products.

Concept Check

1. Which sales promotional tool is most common for new products?

2. What's the difference between a coupon and a deal?

3. Which trade promotion is used on an ongoing basis?

PUBLIC RELATIONS

As noted in Chapter 18, public relations is a form of communication management that seeks to influence the image of an organization and its products and services. Public relations efforts may utilize a variety of tools and may be directed at many distinct audiences. While public relations personnel usually focus on communicating positive aspects of the business, they may also be called on to minimize the negative impact of a problem or crisis. Firestone, for example, recalled 6.5 million tires when National Highway Traffic Safety Administration officials launched an investigation into consumer complaints about the tires. Debates with Ford Motor Company about the tire failures being due to overloading or underinflation created a difficult situation for the public relations department.[81] The most frequently used public relations tool is publicity.

Publicity Tools

In developing a public relations campaign, several methods of obtaining nonpersonal presentation of an organization, good, or service without direct cost—**publicity tools**—are available to the public relations director. Many companies frequently use the *news release,* consisting of an announcement regarding changes in the company or the product line. The objective of a news release is to inform a newspaper, radio station, or other medium of an idea for a story. A recent study found that more than 40 percent of all free mentions of a brand name occur during news programs.[82]

A second common publicity tool is the *news conference.* Representatives of the media are all invited to an informational meeting, and advance materials regarding the content are sent. This tool is often used when negative publicity—as in the cases of the Ford Explorer rollover problem, the NASCAR Daytona 500 accident that killed Dale Earnhardt, and the *Exxon Valdez* oil spill—requires a company response.[83]

Sarah Jessica Parker uses publicity to promote her movies and television programs.

Nonprofit organizations rely heavily on *public service announcements* (PSAs), which are free space or time donated by the media. For example, the charter of the American Red Cross prohibits any local chapter from advertising, so to solicit blood donations local chapters often depend on PSAs on radio or television to announce their needs.

Finally, today many high-visibility individuals are used as publicity tools to create visibility for their companies, their products, and themselves. Richard Branson uses visibility to promote the Virgin Group, Sarah Jessica Parker uses it to promote her movies and television programs, and U.S. senators use it to promote themselves as political candidates. These publicity efforts are coordinated with news releases, conferences, advertising, donations to charities, volunteer activities, endorsements, and any other activities that may have an impact on public perceptions.[84]

INCREASING THE VALUE OF PROMOTION

Today's customers seek value from companies that provide leading-edge products, hassle-free transactions at competitive prices, and customer intimacy.[85] Promotion practices have changed dramatically to improve transactions and increase customer intimacy by (1) emphasizing long-term relationships and (2) increasing self-regulation.

Building Long-Term Relationships with Promotion

Many changes in promotional techniques have been driven by marketers' interest in developing long-term relationships with their customers. Promotion can contribute to brand and store loyalty by improving its ability to target individual preferences and by engaging customers in valuable and entertaining communication. New media such as the Internet have provided immediate opportunities for personalized promotion activities such as e-mail advertising. In addition, technological developments have helped traditional media such as TV and radio focus on individual preferences through services such as TiVo and XM Satellite Radio. Although the future holds extraordinary promise for the personalization of promotion, the industry will need to manage and balance consumers' concerns about privacy as it proceeds.

Changes that help engage consumers have also been numerous. Marketers have attempted to utilize interactive technologies and to integrate new media and technologies into the overall creative process. Ad agencies are increasingly integrating public relations, direct marketing, advertising, and promotion into comprehensive campaigns. In fact, some experts predict that advertising agencies will soon become "communications consulting firms." Further, increasingly diverse and global audiences necessitate multimedia approaches and sensitivity communication techniques that engage the varied groups.[86] Overall, companies hope that these changes will build customer relationships for the long term—emphasizing a lifetime of purchases rather than a single transaction.

Self-Regulation

Unfortunately, over the years many consumers have been misled, or even deceived, by some promotions. Examples include sweepstakes in which the gifts were not awarded, rebate offers that were a terrible hassle, and advertisements whose promises were great, until the buyer read the small print. In one of the worst scandals in promotion history, McDonald's assisted an FBI investigation of the firm responsible for its sweepstakes, because the promotion agency security director was suspected of stealing winning gamepieces.[87]

Promotions targeted at special groups such as children and the elderly also raise ethical concerns. For example, providing free samples to children in elementary schools or linking product lines to TV programs and movies have led to questions about the need for restrictions on promotions.[88] Although the Federal Trade Commission does provide some guidelines to protect consumers and special groups from misleading promotions, some observers believe more government regulation is needed.

To rely on formal regulation by federal, state, and local governments of all promotional activities would be very expensive. As a result, there are increasing efforts by advertising agencies, trade associations, and marketing organizations at *self-regulation*.[89] By imposing standards that reflect the values of society on their promotional activities, marketers can (1) facilitate the development of new promotional methods, (2) minimize regulatory constraints and restrictions, and (3) help consumers gain confidence in the communication efforts used to influence their purchases. As organizations strive for effective self-regulation, marketing executives will need to make sound ethical judgments about the use of existing and new promotional practices.

Concept Check

1. What is a news release?

2. What is the difference between government regulation and self-regulation?

CHAPTER IN REVIEW

1 *Explain the differences between product advertising and institutional advertising and the variations within each type.*

Product advertisements focus on selling a good or service and take three forms: Pioneering advertisements tell people what a product is, what it can do, and where it can be found; competitive advertisements persuade the target market to select the firm's brand rather than a competitor's; and reminder advertisements reinforce previous knowledge of a product. Institutional advertisements are use to build goodwill or an image for an organization. They include advocacy advertisements, which state the position of a company on an issue, and pioneering, competitive, and reminder advertisements, which are similar to the product ads but focused on the institution.

2 *Describe the steps used to develop, execute, and evaluate an advertising program.*

The promotion decision process can be applied to each of the promotional elements. The steps to develop an advertising program include identify the target audience, specify the advertising objectives, set the advertising budget, design the advertisement, create the message, select the media, and schedule the advertising. Executing the program requires pretesting, and evaluating the program requires posttesting.

3 *Explain the advantages and disadvantages of alternative advertising media.*

Television advertising reaches large audiences and uses picture, print, sound, and motion; its disadvantages, however, are that it is expensive and perishable. Radio advertising is inexpensive and can be placed quickly, but it has no visual element and is perishable. Magazine advertising can target specific audiences and can convey complex information, but it takes a long time to place the ad and is relatively expensive. Newspapers provide excellent coverage of local markets and can be changed quickly, but they have a short life span and poor color. Yellow pages advertising has a long use period and is available 24 hours per day; its disadvantages, however, are that there is a proliferation of directories and they cannot be updated frequently. Internet advertising can be interactive, but its effectiveness is difficult to measure. Outdoor advertising provides repeat exposures, but its message must be very short and simple. Direct mail can be targeted at very selective audiences, but its cost per contact is high.

4 *Discuss the strengths and weaknesses of consumer-oriented and trade-oriented sales promotions.*

Coupons encourage retailer support but may delay consumer purchases. Deals reduce consumer risk but reduce perceived value. Premiums offer consumers additional merchandise they want, but they may be purchasing only for the premium. Contests create involvement but require creative thinking. Sweepstakes encourage repeat purchases, but sales drop after the sweepstakes. Samples encourage product trial but are expensive. Loyalty programs help create loyalty but are expensive to run. Displays provide visibility but are difficult to place in retail space. Rebates stimulate demand but are easily copied. Product placement provides a positive message in a noncommercial setting but is difficult to control. Trade-oriented sales promotions include (*a*) allowances and discounts, which increase purchases but may change retailer ordering patterns, (*b*) cooperative advertising, which encourages local advertising, and (*c*) salesforce training, which helps increase sales by providing the salespeople with product information and selling skills.

5 *Recognize public relations as an important form of communication.*

Public relations activities usually focus on communicating positive aspects of the business. A frequently used public relations tool is publicity. Publicity tools include new releases and news conferences. Nonprofit organization often use public service announcements.

FOCUSING ON KEY TERMS

advertising p. 496
consumer-oriented sales promotions p. 514
cooperative advertising p. 519

cost per thousand p. 504
frequency p. 504
full-service agency p. 512

gross rating points p. 504
infomercials p. 506
in-house agencies p. 513
institutional advertisements p. 497
limited-service agencies p. 513
posttests p. 513
pretests p. 512

product advertisements p. 497
product placement p. 518
publicity tools p. 520
rating p. 504
reach p. 504
trade-oriented sales promotions p. 519

DISCUSSION AND APPLICATION QUESTIONS

1 How does competitive product advertising differ from competitive institutional advertising?

2 Suppose you are the advertising manager for a new line of children's fragrances. Which form of media would you use for this new product?

3 You have recently been promoted to be director of advertising for the Timkin Tool Company. In your first meeting with Mr. Timkin, he says, "Advertising is a waste! We've been advertising for six months now and sales haven't increased. Tell me why we should continue." Give your answer to Mr. Timkin.

4 A large life insurance company has decided to switch from using a strong fear appeal to a humorous approach. What are the strengths and weaknesses of such a change in message strategy?

5 Which medium has the lowest cost per thousand?

MEDIUM	COST	AUDIENCE
TV show	$5,000	25,000
Magazine	2,200	6,000
Newspaper	4,800	7,200
FM radio	420	1,600

6 Some national advertisers have found that they can have more impact with their advertising by running a large number of ads for a period and then running no ads at all for a period. Why might such a flighting schedule be more effective than a continuous schedule?

7 Each year managers at Bausch and Lomb evaluate the many advertising media alternatives available to them as they develop their advertising program for contact lenses. What advantages and disadvantages of each alternative should they consider? Which media would you recommend to them?

8 What are two advantages and two disadvantages of the advertising posttests described in the chapter?

9 Federated Banks is interested in consumer-oriented sales promotions that would encourage senior citizens to direct deposit their Social Security checks with the bank. Evaluate the sales promotion options, and recommend two of them to the bank.

10 How can public relations be used by Firestone and Ford following investigations into complaints about tire failures?

11 Describe a self-regulation guideline you believe would improve the value of (*a*) an existing form of promotion and (*b*) a new promotional practice.

GOING ONLINE   Advertising on the Internet

Most websites accept some form of advertising. If you were to advise your college or university to advertise on the Internet, what three sites would you recommend? Visit the Interactive Advertising Bureau web site (www.iab.com) and review the "Standards and Guidelines" section to determine what type of online ad you would recommend.

1 How many types of (*a*) rectangles and pop-ups, (*b*) banners and buttons, and (*c*) skyscrapers does the IAB specify?

2 Describe the profile of the audience for each of the websites.

3 What does the IAB suggest you include in your online advertising privacy policy?

BUILDING YOUR MARKETING PLAN

To augment your promotion strategy from Chapter 18:

1 Use Figure 19–4 to select the advertising media you will include in your plan by analyzing how combinations of media (e.g., television and Internet advertising, radio and yellow pages advertising) can complement each other.

2 Use Figure 19–6 to select your consumer-oriented sales promotion activities.

3 Specify which trade-oriented sales promotions and public relations activities you will use.

VIDEO CASE 19   Fallon Worldwide: In the *Creativity* Business

"Most people think of Fallon as being in the advertising business, but we don't really think of ourselves that way," says Rob White, president of Fallon Worldwide. "We believe that we are a creativity company that happens to do some advertising," he continues. As an example, he points out that Fallon starts upstream of a firm's communication issues to identify the key business problem and uses creativity to help solve it. Sometimes this involves a heavy dose of advertising and other times almost none. But it always takes a very creative flair.

Founded in 1981, Fallon Worldwide—or simply Fallon—has won dozens of advertising awards. This includes two Agency of the Year awards given by *Advertising Age* magazine. "I think Fallon's success is due to two important things," says White. "One is the people and the other one is the culture that bonds the people together. When you create a special kind of culture with collaboration and teamwork from a very high level and people with different backgrounds, amazing things can happen," he explains.

Bruce Bildsten, Fallon creative group director, echoes this focus on creativity: "It's always a challenge as creative director to try to stay at the forefront and come up with something that people haven't seen. I desperately try not to look at other advertising for ideas. I always challenge our people to look at work from other parts of the world—film, novels, music—for inspiration."

A look at two promotional campaigns developed at Fallon show how creativity, teamwork, and not looking at traditional ads from other agencies come together to build award-winning campaigns. Both campaigns discussed below have been recognized for their creativity and their success at achieving the clients' objectives.

CITIBANK: ATTRACTING BALANCE SEEKERS

Citibank approached Fallon because it knew it had a problem. Citi had been successful in the past by being a low cost provider, having great service, and by focusing on direct marketing. Suddenly that wasn't enough. Competition had increased significantly and customer perceptions of banks and credit card companies had changed. Laurel Flatt, Fallon Account Director on the Citibank account, describes the challenge: "New banks were springing up all over the place. There were new credit card companies. Consumers looked at financial services as simply a commodity. Your relationship with your bank, your credit card company was once a very, very special relationship." Now, however, consumers viewed one bank as being no different than another.

When Citibank came to Fallon, it said that it really wanted to be "un-banklike," it wanted to be different. Fallon asked the question, "What is the right way to be un-banklike in a way that will generate results for the Citi brand?" Qualitative and quantitative research identified a segment of consumers that Fallon labeled "balance seekers." This group amounted to about 50 percent of the market for financial services. Balance seekers viewed financial services and money as a means to an end, something that helps them lead the life they live. This segment also shared an attitude that was receptive to the idea of an un-banklike message, though they had different income levels, assets, ages, and other demographic characteristics.

Fallon translated un-banklike to mean very friendly, human, and a little bit quirky—very different from the serious tone of traditional bank and financial services companies. In addition, Fallon wanted the Citi brand to represent a healthy approach to money. Finally, Fallon wanted to communicate that the credit card protects consumers and their purchases.

Fallon's ad executions were funny, and engaging. One ad shows a middle aged woman from Minnesota getting a tattoo. The tag line is "It didn't seem right to us, either" and talks about Citi's Fraud Early Warning system to identify unusual spending behavior. Another ad shows a truck driver from Iowa asleep under a hair dryer at La Petite Lily Day Spa with the same tag line and message about how Citi's identity theft solutions can help make things right. The Citi campaign utilized billboards and wall advertising, bus shelter kiosks, magazines, and television.

Fallon used brand-tracking to chart the degree of differentiation of the Citi brand. Over time, the differentiation climbed as more and more people perceived Citi as different from other banks yet relevant in their lives. Sales results were also positive. Card acquisition and card usage increased dramatically!

BMW: GRABBING ATTENTION WITH "THE HIRE"

Working closely together in the late 1990s, BMW and Fallon brainstormed, talked to consumers, and agonized over what the positioning of BMW should be. Their answer: "Responsiveness"—which means a performance vehicle that includes not only acceleration and braking but also its cornering, its safety.

The only problem with this was that soon major competitors like Mitsubishi and Ford were trying to adopt this "responsiveness" positioning for themselves. "So our first promotional objective was to separate BMW from its competitors as the only true, cool, legitimate, ultimate driving machine," says Ginny Grossman, Fallon Group Director. "We wanted the ownership of the 'responsiveness' position. We wanted people to associate that with BMW and only BMW."

"The target audience for 'The Hire' was BMW's future customer," says Erin Tait, Fallon Senior Account Planner. "Today the average age of a BMW driver is 42. So what we wanted to do was make sure that the future audience, the 20- and 30-year-olds felt as good about the BMW brand as the 40- and 50-year-olds did. So, this campaign 'The Hire' was about making sure that the BMW brand was relevant and attractive to that younger audience."

Overseen by Hollywood directors such as Ang Lee and John Frankenheimer, "The Hire" is the title given to a series of short films launched on the Internet that can be downloaded (www.bmwfilms.com). They feature Clive Owen as the driver and carry provocative titles such as "Ambush," "Chosen," "The Follow," "Star," and "Powder Keg" in the first "season," and "Hostage," "Ticker," and "Beat the Devil" more recently in "The Hire II."

In trying to reach this younger market, a special problem emerged. "When we spoke to 20- and 30-year-olds about the BMW brand and what they thought it meant to them, they talked about things like being really into aggressive driving and risk-taking. That's the kind of person that would choose a BMW. But unfortunately, a lot of those attributes got taken in kind of a negative way," explains Tait.

"So our challenge was to take the positive value of the BMW brand. That's what Clive Owen in 'The Hire' re-

ally helped to do because the decisions he makes and the risks he takes are all for the good and for helping the person he's been hired to drive," says Tait. "You learn about this character through these movies which helps shape your perception of the kind of person that would choose a BMW. Plus it gives you a great sense for how the car performs in treacherous, difficult driving situations."

BMW and Fallon's next challenge was how to use these creative films to attract the attention of 20- and 30-year-olds and achieve "water cooler talk" the next day after they saw them on the Internet.

PUSHING THE CREATIVE BARRIERS

How does Fallon keep the creative juices flowing—from developing new promotional campaigns to using new media like the Internet? This involves continuing to develop award-winning commercials like "It's Time to Fly" for United Airlines and "Havana Nights" for Virgin Mobil, as well as the Citi and BMW campaigns.

Concerning new media, Kevin Flatt, Fallon Creative-Interactive, talks about the increasing importance of the Internet: "A number of our clients are recognizing now that they can get more focused connections to meaningful consumers with the Internet and be able to measure whether it's working or not." For people thinking about going into advertising, he tells what his job means to him: "If you love it, it is the most rewarding job because of how wonderful it is to be able to go and tell somebody 'I love what I do!'"

Questions

1 Fallon Worldwide stresses its creativity, as shown by comments from the Fallon people in the case. In what ways do the Citi and BMW campaigns reflect their creativity? Compare the sources of the ideas in the two campaigns.

2 In the Citi and BMW campaigns how were (*a*) the target markets and (*b*) each brand's positioning changed from the situation prior to the campaign?

3 Compare the media used for the Citi and BMW campaigns. Why were these media chosen? Do you expect the use of these or other media to change in the future?

4 How might Fallon and its clients measure the success of (*a*) the Citi and (*b*) the BMW campaigns?

20 PERSONAL SELLING AND SALES MANAGEMENT

LEARNING OBJECTIVES

After reading this chapter you should be able to:

1 Discuss the nature and scope of personal selling and sales management in marketing.

2 Identify the different types of personal selling.

3 Explain the stages in the personal selling process.

4 Describe the major functions of sales management.

SELLING THE WAY CUSTOMERS WANT TO BUY

Anne Mulcahy has a challenging assignment. As the chairman of the board and chief executive officer at Xerox Corporation, she is in the midst of successfully implementing one of the greatest feats in the annals of business history: restoring Xerox's legendary marketing and financial vitality. Her success can be attributed to staying in sync with Xerox customers and employees. "I believe strongly that my success as a leader is driven by my commitment to understanding and meeting customers' requirements, as well as developing and nurturing a motivated and proud workforce," says Mulcahy (shown on the opposite page). "With the right amount of focus, the two have the potential to drive exceptional results."

Mulcahy is ideally suited to the task. She began her 28-year Xerox career as a field sales representative and assumed increasingly responsible management and executive positions. These included chief staff officer, president of Xerox's General Markets Operations, and president and chief operating officer of Xerox. As chairman and CEO, Mulcahy has to muster the knowledge and experience gained from this varied background. Not surprisingly, her sales background has played a pivotal role.

"We will win back market share one customer at a time, one sale at a time," Mulcahy says. "We'll do that by providing greater value than our competitors—and that means selling the way customers want to buy." She adds that Xerox must offer a broad range of products and services at competitive prices through direct, indirect, Internet, and telephone sales, and customer support. Her approach to sales, coupled with her considerable management experience, has already borne fruit as Xerox positions itself for future sales and profit growth.[1]

This chapter describes the scope and significance of personal selling and sales management in marketing. It first highlights the many forms of personal selling and outlines the selling process. Salesforce management functions are then described, including recent advances in salesforce automation and customer relationship management.

SCOPE AND SIGNIFICANCE OF PERSONAL SELLING AND SALES MANAGEMENT

Chapter 18 described personal selling and management of the sales effort as being part of the firm's promotional mix. Although it is important to recognize that personal selling is a useful vehicle for communicating with present and potential buyers, it is much more. Take a moment to answer the questions in the personal selling and sales management quiz in Figure 20–1. As you read on, compare your answers with those in the text.

Nature of Personal Selling and Sales Management

Personal selling involves the two-way flow of communication between a buyer and seller, often in a face-to-face encounter, designed to influence a person's or group's purchase decision. However, with advances in telecommunications, personal selling also takes place over the telephone, through video teleconferencing and Internet-enabled links between buyers and sellers.

Personal selling remains a highly human-intensive activity despite the use of technology. Accordingly, the people involved must be managed. **Sales management** involves planning the selling program and implementing and controlling the personal selling effort of the firm. The tasks involved in managing personal selling include setting objectives; organizing the salesforce; recruiting, selecting, training, and compensating salespeople; and evaluating the performance of individual salespeople.

Selling Happens Almost Everywhere

"Everyone lives by selling something," wrote author Robert Louis Stevenson a century ago. His observation still holds true today. The Bureau of Labor Statistics reports that almost 14 million people are employed in sales positions in the United States. Included in this number are manufacturing sales personnel, real estate brokers, stockbrokers, and salesclerks who work in retail stores. In reality, however, virtually

FIGURE 20–1
Personal selling and sales management quiz

1. What percentage of chief executive officers in the 1,000 largest U.S. corporations have significant sales and marketing experience in their work history? (check one)

   10% _____   30% _____   50% _____
   20% _____   40% _____   60% _____

2. About how much does it cost for a field sales representative to make a single personal sales call on a business customer? (check one)

   $100 _____ $200 _____ $300 _____
   $150 _____ $250 _____ $350 _____

3. "A salesperson's job is finished when a sale is made." True or false? (circle one)

               True   False

4. About what percentage of U.S. companies include customer satisfaction as a measure of salesperson performance? (check one)

   10% _____   30% _____   50% _____
   20% _____   40% _____   60% _____

Could this be a salesperson in the operating room? Read the text to find why Medtronic salespeople visit hospital operating rooms.

Medtronic
www.medtronic.com

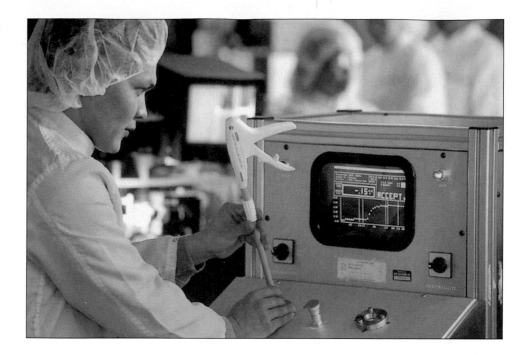

every occupation that involves customer contact has an element of personal selling. For example, attorneys, accountants, bankers, and company personnel recruiters perform sales-related activities, whether or not they acknowledge it. About 20 percent of the chief executive officers in the 1,000 largest U.S. corporations have significant sales and marketing experience in their work history like Anne Mulcahy at Xerox.[2] (What percentage did you check for question 1 in Figure 20–1?) Thus, selling often serves as a stepping-stone to top management, as well as being a career path in itself.

Personal Selling in Marketing

Personal selling serves three major roles in a firm's overall marketing effort. First, salespeople are the critical link between the firm and its customers. This role requires that salespeople match company interests with customer needs to satisfy both parties in the exchange process. Second, salespeople *are* the company in a consumer's eyes. They represent what a company is or attempts to be and are often the only personal contact a customer has with the company. For example, the "look" projected by Gucci salespeople is an important factor in communicating the style of the company's apparel line. Third, personal selling may play a dominant role in a firm's marketing program. This situation typically arises when a firm uses a push marketing strategy, described in Chapter 18. Avon, for example, pays almost 40 percent of its total sales dollars for selling expenses. Pharmaceutical firms and office and educational equipment manufacturers also rely heavily on personal selling in the marketing of their products.

Creating Customer Value through Salespeople: Relationship and Partnership Selling

As the critical link between the firm and its customers, salespeople can create customer value in many ways. For instance, by being close to the customer, salespeople can identify creative solutions to customer problems. Salespeople at Medtronic, Inc., the world leader in the heart pacemaker market, are in the operating room for more than 90 percent of the procedures performed with their product and are on call, wearing pagers, 24 hours a day. "It reflects the willingness to be there in every situation, just in case a problem arises—even though nine times out of ten the procedure goes just fine," notes a satisfied customer.[3] Salespeople can create value by easing the customer buying process. This happened at AMP, Inc., a producer of electrical products. Salespeople and customers had a difficult time getting product specifications and performance data on AMP's 70,000 products quickly and accurately. The company now records all information on CD-ROM disks that can be scanned instantly by salespeople and customers. Customer value is also created by salespeople who follow through after the sale. At Jefferson Smurfit Corporation, a multibillion-dollar supplier of packaging products, one of its salespeople juggled production from three of the company's plants to satisfy an unexpected demand for boxes from General Electric. This person's action led to the company being given GE's Distinguished Supplier Award.

Customer value creation is made possible by **relationship selling**, the practice of building ties to customers based on a salesperson's attention and commitment to customer needs over time. Relationship selling involves mutual respect and trust among buyers and sellers. It focuses on creating long-term customers, not a one time sale. A survey of 300 senior sales executives revealed that 96 percent consider "building long-term relationships with customers" to be the most important activity affecting sales performance. Companies such as Xerox, American Express, Electronic Data Systems, Motorola, and Owens-Corning have made relationship building a core focus of their sales effort.[4]

Some companies have taken relationship selling a step further and forged partnerships between buyer and seller organizations. With **partnership selling**, sometimes called *enterprise selling,* buyers and sellers combine their expertise and resources to create customized solutions; commit to joint planning; and share customer, competitive, and company information for their mutual benefit, and ultimately the customer. As an approach to sales, partnership selling relies on cross-functional business specialists who apply their knowledge and expertise to achieve higher productivity, lower cost, and greater customer value. Partnership selling complements supplier and channel partnering described in Chapters 6, 15, and 16. This practice is embraced by companies such as General Electric, Honeywell, Du Pont, and IBM. For example, on any given day, IBM has 30 information technology hardware and software specialists, business consultants, and engineers working at Charles Schwab, a large brokerage firm, all under the direction of a senior IBM sales executive. Their job? Create and manage a complex state-of-the-art financial planning system that assists Schwab clients with their retirement planning.[5]

Relationship and partnership selling represent another dimension of customer relationship management. Both emphasize the importance of learning about customer needs and wants and tailoring solutions to customer problems as a means to customer value creation.

Concept Check

1. What is personal selling?

2. What is involved in sales management?

THE MANY FORMS OF PERSONAL SELLING

Personal selling assumes many forms based on the amount of selling done and the amount of creativity required to perform the sales task. Broadly speaking, three types of personal selling exist: order taking, order getting, and customer sales support activities. While some firms use only one of these types of personal selling, others use a combination of all three.

A Frito-Lay salesperson takes inventory of snacks for the store manager to sign. In this situation, the manager will make a straight rebuy decision.

Frito-Lay, Inc.
www.fritolay.com

Order Taking

Typically, an **order taker** processes routine orders or reorders for products that were already sold by the company. The primary responsibility of order takers is to preserve an ongoing relationship with existing customers and maintain sales.

Two types of order takers exist. *Outside order takers* visit customers and replenish inventory stocks of resellers, such as retailers or wholesalers. For example, Frito-Lay salespeople call on supermarkets, convenience stores, and other establishments to ensure that the company's line of snack products (such as Doritos and Tostitos tortilla chips) is in adequate supply. In addition, outside order takers often provide assistance in arranging displays. *Inside order takers,* also called *order clerks* or *salesclerks,* typically answer simple questions, take orders, and complete transactions with customers. Many retail clerks are inside order takers. Inside order takers are often employed by companies that use *inbound telemarketing,* the use of toll-free telephone numbers that customers can call to obtain information about products or services and make purchases. In business-to-business settings, order taking arises in straight rebuy situations.

Order takers generally do little selling in a conventional sense and engage in only modest problem solving with customers. They often represent products that have few options, such as confectionary items, magazine subscriptions, and highly standardized industrial products. Inbound telemarketing is also an essential selling activity for more "customer service" driven firms, such as Dell Inc. At these companies, order takers undergo extensive training so that they can better assist callers with their purchase decisions.

Order Getting

An **order getter** sells in a conventional sense and identifies prospective customers, provides customers with information, persuades customers to buy, closes sales, and follows up on customers' use of a product or service. Like order takers, order getters can be inside (an automobile salesperson) or outside (a Xerox salesperson). Order getting involves a high degree of creativity and customer empathy and is typically required for selling complex or technical products with many options, so considerable product knowledge and sales training are necessary. In modified rebuy

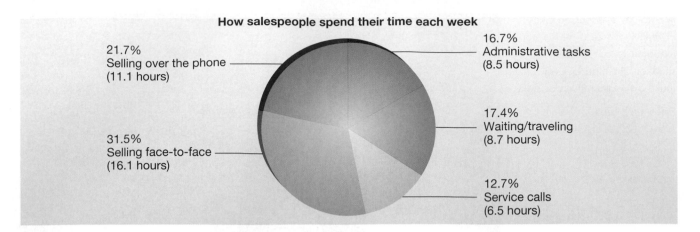

How salespeople spend their time each week

21.7%
Selling over the phone
(11.1 hours)

16.7%
Administrative tasks
(8.5 hours)

17.4%
Waiting/traveling
(8.7 hours)

31.5%
Selling face-to-face
(16.1 hours)

12.7%
Service calls
(6.5 hours)

FIGURE 20–2

How outside order-getting salespeople spend their time each week

or new-buy purchase situations in business-to-business selling, an order getter acts as a problem solver who identifies how a particular product may satisfy a customer's need. Similarly, in the purchase of a service, such as insurance, a Metropolitan Life insurance agent can provide a mix of plans to satisfy a buyer's needs depending on income, stage of the family's life cycle, and investment objectives.

Order getting is not a 40-hour-per-week job. Industry research indicates that outside order getters, or field service representatives, work about 51 hours per week. As shown in Figure 20–2, 53 percent of their time is spent selling and another 13 percent is devoted to customer service calls. The remainder of their work is occupied by getting to customers and performing numerous administrative tasks.[6]

Order getting by outside salespeople is also expensive. It is estimated that the average cost of a single field sales call on a business customer is about $350, factoring in salespeople compensation, benefits, and travel-and-entertainment expenses. (What amount did you check for question 2 in Figure 20–1?) This cost illustrates why outbound telemarketing is popular. *Outbound telemarketing* is the practice of using the telephone rather than personal visits to contact current and prospective customers. A significantly lower cost per sales call (in the range of $20 to $25) and little or no field expense accounts for its widespread appeal. More than 100 million outbound telemarketing calls are made to homes and businesses each year in the United States.[7]

Customer Sales Support Personnel

Customer sales support personnel augment the selling effort of order getters by performing a variety of services. For example, **missionary salespeople** do not directly solicit orders but rather concentrate on performing promotional activities and introducing new products. They are used extensively in the pharmaceutical industry, where they persuade physicians to prescribe a firm's product. Actual sales are made through wholesalers or directly to pharmacists who fill prescriptions. A **sales engineer** is a salesperson who specializes in identifying, analyzing, and solving customer problems and brings know-how and technical expertise to the selling situation but often does not actually sell products and services. Sales engineers are popular in selling business products such as chemicals and heavy equipment.

In many situations firms engage in cross-functional **team selling**, the practice of using an entire team of professionals in selling to and servicing major customers.[8] Team selling is used when specialized knowledge is needed to satisfy the different interests of individuals in a customer's buying center. For example, a selling team might consist of a salesperson, a sales engineer, a service representative, and a financial executive, each of whom would deal with a counterpart in the customer's firm. Selling teams have grown in popularity due to partnering and take different forms.

MARKETING NEWSNET

Creating and Sustaining Customer Value through Cross-Functional Team Selling

CROSS FUNCTIONAL

The day of the lone salesperson calling on a customer is rapidly becoming history. Many companies today employ cross-functional teams of professionals to work with customers to improve relationships, find better ways of doing things, and, of course, create and sustain value for their customers.

Xerox and IBM pioneered cross-functional team selling, but other firms were quick to follow as they spotted the potential to create and sustain value for their customers. Recognizing that corn growers needed a herbicide they could apply less often, a Du Pont team of chemists, sales and marketing executives, and regulatory specialists created just the right product that recorded sales of $57 million in its first year. Procter & Gamble uses teams of marketing, sales, advertising, computer systems, and supply chain personnel to work with its major retailers, such as Wal-Mart, to identify ways to develop, promote, and deliver products. Pitney Bowes, Inc., which produces sophisticated computer systems that weigh, rate, and track packages for firms such as UPS and Federal Express, also uses sales teams to meet customer needs. These teams consist of sales personnel, "carrier management specialists," and engineering and administrative executives who continually find ways to improve the technology of shipping goods across town and around the world.

Efforts to create and sustain customer value through cross-functional team selling have become a necessity as customers seek greater value for their money. According to the vice president for procurement of a Fortune 500 company, "Today, it's not just getting the best price but getting the best value—and there are a lot of pieces to value."

In *conference selling,* a salesperson and other company resource people meet with buyers to discuss problems and opportunities. In *seminar selling,* a company team conducts an educational program for a customer's technical staff, describing state-of-the-art developments. IBM and Xerox pioneered cross-functional team selling in working with prospective buyers. Other firms have embraced this practice and created and sustained value for their customers, as described in the accompanying Marketing NewsNet.[9]

Concept Check

1. What is the principal difference between an order taker and an order getter?

2. What is team selling?

THE PERSONAL SELLING PROCESS: BUILDING RELATIONSHIPS

Selling, and particularly order getting, is a complicated activity that involves building buyer–seller relationships. Although the salesperson–customer interaction is essential to personal selling, much of a salesperson's work occurs before this meeting and continues after the sale itself. The **personal selling process** consists of six stages: (1) prospecting, (2) preapproach, (3) approach, (4) presentation, (5) close, and (6) follow-up (Figure 20–3 on the next page).

FIGURE 20–3

Stages and objectives of the personal selling process

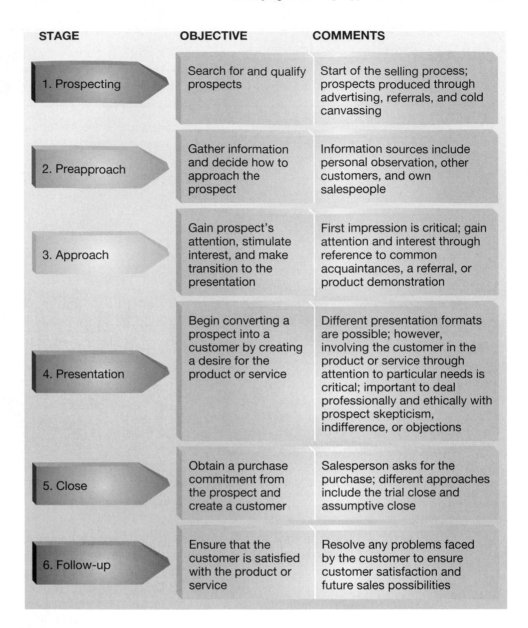

STAGE	OBJECTIVE	COMMENTS
1. Prospecting	Search for and qualify prospects	Start of the selling process; prospects produced through advertising, referrals, and cold canvassing
2. Preapproach	Gather information and decide how to approach the prospect	Information sources include personal observation, other customers, and own salespeople
3. Approach	Gain prospect's attention, stimulate interest, and make transition to the presentation	First impression is critical; gain attention and interest through reference to common acquaintances, a referral, or product demonstration
4. Presentation	Begin converting a prospect into a customer by creating a desire for the product or service	Different presentation formats are possible; however, involving the customer in the product or service through attention to particular needs is critical; important to deal professionally and ethically with prospect skepticism, indifference, or objections
5. Close	Obtain a purchase commitment from the prospect and create a customer	Salesperson asks for the purchase; different approaches include the trial close and assumptive close
6. Follow-up	Ensure that the customer is satisfied with the product or service	Resolve any problems faced by the customer to ensure customer satisfaction and future sales possibilities

Prospecting

Personal selling begins with *prospecting*—the search for and qualification of potential customers. For some products that are onetime purchases, such as encyclopedias, continual prospecting is necessary to maintain sales. There are three types of prospects. A *lead* is the name of a person who may be a possible customer. A *prospect* is a customer who wants or needs the product. If an individual wants the product, can afford to buy it, and is the decision maker, this individual is a *qualified prospect*.

Leads and prospects are generated using several sources. For example, advertising may contain a coupon or a toll-free number to generate leads. Some companies use exhibits at trade shows, professional meetings, and conferences to generate leads or prospects. Staffed by salespeople, these exhibits are used to attract the attention of prospective buyers and disseminate information. Others utilize the Internet for generating leads and prospects. Today, salespeople are using websites, e-mail, bulletin boards, and newsgroups to connect to individuals and companies that may be interested in their products or services. Another approach for generating leads is through *cold canvassing* in person or by telephone. This approach simply means that

Trade shows are a popular source for leads and prospects. Companies like TSCentral provide comprehensive trade show information.

TSCentral

www.tscentral.com

a salesperson may open a directory, pick a name, and contact that individual or business. Although the refusal rate is high with cold canvassing, this approach can be successful. For example, on one occasion, 41 brokers at Lehman Brothers identified 18,004 prospects, qualified 1,208 of them, made 659 sales presentations, and opened 40 new accounts in four working days.[10] However, cold canvassing is frowned upon in most Asian and Latin American societies. Personal visits, based on referrals, are expected.

Cold canvassing is often criticized by U.S. consumers and is now regulated. A recent survey reported that 75 percent of U.S. consumers consider this practice an intrusion on their privacy, and 72 percent find it distasteful.[11] The Telephone Consumer Protection Act (1991) contains provisions to curb abuses such as early morning or late night calling. Additional federal regulations require more complete disclosure regarding solicitations, include provisions that allow consumers to avoid being called at any time through the Do Not Call Registry, and impose fines up to $11,000 for violations.

Preapproach

Once a salesperson has identified a qualified prospect, preparation for the sale begins with the preapproach. The *preapproach* stage involves obtaining further information on the prospect and deciding on the best method of approach. Knowing how the prospect prefers to be approached, and what the prospect is looking for in a product or service, is essential regardless of cultural setting. For instance, a Merrill Lynch stockbroker will need information on a prospect's discretionary income, investment objectives, and preference for discussing brokerage services over the telephone or in person. For business product companies such as Texas Instruments, the preapproach involves identifying the buying role of a prospect (for example, influencer or decision maker), important buying criteria, and the prospect's receptivity to a formal or informal presentation. Identifying the best time to contact a prospect is also important. For example, Northwestern Mutual Life Insurance Company suggests the best times to call on people in different occupations: dentists before 9:30 A.M., lawyers between 11:00 A.M. and 2:00 P.M., and college professors between 7:00 and 8:00 P.M.

This stage is very important in international selling where customs dictate appropriate protocol. In many South American countries, for example, buyers expect salespeople to be punctual for appointments. However, prospective buyers are routinely 30 minutes late. South Americans take negotiating seriously and prefer straightforward presentations, but a hard-sell approach will not work.[12]

Successful salespeople recognize that the preapproach stage should never be short-changed. Their experience coupled with research on customer complaints indicate that failure to learn as much as possible about the prospect is unprofessional and the ruin of a sales call.

Approach

The *approach* stage involves the initial meeting between the salesperson and prospect, where the objectives are to gain the prospect's attention, stimulate interest, and build the foundation for the sales presentation itself and the basis for a working

relationship. The first impression is critical at this stage, and it is common for salespeople to begin the conversation with a reference to common acquaintances, a referral, or even the product or service itself. Which tactic is taken will depend on the information obtained in the prospecting and preapproach stages.

The approach stage is very important in international settings. In many societies outside the United States, considerable time is devoted to nonbusiness talk designed to establish a rapport between buyers and sellers. For instance, it is common for two or three meetings to occur before business matters are discussed in the Middle East and Asia. Gestures are also very important. The initial meeting between a salesperson and a prospect in the United States customarily begins with a firm handshake. Handshakes also apply in France, but they are gentle, not firm. Forget the handshake in Japan. A bow is appropriate. What about business cards? Business cards should be printed in English on one side and the language of the prospective customer on the other. Knowledgeable U.S. salespeople know that their business cards should be handed to Asian customers using both hands, with the name facing the receiver. In Asia, anything involving names demands respect.[13]

Presentation

The *presentation* is at the core of the order-getting selling process, and its objective is to convert a prospect into a customer by creating a desire for the product or service. Three major presentation formats exist: (1) stimulus-response format, (2) formula selling format, and (3) need-satisfaction format.

Stimulus-Response Format   The **stimulus-response presentation** format assumes that given the appropriate stimulus by a salesperson, the prospect will buy. With this format the salesperson tries one appeal after another, hoping to hit the right button. A counter clerk at McDonald's is using this approach when he or she asks whether you'd like an order of french fries or a dessert with your meal. The counter clerk is engaging in what is called *suggestive selling*. Although useful in this setting, the stimulus-response format is not always appropriate, and for many products a more formalized format is necessary.

Formula Selling Format   A more formalized presentation, the **formula selling presentation** format, is based on the view that a presentation consists of information that must be provided in an accurate, thorough, and step-by-step manner to inform the prospect. A popular version of this format is the *canned sales presentation,* which is a memorized, standardized message conveyed to every prospect. Used frequently by firms in telephone and door-to-door selling of consumer products (for example, Kirby vacuum cleaners), this approach treats every prospect the same, regardless of differences in needs or preference for certain kinds of information. Canned sales presentations can be advantageous when the differences between prospects are unknown or with novice salespeople who are less knowledgeable about the product and selling process than experienced salespeople. Although it guarantees a thorough presentation, it often lacks flexibility and spontaneity and, more important, does not provide for feedback from the prospective buyer—a critical component in the communication process and the start of a relationship.

Need-Satisfaction Format   The stimulus-response and formula selling formats share a common characteristic: The salesperson dominates the conversation. By comparison, the **need-satisfaction presentation** format emphasizes probing and listening by the salesperson to identify needs and interests of prospective buyers. Once these are identified, the salesperson tailors the presentation to the prospect and highlights product benefits that may be valued by the prospect. The need-satisfaction format, which emphasizes problem solving, is the most consistent with the marketing concept and relationship building.

Two selling styles are common with this format.[14] **Adaptive selling** involves adjusting the presentation to fit the selling situation, such as knowing when to offer

solutions and when to ask for more information. Sales research and practice show that knowledge of the customer and sales situation are key ingredients for adaptive selling. Many consumer service firms such as brokerage and insurance firms and consumer product firms like Reebok, AT&T, and Gillette effectively apply this selling style. **Consultative selling** focuses on problem identification, where the salesperson serves as an expert on problem recognition and resolution. With consultative selling, problem solution options are not simply a matter of choosing from an array of existing products or services. Rather, novel solutions often arise, thereby creating unique value for the customer. Consultative selling is prominent in business-to-business marketing. Johnson Controls' Automotive Systems Group, IBM's Global Services, and DHL Worldwide Express are often cited for their consultative selling style, as is Xerox. According to a senior Xerox sales executive, "Our business is no longer about selling boxes. It's about selling digital, networked-based information management solutions, and this requires a highly customized and consultative selling process."

Handling Objections   A critical concern in the presentation stage is handling objections. *Objections* are excuses for not making a purchase commitment or decision. Some objections are valid and are based on the characteristics of the product or service or price. However, many objections reflect prospect skepticism or indifference. Whether valid or not, experienced salespeople know that objections do not put an end to the presentation. Rather, techniques can be used to deal with objections in a courteous, ethical, and professional manner. The following six techniques are the most common:[15]

1. *Acknowledge and convert the objection.* This technique involves using the objection as a reason for buying. For example, a prospect might say, "The price is too high." The reply: "Yes, the price is high because we use the finest materials. Let me show you. . . ."

MARKETING NEWSNET

The Subtlety of Saying *Yes* in East Asia

The economies of East Asia—spanning from Japan to Indonesia—almost equal that of the United States and total about four-fifths of the European Union. The marketing opportunities in East Asia are great, but effective selling in these countries requires a keen cultural ear. Seasoned global marketers know that in many Asian societies it is impolite to say *no,* and *yes* has multiple meanings.

Yes in Asian societies can have at least four meanings. It can mean that listeners are simply acknowledging that a speaker is talking to them even though they don't understand what is being said. Or, it can mean that a speaker's words are understood, but not that they are agreed with. A third meaning of *yes* conveys that a presentation is understood, but other people must be consulted before any commitment is possible. Finally, *yes* can also mean that a proposal is understood and accepted. However, experienced negotiators also note that this *yes* is subject to change if the situation is changed.

This one example illustrates why savvy salespeople are sensitive to cultural underpinnings when engaged in cross-cultural sales negotiations.

2. *Postpone.* The postpone technique is used when the objection will be dealt with later in the presentation: "I'm going to address that point shortly. I think my answer would make better sense then."

3. *Agree and neutralize.* Here a salesperson agrees with the objection, then shows that it is unimportant. A salesperson would say, "That's true and others have said the same. However, they concluded that issue was outweighed by the other benefits."

4. *Accept the objection.* Sometimes the objection is valid. Let the prospect express such views, probe for the reason behind it, and attempt to stimulate further discussion on the objection.

5. *Denial.* When a prospect's objection is based on misinformation and clearly untrue, it is wise to meet the objection head on with a firm denial.

6. *Ignore the objection.* This technique is used when it appears that the objection is a stalling mechanism or is clearly not important to the prospect.

Each of these techniques requires a calm, professional interaction with the prospect and is most effective when objections are anticipated in the preapproach stage. Handling objections is a skill requiring a sense of timing, appreciation for the prospect's state of mind, and adeptness in communication. Objections also should be handled ethically. Lying or misrepresenting product or service features are grossly unethical practices.

Close

The *closing* stage in the selling process involves obtaining a purchase commitment from the prospect. This stage is the most important and the most difficult because the salesperson must determine when the prospect is ready to buy. Telltale signals indicating a readiness to buy include body language (prospect reexamines the product or contract closely), statements ("This equipment should reduce our maintenance costs"), and questions ("When could we expect delivery?").

The close itself can take several forms. Three closing techniques are used when a salesperson believes a buyer is about ready to make a purchase: (1) trial close, (2) assumptive close, and (3) urgency close. A *trial close* involves asking the prospect to make a decision on some aspect of the purchase: "Would you prefer the blue or gray model?" An *assumptive close* entails asking the prospect to consider choices concerning delivery, warranty, or financing terms under the assumption that a sale has been finalized. An *urgency close* is used to commit the prospect quickly by making reference to the timeliness of the purchase: "The low interest financing ends next week," or "That is the last model we have in stock." Of course, these statements should be used only if they accurately reflect the situation; otherwise, such claims would be unethical. When a prospect is clearly ready to buy, the final close is used, and a salesperson asks for the order.

Knowing when the prospect is ready to buy becomes even more difficult in cross-cultural buyer–seller negotiations where societal customs and language play a large role. Read the accompanying Marketing NewsNet to understand the multiple meanings of *yes* in Japan and other societies in East Asia.[16]

Follow-Up

The selling process does not end with the closing of a sale; rather, professional selling requires customer follow-up. One marketing authority equated the follow-up with courtship and marriage, by observing, "the sale merely consummates the courtship.[17] Then the marriage begins. How good the marriage is depends on how well the relationship is managed." The *follow-up stage* includes making certain the customer's purchase has been properly delivered and installed and difficulties experienced with the use of the item are addressed. Attention to this stage of the selling process solidifies the buyer–seller relationship. Research shows that the cost and effort to obtain repeat sales from a satisfied customer is roughly half of that necessary to gain a sale from a new customer.[18] In short, today's satisfied customers become tomorrow's qualified prospects or referrals. (What was your answer to question 3 in the quiz?)

Concept Check

1. What are the six stages in the personal selling process?

2. What is the distinction between a lead and a qualified prospect?

3. Which presentation format is most consistent with the marketing concept? Why?

THE SALES MANAGEMENT PROCESS

Selling must be managed if it is going to contribute to a firm's marketing objectives. Although firms differ in the specifics of how salespeople and the selling effort are managed, the sales management process is similar across firms. Sales management consists of three interrelated functions: (1) sales plan formulation, (2) sales plan implementation, and (3) evaluation and control of the salesforce (Figure 20–4).

FIGURE 20–4

The sales management process

Sales plan formulation	Sales plan implementation	Evaluation and control of the salesforce
Setting objectives	Salesforce recruitment and selection	Quantitative assessment
Organizing the salesforce	Salesforce training	Behavioral evaluation
Developing account management policies	Salesforce motivation and compensation	

ETHICS AND SOCIAL RESPONSIBILITY ALERT

The Ethics of Asking Customers about Competitors

ETHICS

Salespeople are a valuable source of information about what is happening in the marketplace. By working closely with customers and asking good questions, salespeople often have firsthand knowledge of customer problems and wants. They also are able to spot the activities of competitors. However, should salespeople explicitly ask customers about competitor strategies such as pricing practices, product development efforts, and trade and promotion programs?

Gaining knowledge about competitors by asking customers for

information is a ticklish ethical issue. Research indicates that 25 percent of U.S. salespeople engaged in business-to-business selling consider this practice unethical, and their companies have explicit guidelines for this practice. It is also noteworthy that Japanese salespeople consider this practice to be more unethical than do U.S. salespeople.

Do you believe that asking customers about competitor practices is unethical? Why or why not?

Sales Plan Formulation: Setting Direction

Formulating the sales plan is the most basic of the three sales management functions. According to the vice president of the Harris Corporation, a global communications company, "If a company hopes to implement its marketing strategy, it really needs a detailed sales planning process."[19] The **sales plan** is a statement describing what is to be achieved and where and how the selling effort of salespeople is to be deployed. Sales plan formulation involves three tasks: (1) setting objectives, (2) organizing the salesforce, and (3) developing account management policies.

Setting Objectives   Setting objectives is central to sales management because this task specifies what is to be achieved. In practice, objectives are set for the total salesforce and for each salesperson. Selling objectives can be output related and focus on dollar or unit sales volume, number of new customers added, and profit. Alternatively, they can be input related and emphasize the number of sales calls and selling expenses. Output- and input-related objectives are used for the salesforce as a whole and for each salesperson. A third type of objective that is behaviorally related is typically specific for each salesperson and includes his or her product knowledge, customer service, and selling and communication skills. Increasingly, firms are also emphasizing knowledge of competition as an objective since salespeople are calling on customers and should see what competitors are doing. In fact, a recent survey indicated that 89 percent of companies encourage their salespeople to gather competitive intelligence.[20] But should salespeople explicitly ask their customers for information about competitors? Read the accompanying Ethics and Social Responsibility Alert to see how salespeople view this practice.[21]

Whatever objectives are set, they should be precise and measurable and specify the time period over which they are to be achieved. Once established, these objectives serve as performance standards for the evaluation of the salesforce, the third function of sales management.

Organizing the Salesforce   Establishing a selling organization is the second task in formulating the sales plan. Three questions are related to organization. First, should the company use its own salesforce, or should it use independent agents such

FIGURE 20–5

Break-even chart for comparing independent agents and a company salesforce

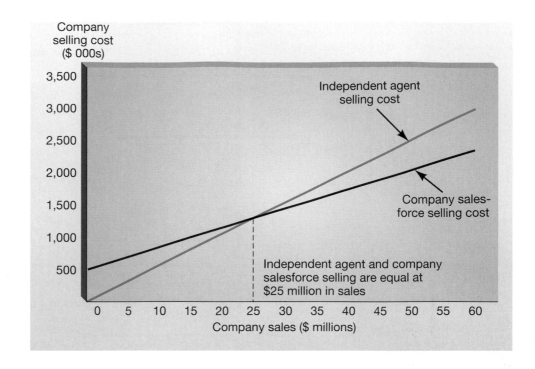

as manufacturer's representatives? Second, if the decision is made to employ company salespeople, then should they be organized according to geography, customer type, or product or service? Third, how many company salespeople should be employed?

The decision to use company salespeople or independent agents is made infrequently. However, Coca-Cola's Food Division recently replaced its salesforce with independent agents (food brokers). The Optoelectronics Division of Honeywell, Inc., has switched back and forth between agents and its own salesforce over the last 25 years and now uses both. The decision is based on an analysis of economic and behavioral factors. An economic analysis examines the costs of using both types of salespeople and is a form of break-even analysis.

Consider a situation in which independent agents would receive a 5 percent commission on sales, and company salespeople would receive a 3 percent commission, salaries, and benefits. In addition, with company salespeople, sales administration costs would be incurred for a total fixed cost of $500,000 per year. At what sales level would independent or company salespeople be less costly? This question can be answered by setting the costs of the two options equal to each other and solving for the sales level amount, as shown in the following equation:

Total cost of company salespeople = Total cost of independent agents

$$[0.03(X) + \$500,000] = 0.05(X)$$

where X = sales volume. Solving for X, sales volume equals $25 million, indicating that below $25 million in sales independent agents would be cheaper, but above $25 million a company salesforce would be cheaper. This relationship is shown in Figure 20–5.

Economics alone does not answer this question, however. A behavioral analysis is also necessary and should focus on issues related to the control, flexibility, effort, and availability of independent and company salespeople.[22] An individual firm must weigh the pros and cons of the economic and behavioral considerations before making this decision.

If a company elects to employ its own salespeople, then it must choose an organizational structure based on (1) geography, (2) customer, or (3) product (Figure 20–6 on the next page). A geographical structure is the simplest organization, where the

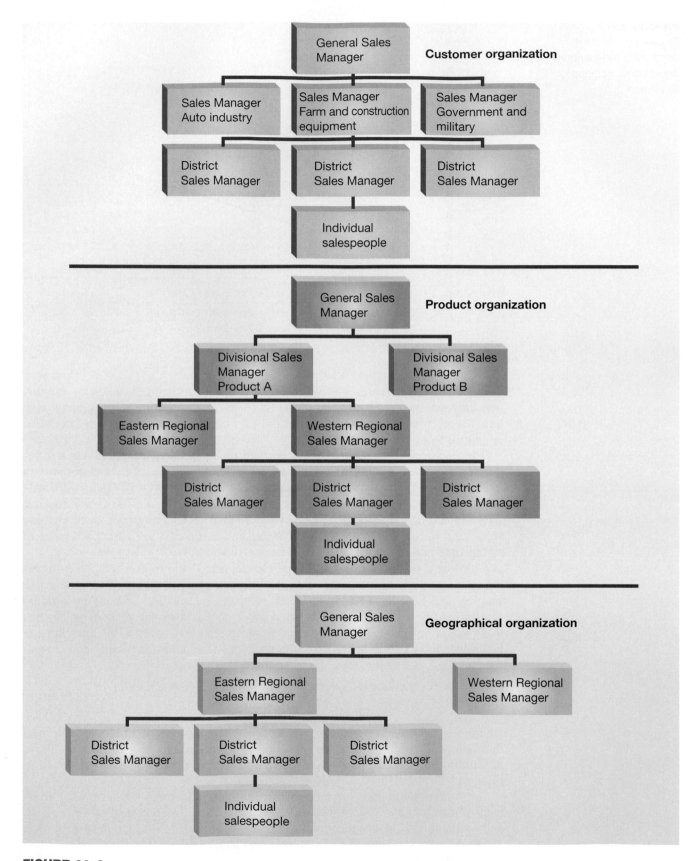

FIGURE 20–6
Organizing the salesforce by customer, product, and geography

United States, or indeed the globe, is first divided into regions and each region is divided into districts or territories. Salespeople are assigned to each district with defined geographical boundaries and call on all customers and represent all products sold by the company. The principal advantage of this structure is that it can minimize travel time, expenses, and duplication of selling effort. However, if a firm's products or customers require specialized knowledge, then a geographical structure is not suitable.

When different types of buyers have different needs, a customer sales organizational structure is used. In practice this means that a different salesforce calls on each separate type of buyer or marketing channel. For example, Kodak recently switched from a geographical to a marketing channel structure with different sales teams serving specific retail channels: mass merchandisers, photo specialty outlets, and food and drug stores. The rationale for this approach is that more effective, specialized customer support and knowledge are provided to buyers. However, this structure often leads to higher administrative costs and some duplication of selling effort, because two separate salesforces are used to represent the same products.

A variation of the customer organizational structure is **major account management**, or *key account management,* the practice of using team selling to focus on important customers so as to build mutually beneficial, long-term, cooperative relationships.[23] Major account management involves teams of sales, service, and often technical personnel who work with purchasing, manufacturing, engineering, logistics, and financial executives in customer organizations. This approach, which often assigns company personnel to a customer account, results in "customer specialists" who can provide exceptional service. Procter & Gamble uses this approach with Wal-Mart, as does Black & Decker with Home Depot.

When specific knowledge is required to sell certain types of products, then a product sales organization is used. For example, Lone Star Steel has a salesforce that sells drilling pipe to oil companies and another that sells specialty steel products to manufacturers. The primary advantage of this structure is that salespeople can develop expertise with technical characteristics, applications, and selling methods associated with a particular product or family of products. However, this structure also produces high administrative costs and duplication of selling effort because two company salespeople may call on the same customer.

In short, there is no one best sales organization for all companies in all situations. Rather, the organization of the salesforce should reflect the marketing strategy of the firm. Each year about 10 percent of U.S. firms change their sales organizations to implement new marketing strategies.

The third question related to salesforce organization involves determining the size of the salesforce. For example, why do you think Frito-Lay has about 17,500 salespeople who call on supermarkets, convenience stores, and other establishments to sell snack foods? The answer lies in the number of accounts (customers) served, the frequency of calls on accounts, the length of an average call, and the amount of time a salesperson can devote to selling.

A common approach for determining the size of a salesforce is the **workload method**. This formula-based method integrates the number of customers served, call frequency, call length, and available selling time to arrive at a figure for the salesforce size. For example, Frito-Lay needs about 17,500 salespeople according to the following workload method formula:

$$NS = \frac{NC \times CF \times CL}{AST}$$

where,

NS = Number of salespeople

NC = Number of customers

CF = Call frequency necessary to service a customer each year

Competitive position of sales organization

	High	Low

High

1
Attractiveness: Accounts offer a good opportunity because they have high potential and the sales organization has a strong position.
Account management policy: Accounts should receive high level of sales calls and service to retain and possibly build accounts.

3
Attractiveness: Accounts may offer a good opportunity if the sales organization can overcome its weak position.
Account management policy: Emphasize a heavy sales organization position or shift resources to other accounts if a stronger sales organization position is impossible.

2
Attractiveness: Accounts are somewhat attractive because the sales organization has a strong position, but future opportunity is limited.
Account management policy: Accounts should receive moderate level of sales and service to maintain current position of sales organization.

4
Attractiveness: Accounts offer little opportunity, and the sales organization position is weak.
Account management policy: Consider replacing personal calls with telephone sales or direct mail to service accounts. Consider dropping account.

Low

(left axis label: **Account opportunity**)

FIGURE 20–7

An account management policy grid grouping customers according to the level of opportunity and a firm's competitive sales position

CL = Length of an average call

AST = Average amount of selling time available per year

Frito-Lay sells its products to 350,000 supermarkets, convenience stores, and other establishments. Salespeople should call on these accounts at least once a week, or 52 times a year. The average sales call lasts an average of 81 minutes (1.35 hour). An average salesperson works 2,000 hours a year (50 weeks × 40 hours a week), but 12 hours a week are devoted to nonselling activities such as travel and administration, leaving 1,400 hours a year. Using these guidelines, Frito-Lay would need

$$NS = \frac{350,000 \times 52 \times 1.35}{1,400} = 17,550 \text{ salespeople}$$

The value of this formula is apparent in its flexibility; a change in any one of the variables will affect the number of salespeople needed. Changes are determined, in part, by the firm's account management policies.

Developing Account Management Policies   The third task in formulating a sales plan involves developing **account management policies** specifying whom salespeople should contact, what kinds of selling and customer service activities should be engaged in, and how these activities should be carried out. These policies might state which individuals in a buying organization should be contacted, the amount of sales and service effort that different customers should receive, and the kinds of information salespeople should collect before or during a sales call.

An example of an account management policy in Figure 20–7 shows how different accounts or customers can be grouped according to level of opportunity and the firm's competitive sales position.[24] When specific account names are placed in each cell, salespeople clearly see which accounts should be contacted, with what level of selling and service activity, and how to deal with them. Accounts in cells 1 and 2 might have high frequencies of personal sales calls and increased time spent on a call. Cell 3 accounts will have lower call frequencies, and cell 4 accounts might be contacted through telemarketing or direct mail rather than in person. For example, Union Pacific Railroad put its 20,000 smallest accounts on a telemarketing program. A subsequent survey of these accounts indicated that 84 percent rated Union Pacific's sales effort "very effective" compared with 67 percent before the switch.[25]

WEB LINK   What Is Your Emotional Intelligence?

A person's success at work depends on many talents, including intelligence and technical skills. Recent research indicates that an individual's emotional intelligence is also important, if not more important! Emotional intelligence (E-IQ) has five dimensions: (1) self-motivation skills; (2) self-awareness, or knowing one's own emotions; (3) the ability to manage one's emotions and impulses; (4) empathy, or the ability to sense how others are feeling; and (5) social skills, or the ability to handle the emotions of other people.

What is your E-IQ? Visit the website at http://ei.haygroup.com and go to the "Learn More" header. Answer the questions to learn what your E-IQ is and obtain additional insights.

Sales Plan Implementation: Putting the Plan into Action

The sales plan is put into practice through the tasks associated with sales plan implementation. Whereas sales plan formulation focuses on "doing the right things," implementation emphasizes "doing things right." The three major tasks involved in implementing a sales plan are: (1) salesforce recruitment and selection, (2) salesforce training, and (3) salesforce motivation and compensation.

Salesforce Recruitment and Selection

Effective recruitment and selection of salespeople is one of the most crucial tasks of sales management. It entails finding people who match the type of sales position required by a firm. Recruitment and selection practices would differ greatly between order-taking and order-getting sales positions, given the differences in the demands of these two jobs. Therefore, recruitment and selection begin with a carefully crafted job analysis and job description followed by a statement of job qualifications.

A *job analysis* is a study of a particular sales position, including how the job is to be performed and the tasks that make up the job. Information from a job analysis is used to write a *job description,* a written document that describes job relationships and requirements that characterize each sales position. It explains: (1) to whom a salesperson reports, (2) how a salesperson interacts with other company personnel, (3) the customers to be called on, (4) the specific activities to be carried out, (5) the physical and mental demands of the job, and (6) the types of products and services to be sold. The job description is then translated into a statement of job qualifications, including the aptitudes, knowledge, skills, and a variety of behavioral characteristics considered necessary to perform the job successfully. Qualifications for order-getting sales positions often mirror the expectations of buyers: (1) imagination and problem-solving ability, (2) honesty, (3) intimate product knowledge, and (4) attentiveness reflected in responsiveness to buyer needs and customer loyalty and follow-up.[26] Firms use a variety of methods for evaluating prospective salespeople. Personal interviews, reference checks, and background information provided on application forms are the most frequently used methods.

Successful selling also requires a high degree of emotional intelligence. **Emotional intelligence** is the ability to understand one's own emotions and the emotions of people with whom one interacts on a daily basis. These qualities are important for adaptive selling and may spell the difference between effective and ineffective order-getting salespeople.[27] Are you interested in what your emotional intelligence might be? Read the accompanying Web Link and test yourself.

The search for qualified salespeople has produced an increasingly diverse salesforce in the United States. Women now represent half of all professional salespeople, and minority representation is growing. The fastest growth rate is among salespeople of Asian and Hispanic descent (see Figure 20–8 on the next page).[28]

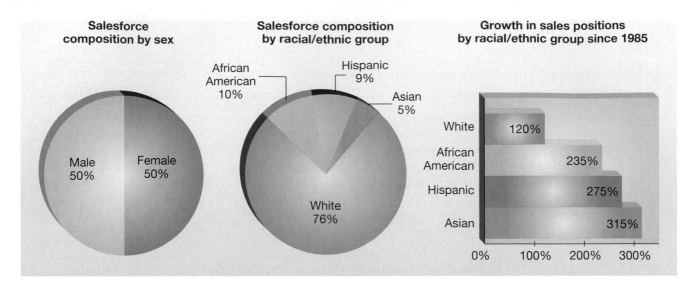

FIGURE 20–8

U.S. salesforce composition and change

Salesforce Training Whereas recruitment and selection of salespeople is a one-time event, salesforce training is an ongoing process that affects both new and seasoned salespeople.[29] Sales training covers much more than selling practices. For example, IBM Global Services salespeople, who sell consulting and various information technology services, take at least two weeks of in-class and Internet-based training on both consultative selling and the technical aspects of business.

Training new salespeople is an expensive process. Almost 5 million U.S. salespeople receive employer-sponsored training annually at a cost of almost $10 billion per year. On-the-job training is the most popular type of training, followed by individual instruction taught by experienced salespeople. Formal classes, seminars taught by sales trainers, and computer-based training are also popular.

Salesforce Motivation and Compensation A sales plan cannot be successfully implemented without motivated salespeople. Research on salesperson motivation suggests that: (1) a clear job description, (2) effective sales management practices, (3) a personal need for achievement, and (4) proper compensation, incentives, or rewards will produce a motivated salesperson.[30]

The importance of compensation as a motivating factor means that close attention must be given to how salespeople are financially rewarded for their efforts. Salespeople are paid using one of three plans: (1) straight salary, (2) straight commission, or (3) a combination of salary and commission. Under a *straight salary compensation plan,* a salesperson is paid a fixed fee per week, month, or year. With a *straight commission compensation plan,* a salesperson's earnings are directly tied to the sales or profit generated. For example, an insurance agent might receive a 2 percent commission of $2,000 for selling a $100,000 life insurance policy. A *combination compensation plan* contains a specified salary plus a commission on sales or profit generated.

Each compensation plan has its advantages and disadvantages.[31] A straight salary plan is easy to administer and gives management a large measure of control over how salespeople allocate their efforts. However, it provides little incentive to expand sales volume. This plan is used when salespeople engage in many nonselling activities, such as account or customer servicing. A straight commission plan provides the maximum amount of selling incentive but can detract salespeople from providing customer service. This plan is common when nonselling activities are minimal. Combination plans are most preferred by salespeople and attempt to build on the advantages of salary and commission plans while reducing potential shortcomings of each. A majority of companies use combination plans today.

Mary Kay Cosmetics recognizes a top salesperson at its annual sales meeting.

Mary Kay Cosmetics, Inc.
www.marykay.com

Nonmonetary rewards are also given to salespeople for meeting or exceeding objectives. These rewards include trips, honor societies, distinguished salesperson awards, and letters of commendation. Some unconventional rewards include the new pink Cadillacs and Pontiacs, fur coats, and jewelry given by Mary Kay Cosmetics to outstanding salespeople. Mary Kay, with 10,000 cars, has the largest fleet of General Motors cars in the world.[32]

Effective recruitment, selection, training, motivation, and compensation programs combine to create a productive salesforce. Ineffective practices often lead to costly salesforce turnover. U.S. firms experience an annual 11.6 percent turnover rate, which means that almost one of every nine salespeople are replaced each year.[33] The expense of replacing and training a new salesperson, including the cost of lost sales, can be high. Also, new recruits are often less productive than seasoned salespeople.

Salesforce Evaluation and Control: Measuring Results

The final function in the sales management process involves evaluating and controlling the salesforce. It is at this point that salespeople are assessed as to whether sales objectives were met and account management policies were followed. Both quantitative and behavioral measures are used to tap different selling dimensions.[34]

Quantitative Assessments   Quantitative assessments are based on input- and output-related objectives set forth in the sales plan. Input-related measures focus on the actual activities performed by salespeople such as those involving sales calls, selling expenses, and account management policies. The number of sales calls made, selling expense related to sales made, and the number of reports submitted to superiors are frequently used input measures.

Output measures often appear in a sales quota. A **sales quota** contains specific goals assigned to a salesperson, sales team, branch sales office, or sales district for a stated time period. Dollar or unit sales volume, last year/current sales ratio, sales of specific products, new accounts generated, and profit achieved are typical goals. The time period can range from one month to one year.

Behavioral Evaluation   Behavioral measures are also used to evaluate salespeople. These include assessments of a salesperson's attitude, attention to customers, product knowledge, selling and communication skills, appearance, and professional demeanor. Even though these assessments are sometimes subjective, they are frequently considered and, in fact, inevitable, in salesperson evaluation. Why? These factors are often important determinants of quantitative outcomes.

About 60 percent of U.S. companies now include customer satisfaction as a behavioral measure of salesperson performance.[35] (What percentage did you check for question 4 in Figure 20–1?) Indianapolis Power & Light, for example, asks major customers to grade its salespeople from A to F. IBM Siebel Systems has been very aggressive in using this behavioral measure. Forty percent of an IBM Siebel salesperson's evaluation is linked to customer satisfaction; the remaining 60 percent is linked to profits achieved. The relentless focus on customer satisfaction by Eastman Chemical Company salespeople contributed to the company being named a recipient of the prestigious Malcolm Baldrige National Quality Award.[36] Eastman surveys its customers with eight versions of its customer satisfaction questionnaire printed in nine languages. Some 25 performance items are studied, including on-time and correct delivery, product quality, pricing practice, and sharing of market information. The survey is managed by the salesforce, and salespeople review the results with customers. Eastman salespeople know that "the second most important thing they have to do is get their customer satisfaction surveys out to and back from customers," says Eastman's sales training director. "Number one, of course, is getting orders."

Salesforce Automation and Customer Relationship Management

Personal selling and sales management are undergoing a technological revolution with the integration of salesforce automation into customer relationship management processes. In fact, the convergence of computer, information, communication, and Internet technologies has transformed the sales function in many companies and made the promise of customer relationship management a reality. **Salesforce automation** (SFA) is the use of these technologies to make the sales function more effective and efficient. SFA applies to a wide range of activities, including each stage in the personal selling process and management of the salesforce itself.

Salesforce automation exists in many forms. Examples of SFA applications include computer hardware and software for account analysis, time management, order processing and follow-up, sales presentations, proposal generation, and product and sales training. Each application is designed to ease administrative tasks and free up time for salespeople to be with customers building relationships and providing service.[37]

Salesforce Computerization   Computer technology has become an integral part of field selling through innovations such as laptop, notebook, palmtop, pad, and tablet computers. Today, 76 percent of companies supply their field salespeople with laptop computers.[38] For example, salespeople for Godiva Chocolates use their laptop computers to process orders, plan time allocations, forecast sales, and communicate with Godiva personnel and customers. While in a department store candy buyer's office, such as Neiman Marcus, a salesperson can calculate the order cost (and discount), transmit the order, and obtain a delivery date within minutes from Godiva's order processing department.[39]

Toshiba America Medical System salespeople use laptop computers with built-in CD-ROM capabilities to provide interactive presentations for their computerized tomography (CT) and magnetic resonance imaging (MRI) scanners. In it the customer sees elaborate three-dimensional animations, high-resolution scans, and video

Computer and communication technologies have made it possible for Hewlett-Packard salespeople to work out of their homes.

Hewlett-Packard
www.hp.com

Toshiba America Medical System salespeople have found computer technology to be an effective sales tool and training device.

Toshiba America Medical Systems
www.toshiba.com

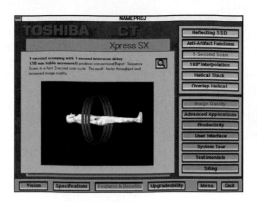
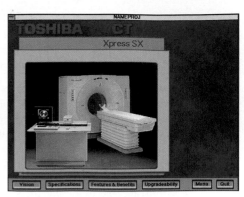

clips of the company's products in operation as well as narrated testimonials from satisfied customers. Toshiba has found this application to be effective both for sales presentations and for training its salespeople.[40]

Salesforce Communication   Technology also has changed the way salespeople communicate with customers, other salespeople and sales support personnel, and management. Facsimile, electronic mail, and voice mail are three common communication technologies used by salespeople today. Cellular (phone) technology, which now allows salespeople to exchange data as well as voice transmissions, is equally popular. Whether traveling or in a customer's office, these technologies provide information at the salesperson's fingertips to answer customer questions and solve problems.

Advances in communication and computer technologies have made possible the mobile and home sales office. Some salespeople now equip minivans with a fully functional desk, swivel chair, light, computer, printer, fax machine, cellular phone, and a satellite dish. Jeff Brown, an agent manager with U.S. Cellular, uses such a mobile office. He says, "If I arrive at a prospect's office and they can't see me right away, then I can go outside to work in my office until they're ready to see me."[41]

Home offices are now common. Hewlett-Packard is a case in point. The company recently shifted its U.S. salesforce into home offices, closed several regional sales offices, and saved $10 million in staff salaries and office rent. A fully equipped home office for each salesperson costs the company about $8,000 and includes a notebook computer, fax/copier, cellular phone, two phone lines, and office furniture.[42]

Perhaps the greatest impact on salesforce communication is the application of Internet technology. Today, salespeople are using their company's Intranet for a variety of purposes. At EDS, a professional services firm, salespeople access its Intranet to download client material, marketing content, account information, technical papers, and competitive profiles. In addition, EDS offers 7,000 training classes that salespeople can take anytime, anywhere.[43]

Salesforce automation is clearly changing how selling is done and how salespeople are managed. Its numerous applications promise to boost selling productivity, improve customer relationships, and decrease selling cost. As applications increase, SFA has the potential to transform selling and sales management.

Concept Check

1. What are the three types of selling objectives?

2. What three factors are used to structure sales organizations?

3. How does emotional intelligence tie to adaptive selling?

CHAPTER IN REVIEW

1 *Discuss the nature and scope of personal selling and sales management in marketing.*

Personal selling involves the two-way flow of communication between a buyer and seller, often in a face-to-face encounter, designed to influence a person's or group's purchase decision. Sales management involves planning the selling program and implementing and controlling the personal selling effort of the firm. The scope of selling and sales management is apparent in three ways. First, virtually every occupation that involves customer contact has an element of personal selling. Second, selling plays a significant role in a company's overall marketing effort. Salespeople occupy a boundary position between buyers and sellers; they *are* the company to many buyers and account for a major cost of marketing in a variety of industries; and they can create value for customers. Finally, through relationship and partnership selling, salespeople play a central role in tailoring solutions to customer problems as a means to customer value creation.

2 *Identify the different types of personal selling.*

Three types of personal selling exist: (*a*) order taking, (*b*) order getting, and (*c*) customer sales support activities. Each type differs from the others in terms of actual selling done and the amount of creativity required to perform the sales task. Order takers process routine orders or reorders for products that were already sold by the company. They generally do little selling in a conventional sense and engage in only modest problem solving with customers. Order getters sell in a conventional sense and identify prospective customers, provide customers with information, persuade customers to buy, close sales, and follow up on customers' use of a product or service. Order getting involves a high degree of creativity and customer empathy and is typically required for selling complex or technical products with many options. Customer sales support personnel augment the sales effort of order getters by performing a variety of services. Sales support personnel are prominent in cross-functional team selling, the practice of using an entire team of professionals in selling to and servicing major customers.

3 *Explain the stages in the personal selling process.*

The personal selling process consists of six stages: (*a*) prospecting, (*b*) preapproach, (*c*) approach, (*d*) presentation, (*e*) close, and (*f*) follow-up. Prospecting involves the search for and qualification of potential customers. The preapproach stage involves obtaining further information on the prospect and deciding on the best method of approach. The approach stage involves the initial meeting between the salesperson and prospect. The presentation stage involves converting a prospect into a customer by creating a desire for the product or service. The close involves obtaining a purchase commitment from the prospect. The follow-up stage involves making certain that the customer's purchase has been properly delivered and installed and difficulties experienced with the use of the item are addressed.

4 *Describe the major functions of sales management.*

Sales management consists of three interrelated functions: (*a*) sales plan formulation, (*b*) sales plan implementation, and (*c*) evaluation and control of the salesforce. Sales plan formulation involves setting objectives, organizing the salesforce, and developing account management policies. Sales plan implementation involves salesforce recruitment, selection, training, motivation, and compensation. Finally, evaluation and control of the salesforce focuses on quantitative assessments of sales performance and behavioral measures such as customer satisfaction that are linked to selling objectives and account management policies.

FOCUSING ON KEY TERMS

account management policies p. 544
adaptive selling p. 537
consultative selling p. 537
emotional intelligence p. 545
formula selling presentation p. 536
major account management p. 543
missionary salespeople p. 532
need-satisfaction presentation p. 537
order getter p. 531
order taker p. 531
partnership selling p. 530

personal selling p. 528
personal selling process p. 533
relationship selling p. 530
sales engineer p. 532
sales management p. 528
sales plan p. 540
sales quota p. 547
salesforce automation p. 548
stimulus-response presentation p. 536
team selling p. 532
workload method p. 543

DISCUSSION AND APPLICATION QUESTIONS

1 Jane Dawson is a new sales representative for the Charles Schwab brokerage firm. In searching for clients, Jane purchased a mailing list of subscribers to *The Wall Street Journal* and called them all regarding their interest in discount brokerage services. She asked if they have any stocks and if they have a regular broker. Those people without a regular broker were asked their investment needs. Two days later, Jane called back with investment advice and asked if they would like to open an account. Identify each of Jane Dawson's actions in terms of the personal selling process.

2 For the first 50 years of business the Johnson Carpet Company produced carpets for residential use. The salesforce was structured geographically. In the past five years, a large percentage of carpet sales has been to industrial users, hospitals, schools, and architects. The company also has broadened its product line to include area rugs, Oriental carpets, and wall-to-wall carpeting. Is the present salesforce structure appropriate, or would you recommend an alternative?

3 Where would you place each of the following sales jobs on the order-taker/order-getter continuum shown below? (*a*) Burger King counter clerk, (*b*) automobile insurance salesperson, (*c*) IBM computer salesperson, (*d*) life insurance salesperson, and (*e*) shoe salesperson.

Order taker	**Order getter**

4 Listed here are two different firms. Which compensation plan would you recommend for each firm, and what reasons would you give for your recommendations? (*a*) A newly formed company that sells lawn care equipment on a door-to-door basis directly to consumers; and

(*b*) the Nabisco Company, which sells heavily advertised products in supermarkets by having the salesforce call on these stores and arrange shelves, set up displays, and make presentations to store buying committees.

5 The TDK tape company services 1,000 audio stores throughout the United States. Each store is called on 12 times a year, and the average sales call lasts 30 minutes. Assuming a salesperson works 40 hours a week, 50 weeks a year, and devotes 75 percent of the time to actual selling, how many salespeople does TDK need?

6 A furniture manufacturer is currently using manufacturer's representatives to sell its line of living room furniture. These representatives receive an 8 percent commission. The company is considering hiring its own salespeople and has estimated that the fixed cost of managing and paying their salaries would be $1 million annually. The salespeople would also receive a 4 percent commission on sales. The company has sales of $25 million dollars, and sales are expected to grow by 15 percent next year. Would you recommend that the company switch to its own salesforce? Why or why not?

7 Suppose someone said to you, "The only real measure of a salesperson is the amount of sales produced." How might you respond?

GOING ONLINE Selling News You Can Use

A unique resource for the latest developments in personal selling and sales management is the Sales Marketing Network (SMN) at www.info-now.com. SMN provides highly readable reports on a variety of topics including many discussed in this chapter, such as telemarketing, motivation, sales training, and sales management. These reports contain concise overviews, definitions, statistics, and reviews of critical issues. They also include references to additional information and links to related material elsewhere on the SMN

site. Registration (at no cost) is required to view some of the reports.

Visit the SMN site and do the following:

1 Select a chapter topic, and update the statistics for, say, sales training costs or the popularity of different salesforce incentives.

2 Select a topic covered in the chapter such as telemarketing, and summarize the critical issues identified for this practice.

BUILDING YOUR MARKETING PLAN

Does your marketing plan involve a personal selling activity? If the answer is no, read no further and do not include a personal selling element in your plan. If the answer is yes:

1 Identify the likely prospects for your product or service.

2 Determine what information you should obtain about the prospect.

3 Describe how you would approach the prospect.

4 Outline the presentation you would make to the prospect for your product or service.

5 Develop a sales plan, focusing on the organizational structure you would use for your salesforce (geography, product, or customer).

VIDEO CASE 20 Reebok: Relationship Selling and Customer Value

"I think face-to-face selling is the most important and exciting part of this whole job. It's not writing the sales reports. It's not analyzing trends and forecasting. It's the two hours that you have to try to sell the buyer your products in a way that's profitable for both you and the retailer," relates Robert McMahon, key account sales representative for Reebok Northeast. As the person in charge of Reebok's largest accounts in New England—including MVP Sports, recently acquired by Decathlon Sports, Modell's, and City Sports—McMahon's job encompasses a myriad of activities, from supervising other sales representatives to attending companywide computer training sessions to monitoring competitors' activities. But it's the actual selling that is most appealing to McMahon. "That's the challenging, stimulating part of the job. Selling to the buyer is a different challenge every day. Every sales call, as well as you may have preplanned it, can change based on shifts and trends in the market. So you need to be able to react to those changes and really think on your feet in front of the buyer."

REEBOK—HOT ON NIKE'S HEELS IN THE ATHLETIC SHOE AND APPAREL MARKET

Reebok is the second-largest athletic shoe manufacturer behind the market leader, Nike. In addition to its athletic shoes, Reebok also sells Rockport, Greg Norman Collection, and Ralph Lauren Footwear shoes. The Reebok sporting goods line remains the flagship brand, though, and distinguishes itself on the market through the DMX cushioning technology in its footwear. Reebok concentrates its resources on getting its footwear and sporting goods gear into a diversified mix of distribution channels such as athletic footwear specialty stores, department stores, and large sporting goods stores. Reebok is unique in that it emphasizes relationships with the retailers as an integral part of its marketing strategy. As an employee at MVP Sports, one of Reebok's major retailers, puts it, "Reebok is the only company that comes in on a regular basis and gives us information. Nike comes in once in a great while. New Balance comes in every six months. Saucony has come in twice. That's been it. Reebok comes in every month to update us on new information and new products. They tell us about the technology so we can tell the customers." Says Laurie Sipples, "vector" representative for Reebok, "There's a partnership that exists between Reebok and an account like MVP Sports that sets us apart. That relationship is a great asset that Reebok has because the retailer feels more in touch with us than other brands."

THE SELLING PROCESS AT REEBOK

Selling at Reebok includes three elements—building trust between the salesperson and the retailer, providing enough information to the retailer for them to be successful selling Reebok products, and finally supporting the retailer after the sale. Sean Neville, senior vice president and general manager of Reebok North America, explains, "Our goal is not to sell to the retailer; our goal is ultimately to sell to the consumer, and so we use the retailer as a partner. The salespeople are always keeping their eyes open and thinking like the retailer and selling to the consumer."

Reebok sells in teams that consist of the account representatives, who do the actual selling to the retailer, and the vector representatives, who spend their time in the stores training the store salespeople and reporting trends back to the account manager. The selling teams are organized geographically so that the salespeople live and work in the area they are selling. This allows the sales team to understand the consumer intuitively. Neville explains, "If you have someone from New York City fly to L.A. and try to tell someone on the streets of Los Angeles what's happening from a trends standpoint and what products to purchase, it's very difficult."

On average, Reebok salespeople spend 70 percent of their time preparing for a sale and 30 percent of their time actually selling. The sales process at Reebok typically follows the six steps of the personal selling process identified in Figure 20–3: (1) Reebok identifies the outlets it would like to carry its athletic gear; (2) the salesforce prepares for the a presentation by familiarizing themselves with the store and its customers; (3) a Reebok representative approaches the prospect and suggests a meeting and presentation; (4) as the presentation begins, the salesperson summarizes relevant market conditions and consumer trends to demonstrate Reebok's commitment to a partnership with the retailer, states what he or she hopes to get out of the sales meeting, explains how the products work, and reinforces the benefits of Reebok products; (5) the salesperson engages in an action close (gets a signed document or a firm confirmation of the sale); and (6) later, various members of the salesforce frequently visit the retailer to provide assistance and monitor consumer preferences.

THE SALES MANAGEMENT PROCESS AT REEBOK

The sales teams at Reebok are organized based on Reebok's three major distribution channels: athletic specialty stores, sporting goods stores, and department stores. The smaller stores have sales teams assigned to

Reebok Unlimited
ARE YOU FEELING IT?

In this sport, accomplishments are measured in hundredths of a second, fractions of an inch, and sometimes, over a century.

In 1895, our founder, Joe Foster, invented the running spike. It changed track and field, and we've been innovating ever since. In the 1999 Reebok track and field collection, you'll find shoes that will help you make the most of your efforts, whatever your event. With 101 years of innovation, they'll give you every advantage you need to accomplish your personal best.

Pro Triple Jump   3D Road Racer   Pro Sprint   Pro Javelin   Pro Distance   Pro Glide   Pro High Jump   Pro Long Jump/Pole Vault

www.reebok.com © 1999 Reebok International Ltd. All Rights Reserved. REEBOK, DMX and the Vector Logo (   ) are registered trademarks of Reebok.

them based on geographical location within the United States (west coast, central, southeast, and northeast). The salesforce is then further broken down into footwear and apparel teams. The salesforce is primarily organized by distribution channel because this is most responsive to customer needs and wants. The salesforce is compensated on both a short-term and long-term basis. In the short term, salespeople are paid based on sales results and profits for the current quarter as well as forecasting. In the long term, salespeople are compensated based on their teamwork and teambuilding efforts. As Neville explains, "Money is typically fourth or fifth on the list of pure motivation. Number one is recognition for a job well done. And that drives people to succeed." Management at Reebok is constantly providing feedback to the salesforce acknowledging their success, not just during annual reviews, and Neville feels this is the key to the high level of motivation, energy, and excitement that exists in the salesforce at Reebok.

WHAT'S NEW ON THE HORIZON FOR THE SALESFORCE AT REEBOK?

Reebok has recently issued laptop computers to its entire salesforce that enable the salespeople to check inventories in the warehouses, make sure orders are being shipped on time, and even enter orders while they're out in the field. Reebok is also focusing more on relationship selling. McMahon describes his relationship with a major buyer as "one of trust and respect. It's gotten to the point now where we're good friends. We go to a lot of sporting events together, which I think really helps." Another recent innovation is for the salesforce to incentivize the stores' sales clerks. For instance, whoever sells the most pairs of Reebok shoes in a month will get tickets to a concert or a football game.

Questions

1   How does Reebok create customer value for its major accounts through relationship selling?

2   How does Reebok utilize team selling to provide the highest level of customer value possible to its major accounts?

3   Is Reebok's salesforce organized based on geography, customer, or product?

4   What are some ways Reebok's selling processes are changing due to technical advancements?

PART 1
Initiating the
Marketing Process

PART 2
Understanding Buyers
and Markets

PART 3
Targeting Marketing
Opportunities

PART 4
Satisfying Marketing
Opportunities

PART 5
Managing the
Marketing Process

MANAGING THE MARKETING PROCESS

HOW PART 5 FITS INTO THE BOOK

The final two chapters of the text show how marketing managers weave a myriad of controllable and uncontrollable factors into both interactive and multichannel marketing programs as well as more traditional marketing programs, often using the steps in the strategic marketing process introduced in Part 1.

CHAPTER 21
Implementing Interactive and Multichannel Marketing

CHAPTER 22
Pulling It All Together: The Strategic Marketing Process

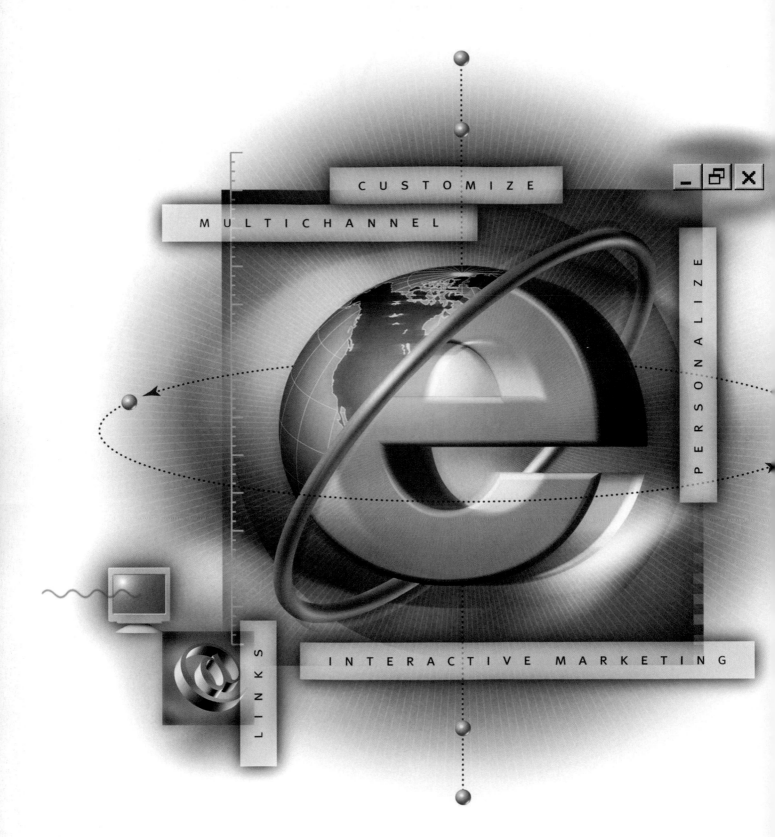

CHAPTER 21

IMPLEMENTING INTERACTIVE AND MULTICHANNEL MARKETING

LEARNING OBJECTIVES

After reading this chapter you should be able to:

1 Describe what interactive marketing is and how it creates customer value, customer relationships, and customer experiences.

2 Identify the demographic and lifestyle profile of online consumers.

3 Explain why certain types of products and services are particularly suited for interactive marketing.

4 Describe why consumers shop and buy online and how marketers influence online purchasing behavior.

5 Define multichannel marketing and the role of transactional and promotional websites in reaching online consumers.

ONE BIKE: YOURS

"One bike: Yours" is the company motto for Seven Cycles, Inc. for a good reason. Seven Cycles is the largest custom bicycle frame builder in the world. The company produces a huge range of road, mountain, cyclo-cross, triathlon, single-speed and tandem bikes annually and no two are alike. At Seven Cycles, attention is focused on each customer's cycling experience through the optimum fit, function, performance, and comfort of his or her very own bike.

The marketing success of Seven Cycles is due certainly to its state-of-the-art bicycle frames. But as company founder and president, Ron Vandermark, says, "Part of our success is that we are tied to a business model that includes the Internet." Seven Cycles uses its website (www.sevencycles.com) to let customers get deeply involved in the frame-building process and the selection of hubs, spokes, and handlebars to complete the bike. It enables customers to design their own bike frames using the company's Custom Kit™ fitting system that considers the rider's size and riding habits. Then, customers can track their custom frame all the way through the development and production process by clicking "Where's My Frame?" on the Seven Cycles website.

This chapter describes how companies design and implement marketing programs that capitalize on the unique value-creation capabilities of Internet technology. We begin by explaining how this technology can create customer value, build customer relationships, and produce customer experiences in novel ways. Next, we describe how Internet technology affects consumer behavior and marketing practice. Finally, we show how marketers integrate and leverage their communication and delivery channels using Internet technology.[1]

CREATING CUSTOMER VALUE, RELATIONSHIPS, AND EXPERIENCES IN MARKETSPACE

Consumers and companies populate two market environments today. One is the traditional *marketplace.* Here buyers and sellers engage in face-to-face exchange relationships in a material environment characterized by physical facilities (stores and offices) and mostly tangible objects. The other is the *marketspace,* an Internet-enabled digital environment characterized by face-to-screen exchange relationships and electronic images and offerings.

The existence of two market environments has been a boon for consumers. Today, consumers can shop for and purchase a wide variety of products and services in either market environment. Actually, many consumers now browse and buy in both market environments, and more are expected to do so in the future as access to and familiarity with Internet technology grows. As an illustration, Figure 21–1 shows the growth trend in online shoppers and estimated online retail sales in the United States.[2]

Marketing in two market environments also poses significant challenges for companies. Companies with origins in the traditional marketplace, such as Procter & Gamble, Wal-Mart, and General Motors, are challenged to define the nature and scope of their marketspace presence. These companies continue to refine the role of Internet technology in attracting, retaining, and building consumer relationships to improve their competitive positions in the traditional marketplace while achieving a marketspace presence.

On the other hand, companies with marketspace origins, including Amazon.com, eBay, E-Trade, and others, are challenged to continually refine, broaden, and deepen their marketspace presence, and consider what role, if any, the traditional marketplace will play in their future. Reflect.com is a case in point. It has recently opened a retail store and has a boutique shop in Marshall Field's flagship department store in Chicago. According to the company's CEO, the marketplace presence is attracting customers who have seen the brand online but want to experience it in a retail store setting. Customers then can replenish their products simply by visiting the Reflect.com website.[3] Regardless of origin, a company's success in achieving a meaningful marketspace presence hinges largely on designing and executing a marketing program that capitalizes on the unique customer value-creation capabilities of Internet technology.

FIGURE 21–1

Trend in online shoppers and online retail sales revenue in the United States

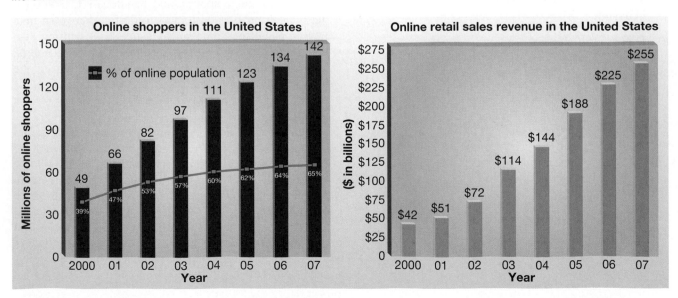

Customer Value Creation in Marketspace

Despite the widespread interest in marketspace, its economic significance remains small compared with the traditional marketplace. Electronic commerce is expected to represent less than 20 percent of total U.S. consumer and business goods and services expenditures in 2007, and less than 9 percent of global expenditures.[4] Why then has the new marketspace captured the eye and imagination of marketers?

Marketers believe that the possibilities for customer value creation are greater in marketspace than in the traditional marketplace. Recall from Chapter 1 that marketing creates time, place, form, and possession utilities for customers, thereby providing value. In marketspace, the provision of direct, on-demand information is possible from marketers *anywhere* to customers *anywhere at any time.* Why? Operating hours and geographical constraints do not exist in marketspace. For example, Recreational Equipment (www.rei.com), an outdoor gear marketer, reports that 35 percent of its orders are placed between 10:00 P.M. and 7:00 A.M., long after and before retail stores are open for business. This isn't surprising. About 58 percent of Internet users prefer to shop and buy in their night clothes or pajamas.[5] Similarly, a U.S. consumer from Chicago can access Marks & Spencer (www.marks-and-spencer.co.uk), the well-known British department store, to shop for clothing as easily as a person living near London's Piccadilly Square. Possession utility—getting a product or service to consumers so they can own or use it—is accelerated. Airline, car rental, and lodging electronic reservation systems such as Orbitz (www.orbitz.com) allow comparison shopping for the lowest fares, rents, and rates and almost immediate access to and confirmation of travel arrangements and accommodations.

The greatest marketspace opportunity for marketers, however, lies in its potential for creating form utility. Interactive two-way Internet-enabled communication capabilities in marketspace invite consumers to tell marketers specifically what their requirements are, making customization of a product or service to fit the buyer's exact needs possible. For instance, at Godiva.com, customers can choose an assortment of their favorite chocolates from an online catalog for a gift or a delectable self-indulgent treat.

Godiva creates form utility in the creation of personal assortments for its customers.

Godiva
www.godiva.com

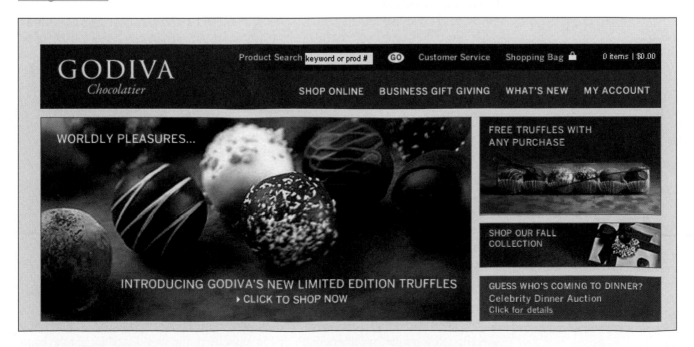

Interactivity, Individuality, and Customer Relationships in Marketspace

Marketers also benefit from two unique capabilities of Internet technology that promote and sustain customer relationships. One is *interactivity;* the other is *individuality.*[6] Both capabilities are important building blocks for buyer–seller relationships. For these relationships to occur, companies need to interact with their customers by listening and responding to their needs. Marketers must also treat customers as individuals and empower them to (1) influence the timing and extent of the buyer–seller interaction and (2) have a say in the kind of products and services they buy, the information they receive, and in some cases, the prices they pay.

Internet technology allows for interaction, individualization, and customer relationship building to be carried out on a scale never before available and makes interactive marketing possible. **Interactive marketing** involves two-way buyer–seller electronic communication in a computer-mediated environment in which the buyer controls the kind and amount of information received from the seller. Interactive marketing today is characterized by sophisticated choiceboard and personalization systems that transform information supplied by customers into customized responses to their individual needs.

Choiceboards

A **choiceboard** is an interactive, Internet-enabled system that allows individual customers to design their own products and services by answering a few questions and choosing from a menu of product or service attributes (or components), prices, and delivery options.[7] Customers today can design their own computers with Dell's online configurator, style their own athletic shoe at Niketown.com, assemble their own investment portfolios with Schwab's mutual fund evaluator, build their own bicycle at SevenCycles.com, and create a diet and fitness program at eDiets.com that fits their lifestyle. Because choiceboards collect precise information about preferences and behavior of individual buyers, a company becomes more knowledgeable about a customer and better able to anticipate and fulfill that customer's needs. To experience the choiceboard system, use the Nike iD Customized Product link described in the accompanying Web Link and style your personalized athletic equipment.

Most choiceboards are essentially transaction devices. However, companies such as Dell have expanded the functionality of choiceboards using collaborative filtering technology. **Collaborative filtering** is a process that automatically groups people with similar buying intentions, preferences, and behaviors and predicts future purchases.[8] For example, say two people who have never met buy a few of the same CDs over time. Collaborative filtering software is programmed to reason that these two buyers might have similar musical tastes: If one buyer likes a particular CD, then the other will like it as well. The outcome? Collaborative filtering gives marketers the ability to make a dead-on sales recommendation to a buyer in *real time.* You see collaborative filtering applied each time you view a selection at Amazon.com and see "Customers who bought this (item) also bought. . . ."

Choiceboards and collaborative filtering represent two important capabilities of Internet technology and have changed the way companies operate today. According to an electronic commerce manager at IBM, "The business model of the past was make and sell. Now instead of make and sell, it's sense and respond."[9]

Personalization

Choiceboards and collaborative filtering are marketer-initiated efforts to provide customized responses to the needs of individual buyers. Personalization systems are typically buyer-initiated efforts. **Personalization** is the consumer-initiated practice of generating content on a marketer's website that is custom tailored to an individual's specific needs and preferences. For example, Yahoo! (www.yahoo.com) allows users to create personalized MyYahoo pages. Users can add or delete a variety of types of information from their personal pages, including specific stock quotes, weather conditions in any city in the world, and local television

WEB LINK

Interactivity and Individuality—Your Nike iD Customized Product

www.mhhe.com/Kerin

Nike is a recognized innovator in the use of choiceboard systems for creating interactivity, individuality, and customer relationships. Its Nike iD Customized Product configurator invites customers to create one-of-kind shoes, messenger bags, and backpacks by simply answering a few questions and viewing the finished product from numerous angles.

Make a few additional clicks and your customized product is ordered and will be delivered in three weeks.

To experience the Nike iD Customized Product configurator, go to www.niketown.com. Click "Nike iD" and begin to design your own personal product right down to the color of Nike's signature swoosh.

schedules. In turn, Yahoo! can use the buyer profile data entered when users register at the site to tailor e-mail messages, advertising, and content to the individual—and even post a happy birthday greeting on the user's special day.

An aspect of personalization is a buyer's willingness to have tailored communications brought to his or her attention. Obtaining this approval is called **permission marketing**—the solicitation of a consumer's consent (called *opt-in*) to receive e-mail and advertising based on personal data supplied by the consumer. Permission marketing is a proven vehicle for building and maintaining customer relationships, provided it is properly used. Companies that successfully employ permission marketing adhere to three rules.[10] First, they make sure opt-in customers only receive information that is relevant and meaningful to them. Second, their customers are given the option of *opting out,* or changing the kind, amount, or timing of information sent to them. Finally, their customers are assured that their name or buyer profile data will not be sold or shared with others. This assurance is important because 70 percent of Internet users have expressed concern about the privacy of their personal information.[11]

Creating an Online Customer Experience

A continuing challenge for companies is the design and execution of marketing programs that capitalize on the unique and evolving customer value-creation

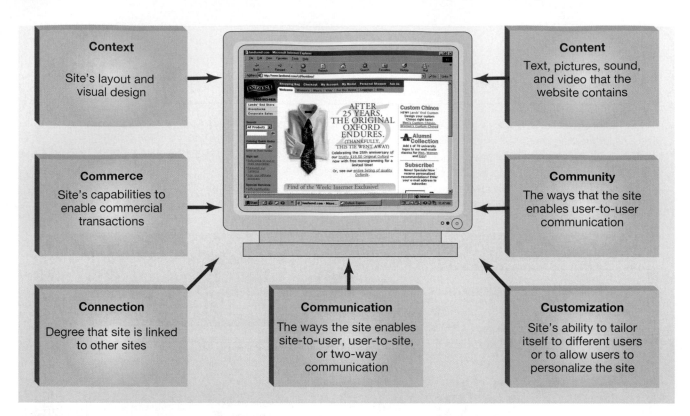

FIGURE 21–2

Website design elements that drive customer experience

capabilities of Internet technology. Companies now realize that simply applying Internet technology to create time, place, form, and possession utility is not enough to claim a meaningful marketspace presence. Today, the quality of the customer experience produced by a company is the standard by which a meaningful marketspace presence is measured.

From an interactive marketing perspective, **customer experience** is defined as the sum total of the interactions that a customer has with a company's website, from the initial look at a homepage through the entire purchase decision process.[12] Companies produce a customer experience through seven website design elements. These elements are context, content, community, customization, communication, connection, and commerce, each of which is summarized in Figure 21–2. A closer look at these elements illustrates how each contributes to customer experience.

Context refers to a website's aesthetic appeal and functional look and feel reflected in site layout and visual design. A functionally oriented website focuses largely on the company's offering, be it products, services, or information. For instance, travel websites tend to be functionally oriented with an emphasis on destinations, scheduling, and prices. In contrast, beauty websites, such as CoverGirl.com, are more aesthetically oriented. As these examples suggest, context attempts to convey the core consumer benefit provided by the company's offerings. *Content* applies to all digital information on a website, including the presentation form—text, video, audio, and graphics. Content quality and presentation along with context dimensions combine to engage a website visitor and provide a platform for the five remaining design elements.

Website *customization* is the ability of a site to modify itself to, or be modified by, each individual user. This design element is prominent in websites that offer personalized content, such as My eBay and MyYahoo. The *connection* element in website design is the network of formal linkages between a company's site and other sites. These links are embedded in the website; appear as highlighted words, a picture, or graphic; and allow a user to effortlessly visit other sites with a mouse click. Connection is a major design element for informational websites such as *The New York Times*. For example,

ENOUGH DREAMING. IT'S TIME TO RIDE.

Harley-Davidson pays close attention to creating a favorable customer experience at its website.

Harley-Davidson
www.harley-davidson.com

users of NYTimes.com can access the book review section and link to Barnes & Noble to order a book or browse related titles without ever visiting a store.

Communication refers to the dialogue that unfolds between the website and its users. Consumers—particularly those who have registered at a site—now expect that communication be interactive and individualized in real time much like a personal conversation. In fact, some websites now enable a user to talk directly with a customer representative while shopping the site. For example, two-thirds of the sales through Dell.com involve human sales representatives. In addition, an increasing number of company websites encourage user-to-user communications hosted by the company to create virtual communities, or simply, *community*. This design element is growing in popularity because it has been shown to enhance customer experience and build favorable buyer–seller relationships. Examples of communities range from the Parenting Community hosted by Kimberly-Clark (www.huggies.com) to the Harley Owners Group (HOG) sponsored by Harley-Davidson (www.harley-davidson.com).

The seventh design element is *commerce*—the website's ability to conduct sales transactions for products and services. Online transactions are quick and simple in well-designed websites. Amazon.com has mastered this design element with "one-click shopping," a patented feature that allows users to place and order products with a single mouse click.

All websites do not include every design element. Although every website has context and content, they differ in the use of the remaining five elements. Why? Websites have different purposes. For example, only websites that emphasize the actual sale of products and services include the commerce element. Websites that are used primarily for advertising and promotion purposes emphasize the communication element. The difference between these two types of websites is discussed later in the chapter.

Concept Check

1. The greatest marketspace opportunity for marketers lies in the creation of what kind of utility?

2. The consumer-initiated practice of generating content on a marketer's website that is custom tailored to an individual's specific needs and preferences is called _____.

3. Companies produce a customer experience through what seven website design elements?

ONLINE CONSUMER BEHAVIOR AND MARKETING PRACTICE IN MARKETSPACE

Who are online consumers, and what do they buy? Why do they choose to shop and purchase products and services in the new marketspace rather than or in addition to the traditional marketplace? Answers to these questions have a direct bearing on marketspace marketing practices.

The Online Consumer

Many labels are given online consumers—cybershoppers, Netizens, and e-shoppers—suggesting they are a homogeneous segment of the population. They are not, but as a group, they do differ demographically from the general population.

Profiling the Online Consumer   Online consumers differ from the general population in one important respect. They own or have access to a computer or an Internet-enabled device, such as a wireless cellular telephone or personal digital assistant. More than 50 percent of U.S. households have a computer in their home with Internet access, although access is often possible at work or school. Figure 21–3 profiles households with Internet access at home.[13]

Online consumers are the subsegment of all Internet users who employ this technology to research products and services and make purchases. Research

FIGURE 21–3

Internet access at home among U.S. households

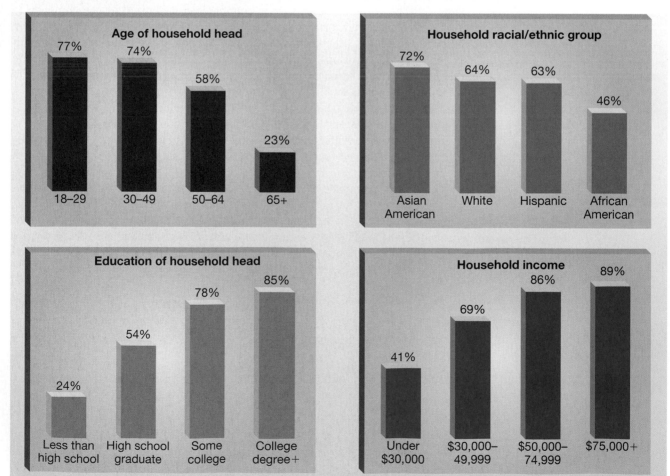

indicates that about 80 percent of all adult Internet users have sought online product or service information at one time or another.[14] For example, some 70 percent of prospective travelers have researched travel information online, even though fewer than 25 percent have actually made online travel reservations. More than 60 percent have researched automobiles before making a purchase, but less than 5 percent of users actually bought a vehicle online. About two-thirds of adult Internet users have actually purchased a product or service online at one time or another.

As a group, online consumers, like Internet users, are about evenly split between men and women and tend to be better educated, younger, and more affluent than the general U.S. population, which makes them an attractive market. Even though online shopping and buying is growing in popularity, a small percentage of online consumers still account for a disproportionate share of online retail sales in the United States. It is estimated that 20 percent of online consumers who spend $1,000-plus per year online account for 87 percent of total consumer online sales.[15] Also, women tend to purchase more goods and services online than men.[16]

Online Consumer Lifestyle Segmentation   Not all Internet users use the technology the same way, nor are they likely to be exclusive online consumers. Numerous marketing research firms have studied the lifestyles and shopping and spending habits of online consumers. A recurrent insight is that online consumers are diverse and represent different kinds of people seeking different kinds of online experiences. As an illustration, Harris Interactive, a large U.S. research firm, has identified six distinct online consumer lifestyle segments.[17]

The largest online consumer lifestyle segment, called *click-and-mortar,* consists of women who tend to browse retailer websites but actually buy products in traditional retail outlets. They make up 23 percent of online consumers and represent an important segment for multichannel retailers that also feature catalog and store operations, such as J. Crew and JCPenney. Twenty percent of online consumers are *hunter-gatherers*—married couples with children at home who use the Internet like a consumer magazine to gather information and compare products and prices. They can be found visiting comparison shopping websites such as dealcatcher.com and mysimon.com on a regular basis. The accompanying Marketing NewsNet provides an in-depth look at today's "Internet mom."[18] Nineteen percent of online consumers are *brand loyalists* who regularly visit their favorite bookmarked websites and spend the most money online. They are better-educated and more-affluent Internet users who effortlessly navigate familiar and trusted websites and enjoy the online browsing and buying experience. Next there are *time-sensitive materialists* who regard the Internet as a convenience tool for buying music, books, and computer software and electronics. They account for 17 percent of online consumers and can be found visiting Amazon.com, dell.com, sony.com, and bmg.com. The *hooked, online, and single* segment consists of young, affluent, and single online consumers who bank, play games, and spend more time online than any other segment. They make up 16 percent of online consumers, enjoy auction websites such as eBay, and visit game websites like Slingo.com, MSN Games, AOL Games, and Jigzone.com. Five percent of online consumers are the *ebivalent newbies*—relative newcomers to the Internet who rarely spend money online but seek product information. Do any of these segments describe your online lifestyle and spending habits?

What Online Consumers Buy

Much still needs to be learned about online consumer purchase behavior. Although research has documented the most frequently purchased products and services bought online, marketers also need to know why these items are popular in the new marketspace.

MARKETING NEWSNET

Meet Today's Internet Mom—All 31 Million!

TECHNOLOGY & E-COMMERCE

Do you have fond childhood memories of surfing the Internet with your mother? Today's children between the ages of 6 and 14 probably will.

Recent research indicates that 31 million mothers are online regularly. They're typically 38 years old and tend to be married, college educated, and working outside the home. A study conducted by C&R Research on behalf of Disney Online has identified four segments of mothers based on their Internet usage. The *Yes Mom* segment represents 14 percent of online moms. They work outside the home, go online 8 hours per week, and value the convenience of obtaining information about products and services. The *Mrs. Net Skeptic* segment accounts for 31 percent of online moms. They tend to be stay-at-home moms, are extremely family-oriented, and go online 6 hours per week for parenting and children's education information and food and cooking tips. The *Tech Nester* mom (32 percent of online moms) believes the Internet brings their family closer together. They average 10 hours per week online and prefer online shopping to in-store shopping. The fourth segment— *Passive under Pressure* moms—tend to be Internet newbies and go online, but infrequently.

The first three segments, which account for 77 percent of online moms, agree that the Internet has simplified their lives. They also say that the Internet has been in invaluable information source for vacation travel, financial products,

and automobiles and providing useful ideas and suggestions on family-related topics. Online moms ranked weather, food and cooking, entertainment, news, health, and parenting as the most popular websites to visit.

There are six general product and service categories that dominate online consumer buying today and for the foreseeable future, as shown in Figure 21–4.[19] One category consists of items for which product information is an important part of the purchase decision, but prepurchase trial is not necessarily critical. Items such as computers, computer accessories, and consumer electronics sold by dell.com fall into this category. So do books, which accounts for the sales growth of Amazon.com and Barnes & Noble (www.barnesandnoble.com). Both booksellers publish short reviews of new books that visitors to their websites can read before making a purchase decision. According to an authority on electronic commerce, "You've read the reviews, you want it, you don't need to try it on."[20] A second category includes items for which audio or video demonstration is important. This category consists of CDs, videos, and DVDs sold by columbiahouse.com and cdnow.com. The third category contains items that can be delivered digitally, including computer software, travel and lodging reservations and confirmations, financial brokerage services, and electronic ticketing. Popular websites for these items include travelocity.com, ticketmaster.com, and schwab.com.

Unique items, such as collectibles, specialty goods, and foods and gifts, represent a fourth category. Collectible auction houses (www.sothebys.com and www.butterfields.com), wine merchant eVineyard (www.wine.com), and flower and gift marketer 1-800-Flowers (www.1800flowers.com) sell these products. A fifth

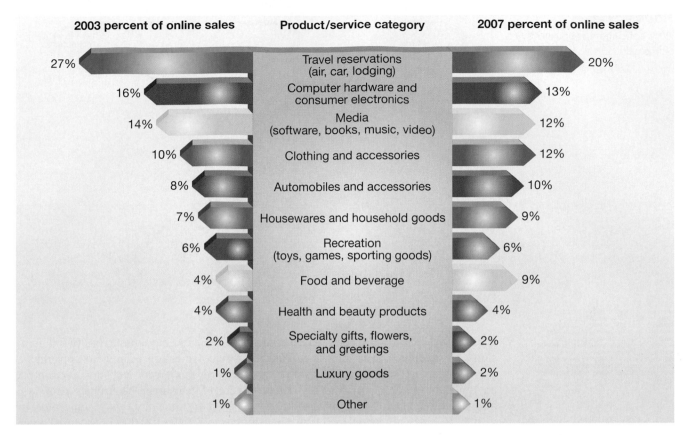

2003 percent of online sales	Product/service category	2007 percent of online sales
27%	Travel reservations (air, car, lodging)	20%
16%	Computer hardware and consumer electronics	13%
14%	Media (software, books, music, video)	12%
10%	Clothing and accessories	12%
8%	Automobiles and accessories	10%
7%	Housewares and household goods	9%
6%	Recreation (toys, games, sporting goods)	6%
4%	Food and beverage	9%
4%	Health and beauty products	4%
2%	Specialty gifts, flowers, and greetings	2%
1%	Luxury goods	2%
1%	Other	1%

FIGURE 21–4

Online consumer retail sales by product/service category: 2003 and 2007

category includes items that are regularly purchased and where convenience is very important. Many consumer-packaged goods, such as grocery products, fall into this category. A final category of items consists of highly standardized products and services for which information about price is important. Certain kinds of insurance (auto and homeowners), home improvement products, casual apparel, and toys make up this category.

Why Consumers Shop and Buy Online

Marketers emphasize the customer value-creation possibilities, the importance of interactivity, individuality and relationship building, and producing customer experience in the new marketspace. However, consumers typically refer to six reasons why they shop and buy online: convenience, choice, customization, communication, cost, and control (Figure 21–5 on the next page).

Convenience   Online shopping and buying is *convenient.* Consumers can visit Wal-Mart at www.walmart.com to scan and order from among thousands of displayed products without fighting traffic, finding a parking space, walking through long aisles, and standing in store checkout lines. Alternatively, online consumers can use **bots**, electronic shopping agents or robots that comb websites to compare prices and product or service features. In either instance, an online consumer has never ventured from his or her computer monitor. However, for convenience to remain a source of customer value creation, websites must be easy to locate and navigate, and image downloads must be fast. A commonly held view among online marketers is the **eight-second rule**: Customers will abandon their efforts to enter and navigate a website if download time exceeds eight seconds. Furthermore, the more clicks and pauses between clicks required to access information or make a purchase, the more likely it is a customer will exit a website.

FIGURE 21–5
Why consumers shop and buy
online

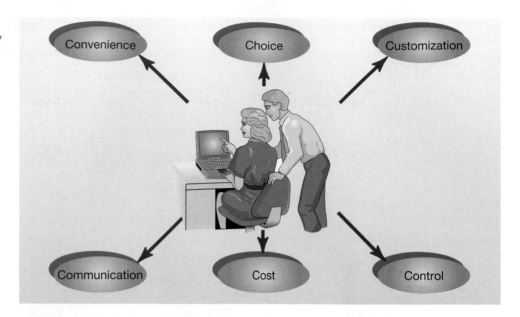

Choice   *Choice,* the second reason consumers shop and buy online, has two dimensions. First, choice exists in the product or service selection offered to consumers. Buyers desiring selection can avail themselves of numerous websites for almost anything they want. For instance, online buyers of consumer electronics can shop individual manufacturers such as Bose (www.bose.com) or Sony (www.sony.com), or visit [QVC.com](QVC.com), a general merchant, that offers more than 100,000 products. Choice assistance is the second dimension. Here, the interactive capabilities of Internet-enabled technologies invite customers to engage in an electronic dialogue with marketers for the purpose of making informed choices. Lands' End (www.landsend.com) provides choice assistance with its "My Virtual Model" apparel service. Men and women submit their body shape, skin color, hair style, height, weight, and other attributes. The model then "tries on" outfits identified by the customer. Like any good salesperson, the service recommends flattering outfits for purchase.

Customization   Even with a broad selection and choice assistance, some customers prefer one-of-a-kind items that fit their specific needs. *Customization* arises from Internet-enabled capabilities that make possible a highly interactive and individualized information and exchange environment for shoppers and buyers. Remember the earlier Reflect.com, Nike, Schwab, Dell, and Seven Cycles examples? To varying degrees, online consumers also benefit from **customerization**—the growing practice of not only customizing a product or service but also personalizing the marketing and overall shopping and buying interaction for each customer.[21] Customerization seeks to do more than offer consumers the right product, at the right time, at the right price. It combines choiceboard and personalization systems to expand the exchange environment beyond a transaction and makes shopping and buying an enjoyable, personal experience.

Communication   Online consumers particularly welcome the *communication* capabilities of Internet-enabled technologies. This communication can take three forms: (1) marketer-to-consumer e-mail notification, (2) consumer-to-marketer buying and service requests, and (3) consumer-to-consumer chat rooms and instant messaging. This communication capability is evidenced in the fact that over 20 trillion e-mail messages are sent annually worldwide and about 800 million instant messages are sent daily on America Online.[22]

Communication has proven to be a double-edged sword for online consumers.[23] On the one hand, the interactive communication capabilities of Internet-enabled technologies increase consumer convenience, reduce information search costs, and make choice assistance and customization possible. Communication also promotes the development of company-hosted and independent **web communities**—websites that allow people to congregate online and exchange views on topics of common interest. For instance, iVillage.com is a web community for women and includes topics such as career management, personal finances, parenting, relationships, beauty, and health. A recent development is the creation of web logs, or blogs. A **blog** is a webpage that serves as a publicly accessible personal journal for an individual. Blogs have grown in popularity because they provide online forums on a wide variety of subjects ranging from politics to car repair.

On the other hand, communications can take the form of electronic junk mail or unsolicited e-mail, called **spam**. The prevalence of spam has prompted some online services such as Hotmail to institute policies and procedures to prevent spammers from spamming their subscribers, and several states have antispamming laws. In 2004, the CAN-SPAM (Controlling the Assault of Non-Solicited Pornography and Marketing) Act became effective and restricts information collection and unsolicited e-mail promotions on the Internet.

Internet-enabled communication capabilities also make possible *buzz,* a popular term for word-of-mouth behavior in marketspace. Chapter 5 described the importance of word of mouth in consumer behavior. Internet technology has magnified its significance. In marketspace, the scope and speed of word of mouth has increased fourfold on average because of consumer chat rooms, instant messaging, and product and service review websites such as epinions.com and consumerreview.com.[24] Buzz is particularly influential for toys, cars, sporting goods, motion pictures, apparel, consumer electronics, pharmaceuticals, health and beauty products, and health care services. Some marketers have capitalized on this phenomenon by creating buzz through viral marketing.

Viral marketing is an Internet-enabled promotional strategy that encourages individuals to forward marketer-initiated messages to others via e-mail. There are three approaches to viral marketing. Marketers can embed a message in the product or service so that customers hardly realize they are passing it along. The classic example is Hotmail, which was one of the first companies to provide free, Internet-based e-mail. Each outgoing e-mail message has the tagline: Get Your Private, Free Email from MSN Hotmail. Today, Hotmail has more than 100 million users. Marketers can also make the website content so compelling that viewers want to share it with others. De Beers has done this at www.adiamondisforever.com, where users can design their own rings and show them to others. One out of five website visitors e-mail their ring design to friends and relatives who visit the site. Similarly, eBay reports that more than half its visitors are referred by other visitors. Finally, marketers can offer incentives (discounts, sweepstakes, or free merchandise) for referrals.

De Beers effectively applied viral marketing in the launch of its custom ring website.

De Beers
www.adiamondisforever.com

How did Procter & Gamble use viral marketing techniques to make Physique shampoo the most successful new shampoo ever launched in the United States? Read the text to find the answer.

Physique

www.physique.com

Procter & Gamble did this for its Physique shampoo. People who referred 10 friends to the shampoo's website (www.physique.com) received a free, travel-sized styling spray and were entered in a sweepstakes to win a year's supply of the shampoo. The response? The promotion generated 2 million referrals and made Physique the most successful new shampoo ever launched in the United States.

Cost   Consumer *cost* is a fifth reason for online shopping and buying. Research indicates that many popular items bought online can be purchased at the same price or cheaper than in retail stores.[25] Lower prices also result from Internet-enabled software that permits **dynamic pricing**, the practice of changing prices for products and services in real time in response to supply and demand conditions. As described in Chapter 14, dynamic pricing is a form of flexible pricing and can often result in lower prices. It is typically used for pricing time-sensitive items like airline seats, scarce items found at art or collectible auctions, and out-of-date items such as last year's models of computer equipment and accessories. A consumer's cost of external information search, including time spent and often the hassle of shopping, is also reduced. Greater shopping convenience and lower external search costs are two major reasons for the popularity of online shopping and buying among women, and particularly for those who work outside the home.

Control   The sixth reason consumers prefer to buy online is the *control* it gives them over their shopping and purchase decision process. Online shoppers and buyers are empowered consumers. They deftly use Internet technology to seek information, evaluate alternatives, and make purchase decisions on their own time, terms, and conditions. Nearly 80 percent of online consumers regularly engage **portals** and search engines, which are electronic gateways to the Internet that supply a broad array of news and entertainment, information resources, and shopping services. Yahoo!, America Online, and MSN.com are well-known portals, and Google is a prominent search engine. To evaluate alternatives, consumers visit comparison shopping websites such as comparenet.com and price.com or employ bots such as Yahoo! Shopping, which provide product descriptions and prices for a wide variety of brands and models. The result of these activities is a more informed consumer and discerning shopper. In the words of one marketing consultant, "In the marketspace, the customer is in charge."[26]

Even though consumers have many reasons for shopping and buying online, a segment of Internet users refrain from making purchases for privacy and security reasons as described in the accompanying Ethics and Social Responsibility Alert.[27] These consumers are concerned about a rarely mentioned seventh C—cookies. **Cookies** are computer files that a marketer can download onto the computer of an online shopper who visits the marketer's website. Cookies allow the marketer's website to record a user's visit, track visits to other websites, and store and retrieve

ETHICS AND SOCIAL RESPONSIBILITY ALERT

Sweet and Sour Cookies in the New Marketspace

ETHICS

Privacy and security are two key reasons consumers are leery of online shopping and buying. A recent Jupiter Research poll reported that 70 percent of online consumers are concerned about threats to their personal privacy on the Internet. Even more telling, 53 percent have stopped shopping a website or forgone an online purchase because of privacy concerns. Industry analysts estimate that low consumer confidence in privacy and security will result in lost sales of $24.5 billion by 2006.

The privacy and security concerns of online consumers are related to the cookies described in the text and how those cookies can be used or misused. A percolating issue is whether the U.S. government should pass more stringent Internet privacy laws. About 70 percent of online consumers favor such action. Companies have adopted initiatives to develop their own privacy standards without government action. The Online Privacy Alliance (www. privacyalliance.org) is a consortium of businesses and associations that aims to promote electronic commerce through online privacy policies and self-regulation. TRUSTe (www.truste.com) awards its trademark to websites that comply with standards of privacy protection and disclosure.

Do you think that governmental or self-regulation is the best way to deal with issues of privacy and security in the new marketspace?

this information in the future. Cookies also contain information provided by visitors, such as expressed product preferences, personal data, passwords, and financial information, including credit card numbers. Clearly, cookies make possible customized and personalized content for online shoppers. The controversy surrounding cookies is summed up by an authority on the technology: "At best a cookie makes for a user-friendly Web world: like a doorman or salesclerk who knows who you are. At worst, cookies represent a potential loss of privacy."[28]

When and Where Online Consumers Shop and Buy

Shopping and buying also happen at different times in marketspace than in the traditional marketplace.[29] About 80 percent of online retail sales occur Monday through Friday. The busiest shopping day is Wednesday. By comparison, 35 percent of retail store sales are registered on the weekend. Saturday is the most popular shopping day. Monday through Friday online shopping and buying often occurs during normal work hours—some 40 percent of online consumers say they visit websites from their place of work, which partially accounts for the sales level during the workweek. Favorite websites for workday shopping and buying include those featuring event tickets, auctions, online periodical subscriptions, flowers and gifts, consumer electronics, and travel. Websites offering health and beauty items, apparel and accessories, and music and video tend to be browsed and bought from a consumer's home.

Consumers are more likely to browse than buy online. Although 9 in 10 online consumers regularly browse in the marketspace of websites, more than half (51 percent) confine most of their purchases to the traditional retail store marketplace.[30] Consumer marketspace browsing and buying in the traditional marketplace has popularized multichannel marketing, which is described next.

Concept Check

1. What is the eight-second rule?

2. Which online consumer lifestyle segment spends the most money online and which spends the most time online?

3. What are the six reasons consumers prefer to shop and buy online?

MULTICHANNEL MARKETING TO THE ONLINE CONSUMER

The fact that a large number of consumers browse and buy in two market environments means that few companies limit their marketing programs exclusively to the traditional marketplace or marketspace. Today, it is commonplace for companies to maintain a presence in both market environments of some kind and measure. This dual presence is made possible by multichannel marketing.

Integrating and Leveraging Multiple Channels with Multichannel Marketing

Companies often employ multiple marketing channels for their products and services as described in Chapter 15. *Dual distribution* is the term used to describe this practice, which focuses on reaching different consumers through different marketing channels. For example, Avon markets its health and beauty products directly through Avon sales representatives, a brochure, kiosks in shopping malls, and an Avon website. The various communication (representatives and brochures) and delivery (kiosks) channels allow Avon to reach different consumers, feature different brands, and provide different shopping and buying experiences.

Multichannel marketing bears some resemblance to dual distribution. For example, different communication and delivery channels are used such as catalogs, kiosks, retail stores, personal selling, and websites. In fact, retailers that employ two or more of these channels are labeled *multichannel retailers* as described in Chapter 17. However, the resemblance ends at this point. **Multichannel marketing** is the *blending* of different communication and delivery channels that are *mutually reinforcing* in attracting, retaining, and building relationships with consumers who shop and buy in the traditional marketplace and marketspace. Multichannel marketing seeks to integrate a firm's communication and delivery channels, not differentiate them. In doing so, consumers can browse and buy "anytime, anywhere, anyway," expecting that the experience will be similar regardless of channel. At Eddie Bauer, for example, every effort is made to make the apparel shopping and purchase process for its customers the same in its retail stores, with its catalog, and at its website. According to an Eddie Bauer marketing manager, "We don't distinguish between channels because it's all Eddie Bauer to our customers."[31]

Multichannel marketing also can leverage the value-adding capabilities of different channels.[32] For example, retail stores can leverage their physical presence by allowing customers to pick up their online orders at a nearby store or return or exchange nonstore purchases if they wish. Catalogs can serve as shopping tools for online purchasing, as they do for store purchasing. Websites can help consumers do their homework before visiting a store. Office Depot has leveraged its store, catalog, and website channels with impressive results. The company, which is the world's largest office supply retail chain, is the second-largest Internet retailer in the world (behind Amazon.com), doing more than $2 billion in online retail sales annually.[33] The benefits of multichannel marketing is also apparent in the spending behavior of consumers as described in the accompanying Marketing NewsNet.[34]

MARKETING NEWSNET   The Multichannel Marketing Multiplier

CUSTOMER VALUE

Multichannel marketing is the blending of different communication and delivery channels that are mutually reinforcing in attracting, retaining, and building relationships with consumers who shop and buy in the traditional marketplace and marketspace. Industry analysts refer to the complementary role of different communication and delivery channels as an *influence effect*.

Retailers that integrate and leverage their stores, catalogs, and websites have seen a sizable lift in yearly sales recorded from individual customers. Eddie Bauer is a case in point. Customers who shop only one of its channels spend $100 to $200 per year. Those who shop in two channels spend $300 to $500 annually. Customers who shop all these channels—store, catalog, and website—spend $800 to $1,000 per year. Moreover, multichannel customers have been found to be *three times* as profitable as single-channel customers.

JCPenney has seen similar results. The company is a leading multichannel retailer and reports that a JCPenney customer who shops in all three channels—store, catalog, and website—spends *four to eight times* as much as a customer who shops in only one channel, as shown in the chart below.

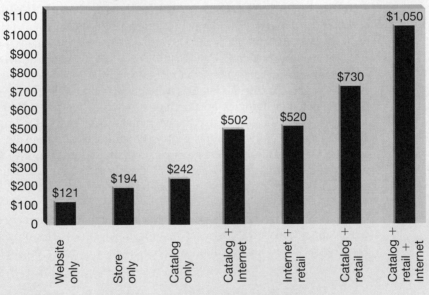

Average annual dollars spent by a JCPenney customer

Website only: $121
Store only: $194
Catalog only: $242
Catalog + Internet: $502
Internet + retail: $520
Catalog + retail: $730
Catalog + retail + Internet: $1,050

Implementing Multichannel Marketing

Not all companies employ websites for multichannel marketing the same way. This should not be surprising. Different companies apply the value-creation capabilities of Internet technology differently depending on their overall marketing program.

Websites play a multifaceted role in multichannel marketing because they can serve as either a communication or delivery channel. Two general applications of websites exist based on their intended purpose: (1) transactional websites and (2) promotional websites.

Multichannel Marketing with Transactional Websites   *Transactional websites* are essentially electronic storefronts. They focus principally on converting an online browser into an online, catalog, or in-store buyer using the website design elements described earlier. Transactional websites are most common among store and catalog retailers and direct selling companies, such as Tupperware. The Gap, for instance, generates more sales volume from its website (www.gap.com) than any one of its stores, save one.[35] Retailers and direct selling firms have found that their websites, while cannibalizing sales volume from stores, catalogs, and sales representatives, attract new customers and influence sales. Consider Victoria's Secret, the well-known specialty retailer of intimate apparel for women age 18 to 45. It reports that almost 60 percent of its website customers are men, most of whom generate new sales volume for the company.[36] Likewise, Sears.com is estimated to account for more than $600 million worth of Sears, Roebuck & Co. merchandise sales. Why? Sears customers first research merchandise online before visiting a store.[37]

Transactional websites are used less frequently by manufacturers of consumer products. A recurring issue for manufacturers is the threat of *channel conflict*, described in Chapter 15, and the potential harm to trade relationships with their retailing intermediaries. Still, manufacturers do use transactional websites, often cooperating with retailers. For example, Ethan Allen, the furniture manufacturer, markets its product line at www.ethanallen.com. Whenever feasible, Ethan Allen retailers fill online orders, and receive 25 percent of the sales price. For items shipped directly from the Ethan Allen factory, the store nearest the customer receives 10 percent of the sales price.[38] In addition, Ethan Allen, like other manufacturers, typically lists stores on their website where their merchandise can be shopped and bought. More often than not, however, manufacturers engage multichannel channels, using websites as advertising and promotion vehicles.

Multichannel Marketing with Promotional Websites   *Promotional websites* have a very different purpose than transactional sites. They advertise and promote a company's products and services and provide information on how items can be used and where they can be purchased. They often engage the visitor in an interactive experience involving games, contests, and quizzes with electronic coupons and other gifts as prizes. Procter & Gamble maintains separate websites for dozens of its leading brands, including Pringles potato chips (www.pringles.com), Vidal Sassoon hair products (www.vidalsassoon.com), Scope mouthwash (www.scope-mouthwash.com), and Pampers diapers (www.pampers.com). Promotional sites can be effective in generating interest in and trial of a company's products and services (see Figure 21–6).[39] General Motors reports that 80 percent of the people visiting a Saturn store first visited the brand's website (www.saturn.com) and 70 percent of Saturn leads come from its website.

Promotional websites also can be used to support a company's traditional marketing channel and build customer relationships. This is the objective of the Clinique Division of Estée Lauder, Inc., which markets cosmetics through department stores.

FIGURE 21–6

Implementing multichannel marketing with promotional websites

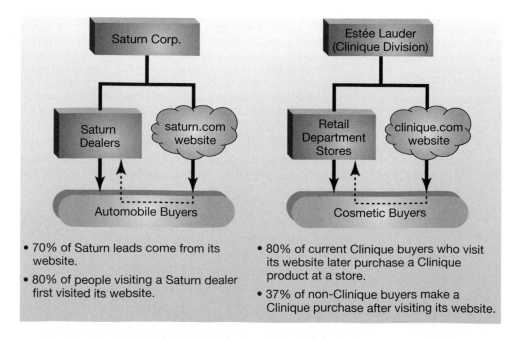

- 70% of Saturn leads come from its website.
- 80% of people visiting a Saturn dealer first visited its website.

- 80% of current Clinique buyers who visit its website later purchase a Clinique product at a store.
- 37% of non-Clinique buyers make a Clinique purchase after visiting its website.

Clinique reports that 80 percent of current customers who visit its website (www.clinique.com) later purchase a Clinique product at a department store; 37 percent of non-Clinique buyers make a Clinique purchase after visiting the company's website.

The popularity of multichannel marketing is apparent in its growing impact on online retail sales.[40] Fully 65 percent of U.S. online retail sales in 2003 were made by companies that practiced multichannel marketing. Multichannel marketers are expected to register about 85 percent of U.S. online retail sales in 2006.

Concept Check

1. Multichannel marketing is _____.

2. Channel conflict between manufacturers and retailers is likely to arise when manufacturers use _____ websites.

CHAPTER IN REVIEW

1 *Describe what interactive marketing is and how it creates customer value, customer relationships, and customer experiences.*

Interactive marketing involves two-way buyer–seller electronic communication in a computer-mediated environment in which the buyer controls the kind and amount of information received from the seller. It creates customer value by providing time, place, form, and possession utility for consumers. Customer relationships are created and sustained through two unique capabilities of Internet technology: interactivity and individuality. From an interactive marketing perspective, customer experience represents the sum total of the interactions that a customer has with a company's website, from the initial look at a homepage through the entire purchase decision process. Companies produce a customer experience through seven website design elements. These elements are context, content, community, customization, communication, connection, and commerce.

2 *Identify the demographic and lifestyle profile of online consumers.*

As a group, online consumers are about evenly split between men and women and tend to be better educated, younger, and more affluent than the general U.S. population. Women tend to purchase more goods and services online than men. The lifestyle profile of online consumers reflects the different kinds of online experiences they seek. Six lifestyle segments have been identified. The click-and-mortar segment consists of women who browse retailer websites but actually buy products at retail outlets. Hunter-gatherers use the Internet like a consumer magazine to gather information and compare products and services. Brand loyalists regularly visit their favorite bookmarked websites and spend the most money online. Time-sensitive materialists regard the Internet as a convenient tool for buying. The hooked, online, and single segment spend more time online than any segment. Ebivalent newbies are relative newcomers to the Internet who rarely spend money online, but seek product information.

3 *Explain why certain types of products and services are particularly suited for interactive marketing.*

Certain types of products and services seem to be particularly suited for interactive marketing. One category consists of items for which product information is an important part of the purchase decision, but prepurchase trial is not necessarily critical. A second category involves items for which audio or video demonstration is important. A third category contains items that can be digitally delivered. Unique items represent a fourth category. A fifth category includes items that are regularly purchased and where convenience is very important. A final category consists of highly standardized items for which information about price is important.

4 *Describe why consumers shop and buy online and how marketers influence online purchasing behavior.*

There are six reasons consumers shop and buy online. They are convenience, choice, customization, communication, cost, and control. Marketers have capitalized on these reasons through a variety of means. For example, they provide choice assistance using choiceboard and collaborative filtering technology, which also provides opportunities for customization. Company-hosted web communities and viral marketing practices capitalize on the communications dimensions of Internet-enabled technologies. Dynamic pricing provides real-time responses to supply and demand conditions, often resulting in lower prices to consumers. Permission marketing is popular given consumer interest in control.

5 *Define multichannel marketing and the role of transactional and promotional websites in reaching online consumers.*

Multichannel marketing is the blending of different communication and delivery channels that are mutually reinforcing in attracting, retaining, and building relationships with consumers who shop and buy in the traditional marketplace and marketspace. In practice, this means that companies simultaneously market their products through personal selling, retail stores, websites, catalogs, and kiosks. Websites play a multifaceted role in multichannel marketing because they can serve as either a delivery or communication channel. In this regard, transactional websites are essentially electronic storefronts. They focus principally on converting an online browser into an online, catalog, or in-store buyer using the website design elements described earlier. On the other hand, promotional websites serve to advertise and promote a company's products and services and provide information on how items can be used and where they can be purchased.

FOCUSING ON KEY TERMS

blog p. 569
bots p. 567
choiceboard p. 560
collaborative filtering p. 560
cookies p. 570
customer experience p. 562
customerization p. 568
dynamic pricing p. 570
eight-second rule p. 567

interactive marketing p. 560
multichannel marketing p. 572
online consumers p. 564
permission marketing p. 561
personalization p. 560
portals p. 570
spam p. 569
viral marketing p. 569
web communities p. 569

DISCUSSION AND APPLICATION QUESTIONS

1 By early 2005, about two-thirds of Internet users had actually purchased something online. Have you made an online purchase? If so, why do you think so many people who have access to the Internet are not also online buyers? If not, why are you reluctant to do so? Do you think that electronic commerce benefits consumers even if they don't make a purchase?

2 Like the traditional marketplace, marketspace offers marketers opportunities to create greater time, place, form, and possession utility. How do you think Internet-enabled technology rates in terms of creating these values? Take a shopping trip at a virtual retailer of your choice (don't buy anything unless you really want to). Then compare the time, place, form, and possession utility provided by the virtual retailer with that you enjoyed during a nonelectronic experience shopping for the same product category.

3 Visit Amazon.com (www.amazon.com) or Barnes & Noble (barnesandnoble.com). As you tour the company's website, think about how shopping for books online compares with a trip to your university bookstore to buy books. Specifically, compare and contrast your shopping experiences with respect to convenience, choice, customization, communication, cost, and control.

4 Suppose you are planning to buy a new car so you decide to visit www.carpoint.com. Based on your experience visiting that site, do you think you would enjoy more or less control in negotiating with the dealer when you actually purchase your vehicle?

5 Visit the website for your university or college. Based on your visit, would you conclude that the site is a transactional site or a promotional site? Why? How would you rate the site in terms of the six website design elements that affect customer experience?

6 One of the benefits that interactive marketing provides for companies is the ability to obtain consumer information that can be used to more effectively manage the marketing mix. Catalina Marketing Corporation, for example, creates profiles of its online customers' product category and brand preferences and uses this information to generate personalized coupons. Some consumers, however, worry about their privacy as companies like Catalina create customer databases. Visit Catalina's website at www.valuepage.com to determine what information you must provide to obtain your own customized coupons. Is the added value of the coupons worth the price of the information you must reveal to get the coupons? Why or why not?

GOING ONLINE Tracking Trends in Interactive Marketing

What are the most recent statistics and trends in interactive and multichannel marketing? Look no further than Clickz.com, an online service that abstracts up-to-date research on Internet usage and applications from around the world. Clickz.com conveniently organizes research by business, social, technical, demographic, and geographical categories for easy inspection.

Visit the Clickz website at www.clickz.com, then click the "Stats" link. Your assignment is as follows:

1 Choose a topic covered in the chapter that interests you, such as the demographics of Internet users. Compare and contrast the most recent research published in Clickz.com with information contained in the chapter. Don't be surprised if you find differences.

2 Choose two regions of the world, such as North America and Europe. How do Internet usage and interactive marketing differ between the two regions based on the most recent research?

BUILDING YOUR MARKETING PLAN

Does your marketing plan involve a marketspace presence for your product or service? If the answer is no, read no further and do not include this element in your plan. If the answer is yes, then attention must be given to developing a website in your marketing plan. A useful starting point is to:

1 Describe how each website element—context, content, community, customization, communication, connection, and commerce—will be used to create a customer experience.

2 Identify a company's website that best reflects your website conceptualization.

VIDEO CASE 21   McFarlane Toys: The Best of Interactive Marketing

"All my life, I've been underwhelmed by the sports action figures sold in the toy aisles," says Todd McFarlane, founder of McFarlane Toys.

This assessment of the marketplace led McFarlane to create his own toy manufacturing company, an entirely new category of toys called "upscale figures," and an extraordinarily sophisticated marketing strategy based on traditional and interactive approaches. McFarlane Toys is now one of the world's largest toy companies. The company's products include action figures of professional athletes, rock stars, NASCAR drivers, and characters from movies such as *The Terminator, The Matrix,* and *Austin Powers.* Its marketing programs have used Internet contests, virtual showrooms, online catalogs, and a variety of other award-winning tools. Overall, McFarlane Toys has transformed a category that used to be just plastic replicas for children into an art collectible for adults. McFarlane explains, "It's about creating a toy that, if you had it on your shelf, somebody wouldn't say, 'Are you collecting toys? How old are you?'"

THE COMPANY

McFarlane started his career as an artist for Marvel/Epic Comics, working on issues of *Incredible Hulk, Amazing Spider-Man, Batman,* and *Coyote.* Eventually he formed Image Comics with six other Marvel artists and began work on his own comic book, *Spawn.* The first issue of *Spawn* sold a record-breaking 1.7 million copies. Since then the series has become a top-selling comic published in 16 languages and sold in more than 120 countries.

The success of *Spawn* soon generated licensing proposals from toy companies, movies studios, and television producers. When Todd met with each of the companies, however, he was concerned about his ability to have creative control over the toy production. As a result, he started his own toy company, McFarlane Toys, in order to guarantee his fans high quality, intricately detailed, and reasonably priced action figures. *Spawn* action figures quickly became one of the most successful toys on the market.

Following the introduction of the Spawn action figures, McFarlane began producing action figures of pop culture icons in film, music, gaming, and sports. The company also signed license agreements with the four major North American sports leagues—football, baseball, basketball, and hockey. In addition, McFarlane Toys produced toys for licensors such as the Beatles, *Shrek,* KISS, *X-Files, Alien,* AC/DC, Jimi Hendrix, and many others. The quality and the collectibility of the figures has given McFarlane Toys a worldwide reputation among retailers and consumers.

When he founded McFarlane Toys, Todd said, "I'm just going to do action figures. I'm going to be the king of Aisle 7." Other opportunities soon appeared, however, and Todd became involved in the production of feature films, music videos, electronic games, and animated television. Some of these projects have included: the live-action film *Spawn* which grossed $50 million in just 19 days; the HBO series *Todd McFarlane's Spawn* which won an Emmy award; and the music video for Korn's *Freak on a Leash* which received a Grammy award. All of these activities have helped expand the growing number of McFarlane Toy fans.

Today McFarlane Toys is ranked among the top five makers of action figures, with sales estimated between $25 and $125 million. McFarlane manages the company as the "creative force" from its headquarters in Tempe, Arizona. The toy designers work in New Jersey and the toys are manufactured in China. Currently, it takes about 12 months for a product idea on paper to make its way through the rigorous process of becoming a toy on the shelf.

THE TOY INDUSTRY

Toys are big business. Worldwide toy sales exceed $59 billion. The United States is the largest toy market and accounts for 35 percent of worldwide industry sales. A child in the United States receives about $242 worth of toys per year on average. By comparison, the average annual expenditure per child outside the United States is

$26. Dolls represent the largest single category of toys, although action figures account for $1.2 billion in sales. Figure 1 shows the dollar sales of individual toy categories in the United States:

CATEGORY	SALES ($ BILLIONS)
Action Figures & Accessories	$ 1.2
Arts & Crafts	2.4
Building Sets	.6
Dolls	2.8
Games/Puzzles	2.4
Infant/Preschool	2.6
Learning & Exploration	.5
Outdoor & Sports Toys	2.4
Plush	1.4
Vehicles	2.0
All Other Toys	2.5
TOTAL	$20.8

FIGURE 1
Toy Category Sales in the United States
(Listed alphabetically)

U.S. mass merchants are the principal retailers of toys. General merchandise and discounters like Wal-Mart, Kmart, and Target register 51 percent of retail toy sales. Toy chains account for 25 percent of retail sales. Other retailers, such as catalog, toy, hobby and game stores, department stores, and food and drug stores, record 24 percent of sales. Wal-Mart stores are the number one toy retailer in the United States.

The worldwide toy industry is dominated by two U.S. toy makers: Mattel and Hasbro. Japan's Bandai Company and Sanrio, and Denmark's LEGO Company are also major toy makers.

E-COMMERCE AND INTERACTIVE MARKETING AT MCFARLANE TOYS

Shortly after forming McFarlane Toys, Todd set up a booth in the annual industry trade show in New York called Toy Fair. Even though the new company didn't have any toys produced yet, an action figure buyer from a toy chain store saw photos of the proposed toys and agreed to place an order. Other traditional retailing opportunities in large discount stores such as Wal-Mart, entertainment outlets such as Sam Goody and Tower Records, and small, local comic book stores such as Diamonds soon followed. McFarlane Toys also utilized traditional forms of marketing, including media interviews

and public relations events, to reach buyers who represented toy stores. McFarland also recently opened its first retail store in Arizona, which showcases current products and prototypes of future releases of the various lines of action figures. Collectors from around the world have visited the store to purchase products, attend artist autograph sessions, and to meet Todd!

Since the target market for McFarlane Toys products is older children and young adults—who make 30 to 40 percent of all action figure purchases—e-commerce and interactive marketing offered another opportunity to reach action figure consumers. The McFarlane Toys website (www.spawn.com) is a good example of the *convenience* online marketing can offer. The site provides a store for purchasing action figures in each of the lines (e.g., movie figures, music figures, baseball figures, comic book figures, etc.). High quality images allow shoppers to view each figure before adding it to a "basket" and then placing the order. The site also offers visitors a *choice* for the location of their purchase. A "Where to Buy" link lists all retailers and other online "e-tailers" such as www.comicsplusonline.com and www.allstarfigures.com.

The website also provides a variety of opportunities for *communication*. Consumer-to-marketer communication is provided through the "Contact Us" link. In addition, marketer-to-consumer information is provided through the McFarlane newsletter, which is sent to visitors who register to receive the update. Finally, consumers can use the spawn.com message board to participate in discussions about action figures, movies, and comics, or to buy, sell, and trade McFarlane products. There are 32,500 registered users of the message board forums, and as many as 690 of them have been online at the same time. A unique way that McFarlane provides *customization* of his offerings for his customers is through the Collector's Club, which offers exclusive, limited-edition action figures to members.

Online consumers are also typically concerned about *cost* and *control*. McFarlane tries to keep the cost of most of his toys between $10 and $15 by keeping production expenses low. Online shoppers also receive special offers when warehouse inventory is being reduced or eliminated. Of course, sales and discounts can often be found by utilizing the links to the many stores and online retailers that carry McFarlane Toys. Online users control their interaction with McFarlane by providing information only through "opt-in" solicitation for purchases, message board use, and newsletter e-mail delivery.

As McFarlane's focus on interactive marketing increased, the importance of the trade show where the first order came in declined. In fact, McFarlane recently stopped attending the trade show and began announcing its new products on its website with an online event called ToyFest. The event generated close to 200 million hits and 600,000 unique visitors. McFarlane explains, "It's always been strange to me that consumers were not allowed at Toy Fair, but with spawn.com our consumers can view our new lines at the same time as everybody else."

ISSUES FOR THE FUTURE

Of course, McFarlane's success has attracted attention from consumers, retailers, and competitors. New small firms such as Palisades Toys, Art Asylum, Playmates, and Mezco are now turning out action figures. Larger firms are also trying to compete. Hasbro, for example, recently won an award for its *Star Wars* figures. As more companies enter the category, obtaining new licensing agreements is also becoming more difficult.

While McFarlane has been heard to comment, "It's just stuff," he is very committed to continuing to develop and grow the category he created. In the future, expect to see additional action figures, movies, music videos, and video games. McFarlane Toys is also working at maintaining the strong relationship with its loyal customers through online contests, customer polls about

potential new products, and a new product idea link to company designers.

Finally, in a move completely unrelated to action figures, McFarlane bought notable home run baseballs, including Mark McGwire's 70th home run ball for $3 million, to create The McFarlane Collection. The collection is touring stadiums and special events to raise money to battle Lou Gehrig's disease. More than 2 million fans have seen the exhibit!

Questions

1 Describe the channels of distribution McFarlane Toys uses to reach its action figure customers.
2 Why have interactive marketing strategies been successful for McFarlane Toys? What unique elements are part of its online experience?
3 How does McFarlane Toys address each of the six C's consumers consider when shopping and buying online?

Chicken Helper
New!
Cheesy Chicken Enchilada

Pork Helper
Pork Fried Rice
NEW!

BerryBurst Cheerios
Triple Berry
Can Help Lower Cholesterol

nouriche
LIGHT
Breakfast Smoothie
Peach

nouriche
Breakfast Smoothie
Rasp

nouriche

Go-GURT
Portable Yogurt

Cascadian Farm
Since 1972
ORGANIC
Purely O's

Betty Crocker
Com
MEAL
Herb St
& Tur

Space Saver Bag!
RESEALABLE BAG

Pillsbury
Home Baked Classics
Sweet Rolls
Cinnamon with Icing

Yoplait
nouriche
Breakfast Smoothie
Mixed Berry

Yoplait
nouriche
LIGHT
Breakfast Smoothie
Raspberry

Yoplait
Whip

Yoplait
Ultra

General Mills
OATMEAL CRISP

Cinnamon Toast

22

PULLING IT ALL TOGETHER: THE STRATEGIC MARKETING PROCESS

LEARNING OBJECTIVES

After reading this chapter you should be able to:

1 Explain how marketing managers allocate their limited resources.

2 Describe three marketing planning frameworks: Porter's generic strategies, profit enhancement options, and market-product synergies.

3 Explain what makes an effective marketing plan and some problems that often exist with it.

4 Schedule a series of tasks to meet a deadline using a Gantt chart.

5 Describe the alternatives for organizing a marketing department and the role of a product manager.

6 Explain how sales and profitability analyses and ROI marketing are used to evaluate and control marketing programs.

MARKETING STRATEGY AT GENERAL MILLS: TOUGH COMPETITION AND CRITICAL DECISIONS

Assume you are a marketing manager at General Mills responsible for introducing successful new brands of cereal. Here are some facts to tell you how difficult your job is:

- Only one out of five new brands succeeds, which is defined as achieving 0.5 percent market share, or half of 1 percent, of the $8 billion-a-year U.S. ready-to-eat (RTE) cereal market.[1]

- A new-product launch typically costs up to $40 million.

- There are more than 300 competing breakfast cereals already sitting somewhere on a supermarket shelf.

- Many Americans on low-carbohydrate diets are avoiding cereals, causing the size of the RTE market to actually decline recently. So new cereal offerings must steal, or cannibalize, sales from existing brands for a successful launch.

- Smaller competitors have entered the U.S. RTE cereal market by introducing "bagged" or generic, private-label versions of well-known General Mills' and Kellogg's brands for about $1 less per bag than their branded counterparts.[2]

Does your job still sound like fun?

To make matters even a bit more complicated, General Mills acquired Pillsbury in late 2001, seeking to leverage Pillsbury's well-known brands using General Mills' marketing expertise to increase revenues.[3] General Mills also sought important marketing, manufacturing, and supply chain efficiencies and synergies in the merged companies, eventually achieved through moving more than 80 million cases of food and 2,400 pieces of equipment.[4]

Since the Pillsbury acquisition, General Mills has introduced more than a hundred new products that respond to what consumers are asking for: greater convenience, being able to eat the product on the go, and healthier eating that goes beyond low-carbohydrate diets.[5] Sometimes it's possible to get all these features in the same new product and other times not. Clinical research studies support General Mills' search for healthier foods. In late 2004 it announced that by early 2005 it would make all its cereals with whole grains, ingredients that can help prevent diabetes, heart disease, cancer, and obesity.[6] Some examples of the new products from General Mills:

- Yoplait® Nouriche® and Nouriche Light nonfat yogurt smoothies with 20 vitamins and minerals, along with protein and fiber, giving them the nourishment of a meal.[7]

- Betty Crocker Pork Helper™ for Pork Fried Rice and Chicken Helper™ for Cheesy Chicken Enchilada, lines that build on the legendary success of its Hamburger Helper introduced three decades ago.

- Go-Bags™, six-to-a-carton pouches of breakfast cereal like Cinnamon Toast Crunch® that can be eaten . . . on the go.

- Pillsbury Home Baked Classics®, a line of frozen biscuits, sweet rolls, and dinner rolls in resealable bags to permit baking only one or two, rather than the entire package, which augments the Pillsbury line of refrigerated dough products.

- Pillsbury Ready to Bake!™ cookies, a line of frozen cookies that just need to be popped into the oven, not even needing to be formed into cookie shapes.

Does all of this look easy? Not necessarily. For example, when General Mills marketing researchers discovered that consumers like actually to *see* the chocolate chips on top of their chocolate chip cookies, it invested in new manufacturing equipment to make this a reality. Putting the chocolate chips on top increased sales 50 percent.[8]

Chapter 22 discusses issues and techniques related to planning, implementation, and control phases of the strategic marketing process, the kind of topics marketing managers face every day. Throughout the chapter, you'll be able to obtain insights into the marketing strategies now emerging at General Mills. You'll also discover why Steve Sanger, its chief executive officer, is focused on a "one-handedness" strategy to achieve growth. The individual elements of the strategic marketing process were introduced in Chapter 2.

MARKETING BASICS: DOING WHAT WORKS AND ALLOCATING RESOURCES

As noted in Chapter 2, corporate and marketing executives search continuously to find a competitive advantage—a unique strength relative to competitors. Having identified this competitive advantage, they must figure out how to exploit it.[9] This involves (1) finding and using what works for their organization and industry and (2) allocating resources effectively.

Finding and Using What Really Works

In a five-year study, researchers Nohria, Joyce, and Roberson conducted in-depth analysis of 160 companies and more than 200 management tools and techniques, such as supply chain management, customer relationship management (CRM), or use of an Intranet. The result? Individual management tools and techniques had no direct relationship to superior business performance in the companies.[10]

What *does* matter? The researchers concluded that four basic business and management practices are what matter—"what really works," to use their phrase. These are: (1) strategy, (2) execution, (3) culture, and (4) structure. Firms with excellence in all four of these areas are likely to achieve superior business performance. And in terms of individual tools and techniques, the researchers concluded that which ones the firm chooses to use is less important than flawless execution of the ones it does use.

Industry leaders like Wal-Mart, Home Depot, and Dell do *all* four of the basic practices extremely well, not just two or three, and are vigilant to keep doing them well when conditions change. Coca-Cola[11] and Kodak[12], superstars a decade ago, are struggling today to get these basics right and regain past success. But let's look at companies that stand out today in each of the four basics:

- *Strategy: Devise and maintain a clearly stated, focused strategy.* While Wal-Mart may be the unstoppable force in mass-merchandise retailing, in warehouse clubs its Sam's Club is not. The winner to date: Costco Wholesale, with 60 percent as many stores as Sam's Club but almost twice the sales revenue. A key reason is its focused strategy based on the knowledge that of all U.S. retail channels, warehouse clubs attract the largest proportion of affluent shoppers. Costco's strategy: Sell a limited selection of branded high-end merchandise at low prices.[13]

- *Execution: Develop and maintain flawless operational execution.* Toyota is generally acknowledged as the best in the world in revolutionizing the design and manufacture of autos. Toyota managers created the doctrine of *kaizen,* or continuous improvement. For example, by speeding up decisions, Toyota reduced the time to get the 2003 Solara from the drawing board to showroom to 19 months, about half the industry average.[14]

- *Culture: Develop and maintain a performance-oriented culture.* The number one spot on *Fortune's* 2004 list of the 100 Best Companies to Work For goes to Smuckers—yes, the "With a name like Smuckers" company. Its straightforward culture is based on four key elements in its code of conduct: "Listen with your full attention, look for the good in others, have a sense of humor, and say thank you for a job well done." The performance result? Company stock had a total return of 100 percent over the previous five years.[15]

- *Structure: Build and maintain a fast, flexible, flat organization.* Successful small organizations often grow into bureaucratic large ones with layers of managers and red tape that slow decisions down. An exception and the unquestioned all-time leader in delivering world-class aircraft with only about 50 engineers and designers and 100 expert machinists: Lockheed's Skunk Works. Discussed later in the chapter, its first director set guidelines for organizational structure

Costco and Smuckers achieve excellence in what really matters.

and implementation. Attempts have been made to try to apply these Skunk Works guidelines to U.S. auto industry projects and operations as far away as France and Russia. Key guidelines are (1) give the director the authority to make quick decisions and (2) use a small number of good people who can talk to anyone in the organization to solve a problem.[16]

Of course, in practice a firm cannot allocate unlimited resources to achieving each of these business basics. It must make choices on where its resources can give the greatest return, the topic of the next section.

Allocating Marketing Resources Using Sales Response Functions

A **sales response function** relates the expense of marketing effort to the marketing results obtained.[17] For simplicity in the examples that follow, only the effects of annual marketing effort on annual sales revenue will be analyzed, but the concept applies to other measures of marketing success—such as profit, units sold, or level of awareness—as well.

Maximizing Incremental Revenue Minus Incremental Cost   Economists give managers a specific guideline for optimal resource allocation: Allocate the firm's marketing, production, and financial resources to the markets and products where the excess of incremental revenues over incremental costs is greatest. This parallels the marginal revenue–marginal cost analysis of Chapter 13.

Figure 22–1 illustrates the resource allocation principle that is inherent in the sales response function. The firm's annual marketing effort, such as sales and advertising expenses, is plotted on the horizontal axis. As the annual marketing effort increases, so does the resulting annual sales revenue, which is plotted on the vertical axis. The relationship is assumed to be S-shaped, showing that an additional $1 million of marketing effort from $3 million to $4 million results in far greater increases of sales revenue in the midrange ($20 million) of the curve than at either end (an increase from $2 million to $3 million in spending yields an increase of $10 million in sales; an increase from $6 million to $7 million in spending leads to an increase of $5 million in sales).

A Numerical Example of Resource Allocation   Suppose Figure 22–1 shows the situation for a new General Mills product such as Berry Burst Cheerios®, an extension of the Cheerios brand targeted at "the grocery shopper," who is typically a 35- to 54-year-old woman. Berry Burst Cheerios contains berries that plump up when milk is added, a technical challenge for scientists.[18]

FIGURE 22–1

Sales response function showing the situation for two different years

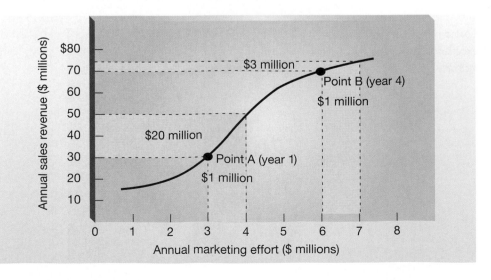

Also assume that the sales response function doesn't change through time as a result of changing consumer tastes and incomes. Point A shows the position of the firm in year 1, whereas Point B shows it three years later in year 4. Suppose General Mills decides to launch new advertising and sales promotions that, let's say, increase its marketing effort for the brand from $3 million to $6 million a year. If the relationship in Figure 22–1 holds true and is a good picture of consumer purchasing behavior, the sales revenues of Berry Burst Cheerios should increase from $30 million to $70 million a year.

Let's look at the major resource allocation question: What are the probable increases in sales revenue for Berry Burst Cheerios in year 1 and year 4 if General Mills were to spend an additional $1 million in marketing effort? As Figure 22–1 reveals,

Year 1

Increase in marketing effort from $3 million to $4 million = $1 million
Increase in sales revenue from $30 million to $50 million = $20 million
Ratio of incremental sales revenue to effort = $20,000,000:$1,000,000 = 20:1

Year 4

Increase in marketing effort from $6 million to $7 million = $1 million
Increase in sales revenue from $70 million to $73 million = $3 million
Ratio of incremental sales revenue to effort = $3,000,000:$1,000,000 = 3:1

Thus, in year 1 a dollar of extra marketing effort returned $20 in sales revenue, whereas in year 4 it returned only $3. If no other expenses are incurred, it might make sense to spend $1 million in year 4 to gain $3 million in incremental sales revenue. However, it may be far wiser for General Mills to invest the money in products in one of its other business units, such as its new Yoplait Nouriche Light. The essence of resource allocation is simple: Put incremental resources where the incremental returns are greatest over the foreseeable future.

Allocating Marketing Resources in Practice   General Mills, like many firms in these businesses, does extensive analysis using **share points**, or percentage points of market share, as the common basis of comparison to allocate marketing resources effectively for different product lines within the same firm. This allows it to seek answers to the question, "How much is it worth to us to try to increase our market share by another 1 (or 2, or 5, or 10) percentage point?"

This analysis enables higher-level managers to make resource allocation trade-offs among different kinds of business units owned by the company. To make these resource allocation decisions, marketing managers must estimate: (1) the market share for the product, (2) the revenues associated with each point of market share (a share point in breakfast cereals may be five times what it is in cake mixes), (3) the contribution to overhead and profit (or gross margin) of each share point, and (4) possible cannibalization effects on other products in the line (for example, new Berry Burst Cheerios might reduce sales of regular Cheerios).[19]

The resource allocation process helps General Mills choose wisely from among the many opportunities that exist in its various products and markets. In the case of Berry Burst Cheerios, it was the most successful launch in General Mills' history, achieving almost $100 million in retail sales its first year.[20]

Resource Allocation and the Strategic Marketing Process   Company resources are allocated effectively in the strategic marketing process by converting marketing information into marketing actions. Figure 22–2 on the next page summarizes the strategic marketing process introduced in Chapter 2, along with some details of the marketing actions and information that comprise it. Figure 22–2 is really a simplification of the actual strategic marketing process: While the three phases of the strategic marketing process have distinct separations in the figure and

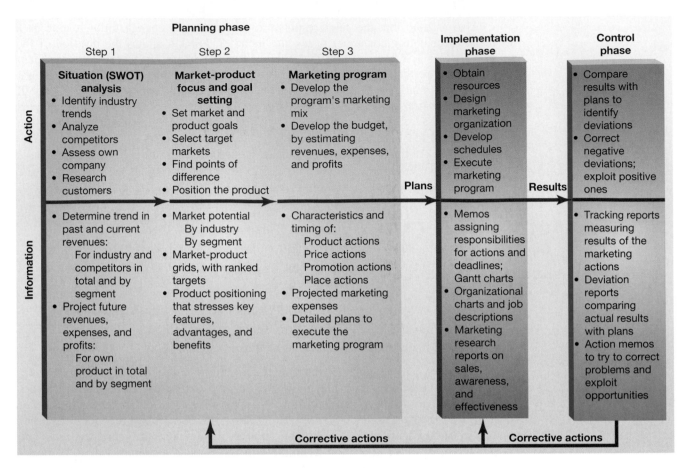

FIGURE 22–2

The strategic marketing process: actions and information

the marketing actions are separated from the marketing information, in practice these blend together and interact.

The upper half of each box in Figure 22–2 highlights the actions involved in that part of the strategic marketing process, and the lower half summarizes the information and reports used. Note that each phase has an output report:

PHASE	OUTPUT REPORT
Planning	Marketing plans (or programs) that define goals and the marketing mix strategies to achieve them
Implementation	Results (memos or computer outputs) that describe the outcomes of implementing the plans
Control	Corrective action memos, triggered by comparing results with plans, that (1) suggest solutions to problems and (2) take advantage of opportunities

The corrective action memos become feedback loops in Figure 22–2 that help improve decisions and actions in earlier phases of the strategic marketing process.

THE PLANNING PHASE OF THE STRATEGIC MARKETING PROCESS

Three aspects of the strategic marketing process deserve special mention: (1) the varieties of marketing plans, (2) marketing planning frameworks that have proven useful, and (3) some marketing planning and strategy lessons.

The Variety of Marketing Plans

The planning phase of the strategic marketing process usually results in a marketing plan that sets the direction for the marketing activities of an organization. As noted earlier in Appendix A, a marketing plan is the heart of a business plan. Like business plans, marketing plans aren't all from the same mold; they vary with the length of the planning period, the purpose, and the audience. Let's look briefly at two kinds: long-range and annual marketing plans.

Long-Range Marketing Plans   Typically, long-range marketing plans cover marketing activities from two to five years into the future. Except for firms in industries such as autos, steel, or forest products, marketing plans rarely go beyond five years into the future because the tremendous number of uncertainties present make the benefits of planning less than the effort expended. Such plans are often directed at top-level executives and the board of directors.

Annual Marketing Plans   Usually developed by a marketing or product manager (discussed later in the chapter) in a consumer products firm such as General Mills, annual marketing plans deal with marketing goals and strategies for a product, product line, or entire firm for a single year. Typical steps that firms take in developing their annual marketing plans for their existing products are shown in Figure 22–3.[21] This annual planning cycle typically starts with a detailed marketing research study of current users and ends after 48 weeks with the approval of the plan by the division general manager, 10 weeks before the fiscal year starts. Between these points there are continuing efforts to uncover new ideas through key-issues sessions with specialists

FIGURE 22–3

Steps a large consumer package goods firm takes in developing its annual marketing plan

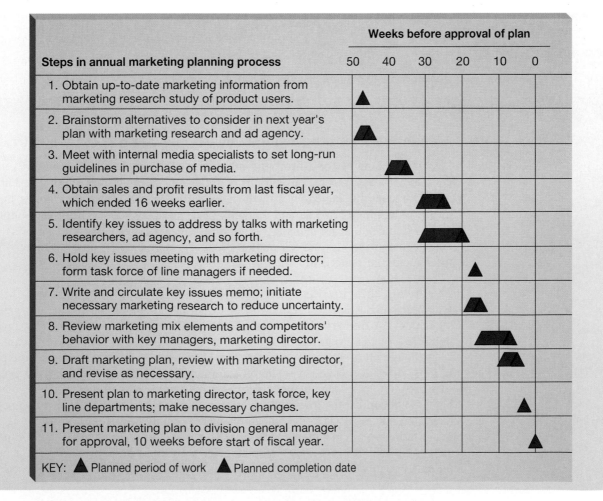

Steps in annual marketing planning process	Weeks before approval of plan					
	50	40	30	20	10	0
1. Obtain up-to-date marketing information from marketing research study of product users.	▲					
2. Brainstorm alternatives to consider in next year's plan with marketing research and ad agency.	▲					
3. Meet with internal media specialists to set long-run guidelines in purchase of media.		◢◣				
4. Obtain sales and profit results from last fiscal year, which ended 16 weeks earlier.			◢◣			
5. Identify key issues to address by talks with marketing researchers, ad agency, and so forth.			◢◣			
6. Hold key issues meeting with marketing director; form task force of line managers if needed.				▲		
7. Write and circulate key issues memo; initiate necessary marketing research to reduce uncertainty.				▲		
8. Review marketing mix elements and competitors' behavior with key managers, marketing director.					◢◣	
9. Draft marketing plan, review with marketing director, and revise as necessary.					◢◣	
10. Present plan to marketing director, task force, key line departments; make necessary changes.					▲	
11. Present marketing plan to division general manager for approval, 10 weeks before start of fiscal year.						▲

KEY: ◢◣ Planned period of work   ▲ Planned completion date

both inside and outside the firm. The plan is fine-tuned through a series of often excruciating reviews by several levels of management, which leaves few surprises and little to chance.

It is easier to talk about planning than to do it well. Try your hand as a consultant to help Trevor's Toys make some strategic marketing decisions, as described in the Web Link.

Concept Check

1. What is the significance of the S-shape of the sales response function in Figure 22–1?

2. What are the main output reports from each phase of the strategic marketing process?

3. What are two kinds of marketing plans?

Marketing Planning Frameworks: The Search for Growth

Marketing planning for a firm with many products competing in many markets is a complex process. Yet in a business firm all these planning efforts are directed at finding the means for increased growth in sales and profits. Three techniques that are useful in helping corporate and marketing executives in such a firm make important resource allocation decisions are: (1) Porter's generic business strategies, (2) profit enhancement options, and (3) market-product synergies. All three techniques relate to elements introduced in earlier chapters.

Porter's Generic Business Strategies   As shown in Figure 22–4, Michael E. Porter has developed a framework in which he identifies four basic, or "generic," strategies.[22] A **generic business strategy** is one that can be adopted by any firm, regardless of the product or industry involved, to achieve a competitive advantage.

Although all of the techniques discussed here involve generic strategies, the phrase is most often associated with Porter's framework. In this framework, the columns identify the two fundamental alternatives firms can use in seeking competitive advantage: (1) becoming the low-cost producer within the markets in which it competes or (2) differentiating itself from competitors by developing points of difference in its product offerings or marketing programs. In contrast, the rows identify the competitive scope: (1) a broad target by competing in many market segments or (2) a narrow target by competing in only a few segments or even a single segment. The columns

FIGURE 22–4

Porter's four generic business strategies

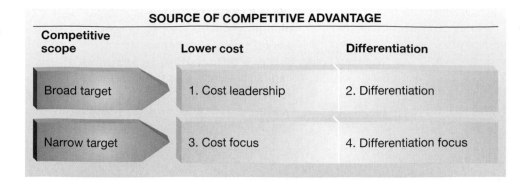

	SOURCE OF COMPETITIVE ADVANTAGE	
Competitive scope	**Lower cost**	**Differentiation**
Broad target	1. Cost leadership	2. Differentiation
Narrow target	3. Cost focus	4. Differentiation focus

and rows result in four generic business strategies, any one of which can provide a competitive advantage among similar business units in the same industry:

1. A **cost leadership strategy** (cell 1) focuses on reducing expenses and, in turn, lowers product prices while targeting a broad array of market segments. One way is by securing raw materials from a lower-cost supplier. Also, significant investments in capital equipment may be necessary to improve the production or distribution process and achieve these lower unit costs. The cost leader still must have adequate quality levels. Wal-Mart's sophisticated systems of regional warehouses and electronic data interchange with its suppliers have led to huge cost savings and its cost leadership strategy that results in lower prices for customers.

2. A **differentiation strategy** (cell 2) requires products to have significant points of difference in product offerings, brand image, higher quality, advanced technology, or superior service to charge a higher price while targeting a broad array of market segments. This allows the firm to charge a price premium. Delphi Automobile Systems has used this strategy to use satellite communications to connect you and your car to 24-hour-a-day emergency services, directions to a destination, and the opportunity to order a movie while on the road.

3. A **cost focus strategy** (cell 3) involves controlling expenses and, in turn, lowering product prices targeted at a narrow range of market segments. Retail chains targeting only a few market segments in a restricted group of products—such as

Which of Porter's generic strategies are Wal-Mart and Volkswagen using? For the answers and a discussion of the strategies, see the text.

Office Max in office supplies—have used a cost focus strategy successfully. Southwest Airlines has been very successful in offering low fares between restricted pairs of cities.

4. Finally, a **differentiation focus strategy** (cell 4) requires products to have significant points of difference to target one or only a few market segments. Volkswagen achieved spectacular success in the late 1990s by targeting the "nostalgia" segment, 35- to 54-year-old baby boomers, with its technology-laden New Beetle whose success helped lead to new VW models like today's Phaeton.[23]

These strategies also form the foundation for Michael Porter's theory about what makes a nation's industries successful, as discussed in Chapter 7.

Profit Enhancement Options

If a business wants to increase, or enhance, its profits, it can (1) increase revenues, (2) decrease expenses, or (3) do both. Among these profit enhancement options, let's look first at the strategy options of increasing revenues and then at those for decreasing expenses.

The strategy option of increasing revenues can only be achieved by using one or a combination of four ways to address present or new markets and products (Figure 22–5): (1) market penetration, (2) product development, (3) market development, and (4) diversification (which are described in Chapter 2).

Procter & Gamble has followed a successful strategy of market penetration (present markets, present products) by concentrating its effort on becoming the market leader in each of its more than 30 product categories. It is currently first in market share in more than half these product categories. In one three-month period in mid-2004, P&G increased its market share in 19 of its 20 largest core brands by introducing product improvements and trimming retail prices.[24]

In contrast, Johnson & Johnson has succeeded with a product development strategy (new products, present markets) to complement popular brands such as Tylenol pain reliever and Accuvue contact lenses. To compete with Bristol-Myers Squibb, American Home Products, and other companies, Johnson & Johnson developed Tylenol PM, a combination pain killer and sleeping pill, and Surevue, a long-lasting disposable contact lens.

Walt Disney Co. pursued a market development strategy (new markets, present products) following the success of the original Disneyland in Anaheim, California. The first market expansion, of course, was to Orlando, Florida, and more recently Disney built theme parks in Tokyo, Paris, and Hong Kong.

Finally, Philip Morris, which depended on Marlboro cigarettes for 60 percent of its profits in the late 1980s, has used a diversification strategy (new markets, new

FIGURE 22–5

Profit enhancement options for increasing a firm's profits

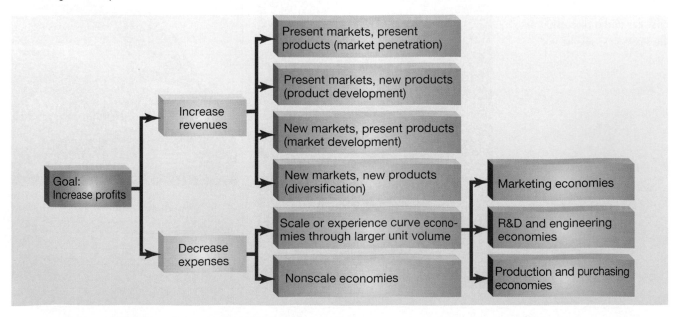

products) to reduce its dependence on a single brand. In recent years, Philip Morris has purchased 7UP, Miller Brewing, General Foods, and Kraft to create a portfolio of consumer products.

Strategy options for decreasing expenses fall into two broad categories (Figure 22–5). One is relying on scale economies from an increased volume of production to drive unit costs down and gross margins up, the best-known examples being electronic devices such as fax or voice-mail machines whose prices fell by half in a few years. Scale economies may occur in marketing, as well as in R&D, engineering, production, and purchasing.

The other strategy option to decrease expenses is simply finding other ways to reduce costs, such as cutting the number of managers, increasing the effectiveness of the salesforce through more training, or reducing the product rejects through improved quality. Procter & Gamble concluded the world didn't really need 31 varieties of Head & Shoulders shampoo. Cutting the number of packages, sizes, and formulas in hair care alone, P&G has slashed the varieties almost in half, reducing expenses and increasing profits in the bargain.[25]

Market-Product Synergies

Using the market-product grid framework introduced in Chapter 9, we can see two kinds of synergy that are critical in developing corporate and marketing strategies: (1) marketing synergy and (2) R&D–manufacturing synergy. While the following example involves external synergies through mergers and acquisitions, the concepts apply equally well to internal synergies sought in adding new products or seeking new markets.

A critical step in the external analysis is to assess how these merger and acquisition strategies provide the organization with synergy, the increased customer value achieved through performing organizational functions more efficiently. The increased customer value can take many forms: more products, improved quality on existing products, lower prices, improved distribution, and so on. But the ultimate criterion is that customers should be better off as a result of the increased synergy. The firm, in turn, should be better off by gaining more satisfied customers.

A market-product grid helps identify important trade-offs in the strategic marketing process. As noted in the Marketing NewsNet, assume you are vice president of marketing for Great States Corporation's line of nonpowered lawn mowers and powered walking mowers sold to the consumer market. You are looking for new product and new market opportunities to increase your revenues and profits.

You conduct a market segmentation study and develop a market-product grid to analyze future opportunities. You identify three major segments in the consumer market based on geography: (1) city, (2) suburban, and (3) rural households. These market segments relate to the size of lawn a consumer must mow. The product clusters are: (1) nonpowered, (2) powered walking, and (3) powered riding mowers. Five alternative marketing strategies are shown in the market-product grids in Figure 22–6.[26] As

FIGURE 22–6
Market-product grid of alternative strategies for a lawnmower manufacturer

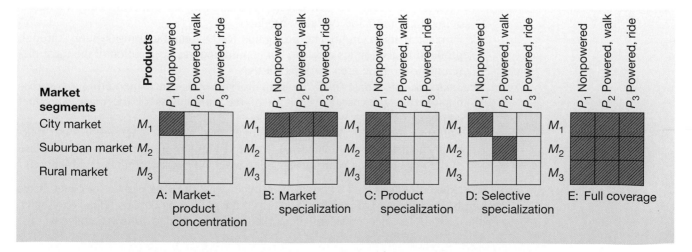

MARKETING NEWSNET

The Strategy Issue for the New Millennium—Finding Synergies

CUSTOMER VALUE

America Online (AOL) acquires Time Warner "to create entertainment synergies." General Mills (Big G) acquires Pillsbury "to get synergy." General Electric (GE) tries to acquire Honeywell (and fails because of antitrust concerns from the European Union) "to realize synergies." With the current emphasis of giant mergers and acquisitions, partners in these ventures look for synergies that for some are realized and for others have often proven elusive or impossible to achieve.

For example, AOL Time Warner believed that it could attain marketing synergies by cross-selling its AOL, Time Warner Cable, CNN, Time, Inc., services, such as promoting a Warner Bros. movie on CNN or placing an AOL ad in *Time* magazine. Big G expects to generate distribution efficiencies by adding refrigerated and frozen products made by Pillsbury to its own lines of refrigerated products like Yoplait and Go-Gurt yogurts. GE sought to integrate Honeywell's avionics business with its jet engine business, creating the potential of offering airplane manufacturers like Boeing a bundled package at a lower price because of sales efficiencies.

To try your hand in this multibillion dollar synergy game, assume you are vice president of marketing for Great States Corp., which markets a line of nonpowered, powered walking, and riding lawn mowers. A market-product grid for your business is shown in Figure 22–7. You distribute your

nonpowered mowers in all three market segments shown and powered and walking mowers only in suburban markets. However, you don't offer powered riding mowers for any of the three markets.

Here are your strategy dilemmas:

1. Where are the marketing synergies (efficiencies)?
2. Where are the R&D–manufacturing synergies (efficiencies)?
3. What would a market-product grid look like for an ideal company that Great States could merge with in order to achieve both marketing and R&D–manufacturing synergies (efficiencies)?

For answers to these questions, read the text and study Figures 22–6 and 22–7.

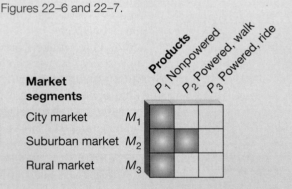

mentioned in Chapter 9, the important marketing synergies, or efficiencies, run horizontally across the rows in Figure 22–6. Conversely, the important R&D–manufacturing synergies, or efficiencies, run vertically down the columns. Let's look at the synergy effects for the five combinations in Figure 22–6.

A. *Market-product concentration.* The firm benefits from focus on a single product line and market segment, but it loses opportunities for significant synergies in both marketing and R&D–manufacturing.

B. *Market specialization.* The firm gains marketing synergy through providing a complete product line, but R&D–manufacturing have the difficulty of developing and producing two new products.

C. *Product specialization.* The firm gains R&D–manufacturing synergy through production economies of scale, but gaining market distribution in the three different geographic areas will be costly.

D. *Selective specialization.* The firm doesn't get either marketing or R&D–manufacturing synergies because of the uniqueness of the market-product combinations.

E. *Full coverage.* The firm has the maximum potential synergies in both marketing and R&D–manufacturing. The question: Is it spread too thin because of the resource requirements needed to reach all market-product combinations?

The Marketing NewsNet posed the question of what the ideal partner for Great States would be if it merged with another firm, given the market-product combinations shown in the box. If, as vice president of marketing, you want to follow a full-coverage

FIGURE 22–7

An ideal merger for Great States to obtain full market-product coverage

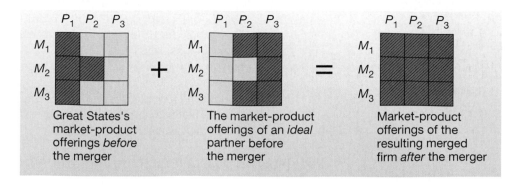

Great States's market-product offerings *before* the merger

The market-product offerings of an *ideal* partner before the merger

Market-product offerings of the resulting merged firm *after* the merger

strategy, then the ideal merger partner is shown in Figure 22–7. This would give the maximum potential synergies—if you are not spreading your merged companies too thin. Marketing gains by having a complete product line in all regions, and R&D–manufacturing gains by having access to new markets that can provide production economies of scale through producing larger volumes of its existing products.

Concept Check

1. Describe Porter's four generic business strategies.

2. What are four alternative ways to increase a firm's profits when considering profit enhancement options strategies?

3. Where do (*a*) marketing synergies and (*b*) R&D–manufacturing synergies appear in a market-product grid framework?

Some Planning and Strategy Lessons

Applying these frameworks is not automatic but requires a great deal of managerial judgment. Commonsense requirements of an effective marketing plan are discussed next, followed by problems that can arise.

Guidelines for an Effective Marketing Plan   President Dwight D. Eisenhower, when he commanded Allied armies in World War II, made his classic observation, "Plans are nothing; planning is everything." It is the process of careful planning that focuses an organization's efforts and leads to success. The plans themselves, which change with events, are often secondary. Effective planning and plans are inevitably characterized by identifiable objectives, specific strategies or courses of action, and the means to execute them. Here are some guidelines in developing effective marketing plans:

Marketing 101 final exam: What is the common feature of these brands that explains General Mills focus on one-handedness? For the answer and its significance, see the text and Marketing NewsNet.

- *Set measurable, achievable goals.* Ideally, goals should be quantified and measurable in terms of what is to be accomplished and by when. So "Increase market share from 18 percent to 22 percent by December 31, 2008" is preferable to "Maximize market share given our available resources." Also, to motivate people the goals must be achievable.
- *Use a base of facts and valid assumptions.* The more a marketing plan is based on facts and valid assumptions, rather than guesses, the less uncertainty and risk are associated with executing it. Good marketing research helps.

- *Utilize simple, but clear and specific, plans.* Effective execution of plans requires that people at all levels in the firm understand what, when, and how they are to accomplish their tasks.
- *Have complete and feasible plans.* Marketing plans must incorporate all the key marketing mix factors and be supported by adequate resources.
- *Make plans controllable and flexible.* Marketing plans must enable results to be compared with planned targets, which allows replanning—the flexibility to update the original plans.

Problems in Marketing Planning and Strategy   From postmortems on company plans that did work and on those that did not work, a picture emerges of where problems occur in the planning phase of a firm's strategic marketing process. The following list explores these problems:

1. Plans may be based on very poor assumptions about environmental factors, especially changing economic conditions and competitors' actions. A Western Union plan failed because it didn't reflect the impact of deregulation and competitors' actions on business.
2. Planners and their plans may have lost sight of their customers' needs. The "better ingredients, better pizza" slogan makes the hair stand up on the back of the necks of Pizza Hut executives. The reason is that this slogan of Papa John's International pizza chain reflects the firm's obsessive attention to detail, which is stealing market share from much-bigger Pizza Hut. Sample detail: If the cheese on the pizza shows a single air bubble or the crust is not golden brown, the offending pizza is not served to the customer.
3. Too much time and effort may be spent on data collection and writing the plans. Westinghouse has cut its planning instructions for operating units "that looked like an auto repair manual" to five or six pages.
4. Line operating managers often feel no sense of ownership in implementing the plans. Andy Grove, when he was CEO of Intel, observed, "We had the very ridiculous system . . . of delegating strategic planning to strategic planners. The strategies these [planners] prepared had no bearing on anything we actually did."[27] The solution is to assign more planning activities to line operating managers, the people who actually carry them out.

Big G plus Pillsbury: Finding Synergies, Segments, and Partners

Combining General Mills and Pillsbury operations resulted in a firm with more than $10 billion in annual sales. Steve Sanger, CEO of the merged firm, gets excited when he talks about carrying his consumer convenience and "one-handedness" synergies into the Pillsbury product line. So on the drawing boards may be a Pillsbury biscuit or cookie dough "wrapped around something," a new product you might be able to buy soon.[28]

As shown in the Marketing NewsNet, General Mills—or "Big G," from its cereal logo—has new products and brands targeted at many segments, some large and others only niche segments. With Big G's Go-Bags, Yoplait Nouriche, and Milk 'n Cereal Bars, commuters on the way to work can try "dashboard dining"—eating breakfast with only one hand and without a bowl or spoon. Sometimes the new introductions involve a leap in technology, but more often they involve incremental innovations that are the lifeblood of successful companies in the food industry.[29] Examples are taking calories out of Trix cereal or introducing Betty Crocker Complete Meals with the meat in the box and with five servings—five because dad wants more than one serving in a family with two children and six servings makes it too pricey.

General Mills is increasing its presence in global and domestic markets through joint ventures and partnering. Its Cereal Partners Worldwide (CPW), a joint venture with Nestlé, now holds 22 percent market share across 75 countries, enabling General Mills food products to reach new segments of international consumers. To

CUSTOMER VALUE

MARKETING NEWSNET

Keeping Planning Simple at Big G: "One-Handed" Convenience plus Cover All the Bases

What do you do if you are the chief executive officer of a firm in the low-growth food industry? This is the problem facing Steve Sanger, CEO of General Mills. His remarkable answers: one-handedness and covering all the bases, both built on a focus on today's consumers and keeping marketing planning simple and clear.

One-Handedness

When Steve Sanger gets proposals for a new food product or a way to reposition an old one, he asks one question, "Can we make it 'one-handed'?" This doesn't mean *build* it one-handed but being able to *eat* it one-handed! This lets

consumers have a free hand while eating and typing or driving. A Go-Bag pouch of Cinnamon Toast Crunch, a Yoplait Nouriche Light yogurt smoothie, and Big G Milk 'n Cereal Bars are examples of Sanger's one-handed strategy.

Cover All the Bases

Big G responds to changing consumer tastes and covers all bases using market and product strategies like those with the brands shown below. This also involves joint ventures with other firms with special expertise, like Nestlé to reach Polish consumers or Du Pont to develop 8th Continent Soymilk.

PRODUCTS

Markets	Current	New
	Market Penetration	**Product Development**
Current	Finding ways to make current products appeal to current customers: Go-Bags, six-to-a-carton pouches of breakfast cereal for snacking	Reaching current customers with a new product: Yoplait Nouriche, a healthy yogurt smoothie with 20 vitamins and minerals
	Market Development	**Diversification**
New	Reaching new customers with a current product: Cini Minis for Polish consumers—known as Cinnamon Toast Crunch in the U.S.	Reaching new customers with a new product: 8th Continent Soymilk, for consumers who can't drink milk or are health conscious

exploit innovative new technology, General Mills has a soy joint venture with Du Pont to develop and introduce 8th Continent™ Soymilk in both regular and light versions, giving nutritious new options for breakfast. Shorter-term marketing partnerships also exist, like that in 2004 with the Dreamworks *Shrek 2* movie. Big G had 20 products tied to *Shrek 2,* from a Shrek cereal with marshmallow pieces shaped like the movie characters to Pillsbury Toaster Strudel with Ogre icing.[30]

Balancing Value and Values in Strategic Marketing Plans   Two important trends are likely to influence the strategic marketing process in the future. The first, *value-based planning,* combines marketing planning ideas and financial planning techniques to assess how much a division or strategic business unit (SBU) contributes to the price of a company's stock (or shareholder wealth). Value is created when the financial return of a strategic activity exceeds the cost of the resources allocated to the activity.

The second trend is the increasing interest in *value-driven strategies,* which incorporate concerns for ethics, integrity, employee health and safety, and environmental safeguards with more common corporate values such as growth, profitability, customer service, and quality. Some experts have observed that although many corporations cite broad corporate values in advertisements, press releases, and company newsletters, they have not yet changed their strategic plans to reflect the stated values.[31] U.S. firms, like firms and governments around the world, are increasingly called on to be good global citizens and to support sustainable development.[32]

THE IMPLEMENTATION PHASE OF THE STRATEGIC MARKETING PROCESS

The Monday morning diagnosis of a losing football coach often runs something like "We had an excellent game plan; we just didn't execute it."

Is Planning or Implementation the Problem?

The planning-versus-execution issue applies to the strategic marketing process as well: A difficulty when a marketing plan fails is determining whether the failure is due to a poor plan or poor implementation.[33]

Effective managers tracking progress on a struggling plan first try to identify whether the problems involve: (1) the plan and strategy, (2) its implementation, or (3) both, and then they try to correct the problems. But as discussed earlier in the chapter, research on what really works shows that successful firms have excellence on both the planning and strategy side and the implementation and execution side. For example, General Electric's continuing leadership in lighting combines strong innovative products (planning and strategy) with excellent advertising and distribution (implementation and execution).

General Electric's army of innovative lights have benefited from having both good planning and implementation of their marketing programs—and by making it into one of Jack Welch's "three circles."

General Electric Company
www.ge.com

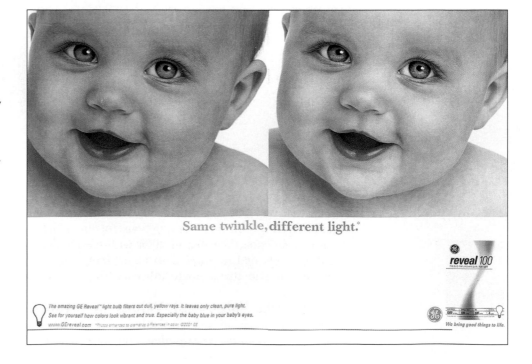

Same twinkle, different light.

The amazing GE Reveal™ light bulb filters out dull, yellow rays. It leaves only clean, pure light.
See for yourself how colors look vibrant and true. Especially the baby blue in your baby's eyes.
www.GEreveal.com

reveal 100

We bring good things to life.

MARKETING NEWSNET

GE's Implementation Strategies—How Neutron Jack Became One of the Most Acclaimed CEOs of the Twentieth Century

CUSTOMER VALUE

Time magazine calls him "one of the most acclaimed CEOs (chief executive officers) of the twentieth century." Yet employees at his company in the 1980s called him "Neutron Jack" because they said his corporate downsizings were alleged to leave the buildings standing with no people in them—like a neutron bomb would. However, his difficult strategy decisions and in-your-face leadership style probably assured the jobs of thousands of his firm's employees today.

He is Jack Welch, General Electric's CEO for two decades, up to mid-2001. Welch's implementation focus emerges in his five-box flowchart below:

- *Three-circle strategy.* In the early 1980s, Welch looked at the 350 businesses in 43 strategic business units he inherited. By focusing GE's businesses in three key areas as shown in the illustration, he set the strategic direction for GE's future.
- *#1, #2.* Welch concluded that GE "winners" would be either #1 or #2 in their industry.
- *Fix, close, or sell.* This became GE's mantra. Coupled with "#1, #2," more than 100 businesses were closed or sold. An example is GE's housewares (small appliance) division that was sold to Black & Decker. The rest were fixed.
- *Delayering.* Welch felt GE was drowning in layers, managers, and red tape. By eliminating a lot of these and "rituals, endless studies, and briefings," he gave employees more personal empowerment and accountability.
- *Downsizing.* Painful as it was to him, Welch thought the only way to create a competitive organization was ultimately to lay off one-third of GE's employees, 150,000 workers.

How important have Jack Welch's ideas become? Today they are studied, and often adapted, by hundreds of chief executive officers around the world.

Core businesses
- Lighting
- Major Appliances
- Motor

High-tech businesses
- Medical Systems
- Industrial Electronics
- Aerospace

Service businesses
- Credit Corporation
- Information Services
- Nuclear Services

Three-circle strategy → #1, #2 → Fix, close, or sell → Delayering → Downsizing

Increasing Emphasis on Marketing Implementation

In the new millennium, the implementation phase of the strategic marketing process has emerged as a key factor to success by moving many planning activities away from the duties of planners to those of line managers.

As described in the Marketing NewsNet, General Electric's Jack Welch became a legend in making GE more efficient and far better at implementation. When Welch became CEO in 1981 he faced an organization mired in red tape, turf battles, and slow decision making. Further, Welch saw GE bogged down with 25,000 managers and close to a dozen layers between him and the factory floor. In his "delayering," he sought to cut GE's levels in half and to speed up decision making and implementation by building an atmosphere of trust and autonomy among his managers and employees. Although there are debates on some Welch strategies, businesses around the world are using his focus on implementation as a benchmark. One measure of GE's global impact: In 2000, *Fortune* magazine named General Electric "the world's most admired company."[34] Another measure is that among the three candidates to replace Welch as CEO of General Electric, one is now CEO of GE, another heads 3M, and the third heads Home Depot.

For the unusual way General Motors avoided the NIH syndrome to help develop the Saturn, see the text.

Improving Implementation of Marketing Programs

No magic formula exists to guarantee effective implementation of marketing plans. In fact, the answer seems to be equal parts of good management skills and practices, from which have come some guidelines for improving program implementation.

Communicate Goals and the Means of Achieving Them   Those called on to implement plans need to understand both the goals sought and how they are to be accomplished. Everyone in Papa John's—from founder John Schnatter to telephone order takers and make-line people—is clear on what the firm's goal is: to deliver better pizzas using better ingredients. The firm's orientation packet for employees lists its six core values that executives are expected to memorize. Sample: Core value 4 is "PAPA," or "People Are Priority No. 1, Always."[35]

Have a Responsible Program Champion Willing to Act   Successful programs almost always have a **product or program champion** who is able and willing to cut red tape and move the program forward. Such a person often has the uncanny ability to move back and forth between big-picture strategy questions and specific details when the situation calls for it. Program champions are notoriously brash in overcoming organizational hurdles. The U.S. Navy's Admiral Grace Murray Hopper not only gave the world an early computer language but also the word *bug,* meaning any glitch in a computer or computer program. This program champion's famous advice for moving decisions to actions by cutting through an organization's red tape: "Better to ask forgiveness than permission."

Reward Successful Program Implementation   When an individual or a team is rewarded for achieving the organization's goal, they have maximum incentive to see a program implemented successfully because they have personal ownership and a stake in that success.

Take Action and Avoid Paralysis by Analysis   Management experts warn against "paralysis by analysis," the tendency to excessively analyze a problem instead of taking action. To overcome this pitfall, they call for a "bias for action" and recommend a "do it, fix it, try it" approach.[36] Conclusion: Perfectionists finish last, so getting 90 percent perfection and letting the marketplace help in the fine-tuning makes good sense in implementation.

Lockheed Martin's Skunk Works got its name from the comic strip *L'il Abner* and its legendary reputation from achieving superhuman technical feats with a low budget and ridiculously short deadlines by stressing teamwork. Under the leadership of Kelly Johnson, in 35 years the Skunk Works turned out a series of world-class aircraft from the world's fastest (the SR-71 Blackbird) to the nation's most untrackable aircraft (the F-117 Stealth fighter). Two of Kelly Johnson's basic tenets: (1) make decisions promptly and (2) avoid paralysis by analysis. In fact, one U.S. Air Force audit showed that Johnson's Skunk Works could carry out a program on schedule with 126 people, whereas a competitor in a comparable program was behind schedule with 3,750 people.[37]

Foster Open Communication to Surface Problems   Success often lies in fostering a work environment that is open enough so employees are willing to speak out when they see problems without fear of recrimination. The focus is placed on trying to solve the problem as a group rather than finding someone to blame. Solutions are solicited from anyone who has a creative idea to suggest—from the janitor to the president—without regard to status or rank in the organization.

Two more Kelly Johnson axioms from Lockheed Martin's Skunk Works apply here: (1) When trouble develops, surface the problem immediately, and (2) get help; don't keep the problem to yourself. This latter point is important even if it means getting ideas from competitors.

In Saturn, General Motors' created a new company where participatory management and improved communications led to a successful product. For example, to encourage discussion of possible cost reductions, each employee receives 100 to 750 hours of training, including balance sheet analysis. To avoid the "NIH syndrome"—the reluctance to accept ideas "not invented here" or not originated inside one's own firm—Saturn engineers bought 70 import cars to study for product design ideas and selected options that would most appeal to their target market.

Schedule Precise Tasks, Responsibilities, and Deadlines   Successful implementation requires that people know the tasks for which they are responsible and the deadline for completing them. To implement the thousands of tasks on a new aircraft design, Lockheed Martin typically holds weekly program meetings. The outcome of each of these meetings is an **action item list**, an aid to implementing a marketing plan consisting of three columns: (1) the task, (2) the person responsible for completing that task, and (3) the date to finish the task. Within hours of completing a program meeting, the action item list is circulated to those attending. This then serves as the starting agenda for the next meeting. Meeting minutes are viewed as secondary and backward looking. Action item lists are forward looking, clarify the targets, and put strong pressure on people to achieve their designated tasks by the deadline.

Related to the action item lists are formal *program schedules,* which show the relationships through time of the various program tasks. Scheduling an action program involves: (1) identifying the main tasks, (2) determining the time required to complete each, (3) arranging the activities to meet the deadline, and (4) assigning responsibilities to complete each task.

Suppose, for example, that you and two friends are asked to do a term project on the problem, "How can the college increase attendance at its performing arts concerts?" And suppose further that the instructor limits the project in the following ways:

1. The project must involve a mail survey of the attitudes of a sample of students.
2. The term paper with the survey results must be submitted by the end of the 11-week quarter.

To begin the assignment, you need to identify all the project tasks and then estimate the time you can reasonably allocate to each one. To complete it in 11 weeks, your team must work on different parts at the same time, and some activities must be independent enough to overlap. This requires specialization and cooperation. Suppose that of the three of you (A, B, and C), only student C can type. Then you (student A) might assume the task of constructing the questionnaire and selecting samples, and

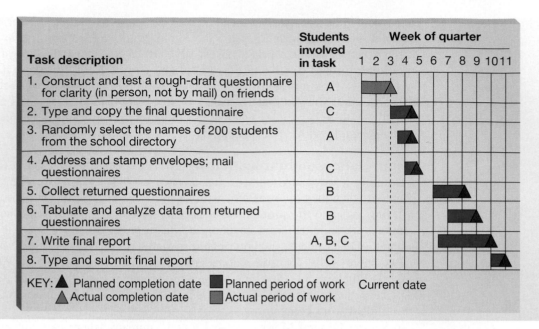

Task description	Students involved in task	Week of quarter
		1 2 3 4 5 6 7 8 9 10 11
1. Construct and test a rough-draft questionnaire for clarity (in person, not by mail) on friends	A	
2. Type and copy the final questionnaire	C	
3. Randomly select the names of 200 students from the school directory	A	
4. Address and stamp envelopes; mail questionnaires	C	
5. Collect returned questionnaires	B	
6. Tabulate and analyze data from returned questionnaires	B	
7. Write final report	A, B, C	
8. Type and submit final report	C	

KEY: ▲ Planned completion date   ■ Planned period of work   Current date
△ Actual completion date   ▢ Actual period of work

FIGURE 22–8

Gantt chart for scheduling the term project

student B might tabulate the data. You must also figure out which activities can be done concurrently to save time.

Scheduling production and marketing activities—from a term project to a new product rollout to a space shuttle launch—can be done efficiently with a *Gantt chart,* which is a graphical representation of a program schedule. Figure 22–8 shows one variation of a Gantt chart used to schedule the class project, demonstrating how the concurrent work on several tasks enables the students to finish the project on time. Developed by Henry L. Gantt, this method is the basis for the scheduling techniques used today, including elaborate computerized methods. The key to all scheduling techniques is to distinguish tasks that *must* be done sequentially from those that *can* be done concurrently. As in the case of the term project, scheduling tasks concurrently often reduces the total time required for a project. Software programs, such as Microsoft Project, simplify the task of developing a schedule or Gantt chart.

<table>
<tr><td>Concept Check</td><td>

1. Why is it important to include line operating managers in the planning process?

2. What is the meaning and importance of a program champion?

3. Explain the difference between sequential and concurrent tasks in a Gantt chart.
</td></tr>
</table>

Organizing for Marketing

A marketing organization is needed to implement the firm's marketing plans. Basic issues in today's marketing organizations include understanding (1) how line versus staff positions and divisional groupings interrelate to form a cohesive marketing organization and (2) the role of the marketing or product manager.

Line versus Staff and Divisional Groupings Although simplified, Figure 22–9 shows the organization of a typical business unit in a consumer packaged goods firm like Procter & Gamble, Kraft, or General Mills. This business unit consists of the Dinner Products, Baked Goods, and Desserts groups. It highlights the distinction between line and staff positions in marketing. Managers in **line positions**, such

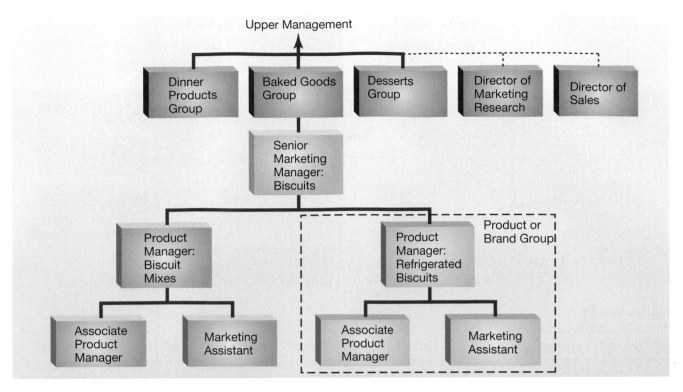

FIGURE 22–9

Organization of a business unit in a typical consumer packaged goods firm, showing two product or brand groups

as the senior marketing manager for Biscuits, have the authority and responsibility to issue orders to the people who report to them, such as the two product managers shown in Figure 22–9. In this organizational chart, line positions are connected with solid lines. People in **staff positions** (shown by dotted lines) have the authority and responsibility to advise people in line positions but cannot issue direct orders to them.

Most marketing organizations use divisional groupings—such as product line, functional, geographical, and market-based—to implement plans and achieve their organizational objectives. Three of these appear in some form in the organizational chart in Figure 22–9. The top of the chart shows organization by **product line groupings** in which a unit is responsible for specific product offerings, such as Dinner Products or Baked Goods.

At higher levels than shown in Figure 22–9, grocery products firms are organized by **functional groupings**—such as manufacturing, marketing, and finance—that represent the different departments or business activities within a firm.

Most grocery products firms use **geographical groupings** in which sales territories are subdivided according to geographical location. Each director of sales has several regional sales managers reporting to him or her, such as western, southern, and so on. These, in turn, have district managers reporting to them, with the field sales representatives at the lowest level.

A fourth method of organizing a company is to use **market-based groupings**, which utilize specific customer segments, such as the banking, health care, or manufacturing segments. When this method of organizing is combined with product groupings, the result is a *matrix organization.*

A relatively new position in consumer products firms is the *category manager* (senior marketing manager in Figure 22–9). Category managers have profit-and-loss responsibility for an entire product line—all biscuit brands, for example. They attempt to reduce the possibility of one brand's actions hurting another brand in the same category. Procter & Gamble uses category managers to organize by "global business units" such as baby care and beauty care. Cutting across country boundaries, these global business units implement standardized worldwide pricing, marketing, and distribution.[38]

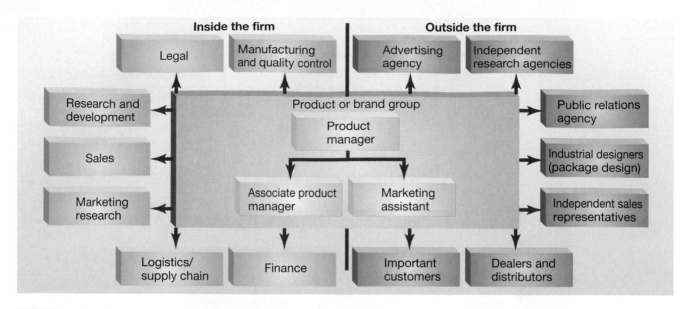

FIGURE 22–10

Units with which the product manager and product group work

Role of the Product Manager The key person in the product or brand group shown in Figure 22–10 is the manager who heads it. As mentioned in Chapter 10, this person is often called the *product manager* or *brand manager*. This person and the assistants in the product group are the basic building blocks in the marketing department of most consumer and business product firms. The function of a product manager is to plan, implement, and control the annual and long-range plans for the products for which he or she is responsible.

There are both benefits and dangers to the product manager system. On the positive side, product managers become strong advocates for the assigned products, cut red tape to work with people in various functions both inside and outside the organization (Figure 22–10), and assume profit-and-loss responsibility for the performance of the product line. On the negative side, even though product managers have major responsibilities, they have relatively little direct authority, so most groups and functions shown in Figure 22–10 must be coordinated to meet the product's goals.[39] To coordinate the many units, product managers must use persuasion rather than orders.

THE CONTROL PHASE OF THE STRATEGIC MARKETING PROCESS

The essence of control, the final phase of the strategic marketing process, is to compare results with planned goals for the marketing program in order to take necessary corrective actions.

The Marketing Control Process

Ideally, quantified goals from the marketing plans developed in the planning phase have been accomplished by the marketing actions taken in the implementation phase (Figure 22–11) and measured as results in the control phase. A marketing manager then uses *management by exception,* which means identifying results that deviate from plans to diagnose their causes and take new actions. Often results fall short of plans, and a corrective action is needed. For example, after 50 years of profits Caterpillar accumulated losses of $1 billion. To correct the problem, Caterpillar focused its marketing efforts on core products and reduced its manufacturing costs. At other times the comparison shows that performance is far better than anticipated, in which case the marketing manager tries to identify the reason and move quickly to exploit the unexpected opportunity.

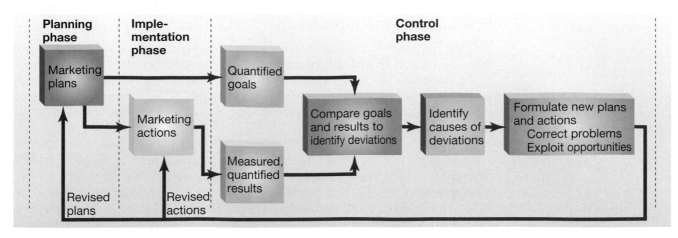

FIGURE 22-11
The control phase of the strategic marketing process

Measuring Results   Without some quantitative goal, no benchmark exists with which to compare actual results. Manufacturers of both consumer and business products are increasingly trying to develop marketing programs that have not only specific action programs but also specific procedures for monitoring key measures of performance. Today, marketing executives measure not only financial targets such as sales revenues and profits but also marketing ones, such as customer satisfaction, time-to-market, and salesforce motivation.

Taking Marketing Actions   When results deviate significantly from plans, some kind of action is essential. Deviations can be the result of the process used to specify goals or can be due to changes in the marketplace. Beaten badly for years in the U.S. toothpaste market by P&G's Crest, in the late 1990s Colgate went on the offensive. It used new technology and aggressive marketing actions to introduce its Total toothpaste, the first "oral pharmaceutical" ever approved by the U.S. Food and Drug Administration. Not only does Total clean teeth, but its germ-fighting feature helps heal gingivitis, a bleeding-gum disease. This has helped Colgate achieve the highest market share in the U.S. toothpaste market.[40]

Sales Analysis

For controlling marketing programs, **sales analysis**—using the firm's sales records to compare actual results with sales goals and identify areas of strength and weakness—is critical. All the variables that might be used in market segmentation may be used in **sales component analysis**, also called *microsales analysis,* which traces sales revenues to their sources, such as specific products, sales territories, or customers. Common breakdowns include the following:

- Customer characteristics: demographics, NAICS, size, reason for purchase, and type of reseller (retailer or wholesaler).
- Product characteristics: model, package size, and color.
- Geographical region: sales territory, city, state, and region.
- Order size.
- Price or discount class.
- Commission to the sales representative.

Today's computers can easily produce these breakdowns, provided the input data contain these classifications. Therefore, it is critical that marketing managers specify the breakdowns they require from the accounting and information systems departments, so they get the needed information for decisions without information overload.

Profitability Analysis and ROI Marketing

To their surprise, marketing managers often discover the 80/20 rule the hard way—on the job. **Profitability analysis** is a tool for controlling marketing programs using the profit attributable to the firm's products, customer groups, sales territories, channels of distribution, and promotions. This leads to decisions to expand, maintain, reduce, or eliminate specific products, customer groups, channels, or promotions.

For example, following the 80/20 rule, a marketing manager will try to find the common characteristics among the 20 percent of the customers (or products, brands, sales districts, salespeople, or kinds of orders) that generate 80 percent (or the bulk) of revenues and profits to find more like them to exploit competitive advantages. Conversely, the 80 percent of customers, products, brands, and so on that generate few revenues and profits may need to be reduced or even dropped entirely unless a way is found to make them more profitable.

Obtaining the detailed data to do this kind of profitability analysis and knowing how to analyze these data are difficult. To bridge these gaps, in the late 1980s researchers started to develop **ROI marketing**, the application of modern measurement technologies and contemporary organizational design to understand, quantify, and optimize marketing spending.[41] ROI, or return on investment, marketing uses computer models on the data collected to determine, for example, the profitability of a coupon directed at a specific market segment. The analysis takes into account factors like the coupon's cost to reach the segment, the revenue generated from the segment the two weeks following the coupon's distribution, the amount of sales taken from competitors and from cannibalizing the company's other products, and so on. Widespread acceptance of ROI marketing will depend on the impact on the demonstrated profitability of its use in key marketing decisions.[42]

Concept Check

1. What is the difference between a line and a staff position in a marketing organization?

2. What are four groupings used within a typical marketing organization?

3. What two components of the strategic marketing process are compared to control a marketing program?

CHAPTER IN REVIEW

1 *Explain how marketing managers allocate their limited resources.*
Marketing managers use the strategic marketing process and marketing information, such as marketing plans, sales reports, and action memos, to effectively allocate their scarce resources to exploit the competitive advantages of their products. Marketers may use either sales response functions or market share (share point) analysis to help them assess what the market's response will be to additional marketing efforts.

2 *Describe three marketing planning frameworks: Porter's generic strategies, profit enhancement options, and market-product synergies.*
Three useful frameworks to improve marketing planning are: (a) Porter's generic business strategies; (b) profit enhancement options; and (c) market-product synergies. Porter identifies four generic business strategies that firms can adopt: a cost

leadership strategy, which focuses on reducing expenses to lower product prices while targeting a broad array of market segments; a differentiation strategy, which requires products to have significant points of difference to charge a premium price while targeting a broad array of market segments; a cost focus strategy, which involves controlling costs to lower prices of products targeted at a narrow range of market segments; and a differentiation focus strategy, which requires products to have significant points of difference to reach one or only a few market segments.

A second marketing planning framework is to use profit enhancement options to increase sales revenues, decrease costs, or both. To increase revenues, marketers can use one or a combination of four strategies to focus on present or new products or markets: market penetration (selling more of a product to existing markets); market development (selling an existing product to new markets); product development (selling a new product to existing markets); and diversification (selling new products to new markets). To reduce expenses, marketers can (*a*) generate additional economies of scale in marketing and production costs and (*b*) reduce personnel and other nonmarketing costs, product rejects through improved quality, and so forth.

The third framework is to use a market-product grid that results in two kinds of synergies: marketing synergies (efficiencies), which run horizontally across the row of the various products offered by the firm to a single market segment; and R&D–manufacturing synergies (efficiencies), which run vertically down a column of the various market segments targeted for a given product or product class. The interactions or synergy effects of these marketing and production efficiencies results in five alternative combinations: market-product concentration, market specialization, product specialization, selective specialization, and full coverage.

3 *Explain what makes an effective marketing plan and some problems that often exist with it.*

An effective marketing plan has: measurable, achievable goals; uses facts and valid assumptions; is simple, clear, and specific; is complete and feasible; and is controllable and flexible. Some problems that arise with marketing plans are that marketers: (*a*) base them on poor assumptions about the marketing environment; (*b*) lose sight of their customers' needs; (*c*) spend too much time and effort on data collection for and writing the actual plan; and (*d*) do not seek ownership of the plan by operating managers and others charged with its implementation.

4 *Schedule a series of tasks to meet a deadline using a Gantt chart.*

Successful implementation of a marketing plan requires that people know the tasks, responsibilities, and deadlines needed to complete it. Once the information for these three areas is generated, a program schedule can be developed. A Gantt chart is a graphical representation of this schedule. The key to this scheduling technique is to identify those tasks that must be done sequentially from those that can be done concurrently.

5 *Describe the alternatives for organizing a marketing department and the role of a product manager.*

A marketing department must be organized to effectively implement a marketing plan. First, marketing organizations must distinguish between line positions, those individuals in the marketing organization who have the authority and responsibility to issue orders to people that report to them to carry out a particular aspect of the marketing plan, and staff positions, those individuals who have the authority and responsibility to advise but not directly order people in line positions to do something.

Second, marketing organizations use one of four divisional groupings to implement marketing plans: product line groupings, responsible for specific product offerings; functional groupings that represent the different departments and business activities (marketing, manufacturing, finance, etc.) within a firm; geographical groupings, in which sales territories are subdivided according to geographical location; and market-based groupings, which utilize specific customer segments.

The role of the product manager is to interact with numerous people and groups both inside and outside the firm to coordinate the planning, implementation, and control of the marketing plan and its budget on an annual and long-term basis for the products responsible.

6 *Explain how sales and profitability analyses and ROI marketing are used to evaluate and control marketing programs.*

The control phase of the strategic marketing process involves measuring the results of the actions from the implementation phase and comparing them with goals set in the planning phase. Sales analysis uses the firm's sales records to compare actual sales with sales objectives. Profitability analysis uses the profit attributable to the firm's products, customer groups, sales territories, distribution channels, and promotions. A specific kind of profitability analysis is ROI marketing, which is the application of modern measurement technologies and contemporary organizational design to understand, quantify, and optimize marketing spending.

FOCUSING ON KEY TERMS

action item list p. 599
cost focus strategy p. 589
cost leadership strategy p. 589
differentiation focus strategy p. 590
differentiation strategy p. 589
functional groupings p. 601
generic business strategy p. 588
geographical groupings p. 601
line positions p. 600
market-based groupings p. 601

product line groupings p. 601
product or program champion p. 598
profitability analysis p. 604
ROI marketing p. 604
sales analysis p. 603
sales component analysis p. 603
sales response function p. 584
share points p. 585
staff positions p. 601

DISCUSSION AND APPLICATION QUESTIONS

1 Assume a firm faces an S-shaped sales response function. What happens to the ratio of incremental sales revenue to incremental marketing effort at the (*a*) bottom, (*b*) middle, and (*c*) top of this curve?

2 What happens to the ratio of incremental sales revenue to incremental marketing effort when the sales response function is an upward-sloping straight line?

3 In 2004, General Mills invested millions of dollars in expanding its cereal and yogurt businesses. To allocate this money between these two businesses, what information would General Mills like to have?

4 Suppose your Great States lawn mower company has the market-product concentration situation shown in Figure 22–6A. What are both the synergies and potential pitfalls of following expansion strategies of (*a*) market specialization and (*b*) product specialization?

5 Are value-driven strategies inconsistent with value-based planning? Give an example that supports your position.

6 The first Domino's Pizza restaurant was near a college campus. What implementation problems are (*a*) similar

and (*b*) different for restaurants near a college campus versus a military base?

7 A common theme among managers who succeed repeatedly in program implementation is fostering open communication. Why is this so important?

8 Parts of tasks 5 and 6 in Figure 22–8 are done both concurrently and sequentially. How can this be? How does it help the students meet the term paper deadline?

9 In the organizational chart for the consumer packaged goods firm in Figure 22–9, where do product line, functional, and geographical groupings occur?

10 Why are quantified goals in the planning phase of the strategic marketing process important for the control phase?

GOING ONLINE   Strategic Actions of Three CEOs

Because of General Electric's reputation for developing good managers, executive search firms often tap its talent to lead other organizations. Three GE executives were the leading candidates to replace Jack Welch, GE's CEO, when he retired in mid-2001.

Today, all three are now CEOs of major corporations: Jeffrey Immelt (General Electric), James McNerney

(3M), and Robert Nardelli (Home Depot). Go to the websites of these three companies (www.ge.com, www.3m.com, and www.homedepot.com). Look at the most recent quarterly press or news release or annual report to identify any strategic actions each CEO initiated to improve the company's performance, such as acquisitions, new products or services, new markets, and so forth.

BUILDING YOUR MARKETING PLAN

Do the following activities to complete your marketing plan:

1 Draw a simple organization chart for your organization.

2 Develop a Gantt chart to schedule the key activities to implement your marketing plan.

3 In terms of the control phases, list (*a*) the four or five critical factors (such as revenues, number of customers,

variable costs) and (*b*) how frequently (monthly, quarterly) you will monitor to determine if special actions are needed to exploit opportunities or correct deviations.

4 Read Appendix A, "Building an Effective Marketing Plan." Then write a 600-word executive summary for your marketing plan using the numbered headings shown in Appendix A.

VIDEO CASE 22 Yoplait® USA: Portrait of a Turnaround

The year is 1992 and Yoplait® USA is in trouble!

This is a far different situation than early years at Yoplait, USA, a subsidiary of General Mills, Inc. But the problems are serious and some difficult, critical decisions must be made.

RESEARCHING THE IDEA

The idea for Yoplait began a decade earlier when top management at General Mills asked Steven M. Rothschild to head a team to investigate yogurt as a new business opportunity for the company. Rothschild's team found that in the United States yogurt had annual sales of $350 million with an annual growth rate of about 18 percent. The team also discovered that about 95 percent of the yogurt consumed in the United States was mixed with fruit or flavoring, and about 5 percent was plain. Also, about 95 percent was consumed in 8-ounce cups. Finally, the team's analysis indicated that the U.S. annual per capita consumption of yogurt was low (5 cups per person) compared with consumption in European countries (27 cups per person a year in France).

Even though General Mills had never before produced and marketed a refrigerated product, Rothschild and the team believed that a yogurt product would be a good match for the company. This was because it was: (1) a high-turnover branded item that would allow a significant profit margin; (2) a product for which the firm's skills in positioning, advertising, packaging, and promotion would provide an advantage over competition; and (3) a business that would capitalize on trends resulting from long-term changes in consumer behavior. Based on the team's analysis, General Mills decided to enter the yogurt market!

LAUNCHING YOPLAIT IN THE U.S.

Estimating that it would take about three years to develop a new brand of yogurt on its own, General Mills saved time by buying the rights to market Yoplait yogurt in the United States from Sodima, a large French company. This decision gave General Mills access to Yoplait's technology and expertise related to producing and distributing a refrigerated product.

At that time Yoplait was the best-selling yogurt in France. Marketing research revealed what consumers perceived as Yoplait's key benefits: (1) 100 percent natural yogurt without artificial sweeteners or preservatives, (2) real fruit mixed throughout, and (3) outstanding taste with a creamy texture. In terms of U.S. competition, there was no national brand of yogurt at the time, but there was a two-tiered group of yogurt producers: (1) premium regional brands such as Dannon and Kraft, and (2) private-label brands produced by local dairies.

Rothschild and his team at Yoplait USA moved quickly to gain acceptance for Yoplait as a national brand among American consumers. In several brilliant marketing decisions, they first packaged Yoplait yogurt in a unique conical shape containing 6 ounces of yogurt—not the conventional 8 ounces—because marketing research showed consumers really didn't want the larger amount. Then, rather than stress Yoplait's taste, the team gained consumer awareness and trial by positioning it exotically as "The Yogurt of France" that used television ads featuring "typical Americans" eating Yoplait and extolling its virtues in French! American consumers were entranced by the ads—overlooking the minor detail the "typical Americans" were actor Loretta Swit (from *M*A*S*H*), who spoke French fluently, and Los Angeles Dodgers' manager Tommy Lasorda. Yoplait USA legend has it Lasorda ate 37 cups of Yoplait in the 37 television takes needed to arrive at his television commercial featuring his rather incomprehensible French.

But there was a temporary glitch. To achieve its good taste, Yoplait contains live cultures, so the product requires continuous refrigeration. But General Mills had never manufactured and distributed a refrigerated product. The live yogurt cultures plus improper refrigeration during shipment proved a bad combination. The result according to Rothschild: "We had little bombs exploding in grocery stores and supermarkets across the country." And these retailers were telling him, "We knew you guys didn't know what you were doing and now you've proven it!"

The refrigeration glitch was solved. Yoplait's quality and taste appealed to consumers. And Yoplait experienced extraordinary success.

COMPLACENCY VS. CONSTRUCTIVE RESTLESSNESS

As the brand grew, however, its managers became complacent and underestimated the competition from other brands such as Dannon. Although Yoplait was No. 2 nationally, its market share and profitability began to decline. In an attempt to manage the product life cycle, Yoplait tried a "Western-style" version of its product with fruit on the bottom and flavored syrup on top. It failed.

Fast forward several years to 1992 and Chap Colucci, Yoplait USA's newly named vice president of marketing and sales. His job: Turn things around at Yoplait USA… and quickly! Soon after Colucci joined the Yoplait USA team, he concluded that while the product had been successful during its introduction, the team was not pursuing strategies that would ensure continued growth.

"A little bit of constructive restlessness is good," says Colucci, "because you can become too satisfied with your own success, with the status quo. You take your foot off the gas and things begin to stall."

Colucci conducted a situation analysis in preparation for developing a new marketing strategy for Yoplait USA. His analysis turned up some serious concerns, including:

1 *High retail prices.* Yoplait's price for a six-ounce cup was actually higher than competitors' eight-ounce cups. For example, the prices on Yoplait's 4 Pack were about 20 percent higher per cup than Dannon's and Kraft's 6 Pack.

2 *Low gross margins.* Margins had declined, at least partly because of high production and overhead costs.

3 *Unbalanced promotion spending mix.* Most promotional expenditures were directed at retailers and wholesalers rather than consumers.

4 *Lack of continued effective advertising.* Yoplait had been living off the great "The Yogurt of France" series of print ads and TV commercials that launched the product without a similar creative follow-up campaign.

5 *Few coupons offered.* Yoplait had cut back on consumer coupons, while its competitors had heavy couponing.

6 *Few new products.* While Yoplait had developed a Lite product line extension, there were very few new products in development.

7 *Geographic marketing organization.* Yoplait was organized geographically with three regions—Eastern, Central, and Western. This organization had caused marketing managers to focus on geography, not basic marketing.

These observations became the basis for Colucci and his team to develop a strategic marketing program.

Colucci's brand management activities involved all elements of the marketing mix: improved pricing, more consumer promotion, new advertising, new product line extensions, and new ways and places in which Yoplait could be consumed. For example, Yoplait introduced a "grab-and-go" product for children, new flavors, a portable yogurt product for adults, and yogurt drinks.

YOPLAIT USA TODAY

Fast forward another dozen years to today. Yoplait USA has an incredible array of product line extensions. Besides Yoplait Original and Yoplait Trix® that have been around for years, recent product line extensions include:

- Go-GURT®, "portable yogurt" for kids
- Yoplait Light, a low-calorie yogurt
- Yoplait Whips®, a fluffy yogurt
- Yoplait Ultra™, a low carb yogurt
- Yoplait Nouriche®, a yogurt smoothie
- Yoplait Nouriche® Light, a low-calorie yogurt smoothie

Some brands in Yoplait's product line are shown in the photo on the opposite page.

Yoplait products are now available in outlets where meals are sold. Regular Yoplait yogurt is a menu choice in many school cafeterias. And Go-GURT, the yogurt-in-a-tube, is now available at McDonald's.

In 2004, sales of Yoplait's refrigerated products totaled $1.01 billion, which represents a 37 percent market share of U.S. yogurt sales, and Yoplait is No. 1 in the yogurt cup category.

Chap Colucci's "constructive restlessness" had helped lay the foundation for today's Yoplait successes.

Questions

1 (*a*) What stages of the product life cycle has yogurt gone through in the United States since General Mills first evaluated it as a business opportunity? (*b*) How might marketing activities have changed at Yoplait USA at different stages of the product life cycle?

2 Chap Colucci's analysis suggested that Yoplait brand managers may have relied too long on the early success of the brand. Analyze each of the seven concerns Colucci faced and (*a*) identify the implementations for Yoplait USA of each concern, (*b*) suggest possible *planning and implementation* actions, and (*c*) describe possible *control* measures that might be used.

3 In light of your answers to questions 1 and 2 above, today what should Yoplait USA's strategy be for its Yoplait product line in terms of (*a*) points of difference, (*b*) target markets, and (*c*) 4 Ps activities?

C

PLANNING A CAREER IN MARKETING

GETTING A JOB: THE PROCESS OF MARKETING YOURSELF

Getting a job is usually a lengthy process, and it is exactly that—a *process* that involves careful planning, implementation, and control. You may have everything going for you: a respectable grade point average (GPA), relevant work experience, several extracurricular activities, superior communication skills, and demonstrated leadership qualities. Despite these, you still need to market yourself systematically and aggressively; after all, even the best products lie dormant on the retailer's shelves unless marketed effectively.

The process of getting a job involves the same activities marketing managers use to develop and introduce products into the marketplace.[1] The only difference is that you are marketing yourself, not a product. You need to conduct marketing research by analyzing your personal qualities (performing a self-audit) and by identifying job opportunities. Based on your research results, select a target market—those job opportunities that are compatible with your interests, goals, skills, and abilities—and design a marketing mix around that target market. *You* are the "product";[2] you must decide how to "position" yourself in the job market. The price component of the marketing mix is the salary range and job benefits (such as health and life insurance, vacation time, and retirement benefits) that you hope to receive. Promotion involves communicating with prospective employers through written and electronic correspondence (advertising) and job interviews (personal selling). The place element focuses on how to reach prospective employers—at the career services office or job fairs, for example.

This appendix will assist you in career planning by (1) providing information about careers in marketing and (2) outlining a job search process.

CAREERS IN MARKETING

The diversity of marketing opportunities is reflected in the many types of marketing jobs, ranging from product management to marketing research to public relations.

The growing interest in marketing by service organizations such as athletic teams, law firms, and banks, and nonprofit organizations such as universities, the performing arts, and government agencies, has added to the numerous opportunities offered by traditional employers such as manufacturers, retailers, and advertising agencies. In addition, e-commerce has created a variety of new opportunities such as product development managers for application service providers, data miners, and permission marketing managers for graduates with marketing skills.[3] Examples of companies that have opportunities for graduates with degrees in marketing include American Express, Coca-Cola, Disney, Ford, Hallmark Cards, John Deere, L'Oréal USA, Office Depot, Philips, Sherwin-Williams, TJ Maxx, Underwriters Laboratories, Verizon, and Xerox.[4] Most of these career opportunities offer the chance to work with interesting people on stimulating and rewarding problems. Comments one product manager, "I love marketing as a career because there are different challenges every day."[5]

Recent studies of career paths and salaries suggest that marketing careers can also provide excellent opportunities for advancement and substantial pay. For example, about one of every five chief executive officers (CEOs) of the nation's 500 most valuable publicly held companies have a career history that is heaviest in marketing.[6] Similarly, reports of average starting salaries of college graduates indicate that salaries in marketing compare favorably with those in many other fields. The average starting salary of new marketing undergraduates in 2003 was $34,628, compared with $27,646 for journalism majors and $30,438 for advertising majors.[7] The future is likely to be even better. The U.S. Department of Labor reports that marketing and sales will be one of the fastest-growing occupations through 2012.[8]

Figure C–1 describes marketing occupations in six major categories: product management and physical distribution, advertising and promotion, retailing, sales, marketing research, and nonprofit marketing. One of these may be right for you. (Additional sources of marketing career information are provided at the end of this appendix.)

PRODUCT MANAGEMENT AND PHYSICAL DISTRIBUTION

Product development manager creates a road map for new products by working with customers to determine their needs and with designers to create the product.

Product manager is responsible for integrating all aspects of a product's marketing program including research, sales, sales promotion, advertising, and pricing.

Supply chain manager oversees the part of a company that transports products to consumers and handles customer service.

Operations manager supervises warehousing and other physical distribution functions and often is directly involved in moving goods on the warehouse floor.

Inventory control manager forecasts demand for goods, coordinates production with plant managers, and tracks shipments to keep customers supplied.

Physical distribution specialist is an expert in the transportation and distribution of goods and also evaluates the costs and benefits of different types of transportation.

SALES

Direct or retail salesperson sells directly to consumers in the salesperson's office, the consumer's home, or a retailer's store.

Trade salesperson calls on retailers or wholesalers to sell products for manufacturers.

Industrial or semitechnical salesperson sells supplies and services to businesses.

Complex or professional salesperson sells complicated or custom-designed products to businesses. This requires understanding of the product technology.

Customer service manager maintains good relations with customers by coordinating the sales staff, marketing management, and physical distribution management.

NONPROFIT MARKETING

Marketing manager develops and directs marketing campaigns, fundraising, and public relations.

ADVERTISING AND PROMOTION

Account executive maintains contact with clients while coordinating the creative work among artists and copywriters. Account executives work as partners with the client to develop marketing strategy.

Media buyer deals with media sales representatives in selecting advertising media and analyzes the value of media being purchased.

Copywriter works with art director in conceptualizing advertisements and writes the text of print or radio ads or the storyboards of television ads.

Art director handles the visual component of advertisements.

Sales promotion manager designs promotions for consumer products and works at an ad agency or a sales promotion agency.

Public relations manager develops written or filmed messages for the public and handles contacts with the press.

Internet marketing manager develops and executes the e-business marketing plan and manages all aspects of the advertising, promotion, and content for the online business.

RETAILING

Buyer selects products a store sells, surveys consumer trends, and evaluates the past performance of products and suppliers.

Store manager oversees the staff and services at a store.

MARKETING RESEARCH

Project manager for the supplier coordinates and oversees the market studies for a client.

Account executive for the supplier serves as a liaison between client and market research firm, like an advertising agency account executive.

In-house project director acts as project manager (see above) for the market studies conducted by the firm for which he or she works.

Competitive intelligence researcher uses new information technologies to monitor the competitive environment.

Data miner compiles and analyzes consumer data to identify behavior patterns, preferences, and user profiles for personalized marketing programs.

SOURCE: Adapted from David W. Rosenthal and Michael A. Powell, *Careers in Marketing,* ©1984, pp. 352–54.

FIGURE C–1

Marketing occupations

Product Management and Physical Distribution

Many organizations assign one manager the responsibility for a particular product. For example, Procter & Gamble (P&G) has separate managers for Tide, Cheer, Gain, and Bold. Product or brand managers are involved in all aspects of a product's marketing program, such as marketing research, sales, sales promotion, advertising, and pricing, as well as manufacturing. Managers of similar products typically report to a category manager and may be part of a *product management team.*[9]

College graduates with bachelor's and master's degrees—often in marketing and business—enter P&G as brand assistants, the only starting position in its product or brand group. Each year students from campuses throughout the United States accept positions with P&G.[10] As brand assistants, their responsibilities consist primarily of selling and sales training.

After one to two years of good performance, the brand assistant is promoted to assistant brand manager and after about the same period to brand (product) manager.

These promotions often involve several brand groups. For example, a new employee might start as brand assistant for P&G's soap products, be promoted to assistant brand manager for Crest toothpaste, and subsequently become brand manager for Folger's coffee, Charmin, or Pampers. The reason, as recruiter Henry de Montebello explains, is that "in the future everybody will have strategic alliances with everybody else, and the executives who thrive will be well-rounded."[11]

Several other jobs related to product management (Figure C–1) deal with physical distribution issues such as storing the manufactured product (inventory), moving the product from the firm to the customers (transportation), and engaging in many other aspects of the manufacture and sale of goods. Prospects for these jobs are likely to increase as wholesalers increase their involvement with selling and distribution activities and begin to take advantage of overseas opportunities.[12]

Advertising and Promotion

Although we may see hundreds of advertisements in a day, what we can't see easily is the fascinating and complex advertising profession. The entry-level advertising positions filled every year include jobs with a variety of firms. Advertising professionals often remark that they find their jobs appealing because the days are not routine and they involve creative activities with many interesting people.

Advertising positions are available in three kinds of organizations: advertisers, media companies, and agencies. Advertisers include manufacturers, retail stores, service firms, and many other types of companies. Often they have an advertising department responsible for preparing and placing their own ads. Advertising careers are also possible with the media: television, radio stations, magazines, and newspapers. Finally, advertising agencies offer job opportunities through their use of account management, research, media, and creative services.

Starting positions with advertisers and advertising agencies are often as assistants to employees with several years of experience. An assistant copywriter facilitates the development of the message, or copy, in an advertisement. An assistant art director participates in the design of visual components of advertisements. Entry-level media positions involve buying the media that will carry the ad or selling air time on radio or television or page space in print media. Advancement to supervisory positions requires planning skills, a broad vision, and an affinity for spotting an effective advertising idea. Students interested in advertising should develop good communication skills and try to gain advertising experience through summer employment opportunities or internships.[13]

Growing interest in integrated marketing programs has increased opportunities for sales promotion managers, public relations managers, and Internet marketing managers. These positions require an understanding of the potential synergy of all promotional tools. Responsibilities include the design and implementation of sweepstakes, sampling programs, events and partnerships, newsletters, press releases and conferences, e-mail promotions, web-content management, and permission marketing campaigns.

Retailing

There are two separate career paths in retailing: merchandise management and store management (Figure C–2). The key position in merchandising is that of a buyer, who is responsible for selecting merchandise, guiding the promotion of the merchandise, setting prices, bargaining with wholesalers, training the salesforce, and monitoring the competitive environment. The buyer must also be able to organize and coordinate many critical activities under severe time constraints. In contrast, store management involves the supervision of personnel in all departments and the general management of all facilities, equipment, and merchandise displays. In addition, store managers are responsible for the financial performance of each department and for the store as a whole. Typical positions beyond the store manager level include district manager, regional manager, and divisional vice president.[14]

FIGURE C–2
Typical retailing career paths

Most starting jobs in retailing are trainee positions. A trainee is usually placed in a management training program and then given a position as an assistant buyer or assistant department manager. Advancement and responsibility can be achieved quickly because there is a shortage of qualified personnel in retailing and because superior performance of an individual is quickly reflected in sales and profits—two visible measures of success. In addition, the growth of multichannel retailing has created new opportunities such as website management and online merchandise procurement.[15]

Sales

College graduates from many disciplines are attracted to sales positions because of the increasingly professional nature of selling jobs and the many opportunities they can provide. A selling career offers benefits that are hard to match in any other field: (1) the opportunity for rapid advancement (into management or to new territories and accounts); (2) the potential for extremely attractive compensation (the average salary of all sales representatives is $111,135);[16] (3) the development of personal satisfaction, feelings of accomplishment, and increased self-confidence; and (4) independence—salespeople often have almost complete control over their time and activities. Many companies now offer two sales career paths—one for people who want to go into management, and another for those who want to remain in sales for their entire career.[17]

Employment opportunities in sales occupations are found in a wide variety of organizations, including insurance agencies, retailers, and financial service firms (Figure C–3 on the next page). In addition, many salespeople work as manufacturer's representatives for organizations that have selling responsibilities for several manufacturers.[18] Activities in sales jobs include *selling duties,* such as prospecting for customers, demonstrating the product, or quoting prices; *sales-support duties,* such as handling complaints and helping solve technical problems; and *nonselling duties,* such as preparing reports, attending sales meetings, and monitoring competitive activities. Salespeople who can deal with these varying activities are critical to a company's success. According to RJR Nabisco, its recruiting priority is "finding quality people who can analyze data from customers, see things from the consumer's eyes, use available sales tools like laptops and syndicated data, and interface with the marketing people at headquarters."[19]

One of the fastest areas of growth in sales is in the direct marketing industry. Interest in information technology, customer relationship management (CRM), and integrated marketing has increased the demand for contact with customers. For many firms this means new or additional telemarketing efforts; for other firms it means increasing the amount of time salespeople spend with clients; for still others it means sophisticated e-mail marketing. "E-mail is the most valuable channel companies have to be interactive with their customers," says Gina Lambright, vice president for client services at marketing consulting firm Quris in San Francisco. At Dell Computer, the company

FIGURE C–3
Employment opportunities in
selected sales occupations
(2002 to 2012)

OCCUPATION	2002 EMPLOYMENT	2012 EMPLOYMENT	PERCENTAGE CHANGE 2002–2012	AVERAGE ANNUAL GROWTH
Insurance sales agents	381,400	413,500	8%	3,210
Real estate brokers and sales agents	406,800	426,700	5	1,990
Retail sales-persons	4,075,800	4,671,700	15	59,590
Manufacturers' sales representatives	1,857,100	2,213,400	19	35,630
Securities and financial services sales agents	299,900	338,900	13	3,900

SOURCE: "The 2002–2012 Job Outlook in Brief," *Occupational Outlook Quarterly* (Washington, DC: U.S. Dept. of Labor, Bureau of Labor Statistics, Spring 2004), pp. 29–30.

recently selected by *Sales & Marketing Management* magazine for its Best E-Business Strategy award, online communication allows salespeople to concentrate on "value-added functions" and "the ultimate direct relationship with no intermediary."[20]

Marketing Research

Marketing researchers play important roles in many organizations today. They are responsible for obtaining, analyzing, and interpreting data to facilitate making marketing decisions. This means marketing researchers are basically problem solvers. Success in the area requires not only an understanding of statistics, computers, and the Internet but also a broad base of marketing knowledge[21] and an ability to communicate with management. Individuals who are inquisitive, methodical, analytical, and solution oriented find the field particularly rewarding.

The responsibilities of the men and women currently working in the market research industry include defining the marketing problem, designing the questions, selecting the sample, collecting and analyzing the data, and, finally, reporting the results of the research. These jobs are available in three kinds of organizations. *Marketing research consulting firms* contract with large companies to provide research about their products or services.[22] *Advertising agencies* may provide research services to help clients with questions related to advertising and promotional problems. Finally, some companies have an *in-house research staff* to design and execute their research projects. Online marketing research is rapidly requiring understanding of new tools such as dynamic scripting, response validation, intercept sampling, and online consumer panels.[23]

Although marketing researchers may start as assistants performing routine tasks, they quickly advance to broader responsibilities. Survey design, interviewing, report writing, and all aspects of the research process create a challenging career. In addition, research projects typically deal with such diverse problems as consumer motivation, pricing, forecasting, and competition. The marketing research field has experienced a shortage of qualified candidates in recent years. Successful candidates, however, "like what they're doing and get excited over their work, whether it be listening to a focus group or running a complex datamining model," according to Carolyn Marconi, director of marketing research for the Vanguard Group, Inc.[24]

International Careers

Many of the careers just described can be found in international settings—in multinational U.S. corporations, small- to medium-size firms with export business, and franchises. The international public relations firm Burson-Marstellar, for example, has offices in New York, Buenos Aires, Sydney, Copenhagen, and Bangkok. Similarly, franchises such as Blockbuster Entertainment are expanding in many other markets outside of the United States. The changes in the European Union and among Asian countries may provide other opportunities. Variations of the permanent international career are also possible—for example, some companies may alternate periods of work at "headquarters" with "field" assignments in foreign countries.[25] Finally, a domestic international career—working for a foreign-owned company with an office in the United States—may be appealing.[26]

Applicants for international positions should first develop a skill that can be applied in an international setting. In addition, however, internationally competent employees will need language and cultural skills. A Conference Board description illustrates the point:

> The successful managers of the future will probably be those who speak both Japanese and English, who have a strong base in Brussels and contacts in the Pacific Rim, and who know the cafes and bars of Singapore.

Further, in many organizations, international experience has become a necessity for promotion and career advancement. "If you are going to succeed, an expatriate assignment is essential," says Eric Kraus of Gillette Co. in Boston. Of Gillette's top 20 executives, 19 have international experience.[27]

THE JOB SEARCH PROCESS

Activities you should consider during your job search process include assessing yourself, identifying job opportunities, preparing your résumé and related correspondence, and going on job interviews.

Assessing Yourself

You must know your product—you—so that you can market yourself effectively to prospective employers. Consequently, a critical first step in your job search is conducting a self-analysis, which involves critically examining yourself on the following dimensions: interests, abilities, education, experience, personality, desired job environment, and personal goals.[28] The importance of performing this assessment was stressed by a management consultant:[29]

> Many graduates enter the world of work without even understanding the fact that they are specific somebodies, much less knowing the kinds of competencies and motivations with which they have been endowed. . . . The tragedy of not knowing is awesome. Ignorant of who they are, most graduates are doomed to spend too much of their lives in work for which they are poorly suited. . . . Self-knowledge is critical to effectively managing your career.

Asking Key Questions   A self-analysis, in part, entails asking yourself some very important and difficult questions (Figure C–4 on the next page). It is critical that you respond to the questions honestly, because your answers ultimately will be used as a guide in your job selection.[30] A less-than-candid appraisal of yourself might result in a job mismatch.

INTERESTS

How do I like to spend my time?
Do I enjoy working with people?
Do I like working with tangible things?
Do I enjoy working with data?
Am I a member of many organizations?
Do I enjoy physical activities?
Do I like to read?

ABILITIES

Am I adept at analysis
What are my hardware, software, and operating system
    skills?
Do I have good verbal and written communication skills?
What special talents do I have?
At which abilities do I wish I were more adept?

EDUCATION

How have my courses and extracurricular activities
    prepared me for a specific job?
Which were my best subjects? My worst?
Is my GPA a good indication of my academic ability?
    Why?
Do I aspire to a graduate degree? Before beginning my
    job?
Why did I choose my major?

PERSONAL GOALS

What are my short-term and long-term goals? Why?
Am I career oriented, or do I have broader interests?
What are my career goals?
What jobs are likely to help me achieve my goals?
What do I hope to be doing in 5 years? In 10 years?
What do I want out of life?

PERSONALITY

What are my good and bad traits?
Am I competitive?
Do I work well with others?
Am I outspoken?
Am I a leader or a follower?
Do I work well under pressure?
Do I work quickly, or am I methodical?
Do I get along well with others?
Am I ambitious?
Do I work well independently of others?

DESIRED JOB ENVIRONMENT

Am I willing to relocate? Why?
Do I have a geographical preference? Why?
Would I mind traveling in my job?
Do I have to work for a large or nationally known firm to be
    satisfied?
Must my job offer rapid promotion opportunities?
If I could design my own job, what characteristics would it
    have?
How important is high initial salary to me?

EXPERIENCE

What previous jobs have I held? What were my responsibil-
    ities in each job?
What internships or co-op positions have I held? What
    were my responsibilities?
What volunteer positions have I held? What were my
    responsibilities?
Were any of my jobs or positions applicable to positions
    I may be seeking? How?
What did I like the most about my previous jobs? Like the
    least?
If I had it to do over again, would I work in these jobs?
    Why?

FIGURE C–4

Questions to ask in your self-analysis

Identifying Strengths and Weaknesses   After you have addressed the questions posed in Figure C–4, you are ready to identify your strengths and weaknesses. To do so, draw a vertical line down the middle of a sheet of paper and label one side of the paper "strengths" and the other side "weaknesses." Based on your answers to the questions, record your strong and weak points in their respective column. Ideally, this cataloging should be done over a few days to give you adequate time to reflect on your attributes. In addition, you might seek input from others who know you well (such as parents, close relatives, friends, professors, or employers) and can offer more objective views. They might even evaluate you on the questions in Figure C–4, and you can compare the results with your own evaluation. A hypothetical list of strengths and weaknesses is shown in Figure C–5.

What skills are most important? The answer, of course, varies by occupation and employer. Recent studies, however, suggest that problem-solving skills, communication skills, interpersonal skills, analytical and computer skills, and leadership skills are all valued by employers. Personal characteristics employers seek in a job candidate include honesty, integrity, motivation, initiative, self-confidence, flexibility, and enthusiasm. Finally, most employers also look for work experience, internship experience, or co-op experience.[31]

Taking Job-Related Tests   Personality and vocational interest tests, provided by many colleges and universities, can give you other ideas about yourself. After

FIGURE C–5

Hypothetical list of a job candidate's strengths and weaknesses

STRENGTHS	WEAKNESSES
I enjoy being with people.	I am not adept at working with computers.
I am an avid reader.	I have minimal work experience.
I have good communication skills.	I have a mediocre GPA.
I am involved in many extracurricular activities.	I am sometimes impatient.
I work well with others.	I resent close supervision.
I work well independently.	I work methodically (slowly).
I am honest and dependable.	I will not relocate.
I am willing to travel in the job.	I anger easily sometimes.
I am a good problem solver.	I lack a customer orientation.
I have a good sense of humor.	I have poor technical skills.

tests have been administered and scored, test takers meet with testing service counselors to discuss the results. Test results generally suggest jobs for which students have an inclination. The most common tests at the college level are the Strong Interest Inventory and the Campbell Interest and Skill Survey. Some counseling centers also administer the Myers-Briggs Type Indicator—a personality measure that helps identify professions you may enjoy.[32] If you have not already done so, you may wish to see whether your school offers such testing services.

Identifying Your Job Opportunities

To identify and analyze the job market, you must conduct some marketing research to determine what industries *and* companies offer promising job opportunities that relate to the results of your self-analysis. Several sources that can help in your search are discussed next.

Career Services Office   Your career services office is an excellent source of job information. Personnel in that office can: (1) inform you about which companies will be recruiting on campus, (2) alert you to unexpected job openings, (3) advise you about short-term and long-term career prospects, (4) offer advice on résumé construction, (5) assess your interviewing strengths and weaknesses, and (6) help you evaluate a job offer. In addition, the office usually contains a variety of written materials focusing on different industries and companies and tips on job hunting. One major publication available in most career services offices is the National Association of Colleges and Employers publication *Job Choices,* which contains a list of employers, kinds of job openings for college graduates, and whom to contact about jobs in those firms. Another publication for students is *jobpostings,* which is published seven times during the academic year and distributed to more than 350 colleges and universities across the United States.

Online Career and Employment Services   Many companies no longer make frequent on-campus visits. Instead, they may use the many online services available to advertise an employment opportunity or to search for candidate information. The National Association of Colleges and Employers, for example, maintains a site on the World Wide Web called JobWeb (www.jobweb.org). Similarly, monster.com and careerbuilder.com are online databases of employment ads, candidate

résumés, and other career-related information. Some of the information resources include career guidance, a cover letter library, occupational profiles, résumé templates, and networking services.[33] Employers may contact students directly when the candidate's qualifications meet their specific job requirements. The advantage of this system for students is that regardless of the size or location of the campus they are attending, many companies have access to their résumé. Some job boards even allow applicants to post audio and video clips of themselves. One advantage for recruiters is that some of the job boards utilize software for performing background verification.[34] Your school's career center may also have a homepage that offers online job search information and links to other Internet sites.

Library The public or college library can provide you with reference material that, among other things, describes successful firms and their operations, defines the content of various jobs, and forecasts job opportunities. For example, *Fortune* publishes a list of the 1,000 largest U.S. and global companies and their respective sales and profits, and Dun & Bradstreet publishes directories of all companies in the United States with a net worth of at least $500,000. *Careers in Marketing,* a publication of the American Marketing Association, presents career opportunities in marketing. The *Occupational Outlook Handbook* is an annual publication of the U.S. Department of Labor that provides projections for specific job prospects, as well as information pertaining to those jobs. A librarian can indicate reference materials that will be most pertinent to *your* job search.

Advertisements Help-wanted advertisements provide an overview of what is happening in the job market. Local (particularly Sunday editions) and college newspapers, trade press (such as *Marketing News* or *Advertising Age*), and business magazines (such as *Sales & Marketing Management*) contain classified advertisement sections that generally have job opening announcements, often for entry-level positions. Reviewing the want ads can help you identify what kinds of positions are available and their requirements and job titles, which firms offer certain kinds of jobs, and levels of compensation.

Employment Agencies An employment agency can make you aware of several job opportunities very quickly because of its large number of job listings available through computer databases. Many agencies specialize in a particular field (such as sales and marketing). The advantages of using an agency include that it: (1) reduces the cost of a job search by bringing applicants and employers together, (2) often has exclusive job listings available only by working through the agency, (3) performs much of the job search for you, and (4) tries to find a job that is compatible with your qualifications and interests.[35] In the past, some employment agencies have engaged in questionable business practices, so check with the Better Business Bureau or your business contacts to determine the quality of the various agencies.

Personal Contacts and Networking An important source of job information that students often overlook is their personal contacts. People you know often may know of job opportunities, so you should advise them that you're looking for a job. Relatives and friends might aid your job search. Instructors you know well and business contacts can provide a wealth of information about potential jobs and even help arrange an interview with a prospective employer. They may also help arrange *informational interviews* with employers that do not have immediate openings. These interviews allow you to collect information about an industry or an employer and give you an advantage if a position does become available. It is a good idea to leave your résumé with all your personal contacts so they can pass it along to those who might be in need of your services.

Student organizations (such as the student chapter of the American Marketing Association and Pi Sigma Epsilon, the professional sales fraternity) may be sources of job opportunities, particularly if they are involved with the business community. Local chapters of professional business organizations (such as the American Marketing Association and Sales and Marketing Executives International) also can provide job information; contacting their chapter president is a first step in seeking assistance from these organizations. In the past decade, small employers have provided the greatest growth in employment, and their most common source of new employees is through personal referrals.[36] Creating a network of professional contacts is one of the most important career planning activities you can undertake.[37]

State Employment Office   State employment offices have listings of job opportunities in their state and counselors to help arrange a job interview for you. Although state employment offices perform functions similar to employment agencies, they differ in listing only job opportunities in their state and providing their services free.

Direct Contact   Another means of obtaining job information is direct contact—personally communicating to prospective employers (either by mail, e-mail, or in person) that you would be interested in pursuing job opportunities with them. Often you may not even know whether jobs are available in these firms. If you correspond with the companies in writing, a letter of introduction and an attached résumé should serve as your initial form of communication. Your major goal in direct contact is ultimately to arrange a job interview.

Writing Your Résumé

A résumé is a document that communicates to prospective employers who you are. An employer reading a résumé focuses on two key questions: (1) What is the candidate like? and (2) What can the candidate do for me?[38] It is imperative that you design a résumé that addresses these two questions and presents you in a favorable light. Personnel in your career services office can provide assistance in designing résumés.

The Résumé Itself   A well-constructed résumé generally contains up to nine major sections: (1) identification (name, address, and telephone number), (2) job or career objective, (3) educational background, (4) extracurricular activities, (5) work experience or history, (6) skills or capabilities (that pertain to a particular kind of job for which you may be interviewing), (7) accomplishments or achievements, (8) personal interests, and (9) personal references.[39] There is no universally accepted format for a résumé, but three are more frequently used: chronological, functional, and targeted. A *chronological* format presents your work experience and education according to the time sequence in which they occurred (i.e., in chronological order). If you have had several jobs or attended several schools, this approach is useful to highlight what you have done. With a *functional* format, you group your experience into skill categories that emphasize your strengths. This option is particularly appropriate if you have no experience or only minimal experience related to your chosen field. A *targeted* format focuses on the capabilities you have for a specific job. This alternative is desirable if you know what job you want and are qualified for it.[40] In any of the formats, if possible, you should include quantitative information about your accomplishments and experience, such as "increased sales revenue by 20 percent" for the year you managed a retail clothing store. A résumé that illustrates the chronological format is shown in Figure C–6 on the next page.[41]

Technology has created a need for a new type of résumé—the electronic résumé. Although traditional versions of résumés may be visually appealing, today most career experts suggest that résumés accommodate delivery through mail, e-mail, and fax machines. In addition, résumés must accommodate employers who use scanning technology to enter résumés into their own databases or who search commercial online databases. To fully utilize online opportunities, an electronic résumé with a popular font

FIGURE C–6
Chronological résumé

SALLY WINTER

Campus address (until 6/1/2005):   Home address:
Elm Street Apartments #2B   123 Front Street
College Town, Ohio 44042   Teaneck, NJ 07666
Phone: (614) 424-1648   Phone: (201) 836-4995
swinter@osu.stu.edu

Education
B.S. in Business Administration, Ohio State University, 2005, cum laude—3.3 overall
GPA—3.6 GPA in major

Work Experience
Paid for 70 percent of my college expenses through the following part-time and summer
jobs:

Legal Secretary, Smith, Lee & Jones, Attorneys at Law, New York, NY—summer 2003
- Took dictation and transcribed tapes of legal proceedings
- Typed contracts and other legal documents
- Reorganized client files for easier access
- Answered the phone and screened calls for the partners

Salesclerk, College Varsity Shop, College Town, Ohio—2002–2004 academic years
- Helped customers with buying decisions
- Arranged stock and helped with window displays
- Assisted in year-end inventories
- Took over responsibilities of store manager when she was on vacation or ill

Assistant Manager, Treasure Place Gift Shop, Teaneck, NJ—summers and Christmas
vacations—2001–2004
- Supervised two salesclerks
- Helped select merchandise at trade shows
- Handled daily accounting
- Worked comfortably under pressure during busy seasons

Campus Activities
- Elected captain of the women's varsity tennis team for two years
- Worked as a reporter and night editor on campus newspaper for two years
- Elected historian for Mortar Board chapter, a senior women's honorary society

Computer Skills
- Word, Excel, PowerPoint, Outlook

Personal Interests
- Collecting antique clocks, listening to jazz, swimming

References Available on Request

(e.g., Times Roman) and relatively large font size (e.g., 10–14 pt.)—and without italic text, graphics, shading, underlining, or vertical lines—must be available. In addition, because online recruiting starts with a key word search, it is important to include key words, focus on nouns rather than verbs, and avoid abbreviations.[42]

Letter Accompanying a Résumé   The letter accompanying a résumé, or cover letter, serves as the job candidate's introduction. As a result, it must gain the attention and interest of the reader or it will fail to give the incentive to examine the résumé carefully. In designing a letter to accompany your résumé, address the following issues:[43]

- Address the letter to a specific person.
- Identify the position for which you are applying and how you heard of it.
- Indicate why you are applying for the position.

FIGURE C–7
Sample letter accompanying a résumé

Sally Winter
Elm Street Apartments, #2B
College Town, Ohio 44042
January 31, 2005

Mr. J. B. Jones
Sales Manager
Hilltop Manufacturing Company
Minneapolis, MN 55406

Dear Mr. Jones:

Dr. William Johnson, Professor of Business Administration at the Ohio State University, recently suggested that I write to you concerning your opening and my interest in a sales position. With a B.S. degree in business administration and courses in personal selling and sales management, I am confident that I could make a positive contribution to your firm.

During the past four years, I have been a salesclerk in a clothing store and an assistant manager in a gift shop. These two positions required my performing a variety of duties including selling, purchasing, stocking, and supervising. As a result, I have developed an appreciation for the viewpoints of the customer, salesperson, and management. Given my background and high energy level, I feel that I am particularly well qualified to assume a sales position in your company.

My enclosed résumé better highlights my education and experience. My extracurricular activities should strengthen and support my abilities to serve as a sales representative.

I am eager to talk with you because I feel I can demonstrate to you why I am a strong candidate for the position. I have friends in Minneapolis with whom I could stay on weekends, so Fridays or Mondays would be ideal for an appointment. I will call you in a week to see if we can arrange a mutually convenient time for a meeting. I am hopeful that your schedule will allow this.

Thank you for your kind consideration. If you would like some additional information, please feel free to contact me at (614) 424-1648. I look forward to talking with you.

Sincerely,

Sally Winter

enclosure

- Summarize your most significant credentials and qualifications.
- Refer the reader to the enclosed résumé.
- Request a personal interview, and advise the reader when and where you can be reached.

A sample letter comprising these six factors is presented in Figure C–7. Some students have tried creative approaches to making their letter stand out—sending a gift with their letter or using creative packaging, for example. Although these tactics may gain a recruiter's attention, most hiring managers say that a frivolous approach makes for a frivolous employee. As a general rule, nothing works better than an impressive cover letter and good academic credentials.[44]

Interviewing for Your Job

The job interview is a conversation between a prospective employer and a job candidate that focuses on determining whether the employer's needs can be satisfied by the candidate's qualifications. The interview is a "make or break" situation: If the interview goes well, you have increased your chances of receiving a job offer; if it goes poorly, you probably will be eliminated from further consideration.

Preparing for a Job Interview To be successful in a job interview, you must prepare for it so you can exhibit professionalism and indicate to a prospective employer that you are serious about the job. When preparing for the interview, several critical activities need to be performed.

Before the interview, gather facts about the industry, the prospective employer, and the job. Relevant information might include: the general description for the occupation; the firm's products or services; the firm's size, number of employees, and financial and competitive position; the requirements of the position; and the name and personality of the interviewer.[45] Obtaining this information will provide you with additional insight into the firm and help you formulate questions to ask the interviewer. This information might be gleaned, for example, from corporate annual reports, *The Wall Street Journal,* Moody's manuals, Standard & Poor's *Register of Corporations, Directors, and Executives, The Directory of Corporate Affiliations,* selected issues of *BusinessWeek,* or trade publications. If information is not readily available, you could call the company and indicate that you wish to obtain some information about the firm before your interview.

Preparation for the job interview should also involve role playing, or pretending that you are in the "hot seat" being interviewed. Before role playing, anticipate questions interviewers may pose and how you might address them (Figure C–8). Do not memorize your answers, though, because you want to appear spontaneous, yet

FIGURE C–8
Questions frequently asked by interviewers

INTERVIEWER QUESTIONS

1. How would you describe yourself?

2. What do you consider to be your greatest strengths and weaknesses?

3. Describe your most rewarding college experiences.

4. What do you see yourself doing in 5 years? In 10 years?

5. What are three important leadership qualities? How have you demonstrated these qualities?

6. What do you really want out of life?

7. What are your long-range and short-range goals?

8. Why did you choose your college major?

9. In which extracurricular activities did you participate? Why?

10. What jobs have you enjoyed the most? The least? Why?

11. How has your previous work experience prepared you for a marketing career?

12. Why do you want to work for our company?

13. What qualifications do you think a person needs to be successful in a company like ours?

14. Describe a creative idea you produced that led to the success of a project.

15. What criteria are you using to evaluate the company for which you hope to work?

16. Describe a project where you worked as part of a team.

17. What can I tell you about our company?

18. Are you willing to relocate?

19. Are you willing to spend at least six months as a trainee?

20. Why should we hire you?

FIGURE C–9

Questions frequently asked by interviewees

INTERVIEWEE QUESTIONS
1. Why would a job candidate want to work for your firm?
2. What makes your firm different from its competitors?
3. What is the company's promotion policy?
4. Describe the typical first-year assignment for this job.
5. How is an employee evaluated?
6. What are the opportunities for personal growth?
7. Do you have a training program?
8. What are the company's plans for future growth?
9. What is the retention rate of people in the position for which I am interviewing?
10. How can you use my skills?
11. Does the company have development programs?
12. What kind of image does the firm have in the community?
13. Why do you enjoy working for your firm?
14. How much responsibility would I have in this job?
15. What is the corporate culture in your firm?

logical and intelligent. Nonetheless, it is helpful to practice how you might respond to the questions. You should also anticipate a substance abuse screening process, now common among a wide variety of organizations.[46] In addition, develop questions you might ask the interviewer that are important and of concern to you (Figure C–9). "It's an opportunity to show the recruiter how smart you are," comments one recruiter.[47]

When role playing, you and someone with whom you feel comfortable should engage in a mock interview. Afterward, ask the stand-in interviewer to candidly appraise your interview content and style. You may wish to videotape the mock interview; ask the personnel in your career services office where videotaping equipment can be obtained for this purpose.

Before the job interview you should attend to several details. Know the exact time and place of the interview; write them down—do not rely on your memory. Get the full company name straight. Find out what the interviewer's name is and how to pronounce it. Bring a notepad and pen along on the interview, in case you need to record anything. Make certain that your appearance is clean, neat, professional, and conservative. And be punctual; arriving tardy to a job interview gives you an appearance of being unreliable.

Succeeding in Your Job Interview   You have done your homework, and at last the moment arrives and it is time for the interview. Although you may experience some apprehension, view the interview as a conversation between the prospective employer and you. Both of you are in the interview to look over the other party, to see whether there might be a good match. You know your subject matter (you); furthermore, because you did not have a job with the firm when you walked into the interview, you really have nothing to lose if you don't get it—so relax.[48]

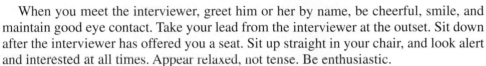
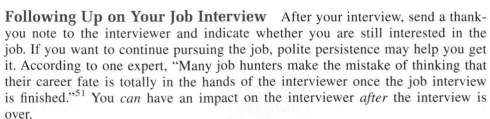

When you meet the interviewer, greet him or her by name, be cheerful, smile, and maintain good eye contact. Take your lead from the interviewer at the outset. Sit down after the interviewer has offered you a seat. Sit up straight in your chair, and look alert and interested at all times. Appear relaxed, not tense. Be enthusiastic.

During the interview, be yourself. If you try to behave in a manner that is different from the real you, your attempt may be transparent to the interviewer or you may ultimately get the job but discover that you aren't suited for it. In addition to assessing how well your skills match those of the job, the interviewer will probably try to assess your long-term interest in the firm. William Kucker, a recruiter for General Electric, explains, "We're looking for people to make a commitment."[49]

As the interview comes to a close, leave it on a positive note. Thank the interviewer for his or her time and the opportunity to discuss employment opportunities. If you are still interested in the job, express this to the interviewer. The interviewer will normally tell you what the employer's next step is—probably a visit to the company.[50] Rarely will a job offer be made at the end of the initial interview. If it is and you want the job, accept the offer; if there is any doubt in your mind about the job, however, ask for time to consider the offer.

Following Up on Your Job Interview   After your interview, send a thank-you note to the interviewer and indicate whether you are still interested in the job. If you want to continue pursuing the job, polite persistence may help you get it. According to one expert, "Many job hunters make the mistake of thinking that their career fate is totally in the hands of the interviewer once the job interview is finished."[51] You *can* have an impact on the interviewer *after* the interview is over.

The thank-you note is a gesture of appreciation and a way of maintaining visibility with the interviewer. (Remember the adage, "Out of sight, out of mind.") Even if the interview did not go well, the thank-you note may impress the interviewer so much that his or her opinion of you changes. After you have sent your thank-you note, you may wish to call the prospective employer to determine the status of the hiring decision. If the interviewer told you when you would hear from the employer, make your telephone call *after* this date (assuming, of course, that you have not yet heard from the employer); if the interviewer did not tell you when you would be contacted, make your telephone call a week or so after you have sent your thank-you note. While e-mail is a common form of communication today, it is often viewed as less personal than a letter or telephone call, so be confident that e-mail is preferred before using it to correspond with the interviewer.[52]

As you conduct your follow-up, be persistent but polite. If you are too eager, one of two things could happen to prevent you from getting the job: The employer might feel that you are a nuisance and would exhibit such behavior on the job, or the employer may perceive that you are desperate for the job and thus are not a viable candidate.

Handling Rejection   You have put your best efforts into your job search. You developed a well-designed résumé and prepared carefully for the job interview. Even the interview appears to have gone well. Nevertheless, a prospective employer may send you a rejection letter. ("We are sorry that our needs and your superb qualification don't match.") Although you will probably be disappointed, not all interviews lead to a job offer because there normally are more candidates than there are positions available.

If you receive a rejection letter, you should think back through the interview. What appeared to go right? What went wrong? Perhaps personnel from your career services office can shed light on the problem, particularly if they are in the custom of having interviewers rate each interviewee. Try to learn lessons to apply in future interviews. Keep interviewing and gaining interview experience; your persistence will eventually pay off.

SELECTED SOURCES OF MARKETING CAREER INFORMATION

The following is a selected list of marketing information sources that you should find useful during your academic studies and professional career.

BUSINESS AND MARKETING PUBLICATIONS

Business Periodicals Index (BPI) (New York: H. W. Wilson Company). This is a monthly (except August) index of almost 527 periodicals from all fields of business and marketing.

Don Doman, Dell Dennison, and Margaret Doman, *Market Research Made Easy,* 2nd ed. (Bellingham, WA: Self-Counsel Press, 2002). This practical, easy-to-read book provides a marketing research process to help select appropriate research methods, identify subjects, design questionnaires, use the Internet, and analyze data.

Jeffrey Heilbrunn, ed., *Marketing Encyclopedia* (Lincolnwood, IL: NTC Business Books, 1995). This book provides a collection of essays by professional and academic marketing experts on issues and trends shaping the future of marketing.

Hoover's Handbook of World Business, 10th ed. (Austin, TX: Hoover's Business Press, 2004). A detailed source of information about companies outside of the United States, including firms from Canada, Europe, Japan, China, India, and Taiwan.

Paige Leavitt, John Prescott, Darcy Lemon, and Farida Hasanali, *Competitive Intelligence: A Guide for Your Journey to Best-Practice Processes* (Houston, TX: American Productivity and Quality Center, 2004). This book provides a five-step model for developing and implementing a competitive intelligence effort; it explains how to collect, coordinate, and interpret actionable information.

Barbara Lewis and Dale Littler, eds., *The Blackwell Encyclopedic Dictionary of Marketing* (Cambridge, MA: Blackwell Publishers, 1999). Part of the 10-volume *Blackwell Encyclopedia of Management,* this book provides clear, concise, up-to-the-minute, and highly informative definitions and explanations of the key concepts and terms in marketing management, consumer behavior, segmentation, organizational marketing, pricing, communications, retailing and distribution, product management, market research, and international marketing.

Jean L. Sears and Marilyn K. Moody, *Using Government Information Sources,* 3rd ed. (Phoenix, AZ: Oryx Press, 2001). An easy-to-use manual arranged by topics such as consumer expenditures, business and industry statistics, economic indicators, and projections. Each chapter contains a search strategy, a checklist of courses, and a narrative description of the sources.

Cynthia L. Shamel, *Introduction to Online Market & Industry Research* (Mason, OH: Thomson Learning, 2004). This comprehensive reference provides search strategies and valuable data source information, including rankings of data sources, for industry researchers.

Betsy-Ann Toffler, *Dictionary of Marketing Terms,* 3rd ed. (Hauppauge, NY: Barrons Educational Series, 2000). This dictionary contains definitions of more than 4000 marketing terms.

Conor Vibert, *Introduction To Online Competitive Intelligence Research* (Mason, OH: Thomson Learning, 2004). This book provides a step-by-step methodology for competitive intelligence research including planning, data collection, analysis, and dissemination. Typical problem scenarios and cases illustrating search strategies are also included in the book.

Garrett Wasny, *World Business Resources.com* (New York: McGraw-Hill, 2000). A directory of over 8,000 international business, economic, and demographic resources online. Organized by topic and by region, this guide also offers more than 200 tips to speed up Internet searches.

James Woy, *Encyclopedia of Business Information Sources,* 18th ed. (Detroit: Gale Group, 2004). A bibliographic guide to over 35,000 citations covering more than 1,100 primary subjects of interest to business personnel.

CAREER PLANNING PUBLICATIONS

Richard N. Bolles, *The 2004 What Color Is Your Parachute? A Practical Manual for Job-Hunters and Career-Changers* (Berkeley, CA: Ten Speed Press, 2004). A companion workbook is also available. See www.jobhuntersbible.com.

Dennis V. Damp and Samuel Concialdi, *The Book of U.S. Government Jobs: Where They Are, What's Available, and How to Get One,* 8th ed. (Moon Township, PA: Bookhaven Press, 2002).

Diane Darling, *The Networking Survival Guide: Get the Success You Want by Tapping into the People You Know* (New York: McGraw-Hill, 2003).

Margaret Riley Dikel and Frances E. Roehm, *Guide to Internet Job Searching* (New York: McGraw-Hill, 2004).

Jack Evans and Barry Berman, *Careers in Marketing,* 2nd ed. (Englewood Cliffs, NJ: Prentice Hall, 1995).

J. Michael Farr and LaVerne L. Ludden, *200 Best Jobs for College Graduates,* 2nd ed. (Indianapolis: JIST Publishing, 2003). See www.jist.com.

Katherine Hansen, *A Foot in the Door: Networking Your Way into the Hidden Job Market* (Berkeley, CA: Ten Speed Press, 2000).

Harvard Business School Career Guide for Marketing—2001 (Cambridge, MA: President and Fellows of Harvard College, 2001). See www.hbsp.harvard.edu.

Fred E. Jardt and Mary B. Nemnich, *Cyberspace Resume Kit: How to Make and Launch a Snazzy Online Resume* (Indianapolis: JIST Works, 2001). See www.jist.com.

The National Job Bank, 19th ed. (Avon, MA: Adams Media Corporation, 2003). See www.adamsmedia.com.

Nina Segal and Eric Kocher, *International Jobs: Where They Are and How to Get Them,* 6th ed. (New York: Perseus Publishing, 2003).

Martin Yate, *Cover Letters That Knock 'Em Dead; and Résumés That Knock 'Em Dead* (Holbrook, MA: Adams Media Corporation, 2002). See www.adamsmedia.com.

Websites: Resources on job searches, résumé writing, interviewing, U.S. and international job postings, and so forth.

www.accessalesjobs.com   www.studentjobs.gov
www.ajb.dni.us   www.hotjobs.com
www.careercity.com   www.monster.com
www.careerXroads.com   www.jobbankusa.com
www.careers.org   www.studentcentral.com
www.careerbuilder.com   www.vault.com
www.careers-in-marketing.com   www.wetfeet.com

SELECTED PERIODICALS

Ad Week, BPI Communications, Inc. (weekly). See www.adweek.com. (subscription rate: $149)

Advertising Age, Crain Communications, Inc. (weekly). See www.adage.com. (subscription rate: $149)

American Demographics, Primedia Inc. (monthly). See www.demographics.com. (subscription rate: $58)

Barron's, Dow Jones & Co., Inc. (weekly). See www.barrons.com. (subscription rates: $145 print; $79 online; $39 online for current print subscribers)

BrandWeek, BPI Communications, Inc. (weekly). See www.adweek.com. (subscription rate: $149)

Business 2.0, Business 2.0 Inc. (monthly). See www.business2.com. (subscription rate: $9.99)

Business Horizons, Indiana University c/o Elsevier Science Publishing (bimonthly). See www.elsevier.com. (subscription rate: $107)

BusinessWeek, McGraw-Hill Companies (weekly). See www.businessweek.com. (subscription rate: $45.97)

Chain Store Age, Lebhar-Friedman, Inc. (monthly). See www.chainstoreage.com. (subscription rate: $105)

eCommerce Times, ECT News Network, Inc. (daily). See www.ecommercetimes.com.

Fortune, Time, Inc. (28 issues). See www.fortune.com. (subscription rates: $19.99 online special; $29.98 regular)

Forbes, Forbes Inc. (17 issues). See www.forbes.com. (subscription rate: $59.95)

Harvard Business Review, Harvard University (monthly). See www.hbsp.harvard.edu. (subscription rate: $118)

Industrial Marketing Management, Elsevier Science Publishing (8 issues). See www.elsevier.com. (subscription rate: $132)

International Journal of Electronic Commerce, M. E. Sharpe Publishing (quarterly). See www.mesharpe.com. (subscription rate: $89)

Journal of the Academy of Marketing Science, Sage Publications, Inc. (quarterly). See www.sagepub.com. (subscription rate: $112)

Journal of Advertising Research, Advertising Research Foundation (quarterly). See www.arfsite.org. (subscription rate: $155)

Journal of Business and Industrial Marketing, Emerald Group Publishing, Ltd. (7 issues). See www.emeraldinsight.com. (subscription rate: $2,369)

Journal of Consumer Marketing, Emerald Group Publishing, Ltd. (7 issues). See www.emeraldinsight.com. (subscription rate: $1,999)

Journal of Consumer Research, University of Chicago Press (quarterly). See www.journals.uchicago.edu. (subscription rates: $145 nonmembers; $55 members; $25 students)

Journal of Interactive Marketing, Direct Marketing Educational Foundation (quarterly). See www.the-dma.org. (subscription rate: $250)

Journal of Marketing, American Marketing Association (quarterly). See www.marketingpower.com. (subscription rates: $90 nonmembers; $53 members)

Journal of Marketing Education, Sage Publications, (three times per year). See www.sagepub.com. (subscription rate: $79)

Journal of Marketing Research, American Marketing Association (quarterly). See www.marketingpower.com. (subscription rates: $90 nonmembers; $53 members)

Journal of Personal Selling & Sales Management, Pi Sigma Epsilon National Education Foundation (quarterly). See www.mkt.cba.cmich.edu/jpssm. (subscription rate: $60)

Journal of Public Policy and Marketing, American Marketing Association (semiannually). See www.marketingpower.com. (subscription rates: $75 nonmembers; $53 members)

Journal of Retailing, Elsevier Science Publishing (quarterly). See www.elsevier.com. (subscription rate: $136)

Marketing Education Review, CTC Press (three times per year). See www.marketingeducationreview.com. (subscription rate: $32)

Marketing Health Services, American Marketing Association (quarterly). See www.marketingpower.com. (subscription rates: $75 nonmembers; $53 members)

Marketing Management, American Marketing Association (six times per year). See www.marketingpower.com. (subscription rates: $59.95 nonmembers; $53 members)

Marketing News, American Marketing Association (biweekly). See www.marketingpower.com. (subscription rates: $100 nonmembers; $39 members)

Marketing Research, American Marketing Association (quarterly). See www.marketingpower.com. (subscription rates: $75 nonmembers; $53 members)

Media Week, Quantum Business Media (50 issues). See www.mediaweek.co.uk. (subscription rate: $149)

Sales & Marketing Management, VNU Business Publications. See www.salesandmarketing.com. (subscription rate: $99)

Stores, National Retail Federation (weekly). See www.nrf.com or www.stores.org. (subscription rates: $120 nonmembers; free for members)

The Wall Street Journal Interactive, Dow Jones & Company, Inc. (weekly). See www.wsj.com. (subscription rates: $198 print; $79 online; $34.95 (15 weeks) for students, both print and online)

PROFESSIONAL AND TRADE ASSOCIATIONS

Alliance for Environmental Innovation
18 Tremont St.
Suite 850
Boston, MA 02108
(617) 723-2996
www.environmentaldefense.org/alliance

American Association of Advertising Agencies
405 Lexington Ave.
New York, NY 10174-1801
(212) 682-2500
www.aaaa.org

American Advertising Federation
1101 Vermont Ave. NW., Suite 500
Washington, DC 20005-6306
(202) 898-0089
www.aaf.org

American e-Commerce Association
2346 Camp St.
New Orleans, LA 70130
(504) 495-1748
www.aeaus.com

American Marketing Association
311 S. Wacker Dr., Suite 5800
Chicago, IL 60606
(800) AMA-1150
www.marketingpower.com

American Society of Transportation and Logistics
1700 N. Moore St., Suite 1900
Arlington, VA 22209
(703) 524-5011
www.astl.org

Association for Interactive Media
1430 Broadway, 8th Floor
New York, NY 10018
(888) 337-0008
www.imarketing.org

Bank Marketing Association
1120 Connecticut Ave. NW
Washington, DC 20036
(800) 433-9013
www.bmanet.org

Business Marketing Association
400 N. Michigan Ave., 15th Floor
Chicago, IL 60611
(800) 664-4BMA (4262)
www.marketing.org

Direct Marketing Association
1120 Avenue of the Americas
New York, NY 10036-6700
(212) 768-7277
www.the-dma.org

Direct Selling Association
1275 Pennsylvania Ave. NW, Suite 800
Washington, DC 20004
(212) 347-8866
www.dsa.org

International Advertising Association
521 Fifth Ave., Suite 1807
New York, NY 10175
(212) 557-1133
www.iaaglobal.org

International Franchise Association
1350 New York Ave. NW, Suite 900
Washington, DC 20005-4709
(202) 628-8000
www.franchise.org

International Mass Retail Association
1700 North Moore St., Suite 2250
Arlington, VA 22209
(703) 841-2300
www.imra.org

Marketing Research Association
1344 Silas Deane Hwy., Suite 306
Rocky Hill, CT 06067-1342
(860) 257-4008
www.mra-net.org

Marketing Science Institute
1000 Massachusetts Ave.
Cambridge, MA 02138-5396
(617) 491-2060
www.msi.org

National Association of Purchasing Management
P.O. Box 22160
Tempe, AZ 85285-2160
(480) 752-6276
www.napm.org

National Association of Wholesale Distributors
1725 K St. NW
Washington, DC 20006-1419
(202) 872-0885
www.naw.org

National Mail Order Association
2807 Polk St. NE
Minneapolis, MN 55418-2954
(612) 788-1673
www.nmoa.org

National Retail Federation
325 7th St. NW, Suite 1100
Washington, DC 20004
(800) NRF-HOW2
www.nrf.com

Product Development and Management Association
17000 Commerce Parkway, Suite C
Mount Laurel, NJ 08054
(800) 232-5241
www.pdma.org

Public Relations Society of America
33 Maiden Lane
New York, NY 10038-5150
(212) 460-1400
www.prsa.org

Sales and Marketing Executives International
P.O. Box 1390
Sumas, WA 98295-1390
(312) 893-0751
www.smei.org

Society for Marketing Professional Services
99 Canal Center Plaza, Suite 330
Alexandria, VA 22314
(800) 292-7667
www.smps.org

U.S. Internet Industry Association (USIIA)
5810 Kingstowne Center Drive
Suite 120, PMB 212
Alexandria, VA 22315-5711
(703) 924-0006
www.usiia.org

Women in Advertising and Marketing of
Metropolitan Washington
4200 Wisconsin Ave. NW, Suite 106-238
Washington DC 20016
(301) 369-7400
www.wamdc.org

ALTERNATE CASES

CASE D–1   Burton Snowboards: Building a Sport

At the age of 23, Jack Burton Carpenter quit a well-paid financial position to pursue his passion for snowboarding. He founded Burton Snowboards with a $20,000 inheritance in Manchester, Vermont, in 1977.

Carpenter first became interested in snowboarding when he received a Snurfer for Christmas in the late 1960s. The Snurfer was essentially two skis bound together with a rope for steering. Although the Snurfer was never a commercial success, Carpenter never forgot the product and it became the basis for the Burton snowboard. The early years were rough. He sold fewer than 1,500 boards in his first three years in business. The big break came in 1983 when Vermont's Stratton Mountain became the first ski resort to allow snowboarding. Burton (he dropped the Carpenter to avoid confusion) sent employees out to more than 300 ski resorts to lobby to allow boarders on the hills. Burton Snowboarding has grown to be the leading snowboard maker, with about 40 percent share of the U.S. market, does business in 35 countries, and has offices in Japan, Austria, as well as Vermont. Estimated 2003 sales were $140 million.

THE INDUSTRY

Snowboarding is a wintertime sport that resembles surfing on a ski hill. The modern snowboard industry began around 25 years ago. According to the National Sporting Goods Association, there were 6.3 million snowboarders in the United States, up from 2.1 million boarders 10 years earlier. Snowboarders represent 2.5 percent of the 2003 U.S. population, up from 0.9 percent in 1993. However, at the same time that snowboarding has been growing in popularity, alpine skiing is declining. There were 6.8 million alpine skiers in 2003, representing 2.6 percent of the population, down from 10.6 million skiers, representing 4.6 percent of the U.S. population in 1993. Snowboarders represent more than 31 percent of all ski passes and are the fastest-growing part of the ski industry. However, growth in snowboarding has slowed from 21 percent growth in the late 1990s to 11 percent in the 2003–2004 season and is expected to be about 5 percent in 2004–2005.

Snowboarding has achieved world-wide attention and acceptance. The International Olympic Committee and the International Ski Federation first accepted snowboarding as a medal sport in the 1998 Winter Olympics, held in Nagano, Japan.

THE COMPETITION

There are many snowboard manufacturers, not to mention companies that produce snowboarding apparel and accessories as well as full-line snowboarding equipment suppliers such as Burton. Barriers to entry are relatively low so new entrants can be expected though there has been consolidation in the industry. One estimate places Burton's market share at 38 percent followed by K2 (which acquired Ride) at 31 percent, Lamar with 7 percent, Salomon with 6 percent, Rossignol with 4 percent, and Gnu with 3 percent.

Snowboard sales have dropped from 30–40 percent annual gains in the late 1990s to just 4 percent for each of the last three years.

Burton is not only the pioneer but has also been the trendsetter for snowboarding. Burton has the product line with the greatest depth and breadth with racing, free riding, park, and pipe boards. Burton's line appeals to novice as well as professional boarders. Retail list prices range from $300 to $800. In addition to boards, Burton offers protective gear (through its wholly owned subsidiary, R.E.D. "Rider Engineered Devices"), bags, bindings, boots, and goggles (Burton's anon.optics). For information on Burton's product line or to take a virtual tour of the Burton factory at www.burton.com.

THE ISSUES

Burton uses print advertisements in such magazines as *Snowboarder* and *Transworld SNOWboarding*. The ads are often tied in with reader service cards at the back of the magazine so that additional information can be requested. Burton also sponsors riders—an important promotional tool and vital to the sport's success. Burton sponsors more than 100 riders worldwide at different levels. The top level of sponsorship—the Global Team—consists of only 17 riders, among the best in the world. These team members are often role models for young boarders. For example, in the 2002 Winter Olympics in Salt Lake City, Burton team riders Kelly Clark won a gold medal for the United States in the women's halfpipe competition, Ross Powers won the gold medal in men's halfpipe, and Chris Klug earned a bronze medal in the parallel giant slalom event. Even well-known celebrity boarders couldn't survive financially without such sponsorship. Burton also sponsors snowboarding events such as the U.S. Open Snowboarding Championships. Other promotional items include posters and stickers.

Snowboard design is constantly changing. Currently boards are becoming longer (for better landings), are trending toward unidirectional styles (rather than the blunt nosed boards that can ride in both directions), and

now have more side cuts and narrower stances than in the past. Sales of freestyle boards have increased 59 percent.

Burton has been very loyal to the distributors that have helped them build the business. While Burton tends to be distributed primarily in specialty shops, there may be increasing pressure to offer the boards at national chains. In general, snowboard sales in sporting goods chains did not do as well as sales through specialty stores during the 2003–2004 season.

Perhaps the biggest challenge facing Burton and the entire snowboarding industry is demographics. Snowboarding is primarily a sport engaged in by younger, male participants. In 2000, more than 80 percent of participants were under the age of 24 with the median age of a snowboarder at 15.7 years. More than 74 percent of snowboarders are male. Can the appeal of snowboarding be expanded to a more diverse audience? Will Grays on Trays, or the over-30 snowboarder, be the next wave of snowboarding growth?

Questions

1 What are the environmental forces influencing the snowboarding industry?

2 What are the differences in marketing goals for Burton Snowboarding in (*a*) its early years while developing the industry and (*b*) today with growing competition?

3 Identify the elements of the marketing mix for Burton currently. What marketing mix would you recommend for Burton given the changes occurring in the snowboarding marketplace?

4 How will the image of snowboarding be affected if more skiers or older participants take up the sport?

CASE D–2   Daktronics, Inc: Global Displays in 68 Billion Colors

"We were looking for a way to provide jobs and keep our graduates at home," said Dr. Aelred (Al) J. Kurtenbach, board chairman of Daktronics, Inc. So in 1968, Kurtenbach, then an engineering professor at South Dakota State University (SDSU), and fellow professor Duane Sander decided to start a business. "We started a biomedical engineering company, mainly because we'd both done research in this area," continued Kurtenbach.

But even college professors make bad decisions occasionally!

THE DAKTRONICS LAUNCH: DOWNSIDE, UPSIDE

"It was a dismal failure," explains Kurtenbach, "because the electronic thermometer and automated blood-pressure gauge we'd developed worked fine but simply cost too

much to produce and sell." Also, he and Sander were concerned that by the time they went through the lengthy process to receive U.S. Food and Drug Administration approval, Daktronics would run out of money.

Enter: A miracle—in the form of the South Dakota State wrestling coach who needed a portable scoreboard near the wrestling mat to tell fans the time and score without blocking their view of action on the mat. At the time, wresting teams had to use basketball displays that couldn't show the right wrestling information and were too high and far from the mat.

In response, Daktronics designed the Matside®, a pyramid-shaped scoreboard that sits on the floor and is still in use at wrestling matches around the United States today, 35 years later. The Matside also established Daktronics' reputation as a company that could get problems solved, and quickly.

From that low-key launch, Daktronics has emerged as the world-class designer of scoreboards and electronic displays used in the United States and around the globe. The reason for Daktronics' success? "Innovation," says Kurtenbach. *Fortune Small Business* describes the company as a "geek-rich workplace," with more than 230 degreed engineers out of its 900 full-time employees in its plant in Brookings, South Dakota—population 18,504.

To start Daktronics in 1968, Kurtenbach and Sander sold shares to family and friends at $5 per share, raising a bit less than $100,000. That limited initial funding also pushed Kurtenbach and Sander into finding products that customers would buy to generate revenues for Daktronics. The company still must stay alert because it faces global competitors like Barco from Belgium and Mitsubishi from Japan.

TODAY'S MARKET SEGMENTS

Daktronics divides its markets into three segments: sports (70 percent of Daktronics' sales), business (20 percent), and government (10 percent). The company reaches these markets today through 35 U.S. regional sales and service offices and a recently opened office in Frankfurt, Germany to reach European and Middle Eastern customers.

In the sports segment, if you watched the last Kentucky Derby at Churchill Downs or the 2004 Olympics in Athens on television, you probably saw a sample of Daktronics electronic scoring and display systems. The same goes for 24 of 30 Major League Baseball parks, 22 of 31 National Football League stadiums, 19 of 28 National Basketball Association facilities, and 19 of 30 National Hockey League arenas, where Daktronics has created some or all of the displays. This also is true of election displays at hundreds of colleges, universities, and high schools, where the prices can vary from millions of dollars to a few thousand.

A surprise to many: Advertising on these displays can often pay for themselves in a year or two. Brad Mayne,

president of the American Airlines Center in Dallas, where the NBA Mavericks and NHL Stars play, says that Daktronics' scoreboard (shown below) paid for itself in advertising by the second season.

Daktronics' largest scoreboard? It's a 36-by-149-foot giant at the Cleveland Indians' Jacobs Field. The nine full-color displays installed throughout Jacobs Field provide live videos and replays, lineups, scores, pitch information, and so on.

In the business segment, probably the biggest and best known are Daktronics' electronic displays in New York City. It recently installed a 65-foot high display in Times Square that shows video, animation, graphics, stock quotes, and news headlines in striking shades of color.

While that may be the best-known business display, hundreds of Daktronics programmable displays dot the United States in shopping malls and outside of stores and churches. These displays show everything from current times and temperatures to financial information, gas prices, and motel room rates. James (Jim) B. Morgan, president and chief executive officer of Daktronics, now puts greater emphasis on the business accounts to make the company less dependent on the sports segment.

Less well known are Daktronics displays for the government segment. Suppose that on the way to class today, a freeway sign told you that a crash in the right lane ahead means you should move to a left lane and slow down. It was probably a Daktronics-built sign, something like that for the Cumberland Gap Tunnel that connects Virginia, Kentucky, and Tennessee, shown on the opposite page. Besides highway signs, the government segment includes airport and train station displays announcing arrival and departure times.

To see what Daktronics sports, business, and government displays have been installed in your state, go to www.daktronics.com.

TECHNOLOGY

Exploiting the latest technology is critical to Daktronics' success. At the level of signage just needed to display words and numbers, a key company innovation is the Glow Cube® pixel, about the size of a Rubik's Cube. Black on one side and reflective yellow on the other, hundreds of these rotate to black or yellow to spell words or create shapes on scoreboards or highway signs. Glow Cube® pixels are the building blocks you also see on traditional signs ranging from those on professional golf tour events to portable soccer scoreboards.

For the giant programmable video displays, the basic building blocks are thousands of LEDs (light emitting diodes). LED color breakthrough in the 1990s led to today's displays capable of showing 68 billion hues of color—largely replacing tiny incandescent lamps in these displays and using only about 10 percent of the electrical power needed for those lamps. Sophisticated computer programs and video and replay systems make these screens come to life at an athletic event. Because of the low power usage and high reliability, the LED pixel has replaced the Glow Cube® pixel in most applications.

COMMUNICATIONS AND MANAGEMENT

With the engineering, manufacturing, and marketing departments housed in the same Daktronics building, many questions can be addressed with simple, direct water-cooler conversations. Kurtenbach sees this open communication as a huge competitive advantage for Daktronics.

Dr. Kurtenbach's transition from academics to business was surprisingly easy. To learn how businesses work and succeed, he checked out histories of large U.S. companies from the library. He uses what he calls his "waterboy" approach in managing—meaning that every manager is like a waterboy for the team, necessary but not the star. Kurtenbach developed this leadership style growing up as one of 13 children in a farm family that often involved his doing the essential tasks none of his brothers or sisters wanted to do.

STUDENT JOBS AND ECONOMIC DEVELOPMENT

How did Kurtenbach's original goal of starting a local business to help keep South Dakota State University graduates in the state turn out? Kurtenbach and Daktronics probably get a grade of A+. Not only does the company employ more than 900 full-time people in its Brookings facility, but it also provides more than 450 *paid* internships each year for students—mostly from SDSU. To help Daktronics continue to enhance its cutting-edge technology, SDSU has also responded by enhancing its graphic- and computer-design offerings.

And that $5 per share investment by family and friends in the disastrous Daktronics "biomedical device launch" in 1968? With stock splits, each share is worth about $2,700 today, probably not a drag on Brookings local economic development either.

Questions

1 What are the reasons or appeals that might cause potential customers in the following markets to buy a Daktronics scoreboard, electronics display, or large screen video? (*a*) A Major League Baseball team, (*b*) a high school for its football field, (*c*) a local hardware store, and (*d*) a state highway department.

2 (*a*) Do a SWOT analysis for Daktronics. (*b*) For one entry in each of the four cells in your SWOT table (strengths, weaknesses, opportunities, and threats) suggest an action Daktronics might take to increase revenues.

3 Using Figure 2–4 as a guide, identify an action Daktronics might take to increase sales in each of the four cells: (*a*) current markets, current products; (*b*) current markets, new products; (*c*) new markets, current products; (*d*) new markets, new products.

CASE D–3   Jamba Juice: Scanning the Marketing Environment

What were you doing in 10th grade? Waiting to get your driver's license? Kirk Perron was thinking about his future and putting together a deal that would help launch the successful Jamba Juice chain. It sounds incredible but Kirk Perron bought the real estate for his first juice bar when he was in 10th grade. He borrowed money from a high school counselor, the librarian, and his school bus driver to put together the $12,000 down payment.

THE COMPANY

Kirk Perron opened up his first operation as The Juice Club in 1990 in San Luis Obispo, California. He hit on the idea for a convenient, delicious, healthful food store on a long weekend bike ride. An avid cyclist with a life-long interest in health and nutrition, he wanted to offer an alternative to typical fast-food fare. The idea was a hit and quickly spread. In 1995, the company changed its name from The Juice Club to Jamba Juice. Today Jamba Juice has more than 445 stores nationwide offering a variety of healthy drinks and snacks. Jamba Juice is considered the industry leader in the smoothie market and Perron predicts that one day Jamba Juice will be as big a brand as Coca-Cola.

THE IDEA

Jamba Juice is all about healthy food and fun. Jamba is from an African word that means "to celebrate." Walk into a Jamba Juice store and customers can choose from a wide variety of Jamba Juice specialties including smoothies, fresh squeezed fruit and vegetable juices, breads, and pretzels. Jamba's commitment to healthy products is reflected in its mission statement, "Enriching the daily experience of our customers, our community, and ourselves through the life-nourishing qualities of fruits and vegetables."

Smoothies are the bulk of the Jamba Juice's business. They are made with juice and fruit and often yogurt, sherbet, or ice milk. A typical smoothie gets most of its calories from carbohydrates and protein providing a low or no-fat, nutritious meal. Jamba smoothies are designed to meet "heart healthy" FDA requirements. Nutritional supplements called "boosts," such as "energy juice boost," containing ginseng and gingko biloba, and "immunity juice boost," with echinacea and antioxidants, are available and can be added to smoothies. Jamba Juice also recently added a new low-calorie drink, the Enlightened Smoothie, to its menu. Learn more about Jamba at www.jambajuice.com.

As you sit at the counter in a Jamba Juice, you can watch friendly, well-trained Jamba Juice employees whip, beat, and blend your smoothie right before your eyes. Stores also feature nutrition centers where customers can get a complete nutritional breakdown for each product. Outlets also feature a merchandising area, which has Jamba Juice juicers, mugs, hats, and T-shirts.

THE COMPETITION

Juice bars have been part of a growing trend. Barriers to entry are fairly low. Single-store outlets and small chains within a city or region are common, although Jamba has several large competitors. New Orleans-based Smoothie King, for example, has 340 locations in 34 states, and Atlanta-based Planet Smoothie has more than 100 stores in 20 states. Other competitors include Juice Stop, Juice It Up!, Surf City Squeeze, and Orange Julius. Jamba Juice has positioned itself as a replacement for typical fast-food fare. This means it also considers fast-food restaurants indirect competitors.

Jamba has had to fight to maintain its trademark in a competitive market. Several years ago a San Francisco Juice bar called Jamm'n Juice was forced to change its name after Jamba complained that Jamm'n Juice and its animated fruit and vegetables were too close to the Jamba trademark and logo.

THE MARKET

Juice bars have existed for decades, often in health-food stores and gyms and were associated with what was a small group of intensely health-conscious customers. That small demographic group boomed in recent years fueling the market for fat-free foods, fitness equipment, and apparel. There has also been an increasing level of health consciousness among society generally. However, "the consumer always talks thin and eats fat" according to Allan Hickock, an industry analyst with Piper Jaffray.

However, Jamba Juice is optimistic about the opportunities for expanding the market by replacing fast food with good-for-you food. Retail sales of juice and smoothies exceeded $1.2 billion in 2004 compared with $552 million in 2000. About two-thirds of Jamba's customers are between the ages of 15 and 25—not exactly the same demographic group as the traditional health-conscious baby boomer. Age and education level are important selection criteria for opening new Jamba Juice outlets. Kirk Perron believes that the more highly educated potential customers are, the more likely they will be to stop in for a nutritious smoothie. In fact, many of current and planned Jamba outlets are in college towns and partnerships have been formed to open outlets in universities and airports. You can find Jamba in both the Los Angeles and San Francisco airports and on campus at the University of North Carolina, George Washington University, and the University of Nevada–Las Vegas, among others. Jamba also has a licensing agreement with Whole Foods Markets, a partner that shares Jamba's values and commitment to healthy living.

THE ISSUES

Purists insist that the best drinks come from completely fresh produce. Fresh produce can be hard to work with to provide consistent-tasting drinks. Also, the price of fresh produce can change drastically throughout the year.

With fairly limited menus, juice bars are considered great as an add-on rather than a stand-alone retail establishment because they are usually not strong enough to draw customer traffic on their own. Personnel are important to the success of a juice bar—described as "bartenders" they have to be able to put on a good show for the customer.

There is a seasonality effect for smoothie and juice operators. For example, in northern climates, operators in enclosed downtown skyways or mall locations often see their business fall off in the summer when people are outdoors walking around. Business surges in the winter.[3]

Questions

1 Conduct an environmental scan for Jamba Juice as it considers a new juice bar to open near your university. Identify factors that you think have an impact on the juice bar market, and indicate whether these factors would tend to enhance opportunities or represent threats.

2 Given your environmental analysis, which environmental force do you believe is most critical for Jamba Juice and why?

3 Examine the competitive environment for juice bars. Consider the likelihood of new entrants, barriers to entry, existing competitors, and substitutes. How would you summarize the current competitive environment?

4 Do you think that the juice bar phenomenon is a fad or rooted in some fundamental environmental and market forces? Why?

CASE D–4   Ford and Firestone: Who's to Blame?

Ford Motor Company and Firestone Tire and Rubber enjoyed one of the longest-running relationships in American business, built upon the friendship and business relationship among the founders, Harvey Firestone and Henry Ford. From 1908 when Firestone first outfitted the Model T Ford until 2000, Firestone was the primary tire supplier to Ford. A well-publicized falling out over the blame for the deaths and accidents occurring in Ford Explorer vehicles equipped with Firestone tires buried the relationship. Firestone variously blamed Ford and consumers while Ford blamed Firestone. Both companies have damaged their credibility and reputation among consumers. What went wrong?

THE FORD EXPLORER

To understand how the entire situation unfolded, it is useful to focus on the development and launch of earlier Ford automobiles. The Ford Pinto was designed in the early 1960s to compete in the lower-priced subcompact segment. Ford engineers located the Pinto's gas tank in a location vulnerable to rear-end collisions to cut costs. A Ford cost-benefit analysis estimated it would cost $11 per car to move the gas tank to a less vulnerable position. Given that it expected to produce 12.5 million Pintos over the life of the model, Ford decided not to redesign the car and spend $137 million to move the gas tank. Using insurance company claim values at the time, Ford estimated that it would "save" about $50 million in insurance claims by relocating the gas tank, netting $87 million loss. Hence, it was cheaper to leave the gas tank in its rear-end position. The decision proved fatal. Ultimately, the recall of the Pinto and related expenses cost Ford at least $1.5 billion.

The Explorer's design was based on the Ford Bronco, essentially a line of light trucks using the twin I-beam suspension to lift up the vehicle to travel over rough terrain. However, this meant that the center of gravity was higher—the vehicle became more prone to stability problems and rollovers. By the late 1980s, Ford faced more than 800 lawsuits from rollovers of the Bronco II and Ranger, forerunners of the Explorer.

Ford developed the Explorer to address a mid-1980s market looking for a rugged vehicle that was primarily image and secondarily performance. Because automobile manufacturing had a four- to five-year lead time for a new model, decisions were made about the Explorer before all the consequences of the earlier decisions on the Bronco and Ranger were in. Among the early decisions made were the use of the same twin I-beam suspension of the Bronco II and manufacturing on the same assembly line used for the Ranger. Internal company documents of tests on the Explorer prototype showed a number of problems with rollovers and a tendency to lift its wheels and tip during turns made at speeds up to 55 mph—even worse performance than the Bronco II. As early as 1987 there were calls from designers to make changes in the design of the vehicle that would improve stability and maintain passenger safety.

Consumer Reports came out with a scathing review of the Bronco II in June 1989, advising consumers to "steer clear" of the product. At this point, the Explorer's design, modeled on the Bronco II, was frozen; parts were ordered and facilities were readied for production for 1990 delivery.

Another important design decision was that of the tires for the Explorer. Both Goodyear and Firestone tires were selected for the Explorer. Examining various Firestone models, a Ford engineer reported that there was a good probability of passing the Consumer's Union testing for the Explorer with Firestone P225 tires and less confidence with the Firestone P235. Ford chose the P235. Ford's engineer, Roger Stornant, claimed that "management is aware of the potential risk with the P235 tires and has accepted that risk. The Consumer's Union test is generally unrepresentative of the real world and I see no 'real' risk in failing except what may result in the way of spurious litigation."

Ford engineers suggested four ways to improve the stability of the Explorer: widening the chassis by two inches, lowering the engine, lowering the tire pressure, and stiffening the springs. Ford chose the latter two, reducing the recommended tire pressure from 30–35 psi to 26 psi. This produced more road gripping, but it also increased friction, increased the heat of the tires, and caused tread separations. The lower tire pressure also reduced fuel economy.

BRIDGESTONE/FIRESTONE

Firestone had its own history of recalls. In 1978, between 13 and 14 million Firestone "500" tires were recalled due to faulty manufacture costing the company more than $200 million. The National Highway Safety Administration (NHTSA) called for tougher new standards for tires and light trucks. If these standards had been in place in the late 1970s, the early and subsequent designs of SUVs would have been quite different, saving lives and money. However, the NHTSA was essentially dismantled by the Reagan administration that slashed the NHTSA's budget and revoked several new regulations, including a warning light for tire inflation problems.

In 1987, Firestone became a subsidiary of Bridgestone Tire Co. Ltd. Bridgestone, a Japanese company, was named for its founder Shojiro Ishibashi, who's name means "stone bridge." Bridgestone was proud of its technological leadership—innovations in tire performance and design—as well as its dedication to quality. The Firestone subsidiary was relabeled the Bridgestone/Firestone Company in 1990, with headquarters in Nashville, Tennessee.

The first tire separation lawsuits hit Firestone in 1992. This was followed by labor disputes and a strike at the Bridgestone/Firestone plant in Decatur, Illinois, following attempts to cut costs. Testing of both Goodyear and Firestone tire models used on the Explorer showed that the Goodyear tires significantly outperformed Firestone. In some instances, Firestone tires wore out twice as fast as Goodyears. The Firestone Wilderness tire earned the lowest-acceptable NHTSA heat resistance rating—a C. The comparable Goodyear tire received a B.

Ford began to pressure Goodyear to lower tire prices in 1995. Goodyear decided it could not manufacture tires at a price that Ford was willing to pay and actually asked for a price increase due to higher material costs. At this point, Ford discontinued using Goodyear tires on its Explorer, relying entirely upon Firestone.

LAUNCH OF THE EXPLORER AND THE LAWSUITS

The Explorer was launched in 1990 and quickly became the best-selling SUV on the market. Granted, few consumers were using it for its off-road capabilities, but they looked adventuresome whizzing down the freeway to the mall. Ford engineers were well aware of the safety risk of the Explorer. Letters to dealerships warned of the dangers of failing to follow precautions on recommended tire usage, stating that ignoring these precautions could lead to loss of control and vehicle rollover, which could result in serious injury or death.

Ford also conducted a survey in 1993 of SUV drivers, finding that these drivers drove faster, were more likely to drive in bad weather, and followed other vehicles more closely, particularly troubling since the Explorer needed 20 to 30 feet more to stop when traveling at 60 mph than a typical family car.

By 1995, a Texas jury found Ford 100 percent at fault for the death of a 20-year-old college student driving a Bronco II that rolled over due to tire separation. The $25 million verdict was the largest SUV rollover verdict at the time. In 1996, a trainee test driver lost control of an Explorer during a lane change at 52.5 mph. The driver, overcorrecting, found the car in a four-wheel slide and then a 360-degree flip.

State Farm Insurance, the largest U.S. automobile insurer, notified Firestone and NHTSA in 1998 that they were experiencing an unusual number of claims on Firestone tires. Ford quietly began replacing Firestone tires on Explorers in Venezuela and Saudi Arabia due to rollover deaths in those countries.

POINTING FINGERS

An investigative report on a Houston television station started to blow the cover off the problems at Ford and Firestone in February 2000. The vice president of public affairs at Firestone accused the television station of unfairly characterizing Firestone Radial ATX tires as dangerous. She stated that the television station would better serve viewers by telling them how to properly maintain their tires and suggested that many of the crashes were caused by external factors such as punctures.

By May 2000, NHTSA belatedly launched an investigation and sent a defect notice to Firestone. Ford accused Firestone of withholding data needed to determine which tires were defective. Ford accused NHTSA of sitting on Firestone data, and it was Ford that pinpointed where the bad tires were being produced and pressed for a recall. By late summer of 2000, the recall was announced.

Ford organized a war room of 500 people dedicated to the crisis—public affairs and media, engineering, legal, regulatory, purchasing, and finance people collecting and analyzing data, operating a 24-hour hotline for the public, and disseminating information with NHTSA and the public.

Meanwhile, Bridgestone executives in Japan had no real appreciation of what was happening with Firestone. There were few Explorers sold in Japan and very few tires subject to recall. The attitude was that the Japanese built better cars, therefore the problem must be with Ford. The first public statement by Firestone's president, Masatoshi Ono, seemed to hold the Ford Explorer responsible and advised car owners to check tire pressure every month, even better, every two weeks.

Ford's CEO, Jacques Nasser, went on the offensive claiming that there were no problems with the design of the Explorer and that there were no data pointing to faults with the Explorer; he insisted that this was a tire problem. Ford rolled out a $5 million advertising campaign to protect its reputation and brand.

In May 2001, a second recall of 13 million Firestone tires was announced by Ford in an attempt to clear the path for the 2002 Explorer. Ford claimed it did not have enough confidence in the Firestone tires, while Firestone countered that the real issue was the safety of the Explorer. Firestone-equipped Explorers accounted for most of the 174 deaths and 700 injuries sustained in accidents reported at that time. In addition, Ford faced lawsuits seeking more than $590 million in damages.

Congressional hearings were launched. Accusations and data flew back and forth. Bridgestone/Firestone announced its intention to close its Decatur, Illinois, plant in December 2001, laying off almost 1,400 people. The president of the local steelworkers union claimed that Ford blamed Firestone and then Firestone made a scapegoat of the Decatur plant.

Ford announced in July 2001 that it had taken an equity position in Top Driver, Inc., the largest chain of driving schools in the country, and would be developing a driver safety course for SUV owners. The implication was that accidents with Ford Explorers were due not only to defective Firestone tires but to driver error as well. Ford was criticized as hypocritical for presenting advertising images of invincible SUVs that can be driven with abandon, weaving in and out of traffic, giving drivers a false sense of security while at the same time claiming that SUV drivers needed safety training.

Questions

1 What moral philosophy appeared to guide the decision making at Ford? At Bridgestone/Firestone? Is there any evidence that either company changed its decision-making model as lawsuits mounted?

2 Do you see Ford's handling of the situation surrounding the development, marketing, and subsequent recall as ethical but illegal, ethical and legal, unethical but legal, or unethical and illegal? Why?

3 What actions would you recommend Ford take to deal with the aftermath of this situation?

CASE D–5   The Jamisons Buy an Espresso Machine

At 4:52 P.M. on Friday, January 28, 2005, Brock and Alisha Jamison bought an espresso machine. There was no doubt about it. Any observer would agree that the purchase took place at precisely that time. Or did it?

When questioned after the transaction, neither Brock nor Alisha could remember which of them first suggested the idea of getting an espresso machine. They do recall that in the summer of 2003 they attended a dinner party given by a friend who specialized in French and Chinese cooking. The meal was delicious, and their friend Brad was very proud of the Krups espresso machine he had used to cap off the evening. The item was expensive, however, at about $900.

The following summer, Alisha noticed a comparison study of espresso machines in *Gourmet* magazine. The performance of four different brands was compared. At about the same time, Brock noticed that *Consumer Reports* also compared a number of brands of espresso machines. In both instances, the Krups brand come out on top.

Later that fall, new models of the Krups were introduced, and a model they liked was selling for $700 in department stores. The Jamisons searched occasionally for Krups in discount houses or in wholesale showroom catalogs, even searching the Internet, hoping to find a lower price for the product. They were simply not offered there.

For Christmas 2004, the Jamisons traveled from Los Angeles to the family home in Michigan. While there, the Jamisons received a gift of a KitchenAid mixer from Brock's grandmother. Although the mixer was beautiful, Alisha immediately thought how much more elegant and useful an espresso machine would be. One private sentence to that effect brought immediate agreement from Brock. The box was (discreetly) not opened, although many thanks were expressed. The box remained unopened the entire time the Jamisons kept the item.

Back home in Los Angeles in January, Alisha again saw that the Krups was sale-priced at $600 at Sur la Table, one of the major gourmet stores in California. Brock and Alisha visited a branch location on a Saturday afternoon and saw the item. The salesperson, however, was not very knowledgeable about its features and not very helpful on explaining its attributes. The Jamisons left, very disappointed.

Two days later, Alisha called a different location for Sur la Table in a more urban location and talked to Dora Mayeur, a seemingly knowledgeable salesperson whose co-worker, Stephanie Wales, claimed to own and love exactly the model the Jamisons had in mind. Furthermore, Dora said that they did carry KitchenAid mixers and would make an exchange of the mixer, which had been received as a gift and for which no receipt was available.

On the following Friday morning, Brock put the mixer in his car trunk when he left for work. That afternoon, Alisha and six-month-old Brock, Jr., rode into town with a friend to meet Brock and make the transaction. After meeting downtown, they drove through uncharacteristic heavy rainy-day traffic to Sur la Table to meet Dora, whom they liked as much in person as they did on the telephone. Dora conducted a brief review of the types and models available.

There was the Nespresso brand, which used Nescafé coffee capsules, for about $400. There were four varieties of the FrancisFrancis brand, priced between $430 and $720. At the top of the price structure, was the multilingual, Swiss-made Jura brand, priced at $2,200. The Krups that they had coveted was also there, selling at $600, but it was much larger than they thought. In fact, the item was the shape (and seemed to be nearly the size) of the Vienna Opera House.

There was a somewhat smaller, less expensive Krups twin-tower model, and the Jamisons toyed with the idea of buying it, but Dora suggested that the more expensive version was well worth the money. The Jamisons then confirmed their initial decision to take the $600 Krups model and asked Dora about exchanging the KitchenAid mixer they had brought with them. "No problem," said Dora.

After making a quick phone call, Dora returned with bad news. Sur la Table had not carried that particular model of mixer. This model mixer was a single-color model that is usually carried at department stores and catalog sales houses. The one carried by the specialized culinary stores, such as Sur la Table, was a two-tone item. She even offered to allow the Jamisons to use her phone to verify the availability of the item. The Jamisons did exactly that.

Alisha dialed several of the suggested stores, looking for a retailer that carried both the Krups and the KitchenAid model, but she quickly learned that they were distributed through different types of retail stores. A young man who answered the phone at one store, however, seemed friendly and helpful, and Alisha was able to obtain his agreement to take the item as a return if she could get there that afternoon.

The store was about one-half mile away. Brock volunteered to brave the elements and return the mixer. He took the shopping shuttle to the store with the still-unopened mixer box under his arm. About an hour later, Brock returned cold and wet, with a refund. Together, the Jamisons bought the Krups espresso machine at 4:52 P.M. and proudly took it home.

Questions

1 Which of the Jamisons decided to buy an espresso machine? The Krups brand?
2 When was the decision to buy made?
3 What were the important attributes in the evaluation of the Krups brand?
4 Would you characterize the Jamisons' purchase decision process as routine problem solving, limited problem solving, or extended problem solving? Why?

CASE D–6   Motetronix Technology: Marketing Smart Dust

"The next 18 months will be critical in getting the word out about our technology and products," says Ajay Gupta, president of Motetronix Technology. "The Dust Storm is on the horizon and companies that capitalize on it early have huge potential."

THE COMPANY AND TECHNOLOGY

Motetronix Technology is a developer and manufacturer of "smart dust," or tiny wireless microelectromechanical sensors that measure temperature, light, and vibration; analyze chemical compounds, including radiation and air quality; and observe surrounding movement. These sensors are powered by AA batteries and controlled by an operating system called Tiny OS. Called *motes* (short for a re*mote* wireless transceiver that both transmits and receives analog or digital signals), these sensors survey the world around them and communicate with each other wirelessly, grapevining down the line until the data get to a personal computer. The "smart dust" name comes from the ultimate goal of making each mote about one cubic millimeter small, or the size of a grain of sand.

SMART DUST APPLICATIONS

Industry analysts are predicting that smart dust will have a host of commercial, military, security, and ecological applications. Along with the Pentagon, the U.S. Department of Homeland Security has already devoted a large portion of its R&D budget to sensor technology for military and security applications. Commercial and ecological applications are still being studied. According to industry analysts, vibration sensors on a factory floor will tell when a machine is about to fail, saving millions of dollars in downtime. Air-pressure sensors on truck tires will prevent accidents and save on fuel. Sensors dropped in a forest fire's path will predict which areas will flame up next. Motes will be able to determine when a building is safe to reenter after an earthquake, monitor the vital signs (and locations) of elderly people, or monitor power consumption of household appliances. A dispersion of motes 10 to 100 feet apart could monitor traffic on a highway or measure moisture levels on farm lands.

Applications for motes are expected to increase with decreasing prices and smaller sizes. In 2005, a single mote was priced in the range of $50 to $100, depending on level of sophistication and was two cubic millimeters in size (smaller than a piece of glitter). By 2010, the price of a mote is expected to fall to $1 and the size will shrink to one cubic millimeter with advances in silicon and fabrication techniques.

MARKETING SMART DUST

Motetronix Technology executives were sensitive to the fact that promising applications of smart dust had to be tempered by the reality of the marketplace and buyer behavior. Therefore, Ajay Gupta charged his marketing team with the responsibility for reviewing buying behavior associated with the adoption of a new technology. The buying process appeared to contain at least six phases: (1) need recognition, (2) identification of available products, (3) comparison with existing technology, (4) vendor or seller evaluation, (5) the decision itself, and (6) follow-up on technology performance. Moreover, there appeared to be several people within the buying organization who would play a role in the adoption of a new technology. For example, top management (such as the president and executive vice presidents) would certainly be involved. Engineering and operations management (e.g., vice presidents of engineering and manufacturing) and design engineers (e.g., persons who develop specifications for new products) would also play a major role. Purchasing personnel would have a say in such a decision and particularly in the vendor-evaluation process. The role played by each person in the buying organization was still unclear to Motetronix. It seemed that engineering management personnel could slow the adoption of smart dust if they did not feel it was appropriate for the products made by the company. Design engineers, who would actually apply fiber-optics in product design, might be favorably or unfavorably disposed to the technology depending on whether they knew how to use it. Top management personnel would participate in any final decisions to use smart dust and could generate interest in the technology if stimulated to do so.

This review of buying behavior led to questions about how to influence an organization's buying process and have its technology used in a company's products or facility. Complicating the discussion was the fact that Motetronix was a comparative unknown in the industry relative to Crossbow Technology and Dust, Inc., two companies that had already commercialized the smart dust technology. In addition, issues still remained related to smart dust reliability, power consumption, and cost/price.

Questions

1 What type of buying situation is involved in the purchase of smart dust, and what will be important buying criteria used by companies considering using smart dust in their products or in their facility?

2 Describe the purchase decision process for adopting smart dust, and state how members in the buying center for this technology might play a part in this process.

3 What effect will perceived risk have on a company's decision of whether to use smart dust in its products or in its facility?

CASE D–7   Callaway Golf: The Global Challenge

Callaway Golf got its start in 1982 when the late Ely R. Callaway invested $400,000 for half interest in a golf club company called Hickory Stick. Callaway-Hickory, later renamed Callaway Golf, had sales of just $22 million in 1990 and was considered a small player as an OEM (original equipment manufacturer) for golf clubs. Callaway Golf made golf history and truly established itself in 1991 with the introduction of a very popular stainless steel driver called the Big Bertha. The Big Bertha driver was soon followed by one of the biggest-selling drivers of all time, the titanium-headed Great Big Bertha. The success of the Big Bertha drivers and fairway woods made Callaway Golf a major player in the golf club business and the oversized titanium driver explosion was on. In 1997, the Biggest Big Bertha was introduced and ahead of its time. This club was so big that many golfers had difficulty making the adjustment to the increased driver head size, and it did not catch on in popularity like the previous Big Bertha products. The Big Bertha name and product line continued with Steelhead, Hawkeye, ERC, C4, and ERC Fusion. By 2003, Callaway sales of drivers, irons, balls, putters, and a very popular line of fairway woods exceeded $814 million, making Callaway Golf one of the big three OEMs in the business of golf.

BUYER BEHAVIOR

Golfers, both pros and amateurs, experiment with drivers, fairway woods, and putters more than other clubs in their golf bags. In fact, many top professionals and amateurs choose to play with their favorite irons for years before changing. Callaway Golf made a cunning decision to enter the club market the way it did in the late 1980s and early 1990s. By introducing drivers and uniquely designed fairway woods, clubs that players often change in the constant quest for distance and accuracy, Callaway Golf quickly became a name and force in the golf club equipment business.

THE GLOBAL GOLF MARKET

The golf industry has a broad and diverse global market. The game is extremely popular around the world. The game and the rules are essentially the same everywhere. Golfers share similar characteristics and interests—a beginning golfer or an avid golfer in the United States is not much different from a beginning golfer or an avid golfer in Australia or Germany.

The professional golf tours have done much to make golf a global sport. Golf enthusiasts from around the world can follow their sport and stars through televised tournaments, daily newspaper coverage, weekly golf journals, monthly golf magazines, and Internet websites. Golf-related websites are among the most popular sites on the Internet. And the Golf Channel on cable television continues to be a strong venue for direct product marketing as well as international event coverage. Golf is truly a global sport. Courses and competitions exist in many countries and on almost every continent—except Antarctica. Professional and amateur players from around the world compete and interact with a high degree of etiquette and sportsmanship. Golfers at all levels share ideas and experiences from the game.

There are differences among global golf markets. Japanese golfers seek out technology and products to compensate for their smaller average stature. Savvy golf equipment manufacturers have developed clubs specifically for the Japanese market with different head shapes, weight, lie angle, and shafts adjusted for the average Japanese golfer's height. And the long or distance ball is very popular. In the United States, distance balls are inexpensive and fairly low-tech. In Japan, distance balls are a premium product, selling for as much as 700 yen, or $70 per dozen. While many U.S. golfers, regardless of ability, seek out the equipment used by professional golfers, Japanese golfers often think they are "not worthy" to use top-caliber equipment.

"In the United States, we talk about the pyramid of influence and how the best players dictate what everyone else wants to buy," says Maki Shinoda of Nike. "But in Japan, you basically need to flip the pyramid upside down." This creates an interesting challenge for golf equipment manufacturers: Technology sells, but what is the best way to position the product for the market so that it does not appear to be "too professional"?

COMPETITION

The golf equipment business is very competitive. Many merchants exist, and the field is constantly changing with new start-ups, mergers, and acquisitions. Major equipment manufacturers include Titleist, TaylorMade, Callaway, and Ping. Adams, Cleveland, Wilson, Mizuno, Nike, and others also compete for a slice of the $4 billion worldwide golf equipment market. Adams Golf has had recent success with product launches, capturing market share in the driver and fairway wood specialty club market. Offering unique technological innovations and premium products, Adams is an example of a company that followed a strategy similar to Callaway. Other well-established club manufacturers have followed Callaway's "bigger is better" philosophy when it comes to the marketing and manufacturing of popular drivers. Cleveland, TaylorMade, Titleist, Ping, and Adams have all designed oversized drivers that have, at one time or another, been the rage with amateurs and professionals around the world. In many respects, today's design and engineering for drivers has been a contest of who can make the longest-driving and most forgiving club that technology and the rules of golf allow. Premium clubs today not only offer technological innovation, forgiveness, power, distance, and accuracy, but they are also pushing the laws of physics and the rules of golf.

CALLAWAY'S INTERNATIONAL MARKETING

For Callaway Golf, the global market is a very big part of its total market for clubs, with about 40 percent of all sales coming from golfers in countries outside of the United States. The severe economic downturn in Japan hit Callaway and other manufacturers hard. Club sales in Japan dropped to 8.2 million in 2003, down from 22 million in 1990. Callaway's first quarter 2004 sales fell behind 2003 quarterly sales in Japan and other Asian countries, though gains were registered in Europe and other non-Asian countries. Still, uncertain economic conditions globally has meant fewer rounds played and, for the most part, relatively little growth in course development and equipment sales. With many avid golfers tempted by new technology and improved products, others choose to forgo new club purchases during periods of tough economic times.

ISSUES

In sports, it is often said that getting to the top is easier than staying there. Callaway Golf is faced with the burdensome task of sustaining its phenomenal growth and market share against competitors in hot pursuit. Fast followers like Adams Golf and others have developed and discounted products that cut into Callaway's mainstay, the driver and fairway wood, or specialty club market. Other big players in the equipment business are also after Callaway's market share and may pose a greater threat to Callaway's long-term success. These companies, including Titleist, TaylorMade, and Ping, are large and strong enough to survive any market slump. They also have the resources to buy up smaller successful companies and the technology to provide popular products.

Technology does drive the industry. In 2004, Adidas-Soloman A.G. (TaylorMade) released a driver with technological innovation unlike any other on the market. TaylorMade's new driver, the r7 Quad, introduced a unique interchangeable weighting system that allows golfers to customize their driver for different course conditions and desired ball flight. International players Sergio Garcia (Spain) and Retief Goosen (South Africa) used TaylorMade's new r7 Quad in early-season victories. Goosen's victory at the 2004 U.S. Open, at the height of the hype of the r7 launch, hit the market like a tidal wave. Callaway and others were left swimming for higher ground as discounting and dumping has changed the market share landscape. Callaway has often resisted discounting its premium product line. Even the success of international LPGA tour star Annika Sorenstam (Sweden), number one in the world, using the innovative carbon composite titanium fusion technology of the ERC Fusion driver and a bag full of Callaway clubs has not helped Callaway win back declining market share in the competitive club market.

Golf's ruling bodies—the United States Golf Association (USGA) in North America and the Royal and Ancient Golf Club of St. Andrews (R&A)—have agreed on limits for driver head size and coefficient of restitution (COR). Adams and Cleveland Golf have recently marketed legal clubs that test right on the limits for head size (460 cc) and COR (.830). Other manufacturers have also released products that have larger head sizes than Callaway products, and thus Callaway has had difficulty competing in the marketplace it once dominated.

The newest and potentially biggest golf market, China, is now emerging, as golf becomes a popular choice for its increasing population of young professionals. Although there are currently only about 1 million Chinese golfers, about 0.1 percent of the population, an annual growth rate of 25 percent is forecast over the next five years. The key to future global growth for the golf equipment industry may be in the budding Chinese market or the growing Indian market, also expected to grow at the same healthy rate as the Chinese market.

Questions

1 What are the pros and cons of a global versus a multidomestic approach to marketing golf clubs for Callaway? Which approach do you feel would have more merit and why?

2 What are some of the significant environmental factors that could have a *major* impact on the marketing of golf clubs internationally? Describe each factor and what the nature of the impact would be.

3 What marketing mix recommendations would you have for Callaway as it attempts to increase its international market share, especially in the Chinese market?

CASE D-8   HOM Furniture: Where Keen Observation Pays

"Some ideas are too good *not* to steal!" The speaker isn't a CIA agent but Wayne Johansen, CEO of HOM Furniture, a group of 13 furniture stores in the upper Midwest. Johansen isn't talking about anything illegal but is describing his approach to doing very practical, commonsense marketing research: visiting dozens of first-class retailers and then weaving the best of the ideas into HOM Furniture's operations. But that gets us ahead of the story.

HOW IT ALL BEGAN

Wayne Johansen's life reads like an entrepreneurial case study. Right out of high school, Johansen started JC Imports, a wholesale import business built around jewelry and leather goods. The decision to add waterbeds to the merchandise mix proved to be a smart one and the import business was soon closed to focus on booming waterbed sales. But all good things must come to an end; waterbeds don't wear out and the target audience of baby boomers was aging. When the market became saturated, Johansen, along with his brother, Rod, and Carl Nyberg converted their Water Bedroom stores to Total Bedroom stores. Ultimately, they wanted to expand into a full-line furniture company, but they needed larger store sizes, more warehouse capacity, and more working capital. So they took the first step in 1991 and HOM Oak and Leather stores were born. In 1997, their ultimate dream became reality as HOM Oak and Leather expanded into HOM Furniture, with sales of $30 million in 1996 growing to over $180 million in 2003.

THE CONSUMER BUYING PROCESS

Success at HOM Furniture has been built upon keen understanding of how consumers buy furniture. Furniture is a product category characterized by "complexity and significant risk," explains Johansen. A furniture purchase must fit into the consumer's overall decorating scheme, coordinating with paint, wallpaper, draperies, and floor coverings. Women are the key decision makers and they believe that their home furnishings make a statement about whether they have good taste and social status. They fear a bad decision, relying more on the expertise of the salesperson and the selection available in the store, rather than on brand names.

HOM Furniture has responded with large and inviting stores in highly visible locations, featuring great selection and knowledgeable salespeople who specialize in a given department. The smell of fresh-baked cookies greets customers as they enter the store, drawing them into a race track–shaped layout of the different store departments. This provides maximum exposure to merchandise and creates an airy, open feeling.

MARKETING INFORMATION AT HOM

Very quickly, Johansen and his partners recognized the value of marketing information. Prior to the launch of HOM Furniture in 1997, they toured 70 of the top 100 U.S. full-line furniture stores to observe the practices that contribute most to success. Some of the successful ideas gleaned from these visits include fresh-baked cookies in the stores, the use of a "house" structure in the center of the stores, and the design of two-level stores.

This benchmarking activity continues today as HOM Furniture participates in a consortium of 14 furniture stores from the United States, Canada, and Mexico. Because the member stores do not directly compete with one another in their geographic area, they are free to share financial statements, sales data, and their best ideas. Meeting three times annually, the participants spend the first day touring the host store and reviewing store advertising. The second day is reserved for the "best idea" contest. Each participant contributes $20 and the best idea takes the pot.

Site location is widely recognized as critical to the success of any retail store. In order to reach a regional audience, HOM Furniture builds stores that are highly visible from the freeways leading into the city from all directions. With analytical assistance from a local newspaper, management can plot the location of all current customers on a map as well as determine the market potential within a given radius for any possible future store location. Assuming that a customer will shop at the HOM store nearest his or her home, HOM management can calculate the extent to which a future store will cannibalize business from existing stores.

This geographic analysis can be merged with MicroVision data from Claritas. MicroVision is a segmentation and consumer targeting system that classifies every U.S. household into 1 of 48 unique market segments, using demographic, lifestyle, socioeconomic, buying, media,

and behavioral characteristics. For any given zip code, MicroVision provides a count of the number of households for each of the 48 market segments identified. This allows HOM's management to build stores in areas that are heavily populated with the types of consumers who like to shop at HOM Furniture stores.

Once the store is in operation, sales and productivity information is closely monitored. Management has easy access to a database that tracks sales by store, by department, by day of the week, and by hour of the day. In addition, the sales generated by each salesperson are recorded on a monthly basis. Productivity analysis is made possible through an electronic sensor mounted on the doorframe of the main entrance to each store to measure "door swings"—a very precise measure of customer visits. With door swing data by store, by day, and by hour, management can use sales per door swing as a measure of productivity and also relate door swings to ads, such as a Sunday insert in the local paper.

After the sale is complete, HOM Furniture wants to make sure that the customer is thoroughly satisfied. On average, a person buys $40,000 of furniture during a lifetime. A satisfied customer is more likely to be a repeat customer, worth thousands of dollars in future business. For that reason, HOM monitors the number of customer calls received and also the percentage of product sold that requires service. Expanding the system for measurement of customer satisfaction is one of Johansen's future priorities.

Questions

1 (*a*) Identify the data sources HOM Furniture uses in its marketing information system. (*b*) Which would you classify as secondary data sources? (*c*) Which would be considered primary data sources?

2 When HOM Furniture advertises, it looks for a resulting spike in sales using their extensive database. (*a*) What are the advantages of this approach? (*b*) What are the possible shortcomings of this approach and how would you address them?

3 Assume that you have been hired as a marketing consultant by HOM Furniture's management. (*a*) What specific types of information should HOM collect to measure customer satisfaction with its stores and services? (*b*) For each type of information you identified in (*a*), how would HOM Furniture make use of that information to improve customer satisfaction?

CASE D–9   The Hummer: A Segmentation Challenge

We've all heard about them—most of us have even seen one. But the odds are that what we've seen on the highway is not the original Hummer or Humvee. The first Hummers were designed for the U.S. Army as a jeep. Constructed of corrosion-proof aircraft aluminum, a chassis made of massive, hollow girders, with hundreds of rivets covering the exterior and interior surface, the original Hummer was a whopping 6 feet 3 inches in height, 15 feet 4 inches long, had giant front tires that were twice the diameter of a passenger car, was capable of splashing through water 30 feet deep, climbing 45-degree inclines, hills, and mountains, and was virtually unstoppable. But let's face it—most consumers do not require this sort of automotive performance.

HISTORY OF THE HUMMER

AM General entered competition for the development of a High Mobility Multi-Purpose Wheeled Vehicle (HMMWV) to meet the demanding standards of the U.S. Army in 1979. At that time, the U.S. Army created a list of objectives for its new vehicle. For instance, the Army wanted a vehicle that could climb a 60-degree grade without bogging down as well as traverse a 40-degree side slope with stability while carrying a two-ton payload. The Army's requirements were for a new kind of vehicle, one that would be versatile, reliable, and easy to maintain. AM General engineers were not told *how* to reach these objectives but rather what was desired in the vehicle. AM General engineers then found unique design solutions to solve the problems created by the performance objectives.

The prototype Hummer was tested in the Nevada desert in July 1980, less than one year after its initial designs were drawn. After extensive testing, the Army awarded three contracts for test vehicles to General Dynamics, Teledyne, and AM General. Within 10 months, AM General delivered its Hummer prototypes to the Army. After five months of testing, the AM General Hummer was judged the superior product and AM General was awarded an initial production contract of 55,000 vehicles over a five-year period.

Since production began in 1983, AM General has sold more than 170,000 Humvees, or Hummers, as it was affectionately nicknamed, to the military. The Hummer replaced several vehicles in the U.S. Army's fleet, including the jeep with its many unique design features. Independent suspension for all four wheels avoids ground clearance limits of most conventional four-wheel drive vehicles. The truck's wide track and well-distributed weight keep the center of gravity low, preventing the truck from tipping over. Tire pressure can be adjusted on the go from 15 psi in soft sand to 30 psi on asphalt to obtain the best traction and handling on changing terrain.

THE CONSUMER MARKET

Arnold Schwarzenegger is reportedly responsible for the consumer version of the Hummer. Shortly after the first Gulf War began, AM General's president received a call from Schwarzenegger expressing interest in buying a Hummer, which eventually spurred development of the first consumer Hummer models.

In December 1999, AM General granted General Motors exclusive worldwide rights to the Hummer brand name as well as all rights to market and distribute the Hummer. The original civilian Hummer was renamed the Hummer H1. H1 sales are about 900 units annually. Today, GM markets the H1, H2, and H2SUT (a pickup version) and is planning to launch the H3 in 2006. AM General continues to manufacture the various military and civilian Hummer models, although newer models, such as the H2, are produced to GM designs and produced by AM General as a contract manufacturer. For example, the H2 is built on a GM Suburban frame.

Consumer prices range from $117,508 for the H1 wagon to the lowest-priced base model H2 that lists for $51,800. Standard equipment on the H2 includes all-wheel drive, ABS 17-inch wheels, heated leather front and second-row seats, power steering, automatic transmission, air conditioning, and a class III trailer hitch with towing capacity of 7,000 lbs. However, even the largest Hummer has limited space. A JD Power and Associates survey of owners complained of scarce passenger and cargo space, cheap workmanship inside, and poor rear-window visibility. And *Consumer Guide* gives the Hummer H1 and H2 low scores in the full-size and luxury SUV categories, respectively. GM plans to make future models more practical, sprucing up interiors and introducing the H3 with a five-cylinder engine that will be more fuel efficient.

What about gas mileage? Dealers say that the military-style vehicle gets 8 to 10 miles per gallon. General Motors states that the Hummer H2 averages 10 to 13 miles per gallon. This compares with 14 to 19 mpg for the Ford Expedition and 13 to 17 mpg for the Chevy Suburban. As one Southern California Hummer dealer put it, "You got a vehicle that weighs 6,500 lbs. and has the aerodynamics of a brick. Fuel economy is not going to be at the top of what it excels at." In fact, gas mileage figures are not posted on Hummer window stickers because the vehicle is so heavy that it is exempt from mileage reporting requirements.

What is the profile of the typical Hummer customer? GM reports that the average H2 buyer is 41, 73 percent are male, 12 percent are Hispanic, and 9 percent African

American. Most buyers have at least two other vehicles. Entrepreneurs (44 percent) and self-employed (50 percent) individuals, not corporate conformists, tend to buy the Hummer. Let's face it. This is not a vehicle to own if you want to be inconspicuous. The Hummer H1 targets a different customer than the H2. The competition for an H1 purchase would include a second home or a big boat.

CHALLENGES

During the summer of 2003, the Hummer H2 was a hot commodity, with buyers willing to pay $10,000 premiums over sticker price and waiting months to take delivery on the vehicles. However, by October 2003, GM was cutting production following five straight months of sales declines. On track to sell 40,000 H2 vehicles in 2004, it now looks as though GM will move just 30,000 units, and inventories have risen to 68 days, about average for the industry but triple what dealers carried in 2003. And the Hummer is not alone. Sales of low-mileage sport utility vehicles such as the Cadillac Escalade dropped 17 percent; the Ford Expedition dropped 33 percent from same month 2003 levels.

With increasing concerns about gas prices and instability in big oil-producing regions such as the Middle East, the popularity of gas-guzzling vehicles is in question. A spokesperson for the Sierra Club put it this way, "The Hummer is the best friend that Exxon ever had." The Union of Concerned Scientists has criticized the automobile industry for not boosting SUV gas mileage when it

has existing technology to do so. Reputedly, the Hummer could be made twice as fuel efficient if GM equipped it with better technology.

In addition, there is a social backlash to SUVs ("selfish urban vehicles") along with the popularity of new, fuel-efficient and very quiet hybrid vehicles as well as a cultural shift about what is cool. The Hummer buyer is the polar opposite of the kind of customer who buys a Toyota Prius, and both are on the margins of U.S. automobile consumers at present. Don't expect to see the kind of customer who has a love affair with SUV performance and its intangible benefits suddenly become a customer who is concerned about the environment and gas mileage.

Questions

1 What types of market segments exist for the Hummer (*a*) in the consumer market and (*b*) in the business-to-business market?

2 What are the pros and cons of the market segments that you identified above? Which market segments should General Motors target given the fall off in demand from the government segment and possibly in some consumer segments?

3 How would GM's marketing mix and positioning differ for its consumer market segments and a business-to-business segment such as targeting the Hummer to logging companies?

CASE D–10   Medtronic in China: Where "Simpler" Serves Patients Better

"I felt tremendous pressure to find markets and technologies to grow the business in other parts of the world," says Bobby Griffin, president of Medtronic Pacing Business. "Ninety-seven percent of Medtronic's products were being sold to 27 percent of the world. I'd read books on China and *BusinessWeek* articles about the success of General Electric and other companies that had gone into China with scaled-down products."

THE MARKET AND THE NEED

Medtronic is the world's leading medical technology company and sells products to alleviate heart arrhythmia and neurological disorders, such as heart pacemakers, defibrillators, and angioplasty balloon catheters. But in the early 1990s, Medtronic sold only a few pacemakers in China, a country of 1.3 billion people. So Griffin interviewed a number of Chinese physicians. Their desires were very clear: They wanted a highly

reliable, basic pacing device that would allow them to serve more people in need. "These doctors were motivated not by greed but by their desire to help and heal their patients," Griffin concluded. "Their relationships with their patients in the hospitals were touching. Instead of talking down to them from a standing position, they would get down on one knee and whisper in the patient's ear."

Griffin also found that only 4,000 cardiac patients a year were implanted with pacemakers in China, a small minority of the patients who needed them. "It was clear that a certain class of people in China could afford almost anything, while most could afford no treatment at all," Griffin said. "Yet more people in China could afford pacing than the populations of Germany and France combined. Of the millions of people living in the coastal cities and provinces of China, those in the middle class had $2,000 in disposable income. Ten thousand television sets were being sold every week, but health care is also vitally important."

THE NEW PACEMAKER FOR CHINA

As Griffin's plane lifted off from the Hong Kong airport, he recalled, "If we could build a pacemaker we could sell in China for $1,000 and still make our margins, we could serve many more people all over the world with a reliable product and still make a profit. I made up my mind to set an audacious goal. I'd shoot for a *radical* cost reduction in the product design."

Back at corporate headquarters, after a "You're crazy, Griffin!" reaction, Medtronic's head of development agreed to support the project. The project also received support from Medtronic's marketing organization: They liked the idea because the company could lead with an inexpensive product that could leverage sales of higher-end products later.

To meet Bobby Griffin's audacious goal, Medtronic chose its Champion pacemaker, a simplified version of the company's existing pacing systems that could meet specifications of cardiologists in China. Mechanical engineering design manager Bill Hooper had been supporting the Champion pacing system through Quest, a special program within the company that funded the work of engineers who wanted to develop projects that wouldn't otherwise receive funding. Hooper observed, "My dream was to see patients in less developed countries restored to full life in ways that had been available for years in more developed countries." His efforts exemplified Medtronic's mission: *To contribute to human welfare by application of biomedical engineering in the research, design, manufacture, and sale of instruments or appliances that alleviate pain, restore health, and extend life.*

Hooper and electrical engineer Larry Hudziak had taken the current sophisticated technology and simplified it. "We wanted to reduce the cost to make it affordable in the Chinese market. By using a proven pacing lead technology for the coil, insulator, electrode and tine, we were able to save substantially. One of the most critical parts of the Champion, the lead wire, needed to flex whenever patients breathed, their hearts beat, or they moved. We chose a lead that had the best reliability of anything we make," Hooper explained.

The Champion design did not include more complex, state-of-the-art features like dual-chamber stimulation, activity sensors, or steroid-eluding leads. The Chinese physicians Bobby Griffin had met with considered these features unnecessary, preferring high quality, low cost, longevity, and ease of use. The design team had to work hard to reduce the cost of the Champion pacemaker, which could translate into a lower selling price. Medtronic engineers also designed the Champion so that it could be programmed externally with a simple magnetic device. By February 1995, the design was complete and the product had been tested.

ON-SITE IN CHINA: A NEW PLANT AND SALESFORCE

Medtronic realized that to ensure quality control, it needed to be directly involved in the production and selling process, and available when physicians implanted the pacemaker. Bill Hooper knew how to design facilities to cut costs, but it required an almost constant presence in Shanghai, where the plant was being built. Over a three-year period, Hooper made 19 trips, and Ron Meyer, vice president of a pacing group, made 26. They reported to each other via e-mail and phone calls. "The routine was grueling," Hooper recalls. "Check into the hotel, unpack, head out to buy water and walk for exercise, then back to your room. It was such a drill."

Building a new plant was not the only challenge facing Hooper and Meyer. Medtronic also needed a salesforce, including experienced heart surgeons, to contact and train Chinese physicians. Furthermore, with the plant located in Shanghai, on the eastern coast of China, they needed a distribution system capable of serving a country roughly the size of the United States (9.6 million square kilometers).

Hooper recalled that these were tough times for both of them: "We both had families. When I was doing algebra with my daughter on the phone in the middle of the night from China, I could remind myself, 'I'm here because of Medtronic's mission and my part in fulfilling that mission.' If I hadn't had that, I would have given up."

Questions

1 Assess Medtronic's decision to develop and market the new Champion heart pacemaker in terms of the following reasons for new-product success: (*a*) points of difference, (*b*) market attractiveness, (*c*) bad timing, and (*d*) economic access to doctors and patients.

2 Discuss the steps of the new-product process as they relate to the Champion Pacemaker.

3 New-product development is important to a company like Medtronic, but it is hard work, and often leads to failure. How can a company encourage its employees to take initiative, make a profit, *and* be ethically and socially responsible?

4 Relate Medtronic's decision to sell pacemakers in China to its corporate mission statement. How does the decision relate to these Medtronic stakeholders: (*a*) shareholders of Medtronic stock, (*b*) Medtronic employees, and (*c*) Chinese patients?

5 Medtronic chose to design and build a new low-priced, highly reliable, reduced-feature heart pacemaker in its Shanghai plant. What are the strengths and weaknesses of this decision from (*a*) a marketing viewpoint and (*b*) an ethical viewpoint?

CASE D–11   Pampered Pooches Travel in Style

Can nothing be too good for man's best friend? Pampered pets can dine on Omaha Steaks' Steak Treats for Pets, 100 percent beefsteak with no additives and preservatives and then finish off with a Frosty Paws soy-based "ice cream" treat for dessert. Fido can recline on a decadent burgundy Versaille loveseat for $285 from Awesome Pet Products while wearing a faux mink coat and rhinestone tiara. If that weren't enough, burgeoning pet services include massage, chiropractic, and even liposuction.

The American Pet Products Marketing Association estimated that $31 billion was spent on pets in 2003, half of that on food. About 62 percent of all U.S. households now own a pet.

Who are these pampered pets? And perhaps more important, who are their owners? There are 77 million cats and 65 million dogs in the United States. Pampered pets are often surrogate children for empty nesters and childless-by-choice couples. In fact, the majority of pet owners (83 percent) consider themselves "mom" or "dad" to their pets. Pets are also considered companions and friends.

American Demographics breaks down pet owners into four key segments: married boomers with no kids, singles/divorced boomer women, young couples with no kids, and seniors. Married boomers without kids are 27 percent more likely than the average American to have a pet and 30 percent more likely than the average American to have more than one pet. More than half (52 percent) of 35–45 married couples without children have a pet; 31 percent have two or more. This segment also spends more money on pets than married couples with children. Among the singles/divorced boomer women segment, 45 percent own a pet. This group is 18 percent more likely than the average American to own a cat.

Young couples with no kids spend more per year on their pets than any other segment. Of young couples with no kids, 52 percent own a pet and 33 percent are more likely than the average American to own more than one pet.

Among seniors, 39 percent of those 55–64 years of age own a pet, and 25 percent of those over 65 own a pet. Seniors are expected to be the group with the fastest expected rate of growth in pet ownership.

Owners of pampered pooches are likely subscribers to such lifestyle magazines as *Animal Fair, Dog Fancy,*

Modern Dog, and *The Bark,* a Berkeley, California–area newsletter started to fight for a leash-free park that has evolved into the *New Yorker* for dog enthusiasts.

One of the hottest parts of the pet market right now is pet travel. Most of these traveling pets are dogs. A 2002 study by the American Pet Products Manufacturers Association found that 16 percent of dog owners travel with their pets, whereas only 2 percent of cat owners do so. The American Animal Hospital Association puts this figure much higher on the basis of a 2001 study that estimated that 68 percent of pets traveled with their pets, a figure more consistent with estimates by specialty pet lifestyle publications. However, readers of pet lifestyle publications are more likely to travel with their pets than pet owners generally.

Websites devoted to identifying pet-friendly accommodations such as pettravel.com and petsonthego.com and books such as AAA's *Traveling with Your Pet* are very popular as devoted pet owners make travel plans.

Traditional hotel and motel companies are increasingly catering to pet owners. Some Hotels and Resorts Worldwide locations (Sheraton, Westin, and W Hotels) offer oversized pet pillows, plush doggie robes, and check-in gift packages that include a pet toy, dog treat, ID tag, bone, and turn-down treat; they even have a licensed dog masseuse on staff. Upscale hotels are more likely to cater to pets and their owners. The Peninsula Chicago has a "pets only" room service menu. At the Beverly Hills Hotel, canine guests get inscribed water bowls, among other amenities.

Pet-products companies are expanding their offerings to move into the pet hospitality area. For example, PetsMart is opening up PetsHotels next to its stores. Starting at $21, PetsHotels provides a private kennel, two walks per day, and supervised playroom time. For a $10 "room" upgrade, you can provide your pet with a television set tuned to the Animal Planet.

Kennels can rival four-star hotels—pet aerobics, manicures, swim lessons—and even conventional kennels have added more upscale services. In fact, kennels have restyled themselves as pet country clubs, pet resorts, or pet care centers. Jim Krack, executive director of the American Boarding Kennel Association, put it this way: "A dog doesn't really care if he's in a place with cement walls or one with wallpaper and a brass bed, but owners today expect the same type of accommodations and services they can get for themselves."

Consider the 31-year-old woman who had her 7-year-old black lab, Daisy, as bridesmaid at her wedding. Then, while the newlyweds were on their honeymoon in Italy, Daisy spent two weeks at the luxurious Paradise Ranch Country Club for Dogs in Sun Valley California at $45 per night. For this bride, nothing is too good for her best friend.

Questions

1 What product attributes and benefits could an upscale hotel provide a pet owner? Are these the same product attributes and benefits provided by an upscale kennel?

2 What strategy would a company like Petco be pursuing by entering the pet hotel market? What strategy would a company like Marriott be pursuing by entering the pet hotel market?

3 What are the pros and cons of (*a*) a multiproduct branding strategy and (*b*) a multibranding strategy in the pet hospitality industry for companies such as (*i*) Petco and (*ii*) Marriott?

4 In what stage of the product life cycle is the pet hospitality industry? An offering such as PetsMart's PetsHotels? Explain and support your answers.

CASE D–12   DigitalThink: Marketing E-Learning Services

"In 1996, two colleagues and I started discussing the possibilities that the Internet was opening up for corporate training," said Umberto Milletti, vice president of marketing and solutions management at DigitalThink. "We realized that we could harness the power of the same technologies that had revolutionized other parts of the business world to help organizations better disseminate skills and knowledge to their people."

Milletti's observation was very insightful. Over the last several decades, computer technology and, more recently, the Internet have changed the way that companies around the world do business. Increasingly powerful computers and software applications help employees work more productively; processes that once were laborious and manual are lightning fast; and geographically dispersed people can communicate and collaborate in cyberspace faster than ever before.

DigitalThink, a company that has grown from 3 employees to more than 400, and was recently ranked twenty-second among the 500 fastest-growing technology companies, is at the forefront of a revolution in corporate training and education services. DigitalThink and other e-learning companies are supplementing, and occasionally replacing, traditional classroom-based training in much of the business world. The effectiveness of e-learning is causing many firms to reconsider their methods of providing training and education to employees, partners, and customers.

MARKET OPPORTUNITIES

Large companies with many locations and dispersed workforces, such as car rental agencies, hotels, airlines, retail stores, banks, and consulting firms, need to train thousands of employees frequently throughout the year.

In the past, employees would gather in central locations for training courses that could last anywhere from a few days to one month. This approach to training and education was very costly and time consuming, and its effectiveness was influenced by inconsistencies in the capabilities of the trainers and the difficulty of requiring the trainers and the students to be in the same location. Using technology-based instruction saves the company time and money by increasing the reliability and effectiveness of the service and by putting the learner in control of the location and the pace of the learning experience. DigitalThink is leading the e-learning movement. Its methods have been shown to compress training time by as much as 50 percent and reduce the cost of development, maintenance, and delivery by 64 percent. A recent study reported that the global market for e-learning has grown at a 100 percent annual growth rate to $33.6 billion in 2005.

HOW DOES DIGITALTHINK ACHIEVE THESE MIRACULOUS RESULTS?

DigitalThink e-learning is tied directly to tangible outcomes. Courses are designed to develop the specific knowledge and skills that employees or salespeople need to do their jobs and to give them the opportunity to test their knowledge and apply what they've learned with a real-world situation or problem that they might encounter on the job. "Learning is most effective when students practice and demonstrate performance in a way that closely matches the performance expected of them," explains Shelly Berkowitz, manager of instructional design at DigitalThink. "We design relevant, realistic practice and assessment activities that require students to solve problems that are as complex as those they encounter in actual work situations."

Trainees can go through the courses at their own pace, allowing people to take as much or as little time as they need. Advanced students can skip over material that they already know and go directly to the exercise or assessment section to test their mastery of the material. DigitalThink e-learning can also be delivered to the learner through different media: on a CD, via a company intranet, or through a browser on the Internet. The Web-based versions of DigitalThink's training courses are the most popular—these allow companies to update and maintain the training program very easily and cost effectively as well as to reach all their employees smoothly and quickly.

THE MARKET

DigitalThink sees its target market as the Global 2000 companies, the largest corporations in the United States and around the world. These companies have the critical mass needed to justify large training programs, as well as continued need for training and retraining. Within these companies, key decision makers with large staffs might include the director of a call center, the vice president of sales, or the chief information officer. Hardware and software manufacturers, travel and leisure companies, major retailers, and other organizations that have typically been dependent on massive instructor-led training efforts are key markets where DigitalThink has had success selling its e-learning products and services. In fact, Digital-Think's current customers include 31 of the Fortune 100 companies and 450 organizations in 158 countries. Specific customer needs vary from ready-made courseware, to custom course development, to comprehensive learning management systems that include virtual classrooms, content management systems, and consulting services.

CUSTOMER EXAMPLES

DigitalThink developed a customized training program for an international airline's baggage and reservations departments. This airline is very geographically dis-

persed, so it did not make sense for it to constantly transport new employees to a central location for training. Also, with the large number of people performing these jobs, the training needs are almost constant. The content of the training is very process oriented, which is one of the best applications for e-learning. The airline and its employees have been pleased with its decision to transition its training program to a technology-based system.

Circuit City is another of DigitalThink's prominent customers. "The e-learning program that we provide to Circuit City is centered around customer service, products that the sales counselors sell, general sales skills, and managerial skills," explains Milletti. DigitalThink has helped Circuit City create more effective, interactive training for its 40,000 associates and managers, which has helped the company realize more than $100 million in cost savings. And the retailer expects to see continued improvement in customer satisfaction and sales.

Questions

1 What are (*a*) the advantages and (*b*) the disadvantages of DigitalThink's technology-based instruction over conventional classroom-based educational services?

2 Given your answer to question 1 above, (*a*) what are the key criteria DigitalThink should use in identifying prospective customers for its service, (*b*) what market segments meet your criteria, and (*c*) what are possible sales objections these segments might have that you have to address?

3 Suppose a large international hotel chain asks Digital-Think to make a proposal to train its thousands of front-desk clerks and receptionists. (*a*) How would you design an e-learning program to train them how to check in a customer? (*b*) How can DigitalThink demonstrate the points of difference or benefits to the hotel chain of its technology-based instruction to obtain a contract to design an e-learning program?

CASE D–13 Health Cruises, Inc.: Estimating Cost, Volume, and Profit Relationships

Health Cruises, Inc., packages cruises to Caribbean islands such as Martinique and the Bahamas. Like conventional cruises, the packages are designed to be fun. But the cruise is structured to help participants become healthier by breaking old habits, such as smoking or overeating. The Miami-based firm was conceived by Susan Isom, 30, a self-styled innovator and entrepreneur. Prior to this venture, she had spent several years in North Carolina promoting a behavior-modification clinic.

Isom determined that many people were very concerned about developing good health habits, yet they seemed unable to break away from their old habits because of the pressures of day-to-day living. She reasoned that they might have a chance for much greater success in a pleasant and socially supportive environment, where good health habits were fostered. Accordingly, she established Health Cruises, Inc., hired 10 consulting psychologists and health specialists to develop a program, and chartered a ship. DeForrest Young, a Miami management consultant, became the chairperson of Health Cruises. Seven of Isom's business associates contributed an initial capital outlay totaling more than $250,000. Of this amount, $65,000 went for the initial advertising budget, $10,000 for other administrative expenses, and $220,000 for the ship rental and crew.

Mary Porter, an overweight Denver schoolteacher, has signed up to sail on a two-week cruise to Nassau, departing December 19. She and her shipmates will be paying an average of $1,500 for the voyage. The most desirable staterooms cost $2,200.

Mary learned of the cruise by reading the travel section of her Sunday newspaper on October 16. On that date, the Pittsford and LaRue Advertising Agency placed promotional notices for the cruise in several major metropolitan newspapers. Mary was fascinated by the idea of combining therapy sessions with swimming, movies, and an elegant atmosphere.

Pittsford and LaRue account executive Carolyn Sukhan originally estimated that 300 people would sign up for the cruise after reading the October 16 ads. But as of November 14, only 200 had done so. Isom and Health Cruises, Inc., faced an important decision.

"Here's the situation as I see it," explained a disturbed Ms. Isom at the Health Cruises board meeting. "We've already paid out more than a quarter of a million to get this cruise rolling. It's going to cost us roughly $200 per passenger for the two weeks, mostly for food. Pittsford and LaRue predicted that 300 people would respond to the advertising campaign, but we've only got 200.

"I see three basic options: (1) we cancel the cruise and take our losses; (2) we run the cruise with the 200 and a few more that will trickle in over the next month; or (3) we shell out some more money on advertising and hope that we can pull in more people.

"My recommendation to this board is that we try to recruit more passengers. There are simply too many empty rooms on that ship. Each one costs us a bundle."

At this point, Carolyn Sukhan addressed the board: "I've worked out two possible advertising campaigns for the November 20 papers. The first, the limited campaign, will cost $6,000. I estimate that it will bring in some 20 passengers. The more ambitious campaign, which I personally recommend, would cost $15,000. I believe this campaign will bring in a minimum of 40 passengers.

"I realize that our first attempt was somewhat disappointing. But we're dealing here with a new concept, and a follow-up ad might work with many newspaper readers who were curious and interested when they read our first notice.

"One thing is absolutely certain," Sukhan emphasized. "We must act immediately if there's any hope of getting more people on board. The deadline for the Sunday papers is in less than 48 hours. And if our ads don't appear by this weekend, you can forget it. No one signs up in early December for a December 18 sailing date."

Isom interrupted, shaking her head. "I just don't know what to say. I've looked over Carolyn's proposals, and they're excellent. Absolutely first-rate. But our problem, to be blunt, is money. Our funds are tight, and our investors are already nervous. I get more calls each day, asking me where the 300 passengers are. It won't be easy to squeeze another $6,000 out of these people. And to ask them for $15,000—well, I just don't know how we're going to be able to justify it."

Questions

1 What is the minimum number of passengers that Health Cruises must sign up by November 20 to break even with the cruise? (Show your calculations.)

2 Should Health Cruises go ahead with the cruise, since 200 passengers had signed up as of November 14?

3 Would it be worthwhile for Health Cruises to spend either $6,000 or $15,000 for advertising on November 20? If so, which figure would you recommend?

4 How realistic are Carolyn Sukhan's estimates of 20 more passengers for the $6,000 advertising campaign and 40 more passengers for the $15,000 campaign?

5 Should Health Cruises consider cutting its prices for this maiden voyage health cruise?

CASE D–14   Little Remedies® Brand: Vetco, Inc.—The Bad News E-mail

Matt Kornberg was a small-business owner with one very large problem—or more precisely—a *very*, very large problem!

As he read the e-mail from one of his best customers and one of the largest discount retail chains in the United States, the news was not good. Two of his best-selling items were on a new list of "discontinued items." In this one brief e-mail, the retailer's digestive-products buyer had just eliminated over $450,000 of his company's annual sales!

Why the sudden decision? This retailer was making room for 45 facings of a new over-the-counter (OTC) anti-gas medicine that was recently "switched" from prescription status. In fact, eight other manufacturers had just received the same bad news from the same retailer: "We need the shelf space and there's just no room left to keep your products in our store."

THE IDEA, THE COMPANY, AND THE MARKET

When Kornberg was a young pharmacist working in Long Island, New York, he was asked many questions by his customers; but a few began to stick out. Frequently, new mothers would ask for saline nasal spray, "because my pediatrician told me to use it for my new baby's stuffy nose." "But I can't seem to find it." "What section of the store is it in?" "Is this the saline that I should buy?" In fact, new mothers were such constant questioners, that Matt kept a small supply of saline right behind the counter.

Saline was a simple product, really just purified salt water. For newborns, saline nasal spray would gently moisten irritated nostrils, promote congestion relief, and help remove nasal mucus. And since most pediatricians avoided prescribing or recommending stronger deconges-tants for infant stuffy noses, saline was clearly the product of choice. The problem was that most saline was packaged in generic looking bottles, and often without an outer carton. Also, package markings were not "mom-friendly." As a re-sult, it was difficult to find the prod-uct on the shelf—and once a mom did find it, she was unsure if this was the product her pediatrician had recommended.

That's how *"Little Noses®* Saline" was born, which led Korn-berg to start his Little Remedies® Company and a whole line of Little Remedies® products. Today there are over 10 different Little Reme-dies products for infants and chil-dren—all of them designed to help mothers (and their kids) with the common ailments of early childhood. Over the years, the brand has distinguished itself by featuring products that contain no unnecessary additives, no artificial coloring dyes, and no artificial flavorings. As shown by the ad on this page, the packaging on the Little Remedies products is attention-getting on a retailer's shelf.

Kornberg may not have known it at the time, but he had a great idea. The pediatric health market was grow-ing, and interest in "natural" products was on the rise—especially from pregnant women. A little research into census data showed that the numbers involved were impressive:

- 4,000,000 babies are born in the United States each year.
- There are 14,000,000 mothers with children 6 years old and under in the United States.

So the market for children's remedies products was huge.

Too Much Gas?
We Make It
All Better!™

When your baby experiences gas pain you want to relieve it as quickly and safely as possible.

Pediatrician recommended Little Tummys® Gas Relief Drops contain the active ingredient *Simethicone*, the #1 choice of pediatricians and pharmacists to safely and quickly relieve gas pain in infants and children.

Best of all, Little Tummys® Gas Relief Drops avoids unnecessary additives and its great berry taste and calibrated dropper ensures easy administration and proper dosing.

Look for Little Tummys® Gas Relief Drops in the gas relief or baby section of your favorite store. You'll both feel better!

- No Alcohol or Saccharin
- No Artificial Flavors or Dyes
- No Harmful Preservatives

Little Remedies® Products
We Make It All Better™
See Our Complete Product Line and *SPECIAL* Offers at www.littleremedies.com

DISTRIBUTION AND PRICING

OTC health products are commonly carried in drug, grocery, and mass-merchant retail stores. OTC products are usually merchandized in "sections" to make it easy for customers to shop and find items quickly and effi-ciently. Little Remedies items are located in the Nasal, Cough/Cold, and Digestive sections of these stores.

Gaining distribution in large retail chains is no easy process—especially for a small company. Getting a retailer to carry a manufacturer's product can often involve "slot-ting fees, advertising allowances, and promotion al-lowances." In today's expensive marketplace, that can mean as much as $30,000 per item with no guarantee that the product will stay on the shelf for any length of time! And once products are approved and actually placed on store shelves, many marketing factors will contribute to their ultimate sales velocity. For Little Remedies prod-ucts, these factors include packag-ing, pricing, advertising support, physician referral, pharmacist re-ferral, and promotion.

Pricing strategies for OTC health products like Little Reme-dies are built around several issues:

- Typical manufacturing margins for the company (and within the industry).
- Typical retail margins for prod-ucts in certain "sections" within the store.
- Retail shelf price of competitive category participants (#1-branded products; secondary branded products; private-label products).

Matt Kornberg's overall strategy was to position the Little Reme-dies line as a "secondary value brand." This meant that the Little Remedies product would be priced less than the #1-branded product, but more than the store's private-label product. In addition, the goal was always to provide "value" through supe-rior product formulation (no unnecessary additives, no artificial coloring or flavoring). Finally, where possible and affordable, the goal was to supply more product—for example, double the ounces per bottle.

THE PROBLEM AND YOUR CONSULTING TASK

Kornberg's two products (*Little Tummys®* Gas Relief Drops and *Little Tummys®* Laxative Drops) each have a good sales history with the retailer. The Gas Relief drops are priced in-between the more expensive #1-branded pediatric gas prod-uct and the retailer's own private-label pediatric gas prod-uct. As a result, many moms find *Little Tummys®* Gas Relief

Drops to be a "good value"—better than private label, and just as good as the #1 brand. And Kornberg is proud of *Little Tummys*® Laxative Drops because they are a unique item in the digestive set: His is the only product available at this retailer for moms with constipated infants and children. Shelf facings of these two Little Remedies products side-by-side will look like the photo on this page.

But what can Kornberg do with this bad news e-mail? How can he get this buyer to change his mind? There is no arguing that the retailer needs the space. And plenty of other manufacturers have quality medicines that are being discontinued. What can he possibly say that will get his items reinstated?

As a consultant to Kornberg and Little Remedies, you need to analyze the situation with the actual data. But you don't have the actual competitive brand names for legal reasons.

The discount retailer that sent the e-mail had reduced the pediatric gas section to just four packages: the #1 brand of pediatric gas relief in 1 ounce and ½ ounce sizes and two facings of its own private-label retail brand (both 1 ounce sizes). The prior year, there had been just one facing of private-label gas relief product. You'll need to assume that shelf space is limited in width to just four packages of shelf facings.

You must also assume that the discount retailer's buyer would *not* totally discontinue the #1 brand or its own private label. Any new scenario you create should assume that there would be at least one package of the #1 brand and one package of private label among the four shelf facings.

Some possible Shelf Set Scenarios (SSS) you might propose include (a) adding back only *Little Tummys*® Gas Relief Drops or (b) adding back both *Little Tummys*® Gas Relief Drops and *Little Tummys*® Laxative Drops—the latter because the discount retailer has neither a #1 laxative drop or its own private-label laxative drop.

Create a compelling selling story for the retailer's digestive buyer that results in reinstatement of at least one of the discontinued items. Your selling story should include a new SSS with rationale for why your proposed new SSS is better than the one currently planned by the buyer.

Questions

1 What is the retailer's goal for the shelf space (a) for this year and (b) for the longer term?
2 What is Little Remedies' goal for the shelf space?
3 Identify (a) the two most logical Shelf Set Scenarios that include Little Remedies products, (b) the corresponding estimated annual profit for the retailer for each, and (c) the estimated annual profit for the retailer from its planned SSS.
4 What impact do the Shelf Set Scenarios have on the consumer (a mother buying these products for her children)?
5 Should the buyer for the discount retail chain add back one or both of the Little Remedies products on the chain's shelves? Why or why not?

PRODUCT	SIZE	RETAILER'S COST	RETAIL PRICE	RETAILER PROFIT PER PACKAGE	RETAILER'S PROFIT MARGIN[†]	12-WEEK ACTUAL UNIT SALES	52-WEEK ESTIMATED UNIT SALES	RETAILER'S ESTIMATED ANNUAL PROFIT
#1 Brand Anti-gas Drops	1 oz	$8.25	$10.90			20,924		
#1 Brand Anti-gas Drops	1/2 oz	$5.25	$6.48			12,187		
Retailer Private-Label Anti-gas Drops*	1 oz	$1.00	$3.68			35,965		
Retailer Private-Label Anti-gas Drops**	1 oz	$1.00	$3.68					
Little Tummys® Gas Relief Drops	1 oz	$4.60	$6.38			17,966		
Little Tummys® Laxative Drops	1 oz	$3.73	$6.43			5,821		

*First Shelf Facing
**Second Shelf Facing (Assume incremental facing increases sales by 10%)
[†]On Retail Price

CASE D–15 Fastenal Company: Bringing Retail Principles to the Wholesale Market

HOW IT ALL BEGAN

The first Fastenal store opened in 1967 in Winona, Minnesota, home town of the company founder and chairman of the board, Bob Kierlin. "We chose the name to indicate our company goal of being a one-stop location for all of a person's threaded fastener needs," said Kierlin. (Threaded fasteners include the wide variety of screws, bolts, and related types of products sold to industrial as opposed to individual homeowner customers.)

"By the end of our first full year of business, we offered roughly 1,000 different items in stock, but most customer inquiries came for items we did not stock for sale. Our first full-year sales were approximately $18,000. We had one delivery vehicle, a 1960 Cadillac with great big tailfins," said Kierlin with a grin.

"It took a while for us to hit our stride, but once we did we grew into a pretty big business," said Kierlin, a humble and unassuming person who is also a master of the understatement. As evidence, consider the following facts and figures that describe Fastenal Company today. What was once a single location company has grown to more than 1,400 store locations, and Fastenal is the largest wholesale fastener distributor in North America. This year, Fastenal's sales will exceed $1 billon, with about 55 percent of sales coming from the threaded fasteners product lines. Furthermore, with its expansion of related industrial and construction product lines, it has become one of the fastest-growing full-line distributors of industrial supply products in North America. Fastenal carries products in 10 broad industrial product categories, including power tools, hydraulic hoses, janitorial supplies, and safety products.

In addition, the company provides support services to complement many of its product lines. For example, if a contractor needs a special length or configuration for a hydraulic hose, they can be custom made by the company's crimping division. Fastenal also provides on-site repair of the power tools it sells and offers its customers

centralized power tool rehabilitation and overhaul service. It also provides a form of fastener-usage consulting service for customers as well. It recently worked with a manufacturer of soda-dispensing equipment and was able to provide assistance in the design phase, eventually cutting the cost of fasteners by nearly 35 percent.

FASTENAL COMPANY OPERATIONS

On a typical day, 140 company-owned trucks and trailers are on the road delivering inventory throughout the company's network, which includes 12 regional hubs located throughout North America. As a general rule, each of the 1,400 stores is supplied by a hub located within 350 miles of the store, but each store has access to any item in the systemwide $250 million inventory on a next-day-delivery basis.

Fastenal currently sells more than 212,000 different threaded fasteners and an additional 236,000 other industrial products and supplies. Individual products within product categories are referred to as stock keeping units, or SKUs. These products are sold to customers in three different markets: the construction market, maintenance repair and operations (MRO) market, and original equipment manufacturer's (OEM) market. Customers in the first two markets either stop by one of the company's stores to make a typical retail type purchase or they are called on by a store outside salesperson, via telephone or an on-site visit. Customers in the OEM market are typically dealt with directly by one of the company's key account sales and support people.

Fastenal also has a number of stores on site for larger customers in each of its three customer categories. For example, "whenever a customer in the construction market has a project over $200 million in size we will install a vendor-managed inventory on site so that project critical supplies will be available when needed," said Fastenal president and CEO Will Oberton.

THE CHALLENGES

"We are in the final stages of completing our branch store conversion project called CSP for customer service project. The remodeled stores will display a selection of our products in a more traditional retail configuration," said Oberton. "This has changed our store site selection process as we are trying to generate more store traffic and drive-by business. As a result of the new site selection process and retail store conversion we may get some nontraditional walk-in customers as well."

How do you manage a business that sells more than 440,000 individual items in 10 broad product categories to a wide variety of buyers, each having a wide range of buying requirements? As Oberton explained,

> You certainly don't try to use a centralized planning approach; instead, decision making is done at the individual store manager level as they know their customers and their customers' needs best. Our store managers actually run their own business. Our goal companywide is to decentralize decision making and put the store manager in charge of everyday decisions involving how to deal with an individual customer. We also expect the store manager to make strategic decisions that affect store operations. Companywide, all stores carry what we call our core offerings, and it is the store manager's job to stock those additional products that their specific customers need. It is the store manager's responsibility to stock those things their customers need in a time critical setting as opposed to what the customer can wait and have brought in from another part of our distribution network. Our motto is "growth through customer service," and our branch managers are the face of Fastenal to our customers and they play a big role in allowing us to continue to grow.

Questions

1   What are the significant marketing and sales opportunities available to Fastenal Company given that it has 1,400 stores located throughout North America? In contrast, Fastenal's major national competitors have stores only in major metropolitan areas and as a result it uses its Internet and catalog divisions to provide sales to customers who are not able to visit its stores in person.

2   Describe three specific things that Fastenal has done to respond to the unique buying requirements of the customers in its three markets.

3   A homeowner who plans to work on a weekend home improvement project comes to the counter late Friday afternoon after spending some time looking at the product displays and asks the store manager the following question—"I have been looking at your cordless drills and I was wondering why all of your drills are so much more expensive [her exact words] than any of the drills I saw advertised in a recent Home Depot ad in the newspaper?" What do you think the store manager should say in response to her question?

CASE D–16 Dell Inc.: A Leader in Supply Chain Management

Dell is the largest direct seller of computers in the world and one of the top global PC manufacturers. Dell had more than $41.4 billion in sales in 2004, a 17.1 percent annual increase in sales. It offers desktops, notebooks, network servers, peripherals, and software. Recently, Dell has added consumer electronics, including digital music players and LCD television/computer monitors. More than 90 percent of Dell's sales are to businesses and governmental customers. The company's success is attributed in large part to its effective use of supply chain management.

Supply chain management is what it's all about at Dell. Dell has closely aligned its suppliers with its direct channel strategy, resulting in dramatic improvements in inventory management and control. Inventories are kept at ultra-low levels, one-tenth that of its competitors. A typical Dell factory runs with about five or six hours worth of inventory on hand. This is important in an industry where component costs can decline 30 to 35 percent per year, which helps Dell take advantage of lower anticipated inventory costs in the future as well as minimizing the risk of holding obsolete parts in inventory. In addition, Dell has a very favorable cash conversion cycle. This means that Dell gets paid faster than it pays out to vendors.

No less significant have been Dell's efforts to work with vendors to reduce vendor cycle times—the time that elapses from Dell placing an order to a supplier to receiving that order in a Dell manufacturing facility. Dell communicates with its suppliers and supply chain partners through "Platinum Supplier" web pages. These pages provide each vendor with information on Dell's forecasted demand for the vendor's products, share production schedules, and allow for e-mail communication to make adjustments and changes.

The Dell website (www.dell.com) allows customers to shop online. Different online stores are available for different types of customers, such as education, government, home/home office, and businesses. Shoppers can select the items they want and place them in their shopping basket. Once the order has been submitted, the website has the capability to check delivery dates and to even monitor the status of the order with its online tracking system. More than 50,000 business customers use the Dell online purchasing and information portal.

Since 1996, Dell has provided its top corporate customers its "Premier Pages" program. Beyond mere customer service or e-commerce, the Dell Premier Page empowers organizations to take control. The Dell Premier Page is a website that is personalized specifically for your company and will include a customized online computer store where you can configure your system; the prices you see are the prenegotiated contract prices already agreed with your organization. You will know instantly what the system will cost, and you can place your order online.

Dell integrates all its electronic commerce and communication systems. It uses browser and Internet/Intranet technology as the interface for all applications. This makes it possible for every PC in the world to interact with Dell.

Dell utilizes decision support applications for modeling and simulating materials and factory scheduling to improve supply chain efficiency. For example, Dell can look out hours or days in advance, match this up with materials flow, and based on this information, optimize a manufacturing plan to execute in the factory.

What does this all mean for the customer? Better service and lower costs—value that gives Dell an edge in the marketplace.

Questions

1 Explain how Dell's approach to supply chain management satisfies the logistical objectives of minimizing logistics costs while maximizing customer service.
2 What are the supply chain management implications for Dell's competitors that primarily utilize an indirect channel strategy? What supply chain and marketing recommendations do you suggest for Dell given the competitive environment?
3 How does supply chain management relate to the marketing concept at Dell?

CASE D–17   Nordstrom, Inc.: Retailing in a Competitive Environment

Company lore says that John Nordstrom founded the department store that bears his name today using his stake from the Alaska gold rush. Whether the story is fact or fiction, the philosophy behind the company has made its success one of the real gold nuggets in U.S. retailing.

THE COMPANY

Started in Seattle in 1901 as a shoe store by Swedish immigrant John Nordstrom and a partner, Carl F. Wallin, the business prospered. In 1928, John Nordstrom sold his stake in the company to his three sons, Everett, Elmer, and Lloyd. Wallin sold his stake the following year. By 1959, Nordstrom was the largest independently owned shoe store in the United States. Nordstrom operated 27 stores in 1963. That same year Nordstrom acquired Best's Apparel, a decision that moved Nordstrom beyond shoes and launched it into women's fashions.

The third family generation took over Nordstrom management in 1970. At that point Nordstrom offered not only shoes but also apparel and accessories for the entire family. Although Nordstrom went public as Nordstrom, Inc., in 1971, the Nordstrom family still retains controlling interest in the company. The fourth generation of the family now manages the company.

Nordstrom has grown from a single shoe store to more than 149 U.S. stores in 27 states, including 93 full-line fashion specialty stores, 49 Nordstrom Rack stores, as well as more than 31 international boutiques and stores. Nordstrom also has an online shopping presence (www.nordstrom.com) to offer additional convenience to current and new customers. Expansion has moved it from the West Coast and Seattle area where Nordstrom has had a major presence to strategic locations throughout the country. Among the many new stores planned to open between 2005 and 2006 are those in Atlanta, Georgia (Phipps Plaza), Dallas, Texas (NorthPark Center), San Antonio, Texas (The Shops at La Cantera), and Palm Beach Gardens, Florida (The Gardens Mall). Nordstrom stores are generally located in major or regional malls and feature a wide selection of apparel and shoes for men, women, and children. Nordstrom stores may include a gift department and often a small restaurant. Nordstrom does not carry furniture, linens, housewares, or electronics—items often found in department stores.

THE IDEA

The hallmark of Nordstrom is service. The initial philosophy of the two founders, still guiding Nordstrom today, was to offer the *very best* service, selection, quality, and value to the customer. This commitment to exceptional customer service has been combined with a managerial orientation that encourages and supports an entrepreneurial spirit among employees to react to customer needs.

Extraordinary tales are told of sales associates who went the extra mile to satisfy the customer. Reportedly a customer fell in love with a pair of Donna Karan slacks that had just gone on sale at the Nordstrom store in downtown Seattle. The salesperson, unable to track down the slacks at any of the other five Seattle area stores, secured some petty cash from her department manager, ran across the street to the Frederick and Nelson department store where she bought the slacks at full price, and returned triumphantly to Nordstrom to sell them to the customer at the Nordstrom sale price.

Another fabled story is of a loyal Nordstrom customer who died with her Nordstrom account $1,000 in arrears. Nordstrom not only settled her account but also sent flowers to the funeral.

Nordstrom salespeople make customers feel special. You won't find Nordstrom customers running to another part of the store to find a gift box (gift boxes are provided, complete with gift card and complimentary bow, in the department in which you make your purchase). One surprised father found that the Nordstrom's men's room had a changing table with complimentary diapers when he went inside to change his young son.

It is not unusual for a customer to receive a thank-you note from your Nordstrom salesperson, or phone calls or notes concerning new merchandise of particular interest to them. Salespeople keep customer books listing customer information such as likes and dislikes, sizes, and past purchases. This allows the salesperson to notify customers when merchandise arrives that could be of interest. One salesperson had the challenge of selling different "looks" to 40 different partners within the same 120 attorney office. It simply wouldn't do for the attorneys to show up in the office with the same suit!

Nordstrom is known not only for its salespeople but also for its generous guarantee return policy and welcoming, comfortable, and hassle-free store designs. One pleased spouse of a devoted Nordstrom customer wrote, "Of all the stores, Nordstrom was best. They gave a husband a place to rest."

THE ISSUES

In an increasingly competitive environment, Nordstrom's emphasis on building customer loyalty and retaining customers provides an advantage. While Nordstrom provides customers with what they consider an unsurpassed commitment to quality and value, increasing price competition and price-conscious consumers may be a threat.

Nordstrom's June 2004 preliminary year-to-date sales were estimated at $2.7 billion, up 13.5 percent. Year-to-date same store sales were up 10.5 percent during this same period compared to 2003.

Primary competition for Nordstrom could come from popular specialty stores such as Talbots or Ann Taylor for women's clothing; Brooks Brothers for men's clothing; Joseph Banks, Abercrombie and Fitch, and J. Crew for both men and women; and Kids Talbot and Gymboree for children. In addition, Nordstrom recognizes The Gap and Banana Republic as competitors. Because apparel specialty stores focus on more narrow product lines such as professional apparel, sportswear, or casual wear or by type of customer, the competition can be very diverse. In addition, traditional department stores such as Marshall Fields, Bloomingdale's, Nieman Marcus, and Saks are primary competitors. Department store competitors and specialty store competitors vary depending on the particular market and geographic location since many are regional rather than national in scope. It is worth noting that Nordstrom will experience competition not only from specialty stores for particular product lines (e.g., shoes) but also from stores offering broader lines such as traditional department stores. Continued geographic expansion can provide Nordstrom with additional opportunities for growth but also expose it to new competitors that may attempt to imitate Nordstrom's famous service and quality.

Questions

1 How would Nordstrom be classified as a retail outlet in terms of form of ownership, level of service, and merchandise line?

2 What type of retail position does Nordstrom occupy? Who do you see as its primary competitors, given this position?

3 How do you reconcile Nordstrom's growth and success with the fact that department stores as a category are in the maturity stage of the retail life cycle? What implications are there for Nordstrom given the maturity of the category as well as the wheel of retailing concept?

CASE D–18 McDonald's Restaurants: An IMC Program to Reach Different Segments

"McDonald's outstanding success in Russia is a tribute to our Russian employees, suppliers, and, of course, our customers," comments George A. Cohon, senior chairman, McDonald's in Russia. It all started in 1976 at the Olympic Games in Montreal with a chance meeting between Cohon, who was then senior chairman of McDonald's Canada, and members of the Soviet Olympic delegation.

Fourteen years and countless meetings later, the 700-seat Pushkin Square restaurant in Moscow opened

on January 31, 1990. The Pushkin restaurant still is the busiest McDonald's in the world, having served more than 77 million customers during the first 11 years since its opening. But competition from Russian quick-service restaurant operators, such as Rostiks and Russian Bistro, is increasing. Therefore, the McDonald's team must continue to develop effective means of communicating with present and prospective customers.

ABOUT McDONALD'S IN RUSSIA

The amount of food McDonald's has served in Russia is staggering. Consider that in its first 11 years of operations in Russia, McDonald's has served:

- More than 300 million customers, over twice the 146 million population of Russia.
- More than 66 million Big Mac™ sandwiches, that if put side by side would be longer than the 3,476-kilometer diameter of the moon!

McDonald's currently has over 100 restaurants in Russia, from Moscow and St. Petersburg to Nizhny Novgorod and Samara. McDonald's employs more than 6,000 Russians, or about 100 for each new restaurant that opens. More than 70 managers have successfully graduated from its "Hamburger University" training course held at McDonald's head office in Chicago, part of the 2,000 hours of training they each receive. McDonald's in Russia also operates McComplex, a one-of-a-kind food-processing and distribution facility located in Moscow, which supplies products to restaurants not only in Russia but also in Germany, Ukraine, Belarus, Austria, and the Czech Republic. It features dairy, bakery, pie, liquid, and meat lines and has its own quality assurance laboratories to ensure that McDonald's strict food quality standards are met. McDonald's in Russia sources more than 75 percent of the raw ingredients it needs from over 100 independent suppliers in Russia and the Commonwealth of Independent States (CIS).

McDONALD'S COMMUNITY EFFORTS

McDonald's has a philosophy of "giving back to the communities in which we serve" in the 120 countries in which it operates. In Russia, Ronald McDonald Children's Charities (Russia) operates the Ronald McDonald Centre, a sports and play facility for physically and mentally challenged children. Located in Moscow, the Ronald McDonald Centre hosts more than 1,500 children a week, conducting music, computer, and gym classes. In addition, McDonald's in Russia contributes to various charitable children's organizations to purchase items such as medical supplies and transportation equipment. Since opening 11 years ago, McDonald's in Russia has contributed more than $5 million U.S. to benefit Russian children in need.

WHAT McDONALD'S MARKETS AND WHAT CUSTOMERS LOOK FOR

McDonald's restaurants were founded and continue to operate worldwide on the basis of the formula, Q, S, C, and V: quality, service, cleanliness, and value. The simple menu ensures convenience and quick service. McDonald's is the favorite restaurant of many Russian families because McDonald's serves a high-quality meal, in a clean environment, with a smile, at a price families can afford.

Customers all over the world count on McDonald's for consistent taste and high-quality products, no matter where the restaurant is located. The McDonald's quality assurance program ensures that only the best quality products are served to its customers. This program begins with ensuring that only top-quality ingredients are used, that each food item is prepared in a consistent manner, and that the final product meets McDonald's exacting quality standards. For example, the components of a McDonald's Big Mac sandwich in Russia will undergo more than 98 quality checks before the final sandwich is presented to the customer. This ensures that every Big Mac sandwich tastes the same whether it is ordered by a customer in London, Tokyo, or Moscow.

McDonald's offers a curious marketing dilemma. Although the same meals are served to all customers, these same customers may be looking for strikingly different eating experiences on their restaurant visits. For example, a busy manager who only has enough time to "grab a quick lunch" is seeking a different eating experience than a young couple with a six-year-old child who is celebrating a special occasion. McDonald's also practices an "act local" strategy, which allows its restaurants to cater to local tastes and laws. For example, its restaurants in Germany and France can serve beer, something prohibited in the United States.

DESIGNING AN INTEGRATED MARKETING COMMUNICATIONS (IMC) PROGRAM

These diverse customer segments, with their very different reasons for visiting a McDonald's restaurant, pose a special challenge for a McDonald's marketing manager responsible for designing and implementing an effective integrated marketing communications (IMC) program. Some of the key initial questions include:

- What are the key market segments that McDonald's might be trying to reach?
- What might each segment look for when it chooses to visit McDonald's?
- What appeals and messages might be used to attract each of these segments?
- What combination of promotional mix elements (advertising, personal selling, public relations, sales promotion, and direct marketing) could be used to reach each segment?

The decisions a McDonald's marketing manager must make become more complicated because the IMC program may vary from city to city. If McDonald's is entering a new city with its first restaurant, an IMC may be very costly. If McDonald's is adding several more restaurants in Moscow, the IMC costs can be spread across the more than 20 outlets it promotes.

Questions

1 Consider these four distinct market segments for McDonald's meals in Russian cities in which it has outlets: a family with young children, busy businesspeople, an older couple, and foreign tourists who are already familiar with McDonald's. For each segment (*a*) identify the special benefit or appeal McDonald's has to offer and (*b*) compose a 10- to 12-word promotional message that might be used to reach it.

2 For the first McDonald's restaurant to open in a city, what element of an integrated marketing communications (IMC) program might be used to reach (*a*) a family with young children and (*b*) busy businesspeople?

3 For the McDonald's restaurants in Moscow, what element of an integrated marketing communications (IMC) program might be used to reach (*a*) an older couple and (*b*) foreign tourists?

CASE D–19   Volkswagen: The Drivers Wanted Campaign

Volkswagen's comeback in the United States is an amazing marketing story. VW demonstrated that it was possible to recover from a poor reputation with exciting new automobile designs combined with a lively and engaging promotional program. The promotional program's success was due to creating a unified image for the umbrella brand while also developing the personalities of each of its separate car models.

VW HISTORY

Volkswagen originally designed the Beetle in pre–World War II Germany as a people's car—*volks* ("people") *wagen* ("car"). It provided dependable, reliable, and economical transportation. The car was first sold in the United States in 1949 with a list price of $800. The car was a commercial success around the world with more than 21 million built, more than any other car in history. It was one of the best-selling and most-loved cars in U.S. auto history. However, by 1979 VW had discontinued sales of the Beetle in the United States. Why?

Volkswagen automobiles had personality—the cuddly Beetle, the counterculture Microbus—but increasingly began to seem dowdy and unpretentious, inconsistent with VW's attempts to reposition itself and its brands as more upscale. Also, many original designs were unlikely to meet growing U.S. safety standards as well as increasing performance standards.

Volkswagen's U.S. sales, at their peak in 1970 at 570,000 cars, fell to only 49,500 in 1993. Many wrote off Volkswagen and expected the company to go the way of Renault and Fiat in the U.S. automotive market. However, by 1999 Volkswagen sales had leapt to 316,000 cars.

THE COMEBACK

VW unveiled its new Beetle concept car at the 1994 Detroit Automobile Show. Although the car wasn't scheduled for shipment for two more years, the excitement and anticipation of the Beetle got buyers into showrooms to check out the redesigned Golfs, Passats, and Jettas.

Redesigning cars wasn't enough. Volkswagen unrolled a dynamite advertising campaign using Boston-based Arnold Worldwide. Arnold Worldwide won countless advertising awards for its Volkswagen "Drivers Wanted" campaign, including honors from the Association of Independent Commerical Producers, Clios, Addys, ANDYs, Effies, and Cannes Lions.

How did Arnold Worldwide reinvigorate the Volkswagen brand? It started with research. Why did people buy Volkswagen? What made Volkswagen buyers unique? Research showed that there was a particular personality type that was predisposed to buying Volkswagen. The "Drivers Wanted" campaign targeted this psychographic: "On the road of life, there are passengers and there are drivers." The Volkswagen customer is a driver. They're different. They like to take a curve, push the speed envelope a little, take the long way home. Volkswagen customers think differently, and they want a driving experience that delivers on both their emotional and performance expectations of an affordable, German-engineered driving experience.

Volkswagen has had a number of notable advertisements under its "Drivers Wanted" campaign. One was the 2002 award-winning classic "Bubble Boy." Accompanied with the ELO music "Mr. Blue Sky," this television ad shows the day-in and day-out grind of a Bill Briggs and the promise of the freedom and blue sky of the new Volkswagen Beetle convertible. The 2004 "Leaf" commercial shows a leaf that hitches a ride on a Passat. Again, the advertisement tells a story without words and to compelling musical accompaniment that engages the viewer. "Squares," features numerous square shapes, such as a clock and a piece of toast, and then finally the unique and different shape of the Beetle; the ad grabs viewers' attention with its rapid fire, artistic "squares" and pulsing music. To view these and other Volkswagen ads, check out www.vw.com/commercials/index.html.

What has the "Drivers Wanted" campaign meant for Volkswagen? Arnold Worldwide estimates that the campaign has created $1 billion in incremental value for Volkswagen—$500 million from incremental unit sales above and beyond Volkswagen's most optimistic sales forecasts, $350 million in profits from price premiums, and $150 million in savings from discounts that Volkswagen did not have to make to move its products. This does not include the value of significant improvements in Volkswagen's unaided brand awareness, brand opinion, unaided purchase consideration, and ad recall. According to proprietary tracking from Volkswagen, unaided purchase consideration is up 225 percent and brand loyalty is up 73 percent. Not only that, but "Drivers Wanted" is the most recognized automotive tag line in North America.

The latest Volkswagen ads extend the "Drivers Wanted" message to the "Drive It. You Get It." These ads are a departure from the arty, "less is more" ads. With dialogue and an enthusiastic VW salesperson riding along with people test driving Volkswagens, the message is "check out the engineering features and driving benefits of the Volkswagen models." The humor is less subtle and the ads are less engaging than the earlier "Drivers Wanted" ads. However, the objective is different. Volkswagen of America sales for 2003 were about 303,000 units, 11 percent lower than in 2002, and 2004 sales are struggling. Volkswagen is offering rare incentives such as 0.9 financing and improved leasing terms to boost sales until the new 2005 Passat and Jettas are available. Even the acclaimed Touareg SUV is included in the incentive program. Good advertising is only part of the formula for a successful marketing effort.

Questions

1 What were the primary promotional objectives for Volkswagen at the beginning of the "Drivers Wanted" campaign? What are Volkswagen's current promotional objectives? How do you expect the promotional objectives for the overall Volkswagen brand and for specific car models, such as the Jetta or Touareg, to change over time?

2 What do you feel are the most valid measures for assessing the success of the Volkswagen advertising campaign? Explain why you feel that these are the best means of determining effectiveness.

3 Volkswagen's promotional program has heavily emphasized a pull promotional strategy versus a push promotional strategy. Why? Is this emphasis likely to change over time?

CASE D–20   Manor Furniture: Making Promotion Trade-Offs

Edward Meadows, president of Manor Furniture, met with representatives of Kelly, Astor & Peters Advertising (KAP) and Andrew Reed, Manor's vice president of marketing and sales, to discuss the company's advertising program for 2004. The KAP representatives recommended that Manor Furniture increase its advertising in shelter magazines (such as *Good Housekeeping* and *Better Homes and Gardens,* which feature home improvement ideas and new ideas in home decorating) by $300,000 and maintain the expenditures for other promotional efforts at a constant level during 2004. The rationale given for the increase in advertising was that Manor Furniture had low name recognition among prospective buyers of furniture, and it intended to introduce new styles of living and dining room furniture. Reed, however, had a different opinion as to how Manor Furniture should spend the $300,000. He thought it was necessary to: (1) hire additional salespeople to call on the 30 new retail stores to be added by the company in 2004, (2) increase the funds devoted to cooperative advertising, and (3) improve the selling aids given to retail stores and salespeople.

THE COMPANY

Manor Furniture is a medium-sized manufacturer of medium- to high-priced living and dining room furniture. Sales in 2003 were $50 million. The company sells its furniture through 1,000 furniture specialty stores nationwide, but not all stores carry the company's entire line. This fact bothered Meadows because, in his words, "If they ain't got it, they can't sell it!" The company employs 10 full-time salespeople, who receive a $50,000 base salary annually and a small commission on sales. A company salesforce is atypical in the furniture industry because most furniture manufacturers use selling agents or manufacturer's representatives who carry a wide assortment of noncompeting furniture lines and receive a commission on sales. "Having our own sales group is a policy my father established 30 years ago," noted Meadows, "and we've been quite successful having people who are committed to our company. Our people don't just take furniture orders. They are expected to motivate retail salespeople to sell our line, assist in setting up displays in stores, coordinate cooperative advertising plans, and give advice on a variety of matters to our retailers and their salespeople."

In 2003, Manor spent $2.45 million for total promotional expenditures, excluding the salary of the vice president of marketing and sales. Promotional expenditures were categorized into four groups: (1) sales expense and administration, (2) cooperative advertising programs with retailers, (3) trade promotions, and (4) consumer advertising. Cooperative advertising allowances are usually spent on newspaper advertising in a retailer's city and are matched by the retailer's funds on a dollar-for-dollar basis. Trade promotion is directed toward retailers and takes the form of catalogs, trade magazine advertisements, booklets for consumers, and point-of-purchase materials such as displays for use in retail stores. Also included in this category is the expense of trade shows. Manor Furniture is represented at two trade shows a year. Consumer advertising is directed to potential consumers through shelter magazines. The typical format used in consumer advertising is to highlight new furniture and different living and dining room arrangements. Dollar allocation for each program in 2003 was as follows:

PROMOTIONAL PROGRAM	EXPENDITURE
Sales expense and administration	$ 612,500
Cooperative advertising	1,102,500
Trade advertising	306,250
Consumer advertising	428,750
Total	$2,450,000

THE INDUSTRY

The household wooden furniture industry is composed of more than 5,000 firms. Industry sales at manufacturers' prices were $10 billion. California, North Carolina, Virginia, New York, Tennessee, Pennsylvania, Illinois, and Indiana are the major U.S. furniture-producing

areas. Although Ethan Allen, Bassett, Henredon, and Kroehler are well-known furniture manufacturers, no one firm captured more than 10 percent of the total household wooden furniture market.

The buying and selling of furniture to retail outlets centers around manufacturers' expositions at selected times and places around the country. At these marts, as they are called in the furniture industry, retail buyers view manufacturers' lines and often make buying commitments for their stores. However, Manor's experience has shown that sales efforts in the retail store by company representatives account for as much as half the company's sales in a given year. The major manufacturer expositions are held in High Point, North Carolina in October and April. Regional expositions are also scheduled in June through August in locations such as Los Angeles, New York, and Boston.

Company research on consumer furniture-buying behavior indicated that people visit several stores when shopping for furniture, and the final decision is made jointly by a husband and wife in about 90 percent of furniture purchases. Other noteworthy findings are as follows:

- Eighty-four percent of buyers believe "the higher the price, the higher the quality" when buying home furnishings.
- Seventy-two percent of buyers browse or window shop in furniture stores even if they don't need furniture.
- Eighty-five percent read furniture ads before they actually need furniture.
- Ninety-nine percent agreed with the statement, "When shopping for furniture and home furnishings, I like the salesperson to show me what alternatives are available, answer my questions, and let me alone so I can think about it and maybe browse around."
- Ninety-five percent get redecorating ideas from shelter magazines.
- Forty-one percent have written to order a manufacturer's booklet.
- Sixty-three percent feel they need decorating advice for "putting it all together."

BUDGETARY ISSUES

After the KAP Advertising representatives made their presentation, Reed again emphasized that the incremental $300,000 should not be spent for consumer advertising. He noted that Manor Furniture had set as an objective that each salesperson would make six calls per year at each store and spend at least four hours at each store on every call. "Given that our salespeople work a 40-hour week, 48 weeks per year, and devote only 80 percent of their time to selling due to travel time between stores, we already aren't doing the sales job," Reed added. Meadows agreed but reminded Reed that the $300,000 increment in the promotional budget was a maximum the company could spend, given other cost increases.

Questions

1 How might you describe furniture buying using the purchase decision process described in Chapter 5?

2 How might each of the elements of the promotional program influence each stage in the purchase decision process?

3 What should Manor's promotional objectives be?

4 How many salespeople does Manor need to adequately service its accounts?

5 Should Manor Furniture emphasize a push or pull promotional strategy? Why?

CASE D–21   Crate and Barrel: Multichannel Marketing

Chicago-based Crate and Barrel started as a one-store operation in 1962. Gordon and Carole Segal returned from their honeymoon in Europe with a variety of unique and affordable designs for their home. Recognizing that there was no one addressing the need for those with "more taste than money," they took out a lease on an old elevator factory and Crate and Barrel was born. The entrepreneurs were so excited about the new venture that only moments before the store opened, they realized that they had forgotten to get a cash register. A simple box had to serve.

THE COMPANY

Crate and Barrel has grown to more than 125 stores with 6,000 sales associates. Its 2003 sales were $865 million, a 12.3 percent annual increase. Crate and Barrel stores, catalogs, and website offer a wide variety of household items: furniture, lighting, rugs, products for bed and bath, dinnerware, flatware, cookware, kitchenware, linens, food, and gifts. In 1998, Otto Versand, the world's largest mail-order merchant, acquired a majority stake in Euromarket Designs Inc., which does business as the Crate and Barrel brand.

Crate and Barrel competes in the retail home furnishings and housewares industry with such well-known names as Pottery Barn, Williams-Sonoma, Pier 1 Imports, and Restoration Hardware. What makes Crate and Barrel special? It carved out a unique niche with more modern styling and brighter colors than its competitors. About one-third of the merchandise is unique to Crate and Barrel. But more important, Crate and Barrel offers a wide selection of well-designed products that provide good customer value.

MULTICHANNELS

Crate and Barrel has successfully utilized multiple channels to make its products available to customers. The company sends out more than 15 million brightly colored catalogs annually. The catalogs are just plain fun to look through. For the most complete selection of products, check out the Crate and Barrel website, www.crateandbarrel.com. Product offerings are arrayed by category so customers can browse or can visit the gift ideas or bridal registry pages to select a purchase. Unlike the catalog, the website allows customers to zoom in on items and check out specs. Crate and Barrel customers can opt-in to e-mail alerts of new product offerings and sales.

Purchase can be made in one of the many retail stores, online, by mail, or by the toll-free phone line. Crate and Barrel even offers its own credit card to facilitate purchases.

The company has made significant investments in enterprise marketing systems to manage its customer database and direct-mail campaigns. The system allows Crate and Barrel to effectively design, execute, and assess the results of cross-channel marketing efforts. A Crate and Barrel customer can spot a set of Marimekko towels in the catalog, order the towels and matching bedding from the website, and easily stop in to a Crate and Barrel store to physically test and compare wood and metal beds to complete a purchase.

Questions

1 How does Crate and Barrel facilitate consumer purchases with its multichannel strategy?

2 What are the six Cs of e-commerce, and how does Crate and Barrel address each of these?

3 Given that all of its major competitors also attempt to utilize multiple channels, in what ways could Crate and Barrel create a competitive advantage for itself with its multichannel strategy?

CASE D–22   BP Connect: Gasoline, Convenience, and . . . Just-Baked Bread

"Before developing BP Connect™, we did extensive research to find exactly what consumers wanted in a convenience and fuel store," says Jack Burdett, senior vice president of retail marketing for BP plc.

Burdett is referring to a full-scale prototype of BP Connect's 4,200-square-foot convenience food-gasoline station constructed in an Atlanta warehouse in July 2000. Reactions of U.S. consumers touring the Atlanta prototype were overwhelmingly positive. BP spent $7 million developing the BP Connect concept and will spend $4.4 billion during the next four years to update old or build new BP Connect stations worldwide. In December 2000, BP Connect outlets opened in London, England, and Lisbon, Portugal, to enthusiastic reviews. The first BP Connect stations in the United States opened in 2001 in Indianapolis, Cleveland, and Atlanta.

THE COMPANY

BP plc—often shortened to simply BP—is the world's largest producer and marketer of petroleum products. BP is also the largest gasoline retailer in the United States with 14,700 stations, or about 15 percent of the market. Since 1998, BP has spent $120 billion to acquire Amoco, ARCO, and Burmah Castrol, making it the largest retailer of petroleum products in the world. At the end of 2004, BP served 13 million customers per day globally with 28,000 branded retail sites, including 950 ampm™ convenience stores.

Initially, Amoco was going to be the brand identity used in the United States. However, according to Doug Ford, BP's CEO for retailing and marketing worldwide, that decision was changed after BP conducted focus groups. Consumers preferred the new BP logo and color scheme but still wanted the quality products that Amoco sells. Therefore, while BP will rebrand its BP and Amoco sites, it will continue to offer branded Amoco gasoline. However, because ARCO's customers are different than BP's or Amoco's, BP will also retain the very successful *ampm* convenience stores and ARCO-branded gasoline stations.

TRENDS IN CONVENIENCE STORE AND GASOLINE RETAILING

Several major trends currently affect both traditional convenience store and petroleum retailing worldwide:

- *Mergers and acquisitions.* During the past several years, BP and other major oil firms, such as Exxon (Mobil) and Total (PetroFina & Elf), have merged with or acquired one or more of their competitors.
- *Convergence.* Since 1977, the percentage of gasoline stations in the United States that are also convenience stores has gone from 5 percent to about 50 percent. To improve profitability, convenience stores and gasoline retailers have encroached on each other's domain by offering products and services typically sold by the other.
- *Competition.* In the United States, large supermarket chains (such as Albertson's, in partnership with BP's ARCO), mass merchandisers (such as Wal-Mart), and wholesale clubs (such as Costco or Sam's Club) have added retail petroleum operations to their product-service mix that are located on their parking lots.
- *Convenience.* Changes in lifestyle and shopping behavior has resulted in a greater demand for time and place convenience by consumers. Gasoline retailers have replaced the old "gas and cigarettes" strategy with a "scrambled merchandising" strategy that offers consumers several unrelated product lines in a single retail outlet, such as food, car washes, ATM banking, and new payment technologies (Exxon Mobil's Speedpass) to speed up the payment transactions.
- *Branding.* A growing number of petroleum retailers are using brand management to create a consistent, global, and proprietary image that enables firms to differentiate their offerings from those of competitors to gain a competitive advantage.
- *Co-branding.* Co-branding involves the pairing of brand names into a coherent image from two or more marketers to capitalize on the strengths of each that appeals to a firm's target consumers. Convenience store and petroleum marketers have developed relationships with fast-food restaurants (such as Taco Bell, Blimpie's, etc.) and other food, beverage, and nonfood firms in order to satisfy more consumer needs immediately, instead of having them buy the same brand elsewhere.

THE BP CONNECT CONCEPT

Based on the results of marketing research—much at the prototype outlet in Atlanta—BP Connect stores will feature:

- *A new logo.* The BP shield and Amoco torch will be replaced by a new "helios" logo that BP hopes will enhance its corporate image as a "green," environmentally friendly company.
- *Solar panels.* BP is the world's largest producer of solar power, so BP Connect will use renewable electricity generated from solar panels in its curved canopy to provide 10 to 20 percent of the power needed to operate the station.
- *High-tech pumps and twenty-first century information technology.* Instead of traditional rectangular pumps, BP Connect stations will have curved ones that include an 8-inch touch screen to display news, weather, sports scores, and promotions; enable consumers to order food inside while pumping gas and to pay with a debit/credit card; and print travel maps from in-store Internet kiosks.
- *Sectional design.* Using a wide, open-aisle design, BP Connect will be divided into five sections: food service, beverage, impulse-buying with snacks, convenience store, and Internet kiosk. Lighting will change with each section. In-store offerings will include fresh fruit and produce, a bakery, and a Wild Bean Coffee quick-serve restaurant. Some stores will have attached car washes.

BP plans on spending $200 million to let its BP Connect stores link to the Internet, which will let drivers check traffic congestion at the gas pumps or go inside and—for a fee—use the Internet at a kiosk. The goal: Help BP generate half its retail sales from nonfuel items within five years.

THE MARKETING ISSUES

The BP Connect rollout strategy for the new stations represents a massive investment. Not only is there huge competition from other petroleum companies, but convenience store, supermarket, and mass-merchandiser chains are moving into the gasoline business.

In answering the following questions, assume you are a marketing consultant to BP, assisting it with its BP Connect global rollout strategy for the next three years.

Questions

1 Conduct a SWOT (strengths, weaknesses, opportunities, threats) analysis for the BP Connect concept.

2 Consider these two elements of the BP Connect concept described above: high-tech pumps and twenty-first century information technology; and the sectional design. Assess these from the point of view of consumers in (*a*) the United States, (*b*) Western Europe, and (*c*) Eastern Europe.

3 In the United States, how might BP conduct marketing research on the two elements of BP Connect identified in question 2 above?

GLOSSARY

80/20 rule   A concept that suggests 80 percent of a firm's sales are obtained from 20 percent of its customers. p. 241

above-, at-, or below-market pricing   Setting a market price for a product or product class based on a subjective feel for the competitors' price or market price as the benchmark. p. 370

account management policies   Specifies whom salespeople should contact, what kinds of selling and customer service activities should be engaged in, and how these activities should be carried out. p. 544

action item list   An aid to implementing a marketing plan, consisting of three columns: (1) the task, (2) the person responsible for completing that task, and (3) the date to finish the task. p. 599

adaptive selling   A need-satisfaction presentation format that involves adjusting the presentation to fit the selling situation, such as knowing when to offer solutions and when to ask for more information. p. 537

advertising   Any paid form of nonpersonal communication about an organization, good, service, or idea by an identified sponsor. pp. 473, 496

all-you-can-afford budgeting   Allocating funds to promotion only after all other budget items are covered. p. 484

attitude   A learned predisposition to respond to an object or class of objects in a consistently favorable or unfavorable way. p. 131

average revenue (AR)   The average amount of money received for selling one unit of a product, or simply the price of that unit. p. 346

baby boomers   The generation of children born between 1946 and 1964. p. 75

back translation   A translated word or phrase is retranslated into the original language by a different interpreter to catch errors. p. 184

balance of trade   The difference between the monetary value of a nation's exports and imports. p. 171

barriers to entry   Business practices or conditions that make it difficult for new firms to enter the market. p. 87

barter   The practice of exchanging goods and services for other goods and services rather than for money. p. 337

basing-point pricing   Selecting one or more geographical locations (basing point) from which the list price for products plus freight expenses are charged to the buyer. p. 379

beliefs   A consumer's subjective perception of how a product or brand performs on different attributes based on personal experience, advertising, and discussions with other people. p. 131

benchmarking   Discovering how others do something better than your own firm so you can imitate or leapfrog competition. p. 36

bidder's list   A list of firms believed to be qualified to supply a given item. p. 160

blended family   A family formed by the merging into a single household of two previously separated units. p. 77

blog   A web page that serves as a publicly accessible personal journal for an individual. p. 569

bots   Electronic shopping agents or robots that comb websites to compare prices and product or service features. p. 567

brand equity   The added value a given brand name gives to a product beyond the functional benefits provided. p. 300

brand licensing   A contractual agreement whereby one company (licensor) allows its brand name(s) or trademark(s) to be used with products or services offered by another company (licensee) for a royalty or fee. p. 302

brand loyalty   A favorable attitude toward and consistent purchase of a single brand over time. p. 130

brand name   Any word, device (design, shape, sound, or color), or combination of these used to distinguish a seller's goods or services. p. 299

brand personality   A set of human characteristics associated with a brand name. p. 300

branding   A basic decision in marketing products in which an organization uses a name, phrase, design, or symbols, or combination of these to identify its products and distinguish them from those of competitors. p. 299

breadth of product line   The variety of different items a store carries. p. 449

break-even analysis   A technique that analyzes the relationship between total revenue and total cost to determine profitability at various levels of output. p. 351

break-even chart   A graphic presentation of the break-even analysis that shows when total revenue and total cost intersect to identify profit or loss for a given quantity sold. p. 353

break-even point (BEP)   The quantity at which total revenue and total cost are equal. p. 351

brokers   Independent firms or individuals whose principal function is to bring buyers and sellers together to make sales. p. 404

bundle pricing   The marketing of two or more products in a single package price. p. 364

business analysis   The stage of the new-product process that involves specifying the product features and marketing strategy and making necessary financial projections needed to commercialize a product. p. 277

business goods   Products that assist directly or indirectly in providing products for resale. Also called *B2B goods, industrial goods,* or *organizational goods.* p. 263

business marketing   The marketing of goods and services to companies, governments, or not-for-profit organizations for use in the creation of goods and services that they can produce and market to others. p. 148

business plan   A road map for the entire organization for a specified future period of time, such as one year or five years. p. 53

business unit   An organization that markets a set of related products to a clearly defined group of customers. p. 31

business unit level   The level in an organization where business unit managers set the direction for their products and markets to exploit value-creating opportunities. p. 31

buy classes   Consists of three types of organizational buying situations: straight rebuy, new buy, and modified rebuy. p. 157

buying center   The group of people in an organization who participate in the buying process and share common goals, risks, and knowledge important to a purchase decision. p. 156

capacity management   Integrating the service component of the marketing mix with efforts to influence consumer demand. p. 327

category management   An approach to managing the assortment of merchandise in which a manager is assigned the responsibility for selecting all products that consumers in a market segment might view as substitutes for each other, with the objective of maximizing sales and profits in the category. p. 460

cause marketing   Occurs when the charitable contributions of a firm are tied directly to the customer revenues produced through the promotion of one of its products. p. 108

caveat emptor   The legal concept of "let the buyer beware" that was pervasive in American business culture prior to the 1960s. p. 101

central business district   The oldest retail setting, usually located in the community's downtown area. p. 459

channel captain   A channel member (producer, wholesaler, or retailer) that coordinates, directs, and supports other channel members. p. 413

channel conflict   Arises when one channel member believes another channel member is engaged in behavior that prevents it from achieving its goals. p. 412

channel of communication   The means (e.g., a salesperson, advertising media, or public relations tools) of conveying a message to a receiver. p. 471

channel partnership   Consists of agreements and procedures among channel members for ordering and physically distributing a producer's products through the channel to the ultimate consumer. p. 407

choice board   An interactive, Internet-enabled system that allows individual customers to design their own products and services by answering a few questions and choosing from a menu of product or service attributes (or components), prices, and delivery options. p. 560

co-branding   A branding strategy that involves the practice of the pairing of two brand names of two manufacturers on a single product. p. 305

code of ethics   A formal statement of ethical principles and rules of conduct. p. 103

cognitive dissonance   The feeling of postpurchase psychological tension or anxiety consumers may experience when faced with two or more highly attractive alternatives. p. 123

collaborative filtering   A process that automatically groups people with similar buying intentions, preferences, and behaviors and predicts future purchases. p. 560

commercialization   The stage of the new-product process that involves positioning and launching a new product in full-scale production and sales. p. 280

communication   The process of conveying a message to others that requires six elements: a source, a message, a channel of communication, a receiver, and the processes of encoding and decoding. p. 470

community shopping center   A retail location that typically has one primary store (usually a department store branch) and often 20 to 40 smaller outlets, serving a population of consumers who are within a 10- to 20-minute drive. p. 459

company forecast   The total sales of a product that a firm expects to sell during a specified time period under specified environmental conditions and its own marketing efforts. Also called *sales forecast*. p. 252

competencies   An organization's special capabilities, including skills, technologies, and resources that distinguish it from other organizations. p. 36

competition   The alternative firms that could provide a product to satisfy a specific market's needs. p. 85

competitive advantage   A unique strength relative to competitors, often based on quality, time, cost, or innovation. p. 36

competitive parity budgeting   Allocating funds to promotion by matching the competitors' absolute level of spending or the proportion per point of market share. Also called *matching competitors* or *share of market*. p. 483

consideration set   The group of brands that a consumer would consider acceptable from among all the brands in the product class of which he or she is aware. p. 122

constraints   In a decision, the restrictions placed on potential solutions to a problem. p. 209

consultative selling   A need-satisfaction presentation format that focuses on problem identification, where the salesperson serves as an expert on problem recognition and resolution. p. 537

consumer behavior   The actions a person takes in purchasing and using products and services, including the mental and social processes that come before and after these actions. p. 120

Consumer Bill of Rights (1962)   A law that codified the ethics of exchange between buyers and sellers, including the rights to safety, to be informed, to choose, and to be heard. p. 101

consumer ethnocentrism   The tendency to believe that it is inappropriate, indeed immoral, to purchase foreign-made products. p. 184

consumer goods   Products purchased by the ultimate consumer. p. 263

consumer socialization   The process by which people acquire the skills, knowledge, and attitudes necessary to function as consumers. p. 136

consumerism   A grassroots movement started in the 1960s to increase the influence, power, and rights of consumers in dealing with institutions. p. 88

consumer-oriented sales promotion   Sales tools used to support a company's advertising and personal selling directed to ultimate consumers. p. 514

convenience goods   Items that the consumer purchases frequently, conveniently, and with a minimum of shopping effort. p. 264

cookies   Computer files that a marketer can download onto the computer of an online shopper who visits the marketer's website. p. 570

cooperative advertising   Advertising programs by which a manufacturer pays a percentage of the retailer's local advertising expense for advertising the manufacturer's products. p. 519

corporate level   The level in an organization where top management directs overall strategy for the entire organization. p. 30

cost focus strategy   One of Porter's generic business strategies that involves controlling expenses and, in turn, lowering product prices targeted at a narrow range of market segments. p. 589

cost leadership strategy   One of Porter's generic business strategies that focuses on reducing expenses and, in turn, lowers product prices while targeting a broad array of market segments. p. 589

cost per thousand (CPM)   The cost of reaching 1,000 individuals or households with the advertising message in a given medium (M is the Roman numeral for 1,000). p. 504

cost-plus pricing Summing the total unit cost of providing a product or service and adding a specific amount to the cost to arrive at a price. p. 366

countertrade The practice of using barter rather than money for making global sales. p. 170

cross-cultural analysis The study of similarities and differences among consumers in two or more nations or societies. p. 181

cross-functional teams A small number of people from different departments in an organization who are mutually accountable to a common set of performance goals. p. 31

cultural symbols Things that represent ideas and concepts. p. 182

culture The set of values, ideas, and attitudes that are learned and shared among the members of a group. p. 78

currency exchange rate The price of one country's currency expressed in terms of another country's currency. p. 187

customary pricing Setting a price that is dictated by tradition, a standardized channel of distribution, or other competitive factors. p. 370

customer contact audit A flowchart of the points of interaction between a consumer and a service provider. p. 325

customer experience The sum total of the interactions that a customer has with a company's website, from the initial look at a home page through the entire purchase decision process. p. 562

customer relationship management (CRM) The process of identifying prospective buyers, understanding them intimately, and developing favorable long-term perceptions of the organization and its offerings so that buyers will choose them in the marketplace. p. 20

customer service The ability of logistics management to satisfy users in terms of time, dependability, communication, and convenience. p. 429

customer value The unique combination of benefits received by targeted buyers that includes quality, price, convenience, on-time delivery, and both before-sale and after-sale service. p. 15

customerization The growing practice of not only customizing a product or service but also personalizing the marketing and overall shopping and buying interaction for each customer. p. 568

customs What is considered normal and expected about the way people do things in a specific country. p. 182

data The facts and figures related to the problem, divided into two main parts: secondary data and primary data. p. 210

data mining The extraction of hidden predictive information from large databases. p. 223

decision A conscious choice from among two or more alternatives. p. 206

decoding The process of having the receiver take a set of symbols, the message, and transform them back to an idea. p. 471

demand curve A graph relating the quantity sold and price, which shows the maximum number of units that will be sold at a given price. p. 344

demand factors Factors that determine consumers' willingness and ability to pay for goods and services. p. 345

demographics Describing a population according to selected characteristics such as age, gender, ethnicity, income, and occupation. p. 74

depth of product line The store carries a large assortment of each item. p. 449

derived demand The demand for industrial products and services is driven by, or derived from, demand for consumer products and services. p. 151

development The stage of the new-product process that involves turning the idea on paper into a prototype. p. 277

differentiation strategy One of Porter's generic business strategies that requires products to have significant points of difference in product offerings, brand image, higher quality, advanced technology, or superior service to charge a higher price while targeting a broad array of market segments. p. 589

differentiation focus strategy One of Porter's generic business strategies that requires products to have significant points of difference to target one or only a few market segments. p. 590

direct channel A marketing channel where a producer and ultimate consumers deal directly with each other. p. 399

direct forecast Estimating the value to be forecast without any intervening steps. p. 252

direct investment A global market-entry strategy that entails a domestic firm actually investing in and owning a foreign subsidiary or division. p. 192

direct marketing A promotion alternative that uses direct communication with consumers to generate a response in the form of an order, a request for further information, or a visit to a retail outlet. p. 475

direct marketing channels Allowing consumers to buy products by interacting with various advertising media without a face-to-face meeting with a salesperson. p. 401

direct orders The result of direct marketing offers that contain all the information necessary for a prospective buyer to make a decision to purchase and complete the transaction. p. 488

discretionary income The money that remains after paying for taxes and necessities. p. 83

disintermediation Channel conflict that arises when a channel member bypasses another member and sells or buys products direct. p. 412

disposable income The money a consumer has left after paying taxes to use for food, shelter, clothing, and transportation. p. 82

downsizing Reducing the content of packages without changing package size and maintaining or increasing the package price. p. 299

dual distribution An arrangement whereby a firm reaches different buyers by employing two or more different types of channels for the same basic product. p. 402

dumping When a firm sells a product in a foreign country below its domestic price or below its actual cost. p. 195

dynamic pricing The practice of changing prices for products and services in real time in response to supply and demand conditions. p. 570

economic espionage The clandestine collection of trade secrets or proprietary information about a company's competitors. p. 102

Economic Espionage Act (1996) A law that makes the theft of trade secrets by foreign entities a federal crime in the United States. p. 173

economy Pertains to the income, expenditures, and resources that affect the cost of running a business and household. p. 80

efficient consumer response Reducing the retailer's lead time so that inventory levels of customers may be minimized and to make the process of reordering and receiving products as simple as possible. Also called *quick response*. p. 430

eight-second rule A view that customers will abandon their efforts to enter and navigate a website if download time exceeds eight seconds. p. 567

electronic commerce Any activity that uses some form of electronic communication in the inventory, exchange, advertisement, distribution, and payment of goods and services. p. 85

electronic data interchanges (EDIs) Combining proprietary computer and telecommunication technologies to exchange electronic invoices, payments, and information among suppliers, manufacturers, and retailers. p. 428

electronic marketing channels Employing the Internet to make goods and services available for consumption or use by consumers or business buyers. p. 400

e-marketplaces Online trading communities that bring together buyers and supplier organizations to make possible the real-time exchange of information, money, products, and services. Also called *B2B exchanges* or *e-hubs*. p. 162

emotional intelligence The ability to understand one's own emotions and the emotions of people with whom one interacts on a daily basis. p. 545

encoding The process of having the sender transform an idea into a set of symbols. p. 471

environmental factors The uncontrollable factors involving social, economic, technological, competitive, and regulatory forces. p. 14

environmental scanning The process of continually acquiring information on events occurring outside the organization to identify and interpret potential trends. p. 72

ethics The moral principles and values that govern the actions and decisions of an individual or group. p. 98

evaluative criteria Factors that represent both the objective attributes of a brand and the subjective ones a consumer uses to compare different products and brands. p. 121

everyday low pricing The practice of replacing promotional allowances with lower manufacturer list prices. p. 377

exchange The trade of things of value between buyer and seller so that each is better off after the trade. p. 8

exclusive distribution A level of distribution density whereby only one retail outlet in a specific geographical area carries the firm's products. p. 409

experience curve pricing A method of pricing based on the learning effect, which holds that the unit cost of many products and services declines by 10 percent to 30 percent each time a firm's experience at producing and selling them doubles. p. 367

exporting A global market-entry strategy in which a company produces goods in one country and sells them in another country. p. 190

Extranets Internet-based technologies used to permit communication between a company and its suppliers, distributors, and other partners. p. 85

failure fee A penalty payment a manufacturer makes to compensate a retailer for sales its valuable shelf space failed to make. p. 281

family life cycle The distinct phases that a family progresses through from formation to retirement, each phase bringing with it identifiable purchasing behaviors. p. 136

feedback The sender's interpretation of the response that indicates whether a message was decoded and understood as intended. p. 472

field of experience A mutually shared understanding and knowledge that a sender and receiver apply to a message so that it can be communicated effectively. p. 472

fixed cost (FC) The sum of the expenses of the firm that are stable and do not change with the quantity of a product that is produced and sold. p. 350

flexible-price policy Setting different prices for products and services depending on individual buyers and purchase situations. Also called *dynamic pricing*. p. 371

FOB origin pricing The price the seller quotes that includes the cost of loading the product onto the vehicle. The seller names the location (warehouse or factory) where the loading is to occur. The buyer is responsible for picking the mode of transportation and paying for all transportation and handling costs. p. 378

Foreign Corrupt Practices Act (1977) A law, amended by the *International Anti-Dumping and Fair Competition Act* (1998), that makes it a crime for U.S. corporations to bribe an official of a foreign government or political party to obtain or retain business in a foreign country. p. 182

form of ownership Distinguishes retail outlets on the basis of whether they are owned by individuals, corporate chains, or contractual systems. p. 446

formula selling presentation A presentation format that consists of information that must be provided in an accurate, thorough, and step-by-step manner to inform the prospect. p. 536

four I's of service The four unique elements to services: intangibility, inconsistency, inseparability, and inventory. p. 317

franchising A contractual arrangement between a parent company (a franchisor) and an individual or a firm (a franchisee) that allows the franchisee to operate a certain type of business under an established name and according to specific rules. p. 406

frequency The average number of times a person in the target audience is exposed to a message or an advertisement. p. 504

full-service agency An advertising agency that provides the most complete range of services, including market research, media selection, copy development, artwork, and production. p. 512

functional groupings Organizational groupings that represent the different departments or business activities within a firm. p. 601

functional level The level in an organization where groups of specialists actually create value for the organization. p. 31

gap analysis A type of analysis that identifies the differences between a consumer's expectations about and actual experience with a service based on dimensions of service quality. p. 324

Generation X The 15 percent of the U.S. population born between 1965 and 1976. Also called *baby bust*. p. 75

Generation Y The 72 million Americans born between 1977 and 1994. Also called *echo boom* or *baby boomlet*. p. 76

generic business strategy A strategy that can be adopted by any firm, regardless of the product or industry involved, to achieve a competitive advantage. p. 588

geographical groupings Organization groupings in which sales territories are subdivided according to geographical location. p. 601

global brand A brand marketed under the same name in multiple countries with similar and centrally coordinated marketing programs. p. 179

global competition Exists when firms originate, produce, and market their products and services worldwide. p. 177

global consumers Consumer groups living in many countries or regions of the world who have similar needs or seek similar features and benefits from products or services. p. 179

global marketing strategy Transnational firms that employ the practice of standardizing marketing activities when there are cultural similarities and adapting them when cultures differ. p. 178

goals These convert the mission into targeted levels of performance to be achieved, often by a specific time. Also called *objectives*. p. 34

government units The federal, state, and local agencies that buy goods and services for the constituents they serve. p. 149

gray market A situation where products are sold through unauthorized channels of distribution. Also called *parallel importing*. p. 196

green marketing Marketing efforts to produce, promote, and reclaim environmentally sensitive products. p. 108

gross domestic product The monetary value of all goods and services produced in a country during one year. p. 171

gross income The total amount of money made in one year by a person, household, or family unit. Also known as *money income* at the Census Bureau. p. 81

gross rating points (GRPs) A reference number used by advertisers that is obtained by multiplying reach (expressed as a percentage of the total market) by frequency. p. 504

hierarchy of effects The sequence of stages a prospective buyer goes through from initial awareness of a product to eventual action (either trial or adoption of the product). The stages include awareness, interest, evaluation, trial, and adoption. p. 482

hypermarket A large store (more than 200,000 square feet) that offers consumers everything in a single outlet, eliminating the need to shop at more than one location. p. 450

idea generation The stage of the new-product process that involves developing a pool of concepts as candidates for new products. p. 273

idle production capacity Occurs when the service provider is available but there is no demand. p. 319

indirect channels Marketing channels where intermediaries are inserted between the producer and consumers and perform numerous channel functions. p. 399

industrial distributor An intermediary that performs a variety of marketing channel functions, including selling, stocking, delivering a full product assortment, and financing. p. 400

industrial firms Organizational buyers that in some way reprocess goods or services they buy before selling them again to the next buyer. p. 149

industry potential The maximum total sales of a product by all firms to a segment during a specified time period under specified environmental conditions and marketing efforts of the firm. Also called *market potential*. p. 252

infomercials Program-length (30-minute) advertisements that take an educational approach to communication with potential customers. p. 506

information technology Involves a computer and communication system to satisfy an organization's needs for data storage, processing, and access. p. 222

in-house agencies Consists of the company's own advertising staff, which may provide full services or a limited range of services. p. 513

institutional advertisements Advertisements designed to build goodwill or an image for an organization rather than promote a specific good or service. p. 497

integrated marketing communications (IMC) The concept of designing marketing communications programs that coordinate all promotional activities—advertising, personal selling, sales promotion, public relations, and direct marketing—to provide a consistent message across all audiences. p. 470

intensive distribution A level of distribution density whereby a firm tries to place its products and services in as many outlets as possible. p. 409

interactive marketing Two-way buyer–seller electronic communication in a computer-mediated environment in which the buyer controls the kind and amount of information received from the seller. p. 560

internal marketing The notion that a service organization must focus on its employees, or internal market, before successful programs can be directed at customers. p. 327

intertype competition Competition between very dissimilar types of retail outlets. p. 450

Intranet An Internet-based network used within the boundaries of an organization. p. 85

involvement The personal, social, and economic significance of the purchase to the consumer. p. 124

ISO 14000 Worldwide standards for environmental quality and green marketing practices developed by the International Standards Organization (ISO). p. 108

ISO 9000 Standards for registration and certification of a manufacturer's quality management and assurance system based on an on-site audit of practices and procedures developed by the International Standards Organization. p. 154

joint venture A global market-entry strategy in which a foreign company and a local firm invest together to create a local business in order to share ownership, control, and profits of the new company. p. 191

just-in-time (JIT) concept An inventory supply system that operates with very low inventories and requires fast, on-time delivery. p. 437

label An integral part of the package that typically identifies the product or brand, who made it, where and when it was made, how it is to be used, and package contents and ingredients. p. 307

laws Society's values and standards that are enforceable in the courts. p. 98

lead generation The result of a direct marketing offer designed to generate interest in a product or a service and a request for additional information. p. 488

lead time The lag from ordering an item until it is received and ready for use or sale. Also called *order cycle time* or *replenishment time*. p. 430

learning Those behaviors that result from (1) repeated experience and (2) reasoning. p. 130

level of service The degree of service provided to the customer, including self-, limited-, and full-service retailers. p. 446

lifestyle A mode of living that is identified by how people spend their time and resources, what they consider important in their environment, and what they think of themselves and the world around them. p. 132

limited-service agencies Advertising agencies that specialize in one aspect of the advertising process such as providing creative services to develop the advertising copy or buying previously unpurchased media space. p. 513

line positions Managers who have the authority and responsibility to issue orders to the people who report to them. p. 600

linear trend extrapolation Using a straight line to extend a pattern observed in past data into the future. p. 253

logistics Those activities that focus on getting the right amount of the right products to the right place at the right time at the lowest possible cost. p. 422

logistics management The practice of organizing the cost-effective flow of raw materials, in-process inventory, finished goods, and related information from point of origin to point of consumption to satisfy customer requirements. p. 422

loss-leader pricing Deliberately selling a product below its customary price, not to increase sales, but to attract customers' attention, in hopes that they will buy other products as well. p. 370

lost-horse forecast Making a forecast using the last-known value and modifying it according to positive or negative factors expected in the future. p. 252

macromarketing The study of the aggregate flow of a nation's goods and services to benefit society. p. 21

major account management The practice of using team selling to focus on important customers so as to build mutually beneficial, long-term, cooperative relationships. Also called *key account management*. p. 543

make-buy decision An evaluation of whether components and assemblies will be purchased from outside suppliers or built by the company itself. p. 160

manufacturer's agents Agents who work for several producers and carry noncompetitive, complementary merchandise in an exclusive territory. Also called *manufacturer's representatives*. p. 404

marginal analysis A continuing, concise trade-off of incremental costs against incremental revenues. p. 351

marginal cost (MC) The change in total cost that results from producing and marketing one additional unit of a product. p. 350

marginal revenue (MR) The change in total revenue that results from producing and marketing one additional unit. p. 346

market People with both the desire and the ability to buy a specific product. p. 13

market modification A strategy in which a company tries to find new customers, increase a product's use among existing customers, or create new use situations. p. 297

market orientation An organization that focuses its efforts on: (1) continuously collecting information about customers' needs, (2) sharing this information across departments, and (3) using it to create customer value. p. 20

market potential The maximum total sales of a product by all firms to a segment during a specified time period under specified environmental conditions and marketing efforts of the firm. Also called *industry potential*. p. 252

market segmentation Involves aggregating prospective buyers into groups, or segments, that (1) have common needs and (2) will respond similarly to a marketing action. p. 44

market segments The relatively homogeneous groups of prospective buyers that result from the market segmentation process. p. 233

market share The ratio of sales revenue of the firm to the total sales revenue of all firms in the industry, including the firm itself. p. 34

market testing The stage of the new-product process that involves exposing actual products to prospective consumers under realistic purchase conditions to see if they will buy. p. 279

market-based groupings Organizational groupings that utilize specific customer segments. p. 601

marketing An organizational function and a set of processes for creating, communicating, and delivering value to customers and for managing customer relationships in ways that benefit the organization and its stakeholders. p. 8

marketing channel Individuals and firms involved in the process of making a product or service available for use or consumption by consumers or industrial users. p. 396

marketing concept The idea that an organization should (1) strive to satisfy the needs of consumers (2) while also trying to achieve the organization's goals. p. 20

marketing mix The marketing manager's controllable factors—product, price, promotion, and place—that can be used to solve a marketing problem. p. 14

marketing plan A road map for the marketing activities of an organization for a specified future period of time, such as one year or five years. p. 42

marketing program A plan that integrates the marketing mix to provide a good, service, or idea to prospective buyers. p. 16

marketing research The process of defining a marketing problem and opportunity, systematically collecting and analyzing information, and recommending actions. p. 205

marketing strategy The means by which a marketing goal is to be achieved, usually characterized by a specified target market and a marketing program to reach it. p. 48

marketing tactics Detailed day-to-day operational decisions essential to the overall success of marketing strategies. p. 48

market-product grid A framework to relate the market segments of potential buyers to products offered or potential marketing actions by the firm. p. 234

marketspace An information- and communication-based electronic exchange environment mostly occupied by sophisticated computer and telecommunication technologies and digitized offerings. p. 85

measures of success Criteria or standards used in evaluating proposed solutions to a problem. p. 208

merchandise line Describes how many different types of products a store carries and in what assortment. p. 446

merchant wholesalers Independently owned firms that take title to the merchandise they handle. p. 403

message The information sent by a source to a receiver in the communication process. p. 471

micromarketing How an individual organization directs its marketing activities and allocates its resources to benefit its customers. p. 21

mission A statement of the organization's scope, often identifying its customers, markets, products, technology, and values. Also called *vision*. p. 33

missionary salespeople Sales support personnel who do not directly solicit orders but rather concentrate on performing promotional activities and introducing new products. p. 532

mixed branding A branding strategy where a firm markets products under its own name(s) and that of a reseller because the segment attracted to the reseller is different from its own market. p. 306

moral idealism A personal moral philosophy that considers certain individual rights or duties as universal, regardless of the outcome. p. 105

motivation The energizing force that stimulates behavior to satisfy a need. p. 126

multibranding A branding strategy that involves giving each product a distinct name when each brand is intended for a different market segment. p. 305

multichannel marketing The blending of different communication and delivery channels that are mutually reinforcing in attracting, retaining, and building relationships with consumers who shop and buy in the traditional marketplace and marketspace. p. 572

multichannel retailers Retailers that utilize and integrate a combination of traditional store formats and nonstore formats such as catalogs, television, and online retailing. p. 463

multicultural marketing Combinations of the marketing mix that reflect the unique attitudes, ancestry, communication preferences, and lifestyles of different races. p. 78

multidomestic marketing strategy Multinational firms that have as many different product variations, brand names, and advertising programs as countries in which they do business. p. 178

multiproduct branding A branding strategy in which a company uses one name for all its products in a product class. p. 304

need-satisfaction presentation A presentation format that emphasizes probing and listening by the salesperson to identify needs and interests of prospective buyers. p. 537

new-product process The stages a firm goes through to identify business opportunities and convert them to a salable good or service. p. 272

new-product strategy development The stage of the new-product process that defines the role for a new product in terms of the firm's overall corporate objectives. p. 272

noise Extraneous factors that can work against effective communication by distorting a message or the feedback received. p. 472

nonprobability sampling Using arbitrary judgments to select the sample so that the chance of selecting a particular element may be unknown or zero. p. 210

North American Industry Classification System (NAICS) Provides common industry definitions for Canada, Mexico, and the United States, which makes easier the measurement of economic activity in the three member countries of the North American Free Trade Agreement (NAFTA). p. 150

objective and task budgeting Allocating funds to promotion whereby the company: (1) determines its promotion objectives, (2) outlines the tasks to accomplish these objectives, and (3) determines the promotion cost of performing these tasks. p. 484

objectives These convert the mission into targeted levels of performance to be achieved, often by a specific time. Also called *goals*. p. 34

observational data Facts and figures obtained by watching, either mechanically or in person, how people actually behave. p. 213

odd-even pricing Setting prices a few dollars or cents under an even number. p. 364

off-peak pricing Charging different prices during different times of the day or days of the week to reflect variations in demand for the service. p. 328

off-price retailing Selling brand-name merchandise at lower than regular prices. p. 458

one-price policy Setting one price for all buyers of a product or service. Also called *fixed pricing*. p. 371

online consumers The subsegment of all Internet users who employ this technology to research products and services and make purchases. p. 564

opinion leaders Individuals who exert direct or indirect social influence over others. p. 134

order getter Sells in a conventional sense and identifies prospective customers, provides customers with information, persuades customers to buy, closes sales, and follows up on customers' use of a product or service. p. 531

order taker Processes routine orders or reorders for products that were already sold by the company. p. 531

organizational buyers Those manufacturers, wholesalers, retailers, and government agencies that buy goods and services for their own use or for resale. pp. 22, 148

organizational buying behavior The decision-making process that organizations use to establish the need for products and services and identify, evaluate, and choose among alternative brands and suppliers. p. 158

organizational buying criteria The objective attributes of the supplier's products and services and the capabilities of the supplier itself. p. 153

organizational culture A set of values, ideas, and attitudes that is learned and shared among the members of an organization. p. 33

packaging A component of a product that refers to any container in which it is offered for sale and on which label information is conveyed. p. 307

partnership selling The practice whereby buyers and sellers combine their expertise and resources to create customized solutions, commit to joint planning, and share customer, competitive, and company information for their mutual benefit, and ultimately the customer. Also called *enterprise selling*. p. 530

penetration pricing Setting a low initial price on a new product to appeal immediately to the mass market. p. 363

perceived risk The anxieties felt because the consumer cannot anticipate the outcomes of a purchase but believes that there may be negative consequences. p. 129

percentage of sales budgeting Allocating funds to promotion as a percentage of past or anticipated sales, in terms of either dollars or units sold. p. 483

perception The process by which an individual selects, organizes, and interprets information to create a meaningful picture of the world. p. 128

perceptual map A means of displaying or graphing in two dimensions the location of products or brands in the minds of consumers to enable a manager to see how consumers perceive competing products or brands relative to its own and then take marketing actions. p. 250

permission marketing The solicitation of a consumer's consent (called *opt-in*) to receive e-mail and advertising based on personal data supplied by the consumer. p. 561

personal selling The two-way flow of communication between a buyer and seller, designed to influence a person's or group's purchase decision, usually in face-to-face communication between the sender and receiver. pp. 474, 528

personal selling process Sales activities occurring before and after the sale itself, consisting of six stages: (1) prospecting, (2) preapproach, (3) approach, (4) presentation, (5) close, and (6) follow-up. p. 533

personality   A person's consistent behaviors or responses to recurring situations. p. 127

personalization   The consumer-initiated practice of generating content on a marketer's website that is custom tailored to an individual's specific needs and preferences. p. 560

points of difference   Those characteristics of a product that make it superior to competitive substitutes. p. 45

portals   Electronic gateways to the Internet that supply a broad array of news and entertainment, information resources, and shopping services. p. 570

posttests   Tests conducted after an advertisement has been shown to the target audience to determine whether it accomplished its intended purpose. p. 513

power center   A huge shopping strip with multiple anchor (or national stores). p. 459

predatory pricing   The practice of charging a very low price for a product with the intent of driving competitors out of business. p. 381

prestige pricing   Setting a high price so that quality- or status-conscious consumers will be attracted to the product and buy it. p. 363

pretests   Tests conducted before the advertisements are placed in any medium to determine whether it communicates the intended message or to select among alternative versions of the advertisement. p. 512

price   The money or other considerations (including other goods and services) exchanged for the ownership or use of a good or service. p. 336

price discrimination   The practice of charging different prices to different buyers for goods of like grade and quality. p. 380

price elasticity of demand   The percentage change in quantity demanded relative to a percentage change in price. p. 348

price fixing   A conspiracy among firms to set prices for a product. p. 379

price lining   Setting the price of a line of products at a number of different specific pricing points. p. 364

price war   Successive price cutting by competitors to increase or maintain their unit sales or market share. p. 373

pricing constraints   Factors that limit the range of prices a firm may set. p. 341

pricing objectives   Specifying the role of price in an organization's marketing and strategic plans. p. 340

primary data   Facts and figures that are newly collected for the project. p. 210

private branding   A branding strategy used when a company manufactures products but sells them under the brand name of a wholesaler or retailer. Also called *private labeling* or *reseller branding*. p. 306

probability sampling   Using precise rules to select the sample such that each element of the population has a specific known chance of being selected. p. 210

product   A good, service, or idea consisting of a bundle of tangible and intangible attributes that satisfies consumers and is received in exchange for money or some other unit of value. p. 262

product or program champion   A person who is able and willing to cut red tape and move the program forward. p. 598

product advertisements   Advertisements that focus on selling a good or service and which take three forms: (1) pioneering (or informational), (2) competitive (or persuasive), and (3) reminder. p. 497

product class   The entire product category or industry. p. 294

product differentiation   A marketing strategy that involves a firm's using different marketing mix activities, such as product features and advertising, to help consumers perceive the product as being different and better than competing products. p. 233

product form   Variations of a product within the product class. p. 294

product life cycle   Describes the stages a new product goes through in the marketplace: introduction, growth, maturity, and decline. p. 288

product line   A group of products that are closely related because they satisfy a class of needs, are used together, are sold to the same customer group, are distributed through the same type of outlets, or fall within a given price range. p. 262

product-line groupings   Organizational groupings in which a unit is responsible for specific product offerings. p. 601

product-line pricing   The setting of prices for all items in a product line to cover the total cost and produce a profit for the complete line, not necessarily for each item. p. 372

product mix   The number of product lines offered by a company. p. 263

product modification   Altering a product's characteristic, such as its quality, performance, or appearance, to try to increase the product's sales. p. 297

product placement   A sales promotion tool that uses a brand-name product in a movie, television show, video, or a commercial for another product. p. 518

product positioning   The place an offering occupies in consumers' minds on important attributes relative to competitive products. p. 249

product repositioning   Changing the place an offering occupies in a consumer's mind relative to competitive products. p. 249

production goods   Items used in the manufacturing process that become part of the final product. p. 265

profit   The reward to a business firm for the risk it undertakes in offering a product for sale; the money left over after a firm's total expenses are subtracted from its total revenues. p. 30

profit equation   Profit = Total revenue minus Total cost; or Profit = (Unit price times Quantity sold) minus Total cost. p. 339

profitability analysis   A tool for controlling marketing programs using the profit attributable to the firm's products, customer groups, sales territories, channels of distribution, and promotions to expand, maintain, or eliminate specific products, customer groups, channels, or promotions. p. 604

promotional allowances   Cash payments or extra amount of "free goods" awarded sellers in the channel of distribution for undertaking certain advertising or selling activities to promote a product. p. 377

promotional mix   The combination of one or more of the communication tools used to: (1) inform prospective buyers about the benefits of the product, (2) persuade them to try it, and (3) remind them later about the benefits they enjoyed by using the product. p. 470

protectionism   The practice of shielding one or more industries within a country's economy from foreign competition through the use of tariffs or quotas. p. 174

protocol   A statement that, before product development begins, identifies: (1) a well-defined target market; (2) specific customers' needs, wants, and preferences; and (3) what the product will be and do. p. 270

public relations   A form of communication management that seeks to influence the feelings, opinions, or beliefs held by customers, prospective customers, stockholders, suppliers, employees, and other publics about a company and its products or services. p. 474

publicity A nonpersonal, indirectly paid presentation of an organization, good, or service. p. 474

publicity tools Methods of obtaining nonpersonal presentation of an organization, good, or service without direct cost. Examples include news releases, news conferences, and public service announcements. p. 520

pull strategy Directing the promotional mix at ultimate consumers to encourage them to ask the retailer for a product. p. 481

purchase decision process The stages a buyer passes through in making choices about which products and services to buy. p. 120

push strategy Directing the promotional mix to channel members to gain their cooperation in ordering and stocking the product. p. 480

quality Those features and characteristics of a product that influence its ability to satisfy customer needs. p. 36

quantity discounts Reductions in unit costs for a larger order. p. 375

questionnaire data Facts and figures obtained by asking people about their attitudes, awareness, intentions, and behaviors. p. 215

quick response Reducing the retailer's lead time so that inventory levels of customers may be minimized and to make the process of reordering and receiving products as simple as possible. Also called *efficient consumer response.* p. 430

quota A restriction placed on the amount of a product allowed to enter or leave a country. p. 175

rating The percentage of households in a market that are tuned to a particular TV show or radio station. p. 504

reach The number of different people or households exposed to an advertisement. p. 504

receivers Consumers who read, hear, or see the message sent by a source in the communication process. p. 471

reciprocity An industrial buying practice in which two organizations agree to purchase each other's products and services. p. 155

reference groups People to whom an individual looks as a basis for self-appraisal or as a source of personal standards. p. 136

regional shopping centers Consists of 50 to 150 stores that typically attract customers who live or work within a 5- to 10-mile range, often containing two or three anchor stores. p. 459

regulation Restrictions state and federal laws place on business with regard to the conduct of its activities. p. 87

relationship marketing Linking the organization to its individual customers, employees, suppliers, and other partners for their mutual long-term benefits. p. 16

relationship selling The practice of building ties to customers based on a salesperson's attention and commitment to customer needs over time. p. 530

resellers Wholesalers and retailers that buy physical products and resell them again without any processing. p. 149

response In the feedback loop, the impact the message had on the receiver's knowledge, attitudes, or behaviors. p. 472

retail life cycle The process of growth and decline that retail outlets, like products, experience. Consists of the early growth, accelerated development, maturity, and decline stages. p. 462

retail positioning matrix A matrix that positions retail outlets on two dimensions: breadth of product line and value added. p. 456

retailing All activities involved in selling, renting, and providing goods and services to ultimate consumers for personal, family, or household use. p. 444

retailing mix The activities related to managing the store and the merchandise in the store, which include retail pricing, store location, retail communication, and merchandise. p. 457

reverse auction In an e-marketplace, an online auction in which a buyer communicates a need for a product or service and would-be suppliers are invited to bid in competition with each other. p. 163

reverse logistics A process of reclaiming recyclable and reusable materials, returns, and reworks from the point of consumption or use for repair, remanufacturing, redistribution, or disposal. p. 438

reverse marketing The deliberate effort by organizational buyers to build relationships that shape suppliers' products, services, and capabilities to fit a buyer's needs and those of its customers. p. 154

ROI marketing A tool for controlling marketing programs using the application of modern measurement technologies and contemporary organizational design to understand, quantify, and optimize marketing spending. p. 604

sales analysis A tool for controlling marketing programs using the firm's sales records to compare actual sales with sales goals to identify areas of strength and weakness. p. 603

sales component analysis A tool for controlling marketing programs which traces sales revenues to their sources, such as specific products, sales territories, or customers. Also called *microsales analysis.* p. 603

sales engineer A salesperson who specializes in identifying, analyzing, and solving customer problems and brings know-how and technical expertise to the selling situation but often does not actually sell products and services. p. 532

sales forecast The total sales of a product that a firm expects to sell during a specified time period under specified environmental conditions and its own marketing efforts. Also called *company forecast.* p. 252

sales management Planning the selling program and implementing and controlling the personal selling effort of the firm. p. 528

sales plan A statement describing what is to be achieved and where and how the selling effort of salespeople is to be deployed. p. 540

sales promotion A short-term inducement of value offered to arouse interest in buying a good or service. p. 475

sales quota Specific goals assigned to a salesperson, sales team, branch sales office, or sales district for a stated time period. p. 547

sales response function Relates the expense of marketing effort to the marketing results obtained. p. 584

salesforce automation (SFA) The use of computer, information, communication, and Internet technologies to make the sales function more effective and efficient. p. 548

salesforce survey forecast Asking the firm's salespeople to estimate sales during a coming period. p. 253

sampling Selecting representative elements from a population. p. 210

scrambled merchandising Offering several unrelated product lines in a single store. p. 449

screening and evaluation The stage of the new-product process that involves internal and external evaluations of the new-product ideas to eliminate those that warrant no further effort. p. 275

secondary data   Facts and figures that have already been recorded before the project at hand. p. 210

selective distribution   A level of distribution density whereby a firm selects a few retail outlets in a specific geographical area to carry its products. p. 410

self-concept   The way people see themselves and the way they believe others see them. p. 127

self-regulation   An alternative to government control where an industry attempts to police itself. p. 91

selling agents   Agents who represent a single producer and are responsible for the entire marketing function of that producer. p. 404

semiotics   A field of study that examines the correspondence between symbols and their role in the assignment of meaning for people. p. 182

service continuum   A range from the tangible to the intangible or good-dominant to service-dominant offerings available in the marketplace. p. 319

services   Intangible activities or benefits that an organization provides to consumers in exchange for money or something else of value. p. 316

share points   An analysis that uses percentage points of market share as the common basis of comparison to allocate marketing resources effectively for different product lines within the same firm. p. 585

shopping goods   Items for which the consumer compares several alternatives on criteria, such as price, quality, or style. p. 264

shrinkage   Breakage and theft of merchandise by customers and employees. p. 458

situation analysis   Taking stock of where a firm or product has been recently, where it is now, and where it is headed in terms of the organization's plans and the external factors and trends affecting it. p. 43

situational influences   The five aspects of the purchase situation that impacts the consumer's purchase decision process: (1) the purchase task, (2) social surroundings, (3) physical surroundings, (4) temporal effects, and (5) antecedent states. p. 125

Six Sigma   A means to "delight the customer" by achieving quality through a highly disciplined process to focus on developing and delivering near-perfect products and services. p. 273

skimming pricing   Setting the highest initial price that customers really desiring the product are willing to pay. p. 362

slotting fee   A payment a manufacturer makes to place a new item on a retailer's shelf. p. 281

social audit   A systematic assessment of a firm's objectives, strategies, and performance in terms of social responsibility. p. 109

social class   The relatively permanent, homogeneous divisions in a society into which people sharing similar values, interests, and behavior can be grouped. p. 138

social forces   The demographic characteristics of the population and its values. p. 74

social responsibility   The idea that organizations are part of a larger society and are accountable to that society for their actions. p. 106

societal marketing concept   The view that organizations should satisfy the needs of consumers in a way that provides for society's well-being. p. 21

source   A company or person who has information to convey. p. 470

spam   Communications that take the form of electronic junk mail or unsolicited e-mail. p. 569

specialty goods   Items that a consumer makes a special effort to search out and buy. p. 264

staff positions   People who have the authority and responsibility to advise people in the line positions but cannot issue direct orders to them. p. 601

stakeholders   The people who are affected by what the company does and how well it performs. p. 33

standard markup pricing   Adding a fixed percentage to the cost of all items in a specific product class. p. 366

statistical inference   Drawing conclusions about a population from a sample taken from that population. p. 210

stimulus-response presentation   A presentation format which assumes that given the appropriate stimulus by a salesperson, the prospect will buy. p. 536

strategic alliances   Agreements among two or more independent firms to cooperate for the purpose of achieving common goals. p. 177

strategic channel alliances   A practice whereby one firm's marketing channel is used to sell another firm's products. p. 402

strategic marketing process   The approach whereby an organization allocates its marketing mix resources to reach its target markets. p. 42

strip location   A cluster of stores to serve people who are within a 5- to 10-minute drive. p. 459

subcultures   Subgroups within the larger, or national, culture with unique values, ideas, and attitudes. p. 139

subliminal perception   Seeing or hearing messages without being aware of them. p. 129

supply chain   A sequence of firms that perform activities required to create and deliver a good or service to consumers or industrial users. p. 422

supply chain management   The integration and organization of information and logistic activities across firms in a supply chain for the purpose of creating and delivering goods and services that provide value to consumers. p. 422

supply partnership   A relationship that exists when a buyer and its supplier adopt mutually beneficial objectives, policies, and procedures for the purpose of lowering the cost or increasing the value of products and services delivered to the ultimate consumer. p. 155

support goods   Items used to assist in producing other goods and services. p. 265

survey of buyers' intentions forecast   Asking prospective customers if they are likely to buy the product during some future time period. p. 253

sustainable development   Conducting business in a way that protects the natural environment while making economic progress. p. 110

SWOT analysis   An acronym describing an organization's appraisal of its internal **S**trengths and **W**eaknesses and its external **O**pportunities and **T**hreats. p. 43

synergy   The increased customer value achieved through performing organizational functions more efficiently. p. 237

target market   One or more specific groups of potential consumers toward which an organization directs its marketing program. p. 14

target pricing   Estimating the price that the ultimate consumer would be willing to pay for a product, working backward through markups taken by retailers and wholesalers to determine what price is charged to wholesalers, and then deliberately adjusting the composition and features of a product to achieve the target price to consumers. p. 364

target profit pricing Setting an annual target of a specific dollar volume of profit. p. 367

target return-on-investment pricing Setting a price to achieve an annual target return-on-investment (ROI). p. 368

target return-on-sales pricing Setting a price to achieve a profit that is a specified percentage of the sales volume. p. 368

tariffs Government taxes on goods or services entering a country, primarily serving to raise prices on imports. p. 174

team selling Using an entire team of professionals in selling to and servicing major customers. p. 532

technology Inventions or innovations from applied science or engineering research. p. 83

telemarketing Using the telephone to interact with and sell directly to consumers. p. 454

third-party logistics providers Firms that perform most or all of the logistics functions that manufacturers, suppliers, and distributors would normally perform themselves. p. 432

total cost (TC) The total expense incurred by a firm in producing and marketing a product. Total cost is the sum of fixed cost and variable cost. p. 350

total logistics cost Expenses associated with transportation, materials handling and warehousing, inventory, stockouts (being out of inventory), order processing, and return goods handling. p. 428

total revenue (TR) The total money received from the sale of a product. p. 346

trade name A commercial, legal name under which a company does business. p. 299

trademark Identifies that a firm has legally registered its brand name or trade name so the firm has its exclusive use, thereby preventing others from using it. p. 299

trade-oriented sales promotions Sales tools used to support a company's advertising and personal selling directed to wholesalers, distributors, or retailers. Also called *trade promotions*. p. 519

trading down Reducing the number of features, quality, or price. p. 299

trading up Adding value to a product (or line) through additional features or higher-quality materials. p. 299

traditional auction In an e-marketplace, an online auction in which a seller puts an item up for sale and would-be buyers are invited to bid in competition with each other. p. 163

traffic generation The outcome of a direct marketing offer designed to motivate people to visit a business. p. 488

trend extrapolation Extending a pattern observed in past data into the future. p. 253

ultimate consumers The people who use the goods and services purchased for a household. Also called *consumers, buyers,* or *customers.* p. 22

uniform delivered pricing The price the seller quotes includes all transportation costs. p. 378

unit variable cost (UVC) Variable cost expressed on a per unit basis. p. 350

unsought goods Items that the consumer either does not know about or knows about but does not initially want. p. 264

usage rate The quantity consumed or patronage (store visits) during a specific period. Also called *frequency marketing.* p. 239

utilitarianism A personal moral philosophy that focuses on the "greatest good for the greatest number," by assessing the costs and benefits of the consequences of ethical behavior. p. 106

utility The benefits or customer value received by users of the product. p. 23

value The ratio of perceived benefits to price; or Value = (Perceived benefits divided by Price). p. 338

value analysis A systematic appraisal of the design, quality, and performance of a product to reduce purchasing costs. p. 160

value consciousness The concern for obtaining the best quality, features, and performance of a product or service for a given price. p. 80

value-pricing The practice of simultaneously increasing product and service benefits while maintaining or decreasing price. p. 339

values A society's personally or socially preferable modes of conduct or states of existence that tend to persist over time. p. 181

variable cost (VC) The sum of the expenses of the firm that vary directly with the quantity of a product that is produced and sold. p. 350

vendor-managed inventory (VMI) An inventory management system whereby the supplier determines the product amount and assortment a customer (such as a retailer) needs and automatically delivers the appropriate items. p. 437

vertical marketing systems Professionally managed and centrally coordinated marketing channels designed to achieve channel economies and maximum marketing impact. p. 405

viral marketing An Internet-enabled promotional strategy that encourages individuals to forward marketer-initiated messages to others via e-mail. p. 569

warranty A statement indicating the liability of the manufacturer for product deficiencies. p. 309

web communities Websites that allow people to congregate online and exchange views on topics of common interest. p. 569

wheel of retailing A concept that describes how new forms of retail outlets enter the market. p. 461

whistle-blowers Employees who report unethical or illegal actions of their employers. p. 105

word of mouth The influencing of people during conversations. p. 135

workload method A formula-based method for determining the size of a salesforce that integrates the number of customers served, call frequency, call length, and available selling time to arrive at a figure for the salesforce size. p. 543

World Trade Organization A permanent institution that sets rules governing trade between its members through panels of trade experts who decide on trade disputes between members and issue binding decisions. p. 175

yield management pricing The charging of different prices to maximize revenue for a set amount of capacity at any given time. p. 365

CHAPTER NOTES

CHAPTER 1

1. Data in Figure 1–1 are based on sports participation statistics published by the National Sporting Goods Association, www.nsga.org; and the Sporting Goods Manufacturers Association, www.sgma.com.
2. Personal interview with Jeremy Stonier, February 2003.
3. See the website of the American Marketing Association, www.marketingpower.com.
4. Richard P. Bagozzi, "Marketing as Exchange," *Journal of Marketing,* October 1975, pp. 32–39; and Gregory T. Gundlach and Patrick E. Murphy, "Ethical and Legal Foundations of Relational Marketing Exchanges," *Journal of Marketing,* October 1993, pp. 35–46.
5. Productscan® Online database of new products, from Marketing Intelligence Service, December 17, 2003, www.productscan.com.
6. Robert M. McMath and Thom Forbes, *What Were They Thinking?* (New York: Times Business, 1998), pp. 3–22.
7. From the NewProductWorks website, "Favorite Failures," www.newproductworks.com.
8. From the Hot Pockets website, www.chefamerica.com and www.hotpockets.com.
9. Eric Pope, "Robotic Vacuum Sweeps Up Holiday Gift Competition," *Detroit News,* December 24, 2003, www.detnews.com/2003/business/0312/24/d02-17664.htm; and the Roomba FloorVac website, www.roombavac.com.
10. From the NewProductWorks website, "Favorite Failures," www.newproductworks.com.
11. Peter Brownfeld, "Groups, States Target Distracted Drivers," Fox News Channel, January 15, 2004, www.foxnews.com; Debbie Howlett, "Americans Driving to Distraction," *USA Today,* March 3, 2004, www.usatoday.com/news/nation/2004-03-04-distracted-usat x.htm; "Cingular Teen Distracted Driving Program Reaches 5.6 Million Students," January 28, 2004, www.cell-phone-plans.net; and numerous resources from the Cellular Telecommunications and Internet Association, www.wow-com.com; the ads were created by the Safe Communities of Wright County, Minnesota, and sponsored by the Minnesota Department of Public Safety, Office of Traffic Safety.
12. E. Jerome McCarthy, *Basic Marketing: A Managerial Approach* (Homewood, IL: Richard D. Irwin, 1960); and Walter van Waterschoot and Christophe Van den Bulte, "The 4P Classification of the Marketing Mix Revisited," *Journal of Marketing,* October 1992, pp. 83–93.
13. James Surowiecki, "The Return of Michael Porter," *Fortune,* February 1999, pp. 135–38; and Kathleen M. Eisenhardt and Shona L. Brown, "Time Pacing: Competing in Markets That Won't Stand Still," *Harvard Business Review,* March–April 1998, pp. 59–69.
14. Werner J. Reinartz and V. Kumar, "On the Profitability of Long-Life Customers in a Noncontractual Setting: An Empirical Investigation and Implications for Marketing," *Journal of Marketing,* October 2000, pp. 17–35; and "What's a Loyal Customer Worth?" *Fortune,* December 11, 1995, p. 182.
15. Michael Treacy and Fred D. Wiersema, *The Discipline of Market Leaders* (Reading, MA: Addison-Wesley, 1995); Michael Treacy and Fred Wiersema, "How Market Leaders Keep Their Edge," *Fortune,* February 6, 1995, pp. 88–89; and Michael Treacy, "You Need a Value Discipline—But Which One?" *Fortune,* April 17, 1995, p. 195.
16. Susan Foumier, Susan Dobscha, and David Glen Mick, "Preventing the Premature Death of Relationship Marketing," *Harvard Business Review,* January–February 1998, pp. 42–51.
17. Leigh Muzlay, "Shoes That Morph from Sneakers to Skates Are Flying Out of Stores," *The Wall Street Journal,* July 26, 2001, p. B1; and The SGMA Report 2000, "The U.S. Athletic Footwear Market Today," published by the Sporting Goods Manufacturers Association.
18. The material on Rollerblade's current marketing strategy is based on personal interviews with Jeremy Stonier and Nicholas Skally in February 2003 and on information from the Rollerblade website and Rollerblade sales materials.
19. Robert F. Keith "The Marketing Revolution," *Journal of Marketing,* January 1960, pp. 35–38.
20. *Annual Report* (New York: General Electric Company, 1952), p. 21.
21. John C. Narver, Stanley F. Slater, and Brian Tietje, "Creating a Market Orientation," *Journal of Market Focused Management,* no. 2 (1998), pp. 241–55; Stanley F. Slater and John C. Narver, "Market Orientation and the Learning Organization," *Journal of Marketing,* July 1995, pp. 63–74; and George S. Day, "The Capabilities of Market-Driven Organizations," *Journal of Marketing,* October 1994, pp. 37–52.
22. The definition of customer relationship management is adapted from Rajendra K. Srivastava, Tasadduq A. Shervani, and Liam Fahey, "Marketing, Business Processes, and Shareholder Value: An Embedded View of Marketing Activities and the Discipline of Marketing," *Journal of Marketing,* special issue (1999), pp. 168–79.
23. Darrell K. Rigby, Frederick F. Reichheld, and Phil Schefter, "Avoid the Perils of CRM," *Harvard Business Review,* February 2002, pp. 101–9.
24. Michael E. Porter and Claas van der Linde, "Green and Competitive Ending the Stalemate," *Harvard Business Review,* September–October 1995, pp. 120–34; Jacquelyn Ottman, "Edison Winners Show Smart Environmental Marketing," *Marketing News,* July 17, 1995, pp. 16, 19; and Jacquelyn Ottman "Mandate for the '90s: Green Corporate Image," *Marketing News,* September 11, 1995, p. 8.
25. Shelby D. Hunt and John J. Burnett, "The Macromarketing/Micro-marketing Dichotomy: A Taxonomical Model," *Journal of Marketing,* Summer 1982, pp. 9–26.
26. Philip Kotler and Sidney J. Levy, "Broadening the Concept of Marketing," *Journal of Marketing,* January 1969, pp. 10–15.
27. Jim Rendon, "When Nations Need a Little Marketing," *The New York Times,* November 23, 2003, p. BU6.
28. "Marketing Museums: When Merchants Enter the Temple," *The Economist,* April 21, 2001, pp. 64–66; and Lisa Snedeker, "Putting Their Money on Monets," *Star Tribune,* August 16, 2001, p. F16.
29. The Web Link is based on "The State Hermitage Museum," a case written by Olga Saguinova, Michael J. Vessey, and William Rudelius appearing in Rudelius et al., *Marketing,* 1st Russian ed. (Moscow: DeNovo Publishing Company, 2001), pp. 594–96; and Peter Baker, "Historically Rich Russia Struggles to Attract Tourists," *Star Tribune* September 9, 2001, p. G5.
30. Bernard Stamler, "Temples of Culture Are Needy, Too. Tai Chi, Anyone?" *The New York Times,* April 23, 2003, p. 2.
31. John A. Byrne, "Caught in the Net," *BusinessWeek,* August 27, 2001, pp. 114–16; and Gary Gentile, "eToast," *Star Tribune,* March 3, 2001, pp. D1, D2.

Rollerblade: This case was written by William Rudelius and is based on personal interviews with Jeremy Stonier and Nicholas Skally and on Rollerblade materials.

CHAPTER 2

1. www.benjerry.com.
2. Blair S. Walker, "Good-Humored Activist Back to the Fray," *USA Today,* December 8, 1992, pp. 1B–2B.

3. Jim Castelli, "Finding the Right Fit: Are You Weird Enough?" *HR Magazine,* September 1990, pp. 38–39.

4. "Ben & Jerry's Homemade, Inc.," news release, Burlington, VT, April 12, 2001.

5. Roger A. Kerin, Vijay Mahajan, and P. Rajan Varadarajan, *Contemporary Perspectives on Strategic Marketing Planning* (Boston: Allyn & Bacon, 1990), chap. 1; and Orville C. Walker, Jr., Harper W. Boyd, Jr., and Jean-Claude Larreche, *Marketing Strategy* (Burr Ridge, IL: Richard D. Irwin, 1992), chaps. 1 and 2.

6. Theodore Levitt, "Marketing Myopia," *Harvard Business Review,* July–August 1960, pp. 45–56.

7. Kenneth E. Goodpaster and Thomas E. Holloran, "Anatomy of Spiritual and Social Awareness: The Case of Medtronic, Inc.," Third International Symposium on Catholic Social Thought and Management Education, Goa, India, 1999, pp. 9–11.

8. Katherine Ellison, "The Bottom Line Redefined," *Nature Conservancy,* Winter 2002, pp. 45–50.

9. Amy Merrick, "Sears Orders Fashion Makeover from the Lands' End Catalog," *The Wall Street Journal,* January 28, 2004, pp. A1, A8.

10. George Stalk, Phillip Evans, and Lawrence E. Shulman, "Competing on Capabilities. The New Rules of Corporate Strategy," *Harvard Business Review,* March–April 1992, pp. 57–69.

11. Roger A. Kerin and Robert A. Peterson, *Strategic Marketing Problems: Cases and Comments,* 10th ed. (Englewood Cliffs, NJ: Prentice Hall, 2004), pp. 2–3; and Derek F. Abell, *Defining the Business* (Englewood Cliffs, NJ: Prentice Hall, 1980), p. 18.

12. Christopher Meyer, *Fast Cycle Time* (New York: Free Press, 1993); and Michael E. Porter, *Competitive Advantage* (New York: Free Press, 1985).

13. Jon Swartz, "EBay Evolves to Serve Small Businesses," *USA Today,* February 23, 2004, p. 1B.

14. Michael Totty, "Making the Sale," *The Wall Street Journal,* September 24, 2001, p. R6.

15. Adapted from "The Experience Curve Reviewed, IV. The Growth Share Matrix of the Product Portfolio" (Boston: The Boston Consulting Group, 1973).

16. Kerin, Mahajan, and Vardarajan, *Contemporary Perspectives,* p. 52.

17. William C. Symonds, "The Kodak Revolt Is Short-Sighted," *Business-Week,* November 3, 2003, p. 38.

18. Jefferson Graham, "Kodak Gives Film Cameras Heave-Ho," *USA Today,* January 14, 2004, p. 5B.

19. "Has Kodak Missed the Moment?" *The Economist,* January 3, 2004, pp. 46–47.

20. James Bandler, "Kodak to Cut Staff Up to 21%, EasyShare up 81% Amid Digital Push," *The Wall Street Journal,* January 23, 2004, pp. A1, A7.

21. Faith Keenan and Cathy Schottenstein, "Big Yellow's Digital Dilemma," *BusinessWeek,* March 24, 2003, pp. 80–81.

22. Ben Dobbin, "Kodak Unveils Photo Kiosk to Develop Film in Minutes," *Star Tribune,* February 9, 2004, startribune.com.

23. Strengths and weaknesses of the BCG technique are based on Derek F. Abell and John S. Hammond, *Strategic Market Planning: Problem and Analytic Approaches* (Englewood Cliffs, NJ: Prentice Hall, 1979); Yoram Wind, Vijay Mahajan, and Donald Swire, "An Empirical Comparison of Standardized Portfolio Models," *Journal of Marketing,* Spring 1983, pp. 89–99; and J. Scott Armstrong and Roderick J. Brodie, "Effects of Portfolio Planning Methods on Decision Making: Experimental Results," *International Journal of Research in Marketing,* Winter 1994, pp. 73–84.

24. H. Igor Ansoff, "Strategies for Diversification," *Harvard Business Review,* September–October 1957, pp. 113–24.

25. Linda Swenson and Kenneth E. Goodpaster, *Medtronic in China (A)* (Minneapolis, MN: University of St. Thomas, 1999), pp. 4–5.

26. Joseph Nocera, "Kodak: The CEO vs. the Gadfly," *Fortune,* January 12, 2004, pp. 85–92.

27. Bandler, "Kodak to Cut Staff," pp. A1, A7.

28. Todd Wasserman, "The Mercenary" (a.k.a 'Super') CMO, *BrandWeek,* June 21, 2004, pp. S6–S18.

29. "Has Kodak Missed the Moment?" *The Economist,* January 3, 2004, pp. 46–47.

30. Ibid.

Specialized Bicycle Components, Inc.: This case was written by Giana Eckhardt and Steven Hartley. Sources: "Industry Overview 2003–04," National Bicycle Dealers Association (see http://nbda.com); Nancy Bouchard, "Above the Rim," *Sporting Goods Business* (October 1, 2003); "A Passion For Cycling Guides Specialized to Repeated New Breakthroughs," Specialized press release (see www.specialized.com); "Humble Origins Set Customer Service Standards" Specialized press release (see www.specialized.com).

APPENDIX A

1. Personal interview with Authur R. Kydd, St. Croix Management Group.

2. Examples of guides to writing marketing plans include William A. Cohen, *The Marketing Plan* (New York: Wiley, 1995); Mark Nolan, *The Instant Marketing Plan* (Santa Maria, CA: Puma Publishing Company, 1995); and Roman G. Hiebing, Jr., and Scott W. Cooper, *The Successful Marketing Plan,* 2nd ed. (Lincolnwood, IL: NTC Business Books, 1997).

3. Examples of guides to writing business plans include Rhonda M. Abrahms, *The Successful Business Plan: Secrets & Strategies,* 3rd ed. (Grants Pass, OR: Oasis Press/PSI Research, 2000); Joseph A. Covello and Brian J. Hazelgren, *The Complete Book of Business Plans* (Naperville, IL: Sourcebooks, 1995); Joseph A. Covello and Brian J. Hazelgren, *Your First Business Plan,* 3rd ed. (Naperville, IL: Sourcebooks, 1998); and Angela Shupe, ed., *Business Plans Handbook,* vols. 1–4 (Detroit: Gale Research, 1997).

4. Abrahms, *The Successful Business Plan,* p. 30.

5. Some of these points are adapted from Abrahms, pp. 30–38; others are adapted from William Rudelius, *Guidelines for Technical Report Writing* (Minneapolis: University of Minnesota, undated). See also William Strunk, Jr., and E. B. White, *The Elements of Style* (New York, Macmillan, 1979).

6. Rebecca Zimoch, "The Dawn of the Frozen Age," *Grocery Head-quarters,* December 2002; see www.groceryheadquarters.com.

7. ACNielsen Strategic Planner as reported to the National Frozen & Refrigerated Foods Association for the week ending April 17, 2004; see www.nfraweb.org.

8. Information Resources 2003 data as reported to the American Frozen Food Institute; see www.affi.com.

9. Chuck Van Hyning, *NPD's National Eating Trends;* see www.npdfoodworld.com.

10. Rebecca Zimoch, "Understanding the Hispanic Consumer," *Grocery Headquarters,* May 2003; see www.groceryheadquarters.com

11. Interview with Don Montouri, *Packaged Facts;* see www.packagedfacts.com.

12. Bob Burgdorfer, "Companies Ready to Square Off in Big-Time Chili Cook-off," *USA Today,* May 26, 2004.

The authors are indebted to Randall F. Peters and Leah Peters for being allowed to adapt elements of a business plan for Paradise Kitchens, Inc., for the sample marketing plan and for their help and suggestions.

CHAPTER 3

1. Peter Burrows, "Show Time!" *BusinessWeek,* February 2, 2004, pp. 57–64; and Devine Leonard, "Songs in the Key of Steve," *Fortune,* May 12, 2003, pp. 52–62.

2. "Coffee Shops in the U.S.," press release from Mintel Group, February 2004; "Java's Hot, Bagels Not," *Restaurant Business,* April 1, 2003; Stephanie Thompson, "Coffee Brands Think Outside of the Can," *Advertising Age,* July 28, 2003, p. 26; and Rebecca Gardyn, "Grounds for a New Strategy," *American Demographics,* June 2001, pp. 115–17.

3. "Starbucks Automates Espresso Preparation," *Restaurant Business,* March 12, 2004; and Jeff Cioletti and Sherry Petersen, "Soda Shakeout," *Convenience Store News Online,* February 9, 2004.

4. Fred Vogelstein, "10 Tech Trends to Bet On," *Fortune,* February 23, 2004, pp. 76–88; Alison Stein Wellner, "The Next 25 Years," *American Demographics,* April 2003, pp. 24–27; Stephen B. Shepard, "You Read It Here First," *BusinessWeek,* March 15, 2004, p. 16; Catherine Arnold, "Anti-Smoking Trend Hits Asia," *Marketing News,* January 15, 2004, p. 4; Arundhati Parmar, "Outlook 2004: Competitive Intelligence," *Marketing News,* January 15, 2004, pp. 16–17; and Steve Jarvis, "Internet Privacy at the Plate, Net Names, Taxes on Deck Too," *Marketing News,* January 1, 2001, pp. 12–14.

5. *World Population Prospects: The 2002 Revision* (2003), United Nations, table A4; and Carl Haub, "2003 World Population Data Sheet," Population Reference Bureau.

6. Haub, "2003 World Population Data Sheet"; "World Population at a Glance: 1998 and Beyond," U.S. Department of Commerce, Bureau of the Census, January 1999; "Global Demographics: The Group of Seven's Senior Moment," *BusinessWeek Online,* March 17, 2003; and "New Facts on Globalization, Poverty, and Income Distribution," International Chamber of Commerce, January 15, 2003.

7. Alison Stein Wellner, "The Next 25 Years," *American Demographics,* April 2003, pp. 24–27.

8. Pamela Paul, "Meet the Parents," *American Demographics,* January 2002, pp. 42–47; and Toddi Gutner, "Generation X: To Be Young, Thrifty, and in the Black," *BusinessWeek,* July 21, 1997, p. 76.

9. Michael J. Weiss, "To Be about to Be," *American Demographics,* September 2003, pp. 29–36; Peter Francese, "Ahead of the Next Wave," *American Demographics,* September 2003, pp. 42–43; and Don O'Briant, "Millenials: The Next Generation," *Atlanta Journal-Constitution,* August 11, 2003, p. 1D.

10. Pamela Paul, "Global Generation Gap," *American Demographics,* March 2002, pp. 18–19; and Allyson L. Stewart-Allen, "EU's Future Consumers: 3 Groups to Watch," *Marketing News,* June 4, 2001, p. 9.

11. James Morrow, "A Place for One," *American Demographics,* November 2003, pp. 25–29; Michelle Conlin, "Unmarried America," *BusinessWeek,* October 20, 2003, pp. 106–116; and Vanessa O'Connell, "Advertisers Are Cautious as Household Makeup Shifts," *The Wall Street Journal,* May 15, 2001, pp. B1, B4.

12. Matthew Grimm, "Hitch Switch," *American Demographics,* November 2003, pp. 34–35; John Fetto, "Till Death," *American Demographics,* September 2002, p. 8; and Joan Raymond, "The Ex-Files," *American Demographics,* February 2001, pp. 60–64.

13. Marc J. Perry and Paul J. Mackun, "Population Change and Distribution," Census 2000 Brief: U.S. Bureau of the Census, April 2001; and Paul Campbell, "Population Projection: States, 1995–2025," Current Population Report, U.S. Department of Commerce, May 1997.

14. Peter Francese, "Top Trends for 2003," *American Demographics,* December 2002–January 2003, pp. 48–51; and Harry S. Dent, Jr., *The Roaring 2000s* (New York: Simon and Schuster, 1998), p. 211.

15. Joshua Bolten, "Update of Statistical Area Definitions and Additional Guidance on Their Use," Office of Management and Budget, OMB Bulletin No. 04–03, February 18, 2004; and "About Metropolitan and Micropolitan Statistical Areas," U.S. Census Bureau, www.census.gov/population/www/estimates/aboutmetro.html.

16. Alison Stein Wellner, "Our True Colors," *American Demographics,* November 2002, pp. S2–S20; Eduardo Porter, "Even 126 Sizes Don't Fit All," *The Wall Street Journal,* March 2, 2001, pp. B1, B4; and William H. Frey, "Micro Melting Pots," *American Demographics,* June 2001, pp. 20–23.

17. Brian Grow, "Hispanic Nation," *BusinessWeek,* March 15, 2004, pp. 58–70; Wellner, "Our True Colors"; Deborah L. Vence, "You Talkin' to Me? *Marketing News,* March 1, 2004, pp. 1, 9–11; and Wellner, "The Next 25 Years."

18. William Frey, "The Diversity Myth," *American Demographics,* June 1998, pp. 39–43; and Jeffery D. Zbar, "In a Diverse Hispanic World, Image Counts," *Advertising Age,* April 3, 1995, pp. 518–19.

19. John Fetto, "Does Father Really Know Best?" *American Demographics,* June 2002, p. 6.

20. Rebecca Gardyn, "Got Game?" *American Demographics,* October 2003, p. 8; Arundhati Parmar, "Not So Fair," *Marketing News,* June 9, 2003, p. 4; Rebecca Gardyn, "Granddaughters of Feminism," *American Demographics,* April 2001, pp. 43–47; and Judith Langer, "Behind the Looking Glass," *American Demographics,* February 2001, pp. 53–59.

21. Edward B. Keller and Thomas A. W. Miller, "Re-mapping the World of Consumers," *American Demographics,* October 2000, pp. S1–S20; and Sandra Yin, "Making a Healthy Choice," *American Demographics,* July 2001, pp. 40–41.

22. Jill Smolowe, "Do You Still Know Me?" *Time,* September 12, 1994, p. 60; and Judann Dagnoli, "Value Strategy to Battle Recession," *Advertising Age,* January 7, 1991, pp. 1, 44.

23. Mortimer B. Zuckerman, "A Truly Cruel College Squeeze," *U.S. News & World Report,* March 8, 2004, p. 80.

24. Michael J. Mandel, "Inventing the Clinton Recession," *BusinessWeek,* February 23, 2004, p. 48; and James Cooper, Kathleen Madigan, and James Mehring, "Welcome to the Growth Recession," *BusinessWeek,* July 2, 2001, pp. 87–90.

25. Michael J. Weiss, "Inside Consumer Confidence Surveys," *American Demographics,* February 2003, pp. 23–29; and Richard T. Curtin, *Surveys of Consumers,* Survey Research Center, University of Michigan, September 5, 2003, pp. 1–4.

26. Carmen DeNavas-Walt, Bernadette D. Proctor, and Robert J. Mills, "Income, Poverty and Health Insurance Coverage in the United States: 2003; "Income in the United States," *Current Population Reports,* U.S. Census Bureau, August 2004, p. 27.

27. Don Carlson, "The Old Economy in the New Economy," *BusinessWeek,* November 13, 2000, p. 42H; Owen Ullmann, "Forget Saving, America. Your Job Is to Spend," *BusinessWeek,* December 28, 1998, p. 54; Gene Koretz, "Savings' Death Is Exaggerated," *BusinessWeek,* September 14, 1998, p. 26; and Marcia Mogelonsky, "No More Food, Thanks," *American Demographics,* August 1998, p. 59.

28. "Consumer Expenditures in 2002," U.S. Department of Labor, Bureau of Labor Statistics, February 2004, pp. 1–4; and "Spending on Necessities," *Monthly Labor Review,* U.S. Department of Labor, Bureau of Labor Statistics, June 24, 2003.

29. John Carey, "Tiny Smart Bombs vs. Cancer?" *BusinessWeek,* March 1, 2004, p. 115; Stephen H. Wildstrom, "Get Ready for an Innovative New Year," *BusinessWeek,* December 29, 2003, p. 28; Herve Gallaire, "Can New Technology Recharge Xerox?" *BusinessWeek,* December 22, 2003, p. IM2; and Fred Vogelstein, "10 Tech Trends to Bet On," *Fortune,* February 23, 2004, pp. 75–88.

30. Michael Krauss, "Young Net Entrepreneurs Leverage Web Anew," *Marketing News,* February 1, 2004, p. 6.

31. Leon Jaroff, "Smart's the Word in Detroit," *Time,* February 6, 1995, pp. 50–52.

32. Clint Willis, "25 Cool Things You Wish You Had and Will," *Forbes ASAP,* June 1, 1998, pp. 49–60.

33. Jim Carlton, "Recycling Redefined," *The Wall Street Journal,* March 6, 2001, pp. B1, B4; Stephanie Anderson, "There's Gold in Those Hills of Soda Bottles," *BusinessWeek,* September 11, 1995, p. 48; Maxine Wilkie, "Asking Americans to Use Less Stuff," *American Demographics,* December 1994, pp. 11–12; and Jacquelyn Ottman, "New and Improved Won't Do," *Marketing News,* January 30, 1995, p. 9.

34. Chris Anderson, "The Wi-Fi Revolution," *Unwired,* supplement to *Wired,* 2003.

35. Henry Goldblatt, "The End of the Long Distance Club," *Fortune,* May 26, 1997, p. 30; and "Wheel of Fortune," *The Economist,* November 21, 1998, p. 53.

36. DeAnn Welmer, "Don't Be Shocked by Surges in the Price of Power," *BusinessWeek,* July 27, 1998, p. 33.

37. Jay Greene, "Microsoft: First Europe, Then. . . ?" *BusinessWeek,* March 22, 2004, p. 86.

38. Michael Porter, *Competitive Advantage* (New York: Free Press, 1985); and Michael Porter, *Competitive Strategy* (New York: Free Press, 1980).

39. Catherine Amst, "For Lucent, a Shining Moment," *BusinessWeek,* April 21, 1997, p. 126.

40. "Small Business Resources for Faculty, Students, and Researchers: Answers to Frequently Asked Questions," Small Business Administration, Office of Advocacy, March 2004.

41. "A New Copyright Law?" *BusinessWeek,* August 3, 1998, p. 45.

42. "Highlights of Food Labeling," *Marketing News,* March 15, 2004, p. 14.

43. Dorothy Cohen, "Trademark Strategy Revisited," *Journal of Marketing,* July 1991, pp. 46–59.

44. Maxine L. Retsky, "Review Int'l Filing Process for Marks," *Marketing News,* September 29, 2003, p. 8.

45. Paul Barrett, "High Court Sees Color as Basis for Trademarks," *The Wall Street Journal,* March 29, 1995, p. A6; Paul Barrett, "Color in the Court," *The Wall Street Journal,* January 5, 1995, p. A1; and David Kelly, "Rainbow of Ideas to Trademark Color," *Advertising Age,* April 24, 1995, pp. 20, 22.

46. Maxine L. Retsky, "Dilution of Trademarks Hard to Prove," *Marketing News,* May 12, 2003, p. 6.

47. Dick Mercer, "Tempest in a Soup Can," *Advertising Age,* October 17, 1994, pp. 25–29.

48. Catherine Arnold, "Law Gives Industry a Buzz," *Marketing News,* February 1, 2004, p. 11; Maxine L. Retsky, "New National 'Do Not Call' Law Becomes Effective, Enforceable," *Marketing News,* August 4, 2003, p. 6; "Who Buys That Stuff?" *Marketing News,* February 1, 2004, p. 11; Arundhati Parmar, "We Said, Do-Not-Call," *Marketing News,* March 15, 2004, p. 4; and Deborah L. Vence, "Less Ringing in the Ear," *Marketing News,* December 8, 2003, p. 14.

49. Maxine L. Retsky, "Stakes Are High for Direct Mail Sweepstakes Promotions," *Marketing News,* July 3, 2000, p. 8; Catherine Arnold, "Picky, Picky, Picky" *Marketing News,* February 15, 2004, p. 17; Catherine Arnold, "No Can Spam," *Marketing News,* January 15, 2004, p. 3; Arundhati Parmar, "Can't Say You Weren't Warned," *Marketing News,* February 15, 2004, p. 4; and James Heckman, "Laws That Take Effect—and Some Likely to Return in 1999 Mean Marketers Must Change Some Policies," *Marketing News,* December 7, 1998, p. 1, 16.

50. Mark McFadden, "The BBB on the WWW," *HP Professional,* September 1997, p. 36.

Flyte Time Productions, Inc.: This case was written by William Rudelius based on personal interviews with Jimmy Jam and Terry Lewis and the following sources: Don Campbell, "In Groove We Trust," *NWA World Traveler,* February 2004, pp. 29–33; Jon Bream, "Flyte Tyme Is Still Ticking after 20 Years of Hits," *Star Tribune,* April 29, 2001, pp. F1, F7; and "Jimmy Jam and Terry Lewis Make Flyte Tyme Studios No. 1," *Business Wire,* August 21, 2001.

CHAPTER 4

1. www.beeresponsible.com, downloaded March 1, 2004; www.beerinstitute.org, downloaded March 1, 2004; Mike Beirne, "In the Name of Responsibility," *BrandWeek,* May 12, 2003, pp. 32–36.

2. For a discussion of the definition of ethics, see Eugene R. Lazniak and Patrick E. Murphy, *Ethical Marketing Decisions: The Higher Road* (Boston: Allyn & Bacon, 1993), chap. 1.

3. Verne E. Henderson, "The Ethical Side of Enterprise," *Sloan Management Review,* Spring 1982, pp. 37–47; see also, Joseph L. Badaracco, Jr., *Defining Moments: When Managers Must Choose between Right and Right* (Boston: Harvard Business School Press, 1997).

4. "Honorable?" *Business 2.0,* February 2000, p. 92.

5. "Exporting Death," *Time,* April 13, 1998, p. 63; Ray O. Werner, "Marketing and the Supreme Court in Transition, 1982–1984," *Journal of Marketing,* Summer 1985, pp. 97–105; and Jane Bryant

Quinn, "Computer Program Deceives Consumers," *Dallas Morning News,* March 2, 1998, p. B3.

6. *The 2003 National Business Ethics Survey* (Washington, DC: Ethics Resource Center, 2003); "Image Issue," *Advertising Age,* December 9, 2002, p. 18; and Patrick J. Gnazzo and George R. Wratney, "Are You Serious about Ethics?" *Across the Board,* July–August 2003, pp. 47–50.

7. See, for example, Lawrence B. Chonko, *Ethical Decision Making in Marketing* (Thousand Oaks, CA: Sage, 1995).

8. Thomas Donaldson, "Values in Tension: Ethics away from Home," *Harvard Business Review,* September–October 1996, pp. 48–62.

9. "Levi Only Comfortable Dealing with Countries That Fit Its Image," *Dallas Morning News,* January 9, 1995, p. D2.

10. These statistics were obtained from Recording Industry Association of America (www.riaa.com), Motion Picture Association of America (www.mpaa.com), and the Business Software Alliance (www.bsa.com).

11. *Internet Piracy on Campus* (IPSOS: Washington, DC, September 16, 2003).

12. Vern Terpstra and Kenneth David, *The Cultural Environment of International Business,* 3rd ed. (Cincinnati: South-Western Publishing, 1991), p. 12.

13. "Carnivore in the Cabbage Patch," *U.S. News & World Report,* January 20, 1997, p. 69.

14. "Three Ad Agencies Settle FTC Charges of Deceptive Car-Leasing Commercials," *The Wall Street Journal,* January 21, 1998, p. B2.

15. Timothy Muris, "Protecting Consumers' Privacy: 2002 and Beyond," www.ftc.gov, downloaded January 3, 2004.

16. For an extensive examination on slotting fees, see Paul N. Bloom, Gregory T. Gundlach, and Joseph P. Cannon, "Slotting Allowances and Fees: Schools of Thought and Views of Practicing Managers," *Journal of Marketing,* April 2000, pp. 92–109. Also see, "FTC Pinpoints Slotting Fees," *Advertising Age,* February 26, 2001, p. 52.

17. "FBI Chief Puts Cost of Economic Espionage at $200 Million," *Bloomberg News,* June 21, 2003.

18. "P&G Expected to Get about $120 Million in Settlement of Chewy-Cookie Lawsuit," *The Wall Street Journal,* September 11, 1989, p. B10.

19. These examples are highlighted in Thomas W. Dunfee, N. Craig Smith, and William T. Ross, Jr., "Social Contracts and Marketing Ethics," *Journal of Marketing,* July 1999, pp. 14–32; and Andy Pasztor, *When the Pentagon Was for Sale: Inside America's Biggest Defense Scandal* (New York: Scribner, 1995).

20. www.transparency.org, downloaded February 21, 2004.

21. Thomas Donaldson, "The Corporate Ethics Boom: Significant, or Just for Show?" Knowledge.Wharton.upenn.edu, downloaded February 25, 2001; and "Doing Well by Doing Good," *The Economist,* April 22, 2000, pp. 65–67.

22. "Coca-Cola Unit Head Resigns after Rigged Test," www.forbes.com, downloaded August 25, 2003.

23. *The 2003 National Business Ethics Survey.*

24. "Workers Who Blow the Whistle on Bosses Often Pay a High Price," *The Wall Street Journal,* July 18, 1995, p. B1.

25. For an extensive discussion on these moral philosophies, see R. Eric Reidenbach and Donald P. Robin, *Ethics and Profits* (Englewood Cliffs, NJ: Prentice Hall, 1989); Chonko, *Ethical Decision Making*; and Lazniak and Murphy, *Ethical Marketing Decisions.*

26. "3M's Big Cleanup," *BusinessWeek,* June 5, 2000, pp. 96–98.

27. James O. Wilson, "Adam Smith on Business Ethics," *California Management Review* (Fall 1989), pp. 57–72.

28. Alix M. Freedman, "Bad Reaction: Nestlé's Bid to Crash Baby-Formula Market in U.S. Stirs a Row," *The Wall Street Journal,* February 16, 1989, pp. A1, A6; and Alix Freedman, "Nestlé to Drop Claim on Label of Its Formula," *The Wall Street Journal,* March 13, 1989, p. B5.

29. Harvey S. James and Farhad Rassekh, "Smith, Friedman, and Self-Interest in Ethical Society," *Business Ethics Quarterly,* July 2000, pp. 659–74.

30. "Cost of Living," *The Economist,* March 1, 2003, p. 60.

31. "Perrier—Overresponding to a Crisis," in Robert F. Hartley, *Marketing Mistakes and Successes,* 9th ed. (New York: John Wiley & Sons, 2004), pp. 153–64.

32. "The Great Firestone/Ford Explorer Tire Disaster," in Hartley, *Marketing Mistakes and Successes,* pp. 139–52.

33. "More about Pollution Prevention Pays," www.3M.com, downloaded February 18, 2004; "Xerox Steps up Successes of Environment, Health, Safety Programs," www.xerox.com/environment, downloaded February 25, 2004; "Boise Cascade Turns Green," *The Wall Street Journal,* September 3, 2003, p. B6; and "FedEx and Brown Are Going Green," *BusinessWeek,* August 11, 2003, pp. 60, 62.

34. *The ISO Survey of ISO 9000 and ISO 14000 Certificates,* Geneva, Switzerland: International Organization for Standardization, 2004.

35. For an extended discussion on this topic, see P. Rajan Varadarajan and Anil Menon, "Causes-Related Marketing: A Coalignment of Marketing Strategy and Corporate Philanthropy," *Journal of Marketing,* July 1988, pp. 58–74. The examples are found in Susan Orenstein, "The Selling of Breast Cancer," *Business 2.0,* February 2003, pp. 88–94; and Christine Bittar, "Seeking Cause and Effect," *BrandWeek,* September 11, 2002, pp. 19–23.

36. "Cause and 'Affect'," *BrandWeek,* October 7, 2002, p. 16; and Bittar, "Seeking Cause and Effect."

37. These steps are adapted from J. J. Carson and G. A. Steiner, *Measuring Business Social Performance: The Corporate Social Audit* (New York: Committee for Economic Development, 1974). See also Sandra Waddock and Neil Smith, "Corporate Responsibility Audits: Doing Well by Doing Good," *Sloan Management Review,* Winter 2000, pp. 75–84.

38. "Sweatshops: Finally, Airing the Dirty Linen," *BusinessWeek,* June 23, 2003, pp. 100–1.

39. "Corporate America's Social Conscience," *Fortune,* May 26, 2003, pp. 147ff.

40. This discussion is based on Wayne D. Hoyer and Deborah J. MacInnis, *Consumer Behavior,* 3rd ed. (New York: Houghton Mifflin Company, 2004), pp. 535–37; "Factoids," *Research Alert,* December 8, 2002, p. 5; and "Penny for Your Thoughts," *American Demographics,* September 2000, pp. 8–9.

41. "A Pirate and His Penance," *Time,* January 26, 2004, p. 60.

42. "A Lighter Shade of Green," *American Demographics,* February 2000, p. 24.

43. "Schism on the Green," *BrandWeek,* February 26, 2001, p. 18.

44. "FTC Stands by Regs for 'Green' Ad Claims," *Advertising Age,* October 7, 1996, p. 61.

Starbucks Corporation: This case is based on information on the company website (www.starbucks.com) and the following sources: "Living Our Values," *2003 Corporate Social Responsibility Annual Report;* "Starbucks Annual Shareholder Meeting," Starbucks press release, March 30, 2004; Ranjay Gulati, Sarah Huffman, and Gary Neilson, "The Barista Principle: Starbucks and the Rise of Relational Capital," *Strategy and Business,* 3rd Quarter 2002, pp. 58–69; and Andy Serwer, "Hot Starbucks to Go," *Fortune,* January 12, 2004, pp. 52ff.

CHAPTER 5

1. "This Volvo Is Not a Guy Thing," *BusinessWeek,* March 15, 2004, pp. 84–86; and "Volvo for Wife," www.forbes.com, downloaded April 1, 2004.

2. Roger D. Blackwell, Paul W. Miniard, and James F. Engel, *Consumer Behavior,* 9th ed. (Mason, OH: South-Western Publishing, 2001).

3. For thorough descriptions of consumer expertise, see Joseph W. Alba and J. Wesley Hutchinson, "Knowledge Calibration: What Consumers Know and What They Think They Know," *Journal of Consumer Research,* September 2000, pp. 123–57.

4. For in-depth studies on external information search patterns, see Sridhar Moorthy, Brian T. Ratchford, and Debabrata Talukdar, "Consumer Information Search Revisited: Theory and Empirical Analysis," *Journal of Consumer Research,* March 1997, pp. 263–77; Joel E. Urbany, Peter R. Dickson, and William L. Wilkie, "Buyer Uncertainty and Information Search," *Journal of Consumer Research,* March 1992, pp. 452–63; and Sharon E. Beatty and Scott M. Smith, "External Search Effort: An Investigation across Several Product Categories," *Journal of Consumer Research,* June 1987, pp. 83–95.

5. "CD Players—Portable," *Consumer Reports 2003 Buying Guide* (Yonkers, NY: Consumers Union, 2003), pp. 225–27.

6. For an extended discussion on evaluative criteria, see Del J. Hawkins, Roger J. Best, and Kenneth A. Coney, *Consumer Behavior,* 9th ed. (Burr Ridge, IL: McGraw-Hill/Irwin, 2004), pp. 562–79.

7. John A. Howard, *Buyer Behavior in Marketing Strategy,* 2nd ed. (Englewood Cliffs, NJ: Prentice Hall, 1994), pp. 101, 128–89. For an extended discussion on consumer choice sets, see Allan D. Shocker, Moshe Ben-Akiva, Bruno Boccara, and Prakesh Nedungadi, "Consideration Set Influences on Consumer Decision Making and Choice: Issues, Models, and Suggestions." *Marketing Letters,* August 1991, pp. 181–98.

8. William J. McDonald, "Time Use in Shopping: The Role of Personal Characteristics," *Journal of Retailing,* Winter 1994, pp. 345–66; Robert J. Donovan, John R. Rossiter, Gillian Marcoolyn, and Andrew Nesdale, "Store Atmosphere and Purchasing Behavior," *Journal of Retailing,* Fall 1994, pp. 283–94; and Eric A. Greenleaf and Donald R. Lehman, "Reasons for Substantial Delay in Consumer Decision Making," *Journal of Consumer Research,* September 1995, pp. 186–99.

9. Ruth N. Bolton, "A Dynamic Model of the Duration of the Customer's Relationship with a Continuous Service Provider: The Role of Satisfaction," *Marketing Science* 17 (1998), pp. 45–65.

10. Jagdish N. Sheth, Banwari Mitral, and Bruce Newman, *Consumer Behavior* (Fort Worth: Dryden Press, 1999), p. 22.

11. Frederick F. Reichheld and Thomas Teal, *The Loyalty Effect* (Boston: Harvard Business School Press, 1996); "What's a Loyal Customer Worth?" *Fortune,* December 11, 1995, p. 182; and Patricia Sellers, "Keeping the Buyers You Already Have," *Fortune,* Autumn–Winter 1993, p. 57. For an in-depth examination of this topic, see Werner J. Reinartz and V. Kumar, "On the Profitability of Long-Life Customers in a Noncontractual Setting: An Empirical Investigation and Implications for Marketing," *Journal of Marketing,* October 2000, pp. 17–35.

12. For an overview of research on involvement, see John C. Mowen and Michael Minor, *Consumer Behavior,* 5th ed. (Upper Saddle River, NJ: Prentice Hall, 1998), pp. 64–68; and Wayne D. Hoyer and Deborah J. MacInnis, *Consumer Behavior,* 3rd ed. (Boston: Houghton Mifflin Co., 2004), pp. 57–59.

13. For an overview on the three problem-solving variations, see Hawkins, Best, and Coney, *Consumer Behavior,* pp. 500–04.

14. Russell Belk, "Situational Variables and Consumer Behavior," *Journal of Consumer Research,* December 1975, pp. 157–63.

15. A. H. Maslow, *Motivation and Personality* (New York: Harper & Row, 1970). Also see Richard Yalch and Frederic Brunel, "Need Hierarchies in Consumer Judgments of Product Design: Is It Time to Reconsider Maslow's Hierarchy?" in Kim Corfman and John Lynch, eds., *Advances in Consumer Research* (Provo, UT: Association for Consumer Research, 1996), pp. 405–10.

16. Joel B. Cohen, "An Interpersonal Orientation to the Study of Consumer Behavior," *Journal of Marketing Research,* August 1967, pp. 270–78; and Rena Bartos, *Marketing to Women around the World* (Cambridge, MA: Harvard Business School, 1989).

17. Terry Clark, "International Marketing and National Character: A Review and Proposal for an Integrative Theory," *Journal of Marketing,* October 1990, pp. 66–79; and John-Benedict E. M. Steenkamp, "The Role of National Culture in International Marketing Research," *International Marketing Review* 18, no. 1 (2001), pp. 30–44.

18. Myron Magnet, "Let's Go for Growth," *Fortune,* March 7, 1994, p. 70.

19. This example provided in Michael R. Solomon, *Consumer Behavior,* 4th ed. (Upper Saddle River, NJ: Prentice Hall, 1999), p. 59.

20. For further reading on subliminal perception, see Anthony G. Greenwald, Sean C. Draine, and Richard L. Abrams, "Three Cognitive Markers of Unconscious Semantic Activation," *Science,* September 1996, pp. 1699–701; Dennis L. Rosen and Surendra N. Singh, "An Investigation of Subliminal Embedded Effect on Multiple Measures of Advertising Effectiveness," *Psychology & Marketing,* March–April 1992, pp. 157–73; and Kathryn T. Theus, "Subliminal Advertising and the Psychology of Processing Unconscious Stimuli: A Review of the Research," *Psychology & Marketing,* May–June 1994, pp. 271–90.

21. August Bullock, *The Secret Sales Pitch* (San Jose, CA: Norwich Publishers, 2004); "GOP Commercial Resurrects Debate on Subliminal Ads," *The Wall Street Journal,* September 13, 2000, p. B10; "I Will Love This Story," *U.S. News & World Report,* May 12, 1997, p. 12; and "Firm Gets Message Out Subliminally," *Dallas Morning News,* February 2, 1997, pp. 1H, 6H.

22. "CPG Brand Loyalty Is up for Grabs," www.forrester.com, downloaded December 2002; and "Customer Loyalty: Going, Going . . . ," *American Demographics,* September 1997, pp. 20–23.

23. Martin Fishbein and I. Aizen, *Belief, Attitude, Intention and Behavior: An Introduction to Theory and Research* (Reading, MA: Addison-Wesley 1975), p. 6.

24. Richard J. Lutz, "Changing Brand Attitudes through Modification of Cognitive Structure," *Journal of Consumer Research,* March 1975, pp. 49–59. See also Mowen and Minor, *Consumer Behavior,* pp. 287–88.

25. "The VALS™ Types," www.sric-bi.com/VALS, downloaded April 16, 2004.

26. This discussion is based on Ed Keller and Jon Berry, *The Influentials* (New York: Simon and Schuster, 2003).

27. "Word of Mouth Is Where It's At," *BrandWeek,* June 2, 2003, p. 26.

28. Linda Tischler, "What's the Buzz?" *Fast Company,* May 2004, pp. 76–77; Melanie Wells, "Kid Nabbing," *Forbes,* February 2, 2004, pp. 84–87; and Marion Salzman, Ira Matathia, and Ann O'Reilly, *Buzz: Harness the Power of Influence and Create Demand* (New York: John Wiley & Sons, 2003).

29. For an extensive review on consumer socialization of children, see Deborah Roedder John, "Consumer Socialization of Children: A Retrospective Look at Twenty-Five Years of Research," *Journal of Consumer Research,* December 1999, pp. 183–213.

30. "Get 'Em While They're Young," *Marketing News,* November 10, 1997, p. 2.

31. This discussion is based on "Marriage Drain's Big Cost," *American Demographics,* April 2004, pp. 40–41; James Morrow, "A Place for One," *American Demographics,* November 2003, pp. 25–31; and J. Paul Peter and Jerry C. Olson, *Consumer Behavior and Marketing Strategy,* 7th ed. (Burr Ridge, IL: McGraw Hill/Irwin, 2005), pp. 342–44.

32. "Co-Masters of Their Domain," *BrandWeek,* September 8, 2003, p. 20; and "Tailor-Made," *Advertising Age,* September 23, 2002, p. 14.

33. "He's in Fashion," *American Demographics,* November 2002, p. 10; and "Look Who's Shopping," *Progressive Grocer,* January 2001, p. 18.

34. "Kids Gaining Voice in How Home Looks," *Advertising Age,* March 29, 2004, p. S4; "Coming of Age in Consumerdom," *American Demographics,* April 2004, p. 14; and www.teenresearch.com, downloaded January 15, 2004.

35. Harold R. Kerbo, *Social Stratification and Inequality* (Burr Ridge, IL: McGraw-Hill, 2000). For an extensive discussion on social class, see Eric Arnould, Linda Price, and George Zinkhan, *Consumers,* 2nd ed. (Burr Ridge, IL: McGraw Hill/Irwin, 2004), chap. 6.

36. For a summary of representative research on African American consumers, see Allison Stein Wellner, "Diversity in America," supplement to *American Demographics,* November 2002; Christine Bittar, "The New Face of Beauty," *BrandWeek,* January 19, 2004, pp. 24–28; William H. Frey, "Revival," *American Demographics,* October 2003, pp. 27–31; and "Race, Ethnicity, and the Way We Shop," *American Demographics,* February 2003, pp. 30–33.

37. "Hispanic Nation," *BusinessWeek,* March 15, 2004, pp. 58–68; "P&G, Sears, GM Top Hispanic Ad Spending Survey," *Advertising Age,* April 19, 2004, pp. 1, 60; Laurel Wentz, "Cross Over," *Advertising Age,* July 7, 2003, pp. S1–S6; and "Campbell Looks to Make Splash with Hispanics," *BrandWeek,* December 8, 2003, p. 22.

38. "Hispanics Wanted," *BrandWeek,* April 12, 2004, p. 22.

39. Wellner, "Diversity in America"; and "Race, Ethnicity, and the Way We Shop."

Ken Davis Products, Inc. This case is based on interviews with Barbara Jo Davis.

CHAPTER 6

1. Interview with Kim Nagele, JCP Media, March 10, 2004.

2. This figure is based on *Statistical Abstract of the United States: 2003,* 123rd ed. (Washington, DC: U.S. Census Bureau, 2003).

3. "FAA Announces Contract for New Workstations," *Dallas Morning News,* April 30, 1999, p. 16H.

4. These examples are based on Dave Nelson, Patricia E. Moody, and Jonathan Stenger, *The Purchasing Machine* (New York: Free Press, 2003); and an interview with Olga Krasnova, Infoservices, March 7, 2004.

5. *2002 NAICS United States Manual* (Washington, DC: Office of Management and Budget, 2002).

6. This listing and portions of the following discussion are based on F. Robert Dwyer and John F. Tanner, Jr., *Business Marketing,* 2nd ed. (Burr Ridge, IL: McGraw-Hill/Irwin, 2002); Michael D. Hutt and Thomas W. Speh, *Business Marketing Management,* 8th ed. (Mason, OH: South-Western, 2004); and Frank G. Bingham, Jr., Roger Gomes, and Patricia A. Knowles, *Business Marketing,* 3rd ed. (Burr Ridge, IL: McGraw-Hill/Irwin, 2005).

7. "Latin Trade Connections," *Latin Trade,* June 1998, p. 72.

8. "Mega Plane," *Business Week,* November 10, 2003, pp. 88–92; and Alex Taylor III, "Lord of the Air," *Fortune,* November 10, 2003, pp. 144–52.

9. These and other examples are found in "The Business Case for Diversity," www.diversity.com, downloaded on February 28, 2004; and "Boise Cascade Turns Green," *The Wall Street Journal,* September 3, 2003, p. B6. Also see Minette E. Drumwright, "Socially Responsible Organizational Buying: Environmental Concern as a Noneconomic Buying Criterion," *Journal of Marketing,* July 1994, pp. 1–18.

10. For a study of buying criteria used by industrial firms, see Daniel H. McQuiston and Rockney G. Walters, "The Evaluation Criteria of Industrial Buyers: Implications for Sales Training," *Journal of Business & Industrial Marketing,* Summer–Fall 1989, pp. 65–75. Also see Dwyer and Tanner, *Business Marketing,* chap. 2.

11. For an overview on ISO 9000 certification, see Thomas H. Stevenson and Frank C. Barnes, "What Industrial Marketers Need to Know about ISO 9000 Certification: A Review, Update, and Integration with Marketing," *Industrial Marketing Management,* November 2002, pp. 695–703.

12. Michael R. Leenders and David L. Blenkhorn, *Reverse Marketing: The New Buyer–Supplier Relationship* (New York: Free Press, 1996).

13. This example is found in Sandy D. Jap and Jakki J. Mohr, "Leveraging Internet Technologies in B2B Relationships," *California Management Review,* Summer 2002, pp. 24–38.

14. "America's Most Admired Companies," *Fortune,* March 8, 2004, pp. 80ff; Brian Milligan, "Medal of Excellence: Harley-Davidson Wins by Getting Suppliers on Board," *Purchasing,* September 2000, pp. 52–65; and "Harley-Davidson Company," *Purchasing Magazine Online,* September 4, 2003.

15. "IBM Plans New Supercomputers," *Dallas Morning News,* November 19, 2002, p. 8D.

16. This discussion is based on www.ibm.com/procurement/html/ principles_practices, downloaded March 10, 2004; and H. Michael

Hayes, Per Jenster, and Nils-Erik Aaby, *Business Marketing* (Burr Ridge, IL: McGraw-Hill/Irwin, 1996).

17. "EDS Jars Rivals, Wins Big Defense Deal," *The Wall Street Journal,* October 9, 2000, p. A4; and "HP Finalizes $3 Billion Outsourcing Agreement to Manage Procter & Gamble's IT Infrastructure," Hewlett-Packard news release, May 6, 2003.

18. This discussion is based on James C. Anderson and James A. Narus, *Business Market Management* (Upper Saddle River, NJ: Prentice Hall, 1999); Neil Rackham, Lawrence Friedman, and Richard Ruff, *Getting Partnering Right* (New York: McGraw-Hill, 1996); and Joseph P. Cannon and Christian Homburg, "Buyer–Supplier Relationships and Customer Firm Costs," *Journal of Marketing,* January 2001, pp. 29–43.

19. Thomas V. Bonoma, "Major Sales: Who Really Does the Buying?" *Harvard Business Review,* May–June 1982, pp. 11–19. For recent research on buying centers, see Morry Ghingold and David T. Wilson, "Buying Center Research and Business Marketing Practices: Meeting the Challenge of Dynamic Marketing," *Journal of Business & Industrial Marketing* 13, no. 2 (1998), pp. 96–108; and Philip L. Dawes, Don Y. Lee, and Grahame R. Dowling, "Information Control and Influence in Emerging Buying Centers," *Journal of Marketing,* July 1998, pp. 55–68.

20. Paul A. Herbig, *Handbook of Cross-Cultural Marketing* (New York: Halworth Press, 1998).

21. Julie M. Bristor, "Influence Strategies in Organizational Buying: The Importance of Connections to the Right People in the Right Places," *Journal of Business-to-Business Marketing* 1 (1993), pp. 63–98.

22. These definitions are adapted from Frederick E. Webster, Jr., and Yoram Wind, *Organizational Buying Behavior* (Englewood Cliffs, NJ: Prentice Hall, 1972), p. 6.

23. "Can Corning Find Its Optic Nerve?" *Fortune,* March 19, 2001, pp. 148–50.

24. Representative studies on the buy-class framework that document its usefulness include Erin Anderson, Wujin Chu, and Barton Weitz, "Industrial Purchasing: An Empirical Exploration of the Buy-Class Framework," *Journal of Marketing,* July 1987, pp. 71–86; Morry Ghingold, "Testing the 'Buy-Grid' Buying Process Model," *Journal of Purchasing and Materials Management,* Winter 1986, pp. 30–36; P. Matthyssens and W. Faes, "OEM Buying Process for New Components: Purchasing and Marketing Implications," *Industrial Marketing Management,* August 1985, pp. 145–57; and Thomas W. Leigh and Arno J. Ethans, "A Script-Theoretic Analysis of Industrial Purchasing Behavior," *Journal of Marketing,* Fall 1984, pp. 22–32. Studies not supporting the buy-class framework include Joseph A. Bellizi and Philip McVey, "How Valid Is the Buy-Grid Model?" *Industrial Marketing Management,* February 1983, pp. 57–62; and Donald W. Jackson, Janet E. Keith, and Richard K. Burdick, "Purchasing Agents' Perceptions of Industrial Buying Center Influences: A Situational Approach," *Journal of Marketing,* Fall 1984, pp. 75–83.

25. See, for example, R. Vekatesh, Ajay Kohli, and Gerald Zaltman, "Influence Strategies in Buying Centers," *Journal of Marketing,* October 1995, pp. 61–72; Gary L. Lilien and Anthony Wong, "An Exploratory Investigation of the Structure of the Buying Center in the Metal Working Industry," *Journal of Marketing Research,* February 1984, pp. 1–11; and Wesley J. Johnston and Thomas V. Bonoma, "The Buying Center: Structure and Interaction Patterns," *Journal of Marketing,* Summer 1981, pp. 143–56. Also see Christopher P. Puto, Wesley E. Patton III, and Ronald H. King, "Risk Handling Strategies in Industrial Vendor Selection Decisions," *Journal of Marketing,* Winter 1985, pp. 89–98.

26. *Machine Vision Market: 2002 Results and Forecasts to 2007* (Ann Arbor, MI: Automated Imaging Association, 2003).

27. "B2B E-Commerce Headed for Trillions," www.clickz.com, downloaded March 1, 2004.

28. This discussion is based on Jennifer Reinhold, "What We Learned in the New Economy," *Fast Company,* March 4, 2004, pp. 56ff; Mark Roberti, "General Electric's Spin Machine," *The Industry Standard,* January 22–29, 2001, pp. 74–83; "Grainger Lightens Its Digital Load," *Industrial Distribution,* March 2001, pp. 77–79; and www.boeing.com/procurement, downloaded February 6, 2004.

29. "B2B, Take 2," *BusinessWeek Online,* November 25, 2003.

30. Michael Krauss, "EBay 'Bids' on Small-Biz Firms to Sustain Growth," *Marketing News,* December 8, 2003, pp. 6, 7; "Ebay Realizes Success in Small-Biz Arena," *Marketing News,* May 1, 2004, p.11; and www.ebaybusiness.com.

31. This discussion is based on Robert J. Dolan and Youngme Moon, "Pricing and Market Making on the Internet," *Journal of Interactive Marketing,* Spring 2000, pp. 56–73; and Ajit Kambil and Eric van Heck, *Marking Markets: How Firms Can Benefit from Online Auctions and Exchanges* (Boston: Harvard Business School Press, 2002).

32. Sandy Jap, "An Exploratory Study of the Introduction of Online Reverse Auctions," *Journal of Marketing,* July 2003, pp. 96–107.

Lands' End: This case is based on information available on the company website (www.landsend.com) and the following sources: Robert Berner, "A Hard Bargain at Lands' End?" *BusinessWeek,* May 28, 2001, p. 14; Rebecca Quick, "Getting the Right Fit—Hips and All—Can a Machine Measure You Better than Your Tailor?" *The Wall Street Journal,* October 18, 2000, p. B1; Stephanie Miles, "Apparel E-tailers Spruce Up for Holidays," *The Wall Street Journal,* November 6, 2001, p. B6; and Dana James, "Custom Goods Nice Means for Lands' End," *Marketing News,* August 14, 2000, p. 5.

CHAPTER 7

1. Lisa Bannon and Carlta Vitzthum, "One-Toy-Fits-All: How Industry Learned to Love the Global Kid," *The Wall Street Journal,* April 29, 2003, pp. A1, A4; "Mattel, Inc.," *Hoover's Online,* www.hoovers.com, downloaded March 25, 2004; and "Mattel Recharges Its Batteries," *NYSE Magazine,* www.nyse.com, downloaded July 3, 2003.

2. These estimates are based on data from *International Trade Statistics 2004* (Geneva: World Trade Organization). Global trade statistics reported in this chapter also came from this source, unless otherwise indicated.

3. Masaaki Kotabe and Kristiaan Helsen, *Global Marketing Management,* 3rd ed. (New York: Wiley, 2004), p. 440.

4. "Bartering Gains Currency in Hard-Hit Southeast Asia," *The Wall Street Journal,* April 6, 1998, p. A10; and Beatrice B. Lund, "Corporate Barter as a Marketing Strategy," *Marketing News,* March 3, 1997, p. 8.

5. Michael E. Porter, *The Competitive Advantage of Nations* (New York: Free Press, 1990), pp. 577–615. For another view that emphasizes cultural differences, see David S. Landes, *The Wealth and Poverty of Nations* (New York: Norton, 1998).

6. Barry Shapiro, "Economic Espionage," *Marketing Management,* Spring 1998, pp. 56–58; and "More Spies Targeting U.S. Firms," *Dallas Morning News,* January 12, 1998, pp. 1D, 4D.

7. Dennis R. Appleyard and Alfred J. Field, Jr., *International Economics,* 4th ed. (Burr Ridge, IL: McGraw-Hill/Irwin, 2001), chap. 15; "A Fruit Peace," *The Economist,* April 21, 2001, pp. 75–76; and Gary C. Hufbauer and Kimberly A. Elliott, *Measuring the Cost of Protection in the United States* (Washington, DC: Institute for International Economics, 1994).

8. This discussion is based on information provided by the World Trade Organization, www.wto.org, downloaded March 17, 2004.

9. "A Survey of EU Enlargement," *The Economist,* November 22, 2003, special section.

10. "Free Trade on Trial," *The Economist,* January 3, 2004, pp. 13–15.

11. www.juniper.net/company, downloaded March 15, 2004; and "Alliances in Consumer and Packaged Goods," www.corporatefinance.mckinsey.com, downloaded Autumn 2003.

12. For an excellent overview of different types of global companies and marketing strategies, see Warren J. Keegan, *Global Marketing Management,* 7th ed. (Upper Saddle River, NJ: Prentice Hall, 2002), chap. 2.

13. Johnny K. Johansson and Ilkka A. Ronkainen, "The Brand Challenge," *Marketing Management,* March–April 2004, pp. 54–55.

14. Kevin Lane Keller, *Strategic Brand Management,* 2nd ed. (Upper Saddle River, NJ: Prentice Hall, 2003), p. 693.

15. "Golden Boys and Girls," *The Economist,* February 14, 2004, pp. 37–38; Elissa Moses, *The $100 Billion Allowance: Accessing the Global Teen Market* (New York: Wiley, 2000); and www.mtv.com/company, downloaded March 22, 2004.

16. For an extensive discussion on identifying global consumers, see Jean-Pierre Jeannet and H. David Hennessey, *Global Marketing Strategies,* 4th ed. (Boston: Houghton Mifflin, 1998).

17. "The Net's Second Superpower," *BusinessWeek,* March 15, 2004, pp. 54–56; "B2B E-Commerce Headed for Trillions," www.clickz.com, downloaded March 27, 2004; and "EU B2B Expected to Explode," www.clickz.com, downloaded March 27, 2004.

18. For comprehensive references on cross-cultural aspects of marketing, see Paul A. Herbig, *Handbook of Cross-Cultural Marketing* (New York: Halworth Press, 1998); Jean-Claude Usunier, *Marketing across Cultures,* 2nd ed. (London: Prentice Hall Europe, 1996); and Philip R. Cateora and John L. Graham, *International Marketing,* 12th ed. (Burr Ridge, IL: McGraw-Hill/Irwin, 2005). Unless otherwise indicated, examples found in this section appear in these excellent sources.

19. This discussion is based on Tipton F. McCubbins, "Somebody Kicked the Sleeping Dog—New Bite in the Foreign Corrupt Practices Act," *Business Horizons,* January–February 2001, pp. 27–32.

20. "Clash of Cultures," *BrandWeek,* May 4, 1998, p. 28. Also see R. L. Tung, *Business Negotiations with the Japanese* (Lexington, MA: Lexington Books, 1993).

21. These examples appear in Del I. Hawkins, Roger J. Best, and Kenneth A. Coney, *Consumer Behavior,* 9th ed. (Burr Ridge, IL: McGraw-Hill/Irwin, 2004), chap. 2.

22. "Greens Protest Coke's Use of Parthenon," *Dallas Morning News,* August 17, 1992, p. D4.

23. "Japanese Products are Popular in the U.S.," *Research Alert,* November 17, 2000, p. 8; and "Buying American," *American Demographics,* March 1998, pp. 32–38.

24. "Marketing by Language: Oracle Trims Teams, Sees Big Savings," *Advertising Age International,* July 2000, pp. 4, 38.

25. Terrence A. Shimp and Subhash Sharma, "Consumer Ethnocentrism, Construction and Validation of the CETSCALE," *Journal of Marketing Research,* August 1987, pp. 280–89.

26. Subhash Sharma, Terrence Shimp, and Jeongshin Shin, "Consumer Ethnocentrism: A Test of Antecedents and Moderators," *Journal of the Academy of Marketing Science,* Winter 1995, pp. 26–37; Joel Herche, "A Note on the Predictive Validity of the CETSCALE," *Journal of the Academy of Marketing Science,* Summer 1992, pp. 261–64; Richard G. Netemeyer, Srinivas Durvasula, and Donald R. Lichtenstein, "A Cross-National Assessment of the Reliability and Validity of the CETSCALE," *Journal of Marketing Research,* August 1991, pp. 320–27; and Jill Gabrielle Klein, Richard Ettenson, and Marlene D. Morris, "The Animosity Model of Foreign Product Purchase: An Empirical Test in the People's Republic of China," *Journal of Marketing,* January 1998, pp. 89–100.

27. "The Net's Second Superpower," *BusinessWeek.*

28. "Betting on a New Label: Made in Russia," *BusinessWeek,* April 12, 1999, p. 122; "Russia and Central-Eastern Europe: Worlds Apart," *BrandWeek,* May 4, 1998, pp. 30–31; and "We Will Bury You . . . with a Snickers Bar," *U.S. News & World Report,* January 26, 1998, pp. 50–51.

29. www.wto.com, downloaded February 15, 2004.

30. "Mattel Plans to Double Sales Abroad," *The Wall Street Journal,* February 11, 1998, pp. A3, A11.

31. These examples are found in Cateora and Graham, *International Marketing,* p. 540; "Honda Takes Currency Hit in Europe," *The Wall Street Journal,* March 28, 2001, p. A16; and "Currency Troubles Halt P&G Shipments to Turkey," *Advertising Age,* March 5, 2001, p. 32.

32. Cateora and Graham, *International Marketing.*

33. For an extensive and recent examination of these market entry options, see, for example, Johnny K. Johansson, *Global Marketing: Foreign Entry, Local Marketing, and Global Management,* 3rd ed. (Burr Ridge, IL: McGraw Hill/Irwin, 2003); Keegan, *Global Marketing Management;* Kotabe and Helson, *Global Marketing Management;* and Cateora and Graham, *International Marketing.*

34. Based on an interview with Pamela Viglielmo, director of international marketing, Fran Wilson Creative Cosmetics; and "Foreign Firms Think Their Way into Japan," www.successstories.com/nikkei, downloaded March 24, 2001.

35. *Small and Medium Sized Exporting Companies: A Statistical Profile* (Washington, DC: International Trade Administration), www.ita.doc.gov/, downloaded March 5, 2004.

36. "Made in Taiwan," *Forbes,* April 2, 2001, pp. 64–66.

37. *McDonald's 2003 Annual Report.*

38. "About Us," www.elitefoods.co.il, downloaded June 5, 2004.

39. "A Survey of Business in China," *The Economist,* March 20, 2004, special section.

40. This discussion is based on Keller, *Strategic Brand Management,* pp. 709–10; "Machines for the Masses," *The Wall Street Journal,* December 9, 2003, pp. A19, A20; "The Color of Beauty," *Forbes,* November 27, 2000, pp. 170–76; "It's Goo, Goo, Goo, Goo Vibrations at the Gerber Lab," *The Wall Street Journal,* December 4, 1996, pp. A1, A6; Donald R. Graber, "How to Manage a Global Product Development Process," *Industrial Marketing Management,* November 1996, pp. 483–98; and Herbig, *Handbook of Cross-Cultural Marketing.*

41. Jagdish N. Sheth and Atul Parvatiyar, "The Antecedents and Consequences of Integrated Global Marketing," *International Marketing Review* 18, no. 1 (2001), pp. 16–29. Also see D. Szymanski, S. Bharadwaj, and R. Varadarajan, "Standardization versus Adaptation of International Marketing Strategy: An Empirical Investigation," *Journal of Marketing,* October 1993, pp. 1–17.

42. This discussion is based on John Fahy and Fuyuki Taguchi, "Reassessing the Japanese Distribution System," *Sloan Management Review,* Winter 1995, pp. 49–61; and Edward Tse, "The Right Way to Achieve Profitable Growth in the Chinese Consumer Market," *Strategy & Business,* Second Quarter 1998, pp. 10–21.

43. "Stores Told to Lift Prices in Germany," *The Wall Street Journal,* September 11, 2000, pp. A27, A30.

44. "Rotten Apples," *Dallas Morning News,* April 7, 1998, p. 14A.

CNS Breathe Right Strips: This case was prepared by Mary L. Brown based on interviews with Kevin McKenna, vice president, International and Nick Naumann, Sr. Marketing Services Manager of CNS, Inc., September 2004.

CHAPTER 8

1. John Horn, "Studios Play Name Games," *Star Tribune,* August 10, 1997, p. F11; and "Flunking Chemistry," *Star Tribune,* April 11, 2003, p. E13.

2. US Entertainment Industry: 2003 MPA Market Statistics; Worldwide Market Research; Motion Picture Association of America, p. 17.

3. Bruce Orwall, "'Commander' Finds Wind in Its Sails," *The Wall Street Journal,* November 17, 2003, p. B10.

4. "Spider-Man 2," www.boxofficemojo.com, downloaded July 31, 2004.

5. Willow Bay, "Test Audiences Have Profound Effect on Movies," *CNN Newsstand & Entertainment Weekly,* September 28, 1998; see www.cnn.com/SHOWBIZ/Movies/9809/28/screen.test/.

6. Thomas R. King, "How Big Will Disney's 'Pocahontas' Be?" *The Wall Street Journal,* May 15, 1995, pp. B1, B8.

7. Helene Diamond, "Lights, Camera . . . Research!" *Marketing News,* September 11, 1989, pp. 10–11; and "Killer!" *Time,* November 16, 1987, pp. 72–79.

8. Joel Ryan, "Gigli 'Razzed'," att.eonline.com/News/Items, downloaded January 26, 2004.

9. Carl Diorio, "Tracking Projectings: B. O. Calculations an Inexact Science," *Variety,* May 24, 2001; see www.variety.com/index.asp?layout=story&articleid=VR1117799996.

10. For a lengthier, expanded 2004 definition, consult the American Marketing Association's website at www.marketingpower.com; for a researcher's comments on this and other definitions of marketing research, see Lawrence D. Gibson, "Quo Vadis, Marketing Research?" *Marketing Research,* Spring 2000, pp. 36–41.

11. Definitions of the three kinds of marketing research are adapted from William R. Dillon, Thomas J. Madden, and Neil H. Firtle, *Marketing Research in a Marketing Environment,* 3rd ed. (Burr Ridge: McGraw-Hill/Irwin, 1994), pp. 40–41.

12. John Cloud, "How the Furby Flies," *Time,* November 30, 1998, pp. 84–85; Joseph Pereira, "To These Youngsters, Trying Out Toys Is Hardly Kids' Play," *The Wall Street Journal,* December 17, 1997, pp. A1, A11; and "Toy of the Year Awards, 2000," *Family Fun,* November 2000; see www.family.go.com/entertain/toys/feature/famf1000toymethod_led/famf1000toymethod_led.html.

13. Lawrence D. Gibson, "Defining Marketing Problems," *Marketing Research,* Spring 1998, pp. 4–12.

14. Joe Schwartz, "Back to the Source," *American Demographics,* January 1989, pp. 22–26; and Felix Kessler, "High-Tech Shocks in Ad Research," *Fortune,* July 7, 1986, pp. 58–62.

15. "What TV Ratings Really Mean," Nielsen Media Research website, pp. 1–8; see www.nielsenmedia.com/whatratingsmean.

16. Network Primetime Averages: week of 09/27/04–10/03/04; see www.nielsenmedia.com.

17. Emily Nelson and Martin Peers, "As Technology Scatters Viewers, Networks Go Looking for Them," *The Wall Street Journal,* November 21, 2003, pp. A1, A6; Emily Nelson and Sarah Ellison, "Nielsen's Feud with TV Networks Shows Scarcity of Marketing Data," *The Wall Street Journal,* October 29, 2003, pp. A1, A6; "Nielsen Adapts Its Methods as TV Evolves," *The Wall Street Journal,* September 29, 2003, pp. B1, B10; and "Nielsen to Market Data Gathered by TiVo," *The Wall Street Journal,* February 5, 2004, p. B4.

18. Robert Frank, "How to Live Large, and Largely for Free, Jennifer Voitle's Way," *The Wall Street Journal,* June 9, 2003, pp. A1, A8.

19. Mark Maremont, "New Toothbrush Is Big-Ticket Item," *The Wall Street Journal,* October 27, 1998, pp. B1, B6; and Emily Nelson, "P&G Checks Out Real Life," *The Wall Street Journal,* May 17, 2001, pp. B1, B4.

20. Gerry Khermouch, "Consumers in the Mist," *BusinessWeek,* February 26, 2001, pp. 92, 94.

21. Jonathan Eig, "Food Industry Battles for Moms Who Want to Cook—Just a Little," *The Wall Street Journal,* March 7, 2001, pp. A1, A10; and Susan Feyder, "It Took Tinkering by Twin Cities Firms to Saver Some Sure Bets," *Minneapolis Star Tribune,* June 9, 1982, p.11A.

22. Constance Gustke, "Built to Last," *Sales and Marketing Management,* August 1997, pp. 78–83.

23. "Focus on Consumers," *General Mills Midyear Report,* Minneapolis, MN, January 8, 1998, pp. 2–3.

24. Michael J. McCarthy, "Stalking the Elusive Teenage Trendsetter," *The Wall Street Journal,* November 19, 1998, pp. B1, B10; and "Teens Spend $155 Billion in 2000," Teenage Research Unlimited press releases, January 25, 2001.

25. Roy Furchgott, "For Cool Hunters, Tomorrow's Trend Is the Trophy," *The New York Times,* June 28, 1998, p. 10; Patrick Goldstein, "Untangling the Web of Teen Trends," *Los Angeles Times,* November 21, 2000, p. F1; and Lev Grossman, "The Quest for Cool," *Time,* September 8, 2003, pp. 48–54.

26. Joshua Grossnickle and Oliver Raskin, "What's Ahead on the Internet," *Marketing Research,* Summer 2001, pp. 9–13; and Gordon A. Wyner, "Life (on the Internet) Imitates Research," *Marketing Research,* Summer 2000, pp. 38–39.

27. The Wendy's questionnaire is adapted from one originally developed by Robert Joffe, now at the University of Redlands.

28. Wendy Zellner, "Look Out, Supermarkets—Wal-Mart Is Hungry," *BusinessWeek,* September 14, 1998, pp. 98–100; Richard McCattery, "Wal-Mart Rumbles in the Supermarket Jungle," The Motley Fool, March 7, 1998, www.fool.com/news/foth/2000/foth000307; and "Our 1,000 Supercenter," Wal-Mart news release, August 22, 2001.

29. Steve Alexander, "Data Mining," *Minneapolis Star Tribune,* August 17, 1997, pp. D1, D5.

30. The step 4 and step 5 discussion was written by David Ford and Don Rylander of Ford Consulting Group, Inc.; the Tony's Pizza example was provided by Teré Carral of Tony's Pizza.

Ford Consulting Group, Inc.: This case was written by David Ford.

CHAPTER 9

1. Joseph Pereira and Stephanie Kang, "Phat News: Rappers Choose Reebok Shoes," *The Wall Street Journal,* November 14, 2003, pp. B1, B4.

2. Ibid., p. B4.

3. Stanley Holmes, "The New Nike," *BusinessWeek* (September 20, 2004), pp. 78–86; and Tim Gray, "The Bounce Is Back for Sneaker Manufacturers," *The New York Times* (May 23, 2004), p. BU8.

4. Material on sneakers is based on the SGMA Report 2002, "The U.S. Athletic Footwear Market Today," which is published annually by the Sporting Goods Manufacturers Association (www.sgma.com) based on a study by the NPD Group (www.npd.com), which polls 35,000 consumers weekly and collects data from over 3,500 retailers to provide this information; and April Y. Pennington "Heeling Art," *Entrepreneur Magazine,* May 2002, www.entrepreneur.com.

5. Information obtained from press releases from www.reebok.com, www.nike.com, www.vans.com, www.footlocker-inc.com, and www.cmax.com, as well as Terry Lefton, "Mike Likes Spite for Nike's New Jordan Line," *Business Journal—Portland,* July 29, 2002, www. portland.bizjournals.com.

6. Jeffrey A. Trachtenberg, "Magic Numbers," *Star Tribune,* June 17, 2003, pp. E1, E3.

7. David Leohnardt, "Two-Tier Marketing," *BusinessWeek,* March 17, 1997, pp. 82–90.

8. "Special Report on Mass Customization: A Long March," *The Economist,* July 14, 2001, pp. 63–65.

9. "Will the U.S. Chicken Out on Russia," *Fortune,* November 23, 1998, pp. 52–53.

10. Amber Holst, "Online Grocer Peapod Feels Chill of Its Rivals' Failures," *The Wall Street Journal,* July 23, 2001, p. B6; Chris Taylor, "E-Grocers Check Out," *Time,* July 23, 2001, p. 65; and Peapod.com news release, July 16, 2001.

11. The discussion of fast-food trends and market share is based on: Patronage of Fast-Food Restaurants by Adults 18 Years and Older: Simmons Market Research Bureau NCS/NHCS Spring 2004 Adult Full-Year Choices System Crosstabulation Report based on visits within the past 30 days.

12. Jennifer Ordonez, "Taco Bell Chef Has New Tactic: Be Like Wendy's," *The Wall Street Journal,* February 23, 2001, pp. B1, B4; and Jennifer Ordonez, "An Efficiency Drive: Fast-Food Lanes Are Getting Even Faster," *The Wall Street Journal,* May 18, 2000, pp. A1, A10.

13. The discussion of Apple's segmentation strategies through the years is based on information from its website, www.apple-history.com/history.html.

14. Dennis Sellers, "Business Journal: Digital Hub Plan Just Might Work," *MacCentral,* January 16, 2001, Mac Publishing, LLC.

15. "The iPod's Big Brother," *BusinessWeek* (September 13, 2004), p. 46.

16. Nicholas Zamiska, "How Milk Got a Major Boost by Food Panel," *The Wall Street Journal* (August 30, 2004), pp. B1, B5.

17. Betsey McKay, "Mooove Over, Milkman," *The Wall Street Journal,* June 9, 2003, pp. B1, B5.
18. Ibid.
19. Rebecca Winters, "Chocolate Milk," *Time,* April 30, 2001, p. 20.
20. Lisa McLaughlin, "This Moo's For You," *Time,* September 22, 2003, p. 77.
21. Patricia R. Olsen, "Adding Fizz to the Dairy Case," *The New York Times,* November 2, 2003, p. BU1.
22. Mark A. Moon, John T. Mentzer, Carlo D. Smith, and Michael S. Garver, "Seven Keys to Better Forecasting," *Business Horizons,* September–October 1998, pp. 44–52.
23. Interview with Bill McKee, manager of Corporate Communications/Public Relations, Xerox Corporation, and annual reports available at www2.xerox.com/go/xix/about_xerox/T_archive.jsp?view=annualreports.

Nokia: This case was written by Michael J. Vessey based on personal and telephone interviews with Keith Nowak of Nokia and David Linsalata of IDC, company data, and the following sources: Information obtained from press releases and other resources from Nokia's website. See www.nokiausa.com; Worldwide Mobile Phone Shipments by Region, 2003–2008; Worldwide Mobile Phone 2004–2008 Forecast Update: July 2004, Doc #31640, IDC, Mobile Devices. See www.idc.com.; Sumner Lemmon, "Chinese Mobile Phone Users Top 310 Million," *The Industry Standard,* August 24, 2004. See www.theindustrystandard.com; "Cracks in the Armor: The Strengths and Weaknesses of the Mobile Phone Market," IDC Telebriefing Report #TB20040930 PowerPoint presentation, September 2004. Information courtesy of David Linsalata IDC, Mobile Devices—Associate Analyst. See www.idc.com; "Wireless Industry Posts Winning Numbers," Cellular Telecommunications & Internet Association (CTIA) Semi-Annual Wireless Data Survey, March 22, 2004. See www.ctia.org; and Kim Tae-gyu, "4G Forum Offers Glimpse of New Telecom Tech," *The Korea Times,* August 22, 2004. See www.koreatimes.co.kr.

CHAPTER 10

1. Personal interview with Dr. George Dierberger, 3M, April 2004.
2. Michael Arndt, "3M's Rising Star," *BusinessWeek,* April 12, 2004, pp. 62–74.
3. Press releases from Motorola, Nokia, Samsung, Apple, and PalmOne; "Portable Media Devices: Beyond Music," e-mail newsletter from Jupiter Research, March 10, 2004; "Gartner: Mobile Phone Sales Grow by 20 Percent," *InfoWorld,* March 10, 2004; "Consumers Win as Turf War Rages over TVs, Cameras," *USA Today,* January 8, 2004, pp. B1, B2; and "Telematics: Coming to a Car Near You," *Technology Review,* Weblog, April 21, 2004, www.technologyreview.com.
4. Jyoti Thottam, "Plasma's Bright Future," *Time,* April 12, 2004, pp. 42–44.
5. Greg A. Stevens and James Burley, "3,000 Raw Ideas = 1 Commercial Success!" *Research-Technology Management,* May–June 1997, pp. 16–27.
6. R. G. Cooper and E. J. Kleinschmidt, "New Products—What Separates Winners from Losers?" *Journal of Product Innovation Management,* September 1987, pp. 169–84; Robert G. Cooper, *Winning at New Products,* 2nd ed. (Reading, MA: Addison-Wesley, 1993), pp. 49–66; and Thomas D. Kuczmarski, "Measuring Your Return on Innovation," *Marketing Management,* Spring 2000, pp. 25–32.
7. Julie Fortser, "The Lucky Charm of Steve Sanger," *BusinessWeek,* March 26, 2001, pp. 75–76.
8. John Gilbert, "To Sell Cars in Japan, U.S. Needs to Offer More Right-Drive Models," *Star Tribune,* May 27, 1995, p. M1.
9. Clayton M. Christensen and Michael E. Raynor, *The Innovator's Solution: Creating and Sustaining Successful Growth* (Cambridge, MA: Harvard Business School Press, 2003); Clayton M. Christensen, *The Innovator's Dilemma: When Technologies Cause Great Firms to Fail* (Cambridge, MA: Harvard Business School Press, 1997);

Clayton M. Christensen and Michael Overdorf, "Meeting the Challenge of Descriptive Change," *Harvard Business Review,* March–April 2000, pp. 67–76; and Clayton M. Christensen and Michael E. Raynor, "Creating a Killer Product," *Forbes,* October 13, 2003, pp. 82–84.
10. See Productscan Online at www.productscan.com.
11. The Avert Virucidal Tissues and Hey! There's A Monster in My Room spray examples are adapted from Robert M. McMath and Thom Forbes, *What Were They Thinking?* (New York: Random House, Inc., 1998).
12. Amy Merrick, "As 3M Chief, McNerney Wastes No Time Starting Systems Favored by Ex-Boss Welch," *The Wall Street Journal,* June 5, 2001, pp. B1, B4; see General Electric's website (www.ge.com) for an in-depth explanation of Six Sigma that 3M and other Fortune 500 companies use to improve quality: "The Road to Customer Impact: What Is Six Sigma?"
13. Morgan L. Swink and Vincent A. Mabert, "Product Development Partnerships: Balancing Needs of OEMs and Suppliers," *Business Horizons,* May–June 2000, pp. 59–68.
14. C. K. Prahalad and Venkat Ramswamy, *The Future of Competition* (Boston: Harvard Business School Press, 2004); Steve Hamm, "Adding Customers to the Design Team," *BusinessWeek,* March 1, 2004, pp. 22–23.
15. Anthony W. Ulwick, "Turn Customer Input into Innovation" *Harvard Business Review,* January 2002, pp. 91–97.
16. Adam Aston and Gail Edmonson, "This Volvo Is Not a Guy Thing," *BusinessWeek,* March 15, 2004, pp. 84–86.
17. Bruce Nussbaum, "The Power of Design," *BusinessWeek,* May 17, 2004, pp. 86–94; the article gives many techniques for idea and concept generation, as do Appendixes A, B, and C in Merle Crawford and Anthony Di Benedetto, *New Products Management,* 7th ed. (Burr Ridge, IL: McGraw-Hill/Irwin, 2003).
18. Personal interview with David Windorski, 3M, April 2004.
19. Steve Hoeffler, "Measuring Preferences for Really New Products," *Journal of Marketing Research,* November 2003, pp. 406–20.
20. Leila Abboud, "The Truth about Trans Fats: Coming to a Label Near You," *The Wall Street Journal,* July 10, 2003, pp. D1, D3; Betsey McKay, "Frito-Lay Puts 'Smart Snack' Label on Baked Chips," *The Wall Street Journal,* August 6, 2003, p. D3; and Bruce Horovitz, "Under Fire, Food Giants Switch to Healthier Fare," *USA Today,* July 1, 2003, pp. 1A, 2A.
21. Gray Hammel, "Innovation's New Math," *Fortune,* July 9, 2001, pp. 130–31.
22. Thomas M. Burton, "By Learning from Failures, Lilly Keeps Drug Pipeline Full," *The Wall Street Journal,* April 21, 2004, pp. A1, A12.
23. Danny Hakim, "Change Coming for Car Safety," *Star Tribune,* December 4, 2003, pp. A1, A8; Jayne O'Donnell, "Automakers Plan to Make Trucks Less of a Threat," *USA Today,* November 28, 2003, p. B1; and Dee-Ann Durbin, "Safety Official Softens Stance on SUVs," *Star Tribune,* February 27, 2003, p. A11.
24. Jack Neff, "White Bread, USA," *Advertising Age,* July 9, 2001, pp. 1, 12, 13.
25. Ben Elgin, "Can Google Hit It out of the Park Again?" *BusinessWeek,* April 19, 2004, pp. 38–39.
26. Tom Molson and George Sproles, "Styling Strategy," *Business Horizons,* September–October 2000, pp. 45–52.
27. Yuhong Wu, Sridhar Balasubramanian, and Vijay Mahajan, "When Is a Preannounced New Product Likely to Be Delayed?" *Journal of Marketing,* April, 2004, pp. 101–13.
28. Jennifer Ordonez, "How Burger King Got Burned in Quest to Make the Perfect Fry," *The Wall Street Journal,* January 16, 2001, pp. A1, A8.
29. Ben Elgin, "Can HP's Printer Biz Keep Printing Money?" *BusinessWeek,* July 14, 2003, pp. 68–70.
30. Peter Burrows, "Architects of the Info Age," *BusinessWeek,* March 29, 2004, p. 22.

3M Greptile Grip Golf Glove: This case was written by Michael J. Vessey based on interviews with Dr. George Dierberger, 3M personnel, and these other published sources: "3M Introduces 3M Golf Glove With Greptile Grip," 3M Press Release, May 5, 2004; "Who We Are," National Golf Foundation. See www.ngf.org; "The Golf 20/20 Vision for the Future Industry Report for 2003, published June 8, 2004. See www.golf2020.com; "Core Golfers Gain Ground in 2003," National Golf Foundation Press Release, May 21, 2004. See www.ngf.org; National Sporting Goods Association e-mail newsletter received June 21, 2004. See www.nsga.org; and 3M Golf Greptile Grip Business Plan.

CHAPTER 11

1. "X-Factor Marks the Spot as Gatorade Boosts Flavors," *BrandWeek,* February 28, 2004, p. 5; "Gatorade Sweats the Visual Details to Refresh Connection with Consumers," *BrandWeek,* March 3, 2003, p. 4; "PepsiCo Asks More of Gatorade Despite Its 85% Market Share," *The Wall Street Journal,* June 11, 2002, p. B4; and "The Gatorade Guys," *Sports Illustrated,* July 2, 2001, pp. 96–97.

2. For an extended discussion of the generalized product life-cycle curve, see David M. Gardner, "Product Life Cycle: A Critical Look at the Literature," in Michael Houston, ed., *Review of Marketing 1987* (Chicago: American Marketing Association, 1987), pp. 162–94; and Donald R. Lehmann and Russell S. Winer, *Product Management,* 4th ed. (Burr Ridge, IL: McGraw-Hall/Irwin, 2005), pp. 261–65.

3. Glenn Rifkin, "Mach3: Anatomy of Gillette's Latest Global Launch," *Strategy & Business,* 2nd Quarter 1999, pp. 34–41.

4. Harper W. Boyd, Jr., Orville C. Walker, John Mullins, and Jean-Claude Larréché, *Marketing Management,* 4th ed. (Burr Ridge, IL: McGraw-Hill/Irwin, 2002), p. 444.

5. Portions of this discussion on the fax machine industry are based on "Brother Wins Gamble in Shifting to Faxes," *The Wall Street Journal,* June 24, 2004, p. B6; "When Your Time Has Come—and Gone," *EDN.com.* November 27, 2003; "Electronics: 2003 Market Share Report by Category," *Reed Business Information,* January 8, 2004; and "Atlas Electronics Corporation," in Roger A. Kerin and Robert A. Peterson, *Strategic Marketing Problems: Cases and Comments,* 8th ed. (Upper Saddle River, NJ: Prentice Hall, 1998), pp. 494–506.

6. "Population Explosion" www.clickz.com, downloaded April 24, 2004; and "There's No Replacement—Not Even E-Mail," *Purchasing Online,* downloaded June 15, 2001.

7. "Why Coke Indulges (the Few) Fans of Tab," *The Wall Street Journal,* April 13, 2001, pp. B1, B4.

8. "Gillette Creates a Little Buzz with its New Razor," *Boston.com,* downloaded January 16, 2004.

9. "How to Separate Trends from Fads," *BrandWeek,* October 23, 2000, pp. 30, 32.

10. "More Guns, More Noise: What's Next for Videogames," *The Wall Street Journal,* May 6, 2004, pp. D1, D5; "Worldwide Videogame Hardware and Software Forecast and Analysis: 2003–2007," *IDC Research,* November 2003; and "Console Wars," *The Economist,* June 22, 2002, pp. 57–58.

11. Everett M. Rogers, *Diffusion of Innovations,* 4th ed. (New York: Free Press, 1995).

12. Jagdish N. Sheth, Banwasi Mitral, and Bruce Newman, *Consumer Behavior* (Fort Worth: Dryden Press, 1999).

13. "When Free Samples Become Saviors," *The Wall Street Journal,* August 14, 2001, pp. B1, B4.

14. For a historical perspective on the product/brand manager system, see George S. Low and Ronald A. Fullerton, "Brands, Brand Management, and the Brand Manager System: A Critical-Historical Evaluation," *Journal of Marketing Research,* May 1994, pp. 173–90.

15. "Hurdles on the Road to Hog Heaven" *BusinessWeek,* November 19, 2003, pp. 96–98; and "Wrinkle-Stain-Resistant Apparel Boost Sales," *DSN Retailing,* June 9, 2003, pp. 25–26.

16. "Dried Plum Print Push Paces Prunes," *BrandWeek,* August 12, 2002, p. 6; and "PlayStation 2 Software Update," press release at www.sony.com, November 15, 2003.

17. www.newbalance.com, downloaded May 6, 2004.

18. "St. Joseph: From Babies to Baby Boomers," *Advertising Age,* July 9, 2001, pp. 1, 38.

19. "Food Marketers Latch on to Health," *Advertising Age,* February 23, 2004, pp. 4, 41; and Daniel Kadlec "The Low Carb Frenzy," *Time,* May 3, 2004, pp. 47–54.

20. "The Shrink Wrap," *Time,* June 2, 2003, p. 81; "Don't Raise the Price, Lower the Water Award," *BrandWeek,* January 8, 2001, p. 19; and "More For Less," *Consumer Reports,* August 2004, p. 63.

21. Matthew Benjamin, "A World of Fakes," *U.S. News & World Report,* July 14, 2003, pp. 46–47.

22. This discussion is based on Kevin Lane Keller, *Strategic Brand Management,* 2nd ed. (Upper Saddle River, NJ: Prentice Hall, 2003).

23. This discussion is based on Kevin Lane Keller, "Building Customer-Based Brand Equity" *Marketing Management,* July–August, 2001, pp. 15–19.

24. This discussion is based on John Deighton, "How Snapple Got Its Juice Back," *Harvard Business Review,* January 2002, pp. 47–53; and "Breakfast King Agrees to Sell Bagel Business," *The Wall Street Journal,* September 28, 1999, pp. B1, B6.

25. "Hummer Markets Shoes for Offroad Set," *Advertising Age,* January 12, 2004, pp. 3, 40; Bruce Orwell, "Disney's Magic Transformation?" *The Wall Street Journal,* October 4, 2000, pp. A1, A15; and Keller, *Strategic Brand Management.*

26. "A Good Name Should Live Forever," *Forbes,* November 16, 1998, p. 88.

27. Rob Osler, "The Name Game: Tips on How to Get It Right," *Marketing News,* September 14, 1998, p. 50; and Keller, *Strategic Brand Management.* Also see Pamela W. Henderson and Joseph A. Cote, "Guidelines for Selecting or Modifying Logos," *Journal of Marketing,* April 1998, pp. 14–30; and Chiranjeev Kohli and Douglas W. LaBahn, "Creating Effective Brand Names: A Study of the Naming Process," *Journal of Advertising Research,* January–February 1997, pp. 67–75.

28. "When Brand Extension Becomes Brand Abuse," *BrandWeek,* October 26, 1998, pp. 20, 22.

29. For an in-depth discussion on co-branding, see Akshay R. Rao and Robert W. Ruekert, "Brand Alliances as Signals of Product Quality," *Sloan Management Review,* Fall 1994, pp. 87–97.

30. This discussion is based on David Aaker, *Brand Portfolio Strategy* (New York: Free Press, 2004); and "To Lure Older Girls, Mattel Brings in Hip-Hop Crowd," *The Wall Street Journal,* July 18, 2003, pp. A1, A6.

31. "Unilever Finally Pares Down to Core Brands," *Mergers & Acquisitions,* February 2004, pp. 6–9.

32. Matthew Boyle, "Brand Killers," *Fortune,* August 11, 2003, pp. 89–100.

33. "Elizabeth Arden Unveils Wal-Mart Only Brand," *Advertising Age,* February 9, 2004, p. 2; and www.Kodak.com/international, downloaded December 3, 2003.

34. www.pez.com, downloaded May 10, 2004; David Welch, *Collecting Pez* (Murphysboro, IL: Bubba Scrubba Publications, 1995); and "Pez Dispense with Idea It's Just for Kids," *BrandWeek,* September 26, 1996, p. 10.

35. "Just the Facts," *Research Alert,* January 2004, p. 2.

36. "L'eggs Hatches a New Hosiery Package," *BrandWeek,* January 1, 2001, p. 6.

37. "Packaging is the Capper," *Advertising Age,* May 5, 2003, p. 22.

38. Theresa Howard, "Frito-Lay's New Stax to Take a Stand," *USA Today,* August 14, 2003, p. 12B.

39. "Asian Brands Are Sprouting English Logos in Pursuit of Status, International Image," *The Wall Street Journal,* August 7, 2001, p. B7C.

40. Stuart L. Hart, "Beyond Greening: Strategies for a Sustainable World," *Harvard Business Review,* January–February 1997,

pp. 66–77; and Ajay Menon and Anil Menon, "Enviropreneurial Marketing Strategy: The Emergence of Corporate Environmentalism as Market Strategy," *Journal of Marketing,* January 1997, pp. 51–67.

BMW: This case was written by Giana Eckhardt and Steven Hartley based on company interviews and the following sources: Claire Billings, "Continuously Building the BMW Brand for 25 Years," *Campaign,* September 24, 2004, p. 16; Larry Armstrong, "BMW's Brand-new 6-series Convertible is Powerful, Elegant, and Eye-catching," *BusinessWeek,* August 9, 2004, p. 73; "BMW Reaches Out To the Affluent Young Urbanites," *Campaign,* July 23, 2004, p. 18; Gail Edmondson, "BMW: Crashing the Compact Market," *BusinessWeek,* June 18, 2004, p. 36; Gail Edmondson, "The Web Smart 50," *BusinessWeek,* November 24, 2003, p. 94; Troy Dreier, "BMW and iPod: Two Exclusive Names That Now Go Well Together," *PC Magazine,* September 21, 2004, p. 176; "Thrill Ride: With Three New BMW Shorts, Fallon Pulls Off Another Creative Coup," *ADWEEK,* October 28, 2002; Scott Donaton, "Cannes Fest Can Recognize Mad + Vine is Not Just a Fad," *Advertising Age,* June 16, 2003, p. 16; and "The New BMW M5," News and Press Release from www.bmwusa.com.

CHAPTER 12

1. "Star Trek: The Experience at the Las Vegas Hilton Announces Opening Date for Borg Invasion 4D Attraction," *PR Newswire,* February 10, 2004; additional information obtained from www.startrekexp.com.

2. Lawrence A. Crosby and Sheree L. Johnson, "Manufacturing Experiences: Tapping Emotions Can Create Value for Your Consumers," *Marketing Management,* January–February 2004, p. 12; Julie Rawe, "Relaunching Planet Earl," *Time,* October 13, 2003, p. A17; Matt Kinsman, "Happy One Hundred," *Promo,* August 1, 2003, p. 9; "Ultimate Electronics and Hard Rock Cafe International Partner to Transform Retailer's Home Theater Rooms in Las Vegas," *PR Newswire,* July 9, 2003; and "One-of-a-Kind Music and Dining Experience Ready to 'Rock' the Live Music Capital of the World," *PR Newswire,* June 25, 2001.

3. B. Joseph Pine and James H. Gilmore, *The Experience Economy,* (Boston: Harvard Business School Press); Rachel Brand, "Selling an Experience," *Denver Rocky Mountain News,* December 10, 2000, p. 1G; "The Personal Touch," *The Economist,* November 11, 2000; Jane E. Zarem, "Experience Marketing," *Folio,* October 2000; and Scott MacStravic, "Make Impressions Last: Focus on Value," *Marketing News,* October 23, 2000, p. 44.

4. Virginia H. Mannering and Kenneth A. Petrick, *BEA News,* Bureau of Economic Analysis, Department of Commerce, March 25, 2004; *World Trade Report 2003,* World Trade Organization, July 2003, table 1A.1; and *News Release No. 373,* World Trade Organization, April 5, 2004.

5. "At Your Service: Clubs Adopt Concierge Concept from Hotel Business," *Club Management,* December 2003, p. 16; Daniel McGinn, "Concierge to the Geek Set," *Newsweek,* December 1, 2003, p. 41; Toddie Gutnerhers, "A Dot-Com's Survival Story," *Business-Week,* May 13, 2002, p. 122; Clara Ogden, "To Name a Tune, Make a Call," *Time,* May 3, 2004, p. 95; Chris Taylor, "Amazon's New Search Service Takes Readers Inside Their Books," *Time,* November 17, 2003, p. 68; and Daren Fonda, "Patently Absurd," *Time,* August 27, 2001, p. 17.

6. Janet R. McColl-Kennedy and Tina White, "Service Provider Training Programs at Odds with Customer Requirements in Five Star Hotels," *Journal of Services Marketing* 11, no. 4 (1997), pp. 249–64; Ellyn A. McColgan, "How Fidelity Invests in Service Professionals," *Harvard Business Review,* January–February 1997, pp. 137–43; and Frederick F. Reichheld and W. Earl Sasser, Jr., "Zero Defections: Quality Comes to Services," *Harvard Business Review,* September–October 1990, pp. 105–11.

7. Christopher Lovelock and Evert Gummesson, "Whither Services Marketing?" *Journal of Services Research* 7 (August 2004),

pp. 20–41; Christopher H. Lovelock and George S. Yip, "Developing Global Strategies for Service Businesses," *California Management Review,* Winter 1996, pp. 64–86.

8. Stephen W. Brown, "The Move to Solutions Providers," *Marketing Management,* Spring 2000, pp. 10–11.

9. Lovelock and Yip, "Developing Global Strategies for Service Businesses."

10. Benny Evangelista, "SBC Park a Hot Spot for Fans Lugging Laptops," *San Francisco Chronicle,* April 26, 2004, p. A1; Tom Lowry, "The Prince of NASCAR," *BusinessWeek,* February 23, 2004, p. 90; Daniel Eisenberg, "The NBA's Global Game Plan," *Time,* March 17, 2003, p. 59; Rich Thomaselli, "National Football League," *Advertising Age,* November 17, 2003, p. S4; and "First Chinese Company Joins Olympic Marketing Program," *Marketing News,* April 15, 2004, p. 14.

11. Matthew L. Meuter, Amy L. Ostrom, Robert I. Roundtree, and Mary Jo Bitner, "Self-Service Technologies: Understanding Customer Satisfaction with Technology-Based Service Encounters," *Journal of Marketing,* July 2000, pp. 50–64.

12. "Nonprofit Activities," *The Nikkei Weekly,* October 30, 2000; and Paul Magnusson, "It's Open Season on Nonprofits," *BusinessWeek,* July 3, 1995, p. 31.

13. Michael Gibb, "Inject New Life into Nonprofits' Marketing Program," *Marketing News,* October 23, 2000, p. 47.

14. "American Red Cross Launches New Marketing Initiative: One Good Reason," *PR Newswire,* December 18, 2003; and "Dunlap Volunteers for Strategic Role at American Red Cross," *Marketing News,* September 29, 2003, p. 30.

15. Gene Del Polito, "Thinking of the P.O. Box," *Advertising Age,* June 11, 2001, p. 22; William Dowell, Chandrani Ghosh, and Bruce van Voorst, "Zapping the Post Office," *Time,* January 19, 1998, pp. 46–47; and Anne Faircloth, "The World Takes on the USPS," *Fortune,* July 24, 1995, p. 28.

16. Keith B. Murray, "A Test of Services Marketing Theory: Consumer Information Acquisition Activities," *Journal of Marketing,* January 1991, pp. 10–25.

17. Dawn Iacobucci, "An Empirical Examination of Some Basic Tenets in Services: Goods-Services Continua," Teresa Swartz, David E. Bowen, and Stephen W. Brown, eds., in *Advances in Services Marketing and Management,* vol. 1 (Greenwich, CT: JAI Press), pp. 23–52; and Valerie A. Zeithaml, "How Consumer Evaluation Processes Differ between Goods and Services," in James H. Donnelly and William R. George, eds., *Marketing of Services* (Chicago: American Marketing Association, 1981).

18. Michael J. Dorsch, Stephen J. Grove, and William Darden, "Consumer Intentions to Use a Service Category," *Journal of Services Marketing* 2 (2000), pp. 92–117; and Murray, "A Test of Services Marketing Theory."

19. Leonard L. Berry and Neeli Bendapudi, "Clueing In Customers," *Harvard Business Review,* February 2003, pp. 100–6.

20. John Ozment and Edward Morash, "The Augmented Service Offering for Perceived and Actual Service Quality," *Journal of the Academy of Marketing Science,* Fall 1994, pp. 352–63.

21. A. Parasuraman, Valerie A. Zeithaml, and Leonard L. Berry, "Reassessment of Expectations as a Comparison Standard in Measuring Service Quality: Implications for Further Research," *Journal of Marketing,* January 1994, pp. 111–24; and Leonard L. Berry, *On Great Service* (New York: Free Press, 1995).

22. Valerie A. Zeithaml, A. Parasuraman, and Leonard L. Berry, *Delivering Quality Service* (New York: Free Press, 1990); and Stephen W. Brown and Teresa Swartz, "A Gap Analysis of Professional Service Quality," *Journal of Marketing,* April 1989, pp. 92–98.

23. Amy Ostrom and Dawn Iacobucci, "Consumer Trade-Offs and the Evaluation of Services," *Journal of Marketing,* January 1995, pp. 17–28; and J. Joseph Cronin, Jr., and Steven A. Taylor, "Measuring Service Quality: A Reexamination and Extension," *Journal of Marketing,* July 1992, pp. 55–68.

24. Deborah L. Vence, "Modify Surveys to Find 'Whys'; Four Tips to Improve Feedback," *Marketing News,* April 15, 2004, p. 17; Stephen W. Brown, "Practicing Best-in-Class Service Recovery," *Marketing Management,* Summer 2000, pp. 8–9; Stephen S. Tax and Stephen W. Brown, "Recovering and Learning from Service Failure," *Sloan Management Review,* Fall 1998, pp. 75–88; Stephen S. Tax, Stephen W. Brown, and Murali Chandrashekaran, "Customer Evaluations of Service Complaint Experiences: Implications for Relationship Marketing," *Journal of Marketing,* April 1998, pp. 60–76; Stephen W. Brown, "Service Recovery Through IT," *Marketing Management,* Fall 1997, pp. 25–27; and Leonard L. Berry and A. Parasuraman, "Listening to the Customer—The Concept of a Service-Quality Information System," *Sloan Management Review,* Spring 1997, pp. 65–76.

25. James G. Maxham III and Richard G. Netermeyer, "A Longitudinal Study of Complaining Customers' Evaluations of Multiple Service Failures and Recovery Efforts," *Journal of Marketing,* October 2002, pp. 57–71.

26. Vicki Clift, "Everyone Needs Service Flow Charting," *Marketing News,* October 23, 1995, pp. 41, 43; Mary Jo Bitner, Bernard H. Booms, and Mary Stanfield Tetreault, "The Service Encounter: Diagnosing Favorable and Unfavorable Incidents," *Journal of Marketing,* January 1990, pp. 71–84; Eberhard Scheuing, "Conducting Customer Service Audits," *Journal of Consumer Marketing,* Summer 1989, pp. 35–41; and W. Earl Sasser, R. Paul Olsen, and D. Daryl Wyckoff, *Management of Service Operations* (Boston: Allyn & Bacon, 1978).

27. Leonard L. Berry, "Relationship Marketing of Services—Growing Interest, Emerging Perspectives," *Journal of the Academy of Marketing Science,* Fall 1995, pp. 236–45; Mary Jo Bitner, "Building Service Relationships: It's All about Promises," *Journal of the Academy of Marketing Science,* Fall 1995, pp. 246–51; Kevin P. Gwinner, Dwayne D. Gremler, and Mary Jo Bitner, "Relational Benefits in Services Industries: The Customer's Perspective," *Journal of the Academy of Marketing Science,* Spring 1998, pp. 101–14; Susan Fournier, Susan Dobscha, and David Glen Mick, "Preventing the Premature Death of Relationship Marketing," *Harvard Business Review,* January–February 1998, pp. 42–51; and John V. Petrof, "Relationship Marketing: The Wheel Reinvented?" *Business Horizons,* November–December 1997, pp. 26–31.

28. Katherine N. Lemon, Tiffany Barnett White, and Russell S. Winer, "Dynamic Customer Relationship Management: Incorporating Future Considerations into the Service Retention Decision," *Journal of Marketing,* January 2002, pp. 1–14.

29. Thomas S. Gruca, "Defending Service Markets," *Marketing Management* 1 (1994), pp. 31–38; and Leonard L. Berry, Jeffrey S. Conant, and A. Parasuraman. "A Framework for Conducting a Services Marketing Audit," *Journal of the Academy of Marketing Science,* Summer 1991, pp. 255–68.

30. Patriya Tansuhaj, Donna Randall, and Jim McCullough, "A Services Marketing Management Model: Integrating Internal and External Marketing Functions," *Journal of Sciences Marketing,* Winter 1998, pp. 31–38.

31. Christian Gronroos, "Internal Marketing Theory and Practice," in Thomas Bloch, G. D. Upah, and V. A. Zeithaml, eds., *Services Marketing in a Changing Environment* (Chicago: American Marketing Association, 1984).

32. Ibid.

33. Stephen W. Brown, "The Employee Experience," *Marketing Management* 12 (March–April 2003), pp. 12–13; Lawrence A. Crosby and Sheree L. Johnson, "Watch What I Do," *Marketing Management* 12 (November–December 2003), pp. 10–11; and March C. Gilly and Mary Wolfinbarger, "Advertising's Internal Audience," *Journal of Marketing,* January 1998, pp. 69–88.

34. Sandy Allen and Ashok Chandrashekar, "Outsourcing Services: The Contract Is Just Beginning," *Business Horizons,* March–April 2000, pp. 25–34.

35. Dan R. E. Thomas, "Strategy Is Different in Service Businesses," *Harvard Business Review,* July–August 1978, pp. 158–65.

36. Haim Oren, "Branding Financial Services Helps Consumers Find Order in Chaos," *Marketing News,* March 29, 1993, p. 6; and Leonard L. Berry, Edwin F. Lefkowith, and Terry Clark, "In Services, What's in a Name?" *Harvard Business Review,* September–October 1998, pp. 28–30.

37. Frederick H. deB. Harris and Peter Peacock, "Hold My Place, Please," *Marketing Management,* Fall 1995, pp. 34–46.

38. Christopher Lovelock, *Services Marketing* (Englewood Cliffs, NJ: Prentice Hall, 1991), pp. 122–27.

39. Kent B. Monroe, "Buyer's Subjective Perceptions of Price," *Journal of Marketing Research,* February 1973, pp. 70–80; and Jerry Olson, "Price as an Informational Cue: Effects on Product Evaluation," in A. G. Woodside, J. N. Sheth, and P. D. Bennett, eds., *Consumer and Industrial Buying Behavior* (New York: Elsevier North-Holland, 1977), pp. 267–86.

40. Tom Abate, "Cellular First Aid," *San Francisco Chronicle,* December 1, 2003, p. E1.

41. Leonard L. Berry, Kathleen Seiders, and Dhruv Grewal, "Understanding Service Convenience," *Journal of Marketing* 66 (July 2002), pp. 1–17; Charles L. Colby and A. Parasuraman, "Technology Still Matters: E-Services Are Alive and Well and Positioned for Growth," *Marketing Management* 12 (July–August), pp. 28–33.

42. Robert E. Hite, Cynthia Fraser, and Joseph A. Bellizzi, "Professional Service Advertising: The Effects of Price Inclusion, Justification, and Level of Risk," *Journal of Advertising Research* 30 (August–September 1990), pp. 23–31; William R. George and Leonard L. Berry, "Guidelines for the Advertising of Services," *Business Horizons,* July–August 1981, pp. 52–56; and Eugene M. Johnson, Eberhard E. Scheuing, and Kathleen A. Gaida, *Profitable Service Marketing* (Homewood, IL: Dow Jones-Irwin, 1986).

43. Kathleen Mortimer, "Services Advertising: The Agency Viewpoint," *Journal of Services Marketing* 2 (2001), pp. 131–46; and Sak Onkvisit and John J. Shaw, "Service Marketing: Image, Branding, and Competition," *Business Horizons,* January–February 1989, pp. 13–18.

44. Joe Adams, "Why Public Service Advertising Doesn't Work," *Ad Week,* November 17, 1980, p. 72.

45. Timothy J. Mullaney, "Online Pics: A Sure Shot," *BusinessWeek* September 3, 2001, p. EB12; Ramin Setoodeh, "Technology: Safer Surfing for Love," *Newsweek,* April 19, 2004, p. 66; and Ginny Parker, "Looking for Prince Charming? In Japan Check Your Cell Phone," *Time,* June 4, 2001; p. 88.

46. Stephen J. Grove, Raymond P. Fisk, and Joby John, "The Future of Services Marketing: Forecasts from Ten Services Experts," *Journal of Services Marketing* 17, no. 2 (2003), pp. 107–21; Stephen L. Vargo and Robert F. Lusch, "Evolving to a New Dominant Logic for Marketing," *Journal of Marketing* 68 (January 2004), pp. 1–17; "Model of Exchange Shifts toward Services," *Marketing News,* January 15, 2004, p. 25; and G. Tomas M. Hult, "Think Global, Act Local in Global Services Marketing," *Marketing News,* March 1, 2004, p. 30.

Philadelphia Phillies: This case was prepared by William Rudelius based on interviews with David Montgomery, David Buck, Marisol Lezcano, and Scott Brandreth; internal company materials; and the Phillies website (www.phillies.com).

CHAPTER 13

1. Wendy Zellner, "Where the Net Delivers: Travel," *BusinessWeek,* June 11, 2001, pp. 142–43.

2. Ibid.

3. Timothy Matanovich, Gary L. Lillien, and Arvind Rangaswamy, "Engineering the Price-Value Relationship," *Marketing Management,* Spring 1999, pp. 48–53.

4. Lisa Gubernick, "The Little Extras that Count (Up)," *The Wall Street Journal,* July 12, 2001, pp. B1, B4; and Donald V. Potter, "Discovering Hidden Pricing Power," *Business Horizons,* November–December 2000, pp. 41–48.

5. www.bugatti-cars.de.

6. Dane Smith, "Plan Would Limit Debt on Student Credit Cards," *Star Tribune,* December 12, 2003, pp. B1, B7; Kristin Tillotson, "Credit-Card Debt Is Pushing Youth into Bankruptcy," *Star Tribune,* June 3, 2001, pp. A1, A20; James Surowiecki, "The Credit Card Kings," *The New Yorker,* November 27, 2000, p. 74; and Theresa Luong, "A Tidy Savings," www.onmagazine.com, July 2001, pp. 58–59.

7. Adapted from Kent B. Monroe, *Pricing: Making Profitable Decisions,* 3rd ed. (New York: McGraw-Hill, 2003), chap. 4. Also see David J. Curry, "Measuring Price and Quality Competition," *Journal of Marketing,* Spring 1985, pp. 106–17.

8. Numerous studies have examined the price-quality-value relationship. See, for example, Jacob Jacoby and Jerry C. Olsen, eds., *Perceived Quality* (Lexington, MA: Lexington Books, 1985); William D. Dodds, Kent B. Monroe, and Dhruv Grewal, "Effects of Price, Brand, and Store Information on Buyers' Product Evaluations," *Journal of Marketing Research,* August 1991, pp. 307–19; and Roger A. Kerin, Ambuj Jain, and Daniel Howard, "Store Shopping Experience and Consumer Price-Quality-Value Perceptions," *Journal of Retailing,* Winter 1992, pp. 235–45. For a thorough review of the price-quality-value relationship, see Valerie A. Ziethaml, "Consumer Perceptions of Price, Quality, and Value," *Journal of Marketing,* July 1998, pp. 2–22.

9. Roger A. Kerin and Robert A. Peterson, "Throckmorten Furniture (A)," *Strategic Marketing Problems: Cases and Comments,* 9th ed. (Englewood Cliffs, NJ: Prentice Hall, 1998), pp. 235–45.

10. Motion Picture Association of America (mpaa.org), a news release dated March 27, 2004; and Bruce Orwall, "Theater Consolidation Jolts Hollywood Power Structure," *The Wall Street Journal,* January 21, 1998, pp. B1, B2.

11. Queena Sok Kim, "Storied FAO Is Casualty of Tough Holiday Toy-Pricing War," *The Wall Street Journal,* December 3, 2003, pp. B1, B11.

12. Donald L. Barlett and James B. Steele, "Why We Pay So Much for Drugs," *Time,* February 2, 2004, pp. 44–52; and "The Benefits of Hypertension," *The Economist,* December 6, 2003, p. 14.

13. Mike Dodd, "Cards Hold 50 Years of Memories," *USA Today,* March 27, 2001, pp. 1A, 2A; and J. C. Conklin, "Don't Throw Out Those Old Sneakers, They're a Gold Mine," *The Wall Street Journal,* September 21, 1998, pp. A1, A20.

14. Prices are as quoted on ebay.com on February 12, 2004.

15. "Cheap and Cheerful," *The Economist,* May 24, 2003, pp. 66–67.

16. Daniel Levy, Mark Bergen, Shautanu Dutta, and Robert Venable, "The Magnitude of Menu Costs: Direct Evidence from Large U.S. Supermarket Chains," *Quarterly Journal of Economics,* August 1997, pp. 791–825.

17. David Wessel, "The Price Is Wrong, and Economics Are in an Uproar," *The Wall Street Journal,* January 2, 1991, pp. B1, B6.

18. Gordan A. Wyner, "New Pricing Realities," *Marketing Research,* Spring 2001, pp. 34–35.

19. Ron Winslow, "How a Breakthrough Quickly Broke Down for Johnson & Johnson," *The Wall Street Journal,* September 18, 1998, pp. A1, A5.

20. Adam Cohen, "No Split but Microsoft's a Monopolist," *Time,* July 9, 2001, pp. 36–38.

21. Akshay R. Rao, Mark E. Bergen, and Scott Davis, "How to Fight a Price War," *Harvard Business Review,* March–April 2000, pp. 107–16.

22. Karen Lundegaard and Shulvin Freeman, "Detroit's Challenge: Weaning Buyers from Years of Deals," *The Wall Street Journal,* January 6, 2004, pp. A1, A2.

23. Frank Bruni, "Price of Newsweek? It Depends," *Dallas Times Herald,* August 14, 1986, pp. S1, S20.

24. Vanessa O'Connell, "How Campbell Saw a Breakthrough Menu Turn into Leftovers," *The Wall Street Journal,* October 6, 1998, pp. A1, A12.

25. Janice Revell, "The Price Is Not Always Right," *Fortune,* May 14, 2001, p. 240; Indrajit Sinha, "Cost Transparency: The Net's Real Threat to Prices and Brands," *Harvard Business Review,* March–April 2000, pp. 43–50; and Walter Baker, Mike Marn, and Craig Zawada, "Price Smarter on the Net," *Harvard Business Review,* February 2001, pp. 122–27.

26. "Airbus Announces $10.6 Billion Worth of Orders During Airshow," July 22, 2004, Press Release on www.airbus.com; "Boeing Outlines Progress on New 7E7 Dreamliner Passenger Plane," July 20, 2004, Press Release on www.boeing.com; Julie Creswell, "Boeing Plays Defense," *Fortune,* April 19, 2004, p. 98; J. Lynn Lunsford, "Boeing's New Baby," *The Wall Street Journal,* November 18, 2003, pp. B1, B8.

27. Ethan Smith, "Universal Slashes CD Prices in Bid to Revive Music Industry," *The Wall Street Journal,* September 4, 2003, pp. B1, B8.

28. Rick Andrews and George R. Franke, "Time-Varying Elasticities of U.S. Cigarette Demand, 1933–1987," *AMA Educator's Conference Proceedings* (Chicago: American Marketing Association, 1990), p. 393.

29. Linda Himelstein, "Webvan Left the Basics on the Shelf," *BusinessWeek,* July 23, 2001, p. 43.

Washburn International: The case is based on information and materials provided by the company.

CHAPTER 14

1. "Gillette Powers up the World's Best Shave with New M3Power: MACH3 Innovation Shaves More Thoroughly and Closer in One Easy Stroke," Gillette press release, January 15, 2004; "Gillette to Launch Vibrating Razor," *The Wall Street Journal,* January 16, 2004, p. A8; "Can Gillette Regain Its Edge?" *BusinessWeek,* January 26, 2004, p. 46; and "Gillette: New Disposable Razor Hums, Makes Hair Stand on End," www.cnn.com, downloaded January 16, 2004.

2. "Hand-to-Hand Combat," *Fortune,* May 31, 2004, p. 60.

3. For the classic description of skimming and penetration pricing, see Joel Dean, "Pricing Policies for New Products," *Harvard Business Review,* November–December 1976, pp. 141–53. Also see Reed K. Holden and Thomas T. Nagle, "Kamikaze Pricing," *Marketing Management,* Summer 1998, pp. 31–39.

4. Jean-Noel Kapferer, "Managing Luxury Brands," *Journal of Brand Management,* July 1997, pp. 251–60.

5. "Good Timing," *BrandWeek,* September 8, 2003, pp. 24–28.

6. "Premium AA Alkaline Batteries," *Consumer Reports,* March 21, 2001, p. 54; Kemp Powers, "Assault and Batteries," *Forbes,* September 4, 2000, pp. 54, 56; and "Razor Burn at Gillette," *BusinessWeek,* June 18, 2001, p. 37.

7. Michael Levy and Barton A. Weitz, *Retailing Management,* 5th ed. (McGraw-Hill/Irwin, 2004), pp. 501–2.

8. "Why That Deal Is Only $9.99," *BusinessWeek,* January 10, 2000, p. 36. For further reading on odd-even pricing, see Robert M. Schindler and Thomas M. Kilbarian, "Increased Consumer Sales Response Through Use of 99-Ending Prices," *Journal of Retailing,* Summer 1996, pp. 187–99; Mark Stiving and Russell S. Winer, "An Empirical Analysis of Price Endings with Scanner Data," *Journal of Consumer Research,* June 1997, pp. 57–67; and Robert M. Schindler, "Patterns of Rightmost Digits Used in Advertised Prices: Implications for Nine-Ending Effects," *Journal of Consumer Research,* September 1997, pp. 192–201.

9. For an overview on target pricing, see Stephan A. Butscher and Michael Laker, "Market Driven Product Development," *Marketing Management,* Summer 2000, pp. 48–53.

10. Thomas T. Nagle and Reed K. Holden, *The Strategy and Tactics of Pricing,* 3rd ed. (Englewood Cliffs, NJ: Prentice Hall, 2002), pp. 243–49.

11. Kent B. Monroe, *Pricing: Making Profitable Decisions,* 3rd ed. (McGraw-Hill/Irwin, 2003), pp. 420–30.

12. Robert J. Dolan and Hermann Simon, *Power Pricing: How Managing Price Transforms the Bottom Line* (New York: Free Press, 1996), p. 249.

13. Peter M. Noble and Thomas S. Gruca, "Industrial Pricing: Theory and Managerial Practice," *Marketing Science* 18, no. 3 (1999), pp. 435–54.

14. George E. Belch and Michael A. Belch, *Introduction to Advertising and Promotion,* 6th ed. (New York: Irwin/McGraw-Hill, 2004), p. 98.

15. For a comprehensive discussion on the experience curve, see Roger A. Kerin, Vijay Mahajan, and P. Rajan Varadarajan, *Contemporary Perspectives on Strategic Market Planning* (Boston: Allyn and Bacon, 1990), chap. 4.

16. "Hewlett-Packard Cuts Office-PC Prices in Wake of Moves by Compaq and IBM," *The Wall Street Journal,* August 22, 1995, p. B11.

17. "Is the Music Store Over?" *Business 2.0,* March 2004, pp. 115–19.

18. "How Dell Fine-Tunes Its PC Pricing to Gain Edge in a Slow Market," *The Wall Street Journal,* June 8, 2001, pp. A1, A8.

19. Rafi A. Mohammed et al., *Internet Marketing: Building Advantage in a Networked Economy,* 2nd ed. (Burr Ridge, IL: McGraw-Hill/Irwin, 2004).

20. "The Web's Role as Equalizer," *Business Week Online,* May 13, 2002; and "Are Minority Shoppers Treated Unfairly? An Expensive Reason to Care," www.diversityinc.com, downloaded May 18, 2002.

21. For an extended discussion on product complements and substitutes, see Allan D. Shocker, Barry L. Bayus, and Namwoon Kim, "Product Complements and Substitutes in Real World: The Relevance of Other Products," *Journal of Marketing,* January 2004, pp. 28–40.

22. Monroe, *Pricing,* pp. 396–97.

23. Jagmohan S. Raju, Raj Sethuraman, and Sanjay K. Dhar, "National Brand-Store Brand Price Differential and Store Brand Market Share," *Pricing Strategy & Practice* 3, no. 2 (1995), pp. 17–24.

24. "The Price Is Not Always Right," *Fortune,* May 14, 2001, p. 240.

25. For an extended discussion about price wars, see Akshay R. Rao, Mark E. Bergen, and Scott Davis, "How to Fight a Price War," *Harvard Business Review,* March–April 2000, pp. 107–16.

26. For an extensive discussion on discounts, see Monroe, *Pricing,* chaps. 16 and 17.

27. Kenneth C. Manning, William O. Bearden, and Randall L. Rose, "Development of a Theory of Retailer Response to Manufacturers' Everyday Low Cost Programs," *Journal of Retailing,* Spring 1998, pp. 107–37; "Everyday Low Profits," *Harvard Business Review,* March–April 1994, p. 13; Stephen J. Hoch, Xavier Dreze, and Mary E. Purk, "EDLP, Hi-Lo, and Margin Arithmetic," *Journal of Marketing,* October 1994, pp. 16–27; and Tibbett Speer, "Do Low Prices Bore Shoppers?" *American Demographics,* January 1994, pp. 11–13. Also see Philip Zerillo and Dawn Iacobucci, "Trade Promotions: A Call for a More Rational Approach," *Business Horizons,* July–August 1995, pp. 69–76; and Barbara E. Kahn and Leigh McAlister, *The Grocery Revolution: The New Focus on the Consumer* (Reading, MA: Addison-Wesley Educational Publishers, 1996).

28. Dorothy Cohen, *Legal Issues in Marketing Decision Making* (Cincinnati, OH: South-Western, 1995).

29. "Six Vitamin Firms Agree to Settle Price-Fixing Suit," *The Wall Street Journal,* October 11, 2000, p. B10.

30. "Price Fixing," *USA Today,* March 7, 2000, p. C1.

31. "Predatory Pricing: Cleared for Takeoff," *BusinessWeek,* May 14, 2001, p. 50.

Stuart Cellars: This case was prepared by Professor Linda Rochford based on information from the company website (www.stuartcellars.com) and the following sources: Dana Nigro, "What's Behind the Bottle Price?" *Wine Spectator,* December 15, 2002, pp. 24–28; and Cyril Penn, ed., "The Hottest Small Brands of 2003," *Wine Business Monthly,* February 1, 2004, p. 8.

CHAPTER 15

1. "Show Time!" *BusinessWeek,* February 2, 2004, pp. 56ff; www.ifoapplestore.com/stores, downloaded June 7, 2004; and Jonah Bloom, "Apple, Song, Hershey Ring Up More than Sales at Their Shops," *Advertising Age,* February 2, 2004, p. 16.

2. Andrew Raskin, "Who's Minding the Store?" *Business 2.0,* February 2003, pp. 70–74.

3. This discussion is based on Bert Rosenbloom, *Marketing Channels: A Management View,* 7th ed. (Cincinnati, OH: South-Western College Publishing, 2004).

4. *2004 Statistical Factbook* (New York: The Direct Marketing Association, 2004).

5. www.generalmills.com, downloaded May 15, 2004; www.nestle.com, downloaded May 15, 2004.

6. For an extensive discussion on wholesaling, see Anne T. Couglan, Erin Anderson, Louis W. Stern, and Adel I. E1-Ansary, *Marketing Channels,* 6th ed. (Upper Saddle River, NJ: Prentice Hall, 2001), chap. 15.

7. For an overview of vertical marketing systems, see Lou Pelton, David Strutton, and James R. Lumpkin, *Marketing Channels,* 2nd ed. (Burr Ridge, IL: McGraw-Hill/Irwin, 2002), chap. 11.

8. Statistics provided by the International Franchise Association, June 10, 2004.

9. For a review of channel partnering, see Robert D. Buzzell and Gwen Ortmeyer, "Channel Partnerships Streamline Distribution," *Sloan Management Review,* Spring 1995, pp. 85–96. Also see Jakki J. Mohr and Robert E. Spekman, "Perfecting Partnerships," *Marketing Management,* Winter–Spring 1996, pp. 35–43.

10. Edwin R. Rigsbee, *The Art of Partnering* (Dubuque, IA: Kendall/Hunt Publishing, 1994), pp. 82–83.

11. Carolyn Hsu, "Party Profits," *U.S. News & World Report,* October 20, 2003, pp. 36ff.

12. Chris Prystay, "At Long Last, Gum Is Legal in Singapore, but There Are Strings," *The Wall Street Journal,* June 4, 2004, pp. A1, A6; and "Gum Marketers Back in Singapore," *Advertising Age,* March 29, 2004, p. 18.

13. For a thorough discussion of distribution intensity, see Gary L. Frazier and Walfried M. Lassar, "Determinants of Distribution Intensity," *Journal of Marketing,* October 1996, pp. 39–51.

14. Joshua Levine and Matthew Swibel, "Dr. No," *Forbes,* May 28, 2001, pp. 72–76.

15. www.radioshack.com/pressreleases, downloaded March 6, 2004.

16. Cliff Edwards, "Boutiques for Flogging the Brand," *BusinessWeek,* May 24, 2004, p. 48.

17. Jonathan Mandell, "Speed It Up Webmaster, We're Losing Billions Every Second," *The New York Times,* September 22, 1999, p. D58.

18. "5 Down, 95 to Go," www.apple.com, downloaded July 25, 2001; and Cliff Edwards, "Sorry, Steve: Here's Why It Won't Work," *BusinessWeek,* May 21, 2001, pp. 44–45.

19. "Gillette Tries to Nick Schick in Japan," *The Wall Street Journal,* February 4, 1991, pp. B3, B4.

20. Ethan Smith, "Why a Grand Plan to Cut CD Prices Went off the Track," *The Wall Street Journal,* June 4, 2004, pp. A1, A6; and "Feud with Seller Hurts Nike Sales, Shares," *Dallas Morning News,* June 28, 2003, p. 30.

21. "Black Pearls Recast for Spring," *Advertising Age,* November 13, 1995, p. 49.

22. Studies that explore the dimensions and use of power and influence in marketing channels include the following: Gul Butaney and Lawrence H. Wortzel, "Distributor Power versus Manufacturer Power: The Customer Role," *Journal of Marketing,* January 1988, pp. 52–63; Kenneth A. Hunt, John T. Mentzer, and Jeffrey E. Danes, "The Effect of Power Sources on Compliance in a Channel of Distribution: A Causal Model," *Journal of Business Research,* October 1987, pp. 377–98; John F. Gaski, "Interrelations among a Channel Entity's Power Sources: Impact of the Exercise of Reward and Coercion on Expert, Referent, and Legitimate Power Sources,"

Journal of Marketing Research, February 1986, pp. 62–67; Gary Frazier and John O. Summers, "Interfirm Influence Strategies and Their Application within Distribution Channels," *Journal of Marketing,* Summer 1984, pp. 43–55; Sudhir Kale, "Dealer Perceptions of Manufacturer Power and Influence Strategies in a Developing Country," *Journal of Marketing Research,* November 1986, pp. 387–93; George H. Lucas and Larry G. Gresham, "Power, Conflict, Control, and the Application of Contingency Theory in Channels of Distribution," *Journal of the Academy of Marketing Science,* Summer 1985, pp. 27–37; and F. Robert Dwyer and Julie Gassenheimer, "Relational Roles and Triangle Dramas: Effects on Power Play and Sentiments in Industrial Channels," *Marketing Letters* 3 (1992), pp. 187–200.

23. "FTC Pinpoints Slotting Fees," *Advertising Age,* February 26, 2001, p. 52; and "Ca-ching," *Forbes,* June 12, 2000, pp. 84–85. Also see Paul N. Bloom, Gregory T. Gundlach, and Joseph P. Cannon, "Slotting Allowances and Fees: Schools of Thought and Views of Practicing Managers," *Journal of Marketing,* April 2000, pp. 92–109; and William L. Wilkie, Debra M. Desrochers, and Gregory T. Gundlach, "Marketing Research and Public Policy: The Case of Slotting Fees," *Journal of Public Policy & Marketing,* Fall 2002, pp. 275–89.

24. For a comprehensive treatment of legal issues pertaining to marketing channels, see Dorothy Cohen, *Legal Issues in Marketing* (Cincinnati, OH: South-Western, 1995), chaps. 12 and 13.

Golden Valley Microwave Foods: This case was written by Thomas J. Belich, Mark T. Spriggs, and Steven W. Hartley based on personal interviews with Jack McKeon and Frank Lynch, company data they provided, and the following sources: "Snagging a Pop Fly," *Snack Food and Wholesale Bakery* (May 2004), p. 48; "Choosing the Right Growth Strategy," *PR Newswire* (November 13, 2003); and "Company Information," from the website (see www.actii.com/company).

CHAPTER 16

1. David Simchi-Levi, Philip Kaminsky, and Edith Simchi-Levi, *Designing and Managing the Supply Chain,* 2nd ed. (Burr Ridge, IL: McGraw-Hill/Irwin, 2003), pp. 101–10; and Eric Young and Mark Roberti, "The Swoosh Stumbles," *The Industry Standard,* March 12, 2001, pp. 47–49.

2. These estimates are given in James R. Stock and Douglas M. Lambert, *Strategic Logistics Management,* 4th ed. (Burr Ridge, IL: McGraw-Hill/Irwin, 2001), p. 5.

3. Simchi-Levi et al., *Designing and Managing the Supply Chain,* p. 6.

4. This discussion is based on Robyn Meredith, "Harder than Hype," *Forbes,* April 16, 2001, pp. 188–94.

5. Major portions of this discussion are based on Sunil Chopra and Peter Meindl, *Supply Chain Management: Strategy, Planning, and Operations,* 2nd ed. (Upper Saddle River, NJ: Prentice Hall, 2004), chaps. 1–3; and Hau L. Lee, "The Triple-A Supply Chain," *Harvard Business Review* (October 2004), pp. 102–12.

6. David Drickhamer, "Supply-Chain Superstars," *Industry Week,* May 1, 2004, pp. 5–7; "Big Blue Flips 'On' New Global Effort," *BrandWeek,* May 24, 2004, p. 15; Brian T. Eck and Murry Mitchell, "Transformation at IBM," *Supply Chain Management,* November–December 2003, pp. 56–62; Daniel Lyons, "Back on the Chain Gang," *Forbes,* October 13, 2003, pp. 114–23; and "Experience: Order for Supply Chains," www.informationweek.com, downloaded February 9, 2004.

7. This discussion is based on Kathryn Jones, "The Dell Way," *Business 2.0,* February 2003, pp. 61–66; Charles Fishman, "The Wal-Mart You Don't Know," *Fast Company,* December 2003, pp. 68–80; and Chopra and Meindl, *Supply Chain Management.*

8. Portions of this discussion are based on "A Perfect Market: A Survey of E-Commerce," *The Economist,* May 15, 2004, special section; Donald J. Bowersox, David J. Closs, and M. Bixby Copper, *Supply Chain Logistics Management* (Burr Ridge, IL: McGraw-Hill/Irwin, 2002), chap. 10; and Chopra and Meindl, *Supply Chain Management.*

9. Simchi-Levi et al., *Designing and Managing the Supply Chain,* p. 6.

10. Toby B. Gooley, "How Logistics Drive Customer Service," *Traffic Management,* January 1996, p. 46.

11. Michael Levy and Barton A. Weitz, *Retailing Management,* 4th ed. (Burr Ridge, IL: McGraw-Hill/Irwin, 2001), pp. 335–36; "A&P Bets the Store," *The Industry Standard,* May 14, 2001), pp. 46–49; and Ursula Y. Alvarado and Herbert Kotzab, "Supply Chain Management: The Integration of Logistics in Marketing," *Industrial Marketing Management,* 30 (2001), pp. 183–98.

12. Jon Bigness, "In Today's Economy, There Is Big Money to Be Made in Logistics," *The Wall Street Journal,* September 6, 1995, pp. A1, A9.

13. Robert J. Bowman, "Pursuing 'On Demand,' IBM Shakes Up Its Supply Chain," www.supplychainbrain.com, April 2003.

14. Erik Schonfeld, "The Total Package," *eCompany,* June 2001, pp. 91–97; and Kurt Hoffman, "Snapple Found Handling Logistics In-House Left a Sour Taste," www.supplychainbrain.com, April 2002.

15. Douglas M. Lambert, James R. Stock, and Lisa Ellram, *Fundamentals of Logistics Management* (Burr Ridge, IL: McGraw-Hill/Irwin, 1998).

16. Eck and Mitchell, "Transformation at IBM"; and David Simchi-Levi, Philip Kaminsky, and Edith Simchi-Levi, *Managing the Supply Chain: The Definitive Guide for the Business Professional* (New York: McGraw-Hill 2004), p. 78.

17. Jeffrey Davis and Martha Baer, "Some Assembly Required," *Business 2.0,* February 12, 2001, pp. 78–87.

18. Simchi-Levi et al., *Managing the Supply Chain.*

19. Marshall Fisher, "What Is the Right Supply Chain for Your Product?" *Harvard Business Review,* March–April 1997, pp. 105–17.

20. "Return to Sender," *Modern Material Handling,* May 15, 2000, pp. 10–11.

21. Harvey Meyer, "The Greening of Corporate America," *Journal of Business Strategy,* January–February 2000, pp. 38–43; and M. Fleischmann, J. van Nunen, and B. Grave, "Integrating Closed-Loop Supply Chains and Spare-Parts Management at IBM," *Interfaces,* November–December 2003, pp. 44–56.

22. Doug Bartholomew, "IT Delivers for UPS," *Industry Week,* August 2002, pp. 25–26.

Amazon.com: This case is based on material available on the company website, www.amazon.com, and the following sources: Robert D. Hof and Heather Green, "How Amazon Cleared That Hurdle," *BusinessWeek* (February 4, 2002), p. 60; Heather Green, "How Hard Should Amazon Swing?" *BusinessWeek* (January 14, 2002), p. 38; Robert D. Hof, "We've Never Said We Had To Do It All," *BusinessWeek* (October 15, 2001), p. 53; "Amazon.com Selects Mercator E-Business Integration Brokers as Key Technology for Supply Chain Integration," *Business Wire* (November 28, 2000); Bob Walter, "Amazon Leases Distribution Center from Sacramento, Calif., Development Firm," *Sacramento Bee* (July 19, 2001).

CHAPTER 17

1. "Reinventing the Store," *The Economist,* November 22, 2003, pp. 65–68; "25 New Targets Aim for the Bull's Eye," *HFN,* April 12, 2004, p. 1; Larry Armstrong, "E-Tune Shopping," *BusinessWeek,* March 29, 2004, p. 108; Robert Berner, "Target: The Cool Factor Fizzles," *BusinessWeek,* February 24, 2003, p. 42; Laura Heller, "Target Gets Mod in Manhattan," *DSN Retailing Today,* August 20, 2001, p. 2; Alice Z. Cuneo, "On Target," *Advertising Age,* December 11, 2000, p. 1; "Target Lets Ads onto the Bag," *HFN,* August 20, 2001, p. 58; and "Target and MJC: Sweet Game Plan," *DSN Retailing Today,* August 20, 2001, p. A4.

2. Kate Betts, "So You Want to Be a Designer," *Time,* May 17, 2004, p. 85.

3. "Fortune 1000 Ranked within Industries," *Fortune,* April 5, 2004, p. F54.

4. *Statistical Abstract of the United States,* 123rd ed. (Washington, DC: U.S. Department of Commerce, Bureau of the Census, 2003), pp. 657–74.

5. "Fortune Global 500," *Fortune,* July 21, 2003, p. 106.

6. "Retail Trade-Establishments, Employees, and Payroll," *Statistical Abstract of the United States,* 123rd ed. (Washington, DC: U.S. Department of Commerce, Bureau of the Census, 2003), p. 660.

7. Daniel Thomas, "Suppliers Will Meet RFID Deadline," *Computer Weekly,* May 11, 2004, p. 14; Laurie Sullivan and Darrell Dunn, "HP, Sun Ramp up RFID Services," *Information Week,* May 10, 2004, p. 16; Irene M. Nunii and Adam Aston, "Radio ID Tags So Cheap They'll Be Everywhere," *BusinessWeek,* October 20, 2003, p. 147; and "Target's RFID Goal Is to Have All Vendors Tagging by 2007," *HFN,* March 22, 2004, p. 26.

8. Don DeBolt, "Franchises Are Key Segment of Nation's Economy," *Franchising Today,* April 2004; also see "Franchise 500" at www.entrepreneur.com.

9. "Franchise 500," *Entrepreneur,* January 2004; Scott Shane and Chester Spell, "Factors for New Franchise Success," *Sloan Management Review,* Spring 1998, pp. 43–50.

10. Charles Haddad, "Delta's Flight to Self-Service," *BusinessWeek,* July 7, 2003, p. 92; "At Your Self-Service," *Hotels,* December 1, 2003, p. 12; and Larry Armstrong, "Digital Photos, on the Double," *BusinessWeek,* June 23, 2003, p. 118.

11. Robert Berner, "Retail: This Rising Tide Won't Lift All Boats," *BusinessWeek,* January 12, 2004, p. 114.

12. Aixa M. Pascual, "Can Office Depot Get Back On Track?" *Business-Week,* September 18, 2000, p. 74.

13. Carol Matlack and Adeline Bonnet, "What's Shackling the Big Chains," *BusinessWeek,* May 17, 2004, p. 26.

14. Anthony Bianco and Wendy Zellner, "Is Wal-Mart Too Powerful?" *BusinessWeek,* October 6, 2003, p. 100.

15. Keith Reed, "Staples Installs Vending Machines at Boston Airport, College Campuses," *Boston Globe,* April 22, 2004; Simone Kaplan, "Earthlink Offices Sprout DVD Vending Machines," *Video Business,* April 12, 2004, p. 8; and "2004 State of the Vending Industry Report," *Automatic Merchandiser,* August 2004, p. 4.

16. Kwan Weng Kin, "Vending Machines in Japan Get 'Smart,' " *The Strait Times* (Singapore), October 26, 2003; and Andy Reinhardt, "A Machine-to-Machine 'Internet of Things,' " *BusinessWeek,* April 26, 2004, p. 102.

17. "U.S. Catalog Sales to Top $175 bn," *Precision Marketing,* May 14, 2004, p. 9; Vito Pilieci, "The IKEA Catalog: It's Bigger than the Bible," *Ottawa Citizen,* August 27, 2003, p. A1; *U.S. Direct and Interactive Marketing Today,* 6th ed. (New York: Direct Marketing Association, October 2000); *Statistical Fact Book 2000* (New York: Direct Marketing Association, 2000); and Ellen Neuborne, "Coaxing with Catalogs," *BusinessWeek,* August 6, 2001, p. EB6.

18. Monica Roman, "You Gotta Have a Catalog," *BusinessWeek,* May 14, 2001, p. 56; and Beth Viveiros, "Catalog and Internet Sales Grow More Quickly than Retail," *Direct,* July 2001.

19. "2004 Annual Catalog Winners," Annual Catalog Conference 2005, see www.catalogconference.com; "Annual Catalog Awards Finalists," *Catalog Age,* April 1, 2004, p. 4; "Intimate Brands Reports August Sales," *PR Newswire,* September 6, 2001; Christopher Palmeri, "Victoria's Little Secret," *Forbes,* August 24, 1998, p. 58; and Dyan Machan, "Sharing Victoria's Secrets," *Forbes,* June 5, 1995, pp. 132–33.

20. Sarah Taylor, "Phoning It In," *FN,* July 29, 2002; "Corporate Facts," from QVC website, www.qvc.com/mainhqfact.html.

21. Shayn Ferriolo, "Home Shopping Network Tunes into Cataloging," *Catalog Age,* November 2002, p. 12; Matt Stump, "Open TV Activates Sports, Shopping Apps," *Multichannel News,* May 3, 2004, p. 129; and Carole Nicksin, "QVC Opens Up in Mall Space," *HFN,* August 20, 2001, p. 6.

22. Heather Green, "Where Did All the Surfers Go?" *BusinessWeek,* August 6, 2001, p. 35; Steve Hamm, David Welch, Wendy Zellner, Faith Keenan, and Peter Engardio, "E-Biz: Down but Hardly Out," *BusinessWeek,* March 26, 2001, pp. 126–30; Lewis Braham, "E-Tailers Are Clicking," *BusinessWeek,* July 23, 2001, p. 73; "Will Wal-Mart Get It Right This Time?" *BusinessWeek,* November 6, 2000, p. 104; and Raymond R. Burke, "Do You See What I See? The Future of Virtual Shopping," *Journal of the Academy of Marketing Science,* Fall 1997, pp. 352–60.

23. "Former Cendant Marketing Chief Will Help Company Leverage Core Media Products while Broadening Member Benefit Offerings," *PR Newswire,* February 21, 2001; Tim Mullaney, "And All the Price Trimmings," *BusinessWeek,* December 18, 2000, p. 68; Mary J. Cronin, "Business Secrets of the Billion-Dollar Website," *Fortune,* February 2, 1998, p. 142; Robert D. Hof, Ellen Neuborne, and Heather Green, "Amazon.com: The Wild World of E-Commerce," *BusinessWeek,* December 14, 1998, pp. 106–19; "Future Shop," *Forbes ASAP,* April 6, 1998, pp. 37–52; Chris Taylor, "Cybershop," *Time,* November 23, 1998, p. 142; Stephen H. Wildstrom, " 'Bots' Don't Make Great Shoppers," *BusinessWeek,* December 7, 1998, p. 14; and Jeffrey Ressner, "Online Flea Markets," *Time,* October 5, 1998, p. 48.

24. Roger O. Crocket, "Let the Buyer Compare," *BusinessWeek,* September 3, 2001, p. EB10.

25. Thomas L. Zeller and David R. Kublank, "Focused E-Tail Measurement and Resource Management," *Business Horizons,* January–February 2002, pp. 53–60.

26. "My Virtual Model Inc. Acquires EZsize," *PR Newswire,* June 21, 2001; Steve Casimiro, "Shop Till You Crash," *Fortune,* December 21, 1998, pp. 267–70; and De' Ann Weimer, "Can I Try (Click) That Blouse (Drag) in Blue?" *BusinessWeek,* November 9, 1998, p. 86.

27. Michael Rogers, "The Future of Internet Cafés," *Newsweek Web Exclusive,* January 21, 2003; also see www.cybercafes.com.

28. "Economic Impact: U.S. Direct Marketing Today Executive Summary—2003," Direct Marketing Association, New York; and Kelly Shermach, "Outsourcing Seen as a Way to Cut Costs, Retain Service," *Marketing News,* June 19, 1995, pp. 5, 8.

29. Catherine Arnold, "Law Gives Industry a Buzz," *Marketing News,* February 1, 2004, p. 11; Scott Reeves, "Back to (Old) School, 'Do-Not-Call' Revives Door-to-Door Sales," *Marketing News,* December 8, 2003, p. 13; and "Direct Marketing," *Marketing News,* January 15, 2004, p. 16.

30. Nanette Byrnes, "The New Calling," *BusinessWeek,* September 18, 2000, pp. 137–48.

31. Bill Vlasic and Mary Beth Regan, "Amway II: The Kids Take Over," *BusinessWeek,* February 1, 1998, pp. 60–70.

32. Mathew Schifrin, "Okay, Big Mouth," *Forbes,* October 9, 1995, pp. 47–48; Veronica Byrd and Wendy Zellner, "The Avon Lady of the Amazon," *BusinessWeek,* October 24, 1994, pp. 93–96; and Ann Marsh "Avon Is Calling on Eastern Europe," *Advertising Age,* June 20, 1994, p. 116.

33. The following discussion is adapted from William T. Gregor and Eileen M. Friars, *Money Merchandizing: Retail Revolution in Consumer Financial Services* (Cambridge, MA: Management Analysis Center, Inc., 1982).

34. Nicole Harris, "Just for Feet Is Making Tracks," *BusinessWeek,* July 20, 1998, pp. 70–72.

35. Gail Tom, Michelle Dragics, and Christi Holdregger, "Using Visual Presentation to Assess Store Positioning: A Case Study of JCPenney," *Marketing Research,* September 1991, pp. 48–52.

36. Francis J. Mulhern and Robert P. Leon, "Implicit Price Bundling of Retail Products: A Multiproduct Approach to Maximizing Store Profitability," *Journal of Marketing,* October 1991, pp. 63–76.

37. Marc Vanhuele and Xavier Dreze, "Measuring the Price Knowledge Shoppers Bring to the Store," *Journal of Marketing,* October 2002, pp. 72–85.

38. Gwen Ortmeyer, John A. Quelch, and Walter Salmon, "Restoring Credibility to Retail Pricing," *Sloan Management Review,* Fall 1991, pp. 55–66.

39. William B. Dodds, "In Search of Value: How Price and Store Name Information Influence Buyers' Product Perceptions," *Journal of Consumer Marketing,* Spring 1991, pp. 15–24.

40. Leonard L. Berry, "Old Pillars of New Retailing," *Harvard Business Review,* April 2001, pp. 131–37.

41. Eric Anderson and Duncan Simester, "Mind Your Pricing Cues," *Harvard Business Review,* September 2003, pp. 96–103.

42. Julie Baker, A. Parasuraman, Dhruv Grewal, and Glenn B. Voss, "The Influence of Multiple Store Environment Cues on Perceived Merchandise Value and Patronage Intentions," *Journal of Marketing,* April 2002, pp. 120–41.

43. Neil Gross, "On beyond Shoplifting Prevention," *BusinessWeek,* October 2, 2000, p. 170; and "A Time to Steal," *BrandWeek,* February 16, 1999, p. 24.

44. Rita Koselka, "The Schottenstein Factor," *Forbes,* September 28, 1992, pp. 104, 106.

45. Wendy Zellner, "Warehouse Clubs: When the Going Gets Tough . . ." *BusinessWeek,* July 16, 2001, p. 60; "Warehouse Clubs Fine-Tune Units," *Chain Drug Review,* June 29, 1998, p. 38; James M. Degen, "Warehouse Clubs Move from Revolution to Evolution," *Marketing News,* August 3, 1992, p. 8; Dori Jones Yang, "Bargains by the Forklift," *BusinessWeek,* July 15, 1991, p. 152; and "Fewer Rings on the Cash Register," *BusinessWeek,* January 14, 1991, p. 85.

46. Ira P. Schneiderman, "Value Keeps Factory Outlets Viable," *Daily News Record,* July 20, 1998, p. 10; Stephanie Anderson Forest, "I Can Get It for You Retail," *BusinessWeek,* September 18, 1995, pp. 84–88; and Adrienne Ward, "New Breed of Mall Knows: Everybody Loves a Bargain," *Advertising Age,* January 27, 1992, p. 55.

47. Anne Faircloth, "Value Retailers Go Dollar for Dollar," *Fortune,* July 6, 1998, pp. 164–66.

48. Barry Brown, "Edmonton Makes Size Pay Off in Down Market," *Advertising Age,* January 27, 1992, pp. 4–5.

49. James R. Lowry, "The Life Cycle of Shopping Centers," *Business Horizons,* January–February 1997, pp. 77–86; Eric Peterson, "Power Centers! Now!" *Stores,* March 1989, pp. 61–66; and "Power Centers Flex Their Muscle," *Chain Store Age Executive,* February 1989, pp. 3A, 4A.

50. Pierre Martineau, "The Personality of the Retail Store," *Harvard Business Review,* January–February 1958, p. 47.

51. Julie Baker, Dhruv Grewal, and A. Parasuraman, "The Influence of Store Environment on Quality Inferences and Store Image," *Journal of the Academy of Marketing Science,* Fall 1994, pp. 328–39; Howard Barich and Philip Kotler, "A Framework for Marketing Image Management," *Sloan Management Review,* Winter 1991, pp. 94–104; Susan M. Keaveney and Kenneth A. Hunt, "Conceptualization and Operationalization of Retail Store Image: A Case of Rival Middle-Level Theories," *Journal of the Academy of Marketing Science,* Spring 1992, pp. 165–75; James C. Ward, Mary Jo Bitner, and John Barnes, "Measuring the Prototypicality and Meaning of Retail Environments," *Journal of Retailing,* Summer 1992, p. 194; and Dhruv Grewal, R. Krishnan, Julie Baker, and Norm Burin, "The Effect of Store Name, Brand Name and Price Discounts on Consumers' Evaluations and Purchase Intentions," *Journal of Retailing,* Fall 1998, pp. 331–52. For a review of the store image literature, see Mary R. Zimmer and Linda L. Golden, "Impressions of Retail Stores: A Content Analysis of Consumer Images," *Journal of Retailing,* Fall 1988, pp. 265–93.

52. Mary Jo Bitner, "Servicescapes: The Impact of Physical Surroundings on Customers and Employees," *Journal of Marketing,* April 1992, pp. 57–71.

53. Jans-Benedict Steenkamp and Michel Wedel, "Segmenting Retail Markets on Store Image Using a Consumer-Based Methodology," *Journal of Retailing,* Fall 1991, p. 300; and Philip Kotler, "Atmospherics as a Marketing Tool," *Journal of Retailing* 49 (Winter 1973–74), p. 61.

54. Carole Nicksin, "Sears' New Ad Campaign to Stress Brand Image, Shopping Convenience," *HFN,* August 27, 2001, p. 4.

55. Kusum L. Ailwadi and Bari Harlam, "An Empirical Analysis of the Determinants of Retail Margins: The Role of Store-Brand Share," *Journal of Marketing,* January 2004, pp. 147–65; Joseph Tarnowski, "And the Awards Went to . . ." *Progressive Grocer,* April 15, 2004; Betsy Spethmann, "Shelf Sets," *Promo,* May 1, 2004, p. 6; and "Study Shows Continued Support for Category Management," *CSNews Online,* March 17, 2004.

56. The wheel of retailing theory was originally proposed by Malcolm P. McNair, "Significant Trends and Development in the Postwar Period," in A. B. Smith, ed., *Competitive Distribution in a Free, High-Level Economy and Its Implications for the University* (Pittsburgh: University of Pittsburgh Press, 1958), pp. 1–25; also see Stephen Brown, "The Wheel of Retailing—Past and Future," *Journal of Retailing,* Summer 1990, pp. 143–49; and Malcolm P. McNair and Eleanor May, "The Next Revolution of the Retailing Wheel," *Harvard Business Review,* September–October 1978, pp. 81–91.

57. Kenneth Hein, "Upfront 2004—The Advertisers: Fast Food," Adweek.com, April 26, 2004; "McDonald's Tests In-Store McCafes," ddimagazine.com, November 14, 2003; and "New McDonald's Ad Pushes Health," restaurantbiz.com, May 12, 2004.

58. Peter Kiekmeyer, "McDonald's Bet Heavily on McCafe," *Montreal Gazette,* August 28, 2001, p. D2; "McDonald's Adds Sourdough Line and Cheesecake to Revolving Menu Offerings," *PR Newswire,* August 9, 2001; and David Farkas, "Drive-Thru in the Fast Lane," *Chain Leader,* July 2001, p. 40.

59. Bill Saporito, "What's for Dinner?" *Fortune,* May 15, 1995, pp. 51–64.

60. William R. Davidson, Albert D. Bates, and Stephen J. Bass, "Retail Life Cycle," *Harvard Business Review,* November–December 1976, pp. 89–96.

61. Gretchen Morgenson, "Here Come the Cross-Shoppers," *Forbes,* December 7, 1992, pp. 90–101.

62. Robert A. Peterson and Sridhar Balasubramanian, "Retailing in the 21st Century: Reflections and Prologue to Research," *Journal of Retailing,* Spring 2002, pp. 9–16.

63. Jim Carter and Norman Sheehan, "From Competition to Cooperation: E-Tailing's Integration with Retailing," *Business Horizons,* March–April 2004, pp. 71–78.

64. Ranjay Gulati and Janson Garino, "Getting the Right Mix of Bricks and Clicks," *Harvard Business Review,* May–June 2000, pp. 107–14; Marshall L. Fisher, Ananth Raman, and Anna Sheen McClelland, "Rocket Science Retailing Is Almost Here: Are You Ready?" *Harvard Business Review,* July–August 2000, pp. 115–24; Charla Mathwick, Naresh Malhotra, and Edward Rigdon, "Experiential Value: Conceptualization, Measurement and Application in the Catalog and Internet Shopping Environment," *Journal of Retailing,* Spring 2001, pp. 39–56; Lawrence M. Bellman, "Bricks and Mortar: 21st Century Survival," *Business Horizons,* May–June 2001, pp. 21–28; Zhan G. Li and Nurit Gery, "E-Tailing—for All Products?" *Business Horizons,* November–December 2000, pp. 49–54; and Bill Hanifin, "Go Forth and Multichannel: Loyalty Programs Need Knowledge Base," *Marketing News,* August 27, 2001, p. 23.

65. Catherine Arnold, "Hot Rod Hot Dogs," *Marketing News,* December 8, 2003, p. 3; Gene Marcial, "Cell Phone Fever Cures Gemplus' Chill," *BusinessWeek,* February 16, 2004, p. 97; "Renesas Combines Smart Card, Flash," *Electronic News,* May 17, 2004; and Carol Matlack, Karim Djemai, and David Fairlamb, "Its Smart Card Could Be the Next Big Thing," *BusinessWeek,* November 11, 2002, p. 55.

66. Beth Karlin, "Manhattan Mall," *Retail Traffic,* February 1, 2004, p. 2; and Kim Kennedy, "The Largest Retail Projects of 2003 and What's ahead for 2004," *Display & Design Ideas,* March 1, 2004.

67. Mary Kuntz, Lori Bongiorno; Keith Naughton, Gail DeGeorge, and Stephanie Anderson Forest, "Reinventing the Store," *BusinessWeek,*

November 27, 1995, pp. 84–96; and David Fischer, "The New Meal Deals," *U.S. News & World Report,* October 30, 1995, p. 66.

Mall of America: This case was written by David P. Brennan and is based on an interview with Maureen Cahill and materials provided by Mall of America.

CHAPTER 18

1. "New England Patriots Quarterback Tom Brady Joins NFL Greats by Being Featured in 2nd Commercial Proclaiming 'I'm Going Back to Disney World!'" *PR Newswire,* February 2, 2004; T.L. Stanley, "Disney World Doubles Spending to $250 Mil.," *Advertising Age,* October 6, 2003, p. 4; Rod Taylor, "Beanie Madness," *Promo,* April 1, 2004, p. 4; "Finding Frito," *Promo,* May 1, 2003, p. 6; "Disney's Toontown Online Lauches in Japan," Disney Online press release, April 19, 2004, see www.psc.disney.go.com; "Mickey to Reward Credit-Card Users," *Columbus Dispatch,* March 8, 2003, p. 1C; and Ian W. Mitchell, "Tokyo DisneySea: How It Translates," *Chicago Sun-Times,* July 27, 2003, p. 1.

2. Wilbur Schramm, "How Communication Works," in Wilbur Schramm, ed., *The Process and Effects of Mass Communication* (Urbana, IL: University of Illinois Press, 1955), pp. 3–26.

3. E. Cooper and M. Jahoda, "The Evasion of Propaganda," *Journal of Psychology* 22 (1947), pp. 15–25; H. Hyman and P. Sheatsley, "Some Reasons Why Information Campaigns Fail," *Public Opinion Quarterly* 11 (1947), pp. 412–23; and J. T. Klapper, *The Effects of Mass Communication* (New York: Free Press, 1960), chap. VII.

4. Cynthia L. Kemper, "Biting Wax Tadpole, Other Faux Pas," *Denver Post,* August 3, 1997, p. G4.

5. Rik Pieters and Michel Wedel, "Attention Capture and Transfer in Advertising: Brand Pictorial, and Text-Size Effects," *Journal of Marketing,* April 2004, pp. 36–50.

6. Adapted from *Dictionary of Marketing Terms,* 2nd ed., Peter D. Bennett, ed. (Chicago: American Marketing Association, 1995), p. 231.

7. Dick Martin, "Gilded and Gelded: Hard-Won Lessons from the PR Wars," *Harvard Business Review,* October 2003, pp. 44–54.

8. Kusum L Ailawadi, Scott A. Neslin, and Karen Gedenk, "Pursuing the Value-Conscious Consumer: Store Brands versus National Brand Promotions," *Journal of Marketing,* January 2001, pp. 71–89.

9. B. C. Cotton and Emerson M. Babb, "Consumer Response to Promotional Deals," *Journal of Marketing* 42 (July 1978), pp. 109–13.

10. Robert George Brown, "Sales Response to Promotions and Advertising," *Journal of Advertising Research* 14 (August 1974), pp. 33–40.

11. Adapted from *Economic Impact: U.S. Direct Marketing Today* (New York: Direct Marketing Association, 1998), p. 25.

12. Siva K. Balasubramanian and V. Kumar, "Analyzing Variations in Advertising and Promotional Expenditures: Key Correlates in Consumer, Industrial, and Service Markets," *Journal of Marketing,* April 1990, pp. 57–68.

13. Don E. Schultz, "Include SIMM in Modern Media Ad Plans," *Marketing News,* May 15, 2004, p. 6; Don E. Schultz, "TV Advertisers Defy Logic, Pay More for Less," *Marketing News,* June 9, 2003, p. 14; Catherine Arnold, "Tech Design," *Marketing News,* January 15, 2004, p. 4; Gail Edmondson and Michael Eidam, "The Mini Just Keeps Getting Mightier," *BusinessWeek,* April 5, 2004, p. 26; Don E. Schultz, "Consumer Marketing Changed by Advent of 29.8/7 Media Week," *Marketing News,* September 24, 2001, pp. 13, 15; Pamela Paul, "Getting Inside Gen Y," *American Demographics,* September 2001, pp. 43–49; Charles Pappas, "Ad Nauseam," *Advertising Age,* July 10, 2000, pp. 16–18; and Dan Lippe, "It's All in Creative Delivery," *Advertising Age,* June 25, 2001, pp. S8, S9.

14. Dunn Sunnoo and Lynn Y. S. Lin, "Sales Effects of Promotion and Advertising," *Journal of Advertising Research* 18 (October 1978), pp. 37–42.

15. John Palmer, "Animal Instincts," *Promo,* May 2001, pp. 25–33.

16. J. Ronald Carey, Stephen A. Clique, Barbara A. Leighton, and Frank Milton, "A Test of Positive Reinforcement of Customers," *Journal of Marketing* 40 (October 1976), pp. 98–100.

17. James M. Olver and Paul W. Farris, "Push and Pull: A One-Two Punch for Packages Products," *Sloan Management Review,* Fall 1989, pp. 53–61.

18. Julia Flynn and Michael Oneal, "A Tall Order for the Prince of Beers," *BusinessWeek,* March 23, 1992, pp. 66–68; and Patricia Sellers, "How Busch Wins in a Doggy Market," *Fortune,* June 22, 1987, pp. 99–111.

19. Fusun F. Gonul, Franklin Carter, Elina Petrova, and Kannan Srinivasan, "Promotion of Prescription Drugs and Its Impact on Physicians' Choice Behavior," *Journal of Marketing,* July 2001, pp. 79–90.

20. Wendy Macias and Lisa Stavchansky Lewis, "A Content Analysis of Direct-to-Consumer (DTC) Perscription Drug Web Sites," *Journal of Advertising,* Winter, 2003; John Carey, "Drug Ads Need Stronger Medicine," *BusinessWeek,* February 9, 2004, p. 84; "Drugstore.com Selected as One of Top 50 Retailing Web Sites for 2004," www.retail-merchandiser.com, November 18, 2003; "Canadians Worry Drug Exports Could Threaten Their Supplies," *Modern Healthcare,* April 12, 2004, p. 36; and "10 Direct-to-Consumer Drugs by Sales," *Advertising Age,* December 22, 2003, p. 28.

21. Robert J. Lavidge and Gary A. Steiner, "A Model for Predictive Measurement of Advertising Effectiveness," *Journal of Marketing,* October 1961, p. 61.

22. Brian Wansink and Michael Ray, "Advertising Strategies to Increase Usage Frequency," *Journal of Marketing,* January 1996, pp. 31–46.

23. "49th Annual Report: 100 Leading National Advertisers," *Advertising Age,* June 28, 2004, p. S2.

24. Don E. Schultz and Anders Gronstedt, "Making Marcom an Investment," *Marketing Management,* Fall 1997, pp. 41–49; and J. Enrique Bigne, "Advertising Budget Practices: A Review," *Journal of Current Issues and Research in Advertising,* Fall 1995, pp. 17–31.

25. John Philip Jones, "Ad Spending: Maintaining Market Share," *Harvard Business Review,* January–February 1990, pp. 38–42; and Charles H. Patti and Vincent Blanko, "Budgeting Practices of Big Advertisers," *Journal of Advertising Research* 21 (December 1981), pp. 23–30.

26. James A. Schroer, "Ad Spending: Growing Market Share," *Harvard Business Review,* January–February 1990, pp. 44–48.

27. Jeffrey A. Lowenhar and John L. Stanton, "Forecasting Competitive Advertising Expenditures," *Journal of Advertising Research* 16, no. 2 (April 1976), pp. 37–44.

28. Daniel Seligman, "How Much for Advertising?" *Fortune,* December 1956, p. 123.

29. James E. Lynch and Graham J. Hooley, "Increasing Sophistication in Advertising Budget Setting," *Journal of Advertising Research* 30 (February–March 1990), pp. 67–75.

30. Jimmy D. Barnes, Brenda J. Muscove, and Javad Rassouli, "An Objective and Task Media Selection Decision Model and Advertising Cost Formula to Determine International Advertising Budgets," *Journal of Advertising* 11, no. 4 (1982), pp. 68–75.

31. Don E. Schultz, "Olympics Get the Gold Medal in Integrating Marketing Event," *Marketing News,* April 27, 1998, pp. 5, 10.

32. Cornelia Pechman, Guangzhi Zhao, Marvin E. Goldberg, and Ellen Thomas Reibling, "What to Convey in Antismoking Advertisements for Adolescents: The Use of Protection Motivation Theory to Identify Effective Message Themes," *Journal of Marketing,* April 2003, pp. 1–18.

33. Jill Kipnis, "Picture This: New Line Breaks Ground with HD Promos," *Billboard,* May 29, 2004; David Finnigan, "The Biz," *BrandWeek,* October 14, 2002; "The Fellowship of the New Line," *Promo,* September 2001, p. 84; and "Sneak Preview of Trailer for New Line Cinema's 'The Lord of the Rings: The Fellowship of the Ring'" *PR Newswire,* September 21, 2001.

34. Claire Atkinson, "Coke Catapults Starcom Media Vest," *Advertising Age,* February 9, 2004, p. S6.

35. Kate Fitzgerald, "Beyond Advertising," *Advertising Age,* August 3, 1998, pp. 1, 14; Curtis P. Johnson, "Follow the Money: Sell CFO on Integrated Marketing's Merits," *Marketing News,* May 11, 1998, p. 10; and Laura Schneider, "Agencies Show That IMC Can Be Good for Bottom Line," *Marketing News,* May 11, 1998, p. 11.

36. Tom Duncan, "Is Your Marketing Communications Integrated?" *Advertising Age,* January 24, 1994, p. 26.

37. Kim Cleland, "Few Wed Marketing, Communications," *Advertising Age,* February 27, 1995, p. 10.

38. "Measure for Measure," *Marketing Management,* January–February 2004, p. 7.

39. Don Schultz, "Objectives Drive Tactics in IMC Approach,"*Marketing News,* May 9, 1994, pp. 14, 18; and Neil Brown, "Redefine Integrated Marketing Communications," *Marketing News,* March 29, 1993, pp. 4–5.

40. *Economic Impact: U.S. Direct Marketing Today* (New York: Direct Marketing Association, 2000), pp. 24–30.

41. "The Columbia House Company Selects Akamai EdgeSuite to Support Growing Online Business," *Business Wire,* September 5, 2001; "Back to College Market Fuels Growth in Internet Commerce and Traffic," *Business Wire,* September 10, 2001; and Carol Krol, "Columbia House Looks Down the Road for Gains from Play," *Advertising Age,* March 1, 1999, p. 20.

42. *Statistical Fact Book '98* (New York: Direct Marketing Association, 1998).

43. Robert Berner, "Going that Extra Inch," *BusinessWeek,* September 18, 2000, p. 84.

44. Adapted from *Economic Impact: U.S. Direct Marketing Today* (New York: Direct Marketing Association, 1998), pp. 25–26.

45. Carol Krol, "Club Med Uses E-Mail to Pitch Unsold, Discounted Packages," *Advertising Age,* December 14, 1998, p. 40.

46. "Rising to the Top," *Promo,* September 2001, pp. 46–62.

47. Jean Halliday, "Taking Direct Route," *Advertising Age,* September 7, 1998, p. 17.

48. Julie Tilsner, "Lillian Vernon: Creating a Host of Spin-offs from Its Core Catalog," *BusinessWeek,* December 19, 1994, p. 85; and Lisa Coleman, "I Went Out and Did It," *Forbes,* August 17, 1992, pp. 102–4.

49. Alan K. Gorenstein, "Direct Marketing's Growth Will Be Global," *Marketing News,* December 7, 1998, p. 15; Don E. Schultz, "Integrated Global Marketing Will Be the Name of the Game," *Marketing News,* October 26, 1998, p. 5; and Mary Sutter and Andrea Mandel-Campbell, "Customers Are Eager, Infrastructure Lags," *Advertising Age International,* October 5, 1998, p. 12.

50. Juliana Koranten, "European Privacy Rules Go into Effect in 15 EU States," *Advertising Age,* October 26, 1998, p. S31; and Rashi Glazer, "The Illusion of Privacy and Competition for Attention," *Journal of Interactive Marketing,* Summer 1998, pp. 2–4.

51. LaToya Deann Rembert, "Will CAN-SPAM Affect You?" *Marketing Research,* Spring 2004, p. 8; Douglas Wood and David Brosse, "Mulling E-Mail Options," *Promo,* September 2001, p. 18; Kathleen Cholewka, "Making E-Mail Matter," *Sales and Marketing Management,* September 2001, pp. 21, 22; "$2.1 Billion Will Be Spent on E-Mail Marketing by Year-End 2001," *Direct Marketing,* August 2001, p. 7; Arlene Weintraub, "When E-Mail Ads Aren't Spam," *BusinessWeek,* October 16, 2000, p. 112; "Opting Out of E-Mail Ads Isn't So Easy to Do," *BusinessWeek,* November 6, 2000, p. 20; and "With E-Mail Marketing, Permission Is Key," eStatNews, www.emarketer.com, September 2001.

UPS: This case was written by Steven Hartley based on taped interviews of company personnel and the following sources: Dean Foust, "Big Brown's New Bag," *BusinessWeek,* July 19, 2004, p. 54; David Rynecki, "Does This Package Make Sense?" *Fortune,* January 26, 2004, p. 132; "The UPS Store and Mail Boxes Etc. Expand to 5000 Worldwide Locations," *Business Wire,* September 13, 2004; Charles Haddad, "The Websmart 50," *BusinessWeek,* November 24, 2003, p. 92; and information contained on the UPS website (www.ups.com).

CHAPTER 19

1. Devin Leonard, "Nightmare on Madison Avenue," *Fortune,* June 28, 2004, pp. 92–108; Gregory Solman, "Wow Factor about to Spike for Ads in Online Games," www.Adweek.com, May 24, 2004; Catherine Arnold, "The New Game in Advergaming," *Marketing News,* June 1, 2004, p. 6; "Virtual Advertising: Digitopia," *New Media Age,* March 18, 2004, p. 25; Alicia Griswold, "BMW Debuts Virtual Hispanic Ad Effort," www.Adweek.com, May 19, 2003; Nancy Coltun Webster, "Now Down To Business: Counting Gamer Thumbs," *Advertising Age,* May 24, 2004, p. S6; Jean Halliday, "Automakers Mix It Up Chasing Young Buyers," *Advertising Age,* April 19, 2004, p. 4; Daniel Eisenberg, "Making Brands Magically Appear," *Time,* July 23, 2001, p. 46; and Christine Y. Chen, "TiVo Is Smart TV," *Fortune,* March 19, 2001, p. 124.

2. David A. Aaker and Donald Norris, "Characteristics of TV Commercials Perceived as Informative," *Journal of Advertising Research* 22, no. 2 (April–May 1982), pp. 61–70.

3. Larry D. Compeau and Dhruv Grewal, "Comparative Price Advertising: An Integrative Review," *Journal of Public Policy & Marketing,* Fall 1998, pp. 257–73; and William Wilkie and Paul W. Farris, "Comparison Advertising: Problems and Potentials," *Journal of Marketing,* October 1975, pp. 7–15.

4. Jennifer Lawrence, "P&G Ads Get Competitive," *Advertising Age,* February 1, 1993, p. 14; Jerry Gotlieb and Dan Sorel, "The Influence of Type of Advertisement, Price, and Source Credibility on Perceived Quality," *Journal of the Academy of Marketing Science,* Summer 1992, pp. 253–60; and Cornelia Pechman and David Stewart, "The Effects of Comparative Advertising on Attention, Memory, and Purchase Intentions," *Journal of Consumer Research,* September 1990, pp. 180–92.

5. Bruce Buchanan and Doron Goldman, "Us vs. Them: The Minefield of Comparative Ads," *Harvard Business Review,* May–June 1989, pp. 38–50; Dorothy Cohen, "The FTC's Advertising Substantiation Program," *Journal of Marketing,* Winter 1980, pp. 26–35; and Michael Etger and Stephen A. Goodwin, "Planning for Comparative Advertising Requires Special Attention," *Journal of Advertising* 8, no. 1 (Winter 1979), pp. 26–32.

6. Lewis C. Winters, "Does It Pay to Advertise to Hostile Audiences with Corporate Advertising?" *Journal of Advertising Research,* June–July 1988, pp. 11–18; and Robert Selwitz, "The Selling of an Image," *Madison Avenue,* February 1985, pp. 61–69.

7. Mary Lou Quinlan, "Women: We've Come a Long Way, Maybe," *Advertising Age,* February 22, 1999, p. 46.

8. Jean Halliday, "Of Hummers and Zen," *Advertising Age,* August 6, 2001, p. 29.

9. "Claritin Springs into Allergy Season with New Consumer Programs," *PR Newswire,* February 20, 2001.

10. Ira Teinowitz, "Self-regulation Urged to Prevent Bias in Ad Buying," *Advertising Age,* January 18, 1999, p. 4.

11. Bob Donath, "Match Your Media Choice and Ad Copy Objective," *Marketing News,* June 8, 1998, p. 6.

12. "TBWA/Chiat/Day Wins the $100,000 Grand Prize Kelly Award for Apple's iPod 'Silhouettes' Magazine Campaign," Magazine Publishers of America press release, June 10, 2004.

13. Kate Maddox, "ARF Forum Examines Internet Research Effectiveness," *Advertising Age,* January 11, 1999, p. 28.

14. Demetrios Vakratsas and Tim Ambler, "How Advertising Works: What Do We Really Know?" *Journal of Marketing,* January 1999, pp. 26–43.

15. "Second Annual Guide to Advertising and Marketing," 2004, a supplement to *Advertising Age,* p. 42; Bob Garfield, "Super Bowl Showdown: Bud's 'Tune Out' Is Pick of an Otherwise Predictable Ad Pack," *Advertising Age,* February 2, 2004, p. 1; Rama Ylkur, Chuck Tomkovick, and Patty Traczyk, "Super Bowl Effectiveness: Hollywood Finds the Games Golden," *Journal of Advertising Research,* March, 2004, pp. 143–59.

16. Jean Halliday, "Entry-Lux Gears Up," *Advertising Age,* June 23, 2003, p. S4; and Kate Macarthur, "$50 Million Push: Predictions for Coke's C2," *Advertising Age,* May 31, 2004, p. 8.

17. Michael S. LaTour and Herbert J. Rotfeld, "There Are Threats and (Maybe) Fear-Caused Arousal: Theory and Confusions of Appeals to Fear and Fear Arousal Itself," *Journal of Advertising,* Fall 1997, pp. 45–59.

18. Bob Garfield, "Allstate Ads Bring Home Point about Mortgage Insurance," *Advertising Age,* September 11, 1989, p. 120; and Judann Dagnoli, "'Buy or Die' Mentality Toned Down in Ads," *Advertising Age,* May 7, 1990, p. S12.

19. Cornelia Pechmann, Guangzhi Zhao, Marvin E. Goldberg, and Ellen Thomas Reibling, "What to Convey in Antismoking Advertisements for Adolescents: The Use of Protection Motivation Theory to Identify Effective Message Themes," *Journal of Marketing,* April, 2003, pp. 1–18; Jeffrey D. Zbar, "Fear!" *Advertising Age,* November 14, 1994, pp. 18–19; John F. Tanner, Jr., James B. Hunt, and David R. Eppright, "The Protection Motivation Model: A Normative Model of Fear Appeals," *Journal of Marketing,* July 1991, pp. 36–45; and Michael S. LaTour and Shaker A. Zahra, "Fear Appeals as Advertising Strategy: Should They Be Used?" *Journal of Consumer Marketing,* Spring 1989, pp. 61–70.

20. Stuart Elliot, "Can Beer Ads Extol Great Taste in Good Taste?" *The New York Times,* April 16, 2004, p. C2; and "Operating Strategy," bebe website, www.bebe.com.

21. Eric Gillin and Greg Lindsay, "The New Puritanism," *Advertising Age,* April 5, 2004, pp. 1, 34; Bruce Horvitz, "Risque May Be Too Risky for Ads," *USA Today,* April 16, 2004, p. 1B; and Rich Thomaselli, "NFL Stops the Music," *Advertising Age,* March 15, 2004, p. 78.

22. Theresa Howard, "Thinking Outside the TV Box Ads Get Creative in Midst of New Media Choices," *USA Today,* June 22, 2004, p. 4B; Anthony Vagnoni, "Best Awards," *Advertising Age,* May 28, 2001, pp. S1–18; Dana L. Alden, Wayne D. Hoyer, and Chol Lee, "Identifying Global and Culture-Specific Dimensions of Humor in Advertising: A Multinational Analysis," *Journal of Marketing,* April 1993, pp. 64–75; and Johny K. Johansson, "The Sense of 'Nonsense': Japanese TV Advertising," *Journal of Advertising,* March 1994, pp. 17–26.

23. Lisa Sanders, "Berlin Cameron Stands on Its Own," *Advertising Age,* January 12, 2004, p. S2.

24. Jeff Manning and Kevin Lane Keller, "Got Advertising That Works?" *Marketing Management,* January–February 2004, pp. 16–20; Stephanie Thompson, "Jacobs Hopes Simpson Can Turn Ice to Gold at Hershey," *Advertising Age,* May 31, 2004, p. 54; "NCP Enlists Simpson Sisters for Ice Breakers," www.Adweek.com, May 18, 2004; "Risky Business: Kobe Sex Scandal Forces Brands to Take a Closer Look," *Business and Industry,* September 29, 2003, p. 1; Alan J. Bush, Craig A. Martin, and Victoria D. Bush, "Sports Celebrity Influence on the Behavioral Intentions of Generation Y," *Journal of Advertising Research,* March 2004, pp. 108–18; "Ronald McDonald Models Milk Mustache," *PR Newswire,* September 11, 2001; "Image of the Week," *Advertising Age,* February 26, 2001, p. 56; Rich Thomaselli, "Air Ball?" *Advertising Age,* October 1, 2001, p. 3; Paul Lukas, "Got Milk? Got Books? Got a Clue?" *Fortune,* September 7, 1998, p. 40; Brian D. Till and Terence A. Shimp, "Endorsers in Advertising: The Case of Negative Celebrity Information," *Journal of Advertising,* March 22, 1998, p. 67; and Alan R. Miciak and William L. Shanklin, "Choosing Celebrity Endorsers," *Marketing Management* 3, no. 3 (1994), pp. 51–59.

25. *2003 Television Production Cost Survey,* American Association of Advertising Agencies, 2003, p. 5; Jean Halliday, "Exotic Ads Get Noticed," *Advertising Age,* April 9, 2001, p. S4.

26. "49th Annual Report: 100 Leading National Advertisers," *Advertising Age,* June 28, 2004, p. S2.

27. Giles D'Souza and Ram C. Rao, "Can Repeating an Advertisement More Frequently than the Competition Affect Brand Preference in a Mature Market?" *Journal of Marketing,* April 1995, pp. 32–42.

28. Vicki R. Lane, "The Impact of Ad Repetition and Ad Content on Consumer Perceptions of Incongruent Extensions," *Journal of Marketing,* April 2000, pp. 80–91.

29. Katherine Barrett, "Taking a Closer Look," *Madison Avenue,* August 1984, pp. 106–9.

30. Joe Mandese, "Out-of-Home TV: Does It Count?" *Advertising Age,* January 18, 1993, p. 53.

31. Claire Atkinson, "Idol Tops TV Price Chart," *Advertising Age,* September 27, 2004, pp. 1, 72.

32. Surendra N. Singh, Denise Linville, and Ajay Sukhdial, "Enhancing the Efficacy of Split Thirty-Second Television Commercials: An Encoding Variability Application," *Journal of Advertising,* Fall 1995, pp. 13–23; Scott Ward, Terence A. Oliva, and David J. Reibstein, "Effectiveness of Brand-Related 15-Second Commercials," *Journal of Consumer Marketing,* no. 2 (1994), pp. 38–44; and Surendra N. Singh and Catherine Cole, "The Effects of Length, Content, and Repetition on Television Commercial Effectiveness," *Journal of Marketing Research,* February 1993, pp. 91–104.

33. Scott Woolley, "Zap," *Forbes,* September 29, 2003, pp. 77–82; Cliff Edwards, "Is TiVo's Signal Fading?" *BusinessWeek,* September 10, 2001, p. 72; Jacqueline M. Graves, "The Fortune 500 Opt for Infomercials," *Fortune,* March 6, 1995, p. 20; and William McCall, "Infomercial Pioneer Becomes Industry Leader," *Marketing News,* June 19, 1995, p. 14.

34. Cara Beardi, "Radio's Big Bounce," *Advertising Age,* August 27, 2001, p. S2.

35. Kate Fitzgerald, "Launches Crowd Already Tough Field," *Advertising Age,* April 5, 2004, p. S2; Catherine Arnold, *Marketing News,* May 1, 2004, p. 3; Jon Fine, "Silicon Valley Spawns New Nascar Lifestyle Magazine," *Advertising Age,* January 12, 2004, p. 8; Jon Fine, "Magazine of the Year: Lucky," *Advertising Age,* October 20, 2003, p. S1; *A Magazine for Everyone,* The Magazine Handbook, The Magazine Publishers Association, 2003, p. 6; R. Craig Endicott, "Past Performance Is Not a Guarantee of Future Returns," *Advertising Age,* June 18, 2001, pp. S1, S6; and George R. Milne, "A Magazine Taxonomy Based on Customer Overlap," *Journal of the Academy of Marketing Science,* Spring 1994, pp. 170–79.

36. Julia Collins, "Image and Advertising," *Harvard Business Review,* January–February 1989, pp. 93–97.

37. Samir Husni, "Good Ideas Gone Awry," *Advertising Age,* October 23, 2000, p. S26.

38. Jon Fine, "Newspaper-Industry Slide Worsens," *Advertising Age,* May 10, 2004, p. 59; Jeffery D. Zbar, "Papers Tackling Sprawl," *Advertising Age,* April 30, 2001, pp. S6, S7; Heather Holliday, "Papers, TV Stations Extend War to Web," *Advertising Age,* April 30, 2001, p. S8; Mary Ellen Podmolik, "Urban Tabloids Snare Hipper Young Readers," *Advertising Age,* April 30, 2001, p. S2; and Kim Cleland, "Online Soon to Snare 100-plus Newspapers," *Advertising Age,* April 24, 1995, p. S6.

39. Lisa Sanders, "Major Marketers Turn to Yellow Pages," *Advertising Age,* March 8, 2004, p. 4; "Yellow Pages Still 'Gold Standard' for Searches," *USA Today,* February 16, 2004, p. 10A; Avery M. Abernethy and David N. Laband, "The Impact of Trademarks and Advertisement Size on Yellow Page Call Rates," *Journal of Advertising Research,* March 2004, pp. 119–25; and "Yellow Pages and the Media Mix," Yellow Pages Publishers Association, Troy, MI.

40. Pierre Berthon and James M. Hulbert, "Marketing In Metamorphosis: Breaking Boundaries," *Business Horizons,* May–June 2003, pp. 31–40.

41. Sandeep Krishnamurthy, "Deciphering the Internet Advertising Puzzle," *Marketing Management,* Fall 2000, pp. 35–39; Judy Strauss and Raymond Frost, *Marketing on the Internet: Principles of Online Marketing* (Englewood Cliffs, NJ: Prentice Hall, 1999), pp. 196–249; and Maricris G. Briones, "Rich Media May Be Too Rich for Your Blood," *Marketing News,* March 29, 1999, p. 4.

42. Kris Oser, "Online Ad Demand Bumps Up Prices," *Advertising Age,* June 7, 2004, p. 3; Normandy Madden, "Levi's Enjoys 'Rebirth' on the Web in Asia," *Advertising Age,* April 29, 2004, p. 52; Heather Green and Ben Elgin, "Do E-Ads Have a Future?" *BusinessWeek,*

January 22, 2001, p. EB46; and Ellen Neuborne, "For Kids on the Web, It's an Ad, Ad, Ad, Ad World," *BusinessWeek,* August 13, 2001, p. 108.

43. Xavier Dreze and Francois-Xavier Hussherr, "Internet Advertising: Is Anybody Watching?" *Journal of Interactive Marketing,* Autumn 2003, pp. 8–23; Timothy J. Mullaney, "E-Biz Strikes Again!" *BusinessWeek,* May 10, 2004, pp. 80–84; Stephen Chen, "The Real Value of 'E-Business Models,'" *Business Horizons,* November–December 2003, pp. 27–33; Deborah L. Vence, "Web Plays Vital Role in Marketing Push," *Marketing News,* April 15, 2004, pp. 15–16; and Stephen Baker, "A Zapper for Online Ads," *BusinessWeek,* December 22, 2003, p. 13.

44. Dana Blankenhorn, "Bigger, Richer Ads Go Online," *Advertising Age,* June 18, 2001, p. T10; Patricia Riedman, "Poor Rich Media," *Advertising Age,* February 5, 2001, p. 26; Heather Green, "Net Advertising: Still the 98-Pound Weakling," *BusinessWeek,* September 1l, 2000, p. 36; and Thom Weidlich, "Online Spots— A New Generation," *Advertising Age,* July 30, 2001, p. S10.

45. Arch G. Woodside, "Outdoor Advertising as Experiments," *Journal of the Academy of Marketing Science* 18 (Summer 1990), pp. 229–37.

46. Ronald Grover, "Billboards Aren't Boring Anymore," *BusinessWeek,* September 21, 1998, pp. 86–90; and Marc Gunther, "The Great Outdoors," *Fortune,* March 1, 1999, p. 150–57.

47. James Betzold, "Jaded Riders Are Ever-Tougher Sell," *Advertising Age,* July 9, 2001, p. S2.

48. Charles R. Taylor and Weih Chang, "The History of Outdoor Advertising Regulation in the United States," *Journal of Macromarketing,* Spring 1995, pp. 47–59; Cyndee Miller, "Outdoor Advertising Weathers Repeated Attempts to Kill It," *Marketing News,* March 16, 1992, pp. 1, 9; Ricardo Davis, "Outdoor Ad Giants Trim Pay to Agencies," *Advertising Age,* January 18, 1993, p. 54; and Patricia Winters, "Outdoor Builds New Areas to Replace Tobacco and Liquor," *Advertising Age,* October 12, 1992, pp. 5–24.

49. Ed Brown, "Advertisers Skip to the Loo," *Fortune,* October 26, 1998, p. 64; John Cortex, "Growing Pains Can't Stop the New Kid on the Ad Block," *Advertising Age,* October 12, 1992, pp. 5–28; Allen Banks, "How to Assess New Place-Based Media," *Advertising Age,* November 30, 1992, p. 36; and John Cortex, "Media Pioneers Try to Corral On-the-Go Consumers," *Advertising Age,* August 17, 1992, p. 25.

50. "It's An Ad, Ad, Ad, Ad World," *Time,* July 9, 2001, p. 17; "Triton, Secora in Alliance for Advertising on ATMs," *Marketing News,* June 5, 2000, p. 12; and Joan Oleck, "High-Octane Advertising," *BusinessWeek,* November 29, 1999, p. 8.

51. Sehoon Park and Minhi Hahn, "Pulsing in a Discrete Model of Advertising Competition," *Journal of Marketing Research,* November 1991, pp. 397–405.

52. Peggy Masterson, "The Wearout Phenomenon," *Marketing Research,* Fall 1999, pp. 27–31; and Lawrence D. Gibson, "What Can One TV Exposure Do?" *Journal of Advertising Research,* March–April 1996, pp. 9–18.

53. Rob Norton, "How Uninformative Advertising Tells Consumers Quite a Bit," *Fortune,* December 26, 1994, p. 37; and "Professor Claims Corporations Waste Billions on Advertising," *Marketing News,* July 6, 1992, p. 5.

54. Ron Benza, "Advertising Looks in the Mirror," *Marketing Management,* March–April 2003, pp. 33–37; Jack Neff, "Feeling the Squeeze," *Advertising Age,* June 4, 2001, pp. 1, 14–15; and Laura Q. Hughes, "Measuring Up," *Advertising Age,* February 5, 2001, pp. 1, 34.

55. The discussion of posttesting is based on William F. Arens, *Contemporary Advertising,* 6th ed. (Burr Ridge, IL: Richard D. Irwin, 1996), pp. 181–82.

56. David A. Aaker and Douglas M. Stayman, "Measuring Audience Perceptions of Commercials and Relating Them to Ad Impact," *Journal of Advertising Research* 30 (August–September 1990), pp. 7–17; and Ernest Dichter, "A Psychological View of Advertising Effectiveness," *Marketing Management* 1, no. 3 (1992), pp. 60–62.

57. David Kruegel, "Television Advertising Effectiveness and Research Innovation," *Journal of Consumer Marketing,* Summer 1988, pp. 43–51; and Laurence N. Gold, "The Evolution of Television Advertising Sales Measurement: Past, Present, and Future," *Journal of Advertising Research,* June–July 1988, pp. 19–24.

58. "Upward Bound," *Promo,* April 2004, p. AR5.

59. Magid M. Abraham and Leonard M. Lodish, "Getting the Most out of Advertising and Promotion," *Harvard Business Review,* May–June 1990, pp. 50–60; Steven W. Hartley and James Cross, "How Sales Promotion Can Work for and against You," *Journal of Consumer Marketing,* Summer 1988, pp. 35–42; Robert D. Buzzell, John A. Quelch, and Walter J. Salmon, "The Costly Bargain of Trade Promotion," *Harvard Business Review,* March–April 1990, pp. 141–49; and Mary L. Nicastro, "Break-Even Analysis Determines Success of Sales Promotions," *Marketing News,* March 5, 1990, p. 11.

60. Natalie Schwartz, "Clipping Path," *Promo,* April 1, 2004, p. 4; Mathew Kinsman, "The Hard Sell," *Promo's 11th Annual Source Book* (2004), p. 19; Betsy Spethmann, "Going for Broke," *Promo,* August 2001, pp. 27–31; and Mathew Kinsman, "Bad Is Good," *Promo,* April 2001, pp. 71–74.

61. Kapil Bawa and Robert W. Shoemaker, "Analyzing Incremental Sales from a Direct-Mail Coupon Promotion," *Journal of Marketing,* July 1998, pp. 66–78.

62. Roger A. Strang, "Sales Promotion—Fast Growth, Faulty Management," *Harvard Business Review* 54 (July–August 1976), pp. 115–24; and Ronald W. Ward and James E. Davis, "Coupon Redemption," *Journal of Advertising Research* 18 (August 1978), pp. 51–58. Similar results on favorable mail-distributed coupons were reported by Alvin Schwartz, "The Influence of Media Characteristics on Coupon Redemption," *Journal of Marketing* 30 (January 1966), pp. 41–46.

63. "Competing with Coupons," *Marketing News,* March 15, 1999, p. 2; and Larry Armstrong. "Coupon Clippers, Save Your Scissors," *BusinessWeek,* June 20, 1994, pp. 164–66.

64. Karen Holt, "Coupon Crimes," *Promo,* April 2004, pp. 23–26, 70.

65. "McD Has Happy Recipe for Kids Meals," www.brandweek.com, March 29, 2004; Carrie MacMillan, "Creature Features," *Promo,* October 2001, p.11; and Dan Hanover, "Not Just for Breakfast Anymore," *Promo,* September 2001, p. 10.

66. Matthew Kinsman, "Riding High," *Promo's 11th Annual Source Book 2004,* p. 26.

67. Lorraine Woellert, "The Sweepstakes Biz Isn't Feeling Lucky," *BusinessWeek,* March 22, 1999, p. 80.

68. Tim Parry, "Instantly Fulfilled," *Promo,* June 1, 2004, p. 7; Betsy Spethmann, "Call It a Win!" *Promo,* May 1, 2004, p. 6; Thomas Lee, "It's an Ad, Ad, Ad, Ad World," *St. Louis Post-Dispatch,* January 26, 2004, p. A1; and Kate MacArthur, "Coke to Use GPS in Contest," *Advertising Age,* October 13, 2003, p. 1.

69. Edward Kabak, "Staking out the States," *Promo,* October 2001, p. 11; Maxine Lans Retsky, "Stakes Are High for Direct Mail Sweepstakes Promotions," *Marketing News,* July 3, 2000, p. 8; Richard Sale, "Sweeping the Courts," *Promo,* May 1998, pp. 42–45; and Fred C. Allvine, Richard D. Teach, and John Connelly, Jr., "The Demise of Promotional Games," *Journal of Advertising Research* 16 (October 1976), pp. 79–84.

70. Lorin Cipolla, "Instant Gratification," *Promo,* April 1, 2004, p. 4; "Best Activity Generating Brand Awareness/Trial," *Promo,* September 2001, p. 51; and "Brand Handing," *Promo's 9th Annual Sourcebook* (2002), p. 32.

71. Kathleen Joyce, "Keeping the Faith," *Promo,* April 2004, p. AR23; and Kelly Shermack, "CPG Marketers Are Developing Loyalty Programs That Benefit Both Manufacturers and Retailers," *Marketing News,* November 10, 2003, p. 13.

72. Cyndee Miller, "P-O-P Gains Followers as 'Era of Retailing' Dawns," *Marketing News,* May 14, 1990, p. 2.

73. Jeff Neff, "Floors in Stores Start Moving," *Advertising Age,* August 20, 2001, p. 15.

74. See www.fordcollegegrad.com.

75. Marvin A. Jolson, Joshua L. Wiener, and Richard B. Rosecky, "Correlates of Rebate Proneness," *Journal of Advertising Research,* February–March 1987, pp. 33–43.

76. M. Ellen Peebles, "And Now, a Word from Our Sponsor," *Harvard Business Review,* October 2003, pp. 31–42; Karl Greenberg, "Tie-Ins: Jaguar Goes Hollywood," www.brandweek.com, May 31, 2004; "Samsung Remaps the Matrix," *Promo,* April 1, 2004, p. 4; Paula Lyon Andruss, "Survivor Packages Make Real-Life Money," *Marketing News,* March 26, 2001, p. 5; Wayne Friedman, "Eagle-Eye Marketers Find Right Spot, Right Time," *Advertising Age,* January 22, 2001, p. S2; David Goetzl, "TBS Tries Virtual Advertising," *Advertising Age,* May 21, 2001, p. 8; and James Poniewozik, "This Plug's for You," *Time,* June 18, 2001 p. 76–77.

77. "Shows Must Go On," *Promo,* January 1, 2004, p. 2; "Sears New Song and Dance," *Promo,* May 1, 2004, p. 6; and Danon Darlin, "Junior Mints, I'm Going to Make You a Star," *Forbes,* November 6, 1995, pp. 90–94.

78. This discussion is drawn particularly from John A. Quelch, *Trade Promotions by Grocery Manufacturers: A Management Perspective* (Cambridge, MA: Marketing Science Institute, August 1982).

79. Michael Chevalier and Ronald C. Curhan, "Retail Promotions as a Function of Trade Promotions: A Descriptive Analysis," *Sloan Management Review* 18 (Fall 1976), pp. 19–32.

80. G. A. Marken, "Firms Can Maintain Control over Creative Co-op Programs," *Marketing News,* September 28, 1992, pp. 7, 9.

81. "Safetyforum.com and Public Citizen Report: NHTSA Forces Firestone to Recall Defective Tires, Expand Wilderness ATs Recall," *PR Newswire,* October 5, 2001; Cindy Skrzycki and Frank Swoboda, "Firestone Refuses Voluntary Recall," www.safetyforum.com, July 20, 2001; Jim Suhr, "Tire Recall Response Time Defended," www.safetyforum.com, August 10, 2000.

82. Scott Hue, "Free 'Plugs' Supply Ad Power," *Advertising Age,* January 29, 1990, p. 6.

83. Mike Harris, "Earnhardt's Lap Belt Was Broken," www.safetyforum.com, February 23, 2001; and Marc Weinberger, Jean Romeo, and Azhar Piracha, "Negative Product Safety News: Coverage, Responses, and Effects," *Business Horizons,* May–June 1991, pp. 23–31.

84. Irving Rein, Philip Kotler, and Martin Stoller, *High Visibility* (New York: Dodd, Mead, 1987); and Steven Colford, "Ross Perot: A Winner after All," *Advertising Age,* December 21, 1992, pp. 4, 18.

85. Michael Treacy and Fred Wiersema, "Customer Intimacy and Other Value Disciplines," *Harvard Business Review,* January–February 1993, pp. 84–93.

86. Gerry Khermouch and Tom Lowry, "The Future of Advertising," *BusinessWeek,* March 26, 2001, p. 139; and D. J., "Outlook 2001: Advertising," *Marketing News,* January 1, 2001, p. 10.

87. Betsy Spethmann, "McFallout," *Promo,* October 2001, pp. 31–38.

88. "Kid Stuff," *Promo,* January 1991, pp. 25, 42; Steven W. Colford, "Fine-Tuning Kids' TV," *Advertising Age,* February 11, 1991, p. 35; and Kate Fitzgerald, "Toys Star-Struck for Movie Tie-Ins," *Advertising Age,* February 18, 1991, p. 3, 45.

89. Herbert J. Rotfeld, Avery M. Abernathy, and Patrick R. Parsons, "Self-Regulation and Television Advertising," *Journal of Advertising* 19, no. 4 (1990), pp. 18–26.

Fallon Worldwide: This case was written by Mark T. Spriggs, William Rudelius, and Linda Rochford based on interviews with Fallon personnel and materials on the Citi and BMW promotional campaigns provided by Citi, BMW, and Fallon.

CHAPTER 20

1. "Xerox Turns a New Page," *CNNMoney.com,* March 16, 2004; "Anne Mulcahy Has Xerox by the Horns," *BusinessWeek Online,* May 29, 2003; and Kathleen Cholewka, "Xerox's Savior?" *Sales & Marketing Management,* April 2001, pp. 36–42.

2. Eilene Zimmerman, "So You Wanna Be a CEO," *Sales & Marketing Management,* January 2002, pp. 31–35.

3. "America's 25 Best Sales Forces," *Sales & Marketing Management,* July 2000, pp. 57–85.

4. Mark W. Johnston and Greg W. Marshall, *Relationship Selling and Sales Management* (Burr Ridge, IL: McGraw-Hill/Irwin, 2005); and David W. Cravens, "The Changing Role of the Sales Force," *Marketing Management,* Fall 1995, pp. 49–57.

5. David Kirkpatrick, "Inside Sam's $100 Billion Growth Machine," *Fortune,* June 14, 2004, pp. 80ff.

6. "Increasing Face Time," *Sales & Marketing Management,* January 2004, p. 12; and Barton A. Weitz, Stephen B. Castleberry, and John F. Tanner, Jr., *Selling: Building Partnerships,* 5th ed. (Burr Ridge, IL: McGraw-Hill/Irwin, 2004), p. 10.

7. "Stop Calling Us," *Time,* April 29, 2003, pp. 56–58.

8. For representative research and commentary on team selling, see Keith A. Chrzanowski and Thomas W. Leigh, "Customer Relationship Strategy and Customer-Focused Teams," in Gerald J. Bauer et al., *Emerging Trends in Sales Thought and Practice* (Westport, CT: Quorum Books, 1998); and Mark A. Moon and Susan Forquer Gupta, "Examining the Formation of Selling Centers: A Conceptual Framework," *Journal of Personal Selling & Sales Management,* Spring 1997, pp. 31–41.

9. Steve Atlas and Elise Atlas, "Team Approach," *Selling Power,* May 2000, pp. 126–28; and Neil Rackman, Lawrence Friedman, and Richard Ruff, *Getting Partnering Right* (New York: McGraw-Hill, 1996), pp. 47–48.

10. Carol J. Loomis, "Have You Been Cold-Called?" *Fortune,* December 16, 1991, pp. 109–15.

11. Jim Edwards, "Dinner, Interrupted," *BrandWeek,* May 26, 2003, pp. 28–32.

12. Paul A. Herbing, *Handbook of Cross-Cultural Marketing* (New York: Holworth Press, 1998).

13. "Japanese Business Etiquette," *Smart Business,* August 2000, p. 55.

14. This discussion is based on Weitz, Castleberry, and Tanner, *Selling,* chap. 6; F. Robert Dwyer and John F. Tanner, *Business Marketing,* 2nd ed. (Burr Ridge, IL: McGraw-Hill/Irwin, 2002), p. 400; and Jeff Golterman, "Strategic Account Management in the Age of the Never Satisfied Customer," *Velocity* 2 (2000), pp. 13–16.

15. For an extensive discussion of objections, see Charles M. Futrell, *Fundamentals of Selling,* 8th ed. (Burr Ridge, IL: McGraw-Hill/Irwin, 2004), chap. 12.

16. Philip R. Cateora and John L. Graham, *International Marketing,* 11th ed. (Burr Ridge, IL: McGraw-Hill/Irwin, 2002), pp. 128, 131; and Herbing, *Handbook of Cross-Cultural Marketing,* p. 60.

17. Theodore Levitt, *The Marketing Imagination* (New York: Free Press, 1983), p. 111.

18. Weitz, Castleberry, and Tanner, *Selling.*

19. *Management Briefing: Sales and Marketing* (New York: Conference Board, October 1996), pp. 3–4.

20. Ellen Neuborne, "Know Thy Enemy," *Sales & Marketing Management,* January 2003, pp. 29–33.

21. Alan J. Dubinsky, Marvin A. Jolson, Ronald E. Michaels, Masaaki Katobe, and Chae Un Lim, "Ethical Perceptions of Field Sales Personnel: An Empirical Assessment," *Journal of Personal Selling & Sales Management,* Fall 1992, pp. 9–21; and Alan J. Dubinsky, Marvin A. Jolson, Masaaki Katobe, and Chae Un Lim, "A Cross-National Investigation of Industrial Salespeople's Ethical Perceptions," *Journal of International Business Studies,* Fourth Quarter 1991, pp. 651–70.

22. See Gilbert A. Churchill, Jr., Neil M. Ford, Orville C. Walker, Jr, Mark W. Johnson, and John F. Tanner, Jr., *Sales Force Management,* 7th ed. (Burr Ridge, IL: McGraw-Hill/Irwin, 2003), pp. 100–4.

23. Churchill et al., *Sales Force Management,* pp. 110–13. Also see Arun Sharma, "Who Prefers Key Account Management Programs? An Investigation of Business Buying Behavior and Buying Firm Characteristics," *Journal of Personal Selling & Sales Management,* Fall

1997, pp. 37–50; Dan C. Weilbaker and William A. Weeks, "The Evolution of National Account Management: A Literature Perspective," *Journal of Personal Selling & Management,* Fall 1997, pp. 49–60; and Christian Homburg, John P. Workman, and Ove Jensen, "A Configural Perspective on Key Account Management," *Journal of Marketing,* April 2002, pp. 38–60.

24. Several variations of the account management policy grid exist. See, for example, Douglas J. Dalrymple, William L. Cron, and Thomas E. DeCarlo, *Sales Management,* 8th ed. (New York: John Wiley & Sons, 2004), chap. 4; and Churchill et al., *Sales Force Management,* chap. 5.

25. "Look Who's Calling?" *Sales & Marketing Management,* May 1998, pp. 43–46.

26. Julia Chang, "Born to Sell?" *Sales & Marketing Management,* July 2003, pp. 34–38.

27. Weitz, Castleberry, and Tanner, *Selling,* pp. 20–21. Also see Daniel Goleman, "What Makes a Leader?" *Harvard Business Review,* November–December 1998, pp. 93–102; A. Fisher, "Success Secret: A High Emotional IQ," *Fortune,* October 26, 1998, pp. 293–98; and Daniel Goleman, *Working with Emotional Intelligence* (New York: Bantam, 1999).

28. *Statistical Abstract of the United States,* 123rd ed. (Washington, DC: U.S. Department of Commerce, 2003). Also see Lucette B. Comer, J. A. F. Nicholls, and Leslie J. Vermillion, "Diversity in the Sales Force: Problems and Challenges," *Journal of Personal Selling & Marketing,* Fall 1998, pp. 1–20; and *Occupational Outlook Quarterly* (Washington, DC: U.S. Department of Labor, Fall, 2003).

29. This discussion is based on Churchill et al., *Sales Force Management,* chap. 10.

30. See, for example, Nora Wood, "What Motivates Best?" *Sales & Marketing Management,* September 1998, pp. 71–78; Melanie Berger, "When Their Ship Comes In," *Sales & Marketing Management,* April 1997, pp. 60–65; William L. Cron, Alan J. Dubinsky, and Ronald E. Michaels, "The Influence of Career Stages on Components of Salesperson Motivation," *Journal of Marketing,* January 1988, pp. 78–82; Pradeep K. Tyagi, "Relative Importance of Key Job Dimensions and Leadership Behaviors in Motivating Salesperson Work Performance," *Journal of Marketing,* Summer 1985, pp. 76–86; and Richard C. Beckerer, Fred Morgan, and Lawrence Richard, "The Job Characteristics of Industrial Salespersons: Relationship of Motivation and Satisfaction," *Journal of Marketing,* Fall 1982, pp. 125–35.

31. Rosann Spiro, William J. Stanton, and Gregory Rich, *Management of the Sales Force* (Burr Ridge, IL: McGraw-Hill/Irwin, 2003), chap. 9.

32. www.marykay.com/recognition, downloaded June 21, 2004.

33. "Number Crunching," *Sales & Marketing Management,* September 2000, pp. 79–88.

34. For further reading, see Goutam N. Challagolla and Tasadduq A. Shervani, "A Measurement Model of the Dimensions and Types of Output and Behavior Control: An Empirical Test in the Salesforce Context," *Journal of Business Research,* July 1997, pp. 159–72; and Gregory A. Rich, William H. Bommer, Scott B. McKenzie, Philip M. Podsakoff, and Jonathan L. Johnson, "Apples and Apples or Apples and Oranges? A Meta-Analysis of Objective and Subjective Measures of Salesperson Performance," *Journal of Personal Selling & Sales Management,* Fall 1999, pp. 41–52.

35. "Measuring Sales Effectiveness," *Sales & Marketing Management,* October 2000, p. 136; and "Quota Busters," *Sales & Marketing Management,* January 2001, pp. 59–63.

36. Melissa Campanelli, "Eastman Chemical: A Formula for Quality," *Sales & Marketing Management,* October 1994, p. 88.

37. "Corporate America's New Sales Force," *Fortune,* August 11, 2003, special advertising section.

38. "Tools of the Trade," *Sales & Marketing Management,* October 2003, pp. 46–51.

39. Cravens, "The Changing Role of the Sales Force."

40. www.toshiba.com/technology, downloaded May 15, 2004.

41. "Going Mobile, Part 2," *Sales & Marketing Management,* June 1994, p. 5.

42. "Supercharged Sell," *Inc.Tech,* November 1998, pp. 42–50.

43. "Intranets Grow Up," *Sales & Marketing Management,* December 2000, p. 105.

Reebok: This case was written by Giana Eckhardt.

CHAPTER 21

1. www.sevencycles.com, downloaded June 8, 2005; Scott Mowbray, "The $5,000 Bike," *Fortune,* November 12, 2001, p. 62; and Lori Valigra, "Why Seven Cycles is Racing Ahead: The Net," *Business Week e-biz,* June 22, 1999, pp. 32–33.

2. "The State of Retailing Online 7.0," www.shop.org, 2004; and "Jupiter Market Forecast Report," Jupiter Research, New York, January 3, 2003.

3. "Internet Retailer's Best of the Web 2004," InternetRetailer.com.

4. "Electronic Commerce," www.wto.org, downloaded May 20, 2004.

5. "Statistics: U.S. Online Shoppers," www.shop.org, downloaded June 26, 2004.

6. Rafi A. Mohammed, Robert J. Fisher, Bernard J. Jaworski, and Gordon J. Paddison, *Internet Marketing: Building Advantage in a Networked Economy,* 2nd ed. (Burr Ridge, IL: McGraw-Hill/Irwin, 2004).

7. Adrian J. Slywotzky, "The Age of the Choiceboard," *Harvard Business Review,* January–February 2000, pp. 40–41.

8. For a description of collaborative filtering and similar types of systems, see Ward Hanson, *Principles of Internet Marketing,* 2nd ed. (Cincinnati, OH: South-Western College Publishing, 2005), pp. 215–30.

9. Michael Grebb, "Behavioral Science," *Business 2.0,* March 2000, p. 112.

10. Alan Rosenspan, "Participation Marketing," *Direct Marketing,* April 2001, pp. 54–66.

11. "Consumers Worried about Online Privacy," Jupiter Media Matrix press release, downloaded June 15, 2003.

12. This discussion is drawn from Jeffrey F. Rayport and Bernard J. Jaworski, *e-Commerce,* 2nd ed. (Burr Ridge, IL: McGraw-Hill/Irwin MarketspaceU, 2004); and Mohammed et al., *Internet Marketing.*

13. "Demographics of Internet Users," www.pewinternet.org/trends, downloaded June 7, 2004.

14. "Statistics: U.S. Online Shoppers"; "Click Here for a New Sedan! (Not Yet, Alas)," *Newsweek,* November 11, 2002, pp. E10–E12; and "The State of Retailing Online 7.0."

15. "The 90/20 Rule of E-Commerce: Nearly 90% of Online Sales Accounted for by 20% of Consumers," Cyber Dialogue press release, September 25, 2000.

16. Michael Weiss, "Online America," *America Demographics,* March 12, 2001, pp. 53–60.

17. "Statistics: U.S. Online Shoppers."

18. "New Study Reveals Internet Is the Medium Moms Rely on Most," Disney Online news release, March 8, 2004; and "On a Mission: The New Internet Mom," FC NOW: The Fast Company Weblog, May 25, 2004.

19. "Jupiter Market Forecast Report."

20. "Branding on the Net," *BusinessWeek,* November 2, 1998, pp. 78–86.

21. Jerry Wind and Arvind Rangaswamy, "Customerization: The Next Revolution in Mass Customization," *Journal of Interactive Marketing,* Winter 2001, pp. 13–32.

22. "Stopping Spam," *The Economist,* April 26, 2003, p. 58.

23. This discussion is based on Lev Grossman, "Meet Joe Blog," *Time,* June 21, 2004, pp. 67–70; "ISP's Band Together to Fight Spam," *Advertising Age,* June 28, 2004, p. 8; and Mohammed et al., *Internet Marketing.*

24. "Pass It On," *The Wall Street Journal,* January 14, 2002, pp. R6, R7; Renée Dye, "The Buzz on Buzz," *Harvard Business Review,*

November–December 2000, pp. 139–46; and "Buzz Marketing," *BusinessWeek,* July 30, 2001, pp. 50–56.

25. "The Price Is Right," *BusinessWeek,* March 31, 2003, pp. 62–68.

26. "Branding on the Net," *BusinessWeek.*

27. "Consumers Worried about Online Privacy"; "Online Privacy and You," www.cyberdialogue.com, downloaded June 10, 2004.

28. Clay Hathorn, "Online Business: Trying to Turn Cookies into Dough," Microsoft Internet Magazine Archive, www.microsoft.com, downloaded February 15, 1999.

29. "Shop Around the Clock," *American Demographics,* September 2003, p. 18; and Nick Wingfield, "The Rise and Fall of Web Shopping at Work," *The Wall Street Journal,* September 27, 2002, pp. B1, B4.

30. "NPD e-Visory Report Shows Offline Sales Benefit from Online Browsing," NPO Group press release, downloaded May 15, 2004.

31. "Eddie Bauer's Banner Time of Year," *Advertising Age,* October 1, 2001, p. 55.

32. For an extended discussion on leveraging multiple channels with multichannel marketing, see Ranjay Gulati and Jason Garino, "Get the Right Mix of Bricks and Clicks," *Harvard Business Review,* May–June 2000, pp. 107–14; and Chao Xiong, "Online Stores Try New Pitch: Fetch It Yourself," *The Wall Street Journal,* November 19, 2003, pp. D1, D4.

33. *Statistical Fact Book 2004* (New York: Direct Marketing Association, 2004).

34. *Multi-Channel Integration: The New Retail Battleground* (Columbus, OH: PricewaterhouseCoopers, March 2001); and Richard Last, "JC Penney Internet Commerce," presentation at Southern Methodist University, February 12, 2001.

35. Michael Krantz, "Click Till You Drop," *Time,* July 20, 1998, pp. 34–39.

36. *Multi-Channel Integration.*

37. *Statistical Fact Book 2004.*

38. *Fighting Fire with Water—from Channel Conflict to Confluence* (Cambridge, MA: Bain & Company, July 1, 2000).

39. *The Next Chapter in Business-to-Consumer E-Commerce: Advantage Incumbent* (Boston: The Boston Consulting Group, March 2001); and Timothy J. Mullaney, "E-Biz Strikes Again," *BusinessWeek,* May 10, 2004, pp. 80–90.

40. "Multichannel Shopping—Projections," www.Forrester.com, downloaded June 2, 2004.

McFarlane Toys: This case was written by Steve Hartley and Roger Kerin. Sources: "McFarlane Toys Launches ToyFest Winter 2003 Online-Only Toy Fair Event Debuting 18 New Lines," *PR Newswire,* February 18, 2003; Bruce Handy, "Small Is Beautiful," *Vanity Fair,* December 2003, p. 208; Wes Orshoski, "McFarlane Adds Hendrix, Elvis to Action-Figure Series," *Billboard,* December 20, 2003, p. 65; Todd McFarlane and Tom Conley, "Toy Fair 2003: Buyers' Market or PR Expense?" *Kidscreen,* February 1, 2003, p. 60; *World Toy Facts and Figures: 2003,* New York: International Council of Toy Industries, 2003.

CHAPTER 22

1. Ann Merrill, "Feeding the Beast," *Star Tribune,* June 2, 2002, pp. D1, D10; and Richard Gibson, "The Cereal Makers Quest for the Next Grape-Nuts," *The Wall Street Journal,* January 23, 1997, pp. B1, B7.

2. David Leonhardt, "Cereal-Box Killers Are on the Loose," *BusinessWeek,* October 12, 1998, pp. 74–77.

3. Ann Merrill, "Pillsbury Acquisition a Done Deal," *Star Tribune,* October 24, 2001, pp. A1, A10.

4. Mike Meyers, "General Mills Expects Fat Future," *Star Tribune,* September 23, 2003, pp. D1, D8.

5. Kate Murphy, "Look! We Can Drive and Snack at the Same Time," *The New York Times,* November 2, 2003, p. BU4.

6. Thomas Lee, "Big G Takes the High Road with Whole Grains," *Star Tribune,* October 10, 2004, pp. D1, D4; Thomas Lee, "More than Just Low Carbs," *Star Tribune,* April 12, 2004, p. D8; and Sonia Reyes, "Category Wars Cereal Battle Takes a Bittersweet Turn," *BrandWeek,* May 24, 2004.

7. *2002 Annual Report* (Minneapolis: General Mills, Inc., 2003), p. 7.

8. *2003 Midyear Report* (Minneapolis: General Mills, Inc., 2004), p. 1.

9. Roger A. Kerin, P. Rajan Varadarajan, and Robert A. Peterson, "First-Mover Advantage: A Synthesis, Conceptual Framework, and Research Proposition," *Journal of Marketing,* October 1992, pp. 33–52; and Pankaj Ghemawat, "Sustainable Advantage," *Harvard Business Review,* September–October 1986, pp. 53–58.

10. Nitin Nohria, William Joyce, and Bruce Roberson, "What Really Works," *Harvard Business Review,* July, 2003, pp. 42–52; and "Who Gets Eaten and Who Gets to Eat," *The Economist,* July 12, 2003, pp. 61–63.

11. Chad Terhune and Betsey McKay, "Behind Coke's Travails: A Long Struggle Over Strategy," *The Wall Street Journal,* May 4, 2004, pp. A1, A6; and Betsy Morris, "The Real Story," *Fortune,* May 31, 2004, pp. 84–98.

12. Faith Arner, "No Excuse Not to Succeed," *BusinessWeek,* May 10, 2004, pp. 96–98.

13. Jack Gordon, "Wall Street Curls Its Lip at Costco's Ungreedy CEO," *Star Tribune,* December 19, 2003, p. A33; and John Helyar, Ann Harrington, and Sol Price, "The Only Company Wal-Mart Fears," *Fortune,* November 24, 2003, pp. 158–63.

14. Kathleen Kerwin and Paul Magnusson, "Can Anything Stop Toyota?" *BusinessWeek,* November 17, 2003, pp. 114–22.

15. Julia Boorstin, "2004 Special Report: The 100 Best Companies to Work For," *Fortune,* January 12, 2004, pp. 56–59.

16. Ben R. Rich and Leo Janos, *Skunk Works* (Boston: Little, Brown and Company, 1994).

17. Murali K. Mantrala, Prabhakant Sirha, and Andris A. Zoltners, "Impact of Resource Allocation Rules on Marketing Investment-Level Decisions and Profitability," *Journal of Marketing Research,* May 1992, pp. 162–75.

18. John Reinan, "Keeping the 'O' Rolling," *Star Tribune,* July 20, 2003, pp. D1, D8.

19. Vanitha Swaminathan, Richard J. Fox, and Srinivas K. Reddy, "The Impact of Brand Extension Introduction on Choice," *Journal of Marketing,* October 2001, pp. 1–15; Deborah Roedder-John, Barbara Loken, and Christopher Joiner, "The Negative Impact of Extensions: Can Flagship Products Be Diluted?" *Journal of Marketing,* January 1998, pp. 19–32; and Akshay R. Rao, Lu Qu, and Robert W. Ruekert, "Signalling Unobservable Product Quality through a Brand Ally," *Journal of Marketing Research,* May 1999, pp. 258–68.

20. *2003 Annual Report* (Minneapolis: General Mills, Inc., 2003), p. 5; *2004 Midyear Report* (Minneapolis: General Mills, Inc., 2004), p. 3.

21. This discussion and Figure 22–3 are adapted from Stanley F. Stasch and Patricis Longtree, "Can Your Marketing Planning Procedures Be Improved?" *Journal of Marketing,* Summer 1980, p. 82; by permission of the American Marketing Association.

22. Adapted with permission of The Free Press, a Division of Macmillan, Inc., from *Competitive Advantage: Creating and Sustaining Superior Performance* by Michael E. Porter. Copyright 1985 by Michael E. Porter.

23. Keith Naughton and Bill Viasie, "The Nostalgia Boom," *BusinessWeek,* March 23, 1998, pp. 58–64; and David Woodruff and Keith Naughton, "Hard Driving Boss," *BusinessWeek,* October 5, 1998, pp. 82–90.

24. Patricia Sellers, "P&G: Teaching an Old Dog New Tricks," *Fortune,* May 31, 2004, pp. 167–80.

25. Zachary Schiller, Greg Burns, and Karen Lowry Miller, "Make It Simple," *BusinessWeek,* September 9, 1996, pp. 96–104.

26. Adopted from Philip Kotler, *Marketing Arrangement* (Upper Saddle River, NJ: Prentice Hall, 2003), p. 299.

27. Stratford Sherman, "How Intel Makes Spending Pay Off," *Fortune,* February 22, 1993, pp. 57–61.

28. Jonathan Eig, "General Mills Intends to Reshape Doughboy in Its Own Image," *The Wall Street Journal,* July 18, 2000, pp. A1, A8; and

Julie Forster, "The Lucky Charm of Steve Sanger," *BusinessWeek,* March 26, 2001, pp. 75–76.

29. "Companies and Innovation: Less Glamour, More Profit," *The Economist,* April 24, 2004, p. 11; and "Don't Laugh at Guilded Butterflies," *The Economist,* April 24, 2004, pp. 71–73.

30. Thomas Lee, "Seeing Green with 'Shrek,' " *Star Tribune,* May 28, 2004, pp. D1, D4.

31. Lee Ginsburg and Neil Miller, "Value-Driven Management," *Business Horizons,* May–June 1992, pp. 23–27; Richard L. Osborn, "Core Value Statement: The Corporate Compass," *Business Horizons,* September–October 1991, pp. 28–34; and Charles E. Watson, "Managing with Integrity: Social Responsibilities of Business as Seen by America's CEOs," *Business Horizons,* July–August 1991, pp. 99–109.

32. Bjorn Lomborg, "Prioritizing the World's To-Do List," *Fortune,* May 17, 2004, p. 60; and Alfred Marcus, Donald A. Geffen, and Ken Sexton, "Business-Government Cooperation in Environmental Decision Making," *International Journal of Corporate Sustainability* 9, no. 4 (2002), pp. 345–55.

33. Charles H. Noble and Michael P. Mokwa, "Implementing Marketing Strategies: Developing and Testing a Managerial Theory," *Journal of Marketing,* October 1999, pp. 57–74.

34. Jeffrey A. Krames, *The Jack Welch Lexicon of Leadership* (New York: McGraw-Hill, 2002), pp. 54–56, 105–8, 187–88; Robert Slater, *Jack Welch and the GE Way* (New York: McGraw-Hill, 1999), pp. 59–68, 77–88, 279–86: Nicholas Stein, "The World's Most Admired Companies," *Fortune,* October 2, 2000, pp. 183–91; and Jim Rohwer, "GE Digs into Asia," *Fortune,* October 2, 2000, pp. 165–78.

35. Daniel Roth, "This Ain't No Pizza Party," *Fortune,* November 9, 1998, pp. 158–64.

36. Thomas J. Peters and Robert H. Waterman, Jr., *In Search of Excellence: Lessons from America's Best-Run Companies* (New York: Harper & Row, 1982).

37. Tom Peters, "Winners Do Hundreds of Percent over Norm," *Minneapolis Star Tribune,* January 8, 1985, p. 5B; and Ben Rich and Leo Janos, *Skunk Works,* pp. 51–53.

38. Peter Galuska, Ellen Neuborne, and Wendy Zeliner, "P&G's Hottest New Product: P&G," *BusinessWeek,* October 5, 1998, pp. 92–96.

39. Robert W. Ruekert and Orville W. Walker, Jr., "Marketing's Interaction with Other Functional Units: A Conceptual Framework and Empirical Evidence," *Journal of Consumer Marketing,* Spring 1987, pp. 1–19. Shikhar Sarin and Vijay Mahajan, "The Effect of Reward Structures on the Performance of Cross-Functional Product Development Teams," *Journal of Marketing,* April 2001, pp. 35–53; and Amy Edmondson, Richard Bohmer, and Gary Pisano, "Speeding Up Team Learning," *Harvard Business Review,* October 2001, pp. 125–32.

40. Nelson D. Schwartz, "Colgate Cleans Up," *Fortune,* April 16, 2001, pp. 179–80.

41. Leslie M. Moeller, Sharat K. Mathur, and Randall Rothenberg, "The Better Half: The Artful Science of ROI Marketing," *Strategy + Business* (Chicago: Booz Allen Hamilton, 2003).

42. James D. Lenskold, "Customer-Centric Marketing ROI," *Marketing Management,* February, 2004, pp. 26–31.

Yoplait USA: This case was prepared by William Rudelius and Steven W. Hartley based on personal interviews with Steven M. Rothschild and Chap Colucci and these other sources: *2004 Annual Report* (Minneapolis, MN, General Mills, Inc., 2004), p. o, p. 6; and the company website (www.generalmills.com).

APPENDIX C

1. Denny E. McCorkle, Joe F. Alexander, and Memo F. Diriker, "Developing Self-Marketing Skills for Student Career Success," *Journal of Marketing Education,* Spring 1992, pp. 57–67.

2. Joanne Cleaver, "Find a Job through Self-Promotion," *Marketing News,* January 31, 2000, pp. 12, 16; and James McBride, "Job-Search Strategies to Begin the Next Millenium," *Planning Job Choices: 1999,* 42nd ed. (Bethlehem, PA: National Association of Colleges and Employers, 1998), pp. 14–18.

3. Julie Rawe, "What Will Be the 10 Hottest Jobs?" *Time,* May 22, 2000, pp. 70–71; and "Five 'New Economy' Careers for Liberal Arts Majors," *Job Choices in Business: 2002,* 45th ed. (Bethlehem, PA: National Association of Colleges and Employers, 2001), pp. 11–13.

4. *Job Choices for Business and Liberal Arts Students,* 47th ed. (Bethlehem, PA: National Association of Colleges and Employers, 2004), p. 114.

5. Nicholas Basta, "The Wide World of Marketing," *BusinessWeek's Guide to Careers,* February–March 1984, pp. 70–72.

6. Paula Lyon Andruss, "So You Want to Be a CEO?" *Marketing News,* January 29, 2001, pp. 1, 10.

7. "Average Yearly Salary Offers," *Salary Survey* (Bethlehem, PA: National Association of Colleges and Employers, 2003), p. 4.

8. Elaine L. Chao and Kathleen P. Utgoff, "Tomorrow's Jobs," *Occupational Outlook Handbook* (Indianapolis: JIST Works, 2004), p. 5.

9. Linda M. Gorchels, "Traditional Product Management Evolves," *Marketing News,* January 30, 1995, p. 4; "Focus on Five Stages of Category Management," *Marketing News,* September 28, 1992, pp. 17, 19; and Sandy Gillis, "On the Job: Product Manager," *BusinessWeek's Guide to Careers,* April–May 1988, pp. 63–66.

10. Phil Moss, "What It's Like to Work for Procter & Gamble," *BusinessWeek's Guide to Careers,* March–April 1987, pp. 18–20.

11. David Kirkpatrick, "Is Your Career on Track?" *Fortune,* July 2, 1990, pp. 38–48.

12. Robin T. Peterson, "Wholesaling: A Neglected Job Opportunity for Marketing Majors," *Marketing News,* January 15, 1996, p. 4.

13. "Advertising," *Career Guide to America's Top Industries* (Indianapolis, IN: JIST Works, 1994), pp. 142–45.

14. "The Climb to the Top," *Careers in Retailing,* January 1995, p. 18.

15. "Playing the Retail Career Game," *Careers in Retailing 2001* (New York: DSN Retailing Today, January 2001), pp. 4, 6.

16. Christine Galea, "The 2004 Compensation Survey," *Sales & Marketing Management,* May 2004, p. 29.

17. Milan Moravec, Marshall Collins, and Clinton Tripoli, "Don't Want to Manage? Here's Another Path," *Sales & Marketing Management,* June 1990, pp. 62–75.

18. Robin T. Peterson, "Startup Careers through Rep Firms," *Marketing News,* August 4, 1997, p. 8.

19. William Keenan, Jr., "America's Best Sales Forces: Six at the Summit," *Sales & Marketing Management,* June 1990, pp. 62–72.

20. Daniel Tynan, "CRM on the Cheap," *Sales & Marketing Management,* June 2004, pp. 37–40; Kathleen Cholewka, "Do No Disturb: A New Way to E-Mail?" *Sales & Marketing Management,* November 2001, pp. 21–22; and "Best E-Business Strategy," *Sales & Marketing Management,* September 2001, p. 28.

21. Michael R. Wukitsch, "Should Research Know More about Marketing?" *Marketing Research,* Winter 1993, p. 50.

22. "Market Research Analyst," in Les Krantz, ed., *Jobs Rated Almanac,* 3rd ed. (New York: Wiley, 1995).

23. Joshua Grossnickle and Oliver Raskin, "What's Ahead on the Internet," *Marketing Research,* Summer 2001, pp. 9–13.

24. Carolyn D. Marconi, "Desperately Looking for New Talent Is a Recurring Theme," *Marketing Research,* Spring 2000, pp. 4–6.

25. Susan B. Larsen, "International Careers: Reality, Not Fantasy," *CPC Annual: A Guide to Employment Opportunities for College Graduates,* 36th ed. (Bethlehem, PA: College Placement Council, 1992), pp. 78–85; and Hal Lancaster, "Global Managers Need Boundless Sensitivity, Rugged Constitutions," *The Wall Street Journal,* October 13, 1998, p. B1.

26. John W. Buckner, "Working Abroad at Home," *Managing Your Career,* Spring 1992, pp. 16–17.

27. Lisa Bertagnoli, "Marketing Overseas Excellent for Career," *Marketing News,* June 4, 2001, p. 4.

28. "Your Job Search Starts with You," *Job Choices: 1996,* 39th ed. (Bethlehem, PA: National Association of Colleges and Employers, 1995), pp. 6–9; Hugh E. Kramer, "Applying Marketing Strategy and Personal Value Analysis to Career Planning: An Experiential Approach," *Journal of Marketing Education,* Fall 1988, pp. 69–73; Alan Deutschman, "What 25-Year-Olds Want," *Fortune,* August 27, 1990, pp. 42–50; and Dawn Richerson, "Personality and Your Career," *Career Woman,* Winter 1993, pp. 46–47.

29. Arthur F. Miller, "Discover Your Design," in *CPC Annual,* vol. 1 (Bethlehem, PA: College Placement Council, 1984), p. 2.

30. Robin T. Peterson and J. Stuart Devlin, "Perspectives on Entry-Level Positions by Graduating Marketing Seniors," *Marketing Education Review,* Summer 1994, pp. 2–5.

31. Callum J. Floyd and Mary Ellen Gordon, "What Skills Are Most Important? A Comparison of Employer, Student, and Staff Perceptions," *Journal of Marketing Education,* August 1998, pp. 103–9; "What Employers Want," *Job Outlook '98* (Bethlehem, PA: National Association of Colleges and Employers); and Andrew Marlatt, "Demand for Diverse Skills Is on Upswing," *Internet World,* January 4, 1999.

32. Diane Goldner, "Fill In the Blank," *The Wall Street Journal,* February 27, 1995, pp. R5, R11.

33. Barbara Kiviat, "The New Rules of Web Hiring," *Time,* November 24, 2003, p. 57; Karen Epper Hoffman, "Recruitment Sites Changing Their Focus," *Internet World,* March 15, 1999; Pamela Mendels, "Now That's Casting a Wide Net," *Business Week,* May 25, 1998: and James C. Gonyea, *The Online Job Search Companion* (New York: McGraw-Hill, 1995).

34. Peter Cappelli, "Making the Most of On-Line Recruiting," *Harvard Business Review,* March 2001, pp. 139–46.

35. Ronald B. Marks, *Personal Selling* (Boston: Allyn & Bacon, 1985), pp. 451–62.

36. Constance J. Pritchard, "Small Employers—How, When and Who They Hire," *Job Choices: 1996,* 39th ed. (Bethlehem, PA: National Association of Colleges and Employers, 1995), pp. 66–69.

37. Leonard Felson, "Undergrad Marketers Must Get Jump on Networking Skills," *Marketing News,* April 8, 2001, p. 14; and Wayne E. Baker, *Networking Smart* (New York: McGraw-Hill, 1994).

38. John L. Munschauer, "How to Find a Customer for Your Capabilities," in 1984–1985 *CPC Annual,* vol. 1 (Bethlehem, PA: College Placement Council, 1984), p. 24.

39. C. Randall Powell, "Secrets of Selling a Résumé," in Peggy Schmidt, ed., *The Honda How to Get a Job Guide* (New York: McGraw-Hill, 1984), pp. 4–9.

40. Ibid., p. 4.

41. Adapted from Powell, "Secrets of Selling a Résumé," pp. 4–9.

42. Joyce Lain Kennedy, "Computer-Friendly Résumé Tips," *Planning Job Choices: 1999,* 42nd ed. (Bethlehem, PA: National Association of Colleges and Employers, 1998), p. 49; and Joyce Lain Kennedy and Thomas J. Morrow, *Electronic Résumé Revolution* (New York: Wiley, 1994).

43. Arthur G. Sharp, "The Art of the Cover Letter," *Career Futures* 4, no. 1 (1992), pp. 50–51.

44. Perri Capell, "Unconventional Job Search Tactics," *Managing Your Career,* Spring 1991, pp. 31, 35.

45. Julie Griffin Levitt, *Your Career: How to Make It Happen* (Cincinnati: South-Western Publishing, 1985).

46. Deborah Vendy, "Drug Screening and Your Career," *CPC Annual* (Bethlehem, PA: College Placement Council, 1992), pp. 61–62.

47. Dana James, "A Day in the Life of a Corporate Recruiter," *Marketing News,* April 10, 2000, pp. 1, 11.

48. Marks, *Personal Selling,* p. 469.

49. Terence P. Pare, "The Uncommitted Class of 1989," *Fortune,* June 5, 1989, pp. 199–210.

50. Robert M. Greenberg, "The Company Visit—Revisited," *NACE Journal,* Winter 2003, pp. 21–27.

51. Bob Weinstein, "What Employers Look For," in Peggy Schmidt, ed., *The Honda How to Get a Job Guide* (New York: McGraw-Hill, 1985), p. 10.

52. Mary E. Scott, "High-Touch vs. High-Tech Recruitment," *NACE Journal,* Fall 2002, pp. 33–39.

APPENDIX D

1. The Burton Snowboards case was prepared by Professor Linda Rochford, University of Minnesota, Duluth, from the following sources: Allen Best, "Growth in Snowboarding Slowing," *Summit Daily News,* April 24, 2004, pp. B7, B8; www.burton.com; Jannell Chester, "Burton Snowboards," www.hoovers.com, downloaded July 5, 2004; Thomas B. Doyle, "Numbers: What Good Are They?" National Ski and Snowboard Retailers Association, www.nssra.com, downloaded July 10, 2004; Thomas B. Doyle, *National Sporting Goods Association Research News,* March 29, 2004; and Cindy Kleh, "Snowboardings Humble Beginnings," *Summit Daily News,* February 23, 2004, p. B2.

2. The Daktronics, Inc., case was prepared by William Rudelius based on conversations with Dr. Al Kurtenbach, internal sources, and these others sources: Bill Syken, "Bright Lights, Little City," *Sports Illustrated,* May 11, 2004; Dick Youngblood, "Signs of Success," *Star Tribune,* April 6, 2003, pp. D1, D2; Marilyn Alva, "Shifting Technology Helps It Score Big Wins," *Investor's Business Daily,* January 12, 2004; Michael Hiestand, "S.D. Company Lights Up Sports World," *USA Today,* May 4, 2004, pp. C1, C2; Cora Daniels, "Bright Lights, Big Future," *Fortune Small Business 100,* July–August, 2001, pp. 60–61.

3. The Jamba Juice case was prepared by Professor Linda Rochford, University of Minnesota, Duluth, and Steven Hartley from the following sources: Jamba Juice Corporation website and press releases: www.jambajuice.com; "Juicy Prospects," *Minneapolis Star Tribune,* August 27, 2001, pp. D1–D2; Louis Trager, "Get Ready for Juice Bars, at a Corner Nearby Soon," *San Francisco Examiner,* 1995; Scott Hume, "Segment Rankings," *Restaurants and Institutions,* July 1, 2004, p. 61; Celeste Ward, "Riney Creates Good Karma for Jamba Juice," *Adweek.com,* March 18, 2004; John Agoglia, "Squeezing Profits," *Club Industry,* December 1, 2003, p. 12.

4. The Ford and Firestone case was prepared by Professor Linda Rochford, University of Minnesota, Duluth, from the following sources: David Barboza, "Bridgestone/Firestone to Close Tire Plant at Center of Huge Recall," *The New York Times,* June 28, 2001, p. C1; Keith Bradsher, "Ford Intends to Replace 13 Million Firestone Wilderness Tires," *The New York Times,* May 23, 2001, p. C1; Keith Bradsher, "Ford Wants to Send Drivers of Sport Utility Vehicles Back to School," *The New York Times,* July 4, 2001, p. A9; John Greenwald, "Tired of Each Other," *Time,* June 4, 2001, pp. 51–56; and Phil Meyerowitz, "SUV Chic: The Rugged and the Reckless," *The New York Times,* July 7, 2001, p. 12.

5. The Jamisons case was prepared by Professor Roy D. Adler, Pepperdine University, Malibu. Used with permission.

6. The Motetronix Technology case was prepared by Roger A. Kerin, based on company sources.

7. The Callaway Golf case was prepared by Professor Linda Rochford, University of Minnesota, Duluth, from the following sources: "Callaway: Average Golfer Has a Right to Make a Choice," *Golfweek,* August 28, 2001, pp. 20–21; James Achenbach, "From Hickory to Callaway, Ely Sought to Please Golfers," *Golfweek,* July 14, pp. 26–27; "China the Largest Growth Market for Equipment," *Today,* March, 2004, pp. 15–18; "Opportunities in Global Golf Market: Market to Grow over 25% in India and China According E-Composites, Inc.," *PR Newswire,* February 18, 2004; "2003 sumer Equipment Purchases by Sport" and "Golf Equipment chases by Age and Gender," National Sporting Goods Associ

www.nsga.org, downloaded June 5, 2004; Jannell Chester, "Callaway Golf Company," www.hoovers.com, downloaded July 20, 2004; Jennifer Davies, "California's Callaway Golf Belatedly Responds to Changes in Market," *San Diego Union Tribune,* July 13, 2004, p. B2; Martin Kaufmann, "Callaway Scrambles after Plans Go Awry," *Golfweek,* June 26, 2004, pp. 42–43; Rob Sauerhaft, "Club '04 Test," *Golf Magazine,* May 2004, pp. 119–92; Dave Seanor, "Major Challenge," *Golfweek,* May 22, 2004, pp. 36–37; and Gene Yasuda, "Unique Challenges Define Equipment Arena," *Golfweek,* May 8, 2004, p. 30.

8. The HOM Furniture case was prepared by Kathy Chadwick based on interviews with Wayne Johansen and internal HOM Furniture materials.

9. The Hummer case was prepared by Professor Linda Rochford, University of Minnesota, Duluth, from the following sources: www.amgeneralcorp.com, downloaded July 3, 2004; "Consumer Guide, New Car Pricing and Reviews: 2005 Hummer H2," www.auto.consumerguide.com, downloaded July 3, 2004; Jennifer Davies, "Hybrid-Car Popularity Shifts into Overdrive," *San Diego Union-Tribune,* May 12, 2004, p. 12; Bob Golfen, "State SUV Sales Up, Bucking U.S. Trend," *Arizona Republic,* July 12, 2004, p. B4; Daniel Gross, "Hummer vs. Prius: The Surprising Winner in the War for America's Auto Soul," www.slate.msn.com, downloaded February 26, 2004; Mark Sauer, "Hum Dinger; Owners' Boxy Behemoths, Reviled and Revered, Are Part of Exclusive Club," *San Diego Union-Tribune,* June 8, 2003, p. E1; Paul Wilborn, "Hummer Drivers Undeterred by Gas Concerns," *Hummer Team News Release,* January 17, 2003; and David Welch, "A Bummer for the Hummer," *BusinessWeek,* February 24, 2004, pp. 36–38.

10. The Medtronic in China case was prepared by Mark T. Spriggs and Kenneth E. Goodpaster based on Medtronic annual reports and three Medtronic cases: *Medtronic in China (A), (B),* and *(C)* prepared by research assistant Linda Swenson under the supervision of Kenneth E. Goodpaster (Minneapolis–St. Paul, MN: University of St. Thomas, 1999).

11. The Pampered Pooches case was prepared by Professor Linda Rochford, University of Minnesota, Duluth, from the following sources: Robyn Gardyn, "Animal Magnetism," *American Demographics,* May 1, 2002; "Cool Canines Beg for Frosty Paws; Frozen Treats for Dogs Have Tails Wagging," *PR Newswire,* downloaded October 15, 2003; Sandra Eckstein, "Buyer's Edge: Toting Toto; Caviar for Furry Friends?" *Atlanta Journal-Constitution,* June 5, 2003, pp. F2ff; Lisa Mclaughlin, "Where Guests with Four Legs Are Pampered," *Time,* February 10, 2003, p. 83; "New Survey Shows America's Love Affair with Pets Stronger than Ever," www.businesswire.com, downloaded September 3, 2003; "Omaha Steaks Launches New Steak Treats for Pets; Highbrow Chow for Pampered Pets," *PR Newswire,* downloaded September 4, 2003; Joel Stein, Jeanne DeQuine, Jeanne McDowell, and Deidre van Dyk, "It's a Dog's Life," *Time,* May 19, 2003, pp. 60–63; Kristen Vinakmens, "Every Dog Has Its Day," Brunico Communications, Inc., December 1, 2003; and Lauren Young, "A Suite for Fido," *BusinessWeek,* April 19, 2004, p. 129.

12. The DigitalThink case was adapted by Monica Noordam and Steven Hartley from a case titled "LearningByte International" written by Giana Eckardt. Sources: Personal interviews with Umberto Milletti and Shelly Berkowitz; DigitalThink's website, www.digitalthink.com; Lisa Vaas, "The E-Training of America," *PC Magazine,* December 26, 2001; DigitalThink press release, "Digital-Think Ranked Number 22 Fastest Growing Technology Company in North America on 2003 Deloitte Technology Fast 500," October 14, 2003; and "Making E-Learning More than 'Pixie Dust,'" *Workforce Management,* March 1, 2003, p. 58.

13. The Health Cruises, Inc., case was prepared by Professors Maurice Mandell and Larry Rosenberg. Reprinted with permission.

14. The Little Remedies, Vetco, Inc., case was prepared by Kirk Hodgdon based on personal interviews with Matt Kornberg and internal company materials.

15. The Fastenal Company case was prepared by Professor Robert Hansen, University of Minnesota, based on company interviews. Used with permission.

16. The Dell case was prepared by Professor Linda Rochford, University of Minnesota, Duluth, from the following sources: "Dell: Build to Order Manufacturing," www.accenture.com, downloaded July 7, 2004; Dell 2004 Annual Report; Lisa Di Carlo, "The TV in the Dell," www.forbes.com, downloaded September 9, 2003; "Factory Floor: Dell Takes Supply Side to Web," www.intech.com, downloaded September 1, 2002; Katie Haegele, "Selling B-to-B Online," www.catalogsuccess.com, downloaded June 1, 2004; and "Dell," www.hoovers.com, downloaded July 1, 2004.

17. The Nordstrom case was prepared by Professor Linda Rochford, University of Minnesota, Duluth, from the following sources: Brian Silverman, "Shopping for Loyal Customers," *Sales & Marketing Management,* March 1995, pp. 96–97; Robert Spector and Patrick D. McCarthy, *The Nordstrom Way: The Inside Story of America's #1 Customer Service Company* (New York: John Wiley and Sons, 1996); www.nordstrom.com, downloaded July 15, 2004; and "Nordstrom," www.hoovers.com, downloaded July 10, 2004.

18. The McDonald's in Russia case was prepared by Sarah Casanova of McDonald's Canada and Michael J. Vessey based on internal McDonald's reports and information from the McDonald's website, www.mcdonalds.com.

19. The Volkswagen case was prepared by Professor Linda Rochford, University of Minnesota, Duluth, from the following sources: "AdForum Creative Hits 2003, 2002," www.adforum.com, downloaded July 20, 2004; "Volkswagen of America," www.hoovers.com, downloaded July 10, 2004; Fran Kelly, "The Incredible Value of Great Campaigns: How Are They Created and How Should They Be Measured?" presentation to the New York American Marketing Association Knowledge+Networking Series event, April 2003; Joe Mandese, "Ad Industry Leaders Explore New Economic Models, Methods of Compensation," *Media Post's Media Daily News,* September 22, 2003, pp. 6–8; Christine Tierney, "Sagging Sales Spur Rare US Incentives," www.detnews.com, downloaded April 19, 2004; "More than Ever, Driving Is Focus of a New Volkswagen Campaign— 'Drive It. You'll Get It,'" www.vw.com, downloaded March 26, 2004; and Rob Walker, "Freed by the Beetle," www.slate.msn.com, downloaded January 6, 2003.

20. The Manor Furniture case was prepared by Roger A. Kerin, based on company sources.

21. The Crate and Barrel case was prepared by Professor Linda Rochford, University of Minnesota, Duluth from the following sources: www.crateandbarrel.com; "Euromarket Designs Inc.," www.hoovers.com, downloaded July 25, 2004; "Home Furnishings Catalogs Freshen Up for Springtime," *Home Furnishings News,* March 22, 2004, p. 20; and "Crate and Barrel Selects Unica Corporation's Affinium to Increase Effectiveness of Its Multichannel Marketing Campaigns," *Business Wire, Inc.,* April 28, 2004.

22. The BP Connect case was prepared by Michael J. Vessey and William Rudelius from the following sources: William Echikson, "When Oil Gets Connected," *BusinessWeek e.biz,* December 3, 2001, pp. EB28–EB30; Martha Hamilton, "Giving Drivers Their Fill: Service Stations Modernized as BP Consolidates Merged Oil Firms," July 25, 2000, downloaded from *The Washington Post;* and Alexei Barrionuevo and Ann Zimmerman, "Latest Supermarket Special— Gasoline," *The Wall Street Journal,* April 30, 2001, pp. B1, B4.

CREDITS

CHAPTER 1

p. 4, Courtesy Rollerblade, Inc.; p. 7 (left), Courtesy Rollerblade, Inc.; p. 7 (right), Courtesy Rollerblade, Inc.; p. 11 (top left), Courtesy of New Product Works; p. 11 (top right), Courtesy Nestlé USA (Solon); p. 11 (bottom left), Photo by Scott Olson/Getty Images; p. 11 (bottom right) ©2003 New Product Works; p. 13 (left), Graphics used by permission of the Minnesota Department of Public Safety Office of Traffic Safety, Office of Communications and the Safe Communities of Wright County, MN; p. 13 (right), Graphics used by permission of the Minnesota Department of Public Safety Office of Traffic Safety, Office of Communications and the Safe Communities of Wright County, MN; p. 15 (left), Courtesy Costco; p. 15 (right), Courtesy Starbucks Coffee Company, ©2004; p. 19 (left), Courtesy Rollerblade, Inc.; p. 19 (right), Courtesy Rollerblade, Inc.; p. 22 (top left), Courtesy Arizona Highways; p. 22 (top right), Courtesy American Library Association; p. 27, Courtesy Rollerblade, Inc.

CHAPTER 2

p. 28, Courtesy Ben & Jerry's; p. 30, AP Photo/Dawn Villella; p. 32, Courtesy Medtronic; p. 35, Courtesy Rick Armstrong; p. 36, These materials have been reproduced with the permission of eBay Inc. COPYRIGHT ©EBAY INC. ALL RIGHTS RESERVED. p. 37 (all), Courtesy Eastman Kodak Company; Agency: Ketchum Communications; p. 38 (all), Courtesy Eastman Kodak Company; Agency: Ketchum Communications; p. 41 (left), Courtesy Ben & Jerry's; p. 41 (top right), Courtesy Ben & Jerry's. Photo ©M. Hruby; p. 41 (bottom right), Courtesy Ben & Jerry's. Photo ©M. Hruby; p. 45, Courtesy Medtronic; p. 48, Courtesy Eastman Kodak Company; Agency: Ketchum Communications; p. 52, Courtesy Specialized Bicycles.

APPENDIX A

pp. 57, 61, 63, 65, 66, ©1996 Paradise Kitchens, Inc. All photos and ads reprinted with permission.

CHAPTER 3

p. 70, Courtesy Apple Computer; p. 75 (left), ©The Procter & Gamble Company. Used by permission; p. 75 (middle), The Donna Karan Company, 2001; p. 75 (right) ©Motorola, Inc. 2003; p. 79, Courtesy Saturn Corporation; p. 83, Select graphic images reprinted courtesy of ESRI Business Information Solutions; Copyright ©ESRI Business Information Solutions. All rights reserved; p. 82, Courtesy Cunard Line Limited/Carnival Corporation; p. 84 (left), TravelDrive™ ad provided courtesy of Memorex

Products, Inc. ©2004 All rights reserved; p. 84 (middle), Napster ad is copyright 2004, Napster, LLC and reprinted with Napster's permission; p. 84 (right), Courtesy LG Electronics U.S.A., Inc.; p. 85 (left), Courtesy Tomra of North America; p. 85 (right), Courtesy of Lever Brothers Company; p. 86, Courtesy T-Mobile; Agency: Publicis Agency/Seattle; p. 89, ©M. Hruby; p. 91, Courtesy of Better Business Bureau, Inc.; p. 94 (top), Courtesy Flyte Time; p. 94 (bottom), Courtesy Flyte Time.

Figure 3.4, from American Demographics, 2002. Reprinted with the permission of PRIMEDIA Business Magazines & Media, Inc. Copyright © 2002. All rights reserved; Figure 3.5, reprinted by permission of the Survey Research Center.

CHAPTER 4

p. 96, Courtesy Anheuser-Busch Companies, Inc.; p. 102, ©2001 Michelle Delsol; p. 103, Courtesy Transparency International; p. 108, Courtesy Susan G. Komen Breast Cancer Foundation; p. 109, Photodisc Blue; p. 110, Courtesy McDonald's Corporation; p. 111, Paula Bronstein/Getty Liaison Agency; p. 114, Michael Newman/Photo Edit.

Figure 4.3, reprinted by permission of the American Marketing Association.

CHAPTER 5

p. 118, Courtesy Volvo of North America; p. 122, Monica Lau/Getty Images; p. 123, Courtesy Kimberly-Clark Worldwide, Inc.; p. 125, ©2004 Tropicana Products, Inc.; p. 128, The Secret Sales Pitch: An Overview of Subliminal Advertising. Copyright ©2004 by August Bullock. All Rights Reserved. Used with permission. SubliminalSex.com; p. 129 (left), FRESH STEPS® is a registered trademark of The Clorox Pet Products Company. Used with permission; p. 129 (right), ©2001 Mary Kay, Inc. Photos by: Grace Huang/for Sarah Laird; p. 131 (left), Courtesy Colgate-Palmolive Company; p. 131 (right), The Bayer Company; p. 132, Courtesy SRI Consulting Business Intelligence (SRIC-BI), Menlo Park, CA. VALS™ is a trademark of SRI Consulting Business Intelligence. Reprinted with permission; p. 133, Courtesy SRI Consulting Business Intelligence (SRIC-BI), Menlo Park, CA. VALS™ is a trademark of SRI Consulting Business Intelligence. Reprinted with permission; p. 134 (left), Courtesy Omega S.A.; p. 134 (right), Courtesy Omega S.A.; p. 135, Courtesy BzzAgent, LLC.; p. 138, Courtesy of Haggar Clothing Co. ©1997 Haggar Clothing Co.; p. 139, Courtesy Bonne Bell, Inc.; p. 141,

Courtesy Target Corporation; p. 144 (top), Courtesy of Ken Davis Products, Inc.; p. 144 (bottom), Courtesy of Ken Davis Products, Inc.; p. 145, Courtesy of Ken Davis Products, Inc.

Figure 5.2, "MP3Compatible Portable CD Players" © 2002 by Consumers Union of U.S., Inc. Yonkers, NY 10703-1057, a nonprofit organization. Reprinted with permission from the September 2002 issue of Consumer Reports® for educational purposes only. No commercial use or reproduction permitted. www.ConsumerReports.org®; VALS™, SRI Consulting Business Intelligence (SRIC-BI), Menlo Park, CA. VALS™ is a trademark of SRI Consulting Business Intelligence. Reprinted with permission.

CHAPTER 6

p. 146, Courtesy JCPenney; p. 149, Courtesy Citidex Long Island On-Line; p. 150, Courtesy U.S. Department of Commerce/Bureau of the Census; p. 153, Courtesy Airbus; p. 154, Lluis Gene/AFP/Getty Images; p. 156, Dan Bosler/Tony Stone; p. 160, Courtesy Allen-Bradley Company, Inc.; p. 162, These materials have been reproduced with the permission of eBay Inc. COPYRIGHT ©EBAY INC. ALL RIGHTS RESERVED; p. 167, ©2004 Lands' End, Inc. Used with permission.

CHAPTER 7

p. 168, ©M. Hruby; p. 173 (left), Courtesy Sharp Electronics Corporation; p. 173 (right), Courtesy of Bruno Magli; p. 176, Frans Lemmens/Getty Images; p. 178, Courtesy ALMAP/BBDO Sao Paulo; p. 179, Courtesy Bartle Bogle Hegarty/Singapore; p. 180, Courtesy Nestlé S.A.; p. 182 (left), The Image Bank; p. 182 (right), PhotoDisc; p. 183 (left), Courtesy Hewlett-Packard/Canada; Publicis Hal Riney; p. 183 (right), Courtesy Hewlett-Packard/Canada; Publicis Hal Riney; p. 183 (right), ©1993 Mary Beth Camp/Matrix International, Inc.; p. 186, Courtesy The Coca-Cola Company; p. 188, Courtesy The PRS Group, Inc. East Syracuse, NY; p. 190, Courtesy Fran Wilson Creative Cosmetics, Inc.; p. 192, Courtesy Elite Industries, Ltd.; p. 191 (left), Courtesy McDonald's Corporation; p. 191 (right), Courtesy McDonald's Corporation; p. 194 (left), Courtesy The Gillette Company; p. 194 (middle), Courtesy The Gillette Company; p. 194 (right), Courtesy The Gillette Company; p. 198, Courtesy CNS, Inc.

Figure 7.5, reprinted with the permission of PRIMEDIA Business Magazines & Media, Inc. Copyright © 2002. All rights reserved.

CHAPTER 8

p. 202, Shooting Star; p. 204, Shooting Star; p. 206, Fisher-Price, Inc. a subsidiary of Mattel, Inc. East Aurora, NY 14052 U.S.A. ©2006 Mattel, Inc. All Rights Reserved; p. 207, Fisher-Price, Inc. a subsidiary of Mattel, Inc. East Aurora, NY 14052 U.S.A. ©2006 Mattel, Inc. All Rights Reserved; p. 208, ©M. Hruby; p. 213, Courtesy Nielsen Media Research; p. 214 (left), Courtesy The Gillette Company; p. 214 (middle), Courtesy 3M; p. 214 (right), Courtesy Skechers U.S.A.; p. 216, Courtesy Teen Research Unlimited; Photo by: M. Hruby; p. 220, Courtesy Wendy's International, Inc.; p. 222, Courtesy Fingerhut Direct Marketing, Inc.; p. 223, Courtesy The Schwan Food Company.

Figure 8.4, source: Nielsen Media Research. Reprinted by permission; Figure 8.5, source: Nielsen Media Research. Reprinted by permission; Figure 8.8, used by permission of Ford Consulting Group; Figure 8.10, used by permission of Tony's Pizza.

CHAPTER 9

p. 230, Photo by Reebok via Getty Images; p. 231, p. 231, ©Brent Jones; p. 232, Photos provided by Heeling Sports, Limited Dallas, TX. ©2004; p. 236 (top), ©M. Hruby; p. 236 (bottom) all courtesy Street & Smith Magazines; p. 239, Microfridge® Courtesy Mac-Gray; p. 243, Courtesy Xerox Corporation; p. 246, Courtesy Wendy's International, Inc.; p. 247 (all), Courtesy Apple Computer; p. 248, Courtesy Apple Computer; p. 249 (all), Courtesy Apple Computer; p. 250, ©M. Hruby; p. 251 (left), ©M. Hruby; p. 251 (right), ©M. Hruby; p. 252, Courtesy Wilson Sporting Goods Co.; p. 256, Courtesy Nokia.

Figure 9.5, National Consumer Survey/NHCS Spring 2004 Adult Full Year Choices System Crosstabulation Report based on visits within the past 30 days (New York: Simmons Market Research Bureau, Inc., Spring 2004). Reprinted with permission; Figure 9.6, National Consumer Survey/NHCS Spring 2004 Adult Full Year Choices System Crosstabulation Report based on visits within the past 30 days (New York: Simmons Market Research Bureau, Inc., Spring 2004). Reprinted with permission.

CHAPTER 10

p. 260, Courtesy 3M; p. 263, Courtesy Vetco Inc., Consumer Healthcare; p. 264, Courtesy Raymond Weil; p. 266 (left), ©Laura Johansen; p. 266 (right), Courtesy Microsoft Corporation; Agency: Edelman Worldwide/Seattle; p. 267, Courtesy of Samsung Telecommunications America; p. 270 (left), New Product Showcase and Learning Center, Inc.; Photograph: Robert Haller; p. 270 (right), Courtesy of the Original Pet Drink; p. 271, Courtesy Canon U.S.A.; Agency: DCA Advertising, Inc.; p. 271, Courtesy Palm, Inc.; p. 271, Courtesy Intuit, Inc.; p. 271, Courtesy Swatch USA.; p. 272 (top), Courtesy New ProductWorks;

p. 272 (bottom), Courtesy NewProductWorks; p. 274 (left and right), Courtesy Volvo of North America; 276 (all top), Courtesy 3M; p. 276 (bottom), ©M. Hruby; p. 278, Jose Azel/Aurora; p. 281 (top), ©M. Hruby; p. 281 (bottom), Courtesy of Hewlett-Packard Company; p. 283, Courtesy NewProductWorks; p. 284, Courtesy 3M; p. 285, Courtesy 3M.

Figure 10.5, reprinted with permission from the July 29, 2001 issue of Advertising Age. Copyright 2001 Crain Communications Inc.

CHAPTER 11

p. 286, Courtesy Element 79 Partners; p. 288, ©M. Hruby; p. 291 (left), Courtesy Ford Motor Company; p. 291 (right), Courtesy Canon USA Corporation; p. 296, ©Ron Kimball; p. 297, Courtesy of the National Fluid Milk Processor Promotion Board; Agency: Bozell/Chicago; p. 300 (left), Courtesy Advanced Research Labs; p. 300 (right), Courtesy Liz Claiborne; Agency: Avrett Free & Ginsberg; Models: Roberto Sanchez & Nadja Scantamburlo; Photographer: J. Westley Jones; p. 302, Courtesy Roper Footwear & Apparel; p. 305 (left), Courtesy of Black & Decker (U.S.), Inc.; p. 305 (right), Courtesy of DeWalt Industrial Tool Company; p. 306, Courtesy of Pez Candy, Inc.; p. 307, Photo by: Arthur Meyerson. "Coca-Cola, the Contour Bottle design and the Coca-Cola Fridge Pack are trademarks of The Coca-Cola Company. Copyright 1994. All rights reserved; p. 308 (top), ©M. Hruby; p. 308 (bottom), ©2001 Susan G. Holtz; p. 312, BMW of North America, LLC.

CHAPTER 12

p. 314, ®,™ & ©Paramount Pictures Corp. STAR TREK and all related titles, logos and characters are trademarks of Paramount Pictures Corp. STAR TREK: THE EXPERIENCE is owned and operated by Paramount Parks, Inc. All rights reserved; p. 317 (left), Courtesy Lufthansa German Airlines; Agency: Gotham/New York; p. 317 (right), Courtesy ANA Airlines; p. 318 (top), Courtesy American Express; Agency: Ogilvy & Mather; p. 318 (bottom), Courtesy Allstate; p. 321, Courtesy Greek Ministry of Tourist Development; p. 322 (left), Courtesy The Nature Conservancy; Agency: Eisner Communications/Baltimore; p. 322 (right), Trademarks and copyrights used herein are properties of the United States Postal Service and are used under license to McGraw-Hill. All Rights Reserved; p. 326, ©2004 Hertz System, Inc. Hertz is a registered service mark and trademark of Hertz System, Inc.; p. 325, 1992. The Ritz-Carlton Hotel Company. All rights reserved. Reprinted with the permission of the Ritz-Carlton Hotel Company L.L.C. The Ritz-Carlton® is a federally registered trademark of The Ritz-Carlton Hotel Company, L.L.C.; p. 327 (top), Used with permission from McDonald's Corporation; p. 327 (middle), Courtesy Sprint; p. 327 (bottom), Logo used with permission of the American Red Cross;

p. 328, Courtesy Laser Vision Institute; p. 329 (left), Courtesy The Princeton Review; 329 (right), Courtesy Accenture; p. 332, Courtesy Philadelphia Phillies; p. 333, Courtesy Philadelphia Phillies.

Figure 12.4, reprinted by permission of Harvard Business Review. An exhibit from "Strategy Is Different in Service Businesses," by Dan R. E. Thomas, July-August 1978. Copyright 1978 by the President and Fellows of Harvard College, all rights reserved; Figure 12.6, adapted with the permission of The Free Press, a Division of Simon & Schuster Adult Publishing Group, from ON GREAT SERVICE: A Framework for Action by Leonard L. Berry. Copyright © 1995 by Leonard L. Berry. All rights reserved.

CHAPTER 13

p. 334, Courtesy Priceline.com, Inc.; p. 336, Courtesy Airbus North America; p. 337, Courtesy Bugatti; p. 338, Michael Krasowitz/Getty Images; p. 341 (top), Courtesy Alexander Global Promotions; p. 341 (bottom left), ©M. Hruby; p. 341 (bottom right), Courtesy of Nike, Inc.; p. 342, Courtesy Territory Ahead; p. 344, ©M.Hruby; p. 348 (left), Courtesy Airbus North America; p. 348 (right), Courtesy Boeing Business Services Company; p. 349 (top), Getty Images; p. 349 (bottom), ©M. Hruby; p. 350, Photo by Chris Hondros/Newsmakers/Getty Images; 351, ©M. Hruby.

CHAPTER 14

p. 360, Courtesy The Gillette Company; p. 365, ©Terry McElroy; p. 366, Courtesy of Rock & Roll Hall of Fame and Museum; p. 367, Courtesy Panasonic Consumer Electronics Company; p. 371, ©Ted Soqui; p. 373, Sharon Hoogstraten; p. 376, Courtesy of The Toro Company; p. 378, Photograph by Monci Jo Williams; FORTUNE; ©1983 Time, Inc. All rights reserved.

APPENDIX B

p. 388, Courtesy The Caplow Company; p. 392, Courtesy The Caplow Company.

CHAPTER 15

p. 394, Jill Braaten/The McGraw-Hill Digital Library. © The McGraw-Hill Companies; p. 402, Courtesy CPW; p. 406 (left), ©M. Hruby; p. 406 (right), Jill Braaten/The McGraw-Hill Digital Library. © The McGraw-Hill Companies; p. 409, Courtesy American Eagle Outfitters, Inc.; p. 411, ©Tim Boyle/Getty Images; p. 412, Courtesy of Dai-Ichi Kikaku Co. Ltd. and Warner-Lambert; p. 410 (left), Courtesy Jiffy Lube International, Inc.; p. 410 (right), ©Amy Etra; p. 417, Courtesy Golden Valley; p. 418 (left), Mark Wilson/Getty; p. 418 (middle), Justin Sullivan/Getty; p. 418 (bottom), Justin Sullivan/Getty.

Figure 15.1, source: American Marketing Association. Used by permission.

CHAPTER 16

p. 420, Reprinted with permission of BusinessWeek; Illustrated by David Cale; p. 424, BMW of North America, LLC; p. 425, Courtesy IBM; p. 426 (left), Courtesy Dell, Inc.; p. 426 (right), Courtesy Wal-Mart Stores, Inc.; p. 437, Courtesy Hewlett-Packard Company; p. 430, PhotoEdit/Mark Richards; p. 432 (left), Courtesy FedEx Corporation; p. 432 (right), Courtesy of Emery Worldwide; p. 434, Courtesy of Maersk, Inc.; p. 435 (left), Courtesy of United Airlines; p. 435 (right), Courtesy of United Airlines, p. 436, Rapistan Demag Corporation; p. 437 (left), Fritz Hoffman/Image Works; p. 437 (right), Fritz Hoffman/Image Works; p. 438, ©John B. Boykin/The Stock Market; p. 441, Courtesy Amazon.com.

CHAPTER 17

p. 442, Reprinted with permission by Target Corporation; p. 445 (bottom), Courtesy Printemps Hausman; 447 (bottom), Reprinted with permission of Tandy Corporation; p. 450 (left), AP Photo/Christoiphe Ena; p. 450 (right), AP Photo/Sue Ogrocki; p. 451, Courtesy Marconi Commerce Systems; p. 452 (left), Courtesy Sears Roebuck & Co.; p. 452 (middle), Courtesy Lillian Vernon Corporation; www.lillianvernon.com; p. 452 (right), Courtesy L.L.Bean 2004 Fly Fishing Catalog; p. 453 (top), Courtesy of QVC Network; p. 453 (bottom), Courtesy MySimon; p. 454, Courtesy My Virtual Model, Inc.; p. 454 (bottom left and right), Easy Everything/Easy Group (UK) Ltd.; p. 462, Courtesy Taco Bell; p. 466 (left and right), Courtesy Mall of America.

CHAPTER 18

p. 468, AP Photo/Peter Cosgrove; p. 471, BMW of North America, LLC; p. 473, Courtesy Best Buy; p. 474, ©M. Hruby; p. 476, Courtesy of Fence Magazine; p. 477 (top), Courtesy MINI USA; p. 477 (bottom), ©M. Hruby; p. 479 (left), Courtesy Gulfstream Aircraft, Inc.; p. 479 (right), Courtesy H.J. Heinz Company; Used with permission; p. 481, Courtesy Novartis Corporation; p. 485, ©M. Hruby; p. 488, Courtesy America Online; p. 493, McGraw-Hill IMC 2nd Edition Educational Video.

Figure 18.7 Reprinted with permission from the September 24, 2001 issue of Advertising Age. Copyright 2001 Crain Communications Inc.

CHAPTER 19

p. 494, Courtesy There.com; p. 496 (left), Used with permission of Verizon Wireless; p. 496 (middle), Courtesy Aventis Pharmaceuticals, Inc.; p. 496 (right), Courtesy FTD; p. 497 (top), Courtesy DDB Worldwide and The Dial Corporation; p. 497 (bottom), Courtesy Lorillard Tobacco Company; p. 498 (left), Courtesy Altria Corp. Services, Inc.; p. 498 (right), Courtesy National Fluid Milk Processor Promotion Board; Agency: Lowe Worldwide, Inc.; p. 499, Courtesy Pepsi Cola Company; p. 500, Courtesy of AdForum.com; p. 501 (left), Office of National Drug Control Policy/Partnership for a Drug-Free America®; p. 505 (top), Courtesy SPEED Channel, 2004; p. 507, TEEN PEOPLE ©2004 Time Inc. All rights reserved; 508 (top), Courtesy Goodby, Silverstein & Partners/San Francisco; p. 509 (left), Courtesy IBM; p. 510, H. Howe/Allsport; p. 511, Courtesy Captivate Network, Inc.; p. 513, Courtesy NOP World; p. 514, Courtesy Val-Pak Direct Marketing Systems; p. 516 (left), ©The Procter & Gamble Company. Used by permission; p. 516 (right), Courtesy Hilton Hospitality, Inc.; p. 518 (left), ©Shooting Star; p. 518 (middle), Photo by Dave Hogan/Getty; p. 518 (right), Courtesy PVI Virtual Media Services; p. 520, ©CBS Broadcasting, Inc. All Rights Reserved; p. 524, Courtesy CIT Group, Inc.; p. 525, Courtesy Fallon McElligott.

Figure. 19.2 Reprinted with permission from the September 24, 2001 issue of Advertising Age. Copyright 2001 Crain Communications Inc.; Figure 19.4 William F. Arens, Contemporary Advertising, 9th ed. Copyright © 2004 by The McGraw-Hill Companies; Figure 19.4 From William G. Nickels, James M. McHugh, and Susan M. McHugh, Understanding Business, 6th ed. Copyright © 2002 by The McGraw-Hill Companies.

CHAPTER 20

p. 526, Courtesy Xerox Corporation; p. 529, Courtesy Medtronic; p. 531, Mitch Kezar/Stone (Getty Images); p. 533, Courtesy Xerox Corporation; p. 535, Einzig Photography; p. 536, CB Productions/Corbis; p. 537, Richard Pasley/Stock Boston; p. 538, Ken Ross/FPG International; p. 540, Color Day Production/The Image Bank; p. 547, Courtesy Mary Kay; p. 548, Jose Peleaz/The Stock Market; p. 549 (left), Courtesy of Toshiba America Medical Systems & Interactive Media; p. 549 (right), Courtesy of Toshiba America Medical Systems & Interactive Media; p. 553, Courtesy of Reebok International Ltd.

CHAPTER 21

p. 556, ©tom white.images; p. 559, Courtesy Godiva Chocolatier; p. 566, ©Paul Barton/ CORBIS; p. 569, Courtesy Diamond Trading Company; Agency: J. Walter Thompson; p. 570, ©The Procter & Gamble Company. Used by permission; p. 571, ©Matt Mahurin, Inc.

Figure 21.2 From Internet Marketing: Building Advantage in a Networked Economy, Mohammad, Fisher et al. Copyright © 2002 by The McGraw-Hill Companies.

CHAPTER 22

p. 580, ©M. Hruby; p. 582, ©M. Hruby; p. 583 (left), Courtesy Costco; p. 583 (right), ©M. Hruby; p. 584, ©M. Hruby; p. 589 (left), Courtesy Wal-Mart, Inc.; p. 589 (right), Courtesy Volkswagen of America; Agency: Arnold Communications; p. 593, ©M. Hruby; p. 594 (top and bottom), ©M. Hruby; p. 595 (all), ©M. Hruby; p. 596, GE Lighting Group; p. 598 (top), Courtesy Saturn Corporation; p. 598 (bottom), Courtesy Lockheed Martin Corp.; p. 603, Courtesy Colgate-Palmolive Company; p. 607, Video still from Marketing, 8/e Video Series. Copyright © 2006 by The McGraw-Hill Companies; p. 608, Video still from Marketing, 8/e Video Series. Copyright © 2006 by The McGraw-Hill Companies; p. 609, ©M. Hruby.

Figure 22.3, Reprinted with permission from Journal of Marketing, published by the American Marketing Association, Summer 1980, p. 82; Figure 22.4, Adapted with permission from The Free Press, a Division of Simon & Schuster Adult Publishing Group, from COMPETITIVE ADVANTAGE: Creating and Sustaining Superior Performance by Michael E. Porter. Copyright © 1985, 1998 by Michael E. Porter. All rights reserved; Figure 22.6, Kotler, Philip, Marketing Management, 11th Edition, © 2003. Adapted by permission of Pearson Education, Inc., Upper Saddle River, NJ; Figure 22.8, Adapted from an Introduction to Contemporary Business, 4th edition, by W. Rudelius, W.B. Erickson © 1985.

APPENDIX C

p. 612 (top), ©Paul Elderidge; p. 612 (bottom), Courtesy The May Department Stores Company; p. 613, Courtesy Xerox Corporation; p. 614, Toyota Motor North America, Inc.; p. 617 (top), Reprinted from Job Choices 2002, with permission of the National Association of Colleges and Emplyers, copyright holder; p. 617 (bottom), Courtesy Monster; 624 (top), Thatch cartoon by Jeff Shesol; Reprinted with permission of Vintage Books; p. 624 (bottom), White Packert/Getty Images.

Figure C-1, Careers in Marketing by David W. Rosenthal and Michael A. Powell © 1984, pp. 352–54, by permission of Pearson Education, Inc., Upper Saddle River, NJ.

APPENDIX D

p. 628, Courtesy Kingpin Snowboarding; p. 630, Courtesy Daktronics, Inc.; p. 631, Courtesy Daktronics, Inc.; p. 640, Courtesy HOM Furniture; p. 644, Photo by Paul Harris/Online USA; p. 648, Courtesy Vetco, Inc. Consumer Healthcare; p. 649, Courtesy Vetco, Inc. Consumer Healthcare; p. 650, Courtesy Faster Company; p. 659, Courtesy British Petroleum

NAME INDEX

A

Aaby, Nils-Erik, 679n
Aaker, David A., 683n, 692n, 694n
Abate, Tom, 685n
Abboud, Leil, 682n
Abell, Derek F., 674n
Abernathy, Avery M., 693n, 695n
Abraham, Magid M., 694n
Abrahms, Rhonda M., 54, 674n
Abrams, Richard L., 678n
Achenbach, James, 699n
Adams, Joe, 685n
Adams, Yolanda, 94
Adler, Roy D., 699n
Aerosmith, 358
Affleck, Ben, 203, 205
Agoglia, John, 699n
Ailawadi, Kusum L., 690n, 691n
Aizen, I., 678n
Alba, Joseph W., 677n
Alden, Dana L., 693n
Alexander, Joe F., 698n
Alexander, Steve, 681n
Allen, Sandy, 685n
Allman, Greg, 358
Allvine, Fred C., 694n
Alpert, Herb, 94
Alva, Marilyn, 699n
Alvarado, Ursula Y., 688n
Ambler, Tim, 692n
Amst, Catherine, 676n
Anderson, Eric, 690n
Anderson, Erin, 679n, 687n
Anderson, James C., 679n
Anderson, Stephanie, 675n
Anderson,Chris, 675n
Andrews, Rick, 686n
Andruss, Paula Lynn, 695n, 698n
Ansoff, H. Igor, 674n
Appleyard, Dennis R., 679n
Arens, William F., 694n
Armstrong, J. Scott, 674n
Armstrong, Lance, 52
Armstrong, Larry, 684n, 688n, 694n
Arndt, Michael, 682n
Arner, Faith, 697n
Arnold, Catherine, 675n, 676n, 689n, 690n, 691n, 692n, 693n
Arnold, Eric, 678n
Arquette, David, 502
Aston, Adam, 682n, 689n
Atkinson, Claire, 691n, 693n
Atlas, Elise, 695n
Atlas, Steve, 695n

B

Babb, Emerson M., 691n
Badarocco, Joseph L., Jr., 676n
Baer, Martha, 688n
Bagozzi, Richard P., 673n
Baker, Julie, 690n
Baker, Peter, 673n
Baker, Stephen, 694n
Baker, Walter, 686n
Baker, Wayne E., 699n
Baksha, Joe, 358–359

Balasubramanian, Siva K., 691n
Balasubramanian, Sridhar, 682n, 690n
Bandler, James, 674n
Banks, Allen, 694n
Bannon, Lisa, 679n
Barboza, David, 699n
Barlett, Donald L., 686n
Barnes, Frank C., 678n
Barnes, Jimmy D., 691n
Barnes, John, 690n
Barrett, Katherine, 693n
Barrett, Paul, 676n
Barrionuevo, Alexei, 700n
Bartholomew, Doug, 688n
Bartos, Rena, 677n
Bartsch, Howard, 690n
Bass, Stephen J., 690n
Basta, Nicholas, 698n
Bates, Albert D., 690n
Bauer, Gerald J., 695n
Bawa, Kapil, 694n
Bay, Willow, 680n
Bayus, Barry L., 687n
Bearden, William O., 687n
Beardi, Cara, 693n
Beatles, 315, 358
Beatty, Sharon E., 677n
Beckerer, Richard C., 696n
Belch, George E., 687n
Belch, Michael A., 687n
Belich, Thomas J., 688n
Belk, Russell, 677n
Bellizzi, Joseph A., 679n, 685n
Bellman, Lawrence M., 690n
Ben-Akiva, Moshe, 677n
Bendapudi, Neeli, 684n
Benjamin, Matthew, 683n
Bennett, Peter D., 685n, 691n
Benza, Ron, 694n
Bergen, Mark E., 686n, 687n
Berger, Melanie, 696n
Berkowitz, Shelly, 645, 700n
Berman, Barry, 625
Berner, Robert, 679n, 688n, 689n, 692n
Berry, Jon, 678n
Berry, Leonard L., 684n, 685n, 690n
Bertagnoli, Lisa, 699n
Berthon, Pierre, 693n
Best, Allen, 699n
Best, Roger J., 677n, 680n
Bettencourt, Nuno, 358
Betts, Kate, 688n
Betzold, James, 694n
Bezos, Jeff, 440–445
Bharadwaj, S., 680n
Bianoco, Anthony, 689n
Bierne, Mike, 676n
Bigne, J. Enrique, 691n
Bigness, Jon, 688n
Bildsten, Bruce, 524
Billings, Claire, 684n
Bingham, Frank G., Jr., 678n
Bird, Larry, 232
Bitner, Mary Jo, 684n, 685n, 690n
Bittar, Christine, 677n, 678n
Blackwell, Roger D., 677n
Blankenhorn, Dana, 694n

Blanko, Vincent, 691n
Blenkhorn, David L., 678n
Blige, Mary J., 93
Bloch, Thomas, 685n
Bloom, Jonah, 687n
Bloom, Paul N., 676n, 688n
Bluestein, Jeff, 154
Boccara, Bruno, 677n
Bohmer, Richard, 698n
Bolles, Richard N., 625
Bolten, Joshua, 675n
Bolter, David, 135
Bolton, Ruth N., 677n
Bombola, Steven, 384
Bommer, William H., 696n
Bonds, Barry, 469
Bongiorno, Lori, 690n
Bonnet, Adeline, 689n
Bonoma, Thomas V., 679n
Booms, Bernard H., 685n
Boorstin, Julia, 697n
Boring, Christopher, 458
Bouchard, Nancy, 674n
Bowen, David E., 684n
Bowersox, Donald J., 688n
Bowman, Robert J., 688n
Boyd, Harper W., Jr., 674n, 683n
Boyle, Matthew, 683n
Boyz II Men, 93
Bradsher, Keith, 699n
Brady, Tom, 469
Braham, Lewis, 689n
Brandreth, Scott, 685n
Branson, Richard, 521
Bream, Jon, 676n
Breen, Brady, 358
Brennan, David P., 691n
Briggs, Bill, 655
Brinegar, Brad, 513
Brione, Maricris G., 693n
Bristor, Julie M., 679n
Brodie, Roderick J., 674n
Brooks, Garth, 467
Brosnan, Pierce, 134, 312
Brosse, David, 692n
Brown, Barry, 690n
Brown, Ed, 694n
Brown, Jeff, 549
Brown, Mary L., 680n
Brown, Neil, 692n
Brown, Robert George, 691n
Brown, Shona L., 673n
Brown, Stephen W., 325, 684n, 685n, 690n
Brownfeld, Peter, 673n
Brunel, Frederic, 677n
Bruni, Frank, 686n
Bryant, Kobe, 503
Buchanan, Bruce, 692n
Buck, David, 685n
Buckner, John W., 698n
Bullock, August, 128, 678n
Bundchen, Gisele, 502
Burdett, Jack, 658
Burdick, Richard K., 679n

Burgdorfer, Bob, 674n
Burin, Norm, 690n
Burke, Raymond R., 689n
Burley, James, 682n
Burnett, John H., 673n
Burns, Greg, 697n
Burrows, Carol, 313
Burrows, Peter, 674n, 682n
Burton, Thomas M., 682n
Bush, Alan J., 693n
Bush, Victoria D., 693n
Butaney, Gul, 687n
Butscher, Stephan A., 686n
Buzzell, Robert D., 687n, 694n
Byrd, Veronica, 689n
Byrne, John A., 673n
Byrnes, Nanette, 689n

C

Cahill, Maureen, 466, 467, 691n
Callaway, Eli R., 637
Campanelli, Melissa, 696n
Campbell, Don, 676n
Campbell, Paul, 675n
Cannon, Joseph P., 676n, 679n, 688n
Cappel, Perri, 699n
Cappelli, Peter, 699n
Carey, J. Ronald, 691n
Carey, John, 675n, 691n
Carey, Mariah, 93, 94
Carlson, Don, 675n
Carlton, Jim, 675n
Carpenter, Jack Burton, 628
Carral, Teré, 223, 224, 225, 681n
Carson, J. J., 677n
Carter, Franklin, 691n
Carter, Jim, 690n
Carter, Shawn, 231
Casanova, Sarah, 700n
Casimiro, Steve, 689n
Castelli, Jim, 674n
Castleberry, Stephen B., 695n, 696n
Cateora, Philip R., 680n, 695n
Catherine the Great, 2
Cellars, Stuart, 687n
Chadwick, Kathy, 700n
Challagolla, Goutam N., 696n
Chandrashekar, Ashok, 685n
Chandrashekaran, Murali, 685n
Chang, Julia, 696n
Chang, Weih, 694n
Chao, Elaine L., 698n
Chen, Christine Y., 692n
Chen, Stephen, 694n
Cher, 315
Chester, Jannell, 699n, 700n
Chevalier, Michael, 695n
Cholewka, Kathleen, 692n, 695n, 698n
Chonko, Lawrence B., 676n
Chopra, Sunil, 688n
Christensen, Clayton M., 682n
Chrzanowski, Keith A., 695n
Chu, Wujin, 679n
Churchill, Gilbert A., Jr., 695n, 696n
Cipolla, Lorin, 694n
Clark, Kelly, 629

Clark, Terry, 677n, 685n
Cleaver, Joanne, 698n
Cleland, Kim, 692n, 693n
Clift, Vicki, 685n
Clique, Stephen A., 691n
Close, Glenn, 204
Closs, David J., 688n
Cloud, John, 681n
Coe, Amy, 443
Cohen, Adam, 686n
Cohen, Ben, 30
Cohen, Dorothy, 676n, 687n, 688n, 692n
Cohen, Joel B., 677n
Cohen, William A., 674n
Cohon, George A., 653
Colby, Charles L., 685n
Cole, Catherine, 693n
Coleman, Lisa, 692n
Colford, Steven, 695n
Collins, John, 321
Collins, Julia, 693n
Collins, Marshall, 698n
Colucci, Chap, 608, 609
Comer, Gary, 166
Comer, Lucette B., 696n
Compeau, Larry D., 692n
Conant, Jeffrey S., 685n
Concialdi, Samuel, 625
Coney, Kenneth A., 677n, 680n
Conklin, J. C., 686n
Conley, Tom, 697n
Conlin, Michelle, 675n
Connelly, John, Jr., 694n
Conway, Sean, 443
Cooper, E., 691n
Cooper, James, 675n
Cooper, Robert G., 269, 682n
Cooper, Scott W., 674n
Copper, M. Bixby, 688n
Corfman, Kim, 677n
Cortex, John, 694n
Costner, Kevin, 203
Cote, Joseph A., 683n
Cotton, B. C., 691n
Couglan, Anne T., 687n
Covello, Joseph A., 674n
Cox, Courtney, 502
Cravens, David W., 695n, 696n
Crawford, Merle, 682n
Creswell, Julie, 686n
Crocket, Roger O., 689n
Cron, William L., 696n
Cronin, J. Joseph, Jr., 684n
Cronin, Mary J., 689n
Crosby, Lawrence A., 684n, 685n
Cross, James, 694n
Cruise, Tom, 518
Cuneo, Alice Z., 688n
Curhan, Ronald C., 695n
Curry, David J., 686n
Curtin, Richard T., 675n

D

D'Souza, Giles, 693n
Dagnoli, Judann, 675n, 693n
Dalrymple, Douglas J., 696n
Daly, Carson, 502
Damo, Dennis V., 625
Danes, Jeffrey E., 687n
Daniels, Cora, 699n
Darden, William, 684n
Dargan, Gayle, 384
Darlin, Damon, 695n

Darling, Diane, 625
Darrell, Dimebag, 358
David, Kenneth, 676n
Davidson, William R., 690n
Davies, Jennifer, 700n
Davis, Barbara Jo, 143–145, 678n
Davis, James E., 694n
Davis, Jeffrey, 688n
Davis, Ken, 143
Davis, Ricardo, 694n
Davis, Scott, 686n, 687n
Dawes, Philip L., 679n
Dawson, Jane, 550
Day, George S., 673n
Dean, Joel, 686n
DeBolt, Don, 689n
DeCarlo, Thomas E., 696n
Degen, James M., 690n
DeGeorge, Gail, 690n
Deighton, John, 683n
Del Polito, Gene, 684n
De Montebello, Henry, 612
DeNavas-Walt, Carmen, 675n
Dent, Harry S., Jr., 675n
DeQuine, Jeanne, 700n
Desrochers, Debra M., 688n
Deutschman, Alan, 699n
Devlin, Stuart, 699n
Dhar, Sanjay, 687n
Diamond, Helene, 680n
Diaz, Cameron, 518
Di Benedetto, Anthony, 682n
Di Carlo, Lisa, 700n
Dichter, Ernest, 694n
Dickson, Peter R., 677n
Dierberger, George, 261–262, 284, 682n, 683n
Dikel, Margaret Riley, 625
Dillon, William R., 681n
Diorio, Carl, 681n
Diriker, Memo F., 698n
Disney, Walt, 316
Djemai, Karim, 690n
Dobbin, Ben, 674n
Dobscha, Susan, 16, 673n, 685n
Dodd, Mike, 686n
Dodds, William D., 686n, 690n
Dolan, Robert J., 679n, 687n
Donaldson, Thomas, 676n
Donath, Bob, 692n
Donaton, Scott, 684n
Donnelly, James H., 684n
Donovan, Robert J., 677n
Dorsch, Michael J., 684n
Douglas, Michael, 204
Dowell, William, 684n
Dowling, Grahame R., 679n
Doyle, Thomas B., 699n
Dragics, Michelle, 689n
Draine, Sean C., 678n
Dreier, Troy, 684n
Dreze, Xavier, 687n, 689n, 694n
Drickhamer, David, 688n
Drumwright, Minnette E., 678n
Dubinsky, Alan J., 695n, 696n
Dubinsky, Donna, 271
Duncan, Tom, 692n
Dunfee, Thomas W., 676n
Dunn, Darrell, 689n
Durbin, Dee-Ann, 682n
Durvasula, Srinavas, 680n
Dutta, Shautanu, 686n
Dwyer, F. Robert, 678n, 688n, 695n
Dye, Renée, 696n
Dylan, Bob, 358

E

Earnhardt, Dale, 520
East, Malcolm, 343
Echikson, William, 700n
Eck, Brian T., 688n
Eckhardt, Giana, 674n, 684n, 700n
Eckstein, Sandra, 700n
Edmondson, Amy, 698n
Edmondson, Gail, 682n, 684n, 691n
Edwards, Cliff, 687n, 693n
Edwards, Jim, 695n
Eidam, Michael, 691n
Eig, Jonathan, 681n, 697n
Eisenberg, Daniel, 684n, 692n
Eisenhardt, Kathleen M., 673n
Eisenhower, Dwight D., 593
El-Ansary, Abdel I., 687n
Elgin, Ben, 682n, 693n
Elliot, Stuart, 693n
Elliott, Kimberly A., 679n
Ellison, Katherine, 674n
Ellison, Sarah, 681n
Ellram, Lisa, 688n
Elway, John, 469
Endicott, Craig, 693n
Engardio, Peter, 689n
Engel, James F., 677n
Eppright, David R., 693n
Etger, Michael, 692n
Ethans, Arno J., 679n
Ettenson, Richard, 680n
Evangelista, Benny, 684n
Evans, Jack, 625
Evans, Phillip, 674n

F

Faes, W., 679n
Fahey, Liam, 673n
Fahy, John, 680n
Faircloth, Anne, 684n, 690n
Fairlamb, David, 690n
Farkas, David, 690n
Farr, J. Michael, 625
Farris, Paul W., 691n, 692n
Felson, Leonard, 699n
Ferguson, Sara, 76, 467
Ferriolo, Sarah, 689n
Fetto, John, 675n
Feyder, Susan, 681n
Field, Alfred J., Jr., 679n
Fine, Jon, 693n
Finnigan, David, 691n
Fireman, Paul, 234
Firestone, Harvey, 633
Firtle, Neil H., 681n
Fischer, David, 691n
Fishbein, Martin, 678n
Fisher, A., 696n
Fisher, Marshall L., 688n, 690n
Fisher, Robert J., 696n
Fishman, Charles, 688n
Fisk, Raymond P., 685n
Fiske, Neil, 443
Fitzgerald, Kate, 692n, 693n, 695n
Flatt, Kevin, 525
Flatt, Laurel, 524
Fleischmann, M., 688n
Floyd, Callum J., 699n
Flynn, Julia, 691n
Fonda, Daren, 684n
Forbes, Thom, 673n, 682n
Ford, David, 228, 681n
Ford, Doug, 658
Ford, Henry, 633

Ford, Neil M., 695n
Forest, Stephanie Anderson, 690n
Forster, Julie, 682n, 698n
Fournier, Susan, 16, 673n, 685n
Foust, Dean, 692n
Fox, Richard J., 697n
Francese, Peter, 675n
Frank, Robert, 681n
Franke, George R., 686n
Frankenheimer, John, 525
Franklin, Aretha, 93
Fraser, Cynthia, 685n
Frazier, Gary L., 687n, 688n
Freedman, Alix M., 676n
Freeman, Shulvin, 686n
Frey, William H., 675n, 678n
Friars, Eileen M., 689n
Friedman, Lawrence, 679n, 695n
Friedman, Milton, 107, 112
Friedman, Wayne, 695n
Frommer, Arthur, 474
Frost, Raymond, 693n
Fullerton, Ronald A., 683n
Furchgott, Roy, 681n
Futrell, Charles M., 695n

G

Gaida, Kathleen A., 685n
Galea, Christine, 698n
Gallaire, Herve, 675n
Galuska, Peter, 698n
Gantt, Henry L., 600
Garcia, Sergio, 639
Gardner, David M., 683n
Gardyn, Rebecca, 674n, 675n
Gardyn, Robyn, 700n
Garfield, Bob, 692n, 693n
Garino, Jason, 697n
Garver, Michael S., 682n
Gaski, John F., 687n
Gedenk, Karen, 691n
Geffen, Donald A., 698n
George, William R., 684n, 685n
Gery, Nurit, 690n
Ghemawat, Pankaj, 697n
Ghermezian Brothers, 466
Ghingold, Morry, 679n
Ghosh, Chandrani, 684n
Gibb, Michael, 684n
Gibson, Lawrence D., 681n, 694n
Gibson, Richard, 697n
Gilbert, John, 682n
Gillin, Eric, 693n
Gillis, Sandy, 698n
Gilly, March G., 685n
Gilmore, James H., 684n
Ginsburg, Lee, 698n
Glazer, Rashi, 692n
Gnazzo, Patrick J., 676n
Goetzl, David, 695n
Gold, Laurence N., 694n
Goldberg, Marvin E., 691n, 693n
Goldblatt, Henry, 675n
Golden, Linda L., 690n
Goldman, Doron, 692n
Goldner, Diane, 699n
Goldstein, Patrick, 681n
Goleman, Daniel, 696n
Golfen, Bob, 700n
Golterman, Jeff, 695n
Gomes, Roger, 678n
Gonul, Fusun F., 691n
Gonyea, James C., 699n
Goodpaster, Kenneth E., 674n, 700n

Goodwin, Stephen A., 692n
Gooley, Toby B., 688n
Goosen, Retief, 639
Gorchels, Linda M., 698n
Gordon, Jack, 697n
Gordon, Mary Ellen, 699n
Gorenstein, Alan K., 692n
Gotlieb, Jerry, 692n
Graber, Donald R., 680n
Graham, Jefferson, 674n
Graham, John L., 680n, 695n
Grave, B., 688n
Graves, Jacqueline M., 693n
Graves, Michael, 443
Gray, Tim, 681n
Grebb, Michael, 696n
Green, Heather, 688n, 689n, 693n, 694n
Greenberg, Karl, 695n
Greenberg, Robert M., 699n
Greene, Jay, 675n
Greenfield, Jerry, 30
Greenleaf, Eric A., 677n
Greenwald, Anthony G., 678n
Greenwald, John, 699n
Gregor, William T., 689n
Gremler, Dwayne D., 685n
Gresham, Larry G., 688n
Grewal, Dhruv, 685n, 686n, 690n, 692n
Griffin, Bobby, 642–643
Grimm, Matthew, 675n
Griswold, Alicia, 692n
Gronroos, Christian, 685n
Gronstedt, Anders, 691n
Gross, Daniel, 700n
Gross, Neil, 690n
Grossman, Ginny, 525
Grossman, Lev, 681n, 696n
Grossnickle, Joshua, 681n, 698n
Grove, Andrew, 594
Grove, Stephen J., 684n, 685n
Grover, Ronald, 694n
Grow, Brian, 675n
Gruca, Thomas S., 685n, 687n
Grundlach, Gregory T., 673n, 676n, 688n
Gubrenick, Lisa, 686n
Gulati, Ranjay, 677n, 690n, 697n
Gunther, Marc, 694n
Gupta, Ajay, 636–637
Gupta, Susan Forquer, 695n
Gustke, Constance, 681n
Gutner, Toddi, 675n
Gutnerhers, Toddie, 684n
Gwinner, Kevin P., 685n

H

Haas, Edward, III, 306
Haddad, Charles, 689n, 692n
Haegle, Katie, 700n
Hahn, Minhi, 694n
Hakim, Danny, 682n
Halliday, Jean, 692n, 693n
Hamilton, Martha, 700n
Hamm, Mia, 287
Hamm, Steve, 682n, 689n
Hammel, Gray, 682n
Hammond, John S., 674n
Handy, Bruce, 697n
Hanifin, Bill, 690n
Hanover, Dan, 694n
Hansen, Katherine, 625
Hansen, Robert, 700n
Hanson, Ward, 696n
Harlam, Bari, 690n

Harrington, Ann, 697n
Harris, Frederick H. deB., 685n
Harris, Mike, 695n
Harris, Nicole, 689n
Harrison, George, 358
Hart, Stuart L., 683n
Hartley, Robert F., 677n
Hartley, Steven W., 674n, 684n, 688n, 692n, 694n, 697n, 698n, 699n, 700n
Hathorn, Clay, 697n
Haub, Carl, 675n
Hawkins, Del I., 677n, 680n
Hawkins, Jeff, 271
Hayes, H. Michael, 678n–679n
Hazelgren, Brian J., 674n
Heckman, James, 676n
Hein, Kenneth, 690n
Heller, Laura, 688n
Helsen, Kristiaan, 679n
Helyar, John, 697n
Henderson, Pamela W., 683n
Henderson, Verne E., 676n
Hennessey, H. David, 680n
Herbig, Paul A., 679n, 680n, 695n
Herche, Joel, 680n
Hernquist, Thomas, 502
Hickock, Allan, 632
Hiebing, Roman G., 674n
Hiestand, Michael, 699n
Himelstein, Linda, 686n
Hite, Robert E., 685n
Hoch, Stephen J., 687n
Hodgdon, Kirk, 700n
Hoeffler, Steve, 682n
Hof, Robert D., 688n, 689n
Hoffman, Karen Epper, 699n
Hoffman, Kurt, 688n
Holden, Reed K., 686n
Holdregger, Christi, 689n
Holliday, Heather, 693n
Holloran, Thomas E., 674n
Holmes, Stanley, 681n
Holst, Amber, 681n
Holt, Karen, 694n
Homburg, Christian, 679n, 696n
Hooley, Graham J., 691n
Hooper, Bill, 643
Hopper, Murray, 598
Horn, John, 680n
Horowitz, Bruce, 682n
Horvitz, Bruce, 693n
Horwath, Mary, 5–6
Houston, Michael, 683n
Howard, Daniel, 686n
Howard, John A., 677n
Howard, Theresa, 683n, 693n
Howlett, Debbie, 673n
Hoyer, Wayne D., 677n, 693n
Hsu, Carolyn, 687n
Hudziak, Larry, 643
Hue, Scott, 695n
Hufbauer, Gary C., 679n
Huffman, Sarah, 677n
Hughes, Laura Q., 694n
Hulbert, James M., 693n
Hult, Tomas M., 685n
Hume, Scott, 699n
Hunt, James B., 693n
Hunt, Kenneth A., 687n, 690n
Hunt, Shelby D., 673n
Husni, Samir, 693n
Hussherr, Francois-Xavier, 694n
Hutt, Michael D., 678n
Hyman, H., 691n

I

Iacobucci, Dawn, 684n, 687n
Immelt, Jeffrey, 606
Imperial, Ernest, 78
Isom, Susan, 646–647

J

Jackson, Donald W., 679n
Jackson, Janet, 93–94, 501, 502
Jackson, Jeanne, 453
Jacoby, Jacob, 686n
Jahoda, M., 691n
Jain, Ambuj, 686n
Jam, Jimmy, 93–95, 676n
James, Dana, 679n, 699n
James, Harvey S., 676n
James, LeBron, 235
Jamison, Alisha, 635–636
Jamison, Brock, 635–636
Janos, Leo, 697n, 698n
Jap, Sandy D., 678n
Jardt, Fred E., 626
Jaroff, Leon, 675n
Jarvis, Steve, 675n
Jaworski, Bernard J., 696n
Jay-Z, 230, 231, 232
Jeannet, Jean-Pierre, 680n
Jensen, Ove, 696n
Jenster, Per, 679n
Jobs, Steven, 247–248, 275, 411
Joffe, Robert, 681n
Johansen, Rod, 639
Johansen, Wayne, 639–640, 700n
Johansson, Johnny K., 680n, 693n
John, Deborah Roeder, 678n
John, Joby, 685n
Johnson, Curtis P., 692n
Johnson, Eugene M., 685n
Johnson, Jonathan L., 696n
Johnson, Kelly, 599
Johnson, Magic, 232
Johnson, Mark W., 695n
Johnson, Sheree L., 684n, 685n
Johnston, Mark W., 695n
Johnston, Wesley J., 679n
Joiner, Christopher, 697n
Jolson, Marvin A., 695n
Jones, Darryl, 358
Jones, John Philip, 691n
Jones, Kathryn, 688n
Jordan, Michael, 287, 469, 502
Joyce, Kathleen, 694n
Joyce, William, 582, 697n

K

Kabak, Edward, 694n
Kadlec, Daniel, 683n
Kahn, Barbara E., 687n
Kale, Sudhir, 688n
Kambil, Ajit, 679n
Kaminski, Philip, 688n
Kapferer, Jean-Noel, 686n
Kaplan, Simone, 689n
Karlin, Beth, 690n
Karp, Daniel, 39, 47, 48–49
Katobe, Masaaki, 695n
Kaufman, Martin, 700n
Keaveney, Susan M., 690n
Keegan, Warren J., 679n
Keenan, Faith, 674n, 689n
Keenan, William, Jr., 698n
Keith, Janet E., 679n
Keith, Robert F., 19, 673n

Keller, Edward B., 675n, 678n
Keller, Kevin Lane, 680n, 683n, 693n
Kelley, David, 275
Kelly, David, 676n
Kelly, Fran, 700n
Kemper, Cynthia L., 691n
Kennedy, Debra, 256, 257
Kennedy, John F., 101
Kennedy, Joyce Lain, 699n
Kennedy, Kim, 690n
Kerbo, Harold R., 678n
Kerin, Roger A., 674n, 683n, 686n, 687n, 697n, 699n, 700n
Kerwin, Kathleen, 697n
Kessler, Felix, 681n
Khermouch, Gerry, 681n, 695n
Kiekmeyer, Peter, 690n
Kierlin, Bob, 649
Kilbarian, Thomas M., 686n
Kim, Namwoon, 687n
Kim, Queena Sok, 686n
Kin, Kwan Weng, 689n
King, Ronald H., 679n
King, Stephanie, 681n
King, Thomas R., 680n
Kinsman, Mathew, 694n
Kinsman, Matt, 684n
Kipnis, Jill, 691n
Kirkpatrick, David, 695n, 698n
Kiviat, Barbara, 699n
Klapper, J. T., 691n
Kleese, Hilary, 167
Kleh, Cindy, 699n
Klein, Jill Gabrielle, 680n
Kleinschmidt, E. J., 269, 682n
Klug, Chris, 629
Knowles, Patricia A., 678n
Kohli, Ajay, 679n
Kohlk, Chiranjeev, 683n
Koranten, Juliana, 692n
Koretz, Gene, 675n
Kornberg, Matt, 647–649, 700n
Koselka, Rita, 690n
Kotabe, Masaaki, 679n
Kotler, Philip, 673n, 690n, 695n, 697n
Kotzab, Herbert, 688n
Kournikova, Anna, 134
Krack, Jim, 644
Krame, Jeffrey A., 698n
Kramer, Hugh E., 699n
Krantz, Michael, 697n
Krasnova, Olga, 678n
Kraus, Eric, 615
Krauss, Michael, 675n, 679n
Krishnamurthy, Sandeep, 693n
Krishnan, R., 690n
Krol, Carol, 692n
Kruegel, David, 694n
Kublank, David R., 689n
Kucker, William, 624
Kuczmarski, Thomas D., 682n
Kuhl, Mike, 285
Kumar, V., 673n, 677n, 691n
Kuntz, Mary, 690n
Kurtenbach, Alfred J., 629–631, 699n
Kydd, Arthur R., 53, 674n

L

Laband, David N., 693n
LaBelle, Patti, 93–94
Laker, Michael, 675n
Lambert, Douglas M., 688n
Lambright, Gina, 613

Lancaster, Hal, 698n
Landes, David S., 679n
Lane, Vicki R., 693n
Langer, Judith, 675n
Larréché, Jean-Claude, 674n, 683n
Larsen, Susan B., 698n
Lasorda, Tommy, 607, 608
Lassar, Walfried M., 687n
Last, Richard, 697n
LaTour, Michael S., 693n
Lauren, Ralph, 302
Lavidge, Robert J., 691n
Lawrence, Jennifer, 692n
Lazniak, Eugene R., 676n
LeBahn, Douglas W., 683n
Lee, Ang, 525
Lee, Choi, 693n
Lee, Don Y., 679n
Lee, Hau L., 688n
Lee, Thomas, 694n, 697n, 698n
Leenders, Michael R., 678n
Lefkowith, Edwin F., 685n
Lefton, Terry, 681n
Lehman, Donald R., 677n, 683n
Leigh, Thomas W., 679n, 695n
Leighton, Barbara A., 691n
Lemmon, Summer, 682n
Lemon, Katherine N., 685n
Lenskold, James, 698n
Leon, Robert P., 689n
Leonard, Devin, 674n, 692n
Leonhardt, David, 681n, 697n
Levine, Joshua, 687n
Levitt, Julie Griffin, 699n
Levitt, Theodore, 32, 674n, 695n
Levy, Daniel, 686n
Levy, Michael, 686n, 688n
Levy, Sidney J., 673n
Lewis, Lisa Stavchansky, 691n
Lewis, Terry, 93–95, 676n
Lezcano, Marisol, 685n
Li, Zhan G., 690n
Lichtenstein, Donald R., 680n
Lillien, Gary L., 679n, 685n
Lim, Chae Un, 695n
Lin, Lynn Y. S., 691n
Lindsay, Greg, 693n
Linsalata, David, 682n
Linville, Denise, 693n
Lippe, Dan, 691n
Lodge, John, 358
Lodish, Leonard M., 694n
Loiaza, Margaret, 229
Loken, Barbara, 697n
Lomborg, Bjorn, 698n
Longtree, Patricia, 697n
Loomis, Carol J., 695n
Lopez, Jennifer, 203, 205
Lovelock, Christopher, 684n, 685n
Low, George S., 683n
Lowenhar, Jeffrey A., 691n
Lowry, James R., 690n
Lowry, Tom, 684n, 695n
Lucas, George H., 688n
Ludden, LaVerne L., 625
Lukas, Paul, 693n
Lumpkin, James R., 687n
Lund, Beatrice B., 679n
Lundegaard, Karen, 686n
Lunsford, J. Lynn, 686n
Luong, Theresa, 686n
Lusch, Robert F., 685n
Lutz, Richard J., 678n
Lynch, Frank, 417, 688n
Lynch, Jack, 677n

Lynch, James E., 691n
Lyons, Daniel, 688n

M

Mabert, Vincent A., 682n
MacArthur, Kate, 692n, 694n
Machan, Dyan, 689n
Macias, Wendy, 691n
MacInnis, Deborah J., 677n
Mackun, Paul J., 675n
MacLaine, Shirley, 518
MacMillan, Carrie, 694n
MacStravic, Scott, 684n
Madden, Normandy, 693n
Madden, Thomas J., 681n
Maddox, Keith, 692n
Madigan, Kathleen, 675n
Madonna, 315
Magnet, Myron, 677n
Magnusson, Paul, 684n, 697n
Mahajan, Vijay, 674n, 682n, 687n, 698n
Malhotra, Naresh, 690n
Mandel, Michael J., 675n
Mandel-Campbell, Andrea, 692n
Mandell, Jonathan, 687n
Mandell, Maurice, 700n
Mandese, Joe, 693n, 700n
Mannering, Virginia H., 684n
Manning, Jeff, 693n
Manning, Kenneth C., 687n
Mantel, Mickey, 342
Mantrala, Murali K., 697n
Marcial, Gene, 690n
Marconi, Carolyn D., 615, 698n
Marcoolyn, Gillian, 677n
Marcus, Alfred, 698n
Maremont, Mark, 681n
Marken, G. A., 695n
Marks, Ronald B., 699n
Marlatt, Andrew, 699n
Marn, Mike, 686n
Marsh, Ann, 689n
Marshall, Greg W., 695n
Martin, Craig A., 693n
Martin, Dick, 691n
Martineau, Pierre, 460, 690n
Maslow, Abraham H., 677n
Masterson, Peggy, 694n
Matanovich, Timothy, 685n
Matathia, Ira, 678n
Mathur, Sharat K., 698n
Mathwick, Charla, 690n
Matlack, Carol, 689n, 690n
Matthews, Dave, 43
Matthyssens, P., 679n
Maxham, James G., III, 685n
May, Eleanor, 690n
Mayeur, Dora, 635–636
Mayne, Brad, 630
McAlister, Leigh, 687n
McBride, James, 698n
McCabe, Lucy, 509
McCall, William, 693n
McCarthy, E. Jerome, 14, 673n
McCarthy, Michael J., 681n
McCarthy, Patrick D., 700n
McCatery, Richard, 681n
McClellan, Anna Sheen, 690n
McColgan, Ellyn A., 684n
McColl-Kennedy, Janet R., 684n
McCorkle, Denny E., 698n
McCubbins, Tipton F., 680n
McCullough, Jim, 685n
McDonald, Ronald, 502

McDonald, William J., 677n
McDowell, Jeanne, 700n
McDowell, Jim, 312
McFadden, Mark, 676n
McFarlane, Todd, 577–579
McGinn, Daniel, 684n
McGraw, Phil, 502
McGwire, Mark, 469
McHugh, James M., 506
McHugh, Susan M., 506
McKay, Betsey, 682n, 697n
McKee, Bill, 682n
McKenna, Kevin, 680n
McKenzie, Scott B., 696n
McKeon, Jack, 417, 688n
McLaughlin, Lisa, 682n, 700n
McMahon, Robert, 552, 553
McMath, Robert M., 11, 673n, 682n
McNair, Malcolm P., 690n
McNierny, James, 273, 606
McQuiston, Daniel H., 678n
McVey, Philip, 679n
Meadows, Edward, 656
Mehring, James, 675n
Meindl, Peter, 688n
Meineke, Steve, 52
Mendels, Pamela, 699n
Menon, Ajay, 684n
Menon, Anil, 677n, 684n
Mentzer, John T., 682n, 687n
Mercer, Dick, 676n
Meredith, Robyn, 688n
Merrick, Amy, 674n, 682n
Merrill, Ann, 697n
Meuter, Matthew L., 684n
Meyer, Christopher, 674n
Meyer, Harvey, 688n
Meyer, Ron, 643
Meyerowitz, Phil, 699n
Meyers, Mike, 697n
Michaels, Ronald E., 695n, 696n
Miciak, Alan R., 693n
Mick, David Glen, 16, 673n, 685n
Miles, Stephanie, 679n
Miletti, Umberto, 645, 646
Miller, Arthur F., 699n
Miller, Cyndee, 694n
Miller, Jim, 445
Miller, Karen Lowry, 697n
Miller, Neil, 698n
Miller, Thomas A. W., 675n
Milletti, Umberto, 700n
Milligan, Brian, 678n
Mills, Robert J., 675n
Milne, George R., 693n
Milton, Frank, 691n
Miniard, Paul W., 677n
Minor, Michael, 677n, 678n
Mitchell, Ian W., 691n
Mitchell, Murry, 688n
Mitral, Banwari, 677n, 683n
Moeller, Leslie M., 698n
Mogelonsky, Marcia, 675n
Mohammed, Rafi A., 687n, 696n
Mohr, Jakki J., 678n, 687n
Mokwa, Michael P., 698n
Molson, Tom, 682n
Monroe, Kent B., 685n, 686n, 687n
Montana, Joe, 469
Montgomery, David, 685n
Montouri, Don, 674n
Moody, Patricia, 678n
Moody Blues, 358
Moon, Mark A., 682n, 695n
Moon, Youngme, 679n

Moorthy, Sridhar, 677n
Morash, Edward, 684n
Moravec, Milan, 698n
Morgan, Fred, 696n
Morgan, James B., 630
Morgenson, Gretchen, 690n
Morris, Betsy, 697n
Morris, Marlene D., 680n
Morrow, James, 675n, 678n
Morrow, Thomas J., 699n
Mortimer, Kathleen, 685n
Moses, Elissa, 680n
Moss, Phil, 698n
Mowen, John C., 677n, 678n
Mudget, Jim, 166–167
Mulcahy, Anne, 527, 529
Mulhern, Francis J., 689n
Mullaney, Timothy J., 685n, 689n, 694n, 697n
Mullins, John, 683n
Munschauer, John L., 699n
Muris, Timothy, 676n
Murphy, Chris, 51–52
Murphy, Kate, 697n
Murphy, Patrick E., 673n, 676n
Murray, Keith B., 684n
Muscove, Brenda J., 691n
Muzlay, Leigh, 673n

N

N Sync, 467
Nagele, Kim, 147, 678n
Nagle, Thomas T., 686n
Nardelli, Robert, 606
Narus, James A., 679n
Narver, John C., 673n
Nasser, Jacques, 634
Naughton, Keith, 690n, 697n
Naumann, Nick, Sr., 680n
Nedungadi, Prakesh, 677n
Neff, Jack, 682n, 694n
Neilson, Gary, 677n
Nelson, Dave, 678n
Nelson, Emily, 681n
Nemnich, Mary B., 626
Nesdale, Andrew, 677n
Neslin, Scott A., 691n
Netemeyer, Richard G., 680n, 685n
Neuborne, Ellen, 689n, 694n, 695n, 698n
New Found Power, 358
Newman, Bruce, 677n, 683n
Nicastro, Mary L., 694n
Nicholls, J. A. F., 696n
Nickels, William G., 506
Nicksin, Carole, 689n, 690n
Nigro, Dana, 687n
Noble, Charles H., 698n
Noble, Peter M., 687n
Nocera, Joseph, 674n
Nohria, Nitin, 582, 697n
Nolan, Mark, 674n
Noordam, Monica, 700n
Nordstrom, Elmer, 652
Nordstrom, Everett, 652
Nordstrom, John, 652
Nordstrom, Lloyd, 652
Norris, Donald, 692n
Norton, Rob, 694n
Nowak, Keith, 255, 682n
Nunii, Irene M., 689n
Nussbaum, Bruce, 682n
Nyberg, Carl, 639

O

Oberton, Will, 650
O'Briant, Don, 675n
O'Connell, Vanessa, 675n, 686n
O'Donnell, Jayne, 682n
Ogden, Clara, 684n
Oleck, Joan, 694n
Oliva, Terence A., 693n
Oliver, James M., 691n
Olsen, Patricia R., 682n
Olsen, R. Paul, 685n
Olson, Jerry C., 678n, 685n, 686n
Olsson, Hans-Olov, 119
Oneal, Michael, 691n
Onkvisit, Sak, 685n
Ono, Masatoshi, 634
Ordonez, Jennifer, 681n, 682n
O'Reilly, Ann, 678n
Oren, Haim, 685n
Orenstein, Susan, 677n
Orshoski, Wes, 697n
Ortmeyer, Gwen, 687n, 690n
Orwall, Bruce, 680n, 683n, 686n
Osborn, Richard L., 698n
Oser, Kris, 693n
Osler, Rob, 683n
Ostrom, Amy L., 684n
Ottman, Jacquelyn, 673n, 675n
Overdorf, Michael, 682n
Owen, Clive, 525
Ozment, John, 684n

P

Paddison, Gordon J., 696n
Palmer, John, 691n
Palmer, Rissi, 94
Palmeri, Christopher, 689n
Palmisano, Samuel J., 425
Pappas, Charles, 691n
Parasuraman, A., 684n, 685n, 690n
Pare, Terrence, 699n
Park, Schoon, 694n
Parker, Ginny, 685n
Parker, Sarah Jessica, 520, 521
Parmar, Arundhati, 675n, 676n
Parry, Tim, 694n
Parsons, Patrick R., 695n
Parton, Dolly, 358
Parvatiyar, Atul, 680n
Pascual, Alixa M., 689n
Patti, Charles H., 691n
Patton, Wesley E., III, 679n
Paul, Pamela, 675n, 691n
Paztor, Andy, 676n
Peacock, Peter, 685n
Pechman, Cornelia, 691n, 692n, 693n
Peebles, M. Ellen, 695n
Peers, Martin, 681n
Pelton, Lou, 687n
Penn, Cyril, 687n
Pennington, April Y., 681n
Pereira, Joseph, 681n
Perron, Kirk, 631–632
Perry, Joe, 358
Perry, Marc J., 675n
Peter, J. Paul, 678n
Peters, Leah E., 56, 674n
Peters, Randall F., 55, 56, 674n
Peters, Thomas J., 698n
Peterson, Eric, 690n
Peterson, Richard A., 686n
Peterson, Robert A., 674n, 683n, 690n, 697n
Peterson, Robin T., 698n, 699n

Petrick, Kenneth A., 684n
Petrof, John V., 685n
Pieters, Rik, 691n
Pilieci, Vito, 689n
Pine, B. Joseph, 684n
Pink Floyd, 358
Piotrovsky, Mikhail, 2
Piracha, Azhar, 695n
Pisano, Gary, 698n
Podaskoff, Philip M., 696n
Podmolik, Mary Ellen, 693n
Poniewozik, James, 695n
Pope, Eric, 673n
Population 1, 358
Porter, Eduardo, 675n
Porter, Mary, 647
Porter, Michael E., 172–173, 588–590, 673n, 674n, 676n, 679n, 697n
Potter, Donald V., 686n
Powell, C. Randall, 699n
Powers, Kemp, 686n
Powers, Ross, 629
Prahalad, C. K., 682n
Presley, Elvis, 94, 315
Price, Linda, 678n
Price, Sol, 697n
Priem, Ron, 154
Prince, 93
Pritchard, Constance J., 699n
Proctor, Bernadette D., 675n
Prystay, Chris, 687n
Ptrova, Elina, 691n
Purk, Mary E., 687n
Puto, Christopher P., 679n

Q

Qu, Lu, 697n
Quam, Steve, 229
Quelch, John A., 690n, 694n, 695n
Quinlan, Mary Lou, 499, 692n
Quinn, Jane Bryant, 676n

R

Rackham, Neil, 679n, 695n
Raju, Jagmohan S., 687n
Raman, Ananth, 690n
Ramswamy, Venkat, 682n
Randall, Donna, 685n
Rangaswamy, Arvind, 685n, 696n
Rao, Akshay R., 683n, 686n, 687n, 697n
Rao, Ram C., 693n
Raskin, Andrew, 687n
Raskin, Oliver, 681n, 698n
Rassekh, Farhad, 676n
Rassouli, Javad, 691n
Ratchford, Brian T., 677n
Rawe, Julie, 684n, 698n
Ray, Michael, 691n
Raymond, Joan, 675n
Raynor, Michael E., 682n
Rayport, Jeffrey F., 696n
Reddy, Srinivas K., 697n
Reed, Andrew, 656, 657
Reed, Keith, 689n
Reeves, Scott, 689n
Regan, Mary Beth, 689n
Rehborg, Mark, 228, 229
Reibling, Ellen Thomas, 691n, 693n
Reibstein, David J., 693n
Reichheld, Frederick F., 673n, 677n, 684n
Reidenbach, R. Eric, 676n

Rein, Irving, 695n
Reinan, John, 697n
Reinartz, Werner J., 673n, 677n
Reinhardt, Andy, 689n
Reinhold, Jennifer, 679n
Rembert, LeToya Deann, 692n
Rendon, Jim, 673n
Resce, Mary Ann, 361
Ressner, Jeffrey, 689n
Retsky, Maxine Lans, 676n, 694n
Revell, Janice, 686n
Reyes, Sonia, 697n
Rich, Ben R., 697n, 698n
Rich, Gregory A., 696n
Richard, Lawrence, 696n
Richerson, Dawn, 699n
Riedman, Patricia, 694n
Rifkin, Glenn, 683n
Rigby, Darrell K., 673n
Rigdon, Edward, 690n
Rigsbee, Edwin R., 687n
Roberson, Bruce, 582, 697n
Roberti, Mark, 679n, 688n
Roberts, Julia, 203
Robin, Donald P., 676n
Rochford, Linda, 687n, 695n, 699n, 700n
Rodenberry, Gene, 33
Roedder-John, Deborah, 697n
Roehm, Frances E., 625
Rogers, Everett M., 683n
Rogers, Michael, 689n
Rohwer, Jim, 698n
Rolling Stones, 358
Roman, Monica, 689n
Romeo, Jean, 695n
Ronkainen, Ilkka A., 680n
Rose, Randall L., 687n
Rosecky, Richard B., 695n
Rosen, Dennis L., 678n
Rosenberg, Larry, 700n
Rosenbloom, Bert, 687n
Rosenspan, Alan, 696n
Ross, William T., Jr., 676n
Rossiter, John R., 677n
Rotfeld, Herbert J., 693n, 695n
Roth, Daniel, 698n
Rothenberg, Randall, 698n
Rothschild, Steven M., 607, 698n
Roundtree, Robert I., 684n
Rowling, J. K., 236
Rubin, Mitchell J., 335
Rudelius, William, 673n, 674n, 676n, 685n, 695n, 698n, 699n, 700n
Ruekert, Robert W., 683n, 697n, 698n
Ruff, Richard, 679n, 695n
Ryan, Joel, 681n
Rylander, Don, 681n
Rynecki, David, 692n

S

Saguinova, Olga, 673n
Sale, Richard, 694n
Salmon, Walter J., 690n, 694n
Salzman, Marion, 678n
Sander, Duane, 629–630
Sanders, Lisa, 693n
Sanger, Steve, 594, 595
Saporito, Bill, 690n
Sarin, Shikhar, 698n
Sasser, W. Earl, Jr., 684n, 685n
Sauer, Mark, 700n
Sauerhaft, Rob, 700n

Schaecher, Phil, 166
Schefter, Phil, 673n
Scheuing, Eberhard E., 685n
Schifrin, Mathew, 689n
Schiller, Zachary, 697n
Schindler, Robert M., 686n
Schmidt, Peggy, 699n
Schnatter, John, 598
Schneider, Laura, 692n
Schneiderman, Ira P., 690n
Schonfeld, Erik, 688n
Schottenstein, Cathy, 674n
Schramm, Wilbur, 691n
Schroer, James A., 691n
Schultz, Don E., 691n, 692n
Schultz, Howard, 114, 115
Schwartz, Joe, 681n
Schwartz, Natalie, 694n
Schwartz, Nelson D., 698n
Schwarzenegger, Arnold, 26, 641
Scott, Mary E., 699n
Seanor, Dave, 700n
Segal, Carole, 657
Segal, Gordon, 657
Segal, Nina, 626
Seiders, Kathleen, 685n
Seligman, Daniel, 691n
Sellers, Dennis, 681n
Sellers, Patricia, 677n, 691n, 697n
Selwitz, Robert, 692n
Serwer, Andy, 677n
Sethuraman, Raj, 687n
Setoodeh, Ramin, 685n
Sexton, Ken, 698n
Shane, Scott, 689n
Shankin, William L., 693n
Shapiro, Barry, 679n
Sharma, Arun, 695n
Sharma, Subhash, 680n
Sharp, Arthur G., 699n
Shaw, John J., 685n
Sheatsley, P., 691n
Sheehan, Norman, 690n
Shepard, Stephen B., 675n
Shermack, Kelly, 689n, 694n
Sherman, Stratford, 697n
Shervani, Tasadduq A., 673n, 696n
Sheth, Jagdish N., 677n, 680n, 683n, 685n
Shimp, Terrence A., 680n, 693n
Shin, Jeongshin, 680n
Shinoda, Maki, 638
Shocker, Allan D., 677n, 687n
Shoemaker, Robert W., 694n
Shulman, Lawrence E., 674n
Shupe, Angela, 674n
Silverman, Brian, 700n
Silverstein, Michael, 443
Simchi-Levi, David, 688n
Simchi-Levi, Edith, 688n
Simester, Duncan, 690n
Simms, Paul, 469
Simon, Hermann, 687n
Sims, Molly, 453
Singh, Surendra N., 678n, 693n
Sinha, Indrajit, 686n
Sinyard, Mike, 51
Sipples, Laurie, 552
Sirha, Prabhakant, 697n
Skally, Nicholas, 27, 673n
Slater, Robert, 698n
Slater, Stanley F., 673n
Slywotsky, Adrian J., 696n
Smidebush, Ed, 167
Smith, A. B., 690n

Smith, Carlo D., 682n
Smith, Dane, 686n
Smith, Ethan, 686n, 687n
Smith, N. Craig, 676n
Smith, Neil, 677n
Smith, Scott M., 677n
Smolowe, Jill, 675n
Snedeker, Lisa, 673n
Solman, Gregory, 692n
Solomon, Michael R., 677n
Sorel, Dan, 692n
Sorenstam, Annika, 639
Spector, Robert, 700n
Speer, Tibbett, 687n
Speh, Thomas W., 678n
Spekman, Robert E., 687n
Spell, Chester, 689n
Spethman, Betsy, 690n, 694n, 695n
Spielberg, Steven, 518
Spiro, Rosann, 696n
Spriggs, Mark T., 688n, 695n, 700n
Sproles, George, 682n
Srinivasan, Kannan, 691n
Srivastava, Rajendra K., 673n
Stalk, George, 674n
Stanler, Bernard, 673n
Stanley, T. I., 691n
Stanton, John L., 691n
Stanton, William J., 696n
Stasch, Stanley F., 697n
Stayman, Douglas M., 694n
Steele, James B., 686n
Steenkamp, Jans-Benedict E. M.,
  677n, 690n
Stein, Joel, 700n
Stein, Nicholas, 698n
Steiner, Gary A., 677n, 691n
Stenger, Jonathan, 678n
Stern, Howard, 502
Stern, Louis W., 687n
Stevens, Greg A., 682n
Stevenson, Robert Louis, 528
Stevenson, Thomas H., 678n
Stewart, David, 692n
Stewart-Allen, Alison L., 675n
Stiving, Mark, 686n
Stock, James R., 688n
Stoller, Chad, 496
Stoller, Martin, 695n
Stonier, Jeremy, 8, 17, 26, 27, 673n
Strang, Roger A., 694n
Strauss, Judy, 693n
Strom, Travis, 285
Strunk, William, Jr., 674n
Strutton, David, 687n
Suhr, Jim, 695n
Sukhan, Carolyn, 647
Sukhdial, Ajay, 693n
Sullivan, Laurie, 689n
Summers, John O., 688n
Sunnoo, Dunn, 691n
Surowiecki, James, 673n, 686n
Sutter, Mary, 692n
Swaminathan, Vanitha, 697n
Swartz, Jon, 674n
Swartz, Teresa, 684n
Swenson, Linda, 674n, 700n
Swibel, Matthew, 687n
Swink, Morgan L., 682n
Swit, Loretta, 607
Syken, Bill, 699n
Symonds, William C., 674n
Szymanski, D., 680n

T

Tae-gyu, Kim, 682n
Taguchi, Fuyuki, 680n
Tait, Erin, 525
Tanner, John F., Jr., 678n, 693n,
  695n, 696n
Tansuhaj, Patriya, 685n
Tarnowski, Joseph, 690n
Tax, Stephen S., 325, 685n
Taylor, Charles R., 694n
Taylor, Chris, 681n, 684n, 689n
Taylor, Elizabeth, 412
Taylor, Rod, 691n
Taylor, Sarah, 689n
Taylor, Stephen A., 684n
Teach, Richard D., 694n
Teal, Thomas, 677n
Teinowitz, Ira, 692n
Terhune, Chad, 697n
Terpstra, Vern, 676n
Tetreault, Mary Stanfield, 685n
Theus, Kathryn T., 678n
Thomas, Dan R. E., 685n
Thomas, Daniel, 689n
Thomaselli, Rich, 684n, 693n
Thompson, Stephanie, 674n, 693n
Thottam, Jyoti, 682n
Tierney, Christine, 700n
Tietje, Brian, 673n
Till, Brian D., 693n
Tillotson, Kristin, 686n
Tilsner, Julie, 692n
TLC, 93
Tom, Gail, 689n
Tomkovick, Chuck, 692n
Totty, Michael, 674n
Trachtenberg, Jeffrey A., 681n
Traczyk, Patty, 692n
Trager, Louis, 699n
Treacy, Michael, 673n, 695n
Tripoli, Clinton, 698n
Tse, Edward, 680n
Tulukdar, Debabrata, 677n
Tung, R. L., 680n
Tyagi, Pradeep K., 696n
Tynan, Daniel, 698n

U

Ullman, Owen, 675n
Ulwick, Anthony W., 682n
Upah, G. D., 685n
Urbany, Joel E., 677n
Usunier, Jean-Claude, 680n
Utada, Hikaru, 94
Utgoff, Kathleen P., 698n

V

Vaas, Lisa, 700n
Vagnoni, Anthony, 693n
Vakratsas, Demetrios, 692n
Van den Bulte, Christophe, 673n
Van der Linde, Claas, 673n
Van Dyk, Deidre, 700n
Van Heck, Eric, 679n
Vanhuele, Marc, 689n
Van Hyning, Chuck, 674n
Van Nunen, J., 688n
Van Voorst, Bruce, 684n
Varadarajan, P. Rajan, 674n, 677n,
  680n, 687n, 697n
Vargo, Stephen L., 685n

Vekatesh, R., 679n
Venable, Robert, 686n
Vence, Deborah L., 675n, 676n, 685n,
  694n, 699n
Vermillion, Leslie J., 696n
Vernon, Lillian, 488
Vessey, Michael J., 673n, 682n,
  683n, 700n
Viglielmo, Pamela, 680n
Vinakmens, Kristen, 700n
Vitzthum, Carlta, 679n
Viveiros, Beth, 689n
Vlasic, Bill, 689n, 697n
Vogelstein, Fred., 675n
Voitle, Jennifer, 214
Voss, Glenn B., 690n

W

Waddock, Sandra, 677n
Wales, Stephanie, 635
Walker, Blair S., 673n
Walker, Orville C., Jr., 674n, 683n,
  695n, 698n
Walker, Rob, 700n
Wallin, Carl F., 652
Walters, Rockney G., 678n
Wanamaker, John, 512
Ward, Adrienne, 690n
Ward, Celeste, 699n
Ward, James C., 690n
Ward, Ronald W., 694n
Ward, Scott, 693n
Warren, Diane, 94
Wasink, Brian, 691n
Wasserman, Todd, 674n
Waterman, Robert H., Jr., 698n
Waterschoot, Walter van, 673n
Watson, Charles E., 698n
Weber, Alexander, 315
Webster, Frederick E., Jr., 679n
Webster, Nancy Coltun, 692n
Wedel, Michel, 690n, 691n
Weeks, William A., 696n
Wehling, Bob, 513
Weidlich, Thom, 694n
Weilbaker, Dan C., 696n
Weimer, De' Ann, 689n
Weinberger, Marc, 695n
Weinstein, Bob, 699n
Weintraub, Arlene, 692n
Weiss, Michael J., 675n, 696n
Weitz, Barton A., 679n, 686n, 688n,
  695n, 696n
Welch, David, 683n, 689n, 700n
Welch, Jack, 597, 606
Wellner, Allison Stein, 675n, 678n
Wells, Melanie, 678n
Welmer, DeAnn, 675n
Wentz, Laurel, 678n
Werner, Ray O., 676n
Wessel, David, 686n
Westerlund, Janes, 386–393
White, E. B., 674n
White, Rob, 524
White, Tiffany Barnett, 685n
White, Tina, 684n
Wiener, Joshua L., 695n
Wiersema, Fred D., 673n, 695n
Wilborn, Paul, 700n
Wildstrom, Stephen H., 675n, 689n
Wilke, Jeffrey, 445
Wilkie, Maxine, 675n

Wilkie, William L., 677n, 688n, 692n
Williams, Venus, 232
Willis, Clint, 675n
Wilson, David T., 679n
Wilson, James O., 676n
Wind, Jerry, 696n
Wind, Yoram, 674n, 679n
Windorski, David, 276, 682n
Winer, Russell S., 683n, 685n, 686n
Wingfield, Nick, 697n
Winslow, Ron, 686n
Winters, Lewis C., 692n
Winters, Patricia, 694n
Winters, Rebecca, 682n
Woellert, Lorraine, 694n
Wolfinbarger, Mary, 685n
Wong, Anthony, 679n
Wood, Douglas, 692n
Wood, Nora, 696n
Woodruff, David, 697n
Woods, Tiger, 232, 284, 502
Woodside, Arch G., 685n, 694n
Wooley, Catherine C., 335
Woolley, Scott, 693n
Workman, John P., 696n
Wortzel, Lawrence H., 687n
Wozniak, Steve, 247
Wratney, George R., 676n
Wu, Yuhong, 682n
Wukitsch, Michael R., 698n
Wyckoff, D. Daryl, 685n
Wyner, Gordon A., 681n, 686n

X

Xiong, Chao, 697n

Y

Yalch, Richard, 677n
Yang, Dori Jones, 690n
Yao Ming, 232
Yasuda, Gene, 700n
Yate, Martin, 626
Yikur, Rama, 692n
Yin, Sandra, 675n
Yip, George S., 684n
Young, DeForrest, 647
Young, Eric, 688n
Young, Lauren, 700n
Youngblood, Dick, 699n

Z

Zahra, Shaker A., 693n
Zaltman, Gerald, 679n
Zamiska, Nicholas, 681n
Zarem, Jane E., 684n
Zawada, Craig, 686n
Zbar, Jeffrey D., 675n, 693n
Zeithaml, Valarie A., 684n,
  685n, 686n
Zeller, Thomas L., 689n
Zellner, Wendy, 681n, 685n, 689n,
  690n, 698n
Zerillo, Philip, 687n
Zhao, Guangzhi, 691n, 693n
Zimmer, Mary R., 690n
Zimmerman, Ann, 700n
Zimmerman, Eilene, 695n
Zimoch, Rebecca, 674n
Zinkham, George, 678n
Zoltners, Andris A., 697n
Zuckerman, Mortimer B., 675n

COMPANY/PRODUCT INDEX

A

A&M Records, 72
A&P, 430
AARP The Magazine, 507
Abbott Laboratories, 163
ABC network, 470, 518
Abercrombie & Fitch, 21, 502
About-Primedia, 215
ABT Lite, 18
Accenture, 321, 329, 330
Accuvue contact lenses, 590
Ace Hardware, 406
ACNielsen, 59, 279
ACNielsen Scan Trak, 212, 228
ACT II popcorn, 417–419
Adams Golf, 638
Adforum.com, 499
Adidas, 25, 231, 303
Adidas-Solomon AG, 639
AdSubtract PRO 3, 510
Advil, 130
Aero, 5–6, 27
Aero 9, 17
Airbus Industrie, 152, 153, 177, 336, 343, 400
    competition with Boeing, 348
Air France, 153
Air Jordan, 235
AirTran, 342
Alamo.com, 401
Alberto-Culver, 291
Albertson's, 659
Alcoa, 343
Alimta, 278
Allegra, 496, 497
Allied Lyons, 186
All My Children, 518
Allstate, 318
All You magazine, 507
Alstarfigures.com, 578
Altria, 498
Amazon.com, 215, 316–317, 396, 401, 453, 454, 463, 558, 560, 563, 565, 566, 572, 576
    case, 440–441
Ambassador greeting cards, 402
American Airlines, 93, 305, 365, 434, 517
American Airlines Center, 630
American Boarding Kennel Association, 644
American Eagle outfitters, 409
American Express Company, 80, 109, 318, 327, 502, 530, 610
American Express Gold Card, 127
American Girl, 169
American Home Products, 590
American Hospital Supply, 413
American Idol, 517
American National Can, 159
American Red Cross, 33, 149, 322, 327, 498, 520
American Thunder, 507
America Online, 21, 136, 444, 488, 499, 509, 510, 568, 570, 592
AM General, 641–642
am New York, 508

Amoco, 658
AMP, Inc., 530
Amway, 455
ANA, 317, 318
Anacin, 303
Anheuser-Busch, Inc., 96, 112, 135, 140, 480, 502
    social responsibility, 97–98
Anheuser-Busch Recycling Corporation, 98
Animal Fair, 644
Animal Planet, 644
Anne Klein Couture, 172
Ann Taylor, 463, 653
AOL Games, 565
AOL Time Warner, 86, 215, 592
Apple Computer, 10, 16, 70, 71, 72, 137, 264, 267, 268, 270, 271, 275, 299, 302, 316, 394, 405, 410, 411, 499, 516
    marketing channels, 395
    product-market strategies, 255
    segmentation strategy, 247–249
Apple I, 247
Apple II, 10, 248, 395
Apple PowerBook, 283
Apple Stores, 411
ARC Group, 257
Archer Farms, 443
ARCO, 658, 659
Arizona Highways, 21, 22
Arm & Hammer, 304
Arnold Worldwide, 655
Arrow shirts, 370
Art Asylum, 579
Arthur D. Little, 275
Ashton Martin, 518
Associated Grocers, 406, 447
Association of Independent Commercial Producers, 655
AstroTurf, 294
AT&T, 86, 183, 517, 537
AT&T Wireless, 122
Atari, 496
Atkin's diet, 276
Audi TT Coupe, 495
Aurora Foods, 214–215, 252, 302
Austad, 284
Austin Powers, 577
Austin's chili, 60
Autobytel.com, 401
Avert Virucidal tissues, 273
Avis Rent-a-Car, 250, 406
Avon Products, Inc., 23, 108, 178, 455, 529, 572
Awsome Pet Products, 644
Awsome Pet Products Marketing Association, 644
AY&Y, 325

B

B. F. Goodrich, 152
Babies "R" Us, 263
Baked Tostitos, 372
Ballpark hotdogs, 502
Banana Republic, 237, 653
Bandai Company, 578

Band-Aid, 89
Bank of America, 506
Bank One, 469
Barbie doll, 169, 187
Barco, 630
Bark, The, 644
Barnes & Noble, 108, 128, 449, 460, 463, 464, 563, 566, 576
Barnesandnoble.com, 454, 463
Barney the TV dinosaur, 208
BarNone, 351
Baseball, 236
Baskin-Robbins, 186
Bassett, 657
Bass Shoe Outlet, 459
Bausch and Lomb, 518
Bayer Corporation, 131, 498
Beach 'n Billboard, 511
Beanie Babies, 341
Beatrice Foods, 430
Behold, 436
Benadryl, 496
Ben & Jerry's Foundation, 51
Ben & Jerry's Homemade, 31, 32, 33, 35, 40–41, 50, 51
    company background, 20–30
    mission statement, 28
    product life, 43
    SWOT analysis, 44
Benetton, 179, 180, 463
Ben Hogan golf clubs, 410
Benjamin Moore, 435
Berlin Cameron, 502, 503
Berry Burst Cheerios, 584–585
Best Buy, 162, 370, 473
Best Foods, 140
Best's Apparel, 652
Best Western International, Inc., 215
Better Homes and Gardens, 656
Betty Crocker, 252
Betty Crocker Complete Meals, 594
Betty Crocker Pork Helper, 582
Beverly Hills Hotel, 644
Bic perfume, 302
Big Bertha golf club, 637
Big G Milk and Cereal Bars, 595
BJ's Wholesale Club, 417, 458
Black & Decker, 177, 193, 194, 283, 305, 543
Black-Flag Roach Ender, 402
Black Pearls, 412
Blimpie's, 659
Blockbuster Entertainment, 417, 447, 615
Bloomberg, 212
Bloomingdale's, 413, 446, 456, 457, 459, 466, 653
Blue Cross-Blue Shield, 491
Bmg.com, 565
BMW, 424, 454, 471, 477, 491, 495, 496, 499
    product life cycle, 312–313
    promotion by, 525
BMX bikes, 51
Boeing Company, 32, 86, 149, 161, 177, 190, 253, 341, 343, 366, 592
    competition with Airbus, 348

Boeing 7E7 Dreamliner, 348
Boeing 737, 342
Boeing 777, 32
Boise Cascade, 108
Bold detergent, 303, 611
Bonne Bell Cosmetics, Inc., 139
Booksamillion.com, 453
Booz, Allen & Hamilton, 321
Borders, 397, 441
Borders.com, 454
Borg Invasion 4D, 315
Bose, 568
Boston Market, 461–462
Boucheron, 410
Boyle-Midway, 402
BP Connect, 659–660
Bratz dolls, 306
Brawny, 298, 516
Breakers, The, 316
Breathe Rite, 198–199
Breyers, 51
Bridgestone/Firestone, 108, 634–635
Bridgestone Tire Company, Ltd., 634
Brillo, 216
Brinks, 321
Bristol-Myers Squibb, 590
British Airways, 122
Broncos, 303
Brooks Brothers Clothiers, 127, 456, 466, 653
Brooks Brothers Outlet Store, 459
Brookstone, 12
Brother, 292
Bruno Magli, 172, 173
Budget Living, 507
Budweiser, 499, 510
Budweiser Light, 130
Bugatti Veyron, 337, 341–342
Buick, 123, 502
Bumble Bee tuna, 378
Burdine's, 446
Burger Chef, 462
Burger King, 104, 241–242, 246, 250, 281, 461, 485, 502, 551
Burlington Coat Factory, 458
Burmah Castrol, 659
Burston-Marstellar, 615
Burton Snowboard Company, 79
Burton Snowboards, case, 628–629
BusinessWeek, 499
Butterfields.com, 566
Byerly's, 464
BzzAgent LLC, 135

C

Cabbage Patch Snacktime Kids doll, 101
Cablevision, 84
Cadbury Schweppes, 184, 251, 302, 432
Cadillac, 128, 130, 237, 310, 412, 547
Cadillac Escalade, 642
Calistoga bottled water, 298
Callaway Golf, case, 637–639
Camay Soap, 305
Campbell Soup Company, 90, 125, 140, 212, 239, 297, 299, 304, 344, 438

C&R Research, 566
Cannes Advertising Festival, 502
Canon, 39, 271, 291, 311, 364
Caplow Company, operating expenses, 386–393
Cap'n Crunch, 275
Careerbuilder.com, 617
CARE International, 115
CarMax, 464
Carnation Company, 106
Carnation Instant Breakfast, 25, 275
Carnegie Deli, 357
Carpoint.com, 576
Carrefour SA, 169, 450
Carroll Shelby's, 60
Cartier, 363
Casera brand, 140
Castleberry's, 60
Catalina Marketing Corporation, 576
Caterpillar, Inc., 155, 179, 400, 602
Ceasar's Palace, 467
Celanese Chemical Company, 416
Celestial Seasonings, 308
Cellular Telecommunications & Internet Association, 13, 256, 257
Century 21, 396
Cereal Partners Worldwide, 178, 402, 594–595
Cerezyme, 107, 112
CGCT, 192
Champion pacemaker, 45, 46, 643
Chanel, 180, 363
Chaps, 302
Charles of the Ritz, 80
Charles Schwab, 322, 530, 550, 560, 568
Charmin, 612
Chatter Telephone, 207, 208, 209
Checkers Drive-In Restaurants, 461
Cheer, 309, 611
Cheerios, 220, 267, 270, 327, 402
Cheesy Chicken Enchilada, 582
Cheetos, 192, 277
Chef America, 12
Chemical Automatics Design Bureau, 149
Cherry Garcia, 30
Chevrolet, 21, 499
Chevrolet Cavalier, 377
Chevrolet Suburban, 641
Chevron, 464
Chicago Cubs, 21
Chicago Symphony Orchestra, 329
Chicago Tribune, 508
Chicken Helper, 582
Chicken of the Sea, 308
Chips Ahoy, 305
Chlor-Trimeton, 496
Christian Dior, 172, 370
Christie's, 180
Chrysler Corporation, 81, 268
Chuck E. Cheese, 316
Church & Dwight, 304
Cigar Aficionado, 499
Cingular Wireless, 13
Cini Minis, 595
Cinnamon Toast Crunch, 582, 595
Circuit City, 441, 449, 465, 646
Cisco Systems, 171
Citibank, 305, 525
    promotion by, 524
City Sports, 552
Claritas, 239, 640
Claritin, 499

Clearasil, 179
Clear Channel radio, 502
Cleveland Golf, 638, 639
Clickz.com, 576
CLIE Handheld, 507
Cling-Free, 303
Clinique, 574–575
Clorox Company, 129, 303
Club Med, 488, 506
Club Wedd, 443
Cluett Peabody & Company, 370
CNN, 592
Coca-Cola Company, 89, 104, 108, 122, 177, 179, 180, 182, 183, 185–186, 193, 197, 251, 270, 292, 300, 308, 321, 398, 409, 447, 499, 502, 503, 516–517, 541, 583, 610, 631
Coca-Cola Venezuela, 486
Coccolino, 178
Coke, 195, 458
Colgate-Palmolive Company, 131, 132, 176
Colts, 303
Columbia House, 487
Comicsplusonline.com, 578
Compaq Computer, 410
ComputerWorld, 9–10
ConAgra, 60, 514
Conservation International, 115
Consumer Reports, 60, 120–121, 142
Consumerreview.com, 569
Converse, 232
Cool Cam camcorder, 136
CoolMax, 26
Coors, 153
Corning, Inc., 149, 157
Corona Extra beer, 135
Correo Argentino, 489
Cosmair, 302
Costco, 659
Costco's, 16, 59, 417, 459, 583
Cost Cutters Family Hair Care, 329
Coupon Information Corporation, 515
Courtyard hotels, 305
Cover Girl Color Match, 296
Craftsman tools, 310, 364
Crate and Barrel, 452
Crate and Barrel, case, 658
Cray, Inc., 263
Create Your Own Shirts program, 445
Crest Neat Squeeze toothpaste, 275
Crest toothpaste, 132, 370, 413, 603, 612
Crossbow Technology, 637
Cub chain, 448
Cunard, 82
Curves, 448
Customatix, 232

D

Daiei, 445
DaimlerChrysler, 134, 192, 399
    promotion expenditures, 483
Daktronics, Inc., 629–631
Dallas Mavericks, 630
Dallas Morning News, 508
Dallas Museum of Art, 23
Dallas Stars, 630
Dannon yogurt, 608
Dasani, 503
Dash, 309
De Beers, 180, 569
Decathlon Sports, 552
Deere & Company, 154

Dell.com, 401, 453, 565
Dell Computer, 16, 163, 191, 371, 401, 427, 531, 560, 583, 613–614
    case, 651–652
    mass customization, 237
    supply chain, 425–426
Dell Premier Page, 651
Del Monte, 430
Deloitte Touche, 329
Delphi Automobile Systems, 589
Delta Air Lines, 364, 434, 448
Dennison chili, 60
DeWalt, 305
DHL Worldwide Express, 537
Dial soap, 303, 496
Die Another Day, 518
Diet Cherry Coke, 267
Diet Coke, 267
Digital Records, Inc., 208
Digital Think, case, 645–646
Digitas.com, 491
Dillard's Department Stores, 412, 449
Disneyland, 316, 590
Disney On Ice, 470
Disney Online, 566
Disney Park, Europe, 418
Disney Sea, Tokyo, 470
Disney World, 469
    marketing communications, 469–470
DKNYKids, 75–76
DMX Shear and Foam cushioning, 235
DNA Copyright Institute, 317
DoCoMo, 451
Dog Fancy, 644
Dog World, 476
Dollar General, 459
Dollar Rent-a-Car, 250
Dollar Tree Stores, 371, 459
Domina Vacanze, 52
Domino's bubble gum, 302
Domino's Pizza, 151, 327
Don Miguel's, 60, 62
Donna Karan, 127, 430, 652
Doritos, 123, 192, 298, 306, 372, 470, 518, 531
Dove, 33
Downy softener, 263
Dr. Care Toothpaste, 11–12
Dreamworks, 595
Dr Pepper, 300
Drugstore.com, 481
DSW Shoe Warehouse, 466
Dulce de Leche, 252
Dun & Bradstreet, 105, 389, 618
Du Pont, 52, 85, 171, 530
    cross-functional team selling, 533
Duracell, 365, 514
Durkee, 60
Dust, Inc., 636

E

E. T., 518
Eagle, 303
Eastman Chemical Company, 547–548
Eastman Kodak, 47–48, 49, 93, 175, 270, 307, 397, 438, 543, 583
    product line, 37–40
Easy Off, 303
eBay, 36, 50, 162, 214, 215, 302, 453, 517, 558, 569
eBayBusiness, 163
Eckerd Drugs, 417
Eddie Bauer, 283, 572, 573
eDiets.com, 560

Ednow.com, 453
Edy electronic cash system, 451
Egghead.com, 401
8th Continent Soymilk, 595
Electrolux, 455
Electronic Data Systems, 155, 530, 549
Eli Lilly & Company, 428
    product development, 277–278
Elite Foods, 192
Elite Industries, 192
Elizabeth Arden, 307, 412
Emery Worldwide, 432
Emirates Airlines, 153
Emporium in San Francisco, 464
Endust, 436
Energizer, 364, 502
    price perception, 365
Energizer Advanced Formula, 365
Epinions.com, 569
Era, 309
ERC Fusion driver, 639
Ericsson, 177, 256
Ernst & Young, 192
ESPN, 26, 477, 496, 505
ESPN Zone, 316
Esquire Sportsman, 507
ESRI, 83
Estée Lauder, Inc., 135, 574
    green marketing, 438
Ethan Allen, 574, 657
eToys, 23
E-Trade, 558
Euromarket Designs, 548
Excedrin, 303
Expedia, 335, 441
Express Bar, 80
Extra Strength Bayer, 131
Extreme Makeover: Home Edition, 518
Exxon, 123, 193, 194, 303, 520
ExxonMobil, 659
E-ZPass, 463

F

Fairfield Inns, 275, 305
Fallon Worldwide, case, 524–525
Family Dollar, 459
FAO Schwartz, 341
Farm Radio Network, 506
Fashionmall.com, 453
FastBreak cards, 463
Fastenal Company, case, 650–651
Fatal Attraction, 204, 205
Federal Express, 108, 151, 153, 322, 325, 327, 375, 398, 432
    sales teams, 533
Federated Department Stores, 446, 456
Fence magazine, 476
Ferrari, 311
Fiat, 655
Fiberwise cereal, 303
Field Furniture, 656
Field Museum, 23
Field of Dreams, 203
Finding Nemo, 470
Fingerhut, 222, 223
Fingos, 270
Firebird, 303
Firestone, 108, 520
Firestone Radial ATX tries, 634
Firestone Tire and Rubber Company, case, 633–635
Firestone Wilderness, 634
Firstgov.gov, 212

Fisher-Price Company, 169, 206–208, 209, 228, 491
FiSonLine, 212
Fitch, 653
Fitness magazine, 80
501 Levi jeans, 407
501 Re-Born jeans, 509
Flava dolls, 306
Flickstation Media, 451
Florida Gators, 287
Florida Orange Growers Association, 297–298
Flyte Time Productions, Inc., 93–95
Folgers coffee, 308, 612
Food Marketing Institute, 517
FootJoy, 262, 284
FootJoy SciFlex, 284
Foot Locker, 412
Ford Bronco, 633
Ford Consulting Group, Inc., 228–229
Ford Expedition, 641, 642
Ford Explorer, 520, 633–635
Ford Motor Company, 119, 123, 135, 159, 177, 192, 265, 291, 303, 305, 355, 399, 406, 447, 518, 520, 525, 610
case, 633–634
promotion expenditures, 483
Ford Pinto, 633
Ford Ranger, 633
Fortune, 133, 154
Fortune Brands, 263
FrancisFrancis brand, 636
Fran Wilson Creative Cosmetics, 190
Freak on a Leash, 577
Frederick and Nelson department stores, 652
FreeMarkets, 162, 164
French's, 60
Fresh Step Crystals, 129, 130
Friends, 213
Frito-Lay, Inc., 123, 192, 276–277, 293, 298, 305, 308, 372, 373, 470, 531
workload formula, 543–544
Frosted Cheerios, 267
FTD, 444, 496, 497
Fuji Photo, 175
Fuller Brush, 455

G

Gain, 611
Gainey Ranch, 316
GameCube, 294
Gap, The, 162, 236–237, 463, 573, 653
Gap.com, 453
GarageBand, 248
Garden Design, 507
Garden Television, 505
Gateway Inc., 268
Gatorade, 286, 287–288, 291, 299, 301, 302, 304, 502
Gatorade Energy Bar, 288
Gatorade Fierce, 304
Gatorade Frost, 304
Gatorade Nutritional Shake, 288
Gatorade X-Factor, 288, 304
Gatorade Xtremo, 288
Geico, 502
General Dynamics, 105, 641
General Electric, 19, 20, 24, 30, 122, 123, 161, 163, 273, 304, 311, 342, 402, 530, 592, 596, 606, 624, 642
implementation strategies, 597
promotion expenditures, 483

General Foods, 55, 591
General Mills, 12, 19, 36, 104, 191, 207–208, 215–216, 220, 270, 274, 297, 305, 430, 485, 587, 593, 594, 600, 606
alliance with Nestlé, 402
case, 607–609
marketing strategy, 581–582
Nestlé joint venture, 177–178, 594–595
resource allocation, 584–585
General Motors, 302, 368, 399, 402, 412, 506, 558, 574, 598, 599, 641, 642
promotion expenditures, 483
Genzyme, 107
Georgia-Pacific, 298
Gerber, 92, 193, 304
Gigante, 177
Gigli, 205
Gillette Company, 179, 194, 215, 302, 447, 537, 615
competition with Schick, 411–412
product introduction, 288–289, 360–363
Gillette for Women Venus razor, 292
Gillette MACH3 razor, 267, 288–289, 292, 294
Gillette razors, 187, 193, 194
Gillette Venus, 267
Gino Marchetti's, 462
Glass Plus, 303
GlaxoSmithKline, 428
promotion expenditures, 483
Global eXchange Services, 163
Global Healthcare Exchange, 163
Global Logistics, 432
Glow Cube, 630
GNB Technologies, Inc., 438
Go-Bags, 582, 594
Godiva, 548, 559
Go-Gurt, 592, 608
Golden Beauty, 194
Goldeneye, 312
Golden Valley Microwave Foods, case, 417–419
Golf Channel, 638
Golfsmith, 262, 284
Good Housekeeping, 656
Good Humor, 51
Good Start infant formula, 106
Goodyear tires, 299, 405
Google, 125, 211, 212, 214, 215, 280
got2b.com, 300
Gourmet magazine, 635
Goya Foods, 60, 140
Great Atlantic & Pacific Tea Company, 88
Great Big Bertha golf club, 637
Great Starts, 239
Green Bay Packers, 337
Greenpeace, 108, 322
Greptile Grip golf glove, 261–262, 284–285
GripShift, 52
Grumman Aircraft, 159
Gucci, 127, 180, 409, 410, 529
Guess jeans, 465
Guggenheim Museum, 22
Gulfstream Aerospace Corporation, 152, 479
Gymboree, 653

H

H. J. Heinz, 21, 340, 364, 430, 479, 514
Haggar Clothing Company, 137
Hallmark Cards, 402, 610
Hamburger Helper, 207, 215–216, 582
H&R Block, 318, 329, 406
Hanes, 502
Hard Rock Cafe International, 315
Hard Rock Cafes and Hotels, 315
Harkman Electric, 400
Harley-Davidson, Inc., 192, 193, 296, 297, 302, 563
supplier collaboration, 154
Harley-Davidson Cafes, 315
HarperCollins, 397
Harris Corporation, 540
Harris Interactive, 565
Harry and David, 452
Harry Potter films, 204, 236
Hart Schaffner & Marx, 370
Hasbro, 578
HBO, 577
Head & Shoulders shampoo, 591
Health Cruises, Inc., case, 646–647
Heartwise cereal, 303
Heeley's sneakers, 17, 232
Heinz ketchup, 308
Helena Rubinstein, 194
Henredon furniture, 302, 410, 657
Herbalife, 455
Hermitage Museum, 22, 23
Hershey Foods, 305, 370, 502, 518
Hertz Rent-a-Car, 25, 250, 325–326
Hewlett-Packard, 36, 39, 72, 155, 183, 188, 281–282, 292, 297, 370, 410, 427, 428, 431, 438, 447, 548, 549
Hickory Stick, 637
Hidden Valley Ranch Low-Fat Salad Dressing, 303
Hidden Valley Ranch Take Heart Salad Dressing, 303
Hilton Hotels, 448
History Channel, 505
Hitachi, 172
Holiday Express, 80
Holiday Inn, 406, 456
Holiday Inn Worldwide, 80
Home Depot, 16, 108, 153, 316, 399, 445, 458, 464, 543, 583, 597, 606
Home Shopping Network, 401, 452–453
Homestyle Pop Secret, 216
HOM Furniture, case, 639–640
HOM Oak and Leather stores, 639
Honda Civic DX, 337
Honda Motors, 188, 281, 304
Honda Motors America, 103
Honey Nut Cheerios, 402
Honeywell, Inc., 530
Optoelectronics Division, 541
Hormel, 60
Hotmail, 569
Hot Pockets, 11, 12, 59
Hot Pockets Pizza Snacks, 12
Hot Pockets Pot Pie Express, 12
Hot Wheels, 169
House of Style, 453
Howlin's Coyote Chili, 42, 56–69
Huggies, 177, 298
Hulk, The, 111
Hummer, 499
case, 641–642
Hummer footwear, 302

I

Ibane, 358
IBM, 23, 103, 155, 184, 191, 196, 248, 268, 271, 303, 304, 319, 370, 400, 431, 435, 438, 496, 509, 530, 551, 560
supply chain, 425
IBM Global Services, 537, 546
IBM Siebel Systems, 547
IBM ThinkPad, 283
Ice Breakers Liquid Ice, 502
Ichiro Suzuki bobble head doll, 341
Ideale, 194
IDEO, 275
iDVD, 248
IGA, 406
IKEA, 180, 452, 467
iLife, 248
iMac G5, 248
iMovie, 248
Incredibles, The, 516
Independent Grocers' Alliance, 447
Indianapolis Power and Light, 547
Information Resources, 212
Information Services, 228
InfoScan, 212, 228
In Her Shoes, 518
Intel Corporation, 155, 156, 179, 297, 301, 594
Intelligent Quisine, 344
Interactive Advertising Bureau, 509
International Company, 273
International Franchise Association, 416, 447–448
International Olympic Committee, 628
International Paper, 147
International Ski Federation, 628
Internet Nonprofit Center, 323
Intuit, 271
Investor's Business Daily, 212
iPhoto, 248
iPod digital music player, 70, 71, 267, 395, 499
Ireland from $60 a Day (Fromer), 474
Ishikawajima-Harima Heavy Industries, 149
iTunes Music Store, 71, 72, 248, 395, 516
iVillage.com, 569

J

J. Crew, 565, 653
Jack in the Box, 462
Jackson Hewitt Tax Service, 448
Jaguar, 454, 518
Jaguar S-type, 499
Jamba Juice, 631–632
James Bond films, 312
Japanese Consumer Cooperative Union, 307
Jazz It Up marinade sauces, 144
JC Imports, 639
JCPenney, 137, 146, 153, 299, 370, 401, 412, 457, 565, 573
organizational buying, 147–148
JCPMedia, 147, 148
JD Power and Associates, 211, 641
Jeep Grand Cherokee, 491
Jeep Liberty, 496
Jefferson Smurfit Corporation, 530
Jenn-Air, 412
Jenny Craig, 80

JetBlue Airlines, 342
Jetta, 656
Jewel Foodstores, 366
Jiffy Lube International, 410
Jif peanut butter, 343
Jigzone.com, 565
JobWeb, 617
John Deere, 154, 610
Johnson & Johnson, 16, 30, 122, 137,
    163, 298, 304, 342–343, 590
    promotion expenditures, 483
Johnson Carpet Company, 551
Johnson Company, 93
Johnson Controls Automotive Systems
    Group, 537
Johnson's baby shampoo, 283
Jolly Joes, 308
Jose Ole, 62
Joseph E. Banks, 653
Joy perfume, 303
Juice Club, 631
Juice It Up!, 632
Juice Stop, 632
Juniper Networks, Inc., 177
Jupiter Research, 571
Jura brand, 636
Just Born, Inc., 308

K

Kanebo, 190, 412
Karstadtquelle, 445
Kazaa, 101
Kellogg Company, 137, 152, 302, 303,
    469, 517
Kellogg's Special K, 220
Kelly, Astor & Peters Advertising,
    656, 657
Ken Davis Products, Inc., 143–145
Kettle Korn, 418
KFC, 464, 472
Kids Talbot, 653
Kimberly-Clark, 123, 177, 273, 298, 563
Kirby vacuum cleaners, 537
Kirin, 412
KitchenAid, 635–636
Kiwi Brands, 435–436
Kleenex, 15, 89, 287, 301
Kleenex diapers, 302
Klondike, 51
Kmart, 135, 364, 412, 448, 450, 578
Kodak digital cameras, 37–39
Kodak film, 37–39
Kodak self-service kiosks, 37–40
Kohler, 339
Komatsu, 179
Kraft American cheese, 299
Kraft Foods, 308, 402, 514, 591, 600
Kraft's 6 Pack, 608
Krispy Kreme, 252
Kroehler, 657
Kroger, 306, 366, 405, 407, 430, 460
Krups espresso machine, 635–636
k2, 628
Kuschelweich, 178

L

Lalique, 363
Lamar, 628
Land Rover, 312
Lands' End, 16, 35–36, 37, 50, 223, 488
    organizational buying, 166–167
Landsend.com, 454, 488
Las Vegas Hilton, 315

Lawrence Livermore National
    laboratory, 155
Lawry's, 60
Lay's Potato Chips, 396, 470
Lay's Stax potato crisps, 308
Lee jeans, 135
L'eggs, 308
LEGO Company, 179, 578
LEGO Land, 467
Lehman Brothers, 535
Lemon Lime, 144
Lender's Bagels, 302
Leo Burnett USA, 513
Lever, 85
Lever Europe, 178
Levi's jeans, 396
Levi Strauss & Company, 100, 110,
    180, 193, 402, 407, 465, 496, 509
Levitra, 499
LexisNexis, 212
Lexmark, 292
Lexus, 518
LG (Lucky Goldstar), 84
Lifetime channel, 505
Lightning, 5–6
Lillian Vernon Corporation, 452, 488
Limited, The, 463
Lipitor, 481
Lipton, 33
Liquid Paper, 292
Little Colds Saf-T-Pops, 263
Little Noses Decongestant Nose
    Drops, 263
Little Noses Saline, 648
Little Remedies, 263
Little Remedies Company, case,
    647–649
Little Tummys Gas Relief, 648–649
Little Tummys Laxative Drops,
    648–649
Liz Claiborne, 50, 110
L.L. Bean, 401, 452, 465
Lockheed Martin, 86, 149, 400
    action item list, 599
    Skunk Works, 583–584,
        598–599
Loehman's, 448
Lone Star Steel, 543
Look-Look, 216
Lord of the Rings trilogy, 204, 485
L'Oreal, 179, 194
L'Oreal USA, 610
L'Orient dinners, 239
Lorillard Tobacco Company, 496
Louis Vuitton, 171, 301
Louvre, 23
Love to Dance Bear, 208
Lowe's home centers, 108, 153, 402
Lucent Technologies, 87
Lufthansa, 153, 317, 318
Luvs, 298
Lycos Network, 215

M

MAB, 172
Mac-Gray Corporation, 239
MAC Group Inc., 456
MACH3 line of shavers, 361
Macintosh computer, 395
MacManus Group, 499
Macy's, 446, 449, 466
Macy's Home Stores, 456
Maersk, 434
Magazine Publishers of America, 499

Major League Baseball, 232, 469, 630
Mall of America, 453
    case, 466–467
Mambo, 300
M&Ms, 13, 374
Manor Furniture, case, 656–658
Mansar Products, Ltd., 399
Marimekko, 548
Marks & Spencer, 445–446, 559
Marlboro, 590
Mars Candy Company, 186, 399, 517
Marshall Field's, 449, 558, 653
Marshall's, 466
Marvel/Epic Comics, 577
Mary Kay Cosmetics, Inc., 129, 130,
    455, 547
MasterCard, 108, 181, 305
Match.com, 329
Matrix, The, 204, 518, 577
Matside, 629
Matsushita, 172, 292, 412
Mattel, Inc., 101, 110, 168, 179, 187,
    278, 306, 506, 578
    global marketing, 169
Maybelline, 193, 296
May Company, 412
Mayo Clinic, 263, 323
Mazola Corn Oil, 140
McCormick spices, 60
McDonald's, 23, 128, 135, 179, 181,
    191, 241–242, 245, 246, 250, 275,
    281, 309, 321, 327, 406, 447, 448,
    456, 461, 462, 463, 470, 516,
    521, 536
    case, 653–655
    Ronald McDonald Houses,
        109–110
McFarlane Toys, case, 577–579
MCI Communications, 86
McKesson, 413
Medtronic, Inc., 33, 35, 36, 44–45,
    53, 529
    case, 642–643
    five-year plan, 45
Mello Yello, 502, 503
Memorex, 84
Mercedes-Benz, 192, 196, 237, 454, 491
Merck & Company, 197
Merrill Lynch, 319, 329, 535
Mesquite, 144
MetLife.com, 401
Metro, 508
Metropolitan Life Insurance, 140,
    141, 531
Metropolitan Museum of Art, 23, 93
Metropolitan Opera, 318
Mezco, 579
MGA Entertainment, 306
Michelin, 127, 177, 299, 301
Micro Age, 409
Microblade XT, 5–6, 17–19, 27
MicroFridge, 239
Microsoft Corporation, 16, 72, 86, 215,
    266, 294, 301, 343, 413, 454, 510
Microsoft Excel, 354
Microsoft Office, 268
Microsoft Project, 600
Microsoft Windows, 268
Microvision, 640
Mike and Ike Treats, 308
Milk-Bone, 516

Milk 'n Cereal Bars, 594
Milk Processor Education Program,
    297, 298
Milky Way Dark, 517
Milky Way Midnight, 517
Miller Brewing Company, 591
Milsco Manufacturing, 154
Mimosin, 178
MINI Cooper, 495
Minnesota Vikings, 26
Minute Maid Squeeze-Fresh, 270
Miracle Whip, 308
Miramax, 305
Mission Foods, 60, 62
Mitsubishi, 488, 525, 630
Mizuno, 638
Modell's Sporting Goods, 262, 407, 552
Model T Ford, 633
Modern Dog, 644
Monster.com, 135, 617
Moodmatcher lip covering, 190
Moody's Investor Services, 622
Morpheus, 101
Mossimo clothing, 443
Motetronix Technology, case, 636–637
Motorola, Inc., 151–152, 179, 192, 256,
    267, 530
Mountain Dew, 518
Mouth 2 Mouth, 507
Mr. Clean, 178
Mr. Culver's Sparklers, 291
MSN, 215, 509, 570
MSN Games, 565
MSN Hotmail, 569
MSN Search, 125
MSN TV, 454
M3Power shaver, 361–363
MTV, 505
Music Boulevard, 491
MusicID, 316
Mustang, 303
MVP Sports, 552
My eBay, 562
Mysimon.com, 453
My Yahoo!, 560

N

Nabisco Company, 137, 305, 404,
    517, 551
Name Conservancy, 322
Napster, 71–72, 84, 444
National Association for Plastic
    Container Recovery, 84
National Basketball Association, 232,
    469, 485, 503, 630
National Football League, 232, 321, 630
National Geographic, 25
National Golf Foundation, 284
National Hockey League, 469, 630
National Milk Processor Promotion
    Board, 130
National Research Group, 204
National Semiconductor, 429
Nature Valley Granola Bars, 274, 283
Neighborhood Markets, 426
Neiman Marcus, 370, 413, 449,
    548, 653
Nellie Mae, 338
Nescafé, 194, 636
Nestlé Food Corporation, 12, 53, 106,
    180, 194, 298, 401, 430, 451,
    469, 514
    General Mills joint venture, 177–178,
        402, 594–595

netMarket.com, 453
Nevada Bob's, 284
NeverScratch soap, 216
New Balance, Inc., 298, 552
New Line Cinema, 485
NewProductWorkshowcase, 283
Newsweek, 343–347
Newton PDA, 270, 271
New Yorker, 137, 644
New York Giants, 25, 469
New York Times, 508, 562
Nexcare bandages, 284
Nexcare Tattoo Waterproof
    Bandages, 262
NFL Collection, 235
Nielsen Media Research, 211, 213, 214,
    228, 509
Nielsen/NetRatings, 214
Nike, Inc., 16, 110, 179, 184, 235, 262,
    263, 284, 298, 301, 302, 316, 341,
    421, 496, 502, 561, 568, 638
    competition with Reebok, 552
    in sneaker wars, 231–233
Nike DriFit glove, 284
Nike Dunks, 343
Nike iD Customized Product, 560, 561
Nike Shox NZ, 412
Niketown, 316
Niketown.com, 560
Nikon, 264
99 Cents Only Stores, 371
Nine West, 380
Nintendo, 294, 363, 372
Nippon Gakki, 412
Nissan Motor Company, 153, 187,
    192, 412
Nokia, 39, 193, 267, 302
    company background, 255–256
    market segmentation, 256–257
Nordica, 18
Nordstrom, 237, 316, 413, 449, 466
Nordstrom, Inc., case, 652–653
Nordstrom Rack, 459, 652
Nortel, 177
Northwest Airlines, 434
Northwestern Mutual Life Insurance
    Company, 535
NPD Group, 220, 232
Nuprin, 303
NutraSweet, 89

O

Obsession perfume, 303
Ocean Spray Cranberries, 308
Office Depot, 162, 413, 463, 572, 610
Office Max, 452, 590
Olay's Total Effects, 75
Old Navy, 50, 237
Olympus cameras, 196, 222
Omaha Steaks, 644
Omega watches, 134
1800flowers.com, 566
Oneida Factory Store, 459
One Sweet Whirled, 30
Online Privacy Alliance, 571
Opium perfume, 410
Oracle Corporation, 184
Oral-B CrossAction toothbrush, 215
Oral-B Laboratories, 214
Orange Citrus, 144
Orange Julius, 632
Orbitz, 335–336, 351, 357, 401, 559
Original Ken Davis Barbecue Sauce, 144

Orkin, 402
Oscar Mayer, 137
Oshman's sporting goods, 449
Otto Versand, 548
Outdoor Life Network, 505
OUT! Hey! There's A Monster In My
    Room, 272
Outward Bound, 322
Owens-Corning Fiberglass Corporation,
    89, 530

P

Palisades Toys, 579
Palm handheld, 510
PalmOne, 267, 410
Palm Pilot PDA, 271
Palm V PDA, 275
Palo Alto Research Center, 275
Pampers, 177, 298, 413, 574, 612
Panasonic, 121, 123, 142, 367, 397
Panasonic Diagonal HDTV Plasma
    Displays, 7
Pantene shampoo, 297
Papa John's International, 594, 598
Paradise Kitchens, Inc., 42, 51
    company background, 55
    marketing plan, 56–69
Paradise Ranch Country Club
    for Dogs, 645
Paragon Trade Brands, 306
Paramount Parks, 315
Passat, 656
Patagonia, 452
Payless ShoeSource, 456, 457, 465
PCjr., 303
Peapod.com, 239, 453
Pearson publishers, 397
Penguin Books, 135
Peninsula Hotel, Chicago, 644
Penske, 432
People, 139
People en Espanol, 140
Pepsi, 179, 195, 499, 516, 518
PepsiCo, 75, 132, 153, 177, 178, 192,
    275, 297, 300, 398, 406, 467, 489
    purchase of Quaker Oats, 288
Perrier, 107
Pert shampoo, 184
PETCO Animal Suppliers, 410, 411
PetroFina & Elf, 659
Pets.com, 350, 351
PetsHotels, 644
PetsMart, 411, 644
Pez Candy, Inc., 306, 307
Pfizer, 496
    promotion expenditures, 483
Philadelphia Phillies, 318, 332–333
Philip Morris, 498, 590–591
Philips Electronics, 121, 122, 123, 610
PhoCusWright, 335
Phoenix automobile model, 303
Phoenix Suns, 489
Physicians' Network, 506
Physique shampoo, 570
Pier I Imports, 548
Pillsbury Company, 19, 24, 55, 61, 252,
    581–582, 592, 594
Pillsbury Home Baked Classics, 582
Pillsbury Ready to Bake! Cookies, 582
Pinault-Printemps, 445
Ping, 638
Pinto, 303
Pitney Bowes, Inc., 153, 533

Pittsford and LaRue Advertising
    Agency, 647
Pixar, 72
Pizza Hut, 594
Planet Hollywood, 315–316
Planet Smoothie, 632
Planters peanuts, 404
PlasticsNet, 162
Plaxo, 84
Playboy, 302
Playmates, 579
PlayStation, 266, 294, 297
Pleasin' Punch, 251
Pocahontas, 204
Poland Spring, 298
Polaroid, 136
Polo, 302
Polo/Ralph Lauren, 405, 444, 445
Pond's, 489
Pontiac, 547
Poo-Chi, 208
Popular Mechanics, 134
Pork Fied Rice, 582
Porsche, 142, 303
Post-It Flag Highlighter, 276
Post-It Flag Pen, 276
Post-It Flags, 276
Post-It Notes, 262, 284
Pottery Barn, 548
PowerBook, 248, 303
Power Mac G5, 248
Pratt & Whitney, 149
Premier Control sneaker, 235
Pretty Woman, 203
Prevacid, 481
Priceline.com, 335–336, 357
Princeton Review, 329, 330
Pringles, 308, 574
Prius, 45
Procter and Gamble, 102–103, 108, 137,
    155, 157, 177, 178, 179, 184, 185,
    188, 195, 211–212, 296, 298, 305,
    308, 309, 377, 407, 413, 422, 447,
    513, 514, 543, 558, 570, 574, 590,
    591, 600, 601, 603, 611, 612
    promotion expenditures, 483
Promotion Marketing Association, 514
Propel Fitness Water, 288
ProQuest, 212
PRS Group, 188
Publisher's Clearing House, 516
Purina Dog Chow, 476–478

Q

Qantas Airways, 153
Qtips, 89
Quaker Oats, 287–288, 299, 302, 612
QuickBooks, 271
Quizno's, 448
Quris, 613
QVC, 452–453

R

Radio Disney, 470
Radio Shack, 162, 306, 410, 447
Ralcorp Holding, 306
Ralph Lauren, 302, 413
Ralston Purina, 299
Random House, 397
Rapunzel Barbie, 169
Ray-Ban, 518
Raymond Weil, 264
Rayovac, 306, 365, 502

RCA brand, 121, 410
Reader's Digest, 133, 516
RealNetworks, 72
Recording Industry of America, 71–72
Recreational Equipment, 559
Redbook, 137
Red Cross, 32
Red Herring, 499
Red Lobster, 126–127
Reebok International, 110, 111, 236,
    298, 537
    case, 552–553
    product line, 234
    segmentation strategy, 233–235
    in sneaker wars, 231–233
Reebok NFL Game Day DMX, 235
Reebok Russia, 192
Reese's Peanut Butter Puffs, 305
Reese's Pieces, 518
Reflect.com, 557, 558, 568
Renault, 655
rePlanet, 84
Restoration Hardware, 548
Revlon, 80, 370, 506, 518
Reynolds Aluminum, 343
Ricoh Company, Ltd., 408
Ride, 628
Risky Business, 518
Rite-Aid, 417
Ritz-Carlton Hotels, 316, 325
RJR Nabisco, 613
Roadrunner, 18, 27
Roadway Logistics, 431, 432
Robert Mondavi, 384–385
Rock and Roll Hall of Fame, 366
Rock Bottom Restaurants, 135
Rockport, 302
Rolex watches, 265, 370, 410
Rollerblade, 4, 7–8, 13, 15, 299
    marketing by, 26–27
    marketing program, 16–19
    product launch, 5–6
Rolling Stone, 507
Rolls-Royce, 180, 265, 363
Ronald McDonald Centre, 654
Ronald McDonald Children's
    Charities, 654
Ronald McDonald Houses, 109–110
Roomba's Robotic Floor Vac, 11, 12
Root Beer Float, 251
Rossignol, 628
Rossimoda, 172
Ross Stores, 458
Rostiks, 653
Rotisserie Grill, 462
Royal and Ancient Golf Club of St.
    Andrews, 639
Royal Mail (UK), 323
Ruffles potato chips, 123, 192, 276
Ruiz Foods, 60, 62
Runner's World, 80, 507
Russian Bistro, 653
Ryder Integrated Logistics, 436
Ryder System, Inc., 432, 436

S

S. Carter Collection, 231, 235
Saab, 402
Safeway, 156, 162, 366, 399, 430,
    460, 488
Sainsbury, 309
St. Croix Venture Partners, 53
St. Joseph Aspirin, 298
St. Louis Rams, 463

Saks Fifth Avenue, 430, 449, 456, 459, 653
Salomon, 628
Salvation Army, 322
Sam Goody, 578
Sam's Club, 417, 426, 458, 583, 659
Samsung, 121, 122, 171, 267, 367, 518
San Diego Padres, 486
San Francisco Giants, 321
San Francisco Opera, 21
San Jose Mercury News, 508
Sanrio, 578
Santitas, 305
Sanyo, 172, 303
Saturn Corporation, 79, 371, 402, 436, 444, 574, 598, 599
Saucony, 552
SBC Communications, 483
Scandinavian Airlines, 342
Schick, 411–412
Schwab.com, 401
Schwan Food Company, 399
Schweppes Tonic Water, 184
Scope mouthwash, 574
Scotch-Brite, 21, 182, 216, 284
Scotchgard, 106
Scotch tape, 284
Scripto, 309
Sears, Roebuck & Company, 36, 156, 299, 306, 310, 321, 364, 396, 397, 399, 412, 452, 459, 460, 466, 518, 574
    promotion expenditures, 483
Sears.com, 574
Segway Human Transporter, 25
Seiko, 179, 196
Seinfeld, 518
Sergio Rossi, 410
SevenCycles.com, 560, 568
7-Eleven Stores, 399, 153, 156, 316, 396, 410, 448, 456
Seventeen, 477
7-Up, 303, 591
Sharp, 292, 303
Sharper Image, 12, 401, 452, 466
Shell, 13
Sheraton Four Points hotels, 86
Sheraton Hotels, 644
Sherwin-Williams, 302, 405, 406, 435, 610
Shiseido, 179, 190, 412
Shoeless Joe, 203
ShopNBC, 452
Shops at Columbus Circle, 464
Shrek 2, 595
Siemens, 159–160, 177
Sierra Club, 642
Signature jeans, 402
Simmons Market Research Bureau, 240–242
Sing & Snore Ernie, 208
Singapore Airlines, 153
Sirius Satellite Radio, 507
Skechers USA, Inc., 214
Skiing, 499
Skippy peanut butter, 343, 370
Skippy Squeez'It, 308
Slingo.com, 565
Slowfire Classic Chunky Beef & Bean Chili, 60
Smith & Street, 236
Smithsonian, 143
Smooth and Spicy Barbecue Sauce, 144
Smoothie King, 632

Smucker's, 469, 583
Smurfer, 628
Snake Light Flexible Flashlight, 193
Snapple Beverage Corporation, 302, 432
Snelling and Snelling, Inc., 406
Snickers, 135, 499
Snowboarder, 629
Snow Master, 129
Snow Pup, 129
Snuggle fabric softener, 178
Soap Pads, 21
Sodima, 191, 607
Sonia Kashuk makeup, 443
SonicBlue, 121, 122
Sonic Cruiser, 348
Sony.com, 565
Sony Corporation, 72, 121, 122, 123, 136, 172, 173, 179, 193, 266, 268, 273, 275, 281, 294, 304, 342, 367, 397, 410, 451, 507, 510, 568
    promotion expenditures, 483
Sony PSP player, 363
Sony TV, 465
Sony Walkman, 268, 275, 342
SOS pads, 216
Sotheby's, 180
Sotheby's.com, 566
Source Perrier, 107
Southwest Airlines, 16, 342, 590
Southwestern sauce, 144
Spawn, 577
Specialized Bicycle Components, Inc., 51–52
Specialized USA, 52
Speed Channel, 505
Spider-Man 2, 203, 204
Spiegel, 223
Spin, 499
Sporting Goods Manufacturers Association, 232
Sporting Manufacturing Association, 628
Sportmart, 262
Sports Authority, 444, 445
Sports Illustrated, 477
Sports Illustrated for Kids, 136
Sportster motorcycles, 297
Sprint, 86, 122, 327
Sprite ReMix, 495
SRI Consulting Business Intelligence, 132–133
Stagg chili, 60
Stake Fastener Company, 400
Standard and Poor's *Register of Corporations,* 622
Staples, 449, 451, 499
Starbucks Coffee Company, 15, 16, 86, 316, 402, 443, 464
    company background, 113
    and Conservation International, 115
    social responsibility, 114–115
    Urban Coffee Opportunities, 114
Starcom MediaVest, 485
Starkist, 298
Star Trek: The Experience, 315, 316
State Farm Insurance, 634
STAT-USA, 212
Steak Treats for Pets, 644
Steelcase, 275
Steinway, 316
Stokely-Van Camp Company, 287
Stora Enso, 147
Stouffer's, 60
Stouffer's Lean Cuisine, 80

Streetbeam, 510
Stuart Cellars, case, 384–385
Subway, 448
Sunbird, 303
Sun Chips, 276
Sunkist, 300, 401
Sun Microsystems, 447
Sunshine Biscuits, 396
Supercenters, 426
Surf City Squeeze, 632
Sur la Table, 636
Survivor, 518
Swank Jewelry, 404
Swanson frozen dinners, 212
Swatch watches, 179, 268, 271, 370
Swingline staplers, 263
Sylvania, 153

T

Tab diet cola, 292
Taco Bell, 462, 464, 659
TAG Heuer, 363
Talbots, 653
Target Stores, 21, 59, 141, 156, 162, 169, 341, 370, 412, 417, 442, 445, 446, 447, 448, 450, 460, 495, 578
    retailing at, 443–444
Tastee Yogurt, 491
TaylorMade, 638, 639
TDK tape company, 551
Team Rollerblade Series, 18
Tecnica, 18
Teenage Research Unlimited, 216
Teen People, 507
Teledyne, 641
Terminator, 577
Terminex, 402
Territory Ahead, The, 342
Texaco, 398, 496, 506
Texas Instruments, 179, 355, 535
There, 496
Therebucks, 496
ThinkPad, 304
Thirsty Cat, 270
Thirsty Dog, 270, 271
Thomson SA, 410
3 Com, 177
3M Corporation, 21, 34, 36, 106, 108, 154, 182, 214, 216, 273, 276, 281, 290, 429, 491, 597, 606
    Greptile Grip golf glove, 284–285
    new product development, 261–262
3000, 203
Thump, Inc., 294
Thunderbird, 303, 518
Tickle Me Elmo, 208
Tide, 309, 413, 518, 611
Tidy Bowl, 303
Tidy Cat, 502, 503
Tiffany & Company, 183, 405, 456, 457, 465
Tiger Electronics, 208
Time, 236, 344, 473, 484, 507, 597
Time, Inc., 136, 140, 592
Time Warner, 592
    promotion expenditures, 483
Time Warner Cable, 592
Timex, 179
Titanic, 204
Titleist, 262, 263, 284, 502, 638
Titleist Perma-Tech, 284
TiVo, 495, 506, 521
TJ Maxx, 458, 610
Todd McFarlane's Spawn, 577

Tohmatsu, 329
Tommy Hilfiger, 21, 76
Tomra Systems, 84
Tony Hawk Underground, 496
Tony's Pizza
    marketing research, 223–226
    and research company, 228–229
Top Driver, Inc., 635
Top Gun, 518
Top Model, 507
Toro Company, 129, 373, 375–376
Toshiba America Medical System, 548–549
Tostitos, 123, 276, 306, 372, 531
Total, 659
Total Bedroom Stores, 639
Total cereal, 582
Total toothpaste, 603
Touchstone Pictures, 305
Tough Love, 203
Tower Records, 412, 578
Town Place Suites, 305
Toyota Camry, 377
Toyota Motors, 20, 45, 412, 489, 583, 614
    promotion expenditures, 483
Toyota Prius, 642
Toyota Solara, 583
Toys "R" Us, 441
Transderm Scop, 481
Transworld SNOWboarding, 629
Travelocity, 335, 357
Trevor Toys, 588
Triarc Companies, 302
True Romance, 143
TRUSTe, 571
Tryst Coffeehouse, 86
TSCentral, 535
Tupperware, 407, 573
Tylenol, 496, 590
Tylenol Cold & Flu, 130, 304
Tylenol PM, 130, 304, 590
Tyson Foods, 60

U

Ultralife lithium battery, 270
Uncle Ben's Calcium Plus rice, 299
Underwriters Laboratories, 610
Unilever, 30, 33, 40, 43, 44, 178, 298, 306, 447, 509
Union Pacific Railroad, 544
United Airlines, 434, 435, 525
United Parcel Service, 108, 322
    sales teams, 533
United Parcel Service Logistics, 432, 438
United States Golf Association, 639
United States Postal Service, 297, 322, 379, 467
United Technologies, 86, 104
United Way, 322
Universal Music Company, 412
UPM-Kymmene, Inc., 147
USA Network, 477
U.S. Bancorp Piper Jaffray, 632
U.S. Cellular, 549
U.S. Rice Millers' Association, 174
U.S. Surgical, 163

V

Vanguard Group, Inc., 615
Van Heusen Factory Store, 459
Vanity Fair, 137

Vans sneakers, 235
V-8 vegetable juice, 125
Velocity brand, 129, 130
Verizon Communications, 496, 497, 610
    promotion expenditures, 483
Verizon Wireless, 86
Veteo, Inc., 263
    case, 647–649
ViaVoice speech recognition, 268
Vicaom, 86
Vicks, 184
Victoria's Secret, 449, 489, 502, 574
Vidal Sassoon, 370, 574
Vipdesk.com, 316
Virgin Atlantic Airways, 153
Virgin Group, 521
Virgin Mobil, 525
Virtual City, 507
Visa, 305, 321, 409, 469, 470
Visa-USA, 467
Vivendi International, 349
Volkswagen, 140, 187, 192, 343,
    589, 590
    case, 655–656
Volvo, 118, 274, 506, 509
    purchasers of, 119–120
Volvo Aero, 149
Volvo of North America, 171
Vonage, 84

W

W. W. Grainger, 161
Walgreen's, 163, 417
Walking, 80
Wall Street Journal, 143, 212, 508

Walmart.com, 453, 567
Wal-Mart Stores, 15, 16, 50, 59, 169,
    177, 195, 220, 237, 262, 263, 306,
    341, 370, 402, 407, 413, 417, 425,
    427, 444, 445, 446, 447, 448, 450,
    455, 456, 457, 458, 460, 464, 465,
    470, 502, 507, 543, 558, 567, 578,
    583, 589
    supply chain, 426
Walt Disney Company, 32–33, 72, 86,
    204, 300, 302, 305, 326, 516,
    590, 610
    promotion expenditures, 483
Walt Disney Internet Group, 215
Walt Disney World Alliance
    Marketing, 469
Wanamakers's Department Store, 512
Washburn International, case, 358–359
Washington Post, 508
Water Bedroom stores, 639
Waterford crystal, 171
Webvan, 351
We channel, 505
Welch's grape jelly, 223
Wells Fargo, 444, 445
Wendy's, 218–220, 238, 241–242,
    250, 462
    target markets, 244–247
West Edmonton Mall, 459
Westinghouse, 594
Westin Hotels, 644
West Wing, 213
Weyerhaeuser, 151
Wheaties, 208, 220
Wheaties Dunk-a-Balls, 11, 12

Whirlpool Corporation, 151, 177, 180,
    187, 194, 274, 411
WhirlpoolWebWorld, 428
Whole Foods Markets, 632
W Hotels, 644
Who Wants to Be a Millionaire, 486
Wick Fowler, 60
Wild Bean Coffee, 659
Wilkinson Sword, 337
Williams-Sonoma, 548
Wilson Sporting Goods, 252, 638
Wilson Sting tennis racket, 371
Wilson tennis rackets, 465
Windex, 364
Wine.com, 566
Winnie the Pooh, 302
Wired, 25, 499
Wisk, 33
Wolf chili, 60
Woolite, 298
Worldcom, 177
WorldOpinion, 228
Worldwide Retail Exchange, 162, 164
WOW potato chips, 293
Wrigley's gum, 193, 264, 491
    in Singapore, 408

X

Xbox, 266, 294
Xerox Corporation, 13, 84, 89, 93, 108,
    162, 242, 243, 244, 253, 271, 290,
    325, 438, 530, 531, 537, 610, 613
    cross-functional team selling, 533
    Palo Alto Research Center, 275
    sales management, 527–528, 529

XM Satellite Radio, 507, 521
XSAg.com, 162
Xtreme Games, 18

Y

Yachting, 507
Yahoo!, 136, 215, 509, 560, 561, 570
Yahoo! Shopping, 570
Yamaha, 358
Yellow Pages, 149–150, 499, 508
Yoplait, 191, 592
Yoplait Light, 608
Yoplait Nouriche, 582, 594, 608
Yoplait Nouriche Light, 582, 585,
    595, 608
Yoplait Original, 608
Yoplait Trix, 608
Yoplait Ultra, 608
Yoplait Whips, 608
Yopliat USA, case, 607–609
Yves St. Laurent, 127, 410

Z

Zenith, 367
Zetrablade, 5–6, 18, 19, 27
Zippo, 310
Zip the Car Beanie Baby, 343
Zocor, 481
Zoecon Corporation, 402
Zyliss slicer, 275

SUBJECT INDEX

A

Above-, at-, or below-market pricing, 370
Accessory equipment, 266
Account executive, 611
Account management policies, 544
Achievers, 133
Action item list, 599
Adaptive selling, 537
Administered vertical marketing system, 407
Administrative expenses, 388
Adoption, 482
Advergramming, 496
Advertisers, 612
Advertising, 485, 495–514, **496**–497
  careers in, 611, 612
  case, 524–525, 646–647
  celebrity spokespersons, 502–503
  characteristics, 473
  cooperative, 519
  corrective, 90
  deceptive, 90
  by e-mail, 489
  expenditures in U.S., 504
  for growth stage, 477
  institutional, 497–498
  in introduction stage, 289
  new world of, 495–496
  nonpersonal element, 473
  objectives, 499
  paid, 473
  permission-based, 509
  placement and audience, 499
  in postpurchase stage, 480
  posttesting, 513–514
  in prepurchase stage, 479
  pretesting, 512
  product advertising, 497
  in promotional mix, 473–474
  to reach target segments, 246–248
  regulation of, 90–91
  scheduling, 511
  teaser campaigns, 135
  types of, 496–498
  virtual, 496
Advertising Age, 485, 502, 524, 618
Advertising agencies
  careers in, 612, 614
  case, 524–525, 655–656
  communications consulting firms, 521
  full-service, 512–513
  in-house, 513
  limited-service, 513
Advertising budget, 499
Advertising department, 470
Advertising media
  cost per thousand, 504
  frequency, 504
  gross rating points, 504
  Internet, 508–510
  magazines, 507
  newspapers, 507–508
  outdoor, 510
  personalized promotion, 521
  place-based media, 511
  radio, 506–507

rating, 504
reach, 504
scheduling, 511
selection, 503–504
selection criteria, 511
television, 505–506
terminology, 504
Yellow Pages, 508
Advertising message
  content, 500–502
  creating, 502–503
  fear appeals, 501
  humorous appeals, 502
  sex appeals, 501
Advertising program
  carrying out, 512–513
  creating message, 502–503
  design of messages, 500–502
  evaluating
    making needed changes, 514
    posttesting, 513–514
  identifying target audience, 498–499
  media alternatives, 505–511
  media selection, 503–504
  pretesting, 512
  scheduling, 511
  setting budget, 499
  specifying objectives, 499
Advertising Research Foundation, 499
Advocacy advertisements, 497–498
Ad Week, 113
African American buying power, 139–140
Agents, 396, 400, 404
Age segments, 232
Aging of population, 74
Aided recall test, 513
Air carriers, 434
Air freight, 434
Air freight forwarders, 434
Airline industry pricing strategies, 364–365
Airplane industry, 348
Allowances, 386
  definition, 377
  promotional, 377
  trade-in, 377
  trade promotion, 519
All-you-can-afford budgeting, 484
Alternative evaluation
  consumer purchases, 121–122
  organizational buying, 160
American household, 76–77
Americanization of fashion, 179
American Marketing Association, 619
  Careers in Marketing, 618
  Code of Ethics, 104–105
  definition of marketing, 8
  publications, 210, 331
  website, 331
American Teleservices Association, 455
Anchor stores, 459
Ancillary services, 478
Annual Catalog Awards, 452
Annual marketing plans, 587–588
Antecedent states, 125
Antitrust laws, and pricing, 379–382

Approach, 536
Art director, 611
Asian American buying power, 140–141
Asian free trade agreements, 177
Aspiration group, 136
Assimilated Asian Americans, 140
Assumptive close, 539
At-market pricing, 370
Attendant services, 411
Attitude, 131
Attitude change, 131–132
Attitude formation, 131
Attitude tests, 513
Automatic vending, 451
Automobile accidents, 278
Automobile industry
  BMW, 312–313
  case, 641–642
  excess inventory, 436
  Ford-Firestone case, 633–635
  hybrid automobiles, 291
  sport utility vehicles, 278
  supply chain, 423–424
  technology, 84
  Volkswagen case, 655–656
Automobile sales
  discrimination in, 372
  trade-in allowances, 377
  women customers, 119–120
Average revenue, 346
Awareness, 482

B

Baby boomers, 75
Backorder, 435
Back translation, 184
Backward integration, 405–406
Bait and switch pricing, 381
Balance of trade, 171
Barriers to entry, 87
Barter, 337
Basing-point pricing, 379
  legality, 381
Behavioral learning, 130
Behavioral salesforce evaluation, 547–548
Beliefs, 131
Believers, 133
Below-market pricing, 370
Benchmarking, 36
Benchmark items, 458
Benefits sought
  consumer markets, 239
  in organizational markets, 243–244
Better Business Bureau, 91
Bicycle components business, 51–52
Bicycle industry, 52
Bicycle sales, 52
Bidder's list, 160
Bidding, 265
  online auctions, 163
Billboards, 510
Blended family, 77
Blog, 569
Boston Consulting Group, 38, 40
  website, 588

Bots, 567
Brainstorming, 275
Brand assistant, 611–612
Brand awareness, 301
Brand development, 288
Brand equity, 300–301
  and brand licensing, 302
  creating, 301–302
  valuing, 302
Brand extension, 304
Brand identity, 301
Branding, 299
  consumer benefits, 300
  of services, 327
Branding strategies
  co-branding, 305
  mixed branding, 306–307
  multibranding, 304–305, 305–306
  multiproduct, 304
  private branding, 306
Brand licensing, 302
Brand loyalists, 565
Brand loyalty, 130
Brand management, 299–307
  brand equity, 300–302
  branding strategies
    co-branding, 305
    mixed branding, 306–307
    multibranding, 305–306
    multiproduct, 304–305
    private branding, 306
  brand licensing, 302
  brand personality, 300–302
  case, 312–313
  choosing brand names, 303
  Gatorade, 282–288
Brand manager, 296–297, 602, 611–612
Brand meaning, 301
Brand names, 299
  and brand equity, 300–301
  criteria for selecting, 303
  and language differences, 183–184
  number of, 303
Brand personality, 300
Brands
  consideration set, 122
  demand for, 341–342
  evaluative criteria, 121–122
  fighting, 305–306
  global, 179
  perceptual maps, 250–251
Breadth of product line, 449–450, 456
Break-even analysis, 351–353
  applications, 354–355
  case, 358–359
Break-even chart, 353, 541
Break-even point, 351
  calculating, 352–353
Bribers, 103
Bribery, 182
Brokers, 396, 404
B2B exchange, 162
B2B goods, 263
Build-to-order manufacturing, 237
Bundle pricing, 364–365
Bureau of Labor Statistics, 83, 93, 528
Burst schedule, 511

Business activities, 32–33
Business analysis, 277
Business culture
   bribes and kickbacks, 103
   economic espionage, 102–103
   ethics of competition, 102–103
   ethics of exchange, 100–102
Business Ethics magazine, 113
Business forms, 30
Business goods, 263–264
   characteristics, 265
   production goods, 265
   support goods, 265–266
Business goods and services, 400
Business marketing, 148
Business plan, 53
   compared to marketing plan, 53–54
   elements of, 53–54
   questions asked about, 54
   style suggestions, 54–55
Business portfolio analysis, 38–40
Business publications, 625
Business-to-business franchises, 447
Business-to-business marketing; *see*
      B2B exchange
Business unit, 31
Business unit level, 31
BusinessWeek, 262, 335–336, 622
Buy classes, 157
Buyer requirements
   attendant services, 411
   convenience, 410
   information, 410
   variety, 410–411
Buyer (retail), 611, 612
Buyers, 157
   lack of access to, 271
   power of, 87
Buyer-seller relationships, 155–156
Buyer turnover, 511
Buying center, 156, 158
   buying situation, 157
   composition of, 156
   importance of, 156
   roles, 157
Buying committee, 156
Buying situation, 157
   consumer markets
      benefits sought, 239
      usage rate, 239
   organizational markets, 243
   usage rate data, 240–241
   at Wendy's, 241–242
Buzz marketing, 477, 569

C

Campbell Interest and Skill Survey, 617
Canned sales presentation, 537
Capacity management, 327–328
Capital costs, 436–437
Career paths, 610
   retailing, 613
   sales, 613
Career planning publications, 625–626
Career service office, 617
Careers in marketing
   advertising, 611, 612
   career paths, 610
   diversity of, 610
   domestic international, 615
   identifying opportunities, 617–619
   information sources, 625–627
   international, 615
   job interview, 621–625

job search process, 610, 615–725
marketing research, 611, 614–615
nonprofit organizations, 611
physical distribution, 611–612
product management, 611–612
promotion, 611, 612–613
salaries, 610
sales, 611, 613–614
service organizations, 610
Careers in Marketing, 618
Car rental, 325–326
Carrying costs of services, 319
Case allowance, 519
Cash and carry wholesalers, 404
Cash cows, 38
Cash discounts, 376–377
Cash rebate, 518
Catalog Age, 452
Catalog sales, 451–452
Catalogs for online shopping, 572
Category killers, 449
Category management, 460
Category managers, 601
Causal research, 208
Cause marketing, 108–109
Caveat emptor, **101**
Cease and desist order, 90
Celebrity endorsements, 130, 502–503
Cellular phones, 267
   and distracted driving, 13
   market, 256
Census 2000, 211
Central business district, 459
Central Product Classification
      system, 151
Cereal market, 581–582
Channel captain, 413
Channel conflict, 412
   multichannel marketing, 574
   regulation of, 413–414
Channel influence, 413
Channel of communication, 471
Channel partnership, 407
Channels of distribution; *see also*
      Marketing channels
   bicycle industry, 52
   gray market, 196
Charitable contributions, 108–109
Chief marketing officer, 47
Child Protection Act, 89
Children
   consumer socialization, 136
   in family decision making, 138
Children's Online Privacy Protection
      Act, 91, 102
China, 74
   infrastructure, 185–186
   Levi Strauss in, 100
   smoking-related deaths, 98
Choiceboard, 560
Choice in online shopping, 568
Chronological résumé format, 619
Clayton Antitrust Act, 88, 90, 380, 414
Clean Airwaves Act, 502
Click-and-mortar consumers, 565
Clickstream, 371
Click-through rate, 510
Closed-end question, 218
Closing stage, 538
Co-branding, 305
Cognitive dissonance, 123
Cognitive learning, 130
Cohabitation, 76–77
Cold canvassing, 534–535

Collaborative filtering, 560
Collectibles business, 343
Combination compensation plan, 546
Combined statistical areas, 77
Commerce, websites, 563
Commercialization, 280
   complexities of, 281
   hazards, 280–281
   regional rollouts, 281
   risks and uncertainties, 281
   speed factor, 281–282
   time-to-market, 281–282
Commission, 336
Communication, 10, 470
   in advertising, 473–474
   decoding, 471–472
   in direct marketing, 475
   at Disney World, 469–470
   encoding, 471–472
   feedback, 472
   field of experience, 472
   in marketing program, 599
   noise, 472
   in online shopping, 568–570
   by packaging and labeling, 307–308
   in public relations, 474–475
   response, 472
   in retailing mix, 460
   salesforce, 549
   in sales promotion, 475
   in supply chain, 430–431
   terminology, 470–471
   web communities, 569
   websites, 563
Communication infrastructure, 186
Communications-based electronic
      interchange, 85
Communications consulting firms, 521
Community, websites, 563
Community shopping center, 459
Company, 30
Company effects of pricing, 372
Company forecast, 252
Company image, 303
Company protection law, 88
Company salespeople, 541
Company strategy, structure, and
      rivalry, 172
Comparable value comparisons, 381
Comparative advertising, 497
Comparison shopping, 465
Compensation of salesforce, 546–547
Competencies, 36
Competition, 85
   alternative forms, 85–86
   components, 86–87
      barriers to entry, 87
      existing competitors, 87
      power of suppliers and buyers, 87
      substitutes, 87
   ethics of, 102–103
   factor in marketing, 6
   global, 15–16
   golf equipment, 638–639
   inspiration for new products, 275
   intertype, 36
   laws to protect, 88
   music industry, 94–95
   predatory pricing, 381–382
   and price war, 373
   and product differentiation, 291
   reacting to, 298
   in retailing, 652–653
   trends in sneaker industry, 232–233

Competition-oriented pricing
   above-, at-, or below market, 370
   customary pricing, 370
   loss-leader pricing, 370
Competitive advantage, 36
   exploiting
      allocating resources, 584–586
      finding what works, 582–584
Competitive advantage of nations,
      171–173
   and economic espionage, 173
   key elements, 172
Competitive bids, 152, 265
Competitive effects of pricing, 373
Competitive forces, 73
Competitive institutional
      advertisements, 498
Competitive intelligence researcher, 611
Competitive markets, 342–344
Competitive parity budgeting, 483
Competitive position, 245
Competitors
   ethics of asking about, 540
   prices of, 344
Complexity of product, 478
Complex salesperson, 611
Computer technology, 548–549
Concepts, 209
Conditional bargains, 381
Conference Board, 81, 615
Conference selling, 533
Connection, websites, 562–563
Consideration set, 122
Constraints, 209
Consultative selling, 537
Consumer-based brand-equity
      pyramid, 301
Consumer behavior, 120
   African American buying power,
      139–140
   Asian American buying power,
      140–141
   automobile purchase, 119–120
   case, 143–145, 635–636
   Hispanic buying power, 140
   involvement, 124–125
   multitasking, 477
   online consumers, 564–572
   psychological influences
      learning, 130
      lifestyles, 132–133
      motivation, 126–127
      perception, 128–130
      personality, 127–128
      values, beliefs, and attitudes,
         131–132
   purchase decision process
      alternative evaluation, 121–122
      information search, 120
      postpurchase behavior, 122–123
      problem recognition, 120–121
      purchase decision, 122
   purchase decision stages, 478–480
   situational influences, 125
   sociocultural influences
      culture/subcultures, 139–141
      family, 136–138
      opinion leaders, 134
      reference groups, 136
      social class, 138–139
      word of mouth, 135–136
Consumer Bill of Rights, 101, 106
Consumer brand resonance, 302
Consumer Confidence Index, 81

Consumer ethnocentrism, 184
Consumer expectations, 81
Consumer Expenditure survey, 83
Consumer goods, 263–264
  classification of, 264–265
Consumer goods and services, 398–399
Consumer Goods Pricing Act, 380
Consumer income
  discretionary income, 83
  disposable income, 82
  gross income, 81–82
Consumer involvement
  and marketing strategy, 125
  problem solving, 124
Consumerism, 88–89
Consumer market
  demographic characteristics, 239
  geographic characteristics, 239
  psychographic characteristics, 239
  segmentation variables, 240
  segmenting
    buying situation, 239–242
    customer characteristics, 239
Consumer needs
  ability to satisfy, 10
  discovering, 10–14
  and marketing program, 16
  and new product development, 10–12
  satisfying, 14–15
  unsatisfied, 9–10
  versus wants, 12–13
**Consumer-oriented sales
    promotion, 514**
  advantages and disadvantages, 515
  contests, 516
  coupons, 514–515
  deals, 516
  loyalty programs, 517
  point-of-purchase displays, 517–518
  premiums, 516
  product placement, 518
  rebates, 518
  samples, 517
  sweepstakes, 516–517
Consumer Product Safety Act, 89
Consumer Product Safety Commission,
    89, 101
Consumer promotions, 514
Consumer protection
  government role, 12–13
  laws, 88–89
Consumer Reports, 633, 635
Consumer responsibility, 110–111
Consumers; *see also* Customer *entries;*
    Online consumers
  achievers, 133
  advertising sources, 495–496
  believers, 133
  benefits of branding, 300
  benefits of intermediaries, 397–398
  benefits of marketing, 22–24
  changes in shopping behavior, 464
  changing trends, 299
  cognitive dissonance, 123
  and digital products, 71–72
  expectations *versus* experience,
    324–325
  experiencers, 133
  focus on, 27
  global, 179–180
  hierarchy of effects, 482
  income in global marketing, 186–187
  innovators, 133
  interaction with service provider, 319

makers, 133
market environments, 558
marketing at retail, 460
and marketing channel
    management, 408
observing, 214–215
perceptions of value, 384–385
precision shopping, 464
product life cycle, 294–296
profiles of product adopters, 295
purchase of services
  assessing quality, 324–325
  complaints, 325
  customer contact, 325–326
  gap analysis, 324–325
  purchase process, 323
  relationship marketing, 325
right to accurate information, 102
right to be heard, 102
strivers, 133
survivors, 133
thinkers, 132–133
understanding, 6
utility, 23–24
value consciousness, 80
value of direct marketing, 487–488
Consumer safety, 633–635
Consumer satisfaction, 34
Consumer socialization, 136
Consumer's Union, 634
Consumer tastes, and demand
    estimation, 345
Consumer tests, 17
Consumer utilities, 444, 445
Consumption, effect of new
    products, 268
Consumption orientation change, 80
Containers, 433
Content, websites, 562
Contests, 516
Context, websites, 562
Continuous innovation, 268
Continuous schedule, 511
Contract assembly, 191
Contract manufacturing, 191
Contractual retail systems, 447–448
Contractual vertical marketing
    system, 406
Control, online shopping, 570–571
Controlling the Assault of Non-Solicited
    Pornography and Marketing Act,
    91, 489, 569
Control phase of strategic marketing
    process, 48–49
Convenience, 410
  online shopping, 567
  of supply chain, 431
Convenience goods, 264–265
Convenience stores, case, 658–660
Cookies, 570–571
Cooperation in marketing channels,
    412–413
Cooperative advertising, 519
Cooperatives, retailer-sponsored,
    406, 447
Copyright law, 88
Copyright protection, 72
Copywriter, 611
Corporate branding, 304
Corporate culture
  code of ethics, 103–104
  definition, 103
  manager/co-worker behavior,
    104–105

Corporate level, 30–31
Corporate retail chains, 446–447
Corporate vertical marketing system,
    405–406
Corporation, 30
Corrective advertising, 90
Corruption Perceptions Index, 103
Cost effective flow, 422
Cost focus strategy, 589–590
Cost justification defense, 380
Cost leadership strategy, 589
Cost of goods sold, 386–388
Cost-oriented pricing, 365–367
  cost-plus pricing, 366–368
  experience curve pricing, 368
  standard markup, 366
Cost per thousand, 504, 505
Cost-plus-fixed-fee pricing, 366
Cost-plus-percentage-of-cost
    pricing, 366
Cost-plus pricing, 366–367
Costs
  break-even analysis, 351–355
  importance of controlling, 350–351
  incremental, 584
  of inventory, 436–437
  kinds of, 350
  marginal analysis, 351, 374
  of marketing, 343
  of marketing channels, 411
  of multibranding, 306
  online shopping, 570
  in operating statement, 386–387
  of packaging and labeling, 307
  of production, 343
  of reaching segments, 245
  of single field sales call, 532
Cost trade-off, 354
Counterfeit products, 299–300
Countertrade, 170–171
Coupons, 514–515
Co-workers
  ethical behavior, 104–105
  new product ideas from, 274
Credence properties, 323
Credit cards
  for college students, 338
  versus smart cards, 463
Cross-cultural analysis, 181
Cross-docking, 426
Cross-functional conflict, 32
Cross-functional teams, 31–32, 273
Cross-functional team selling, 533
Cultural diversity
  back translation, 184
  cross-cultural analysis, 181
  cultural symbols, 182–183
  customs, 182
  ethnocentrism, 184
  language, 183–184
  nonverbal behavior, 182
  values, 181
Cultural symbols, 182–183
Culture, 78–79
  Americanization of, 179
  attitudes and roles of men and
    women, 79–80
  changing values, 80
  influence on consumer behavior,
    139–141
  as socializing force, 100
Cumulative quantity discounts, 375
Currency exchange rate, 187–188
Current Industrial Reports, 211

Current profit maximization, 340
Customary pricing, 370
Customer characteristics, organizational
    markets, 242–244
Customer contact audit, 325–326
Customer effects of pricing, 373
Customer era, 20
Customer experience, 561–563, 562
Customerization, 568
Customer needs, lack of sensitivity to,
    270–271
Customer relationship management, 20
Customer-relationship marketing, 237
Customer relationships in marketspace
  choiceboard, 560
  collaborative filtering, 560
  permission marketing, 561
  personalization, 560–561
Customer retention, 123
Customers
  asked about competitors, 540
  demand patterns, 427–428
  80/20 rule, 241
  environmental forces affecting, 72
  fast-food industry, 241–242
  knowledge of, 35–36
  lack of access to, 271
  new product ideas from, 274
  organizational buyers, 22
  perspective on new products, 268
  protected by packaging, 308
  relationship marketing, 16
  repeat purchases, 290–291
  in supply chain management, 424–425
  trial purchases, 288–289
  ultimate consumers, 22
Customer sales organization, 543
Customer sales support personnel,
    532–533
Customer satisfaction, 123
Customer service, 429
  and logistics, 422
Customer service manager, 611
Customer service standards, 431
Customer value, 15–16, 237
  case, 552–553
  creation in marketspace, 559
  and everyday low pricing, 378
  impact of technology, 84–85
  by packaging and labeling, 307–309
  through personal selling, 529–530
Customization
  choice board, 560
  mass, 236–237
  online shopping, 557
  in sneaker industry, 232
  websites, 562
Customized interaction, 473
Customs, 182
Cybershoppers, 564

D

Dairy industry
  product positioning, 250–251
  product repositioning, 251–252
Data, 210
  analysis of, 223
  versus information, 222
Databases
  for direct marketing, 488
  test-result, 486
Data collection
  concepts, 209
  methods, 209–210

sampling, 210
statistical inference, 210
Data identification, 209
Data miner, 611
Data mining, 222–233
Data warehouse, 222
Dealer, 396
Deals, 516
Deceptive advertising, 90
Deceptive Mail Prevention
Enforcement, 90
Deceptive pricing, 381
Deciders, 157
Decision, 206
evaluation of, 225
Decision maker forecasts, 252–253
Decline stage
characteristics, 292
harvesting strategy, 292
product deletion, 292
and promotion, 477–478
Decoding, 471–472
Delivery of services, 321–322
Demand
elastic, 349
inelastic, 349
in organizational buying, 151
price elasticity of, 348–349
pricing constraint, 341–342
primary, 289
selective, 289
unitary, 349
Demand conditions, 172
Demand curve, 344–345
effect on revenue, 437
movement *versus* shifts, 345–346
and revenue, 436–437
Demand elasticity, 374
Demand estimation, 344–346
Airbus Industrie, 348
Boeing Company, 348
consumer tastes, 345
income, 345
price and availability, 345
Demand factors, 345
Demand-oriented pricing
bundle pricing, 364–365
odd-even pricing, 364
penetration pricing, 363
prestige pricing, 363–364
price lining, 364
skimming pricing, 362–363
target pricing, 364
yield management pricing, 365
Demand patterns, 427–428
Demographics, 74
American household, 76–77
consumer markets, 239
generational cohorts, 75–76
of online consumers, 564–565
population shifts, 77
racial and ethnic diversity, 77–78
shifting age structure, 74
statistical areas, 77
United States population, 75
world population, 74
Department, 31
Department of Commerce, 93, 212
Department of Defense, 103
Department of Justice, 155
channel practices, 414
Department of Labor
Consumer Expenditure Survey, 83
Occupational Outlook Handbook, 618

Dependability of supply chain, 430
Depth of product line, 449
Derived demand, 151
for business goods, 265
Descriptive research, 208
Desk jobbers, 404
Developing countries, income
growth, 187
Development, 277–278
fast prototype, 282
parallel, 281–282
Deviations
acting on, 49
identifying, 48–49
Dichotomous question, 218
Differentiation focus strategy, 590
Differentiation positioning, 250
Differentiation strategy, 589
Diffusion of innovation, 294–295
Digital devices, 267
Digital entertainment, 71–72
Digital Millennium Copyright Act, 88
Digital products, 248
Direct channel, 399
Direct contact, job information, 619
Direct exporting, 190
Direct forecast, 252
Direct investment, 192
Directional medium, 508
Direct labor, 387
Direct mail, 451–452
advantages and disadvantages, 506
expenditures, 504
Direct marketing, 475, 486–489
careers in, 613
characteristics, 473
direct orders, 488
ethical issues, 488–489
expenditures and media, 487
forms of, 486–487
global issues, 488–489
growth of, 487
lead generation, 488
for maturity stage, 477
technological issues, 488–489
traffic generation, 488
value of, 487–488
Direct Marketing Association, 452, 454
Direct marketing channels, 401
Direct orders, 488
Directory of Corporate Affiliations, 622
Direct salesperson, 611
Direct selling, 455
Direct-to-consumer drug
advertising, 491
Discontinuous innovation, 268
Discounts, 457–458
cash discounts, 376–377
definition, 375
quantity discounts, 375
seasonal discounts, 375–376
trade discounts, 476
trade promotion, 519
Discount stores, 463
Discretionary income, 83
Discrimination, 371
Disintermediation, 412
Disposable income, 82
Dissociative group, 136
Distribution; *see also* Logistics
management; Marketing channels;
Supply chain management
in growth stage, 291
in introduction stage, 289

music industry, 94–95
regular, 267
of services, 329
strategies for global marketing,
194–195
Distribution centers, 435
Distribution-related legislation, 90
Distributor, 396
Diversification, 41
Diversification strategies, 590–591
Divisions, 178
Divorce rate, 76–77
Dogs, 39
Domestic international career, 615
Do Not Call Registry, 90–91, 103
Door-to-door selling, 455
Dot-com pricing, 351
Downsizing, 299
Drivers; *see* Likert scale; Marketing
drivers; Observational data;
Sales drivers
Drives, 130
Drop shippers, 404
Dual distribution, 402, 572
and law, 414
Dues, 336
Dumping, 195
Durable goods, 264
Dynamically continuous
innovation, 268
Dynamic pricing, 371, 570

E

Early adopters, 295
Early majority, 295
East Asia, effective selling in, 539
Ebivalent newbies, 565
E-commerce, percent of total
expenditures, 559
Economic Census, 211
Economic development stages, 185
Economic espionage, 102–103
Economic Espionage Act, 103, **173**
Economic forces, 73
Economic infrastructure, 185–186
Economic integration
Asian trade agreements, 177
European Union, 176–177
North American Free Trade
Agreement, 177
Economies of scale, 237
Economy, 80
consumer income, 81–83
and global marketing
currency exchange rates, 187–188
income and purchasing power,
186–187
infrastructure, 185–186
stage of development, 185
macroeconomic conditions, 80–81
sustainable development, 110
EDA; *see* Electronic data interchange
Education marketing, 645–646
Efficient consumer response, 430
Eight-second rule, 567
80/20 rule, 241, 604
Elastic demand, 349, 374
Electronic commerce, 85
Electronic data interchange, 428,
436–438
Electronic displays, 629–631
Electronic funds transfer, 436
**Electronic marketing channels,
400–401**

Electronic messaging, 437
Electronic order processing, 435–436
Electronic résumé, 619–620
E-mail
versus fax machines, 293
number of messages, 568
opt-out system, 489
spam, 569
E-marketplaces, 162–163
Embedded recall test, 513
Emotional intelligence, 545
Employees
market size and number of, 243
new product ideas from, 274
Employee welfare, 34
Employer-sponsored training, 546
Employment agencies, 618, 619
Encoding, 471–472
Endorsements, 130
in sneaker industry, 232
Enterprise resource planning, 428
Enterprise selling, 530
Entrepreneur magazine, 448
Entry, 87
Environment, marketing channel
management, 407–408
Environmental factors, 14
Environmental forces, 9, 72
case, 93–95, 628–629
competition, 85–87
economic forces, 80–83
kinds of, 73
regulation, 87–91
social forces, 74–80
technology, 83–85
Environmental issues, packaging, 309
Environmental scanning, 72
case, 631–633
global market
cultural diversity, 181–184
economic considerations, 184–188
political stability, 188
trade regulations, 188–189
information sources, 93
today's marketplace, 73
tracking trends, 72–73
Environmental trends, 72–73
Equipment-based services, 322
E-shoppers, 564
Espionage, 102–103, 173
Ethical behavior
business culture, 102–103
corporate culture and expectations,
103–105
co-workers, 104–105
current perceptions, 99
industry practices, 102–103
in marketing, 99–106
personal moral behavior, 105–106
societal culture and norms, 100
top management, 104–105
whistle-blowers, 105
Ethical duties, 106
Ethical framework, 98–99
Ethics, 20–21, 98
asking about competitors, 540
car buying discrimination, 372
cell phone use, 13
code of ethics, 103–104
compared to laws, 98
of competition, 102–103
of direct marketing, 488–489
of exchange, 100–102
Internet cookies, 571

Ethics (*continued*)
in organizational buying, 155
of protectionism, 175
retail theft, 458
student credit cards, 338
of subliminal messages, 128
Super Bowl show, 502
sustainable development, 34
and telemarketing, 91
Ethnic diversity, 77–78
African Americans, 139–140
Asian Americans, 140–141
Hispanics, 140
Ethnocentrism, 184
Ethnographic research, 215
Euro, 176
European Union
Data Protection Directive, 489
description, 176–177
trade regulations, 189
Evaluation, 482
Evaluative criteria, 121–122
Everyday fair pricing, 458
Everyday low pricing, 377, 378, 458
Exchange, 8, 10
by barter, 337
ethics of, 100–102
by money and price, 336–338
Exchange rate fluctuations, 187–188
Exclusive dealing, 90, 414
Exclusive distribution, 409–410
Exclusive territorial distributorships, 90
Exclusivity of services, 327
Expenses, decreasing, 590, 591
Expense-to -sales ratio, 389
Experience curve pricing, 367
Experience economy, 315–316
Experience properties, 323
Experiencers, 133
Experiments, 220–221
Exploratory research, 207
Exporting, 190
Exports, 171
Express companies, 434
Express warranty, 309
Extended problem solving, 124
External screening and evaluation,
276–277
External search, 120
External secondary data, 211–212
Extranets, 85, 428
Extreme-value retailers, 459

F

Facilitating function, 397, 398, 403
Factor conditions, 172
Fads, 294
Failure analysis
examples of product failures, 272
marketing reasons, 269–271
for new products, 11–12
pharmaceutical industry, 277–278
test marketing, 280
Failure fee, 281
Fair Packaging and Labeling Act, 88
Family branding, 304
Family decision making, 137–138
Family influences
consumer socialization, 136
decision making, 137–138
life cycle, 136–137
Family life cycle, 136–137
Family Talk about Drinking, 97

Fare, 336
Fashion
Americanization of, 179
merchandising, 430
Fashion product, 294
Fast-food industry survey, 241–242
Fast prototype, 282
Fax machines
versus e-mail, 293
product life cycle, 290
Fear appeals, 501
Federal Bureau of Investigation, 110
Federal Communications Commission,
128, 499
on advertising control, 502
Federal Dilution Act, 89
Federal Trade Commission, 90, 91, 102,
111, 267, 309, 455, 489
channel practices, 414
and geographical pricing, 381
Guide Concerning Use of the Word
"Free" and Similar
Representation, 380
guidelines on promotion, 521
Guides Against Deceptive Pricing, 381
on sweepstakes, 517
Federal Trade Commission Act, 90, 382
Federation of European Direct
Marketing, 489
FEDSTATS, 93
Fee, 336
Feedback, 472
Feedback loop, 472
Field of experience, 472
Fighting brands, 305–306
Finance allowances, 519
Financial risk, 478
Financial systems, 186
Firms, 30
marketing channel management,
408–409
with marketspace origins, 558
First Amendment, 91
Fixed alternative question, 218
Fixed costs, 350, 352
versus variable cost, 354
Fixed pricing, 371
Flighting schedule, 511
Floor graphics, 518
FOB buyer's location, 378
FOB origin pricing, 378, 381
FOB with freight allowed pricing,
378, 379, 381
Focus groups, 216
Follow-up, 539
Food and Drug Administration, 106,
144, 303
Food brokers, 404
Food-gasoline stations, 650–660
Food merchandising, 430
Foreign Corrupt Practices Act,
103, **182**
Forgetting rate, 511
Former price comparisons, 381
Forms of ownership, 446
contractual system, 447–448
corporate chain, 446–447
independent retailers, 446
Formula selling presentation, 536–537
Form utility, 23–24, 398
in retailing, 444, 445
Fortune, 113, 597, 618
Forward integration, 405–406
Four I's of services, 312

Four Ps of marketing, 14
for services, 327–329
Franchise fees, 448
Franchises, 447–448
Franchising, 191, 406
examples, 448
exclusive dealing, 414
tying arrangements, 414
websites, 416
Franchisor, 447
Franshisee, 447
Fraud by consumers, 110–111
Free trade agreements
Asian, 177
European Union, 176–177
North American Free Trade
Agreement, 177
trade regulations, 189
Free Trade Area of the Americas, 177
Freight absorption pricing, 379
Freight forwarders, 434
Frequency, 504, 505
Frequency marketing, 239
Frequent-flyer programs, 517
Full coverage, 592
Full-line pricing, 414
Full-line wholesalers, 403
Full-service agency, 512–513
Full-service merchant wholesalers, 403
Full-service retailers, 449
Full warranty, 310
Functional discounts, 376, 377
Functional groupings, 601
Functional level, 31
Functional résumé format, 619

G

Gantt charts, 600
Gap analysis, 324
Gatekeepers, in buying center, 157
Gender discrimination, 371
Gender role changes, 79–80
Gender segments, 232
General Agreement on Tariffs and
Trade, 175
General expenses, 388–389
Generalized life cycle, 293
General merchandise stores, 448, 449
General merchandise wholesalers, 403
Generational cohorts, 75–76
Generational marketing, 76
Generation X, 75–76
Generation Y, 76, 79, 477
Generic business strategy, 588
cost focus, 589–590
cost leadership, 589
differentiation, 589
differentiation focus, 590
Geographical groupings, 601
Geographical price adjustments
basing-point pricing, 379
FOB origin pricing, 378
uniform delivered pricing,
378–379
Geographical pricing, 381
Geographic characteristics, consumer
markets, 239
Geographic salesforce organization,
541–543
Germany, price regulation, 195
Global brand, 178
Global business units, 601
Global competition, 15–16, 177
Global consumers, 179–180

Global economy
and direct marketing, 488–489
direct selling in, 455
franchising in, 448
impact of retailing, 445–446
services component, 316
services in, 329–330
Global market-entry strategies, 189–192
direct investment, 198
exporting, 190
joint ventures, 191–192
licensing, 191
Global marketing
case, 198–199
competition in, 177–178
decline of protectionism, 174–175
economic considerations
communication infrastructure, 186
currency exchange rate, 187–188
financial system, 186
income and purchasing power,
186–187
infrastructure, 185–186
legal system, 186
stage of development, 185
economic integration
Asian trade agreements, 177
European Union, 176–177
North American Free Trade
Agreement, 177
environmental scan
cultural diversity, 181–184
economic considerations,
184–188
political stability, 188
trade regulations, 188–189
global brands, 179
global companies, 178–179
global consumer, 179–180
marketing channels, 411–412
Mattel, Inc., 169
networked marketspace, 180–181
teenagers, 179
Global marketing program
distribution straetgies, 193–195
pricing strategy, 195–196
product and promotion strategies,
193–194
Global marketing strategy, 178–179
contract assembly, 191
contract manufacturing, 191
franchising, 191
strategic alliances, 177–178
Global organizational markets, 149–150
measuring, 150–151
Global teenager, 179
Goals, 34–35
Goal setting, 44–45
Golden Raspberry Awards, 205
Golf equipment industry, 637–639
Golf market, 284–285
Good Housekeeping seal, 130
Goods; *see also* Product *entries*
business goods, 265–266
consumer goods, 264
durable, 264
marketing of, 22
nondurable, 264
unsought, 264–265
Government markets, 149
measuring, 150–151
Government regulation
advertising/promotion-related, 90–91
consumer protection, 12–13

distribution-related, 90–91
pricing-related, 88–89
product-related, 88–89
to protect competition, 88
of telemarketing, 102
Government-sponsored services, 322–323
Government units, 149
Gray market, 196
Green marketing, 108
Green products, 111
Gross Domestic Product, 81, 171
services percentage, 316, 317
small business percentage, 87
Gross income, 81–82
Gross margin, 387, 389–391, 457
Gross profit, 387
Gross rating points, 504, 505
Gross sales, 386
Growth criterion, 245
Growth stage, 290–292
and promotion, 476–477
Growth strategies
business portfolio analysis, 38–40
market-product analysis, 40–41
Guarantees, 130
Guide Concerning Use of the Word
"Free" and Similar Representation
(FTC), 380
Guides Against Deceptive Pricing
(FTC), 381

H

Harley Owners Group, 563
Harvesting strategies, 292
Head-to-head positioning, 250
Health, packaging, 309
Health concerns, 80
Hierarchy of needs, 126–127
Help-wanted ads, 618
Hierarchy of effects, 482, 499
High-involvement purchase decisions,
124–125
High-learning products, 293
Hi-Lo pricing, 378
Hispanic buying power, 140
Home offices, 549
Hooked online, single segment, 565
Horizontal conflict, 412
Horizontal price fixing, 379–380
Households
current characteristics, 76–77
family decision making, 137–138
income distribution, 81
Hunter-gatherer consumers, 565
Hybrid automobiles, 291
Hypermarkets, 450

I

Idea generation, 273–274
brainstorming, 275
competitive products, 275
co-worker suggestions, 274
customer suggestions, 274
employee suggestions, 274
research and development
breakthroughs, 275
supplier suggestions, 274
Idle production capacity, 319
Implementation of strategic marketing
process, 46–48
Implied warranty, 310
Imports, 171
Inbound telemarketing, 531, 532

Income
of consumers, 81–83
and demand, 345
Income distribution, 186–187
Income statement, 386
Inconsistency of services, 318
Incremental cost, 584
marginal analysis, 374
Incremental revenue, 584
marginal analysis, 374
Independent retailers, 446
Independent salespeople, 541
Index of Consumer Sentiment, 81
India, 74
Indirect channel, 399
Indirect exporting, 190
Individual interviews, 215–216
Individuality, 560
Industrial distributors, 400
Industrial espionage, 173
Industrial firms, 149
Industrial goods, 263–264
Industrial markets, 149
measuring, 150–151
Industrial salesperson, 611
Industrial services, 266
Industry potential, 252
Industry practices
bribes and kickbacks, 103
economic espionage, 102–103
ethics of competition, 102–103
ethics of exchange, 100–102
Industry structure, 85–86
Inelastic demand, 349
Infant Formula Act, 88
Inflation, 81
Influencers, 157
Infomercials, 506
Information
for buyers, 410
versus data, 222
in supply chain efficiency, 427–428
supply chain objective, 427–431
Information search, 120–121
organizational buying, 160
Information systems, 222
Information technology, 16, 85, 222
for direct marketing, 488–489
for marketing actions, 221–223
radio frequency identification
tags, 447
supply chain management, 427–428
Informative advertising, 497
Infrastructure, 185–186
In-house agency, 513
In-house project director, 611
In-house research staff, 614
In-line skate industry, 5–8
Innovation
diffusion of, 294–295
kinds of, 268
Innovators, 133
Input-related objectives, 540
Inquiry test, 513
Inseparability of services, 318–319
Inside order takers, 531
Installations, 265
Instant messaging, 568
Institutional advertisements, 497
advocacy, 497–498
competitive, 498
pioneering, 498
reminder, 498

Intangibility of services, 264, 317–318
**Integrated marketing
communication, 470**
case, 492–493
channel strategies
pull strategy, 481
push strategy, 480
at Disney World, 469–470
product characteristics, 478
product life cycle, 476–478
stages of buying decisions,
478–480
target audience, 476
Integrated marketing communication
program
executing and evaluating, 485–486
identifying target audience, 482
promotional tools, 484–485
promotion budget, 483–484
scheduling promotion, 485
specifying objectives, 482
test-result databases, 486
Integrated retail channels, 463
Intellectual property, 100
Intelligent agent software, 465
Intensive distribution, 409
Interactive marketing, 560
case, 577–579
consumer profile, 564–565
cookies, 570–571
creating customer value, 558–559
customer experience, 561–563
customer relationships, 560–561
dynamic pricing, 570
kinds of purchases, 565–567
reasons for using, 567–571
at Reflect.com, 557
times and sites, 571–572
tracking trends, 576
Interactivity, 560
Interest, 482
Intermediaries
agents, 400
backward integration, 405–406
brokers, 404
consumer benefits, 397–398
definition, 396–397
electronic, 401
facilitating function, 397, 398
forward integration, 405–406
industrial distributors, 400
logistical function, 397, 398
manufacturer's agents, 404
manufacturer's branch offices,
404–405
merchant wholesalers, 403–404
minimizing transactions, 397
profitability, 411
satisfying buyer requirements,
410–411
selling agents, 404
target market coverage, 409–410
transactional function, 397, 398
value created by, 397–398
wholesaling activities, 402–403
Intermittent schedule, 511
Intermodal transportation, 433
Internal marketing, 327
Internal screening and evaluation, 276
Internal search, 120
Internal secondary data, 211
International Anti-Dumping and Fair
Competition Act, 182
International firms, 178

International Franchise Association,
416, 447–448
International marketing
careers, 614
case, 638–639, 642–643, 653–654
International personal selling, 536
International Standard Industrial
Classification for All Economic
Activities, 150
International Standards Organization,
108, 154
International trade, 149–150
balance of trade, 171
competitive advantage, 171–173
and countertrade, 170–171
decline of protectionism, 174–175
dollar value, 170
dumping, 195
exporting, 190
exports and imports, 171
flows
global perspective, 170–171
United States perspective, 171
regulations, 188–189
in services, 316
and World Trade Organization, 175
Internet
choice board, 560
collaborative filtering, 560
communication hazards, 569
cookies, 570–571
data on user behavior, 214, 215
direct marketing on, 487
direct-to-consumer marketing, 491
individuality, 560
instant messaging, 568
interactivity, 560
marketing channel opportunities,
407–408
for marketing research, 212
marketspace, 557
multichannel marketing, 572–575
networked global marketspace,
180–181
number of e-mails, 568
online auctions, 163–164
online newspapers, 508
online organizational buying, 161–164
online retailing, 453–454
portals, 570
privacy/security issues, 571
for salesforce communication, 549
search engines, 570
use by mothers, 566
website design elements, 562–563
and word of mouth, 136
Internet access in United States, 564
Internet advertising, 508–510
advantages and disadvantages, 506
click-through rate, 510
disadvantages, 509
expenditures, 504
options, 509
viability, 510
Internet cafés, 454
Internet marketing, 16; *see also*
Marketspace; Online *entries*
by Lands' End, 36–37
Internet marketing manager, 611
Internet privacy, 101
Intertype competition, 36, 450
Interviews
individual, 215–216
mall intercept, 217
by telephone, 217

Intranet, 85, 549
Introduction stage, 288–290
  and promotion, 476
Inventory, 387
  carrying costs, 319
  costs of, 436–437
  reasons for carrying, 436
  of services, 319
  stockturn rate, 392–393
Inventory control manager, 611
Inventory levels, 428–429
Inventory management
  case, 440–441
  costs involved, 436–437
  just-in-time systems, 155, 437
  reasons for inventory, 436
  vendor-managed, 437–438
Inventory service costs, 437
Inventory systems
  efficient consumer response, 430
  quick response, 430
Investment, 393
Involvement, 124
ISO 9000 standards, 154, 189
ISO 14000 standards, 108

J

Japan
  exporting to, 190
  keiretsu, 412
Job analysis, 545
Job Choices, 617
Job interview, 621–625
  follow-up, 624–625
  handling rejection, 625
  preparation for, 622–623
  questions, 622–623
  role playing, 622–623
  succeeding in, 623–624
Job postings, 617
Job-related tests, 616–617
Job search process, 610
  job interviews, 621–625
  job opportunities, 617–619
  résumé writing, 619–621
  self-assessment, 615–617
Joint operating agreement, 508
Joint venture, 191–192
Journal of Marketing, 210
Journal of Marketing Research, 210
Jury tests, 512
Just-in-time systems, 155, 437

K

Keiretsu, 412
Kelley Blue Book, 337
Key account management, 543
Kickbacks, 103, 182
Knowledgeable groups, forecasts by, 253

L

Label, 307
Labeling
  annual costs, 307
  communication benefits, 307–308
  for customer value, 307–309
  functional benefits, 308
  perceptual benefits, 308–309
  regulation, 88
Laboratory test markets, 279–280
Laggards, 295
La Guardia Airport, 511
Language differences, 183–184

Lanham Act, 89, 299
Late majority, 295
Laws, 98
  deceptive pricing, 381
  dual distribution, 414
  geographic pricing, 381
  marketing channels, 413–414
  predatory pricing, 381–382
  price discrimination, 380–381
  price fixing, 379–380
  vertical integration, 414
Lead, 534
Lead generation, 488
Lead time, 430
Learning, 130
  behavioral, 130
  and brand loyalty, 130
  cognitive, 130
Learning effect, 367
Legal framework, 98–99
Legality of new products, 267
Legal restrictions, 303
Legal systems, 186
Less-than-truckload shipments, 434
Levels of service, 446, 448–449
Library job research, 618
Licensing, 191
Life-cycle analysis, 309
Lifestyle, 132–133
Lifestyle segmentation, 239–242
  online consumers, 565
Lifestyle segments, 233
Likert scale, 219
Limited-coverage warranty, 309–310
Limited-line stores, 449
Limited-line wholesalers, 403–404
Limited problem solving, 124
Limited-service agency, 513
Limited-service retailers, 448
Limited-service wholesalers, 404
Linear trend extrapolation, 253
Line extensions, 304
Line positions, 600–601
List price; *see* Quoted price
Litigation, Ford Explorer suits, 634–635
Logistics, 422
  automobile marketing, 424
  reverse logistics, 438
  total logistics cost, 428–429
Logistics functions, 397, 398, 403
  inventory management, 436–438
  materials handling, 434–435
  order processing, 435–436
  third-party providers, 432–438
  transportation, 432–434
  warehousing, 434–435
Logistics management, 422
  case, 440–441
  customer service, 429
  at Nike, 421
  supply chain objective, 427–431
Logotype/logo, 299
Long-range marketing plans, 587
Long-run profit, 340
Lost-horse forecast, 252–253
Lost-leader pricing, 370
Low-involvement purchase decisions, 124–125
Low-learning products, 293–294
Loyalty programs, 517

M

Machine vision systems, 159–161
Macroeconomic conditions, 80–81

Macromarketing, 21
Madrid Protocol, 89
Magazine advertising
  advantages and disadvantages, 506
  costs, 507
  expenditures, 504
  specialization, 507
Magnusson-Moss Warranty/FTC
  Improvement Act, 310
Mail surveys, 217
Maintained markup, 458
Major account management, 543
Make-buy decision, 160
Makers, 133
Malcolm Baldrige National Quality
  Award, 547
Mall intercept interviews, 217
Management by exception, 602
Managing for long-run profit, 340
Manufacturers
  build-to-order, 237
  contract assembly, 191
  contract manufacturing, 191
  coupon use by, 515
  economies of scale, 237
  ISO 9000 standards, 154
  machine vision systems, 159–161
  offshore facilities, 110
  organizational buyers, 148
  organizational structure, 47
  outsourcing logistics functions, 432
  and relationship marketing, 16
  and slotting allowances, 102
  target pricing, 364
  trade promotions, 519–520
Manufacturer's agents, 404
Manufacturer's branch office, 404–405
Manufacturer-sponsored retail
  franchise, 406
Manufacturer-sponsored wholesale
  systems, 406
Manufacturer's representatives, 404
Manufacturer's sales office, 404–405
Manufacturer's suggested retail
  price, 380
Marginal analysis, 351–352
  for costs and revenues, 374
  and profit maximization, 352
Marginal cost, 350, 351, 374
Marginal revenue, 346, 351, 374, 437
Marginal revenue equals marginal
  cost, 352
Maricopa County Medical
  Association, 98
Markdown, 391, 457–458
Market(s), 13
  estimating size of, 244, 245
  identifying, 273
  in organizational buying, 152
Market attractiveness, 270
Market-based groupings, 601
Market challengers, 125
Market development, 40
Market development strategy, 590
Market environments, 557
Marketer-dominated information
  sources, 121
Market growth rates, 38
Marketing, 7–10, **8**
  benefits of, 22–24
  breadth and depth of, 21–24
  buyers and users, 22
  and competition, 6
  costs of, 343

direct marketing, 486–489
discovering consumer needs, 10–14
ethical behavior
  business culture, 100–103
  corporate culture and expectations,
    103–105
  industry practices, 100–103
  personal moral philosophy,
    105–106
  societal culture and norms, 100
ethical/legal framework, 98–99
ethics, 21
evolution of
  customer era, 20
  marketing concept era, 20
  production era, 19, 20
  sales era, 19, 20
financial aspects
  markdown, 391
  markup, 389–391
  operating ratios, 389
  operating statement, 386–389
  ratios for setting prices, 389–393
  return on investment, 393
  stockturn rate, 392–393
four Ps of, 14
frequency marketing, 239
generational, 76
of goods and services, 22
by Hermitage Museum, 23
multichannel, 572–575
multicultural, 78
multidomestic, 637–639
music industry, 94–95
new product failures, 11–12
for organizational buyers, 22
periodicals related to, 626
prestige-niche strategy, 358
providing accurate information, 102
requirements for
  communication, 10
  exchange, 10
  satisfying needs, 10
  unsatisfied needs, 9–10
role of personal selling, 529
by Rollerblade, 6–8
satisfying consumer needs, 14–15
social responsibility, 21, 107–111
sports events, 321
in two environments, 557
for ultimate consumers, 22
utility created by, 23–24
Marketing actions/activities, 598–599
  in control phase, 603
  data for, 209–210
  evaluating results, 225–226
  factors affecting, 8–19
  identifying, 208–209
  implementing, 225
  information technology for,
    221–223
  making recommendations, 225
  in market segmentation, 233–234
  measures of success, 208–209
  persons and organizations in, 21–22
  from product classification, 264
  regional, 78
Marketing channel management
  company factors, 408–409
  consumer factors, 408
  environmental factors, 407–408
  factors affecting choice, 408
  product factors, 408
  regulatory factors, 408

Marketing channels, 396–397; *see also*
Logistics management; Supply
chain management
Apple Computer, 395, 411
business goods and services, 400
case, 417–419
channel captain, 413
channel conflict, 412
channel influence, 413
consumer goods and services, 398–399
cooperation, 412–413
design considerations
profitability, 411
satisfying buyer requirements,
410–411
target market coverage, 409–410
direct, 401, 499
disintermediation, 412
electronic, 400–401
exclusive distribution, 409–410
functions of intermediaries, 396–398
global dimensions, 411–412
in global marketing, 194–195
indirect, 499
intensive distribution, 409
in Japan, 412
kinds of intermediaries, 402–405
legal considerations, 413–414
multiple, 402
and personal selling, 477
selective distribution, 410
strategic channel alliances, 402
terminology, 396
vertical marketing systems, 405–407
Marketing channel strategy
pull strategy, 481
push strategy, 480
Marketing concept, 20
societal, 21
Marketing concept era, 20
Marketing control process
measuring results, 603
taking actions, 603
Marketing department, 9
and cross-functional teams, 31–32
environmental factors, 14–15
and four Ps of marketing, 14
function, 14
Marketing drivers, 220
Marketing environment
competitive forces
barriers to entry, 87
components of competition, 86–87
existing competitors, 87
forms of competition, 85–86
power of suppliers and buyers, 87
small business, 87
substitutes, 87
economic forces
consumer income, 81–83
macroeconomic conditions, 80–81
regulatory forces
advertising-related laws, 90–91
distribution-related laws, 90
price-related laws, 89–90
promotion-related laws, 90–91
and self-regulation, 91
social forces
culture, 78–80
demographics, 74–78
technological forces
electronic business technologies, 85
impact on consumer value, 84–85
technology of tomorrow, 83–84

today's marketplace, 73
tracking trends, 72–73
Marketing expert test, 7
Marketing information systems, case,
629–640
Marketing management
case, 631
for services
branding, 327
capacity management, 327–328
case, 332–333
distribution, 329
exclusivity, 327
internal marketing, 327
off-peak pricing, 328
price, 328
promotion, 329
Marketing managers, 611
break-even analysis, 352–355
controlling costs, 350–351
information technology use, 221–223
management by exception, 602
marginal analysis, 351–352, 374
role of, 602
view of sales drivers, 221–222
Marketing mix, 14
case, 628–629
elements of, 45–46
in introduction stage, 289–290
organizational buying, 152
poor execution, 270
price in, 339–340
for services, 327–329
Marketing News, 618
Marketing organization
category managers, 601
chart, 602
designing, 47
functional groupings, 601
geographical groupings, 601
line and staff positions, 600–601
market-based groupings, 601
product-line groupings, 601
Marketing plan, 42, 53–54
achievable goals, 593
annual, 587–588
clear and specific, 594
compared to business plan, 53–54
controllable and flexible, 594
elements of, 53, 54
feasible, 594
guidelines, 593–594
long-range, 587
at Medtronic, 45–46
for Paradise Kitchens, Inc., 55–69
questions asked about, 54
steps, 42–46
style suggestions, 54–55
valid assumptions, 593
Marketing planning
finding what works, 582–584
problem areas, 594
sales response function, 584–586
value-based, 595–596
Marketing planning framework
generic business strategy, 589–590
guidelines, 593–594
market-product synergies, 592–593
problems, 594
profit enhancement options, 590–591
Marketing planning process, 587
Marketing program, 15–19, **16**
case, 51–52
components, 45–46

customer tastes, 17
customer value, 15–16
executing, 48
focus of, 17–18
global marketing, 15–16
improving implementation
action item list, 599–600
communicating goals, 598
open communication, 599
product/program champion, 598
rewarding success, 598
scheduling, 599–600
taking action, 598–599
planning gap, 49
relationship marketing, 16
at Rollerblade, 16–19
technology strengths, 18
worldwide, 193–196
Marketing publications, 625
Marketing research, 205–206
action recommendations, 225
base business practices
operational execution, 583
organizational structure, 583–584
performance-oriented culture, 583
strategy, 583
careers in, 611, 614–615
case, 228–229
causal, 208
for decision making, 206
descriptive, 208
developing findings
data analysis, 223
presenting findings, 223–225
difficulty in, 206
evaluating results, 225–226
experiments, 220
exploratory, 207
implementing, 225
and information technology, 221–223
for movies, 204–205
observational data, 213–215
online, 614
online databases, 212
panels, 220–221
plan development
collecting data, 209–210
constraints, 209
identifying data, 209
primary data, 213–221
problem definition
identifying possible actions,
208–209
measures of success, 208–209
setting objectives, 207–208
questionnaire data, 215–221
role of, 205–206
secondary data, 210–212
Marketing research consulting firms, 614
Marketing research organization,
211–212
case, 228–229
Marketing research plan
constraints, 209
data collection, 209–210
data identification, 209
Marketing resources allocation
maximizing incremental revenue, 584
numerical example, 584–585
in practice, 585
share points, 585
and strategic marketing process,
585–586
Marketing schedule, 47–48

Marketing strategy, 48; *see also*
Strategic marketing process
allocating resources, 584–586
in buying centers, 157
case, 607–609, 644–645
and consumer involvement, 125
at Dell Computer, 425–426
differentiation, 41
diversification, 590–591
finding what works, 582–584
focused, 583
at General Mills, 581–582
global, 178–179
market development, 40, 590
market penetration, 40, 590
multidomestic, 178
product development, 40–41, 590
product differentiation, 233
sneaker companies, 235
and supply chain management,
424–425
at 3M Corporation, 260–262
value-driven, 596
at Wal-Mart, 426
Marketing synergy, 248–249
Marketing tactics, 48
Market leaders, 125
Market modification, 297
creating new use situation, 298
finding new users, 297
increasing product use, 297–298
Market orientation, 20
Market penetration, 40
Market penetration strategy, 590
Marketplace, 557
Market potential, 252
Market-product analysis, 40–41
Market-product focus, 44–45
Market-product grid, 234–235, 591–592
developing, 244–245
Market-product specialization, 592
Market-product synergies, 248–249,
691–693
Market segmentation, 44–45, **233**
case, 255–257, 641–642
executing marketing program, 233
grouping buyers into segments,
238–244
grouping products into categories, 244
identifying needs, 233
linking needs to actions, 233–234
marketing actions, 246–248
market-product grid, 234–235, 244
market-product synergies, 248–249
market size estimation, 244
mass customization, 237
meaning of, 233
multiple products/multiple segments,
236–237
reasons for, 233–237
Reebok strategy, 234
selecting target markets, 244–246
single product/multiple segments, 236
situations for, 235–237
strategy at Apple Computer,
247–248, 248
strategy at Wendy's, 246–247
synergy, 237
variables for consumer markets,
239, 240
Market segments, 233
advertising to reach, 246–247
buying situation, 239–242
case, 26–27, 358–359, 630, 653–654

Market segments (*continued*)
consumer markets, 239–242
criteria for forming, 238–239
of global companies, 180
lifestyle segments, 233
mass customization, 237
multiple
with multiple products, 236–237
with one product, 236
organizational markets, 242–244
potential buyers, 238–244
sneaker industry, 232–237
synergy, 237
at Wendy's, 242
Market share, 34
pricing objective, 341
relative, 38
share points, 585
Market size criterion, 245
Marketspace, 85; *see also* Online
entries
choiceboard, 560
collaborative filtering, 560
customer value creation, 559
customer relationships, 560–561
definition, 558
individuality and interactivity,
560–561
number of shoppers, 558
online consumers, 567–571
kinds of purchases, 565–567
lifestyle segmentation, 565
profile of, 564–565
online customer experience, 561–563
personalization, 560–561
reasons for online shopping, 567–571
revenues, 558
times and sites, 571–572
Market specialization, 592
Market structure, 85–86
monopolistic competition, 344
oligopoly, 343
pure competition, 344
pure monopoly, 342–343
Market testing, 279
failure, 280
preliminary, 276–277
simulated test marketing, 279–280
test marketing, 279
Markup, 389–391
maintained, 458
original, 458
Mass customization, 236–237
Mass selling, 472
Matching-competition budgeting, 483
Materials handling, 434–435
Matrix organization, 601
Maturity stage, 292
and promotion, 477
Maximizing current profit, 340
Measures of success, 208
Media; *see* Advertising media
Media buyer, 611
Media company careers, 612
Meet-the-competition defense, 380
Membership group, 136
Men
changing attitudes and goals, 79–80
in family decision making, 137–138
Merchandise allowances, 519
Merchandise line, 446
breadth of, 449–450
depth of, 449
scrambled merchandising, 449–450

Merchandise management, 612
Merchandise offering, 460
Merchandise trade, world value, 316
Merchant wholesalers, 403
functions, 403
kinds of, 403–404
Message, 470; *see also* Advertising
message
Methods, 209
Metropolitan statistical area, 77
Micromarketing, 21
Micropolitan statistical area, 77
Microsales analysis, 603
Middlemen, 396
Millennials, 76
Minority, 75
Minority-owned firms, 153
Mission, 33
Missionary salespeople, 532
Mission statements
Ben and Jerry's, 29
communicating, 33
comparison of, 51
definition, 33
examples, 33
Starbucks, 114
Mixed branding, 306–307
Mobile phones, 267
Modified rebuy, 157
Money income, 80
Monopolistic competition, 86, 344
Monopoly, 86, 342–343
Moral idealism, 105–106
Motivation, 126–127
in lifestyle analysis, 132–133
of salesforce, 546–547
Motor carriers, 433–434
Movement along a demand curve,
345–346
Movie industry, 203–205
costs of production, 203–204
market segmentation by, 237
product placement, 518
profits, 340
promotion scheduling, 485
MP3-capable CD players, 121
Multibranding, 305–306
Multichannel marketing, 572
case, 657–658
channel conflict, 574
characteristics, 572
impact on retail sales, 575
implementing
promotional websites, 574–575
transactional websites,
573–574
leveraging multiple channels, 572
multiplier, 573
Multichannel retailers, 463, 572
Multicultural marketing, 78
**Multidomestic marketing strategy,
178,** 637–639
Multimarket firm, 30–31
Multinational corporations, 178
Multiple marketing channels, 402
Multiple-zone pricing, 378, 379
Multiproduct branding, 304–305
Multiproduct firm, 30–31
Multiracials, 77–78
Multitasking, 477
Music downloading, 101
Music industry, 93–95
Myers-Briggs Type Indicator, 617
Mystery shopper, 214

N
National Aeronautics and Space
Administration, 366
National Association of Colleges and
Employers, 617
National Bureau of Economic
Research, 372
National character, 127
National Do Not Call Registry, 90–91,
103, 455, 535
National Highway Traffic Safety
Administration, 520, 634
National TV ratings, 213–214
Needs
ability to satisfy, 19
hierarchy of, 126–127
unsatisfied, 9–10
Need-satisfaction presentation, 537
Netizens, 564
Net sales, 386
Networked global marketspace, 180–181
Networking, 618–619
Network technologies, 85
New buy, 157
New market, 298
New-product concept, 209
New product process, 40–41, 272
at Apple Computer, 248
business analysis, 277
case, 284–285, 636–637, 642–643
commercialization, 280–282
and consumer needs, 10–12
cross-functional teams, 31–32
development stage, 277–278
fast prototype, 282
idea generation, 273–275
at IDEO, 275
incomplete definition, 270
marketing information methods, 280
market testing, 279–280
parallel development, 281–282
prototype, 277
quality assurance, 273
screening and evaluation, 275–277
services, 264
strategy development, 272–273
at 3M Corporation, 260–262
at Volvo, 274
New products
continuous innovation, 268
discontinuous innovation, 268
dynamically continuous
innovation, 268
examples of failure, 11–12, 272
extent of failure, 11
factors affecting success rate, 269
newness
company perspective, 267–268
customer perspective, 268
versus existing products, 267
in legal terms, 267
overcoming resistance to, 296
product positioning, 249–252
reasons for success or failure, 268–271
simplifying, 271
**New product strategy development,
272**–273
cross-functional teams, 273
identifying markets, 273
Six Sigma process, 273
News conference, 520
Newspaper advertising
advantages and disadvantages, 506
expenditures, 504

joint operating agreement, 508
local-national appeal, 507–508
trends, 508
News release, 520
Newsweek, 344–347
New use situation, 298
New York City Metropolitan
Transportation Authority, 510
Niche markets, 75
Noise, 472
Nonassimilated Asian Americans, 140
Noncumulative quantity discounts, 375
Nondurable goods, 264
Nonpersonal advertising, 473
Nonprobability sampling, 210
Nonprofit organizations, 30
careers in, 611
segmentation by, 233
services by, 322, 323
Nonselling duties, 613
Nonstore retailing, 450–455
automatic vending, 451
catalogs, 451–452
direct mail, 451–452
direct selling, 455
forms of, 451
online, 453–454
telemarketing, 454–455
television home shopping, 452–453
Nonverbal behavior, 182
Norms, 100
North American Free Trade
Agreement, 150
description, 177
**North American Industry
Classification System, 150**–151,
165, 211
and market segments, 242
North American Product Classification
System, 151, 211
Not-invented-here syndrome, 599
Nutritional Labeling and Education
Act, 88

O
Objective and task budgeting, 484
Objectives, 34–35
of advertising, 499
compatibility with target
segment, 245
handling, 537–538
of marketing research, 207–209
of new product strategy
development, 273
of organizational buying, 152–153
of promotion, 482
of sales management, 540
Observational data, 213
ethnographic research, 215
Likert scale, 219
mystery shopper, 214
panels and experiments, 220–221
television ratings, 213–214
unusual methods, 216
watching consumers, 214–215
Occupational Outlook Handbook, 618
Odd-even pricing, 364
Off-peak pricing, 328
Off-price retailing, 458–459
Offshore manufacturing facilities, 110
Oligopoly, 86, 343
Olympic Games, 484
Olympics, 321
Online advertising, 508–510

Online auctions, 163–164
Online career and employment services, 617–618
Online consumers, 564
  lifestyle segmentation, 565
  multichannel marketing to, 572–575
  privacy/security issues, 571
  profiling, 564–565
  purchases by, 565–567
  reasons for shopping
    choice, 568
    communication, 568 570
    control, 570–571
    convenience, 567
    cost, 570
    customerization, 568
    customization, 568
    times and sales, 571–572
Online customer experience, 561–563
Online databases, 212
Online marketing; *see also* Marketspace
  number of shoppers, 558
  percent of total expenditures, 559
  at Reflect.com, 557
  retailing, 453–454
  sales revenue, 558
Online marketing research, 614
Online music, 71
Online newspapers, 508
Online organizational buying
  auctions, 163–164
  e-marketplaces, 162–163
  prominence of, 161–162
Online shopper's clickstream, 371
On-the-job training, 546
Open-ended question, 218
Operating statement, 369, 389
  cost elements, 386–389
  definition, 386
  example, 387
  operating ratios, 389
  profit element, 389
  sales elements, 386
Operational execution, 583
Operations manager, 611
Opinion leaders, 134
Opportunities, 43–44
Opt-in, 561
Opt-out-e-mail system, 489
Order clerks, 531
Order cycle time, 430
Order getter, 531–532
Order processing, 435–436
Orders, in organizational buying, 151–152
Order takers, 531
Organizational buyers, 22, 148
  global markets, 149–150
  government markets, 149
  industrial markets, 149
  reseller markets, 149
  service market, 149
Organizational buying
  bidding list, 160
  buyer-seller relationships, 155–156
  buying center, 156–158
  buying process characteristics, 152
  case, 166–167
  criteria, 153–155, 160
  demand characteristics, 151
  ethics, 155
  by Harley-Davidson, 154
  ISO 9000 standards, 154
  at JCPenney, 147–148

market characteristics, 152
marketing mix, 152
from minority/women-owned firms, 153
number of potential buyers, 152
objectives, 152–153
product/services, 152
reciprocity, 155
reverse marketing, 154
size of order and purchase, 151–152
supply partnerships, 155–156
Organizational buying behavior, 158
  alternative evaluation, 160
  information search, 160
  make-buy decision, 160
  postpurchase behavior, 161
  problem recognition, 159–160
  purchase decision, 161
  value analysis, 160
Organizational buying criteria, 153–155
Organizational buying process, 158–161
Organizational culture, 33
Organizational goods, 263–264
Organizational marketing
  cost-plus pricing, 366–367
  marketing channels, 400
  trade promotions, 519–520
Organizational markets
  benefits sought, 243–244
  business marketing, 148
  buying situation, 243
  demographic characteristics
    NAICS code, 242
    number of employees, 243
  geographic characteristics, 242
  global, 149–150
  government, 149
  industrial, 149
  nature and size of, 148–150
  online buying, 161–164
  organizational buyers, 148
  production goods, 265
  reseller, 149
  segmentation variables, 243
  support goods, 265–266
Organizational structure, 47
  flat and flexible, 583–584
  matrix organization, 601
Organizations
  benchmarking, 36
  business activities, 32–33
  business portfolio analysis, 38–40
  business unit level, 31
  competencies, 36
  competitive advantage, 36
  corporate level, 30–31
  cross-functional teams, 31–32
  customer relationship management, 20
  departments, 31
  environmental forces affecting, 72
  ethics, 20–21
  functional level, 31
  global companies, 178–179
  global competition, 177–178
  global marketing strategies, 189–192
  goals and objectives, 34–35
  knowledge of competitors, 36–37
  knowledge of customers, 35–36
  losses to counterfeiting, 300
  market orientation, 20
  market-product analysis, 40–41
  mission, 33

mission and objectives, 8–19
perspective on new products, 267–268
profit responsibility, 107
profit *versus* nonprofit, 30
reasons for market segmentation, 233–237
relationship marketing, 16
social audit, 109–110
social responsibility, 20–21
societal responsibility, 108–109
stakeholder responsibility, 107–108
stakeholders, 33
strategic alliances, 177–178
strategic business units, 30–31
Original equipment manufacturers, 159
Original markup, 458
Orlando Transportation Authority, 510
Outdoor advertising
  advantages and disadvantages, 506
  expenditures, 504
  types of, 510
Outlet stores, 459
Out-of-home television viewing, 505
Output-related objectives, 540
Output reports, 586
Outside order takers, 531

P

Packaging, 84–85, 307
  adult chocolate milk, 252
  annual costs, 307
  communication benefits, 307–308
  convenience of, 308
  customer protection, 308
  for customer value, 306, 307–309
  downsizing, 299
  environmental sensitivity, 309
  functional benefits, 308
  global trends, 309
  health and safety concerns, 309
  life-cycle analysis, 309
  perceptual benefits, 308–309
  regulation, 88
Paid advertising, 473
Panels, 220–221
Parallel development, 281–282
Parallel importing, 196
Parenting Community, 563
Partnership for a Drug-Free America, 501
Partnership selling, 529–530
Patent law, 88
Payoffs, 182
Penetration pricing, 290, 363
Penturbia, 77
People meter, 213–214
Per capita income, 74
Perceived risk, 129–130
Percentage of sales budgeting, 483
Perception, 128
  selective, 128–129
  subliminal, 129
Perceptual maps, 250–251
Performance contracts, 519
Performance-oriented culture, 583
Permission-based advertising, 509
Permission marketing, 561
Per se illegal, 90, 381–382
Personal influences
  opinion leaders, 134
  word of mouth, 134–135
Personal information sources, 120
Personal interviews, 217
Personality, 127–128
Personality tests, 616–617

Personality traits, 127–128
Personalization, 560–561
Personalization software, 496
Personal job contacts, 618–619
Personal moral philosophy
  moral idealism, 105–106
  utilitarianism, 106
Personal needs, 127
Personal selling, 474, 485, 528
  case, 552–553
  characteristics, 473
  conference selling, 533
  cross-functional teams, 533
  customer sales support, 532–533
  customized interaction, 472–473
  in East Asia, 539
  forms, 530–533
  international, 536
  in marketing, 529
  marketing channel, 477
  missionary salespeople, 532
  order getters, 531–532
  order takers, 531
  partnership selling, 529–530
  in postpurchase stage, 480
  in purchase stage, 479
  relationship selling, 529–530
  sales management quiz, 528
  sales opener, 532
  scope of, 528–529
  stages, 533–534
  team selling, 532
  technological revolution, 548
  at Xerox, 527
Personal selling process, 533
  approach, 536
  case, 552–553
  close, 538
  follow-up, 538–539
  preapproach, 535–536
  presentation, 536–538
  prospecting, 534–535
Pet products, 644–645
Pharmaceutical industry, 277–278
  case, 647–649
  information technology, 427–428
Physical distribution specialist, 611–612
Physical risk, 478
Physical surroundings, 125
Physiological needs, 126–127
Piggyback trains, 433
Pioneering advertising
  institutional, 498
  for products, 497
Pipelines, 433
Pi Sigma Epsilon, 619
Place-based media, 511
Place strategy, 46
Place utility, 14, 23–24, 398
  in retailing, 444, 445
Planning gap, 49
Planning phase of marketing strategy, 42–46
Point-of-purchase displays, 517–518
Points of difference, 45
Political-regulatory climate, 188–189
Political risk, 188
Political stability, 188
Pollution, Soviet Union, 34
Population
  shifting age structure, 74
  of United States, 75
  world, 74

Population explosion, 74
Population Reference Bureau, 74
Population shifts, 77
Population (statistical), 210
Portals, 570
Portfolio tests, 512
Positioning; *see also* Product positioning
   retail stores, 455–457
Possession utility, 23–24, 398
   in retailing, 444, 445
Postage stamp pricing, 379
Postpurchase behavior
   consumer products, 122–123
   organizational buying, 161
Postpurchase stage, 480
Posttests, 513–514
Power center, 459
Preapproach, 535–536
Precision shoppers, 464
Precycling, 84
Predatory pricing, 381–382
Preliminary market testing, 276–277
Premium, 336
   in sales promotion, 516
Prepurchase stage, 479
Presentation
   adaptive selling, 537
   consultative selling, 537
   formula selling, 536–537
   handling objections, 537–538
   need satisfaction, 537
   stimulus-response, 536
Prestige-niche strategy, 358
Prestige pricing, 363–364
Pretesting, 472
Pretests, 512
Price(s), 336–337; *see also* Quoted
   price
   applicable time period, 342
   based on spreadsheet results, 369
   benchmark items, 458
   of collectibles, 343
   of competitors, 344
   costs of changing, 342
   definition, 14
   and demand estimation, 345
   factors increasing or decreasing, 337
   indicator of value, 338–339
   markdown, 391
   in marketing mix, 339–340
   marketing view of, 336–338
   markup, 389–391
   and perception of services, 328
   and quality, 339
   ratios for calculating, 389–393
   short-term reduction, 516
   signpost items, 458
   steps in setting, 339–340, 362
   suggested by manufacturers, 380
   terms for, 336
Price changes, costs of, 342
Price comparisons, 381
Price discounting, 90
Price discrimination, 380–381
   litigation, 383
Price elasticity of demand, 348–349
Price equation, 337, 338
Price fixing, 89–90, **379**–380
Price-level approximation
   competition-oriented approach, 376
   cost-oriented approach, 365–367
   demand-oriented approach, 362–365
   profit-oriented approach, 367–369

Price lining, 364
Price segments, 232
Price strategy, 46
Price war, 373
Pricing
   and antitrust laws, 379–382
   deceptive, 381
   and dumping regulations, 195
   FOB origin, 378
   FOB with freight allowed, 378, 379
   geographical, 381
   of installations, 265
   multiple zone, 378, 379
   off-price retailing, 458
   penetration, 290
   predatory, 381–382
   profit maximization, 351
   in retailing, 457–459
      maintained markup, 457
      markdown, 457–458
      original markup, 457
   for services, 328
   and shrinkage, 458
   single-zone, 378–379
   skimming strategy, 290
   uniform delivered, 378–379
Pricing constraints, 341
   cost of changing prices, 342
   costs of production/marketing, 342
   demand, 341–342
   newness of product, 342
   single product *vs.* product line, 342
Pricing objectives, 340
   market share, 341
   profit, 340
   sales, 340–341
   social responsibility, 341
   survival, 341
   unit volume, 341
Pricing-related legislation, 89–90
Pricing strategies
   above-, at-, or below-market
      pricing, 370
   battery manufacturers, 365
   break-even analysis, 351–355
   bundle pricing, 364–365
   case, 358–359
   and competitor prices, 344
   and controlling costs, 350
   cost-plus pricing, 366–368
   customary pricing, 370
   dot-com failures, 351
   dynamic pricing, 570
   estimating demand, 344–346
   estimating revenue, 346–350
   everyday fair pricing, 458
   everyday low prices, 377, 378, 458
   experience curve pricing, 368
   flexible-price policy, 371–372
   at Gillette, 361–362
   in global marketing, 195–196
   Hi-Lo pricing, 378
   identifying constraints, 342–344
   identifying objectives, 340–341
   loss-leader pricing, 370
   marginal analysis, 351–352
   market pricing, 370
   odd-even pricing, 364
   off-peak pricing, 328
   one-price policy, 371
   penetration pricing, 363
   prestige pricing, 363–364
   and price elasticity of demand, 349

price lining, 364
   product-line pricing, 372
   profit equation, 339
   skimming pricing, 362–363
   standard markup, 366
   target pricing, 364
   target profit pricing, 367–368
   target return-on-investment, 368–369
   target return-on-sales pricing, 368
   travel dot-coms, 335
   types of competitive markets, 342–344
   value pricing, 339
   wine industry, 384–385
   yield management pricing, 365
Primary data, 210
   advantages and disadvantages, 221
   observational data, 213–215
   panels and experiments, 220–221
   questionnaire data, 215–221
Primary demand, 289
Princeton Review, 329
Privacy, Internet, 571
Private branding, 306
Private labeling, 306
Probability sampling, 210
Problem children, 39
Problem definition, 207–209
Problem recognition
   consumer products, 120
   organizational buying, 160
Problem solving, 124
Product adaptation, 193
Product adopters, 295
Product advertisements, 497
Product availability, 345
Product benefits, 303
Product champion, 598
Product class, 294
   demand for, 341–342
Product counterfeiting, 299–300
Product deletion, 292, 306
Product development, 40–41
Product development manager, 611
Product development strategy, 590
Product differentiation, 233
   and competition, 291
   in sneaker industry, 232
   synergy, 237
Product-distribution franchise, 447
Product diversification, 41
Product extension, 193
Product form, 294
Product image, 303
Product imitation, 6
Product invention, 193–194
Production costs, 343
Production era, 19, 20
Product item, 263
Product liability, 633–635
Product liability claims, 310
Product life cycle, 288
   alternatives, 293–294
   case, 312–313
   and consumers, 294–296
   decline stage
      characteristics, 292
      deletion, 292
      harvesting, 292
   fax machines, 290
   generalized, 293
   growth stage, 290–292
   introduction stage, 288–290
   length of, 293

managing
   changing value offered, 299
   market modification, 297–298
   product modification, 297
   repositioning, 288–299
   role of product managers, 296–297
  maturity stage, 292
  pricing constraint, 342
  product class, 294
  product form, 294
  in promotional mix, 476–478
  shape of, 293–294
Product line, 262–263
   at Apple computer, 248–249
   Ben and Jerry's, 29
   breadth of, 449–450
   depth of, 449
   full-line pricing, 414
   general merchandise stores, 449–450
   at Nokia, 256–257
   product item, 263
   versus single product, 342
   stockkeeping units, 263
Product line extensions, 304
Product-line groupings, 601
Product line pricing, 372
Product management
   careers in, 611–612
   case, 312–313
   Gatorade, 287–288
Product management teams, 611
Product manager, 296–297, 602, 611
Product-market units, 31
Product mix, 263
Product modification, 297
Product newness, 342
Product placement, 518
Product positioning, 249
   differentiation, 250
   head-to-head, 250
   milk, 250–251
   perceptual maps, 250–252
Product-related legislation
   company protection, 88, 89
   consumer protection, 88–89
Product repositioning, 249
   case, 655–656
   chocolate milk, 251–252
   in product life cycle, 298–299
      catching rising trend, 299
      changing value offered, 299
      reaching new markets, 298
      reacting to competitors, 298
Products, 262
   acting on deviations, 49
   ancillary services, 478
   business goods, 265–266
   classifying
      degree of tangibility, 264
      new products in services, 264
      user types, 263–264
   complexity, 478
   consumer goods, 264–265
   customization, 557
   definition, 14
   demand for, 341–342
   environmentally safe, 111
   fads, 294
   fashion, 294
   grouped for market, 244
   high-involvement, 125
   high-learning, 293
   identifying deviations, 48–49

low-involvement, 125
low-learning, 293–294
and marketing channel
    management, 408
mass customization, 237
multiple, and multiple market
    segments, 236–237
new *versus* existing, 267
in organizational buying, 152
recycling, 84
risk, 478
search properties, 323
single, and multiple market
    segments, 236
single *versus* product line, 342
variations of, 262–264
Product safety, 101, 633–635
Product sales organization, 543
Product schedule, 47–48
Product specialization, 592
Product strategy, 45
    for global marketing, 193–194
    at Rollerblade, 17–19
Product synergy, 248–249
Product trials, 130
Product warranties, 309–310
Professional organizations, 626–627
Professional sales person, 611
Profit, 30
    goal, 34
    measures of, 340
    pricing objective, 340
Profitability, in marketing
    channels, 411
Profitability analysis, 604
Profit-and-loss statement, 386
Profit before taxes, 389
Profit enhancement options, 590–591
Profit equation, 339
Profit maximizing pricing, 352
Profit organizations, 322
Profit-oriented pricing
    target profit pricing, 367–368
    target return-on-investment pricing,
        368–369
    target return-on-sales pricing, 368
Profit responsibility, 107
Program champion, 598
Program schedules, 599–600
Project manager, 611
Promotion
    aimed at Generation Y, 477
    building long-term relationships, 521
    buzz marketing, 477
    careers in, 611, 612
    case, 646–647, 656–657
    costs of multibranding, 306
    definition, 14
    designing, 485
    at Disney World, 470
    expenditures in United States, 483
    integrated, 521
    in introduction stage, 289
    regulation of, 90–91
    scheduling, 485
    selecting right tools, 484–485
    self-regulation, 521–522
    of services, 329
    specifying objectives, 482
    target audience, 482
    tools of, 470
Promotional allowances, 90, 377
    and Robinson-Patman Act, 381

Promotional mix, 470, 472–475
    advertising, 473–474
    changes in product life cycle,
        476–478
    channel strategies
        pull strategy, 481
        push strategy, 480
    direct marketing, 475
    integrated marketing
        communications, 476–481
    main issues, 476
    mass *versus* customized, 472–473
    personal selling, 474
    product characteristics, 478
    public relations, 474–475
    sales promotion, 475
    stages of buying decision, 478–480
    target audience, 476
    variations in purchase decision,
        478–480
Promotional websites, 574–575
Promotion budget
    all-you-can-afford budget, 484
    competitive parity budget, 483
    objective and task budget, 484
    percentage of sales budget, 483
Promotion Marketing Association, 514
Promotion strategies, 46
    for global marketing, 193–194
Prospect, 534
Prospecting, 534–535
Protectionism
    decline of, 174–175
    ethics of, 175
    quotas, 175
    tariffs, 174
Protocol, 270
Prototype, 277
Psychographics, 132–133
    consumer markets, 239
Psychological influences; *see* Consumer
    behavior
Public information sources, 120–121
Publicity, 329, **474–475**
Publicity tools, 520–521
Public relations, 474–475, 485
    characteristics, 473
    by company representatives, 521
    news conferences, 520
    news releases, 520
    publicity tools, 520–521
    public service announcements,
        520–521
Public relations manager, 611
Public service announcements,
    329, 520–521
Pull strategy, 480, 481
Pulse schedule, 511
Purchase decision, 122, 478–480
    case, 635–636, 636–637
    high-involvement, 124, 125
    low involvement, 124, 125
    by online shoppers, 565–567
    in organizational buying,
        151–152, 161
    postpurchase stage, 480
    prepurchase stage, 479
    purchase stage, 479
Purchase decision process, 120
    alternative evaluation, 121–122
    buying value, 122
    characteristics, 124
    information search, 120–121

postpurchase behavior, 122–123
    problem recognition, 120
Purchase discounts, 387
Purchase frequency, 511
Purchase stage, 479
Purchasing power
    in global marketing, 186–187
    regional comparisons, 187
Pure competition, 85–86, 344
Pure monopoly, 86, 342–343
Push strategy, 480

Q

Qualified prospect, 534
Quality, 36
    aided by packaging, 308
    goal, 34
    poor, 270–271
    and price, 339
    of services, 324–325
    Six Sigma process, 273
Quantitative salesforce evaluation, 547
Quantity discounts, 373
Question marks, 39
Questionnaire data, 215
    electronic technology for, 219
    focus groups, 216
    individual interviews, 215–216
    mall intercept interviews, 217
    methods, 217
    open-ended questions, 218
    semantic differential scale, 218–219
    wording problems, 217
Quick response, 430
Quotas, 175
Quoted price
    balancing incremental costs and
        revenues, 374
    company effects, 372
    competitive effects, 373
    customer effects, 373
    flexible-price policy, 371–372
    one-price policy, 371
    and price war, 373
    special adjustments, 374–382
        allowances, 377
        discounts, 375–377
        geographical, 378–379
        legal/regulatory aspects, 379–382

R

Race discrimination, 371
Racial diversity, 77–78
Rack jobbers, 404
Radio advertising
    advantages and disadvantages, 506
    expenditures, 504
    satellite services, 507
    scope of, 506–507
Radio frequency identification tags, 447
Railroads, 433
Rating, 504, 505
Ratio analysis
    expense-to-sales ratios, 389
    markdown, 391
    markup, 389–391
    return on investment, 393
    stockturn rate, 392–393
Raw materials
    cost-effective flow, 422
    handling costs, 422
Reach, 504, 505
Real time, 560

Rebates, 518
Receivers, 471
Recession, 81
Reciprocity, 155
Recruitment of salesforce, 545
Recycling, 84
    by Anheuser-Busch, 97–98
    by reverse logistics, 438
Reference groups, 135
Reference value, 339
Refusal to deal, 414
Regional marketing activities, 78
Regional rollouts, 281
Regional shopping center, 459
Regional trade agreements, 175
*Register of Corporations, Directors,
    and Executives,* 622
Regular distribution, 267
Regulation, 87–88; *see also*
    Government regulation
    deceptive pricing, 381
    geographic pricing, 381
    predatory pricing, 381–382
    price discrimination, 380–381
    price fixing, 379–380
    of pricing, 379–382
Regulatory restrictions, 303
Reinforcement, 130
Reinforcement ads, 497
Relationship marketing, 16
    in service industry, 326
Relationship selling, 529–530
Relative market share, 38
Reminder advertising
    institutional, 498
    for products, 497
Repeat purchases, 290–291
Replenishment time, 430
Repositioning; *see* Product repositioning
Requirement contracts, 90
Resale price maintenance, 380
Resale restrictions, 414
Research, 207–208; *see also* Marketing
    research
Research and development, 273
Research and development-
    manufacturing synergy, 591, 592
Reseller branding, 306
Reseller markets, 149
    measuring, 150–151
Resellers, 149
Resources, obtaining, 47
Response, 130, **472**
Résumé
    accompanying letter, 620–621
    electronic, 619–620
    formats, 619–620
Retail communication, 460
Retailers, 148
    definition, 396
    failure fee, 281
    in global marketing, 194–195
    impact of multichannel marketing, 575
    loss-leader pricing, 370
    multichannel, 572
    number of, 149
    and online orders, 572
    shelf space, 647–649
    standard markup pricing, 366
    supply partnerships, 156
    transactional websites, 573–574
    wholesaler-sponsored voluntary
        chains, 406

Retailer-sponsored cooperative, 406, 447
Retailing, 443–467, 444
  career paths, 613
  careers in, 611, 612–613
  case, 466–467, 649–651, 652–653
  changing nature of, 461–463
  consumer utilities offered by, 445
  food-gasoline stations, 650–660
  future changes
    impact of technologies, 463
    multichannel retailers, 463
    shopping behavior, 464
  global economic impact, 445–446
  life cycle, 462–463
  nonstore, 450–455
  sales volume in United States, 445
  at Target Stores, 443–444
  and utilities, 444, 445
  value of, 444–446
  wheel of, 461–462
Retailing mix, 457
  category management, 460
  communication, 460
  functional, 460
  merchandise, 460
  off-price retailing, 458
  pricing, 457–459
  psychological attributes, 460
  store location, 459
Retailing strategy
  category management, 460
  communication, 460
  elements of, 456
  merchandise, 460
  positioning, 455–457
  pricing, 457–459
  retailing mix, 457–460
  retail positioning matrix, 456, 457
  store location, 459
Retail life cycle, 462–463
Retail outlets
  anchor stores, 459
  atmosphere/ambience, 460
  category killers, 449
  discount stores, 463
  extreme-value retailers, 459
  forms of ownership
    contractual, 447–448
    corporate, 446–447
    independent, 446
  franchises, 447–448
  general merchandise, 448, 449
  hypermarkets, 450
  intertype competition, 450
  level of service, 448–449
  limited-line, 449
  losses to theft, 458
  merchandise lines, 449–450
  multichannel, 463
  outlet stores, 459
  positioning, 455–457
  retail positioning matrix, 456
  single-line, 449
  single-price, 459
  specialty outlets, 449
  store location, 459
  supercenters, 450
  warehouse stores, 448, 458–459
Retail positioning matrix, 456
Retail sales, 445
Retail salesperson, 611
Return on assets, 340
Return on investment, 340, 393, 604
Returns, 386

Revenue
  break-even analysis, 351–355
  demand curve, 436–437
  increasing, 590, 591
  incremental, 584
  kinds of, 346
  marginal analysis, 351, 374
  from sales, 340–341
Revenue estimation
  demand curves, 346–348
  price elasticity of demand, 348–349
Reverse auction, 163
Reverse logistics, 438
Reverse marketing, 154
Rich media, 508–509
Risk
  in blockbuster films, 203–204
  kinds of, 478
Risk costs, 437
Robinson-Patman Act, 88, 380–381, 383
ROI marketing, 604
Role playing, 622–623
Routine problem solving, 124
Rule of reason, 380, 414
Rumor, 135–136

S

Safety, packaging, 309
Safety needs, 127
Safety standards, 101
Sales
  careers in, 611, 613–614
  80/20 rule, 241
  employment opportunities, 614
  goal, 34
  in growth stage, 290–292
  in introduction stage, 288–290
  in maturity stage, 292
  pricing objective, 340–341
  terminology, 386
  in test marketing, 279
Sales analysis, 603
Sales and Marketing Executives
    International, 619
Sales and Marketing Management,
    614, 618
Salesclerks, 531
Sales component analysis, 603
Sales drivers, 221–222
Sales engineer, 532
Salesforce
  chart, 542
  communication, 549
  compensation, 546–547
  computerized, 548–549
  customer organization, 543
  emotional intelligence, 545
  evaluation and control
    behavioral evaluation, 547–548
    quantitative assessment, 547
  geographic structure, 541–543
  job analysis, 545
  job description, 545
  major account management, 543–544
  motivation, 546–47
  nonmonetary rewards, 547
  organizing, 540–544
  product organization, 543
  recruitment and selection, 545
  training of, 519–520, 546
  workload method of organization,
    543–544

Salesforce automation, 548
  communication, 549
  computerization, 548–549
Sales force survey forecast, 253
Sales forecasting techniques
  judgments by decision makers,
    252–253
  statistical methods, 253
  survey of knowledgeable groups, 253
Sales forecasts, 253
  direct forecast, 253
  industry potential, 253
  linear trend extrapolation, 253
  lost-horse forecast, 252–253
  market potential, 252
  salesforce survey, 253
  survey of buyers' intentions, 253
  trend extrapolation, 253
Sales management, 528, 539–549
  account management policies, 544
  break-even chart, 541
  organizing salesforce, 540–544
  process stages, 539
  sales plan formulation, 540–544
  sales plan implementation
    customer relationship
      management, 548–549
    evaluation, 547–548
    motivation and compensation,
      546–547
    recruitment and selection, 545
    salesforce automation, 548–549
    training, 546
  setting objectives, 540
  technological revolution, 548
  at Xerox, 527
Sales management quiz, 528
Salespeople
  asking about competitors, 540
  company *versus* independent, 541
  workweek divisions, 532
Sales plan, 540
Sales plan formulation, 540–544
  account management policies, 544
  sales organization, 540–544
  setting objectives, 540
Sales plan implementation
  customer relationship management,
    548–549
  motivation and compensation, 546–547
  recruitment and selection, 545
  salesforce automation, 548–549
  salesforce evaluation, 547–548
  training program, 546
Sales promotion, 475, 485
  characteristics, 473
  consumer-oriented, 514–518
  expenditures, 514
  for maturity stage, 477
  in prepurchase stage, 479
  trade-oriented, 519–520
Sales promotion manager, 611
Sales quota, 547
Sales response function, 584
  maximizing incremental revenue, 584
  numerical example, 584–585
  share points, 585
  strategic marketing process, 585–586
Sales-support duties, 613
Sales tests, 513–514
Sample, 210
Samples, sales promotion, 517
Sampling, 210
SBU; *see* Strategic business units

Schedules, 47–48
Scheduling
  of advertising, 499
    approaches, 511
    factors in, 511
    tasks, responsibilities, and deadlines,
      599–600
Scoreboards, 629–631
Scrambled merchandise, 449–450
Screen Actors Guild, 503
Screening and evaluation, 275
  external approach, 276–277
  internal approach, 276
Seals of approval, 130
Search engines, 570
Search properties, 323
Seasonal discounts, 375–376
Secondary data, 210
  advantages and disadvantages, 212
  external, 211–212
  internal, 211
Secret Sales Pitch (Bullock), 128
Security, Internet, 571
Segmentation variables
  consumer market, 240
  organizational markets, 243
Selection of salesforce, 545
Selective comprehension, 129
Selective demand, 289
Selective distribution, 410
Selective exposure, 128
Selective perception, 128–129
Selective retention, 129
Selective specialization, 592
Self-actualization needs, 127
Self-concept, 127–128
Self-liquidating premiums, 516
Self-regulation, 91
  of promotion, 521–522
Self-service retailers, 448
Selig Center for Economic Growth, 143
Selling agents, 404
Selling duties, 613
Selling expenses, 388
Semantic differential scale, 218–219
Semiotics, 182–183
Semitechnical salesperson, 611
Sensitivity analysis, 222
Service continuum, 319–321
Service industry, future of, 329–330
Service organizations, 315–316
Services, 316
  assessing quality, 324–325
  classifications, 320
    delivery mode, 321–322
    government sponsored, 322–323
    profit/nonprofit organizations, 322
  consumer contact, 325–326
  credence properties, 323
  customer complaints, 325
  customer contact audit, 325–326
  customer education, 324
  definition, 264
  dimensions of quality, 324–325
  experience economy, 315–316
  experience properties, 323
  four I's of, 317–319
  future of, 329–330
  in global economy, 316
  growth sector, 316–317
  inconsistency, 318
  inseparability, 318–319
  intangibility, 317–318
  in international trade, 316

inventory, 319
marketing channels, 398–400
marketing management
   case, 332–333
marketing mix, 327–329
marketing of, 22
   branding, 327
   capacity management, 327–328
   distribution, 329
   exclusivity, 327
   internal marketing, 327
   pricing strategies, 328
   promotion, 329
new product development, 264
online purchases, 565–567
in organizational buying, 152
purchase process, 323
relationship marketing, 326
sports events, 321
supplementary, 320–321
Services market, 149
Service-sponsored franchise, 406
Service-sponsored retail franchise
   systems, 406
Share-of-market budgeting, 483
Share points, 585
Shelf life, 309
Shelfscents, 518
Shelf space, 271
Sherman Antitrust Act, 88, 89–90,
   379, 414
Shift in the demand curve, 346
Shoplifting, 458
Shopping centers/malls, 459
Shopping goods, 264–265
Shrinkage, 458
Signpost items, 458
Simulated, 279–280
   reasons for failure, 280
Simulated test markets, 279–280
Singapore, Wrigley's gum in, 408
Single-line stores, 449
Single-price retailers, 459
Single-zone pricing, 378–379
Situational influences, 125
Situation analysis, 43–44
Six Sigma process, **273**
Skimming pricing, 362–363
Skimming strategy, 290
SKU; see Stockkeeping units
Skunk Works, 584, 598–599
Slotting allowances, 102
Slotting fee, 281
Small businesses as competitors, 87
Smart cards, 463
Smoking-related deaths, 98
Sneaker industry
   competitive trends, 232–233
   marketing strategies, 235
   marketing wars, 231–233
   segments and strategies, 231–232
Snowboarding companies, 628–629
Social audit, 109–110
Social class, 138–139
Social forces, 73, 74
   culture, 78–80
   demographics, 74–78
Social needs, 127
Social responsibility, 20–21,
   34, 106
   at Anheuser-Busch, 97–98
   case, 113–114
   cause marketing, 108–109
   cell phone use, 13

concepts
   profit responsibility, 107
   societal responsibility, 108–109
   stakeholder responsibility,
      107–108
consumer responsibility, 110–111
green marketing, 108
Internet cookies, 571
pricing objective, 341
reverse logistics, 438
social audit, 109–110
student credit cards, 338
Super Bowl show, 502
sustainable development, 34
and telemarketing, 91
Social risk, 478
Social surroundings, 125
Societal culture, 100
Societal marketing concept, 21
Societal responsibility, 108–109
Sociocultural influences; *see* Consumer
   behavior
Source, 470–471
South Dakota State University, 629
Spam, 569
Spam e-mail, 489
Special fees, 337
Specialty goods, 264–265
Specialty merchandise wholesalers,
   403–404
Specialty outlets, 449
Sports segments, 232
Sports teams, 321
Sport utility vehicles, 278
Spreadsheets for operating
   statements, 369
Staff position, 601
Stakeholder responsibility, 107–108
Stakeholders, 8, 33
Standard Industrial Classification
   System, 150
Standard markup pricing, 366
Starch test, 513
Stars, 38
State employment office, 619
Statistical areas, 77
   and market segments, 242
Statistical forecasting methods, 253
Statistical inference, 210
Steady schedule, 511
Stimulus discrimination, 130
Stimulus generalization, 130
Stimulus-response presentation, 536
Stockkeeping units, 263
Stockturn rate, 392–393
Storage costs, 437
Storage warehouses, 434–435
Store location, 459
   case, 466–467
Store management, 612
Store manager, 611
Straight commission compensation
   plan, 546
Straight rebuy, 157
Straight salary compensation plan, 546
Strategic alliances, 177–178
Strategic business units, 30–31
   business portfolio analysis, 38–40
   cash cows, 38
   dogs, 39
   at Kodak, 38, 39–40
   question marks, 39
   stars, 38
Strategic channel alliances, 402

Strategic directions
   current company status
      competencies, 36
      competitors, 36–37
      customers, 35–36
   future
      business portfolio analysis, 38–40
      market-product analysis, 40–41
Strategic marketing process, 41–49, 42
balancing value and values, 595–596
case, 51–52, 607–609
control phase, 602–604
   acting on deviations, 49
   comparing results, 48–49
example, 594–595
at General Electric, 597
implementation phase, 46–48,
   586, 596–602
   designing marketing
      organization, 47
   developing schedules, 47–48
   executing program, 48
   obtaining resources, 47
marketing control process, 602–603
output reports, 586
phases, 585–586
planning phase, 42–46, 586–596
   goal setting, 44–45
   marketing program, 44–46
   market segmentation, 44–45
   situation analysis, 43–44
   SWOT analysis, 43–44
problem areas, 594
profitability analysis, 604
ROI marketing, 604
sales analysis, 603
Strategies
   business activities, 32–33
   business unit level, 31
   company mission, 33
   corporate level, 30–31
   diversification, 41
   functional level, 31
   goals and objectives, 34–35
   market development, 40
   market penetration, 40
   organizational culture, 33
   product development, 40–41
Strengths, 43–44
Strict liability rulings, 310
Strip location, 459
Strivers, 133
Strong Interest Inventory, 617
Student credit cards, 338
Student organizations, 619
Subbranding, 304
Subcultures, 139
   African Americans, 139–140
   Asian Americans, 140–141
   Hispanics, 140
   influence on consumer behavior,
      139–141
   information sources on, 143
Subliminal messages, 128
Subliminal perception, 129
Subsidiaries, 178
Successful Business Plan (Abrahms), 54
Suggested-price comparisons, 381
Suggestive selling, 536
Super Bowl
   advertising costs, 499
   favorite ads, 500
   half-time show of 2004, 501–502
   record of advertising costs, 500

Supercenters, 450
Supermarkets
   failure fee, 281
   floor displays, 518
   number of stockkeeping units, 271
   slotting allowances, 102
   slotting fee, 281
   standard markup pricing, 366
Supplementary services, 320–321
Suppliers, 87
   environmental forces affecting, 72
   new product ideas from, 274
Supplies, 266
Supply chain, 422
   aligned with strategy, 424–425
   in auto industry, 423–424
   communication in, 430–431
   convenience, 431
   customer service standards, 431
   at Dell computer, 425–426
   dependability, 430
   information in, 427–431
   inventory strategies, 437–438
   logistics functions, 432–438
   logistics in, 427–431
   responsiveness and efficiency,
      427–428
   reverse logistics, 438
   at Wal-Mart, 426
Supply chain management, 422–423
   case, 440–441, 651
   cross-docking, 426
   customer service concept, 429
   efficient customer response, 430
   electronic data interchange, 428
   enterprise resource planning, 428
   extranets, 428
   information technology, 427–428
   inventory management in, 436–438
   lead time, 430
   and marketing strategy, 424–425
   at Nike, 421
   number of warehouses, 428–429
   quick response, 430
Supply chain manager, 424, 611
Supply partnerships, 155–156
Support goods, 265
   accessory equipment, 266
   industrial services, 266
   installations, 265
   supplies, 266
Supporting industries, 172
Surcharges, 337
Survey of buyers' intentions, 253
Survey Research Center, 81
Survival, pricing objective, 341
Survivors, 133
Sustainable development, 34, 110
Sweepstakes, 516–517
SWOT analysis, 43–44
Synergy, 237
   product-market, 248–249

T

Tamper-resistant packaging, 308
Tangibility, 264
Target audience, 482
   for advertising, 498–499
   for promotion, 476
Targeted résumé format, 619
Target market, 14
   advertising for, 246–247
   case, 26–27
   choosing segments, 245–246

Target market (*continued*)
exclusive distribution, 409–410
intensive distribution, 409
in introduction stage, 288–290
marketing actions for reaching,
246–248
product differentiation, 248
selection criteria, 244–245
compatibility with company
objectives, 245
competitive position, 245
cost of reaching segments, 245
expected growth, 245
market size, 245
selective distribution, 410
Target marketing
grouping buyers into segments,
238–244
grouping products into
categories, 244
marketing actions, 246–248
market-product grid, 244
market-product synergies, 248–249
market size estimation, 244
selecting target markets, 244–246
Target pricing, 364
Target profit pricing, 367–368
Target return objective, 340
**Target return-on-investment pricing,
368**–369
Target return-on-sales pricing, 368
Tariffs, 174
Tastes, and demand estimation, 345
Team promotion, 470
Team selling, 532
Teaser advertising campaigns, 135
Technological forces, 73
Technological services, 329
Technology, 83
for advertising, 495–496
case, 630–631
declining cost of, 84
for direct marketing, 488–489
electronic business, 85
exploiting strengths in, 18
impact on consumer value, 84–85
impact on retailing, 463
salesforce automation, 548–549
of tomorrow, 83–84
Teenagers
consumer spending, 138
in global market, 179
Telemarketing, 454–455
and First Amendment, 91
inbound, 531, 532
National Do Not Call Registry, 535
regulation, 90–91, 102
Telephone Consumer Protection Act,
90, 103, 535
Telephone interviews, 217
Television, product placement, 518
Television advertising, 505–506
advantages and disadvantages, 506
cost disadvantage, 505
expenditures, 504
infomercials, 506
out-of-home viewing, 505
on Super Bowl, 499
wasted coverage, 505
Television guidelines, 91
Television home shopping, 452–453
Television ratings, 213–214
Temporal effects, 125
Test marketing, 279

Test markets, 220
demographic characteristics, 279
Test-result databases, 486
Theater tests, 512
Thinkers, 132–133
Third-party logistics providers, 432
inventory management, 436–438
materials handling, 434–435
order processing, 435–436
for reverse logistics, 438
transportation, 432–434
warehousing, 434–435
Threats, 43–44
Tiffany/Wal-Mart strategies, 236–237
Time, 344, 345
Time-sensitive materialists, 565
Time-to-market, 281–282
Time utility, 23–24, 398
in retailing, 444, 445
Timing of new products, 271
Top management, ethical behavior,
104–105
Total assets, 393
Total cost, 350
Total logistics cost, 428–429
Total quality management, 36
Total revenue, 346, 437
Toy industry, 169
Track jobbers, 404
Trade associations, 626–627
Trade discounts, 376, 377
Trade-in allowances, 377
Trademark, 299
Trademark Counterfeiting Act, 300
Trademark Law Revision Act, 89
Trademark registration, 89
Trade name, 299
Trade-oriented sales promotion
allowances and discounts, 519
cooperative advertising, 519
training distributor salesforce, 519–520
Trade promotions, 519
Trade regulations, 188–189
Trade salesperson, 611
Trading down, 299
Trading up, 299
Trading Up: The New American Luxury
(Silverstein & Fiske), 443
Traditional auction, 163
Traffic generation, 488
Trailer on flatcar trains, 433
Training
of distributor salespeople, 519–520
employer-sponsored, 546
on-the-job, 546
of salesforce, 546
Transactional function, 397, 398, 403
Transactional websites, 573–574
Transactions, 10
Transit advertising, 510
Transnational firms, 178–179
Transparency International, 103
Transportation
air carriers, 434
basic service criteria, 432
comparison of modes, 433
express companies, 434
freight forwarders, 434
motor carriers, 433–434
railroads, 433
Transportation costs, 378–379, 422
Travel dot-coms, 335
Trend analysis, 72–73
Trend extrapolation, 253

Trends, repositioning for, 299
Trial, 482
Trial close, 538
Trial purchasers, 288
Trucking industry, 433–434
Tuition, 336
Tying arrangements, 90, 414

U

Ultimate consumers, 22
Unethical behavior by consumers,
110–111
Unfair business practices, 90
Uniform delivered pricing, 378–379
Unitary demand, 349
United Nations, 74, 93, 151
on bribery, 103
United States
advertising expenditures, 504
annual franchise sales, 406
balance of trade, 171
changing attitudes of men and
women, 79–80
company promotion expenditures, 483
consumer income, 81–83
consumer market segments,
239–242
generational cohorts, 75–76
Gross Domestic Product, 171
household makeup, 76–77
Internet access, 564
macroeconomic conditions, 80–81
major trading partners, 171
niche markets, 75
number of government units, 149
number of retailers, 149
number of small businesses, 87
number of wholesalers, 149
online retail sales revenue, 558
online shoppers, 558
organizational customers, 148
population, 75
population shifts, 77
racial and ethnic diversity, 77–78
retail sales volume, 445
services in Gross Domestic Product,
316, 317
supercenters, 450
sustainable development, 34
volume of direct marketing, 487–488
United States Census Bureau, 74, 77,
80, 93, 143, 211, 212
United States Census of
Manufacturers, 211
United States Census of Retail
Trade, 211
U.S. News and World Report, 344
United States Open Snowboarding
Championships, 629
United States Patent and Trademark
Office, 299, 303
United States Supreme Court, 455
on trademarks, 89
Unit train, 433
Unit variable costs, 350, 352
Unit volume, pricing objective, 341
University of Florida, 287
University of Georgia, 143
University of Michigan, 81
Unsought goods, 264–265
Urgency close, 539
Usage instructions, 130

Usage rate, 239
data, 240–241
80/20 rule, 241
User fee, 337
Users, 157
new, 298
Utilitarianism, 106
Utility, 23–24
forms of, 398
from marketspace, 559
in retailing, 444, 445

V

VALS system, 132–133
Value added, 456
Value analysis, 160
Value-based planning, 595–596
Value consciousness, 80
Value-driven strategies, 596
Value (economic), **338**
assessing, 121–122
from brand equity, 300–301
buying, 122
changing, 299
consumer perceptions, 384–385
seeking, 120–121
Value pricing, 339
Values (cultural), 100, 131, **181**
changing, 80
Variable cost, 350
versus fixed cost, 354
Variety, 410–411
Vending machines, 451
Vendor-managed inventory, 437–438
Vertical conflict, 412
Vertical integration, legality of, 414
Vertical malls, 464
Vertical marketing systems, 405
administered, 407
channel partnerships, 407
contractual, 406
corporate, 405–406
Vertical price fixing, 380
Viral marketing, 569
Virtual advertising, 496
Vision, 33
Vocational interest tests, 616–617
Voice over Internet protocol, 86

W

Wages, 336
Wall Street Journal, 622
Wants *versus* needs, 12–13
Warehouse club, 458–459
Warehouses, 428–429
Warehouse stores, 448
Warehousing, 434–435
Warranty, 130, **309**–310
Wasted coverage, 474, 505
Water transportation, 433
Weaknesses, 43–44
Websites
blogs, 569
bots, 567
commerce, 563
community, 563
connection, 562–563
content, 562
context, 562
customization, 562–563
design elements, 562–563
eight-second rule, 567

Nielsen ratings, 215
promotional, 574–575
transactional, 573–574
Wheel of retailing, 461–462
Whistle-blowers, 105
Wholesalers, 148, 396
in global marketing, 194–195
number of, 149
types of, 403–404
Wholesaler-sponsored voluntary
chains, 406, 447

Wichita Falls, Texas, 279
Wired magazine, 471
Women
automobile purchase, 119–120
changing attitudes and roles, 79–80
in family decision making,
137–138
Women-owned firms, 153
Word of mouth, 134–135, 569
Working conditions, 110
Workload method, 543–544

World population, 74
World trade; *see* International trade
World Trade Organization, 175,
197, 316

Y

Yellow Pages
advantages and disadvantages, 506
directional medium, 508
expenditures, 504

Yellow Pages Integrated Media
association, 508
Yield management pricing, 365, 371

Z

Zero-defects goal, 273

The *Marketing* Student CD-ROM:

Marketing includes more than just great writing, interesting examples, and helpful pedagogy. We've also prepared an interactive **Student CD-ROM** loaded with helpful study aids as well as software to aid you in creating your own marketing plan, a key component to the course.

Doing a little studying? Don't forget your laptop.

The Student CD's study tools will quickly become an indispensable companion as you progress through the course.

- Reinforce your reading while it's still fresh with our multiple-choice Chapter Quizzes.

- Internet Links give you plenty of opportunities to expand your understanding with a quick visit to a relevant Website.